DAILY DEVOTIONAL EVENTS CALENDAR

A STUDY OF SCRIPTURE FOR EVERY DAY OF THE YEAR

Andrew V. Barber, PhD

ISBN 978-0-9669702-6-5

LCCN 2023941084

Copyright © 2023 Andrew V. Barber

All rights reserved. No part of this publication may be reproduced, distributed, or transmitted in any form or by any means, including photocopying, recording, or other electronic or mechanical methods without expressed written permission of the publisher. For permission requests contact the publisher at the following address.

Special Delivery Press

7121 Tierra Alta Ave.

El Paso, TX 79912

https://www.andrewvbarberphd.com

Printed in the USA

TABLE OF CONTENTS

Books of the Bible and Abbreviations	iv
Foreword	v
About the Author	v
Origin of Modern Calendars	vi
Christian Liturgical Calendar	vii
Jewish Feasts and Festivals	x
National and International Holidays and Events	xiii
References	xiii
The Year of Our Lord	xiv
January	1
February	74
March	145
April	200
May	256
June	329
July	398
August	468
September	540
October	599
November	669
December	740
Index	805

BOOKS OF THE BIBLE AND ABBREVIATIONS

Old Testament

BOOK	ABBREV.	BOOK	ABBREV.
Genesis	GEN	Ecclesiastes	ECC
Exodus	EXO	Song of Solomon	SOS
Leviticus	LEV	Isaiah	ISA
Numbers	NUM	Jeremiah	JER
Deuteronomy	DEU	Lamentations	LAM
Joshua	JOS	Ezekiel	EZE
Judges	JDG	Daniel	DAN
Ruth	RUT	Hosea	HOS
1 Samuel	1 SA	Joel	JOE
2 Samuel	2 SA	Amos	AMO
1 Kings	1 KI	Obadiah	OBA
2 Kings	2 KI	Jonah	JON
1 Chronicles	1 CH	Micah	MIC
2 Chronicles	2 CH	Nahum	NAH
Ezra	EZR	Habakkuk	HAB
Nehemiah	NEH	Zephaniah	ZEP
Esther	EST	Haggai	HAG
Job	JOB	Zechariah	ZEC
Psalms	PSA	Malachi	MAL
Proverbs	PRO		

New Testament

BOOK	ABBREV.	BOOK	ABBREV.
Matthew	MAT	1 Timothy	1 TI
Mark	MAR	2 Timothy	2 TI
Luke	LUK	Titus	TIT
John	JOH	Philemon	PHM
Acts	ACT	Hebrews	HEB
Romans	ROM	James	JAM
1 Corinthians	1 CO	1 Peter	1 PE
2 Corinthians	2 CO	2 Peter	2 PE
Galatians	GAL	1 John	1 JO
Ephesians	EPH	2 John	2 JO
Philippians	PHP	3 John	3 JO
Colossians	COL	Jude	JDE
1 Thessalonians	1 TH	Revelation	REV
2 Thessalonians	2 TH		

FOREWORD

In putting together this book I discovered hundreds of holidays, events, and observances that I'd never heard of: some were celebrated in other countries; many were unofficial, redundant, or idiotic; some I liked the sentiment and some I rejected outright. Many days in the year have several observances and many days have no observances, so I was selective. I eliminated many duplicate holidays and observances that differed only in title, date, or origin; for example, some holidays can be national as well as international. I preferred observances that were unique, made sense, or deemed a better fit for that date or season.

It is recommended that the reader read at least one lesson each day. Lessons range from one page to seven pages in length; the average is a little over two pages. The calendar is based on the year 2024, but the same observances occur every year, some on the same day of the week and some on a different day. The total number of lessons is 366, because 2024 is a leap year. These Bible lessons can be applied to any year, as the book is designed to follow events and observances that occur annually. An index is provided for rapid reference to topics, events, and holidays.

The scriptures relate either directly or indirectly to the title or topics associated with the observance. Some scriptural passages are repeated because they can be applied to multiple holidays. Bible verses are based primarily on the King James Version (KJV), though other translations were used to ensure the accuracy of the citation and to adjust the grammar. Thus, Bible verses may be paraphrased; the reader is encouraged to look up the cited scriptures in your favorite Bible. The point of this book is to get people to open their Bible and read it for themselves, and to read it often, preferably daily. Discuss the lessons and passages with your family and friends.

ABOUT THE AUTHOR

After honorably completing military service with the 82nd Airborne, Andrew Barber enrolled in college, earning a BA in Art and an all-levels teaching certificate. While working with and conducting research on runaway adolescents, he finished his MEd in Counseling, landing him into the field of scientific research. While a defense analyst he obtained a PhD in Psychology, progressing to Senior Research Psychologist and later to defense industry Consultant. He held security clearances up to Top Secret and NATO Secret. Dr. Barber returned to academia and counseling, establishing a private clinical practice which he maintained for twenty-five years. He was Professor of counseling, psychology, statistics, and religion, serving also as Campus Chair for the college of Social and Behavioral Sciences before becoming Director of Academic Affairs at a major university. His next position was Director of Clinical Support Services at a community health center, where he served as Lead Psychotherapist and head of Mental Health and Health Education operations for three clinics including the city homeless shelter. Then he became Lead Therapist and Program Manager for adult units at a large psychiatric hospital. Promoted to Program Director, he built and ran the addictions unit, managed the psychiatric intensive care and rapid crisis stabilization units, and was in charge of the pain management program; he also served as the Director of Intake and Assessment Services. He trained and mentored numerous practitioners, and provided clinical supervision for eight years. He returned to private practice before retiring. Andy is a scholar, writer, publisher, educator, counselor, consultant, coach, researcher, evaluator, and Christian apologist. He has authored over thirty technical publications, conducted high-level briefings, presented research papers at professional conferences, and facilitated workshops. He has been studying and researching the Holy Bible since he was a child and has authored several Christian books, and also a textbook on research and statistics. Dr. Barber was raised in a Christian home and has been active in the same church for over sixty years.

ORIGIN OF MODERN CALENDARS

Almost all modern and ancient calendars, with their associated months, progressions, seasons, and time zones, are based on four important phases of the sun which occur annually. Each phase is based on the proportion of daylight to nighttime, with respect to the position and tilt of the earth relative to the sun. In ancient times, the hours for labor were largely determined by the rising and the setting of the sun, this is how they divided the day. It was difficult to work at night due to insufficient lighting (JOH 9:4). Additionally, they divided the year into four equal parts: two equinoxes and two solstices. One can count the days between these periods and estimate the length of one earth year, which equals one orbit around the sun, determined to be approximately 365.25 days. Days were grouped into weeks and months making for an accurate means of keeping track of dates. The Old Testament Jews based their timelines on lunar phases, which was not as accurate, but was in accordance with certain feasts which God commanded them to observe.

Thus, calendars are based primarily on the solstices and equinoxes. Equinox means the proportion of day and night are relatively equal. The summer solstice and winter solstice represent the longest day and the longest night, respectively. The year is partitioned into four quarters, lasting about three months, relating to the four seasons. Keep in mind that the season occurring in the northern hemisphere will be the opposite season in the southern hemisphere, the equator being the latitudinal dividing line. The prime meridian is a longitudinal boundary which runs from pole to pole, separating the eastern and western hemispheres, and is the basis for time zones.

Gregorian Calendar is used in most modern nations, to include the USA. Named for Pope Gregory XIII, it was introduced in 1582 after adjusting the previously used Julian calendar in order to better stabilize the Easter season. It was known that Holy Week followed soon after the vernal equinox, which was a predictable occurrence; but Easter Sunday kept slipping forward on the Julian calendar. Leap year adjustments were incorporated, and the first of January was designated the beginning of the new year. The twelve months had been named mostly after Roman gods and goddesses, except those changed by emperors Julius and Augustus, who exalted themselves by naming months after them, and adding an extra day by lifting them from February.

The Anno Domini (AD) dating scheme, meaning after the dominion of Christ, was the scholarly work of a monk named Dionysius Exiguus who was commissioned by Pope John I in the year 525. He sought to determine the date of the first Easter and track backwards to the date of Jesus's birth. As a result of his calculations, the numbering of years was modified in accordance with the Julian calendar. Historical dates were ascertained with the cutoff at year one, to denote dates occurring after Christ's birth versus before Christ (BC). While a very intuitive guess, modern theologians estimate the actual birth of Christ to be closer to 5 BC. That estimate is supported by additional historical findings, such as the apparent death of Herod the Great in 4 BC, who died shortly after Christ was born; and astronomical data such as the consecutive alignments of Saturn and Jupiter in the sixth century BC, and lunar eclipses occurring during this time period. The postmodernists dropped AD and BC in favor of CE (common era) and BCE (before common era) to disconnect historical dating from Jesus Christ, though these were determined based on His birth.

The Christian and the Jewish liturgical calendars overlap to some degree, but the Jewish lunar calendar has fewer days than the Gregorian calendar. Therefore, some observances can vary widely in a given year, being linked to seasons and times in accordance with the Biblical narrative. You will find it interesting how Old Testament Jewish feasts and festivals correspond to those practiced by Christians in accordance with New Testament events. Therefore, it is unwise to use only one testament of the Bible because the two testaments cross-validate each other.

CHRISTIAN LITURGICAL CALENDAR

A number of special seasons and holidays are organized throughout the year as a guide to Christian church teachers and pastors. Bible readings, services, and sermons are tailored to commemorate significant historical events recorded in both testaments. Key events and seasons are listed chronologically below. Look up the cited scriptures in this section to get the big picture of God's plan and our response to His promises. Liturgical observances are discussed in greater detail on the actual day or week of the year when it occurs on the calendar.

Advent is a period of four consecutive Sundays which lead up to Christmas Day. Advent marks the beginning of the church calendar year. The term advent connotes coming. Christians anticipate the coming of Christ by acknowledging his birth and by looking forward to His return. An advent wreath of four candles is displayed in church and a candle is lit each Sunday until Christmas; most wreaths have a fifth candle in the middle to be lighted on Christmas Day. Advent is a season for fasting, prayer, and preparation; the same is true for the season of Lent which leads up to Christ's crucifixion and resurrection during Holy Week. Christians recognize Jesus as the light of the world, who brought with Him the free gift of eternal life, represented in His first and second advents. For a prelude to Christmas, read the first chapter of Luke.

Christmas Day was assigned to December 25, presumably to interfere with pagan holidays celebrated in honor of the sun god and the winter solstice. The setting of that date is often ascribed to the Roman emperor Constantine who reigned during the fourth century AD, whereby worshipping the sun was changed to worshipping the Son of Righteousness (see MAL 4:1–2). While the exact day and month of Christ's birth is unknown, scholars assert that it was likely earlier, in the fall when shepherds would be watching their flocks. This reconciles with the rules of priesthood, because Jesus Christ began his ministry at age 30 (see NUM 4:3; 1 CH 23:2–3; LUK 3:21–23). It is understood that Jesus preached His Gospel for 3.5 years. Since Jesus was murdered during Passover (springtime), that would place His birth, as well as the initiation of His ministry, on the day of His baptism, around October during the Jewish Feast of Tabernacles. The Jewish Feast of Passover occurs in March or April corresponding with the Christian Holy Week, whereby Passover coincides with Jesus's trial and execution.

Certainly, it makes sense to cherish the birth, death, and resurrection of Christ every day. It also is sensible to choose a special day to recognize the consequential and miraculous occurrence of the virgin birth. So, December 25 works, since the Christmas season has dominated over previous pagan observances. Read the following scriptures for a full understanding of the prophecy and accounts of the birth of Messiah: ISA 7:14; ISA 9:1–7; MIC 5:2–4; MAT 1:18–25; LUK 2:1–20; JOH 1:1–14.

Epiphany designates the twelfth day after Christmas to commemorate the worshipping of the Christ child by the magi. That day traditionally falls on January 6. These wise men acknowledged Christ's kingship, presenting precious gifts of gold, frankincense, and myrrh. This tradition is carried on when we exchange gifts and worship Christ during the special season known as the twelve days of Christmas, in response to the precious gift God gave to us of His only Son. Note that the word epiphany comes from the Greek, meaning to appear or manifest. Epiphany Sunday is generally celebrated the first Sunday after or on 01/06. For a detailed account of the visit by the three wise men read ISA 60:1–6; MAT 2:1–12; LUK 2:21–38.

Baptism of Christ Sunday is held the Sunday after Epiphany Sunday. It is a solemn occasion in remembrance of when Christ began His ministry by endorsing the sacrament of Holy Baptism through His personal participation. The entire godhead of the Trinity was present at that event, when the Holy Spirit descended like a dove and rested on Jesus, and the voice of the Father announced from heaven, "This is my beloved Son in whom I am well pleased" (MAT 3:13–17; MAR 1:9–11). Baptism represents a commitment to Christ; we follow the example He set for us as we begin our baptismal journey on a path that leads to heaven (MAT 28:18–20). For the entire episode surrounding Jesus's baptism read the following scriptures: MAL 3:1–3; MAT 3:1–17; MAR 1:2–11; LUK 3:1–22; JOH 1:15–37. Recall that Jesus's baptism was likely near or on His thirtieth birthday.

Transfiguration Sunday is the day Christians contemplate a spectacular supernatural event recorded in the New Testament. Christ and the prophets Elijah and Moses miraculously appeared in the sky before Peter, James, and John who were atop a high mountain with Jesus. Although different churches recognize this event during different times of the year, Protestant denominations generally choose the last Sunday of the Epiphany season, or the week before Ash Wednesday. Details of Christ's transfiguration can be found in the following verses: MAT 17:1–13; MAR 9:2–9; LUK 9:28–36; 2 PE 1:16–21.

Ash Wednesday is the seventh Wednesday before Easter and the beginning of the season of Lent. It is the initiation of fasting, prayer, and reflection to honor the forty days that Jesus wandered the wilderness following His baptism, where He was tempted by Satan This was a daunting induction into His ministry, and a prelude of things to come. It also is reasoned that the Transfiguration of Christ occurred roughly forty days before His crucifixion. During the Lenten season we look forward to the completion of Christ's ministry, culminating with His horrible death and glorious resurrection. The blessing of ashes corresponds to our mortality, as in the phrase often spoken at funerals: "ashes to ashes, dust to dust" (GEN 3:19). The placing of ashes on the forehead is a symbol of humility and penance. This Catholic tradition is not from the Bible but is nonetheless spiritual and personal.

Palm Sunday is the day we recall Jesus Christ riding triumphantly into Jerusalem on a donkey. As He entered the city the crowds dropped palm branches and coats into His path and praised Him, singing "Hosanna to the Son of David. Blessed is He that comes in the name of the Lord. Hosanna in the highest." Palm Sunday concludes the season of Lent and commences Holy Week which ends on Easter Sunday. Read these Bible verses to get the full picture of that distinguished juncture in Jesus's ministry: ZEC 9:9–10; MAT 21:1–16; MAR 11:1–11; LUK 19:29–46; JOH 12:12–16. The Christian Holy Week culminates in the three episodes below.

Maundy Thursday was a pivotal day as it commemorates when Jesus washed the feet of His disciples. Then Jesus participated in the last Passover supper with His apostles and administered the first Holy Communion to them. Hence the term *Maundy* which means commandment ("do this in remembrance of me"). Later that night Jesus was betrayed by Judas Iscariot. Our participation in the sacrament of Holy Communion (Eucharist) is in tribute to Jesus and His sacrifice for sins, which He commanded us to observe often. Note the association with Maundy Thursday and the Jewish Feast of Unleavened Bread. References for this event are found in MAT 26:1–75; MAR 14:1–31; LUK 22:1–38; JOH 13—17.

Good Friday coincides with the trial, sentencing, and crucifixion of Christ. It also connects with the Jewish Feast of Passover. Jesus's sinless body was broken, represented by breaking bread without yeast, when He endured the punishment that was due the rest of us. His blood was spilled, reflected in the sacrifice of the Passover lamb, to pay for the sin of the world, the price being death. Review the section below on Jewish Feasts to better understand how God's plan is confirmed in the Old and New Testaments. What does the word good denote in Good Friday, you may ask? What is good about what happened to Jesus? The Bible teaches that only God is good, meaning holy; therefore, the distinction of being good also belongs to Christ (MAR 10:18; LUK 18:19). Humans can be made good and holy only by the imputing of Christ's righteousness in exchange for our sin (PHP 3:9; 2 CO 5:21), which is the very work He performed on the cross of Calvary, and is the basis of our Christian faith. We cannot enter the kingdom of God unless we are made pure and free of sin (JOH 3:1–21; 1 CO 15:49–58), cleansed of all unrighteousness by the blood of the Lamb of God (EPH 1:8; HEB 9:13–22). Until His second advent, the words good and holy can apply to only one human that ever walked the planet: Jesus Christ. For greater clarity concerning this mystery, read ISA 53; ZEC 11:12–13; ZEC 12:10; ZEC 13:6–7; MIC 6:6–7; MAT 26:36–75; MAT 27; MAR 14—15; LUK 22—23; JOH 18—19; HEB 9:11–28; REV 5:22.

Easter Sunday was the day Jesus arose from the dead. The resurrection of Christ is the most critical event of all history, and the foundation of Christianity. Easter is the source for our joy of salvation, our trust in God's promises, and our hope of eternal life. Christ told His followers He would be tortured and killed, and then come back to life in three days. That is exactly what happened: He gave his life and he took it back again (JOH 10:11–18). It is a good thing He did, otherwise our faith would be in vain. Easter is the single most identifying fact that separates Christianity from all other world religions. Only Christ can guarantee our resurrection; only He can raise us from the dead on the last day. On Maundy Thursday we see Christ living in obedience to the law which we failed to do; on Good Friday we see Christ paying the price for our sin with His death on the cross. On Easter Sunday we see Christ's victory over death through His resurrection. These events occurred in concert with Jewish feasts celebrated during the same week. This is not a coincidence; it was planned by God to provide a foreshadowing of things to come, forming a solid link between the Old and New Testaments of the Bible. Christ has conquered the law, sin, and death for anyone who will believe, which is why Holy Week is the central theme of Christianity and the cornerstone of our faith, as it also is for the Jews. Read these scriptures to better appreciate God's plan for humanity: ISA 9:6; ISA 11:1–2; MAL 4:2; MAT 28:1–15; MAR 16:1–13; LUK 24:1–32; JOH 11:25–26; JOH 20:1–18; 1 PE 1:18–23.

Ascension of Christ Sunday is recognized on the first Sunday after counting forty days from Easter, because Jesus walked the earth forty days after His resurrection, one for each day He spent in the wilderness. Since Easter occurred on Sunday, then Christ's ascension was on a Thursday. The Sunday after that Thursday is Ascension Sunday. Christ told His apostles that He was going to the Father to prepare a place for believers, and that He would return someday to bring them home (JOH 14:1–3). The angels told the apostles that Christ would return the same way He departed. All Christians look forward to His second advent. It is common to look into heaven when pondering God; one of these days you will see Him there, coming to gather His flock (MAT 28:16–20; MAR 16:14–20; LUK 24:33–53; JOH 21; ACT 1:1–11).

Pentecost began as a Jewish feast and is a significant day throughout both testaments of the Holy Bible. It is a time of anointing by the Holy Spirit. Christians remember that day as the one in which the apostles of Christ received the gift of His Holy Spirit and prophesied in foreign tongues. On that day, everyone heard the words and promises of God in their native language. Thousands were baptized in the name of Jesus, thereby receiving the gift of the Holy Spirit (read the second chapter of Acts). Pentecost is a time for giving to God all honor and glory, sharing the good news of salvation with others, and receiving the anointing of the Holy Spirit. Please refer to Jewish Feasts for complimentary information about Pentecost.

Holy Trinity Sunday occurs the first Sunday after Pentecost to honor our glorious Triune God: Father, Son, and Holy Spirit. The doctrine of the trinity is one of the essential truths of Christianity that must never be compromised. Along with the resurrection of Jesus Christ, it is a concept unique to Christianity, setting it apart from all other world religions. Difficult to comprehend yet understood nevertheless, the mystery of God in three persons provides a spiritual uplifting that is as unexplainable as it is real. This crucial dogma has been included in Christian confessions originating with Christ's apostles, and reaffirmed periodically, notably at the Council of Nicaea in the year AD 325. Read the following scriptures to better comprehend the Holy Trinity: ISA 6:3; ISA 11:2; ISA 43:10–15; ISA 48:16; MAT 28:18–20; 2 CO 13:14; COL 2:20; 1 PE 1:1–2; 1 JO 5:6–8.

Reformation Day commemorates Martin Luther nailing ninety-five theses to the church door at Wittenberg castle on October 31, 1517. Some of the objections included in that decree were the concepts of purgatory, paying penance through monetary indulgences, and praying to saints. Luther openly contested unscriptural practices by the Roman Catholic Church, and was instrumental in advancing the Protestant Reformation. He believed we must trust in the Holy Bible exclusively as the only source of absolute truth (*sola scriptura*), and not depend solely on the clergy or the pope for their explanations. Reformation Sunday is an important observance in the Protestant liturgy, scheduled for the last Sunday in October, so it can occur the week before All Saints Day.

All Saints Day, or All Hallows Day, occurs the first of November and is a day to hallow or revere those Christian saints that have preceded us in death. The feast falls the day after All Hallows Eve (namely, Halloween). The current date is associated with Pope Gregory III (eighth century AD) who dedicated November 1 to venerate past apostles, martyrs, and confessors of Jesus Christ; he likely changed the previous date from March because it was too close to Holy Week. Another possibility is that the date was selected to challenge pagan rituals associated with All Hallows Eve. Not to be confused with All Souls Day, these days correspond to long held traditions (*Dia de los Muertos*, or Day of the Dead) and may suggest opposite ends of the spiritual spectrum.

JEWISH FEASTS AND FESTIVALS

The Jewish Feasts assigned to the Israelites by God Almighty were sacred seasons occurring at certain times of the year (read Leviticus, chapter three). Each event commemorated a special occurrence and was accompanied by fasting, worship, and celebration. The primary seven feasts are represented in the seven candles of the menorah. You will notice deliberate parallels between the commands given to the Hebrews by God in the practicing of their faith, and Christian practices and services. This connects the Old Testament and New Testament, and the Old Covenant of the Law of Moses with the New Covenant of Grace in Jesus Christ.

Note that the Jewish calendar and the division of seasons, months, and times are based on Old Testament customs. For example, the day is divided into two parts: nighttime and daytime. Notice that the first part of the twenty-four-hour day is night and the second part is day. In the book of Genesis (GEN 1:3–5), when God created light and divided the night from the day, the evening and the morning comprised the first day, as well as subsequent days in the creation week. Therefore, a holiday, festival or feast began in the evening at dusk. You may recall, the Jews implored the Roman authorities that a crucified person should be verified as dead and removed from the cross before sundown if the next day was a Sabbath day. Since the High Sabbath of the Feast of Unleavened Bread was the next day, it would have been a sacrilege to leave Christ on the cross after sundown (JOH 19:31).

Passover (*Pesach*) represents salvation through the blood of the lamb which is a symbol of the sacrifice of Christ on the cross. It memorializes the freeing of the Hebrews from Egyptian slavery, when the angel of death passed over those households that were faithful to God. In accordance with God's instruction, they sacrificed a lamb, painted the door jamb with its blood, and ate the lamb for dinner. The next day, the Hebrews obtained their freedom from Egyptian bondage. Clearly, this lamb typifies the Lamb of God who gave His life for all humankind to free them from the slavery of sin. Passover begins at dusk on the first full moon following the vernal equinox, making it late March to early April. Interestingly, a most sacred time for Jews and Christians alike is Holy Week, occurring in early spring when Passover is celebrated, as well as the two feasts that follow it (LEV 23:5–8). To better understand the significance of Passover read GEN 22:1–17; EXO 13:3–13; EXO 24:7–8; MAT 26:2–30; ACT 2.

Unleavened Bread (*Matzah*) spans one week following Passover, when unleavened bread (matzoth) is eaten. It is prohibited to eat any other kind of bread. The yeast (leaven) in the bread represents sin in one's body. Unleavened bread symbolizes the bread of life and is a reference to the body of Christ which was without sin. Christ was executed for the sin of humanity; His broken body was buried in a freshly cut tomb. The breaking of bread foretells the breaking of Christ's body on the cross. Believers will receive a glorified body, without sin like His, when He returns for His people. See how unleavened bread represents the body of Christ, wherein the leaven, or yeast, represents sin in the following passages: LEV 23:5–8; JOH 6:30–58; 1 CO 5:7–8.

First Fruits (*Reshit Katzir*) is a feast which occurs after the high sabbath which initiated the Feast of Unleavened Bread. First Fruits reflects the prosperity that God provides and our obligation to return to Him a tenth, namely the first fruits or tithe of our increase. An offering to God during the first harvest was required. This festival corresponds to Easter, when Christ arose from the dead, being the first fruits of God. The first fruits of Christ will be resurrected upon His return to be presented to the Father blameless and holy. Thus, we give the best of our first fruits to the Father, and in return He will gather unto Himself the first fruits of Christ's own at the resurrection of the just (LEV 23:9–14; NUM 28:25–26; 1 CO 15:12–23).

Pentecost (*Shavuot*) uses the prefix *pent* (five) to represent fifty days from the day of Passover. Known as the Feast of Weeks, seven weeks (forty-nine days) are counted and the next day is Pentecost. It is linked to the anointing of Christ's apostles after the great commission (MAT 28:19–20). The event coincided with the summer harvest when offerings were given; and the Holy Spirit endowed God's people with grace and power. The Holy Spirit is the truth communicated in God's Word. This timeframe is often associated with the receiving of the Ten Commandments by Moses on Mount Sinai. It is primarily connected with the bestowing of the Holy Spirit to those who sought God in the Old Testament and trusted Jesus Christ in the New Testament. And God will pour that Spirit upon you if you believe in His Word and His works and follow His instructions recorded in the Bible (LEV 23:15–16).

Trumpets (*Rosh Hashana*) occurs in autumn and signifies proclamation; it also ushers in the Jewish New Year (LEV 23:23–25; NUM 29:1–2). In olden days it was a common practice to blow trumpets when an important message or person was declared. The Israelites would hear the trumpets and drop what they were doing to attend a worship service at the temple, complete with psalms, proclamations, and celebration. When Christ reappears to collect His people, the trumpet will sound and all who bear His name will be called to heaven to be with God, to worship, celebrate, and serve Him for eternity. Thus, this Jewish feast recognized not only the coming of God's Messiah, but also His return. This is a time to examine oneself, and establish where the heart is: with God or the world.

Atonement (*Yom Kippur*) occurs ten days after the Feast of Trumpets in September or October. It is a most holy day for the Jews: a solemn time of prayer, confession, repentance, and sacrifice, acknowledgement and recompense for sins (LEV 16:29; LEV 23:27–36; NUM 29:7–11). Of course, the imposed sacrificial offerings given routinely by the Israelites provided only temporary compensation as they had to be repeated throughout the year. God's plan of salvation always included an atoning sacrifice that would be offered for the sins of the world, once and for all time

(HEB 9:6–28; HEB 13:11–13). Hence, we have another link between the sacrificial offerings of the Israelites and the sacrifice of Christ on the cross which will stand forever (HEB 10:5–18).

Tabernacles (*Sukkot*) is another holy week of praise and celebration. This feast makes reference to the church on earth. The Jews would build shelters or booths (the meaning of *sukkot*) as a personal sanctuary unto God for worship and prayer. Worship is an essential element of our faith, a demonstration of a commitment to God, and a dedication of our lives to Him. Christians define a church as being any number of faithful believers gathered together to worship and adore our Savior. The Church symbolizes the body of Christ, as well as the New Jerusalem, which is the city of the Lord in the kingdom of heaven where we will reign with God and Christ eternally as adopted children of the most-high God. We see elements of water and light in the Feast of Tabernacles: light reflects Christ, and water reflects the Holy Spirit. During worship we acknowledge all three persons of the Holy Trinity (ISA 45:11–22; EPH 5:23–27; 1 TI 3:16). Read also LEV 23:34–43; NUM 29:12–40; DEU 16:13–15; EXO 23:16; EXO 34:22; ISA 60:1–2; EZR 3:4; NEH 8:13–18; EPH 2:13–22; REV 21:1–3).

Lots (*Purim*) is not one of the original seven feasts but it is still important to Jews as it memorializes deliverance of the Jews from annihilation. Haman, the right-hand man serving Xerxes, king of Persia, tricked the king into issuing a decree to eradicate the Jews (*pur* means to cast a lot, or gamble). His queen Esther was a Jewess raised by her cousin Mordecai; she appealed to the king on behalf of her people by arranging three banquets for him. Xerxes (aka Ahasuerus) responded by hanging Haman and exalting Mordecai who became the king's principal advisor, thereby saving the Jews from genocide. In celebration, people dress in costumes and enjoy good food and desserts, to depict the feast that Esther prepared for her husband the king. Read the book of Esther to get the whole story; it is a beautiful account of faithfulness.

Dedication (*Hanukkah*) also is not one of the original seven feasts. It was added from the period of the apocrypha when control of the temple in Jerusalem was recaptured by the Maccabees. Unlike other feasts, it was not specifically ordained by God in either testament of the Bible. Legend has it that the temple lamp burned for eight days, though there was oil enough for only one day. It is a feast of devotion commemorating the rededication of the temple in Jerusalem. There is no Christian equivalent although the festival occurs around Christmastime (JOH 10:22–30). Reformed Jews who recognize this celebration will display a menorah with nine candles: one each for this feast and the principal seven feasts, and one candle in the middle for God.

Sabbath (*Shabbat*, meaning to stop and rest) is observed by Jews, Catholics, and Protestant denominations. It was traditionally the seventh day of the week (Saturday) in accordance with the six days of creation when God conducted His creation work, after which He rested the seventh day (GEN 1—2). God's command to the Jews was to cease from all work and attend a weekly convocation (church service) at the end of each week. There also were special sabbath days which corresponded to certain feasts of celebration; for example, it was noted earlier that the week of unleavened bread began and ended with a high sabbath which followed the same rules as the weekly sabbath (LEV 23:3–8; JOH 19:31). Christians acknowledge the Sabbath day of rest and a holy convocation every week. Most Protestants celebrate the Sabbath on Sunday, however, beginning the week with worship rather than ending it with worship, because Christ ushered in a new era with His resurrection on Easter Sunday (MAR 2:27–28). Regardless, we owe a day each week to God for worship and fellowship, but it is clear in the Bible that it doesn't always have to be on Saturday or Sunday (ACT 20:7; ROM 14:5–19). Protestants also recognize "high" days of worship such as Maundy Thursday, Good Friday, and Ash Wednesday.

NATIONAL AND INTERNATIONAL HOLIDAYS AND EVENTS

The calendar that follows provides observances, events, and holidays which are routinely celebrated each year; dates are listed by month. Some observances are religious in nature; some were designated by US presidents or Congress to highlight a virtue, victory, or purpose; some are traditions unique to Judeo-Christian nations; some were established by the United Nations to draw attention to world issues and problems; some were adopted from other countries; some were derived from pagan observances; and some simply evolved over the years to make life fun and interesting. The actual dates ascribed to these observances are provided. Note that many of the dates will change year to year, since they connote celestial events that are subject to variation due to inexactness of calendars.

A Bible study is provided for each day, tying the observance to Biblical references that make the event more meaningful. Thus, while the calendar itself represents the year 2024, one can continue to use the Bible lessons indefinitely, as they will always be applicable to yearly events, seasons, and phases. This book is intended to provide a daily devotional complete with secular explanations combined with Biblical truth. Ideally, the reader will want to complete a lesson every day of the year, and possibly repeat them in subsequent years. Studying the Bible each day will keep the devil at bay, as well as open the gates of heaven to those who believe the scriptures.

The format for each lesson follows a template: narrative, research and Bible study, thanks, praise, and prayer, and commentary. Much like the liturgy used for public Christian worship services, it is a process that will keep the reader focused on the right path which leads to freedom in Christ. It is imperative that we make time for God every day, not just once a week. This book will facilitate that objective and can be used by individuals, families, groups, Bible classes, teachers, and preachers. Therefore, the book can be useful to anyone who wants to delve more deeply into God's Word, the Holy Bible, or to instruct others. An exhaustive study of scripture reveals how the Old Testament is validated by the New, and vice-versa. Scriptural references are provided with each lesson, and ordered from Genesis to Revelation. Again, the reader is encouraged to look up the Bible verses cited in the text using their preferred Bible translation.

Some of the information provided in this book has been gleaned from previous works listed below. These books are excellent references if the reader is interested in researching in greater depth the concepts and scriptures provided in these daily lessons. The keyword index in *Fundamentals* enables rapid cross-reference to literally hundreds of subjects and thousands of passages found in the Bible, many of which are discussed and quoted herein. Lastly, since many days of the year do not have a noteworthy observance, I invented some holidays, indicated on the calendar with an asterisk (*). These are special days for in-depth scriptural study and spiritual reflection.

REFERENCES

Barber, A. V. (2020a). *Fundamentals of Christianity: A Bible Study and Guide* (Fourth Edition). El Paso, TX: Special Delivery Press. ISBN 9780966970234.

Barber, A. V. (2020b). *Message of Truth: The History, Science, and Politics of Christianity* (Second Edition). El Paso, TX: Special Delivery Press. ISBN 9780966970272; ISBN 9780966970227 (e-book).

Barber, A. V. (2016). *Faithbook for Christian Counselors.* El Paso, TX: Special Delivery Press. ISBN 9780966970241.

CALENDAR

THE YEAR OF OUR LORD (2024)

JANUARY

PG	CALENDAR		GENERAL SCHEDULE OF OBSERVANCES
1	Mon	01	Emancipation Proclamation Day (1863)
3	Tue	02	Science Fiction Day 01/02
5	Wed	03	National Humiliation Day 01/03
9	Thu	04	National Trivia Day 01/04
11	Fri	05	National Bird Day 01/05
13	Sat	06	Epiphany 01/06
16	Sun	07	Old Rock Day 01/07; Epiphany Sunday
19	Mon	08	War on Poverty Day 01/08
21	Tue	09	National Law Enforcement Appreciation Day 01/09
23	Wed	10	League of Nations Day (1920)
25	Thu	11	International Thank You Day 01/11
26	Fri	12	First Public Museum (1773)
28	Sat	13	Make Your Dream Come True Day 01/13
30	Sun	14	Baptism of Christ Sunday (Sun. after Epiphany)
32	Mon	15	Martin Luther King Day (3rd Mon.)
33	Tue	16	National Religious Freedom Day 01/16
35	Wed	17	National Kid Inventors Day 01/17
37	Thu	18	Week of Prayer for Christian Unity (01/18–25)
40	Fri	19	First Overhead Lighting System (1883)
44	Sat	20	International Day of Acceptance 01/20
46	Sun	21	World Religion Day (3rd Sun.)
48	Mon	22	Sanctity of Human Life Day 01/22
50	Tue	23	Anointing By the Holy Spirit Day*
55	Wed	24	International Day of Education 01/24
57	Thu	25	Canonization of Scripture Day*
60	Fri	26	National Spouse's Day 01/26
63	Sat	27	International Holocaust Remembrance Day 01/27
66	Sun	28	National Data Privacy Day 01/28
68	Mon	29	National Puzzle Day 01/29
69	Tue	30	Assassination of Mohandas Gandhi (1948)
71	Wed	31	National Inspire Your Heart with Art Day 01/31

DAILY DEVOTIONAL EVENTS

FEBRUARY

PG	CALENDAR		GENERAL SCHEDULE OF OBSERVANCES
74	Thu	01	National Freedom Day (1865)
77	Fri	02	Groundhog Day 02/02
79	Sat	03	Day the Music Died (1959)
81	Sun	04	World Cancer Day 02/04
83	Mon	05	National Girls and Women in Sports Day (1st week)
84	Tue	06	Zero Tolerance for Female Mutilation Day 02/06
86	Wed	07	Beginning of Sorrows Day*
90	Thu	08	National Boy Scouts Day 02/08
93	Fri	09	Army Institute for Religious Leadership (1917)
95	Sat	10	Lunar New Year
97	Sun	11	Make a Friend Day 02/11
99	Mon	12	Sticks and Stones Day*
105	Tue	13	Mardi Gras (Fat Tuesday)
106	Wed	14	Valentine's Day 02/14; Ash Wednesday
109	Thu	15	Susan B. Anthony Day 02/15
110	Fri	16	National Caregivers Day (3rd Fri.)
112	Sat	17	Random Acts of Kindness Day 02/17
114	Sun	18	Two Testaments Day*
119	Mon	19	Presidents' Day (3rd Mon.)
122	Tue	20	World Day of Social Justice 02/20
123	Wed	21	Marx and Engels Published Communist Manifesto (1948)
128	Thu	22	Be Humble Day 02/22
131	Fri	23	World Understanding and Peace Day 02/23
134	Sat	24	Gregorian Calendar Introduced (1582)
136	Sun	25	Samuel Colt Patented the Revolver (1836)
138	Mon	26	Amendment Limiting President to Two Terms (1951)
140	Tue	27	Emperor Theodosius Affirmed Christianity (AD 380)
142	Wed	28	Watson and Crick Discovered Structure of DNA (1953)
144	Thu	29	Leap Year Day 02/29

MARCH

PG	CALENDAR		GENERAL SCHEDULE OF OBSERVANCES
145	Fri	01	Employee Appreciation Day (1st Fri.)
147	Sat	02	World Day of Prayer (1st Fri.)
148	Sun	03	World Hearing Day 03/03
150	Mon	04	Holy Experiment Day 03/04
152	Tue	05	Boston Massacre Occurred (1770)
154	Wed	06	Thirteen Day Siege at the Alamo Ended (1836)
156	Thu	07	Alexander Graham Bell Patented the Telephone (1876)
158	Fri	08	International Women's Day 03/08
159	Sat	09	Battle of the Ironclads Occurred (1862)
161	Sun	10	Transfiguration of Christ Sunday
163	Mon	11	National Johnny Appleseed Day 03/11
164	Tue	12	National Girl Scouts Day 03/12
165	Wed	13	National Good Samaritan Day 03/13
166	Thu	14	Scientists Day (birthday of Einstein 1879)
168	Fri	15	Assassination of Julius Caesar Occurred (44 BC)
170	Sat	16	Freedom of Information Day 03/16
171	Sun	17	Saint Patrick's Day 03/17
174	Mon	18	National Supreme Sacrifice Day 03/18
176	Tue	19	Vernal Equinox (3rd week)
178	Wed	20	International Day of Happiness 03/20
180	Thu	21	World Poetry Day 03/21
182	Fri	22	World Water Day 03/22
184	Sat	23	Feast of Lots (Adar 14)
186	Sun	24	Palm Sunday and first day of Holy Week
187	Mon	25	Feast of the Annunciation 03/25
189	Tue	26	Peace Treaty Signed Between Israel and Egypt (1979)
191	Wed	27	World Theater Day 03/27
192	Thu	28	Maundy Thursday
193	Fri	29	Good Friday
195	Sat	30	National Doctors Day (1933)
196	Sun	31	Easter Sunday

APRIL

PG	CALENDAR		GENERAL SCHEDULE OF OBSERVANCES
200	Mon	01	April Fools' Day 04/01
202	Tue	02	International Children's Book Day 04/02
204	Wed	03	Pony Express Began Operations (1860)
206	Thu	04	National Walking Day (1st Wed.)
208	Fri	05	Gold Star Spouses Day 04/05
209	Sat	06	USA Entered World War I (1917)
211	Sun	07	World Health Day 04/07
213	Mon	08	National Library Week (2nd full week)
215	Tue	09	US Civil War Ended (1865)
217	Wed	10	National Siblings' Day 04/10
219	Thu	11	National Pet Day 04/11
221	Fri	12	International Day of Human Space Flight 04/12
223	Sat	13	International Plant Appreciation Day 04/13
225	Sun	14	World Art Day (observed 04/15)
226	Mon	15	Patriots' Day (3rd Mon.)
228	Tue	16	National Tax Day (observed 04/15)
230	Wed	17	Spain Commissioned Columbus (1492)
231	Thu	18	World Heritage Day 04/18
233	Fri	19	Humorous Day 04/19
234	Sat	20	Husband Appreciation Day (3rd Sat.)
236	Sun	21	World Creativity and Innovation Day 04/21
237	Mon	22	Earth Day 04/22
239	Tue	23	Feast of Passover (Nisan 14)
240	Wed	24	Feast of Unleavened Bread (Nisan 15–21)
242	Thu	25	Feast of First Fruits (Nisan 16)
244	Fri	26	Arbor Day (last Fri.)
247	Sat	27	Morse Code Day (1836)
249	Sun	28	International Workers Memorial Day 04/28
251	Mon	29	International Dance Day 04/29
253	Tue	30	Honesty Day 04/30

MAY

PG	CALENDAR		GENERAL SCHEDULE OF OBSERVANCES
256	Wed	01	Law Day 05/01
258	Thu	02	National Day of Prayer (1st Thu.)
260	Fri	03	National Space Day (1st Fri.)
262	Sat	04	International Firefighters Day 05/04
263	Sun	05	World Laughter Day (1st Sun.)
264	Mon	06	Knowing that You Know Day*
270	Tue	07	National Tourism Day 05/07
272	Wed	08	World Red Cross Day 05/08
274	Thu	09	Ascension of Christ Day 05/09
277	Fri	10	Clean Up Your Room Day 05/10
279	Sat	11	American Bible Society Was Founded (1816)
281	Sun	12	Mother's Day (2nd Sun.)
283	Mon	13	International Nurses' Day (observed 05/12)
285	Tue	14	National Police Week (week of May 15th)
286	Wed	15	International Family Day 05/15
288	Thu	16	National Biographer's Day 05/16
291	Fri	17	Dinosaur Day 05/17
293	Sat	18	Armed Forces Day (3rd Sat.)
295	Sun	19	Pentecost Sunday (50th day after Easter)
296	Mon	20	Flower Day 05/20
297	Tue	21	World Meditation Day 05/21
299	Wed	22	National Maritime Day 05/22
301	Thu	23	Bank Robbers Bonnie and Clyde Met Their Doom (1934)
303	Fri	24	John Wesley Established Methodism (1738)
306	Sat	25	National Missing Children's Day 05/25
309	Sun	26	Holy Trinity Sunday (1st Sun. after Pentecost)
313	Mon	27	Memorial Day (last Mon.)
315	Tue	28	Nothing to Fear Day (observed 05/27)
319	Wed	29	Constantinople Fell to the Turks (1453)
321	Thu	30	Joan of Arc Burned at the Stake (1431)
323	Fri	31	Worst Flash Flood in US History (1889)

JUNE

PG	CALENDAR		GENERAL SCHEDULE OF OBSERVANCES
324	Sat	01	National Pen Pal Day 06/01
328	Sun	02	Indian Citizenship Act Became Law (1924)
329	Mon	03	National Love Conquers All Day 06/03
331	Tue	04	Audacity of Hope Day 06/04
333	Wed	05	World Environment Day 06/05
335	Thu	06	National Higher Education Day 06/06 (also D-Day)
338	Fri	07	Daniel Boone Day (1769)
341	Sat	08	National Best Friend's Day 06/08
344	Sun	09	Inoculate Against Sin Day*
347	Mon	10	Alcoholics Anonymous Was Founded (1935)
350	Tue	11	Beware the Second Death Day*
354	Wed	12	Feast of Weeks (Sivan 6–7)
355	Thu	13	Supreme Court Ruled in Favor of Miranda Rights (1966)
357	Fri	14	National Flag Day (1777)
359	Sat	15	King John Signed the Magna Carta (1215)
362	Sun	16	Father's Day (3rd Sun.)
364	Mon	17	Supreme Court Banned Prayer, Bible in School (1963)
366	Tue	18	Napoleon Was Defeated at Waterloo (1815)
368	Wed	19	Juneteenth (1865)
370	Thu	20	Summer Solstice (06/20, 21, or 22)
372	Fri	21	World Music Day 06/21
374	Sat	22	GI Bill of Rights Became Law (1944)
376	Sun	23	Public Service Day 06/23
378	Mon	24	Roe Vs. Wade Was Ruled Unconstitutional (2022)
380	Tue	25	Melanchthon Presented Augsburg Confessions (1530)
384	Wed	26	Day Against Drug Abuse and Trafficking 06/26
386	Thu	27	Helen Keller Day (1880)
388	Fri	28	Early Church Father Irenaeus Died (AD 195)
390	Sat	29	National Camera Day 06/29
394	Sun	30	Don't Worry Day*

JULY

PG	CALENDAR		GENERAL SCHEDULE OF OBSERVANCES
398	Mon	01	Devotion to Duty Day 07/01
400	Tue	02	World UFO Day 07/02
404	Wed	03	North Defeated South at Gettysburg (1863)
406	Thu	04	Independence Day 07/04
408	Fri	05	Sir Isaac Newton Published *Principia* (1687)
409	Sat	06	Sir Thomas More Was Executed for Treason (1535)
411	Sun	07	International Forgiveness Day 07/07
413	Mon	08	American Psychological Association Formed (1892)
415	Tue	09	Avoid the Occult Day*
418	Wed	10	Be Still My Soul Day*
422	Thu	11	Cheer Up the Lonely Day 07/11
424	Fri	12	National Simplicity Day 07/12
426	Sat	13	International Rock Day 07/13
428	Sun	14	Bastille Day (1789)
430	Mon	15	First Crusade Reclaimed Jerusalem (1099)
432	Tue	16	First Detonation of Atomic Bomb (1945)
434	Wed	17	International Justice Day 07/17
435	Thu	18	Rome Burned Under Emperor Nero (AD 64)
436	Fri	19	Five Women Were Hanged for Witchcraft (1692)
438	Sat	20	Apollo 11 Crew Landed on the Moon (1969)
440	Sun	21	Scopes Convicted for Teaching Evolution (1925)
441	Mon	22	World Brain Day 07/22
442	Tue	23	Give God the Glory Day*
446	Wed	24	National Cousins Day 07/24
448	Thu	25	Learn How to Win Day*
452	Fri	26	National Aunt and Uncle Day 06/26
454	Sat	27	National Day of the Cowboy (4th Sat.)
455	Sun	28	National Parents Day (4th Sun.)
457	Mon	29	Revelation Day*
461	Tue	30	In God We Trust Became the National Motto (1956)
464	Wed	31	Women in Ministry Day*

AUGUST

PG	CALENDAR		GENERAL SCHEDULE OF OBSERVANCES
468	Thu	01	Worldwide Web Day 08/01
470	Fri	02	Rejoice in the Lord Day*
472	Sat	03	Jesse Owens Won First of Four Gold Medals (1936)
473	Sun	04	Don't Lose Your Mind Day*
477	Mon	05	God's Law Day*
482	Tue	06	Angels of the Lord Day*
484	Wed	07	National Purple Heart Day 08/07
485	Thu	08	International Infinity Day 08/08 (8th of the 8th)
488	Fri	09	National Book Lovers Day 08/09
489	Sat	10	Waiting for Heaven Day*
494	Sun	11	Mountain Day 08/11
497	Mon	12	IBM Introduced the Personal Computer (1981)
499	Tue	13	Construction Began on Berlin Wall (1961)
501	Wed	14	Social Security Act Signed into Law (1935)
502	Thu	15	National Relaxation Day 08/15
504	Fri	16	National Airborne Day 08/16
506	Sat	17	National Nonprofit Day 08/17
508	Sun	18	Never Give Up Day 08/18
510	Mon	19	World Humanitarian Day 08/19
512	Tue	20	National Radio Day 08/20
514	Wed	21	Senior Citizens Day 08/21
516	Thu	22	First Geneva Convention (1864)
519	Fri	23	Children of Abraham Day*
523	Sat	24	First Printing of the Gutenberg Bible (1456)
525	Sun	25	Council of Nicaea Affirmed Key Doctrines (AD 325)
526	Mon	26	Women's Equality Day 08/26
527	Tue	27	Krakatoa Volcano Erupted in Indonesia (1883)
529	Wed	28	I Have a Dream Speech by Martin Luther King (1963)
531	Thu	29	Armor of God Day*
536	Fri	30	Titus of Rome Destroyed Second Temple (AD 70)
538	Sat	31	Jack the Ripper's Murderous Spree in London (1888)

SEPTEMBER

PG	CALENDAR		GENERAL SCHEDULE OF OBSERVANCES
540	Sun	01	Billy Graham Crusade Attracted Two Million (1957)
542	Mon	02	Labor Day (1st Mon.)
545	Tue	03	Territories Added to the Union with Treaty of Paris (1783)
546	Wed	04	National Wildlife Day 09/04
547	Thu	05	International Day of Charity 09/05
549	Fri	06	Reconciliation Day*
551	Sat	07	International Day of Clean Air for Blue Skies 09/07
552	Sun	08	National Grandparent's Day (Sun. after Labor Day)
554	Mon	09	First Settlement in St. Augustine, FL (09/08/1565)
556	Tue	10	World Suicide Prevention Day 09/10
558	Wed	11	National Day of Service and Remembrance 09/11
560	Thu	12	National Day of Encouragement 09/12
562	Fri	13	International Chocolate Day 09/13
563	Sat	14	Handel's Masterpiece *Messiah* Was Completed (1741)
565	Sun	15	International Day of Democracy 09/15
568	Mon	16	Wife Appreciation Day (3rd Sun.)
570	Tue	17	Constitution Day (aka Citizenship Day) 09/17
572	Wed	18	National First Love Day 09/18
574	Thu	19	Steadfastness Day*
578	Fri	20	War Was Declared Against Terrorism (2001)
579	Sat	21	International Day of Peace 09/21
582	Sun	22	Autumnal Equinox (3rd week)
584	Mon	23	Obedience to God Day*
587	Tue	24	Harvard College Held First Graduation (1642)
588	Wed	25	Peace at Augsburg with Lutherans and Catholics (1555)
591	Thu	26	National Situational Awareness Day 09/26
593	Fri	27	Ford Motor Company Assembled First Model T (1908)
594	Sat	28	National Good Neighbor Day 09/28
596	Sun	29	World Heart Day 09/29
598	Mon	30	Gold Star Mother's and Family's Day (last Sun.)

OCTOBER

PG	CALENDAR		GENERAL SCHEDULE OF OBSERVANCES
599	Tue	01	International Day of Older Persons 10/01
601	Wed	02	International Day for Nonviolence 10/02
603	Thu	03	Feast of Trumpets (Tishrei 1–2)
605	Fri	04	World Smile Day (1st Fri.)
607	Sat	05	World Teacher's Day 10/05)
609	Sun	06	World Communion Sunday (1st Sun.)
611	Mon	07	World Habitat Day (1st Mon.)
612	Tue	08	Great Chicago Fire Burned (1871)
613	Wed	09	Fire Prevention Day 10/09
615	Thu	10	World Mental Health Day 10/10
620	Fri	11	Day of Atonement (Tishrei 10)
623	Sat	12	National Farmer's Day 10/12
624	Sun	13	National Train Your Brain Day 10/13
627	Mon	14	Indigenous Peoples' Day (2nd Mon.)
629	Tue	15	Spread the Word Day*
632	Wed	16	Boss's Day 10/16 (or nearest workday)
633	Thu	17	Feast of Tabernacles (Tishrei 15–21)
635	Fri	18	Crown of Life Day*
639	Sat	19	Cornwallis Surrendered to Washington (1781)
640	Sun	20	International Human Solidarity Day 10/20
641	Mon	21	Magellan Found Passage Between Atlantic, Pacific (1520)
642	Tue	22	Beware the Son of Perdition Day*
646	Wed	23	Repel the Devil and Demons Day*
650	Thu	24	United Nations Day (1945)
652	Fri	25	International Artist Day 10/25
654	Sat	26	Make a Difference Day (4th Sat.)
657	Sun	27	Reformation Sunday (Sun. before 10/31)
660	Mon	28	National First Responders Day 10/28
662	Tue	29	Stock Market Crashed (Black Tuesday, 1929)
664	Wed	30	Internet Day 10/30
667	Thu	31	Halloween (also Reformation Day) 10/31

NOVEMBER

PG	CALENDAR		GENERAL SCHEDULE OF OBSERVANCES
669	Fri	01	All Saints Day 11/01
671	Sat	02	National Author's Day (observed 11/01)
674	Sun	03	Keep Your Promise Day*
678	Mon	04	Use Your Common Sense Day 11/04
680	Tue	05	Election Day (Tue. after the 1st Mon.)
682	Wed	06	National Stress Awareness Day (1st Wed.)
685	Thu	07	Lewis and Clark Spotted the Pacific Ocean (1805)
687	Fri	08	Rontgen Discovered the X-ray (11/09/1895)
690	Sat	09	World Freedom Day 11/09
692	Sun	10	First Bibles Placed by Gideons in Montana (1908)
693	Mon	11	Veteran's Day 11/11
695	Tue	12	Billy Sunday Preached to 70,000 in Boston (1916)
697	Wed	13	Birth of Augustine (AD 354)
699	Thu	14	Choose Wisely Day*
702	Fri	15	National Philanthropy Day 11/15
703	Sat	16	Your Birthday Day*
705	Sun	17	International Students Day 11/17
707	Mon	18	Women Arrested for Voting (1872)
708	Tue	19	International Men's Day 11/19
709	Wed	20	World Children's Day 11/20
711	Thu	21	World Television Day 11/21
713	Fri	22	National Bible Week (week of Thanksgiving)
715	Sat	23	Pascal Converted After Vision of Crucifixion (1654)
717	Sun	24	Celebrate Your Unique Talent Day 11/24
719	Mon	25	Expose the Grand Delusion Day*
726	Tue	26	Admonition Day*
730	Wed	27	Thanksgiving Day (4th Thu.)
732	Thu	28	Black Friday (day after Thanksgiving)
734	Fri	29	Kennedy Assassination Investigated (1963)
736	Sat	30	Presence of the Lord Day*

DECEMBER

PG	CALENDAR		GENERAL SCHEDULE OF OBSERVANCES
740	Sun	01	National Christmas Lights Day 12/01
743	Mon	02	International Day for the Abolition of Slavery 12/02
744	Tue	03	International Day of Persons with Disabilities 12/03
746	Wed	04	Extraordinary Work Team Recognition Day 12/04
748	Thu	05	International Volunteer Day 12/05
750	Fri	06	Saint Nicholas Day 12/06
751	Sat	07	Pearl Harbor Day 12/07
752	Sun	08	National Christmas Tree Day 12/08
754	Mon	09	International Anti-Corruption Day 12/09
756	Tue	10	Human Right's Day 12/10
758	Wed	11	Hawking Won Fundamental Physics Prize (2012)
760	Thu	12	Washington DC Became US Capitol (1800)
763	Fri	13	Body, Mind, and Spirit Day*
768	Sat	14	Responsibility Day*
771	Sun	15	National Cat Herders Day 12/15
773	Mon	16	Boston Tea Party (1773)
775	Tue	17	Wright Brothers Day 12/17
776	Wed	18	Salt of the Earth Day*
778	Thu	19	First Christian Revival (1734)
781	Fri	20	National Underdog Day (3rd Fri.)
783	Sat	21	Winter Solstice (12/21 or 22)
784	Sun	22	Forefathers' Day (1620)
786	Mon	23	Image of God Day*
790	Tue	24	Christmas Eve 12/24
791	Wed	25	Christmas Day 12/25
792	Thu	26	Saint Stephen's Day 12/26
794	Fri	27	Feast of Dedication (Kislev 25–Tevet 3)
795	Sat	28	Holy Innocents Day 12/28
797	Sun	29	Still Need to Do Day 12/29
799	Mon	30	True Wisdom Day*
803	Tue	31	New Years' Eve 12/31

DAILY DEVOTIONAL EVENTS

January 1

New Year's Day has been the start of the year since the Gregorian calendar began; that day was selected because it coincided with the circumcision of Christ (when He was eight days old). The date is rather arbitrary as it is probable that the birth of Christ was earlier in the year than December 25. But the calendar was set centuries ago and it doesn't make sense to change it again. Many Jews continue to follow the lunar calendar by celebrating the new year in autumn. It is unnecessary to explain what the beginning of a new year signifies to everyone, as it means different things to different people. For most people, it is a day of recuperation from the festivities, travel, and extracurricular activities the previous two weeks. Since most people have the day off it follows that the majority will be glued to the television set to watch parades, sports, special programming, etc. For God-fearing people, a new year represents a new start, and an occasion to celebrate life itself, thanking God that we have made it through another year and are still here to glorify Him.

Emancipation Proclamation Day is also recognized on this date. It was 01/01/1863 when Abe Lincoln formally announced that all people held as slaves be set free (the declaration was issued on 09/22/1862). This decree was aimed primarily at the southern states where slavery was most prevalent, thereby altering the impetus of the Civil War from state secession to nationwide freedom. Thomas Jefferson's original draft of the Declaration of Independence initially included the Negro slaves: he reasoned that life, liberty, and pursuit of happiness was meant for all Americans. Unfortunately, this verbiage was removed from that manuscript in order to get all of the thirteen colonies to ratify the document, which they did on 07/04/1776. Still, though some of the founders and framers owned slaves, a great many set them free with the hope that future lawmakers would recognize this error. Patriots have fought for the unalienable rights of our citizenry ever since, as well as for people abroad; and the fight continues. Many lives have been lost as a result; undoubtedly, many more will die in pursuit of emancipation from slavery. Meanwhile, the battle against human trafficking continues; it is rampant, even here in the USA.

To be sure, the Lord Jesus Christ died for freedom from slavery, that is, the slavery of sin and the penalty of death. Those who believe they are free but have not accepted Christ as their Lord and Savior, are not free at all. Those who routinely engage in immoral, devious, deceitful, and self-indulgent activities are not putting God first in their lives and are flirting with eternal damnation. Christians regard true freedom in terms of eternal life. We trust in Christ for all things, because God has promised to meet our every need if we seek Him and His righteousness (MAT 6:19–34). The salvation of Christ is a free gift to all who believe in Him and trust in His Word; and that freedom can never be taken away. Freedom is worth fighting for and dying for (JOE 3:9–14). This is the good fight of faith, that we fight against evil and for the freedom that faith brings, not just for our country but for all people of the world.

God has given every human being the right and the freedom to choose. If you choose God, you choose life; if you choose the world, you choose death. Everyone has a conscience telling them what is wrong and what is right. So, we know in advance whether we are choosing right or wrong, good or evil, God or the world, live or death. The choice is yours.

- LEV 25:38–42 ~ I am the Lord your God, who brought you out of Egypt to give you the land of Canaan, where I will abide with you as your God. If your brother becomes poor and sells himself to you, you are not to treat him as a slave but as a hired worker and a visitor. He will serve you six years until the year of jubilee (seventh year). Then he will leave with his family and return to his home and relatives, to the land his fathers. For they are my servants who were freed from the Egyptians and are not to be sold as slaves. (See also DEU 15:12–15.)

- DEU 30:19–20 ~ Moses said, "I have presented you with life and death, blessing versus cursing. I recommend that you choose life so that you and your descendants may live. I hope you choose to love God, obey his Law, and cling to Him, for He is your life and He is your time; and you will live in the land which He promised to you and your ancestors."

- JOS 14:7–13 ~ Caleb said to Joshua and the heads of the tribes of Israel, "I was forty years old when I went out to spy for Moses, and I brought him a good report. Moses assured me that I would inherit the land where I had done my reconnaissance. And now, forty-five years later, I am still alive to see God's promises come to pass. And I feel as strong now as I did then; and I am still ready to go to war for the Lord." Joshua blessed Caleb, and gave him the inheritance that was promised.

- PSA 119:44–47 ~ I will obey God's laws continuously and forevermore; I will walk in freedom, for I have sought His rules. I will boldly testify before kings, and I will delight in God's commandments that I have loved.

- JOH 8:31–32, 36 ~ Jesus said, "If you believe in my words then you are indeed my disciples; and you will know the truth and the truth will set you free. If the Son of God sets you free, you will be free indeed."

- ROM 6:14, 17–18 ~ Now sin has no hold over you, for you are not under the Law you are under Grace. Thank God that we, who were servants of sin, have obeyed in our hearts that doctrine which delivers us, being made free from sin, and now serving righteousness instead.

- ROM 8:1–6, 15 ~ Now there is no condemnation for those who belong to Christ and walk according to the Spirit and not the flesh. For the law of the Spirit of life in Christ has set us free from the law of sin and death. What the law could not do, since its weakness was in the flesh, God made right by sending His Son in the likeness of sinful flesh, to condemn the sin of the flesh. Therefore live, not according to the flesh, but according to the spirit. Those who live according to the flesh set their minds on evil, but those who live according to the spirit set their minds on God. To set the mind on flesh results in death, but to set the mind on God results in peace and life. You have not received the spirit of slavery and fear, you have received the Spirit of adoption, and for this we cry, "Abba Father."

- 1 TI 6:12–13 ~ Fight the good fight of faith. Keep a firm grasp on eternal life, for this is why you were called, and why you testified before many witnesses and before God.

- 2 PE 2:1–3, 14, 18–20 ~ False prophets will come bringing damnable heresies, denying the Lord and deceiving many. They will exploit you with false words and entice you with lusts of the flesh. They have eyes full of adultery, insatiable for sin. Their hearts are greedy, and they gain through dishonesty. They promise freedom but are themselves slaves to corruption, and are condemned. They will get perpetually worse.

Dear Heavenly Father, we thank and praise you for the liberties that we enjoy in this country and we pray that you will bless and heal our land so we can remain free. Please help and guide our nation and our leaders, as you have since our inception. In particular, help us always to remember and proclaim that the reason our rights are inalienable is because they come from you, not from people or government. Be with those who fight the good fight of faith, whether here or in foreign lands. Help us to be bold in proclaiming your peace, freedom, and love to lost or wandering souls. Guide us to choose leaders who will maintain our constitutional republic and the freedoms we enjoy in accordance with our founding documents. May your will be done in our lives and in our land, and may we continue to choose you first, and heaven as our heritage. In the name of Jesus, Amen.

January 2

Science Fiction Day is not a formal holiday but it is observed nationally to celebrate the art of incorporating imaginative science into literature, film, and television. Some of the science is real, some inventive, some downright bogus, but it is the thrill of being in another world for the length of time it takes to watch or read a well-presented story. The nice thing about this genre is the sky is, literally, the limit. These days it is hard to find an original story that doesn't have some element of science; with increased demand for bizarre effects and alien worlds it needn't be real to be fun. Science fiction appeals to me as a scientist as well as me as an artist; and if the technology is creative and plausible, I like it even more. Of course, it helps to have a good plot and some drama, mystery, and thrilling aspects. The draw is the vast unknown, from which unlimited possibilities exist; thus, there is plenty of material, although coming up with new ideas seems to be lacking lately, because it is easier to repackage old ideas. What really makes the genre entertaining is when they put in some unusual and amazing special effects. Anything that stimulates your imagination can't be bad until it crosses the line of moral appropriateness.

This date was chosen as a tribute to Isaac Asimov (1920–1992) though nobody knows for sure if this was actually his birthday. Asimov was a prolific writer who penned hundreds of works. Born in Russia, his family emigrated to the USA where he was highly educated and worked as a scientist and professor, until his writing became a lucrative venture. He was rewarded for his science fiction in 1966, receiving a lifetime achievement award, as well as other honors. He was known for his series works such as *Foundation* and *Robot*.

But the genre really got kickstarted when sci-fi books were made into full length motion pictures; this brings to mind great authors such as Mary Shelley (*Frankenstein*, 1818); Jules Verne (*Journey to the Center of the Earth*, 1864; *20,000 Leagues Under the Sea*, 1869); H.G. Wells (*Time Machine*, 1895); George Orwell (*1984*, 1949). Honorable mention goes to Gene Roddenberry who created the TV series *Star Trek* (1966); George Lucas who created the movie series *Star Wars* (1971); and Philip Dick (1928–1982), who died rather young but probably had more successful movies made from his stories than anyone, though his titles were often changed; here is the short list of movies based on his work: *Bladerunner, Paycheck, Screamers, Minority Report, Total Recall, Adjustment Bureau*. Okay, so you probably can tell I enjoy sci-fi.

You might ask, how can we relate this to the Bible? For starters, the Bible is one hundred percent accurate, though a great many people think it is a work of fiction. Well, it isn't, and this actually can be proven scientifically (Barber, 2020a). You may recognize these names of famous Biblical figures who were, themselves, knowledgeable men of science: Daniel, Shadrach, Meshach, Abednego (DAN 1:1–21), the three wise men (MAT 2:1–12), and Luke (LUK 1:1–4). I have grouped the primary elements of proof that the Bible is true into an acronym (HARP); they include history, authenticity, reliability, and prophecy. The following scriptures come from the Bible and reveal many things from various fields of science that have been validated. The reader is encouraged to look up these scriptures and compare them with current scientific knowledge. (For a more comprehensive analysis see Barber, 2020b.)

- Cambrian explosion of the vast majority of unique types or lifeforms (phyla) found on this planet (GEN 1:11–25); there are the four classifications of phyla, in order of appearance: birds, fish, animals, humans (GEN 1; 1 CO 15:39).

- Wind cycles, sea currents, and shipping channels are described (PSA 8:8; PSA 18:15; PSA 77:16–19; ECC 1:6–7).

- States of water (gas, liquid, solid) are fully explained (JOB 26:5–12; JOB 28:22–27; JOB 36:26–30; JOB 37:9; PSA 135:6–7; JER 10:13).

- Photosynthesis and chlorophyll are mentioned (JOB 8:16).

- Irreducible complexity of the universe is implied (JOB 10:9–12; PSA 139:14; PRO 20:12).

- Bloodborne diseases, sanitation, quarantine, contagious diseases, and additional medical knowledge were understood (LEV 13:45–46; LEV 17:11–15; LEV 23:12–13; NUM 19:22).

- The universe began at an instant like a "big bang" (GEN 1:3–5) and continues to expand (GEN 1; JOB 9:4–9; JOB 37:18; ISA 40:12; ISA 42:5; ISA 45:12; JER 10:12–13).

- Layers of atmosphere are mentioned (GEN 1:6; DEU 10:14; PSA 8:1; AMO 9:6).

- The earth is round not flat (JOB 26:10; ISA 40:21–26).

- Refraction of light is described (JOB 38:24).

- The anthropic principle stating the universe was designed for human life is upheld (GEN 1:26–30; GEN 2:9; PSA 8:4–8; ISA 46:9–11).

- The existence of dinosaurs is suggested (JOB 40:15–18; JOB 41:1–7; PSA 74:13; ISA 27:1; JER 51:34; MAL 1:3).

Archaeology has produced enormous insight into the Bible and its historical accuracy, to include the discovery of Jericho (JOS 6); the palace of King Saul (1 SA 9—10); King Ahab's palace (1 KI 16); the Assyrian conquest of Israel (1 KI 19); a reference to King David (2 SA 3); the aqueduct of King Hezekiah (2 KI 20; 2 CH 32); the seals used by Jeremiah's scribe Baruch (JER 36, 39, 45); King Herod's obituary circa 4 BC (MAT 2); the ossuary of Caiaphas, high priest (MAT 26); stone marker stating the names of emperor Tiberius and "Pilate prefect of Judea" (MAT 27; MAR 27); the Dead Sea Scrolls; the ancient ruins of the seven churches of Asia Minor where St. John sent the Revelation of Jesus Christ (REV 2—3); names of Roman governors and officials mentioned by St. Luke (LUK 2:1–2, LUK 3:1–2), and dozens more.

The Holy Bible has a little bit of everything, to include science, history, drama, romance, prophecy, self-help, allegory, suspense, mystery, you name it. Just about every type of literary genre can be found in God's Word, except fairy tales and cartoon characters. As hard as many scientists, historians, and theologians have tried to proffer evidence dismissive of the Bible, in the long run what they ended up doing is confirming it.

Thank you, gracious Father, for your Word of truth; it is truly a remarkable book because it was transmitted via your Holy Spirit and your Son Jesus. Without it there would be no hope of redemption and salvation, and for this we thank you again. We are thankful for so many things it would take a lifetime to enumerate them; and we are guilty of so many sins it would take a lifetime to enumerate them. The best we can do, Father, is to come to you in godly sorrow for the evil things we have thought, said, and done, or failed to do; we confess our sins of omission and commission, those we can remember and those we cannot remember. We are truly ashamed of ourselves and appeal to your loving kindness to forgive us again and again, as we come to you in prayer every day. You are a loving Father and we know we can come to you any time, and you will listen, and you will answer our prayers. We love you; help us to reflect the love of your Son who lives in us through your Holy Spirit who spoke your words into our hearts. Help us to be diligent in the study of your Word so we can share the truth to anyone who is ignorant of Biblical truth. Let your truth prevail, defeating the deceit, trickery, and propaganda being disseminated throughout the world in an attempt to cancel you, those who seek you, and those who follow Christ. Help your chosen people to overpower them with the power of your Word and your Spirit which dwell within us, for your truth will always unmask the lies, whereas the liars have no defense but to flee. These things we ask in the name of Jesus Christ, Amen.

January 3

National Humiliation Day is a day for us to swallow our pride and humble ourselves before God in thanks for His saving grace and undying support in times of war and disaster. Even if you are not religious you can benefit from being grateful and humble, especially when things that looked bad turned out to be good. In the summer of 1775, the Continental Congress issued a proclamation declaring a day of "humility, fasting, and prayer" for the United Colonies in deference to King George III; they were hoping for a peaceful reconciliation of differences between England and the colonists after the battles of Lexington and Concord. Though it did not result in the desired effect, this observance periodically continued. In 1779, General Washington declared a cessation of labor for "humility, fasting, and prayer" by the soldiers. In 1798, President Adams resumed this tradition so the nation could take a day off and humble themselves before God. In 1854, Queen Victoria declared a day of national humiliation, fasting and prayer in England to stifle the cholera outbreak. In 1861, President Lincoln issued a declaration for a day of "public humiliation, fasting and prayer" and the "offering of fervent supplications to Almighty God for the safety and welfare" of the United States. Lincoln feared the country had been forgetting God and the peace that He offers; he wanted the people to "acknowledge and revere the supreme government of God". The USA was a privileged nation, despite all of its flaws, and people needed to remember this in the midst of conflict. There was no particular date when this observance was officially recognized. However, in 1923, Chinese-Canadian immigrants declared a day of humiliation in protest of the Canadian Chinese Exclusion Act prohibiting further immigration from China and causing the splitting up of their families. These protesters hijacked Canada Day which occurred the first of July in lieu of Humiliation Day. Fortunately, that law was repealed in 1947, and Humiliation Day has been celebrated on the third of January ever since. This holiday is now being observed around the world.

What does the Bible say about humility?

- PRO 11:2–4 ~ With pride comes shame; with humility comes wisdom. The integrity of the upright will guide them, but the perseverance of the transgressors will destroy them. Riches are of no use in the day of wrath, but righteousness delivers one from death.

- PRO 15:33 ~ The fear of the Lord is the instruction of wisdom, and before honor comes humility.

- PRO 16:18–19 ~ Arrogance and a proud spirit are followed by destruction. It is better to share a humble spirit with the lowly than to share the wealth of the proud.

- PRO 22:4 ~ Through humility and the fear of God we receive riches, honor, and life.

- PRO 28:25 ~ People with proud hearts serve only to create conflict, but those who trust in God will prosper.

- PRO 29:23 ~ Pride brings a person down, but honor lifts the humble in spirit.

- ISA 57:15 ~ God says, "I will live in the high holy place as will all people having a humble and repentant spirit, because I will revive the spirits of those who are humble."

- LUK 14:7–11 ~ Jesus told a parable to address those who sought the best seats in the house. When you are invited to a formal affair like a wedding, do not choose the seat with the highest honor, for that seat may be reserved for someone else who is more important than you. It will be embarrassing when you are asked to move to a seat of lesser honor. Instead, sit at the seat with the lowest honor; if a seat of higher honor has been reserved for you, you will be shown respect by being asked to move to a seat of higher honor. The moral of the story is this: Those who exalt themselves will be humbled and those who humble themselves will be exalted.

JANUARY

- GAL 6:1–2 ~ Brothers, if someone is overtaken by sin, you who are spiritual need to restore that person in the spirit of humility, considering that you also can be tempted. Bear one another's burdens to fulfill the law of Christ.

- PHP 2:3–8 ~ Do not do anything through strife or vanity; instead, be humble, and regard others as better than yourselves. Do not focus on yourself, focus on others like Christ did, who although He was equal with God, He took on the form of a man. Instead of exalting Himself He became the servant of all. He humbled Himself before others and was obedient unto death, even death on the cross.

- 1 PE 3:8–9 ~ Live in harmony with one another with love, sympathy, compassion, and humility. Do not repay evil with evil or insult others, but repay with blessings. Be a blessing to others for you were called to inherit a blessing.

- 1 PE 5:5–6 ~ Show respect to your elders. Serve each other. Clothe yourselves in humility. For God resists the proud and gives grace to the humble. Therefore, humble yourself before God and He will exalt you in due time.

What does the Bible say about fasting?

- 2 SA 1:12 ~ The people mourned, wept, and fasted until evening, for Saul, his son Jonathan, and the army of Israel who had fallen by the sword.

- 2 CH 7:14 ~ God says, "If my people, who are called by my name, humble themselves, pray and seek my face, and turn from their wicked ways, I will hear them, and I will forgive their sins and heal their land."

- DAN 9:3–6, 16 ~ I looked up to the Lord in prayer and supplications, with fasting, and in sackcloth and ashes. I prayed to Him and confessed, saying, "Oh Lord, great and powerful God, who keeps the covenant and is merciful to those who love Him and keep His commandments. We have sinned and have done wickedly; we have rebelled by disregarding your laws and judgments. We have not listened to your servants and prophets who spoke your name before kings and princes, and our forefathers, and to all the people of Israel. Oh Lord, in accordance with your righteousness, I beg you, let your anger pass and your fury be turned away from Jerusalem and your holy mountain, because of our sins and those of our fathers; for Jerusalem and your people have become a reproach to all the nations."

- JOE 2:12–13 ~ The Lord says to turn to Him with all your heart, in fasting and prayer, with weeping and mourning. Rend your heart, not your garments and turn back to God. For He is gracious and merciful, slow to anger, with great kindness, and He will forgive those who repent of evil.

- MAT 6:5, 16 ~ Jesus said, "Do not pray or fast like the hypocrites do, who pretend to be pious, praying and fasting in public places and before the congregations so everyone can see them. That display is the only reward they will ever receive for their efforts."

- MAR 2:19 ~ Should the wedding guests fast while the groom is with them? When the groom goes away, then it will be time to fast.

- LUK 18:9–14 ~ Jesus told the parable of the Pharisee and the publican. Two men went to the temple to pray: a Pharisee and a publican. The Pharisee said, "Thank you Lord that I am not a sinner like other men, such as that tax collector, because I give tithes and I fast twice a week." The publican bowed low before the altar and beat on his breast saying, "God be merciful to me a sinner." Only the publican returned home justified by God. Those who exalt themselves will later be humbled, and those who humble themselves will later be exalted.

- ACT 14:23 ~ And they (Saul and Barnabas) ordained elders in every church, praying and fasting as they commended them to the Lord in whom they believed.
- ROM 14:5–8 ~ One person considers a particular day more sacred than other days; another person considers each day alike. Both should be completely confident in their decision. Those who regard one day as special, do so to the Lord. Those who feast, eat to the Lord and give Him thanks. Those who fast, do so to the Lord and give Him thanks. Nobody lives totally to themselves and nobody dies totally to themselves. If we live, we live to the Lord, and if we die, we die to the Lord. Whether we live or die, we belong to the Lord.
- 1 CO 7:5 ~ Do not deprive one another, unless it is during a time of fasting and prayer; then come together again so that Satan does not tempt you when you are vulnerable.

What does the Bible say about prayer?

- PSA 19:14 ~ David prayed, "Let the words of my mouth and the meditation of my heart be acceptable to you, oh Lord, my strength and my redeemer."
- PSA 50:15 ~ The Lord says, "Call upon me in the day of trouble, and I will deliver you, and you shall glorify me."
- PSA 119:18, 27, 33, 35–39, 41 ~ Open my eyes so that I can see wondrous things from your Law. Make me understand your rules of conduct and I will meditate upon your wondrous works. Teach me your statutes and I will keep them until the end. Lead me in the paths of righteousness. Incline my heart to your testimonies and not to personal gain. Turn my eyes from vanity and give me life in your ways. Let your steadfast love and salvation come to me.
- ISA 65:24 ~ God says, "I will answer you before you even call; I will hear you before you even speak."
- JER 33:3 ~ The Lord says, "Call on me and I will answer you, and show you great and wonderful things that you have never known."
- MAT 6:6–7 ~ Jesus taught: When you pray, do so in private. Pray to the Father in your mind and He will know what you are thinking. Pray to Him secretly, and He will reward you openly. Do not use vain repetitions like the unbelievers do, for they think they will be heard for their many words.
- MAT 7:7 ~ Jesus taught: Ask and you will receive. Seek and you will find. Knock and the door will be opened.
- MAR 11:23–24 ~ Jesus taught: Whatever you ask in prayer, believe that you will receive it and you will. If you pray without doubting, you can make the mountain fall into the sea.
- MAR 14:38 ~ Jesus said, "Watch and pray that you do not enter into temptation."
- JOH 14:13 ~ Jesus said, "Whatever you pray for in my name, the Father will do it, so He may be glorified in the Son."
- ROM 8:26 ~ The Holy Spirit intercedes for us when we pray. We do not know what we should pray for all the time. But through the act of prayer, God analyzes our needs and answers our prayers in a way that benefits us.
- EPH 6:18–19 ~ Pray all the time in the Spirit. Keep alert and persevere. Pray for Christians, prophets, and priests, that their words will proclaim the mystery of the Gospel.

JANUARY

- PHP 4:6–7 ~ Do not have anxiety about anything, but pray for everything. With thanksgiving let your requests be known to God. And the peace of God that surpasses all understanding will keep your heart and mind in Jesus Christ.

- COL 4:2 ~ Continue to pray and wait for the answer, giving thanks for the result.

- 1 TH 5:17–18 ~ Pray constantly. Give thanks in all circumstances.

- 2 TH 3:1 ~ Pray for Christian teachers and ministers, and pray for the freedom to openly speak God's Word.

- 1 TI 2:1–2, 8 ~ I urge that supplications, prayers, intercessions, and thanksgiving be made to God for all people, for leaders, and for all who are in authority, so that we can lead an honest and peaceful life of godliness and truth. People should pray everywhere, lifting up holy hands, without being doubtful or angry.

- JAM 1:6 ~ Ask in faith without doubting.

- JAM 5:16 ~ Confess your faults to each other and pray for each other so you can be healed. The fervent prayer of a righteous person yields high returns.

- 1 JO 5:14–15 ~ If we ask Him anything according to His will, He will give it to us. If we believe that He hears us, He will hear us and He will fulfill our desires.

As you can see, humility, fasting, and prayer go together, in that they are performed simultaneously as a response to catastrophic events, during times of war and conflict, and when sinning and depravity have caused a departure from God and His will for our lives. This is a demonstration of personal reliance on God and sincere godly sorrow for sins. While it is not necessary to always pray in this manner, the practice was common during Biblical times, and the reference to this practice by former presidents and leaders was a call to corporate prayer, in which the whole of society would join together with a contrite heart to make a humble appeal to the Lord for peace and mercy.

It is required when we go before the throne of Grace in prayer to petition the Lord God, that it be done with a humble heart; ashes, sackcloth, and fasting are optional. Further, fasting doesn't always require the rejection of food and sustenance. It can be a personal sacrifice whereby the individual gives up something, using that time to meditate with God. For example, spouses may choose to refrain from sex during Holy Week, or an individual may give up alcohol during Lent or Advent. Or, a person may refrain from interacting with others during times when they feel compelled to remain in prayer and meditation without interruption. The duration of the fast is up to the person, but a food fast should not include water. It is unadvisable fasting for forty days and nights like the Lord Jesus did in the wilderness; most men and women would be risking serious illness if not death. God does not request that we push ourselves to the brink of death to demonstrate how serious we are, because He can tell by reading our hearts.

Heavenly Father, we lift up our hearts to you and we give our lives to you. Help us to be ready to make personal sacrifices for you and for the body of Christ, even as your Son made a personal sacrifice for us when He took our place in death. We bring our petitions to you this day, pleading for your mercy upon our land, and praying for peace among your people. There is considerable conflict and division in this country, as well as between ours and other countries. With humility we kneel before you and pray that you would bring us back to you in unity of spirit, and help us gather the sheep who have strayed into dangerous places. Restore to us and the nations of the world a sense of brotherhood, where we communicate honestly, we employ integrity, and we show genuine love and respect. In Jesus's name we pray, Amen.

January 4

National Trivia Day was a response to the immensely popular trivia board games, and radio and television quiz shows; as a result, a day was dedicated to sharing tidbits of factual information beginning in 1980. This was about the time the game *Trivial Pursuit* was conceived; though it didn't hit the stores until 1981. The notion got traction, boosting sales of trivia games and variants on that theme. The actual history dates back to a 1940s radio quiz program *Take It or Leave It*. Surely, everybody has a favorite game show; the longest running game show is *Jeopardy*, which has been televised, off and on, since 1964 to now. Trivia Day can be celebrated in groups at work or school, with family or friends. It is a fun way of passing the time while increasing factual knowledge, encouraging competition, and challenging everyone's memory. Learning can and should be entertaining; it does not need to be laborious or exhausting all of the time. Plus, anybody can benefit, from the oldest to the youngest, because learning exercises the brain. Interesting facts generate discussions, ideas, and further research.

Trivia quizzing is an effective means of teaching students, training employees, and spreading the truth. Such games and quizzes make learning fun and enhance participation and retention for all members in the group. It is certainly more useful than indoctrinating students with political propaganda. Trivia games are recommended as a tool for teachers of the Bible. For example, how many applications from the Bible can you think of that are based on the number twelve? Ishmael was the progenitor of twelve nations (GEN 25:13–16). Jacob had twelve sons, the twelve tribes of Israel (GEN 35:22–26). Twelve judges presided over the affairs of Israel (JDG 3—13; ACT 13:20). Jesus had twelve apostles (MAT 10:2–4; MAR 3:14–19; LUK 6:13–16; ACT 1:13). After feeding over 5000 people, twelve baskets of leftovers were gathered (MAT 14:20; MAR 8:19). The tree of life bears twelve types of fruit each month (REV 22:1–2). There are many other significant references to the number twelve (for example, read REV 21:9–16).

Another great exercise for Sunday School and other church activities is for participants to recite their favorite Bible verses. Below are some of my favorites. Take turns reading aloud favorite stories or prophecies from the Bible, such as found in these chapters: GEN 22; EXO 20; JOS 6; 1 SA 17; ISA 53; DAN 3; JOH 3; JOH 11; ACT 2; 1 CO 13; HEB 11; REV 21.

- NUM 6:24–26 ~ May the Lord bless and keep you; may the Lord make His face shine upon you and be gracious to you; may the Lord smile upon you and give you His peace.

- DEU 6:2–7 ~ Fear the Lord and keep all His commandments and laws. Ensure that your children and your children's children obey God. Do this and you will prosper and your life will be prolonged. Love God with all your heart, soul, and might. Keep God's Word in your heart and teach His ways carefully and thoughtfully to your children. Talk with your family all the time about God, every day and night, whenever you are together.

- JOB 14:14 ~ When a man dies, will he live again? All the days of my appointed time I will wait, until my change comes.

- JOB 19:25–26 ~ I know that my Redeemer lives and that He shall stand upon the earth on the last day. And though worms will destroy my body in the grave, yet in my flesh I will see God.

- PSA 51:10–12 ~ Create in me a clean heart, Lord, and renew an upright spirit within me. Do not remove me from your presence and do not take your Holy Spirit from me. Restore to me the joy of your salvation, and uphold me with your free Spirit.

- PRO 16:2–3 ~ All the ways of man are clean in his own eyes, but the Lord weighs the spirits. Commit your acts to God and He will establish your thoughts.

JANUARY

- MAT 6:31–34 ~ Jesus said, "Do not worry about what you will eat or drink, or wear; for your heavenly Father knows that you need these things. Instead, seek first the kingdom of God and His righteousness, and He will provide everything you need in addition."

- JOH 1:1, 14, 17 ~ In the beginning was the Word, and the Word was with God, and the Word was God. And the Word became flesh and lived among us; and we saw His glory, the glory of the Father's only Son, full of grace and truth. For the Law was given to us by Moses, but Grace and Truth came by Jesus Christ.

- JOH 11:25–26 ~ Jesus said, "I am the resurrection and the life; those who believe in me, though they were dead, yet shall they live; whoever believes in me will never die."

- ACT 10:34–35 ~ Peter said, "Truly, God does not show favoritism for any person. Within every nation, anyone who fears the Lord and endeavors to be righteous is accepted by Him."

- ROM 8:28–31 ~ All things work together for good, for those who love God and are called according to His purpose. For those He foreknew he predestined to be conformed into the image of His Son, that He might be the firstborn of many brothers. Moreover, those He predestined, He also called to be justified; and those He justified also will be glorified. Therefore, if God is with us, who can be against us?

- ROM 13:12–14 ~ The night is gone and the day is at hand. Let us cast away the works of darkness and put on the armor of light. Let us behave honorably as in the day, not in carousing or drunkenness, not in immorality or depravity, not in strife or envy. Clothe yourself in Christ, and do not dwell on desires of the flesh.

- GAL 5:22–23 ~ The fruits of the Spirit include love, joy, peace, patience, kindness, goodness, faithfulness, humbleness, and restraint; there is no law against these things.

- PHP 4:13 ~ I can do all things through Christ who strengthens me.

- COL 3:5–10 ~ Put to death the worldly part of you, such as sexual immorality, evil desires, covetous, and idolatry. Because of these the wrath of God will come. You once walked in these ways and lived among such people, but now you must eliminate anger, rage, malice, slander, obscenity, and lies. For you have abandoned the old self and its impure practices and put on the new self, which is being renewed in knowledge after the image of our Creator.

- 1 PE 3:15 ~ Sanctify the Lord in your hearts, and always be ready to give an answer, with humility and respect, to anyone who asks about the hope that is within you.

- 1 JO 5:6–8, 20 ~ Three are recorded in heaven: the Father, the Word, and the Holy Spirit. These three are one. The same bear witness: the Spirit, the Water, and the Blood. The Spirit is the Witness, because the Spirit bears the Truth. We know Jesus Christ who is true so we may know God who is true; we live in Him who gave us His Son, the source of eternal life.

- REV 3:20 ~ Behold, I stand at the door and knock. Everyone who hears my voice and opens the door, I will come to them, and I will abide (dine) with them, and they with me.

Dear Father in heaven, thank you for the Holy Bible and your priceless words of truth. Prepare us to give an answer, with humility and respect, to anyone who asks about the love, faith, and hope within us. Help us to be steadfast in the study of your Word, able to reveal to others hidden truths, miracles, promises, and trivia which are life changing and will grab their attention, motivating them to likewise become steadfast in the study of your Word. Let us be witnesses to the truth, enabling people to know the truth that can set them free through faith in Christ Jesus, in whose name we pray, Amen.

January 5

National Bird Day recognizes the importance of birds which are dear to our hearts. Birds are not only cool they also make good companions. Some birds can actually learn to talk, so be careful what you say, lest your bird repeat it. In recent years many bird species have become endangered due to human predators, carelessness, greed, and indifference. The global ecology holds together in a synergy that, if it gets upset, the system begins breaking down. We must protect our birds, or the ecology might get out of balance. What is your favorite bird, or least favorite bird? For some reason we would choose one bird over another, but rest assured, God loves them and feeds them all the same (MAT 10:29). The Avian Welfare Coalition loves birds; this organization has given Bird Day some momentum, as it is being observed by more people each year. Some of the more radical advocates believe you shouldn't even have a bird for a pet.

Yes, not all birds are for pets; in fact, exotic birds, being in high demand for the sake of vanity, are the most abused. Songbirds make the best pets, but large birds are generally not for indoors. Birds are smart, and can be trained to do chores; and we can live in harmony with those birds. This cannot be equated with keeping captive certain species of birds. A wild bird cannot be domesticated; for example, a bird living in a jungle is not able to tolerate the jungle we call civilization. Even if trainable, it is a disservice to the bird. This day calls out the exploitation of birds for sport, confinement, sacrifice, or sale. That doesn't mean you cannot hunt birds, for there are types designated by authority that can be hunted in season for use as food. I used to hunt, but I quit. I'm glad I don't have to hunt and clean my own chicken or turkey. By the way, there are regulations about chicken and egg farms, but some are far more humane than others. If mistreatment of these birds concerns you, you might research this topic in more depth.

Speaking of birds, they can represent a particular type of symbolism in the Bible. Sometimes birds refer to humans that God loves; sometimes birds refer to the demonic. Of course, birds also are represented as actual birds, highlighting their particular characteristics. All kinds of birds are mentioned in the Bible, to include eagle, vulture, raven, sparrow, pigeon, dove, partridge, peacock, hawk, stork, owl, chicken. Their unique characteristics are sometimes highlighted in the Bible. Here are examples where the Bible compares birds to humans.

- JOB 38:41 ~ Who provides food for the raven, when his young cry to God and wander away from lack of food?

- JOB 39:26–27 ~ Is it by your understanding that the hawk soars and spreads his wings toward the south? Is it at your command that the eagle makes his nest on high?

- JER 8:7 ~ Even the stork in the sky knows her appointed season for migration, and likewise the dove, swallow and crane. And they return at the designated time of year. But not the people; for they do not know God's laws.

- MAT 6:25–27 ~ Jesus taught, "Do not worry about your life, what you will eat or drink, or what you will wear. Is there not more to life than food and clothing? Look at the ravens; they do not sow or reap, or gather food into the barn, yet our heavenly Father feeds them. Are people not more important than birds? Can anyone add a single foot to their stature by worrying about these things?"

- MAT 10:16 ~ Jesus said, "I am sending you out like sheep among wolves. Therefore, be as shrewd as snakes and as innocent as doves."

- MAT 13:31–32 ~ Jesus taught, "The kingdom of heaven is like the mustard seed. It is one of the smallest of seeds yet it grows into one of the largest of trees. Then the birds come and build homes in its branches."

- MAT 23:37–38 ~ Jesus said, "Oh, Jerusalem; you have killed the prophets and stoned those who I sent to you. How I would have gathered your children together as a hen gathers her chicks under her wings, but you refused! Look, now your house has become abandoned and desolate."

Here are some examples where birds might represent the demonic.

- DEU 28:26–27~ The Lord will cause you to be beaten by our enemies; you will attack them with all your force and flee from them in seven different directions, into all the kingdoms of the earth. Your carcasses will be meat for the birds and beasts of the earth, and nobody will chase them away.
- PSA 79:2–3, 7 ~ Your dead bodies will become meat for the wild birds and animals. Blood will be shed like water and there will be nobody to bury them, when Israel is devoured and the land is devastated.
- PRO 30:17 ~ The eye that mocks his father and refuses to obey his mother will have his eyes plucked out by ravens and eaten by vultures.
- JER 7:32–33 ~ In the valley of slaughter, their dead bodies will become food for the birds and beasts.
- MAT 13:3–4, 19 ~ Jesus told a parable about sowing to the Spirit: A sower of seeds left some seeds by the wayside where the birds ate them. The seeds represent the Word of God. If the Word is left by the wayside, it will be snatched away by the wicked one.
- REV 18:1–2 ~ I saw another angel descend from heaven with great power, and the earth was illuminated with his glory. With a mighty voice the angel shouted, "Babylon the great has fallen, fallen. It has become the habitation of devils and every foul spirit, like a cage for unclean and hateful birds."
- REV 19:11, 19–21 ~ I saw heaven open and beheld a white horse whose rider was called Faithful and True. And I saw the beast, the kings of the earth, and their armies, gathered for battle against the King of kings. The beast was taken, and with him the false prophet that worked miracles in his sight and deceived those who had the mark of the beast and worshipped his image; both were thrown into the lake of fire. The rest were slain by the sword that issued from the mouth of the One riding the white horse. And the birds feasted upon carrion of flesh.

It would seem that birds are important in the Holy Bible and to God. God gave to humanity birds and other animals and commanded that we care for them (GEN 1:28). Birds are important to us; we need them. If God loves them, we should love them too. It is a good idea to dedicate a day to birds, and now you know why.

Dear glorious Father, who provides for every living thing on the earth; you give us everything we need to sustain us and prosper us. And if we are obedient, you will give us wings like eagles to soar through the heavens. Today we thank you for birds, and we advocate for birds being abused and exploited by ignorant humans, asking that you would enlighten them so they can see the error of their ways and repent. Bring to justice anyone who abuses a bird or any other animal for the sake of entertainment, for their minds are warped and they do not know you. Perhaps they may think twice if they were to be caught and punished. Help us to be adequate overseers of your creation and living creatures, treating them with respect and allowing them to find sanctuary in their natural habitat. Help us to think of you whenever we see a bird in flight, reminding us of that day when we will receive our wings in your heavenly kingdom. In the name of Jesus, our Lord, Amen.

January 6

Epiphany is the season in which the church recognizes a visit from the magi with the baby Jesus and His parents. The experience opened the eyes of these wise men from Gentile nations, for they acknowledged His kingship. They had traveled great distances following the Star of Bethlehem. Announcing their arrival to the local authority, who was King Herod, they found out where the prophesied Messiah would be born. Herod lied about wanting to worship Messiah, for his intention was to destroy the Christ child. God made the wise men aware of the danger so they departed for home taking another route. We know about the gifts they presented: gold, frankincense, and myrrh, valuable as well as symbolic; gifts meant for a king. Gold represents royalty and prosperity; frankincense was burned during prayer and meditation; and myrrh was used to embalm a dead body, thereby depicting Jesus's death as they celebrated His birth. The wise men got a glimpse of God's heavenly kingdom, and the price of admission which they had found in a child (it is often assumed that the family was still residing in a stable with livestock but this is not confirmed in the scriptures). They knelt before Jesus and presented gifts. This is why we exchange gifts during the Christmas season, because of the precedent the magi established, and the realization that the gift of the baby Jesus was the most valuable gift imaginable.

- ISA 49:7 ~ Kings and princes will see the sign and will come to worship.

- ISA 60:6 ~ They come with caravans of camels from Midian, Ephah, and Sheba, bringing gold and incense and praising God.

- MAT 2:1–12 ~ Jesus was born in Bethlehem of Judea in the days of Herod the king. Wise men came from the east into Jerusalem asking Herod, "Where is He who is born king of the Jews? From the east we have seen His star and we have come to worship Him." Herod was troubled by this. He gathered together the chief priests and scribes, demanding to know where the Messiah would be born. They replied that it would be Bethlehem of Judea, for it was written: Bethlehem is not insignificant among the cities of Judea, for from there will come a governor who will rule my people, Israel. Herod called his visitors aside and asked them what time the star appeared, sent them on their way to Bethlehem, and told them to report back to him because he wanted to worship the child too. After leaving Herod they followed the star toward the east until they stood directly under its light. There they found the young Christ child with Mary, His mother, and worshipped Him. They opened their treasures and presented to Him gifts of gold, frankincense, and myrrh. Being warned in a dream not to return to Herod they departed to their home countries another way.

- MAT 2:16–18 ~ Herod killed all the babies in Bethlehem who were two years old and younger. This fulfilled the prophecy of Jeremiah who wrote: In Ramah was heard the bitter weeping and mourning over the children who were killed (JER 31:15).

    Epiphany means manifestation or revelation; this day is considered to be the first manifestation of Christ to the Gentiles; He had revealed Himself to Jews on the night of His birth. Messiah was prophesied to be the glory of Israel and a light to the Gentiles. The Star of Bethlehem signifies this light. The wise men followed it to their destination, where the light shined on the baby Jesus. No doubt, the Christ child gleamed with the light of life.

- ISA 2:3; ISA 11:1–4, 10; ISA 42:1, 6 ~ God said to Isaiah: From Zion I have sent the Law. From Jerusalem I will send the Word. I will raise up a descendant of Jesse, and the Spirit of the Lord will be upon Him. He will possess the Spirit of wisdom, understanding, counsel, and might. He will be faithful to God and will judge with righteousness. I have given Him to you as a covenant to the people, to be a light to all nations; and all nations, including Jews and Gentiles alike, shall seek Him.

- ISA 49:6 ~ The Lord said to Isaiah, "It is no small thing sending my servant and reconciling the tribes of Jacob, restoring the nation of Israel with those I have kept. Because I also will make Him a light to the Gentiles so that my salvation can reach the ends of the earth."

- LUK 2:29–32 ~ Simeon prayed, "Lord, let me die in peace, for I have seen living proof of the salvation you promised to all people: Your light to the Gentiles and the glory of Israel."

- ROM 1:16–17 ~ I am not ashamed of the Gospel of Christ, for it is the power of God unto salvation given to everyone who believes; to the Jew first and then the Gentile.

- ROM 3:9, 23–25, 29 ~ Are Jews better than Gentiles? No! Everyone has sinned and fallen short of God's glory, and everyone is justified by the grace of Jesus Christ who died for the sins of the world. Therefore, God is not only a God of the Jews but of the Gentiles as well.

- 1 CO 12:13 ~ By one Spirit we are baptized into one body, whether we are Jews or Gentiles, bond or free; because we all have received water from the one true Spirit.

You probably have heard of the twelve days of Christmas (12/25–01/06). Epiphany represents the twelfth day. We see artwork and exhibits showing the three wise men with gifts, and shepherds with staffs; but the shepherds came to see the baby Jesus on the night of His birth, and the wise men came later. Their appearance likely occurred after the circumcision of Christ which was conducted on the eighth day. We do not know for sure if the wise men visited before or after the day of purification and dedication occurring on the fortieth day, but the twelfth day has been the tradition. Since the family had to escape the evil decree of Herod, it seems reasonable that the visit of the magi was before the dedication because the family had to flee to Egypt posthaste to avoid King Herod's evil decree. Then, having received word that Herod was dead, they returned to their home in Nazareth. On the day the family arrived at the temple to dedicate Jesus, there were two witnesses: Simeon and Anna.

- LUK 1:79 ~ The baby Jesus was born to give light to those who sit in darkness and in the shadow of death, and to guide their feet into the way of peace.

- LUK 2:21–38 ~ Eight days passed and it was time for the circumcision of the child, during which He was called Jesus, the name that the angel gave to Mary before the baby was conceived in her womb. Once the days of her purification had passed, they brought Jesus to Jerusalem; they presented the infant to the Lord and offered a sacrifice of two turtledoves in accordance with the law of Moses. Meanwhile, there was an honest and devout man in Jerusalem named Simeon, who had been waiting for the consolation of Israel; and the Holy Spirit was upon him. It was revealed to Simeon by the Spirit that he would not see death before seeing the Lord's Christ. He was led to the temple by the Spirit as the family arrived. Simeon took the baby in his arms and blessed God, saying, "Lord now you can let your servant depart in peace according to your Word, for my eyes have seen your salvation which you prepared for all people; a light to enlighten the Gentiles and the glory of your people Israel." Joseph and Mary marveled at the things he said. Simeon blessed them and said to Mary, "Your child will cause the falling and rising of many in Israel. He will be a sign which some people will speak against (like a sword it will pierce your soul) whereby the thoughts of many hearts shall be revealed." Also present was Anna, a Jewish prophetess; she had lived with her husband seven years until his death, after which she remained chaste all of her days, and now was eighty-four years old. She was at the temple day and night, fasting and praying. She entered the sanctuary at that moment and gave thanks to the Lord, declaring to all that this is the answer for those who had been looking forward to redemption in Jerusalem.

- JOH 8:12 ~ Jesus said, "I am the light of the world. Whoever follows me will not walk in darkness but will have the light of life."
- JOH 12:35 ~ Jesus said, "The light will be with you a little longer. Walk while you have the light, before the darkness overtakes you; those who walk in darkness do not know where they are going."
- 1 JO 1:5 ~ God is light; in Him is no darkness at all.

What a powerful event that was, right? Can you imagine being present at the visit of the magi, or at the birth of God's Son, or His dedication, or His crucifixion, or His resurrection, or His ascension? Well, that's why we celebrate these events. Now, consider this: maybe you will be present at His second coming. What do you think of that? It very well could occur in your lifetime, so you best get your house in order, if you haven't yet. Just as the magi followed the light to where the Christ child was born, all people can seek God and He will show them the light, and that light will lead them to Jesus who is the light of the world.

- ISA 5:20 ~ Woe to those who call evil good and good evil, who put darkness for light and light for darkness, who put bitter for sweet and sweet for bitter.
- MAT 5:16 ~ Let your light shine before others, so they may see your good works and glorify your Father who is in heaven.
- MAT 6:22–23; LUK 11:34 ~ Jesus said, "The eye is the lamp of the body. If your eye is sound, your whole body will be full of light. If your eye is not sound, your whole body will be full of darkness. So, if the light in you is darkness, how great is that darkness."
- LUK 11:35–36 ~ Be careful, that the light in you does not become dark. If your whole body is full of light with no darkness, it will be wholly bright like a lamp that shines.
- JOH 3:19 ~ The light came into the world, but men loved darkness rather than light, because their deeds were evil.
- 2 CO 4:5–6, 13 ~ Paul wrote: What we preach is not about ourselves but Jesus Christ our Lord. We are your servants for His sake. God commanded the light to shine out of darkness, and that light has shined in our hearts. We shine the light of the knowledge of the glory of God whose face is Jesus Christ. We have the spirit of faith. As it is written: I believed, and therefore I have spoken; we also believe, and therefore speak.
- EPH 5:8–14 ~ You were once in darkness, but now you are in the light of the Lord. Live as children of light and discover what pleases God, for the fruit of the light consists of goodness, righteousness, and truth. Have nothing to do with the fruitless deeds of darkness, but rather expose them. For it is shameful to mention what the disobedient do in secret. But everything exposed by the light becomes visible for all to see. This is what is meant by the saying, "Wake up sleepers; rise from the dead and Christ will shine on you."

Father in heaven, we thank you for the light of life which is found in Jesus Christ your Son. Let that light shine in us forever; let it be a beacon of hope to people that we come into contact with. Allow your love to shine in our hearts and your light to shine in our eyes. Help people to follow that light, and receive it into their hearts, so they too can shine; and they will find their way home to you in your kingdom, along with the rest of the saints who believe that Christ is the light of life. Praise be to Him who will lead us to the promised land. In His glorious name we pray, Amen.

January 7

Epiphany Sunday is when the church has a special service about the visit of the magi. It is always the first Sunday after Epiphany, so the date will vary each year while Epiphany Day will remain January 6. Epiphany was already discussed in detail in the previous lesson, along with many of the relevant scriptures. There are a lot of other observances on this date, so I have chosen one that I think you may find interesting.

Old Rock Day is for understanding the significance of certain kinds of rocks, each giving us a snapshot in time. For example, fossils show us what lifeforms looked like a long time ago. Many of these lifeforms look the same today, but some do not look like anything we see today. This is a good day to go rock hunting; take your kids anywhere rocks may be found in abundance. You and your children or parents might enjoy exploring an area and rummaging through old rocks that lay on the surface or are slightly buried. Help each other to start a rock collection.

I've been a rockhound since I was a small child; rocks fascinated me then and still do. There are many differences in their luster, color, cleavage, hardness, age, and type: igneous, metamorphic, sedimentary. Then there are rocks that fall from outer space which are very valuable, and extraordinary; not to mention precious stones like diamonds, which is highest on the hardness scale. Even nuggets of gold can be found, and certain ores can be refined into metal. I still have much of my old rock collection, some rocks have sentimental value, some have monetary value, and they all have scientific value. Teach children about geology, why and where rocks are found; how rocks are formed over thousands of years, while others are formed rather quickly. Either way, rocks are older than we are; unless made in a lab (yes you can speed up the process and produce a rock). How do we know the actual age of a rock? Well, there are scientific ways of determining age; some are more accurate than others, and all have limitations. But for the most part, rocks are old. I was lucky growing up in a part of the country where old rocks are plentiful; sometimes one must travel a few hours to find such a spot. You may have to hike or climb to get to the best rocks; it is good exercise, rock hunting.

Investigating rocks began in ancient Greece and continues to this day. But geology didn't become a major field of science until the 1600s. Geological maps didn't exist until the 1700s. The old earth theory didn't become popular until the 1800s. Radiometric dating didn't come about until the twentieth century; that process involves identifying the radioactive impurities and determining the decay found in the specimen. Plate tectonics became understood, but wasn't validated until recently, geologically speaking (1960s). We can explain how rocks were formed; some of these rocks formed quickly as a result of earthquakes and volcanoes. That's how we get a lot of our precious metals and jewels. Some rocks took a long time to form, as layers of sediment crushed them under tons of rock and dirt. This is how fossils are formed: the organism is buried under tons of mud, volcanic ash, or other sediment. Organic material can become petrified, where the outer material piles up, forming a mold around the organism which rots away; over time, the inner area is filled with other minerals that mix with water and form a stone in the shape of that organism. A great example of this is trilobite fossils.

Geologists and cosmologists believe the earth to be 4.5 billion years old. Not all scientists ascribe to that notion, and a great many theologians reject it outright. It really doesn't matter to a rockhound as long as the rock is attractive. It doesn't matter concerning your salvation either. Whether you are an old earther or a new earther, that opinion is not a core belief of Christianity. What is important to Christianity is the rock of our salvation, which is Christ. If you want to talk about old rocks, don't forget the Rock of Ages.

- EXO 17:6 ~ God told Moses, "I will stand before you upon the rock in Horeb, and you will strike the rock, and from it will flow pure water so that the people may drink. And the elders of Israel witnessed this.

- NUM 20:8–11 ~ God empowered Moses to bring water from a rock. That water flowed in abundance, sufficiently quenching the thirst of the Israelites in the desert.

- DEU 32:3–4, 15, 31 ~ God is the Rock, perfect, just, righteous and true. He is the Rock of our salvation.

- 2 SA 22:2–3 ~ David said, "The Lord is my rock, my fortress, and my deliverer. In Him I place my trust. He is my shield, the horn of my salvation, my high tower, my refuge, and my Savior. He saves me from violence."

- 2 SA 23:3 ~ God, the Rock of Israel, spoke saying, "Whoever rules others must be just, ruling in the fear of God."

- PSA 95:1–3 ~ Let us sing to the Lord, the rock of our salvation. Let us come before Him with thanks, praise, and psalms. For He is a great God, and a great King above all gods.

- PSA 105:41; PSA 114:8 ~ God opened the rock and the water gushed out, creating a fountain of water which poured out over the dry land.

- ISA 17:10–11 ~ You, who have forgotten about the rock of your strength, will sow your seeds and they will flourish, but you will reap only grief and sorrow.

- DAN 2:34–35 ~ A stone was cut but not by human hands, and it struck the image (the statue in Nebuchadnezzar's dream) on the feet of iron and clay and broke them into pieces. And they (the four empires) became like the chaff on the summer threshing floor, blown away by the wind.

- MAT 7:24–27 ~ Jesus said, "A wise man builds his house upon a rock, not upon the sand. A house built upon a rock will stand against the elements, but one built upon the sand will fall."

- MAT 16:18 ~ Jesus told Simon, "You are now Peter, and upon this rock I will build my church. And the gates of hell will not prevail against it."

- ROM 9:33 ~ Behold, I am placing in Zion a stone that will make men stumble and fall. Those who believe in Him will never be put to shame.

- REV 2:17 ~ This is what the Spirit has to say to the churches, "I will give the heavenly food to those who overcome. I will give each one of them a white stone (indicating "not guilty"). On the stone their new name will be engraved (their passport to heaven)."

The Rock of Ages is our foundation in the faith. When Jesus told Simon Peter he would be dubbed the rock, it was because he had a solid faith; when Jesus said He would build His church on that rock, He was talking about faith in Him. The rock of our salvation is the faith we have in the atoning sacrifice of Christ, the *Rock of Ages* of whom we sing. Try rock hunting in church and you just might hear that famous hymn. The chief cornerstone is the rock that holds up the entire church, which brings to mind another great hymn, *The Church's One Foundation*.

- PSA 118:22 ~ The stone rejected by the builders has become the chief cornerstone.

- ISA 28:16 ~ God says, "I have placed in Zion a tested and precious cornerstone to ensure a sound foundation."

- ZEC 3:8–9 ~ God says, "Listen all you high priests sitting before me, for I am going to bring my servant the Branch. See the stone I have set before you. There are seven eyes on that one stone. On that stone I have engraved an inscription which states that I have removed the sin of this land in a single day."

- ZEC 4:7 ~ What are you, great mountain? You will become a plain when the capstone comes forth.

- MAT 21:42; MAR 12:10; LUK 20:17–18 ~ Jesus quoted Isaiah (ISA 28:16) to the crowd saying, "Is it not marvelous? But whoever falls on that stone will be broken, and whoever the stone falls on will be crushed."

- ACT 4:10–12 ~ Let everybody know that it was Jesus Christ, whom you crucified but whom God raised from the dead, who has become the chief cornerstone. There can be salvation in nobody else, for there are no other names under heaven that can save us except Christ alone.

- EPH 2:18–21 ~ We have access through Jesus Christ to God the Father. We are not foreigners, but fellow citizens with the saints in the household of God. His house is built upon the foundation placed by the apostles and prophets, with Jesus Christ being the chief cornerstone of that foundation.

- 1 PE 2:4–8 ~ He is a living stone, rejected by men, but chosen by God and precious to Him. That is the stone of offense that makes men stumble and fall. You also are like living stones, built into a spiritual house to be a holy priesthood.

Hopefully, you know a bunch more about rocks than you did before this teaching. You cannot argue with the Bible because it provides truth that is absolute. It is rock solid in its validity and reliability, both of which have been empirically validated. However, scientific truth is not necessarily absolute as there is an element of error, just like when dating rocks. Unless, of course the Bible and the science converge on the same truth, then you could say the science has been absolutely validated. Otherwise, the standard error accepted in most empirical studies is five percent at best. I would rather be 100% sure; those odds are much better than 95%.

- PRO 30:5–6 ~ Every word of God is true. Do not attempt to add to His words or He will rebuke you and you will be proven false.

- 2 TI 3:16 ~ All scripture is inspired by God. God's Word provides the doctrine of truth, refutes that which is false, and instructs all people in the ways of righteousness.

- 2 PE 1:16, 21 ~ We did not follow cleverly devised fables when we told people about the power and coming of Jesus Christ, for we were eye witnesses to His majesty. No prophecy ever came from the impulse of man, but holy men spoke as they were directed by God.

- REV 22:18–19 ~ For I testify to everyone who hears the words of the prophecy of this book, that if anyone adds to these words, God will add unto that person the plagues mentioned in this book. If anyone subtracts from the words of this prophecy, God will take away their name from the Book of Life, and they will not share in the inheritance.

Dear Father, our faith is built on the rock of our salvation, who is Christ the Lord. Let us glean our strength from Him, the cornerstone of our faith. Let us be solid as a rock in our faith, so that it cannot decay, erode, or be crushed into sand. Help our faith to hold up against the windstorms, earthquakes, and tidal waves that come from the world to break us; for they cannot put a dent in the Holy Spirit who is our fortress and our shield. Again, we rely on all three persons of your Holy Trinity, to answer this prayer offered in your name, Amen.

January 8

War on Poverty Day received impetus after President Johnson announced the initiative in 1964. The date of 01/08 is arbitrary, since this is not an official holiday. Johnson sought to improve our image in the world by eliminating poverty in the USA and helping reduce poverty worldwide, in order to "cure it and prevent it". It was intended to make us look equitable and charitable, but while you can help prevent poverty to some degree you cannot cure it. Regardless, this was the right thing to do but it was for the wrong reason. The idea of educating and training the poor to help themselves was one good idea that came out of this initiative. The Economic Opportunity Act of 1964 created vocational training programs like Job Corps which helped troubled or forgotten youths to learn a trade; and VISTA (Volunteers in Service to America), which was a type of national peace corps; and Head Start, which was an early childhood education program for poor families. These were good initiatives, but the creation of the Office of Economic Opportunity was nothing but a bureaucracy booster; the government should not have been running these programs. Such programs are better handled by the private sector. Instead of the government shelling out billions to help ours and other nations, and trying to run the program as well, they should have been using that money to hire capable Americans to do the jobs and run these organizations. This would have ensured the job was completed efficiently and effectively, meaning well-timed and accurately executed. Note that robust scientific studies always measure those two factors; a trade-off can be determined whereby both indices (timing and accuracy) are maximized for the greatest benefit. If the government tries to handle this level of analysis, knowhow, and logistics you can expect the program to cost double and yield half. Proven charities that help the poor are more worthy of your money.

The purpose of today's holiday is self-explanatory. We can and should help the poor. If you are not giving any of your income to help the poor you are robbing God (MAL 3:6–8). Giving to the poor should not be a partisan issue; it deserves bipartisan support no matter which party is in control. But when we give, we should expect no external reward; if you expect a gift, credit, or praise you give for the wrong reason and you receive no reward. Give the credit to God; if you receive a reward at all it should come from Him, and you will know it and it will remain between you and God. The idea of giving generously means you do not take credit and you do not do it to look good. Jesus chastised the Pharisees for acting high and mighty when they announced their generosity with arrogance.

- DEU 16:17 ~ Everyone should give as they are able, in accordance with the blessings which God has given them.

- PSA 10:2–4 ~ The wicked in their pride persecute the poor. They will be taken in by their own imaginations. The wicked brag about their hearts' desires, and praise those who envy them. The Lord despises arrogant people who do not seek Him.

- ISA 10:33 ~ Those who appear to be high and mighty will be cut down, and those who are proud will be humbled.

- ISA 32:5–8 ~ Vile people will no longer be called honorable, nor will the scoundrel be called respectful. The vile person speaks villainy, plots evil, practices ungodliness, and deprives the needy. His instruments are evil. He devises wicked plans to destroy the poor and the just with his lies. But honorable people make noble plans, and they stand firm in their honor.

- MAT 6:2 ~ When you help the needy, do not sound your trumpet as the hypocrites do in the churches and in the streets, so that they can receive praise from others. The truth is, that is all the reward they will ever receive.

JANUARY

- MAT 23:23–25 ~ Jesus said, "Woe to you hypocritical scribes and Pharisees. You make tithes of your goods, yet you ignore the more important matters of the law: justice, mercy, and faith. You are like the blind guide, who would strain at a gnat but easily swallow a camel. Woe to you hypocrites, for you make the outside appear clean while the inside is full of extortion and excess."

- LUK 20:46–47 ~ Jesus said, "Beware of the Pharisees. They enjoy wearing fancy robes, being greeted in the marketplace, sitting in the places of honor in church, and reserving the nicest rooms for their banquets; yet they cheat widows out of their homes, and for a show, say long prayers. They will receive the greater damnation." (also MAT 23:14)

- ACT 3:11–16 ~ After Peter healed the lame man the people marveled. And when Peter saw this, he responded, "Men of Israel, why does this amaze you? Why do you look at us as if, because of our own holiness or power, we were able to make this man walk? The God of Abraham, Isaac, and Jacob, yes, the God of our fathers has glorified His Son Jesus, the same man you delivered to Pilate to be crucified. It was by the name of Jesus Christ, and through faith in His name, that this man became strong. Faith in Christ has healed this man before your very eyes."

- ACT 20:35 ~ In your labors, give to the needy, remembering the words of Jesus Christ, "It is more blessed to give than to receive."

- ROM 12:6–8 ~ Use those gifts God has given you. If you have the gift of prophecy, exercise that gift according to the proportion of your faith. If your gift is ministry, then minister; if it is teaching, then teach; if it is encouraging, then encourage; if it is giving to the needy, then give generously; if it is leadership, then lead diligently; if it is showing mercy, then do so cheerfully.

- 2 CO 3:5 ~ We are not self-sufficient enough to claim responsibility for what we have, because all of our sufficiency comes from God.

- 2 CO 12:6–10 ~ Even if I had something to brag about I would not. I do not want people to think more highly of me than they ought. To keep me from getting self-centered, I was given a thorn in the flesh. I asked God three times to take it from me, but He replied, "My grace is enough for you, for my power is made perfect in weakness." Therefore, I boast gladly about my weaknesses, so that the power of Christ may rest upon me. I delight in my hardships, insults, persecutions, and difficulties, because when I am weak, then I become strong.

The idea of separation of church and state is hogwash. We need our government officials to heed the Word of God. If they took the time to read this lesson, they might be able to give our citizenry more bang for the buck. The amount of money the government spends on charitable programs is not equitable and it is extremely wasteful. If they followed the advice of the scriptures above rather than pocketing some of that money, they actually could cure poverty, at least in this land. Unfortunately, many other governments won't even let aid workers in the door and often steal the funds that our government takes from the taxpayers.

Blessed Father and Savior, we owe you so much. Thank you for cancelling our debts. Help us to likewise be forgiving of others and cancel their debts. Let us be generous, for all that we give is yours, because all that we have is yours. Help us to give cheerfully in order to cheer up those less fortunate, and help us remember to give the credit and praise to you for what they receive from us. That way our giving will not be merely a physical gift, but also a spiritual one, whereby the recipient will have an opportunity to receive you along with the gift. In the name of Christ who gave His life for all that choose to believe in Him, Amen.

DAILY DEVOTIONAL EVENTS

January 9

National Law Enforcement Appreciation Day is an opportunity to support your local police. Buy them a cup of coffee, thank them for their service, wear blue clothes, put a blue ribbon on your vehicle, or support them in peaceful rallies. The events of 08/09/2014 triggered a nationwide discussion about police when a young black man was shot and killed by a white security officer in Ferguson, MO. Protests broke out calling foul, but the investigation and live video made it clear that the officer shot the man in self-defense. But that didn't matter to radical anarchists. Further, leaders of government injected personal bias into the fray. In response to those who chose to use this as an excuse for violence, a countermovement arose in support of the police who lay their lives on the line every day, and often are forced to make life and death decisions. Police do not pull their guns very often, and when they do it is because the situation has escalated into a kill or be killed scenario; that is, if a perpetrator brandishes a weapon, they must point the gun and be on high alert. A split second is the time they have to react to potential violence or death.

Police involved shootings and incidents that followed Ferguson got elevated media attention by the far left which further fueled the fire, sparking a wave of violence; with looting, arson, assault, and worse, which continued due to overreaction from politicians and propagation by news sources. Governors and mayors began defunding police, relaxing rules of engagement, enacting cash-free bail, commuting sentences for hardcore criminals, changing procedures from stop and frisk to do not chase, and refusing to prosecute misdemeanor offenses while downgrading felonies. This slackening of the law was prophesied: The law has been slackened and sound judgment cannot be found; for the wicked have encompassed the righteous causing wrong judgment to proceed (HAB 1:4).

What do you think this did for law enforcement? It caused many officers to resign, quit, or transfer; consequently, the force has been sliced across many precincts to the point that some cities and suburbs are no longer safe, because there aren't enough police, and their hands are tied from taking proactive measures. Recruitment is way down and voters are leaving states for places where there is adequate policing, criminals are prosecuted to the fullest extent of the law, and all laws are enforced equitably, not just violations that politicians want publicized or prosecuted. Yes, there are bad apples in most every institution or organization; when these people cross the line they need to be fired with cause, and prosecuted if they broke the law. It is unnecessary to vilify the entire police department or officers that are doing their jobs by the book to the best of their ability.

- ROM 2:14–15 ~ When the Gentiles, who were not given the law, do by nature the things required of the law, though they have not the law they are a law unto themselves. They exhibit the work of the law written upon their hearts, their consciences also bearing witness; because their thoughts either accuse them or excuse them for things they say and do.

- ROM 13:1–6 ~ Everyone is subject to the higher powers, for all power comes from God; that is, all powers that exist have been ordained by God. Anyone who resists these powers are resisting the ordinance of God, and those who resist God receive damnation as punishment. Those who do what is right have no fear of the authorities, only those who do wrong are afraid of them. Do what is right and the authorities will commend you. Governments are God's servants; they are there to make sure you do what is right. But if you do what is evil, beware, for they do not carry a sword in vain, but to execute judgment on those who are evil. Submit to those who are in authority, not just because you will be punished if you do not, but also as a matter of keeping a clear conscience. This is why you should pay your taxes, because governments are God's servants who work fulltime in governing.

- 1 JO 3:4 ~ Whoever commits sin transgresses the law, for sin is the transgression of the law.

Without police, citizens are forced to take the law into their own hands; and while they have every right to do so, they are untrained and vulnerable. In states that support the second amendment, you find far less crime because they support their police; and the citizens that bear arms know how to use them, better than the criminals usually. Vigilantes that want to punish others to make a statement always pick soft targets where there is little to no chance of retaliation by cops or civilians. Though an unofficial holiday, Law Enforcement Appreciation Day (LEAD) is catching on. Do you support your local police? If not, why is that? Most people that do not support their police are just going with the flow, and don't even have a personal beef with law enforcement. But they will not hesitate to call 9-1-1 for whatever the reason.

The Bible teaches us to support the authorities who enforce the law and keep the peace. They are given their power by God, and the people who elected them. Those who violate the law should expect to be punished, as long as a system is in place that works. History has proven what works and what doesn't. Anyone with a moral compass and a brain can tell what is or is not okay. If we recruit men and women with this ethic, we won't need to worry about law enforcement, because everything will be done by the book, chiefly, God's book the Holy Bible. But when leaders throw away the rule book, there should be repercussions.

- DEU 1:13 ~ Take the wise men of understanding and notoriety, and make them rulers.
- EZR 7:25 ~ Ezra, since you have the wisdom of God, you will select magistrates and judges to govern those beyond the river. They must know the laws of your God, and if they do not, you must teach them.
- JOB 34:17 ~ Shall someone who hates what is right govern others? Can a just person be condemned?
- 1 TI 1:8–9 ~ Laws are good if used lawfully. Laws are not made for the righteous, they are made for the lawless, profane, and disobedient; laws are for ungodly people and for sinners.
- 1 TI 2:2 ~ Pray for your leaders and all who are in authority.
- HEB 13:17 ~ Obey those who rule over you, and submit yourselves to them; for they will be watching you and will give an account, and you will want them to give a good report.
- 1 PE 2:13–14 ~ Submit to every ordinance of society for the Lord's sake, whether to the king, or to his governors who are given the authority to punish evildoers and to commend those who do right.

Father in heaven, you are the lawgiver and law enforcer. You make it clear what is right and proper and what is not. Your Word is a handbook for all people, including police, investigators, and judges. All laws promulgated by governments are based on your laws and precepts. Help us to obey these laws and the laws of the land, for you have placed authorities over us to enforce the law and keep the peace. Help this nation to elect people that love your Law and that are pro law enforcement. Help our legislators, leaders, and law enforcement agencies govern, serve, and protect in accordance with the truth and the law, and help us to remove those who are slacking the law, who are unsupportive of the people that enforce the law, or who use law enforcement for their personal exploitation and agenda. We were once a nation of laws and those laws were enforced to ensure our liberties remained intact; help us to return to that status, so people can feel free to leave their homes, take their kids on outings, and walk the streets any time of day. Help police to remain loyal to the citizenry, conducting themselves with restraint, understanding, honesty, and fairness; not succumbing to political ideologies. These things we ask in the name of Jesus, who placed His life on the line to protect, defend, and save us from calamity and death, Amen.

January 10

League of Nations Day commemorates a coming together of forty-two nations who agreed to establish an international organization on this day in 1920. Their charter was the result of the Treaty of Versailles in 1919. The organization grew to fifty-eight members before disbanding after two decades, largely due to the wars being waged in Europe. But the idea stuck and led to the United Nations being inaugurated in 1945, with fifty member nations. There are currently 193 member states in the UN today. Their hope was that further world wars could be curtailed by the coming together of diverse countries and cultures. It is the commission of the UN to promote world peace, human rights, and international law. Unfortunately, in recent years the UN has become a political tool for rich and powerful people, and much of their work leads to resolutions that are nonbinding, because they have no enforcement authority per se inside member borders. To their credit, there have been times when the UN helped with certain humanitarian crises around the world. But in recent years, they have become another vehicle for self-aggrandizement by delegates, politicians, and administrators. It would be a great idea, if it wasn't for the fact that many member nations and their diplomats are breaching the very principles listed above.

We are living in an era of globalism; this new world ideology has seeped into every institution, to include government, law enforcement, mass media, public education, even the military to some extent. This has been prophesied from days of old. The idea of a world community is nothing more than propaganda to mask socialism, tyranny, and slavery. But it all turns to corruption. Let's see what the Bible says about this predicament.

- DEU 30:15–19 ~ I have set before you this day life and goodness or death and evil. You are commanded to love the Lord your God, walk in His ways, and keep His commandments, statutes, and judgments, so that you can live and multiply; and the Lord will bless you in the land where I am sending you. But if you turn your heart away, and do not listen, straying from the right path and worshipping foreign gods to serve them, then I will denounce you on that day, and you will surely perish; and your days will not be prolonged in this land. I call upon heaven and earth to record this day upon you; for I have set before you, life or death, blessing or cursing. I recommend choosing life, so that you and your offspring can live.

- PRO 1:18–19 ~ Those who are greedy for riches and oppress others to obtain riches are ambushing their own lives and will succeed in destroying themselves.

- ECC 4:1 ~ I saw the oppression that occurred under the sun; I saw the tears of those that were down and out and noticed that they had no comforter. Even though they had power, they had no comforter.

- ISA 3:5, 9, 11 ~ The people will oppress each other. Youth will be insolent to their elders. They proclaim their sin like Sodom, they do not hide it. Woe to them. What they have done to others will be done to them.

- ISA 30:1 ~ Woe to the rebellious children, declares the Lord. Woe to those who carry out plans that are not mine, who form alliances but not with my Spirit, and who heap sin upon sin.

- JER 7:24; JER 23:22 ~ They did not listen or pay attention, but followed the imagination of their evil hearts, going backward not forward. If they had listened to my advice, and proclaimed my words to the people, they would have turned from their evil ways.

- DAN 9:26 ~ The followers of the evil prince will destroy the city and the sanctuary. The end will come like a flood; the wars will continue until the desolations have run their course.

- DAN 11:38 ~ He will honor the power of forces.

- MAT 24:7 ~ Jesus said, "Nations and kingdoms will be at war. This is only the beginning of sorrows."

    Global empires have been tried, and they failed every time, due to lust, greed, pride, and countless evils. Corruption seeps in and incompetence abounds; drunkenness and debauchery become the norm. Consider the great empires of the world: Egypt, Assyria, Babylonia, Media-Persia, Greece, and Rome. They rose to power and fell from power, only to concede that power to another empire which would fail for the same reasons. There will be a final empire during the end days, which will be commandeered by the beast, who is Satan. St. John had called it the new Babylon probably because it will have a lot in common with the old one. Note that some will refer to the last kingdom as the revived Roman Empire. Despots, tyrants, and dictators are pawns of Satan who is the chief of tyrants. And like Satan, they think of themselves as a god, believing they should be in charge of everything; it is the epitome of narcissism and egoism. When these control freaks lose power, they go berserk; but they already were crazy with their delusions of grandeur.

- JER 6:14; JER 8:11, 15 ~ They kept saying "peace, peace" but there was no peace. We looked for peace but none came; we hoped for health but got trouble instead.

- EZE 16:15–20 ~ You trusted in your beauty, and played the harlot, fornicating with anyone and everyone. You took the riches and fine things, made images and had sex with them. You sacrificed your sons and daughters to your idols. Do you think this is a small matter?

- DAN 8:25 ~ The evil king will exalt himself. He will destroy many in the name of peace. He will oppose the Prince of princes but will be destroyed.

- DAN 9:26 ~ The followers of the evil prince will destroy the city and the sanctuary. The end will come like a flood; the wars will continue until the desolations have run their course.

- NAH 3:1–6 ~ Woe to the bloody city, full of lies and robbery. You prey on everyone; always present are the sounds of battle. Look at all the corpses. Because of the multitude of your abominations with the well-known prostitute, that witch who buys and sells nations and families, I will pour abominable filth upon you for everyone to see.

- 1 TH 5:3 ~ When they talk of peace and safety, total destruction will come.

- REV 13:1, 7 ~ I saw an evil beast rise from the sea. He was given power to make war with the saints and to subdue them. He gained power over all races, tongues, and nations.

- REV 17:5, 9–11 ~ On her head was written: Mystery, Babylon the great, the mother of prostitutes and all earthly abominations. The angel explained the mystery of the beast with the seven heads as follows: The seven heads represented seven mountains on which the new Babylon sits. And there are seven kings, five have fallen, one is currently in power, and one is yet to come; and the seventh will reign for a short time. The beast is the eighth king and was also one of the seven.

    Heavenly Father, who is ruler over all nations, tribes, and tongues; you are the one in charge and we are your subjects. We pray for peace in our land and between nations. The world is becoming a volatile powder keg, ready to explode at any time. Please protect your people who cannot escape what is coming unless you rescue us first. Please do not let the globalists, socialists, and communists bring this country down; they are trying to indoctrinate our children and sway the people with false promises. Their goal is to destroy our republic and cancel our founding documents. We pray that you would block these efforts and help conscientious people of God regain control, and restore democracy and our constitutional republic. In Jesus's name, who is the King of kings, we pray, Amen.

January 11

International Thank You Day is a day of thankfulness and gratitude for those who have had a positive impact on our lives. It is so easy to say "thank you" and yet people find it very hard. I was taught to send thank you cards to everyone that helped me or gave me a gift. I seldom see that simple act of kindness anymore. We send gifts to charities, relatives, graduates, and churches, out of the kindness of our hearts; this is a command of the Lord to give cheerfully and generously in proportion to the degree to which God has prospered us. When was the last time you received a thank-you note for any of these things? The best people can do these days is text "thanks". Yes, it takes time to write to someone, but that is what makes a card or a letter special; because you know they took time out of their schedule to think of you. On this day, we are encouraged to reach out to special persons and thank them. This simple act will bring a smile to their faces, even when they are feeling down. It's a good feeling being appreciated, if just for a moment. The idea of a day dedicated to thanking people has lingered hundreds of years. But in 2015 it got attention from social media platforms persuading people to give thanks to family or friends for their acts of kindness. Users were adding a hashtag to their correspondence (#thankyouday). The day has been observed on 01/11 ever since, and also before; there really is no single author or authority designating this special occasion, it simply caught on. And why not?

We need to be thanking our parents, our favorite teachers, the police, the military, everybody that has influenced us and inspired us to be honorable, optimistic, hard-working, and caring. Most of all, we should be thanking God; every day should be Thank You God Day.

- 1 CH 16:8–12 ~ Give thanks to the Lord; call upon His name; make known His wondrous deeds to everyone. Sing praises to Him and rejoice. Continuously seek the Lord with all your strength. Remember all the great things He has done.
- 1 CH 23:30 ~ Give thanks and praise to the Lord every morning and every evening.
- PSA 118:1 ~ Give thanks to the Lord for He is good, and His steadfast love endures forever.
- ISA 12:2–5 ~ God is my salvation. In Him I put my trust; I am not afraid for He is my strength and my song. With joy, the righteous will draw water from the well of His salvation. Give thanks to the Lord and call upon His name. Make known among the nations all He has done and proclaim that His name is exalted. Sing to the Lord, for He has done glorious things; let everyone in the world know that He alone is God.
- LUK 17:11–18 ~ Jesus healed ten lepers. After showing themselves to the priest that they were healed, only one of them returned to thank and praise Jesus. Jesus questioned why the other nine had not returned to give thanks to God.
- PSA 30:4 ~ Sing to the Lord all you saints; give thanks at the remembrance of His holiness.
- 1 TH 5:17–18 ~ Pray without stopping. Give thanks for everything.
- 2 TH 2:13–14 ~ Give thanks always to God for choosing you from the beginning to be saved through sanctification of the Spirit and belief in the truth. He called you by His Gospel to share in the glory of our Lord Jesus Christ.

Dear Heavenly Father, we give thanks to you for all things good, especially your love and peace. We thank you for people who have been examples worth following in our lives. We thank you Holy Spirit for the sacred Word that teaches us the truth. We thank you Jesus for the gifts of salvation and eternal life which we have been given through your sacrifice. We thank you, Holy Trinity, for all of our blessings and we pray your blessings upon our nation and the world, that people will see the light and follow the guidance of your Word. In Jesus's name we pray, Amen.

January 12

First Public Museum was established in America on this day in Charleston, SC, 1773. The Charleston Library Society was organized in 1748 when a group of men donated money to buy land for a library. They started collecting books, as well as museum pieces. On this day in 1773 the museum was opened, inspired by the opening of a British Museum in 1753. A fire destroyed much of the museum in 1778, but it was rebuilt, restocked, and reopened about a decade later. The museum was closed during the Revolutionary War and again during the Civil War.

Museums are great learning tools, because they are fun. Whenever learning can be fun it's a good thing. I always liked museums, especially art and science. If you like museums, go to Washington DC and check out the Smithsonian Institution, where there are seventeen different museums, and the admission is free. They have been around since 1846. James Smithson willed his fortune (about half a million dollars) to the US when he died in 1829. President Jackson ordered Congress to collect the money and place it into the treasury. In 1846 the Smithsonian was founded using that money. The institution obtained fame in 1964 when Sidney Ripley began to manage it; he added eight museums. I used to enjoy his "believe it or not" books. Smithsonian museums are also located in New York and Virginia. These museums feature works of art, historical artifacts, cultural relics, scientific exhibits such as rocks, dinosaur bones, aviation and space, something for everybody. They operate with federal funds and donations. Twenty-five million people visit these museums annually.

Do you like museums? I've enjoyed museums ever since I was a tot. I have yet to visit the Museum of the Bible, recently installed in DC, 2017. I like Biblical memorabilia. I have been fascinated by Biblical archaeology and its contribution to the body of evidence proving the historicity of the Bible. Biblical records and archaeological science converge on numerous points of reference. I have written about this often, outlining the findings and where associated citations can be found in the Bible (see References). Below are but a few tidbits for you to peruse.

- GEN 19:24–25 ~ God rained fire and brimstone upon Sodom and Gomorrah. He destroyed those cities, the plains, the inhabitants, and everything that was alive or growing.

- JDE 1:7 ~ Sodom and Gomorrah, and other cities and peoples who were destroyed because of their wickedness, are examples of the vengeance of eternal fire that awaits the wicked.

- Finding: Ruins buried in brimstone (i.e., sulfur) and ash alongside the Dead Sea and the banks of the Jordan River indicate multiple cities were razed to the ground thousands of years ago.

- EXO 14:13–31 ~ Moses told the people, "Do not be afraid of the Egyptians. Stand and watch, and you will see the salvation of the Lord; for after this day you will never see the Egyptians again." Moses lifted up his rod and the Red Sea parted, then the Israelites crossed on dry land. The Egyptian charioteers gave chase, but the wheels got stuck in the mud. Then the Red Sea closed in on them and the army was drowned. The people saw what the Lord did to the Egyptians and they feared the Lord and believed in God and His servant Moses.

- Finding: Intact Egyptian chariot wheels (circa 1500 BC) were found covered with coral at the bottom of the Red Sea, from the time of Moses and the exodus of the Hebrews.

- PSA 21:1–4 ~ King David wrote: Oh Lord, I rejoice in your strength and in your victories. You have given me the desires of my heart and you have satisfied all the requests of my lips. You have welcomed me with rich blessings and placed a crown of pure gold on my head. I asked for life and you provided it, to last forever and ever.

- 2 SA 23:5 ~ David proclaimed as he was dying, "Is my house right with God? Has He not provided to me an everlasting covenant that will bring salvation and fulfill all my desire?"

– Finding: Tel Dan stele from Aram (dated approximately 775 BC) was found with this Aramaic inscription: *House of David*. This is one of few ancient references to King David. Most records of what he accomplished were destroyed by the Assyrians and the Babylonians, wanting to wipe out any record of David, his accomplishments, and their own defeats.

- 2 KI 20:20 ~ The rest of the acts of Hezekiah and his might, and how he made the pool using a conduit—are they not written in the book of the chronicles of the kings of Judah?

- 2 CH 32:30 ~ Hezekiah stopped the upper watercourse of Gihon and diverted it to the west side of the city of David. King Hezekiah prospered in all of his works.

- JOH 9:1–7 ~ Jesus came across a man who was blind from birth. His disciples asked Him whose sin caused the man to be born blind. Jesus said not his sin or his father's sin, but that the power of the Lord would be manifested through him. Jesus proceeded to make paste from his spittle mixed with dirt. He took the clay and put it over each eye and instructed the man to wash in the pool of Siloam. He did as Jesus instructed and returned with perfect vision.

– Finding: Siloam tunnel (circa 700 BC) exists in Akra, a suburb of Jerusalem. It still brings water from the Gihon Spring into the city. A Hebrew inscription in the wall chronicles King Hezekiah who commissioned the project. Jesus healed a man born blind by instructing him to wash the clay from his eyes in the pool of Siloam.

- JOH 5:1–10 ~ Jesus was going to Jerusalem for a feast of the Jews. Close to the sheep market was the pool of Bethesda, having five porches. Folks who were handicapped, whether blind, lame, or emaciated, would wait for the water to stir; the first to step into the water was healed of their disease. There was a man who had been waiting eight years, having lived with his infirmity thirty additional years. Jesus asked him if he would like to be made whole. He said yes, but he had nobody to lead him to the pool when it stirred; somebody would always jump in front of him. Jesus said to the man, "Rise, take up your bed and walk." Immediately the man got up, grabbed his bedding and walked away. Some of the Jews rebuked the man saying, "It is unlawful for you to carry your bed on the sabbath."

– Finding: The pool of Bethesda (third century BC) where Jesus healed the lame man, was described as having five porches. This landmark is a very popular tourist attraction in Jerusalem.

    Father in heaven, you are wise beyond human understanding. We are ignorant and need to be guided like sheep to green pastures and still waters. We thank you, Jesus, our shepherd who protects us and nurtures us, and who will lead your flock through the gates of heaven on the last day. We thank you for your Word, dictated by your Holy Spirit to the authors of the Bible, so we would know the truth. And still, we have doubts and questions. But you provided external evidence for our kind to find which confirmed your Word as true, and for this we are grateful, for it surely alleviates doubt knowing there is forensic proof. Some of us need more convincing than others; help everyone to be convinced of the truth whether they find it in your book of nature or in your book of scripture. Truly, truth will not contradict either one for you are the author of the universe. Thank you for providing artifacts from the past to help us realize that Bible history is not a collection of tall tales, but real stories that happened to real people; such findings convince many who seek to refute the Word. You have made things known to us about your works and ways, and they are still applicable now and until the end of time. Thank you for everything; we are so blessed and we love you, your Spirt and your Son, Abba Father.

January 13

Make Your Dream Come True Day reminds us never to give up on our aspirations and ambitions. It is uncertain when people started celebrating this day, or how 01/13 became the designated date; but the idea has been around for decades. We do know that with God all things are possible, but not all things are in accordance with the will of God. Any reasonable person will not dream of something crazy, evil, or stupid. For example, winning a billion dollars is not a dream or a vision, it is a wish for material riches; the fact is, winning the lottery doesn't always turn out to be a blessing. But here in the USA, people have the freedom to pursue their dreams and wishes as long as they are legal. Dreams can be large or small; they can be stepping stones or an ultimate goal. Either way, they give us hope; and if your hope is in God, He will help you make those dreams come true. However, you must be committed to your goals in order to make the necessary effort. Desire mixed with effort bring about the best results (Barber, 2020b).

Everyone dreams when they are asleep; most of the time we do not remember them unless they are vivid or we wake up and the dream is still fresh in our minds. Occasionally, God or His angels will give us messages in our dreams; but beware, because evil spirits may also try to embed information while you are inside of the deepest furrows of consciousness. You dream while you are asleep and daydream when you are awake, and the content may be interesting enough to make a note of it in your journal or diary. I recommend everyone have a dream diary, making notes, diagrams, and pictures of what comes to mind; there is much to be learned about oneself and the trends emanating from the unconscious mind. Even nightmares are worth analyzing. As a student of psychology, I studied dreams and dream analysis extensively; I learned to analyze dreams, which I would do with my own dreams, as well as certain clientele who wished to explore their dreams more fully. There is insight and inspiration to be found by exploring your mind, which in the Greek is *psyche* meaning soul.

I often conducted a group therapy session which I called *Vision of Hope*. We explored ways of creating a vision of hope and breaking down the steps, tasks, and objectives of reaching a specific goal, to include a workable timeline. The purpose was for the participants to imagine what hope would look like, sound like, feel like, even taste or smell like: experiencing it with all their senses, and giving them a framework to be illustrated or described. Putting it on paper made the vision real and not merely imaginary; and by breaking the hope down into goals and associated steps, it made the vision possible. Building hope in this manner raises faith, which defeats uncertainty; that is, the individual can start believing in the things for which they hope.

- JOB 8:13–14 ~ The destiny of those who forget God is the loss of hope, for their trust in worldly things is a fragile one.

- JOB 11:18, 20 ~ You will be confident because there is hope; you will be protected, so take rest in your safety. But the wicked will not escape; their hope will be like taking their last breath.

- PSA 130:5 ~ I wait for the Lord, my soul waits; and in His Word I have hope.

- PRO 26:12 ~ Do you see a man who is wise in his own eyes? There is more hope for a fool than for him.

- HAB 2:2–3 ~ The Lord answered me: "Write the vision; make it plain on tablets, so he may run who reads it. For the vision awaits its appointed time, hastening to the end; it will not lie. If it seems slow, wait for it; it will surely come without delay."

- JER 29:11 ~ For I know the plans I have for you, declares the Lord, plans for welfare and not for evil, to give you a future and a hope.

- ROM 15:13 ~ May the God of hope fill you with all joy and peace in believing, so that by the power of the Holy Spirit you may abound in hope.
- 1 CO 12:31 ~ If you eagerly desire the greater gifts, I will show you the most excellent way.

The cure for hopelessness and despair is hope. They are opposites, but hope is the greater power because it is from God and lives inside the heart; whereas despair comes from a lack of hope, originating from the worries of the world. Hope is a fruit of the spirit; hopelessness is fruitless. When a person gives up on their dreams or goals it is because they are experiencing despair which leads to clinical depression. Rejoicing in hope will defeat them both.

- JOB 4:6 ~ Is the fear of God your confidence, and the integrity of your ways your hope?
- JOB 31:24–28 ~ If I placed my hope and confidence in wealth, and I rejoiced in how much of it I had attained, or if I was enticed by the beauty of the sun and moon such that they became an object of my affection, I would be guilty of disregarding God.
- PSA 130:5 ~ I wait for the Lord, my soul waits; and in His Word I have hope.
- LAM 3:21–22 ~ I have hope because the steadfast love of the Lord never ceases and His mercies never end.
- ROM 5:2–5 ~ Through Jesus we have obtained access to His grace in which we stand, and we rejoice in our hope of sharing the glory of God. We rejoice in our sufferings knowing that they produce endurance, which produces character, which produces hope. And hope does not disappoint us, because God's love has been poured into our hearts through the Holy Spirit.
- ROM 8:19–20, 24–25 ~ All creation waits eagerly for the revealing of the children of God. For the creation was subjected to futility, not of its own will, but by the will of Him who subjected it in hope. In this hope we were saved. However, hope that is seen is not really hope; for who hopes for what one has? But if we hope for what we do not see, we must wait for it patiently.
- 1 TI 6:17 ~ Tell the rich people in the world not to act so proud or to set their hopes on uncertain earthly riches. Tell them to set their hope and trust in God, who furnishes everything in this world for us to enjoy.

Make Your Dream Come True Day is a great time to reconsider what is important in life, and where or who you want to be a year or five years from today. It is a time to renew hope and provide encouragement to those who have all but given up. The best way to meet your goals is first to ensure they are in alignment with the will of God. If you believe in Him, you have hope for your future, even your eternity. You also need to believe in yourself. Abandon the negativity, such as "I can't" "it's too hard" "it's taking too long" or "I'm too old or young". Change the self-message to "I can do all things through Christ who strengthens me" (PHP 4:13). Repeat that often enough until you believe it, seeing how it is the truth; or remember the words, "I have a dream," uttered by Martin Luther King at the Washington DC mall in 1963; his dream came true.

Dear Father, who makes our deepest dreams come true; you have guaranteed eternal life to all who would believe in your Word and your Son who lived for us so that we could live in your kingdom. And though we do not deserve such royal treatment, you have promised it because of what Jesus accomplished through His life, death, and resurrection. Now we have hope for the resurrection, that we will be raised to receive a glorified body like Christ, free from sin, worry, despair, or gloom. Help us to look forward to that day with new hope, and believe without wavering. Help us to develop righteous goals, and help us to stay on track by the power of your Holy Spirit who inspires us and enables us to achieve these goals. In the name of Jesus Christ we pray, Amen.

January 14

Baptism of Christ Sunday is a church observance that takes place the week after Epiphany Sunday. We do not know the day or month when Jesus was baptized in the Jordan River by John the Baptist. But it was likely close to His thirtieth birthday; for it was the Jewish practice that a priest or prophet had achieved maturity for such a responsibility at age thirty. It is reasonable to assume that the Lord's baptism was closer to the date of His birth, which was probably in the fall during the Feast of Tabernacles. Like Christmas, this date is arbitrary but the meaning is crucial. I mean, why would Jesus need to be baptized? He did not carry original sin for He was sinless, conceived by the Holy Spirit. The answer is rather simple: Jesus lived by example and baptism was an example He wanted us to follow. This is why it is called a sacrament, because Christ endorsed it with His own participation. The only other sacrament that Jesus participated in personally, was the Eucharist. Though, the Catholics list seven sacraments including marriage and confirmation, only two sacraments did Jesus participate in. Thus, Protestant denominations include Holy Baptism and Holy Communion as sacraments. Marriage, confirmation, confession and other acts of faith are regarded as rites, rituals, or rules, because they do not employ physical elements to confer forgiveness or sanctification, though they surely can be spiritually relevant.

Jesus was baptized by His cousin, John, the son of Elisabeth who jumped for joy inside her womb when hearing mother Mary's voice as she carried Jesus in her womb (LUK 1:41). It was prophesied that a forerunner would declare the Messiah, and that man was John the Baptist. Note, on the day of Jesus's baptism, all three persons of the Holy Trinity were present. After being baptized, Jesus went across the river into the wilderness where He was tempted by Satan. After rebuking Satan, Jesus returned across the Jordan where John was baptizing; John immediately declared, "Behold the Lamb of God who takes away the sin of the world" (JOH 1:29). Disciples following John were handed off to Jesus right then and there, just as John himself had prophesied as well as Old Testament prophets.

- ISA 40:3 ~ The one crying in the wilderness will prepare the way for the Lord; he will clear a straight path in the desert to be a highway for our God.

- MAL 3:1–3 ~ God will send a messenger to prepare the coming of Messiah. But who can endure His coming? For He is like a refiner's fire which completely removes all impurities and imperfections.

- MAT 3:1–3, 11 ~ John the Baptist came preaching in the wilderness of Judea, saying, "Repent for the kingdom of heaven is near." This man is the person spoken of by Isaiah who said, "The voice of the one crying in the wilderness will prepare the way of the Lord, making straight a pathway to Him." John told the people, "Indeed, I baptize you with water unto repentance. But He who comes after me is mightier than I; I am not worthy of untying His shoes. He will baptize you with the Holy Spirit, and with fire."

- MAT 3:14–17; LUK 3:21–22 ~ Jesus came to John to be baptized and John said, "Why do you come to me for baptism? It is I who needs to be baptized by you." Jesus replied, "Let it be this way for now to fulfill all righteousness." So, John baptized Jesus. When Jesus arose from the water the heavens were opened and the Spirit of God descended like a dove, lighting upon Christ. And a voice from heaven declared, "This is my beloved Son, who pleases me immensely." (See also LUK 9:35.)

- LUK 1:11–20, 26–38 ~ The angel Gabriel told Zechariah he would have a son in his old age (John the Baptist). Gabriel told Mary that she would give birth to the Son of God (Jesus Christ).

- LUK 1:76–77 ~ John the Baptist, a prophet of the most high God, went before the Lord to prepare the way for Him, and to give His people knowledge of salvation through forgiveness of sins.

- JOH 1:15, 18, 30 ~ John the Baptist said that Jesus would come after him, that He ranks above him, and that He existed before him. He said that only the Son, who is in the Father's bosom, knows the Father.

Different denominations have different processes and age requirements for baptism. Either way, baptism is a sacrament involving public witness of a commitment to Jesus Christ. It is a solemn event whereby the Holy Spirit is conveyed through the elements, and forgiveness of sins is bestowed. When a person first believes he or she is saved by Jesus, it is advisable that he or she be baptized once, whatever the age.

- EZE 36:24–28 ~ I will remove you from among the heathen, gather you out of all countries, and bring you into your own land. Then I will sprinkle clean water upon you, and you will be cleansed of all filth; from your idols I will I cleanse you. A new heart I will give you; and a new spirit I will put inside you. I will take away the heart of stone and place my Spirit within you. And you will walk in my statutes and keep my judgments. You will live in the land I gave to your fathers; and you will be my people and I will be your God.

- JOH 3:3–6 ~ Jesus said, "Unless a person is born again, he cannot see God's kingdom." Nicodemus asked, "How can someone be born when they are old?" Jesus answered, "Unless a person is born of water and of the Holy Spirit he cannot enter into God's kingdom. Those who are born of the flesh are flesh, and those who are born of the Spirit are Spirit."

- ACT 2:38–41 ~ Peter said, "Repent and be baptized every one of you, in the name of Jesus Christ for the remission of sins, and you will receive the gift of the Holy Spirit. This promise pertains to you, to your children, and to people everywhere: to whomever the Lord calls." Those who gladly listened to Peter's testimony were baptized, numbering about three thousand souls.

- ROM 6:3–4 ~ Paul wrote: Do you not know that anyone who is baptized into Jesus Christ has been baptized unto death? Therefore, we who were baptized will be buried with Him, and as He was raised from the dead, so we shall receive a new life.

- 1 CO 12:13 ~ By one Spirit we are baptized into one body, regardless of our race or economic status; therefore, we all are nourished by one Spirit.

- GAL 3:27 ~ Whoever has been baptized into Christ has put on Christ like a suit of armor.

- EPH 4:4–5 ~ There is only one body, one Spirit, one Lord, one faith, and one baptism.

- EPH 5:26 ~ We are cleansed from sin by the washing of water and the Word (Christ's blood).

- 1 PE 3:21 ~ Baptism will also save us through the resurrection of Jesus Christ. Baptism does not mean washing a dirty body, but rather establishing a clean conscience toward God.

Dear Father in heaven, whose Spirit came down to earth landing upon Jesus as He was being baptized saying, "This is my beloved Son in whom I delight." Please have your Spirit cover us with His comfort and speak your truth into our ears; let those words be written upon our hearts and minds. We have been cleansed through baptism and purified by Christ's blood. As we grow in our faith through baptism, prayer, learning, communion, public worship and fellowship, help us to be refreshed each time by your Spirit, and grow that much stronger in our faith, all the while strengthening others in their faith in Jesus, whose example we try to follow, Amen.

January 15

Martin Luther King Day is a federal holiday commemorating the birthday of the famous civil rights leader and evangelist. His actual birthday was 01/15/1929, but the holiday is observed the third Monday of the month, which in 2024 will be the same date. The Nobel Prize laureate was assassinated in 1968 in Memphis, TN. In 1983, President Reagan signed into law the official day of recognition for this patriotic man of God. The first year that all fifty states celebrated the holiday together was on 01/15/2000. See also the lesson on his dream speech (08/28)

Dr. King was influenced by the nonviolent methods of Gandhi, peacefully marching and protesting the mistreatment and segregation of blacks. Many establishment politicians and law enforcement officials saw him as a threat, particularly in the south, and he was constantly harassed, jailed, and in danger from repeated death threats. But a large movement got behind him, so many antagonists were hesitant to act out on their disdain. One year after the dream speech, the Civil Rights Act of 1964 was passed. King also was awarded the Nobel Peace Prize that year. In 1965, Congress passed the Voting Rights Act to stop discrimination against black voters by using literacy tests, poll taxes, and other atrocities. King continued his crusade and his popularity grew, as did the ire of diehard racists. King was assassinated on 04/04/1968 by James Earl Ray, mostly for the fame; Ray was finally captured in London, returned to the US for trial, and sentenced to life in prison where he died shortly thereafter.

King was quoted often, most notably for a speech in Washington DC, 1963, where before a quarter of a million people he said, "I have a dream that my four little children will one day live in a nation where they will not be judged by the color of their skin but by the content of their character." King did not realize that dream in his lifetime, which was cut short by an assassin. And, although it took years for equality to spread throughout America, King gave the movement the impetus it needed. Electing a black man as president proved that this country is not racist. Yes, many people still hate other people for no good reason when they do not have the love of God.

- PRO 26:24–28 ~ Hateful people conceal their hatred with deceitful words, but in their heart lives anger. They may try to disguise their hate, but eventually it will become exposed to everyone. They are digging a hole that they will fall into themselves; they are rolling a stone that eventually will crush them. Those who lie also hate the people they lie about; while their flattering words create only ruin.

- ISA 3:9 ~ It shows on their faces that they are guilty; they declare their sin like Sodom, they do not hide it. Woe unto their souls for they have recompensed evil unto themselves.

- ROM 12:16–18 ~ Do not be high-minded, but humble yourselves to others who are lowly; do not consider yourself wise by your own conceit. Never reward evil for evil; be honest and peaceful with all people.

- JAM 3:17 ~ Wisdom from heaven is pure, merciful, gentle, peaceful, and easily obtained. It always produces positive results that are impartial, straightforward, and sincere.

Father of humankind and author of the universe, we have been a free nation since the beginning of our founding, though it took a long time for that freedom to be extended to all Americans. Let us never return to enslaving, discriminating, intimidating, or subordinating any group of people; help us to cancel the so-called cancel culture gripping this land. Let us ensure that the friendly hand of freedom is extended to everyone who enters and leaves this beautiful land. Let freedom ring for all Americans regardless of their demographics. Regarding those who continue to subordinate, enslave, and abuse others, have your justice fall upon them swiftly. In the name of your Son, Jesus Christ, who makes all people free through faith in Him, Amen.

January 16

National Religious Freedom Day commemorates the passage of Thomas Jefferson's statute in the commonwealth of Virginia on 01/16/1786. This legislation became the foundation of the First Amendment to our Constitution. In 1993, the Congress of the United States under President George H. W. Bush, issued a joint resolution by both houses to recognize January 16 as Religious Freedom Day, in appreciation of this important freedom which is particularly unique to the USA. The following are excerpts from the original statute penned by Jefferson himself.

"The impious presumption of legislators and rulers, civil as well as ecclesiastical, who, being themselves but fallible and uninspired men have assumed dominion over the faith of others, setting up their own opinions and modes of thinking as the only true and infallible, and as such endeavoring to impose them on others, hath established and maintained false religions over the greatest part of the world and through all time... Truth is great, and will prevail if left to herself, that she is the proper and sufficient antagonist to error, and has nothing to fear from the conflict... Be it enacted by General Assembly that no man shall be compelled to frequent or support any religious worship, place, or ministry whatsoever, nor shall be enforced, restrained, molested, or burdened in his body or goods, nor shall otherwise suffer on account of his religious opinions or belief, but that all men shall be free to profess, and by argument to maintain, their opinions in matters of Religion."

Who can say it better? There are many places in the world where one religion is forced upon the populace. There are many places in the world where religion of any kind is forbidden. There are very few places in the world where religious freedom is guaranteed in their founding documents or through legislation. And yet, without this freedom, our nation would not have survived; in fact, our founders fled other nations because they were denied that freedom. Our forefathers chose overwhelmingly to follow the teachings of the Holy Bible; the USA has leaned principally on that Judeo-Christian foundation. Yes, we welcome people of faith, without discrimination. We also stand for truth and justice. Combined with morality, these are the tenets that hold this republic together: faith, liberty, justice, and truth. They are gifts from God. If we lose any one of them, we lose the American Dream.

In the Old Testament, God chose rulers (DEU 17:15; 1 SA 10:24; 1 KI 3:8), judges (JDG 2:16–18; JDG 13:5), ministers (NUM 1:50; DEU 21:5), and prophets (NEH 9:7; ISA 6:8; JER 1:5). In the New Testament, Jesus chose His apostles (JOH 6:70; ACT 1:2; ACT 9:15). Jesus also chooses us to be His disciples and to serve one another (MAT 20:1–16). We need leaders and governors who love God, His Word, this country, and our Constitution. We need to dismiss leaders and governors who place themselves, their party, or the desires of special interest groups before those tenets listed above. It is advised that you consider these things, and the weight they carry among the assortment of candidates running for office, the next time you cast your vote.

- JOB 36:11–12 ~ If they obey and serve God, they will spend their days in prosperity, and their years in pleasure. But if they do not obey, they will perish by the sword, and they will die without knowledge.

- PRO 29:26–27 ~ Many people seek favor from their rulers, but all judgment comes from God. An unjust person is loathsome to a just person; an upright person is loathsome to an evil person.

- ISA 32:17–18 ~ The effect of righteousness will be peace, and the result of righteousness, calmness and assurance forever. My people will abide in a peaceful habitation, in secure dwellings, and in quiet resting places.

JANUARY

- ROM 5:14–18 ~ Just as the sin of one man (Adam) brought judgment and condemnation to all, so has the righteousness of one man (Christ) brought the free gift of grace, providing justification of life to all believers.

- 1 CO 2:10–13 ~ God reveals His mysteries to us through His Spirit, for the Spirit searches all things, even the deepest things of God. Nobody can know the deepest thoughts of another, only the spirit within that person can know them. Similarly, nobody can know the deepest thoughts of God except His Holy Spirit. We have received the Spirit of God, not the spirit of the world, so that we might know the things that God has given to us for free. This is why we teach in accordance with the wisdom of the Spirit, not the wisdom of this world, for you cannot compare spiritual things with worldly things.

- GAL 1:8 ~ Anyone, including angels, who preaches anything contrary to what Jesus and the apostles preached are cursed.

- GAL 5:13 ~ You have been called to be free; but do not use freedom as an excuse to live according to the flesh; but through love, serve one another.

- EPH 6:7–8 ~ Render service with good will as to the Lord and not to man, knowing that whatever good anyone does, this he will receive back from the Lord, whether he is a bondservant or is free.

- 2 PE 1:1–8 ~ Simon Peter, a servant and apostle of Jesus Christ, to those who have obtained a faith of equal standing with ours by the righteousness of our God and Savior Jesus Christ: May grace and peace be multiplied to you in the knowledge of God and of Jesus our Lord. His divine power has granted to us all things that pertain to life and godliness, through the knowledge of Him who called us to His own glory and excellence by which He has granted to us His precious and very great promises, so that through them you may become partakers of the divine nature, having escaped from the corruption that is in the world because of sinful desires. For this very reason, make every effort to supplement your faith with virtue, and virtue with knowledge, and knowledge with self-control, and self-control with steadfastness, and steadfastness with godliness, and godliness with brotherly affection, and brotherly affection with love. For if these qualities are yours and are increasing, they will keep you from being ineffective or unfruitful in the knowledge of our Lord Jesus Christ.

- JAM 1:22–27 ~ Do not just listen to the Word, but do what it says. Whoever listens but does not act is like a person who looks in the mirror and later forgets what they look like. But those who look intently into the perfect law of liberty, and who act on this, they will be blessed in all they do. Those who consider themselves to be religious, but do not control their tongue, deceive themselves and their religion is worthless. God accepts the religion of those who look after the poor, widows and orphans, and who keep themselves from becoming polluted by the world around them.

Dear Heavenly Father, we thank you for the freedoms we enjoy in this land which you have so richly blessed. Expressly, we thank you for the right to worship you in whatever manner we choose. Lead us, therefore, to choose your path; indeed, it is you who set this great nation on that very path, leading to our prosperity and purpose. Let us remain steadfast in the faith so we can keep our nation free, to fearlessly serve, praise, and worship you collectively. Let it be so until we are brought to your perfect kingdom, to serve, praise, and worship you for eternity. Unite us in the one true faith, ever trusting in your mercy. Make us diligent in the study of your Word, your works and your ways, in pursuit of truth and justice. In the name of your Son who set us free from sin and death to be your children and fellow heirs to your kingdom, Amen.

DAILY DEVOTIONAL EVENTS

January 17

National Kid Inventors Day recognizes innovative kids. You'd be amazed at some of the inventions that kids have created. Everyone has unique talents that they are born with, but many other abilities can be realized if there is sufficient interest. Not everyone has a knack for science but it is a required subject for good reason: because we need excellent scientists in every discipline. That's why we have science fairs in the public schools. On this day, many local schools and community centers provide an opportunity for ingenious kids to share their inventions and ideas. If you want to boost their imagination, take your kids to one of these symposia. There also are summer camps and science conventions around the globe at different times of the year to stimulate the ingenuity of children. January 17 was selected because one of the great inventors, Ben Franklin was born on this day in 1706. At the age of eleven he invented flippers for the hands in order to swim faster. He would later invent a fireplace stove insert, bifocal lenses, lightning rod, odometer, and more. A lot of inventions come out of necessity and others are simply the result of a vivid imagination.

One of the great kid inventions came from Louis Braille, who was blinded by a freak accident when he was a young lad. Despite his handicap he studied hard and excelled; meanwhile he developed a system enabling him to read, which bears his name: braille. He was about fifteen years old when he introduced his process. As an adult, he served as a professor, while also perfecting his invention. It wasn't used widely until well after his death, but Braille's basic method is still used to this day by the blind. Here are some other examples of resourceful kids (listed chronologically).

- Blaise Pascal, 1642 (age 18): Invented the digital calculator to help his accountant father reconcile the books. The prolific inventor would become a famed Christian philosopher.
- Chester Greenwood, 1873 (age 15): Got his mother to help sew patches on a wire frame to cover his ears while ice skating. His patent for earmuffs was approved in 1877.
- Frank Epperson, 1905 (age 11): Invented a type of popsicle which he patented in 1923 and made a bundle selling them.
- Albert Sadacca, 1917 (age 15): Invented battery powered stringed Christmas lights after a large fire occurred in New York from candles on a tree. He started a company selling his invention in 1925.
- Philo Farnsworth, 1921 (age 15): Diagrammed a way of transmitting a series of pictures electronically, transmitting his first image six years later; this evolved into the modern-day television and motion pictures.
- Ralph Samuelson, 1922 (age 18): Invented water skis mimicking snow skis; though the invention was patented by someone else, he was the one who came up with the idea.
- Joseph-Armand Bombardier, 1926 (age 19): Attached a car engine to four skis to make a gas-powered snowmobile. He started selling them in 1936; they were mass produced by 1940.
- George Nissen, 1930 (age 16): Invented the trampoline after visiting the circus. He was on the gymnastics team in college when he and his gym instructor perfected the invention.
- Robert Patch, 1963 (age 6): Patented a toy truck that could be disassembled and reassembled into different types of trucks.
- Tom Sims, 1963 (age 13): Designed the first ski-board, improving on the design in 1969 to become the full-sized snowboard still used today. He founded his own brand in 1976, becoming the industry expert in different kinds of snowboards and skateboards.

There were several innovators in the Bible that deserve mentioning who performed amazing feats; some were kids, others were adults. Using specifications given to him by God, Noah built an enormous ark which took him about 100 years to complete (GEN 6:14–16; HEB 11:7); never before had a project of this magnitude been attempted. King David was barely a teen with a sling when he defeated Goliath who was armed to the teeth (1 SA 17). David invented a variety of musical instruments that were used while singing praises and worshipping God (1 CH 23:5; 2 CH 7:6; 2 CH 29:26; AMO 6:5); he was quite the songwriter and lute player as well. David's son Solomon succeeded him as king; Solomon was commissioned by God to build the temple of the Lord incorporating unique artistry and designs (1 KI 6:1; CH 22:6–10; 2 CH 2:7; 2 CH 28:6). Solomon also established the largest navy of ships during his time (1 KI 9:26–27; 1 KI 10:22–23), and developed a formidable cavalry with thousands of stables for chariots and horses (1 KI 4:26). King Hezekiah of Judah commissioned his engineers to reroute the Gihon River to divert fresh water into the city of Jerusalem (2 KI 20:20; 2 CH 32:30). King Uzziah mass produced weapons of war: shields, helmets, spears, bows, slings, and chained overcoats. He also commissioned his engineers to build machines to be placed on towers and fortifications, which would shoot arrows and fling large rocks great distances. This made the king mighty and powerful, but he relished in destruction and he dishonored God by burning incense in the temple (2 CH 26:14–16). Jeremiah was called to be a prophet of God when he was a teen (JER 1:1–7). Daniel was a teen when he refused to defile himself with food served by the Babylonian emperor Nebuchadnezzar; Daniel and his friends initiated a vegetarian diet and showed themselves to be healthier and more fit than the king's own children (DAN 1:8–15). Of course, all knowledge and ingenuity come from God, because He is the inventor of the universe.

- EXO 35:31–35 ~ Through His Spirit, God filled artisans with wisdom, understanding, and knowledge and all manner of craftmanship to create remarkable works out of gold, silver, and brass; cutting of stones to set them into jewelry; and the carving of wood. And they taught these trades to others. And many were likewise filled with the Spirit of wisdom to design and create engravings, embroideries, weavings, and other artistic masterpieces (see also 2 CH 2:7 regarding the building of the temple).

Kids have a knack for coming up with fixes to perceived problems. And they get younger and more innovative each generation. There are numerous inventor kids from this century who are leading the way. It is recommended that parents research these boys and girls on the internet with their own kids; it may open their eyes to the possibilities. It also may increase their self-esteem, proving to them that they are not worthless or helpless, but rather possess the potential for greatness. This potential is in every single human being that has lived on the planet. In many cases, all that is necessary is for the individual to recognize that he or she is unique, talented, and important, not just to their parents but to God the Father. Encourage them to try new things, explore different subject matter, master everything that motivates them, and use their imagination; explore science, do arts and crafts, and build things using anything. Consult them when you are problem solving and show them you value their opinions; they might just solve your problem for you. Most of them are already whiz kids when it comes to electronic devices.

Our Father, you came from heaven above down to earth so that we could know you. We understand that all wisdom, knowledge, and creativity come from you. Help us to realize our full potential, especially that of our kids and grandkids. Open the eyes of parents to see the potential of their kids, and support their children's ideas, opinions, and projects. Give parents the desire to discover things with their children, exploring together, going to museums, art galleries, and science fairs, and doing things their kids like to do. Help children to be given the freedom to discover, ask questions, learn about things that intrigue them, and cultivate their unique gifts. In the name of Christ we pray, who gave His life and took it back again, Amen.

January 18

Week of Prayer for Christian Unity has been around for over a century. During this week we pray for unity, not only among Christian congregations and denominations, but also in the entire body of Christ, who is our head. The week runs from 01/18 to 01/25, regardless of what day of the week it starts on. Church services during the weekend often have a special presentation about unity and solidarity. Whenever a large number of Christians are collectively praying and feeling the Spirit, there is a great deal of power exuded against Satan and his demons. Such prayerful power can drive out evil and subdue the wicked. Unity is something we should pray for every single day. Traditionally, the feasts of St. Peter and St. Paul are observed during this week, depending on denominational norms. A collaboration of ecumenical bodies selects theme, text, and prayer requests. A Roman Catholic slant is added to the material for distribution among their congregations; other denominations are free to do the same.

Though it started out a Catholic observance, Protestants soon established their own version. In 1948 the World Council of Churches was established to consolidate all faiths which are centered on Jesus Christ. The Catholics have a similar council. There are essential doctrines of the true Christian faith which Catholics and Protestants agree upon. Regardless of which church a person attends, these truths should not be compromised. If a church does not adhere to the major tenets of the faith, they cannot be Christian. Deviations from Biblical truth and Christian dogma would be a red flag for those of you looking for a good Bible-based church.

What then are the essential doctrines? Well, it's good to begin with God the Father, creator and lawgiver. Then there is God the Holy Spirit who communicated His law to the authors and prophets of the Old Testament, and that Law was fulfilled through Jesus Christ, recorded by authors and apostles in the New Testament. These two testaments, which are God-breathed by the Holy Spirit, reconcile each other. The truth and directives of the Holy Bible are therefore communicated to all who read it, listen to it, and digest it. The Word of God became flesh, who is God the Son; He came among us to further reveal God's plan, and to show the Father's grace and love to all who seek Him. And since He loved us unconditionally, it is our response to love Him back, and to love one another as much as ourselves. Because we were unable to adhere strictly to God's commandments, Christ died for us; otherwise, we would die in our sins. Christ paid for them; therefore, He is our Redeemer. Since Christ was without sin, death could not hold Him, and He remains alive. Thanks to His resurrection, Christians likewise will be raised to receive a body without sin that will never die. This enables us to live forever with God our Father, and Jesus who is our brother thorough adoption as children of God our Father. The gift of faith given and sustained by the Holy Spirit compels us to live a life for Christ; faith should be revealed in our behavior and our love. But our works cannot earn salvation, for it is free by the grace of God; this is good since one more sin would condemn us all over again. We cannot earn our freedom, but Christ can and did; His shed blood was the cost. Our trust in this atoning sacrifice sets us free from sin and death forever.

For a clear statement of faith, get a copy of the Apostles Creed; it was handed down by the apostles to St. Paul and other evangelists, who passed them along to the early church fathers. Another excellent statement of faith is the Nicene Creed which clarified key truths like the Holy Trinity. These two are great confessions; but confession of faith alone is not a substitute for studying the Holy Bible and worshipping publicly, all of which are acts of faith that will surely raise your scriptural knowledge, moral stance, and spiritual competence. Christians believe in both testaments of the Bible, particularly the Gospel of Jesus Christ which is still spreading throughout the world. These proofs of faith equip a person to spread the Word further, which is the great commission (MAT 28:16–20).

The objective of the Week of Prayer for Christian Unity can be summed up in the last prayer that Jesus prayed with His apostles, on the night before His crucifixion (JOH 17). One passage from that prayer is often quoted during this observance (JOH 17:21). "I pray that they all may be united as one—as you Father are in me and I am in you—and that they also may be one in us, so the world might believe that you sent me."

The church on earth is the body of Christ. It is necessary for us to unite as one with Christ if we are to have a noticeable impact countering the backsliding ways of the world. The people of the world are divided in so many ways it is near impossible to enumerate these divisions. There is only one factor that is able to unite such a diversity of people, and that is Jesus Christ. For there is only one true faith and that should be the defining attribute of Christians around the world. When Christians are joined together in spirit, in unison with the Holy Spirit, there is nothing on earth that can prevail against us.

- PSA 133:1 ~ Behold, how good and how pleasant it is for brothers and sisters of the faith to live together in unity!

- JER 32:39 ~ I will give them one heart, and one way, so that they will fear me forever for their own good, and for the good of their children after them.

- EZE 11:19–20 ~ I will give them an undivided heart, and I will place a new spirit within them. I will remove their heart of stone and replace it with a heart of flesh. Then they will follow my decrees and carefully obey my commandments. They will be my people and I will be their God.

- ACT 1:14 ~ All of them continued with one accord in prayer and meditation.

- ACT 2:44–47 ~ And the believers were as one, for they had everything in common. They sold their possessions and goods and gave generously to the needy. Every day they met with one accord in the temple courts. They took turns breaking bread at the various homes, and they ate together with gladness and unity of heart, praising God and enjoying each other's hospitality. And the Lord added to their number daily, those who were being saved.

- ROM 15:5–6 ~ May the God who gives endurance and encouragement give you oneness of spirit as you follow Christ, so that with one heart and mouth you may glorify God the Father of our Lord Jesus Christ.

- 1 CO 1:10 ~ I urge you, my brothers, in the name of our Lord Jesus Christ, to be in agreement with one another so that there will be no divisions among you. Be perfectly joined together in mind and thought.

- EPH 2:19–22 ~ You are no longer foreigners but fellow citizens of God's kingdom and members of His household, built on the foundation laid by the prophets and apostles with Jesus Christ as the chief cornerstone. In Him the entire building is joined together and grows into a holy temple. In Him you also are being built together to become a place for God's Holy Spirit to live.

- PHP 2:2 ~ Make my joy complete by being like-minded, having the same love and being one in spirit and in purpose.

- 1 JO 5:4–5 ~ Everyone who is born of God overcomes the world; this is the victory, that by faith we can overcome the world. So, who can overcome the world? Anyone who believes that Jesus Christ is the Son of God.

Although we are to unite as members of the body of Christ, we are also supposed to separate ourselves from the world, from evil, and from wicked people. Sure, witness to those who will listen, but stay away from people who hate God and promote wickedness; there is nothing you can do for them except pray for them. There are two things that the enemy has in common, and that is their disdain for Christians and their desire to be their own gods. Since they are of the world, they do not want to face judgment, so they deny the truth and they deny accountability. They believe in a higher power and it is them; this is how they defend their position to accept no blame or responsibility for anything.

- EZR 9:14 ~ Should we break God's commandments again, and join in affinity with the kinds of people who commit such abominations? Would God not be angry with us until He consumed us, so that nobody would remain or escape?

- ISA 59:13 ~ They know they are being disobedient to God; they carefully plan their lies.

- ROM 16:17 ~ I urge you, my brothers, identify those who cause divisions among you, and who place obstacles in your way that are contrary to the doctrine that you have learned. Avoid them completely.

- 1 CO 5:11, 13 ~ Do not associate with someone who claims to be a Christian but who is sexually promiscuous, greedy, idolatrous, slanderous, or who is a drunkard or a swindler; do not even eat at the same table with such a person. You must expel the wicked from among you.

- 1 TI 1:3–7 ~ Do not teach false doctrine, or recognize any myths or irrelevant genealogies, which only serve to raise questions, without providing any answers concerning the faith. The goal is to love with a pure heart, a right conscience, and a sincere faith. Some have wandered away from these principles and turned to meaningless jabber; desiring to be teachers of the Law yet knowing nothing about the Law or about what they purport to be true.

- 2 TI 4:3–4 ~ People will seek teachers who conform to their own likes and dislikes; they will turn away from the truth and wander into myths.

- TIT 1:11 ~ They must be silenced, those who would ruin entire households, teaching things that are wrong for the sake of ill-gotten gain.

- JAM 1:8 ~ A double-minded man is unstable in all his ways.

- JDE 1:17–19 ~ Dear friends, remember what the apostles told us before. They said that in the latter days there would be scoffers who follow their own ungodly desires. These people have come to divide you; they follow the instincts of their flesh and do not have the Spirit within them.

Dear loving Father, we give thanks to you for inviting us to live with you, and we are proud to call you our Father and Jesus our brother. For we are one with you through your Holy Spirit, and we are one with our fellow Christians as members of the body of Christ. Help us to unite under the banner of your Son, as an army of Christian soldiers, to come against wickedness in this world. Help us to boldly proclaim your works and your Word to anyone who is inclined to listen and possibly join with us. Help us to avoid those who would dissuade us or turn us towards the evil intentions they are pursuing. Please remove the barriers that divide us as Christians and bring us together under the umbrella of your grace. We pray for your people everywhere, that they would be protected and keep the faith, especially those who are struggling with persecution and oppression. In the name of Jesus Christ, who is our head, we pray, Amen.

January 19

First Overhead Lighting System designed by Thomas Edison was installed in Roselle, New Jersey. We tend to take for granted many things in our lives. What would you think if you flipped the light switch and got nothing, and there was nothing wrong with the bulbs, and the circuit breaker was not in the off position? I would probably panic, thinking: what, now I have to call an electrician and see if there's something wrong with the wiring? Well, that actually happens in old houses sometimes, but you get the point. The world has had overhead lighting systems since this day in 1883. It seems like a long time ago because it is.

Edison had a storied career, being the inventor of the light bulb, telegraph, alkaline batteries, and phonograph; he held over a thousand patents. Being able to provide light for an entire city was a milestone. The system was powered by a steam-driven generator; we have come a long way from steam generators: nuclear, wind and solar, hydroelectric, and gas-powered plants. So, if the lights won't turn on, should you call your local electric company? Good luck with that. Then again, what if we lost the electrical grid? This is a serious vulnerability: our grid system could become the target of attack by bad actors around the world. There have been attacks, usually small scale, low impact; the big one could disable us for weeks on end. There are other vulnerabilities such as electromagnetic pulse and microwave warfare which could disable our electronic devices. Imagine living without your phone and computer for a while, or for good.

We are so dependent on electricity that people have a hard time managing things when there is none: for example, a blackout affects large service areas due to severe weather or power plant failures, and a brownout is caused when the demand exceeds the capacity. Such anomalies are becoming relatively common due to systems being overloaded by consumers. Sometimes the power company has to create brownouts deliberately for brief periods of time, asking customers to turn their coolers off, and such. By the way, are you the one who turns out lights not in use or the one that leaves them on? Just wondering. Hint, if you considered the cost of all the electricity and other forms of energy being wasted every year you might become part of the former group. Incidentally, when you see lights dimming and flickering, you might want to turn off your computer, because an outage can be followed by a surge when the power is restored. This could cause irreparable damage to electronic devices not plugged into a surge-protected power strip.

How is this related to the Bible then? We could look at electricity as something not to be taken for granted, not to mention the electrical grid. Or worse, do you ever take for granted your salvation? Is your faith a proactive one or an inactive one? Or, look at it from the standpoint of wastefulness, dependency, or unpreparedness. The return of Jesus could come before our systems start breaking down. Are you ready for that? Pretty much the entire book of Revelation is dedicated to the fact that we've had fair warning that His second coming is nigh. Jesus's last words quoted in the Bible were, "I come quickly." And John's reply, "Amen, come Lord Jesus." This can be considered a warning, to take caution, and not be caught off-guard.

- EZE 18:24, 26–27; EZE 33:13–19 ~ If a righteous person turns away from righteousness, and engages in the sin of the wicked, will that person live? All the righteousness that person did will no longer be remembered, but only the sin, which will cause that person to die. When a wicked person turns from evil and does what is lawful and right, that person will live.

- ROM 6:1–2, 12–16 ~ Shall we continue to sin, so that God's grace can continue to abound? God forbid it! How can we, who were dead in our sins, continue to live a life of decadence? Do not allow sin to reign in your mortal body, influencing you to pursue the desires of the flesh. Do not use your body parts as instruments of unrighteousness and sin, but yield to God, and use your body to glorify Him. Sin cannot control you for you are no longer under the Law, but under the grace of God. Does that mean we can sin, because we are under Grace and not the Law? No way! A person obeys whomever they yield to; you can yield to sin unto death, or you can yield to obedience unto righteousness.

- 2 PE 2:20–21 ~ If, after a person has escaped the wickedness of this world through the knowledge of our Lord and Savior Jesus Christ, they allow themselves again to be entangled and overcome by the world, their end will be worse than their beginning. For it would have been better for them not to have known the ways of righteousness, than to have understood and yet turned away from the holy commandment given to them.

We feeble humans take much for granted: our livelihood, freedom, functionality, health, electricity, salvation. Take your pick, for you will probably have taken them all for granted more than a few times; me too. What can we do about it? There is a certain book that has all the answers, you know. How often should you pick it up and read? Answer: More.

- 1 CO 6:19–20 ~ Do you not realize that your body is the temple of God's Holy Spirit which He has given to you? Your body no longer belongs to you for you were bought with a great price. Therefore, glorify God in your body and in your spirit, both of which belong to God.

- HEB 3:14 ~ We are partakers of Christ if we keep the same confidence we had in the beginning, steadfast until the end.

- HEB 6:4–7 ~ For those who were once enlightened, who tasted the eternal gift, were made partakers of the Holy Spirit, were aware of the good news and the powers of the world to come, and who then fell away, it is impossible to renew them unto repentance since they will be crucifying Christ all over again, putting Him to open shame.

- HEB 10:26–29 ~ If we sin willingly, after having received the knowledge of the truth, there can be no further sacrifice for sins, but only the expectation of judgment and raging fire. A worse punishment awaits those who think themselves worthy, yet have walked over the Son of God, insulted the Spirit of Grace, and treated as unholy the blood of the covenant that sanctified them.

- 2 PE 1:5–8 ~ In diligence, add virtue to your faith, knowledge to your virtue, temperance to your knowledge, patience to your temperance, godliness to your patience, kindness to your godliness, and charity to your kindness. If these things abound in you, you will never be barren or unfruitful in the knowledge of our Lord Jesus Christ.

- JDE 1:4 ~ Certain ungodly people, whose condemnation was written about long ago, have sneaked in without anyone noticing, attempting to turn God's grace into lust, and denying the only God and our Lord, Jesus Christ.

How active is your faith life? The big three are prayer, Bible study, and worship. How often do you fellowship with other Christian friends or your church family? To what degree are your natural abilities and knowledge being used to serve God and others? How much should I give back to God? Answer: More.

- DEU 16:17 ~ Everyone should give as they are able, in accordance with the blessings which God has given them.

- PSA 96:8 ~ Give God the glory He deserves. Bring your offerings and worship Him.

- PRO 3:9–10 ~ Honor the Lord with your profits, and with the first fruits of your income, and your barns be filled and your winepresses will burst with new wine.

JANUARY

- ISA 12:4 ~ Praise God, call on His name, declare His works everywhere, and tell everyone His name is exalted.

- MAT 25:40, 45 ~ Jesus said, "Whenever you have done something to help another person, you have done it to me as well; whenever you have not done something to help another person, you have not done it to me."

- LUK 6:38 ~ Give and it shall be given to you in abundance, overflowing; for the same measure that you give is returned unto you.

- JOH 4:24 ~ Jesus said, "God is Spirit and should be worshipped in spirit and in truth."

- ROM 12:6–8 ~ Use those gifts God has given to you. If you have the gift of prophecy, exercise that gift according to the proportion of your faith. If your gift is ministry, then minister; if it is teaching, then teach; if it is encouraging, then encourage; if it is giving to the needy, then give generously; if it is leadership, then lead diligently; if it is showing mercy, then do so cheerfully.

- 1 CO 16:1 ~ On the first day of each week everyone should set aside something for the Lord in accordance with the degree to which they have prospered by His grace, so it will not be necessary to take a collection.

- GAL 5:13 ~ You have been given the freedom to love and serve one another.

- PHP 4:6 ~ Do not worry about anything, but in everything, through praise and thanksgiving, make your needs known to God.

- 1 TI 2:1 ~ Prayers, intercessions, and thanks should be given to God by all people.

- HEB 10:24–25 ~ Let us encourage one another to promote love and good works. Let us never cease to fellowship with one another in God's house as others are in the habit of doing.

Dependency on the world is materialism; we are to be dependent on God for He made all things and gives us all things to sustain our lives. Do not waste or abuse these things. You wouldn't be wasting your time if you knew the day of your death was near; and it always is. You wouldn't waste your resources if you knew you could not replace them, or they could be shut off.

- PSA 49:17 ~ When you die you take nothing with you; your glory does not go with you.

- ECC 7:18 ~ Those who fear God will avoid all extremes.

- LUK 21:34–35 ~ Jesus said, "Be careful. Do not let overindulgence, drunkenness, and the worries of life get the better of you, so when that fateful day comes you will not be caught by surprise. That day will be like a snare that catches the whole earth in its trap."

- ROM 13:13–14 ~ Be honest, as in the daylight; do not engage in rioting, drunkenness, overindulgence, promiscuity, fighting, and jealousy. Build your life around Jesus Christ, do not indulge in the lusts of the flesh.

- 1 CO 6:12; 1 CO 10:23 ~ Something that is permissible is not necessarily beneficial or constructive. It is all right to enjoy something but I will not let it control me.

- 2 CO 4:7 ~ We keep treasure in jars of clay, that shows the unsurpassed power which belongs to God and is not from us.

- GAL 5:19–21 ~ The works of the flesh include adultery, fornication, perversion, lust, idolatry, witchcraft, hatred, quarreling, rivalry, dissension, rage, fighting, sedition, heresy, jealousy, murder, drunkenness, orgies, and the like. Those who engage in such activities will not inherit the kingdom.

- EPH 5:18, 29 ~ Do not get drunk, which is excess; instead, fill yourself with the Holy Spirit. Nobody hates their own bodies; instead, they nourish and cherish their bodies, just as Christ nourishes and cherishes the church.

- PHP 4:5 ~ Let your moderation be an example to others.

Nobody knows how close we are or how far, but we always should be ready to take action, because we could be there before you know it. There is no hope when it's over, and hope is the last thing you lose right before it's too late. Don't put it off, whatever you are keeping on the back burner. Don't give up if you still have unexpended energy; the finish line might be right around the bend. Exercise your brain with cognitive skills, condition your body too. Stay in the spirit and you will win the human race.

- PRO 27:23–24 ~ Pay attention to your business, for riches do not endure forever, and an earthly crown does not endure to every generation.

- 1 CO 9:24–27 ~ Do you understand that there are many competitors in a race but only one will receive first prize? Therefore, run with the intention of winning that prize. Those who strive to master a task must train hard and discipline themselves. However, they do so to obtain an earthly crown that will not last; but we strive for a crown that will last forever. Therefore, I run like a man with a purpose. I do not fight like a boxer beating the air. Instead, I beat my body into shape, making it serve God's purpose, so that my preaching will not cause me to be disqualified for the prize.

- JAM 1:12 ~ Blessed be those who persevere despite their trials and temptations, because they will receive the crown of life which the Lord has promised to anyone who loves Him.

Heavenly Father, we are so richly blessed; thank you so very much. Let us never take for granted all the goodness you have bestowed upon us. Let us never be caught off guard or unprepared, but let us train hard, to be ready for anything the world might throw at us, using the quintessential training manual, the Holy Bible. Help us to be good stewards of your grace, your creation, worldly possessions, and spiritual gifts. Let us be generous with ourselves, our time, and our riches, even as you are generous with us. We are so grateful for our faith, health, comfort, home, and family; ensure that we never take anything for granted and to always be available to those who ask. Help us to always be available to you, to perform our duties as faithful servants, glorifying your name in our lives. We love you Father, your Holy Spirit, and your Son whose light is always shining upon us and within us, which will never burn out or be shut off. In His holy name we pray, Amen.

January 20

International Day of Acceptance is an annual commitment to acceptance, period. Some things we can change, some we cannot; the trick is to know the difference. Either way it does no good to delay acceptance of the ups and downs. All of us have hang-ups, handicaps, hardships, and history that impede our thoughts or result in negative self-messages. These are destructive and should be abandoned; that is, let go of it. There are benefits to letting go; mainly, you needn't carry it anymore. Give it to God that's what Jesus said: If you are heavy laden with guilt, pain, setbacks, rejection, whatever—take it to Calvary and lay it at the foot of the cross. This is the most effective means of acceptance by far. But people tend to hang onto baggage though it only slows them down. Often, we carry a grudge which worsens the situation. Again, today is about letting go: let go and let God as they say. Jesus will carry your load for you, while you get a breather.

This idea was hatched by Annie Hopkins to draw attention to the courage and love of the handicapped; her logo was a wheelchair in a heart. Acceptance was not only about how she accepted her condition but also about being accepted by others, particularly those who disrespect handicapped people, often unknowingly. Annie spoke out about equality, understanding, and respect; these go both ways. The handicapped do not want to be treated any differently than any other human being. We are all God's children and God sees us alike. Annie empowered many others, before her untimely death in 2009; her legacy lives on in this holiday. Today we embrace who we are outside and inside; we enjoy life, encouraging others to do the same. We are sensitive to the needs and disabilities of others, mentally and physically. We also should be concerned about people who are dysfunctional spiritually. A society that accepts one and all, this is the impetus of equality, liberty, and opportunity, ethics which once made our land great.

As you can see, acceptance covers a wide range of applications, especially loss. There are losses that affect a person permanently, be it loss of vision or hearing, loss of mobility, loss of sanity, loss of a loved one, loss of employment, and loss of life in general. In all these cases, the process of grieving must occur, which is similar for any debilitating loss, though people will experience it differently. You may have heard of Dr. Kubler-Ross who originated the stages of grieving in her famous book, *Death and Dying*. The model below is based on hers, with stages listed in a similar order (Barber, 2016). This is not to imply that all people go through the same stages in the same order; sometimes they go back and forth between stages, or do not experience one or more stages. The model is a guide that one can use to see where they are in the process of dealing with a loss; the final stage in their bereavement process will be acceptance.

1. Shock and Denial (disbelief)
2. Depression (comes and goes)
3. Isolation and Withdrawal (feeling overwhelmed)
4. Anger or Blame (unearned guilt or shame)
5. Unfinished Business (should have, would have, could have)
6. Bargaining (sometimes with God)
7. Acceptance (renewed strength)

Mental health treatment facilitates this process, by focusing on whichever phase is being experienced, where roadblocks exist, things to let go of or to hold onto, tying up loose ends, and/or addressing what to expect next. Therapy is an option for anyone having difficulty coping, in order to gain acceptance of oneself and the situation.

- JOB 16:6 ~ If I speak, my pain is not appeased, and if I refrain, how much of it leaves me?

- JOB 42:10, 12 ~ The Lord restored the fortune of Job, after he prayed for his friends. And God gave Job twice that of before, blessing the latter days of Job more than his beginning…

- ECC 3:1–2 ~ For everything there is a season, and a time for every purpose under heaven: a time to be born, and a time to die…

- ISA 53:4–6 ~ Surely, He has borne our griefs and carried our sorrows; yet we esteemed Him stricken, smitten by God, and afflicted. But He was wounded for our transgressions; He was bruised for our iniquities; upon Him was the chastisement that brought us peace, and by the stripes on His back we are healed. All we like sheep have gone astray; everyone has turned away and gone their own way, while the Lord has laid on Him the iniquity of us all.

- LAM 3:31–33 ~ Men are not pushed aside by the Lord forever. Though He allows grief He shows compassion, because great is His unfailing love. For God does not deliberately bring affliction or grief upon the children of men.

- JOH 16:20, 22, 33 ~ Jesus said, "Truly, truly, I say to you, you will weep and lament, but the world will rejoice. You will be sorrowful, but your sorrow will turn into joy… You have sorrow now, but I will see you again, and your hearts will rejoice, and no one will take your joy from you… I have said these things to you so that in me you may have peace. In the world you will have tribulation. But take heart; I have overcome the world."

- ROM 5:1–5 ~ Since we have been justified by faith, we have peace with God through our Lord Jesus Christ. Through Him we have obtained access by faith into His grace in which we stand, rejoicing in our hope of the glory of God. Not only that, but we rejoice in our sufferings, knowing that suffering produces endurance, and endurance produces character, and character produces hope; and hope does not disappoint us, because God's love has been poured into our hearts through the Holy Spirit who has been given to us.

- 2 CO 12:9–10 ~ God said to Paul, "My grace is sufficient for you, for my power is made perfect in weakness." Therefore, I will boast in my infirmities, so that the power of Christ may rest upon me. For the sake of Christ, I am content with weaknesses, insults, hardships, persecutions, and calamities. Because when I am weak, then I become strong.

- JAM 1:2–4 ~ Rejoice when you have trials of various kinds, for you know that the testing of your faith produces patience. And let patience have its full effect, so you may feel perfect and complete, lacking in nothing.

- 1 PE 1:3–6 ~ Blessed is God the Father of our Lord Jesus Christ, who according to His abundant mercy has given us rebirth in a living hope, through the resurrection of Christ from the dead, to receive an inheritance that is incorruptible and undefiled, and that will never fade away. This is reserved for you who are kept by the power of God through faith in salvation, ready to be revealed on the last day. In this you greatly rejoice, though for now you are grieved by various trials.

I deem it appropriate to close with the serenity prayer by Reinhold Niebuhr (1892-1971).

God, give me grace to accept with serenity the things that cannot be changed, courage to change the things which should be changed, and the wisdom to distinguish the one from the other. Living one day at a time; enjoying one moment at a time; accepting hardships as the pathway to peace. Taking, as He did, this sinful world as it is, not as I would have it; trusting that He will make all things right if I surrender to His will; that I may be reasonably happy in this life and supremely happy with Him forever in the next. Amen.

January 21

World Religion Day is observed the third Sunday in January. The original purpose was to promote harmony among people of different faith systems. The idea arose from the Bahais in the late forties to early fifties. The assertion was, all religions lead to the same god, making all prophets equal to include Moses, Jesus, Buddha, Mohammed, Zoroaster, etc. The assumption is that we are of one mind, those who believe in one God, one religion, and one people. The Bahai faith originated in Persia in the mid-1800s to bring together monotheistic faith systems such as Christianity, Judaism, Islam, and Zoroastrianism (the ancient religion of Persia). There are commonalities in these religions, for they glean knowledge and dogma from the Old Testament; but they diverge with respect to the New Testament. Further, religions with polytheistic foundations such as Shintoism, Taoism, Hinduism, even Paganism are welcome, plus religions that do not require belief or worship of any god. The notion of religious freedom has become universal, being celebrated worldwide on this day in various cities, with events designed to bring people together. This could be a way to unite with other cultures, but it is not a good idea to consider religions alike or equal regarding their faith in God when they have different definitions of God. The problem with unification philosophy is their views of Christ differ widely, and salvation can be earned by works, and nobody accepts the Holy Trinity but Christians.

The opportunity for faith communities around the world to come together, enhance solidarity, and exchange cultural customs seems okay. Despite secularist attacks on religion of any kind, the majority of people in the world believe there is a God, a higher power, a creator, a supreme being, and/or life after death. This holiday has grown in recognition for its unifying message of togetherness, faith, and peace. The assumption is that religions needn't divide over doctrines which are incongruent; the only requirement is that you believe in something.

Alas, there are irreconcilable differences between Christianity and other religions. Some people are turned-off by Christianity precisely because of its exclusivity. And what makes Christianity exclusive? It excludes everyone or every religion that denies Jesus's resurrection from the dead, through which we are given new life after we die. Without the resurrection, there would be no Christianity. Thus, all great religions of the world are not from God. It is fine when people of different persuasions come together in unity, but it is not a unity of faith, not by a long shot. Sure, come together and share cultural and religious points of view. But beware of the underlying effect which is to isolate Christians. However, this might be a golden opportunity to witness to those who are not saved because they have yet to find the truth in the Holy Bible.

- DEU 12:32 ~ Do what God has commanded you, and do not add to it or diminish from it.

- ISA 2:3 ~ People will say, "Come, let us go to the mountain of the Lord to the house of the God of Jacob, and He will teach us His ways and we will walk in His paths. For out of Zion will come the Law; out of Jerusalem will come the Word." (See also MIC 4:2.)

- MAT 12:32 ~ Jesus said, "Whoever speaks against the Holy Spirit will not be forgiven, neither in this world nor in the world to come."

- ROM 1:25 ~ They changed God's truth into a lie and worshipped and served the creature rather than the Creator who is blessed forever, Amen.

- GAL 1:8 ~ Anyone, including the angels, who preaches anything contrary to what Jesus Christ and the apostles preached are cursed.

- 1 TH 2:13 ~ We thank God that you received His Word and accepted it as the Word of God and not the word of men. The Word of God is at work in believers like you.

The subject of essential doctrines comes up a lot in these daily devotionals, to highlight the absolute minimum requirements to be a Christian. In fact, every study will be focused on Christian living and our core values and beliefs. Enjoy and celebrate World Religion Day out of respect for all religions and peoples, for this is the American way and this particular freedom is listed in the First Amendment to the Constitution. Here is a chance for everyone to discuss their beliefs; so share the Gospel when it is your turn, and provide the evidence proving the Bible to be true, as we are commanded in the Bible to do.

- JOB 9:20 ~ If I justify myself, my own mouth will have condemned me. If I say I am perfect, then I have proven myself to be perverse.

- ISA 55:7 ~ Let evil and wicked people everywhere change their evil ways, forsake their immoral thoughts, and turn to the Lord, and He will have mercy on them; for the Lord will abundantly pardon those who seek Him.

- MIC 7:18 ~ Who is like you, God, who pardons sin and ignores the evil done by your people? God does not stay angry forever, but finds pleasure in giving mercy.

- MAT 28:18–20 ~ Jesus said to His apostles just before leaving them, "All power in heaven and earth is given to me. Go and teach all nations the things I have taught you, baptizing them in the name of the Father, Son, and Holy Spirit. And remember, I will be with you always, even until the end of time."

- ROM 8:16 ~ The Holy Spirit is a witness with our spirits that we are the children of God.

- ROM 12:1–3 ~ I implore you therefore, by the mercies of God, that you present yourselves as a living sacrifice, holy and acceptable to God, which is a reasonable response to His love. Do not conform to the ways of this world, but be transformed by the renewing of your mind, so you can determine what is good, acceptable, and perfect according to God's will. For I say to everyone, through the grace given to me, do not think of yourself more highly than you ought, but think soberly, in accordance with the measure of faith God has dealt to you.

- PHP 2:11 ~ Every tongue should confess that Jesus Christ is Lord, to the glory of God the Father.

- 1 PE 4:10–11 ~ Whoever has received the gift of salvation in Christ should share that gift as a steward of God's eternal grace. If you preach, do so as a messenger of God. If you minister, do so with the ability God gives you. Do this to glorify God through His Son Jesus Christ.

- 1 JO 2:6 ~ Whoever says they are a Christian should show they are following Christ by the way they conduct their lives.

- 1 JO 5:9–10 ~ If we believe a person witnessing for another, we should believe God's witness even more; and God has given witness of His Son. Those who believe that Jesus is God's Son have God's witness in themselves; those who do not believe are calling God a liar, because they do not believe God's testimony concerning His Son.

    We thank you Father, that your Holy Spirit has conveyed to us the Holy Bible, that we could know the truth and be set free by your Son, who in His deity came to earth as a man to make atonement for the sins of the world. We implore that His witness will forever reign in our hearts, compelling us to eagerly witness to the world, especially those who are ignorant of the Bible and its truth or are following false gods or belief systems. We pray for unity of faith among all people of God, through Jesus Christ by the power of the Holy Spirit, so everyone could be set free and be saved. This is the best way; indeed, it is the only way that the world can ever unite peacefully as one. In Jesus's name, Amen.

January 22

Sanctity of Human Life Day is a day to love life. From conception to death, every life is known and loved by God even before they were born. In 1973 the Supreme Court decided to allow women the right to an abortion (*Roe vs. Wade*). The observance of this day is a rebuttal against that ruling; for our founders recognized the value of all human life. In 1984, President Reagan proclaimed that the closest Sunday to 01/22 would be a day to recognize human life, while taking a strong stance against abortion. Other presidents have refused to observe this as a national holiday because they were pro-choice. Conservatives are more apt to oppose abortion and liberals to defend it; this has caused considerable division between political parties. Little did we know that about fifty years later the Supreme Court would overturn *Roe vs. Wade*, because abortion is a state's rights issue, not a constitutionally-preserved right. Now it is up to every state legislature to pass the type of abortion law that the residents will accept; approximately 75% of Americans favor restrictions when it comes to abortion. But when it comes to God, He surely does not accept abortion of any kind since He is the creator of all things including life, and He instructed us to respect all human life in the sixth commandment. This observance is often accentuated in the liturgy of the Lutheran Church as Sanctity of Human Life Sunday; it also has become a Texas state observance since 2018. In 2021, President Trump signed an executive order to make today a national holiday. Since 1973, over sixty million abortions have taken place in the USA, not counting unrecorded abortions.

Every human life, born or unborn, is made in the image of God. For example, we have a discerning mind that discriminates right from wrong, a capability not shared by other lifeforms indigenous to planet Earth. We have a soul which is the essence of our being; and that soul hangs in the balance with respect to whether we choose God and keep our soul (HEB 10:39), or choose the world and forfeit our soul (MAT 10:28). Animals do not think about the moral aspects of a decision, nor do they get saved or condemned. Humans were made by God to be unique, which is why He loves us unconditionally and absolutely, just as He loves His Son whom He gave for us. We love the Father and the Son equally with the Holy Spirit. We comprehend this, as do angels who had free will to choose God; but many took the side of Satan, to their condemnation.

- GEN 1:26–27 ~ God said, "Let us make humans in our image, after our likeness. And let them have dominion over the fish of the sea, over the fowl of the air, over the cattle, and over all the earth and everything that creeps upon the earth." So, God created humankind in His own image; in the image of God, He created us all, males and females alike.

- GEN 2:7 ~ God formed man from the dust of the earth, and breathed into his nostrils the breath of life, and man became a living soul.

- GEN 9:6 ~ Whoever sheds the blood of another human being must have their blood shed also; for everyone was made in the image of God.

- 2 CO 4:4 ~ The prince of this world has blinded the minds of the unbelievers, preventing the light of the glorious Gospel of Christ, who is the image of God, from shining down upon them.

- EPH 4:23–24 ~ Be renewed in the spirit of your mind and put on the new person, created after God in true righteousness and holiness.

- COL 1:15–17 ~ Christ is the image of the invisible God, and the firstborn of every creature. By Him all things were created in heaven and earth, visible or invisible, including thrones, powers, rulers, and authorities. All things were created by Him and for Him. He is before all things, and only because of Him does anything exist at all.

- 1 JO 2:23 ~ Whoever denies the Son denies the Father. Whoever acknowledges the Son acknowledges the Father.

Abortion is murder. Life begins at conception, this is a scientific fact, as well as a Biblical fact, thereby establishing an absolute truth. Back in the seventies I didn't think much about abortion. It took years before I understood this, after I became more educated in both science and the Bible. Another truth is that we have a physical component (body), a mental component (soul), and a spiritual component (life force, conscience). God also has a physical, mental, and spiritual component which are inseparable; not so for humans. In our case, we can lose our body and soul in hell, and relinquish our spirit and life force, which goes back to God who leased it to us (ECC 12:7). Believers will get a new lease on life and keep their souls.

- JOB 31:15 ~ Did God who formed me in the womb make others the same way? Was it not the same God who formed every one of us within our mother's womb?

- PSA 22:10 ~ The Lord called me, even as I was in the womb, and I have been His since I was born.

- PSA 100:3 ~ The Lord is God. He is the One that made us, not we ourselves. We are His people and the sheep of His pasture.

- PSA 139:13–16 ~ The Lord controlled my very being, even when I was in my mother's womb. I praise God for I was fearfully and wonderfully made. My essence was never concealed from Him, for He knew me even as I was being secretly made and developed inside my mother. He saw me when I was still imperfect, and in His book were written all the members of my body while they were being formed and were yet undeveloped.

- ISA 44:2, 24; ISA 49:5 ~ The Lord made you and formed you in the womb. The Lord formed me from the womb to be His servant.

- ISA 46:3–4 ~ God says, "Listen all of you in the house of Jacob and the remnants of Israel, for you were mine since you were conceived and lived in the womb; when you are old and gray, I still will be the one who keeps you. I made you, I sustain you, and I will deliver you."

- JER 1:5 ~ God said to Jeremiah, "I knew you before I formed you in your mother's womb; I sanctified you before you were delivered from your mother's womb. I ordained you to be a prophet to all nations."

- LUK 1:13–15, 44 ~ God told Zachariah that his wife Elisabeth would bear a son, and to call him John. That son would be filled with the Holy Spirit, even from his mother's womb. Elisabeth said to Mary, "The moment you said hello, the baby in my womb leaped with joy."

- 1 CO 7:4 ~ The wife does not have exclusive power over her body and neither does the husband.

Dear Father of life, who breathed His Holy Spirit into our bodies and we became living souls. Thank you for creating us, sustaining us, and redeeming us. Help us in our understating of your bounteous goodness and mercy, that we may grow in truth and hope, knowing that you will provide all good things, to include the gifts of life, faith, salvation, and everlasting life, simply for trusting in your Son, Jesus Christ. We love Him and we pledge to trust and follow Him all the days of our lives on the way to our heavenly home. Help us always to look forward to that day when we will see you face to face. Help us to cherish life, all life, but especially human life, for life is sacred to you. You allow your Spirit to indwell those who believe and for this we are immensely grateful. Your lifeforce combines with ours to produce a soul like that of Christ, sanctified through faith in Him and cleansed of sin by His blood. We petition you in the name of Christ, oh Father of life, that we remain faithful always and forevermore, Amen.

January 23

Anointing By the Holy Spirit Day is proffered to remind everyone of the importance of the work by the Holy Spirit in our everyday lives and our Christian walk. To anoint literally means to pour oil or smear ointment on someone. In Biblical terms it represents a divine appointment. During Old Testament times, prophets, priests and kings often were selected in this manner; for example, Samuel anointed kings Saul and David to rule over Israel (1 SA 10 and 1 SA 16). In the New Testament Jesus Christ was anointed by the Holy Spirit to be our prophet, priest, and king. In fact, "Christ" means "anointed one" (hence the verb "to christen"). Jesus likewise anointed His disciples with the same Holy Spirit. Lucifer was anointed by God to be worship leader, prior to rebelling against God and being tossed out of heaven (EZE 28:14–19). Do not align yourself with evil, Lucifer, or his demonic soldiers, which are destined for the lake of fire! Be a Christian soldier and defeat them as a member of God's army!

- LEV 20:7–8 ~ God said, "Consecrate yourselves and be holy, because I am the Lord your God. Keep my decrees and follow them. I am the Lord who makes you holy."

- NUM 15:38–40 ~ God commanded Moses: Put tassels on your garments, so that when you see the tassels you will remember my commandments and obey them, and so you do not corrupt yourselves by seeking after your own hearts and your own eyes. Then you will remember and obey, and you will be consecrated unto me.

- PSA 23:1–6 ~ The Lord is my Shepherd; He provides everything I need. He lets me graze in green pastures and beside still waters. He restores my soul. He leads me in paths of righteousness for His namesake. Even when I walk through the valley of the shadow of death, I will fear no evil, for God is with me; His rod and staff protect and comfort me. He prepares a table before me in the presence of my enemies. He anoints my head with oil; my cup overflows. Surely goodness and mercy will follow me all of my days, and I will live in the house of the Lord forever.

- ISA 44:28 ~ He (Messiah) is my appointed Shepherd and He will do everything I ask. He will build Jerusalem, and lay the foundation of the temple.

- LUK 4:16–20 ~ Jesus read from Isaiah about the prophecy which identified Him as the Anointed One who would bring the good news of salvation.

- ACT 10:36–41 ~ Peter preached: The Word that God sent to Israel is Jesus Christ; in Him God's peace can be found. The Word began in Galilee and became known throughout Judea, after the baptism preached by John. God anointed Jesus of Nazareth with the Holy Spirit and His power. Jesus spent His time doing good and healing the demon possessed, for God was with Him. We are witnesses of the things He did in the land of the Jews, and in Jerusalem where He was crucified on a cross. God raised Him from the dead after three days. Many people chosen by God to be witnesses saw Him, and we are among those witnesses.

Have you been anointed by the Holy Spirit? If you answered yes, it follows that you are using your spiritual gifts to edify the church and to spread the good news of the Gospel of Jesus Christ to the world. This is what is meant by being baptized by the Holy Spirit: equipped and called into service by God Himself.

- JOH 20:21–23 ~ Jesus addressed them once again, "Peace be unto you. As my Father sent me, now I am sending you." After saying this, He breathed on them and announced, "Receive the Holy Ghost. Those who's sins you remit, they are remitted; and those who's sins you retain, they are retained."

- ACT 8:17–20 ~ The apostles laid their hands on the converts, and they received the Holy Spirit. And when Simon the sorcerer saw how through the laying of hands the Holy Spirit was bestowed, he offered money saying, "Give me this power, so I can lay hands on others and bestow the Spirit." Peter admonished him, "Your money will perish with you because you think the gift of God can be purchased."

- ACT 20:28 ~ Keep watch over yourselves and the flock of which the Holy Spirit has made you overseers. Feed the church of God which He purchased with his own blood.

- ROM 1:16–17 ~ I am not ashamed of the Gospel of Christ, for it is the power of God unto salvation given to everyone who believes; to the Jew first and also the Gentile [to those who spoke Hebrew as well as those whose native language was Greek]. Therein is the righteousness of God revealed from faith to faith as it is written: the just will live by faith. [Note, the Old Testament was written in Hebrew and the New Testament was written in Greek.]

True believers are anointed by God via the Holy Spirit, to be sealed until the time heaven is opened for eternity. God will place His mark on everyone who has dedicated their lives to Him, having made the commitment of faith. It is guaranteed that God will preserve, protect, and deliver His own from the forces of evil in this world (PSA 91:11; EPH 6:10–18). "Fear not," He says, "for I will be with you always" (JOS 1:9; PSA 41:12; PSA 73:23; HEB 13:5).

- EZE 9:4–6 ~ God commanded His servant to set a mark on the foreheads of those who grieved because of the wickedness around them. The others were to be slain by the sword; all were to be slain except those with God's mark.

- MAT 28:19–20 ~ Jesus told His disciples, "Go into every nation and teach the people everything I have taught you. Baptize them in the name of the Father, Son, and Holy Spirit. Remember, I will always be with you, even until the end of time."

- JOH 3:31–34 ~ He who comes from above is above all others, but he who is of the earth speaks only of worldly things. The witness from heaven testifies of things seen and heard, though nobody accepts it, except those who certify it as true, having been sealed by God. He who was sent speaks the words of God, wherein God gives His Holy Spirit without limit.

- JOH 6:26–27 ~ Jesus pronounced, "Truly I tell you, the reason you follow me is not for the miracles, but because you have partaken of the bread and are filled. Therefore, work not for meat that perishes but for meat which endures unto everlasting life [i.e., the bread of life, which is the body of Christ]. This is the Son of man who carries the seal of God the Father."

- 2 CO 1:21–22 ~ He who established us and you in Christ, and anointed us, is God who has sealed us and placed into our hearts His Spirit as insurance that we remain in Him and receive the promise.

- EPH 4:30 ~ Do not grieve the Holy Spirit of God, who has sealed you for the day of redemption.

- REV 7:2–3 ~ An angel appeared in the east carrying God's seal. He shouted to the four angels who were given charge to harm the earth and the sea, warning them to hold off until God's servants had been sealed.

- REV 9:1–4 ~ The angel blew the trumpet and I saw a star falling to the earth from heaven; he opened the bottomless pit from which bellowed smoke like a furnace, blocking out the sun. From the smoke arose locusts who would sting like scorpions. They were commanded to hurt anyone or anything except those with God's seal on their foreheads.

If you are not sealed by God, you will be vulnerable to the mark of the beast. However, if sealed by the Holy Spirit, you are immune from the mark of the beast and cannot become possessed by any evil spirit including Satan.

- REV 13:11–18 ~ Then another beast with two horns arrived, speaking like the dragon. He exercised the same power as the first beast, performing magic feats such as bringing fire down from heaven. He convinced everyone to worship the first beast, and to make a graven image of it. And the second beast brought the image to life. He caused everyone to receive the mark of the beast on their right hand or forehead; only those with the mark could buy and sell goods. They tracked down and murdered anyone who did not receive the mark and worship the beast. The beast's number is the number of a man: 666.

- REV 14:9–10 ~ The angel warned them that anyone worshipping the beast or receiving the mark of the beast would face God's wrath.

- REV 19:20 ~ But the beast was captured, and with him the false prophet that performed miraculous signs on his behalf, with which he deceived those who had received the mark of the beast and worshipped its image. They were thrown alive into the lake of fire.

Perfect freedom is to be cleansed of sin, freed from its bondage to serve the living God. Jesus will give you a freedom that lasts forever (JOH 8:31–47), from the moment you confess and repent, trusting in the salvation of Christ that through faith in Him you might be set free. This includes a life insurance policy promising that death is not the end, and life will never end (1 JO 5:11). So, while most life insurance policies go into effect once a person dies, yours goes into effect immediately (JOH 5:24; HEB 9:13–22), insofar as Christ has saved you from death and hell and awarded you a place in the Kingdom of Heaven to reign with Him (2 TI 2:12).

- PSA 119:44–47 ~ I will obey God's laws continuously and forevermore; I will walk in freedom, for I have sought His rules. I will boldly testify before kings, and I will delight in God's commandments that I have loved.

- ROM 5:14–18 ~ Just as the sin of one man (Adam) brought judgment and condemnation to all, so has the righteousness of one man (Christ) brought the free gift of grace, providing justification of life to all believers.

- 1 CO 7:22 ~ Those who were servants when called by Christ have become free, and those who were free when called by Christ have become servants. You were bought with a great price, so do not become a slave to humankind, but remain responsible to God and the purpose for which He called you.

- GAL 5:13~ Brothers, you have been called to be free men, but do not use that freedom as an excuse to engage in lusts of the flesh, but in love serve one another.

- 2 TI 2:12 ~ If we suffer with Him, we also will reign with Him; if we deny Him, He also will deny us.

To consecrate is to render something as holy. Biblical sacrifice is to offer something that is considered consecrated (deemed holy) by God. We become a living sacrifice once we have been anointed, consecrated by God as an offering unto death. But we do not have to suffer death because Jesus died in our place to pay the debt of sin. We have had our sins removed from the record, rendering us holy before God so we can instantly join Him in heaven. Thus, the grave is not our destiny, not even a bypass (1 CO 15:44; 2 CO 5:6–8). Satan and death have no power over us, for God has given us the free will to choose life (DEU 30:19). That, my friends, is absolute freedom.

- MAL 3:2–4 ~ Who can endure the day of His coming, and who can stand when He appears? He is like the refiner's fire or the launderer's detergent. He will act as a refiner, purifying the Levites and refining them like precious metal. Then the Lord will have qualified men to bring offerings in righteousness, and those offerings will be acceptable as in times past.

- LUK 3:16–17 ~ John the Baptist answered them saying, "I baptize you with water. But One comes after me whose shoes I am unworthy to untie. He will baptize you with the Holy Spirit and with fire. He has the winnowing fork in hand, ready to clear the threshing floor. He will gather the wheat into the barn, and He will burn up the chaff with unquenchable fire."

- JOH 17:16–19 ~ Jesus prayed to the Father, "They are not of the world even as I am not of the world. Sanctify them by the truth, for your Word is truth. As you have sent me into the world, so I have sent them into the world. For these, I sanctify myself so that they too may be truly sanctified."

- HEB 10:26–27, 31 ~ If you deliberately continue sinning after you have received the knowledge of truth, there will remain no sacrifice for sins. The only thing you will receive is the fearful expectation of judgment and a raging fire that will consume the enemies of God. Yes, it is a dreadful thing to fall into the vengeful hands of the living God.

How on earth would anyone choose death? But they have, and they do, and they will. It's up to God's chosen, made saints by the sanctification of the Holy Spirit, to persuade people to embrace peace, love, faith, truth, and life through Christ who is the way, the truth (Word), and the life. Teach others so that they also can be free indeed! Help in the harvest of the saints by bringing the lost sheep back into the fold, which is God's church on earth, the body of Christ. If you are a member of this body, you will exercise your talents, gifts, knowledge, and skills to spread the words and the love of God to everyone you meet, whenever an opening presents itself. Having received an anointing, you are now appointed to this higher cause as you go about your routine chores and responsibilities.

- MAT 10:32–33 ~ Jesus said, "Anybody who confesses me before others, I will confess them before my Father in heaven. Anybody who denies me to others, I will deny them before my Father in heaven."

- LUK 10:16 ~ Those who listen to my disciples whom I have sent will listen to me; whoever rejects those who I have sent reject me. And those who reject me reject Him who sent me."

- EPH 4:10–16 ~ He that descended from heaven is the same that ascended far above the heavens, that He might fulfill all things. He appointed apostles, prophets, evangelists, pastors and teachers for the perfecting of the saints, for the work of the ministry, and for the edifying of the body of Christ. This He did so we might become unified in the one true faith, and in the knowledge of the Son of God, to become like Him, perfect in righteousness. He wants us to grow into mature Christians and not be like little children who are easily influenced by deception and trickery. He wants us to become more like Christ who joins together the entire body, according to the effectual working of every part, and the strengthening of all in love.

Being anointed will empower you to boldly proclaim the Lord: His words, works, and ways. Initially, one may feel apprehensive, unprepared, or uncertain; but the Holy Spirit will help you gather your words, lead you in your walk, and fulfill your mission (MAT 10:19–20). The Holy Spirit provides the confidence (PRO 2:2–6, 10–12), guidance (PRO 16:9; MAT 7:7), direction (PSA 32:8; PRO 3:5–6; ISA 30:21), power (MAT 10:1; LUK 10:17–20; ACT 1:8), ability (2 CO 9:8; EPH 3:20), and authority (MAT 16:19; MAT 28:19–20) to equip you to perform amazing acts of faith, and possibly even miracles (MAR 16:19–20; JOH 14:12). These things you cannot do on your own; it will be the Holy Spirit working through you. And you will be motivated to learn, teach, edify, and encourage as you gain confidence and power directly from Almighty God.

- PSA 32:8 ~ I will instruct you and teach you in the way you should go. I will guide you with my eye.
- PRO 16:3 ~ Commit your works to God and He will establish your thoughts.
- 2 TI 3:14–16 ~ Continue in the things you have learned and are convinced of, knowing from whom you have learned them. From a child you have known the holy scriptures, which are able to make you wise unto salvation through faith in Jesus Christ. All scripture is given by inspiration of God and is effective for doctrine, for guidance, for correction, and for instruction in righteousness.
- 1 PE 3:15 ~ Sanctify the Lord in your hearts, and always be ready to give an answer, with humility and respect, to anyone who asks about the hope that is within you.
- 1 JO 2:6 ~ Whoever says they are a Christian should show they are following Christ by the way they conduct their lives, walking in the way Christ walked.

Dear Heavenly Father, we pray to you in the name of your Son Jesus Christ, and on behalf of your Holy Spirit. Our prayer is that we daily acknowledge the presence of your Spirit and invite Him into our hearts so that we can face every challenge every day applying His counsel. Guide and lead us along the road that Christ paved with His blood. Help us to hear the voice of the Holy Spirit more clearly before we stray too far in the wrong direction. Teach us your Word of truth, which the Holy Spirit conveys in the Holy Bible and through your Son, the Word made flesh. Equip us to serve using our God-given talents and abilities, and with the additional knowledge and skills that you bestow to help us succeed in our mission as Christian soldiers. We know that the Holy Spirit will show us where to go and what to say, and will prepare us for whatever comes our way if we will only listen and take heed. Open our eyes, our ears, and our hearts making us wise unto enlightenment, understanding, and salvation. Let us be your example and your servant for others to see and hear, so they too will be open to receive your Spirit of grace and love. Increase in this world true knowledge of you, Father, Son, and Holy Spirit, Amen.

January 24

International Day of Education is based on the assertion that everyone has the right to a good education, with the belief that education improves the quality of life for everyone. There are a number of goals associated with this holiday, such as saving the planet, supporting public education and teachers, improving performance of students and teachers, and enabling students to realize their full potential. The Convention on the Rights of the Child first convened in 1989 to promote education worldwide so that all kids would be educated the same, regardless of where they live, which is a tall order for underdeveloped nations. In 2018, the United Nations declared an International Day of Education to be observed on 01/24 every year. The objective was to bring together planners, decision makers, societies, financial aid, and educators to determine the educational needs of different countries and help them to meet goals. The movement received impetus with the bipartisan No Child Left Behind Act, signed into law by President Bush in January, 2002. The purpose was to standardize education in the USA by establishing proficiencies for every age group as well as for teachers. Schools that failed to meet these levels could be sanctioned, closed, or required to find replacement administrators or teachers. A primary objective was to raise test scores for minorities, in what Bush regarded as "the soft bigotry of low expectations." In 2015, President Obama reversed or relaxed many of the requirements of the Bush bill, giving schools more freedom in performance testing, measuring success, making improvements, and holding teachers and administrators accountable. The Obama legislation was called Every Student Succeeds Act, of 2015. This pretty much took the wind out of the sails of the Bush law, such that nothing proactive came from it. Then when Covid 19 hit the country, many schools closed, though most teachers continued to receive their salary; eventually school districts incorporated distance learning via different internet platforms. Unfortunately, these measures served to significantly reduce student performance and participation levels, not to mention teacher performance.

It seems the school systems are still dragging their feet to get schools up and running; plus, some are getting overwhelmed by the insurgency of illegal immigrants who cannot speak English but their kids get to go to public schools anyway at the expense of taxpayers. It might take another act of Congress to help kids catch up in the USA, but so far, the only bills passed are spending bills which have done nothing to improve the quality of education anywhere. And those countries which left open their schools during Covid now outscore us on every critical measure. Given the gobs of money being thrown at the problem while yielding negative results, many parents are choosing to find alternatives for the schooling of their children, making school choice legislation a very attractive option. It is unlikely that public schools will improve any time soon, particularly because of the watered-down curricula being proposed for K–12, as well as in institutions of higher learning.

What will it take to return to normal? Well for starters, maybe we should allow God back into our schools, and allow kids to pray if they want to, and start teaching morality again. Many of our founding fathers proposed that the Holy Bible be the primary primer for schoolkids, but I don't expect that to happen anytime soon, though the Bible is the best textbook ever written.

- DEU 4:9 ~ Be careful and keep close watch over your soul, so you do not forget the miracles that you have witnessed, or let them slip away from your heart. Teach these things to your children and your children's children.

- DEU 6:2–7 ~ Fear the Lord and keep all His commandments and laws. Ensure that your children and your children's children obey God. Do this and you will prosper and your life will be prolonged. Love God with all your heart, soul, and might. Keep God's Word in your heart and teach His ways carefully and thoughtfully to your children. Talk with your family all the time about God, every day and night, whenever you are together.

- PSA 32:8 ~ God says He will instruct you and teach you in the way you should go, and will guide you with His eye.

- PRO 1:2–10 ~ Try to know wisdom and instruction; to perceive the words of understanding; to receive the instruction of wisdom, justice, judgment, and equity; to give subtlety to the simple; to give knowledge and discretion to the young. A wise person will listen and will increase in learning; a person of understanding will seek wise counsel, and will try to understand a proverb and its interpretation, or the words of the wise and the hidden meaning of what they say. Remember, the fear of God is the beginning of understanding; only fools despise wisdom and instruction. Children, listen to the instruction of your parents; if sinners entice you, do not give in.

- PRO 11:3, 14 ~ The integrity of righteous people can guide them, but the perverseness of wicked people will destroy them. For lack of guidance a nation falls, but many advisors assure the victory.

- ECC 7:12, 25 ~ Wisdom is a defense, and money is a defense; but wisdom gives life to those who possess it. I applied my heart to know, to search, and to seek wisdom, and the reasons for things, and to know the wickedness of folly, foolishness, and madness.

- ROM 2:21–22 ~ If you teach others, do you not teach yourself also? Do you not practice what you preach?

- 1 TI 6:3:5 ~ If anyone teaches false doctrines, and disagrees with the true and godly teachings of Christ, they are arrogant and lack understanding. Their contrary positions cause envy, strife, insulting, skepticism, and controversy. They are devoid of the truth, supposing that financial gain is a godly pursuit. Avoid such people.

- 2 TI 2:24 ~ A servant of the Lord does not waste time arguing, but is gentle to everyone, able to teach, and not resentful.

People are concerned about the education of their children, and rightfully so. Public schools, colleges, and universities are not doing a very good job. In many cases, these schools are indoctrinating students into a philosophy that is antichristian. Further, they are introducing topics to kids well before they are old enough to comprehend them, to include gender dysphoria, homosexuality, systemic racism, and anti-American agendas. Parents would be well advised to investigate the things their kids are being taught, and become more actively involved in school activities and meetings. Get the teacher to share their lesson plans; get the kids to explain what they learned in every class at least once a week if not every day. And teach your kids about God and the Bible because they will not get this training in public schools, or most private schools.

Heavenly Father, we pray for the education of our children, that they would be taught the basics and not get brainwashed by evil-minded educators. Help parents to oversee the education of their kids, to participate in school functions, and to teach kids your words and your ways. Enable the kids to recognize wrong or immoral teachings, and to call it out with their parents. Help us to defund schools and discharge instructors that are propagandizing our children. Help us to obtain godly leaders and politicians that will pass appropriate legislation to reestablish strict standards of performance for students and teachers; to have fair evaluations and grading systems; and to provide necessary training and instruction in ethics and civics, math and science, language arts, as well as proper behaviors to exhibit in various circumstances. In the name of Jesus who always taught the truth and the right way to go, Amen.

January 25

Canonization of Scripture Day is being introduced because it recognizes the meticulous work done by scholars and theologians to authenticate all sixty-six books of the Holy Bible. The word canon comes from the Greek word *kanon*, meaning standard or rule. The Bible was standardized early and has not changed since. The process involved meticulously scrutinizing the scriptures, manuscripts, and scrolls to weed out those not inspired by the Holy Spirit. Ways of validating the authenticity of the written word included determining authorship, fact-checking propositions and points, examining the hermeneutics of the work and its consistency with history and associated external sources; establishing the dates and times of the work, its location, intended audience, reasons the work was produced, cultural relevance, and accuracy of translation with respect to context; identifying literal and symbolic representations, internal and external consistency, applicability to the body of knowledge of God, overall accuracy and consistency with other scripture, and more. As you can see, this was not a small task, and it is complicated to explain in great detail.

Councils comprised of Biblical experts in theology, history, literary analysis, exegesis and hermeneutics were assembled to ensure that every book in the canon was true and inerrant. The Old Testament was written in Hebrew. Jewish leadership, scholars, and academia worked tirelessly to recopy material with exactitude, establishing a canon of thirty-nine books. The Old Testament canon was well-established before Christ who quoted from it often.

The twenty-seven books of the New Testament underwent a series of canonical examinations, beginning with the works of the apostles and Jesus's inner circle. This resulted in the original twenty-seven books being authenticated by the end of the first century AD. Because there was a plethora of counterfeits purported to be inspired, the early church fathers preached and wrote what they learned directly from the inner circle of Christ who were eyewitnesses and authored the New Testament. Many manuscripts could not be authenticated since it was unclear who wrote the work, or when and where it was written; they were incongruent with other books in the canon, and many were found to be written centuries after New Testament authors had passed. The original twenty-seven books met all of the standards enumerated above. Numerous ecumenical councils were convened with the emergence of the Holy Catholic church to further validate the scriptures and reach consensus concerning the meaning of certain doctrines. The New Testament was primarily written in Greek, but it had been translated into several other languages including Latin, Coptic, Syriac, Armenian, Ethiopic, Arabic, and Slavonic. Thus, it was relatively easy to derive consistency in the meaning of the words, given the countless versions available. No doubt, this was God's way of ensuring His Word would not be diluted, exaggerated, misrepresented, stifled, or destroyed. In total, some 4700 manuscripts were authenticated. For more on canonization see lesson on 08/25 regarding the Council of Nicaea.

- DEU 29:29 ~ The secret things belong to the Lord, but those things that He reveals belong to us and to our children forever, so that we may follow the words of His Law.

- ACT 26:20, 23; ACT 28:28 ~ God asked me to tell the truth in Damascus, Jerusalem, throughout the coast of Judea, and then to the Gentiles. I came to tell them that they should repent and turn to God, that they should perform good deeds, and that Christ had to suffer and rise from the dead to show everyone the way of righteousness. Know this: that the salvation of God has been sent to the Gentiles and they will hear it.

- 2 PE 1:16, 21 ~ We did not follow cleverly devised fables when we told people about the power and coming of Jesus Christ, for we were eye witnesses to His majesty. No prophecy ever came from the impulse of man, but holy men spoke as they were directed by God.

JANUARY

- 1 JO 1:1–3 ~ That which was from the beginning, the very Word of life, we heard, we saw, and we touched. For life was revealed, and we have seen it, and bear witness, and show you that eternal life, which was with the Father, visited us. That which we have seen and heard we declare to you, so that you can become one of us; for truly our fellowship is with the Father, and with His Son Jesus Christ.

- 1 JO 4:1–3 ~ Test the prophets by asking them if they acknowledge Jesus Christ as God's Son who came as a human being to save humankind from sin.

The Bible we have today has remained intact over centuries precisely because of the diligent work of scholars appointed by God to get the Word out. Any versions containing additions or deletions from the existing canon are not going to be reliable. For example, the inclusion of apocryphal works that were not canonized were included in early Bibles, though they were considered to be separate and not equal in value. Jewish theologians already had excluded from the canon many of those works. Martin Luther dismissed the apocryphal works that the Catholics were using to support doctrines which he deemed unscriptural. Luther promoted the idea of *sola scriptura*, meaning that scripture alone is all that we need because the Bible interprets itself. He advocated making the scriptures available to everybody, and that those who take the time to thoroughly study the scriptures will come to the same truths. Though never part of the original canon, some Catholics include apocryphal books while Protestants do not. Reputable translations of the Bible omit the apocrypha. The Holy Bible itself provides warnings about adding to or subtracting from the original text. It is easy to see the importance of keeping truth pure, and not changing the Bible.

- MAT 10:26–27; LUK 12:3 ~ Jesus said, "Do not fear those who hate you, for everything that is hidden now will be revealed later; everything that is unknown will become known. What I tell you in darkness you will speak in the light. What you hear in private will be proclaimed from the rooftops."

- 1 TI 1:3–10 ~ Do not teach false doctrine, or recognize any myths or irrelevant genealogies, which only serve to raise questions and do not provide answers concerning the faith. The goal is to love with a pure heart, a right conscience, and a sincere faith. Some have wandered away from these principles and turned to meaningless jabber; desiring to be teachers of the Law yet knowing nothing about the Law or about what they purport to be true. But we know that the law is good when it is applied lawfully. For the law was not implemented for the righteous, but for the lawless and disobedient, for the ungodly, for sinners, for the unholy and profane, for murderers and killers; for whoremongers and defilers, for spouse stealers, for liars and perjurers, and everything that goes against sound doctrine.

- HEB 3:12, 19; HEB 4:6 ~ Brothers beware, in case any of you have an evil heart of unbelief that strays from the living God; for they will not enter the kingdom because of their unbelief.

- JAM 4:17 ~ To anyone who knows to do good and does not do it, that for them is sin.

- 1 JO 5:20–21 ~ Remain in Christ who is true. Stay away from anything or anyone who would distort God's truth or attempt to take God's place in your heart.

God communicates His Word through the Holy Spirit, and the Word made flesh who is Jesus Christ. Notice that all persons of the Holy Trinity are involved in our salvation, which is why we worship them equally. God's witness is the Holy Spirit who lived fully in Christ. He became a witness of God's truth to the world; He sends those who believe the truth to spread the Word. The Bible was confirmed to be the true Word of God time and again, so that it would not change; no doubt God was responsible for this because He never changes, and neither does the truth.

DAILY DEVOTIONAL EVENTS

Therefore, God is the author of the Bible; His Holy Spirit spoke to the authors about what to write. God cannot lie; He ensured that the Bible would not be corrupted because it is His Word. Therefore, it must be true. And this assumption was upheld at the Council of Nicaea.

- DEU 4:2 ~ Do not add to or subtract from the commandments God gave to you.
- DEU 11:16 ~ Guard your heart from deceptions that would cause you to turn aside and serve other gods and worship them. Otherwise, the Lord's wrath will be kindled against you, and He will stop the heavens from giving rain, and your land will not bear fruit, and you will perish from the face of the earth.
- ZEC 8:16–17 ~ Always tell the truth to your neighbor; always execute judgments of truth and peace. Do not imagine evil in your hearts against another.
- 1 CO 2:13 ~ We teach using words taught by the Holy Spirit, not by human wisdom. Spiritual truths can only be interpreted by those who possess the Spirit.
- 1 TH 2:13 ~ We thank God that you received His Word and accepted it as the Word of God and not the word of men. The Word of God is at work in believers like you.
- REV 22:18–19 ~ For I testify to everyone who hears the words of the prophecy of this book, that if anyone adds to these words, God will add to that person the plagues mentioned in this book. If anyone subtracts from the words of this prophecy, God will take away their name from the Book of Life, and they will not share in the inheritance.

Heavenly Father, we thank you that your Word has remained pure and untarnished, for it is the best way for us to know you, your mighty works, and your plans for our lives. Help us to be witnesses of the truth, and rebuke those who would distort your words, or dismiss and discredit the Holy Bible. Amplify the voices of those who speak the truth, and teach your Word, that they may be heard; cause those who refute your Word or tell lies in your name to be silenced. Let there be revival among your people to stand together for truth, justice, and morality; help us overcome those who spread false doctrine, who hate the truth of the Bible, or who would indoctrinate children with messages contrary to your Word. Bring to light the true canon of scripture to anyone who would presume to know the Holy Bible, whether they are evangelists, preachers, church leaders, or laypersons, so they do not lead anyone astray with false teachings and doctrines. Praise be to you, Father, Son, and Holy Spirit, for validating and standardizing your holy Word, making it available to anyone who seeks you and your truth, Amen.

January 26

National Spouse's Day is observed this day each year to honor marriage. It probably evolved out of Military Spouse's Day which was introduced in 1984; there is no actual date when National Spouse's Day began but it has been recognized for twenty to thirty years. Originally, it was a celebration of traditional marriage, a monogamous union between one man and one woman. Unfortunately, the progressives have come up with different meanings for this day, because they want marriage redefined. These days it is about intimate relationships of any kind.

When it comes to marriage and spouses, it is advised that we stick to the Biblical definition. Marriage is a union between husband and wife in holy matrimony, meaning it is blessed and sanctioned by God, which is why it is usually conducted before the altar of the Lord. Marriage is a gift from God, for sharing and expressing emotional and physical passions while still obeying His Law. Marriage represents a commitment to one's spouse until death, just like Christ was committed to His church on earth until death, meaning all of His followers.

- GEN 2:18, 21–23 ~ God said, "It is not good for man to be alone so I will make a helper for him." God took a rib from man and made woman. Adam said, "This woman is bone of my bones and flesh of my flesh; she will be called woman for she was taken out of man."

- GEN 2:24 ~ A man will leave his parents and cling to his wife and become one flesh.

- PRO 5:18 ~ Rejoice with the wife of your youth.

- PRO 18:22 ~ Whoever finds a virtuous wife finds a good thing and obtains favor from God.

- ECC 9:9 ~ Always be happy with your spouse, and love him or her the rest of your life.

- JER 29:6 ~ Get married and have children, and encourage your children to get married and have children, so your family can increase and not diminish.

- MAL 2:14–16 ~ The Lord has formed a husband and wife into one flesh. In both flesh and spirit, they belong to Him. But why is this so? Because He wishes godly offspring from them. Guard your spirit, and do not break the covenant with your wife or husband by getting divorced.

- 1 CO 11:3 ~ I want you to know that the head of every man is Christ; and the head of the woman is the man; and the head of Christ is God.

- COL 3:18–19 ~ Wives, submit to your husbands, as long as it is within the Law. Husbands, love your wives and do not be bitter with them.

Any sex outside of marriage violates the seventh commandment: do not commit adultery. Once married, we are required to cherish our spouses and never have sex with another. Intimacy among married couples is fair game as long as it is not in violation of God's commands. If you are attracted to the opposite sex, and you fall in love with someone, get married and you can have all the sex you want together. And it will always be good because the commitment is love.

- MAT 5:27–28 ~ Jesus said, "You know that you should not commit adultery. I tell you that whoever looks at a woman with lust has committed adultery in his heart."

- MAT 19:6, 9 ~ Jesus said, "Once you are joined in marriage you are no longer two separate persons, because you have become one flesh. Whatever God has joined together, nobody should split apart. You cannot divorce your spouse unless he or she has committed adultery against you. If you divorce your spouse and marry another you are guilty of adultery. If you marry someone who is divorced you are guilty of adultery."

- 1 CO 7:1–5, 8–10, 28, 39 ~ It is fine if you never touch a member of the opposite sex. But if you cannot contain your emotions then marry, for it is better to marry than to burn with passion. Get married if you want to avoid the sin of fornication. However, if you marry you must be charitable to your spouse. A husband should have power over the wife's body and the wife should have power over the husband's body. Do not lie to your spouse, and do not split apart. It is not a sin to marry, but married people will have problems associated with their sinful and weak nature. Once married, you are bound together until one of you dies.
- GAL 5:19 ~ The actions of one's evil flesh include adultery, fornication, uncleanness, and lewdness.

God intended marital relationships to reflect the love between Christ who represents the groom, and His church which represents the bride. The husband is the head of the wife just as Christ is the head of the church. The church's message is to love and serve Christ, as He loves and serves His bride. This is why other definitions of marriage are not really marriage. In 2015, the Supreme Court ruled in favor of same-sex marriages, though making law was not within their purview. This was a bad decision, since same sex relationships constitute adultery not marriage.

- DEU 17:15–17 ~ You may have a king from among your people that the Lord will choose. That king must not seek to acquire great numbers of horses, gold or silver; neither should he seek to multiply wives unto himself, for that could cause his heart to become distracted
- ISA 61:10 ~ I will greatly rejoice in the Lord; my soul will be joyful in my God. For He has clothed me with the garments of salvation, he has covered me with the robe of righteousness; just like the groom is adorned with ornaments and the bride is adorned with jewels. Blessed be those whose sins are not counted against them.
- ISA 62:5 ~ As the groom rejoices over the bride, so God rejoices over His people.
- HOS 2:19–20 ~ I will be married to you forever. I will take you as my spouse in righteousness, judgment, loving kindness, mercy, and faithfulness.
- ROM 8:5–7, 13 ~ Those who pursue things of the flesh belong to the flesh; those who pursue things of the spirit belong to the Spirit. To have a carnal mind is death; to have a spiritual mind is life and peace. The carnal mind hates God; it disregards God's Law for it is in complete opposition to it. If you live for the flesh you will die. If you live for the Spirit, you can control the flesh, and you will live.
- 1 CO 7:2, 10–11 ~ Nevertheless, let every man have his own wife, and let every woman have her own husband. God requires that a wife must not leave her husband and the husband must not divorce his wife.
- 2 CO 11:2 ~ I have a godly jealousy toward you, for I have promised you to one husband, so that I can present you (the church) to Him (Christ) as a chaste virgin.
- EPH 5:23–27 ~ The husband is the head of the wife just as Christ is the head of the church. Christ loved the church so much He gave Himself for it, so that He could sanctify it and cleanse it with the washing of water by the Word. He has presented His church to Himself, a church without any imperfections, a church that is holy like Him.
- 1 PE 2:11 ~ Dearly beloved, I implore that while you are strangers and pilgrims on this earth, you abstain from lusts of the flesh which war against your soul.
- REV 19:6–9 ~ I heard the sound of a great multitude, as the rushing of many waters, with a thundering of voices singing "Alleluia, for the omnipotent Lord God reigns. Let us be glad and

rejoice, and give honor to Him; for the marriage of the Lamb has come, and His wife has made herself ready." The bride was dressed in fine linen, clean and white, representing the righteousness of the saints. Then the angel told me to write, "Blessed are those who are invited to the marriage feast of the Lamb," continuing, "These are the true words of God."

Today is a good day for parents to do something together without the kids. Take time to appreciate each other, and reaffirm your love and trust. Help each other with the chores to free up some time to be alone together. When I conducted couples counseling, I recommended that parents establish a date night every week (or month depending on their schedules); maybe pick a different restaurant each time. Celebrate your marriage and the partnership you have developed; and continue advancing as a team, not independently of one another.

Teamwork is essential in a marriage; you become partners in every aspect: emotional, sexual, social, financial, and spiritual. Relationships require two-way communication in order to avoid misunderstandings, strengthen the bonds, and resolve conflicts. You should collaborate on all important decisions. Collaboration results in a decision that is acceptable to both partners as well as the children. If this is unreachable, then compromise: meet each other half way so that each has to give up something to get something they want. Compromise restores the equity in a relationship: balancing the amount of give and take. If there is an imbalance in the equity, with one getting their needs met but not the other, this relationship is doomed to fail. This is what is meant by being equally yoked: joined together like a team of oxen, sharing the load, heading in the same direction, without pulling away or pushing back, and no lagging or dragging.

- PRO 27:17 ~ Iron sharpens iron as one man sharpens another.
- 1 CO 1:10 ~ By the name of Christ, be united in one mind and be of one opinion.
- 1 CO 7:15 ~ If an unbelieving spouse departs, let him or her go. A brother or sister is not bound under such circumstances.
- 2 CO 6:14 ~ Do not be unequally yoked together with unbelievers; for what fellowship can there be between righteousness and unrighteousness, and what communion has light with darkness?
- EPH 4:15–16 ~ By speaking the truth in love, we will become continuously more like Him; in every way, Christ becomes our head. Through Him the entire body is joined and held together, and grows, being built up in love as each part does its job.

Lord God, you make things clear in your Word: your will, laws, and precepts. You have made provision in your Law allowing for marriage, wherein we can enjoy intimacy with our spouse. What a blessing marriage can be; thank you for this privilege. All too often, people seek intimacy but are unwilling to make a commitment; this is true today more than ever, with fewer couples getting married, and lawmakers attempting to redefine marriage when it is already clear in your Word. And though there are responsibilities and problems that we might not experience staying single, the benefits far outweigh the costs. One of those benefits is to raise children to glorify your name. Help parents ensure that their children learn the truth because society will try to indoctrinate them with lies. Enable us to remove bad influences from our schools, churches, and society as best we can, and teach our youth what to watch out for and stay away from. Help our kids learn that your way works the best; that marriage can be a blessing, while engaging in promiscuous sex outside of marriage can be a curse. Help us love our spouses the way your Son loves His church: unconditionally. Whether right or wrong, good or bad, we are loved by you Father; help us to share that love and show it genuinely in our marriages and parenting. Through your Son, Jesus Christ, whose love for humankind was unmatched on earth, we pray, Amen.

January 27

International Holocaust Remembrance Day honors the lives of those tortured and murdered in the Nazi concentration camps. An estimated six million Jews were exterminated between 1941 and 1945 in a cruel attempt at genocide; millions of other innocent minorities also were slain. This was a human atrocity that must be remembered so that it will never be repeated. The United Nations chose this date to annually commemorate the liberation of Auschwitz by the Russian (Red) Army. To ensure we never forget, a resolution was passed to educate people who are unaware or who deny the holocaust ever happened. The first commemorative gathering was on this date in New York at the UN, 2006. Countless more viewed it on television, worldwide. Different countries have their own proceedings on this solemn occasion. It is a good time to reflect on the horrors of two world wars in Europe, no matter what your ethnicity or ancestry. For most of us, this day necessitates a response of prayer to God, motivated by hope that this never happens again.

    The Jews have had their share of suffering; it goes back to Old Testament days when they came in and out of favor with the Lord. Christians have undergone the same kinds of suffering; from the New Testament times till now, we are a people most hated in the world. We could receive the same fate as the Jews, for we have been in and out of the Lord's favor, and we need to find our way back quickly or else. God will prosper you when you are obedient to His will and destroy you if you give up on Him. But God promised the Jews they would someday return to their homeland and reunite as a nation, and they did in 1948. The USA had better get back into God's grace or we will lose our nation just like when God gave Israel over to the Assyrians and Babylonians.

- 2 CH 7:14 ~ God says, "If my people, who are called by my name, humble themselves, pray, seek my face, and turn from their evil ways, I will hear them and forgive their sins, and I will heal their land."

- 2 CH 7:19 ~ But if you turn away from me, and forsake the statutes and commandments that I have set before you, and go and serve other gods and worship them, I will uproot Israel from the land that I have given them, and I will reject this temple I have consecrated for my name. I will make it a byword and an object of ridicule among all nations.

- NEH 9:32–33 ~ Our God is great, mighty, and awesome, who keeps His covenant of mercy. Do not think our problems are trivial, those hardships that came upon our nation since the Assyrians ruled. God has been fair in punishing us in this manner, for we have been wicked.

- JOB 14:14 ~ If a person dies, can he or she live again? All the days of my appointed time I will wait, until my change comes.

- ISA 26:3 ~ The Lord will keep those in perfect peace, whose mind consistently trusts in Him.

- JER 25:11–12 ~ The land will be desolated, and the nations will serve Babylon for seventy years. After the seventy years are over, God will punish the king of Babylon and that nation for their wickedness, and will utterly destroy everything.

- EZE 32:4–12 ~ I will toss you out upon the land, where the beasts and fowl will feed on your carcasses. The land will be darkened beneath a gloomy sky. I will bring destruction upon all nations; the sword of the king of Babylon will terrorize you.

- MAR 13:13 ~ Jesus said, "People will hate you because of me, but those who endure until the end will be saved."

- LUK 21:17–19 ~ Jesus said, "People will hate you because of me; but be patient and you will keep your soul."

JANUARY

- REV 2:10 ~ Jesus said, "You will suffer and be imprisoned because of me. But, be faithful unto death and I will give you a crown of life."

    The Nazi movement was one of several attempts at world domination. They wanted to create a superior race by eradicating ethnicities and intruders they didn't want in their neighborhood. For globalists like them, this constitutes the world; that's why we call them globalists. They want it all for themselves, so don't fall for their line that it's for the welfare of everyone. This scam started in Egypt, next Assyria, Babylon, Media-Persia, Greece, and Rome.

    Did you know that Old Testament prophets forecasted these great empires in advance of them seizing power? They also prophesied about their fall; and when it comes to empires, they fall hard. There will be a final world empire like the others, only worse; this is what is referenced in Revelation as the new Babylon. Theirs will be the fall heard around the world.

- JER 50:40–46 ~ As God destroyed Sodom and Gomorrah and the neighboring cities, so will nobody remain in your cities. Behold says the Lord, a great nation from the north with many kings will rise up from the coasts. They are armed and dangerous, cruel and merciless. And they are coming for you, oh daughter of Babylon. Who have I appointed to perform this task? Is there anyone like me; is there a shepherd that can stand before me? Listen to the words of the Lord, for He is against Babylon in the land of the Chaldeans. The youngest of the flock will be carried away and the land made desolate. The sound of the fall of Babylon will be heard around the world and the earth will shake.

- DAN 2:32–33, 39–44 ~ Daniel interpreted King Nebuchadnezzar's dream of an image having a head of gold, breast and arms of silver, belly and thighs of bronze, legs of iron, and feet of iron mixed with clay. The image represented the kingdoms that would follow. The first kingdom of gold represented the existing kingdom of Babylon; the next kingdom of silver (Media-Persia) would be inferior to the one of gold. The third kingdom of bronze (Greece) would rule the world. The fourth kingdom would be strong as iron (Rome); but that kingdom would split into two kingdoms and would eventually fall apart since iron and clay do not mix. Eventually, God will set up a kingdom which will never be destroyed, and whose sovereignty will never change.

- DAN 2:34–35 ~ A stone was cut but not by human hands, and it struck the image (the statue in Nebuchadnezzar's dream) on its feet of iron and clay and broke them into pieces. And they (the kingdoms) fell, becoming as chaff on the summer threshing floor, blown away by the wind.

- DAN 7:3–13 ~ Four beasts arose from the sea. The first was like a lion with eagle's wings, which were plucked; the second was like a devouring bear; the third was like a leopard, with four wings of a bird and four heads. The fourth was dreadful, with iron teeth and ten horns; one horn rose up and replaced three. I watched until these thrones were thrown down before the Ancient of Days, who was dressed in pure white and sat on a throne of fire (see REV 13:1–4).

- DAN 8:20–25 ~ The ram with two horns represents the kings of Media and Persia. The male goat with one horn represents the first king of Greece. The goat's horn breaks, and is replaced by four others representing four kingdoms. After their rule will begin the rule of the terrible king, who understands riddles, and possesses great power. Through his cunning he will cause the destruction of mighty men and saints. He will magnify himself and deceit will prosper.

- EZE 16:28–30, 36–38 ~ You played like a prostitute with the Assyrians, with your insatiable lust which could never be satisfied. You further multiplied your sinful lust in the lands of

Canaan and Chaldea, and still were not satisfied. You obviously have a weak heart because you behave like an arrogant prostitute. Since you were so terribly filthy, with fornication, idol worship, and the sacrificing of your children, God will gather those you had sex with, along with those you hate, so they can see you naked and ashamed. And God will judge you the way he judges murderers and adulterers.

- REV 17:9–11 ~ The angel explained the mystery of the beast with seven heads as follows. The seven heads represented seven mountains on which the new Babylon sits (the great whore that sits over many waters). And there are seven kings, five have fallen, one is currently in power (Rome), and one is yet to come; and the seventh will reign for a short time (perhaps the Nazis). The beast is the eighth king and was also one of the seven.

- REV 18:2–7, 21 ~ With a mighty voice the angel shouted, "Babylon the great has fallen, fallen. It has become the habitation of devils and every foul spirit, like a cage for unclean and hateful birds. All nations have drunk the wine of the wrath of her fornication; kings of the earth have committed fornication with her, and merchants have become rich through the excess of her luxuries." I heard another voice from heaven saying," Come out of her my people, do not partake of her sins and contract her diseases; for her sins are piled up to heaven, and God has remembered her sins. Give back to her what she has done; pay her back double from her own cup. Give her as much torture and grief as she gave glory and luxury to herself." A mighty angel picked up a gigantic stone and cast it into the sea saying, "With such violence Babylon will be thrown down and disappear."

Tyrants making a power-grab to control the world has been a demented idea since the human race began. And though world empires have had a modicum of success, they collapsed due to that internal corruption which they never escape. Unquenchable lust, greed, pride, and genocide was their downfall. Global empires represent an attempt to proclaim oneself a god to justify their sinful ways, and cancel those who oppose them. Does that sound familiar?

This is the oldest sin in the book. It started with Lucifer, who wanted to be a deity so bad he recruited one third of the angels in mutiny against God Almighty. They were promptly cast out of heaven, falling to earth; some were so bad they went straight to hell (2 PE 2:4; JDE 1:6–8). The rest will meet them shortly when Christ returns in judgment. The last (eighth) global kingdom to fall will be that of Satan, the Beast, and his followers; they will join the fallen to burn in hell, not to rule. This is the fate of all who would be their own god or who reject God.

- HAB 1:11 ~ They are blown with the wind and pass on, those guilty men who relish in their own power as their god.

Omnipotent God, who reigns supreme over every kingdom, nation, tongue, and ethnicity, we worship you alone as there are no other gods but you. Help us to stay loyal to you and not go the way of the globalists, tyrants, power mongers, and deceivers, for their wealth will disintegrate, their empires will be short-lived, and their fall will be forever. Help our nation to return to your grace and veer from the path which leads to destruction. Help us to get back to believing in your awesome power and not defer to the meager power of globalists and other power mongers; please drive them out so we can be free of them, and free to worship you. We were a nation founded on a Judeo-Christian philosophy handed down in the Old and New Testaments of your winsome Word. Let us to get back to the Bible, for it will tell us what to do and when. In the meantime, may our hope and trust always be in Jesus Christ, in whose name we pray, in combination with your Holy Spirit who uplifts and supports all of your people, Amen

January 28

National Data Privacy Day was established by Congress to increase awareness about data piracy and the need to take preventive measures to ensure your data are not stolen or otherwise used without your permission. This day commemorates an international treaty signed in 1981 to protect data privacy. Beginning in 2022, Data Privacy Week ran from January 24–28. Cyber security is one of the greatest threats to society; cyber warfare is already being conducted as part of a cold war which the USA also engages in. Social media data and shared communications are not protected from use by the proprietors of the medium itself, which they sell to businesses, political entities, advertising agencies, credit companies, and so forth. They track your physical movements via your phone and car; and your browsing movements over the internet, including the sites that you visit, the things that you post, the items that you click on, and the people you connect with. Remember, big technology companies sell your data for a profit. They are not obligated to safeguard your data, you are. Today's observance is about protecting your privacy and respecting the privacy of others. All information is valuable, especially personal and sensitive information. There are a number of ways one can safeguard their digital information.

- Confirm that you are using a secure website before ordering any products (the address will show *https*, not *http*; the *s* stands for "secure"). If the data are encrypted it will be extremely difficult for a hacker to obtain your credit card, or other identity information.

- Be careful what data you share and who you share it with, because once it is on the internet it can be accessed, shared, and used for marketing and targeting purposes. There are ways to protect yourself through your security settings and application preferences.

- Antivirus software, firewalls, and Virtual Private Networks (VPN) protect you from hacking, spam, spyware, adware, computer viruses, and other intrusions; keep in mind, these products are not infallible, especially when sold by foreign countries that are not exactly our friends.

- Do not click on third party links. Sometimes the site tries to distract you, or get you to click on an ad or link; advertisers pay to put their stuff on other sites. Many websites reveal what you are looking for but force you to click on another icon to get there. Rather than click on the ad or popup, cut and paste the headline into your browser and search for it that way.

- When you are in your email or social media and notice an attachment that you are not expecting, message the person to see if it is legit before opening it. Or you can cut and paste an address into your browser as stated in the previous bullet and see what comes up.

- It is a good practice to disable applications on your electronic devices that you do not use. Oftentimes, these applications are used by third parties even if you are not using them. Go through the settings for applications you are unfamiliar with or do not need; uninstall them or disable them from interacting with your device. Applications that you use often employ "fingerprinting" to automatically collect data and analyze your habits.

- Disable popups; manually enable the ones you are expecting in your popup settings. Turn off cookies; if you must, specify the type of cookies you will allow for that site. Also, clear your history, cookies, and other temporary data files regularly. Note that your plug and play devices also may have tracking software built into the program or game.

- Back up data files regularly, in the event there is a system crash or pesky malware that gets through all of your roadblocks. Hackers make a fortune keeping captive your data, then making you pay a ransom to access your files. If your information is backed up, you can reimage or reformat your machine and copy the information back to your hard drive.

- Use double or triple verification methods when logging onto secure data sites, where sensitive information like financial, medical, vocational, and purchasing can be accessed. This will weed out the majority of hackers; serious unscrupulous hackers will bypass the precautions taken by the average person. Elite hackers get through most everything.

- Never provide information over the phone or to unknown solicitors. Don't respond to their messages, else you confirm your phone number or email address. Sometimes your device lets you block spam and robots. Bad actors use your data against you or to hack others.

- Understand that information searches over the internet are biased, because the server lists sites and promotes data in accordance with their agenda, political persuasion, or fees. You may have to sift through dozens of sites before finding the truth, whereas the false information will have several sources. University libraries are still the safest places to research refereed journals, which also can be accessed online if you are a student or patron.

Protect yourself, because people will come against you or try to do you harm, especially if you are honest and trust in the Lord. They would rather you trust in them so they can abuse you, seduce you, and subject you. Guard your heart and mind from those who wish to gain influence over you by using your personal information against you or by spreading false information about you. Investigate sources of information to determine which ones are reliable. When it comes to trustworthy information, you can't go wrong with the Holy Bible; any information contradicting God's Word will not be accurate.

- DEU 11:16 ~ Guard your heart from deceptions that would cause you to turn aside, to serve other gods and worship them.

- JOB 11:18, 20 ~ You will be confident because there is hope; you will be protected, so take rest in your safety. The wicked will not escape; their hope will be like taking their last breath.

- PSA 12:2 ~ They speak vainly about others; with flattering lips and two faces they speak.

- PSA 101:5 ~ Whoever privately slanders another, whoever has a conceited look and a proud heart, they will be cut off from God.

- PSA 122:6–7 ~ Pray for peace; may those prosper who love God. Peace be within your walls and security within your towers.

- PRO 4:23 ~ Guard your heart with all diligence, for from it flow the issues of life.

- 1 TH 5:3 ~ When they talk of peace and safety, total destruction will come.

- 1 TI 6:20–21 ~ Guard everything that has been entrusted to your care. Turn away from godless chatter and the opposing ideas of what is falsely called knowledge, which some have professed and in doing so have wandered from the faith.

- 1 PE 5:8–9 ~ Be sober and vigilant; your enemy the devil roams about like a lion searching for someone to devour. He will attempt to consume anyone who is not steadfast in their faith.

Most merciful Father, we feel so vulnerable and forget that you are protecting us like a mother hen gathering her chicks; help us to keep you in mind as we journey into places where people take advantage. Help us to take all due precautions, and not take for granted that data platforms or information sources are truthful, dependable, and transparent. Protect us with your presence, and open our ears to the advice of your Holy Spirit who is omnipresent. Alert us to any danger before we make a selection or request from unfamiliar locations in the world or the worldwide web. Remind us to be diligent in checking out sources, and whether they adhere to the truth or not. In the name of Jesus, the Word, the most truthful witness to humanity, Amen.

January 29

National Puzzle Day is a day for exercising your brain; the date was suggested by game and quiz inventor Jodi Jill in 2002. Brain games are fun and educational. The daily newspaper has several games and puzzles: crossword, jumbled words, missing numbers, searches, and mazes. Word games like Scrabble and others are abundant. Jigsaw puzzles never get old; they have varying difficulty and some are even three-dimensional. Building things with blocks or other shapes are great for little kids. Organizing things and filing things are effective ways of keeping your mind focused. Games and puzzles work both the verbal side and visual side of your brain.

It is important for all people to exercise their cognitive abilities, particularly old people who will lose these functions more quickly if they are not employing them often. Word, board, video, and trivia games and quizzes enhance competition as well as hone perceptual and psychomotor skills. Puzzle solving improves problem solving and decision making. If you struggle with memory, perception, vocabulary or math, puzzles and mind benders may help sharpen these abilities. With the evolution of electronic devices, you can access games and puzzles any time using a phone or computer. Families can work puzzles, play games, teach children, challenge youth, and engage the elderly when coming together on this day, to spend quality time in a way that will interest and instruct everyone, and enhance communications. Puzzles make great gifts too, when you can't think of what to get someone.

Bible games, trivia, and mysteries are great family activities. Putting together diverse passages or prophecies brings clarification to them, by using scripture to interpret other scripture. The Bible is like an enormous jigsaw puzzle; once you put the pieces together you can see the big picture. That's when things really come into the light and make sense. Continue reading the entire Bible, and you will discover what I mean. For example, prophecy in the Old Testament came true in the New Testament; and quotes by Christ and the apostles in the New Testament can be located in the Old Testament. Thus, the Bible references itself and is internally consistent.

- JER 33:3 ~ The Lord says, "Call to me and I will answer you, and tell you great and hidden things that you have not known."

- ZEC 8:16, 19 ~ Do these things: Speak the truth and render decisions that bring truth and peace; exercise love, truth, and peace.

- 1 TI 4:1–3, 7 ~ In the end times some will depart from the faith, acknowledging evil spirits, following the doctrine of devils, telling lies of hypocrisy, forbidding marriage, and prohibiting the eating of meat which God created for us to be received with thanksgiving. Refuse to accept such profane traditions and old wives' tales, and exercise godliness.

- 2 TI 3:14–15 ~ Continue in the things you have learned and are convinced of, knowing from whom you have learned them. From a child you have known the Holy Scriptures, which are able to make you wise unto salvation through faith in Jesus Christ.

- 1 PE 2:5–9 ~ You are living stones, built into a spiritual house; a holy priesthood, to offer spiritual sacrifices acceptable to God through Jesus Christ. You are a chosen generation, a royal priesthood, a holy nation, a special people; for you have been selected to give praise to Him who called you out of darkness into His marvelous light.

Heavenly Father, we pray for health in body, mind, and spirit. Help us to respect ourselves by ensuring that all three components of our being are exercised regularly, to achieve holistic health. Especially, help us not to neglect our spiritual wellbeing which can be exercised through Bible study, prayer, and worshipping with others. Thank you for making your mysteries known and understood through in-depth researching of your Holy Word. In Jesus's name, Amen.

January 30

Assassination of Mohandas Gandhi occurred this date in 1948; it would become Martyr's Day in India. Gandhi was instrumental in popularizing nonviolent protest to realize social reforms. His mother instilled a moral purpose, making him uniquely sensitive to racism and civil rights abuses. He experienced inhumanity firsthand while working in South Africa; he sought to combat legislation there which discriminated against Indians, resulting in a compromise. He returned to India and became involved in politics, supporting the British in the first world war, until they started drafting into service Indian civilians. At that point, he was protesting against the British, calling for national independence and the boycotting of British goods and enterprises. But some of his followers were violent so he retreated. Shortly thereafter, Gandhi was arrested for sedition, tried and imprisoned. Once freed, he resumed the protest, this time against the British salt tax, which really hurt the poor. The movement took them to the sea where they extracted salt from saltwater. Gandhi was arrested and imprisoned again, which was a regular thing. Even in prison he organized a protest against the mistreatment of the lower caste people in India. He championed this cause upon his release. When the second world war erupted, he agreed to support the British in exchange for independence. They refused, only to prompt Gandhi to advocate for the total withdrawal of the Brits from India. The response was to divide the nation into Pakistan and India; this discouraged Gandhi because he wanted to unite all people in India, including the Muslims (he was raised into Jainism which respects both Hinduism and Islam). A Hindu zealot did not agree with his tolerance of Muslims and shot Gandhi dead. A day of mourning was declared by Premier Nehru. Gandhi has been the poster child for civil disobedience, becoming an inspiration to Martin Luther King in his civil rights movement.

    Many people have been martyred for taking a stand against racism, tyranny, and injustice. This includes numerous prophets of the Bible, not to mention Jesus and His apostles. The early church fathers also were martyred for proclaiming the Gospel, as were Protestant reformers. Christians are still being persecuted and murdered all over the globe, and even here at home; and it will get worse before Christ returns (MAT 24:37; LUK 17:26–30).

- ACT 7:55–60 ~ Stephen, being enthralled by the Holy Spirit, gazed into heaven and saw the glory of God, with Jesus standing at His right hand. Stephen proclaimed, "Behold, I see an opening in the heavens and the Son of man standing at God's right hand." The crowd cried out loud and cupped their ears, charging towards Stephen. They dragged him out of the city and stoned him to death. Their coats were lying at a young man's feet, whose name was Saul (who became Paul). Stephen called out saying, "Lord Jesus receive my spirit." He knelt and prayed aloud, "Lord, do not charge this sin to their account," and then he died.

- ACT 12:1–10 ~ Herod the king intended to persecute the church by killing James the brother of John with the sword. When Herod discovered that the Jews approved of this violence, he proceeded to arrest Peter and throw him into prison (during the Feast of Unleavened Bread). He was going to make a public spectacle out of Peter, while the entire Christian church prayed for his welfare. The night before his trial, Peter was sleeping chained between two guards when an angel appeared telling him to get up, at which time the chains fell off his wrists. He put on his cloak and scandals as directed by the angel and the two of them walked out of the prison. Peter thought he was dreaming as they came to the city gate which opened automatically, after which the angel disappeared.

- 2 CO 11:24–27 ~ I (Paul) received thirty-nine lashes at the hands of the Jews on three occasions. Three times I was beaten with rods, and I was stoned once. Three times I was shipwrecked, and I spent a night and a day in the deep sea. I suffered many perilous events; I experienced substantial weariness, pain, cold, hunger and thirst.

JANUARY

- 2 TI 2:9; 2 TI 3:11 ~ Although I endured much hardship, persecution, and affliction, God always delivered me.

- 2 TI 4:22 ~ Paul's last words to Timothy as he awaited execution in Rome by emperor Nero: "May the Lord Jesus Christ be with your spirit."

- REV 2:10 ~ Jesus said, "Be faithful unto death, and I will give you a crown of life."

Anyone who takes a stand for Christ may suffer the same fate as the apostles, but their suffering will turn to glory in the end. It is inevitable that the world will go the way of evil. Make sure you do not go with them. Even if you lose your life protesting evil, you will gain it back.

- LAM 3:31–33 ~ Men are not pushed aside by the Lord forever. Though He allows grief He shows compassion, because great is His unfailing love. For God does not deliberately bring affliction or grief upon the children of men.

- JER 8:11–12 ~ To heal your pain they came saying "peace, peace" but there was no peace. Were they ashamed of their atrocities? Not in the least; they did not even blush. But they will join the fallen. When the Lord comes, they will be cast down.

- ACT 14:22 ~ Paul informed the disciples that they would endure considerable tribulation before entering the kingdom of God.

- ROM 5:2–5 ~ Through Jesus we have obtained access to His grace in which we stand, and we rejoice in our hope of sharing the glory of God. We rejoice in our sufferings knowing that they produce endurance, which produces character, which produces hope. And hope does not disappoint us, because God's love has been poured into our hearts through the Holy Spirit.

- ROM 8:35, 38–39 ~ Who can separate us from the Lord? Can tribulation, distress, persecution, famine, nakedness, peril, or sword? I am convinced that neither death nor life, nor angels, principalities, or powers, nor things present or future, nor height or depth, nor any other created thing, can separate us from the love of God which is in Jesus Christ our Lord.

- JAM 1:2–3, 12 ~ Brothers, rejoice when you fall into various trials, knowing that the testing of your faith produces patience. Blessed be those who endure temptation, for when they are proven, they will receive a crown of life which the Lord has promised to all who love Him.

- 1 PE 2:19–21 ~ It is commendable when you patiently endure grief and sufferings for Christ, because for this you were called; and Christ also suffered on our behalf, leaving us His example to follow.

- 1 PE 3:17–18 ~ It is better, given the will of God, to suffer for doing good than to suffer for doing evil. For Christ also suffered once for sins, the just for the unjust, so He could bring us to God; being put to death in the flesh but made alive by the Spirit.

- 1 PE 4:12–13, 16–17 ~ Do not consider it strange, the fiery trial that you must endure, but rejoice when you partake of the sufferings of Christ; when His glory is revealed you will be exceedingly glad. If you suffer for being a Christian do not be ashamed, but glorify God in the process; for judgment will begin with God's house. And if it begins with us first, what will be end for those who do not obey the Gospel of the Lord?

Dear Father, let us never be ashamed to confess our faith in you, your Son, and your Holy Spirit. Help us to share your truth and witness for Christ. If necessary, help us to endure suffering and abuse, never recanting our faith in your Word and our love for you. Help us to have courage in defending the faith, and protesting the persecution of Christians and the confiscation of our liberties. In the name of Jesus who is the epitome of love in human flesh we pray, Amen.

January 31

National Inspire Your Heart with Art Day recognizes the importance of fine arts in our lives to inspire, communicate, and motivate, and possibly create. It is unclear the origin of this holiday, though the arts have been around since the creation of human beings. In olden days, art and science were partners, and almost interchangeable; case in point, Leonardo da Vinci who illustrated his inventions and ideas, as well as experimenting with different media and subject matter in his artwork. Do you like to view unique works of art, listen to different kinds of music, attend a live performance, read a great story or biography, watch a well-done theater production or movie? Not only is it entertaining to observe fine art and performance art, it can be fun to produce a work of art.

Not everyone has natural artistic talent, but everyone can benefit from using various media to express themselves, and possibly process or vent emotion material, or illustrate thoughts that are difficult to put into words. Besides you do not have to be an artist to engage in art, appreciate it, or learn from it. You may think you lack natural talent in art, music, or writing; well, it depends on what you find beautiful and extraordinary. Art is a subject that covers a lot of disciplines and art can be learned and mastered regardless of your indecision about it.

- 1 CO 3:8–14 ~ The one who plants and the one who waters is the same; everyone receives a yield commensurate with their labor. We are laborers working together with God. You are the mission field; you are God's building. In accordance with God's grace given to the wise master builder, God has laid the foundation, and another will build upon it. But everyone must be aware of what they are building upon. There is no other foundation that can be laid, but that of Jesus Christ. Those who build on Him can proceed to add gold, jewels, wood, hay, or stubble. Everyone's work will be made manifest for all to see on the day it is revealed by fire: the fire that tries every soul to determine what sort it is. If that which is built endures, the builder will be rewarded. If it burns down, the builder will suffer the loss but will be saved from the flames.

- HEB 3:4–6 ~ Every house is built by someone, but God is the builder of everything. Moses was a faithful servant in God's house, testifying of things to be repeated in the future. Christ is the faithful Son who governs over God's house.

- JAM 1:4 ~ Let patience have her perfect work, that you may be complete, wanting nothing.

This is a day to engage your children and explore the various forms of art. Determine what kinds of projects your kids like or would be willing to try. Encourage them to learn to draw, play an instrument, or take a class in drama. Take your kids to a concert or a theatrical event; or to the library or a museum. Ask them what they think of a particular work of art or performance. What do they think the artist was trying to convey or what was their opinion of the work? Any foundation or institution of the arts will be willing to help your kids discover themselves, to bolster their imaginations and creative instincts. Such learning will be useful in their professional lives as well. Actually, everything has an element of art or beauty. Have you ever heard of the art of teaching, the art of science, the art of communicating, the art of leadership, the art of war? Other forms of art would include designing cars, landscaping, architecture, interior decorating, even fishing. Mastering any task makes one an artisan in that field.

- 1 CO 12:7 ~ The manifestation of the Spirit is given to everyone for the common good.

- 1 TH 5:21 ~ Examine all things and hold onto the good.

I remember in elementary school having music and art classes, and going on field trips to the symphony or the art museum; sometimes we went to the auditorium for live performances, and sometimes we ourselves practiced and performed before teachers, family and friends. Personally,

I enjoyed these activities a lot more than the classroom. Recently, there has been less emphasis on art, literature, and music and more emphasis on teaching personal opinions or some political ideology. It is disheartening to see how the fine arts have been marginalized in public schools, with fewer teachers and courses being offered. When I completed my military service, I went to college and majored in art because I wasn't interested much in academics. I never encountered an art medium I didn't like, and in some I excelled; I earned a bachelor degree in art and a teaching certificate to teach art in K–12.

I ended up getting additional degrees in counseling and psychology. I found that things I learned in art were not only valuable but were applicable to other fields of study. For example, the fundamentals of artistic design, composition, and movement helped me considerably in designing tests and experiments, composing lesson plans and test plans, and maintaining flow during lecturing, public speaking, and group therapy. I began introducing art, journaling, and music as counseling interventions as far back as 1979, up until my retirement five years ago. These techniques are widely used today in occupational therapy and psychotherapy. These days there are expressive arts counseling centers, and one can become licensed as a specialist in art therapy. Art is good for the soul and is food for the spirit.

We can learn a lot about the Bible through arts and artifacts; there are paintings and sculptures which represent stories from the Bible, there are illustrated storybooks for kids to learn the Bible, and there is an enormous amount of evidence supporting the Bible to be found in archaeology and other physical sciences. Consider the Shroud of Turin and the matching Sudarium of Oviedo, which show a crucified victim with the exact same wounds that Christ endured. I guess God is a master photographer, leaving us a photographic negative of the resurrection. Do a search on the recent authentication of these artifacts and you might be surprised what you find. It is apparent that God left behind tons of historical evidence for people to find which illustrate His works in general and the Holy Bible in particular. The Bible itself is an excellent work of literature, history, philosophy, and science; and the prophecy is miraculous.

God Himself is quite the artist; if you don't believe that, just take a look around you.

- GEN 1:3–5 ~ On the first day, God said, "Let there be light."

- GEN 1:6–8 ~ On the second day, God placed a firmament, or expanse, above and below the waters to divide them.

- GEN 1:9–13 ~ On the third day, God separated the dry land from the waters below the heavens, and let the earth generate seed-bearing fruit, herbs, and plants.

- GEN 1:14–19 ~ On the fourth day, God placed lights above the firmament (atmosphere) to include the sun, moon, and stars to divide time by years, seasons, and days which were divided into daytime and nighttime.

- GEN 1:20–23 ~ On the fifth day, God created marine life and birds, male and female, so they could reproduce after their own kind.

- GEN 1:24–31 ~ On the sixth day, God created animals and humans, male and female, so they could reproduce after their own kind.

- GEN 2:2–3 ~ On the seventh day, God finished His work and rested. And He blessed the seventh day and sanctified it (made it holy).

There were many artisans, craftsmen (and women), architects and engineers mentioned in the Bible; no doubt inspired by the works of God from His creation. Consider the fact that Jesus was a carpenter (MAR 6:3), Noah was a carpenter (GEN 6:14–16), Paul was a tentmaker (ACT

18:1–4), David was a poet and musician (1 SA 16:14–23): all master craftsmen. We are much more than our art. Artistry is in all of us, though in different specialties and proportions. Find your inner creative urge; if it's in you, it'll want to come out.

- EXO 35:26–27, 31–33 ~ Talented women made beautiful colored fabrics and linens by spinning hair from goats and sheep. People were filled with the Spirit of God in wisdom, understanding, knowledge, and in all kinds of craftsmanship, to create interesting works in metal, stone, and wood.
- 1 CH 22:15 ~ There were an abundance of workmen who cut wood and stone for all kinds of applications, as well as workers in gold, silver, brass, and iron. Arise and get busy, and the Lord will be with you.
- 1 CH 25:1–31 ~ There were twelve times twenty-four people assigned to make music in God's house with twelve brothers and sons per tribe.
- 2 CH 5:13–14 ~ As the orchestra and choir joined in musical harmony to thank and praise God, the church was filled with a cloud, for the glory of God had encompassed the church.
- ECC 3:11 ~ God has made everything beautiful in its time; He has placed eternity into the heart. Yet nobody can imagine what God accomplishes from the beginning to the end.
- ISA 64:8 ~ Oh Lord, you are our Father. We are the clay and you are the potter, for we are the work of your hands.
- JER 18:1–6 ~ The word of the Lord came to Jeremiah telling him to go visit the potter and receive a message. So, he went to the potter's house and found him working at the wheel. The potter formed a bowl, but he was not happy with it so he formed another bowl that he liked better. Then the message came to Jeremiah, "House of Israel, can I not do with you as the potter has done? Behold, as the clay is in the hand of the potter so are you like clay in my hands."
- JOH 5:17 ~ Jesus answered them, "My Father has been at work all the while, and I work too."
- EPH 2:10 ~ We are His workmanship, created in Jesus Christ to do good works, which God has ordained in advance.
- COL 3:23–24 ~ Whatever you strive to do, do it wholeheartedly as to the Lord and not unto men, knowing that from God you will receive the reward of inheritance because you serve Christ.

Heavenly Father, creator of all things good, who inspires us to do good works and to create things of beauty; we thank you for the many talents and abilities you have given to us. We pray for the motivation to learn more skills and to give back using those same skills, abilities, and talents. Help us to learn how to serve you in all these ways, while we serve others. Help us to teach children to appreciate your creation, and the artistic creations of others; and to appreciate the talents and abilities you have given to them. Enlighten school administrators and boards that they include the arts in their curricula. Help us also to get prayer and your Word back into the schools, or at least provide the opportunity for parents to change schools that do not teach the truth or the basics of the Holy Bible. Please do not let boards and bureaucrats dictate what our children must learn, but let that be up to the parents; and help parents to be proactive in the physical, mental, and spiritual development of their children. Help us as parents to look to you for our guidance, and to shine as an before others, which is the light within us reflecting Christ the Lord. In His name we pray, Amen.

February 1

National Freedom Day commemorates this date in 1865 when President Lincoln signed into law antislavery legislation which soon would become the Thirteenth Amendment to the Constitution. The push to memorialize the event arose from a former slave named Richard Wright who was freed after the Civil War, and was a veteran of the Spanish-American War. The US army major arranged a conference in Philadelphia to garner support for his idea. In 1948, the year after Wright died, President Truman signed a bill making National Freedom Day in the USA official.

Schools often acknowledge this historic event; additional events include luncheons, festivals, speeches, and local observances to remind us that freedom is nothing to take for granted. Traditionally, a ceremonial wreath is draped over the Liberty Bell in Philadelphia. Today is a day to praise God for living here in the land of the free; it is also a good time to pray for people around the world who are not free. Take time to enumerate your freedoms as a family; bring plenty of paper because these blessings outnumber the setbacks.

You might first consider your freedom from sin and death. Thanks to Jesus Christ, we need not fear death because He overcame it. And we need not worry about being condemned for our sin because He paid the penalty in full. We are free to do whatever we want, but we are limited by our own conscience which knows in advance what is allowed and what is not allowed. There is no excuse for disobedience (ROM 2:15), though we all fall short (ROM 3:23). Freedom makes everybody equal, so does sin. Which one is worth fighting and dying for?

- PSA 51:10–12 ~ Create in me a clean heart, Lord, and renew an upright spirit within me. Do not remove me from your presence and do not take your Holy Spirit from me. Restore to me the joy of your salvation, and uphold me with your free Spirit.

- PSA 119:44–47 ~ I will obey God's laws continuously and forevermore; I will walk in freedom, for I have sought His rules. I will boldly testify before kings, and I will delight in God's commandments that I have loved.

- JER 8:11–12 ~ To heal your pain they came saying "peace, peace" but there was no peace. Were they ashamed of their atrocities? Not in the least; they did not even blush. But they will join the fallen. When the Lord comes, they will be cast down.

- MAT 10:8 ~ Jesus said, "Freely you have received and freely you should give."

- JOH 8:31–32, 36 ~ Jesus said, "If you believe in my words then you are indeed my disciples; and you will know the truth and the truth will set you free. If the Son of God sets you free, you will definitely be free."

- ROM 3:23–24 ~ All people have sinned and come short of God's glory. All are justified for free by God's grace through the redemption found in Jesus Christ.

- ROM 6:14, 17–18 ~ Now sin has no hold over you, for you are not under the Law you are under Grace. Thank God that we, who were servants of sin, have obeyed in our hearts that doctrine which delivers us, being made free from sin, and now serving righteousness instead.

- 1 CO 2:12–13 ~ We have received, not the spirit of the world, but the Spirit of God, so that we may know the things that God has given to us for free. We speak of these things, not in the words that the world teaches, but in words that the Holy Spirit teaches, comparing spiritual things with spiritual.

- GAL 5:13 ~ You have been given the freedom to love and serve one another.

FEBRUARY

- 2 TH 3:1 ~ Pray for Christian teachers and ministers, and pray for the freedom to openly speak God's Word.

- 1 PE 1:18–19 ~ You were redeemed, not with corruptible things such as gold and silver, but with the precious blood of Christ, a Lamb without any imperfections.

Many freedoms that we enjoy are guaranteed by our Constitution, and most of those are given by God Himself. These are called unalienable rights in the Declaration of Independence because they are not to be taken away (alienated) from anyone since they were not given by government or humans. Of course, if you violate the law you can expect to lose your freedom, because, in a free society, citizens are obligated to respect the freedom of others. If you do not respect freedom, you do not deserve freedom. If you do not have freedom, you'll seek it; and once you obtain it, you will do whatever it takes to keep it. Guard it carefully; do not lose it, for it will be very difficult getting it back if you do.

- JER 2:31–32; JER 14:10 ~ God says, "Why do my people say that they are free to roam? Does a maiden forget her jewelry? Does a bride forget her wedding ornaments? Yet my people have forgotten me for days without number." The Lord says this to the people: "They love to wander; they cannot keep their feet from straying. Therefore, the Lord does not accept them; He will now remember their iniquity, and punish them for their sins."

- ISA 61:1–3 ~ The Spirit of God is upon me, because He has directed me to preach His good news to the humble, to heal the broken hearted, to free the slaves, and to release those who are bound in chains and in prison; to proclaim the Lord's favor and His vengeance, to comfort all who mourn, and to tell those who mourn to exchange their ashes for beauty; to replace mourning with joy, and to don the garment of praise in exchange for the spirit of sorrow, so that they may be trees of righteousness, planted by the Lord for His glorification [Jesus quoted this passage early in His ministry in His hometown (LUK 4:14–20).

- HOS 10:2, 10 ~ Their heart is divided; they have been found guilty. God will break down their altars and destroy their graven images. When it pleases God, He will punish them; nations will gather against them and enslave them because they betrayed the Lord.

- GAL 5:13–18 ~ Brothers, you have been called to be free men, but do not use that freedom as an excuse to engage in lusts of the flesh, but in love serve one another. For all the Law is fulfilled by loving your neighbor as yourself. So, walk in the Spirit not in the flesh. For the Spirit and the flesh oppose one another. If you are led by the Spirit, you are not under the Law.

- 1 PE 2:13–17 ~ Submit to the laws of the land, for it is God's will that you are lawful and upright, thereby silencing those ignorant people who would talk behind your back. Be free, but do not use your freedom to conceal evil. Instead, you must serve the Lord, respect all people, love your fellow Christians, fear God, and honor those in authority.

What is the opposite of freedom? Slavery, of course. If you are not free from something, chances are you are apt to becoming a slave to it: case in point, sin. We are not free to do whatever we want, and that makes sin all the more attractive to our sullied flesh. Such sins can become habitual, after which it is very difficult to stop. Even things that are allowed are not to be abused; overindulgence in anything leads to addiction and is harmful to one's health. Any worldly addiction means the person does not have God first in their lives since the world and the flesh are in control. Let the spirit inside you govern your thoughts, and you will be free. That kind of freedom lasts forever; hold fast to it, else someone snatch it from your hand, like Satan.

- ECC 1:8 ~ The eye never has enough of seeing, nor the ear its fill of hearing.

FEBRUARY

- MAT 24:8–11 ~ Jesus warned everyone that those who follow Him will often be hated by others and that being a Christian will be offensive to many. Some Christians will be assaulted, imprisoned, and even killed for following Christ, but those who endure until the end will receive a crown of life.

- JOH 8:34 ~ Jesus said, "Whoever commits sin becomes a slave to sin."

- ROM 7:19–25 ~ The good I want to do I do not do, and the evil I do not want to do I do. If I do that which I wish not to do, it is not I that do it but sin that dwells in me. And even when I do good, evil is still present within me. Although I delight in God's law in my mind, I see another law working in my body, warring against the law of my mind and making me a slave to the sin which is inherent in my body. What a wretched man am I; who will deliver me from this body of death? I thank God through Jesus Christ our Lord, for with my mind I serve the Law of God, but with the flesh I serve the law of sin.

- 1 CO 6:12; 1 CO 10:23 ~ Something that is permissible is not necessarily beneficial or constructive. It is all right to enjoy something but I will not let it control me.

- PHP 3:8–9 ~ Without a doubt, I count everything loss except the excellent knowledge of Christ Jesus my Lord, for whom I have suffered the loss of all worldly things, which to me are as garbage because of what I have gained in Christ; finding righteousness from Jesus, though not having any of my own in accordance with the law, but possessing the righteousness of God by faith in His Son.

- PHP 4:5 ~ Let your moderation be an example to others.

- GAL 3:28 ~ There is no such thing as Jew or Greek, slave or free, male or female, for we all are equal in Jesus Christ.

- HEB 13:3 ~ Continue to love each other as brothers and sisters. Do not forget to entertain strangers, for by doing so some have entertained angels without knowing it. Remember those who are in prison as if you were there with them, and remember those who are mistreated as if you yourselves were suffering.

- REV 2:10 ~ Jesus said, "You will suffer and be imprisoned because of me. But, be faithful unto death and I will give you a crown of life."

- REV 3:11–13 ~ Jesus said, "Behold, I am coming soon. Hold onto your crown of faith; do not let anyone take it away from you. For those who overcome I will make them a permanent pillar in God's temple; they will have the name of my God and His city, which is the new Jerusalem, written on them. The city will descend from heaven and from God, and I will write my new name on them. Listen to what the Spirit says to the churches on earth."

Heavenly Father, we are thankful for the freedoms we enjoy and we pray for those who are not free. Let your Holy Spirit touch those who are enslaved, either by others or by their own misdeeds. Help them to see that your saving grace is free, and it sets us free from those things that would otherwise try to control our minds. Help us to continuously relinquish control of our thoughts to you, bringing them into alignment with your will. If we think of you before we think of what to do next, we can control ourselves and refrain from sin; but we are weak and feeble-minded, forgetting that you are in control. We need to be mindful of you, but we need your help remembering. Give us signs in our daily life to remind us where we are heading during every moment, all the way to the end, which is home in your kingdom to live as your adopted sons and daughters, along with Jesus our brother. We ask this prayer in His name, Amen.

February 2

Groundhog Day is a tradition in North America, based on an old Dutch myth: observe the groundhog and determine if he sees his shadow or not. If he sees a shadow, it means the skies are clear, and he will return to his burrow for six more weeks of winter. If not, spring will come early. Coincidentally, the observance of Candlemas is also observed, which is a Christian mass commemorating the day the baby Jesus was presented by His mother Mary at the temple, once her purification period had passed; this was a Jewish ceremony and it occurred roughly a month after Jesus's circumcision (LEV 12:1–5; LUK 2:21–38). A church service usually is conducted around the first week of February. This doesn't add any legitimacy to Groundhog Day, which is a "just for fun" holiday. Incidentally, there is no scientific correlation between the weather on one day and what happens six weeks after that.

It can be entertaining, glorifying groundhogs and making movies about them. It distracts from reality in a way, and I suppose we all need a break from that occasionally. But invented portents do not predict anything. People like to look for signs in just about any anomaly, thinking it might have some hidden meaning. As for me, I prefer reality which is every bit as interesting, if not more so. And regarding signs, there are such things in the Bible, but the difference is this: those signs actually are portents of real things that will happen in accordance with God's timing.

There were plenty of Old Testament signs that Messiah would come, and hundreds of prophecies that corroborate their accuracy about Jesus Christ: His birth, character, ministry, sacrifice, and resurrection. Then there are hundreds of New Testament signs that Messiah will come a second time. Curiously, shouldn't we be equally convinced that these signs will be every bit as accurate as those forecasting His first coming, given that they all were confirmed in Christ? Jesus Himself gave a detailed account of many of these signs, while teaching about the end times as the conclusion of His ministry neared (MAT 24–25; MAR 13; LUK 21).

- ISA 32:6–7 ~ The vile person speaks villainy, plots evil, practices ungodliness, and deprives the needy. His instruments are evil. He devises wicked plans to destroy the poor and the just with his lies.

- JER 23:14, 17 ~ I have seen horrible things. They commit adultery, tell lies, and support evildoers so that nobody returns to being good. They have become like Sodom and Gomorrah. They say you will find peace for being evil and following your fantasies.

- JER 30:7 ~ That will be a great time of tribulation; there will be no others like it. It is the time of Jacob's trouble; but he (Israel) shall be saved out of it.

- LAM 2:14 ~ Your prophets have seen false and deceptive visions.

- EZE 5:17 ~ I will send famines, pestilence, and wild beasts; and you will be destroyed by the sword.

- DAN 9:27 ~ During the last half of the week (3.5 years) the abomination that causes desolation will continue, until the terrible end that awaits is poured out upon them.

- DAN 12:11 ~ The abomination that makes desolate will be set up for 1,290 days.

- MIC 6:12 ~ The rich men are full of violence and lies.

- MAT 24:1–18, 22 ~ As they left the temple, Jesus told His disciples that the temple buildings would be thrown down, and every single brick would be ejected. Later, Jesus sat down on the top of the mount of Olives, at which time the disciples asked Him privately about when that would be and what signs would indicate His second coming. Jesus answered, "Do not be fooled, for frauds will come in my name saying they are the Christ, deceiving many. You will hear of wars and rumors of war, but do not be troubled, for the end is not yet. For nation will rise against nation and kingdom against kingdom. There will be famines, pestilences, and earthquakes in different places. This is the beginning of sorrows. They will accost you, torture and kill you for my namesake. Many will be offended and betray one another, and hate will abound. There will be false prophets, seeking to deceive; and iniquity will be everywhere because love will have waxed cold. Those who endure until the end will be saved. The Gospel will be preached in all the world as a witness to the nations; then the end will come. When you see the abomination of desolation stand in the holy place, as spoken of by the prophet Daniel, flee to the mountains. Do not pack or gather your belongings. Unless those days of tribulation are shortened, none will survive. But only for the elect's sake, those days will be shortened.

- MAT 25:13 ~ Watch therefore, because you know neither the day nor the hour.

- 2 TH 2:3–4 ~ Do not be deceived by anyone, for that day will not come before there is a falling away from the faith, when that man of sin, the son of hell, is exposed. He opposes God, exalting himself, and sitting in the holy temple claiming to be God.

- 2 TI 3:1–6, 13 ~ There will be a time of great distress. People will love themselves and money. They will be abusive, arrogant, conceited, disobedient, treacherous, slanderous, ungrateful, unholy, inhumane, haters of good and lovers of pleasure. They will capture weak and wayward women, swayed by impulses. Evil people and impostors will progress from bad to worse, as will the deceivers and the deceived.

- REV 2:10 ~ The devil will throw you into prison to test your faith; you will be tormented in captivity for ten days.

- REV 19:19 ~ I saw the beast, the kings of the earth, and their armies gathered for battle against the King of kings.

The Bible is filled with prophecy, which makes it unique from any other book. The amazing thing is that the prophecies in the Bible always come true to the finest detail. The reliability of scripture exceeds anything ever predicted by science. I mean, you will never get hundreds of experimental results that converge upon one finding using science; but that is precisely what you will find in Biblical prophecy. Another amazing thing about Biblical prophecy are the particulars provided, leaving no question when that prophecy is fulfilled. You can flip a fair coin and expect heads and tails will come up equally as often, but it may take thousands of flips (or more) before the odds come out exactly 50-50. Scientists have contemplated the likelihood of all Old Testament messianic prophecies coming true in one man. Though there were roughly 330 such prophecies, one study was done on seventeen of the principal prophecies: like Messiah being born of a virgin in Bethlehem, to be betrayed and executed, and in three days to rise from the dead (see Peter Stoner, *Science Speaks*, 1958). The probability was one chance out of 100 quadrillion (1/10 followed by sixteen zeroes).

Our Father in Heaven, whose perfection is absolute and forever, we praise and worship you, and we thank you for creating us, preserving us, and saving us. We thank you for your Word which informs us about you and your plan of salvation, which was foretold since the world began, and fulfilled in your only begotten Son, Jesus Christ. Thank you, Jesus! Praise the Lord! We have been duly warned to get our hearts right with you because we know that Jesus will be returning, and by the look of the signs, it might be very soon. Prepare our hearts to receive Him, oh Father, and remind us to be watchful so we are not caught off guard. Let us be as the sentry, ready to sound the alarm that our Master is on His way. In His name we pray, Amen.

February 3

Day the Music Died makes reference to a terrible plane crash claiming the lives of three up-and-coming rock stars on this date in 1959. I actually remember these artists; each had a top forty hit at the time. Their names were Buddy Holly, Ritchie Valens, and J. P. Richardson. They were memorialized in the 1971 Don McLean hit, *American Pie*. The three were touring with various bands and chartered a plane rather than bear the unpleasant and cold conditions on the buses. Richardson was ill and managed to convince Waylon Jennings to give up his seat on the plane. The rest is history; shortly after takeoff on a stormy night, the plane went down, killing the pilot and three stars on impact. Actually, the music didn't die but three musicians did, and this shook the music world, which is why the date is recognized, mostly by baby boomers. However, each year is a gathering in Clear Lake, IA at the cornfield where they met their maker.

Unfortunately, it seems that pop/rock stars and small planes do not mix, because many musical artists have passed in the same manner. Others burned themselves out. Either way they crash and burn. Many will die young and in their prime, with a rosy future just beyond their reach. This same fate besets all who push the limits too far or too often. St. Paul preached moderation in all things and this is excellent advice. Take it easy, be patient; life will get there before you anyway, while death catches most people by surprise.

The majority of risks that people take are unnecessary. Consider the odds and evaluate the situation. Maybe you shouldn't get on a plane in the Midwest in the dead of winter on a night with poor visibility. Maybe you won't have one more for the road; maybe you will refrain from going back to the buffet for yet another plateful. Keep in mind, there isn't a single natural element, plant, or organism on this planet that won't kill you if you ingest too much; even excessive air or water can kill you.

- ECC 7:18 ~ Those who fear God will avoid all extremes.
- MAT 16:26 ~ Jesus asked, "What does it profit a person who gains the world but loses their soul? What can a person give in return for their soul?"
- MAT 23:25 ~ Jesus said, "Woe to you hypocrites, for you make the outside appear clean, while the inside is full of extortion and excess."
- 1 CO 5:11; 1 CO 6:9 ~ Do not associate with people who are fornicators, adulterers, sexually immoral, greedy, idolatrous, flirtatious, extortionists, drunkards, corrupt, and abusive. They are the unrighteous and they will not inherit the kingdom of heaven.
- EPH 5:18 ~ Do not get drunk, which is excess; instead, fill yourself with the Holy Spirit.
- 1 PE 2:11 ~ Abstain from the passions of the flesh which wage war against your soul.
- 1 PE 4:1–3 ~ Though Christ has done away with sin, you must not continue to sin as before, when you practiced lewdness, lust, drunkenness, overindulgence, orgies, and idolatry.
- 1 JO 2:15–16 ~ Do not love the world or worldly things. If a person loves the world, he or she cannot love God. All that is in the world, the lust of the flesh, the greed of the eyes, and the pride of humanity, do not come from the Father but are of this world.

I remember those days of being carefree, feeling invincible, taking stupid risks, doing things on a dare, almost defying death. But I never denied God's presence, and I knew when I was being disobedient to Him and my parents. I believe that God's angels were protecting me, because I cheated death on too many occasions to have beaten the odds; unfortunately, some of my friends did not survive. Those not acknowledging that God is in control probably don't believe in angels either. Then again, some people believe in angels but not God. But everyone believes in death; it is inevitable. Regarding those who do not believe in God, and maintain that it is over when we die, that will be the truth for them. They are more inclined to push the limits and get all they can out of life, thereby hastening death. Perhaps they don't care, because they usually don't believe in hell either. But they will when Jesus returns, though it will be too late.

- PSA 49:17 ~ When you die you take nothing with you; your glory does not go with you.

- ECC 5:10–12 ~ Whoever loves money will never be satisfied with it, and whoever strives for abundance will never have enough. Therefore, it is futile to strive for wealth. When riches increase so do expenditures. What good is it to have a lot of money if all you can do with it is look at it? People who work hard have restful sleep; but the abundance of the rich prevents them from sleeping peacefully.

- ISA 57:1–2 ~ The righteous man dies and nobody takes it to heart; the merciful man is taken away and nobody considers that he is spared from the evil to come. The righteous will enter into peace and will rest in their beds, each one walking in uprightness.

- EZE 7:19 ~ Their silver and gold will not be able to deliver them in the day of God's wrath. They will not satisfy their souls and they will not fill their stomachs, because this has become the obstacle of their iniquity.

- LUK 12:19–20 ~ The greedy man said to his soul, "Soul, you have ample goods; take it easy; eat, drink and be merry." But God said to him, "Fool, tonight your soul is required of you. And all your goods, who will possess them now?"

- LUK 21:34–35 ~ Jesus said, "Be careful. Do not let overindulgence, drunkenness, and the worries of life get the better of you, so when that fateful day comes you will not be caught by surprise. That day will be like a snare that catches the whole world in its trap."

- GAL 5:17–18 ~ The desires of the flesh are against the spirit, and vice-versa, for they are opposed to each other. If you are led by the Holy Spirit, you are not under the Law.

- HEB 9:27 ~ It is appointed for a person to die once and then comes the judgment.

It is upsetting when people die young; it's as if life has cheated them, but maybe they have cheated death. It is particularly troublesome for the loved ones who have suffered such a loss. It is crucial that we look to God during these circumstances so that death doesn't catch us off guard. If you fear God, you will not fear death, because it is but a steppingstone to a better life. If you fear death, you will worry about everything; and your worldly enchantments will not satisfy for long. If you want to get addicted to something that is actually healthy for you, try God's love; it comes with everything, and it's free!

Dear loving Father, who watches continuously and protects us; who sends angels to lift us up lest we dash our foot against a stone—help us remember that you are there and your angels are guarding us from evil and calamity; otherwise, everybody might die young. Thank you for constant care and compassion; likewise help us to be caring and compassionate. Let us be a comfort to others, with the same comfort that you have given us. Help us to be careful, aware, and prepared, deriving our counsel from your Holy Spirit and not our gut instincts. Help us to rely on integrity and honesty, not foolishness and instant gratification. Help us to teach our children to be mindful of what they are about to do, and have courage to walk away when it is wrong, bad for them, or otherwise dangerous. Let us keep in mind that there is nothing to fear if we possess a godly fear of you: awesome Father, Son, and Holy Spirit. Jesus conquered death for us, and will bring us back to life, just as death had no hold on Him. In the name of our living Lord we pray, Amen.

February 4

World Cancer Day is a day for amplifying the voices of cancer patients worldwide, to bring attention to their plight, to learn the risks and preventive measures, and to provide ways people can help with their time and monetary donations. The short-term objective is to reduce deaths from cancer. The long-term objective is to defeat cancer and eradicate it from the face of the earth. Research indicates as much as forty percent of cancer is preventable with early detection.

World Cancer Day was instituted on this date in 2000 at the World Cancer Summit in Paris. The Union for International Cancer Control issued a proclamation in 2008 to further increase knowledge of prevention, treatment, and detection. The United Nations and World Health Organization championed this initiative. There also is a World Cancer Research Day, designated by the American Society of Clinical Oncology on 09/13/2016. This day was established to create an annual campaign to fight cancer. Major cities of the world will illuminate landmarks with orange and blue lights tonight.

Oftentimes, cancer can be avoided by simply making healthy choices and necessary lifestyle changes. Cancer risk can be lowered further by routine visits to the doctor, applicable testing, and early diagnosis. Naturally, we mourn for those who will not escape cancer or will die from it. But the principal decisions made by individuals is the most critical factor for avoiding disease and death. And it isn't just cancer, there are a myriad of diseases and pestilences that we are vulnerable to, which is why visibility is important and why today is a good day to examine your own protective field. Of course, God is the ultimate factor, since the decision as to when we pass is up to Him. This creates uncertainty in humans which is the equivalent of risk: the more certain you are the less the risk. Be certain with God; it is best to risk everything on Him.

Coincidentally, lifestyle changes were addressed in the previous lesson and on other dates. Changes probably need to be added to your preparedness and readiness if you want to avoid diseases and parasites. Again, it's about being on guard, so that the enemy can be sighted far off, giving you more time to muster a defense, and if necessary, to retreat and strategize. If you must take a stand and fight, God will be on your side as long as it is a just cause.

- DEU 31:6 ~ Be strong and take courage; do not be afraid, for the Lord goes with you. He will neither fail you nor forsake you.

- PRO 13:11; PRO 23:4 ~ Wealth obtained by pride will diminish; but those who achieve by way of hard work will see their wealth increase. Do not labor to become rich, and do not concentrate on your own feeble wisdom.

- PRO 21:31 ~ The horse is prepared for the day of battle, but safety is from the Lord.

- ECC 8:8 ~ Nobody has the power to retain the spirit when they die, and nobody has authority over death.

- ISA 28:18 ~ Any covenant made with death will be nullified; any agreement made with hell will be void.

- MAT 7:13–14 ~ Jesus said, "Wide is the gate that leads to destruction, and many will go through it. Straight and narrow is the gate that leads to life, and few will find it."

- ROM 6:23 ~ The risk of sin is death. But God's gift of eternal life is available to everyone through Jesus Christ our Lord.

If you haven't given yourself to the Lord, there is still time. When you do, He will change you from the inside out. And He will empower you to get treatment for your addiction, to overcome irresistible temptations in your environment, to refrain from engaging in foolish or risky behavior, to regain lost confidence, or to remove obstacles in your path causing you to stumble. God will make everything new, including you, incentivizing you to forsake your old ways.

- JOB 8:13–14 ~ The destiny of those who forget God is the loss of hope, for their trust in worldly things is a fragile one.

- PSA 119:165 ~ Those who love God's Law have great peace; nothing can make them stumble.

- ISA 42:9 ~ God says, "Behold, the former things have come to pass, and new things I will declare; before they happen, I will tell you."

- EZE 18:31 ~ God says, "Forsake all your transgressions and get a new heart and a new spirit. Why should you die? I take no pleasure in anyone's death; I prefer that you repent and live!"

- 2 CO 5:17 ~ Therefore, if any man be in Christ, he is a new creature. Old things have passed away; behold, all things have become new.

- 2 PE 3:10 ~ The day of the Lord will come as a thief in the night.

God is the only certainty in this world which will pass away. This is what is meant by entropy (heat death), which will be the fate of this expanding universe; in other words, the earth and everything you see will pass away. Those who expect to live down here in the afterlife are confused; for God will create a new heaven and earth, which will not resemble the old ones.

- DAN 7:14 ~ To the Son of man was given all dominion, glory, and kingdom, which would never pass away or be destroyed.

- MAT 5:18 ~ Jesus said, "Truly I say unto you, before heaven and earth pass away, not one bit of the Law will pass until all has been fulfilled."

- MAT 24:35 ~ Jesus said, "Heaven and earth will pass away, but my words will remain forever."

- COL 3:4, 10–11 ~ When Christ appears, who is our life, all Christians will appear with Him in glory. For we have become new people, renewed in God's image by our knowledge of Him through Christ. There are no longer Jews or Greeks, circumcised or uncircumcised, civilized or uncivilized, slave or free, because Christ is all and in all.

- 1 JO 2:17 ~ The world will pass away along with its lust, but whoever does the will of God lives forever.

Holy Father of the living and the dead, we glorify your name; we are awestruck by your mighty works. You created the universe and everything in it; and you will create it all anew so that there is no memory of the old. We look forward to being there to live with you forever. Help us to trust in this your promise and the hope it gives us, and not be sidetracked by the ways of the world, all of which lead to death. We have chosen life, which you showed to us in your Son who is the light of life. Help others who are lost to see the light; illuminate the path for them with your Word, so they will return to it and depart from the pathway to hell that they are on. Remind us to cherish our bodies, and take care of them, and make healthy choices, and consult with specialists, and take all due precautions to ward of diseases and calamities. Help those who are suffering with diseases like cancer, as well as other infirmities, to be strong in your Spirit; heal them if it be your will so they can share their experience and their story of your healing love continuously. Shield us all with the umbrella of your love and peace so we can live to serve and love you for all of our days. In the name of Jesus Christ whose love is pure and powerful, Amen.

February 5

National Girls and Women in Sports Day was signed into law on February 4, 1987 by President Reagan, to be observed annually during the first week in February (the date varies yearly). Women in sports got their first boost in 1972 with Title IX which states, "No person in the United States shall, on the basis of sex, be excluded from participation in, be denied the benefits of, or be subjected to discrimination under any education program or activity." The Women's Sports Foundation (WSF) was established in 1974 by professional tennis player Billie Jean King, to assist female athletes to "reach their full potential in sports and in life." The WSF helps to organize annual events, speakers, and awards for this holiday. Today we celebrate female athletes of all ages, with organized sporting events, community-based projects, famous athlete presentations, and recognizing achievements of women in sports to include participants, coaches, announcers, and administrators. The day commemorates Flo Hyman, a female Olympian who passed in 1986 from a rare disorder during a volleyball competition.

Lately, wacko executives, promoters, and politicians have been allowing men to compete in women sports because they "identify" as a female. They undergo some treatments and declare themselves a woman to contend against real women who are physically inferior, since these men are not talented enough to compete against men. This is preposterous, but media and government will not take a stand, and many sports organizations have sold out to this nonsense. This is actually illegal for it violates Title IX. It is a conspiracy to dilute the importance of sex, and introduce a flood of new sexual identities by brainwashing children and exposing them to illicit sexual images and demonstrations as early as elementary school. The Bible teaches that there are two, and only two, sexes: male and female. They are different for a reason. To dissolve these two into a melting pot of sexual misidentification is evil, and no doubt the intention of perverts and Satan.

- GEN 1:26–27 ~ God made Eve so that Adam would have a companion, and so that they could be fruitful and multiply.
- GEN 2:24 ~ Children eventually will leave their parents and get married themselves. Once married you become one flesh with your spouse.
- GEN 6:19 ~ God instructed Noah to collect a male and female of each kind of animals so that they could replenish the earth.
- ECC 9:9 ~ Always be happy with your spouse, and love him or her the rest of your life.
- JER 29:6 ~ Get married and have children, and encourage your children to get married and have children, so your family can increase and not diminish.
- MAL 2:14–16 ~ The Lord has formed a husband and wife into one flesh. In both flesh and spirit, they belong to Him. But why is this? Because He wishes godly offspring from them. Guard your spirit; do not break the covenant with your wife or husband by getting divorced.
- MAT 5:28 ~ To lust after someone with your eyes is to commit adultery in your heart.
- MAR 10:6 ~ From the beginning of creation God made them male and female.
- 1 CO 7:2, 10–11 ~ Let every man have his own wife, and every woman her own husband. God requires the wife not to leave her husband and the husband not to divorce his wife.

Dear Heavenly Father, please stifle those who would confuse the sexes or who teach aberrant lifestyles to children. Guard our children from deviant adults that would corrupt them, or try to alter societal norms to suit abnormal impulses. Do not let these idiots get away with this any longer. Embolden parents and decent adults to thwart such lunacy. In Jesus's name, Amen.

February 6

Zero Tolerance for Female Mutilation Day is an international UN observance protesting the abomination called female circumcision, which involves the forcible maiming of a girl's clitoris, labia, and/or other external genitalia. This atrocity is still being practiced in underdeveloped regions of Africa and the Middle East. While no longer a mainstream Muslim rite, some sects still perform this abhorrent procedure and it has spread to other countries. Some cults (e.g., Satanic) also perform the ritual. The United Nations introduced an initiative in 2003 to eradicate such brutality by 2030, by increasing awareness and sponsoring prevention, obtaining funds for intervention and aftercare, and supporting international laws banning the practice including severe penalties for violators. Though such laws exist in the USA, young Muslim women are often carried out of the country by these despicable men in order to avoid prosecution, making it very difficult to bring the perpetrators to justice, while the girls risk death if they speak of it. There is no medical reason for mutilating female genitalia, while male circumcision is safe and there are health benefits to the procedure. Primitive tools and unsanitary conditions are often present, though illicit health professionals are sometimes hired to assist.

Since females have no rights over their bodies in many countries, they are abused and enslaved at the will of the men. Girls are mutilated in this fashion so they cannot enjoy sex. Presumably, this is to ensure they cannot reach orgasm so they will be less inclined to cheat on their husbands; of course, that doesn't keep the men from being unfaithful. Obviously, this is unhealthy for a number of reasons: the victims experience a lifetime of complications to include post-traumatic stress disorder, recurring pain and bleeding, reproductive issues, menstrual issues, and urinary tract problems. The immediate dangers are infection, severe trauma (physical and mental), hemorrhaging, and death. I can think of nothing more repulsive, knowing that hundreds of thousands of girls are subjected to this terror every year.

This is yet another form of slavery, subjecting women to a lifetime of torment and abuse. You can bet that God will deal with these hellions harshly. When they get caught, they deserve the death penalty. But God says vengeance belongs to Him. If it were up to me, they would have their genitals chopped, then spend the rest of their lives in prison.

- DEU 32:35 ~ God says, "Vengeance and recompense are mine. The wicked will fall, for the day of their calamity is near."

- PSA 7:16 ~ The mischief and violence of the wicked will come back on their own heads.

- ECC 12:14 ~ God will judge each act of every person, every secret thing, to determine whether it is good or evil.

- ISA 33:1 ~ Woe to you who plunder but were not plundered; who dealt treacherously though you were not dealt this way. When you cease to plunder you will be plundered; when you stop dealing treacherously, you will be dealt treachery.

- JER 11:14–15 ~ God says, "Do not bother to pray for those people; I will not listen to them when they finally cry to me about their troubles. They have no business in my house with their lewdness, for they enjoy being evil."

- EZE 7:3 ~ God will judge everyone according to their ways, and will recompense the abominations of the wicked back upon them.

- ROM 1:32 ~ People commit evil acts, knowing full well that their acts are worthy of the death penalty. Yet they continue to be evil and to find pleasure in others who do the same.

- 1 TI 5:24–25 ~ Some people's sins will be exposed and they will be punished; for others, their punishment will come later. Likewise, some people's good deeds will be exposed and they will be rewarded; others will be rewarded later.
- JDE 1:4 ~ Certain ungodly people, whose condemnation was written about long ago, have sneaked into the church without anyone noticing, attempting to turn God's grace into lust, and denying the only God and our Lord Jesus Christ.

Mutilated girls suffer severe trauma. Sure, everybody has to deal with traumatic experiences from time to time. But few have to endure it for their entire lives; and for many of these girls, those lives are cut short. This kind of trauma is very hard to treat, but it can be done with special types of professionals who possess unique knowledge and skills. But the men who engage in these abominable practices are untreatable; they cannot be helped for they have deceived themselves and will never turn from their ways. The Bible says they don't even deserve our prayers. I'll bet God has a special place in hell for adults who do this to young ladies.

Most of the prophets in the Bible suffered greatly, but none more than the Lord Jesus. They were stoned, crucified, beaten, jailed, shipwrecked, and more. We who belong in Christ will suffer too, just for loving God. Things will get progressively worse as the last day nears, and it is getting closer, faster.

- PRO 6:16–19 ~ There are seven things that the Lord hates: arrogance, lying, malicious assault, an evil imagination, mischief makers, perjury and slander, and those who deliberately create trouble.
- JER 45:3 ~ Job said, "Woe is me! For the Lord has added sorrow to my pain. I am weary with my groaning, and I find no rest."
- MAT 11:28 ~ Jesus said, "Come to me all who are weary and troubled and I will give you rest."
- JOH 16:22 ~ Jesus said, "You may have sorrow now, but I will see you again and your heart will rejoice, and nobody can take that joy from you."
- JAM 5:10 ~ Brothers, as an example of suffering and patience, consider the prophets who spoke in the name of the Lord.
- 1 JO 3:8 ~ Whoever commits sin is of the devil, who sinned from the very beginning. The Son of God was manifested to destroy the works of the devil.
- REV 2:10 ~ Jesus said, "Do not be afraid of any of the things you may suffer. The devil will throw some of you into prison to be tried; you will have tribulation for ten days. Be faithful unto death and I will give you a crown of life."

All-seeing Father, you know the atrocities that people do in the name of religion, especially to your little daughters. Protect them from monsters who enslave and abuse their women; cause these fools to be found out and removed from society wherever they may be. Bring to awareness the abomination of female mutilation, especially where it remains a tradition among men who believe you allow it; they think they know you but are far from you. We pray for the victims and we pray for the children who are in danger, that your angels would shield them. We pray for all who are dealing with trauma or living in fear, that your Holy Spirit, the Comforter, would bring them peace; and that they would find joy in the salvation of Jesus Christ despite being indoctrinated into a false belief system. In the name of Jesus we pray, Amen and Amen.

February 7

Beginning of Sorrows Day is declared as a reminder that Christ's coming is nigh; it is a day of mourning or rejoicing depending on how you look at it. The text for this study is taken primarily from the Olivet Discourse, a sermon Jesus preached while He stood on the Mount of Olives (MAT 24; MAR 13; LUK 21). Jesus was responding to followers who asked how they would know when His return was nigh. Like always, people want signs, then and now; that is, we prefer to know in advance what to expect. Of course, the Lord wants you to get ready without delay, which is why the actual timeline of the Second Coming is deliberately imprecise (MAT 25:13; 2 PE 3:10). Information is provided in the Holy Bible to suggest this can happen soon. While many theories exist concerning eschatology, it is not the intent of this study to entertain any particular one. However, a list of episodes associated with the last days is provided at the conclusion of this lesson; keep in mind it is not an exhaustive list, and the chronology can only be approximated.

- MIC 6:12 ~ The rich men are full of violence and lies.

- MAT 24:5–34; MAR 13:30; LUK 21:32 ~ Jesus said, "Many shall come in my name, claiming to be me, and deceiving many. There will be wars, famines, pestilence, and earthquakes. These are only the beginning of sorrows. They will capture you, torture you, and kill you; you will be hated for following me. People will offend, betray, and despise each other. When you see the abomination of desolation stand in the holy place, as prophesied by Daniel, escape into the mountains. There will be great tribulation, worse than ever before or ever again. Then a sign in heaven will appear. The whole earth will be in mourning when the Son of God returns in a cloud, with all His power and glory. This generation will not pass away until these things have happened."

- 2 TI 3:13 ~ Evil men and seducers will get progressively worse, deceiving and being deceived.

- REV 22:18–20 ~ For I testify to everyone who hears the words of the prophecy of this book, that if anyone adds to these words, God will add unto that person the plagues mentioned in this book. If anyone subtracts from the words of this prophecy, God will take away their name from the Book of Life, and they will not share in the inheritance. He who testified of these things says, "Surely I am coming soon." Let it be so: come Lord Jesus.

Apparently, there will be a period of great sorrow the likes of which nobody will have experienced before or after (MAT 24:21; LUK 17:26). Sorrowful and evil times have occurred throughout history, affecting both righteous and unrighteous people. During the Old Testament era, God obliterated wicked people during the times of Noah and Lot. God instructed the Israelites to annihilate pagan nations when taking possession of lands east of the Jordan River. The New Testament also recorded troubled times in the lives of Jews and Christians who were oppressed and persecuted by the Roman Empire, which would eventually collapse into pieces like every world empire before it. Certainly, it was a sorrowful time for Jesus's followers who witnessed Him being tortured to death, yet joyful when He reappeared alive. They were bold to confess Christ and glad to endure torture and execution on His behalf.

God's vengeance will rain upon the wicked and the unbelievers when Christ returns in judgment; this will be a very bad end for those who rejected Christ and His emissaries. Prior to His return, the burdens on planet Earth will get increasingly crueler. If you ask me, it's getting pretty bad already, the global sufferings, trials, disasters, and chaos. It is a gloomy prospect knowing that such things will multiply as we get closer to the end. Yet we know that the end will be a new beginning of happiness and bliss for believers, in a place where all pain and suffering will have been extinguished.

- NUM 32:22–23 ~ When the land is subdued before the Lord, you can return guiltless and free before God and Israel. This land will be your possession before the Lord. But if you do not comply you will have sinned against the Lord and you can be sure that your sin will find you out.

- PSA 69:27–28 ~ By adding more sin to sin, one can never know righteousness. Let their names be obliterated from the Book of Life.

- ISA 28:15–19 ~ All covenants of death and agreements with hell will be null and void. Those that trusted in these lies will be trampled by the overwhelming scourge that passes through.

- DAN 9:27 ~ During the last half of the week [often interpreted as half of seven years of tribulation], the abomination that causes desolation will continue, until the terrible end that awaits is poured out upon them.

- JOE 2:28–32 ~ I will pour out my Spirit on humankind. Your sons and daughters will prophesy and will see visions; old men will dream dreams. There will be signs in the heavens and on earth: blood, fire, and smoke. The sun will turn dark and the moon will turn to blood, before that great and terrible day of the Lord. All who call upon the Lord will be delivered.

- ZEP 1:14–15 ~ The great day of the Lord is coming quickly, when mighty men will cry. It is a day of wrath, trouble, and distress, of destruction and desolation, of gloom, clouds, and darkness.

- REV 6:12–17 ~ There was a great earthquake; the sun became black and the moon became like blood. Stars fell from the sky. They tried to hide in the rocks and caves, praying that the mountain would bury them, for the great day of God's wrath had come upon them.

So, how exactly can we prepare for the culmination of such unfathomable events? Well, start with God's Word and end with it. God's Word is Truth so spread the Word! God tells us everything we need to know and He provides everything we need to survive (MAT 6:31–34). God the Father spoke aloud (MAT 17:5), "This is my beloved Son, listen to Him!" Whenever you study God's Word, you are listening.

- ECC 1:17–18 ~ I gave my heart to know wisdom, and to know madness and folly. I perceived this as a vexation of spirit. For with much wisdom comes much grief; and he that increases knowledge increases in sorrow.

- ISA 14:3 ~ It will come to pass, the day the Lord gives you rest from your sorrow and fear and from the hard bondage forced upon you, that you will speak a proverb against Babylon, "See how the oppressor and the golden city have ceased!"

- ISA 51:11 ~ The redeemed of the Lord will return to Zion with singing; everlasting joy will be upon their heads, gladness in their hearts, while sorrow and mourning flee.

- JER 51:29 ~ The land will tremble with sorrow; for every purpose of the Lord will befall Babylon, making the land desolate and without inhabitants.

- JOH 16:20–22 ~ Jesus said, "Truly I say, you will weep and lament while the world rejoices; you will experience much sorrow. But that sorrow will turn to great joy. Just like a woman in the throes of childbirth feels profound joy when her baby is born: she does not remember the anguish but rejoices for the new life being brought into the world. You may have sorrow now, but I will see you again, and your heart will jump for joy, and nobody can take that from you."

- 2 CO 7:9–10 ~ I am glad that you were sorry for your sins and repented. Spiritual sorrow for one's sins works repentance unto salvation; but the sorrow of the world works death.

- REV 17:5, 9, 15 ~ On her head was written: Mystery, Babylon the great, the mother of prostitutes and all earthly abominations. This is the great city that sits on seven mountains and over many waters, nations, and peoples.

- REV 18:2, 10 ~ The angel cried, "Babylon has become the habitation of devils and every foul spirit. That mighty city will receive judgment in one hour."

- REV 21:4 ~ God will wipe away your tears; He will remove all death, sorrow, crying, and pain. Every unpleasant thing from your previous life will be gone forever.

One can make a reasonable case that the world has entered the time of sorrows, implying the end has begun. If true, things will get continually worse from here on out. Thankfully, God will bring His people home prior to pouring out seven vials of wrath at the finale.

- JER 30:7 ~ That will be a great time (of tribulation); there will be no others like it. It is the time of Jacob's trouble; but he shall be saved out of it.

- DAN 12:1 ~ Michael the great prince will stand for God's people. There will be a time of tribulation worse than ever before or ever again, but God's elect will be delivered, all whose names are written in the Book of Life.

- 1 CO 15:51–52, 54 ~ Here is a mystery of God: We will not all sleep (die) but we will all be changed. Suddenly, when the last trumpet sounds, Christ's own, whether dead or alive, will arise without corruption and be changed. Hence, the corruptible will have become incorruptible and the mortal will have become immortal. Then the statement "death is swallowed up in victory" will be true.

- 1 TH 4:16–17 ~ The Lord will descend from heaven with a shout, with the voice of the archangel, and with a blast from the trumpet of God. Then the dead in Christ will rise first. Those who remain alive in Christ will rise to join the others in the clouds, meeting the Lord in the sky. Those chosen by Christ will live with Him forevermore.

- REV 20:4–6, 13–15 ~ I saw thrones, and sitting on them were judges. I saw the souls of those who had been beheaded for their testimony of Jesus, who had not worshipped the beast or its image, nor received its mark on their foreheads or hands. They came to life again and reigned with Christ one thousand years. This was the first resurrection. The rest of the dead did not live again until after the thousand years. Blessed and holy are those who share in the first resurrection for they will not be victims of the second death. At the second resurrection the rest of the souls were raised to be judged by God. Death and Hell, and those not recorded in the Book of Life, were cast into the Lake of Fire; this was the second death.

The following list of end times events is based on a consolidation of relevant scripture and is largely gleaned from prior works. Jesus could return in your lifetime, so you might experience many of them. Arguably, some of these things already are taking place, indicating we indeed have entered a significant time of sorrows, and perhaps the beginning of the end.

Peruse the list and check the number of items which have already happened or are happening now (Barber, 2020b). This exercise should raise your level of awareness profoundly. Hopefully, you will be compelled to repent of your sins more sincerely, study the scriptures more diligently, proclaim the truth more boldly, serve others more compassionately, and talk to, worship, praise, and thank God more frequently. These are things we can do to prepare so that we are not caught off guard. This topic generates good discussions among people who are interested in end times prophecy.

Wars and rumors of wars	Worst of times
Earthquakes, tornadoes (tectonic activity)	Economic collapse
Floods (including tsunamis, hurricanes)	Judgments (war, famine, plagues, beasts)
Pestilence, disease (plagues, pandemics)	Global war
Christians are hated and persecuted	Natural disasters abound
Worldwide famine, hunger	Uncommon celestial occurrences
False prophets proliferate	Mass death, martyrdom
Lawlessness and disorder	Depleted resources, rations
Antichrist arrives on scene	Poisoned water, air
Rebuilding the temple in Jerusalem	Heavenly signs, wonders
Corruption in the church	Evil spirits, demons
Synagogues of Satan	Stinging creatures
Global economy, society	Cavalry of 200,000,000
Sealing of 144,000 (mark of Christ)	First Resurrection
Mark of the Beast	Rapture of saints
Gog, Magog (coalition of Mideast nations)	Armageddon
Final empire of evil (New Babylon)	Vials of wrath
Wicked generation	New Babylon falls
Fake miracles	Judgment Day
Abomination of Desolation	Millennial Reign
Two witnesses will prophesy	Second Resurrection
Beast comes back to life	Second Death, Lake of Fire

- PSA 32:5 ~ I acknowledged my sin to you Lord, and my iniquity I did not hide. I said, "I will confess my transgressions to the Lord." And you forgave the guilt of my sin. Amen.

- ROM 12:1–2 ~ I implore you, by the mercies of God, that you present yourselves as a living sacrifice, holy and acceptable to God, which is a reasonable response to His love. Do not conform to the ways of this world, but be transformed by the renewing of your mind, and you will be able to determine what is good, acceptable, and perfect according to God's will.

- 2 CO 4:16 ~ Therefore we do not lose heart. Though outwardly we continue to deteriorate, yet inwardly we are constantly renewed.

Dear Heavenly Father, create in us a clean heart and an upright spirit daily. Help us remember you are always there with us. Strengthen us each day in our faith and let our works and sacrifices be a reasonable response to your loving kindness. Transform our minds into conformance with your will and renew us by your Holy Spirit when we falter. Help us to never lose heart when we face adversity, calamity, or loss. Let us be ready for the end by studying your Word often while alone or with our families. May we stand strong as catastrophes and atrocities increase, until the end. Thank you for answering our prayers, in the name of Jesus, Amen.

February 8

National Boy Scouts Day honors boy scouting past, present, and future. The boy scouts started in England in 1908 with General Baden-Powell, after the publication of his book, *Scouting for Boys*. It began in the USA with William Boyce on this day in 1910. Apparently, a British boy scout escorted Boyce to his hotel in London after losing his way. He was inspired by this young lad who refused payment saying it was his duty to serve. The Boy Scouts of America (BSA) was incorporated shortly thereafter. The first Boy Scout Handbook was published in 1911. By 1925 membership had grown to over a million boys; to date, more than 100 million American boys have been mentored through the BSA.

The Boy Scout motto is "be prepared." The Boy Scout slogan is "do a good turn daily." These are commitments to service, which is why there are countless heroic deeds recorded by these young men. Many US presidents were scouts, as well as other icons. The scout oath is, "On my honor I will to do best to do my duty to God and my country and to obey the Scout Law; to help other people at all times; to keep myself physically strong, mentally awake, and morally straight." The Scout Law is, "A scout it trustworthy, loyal, helpful, friendly, courteous, kind, obedient, cheerful, thrifty, brave, clean, and reverent."

Do you see anything wrong with these tenets? Does any of their philosophy contradict the Holy Bible? The answers are no and no. In fact, the Boy Scouts was established precisely to reflect a posture of service, strength, and selflessness in young men; further, most scout troops are sponsored by churches. Plainly, the BSA is an example of stewardship and sacrifice, mentoring boys to wear a uniform that portrays loyalty, honesty, and self-sacrifice; not unlike others in uniform who are examples of service to God, country, and strangers.

- ECC 11:9 ~ Rejoice in your youth and let your heart cheer you. Walk in the ways of your heart and the sight of your eyes. But remember, for all these things God will judge you.

- LUK 6:31 ~ Do unto others as you would like them to do unto you.

- 1 CO 12:4–8 ~ There are a variety of spiritual gifts, but only one Spirit. There are different ways of administering but only one Lord. There are different operations, but the same God who works through them. The Spirit is manifested in some way for everyone to use productively. Some people have received wisdom, some knowledge, some faith, all from the same Spirit.

- PHP 4:8 ~ Whatever is true, honorable, just, pure, lovely, and gracious, if there is any excellence, if there is anything worthy of praise, think on these things.

- EPH 6:7–8 ~ Serve wholeheartedly, as if you were serving the Lord and not people, because you know that the Lord will reward everyone for whatever good he or she does, regardless of whether slave or free.

- COL 3:5–10 ~ Put to death the worldly part of you, such as sexual immorality, evil desires, covetous, and idolatry. Because of these the wrath of God will come. Though you once walked in these ways and lived among such people, you must put all of this away from you: anger, rage, malice, slander, obscene talk, and lies. For you have abandoned the old self and its impure practices and put on the new self, which is being renewed in knowledge after the image of our Creator.

- HEB 13:1–2 ~ Let brotherly love continue. Do not forget to help strangers, for you may be ministering to angels for all you know.

Back in my day, the Boy Scouts constituted a worldwide brotherhood of brave young men of which I was proud to be a part. We learned valuable skills such as camping, survival, fire safety, and orienteering, as well as integrity, patriotism, confidence, kindness, and ethics. I regret dropping out as a life scout just shy of attaining the rank of eagle; I did manage to receive the Pro Deo et Patria (God and Country) award. Unfortunately, I was unimpressed by a new scoutmaster who did not follow the rules. Though another replaced him who was a decent leader, I already had discovered new interests which were not so honorable. But I held the same moral principles when I became a responsible adult, the same principles that can be instilled in a good church.

What is the climate now? Secularists and progressives have sought to eliminate boy scouting for disingenuous reasons. The cancel culture does not want to acknowledge the two sexes but to redefine them; they abhor exclusionism based on gender. An assault on the Boy Scouts was triggered by a report in a mainstream newspaper claiming numerous lawsuits had been filed against the BSA charging molestation of boys, discrimination of gays, and what have you. While the allegations were unsubstantiated at the time, the effect was immediate; radicals started coming out of the woodwork to jump on the anti-scouting bandwagon.

Admittedly, there are bad people in every aspect of society; for example, it is known that pedophiles seek jobs in education, medicine, counseling, and churches, precisely to gain access to vulnerable kids. The Boy Scouts is prime pickings to plant people like that, which is why BSA leaders and scoutmasters are vetted. Yeah, many bad actors will slide through the cracks, but that doesn't discredit an entire organization. Yet this is the goal of activists. Their aim has been to eliminate anything Christian, patriotic, or spiritual. The infiltration of evil into our sacred traditions and our churches will be a sign that the end is near; already this is getting out of hand.

- PRO 30:11–14 ~ There is a proud and arrogant generation that thinks they are pure and guiltless, yet they curse their parents and they take advantage of those less fortunate.
- JER 8:12 ~ They were not ashamed when they committed their abominations. They will be among those who fall; at the time of their judgment, they will be cast down.
- MIC 7:3 ~ They are skilled at doing evil. Rulers require gifts and judges require bribes for their services. Those in power dictate their desires; together they conspire against others.
- LUK 16:8 ~ People are commended for being dishonest. The dishonest people of this evil generation are shrewder than the honest people.
- LUK 21:12 ~ They will persecute you for following Christ.
- ACT 20:30 ~ From among yourselves people will come speaking perverse things to draw disciples after them.
- EPH 5:11–12 ~ Do not take part in their evil schemes but expose them instead. It is shameful to even speak about the evil that they do in secret.
- 2 TI 3:1–5, 13 ~ There will be a time of great distress. People will love themselves and money. They will be abusive, arrogant, conceited, disobedient, treacherous, slanderous, ungrateful, unholy, inhumane, haters of good and lovers of pleasure more than God; appearing to be honorable but denying its power. Evil people and impostors will progress from bad to worse, as will the deceivers and the deceived.
- JDE 1:7–8, 18–19 ~ It will be just like Sodom and Gomorrah, indulging in unnatural lust. In their dreams they defile the flesh, reject authority, and abuse the righteous. They are complainers, boasters, scoffers, deceivers, lewd and disgusting, and devoid of the Spirit.

What would be the purpose of using devious tactics to blur lines of decency, to confuse children about right and wrong, to destroy all that is good and righteous? Because, troublemakers love sin so much, they want it legalized. They don't want safety nets for children, institutions of faith, standards of morality, government checks and balances, and traditional educational systems. The more they can peddle chaos and fear, the easier for them to engage in nefarious operations, activities, and enterprises, and the less likely they'll be held accountable or liable.

- JOB 9:20 ~ If I justify myself, my own mouth will have condemned me. If I say I am perfect, then I have proven myself to be perverse.

- ISA 5:20–24 ~ Woe to those who call evil good and good evil; who put darkness for light and light for darkness; put bitter for sweet and sweet for bitter. Woe to those thinking themselves wise and prudent, who are mighty in their ability to drink alcohol, who justify and reward the wicked, and who take righteousness away from the righteous. Just as the fire devours the stubble and chaff, so will their roots become rotten and their blossoms wither; for they have thrown away God's laws and despised the Word of the Holy One of Israel.

- HAB 1:4 ~ The law has been slackened and sound judgment cannot be found; for the wicked have encompassed the righteous causing wrong judgment to proceed.

- MAT 5:18 ~ Jesus said, "Not one rule or statute of the Law will be removed, until earth and heaven pass away and all things have been fulfilled."

- ROM 6:1–2, 12 ~ Shall we continue to sin, so that God's grace can continue to abound? God forbid this! How can we, who were dead in our sins, continue to live a life of decadence? Do not allow sin to reign in your mortal body, influencing you to pursue the lust of the flesh.

- JAM 4:17 ~ To anyone who knows to do good and does not do it, that for them is sin.

- 1 JO 3:4 ~ Whoever commits sin transgresses the law, for sin is the transgression of the law.

Although a Supreme Court decision in 2000 restricted membership to boys, another ruling in 2013 required the BSA to admit gay boys, and in 2015 to admit gay scoutmasters. Then there became a fake push to admit girls, while Girl Scouts kept their standards of decency and morality. What a joke! The gay rights activists lost this case in the court, but continued to pressure governments, corporations, and social justice reformers to maintain the attack on the Boy Scouts and other organizations dedicated to faith, duty, and righteousness. They succeeded in getting the BSA to declare bankruptcy in 2020, as scout membership dropped dramatically; this likely will continue until the BSA has to close up shop or change into a private entity.

The greatest weapon against this kind of evil is Christ's church on earth; it seems we cannot count on the government, since extreme progressives would rather defund police than enforce the law. These same politicians would rather spend money on radical and underhanded causes and activities. People like that need to be removed from office or any positions of authority before they can do further damage to our society, culture, institutions, and kids.

Almighty Father, we are desperately in need of your divine intervention to save this nation from anyone who would destroy our fundamental Judeo-Christian framework, our institutions of worship and learning, our founding documents, our justice and laws, our public and private educational and youth development programs, and our patriotic duty to unseat them. Still, we will fight for you in this matter, and we appeal to you to ensure we are right in standing against those who would dismantle our sacred institutions, so that your Holy Spirit will be there to fight with us. Who can be against us if you are for us? We ask these things in the name of your Son, on whom our faith is founded, as we fight the good fight of faith, Amen.

February 9

Army Institute for Religious Leadership was created on this day in 1917 to train chaplains to serve US forces during World War I. The plan, developed by Chaplain and Major A. A. Pruden, was approved by the war department and commenced the following year at Ft. Monroe, VA. A variety of combat proficiencies were taught including military operations. A number of attendees were civilian clergymen, most of whom were commissioned and deployed. Upon the end of the war, the school was deactivated, then promptly reactivated given the instability around the world, after which the training center was relocated several times, and is now located at Ft. Jackson, SC.

The US military has routinely enlisted help from men of the cloth. Most of the founders and framers believed in Christ, including George Washington who employed chaplains, and attended church services wherever he traveled, and at every chance. In the Old Testament, God appointed the tribe of Levi to be the church leaders; among them was Aaron, elder brother and close confidant of Moses. Warriors and kings in Israel employed prophets, usually the wisest men in their cabinet; David was the warrior and Nathan was the prophet in his time. In the case of King Charlemagne, he was a military leader and a religious leader. Even the Nazis had chaplains (not sure how they got recruited). Though known by different titles, these military men must be trained, not only about the Bible and religious rites, but also military tactics and law, first aid, compass and map reading, and the list goes on; one thing they are not required to do is carry a weapon or engage the enemy (note that in battle, there are exceptions to the last rule).

Being trained in both the clergy and military is a good thing. We know it is smart to be trained in God's ways; being trained in the ways of war is beneficial too. The military is an honorable vocation, and they recruit good people of the cloth. But the religious foundation of the chaplaincy is varied now, for the military is quite diverse. In all branches, chaplains used to have a Judeo-Christian foundation; now they come from different religions, some that depart or distract from the Holy Bible. God tells us in His Word what kind of religious training everybody needs.

- EXO 19:5–6 ~ God said, "If you obey me and keep my covenant you will be a precious treasure to me, above all other peoples. You will be to me a holy nation of priests."

- LUK 10:2–3 ~ Jesus said, "The harvest is plentiful but the laborers are few. Pray that the Lord of the harvest would send more laborers to help. Keep in mind, I am sending you out like lambs among wolves."

- 1 PE 2:5–9 ~ You are living stones, built into a spiritual house; a holy priesthood, to offer spiritual sacrifices acceptable to God through Jesus Christ. You are a chosen generation, a royal priesthood, a holy nation, a special people; for you have been selected to give praise to Him who called you out of darkness into His marvelous light.

- 1 PE 5:2–3 ~ Feed God's flock which is among you; be overseers of the kingdom. Do this, not out of obligation but willingly; do this not for ill-gotten gain but with a clear conscience. Do not act like lords over God's heritage but set an example to the flock.

- REV 1:5–6 ~ Jesus Christ is the faithful witness, the firstborn of the dead, and the prince over the kings of the earth, who loved us and washed away our sins with His own blood. He has made us kings and priests before God the Father. To Him be all glory and dominion forever and ever. Amen.

I was trained as a warrior in the US Army, and later worked as a defense analyst. I also am trained by God's Holy Word. I can tell you, the two are not incompatible. Except there are warriors not from God who claim to know Him; they wage war in the name of religion but do not honor God. I suppose they have their religious advisors, but they do not believe in the same God and are therefore fighting on the wrong side. God has given us examples of great military men who were religious advisors. Consider Caleb, a man of God, a great warrior, and a spy. Israel was always at war, practically every time they disobeyed God, as well as when they claimed the land God promised them. God never gave up on the Israelites; they were victorious when they were on the right side of God, but they were defeated when leaders and religious advisors were on the wrong side of Him, sometimes defying true prophets of God in order to do it their own way.

- NUM 13—14 ~ Moses sent spies into the land with orders to return and report. Of the twelve, ten returned with an unfavorable report which engendered fear concerning the strength of the inhabitants there. Two spies, Caleb and Joshua. returned with a favorable report. They believed God's words and were eager to take the land He promised Israel. Caleb quieted the crowd saying, "Let us go immediately and possess the land, for we can overcome those people." But the others were afraid, and saw themselves as grasshoppers compared to the mighty giants living in the land. Joshua and Caleb pleaded with the people saying, "This is a great land, flowing with milk and honey. Let us not rebel against the Lord or be afraid of the occupants there, for we will eat them alive." But the people would not listen. And God cursed Israel, telling Moses how the adults would never make it to the promised land except for Joshua and Caleb. God said, "My servant Caleb has another Spirit within him, and because he followed my advice completely, he will enter the land and possess it."

- JOS 14:7–13 ~ Caleb said to Joshua and the head of the tribes of Israel, "I was forty years old when I went out to spy for Moses, and I brought him a good report. Moses assured me that I would inherit the land where I had done my reconnaissance. And now, forty-five years later, I am still alive to see God's promises come to pass. And I feel as strong now as I did then; and I am every bit as ready to go to war for the Lord." Joshua blessed Caleb, and gave him the inheritance that was promised.

We are all Christian soldiers to some extent, and we always can use more training.

- ISA 59:17 ~ He has put on righteousness as a breastplate and salvation for a helmet. His clothing consists of the garments of vengeance and zeal is his cloak.

- JOE 3:9–10, 14 ~ Go, tell the Gentiles to prepare for war. Wake the mighty warriors and tell them to come. Beat your plowshares into swords and your pruning hooks into spears. Let the weak say, "I am strong." Multitudes are gathered in the valley of decision, for the day of the Lord is getting closer.

- MAT 10:34, 38–39 ~ Jesus said, "Do not think I came to send peace to the earth, because I am sending a sword. You must take up your cross and follow me if you want to be counted worthy. Those who wish to keep their lives will lose their lives; but those who lose their lives for my sake will be given back their lives."

- 1 TI 6:12–13 ~ Fight the good fight of faith. Keep a firm grasp on eternal life, for this is why you were called, and why you testified before many witnesses and before God.

- 2 TI 2:3–4 ~ Endure hardship like a good Christian soldier. Those who fight wars need not get caught up with the affairs of this life, but rather should concern themselves with the affairs of Jesus Christ who chose them to be a soldier.

Lord God Almighty, help us to be soldiers for Christ and fight with our might; please give us all the training we need to increase in our ability to thwart the enemy. Let us be ever ready to learn, and if necessary, to march into battle carrying the banner of Christ. Remind us to credit you with every victory. As for believers in your perfect Word, we praise you that our victory already has been won by your Son Jesus Christ, in whose name we pray, Amen.

February 10

Lunar New Year is also the Chinese New Year; it is a day of celebration, festivities, and fireworks in China. Many Islamic and Asian cultures observe this day as well, since their calendars are linked with phases of the moon. The first new moon after the winter solstice is the new year in some places. The Jewish new year occurs during their seventh month, in the fall (Tishri 1) rather than the first day of the first month, in the spring (Nisan 1). Their new year celebrates God's creation, which falls on Rosh Hashanah, the Feast of Trumpets. It's a calendar thing; lunar calendars are used mostly for agricultural purposes as they reflect harvest seasons.

Every country, people, and group have reasons to celebrate certain days or mourn on other days. Probably, the time of year is irrelevant when it comes to celebrating or mourning, unless it is to celebrate life, in which case every day of the year should be celebrated. Let's celebrate the salvation which God has given to us through His Son Jesus Christ; this should be celebrated every year, month, day, and minute. We don't need a special day to celebrate God when we awake to a new day. Every day, He is there! To a Christian, all days are equally important, for we are to glorify God regardless. Yes, we should dedicate the Sabbath to the Lord, taking a day off to worship Him and thank Him, whether you do that on Saturday, Sunday, or whichever day fits your schedule.

- PSA 118:24 ~ This is the day that the Lord has made; let us rejoice and be glad in it.

- ROM 14:5, 18–19 ~ One person may esteem one day above another while another person esteems every day equally. Let everyone be fully persuaded in his or her mind.

- ROM 14:7–10 ~ None of us lives to himself, and none of us dies to himself. For if we live, we live unto the Lord; and if we die, we die unto the Lord. Whether we live or die, we are the Lord's. Christ died, revived, and arose so that He might be Lord over both the dead and the living. But why do you judge your brother? And why do you call him out? Because everyone will stand before the judgment seat of Christ.

- ROM 14:18–19 ~ He who serves Christ in these things is acceptable to God and approved of men. Let us therefore follow after the things which promote peace and edify one another.

It can be very difficult reconciling dates with so many calendars. Most calendars employ the solstices and equinoxes, the positions of the sun and moon, and the tilt of the earth to some degree. But it is easy to be confused; for example, the Jewish calendar uses lunar phases making it necessary to add more days after the end of the year or multiple years; while with the Gregorian calendar we add one day every four years. Like many nations, we divide the day equally into two twelve-hour periods, instead of dividing the day according to proportions of day and night as in other cultures. Further, the Jewish calendar begins the new day at sundown in accordance with Genesis, whereas most cultures start the day at sunup. We start the day at midnight. Our calendar year is based on an approximation of Christ's birth year (AD 1); this calculation was off by four or five years. So those who thought computers were going to go haywire in the year 2000 (Y2K) were about four years too late.

People get confused about Holy Week, because it is impossible for Christ to die on Friday, and be in the grave three days, and then arise from the grave on Sunday. The error in believing that Christ died on Friday began with the fact that He had to be removed from the cross before the Jewish Sabbath, which started at sundown, presumably Saturday. But if you read the Bible carefully, you will see that the day after Christ's death was a "high" sabbath, occurring the first day of the Feast of Unleavened Bread. In fact, during the week of unleavened bread there are two high sabbaths, in addition to the weekly sabbath. This means Christ died on the day of Passover, which makes sense since He is the Passover Lamb. That would place His death Thursday on the

Gregorian calendar, or just before sundown Friday night on the Jewish calendar. Christians celebrate Maundy Thursday, which is a reference to the commandment of Christ to participate in Holy Communion often. It just so happens that this event did happen on Thursday. Remember, on the Jewish calendar Thursday started at nightfall. Jesus probably administered the Eucharist, went to Gethsemane where He was betrayed, then He was tried, crucified, and taken off the cross prior to Friday which began at dusk, the first high sabbath (see Barber, 2020a for a full explanation).

- EXO 20:8–10 ~ God commanded the Israelites to remember the Sabbath Day and keep it holy. "Six days you will labor and complete your work. But the seventh day is the Sabbath of the Lord your God; in it you will not do any work, and this includes your family, servants, strangers, and beasts of burden; all which reside within your gates."

- LEV 23:3–8 ~ Six days shall work be done, but the seventh day is the Sabbath of rest, a holy convocation. You will do no work because it is the Lord's Sabbath in all your dwellings. There are feasts of the Lord, also holy convocations, which you will observe in their seasons. The fourteenth day of the first month (Nisan) is the Lord's Passover. The fifteenth day of Nisan begins the feast of Unleavened Bread; seven days you must eat unleavened bread. The first day of that period will be a holy convocation: you will do no work on that day. You will present burnt offerings to the Lord throughout the celebration. The seventh day will be another holy convocation: you will do no work on that day.

- JOH 2:18–19 ~ The Jews answered Jesus, "What sign can you show us to prove it is you doing these things?" Jesus replied, "Destroy this temple [His body], and in three days I will raise it up."

- JOH 19:31 ~ The Jews therefore, because it was the day of preparation (for a feast of celebration), implored that the bodies should not remain upon the cross during the Sabbath, for that sabbath day was a high day. They appealed to Pilate that the legs of the crucified be broken (to hasten death) so their bodies could be taken down prior to nightfall.

- JOH 19:42 ~ They laid Jesus in a sepulcher which had been prearranged in observance of preparation day.

- MAR 2:27–28 ~ Jesus announced, "The Sabbath was made for man, not man for the Sabbath. Therefore, the Son of man is Lord even of the Sabbath."

People also get confused about end time events and when they will happen, how long it will take, and the order in which the events will occur. Well, if God wanted us to have a complete game plan with dates and times, He would have given us one. The only end time event that we need to keep track of is today; because it could end before tomorrow, either by death or by Christ's return.

- REV 7:9 ~ I saw a giant multitude, too many people to even count. There were people from every nation, race, and tongue standing before the throne and the Lamb with palm branches in their hands.

- REV 20:12 ~ In John's vision he saw the dead, both small and great, standing before God. The books were opened, along with another book called the Book of Life. And everyone was judged according to the things written in the books about their actions during their lifetimes.

Heavenly Father, help us to praise your name and thank you for all you have done on our behalf every day of our lives, until we come to your kingdom where we can praise and thank you, and celebrate with you for the rest of eternity. Let us remember you in our rising in the morning, and our retiring in the evening, and all points in-between. In the name of Jesus, we pray, Amen.

February 11

Make a Friend Day reminds us of the importance of friends; we always can benefit from making new friends, though it's not that easy to make lasting friends. This holiday, though unofficial, has been observed in recent years to encourage friendliness. There also is an International Day of Friendship on 07/30 dedicated to friendships in general, especially among nations, and is one of many United Nations observances. Probably, Make a Friend Day is related to Valentine's Day, when we celebrate our spouse or honey, who possibly is also our best friend.

According to social psychologists, we pick our friends after considerable proximity and commonality. For example, you may have made friends with the kid that sat near you in school. In places that you frequent, you often see people around but never have a chance to meet. It may be necessary for you to create an opportunity to meet: approach them and introduce yourself. That is actually the easy part; making a good friend is the hard part. It takes time, effort, and sacrifice. A true friend is somebody you can trust, plain and simple. These friends are the closest we get in relationship, outside of Jesus Christ who is our dearest friend forever. We come to love them like brothers and sisters. You've heard it said, "smile and the world smiles with you" which is partially true. I say, cry and your friends will cry with you.

- EXO 33:11 ~ The Lord spoke with Moses, face to face like speaking to a friend…
- JOB 2:13 ~ Job mourned with his friends, without speaking for seven days and nights.
- PRO 18:13 ~ If you want to have friends you have to act friendly; some friends stick closer than a brother.
- PRO 27:17 ~ Iron sharpens iron like one man sharpens another.
- SOS 5:16 ~ She is my beloved and she is my friend.
- ISA 41:8 ~ God said, "You Israel, are my servants, the children of Jacob whom I have chosen, and the seed of my friend Abraham."
- JOH 15:12–13 ~ Jesus said, "Love each other as I have loved you. There is no greater love than to give your life for friends. You are my friends if you do as I have commanded. Henceforth I will not call you servants, for a servant does not know what His master is up to; but I have called you friends, for I shared with you everything you heard about my Father."
- 1 TH 5:11 ~ Encourage one another and build one another up, just as you are doing.
- JAM 2:23 ~ The scripture was fulfilled stating that Abraham had faith in God and it was imputed to him as righteousness; and he was called a friend of God (ISA 41:8).

Today is a good day to call a friend or two. Or, if you are out and about, smile at and/or say hello to a few people. Maybe strike up a conversation, if you have a little time to spare. For who knows? It could lead to something more than just two ships passing in the night. Naturally, there also are people who you should stay away from; albeit, there are circumstances in which you should not make friends. But that is not a reason to act unfriendly.

- PRO 1:10 ~ If sinners entice you, do not consent.
- PRO 22:24–25 ~ Do not make friends with an angry person or associate with someone who has a quick temper, for you risk learning their ways and falling into the same trap.
- MAT 15:14 ~ Stay away from false teachers, for they are like the blind leading the blind. And when the blind lead the blind, both fall into the ditch.

FEBRUARY

- ROM 16:17 ~ I appeal to you, brothers, to watch out for those who cause divisions and create obstacles, contrary to the doctrine that you have been taught; avoid them.

- 1 CO 5:11, 13 ~ Do not associate with someone who claims to be a Christian but who is sexually promiscuous, greedy, idolatrous, slanderous, or who is a drunkard or a swindler; do not even eat at the same table with such a person. You must expel the wicked from among you.

- 2 TH 3:14–15 ~ If there are people among you who fail to conform to the Word as we have taught it to you, make note of them and stay away from them, so that they will feel ashamed of their behavior. However, do not consider them as an enemy, but admonish them as you would a brother or sister.

- 1 TI 6:5 ~ Those who teach that material wealth is godly have perverse minds, devoid of the truth. They would exploit the truth to gain riches. Stay away from them.

- JAM 4:4 ~ Do you not know that friendship with the world is enmity with God? Therefore, whoever wishes to be a friend of the world will soon become an enemy of God.

- 1 JO 5:20–21 ~ Remain in Christ who is true. Stay away from anything or anyone who would distort God's truth or attempt to take God's place in your heart.

Notice how developing friendships has no restrictions based on age, sex, race, language, social status, economic status; all that is required is genuine love. Jesus loved everybody; he taught us to love everybody, even our enemies. Yes, we all are created in God's image, and that fact alone means people are deserving of our love. But this doesn't mean we need to become friends with them, and it doesn't mean we never will be friends either.

- ACT 2:38–39 ~ Peter said, "Repent and be baptized every one of you, in the name of Jesus Christ for the remission of your sins, and you will receive the gift of the Holy Spirit. This promise pertains to you, your children, and people everywhere: to whomever the Lord calls."

- ACT 10:34–35 ~ Truly, God does not show favoritism for any person. Within every nation, anyone who fears the Lord and endeavors to be righteous is accepted by Him.

- ROM 12:16–21 ~ Be of the same mind one toward another. Do not be high-minded, but humble yourself before others, even those of low estate. Do not pretend to be wise in your own conceit. Do not recompense evil for evil. Always be honest in all things. Live peaceably with all people. Do not seek revenge when someone has done you wrong but rather hold back your wrath. For it is written: Vengeance is mine; I will repay, says the Lord. Therefore, if your enemy is hungry, feed him; if he is thirsty, give him a drink; in doing so you heap hot coals upon his head. Do not be overcome with evil, but overcome evil with goodness.

- 1 CO 12:13 ~ By one Spirit we are baptized into one body. Whether Jews or Gentiles, free men or slaves, all Christians have become members of one Spirit.

- JAM 2:1–9 ~ Do not be partial to people just because you like the way they look or act. Do not give the rich or the famous more respect than anyone else, and do not give the poor and lowly less respect. If you abide by the royal law according to the scripture, "Love your neighbor as yourself," you are doing the right thing. But if you show favoritism to certain persons, you commit sin and are convicted of the law as a lawbreaker.

Dear Father in heaven, we are very thankful—for what a great friend we have in your Son Jesus! He has shown us your love and taught us how to love one another. Help us obey your laws, especially loving you above all others, and loving our neighbors as ourselves. In Jesus's name, who gave Himself for us, after obeying all the commandments that we couldn't, Amen.

DAILY DEVOTIONAL EVENTS

February 12

Sticks and Stones Day is proposed to remind us not to be swayed or damaged by the negativity, unfriendliness, and meanness of others. Words hurt; I learned this the hard way. As a child, I was brainwashed to believe the often-repeated rhyme, "sticks and stones can break my bones but words can never hurt me." I discovered that words can hurt longer than a beating; because bruises to the body heal, but not so much battery to the psyche. Verbal abuse is akin to other types of abuse, and can have long-lasting effects on one's behavioral health—not just for victims of abuse but also abusers. I have treated victims of repeated emotional abuse and repeated physical abuse, and their symptoms are not markedly different; but when sexual abuse is thrown into the mix much worse problems become evident. Children are especially susceptible to psychological pain from verbal and emotional abuse, as well as neglect.

If only people would think carefully before speaking, but that takes tremendous effort. Make no mistake, everyone has difficulty controlling their mouths. But anyone can learn self-control (temperance), which is listed among the most valuable of spiritual gifts (GAL 5:22–23). Self-control also increases confidence which will raise a person's self-esteem. Inviting the Holy Spirit to guide your life enables higher-order thinking, to include seizing control over your thoughts, which will help you control your words and deeds.

These days you really have to be careful what you say publicly if you want to avoid being vilified or worse, despite the constitutional right to speak one's mind. I recommend that you judiciously choose your words before you speak, text, or email. Chances are someone somewhere will keep a record. Of course, God keeps a record, don't you know? Wouldn't it be great if we could expunge the record of all the nasty things we have uttered? Well, Christ already has if you have turned your life over to Him.

- PSA 139:1–2 ~ Oh Lord, you have searched me and you know me. You know my sitting down and my standing up. You understand my thoughts from afar.

- ISA 66:18 ~ God knows their works and their thoughts. The day will come when He will gather all nations and tongues; everyone will see His glory.

- JER 17:9–10 ~ The heart is deceitful and desperately wicked. Who can understand it? I search the heart, I analyze the mind, and I reward people according to their ways and according to their fruit.

- LUK 5:21–26 ~ The scribes and Pharisees began to reason amongst themselves saying, "Who does this man think he is, speaking blasphemies? Can anyone forgive sins but God alone?" Jesus perceived their thoughts and answered them saying, "I know what are you thinking, so I ask you: which is easier, to say 'your sins are forgiven' or to say 'rise up and walk'? But that you might know the Son of man has power upon earth to forgive sins..." Jesus turned to the paralyzed man declaring, "I say unto you, arise, collect your bed, and return to your home." Immediately the man rose up before them, took his bedding, and departed to his own house, glorifying God. Those who saw this were amazed, and glorified God; some were equally filled with fear, saying to one another, "We have seen extraordinary things today."

- 1 CO 4:1–5 ~ St. Paul wrote: Consider us as ministers for Christ and stewards of the mysteries of God. Those who are entrusted as stewards must show faithfulness. It is nothing to me to be judged by you, or by a jury of my peers. Actually, I do not even judge myself, for who am I to judge anybody? I am not so innocent, but the one who will judge me is the Lord. Therefore, judge nothing until the appointed time. Wait for the Lord to come. He will bring to light the hidden things of darkness, and will expose the motivations of every heart. Then all will receive God's just rewards.

- HEB 4:12–13 ~ The Word of God is alive and powerful; sharper than any double-edged sword, it pierces deeply to divide the soul and spirit, and the joints and marrow. It can discern the thoughts and intents of every heart. No creature alive is hidden, because all things are exposed before the eyes of Him to whom we must give an account.

Resolved, some words should be prohibited from use under most if not all circumstances. For example, it is never okay to use the Lord's name in vain, to curse someone, or to testify falsely. It is also unnecessary to use foul language, to emphasize a point with "by God" or "by heaven", or to swear an oath unless it is before the altar of the Lord or in a court of law. These major tenets of God's Law specifically illustrate improper communication (read EXO 20:7, 16; LEV 20:9; ECC 7:21–22; ECC 10:20; MAT 5:34–37; EPH 4:29; JAM 5:12).

Undoubtedly, everyone should remove certain words from their vocabulary. When I was a youngster, I heard people using a particular N-word when referring to black people. I soon discovered that every ethnicity had a denigrating nickname which people tossed about carelessly, and many still do. When I was in the Army, I sometimes was called "cracker" and yes, I found it offensive. I figured, this person doesn't even know me, nor does he want to know me. As I matured, I became more determined to eliminate distasteful verbiage and cursing from my vocabulary. I'm still working on it by the way; I occasionally get angry and emit bad words. It may take quite a while to unlearn decades of social and behavioral conditioning, but if you work hard at it, you will notice improvement.

I pondered, would it be racist to call someone other than dark-skinned the N word, or was it reserved for blacks? Besides, I often heard black people addressing one another using that word. Apparently, it was a term of endearment to them, much like when my friends would address me as "fart face." In that context it wasn't an insult, neither did I find it hateful. My confusion was further exacerbated because certain words or phrases meant different things depending on who was saying them and to whom. Plus, there were opposite meanings for some words like "really" and "gross" and "tight" depending on context. Add to that socially dictated grammatical rules regarding places, people, things, and every human demographic in the book. I deemed it necessary to weed out idle and feckless speech and attach meaning to a conversation, if there was any meaning to be had. I bet you could list twenty different ways to interpret the word "no" from various experiences. It makes more sense to speak clearly and to the point.

Returning to the present, have you noticed pundits referring to political adversaries as Nazis? Obviously, they mean it as an affront, for it is always uttered out of disdain for someone that disagrees with them. Here is yet another N-word being used to denigrate a person just for looking, acting, or thinking differently. Nowadays, if you dislike someone, insult them; for what can they do about it? If they bust you in the chops, they are the ones who get arrested. That's why miscreants get in your face—to provoke you into anger. People doing such things are as bigoted as any racist, sexist, xenophobe, and the rest of the names they call other people. Of course, those in authority regardless of political party, religion, or ethnicity deserve respect. In fact, everybody deserves the utmost of respect; but you seldom see that in politics, or even society for that matter. When respect is given, is it being returned? Many will openly display their dislike for others; and much of the time they are not even accurate in their knowledge of the person's beliefs, feelings, or opinions. So, what is their prejudice? Do they even know? Or is this a calculated means to an evil end? That's right, verbally abuse them until you get your way, that'll work. Then there are those insisting that you use certain words to include invented words, or alter the language of the people to suit their preferences. I mean, how ridiculous can it get?

It is not for us to judge others (MAT 7:1–5). Instead, we are to love others, even our enemies (LUK 6:26–36). We are not to think evil of others, or speak evil about them or to them. This is easier said than done, right?

- PRO 4:23–24 ~ Guard your heart with all diligence, for out of it flow the issues of life. Silence your perverse tongue, and eliminate distasteful speech.

- PRO 12:15–20 ~ The way of fools seems right in their eyes; but those who seek counsel are wise. A fool's anger becomes immediately apparent; but a prudent person overlooks an offense. Those who speak the truth exhibit righteousness; only a false witness tells lies. Careless words pierce like a sword; but the words of the wise bring healing. When truth is spoken it lasts forever; but a lying tongue lasts for a moment. Deceit is in the heart of those imagining evil; joy is in the heart of those promoting peace.

- PRO 24:17–19 ~ Do not rejoice when your enemy falls and do not be glad when others stumble. For the Lord will see this and He will be displeased with you; and He might withhold His hand from punishing them.

- MAT 15:19; MAR 7:20–23 ~ That which proceeds out of the mouth flows from the heart and defiles a person. For out of the heart come evil thoughts that lead to murder, adultery, fornication, theft, lying, blasphemy, covetousness, wickedness, lasciviousness, foolishness, pride, and an evil eye. All these wicked things come from within a person.

- ROM 12:14–18 ~ Jesus taught, "Bless those who persecute you; do not curse them. Rejoice with those who rejoice, and mourn with those who mourn. Live in harmony with one another. Do not act high-minded but humble yourselves, even before people of low estate. Do not act haughty or self-centered. Do not return evil for evil. Display honesty to others; and to the best of your ability, live peaceably with all people.

- EPH 4:31–32 ~ Put away bitterness, rage and anger, fighting and insulting, evil speech, and all maliciousness. Be kind one to another, tenderhearted, and forgiving even as God for Christ's sake has forgiven you.

- JAM 1:26 ~ If anyone purports to be religious, but cannot hold their tongue, they deceive themselves and their religiosity is in vain.

- JAM 4:10–12 ~ Humble yourselves in the sight of the Lord, and He will lift you up. Brothers, do not speak evil one of another. Anyone speaking evil of his brother and judging him speaks evil of the law and judges the law. Anyone who judges the law cannot be keeping the law. There is one lawgiver and there is one judge who is able to save and to destroy. So, who do you think you become when you judge another?

- 1 PE 2:1 ~ Put aside all malice, all treachery, all hypocrisy, all envy, and all evil speech.

We are to humble ourselves before others like Jesus did. We also are to hold our tongues, especially if we have nothing constructive to say. These behaviors take a lot of practice. I think I'm getting better with the humility part. And though I stop myself from saying things that I know are wrong, I still think them before stopping the evil word from escaping from my heart. I have concluded that it is considerably more difficult to stop the evil thought, although that is the best way to control the tongue. You basically have to think before you think.

- PRO 11:2 ~ With pride comes shame; with humility comes wisdom.

- PRO 18:12 ~ Before the destruction of one's heart comes arrogance, and before honor comes humility.

FEBRUARY

- ISA 64:6 ~ All of us have become unclean, and our acts of righteousness are as filthy rags. We shrivel like a leaf, and like the wind, our sins sweep us away.

- LUK 14:11 ~ Whoever exalts themselves will be humiliated; whoever humbles themselves will be exalted.

- ROM 12:3 ~ By the grace given to me I discourage everyone from thinking of themselves more highly than they ought. Instead, think soberly in accordance with the measure of faith God has bestowed upon you.

- 1 CO 13:4–5 ~ Love endures; love is kind. Love is not envious, haughty, or conceited. Love does not behave unseemly, does not seek self-satisfaction, is not easily provoked, and does not think about evil things.

- PHP 2:3–5, 8 ~ Do nothing through strife or vanity; but in humbleness of mind esteem others above yourselves. Do not focus exclusively on your own interests, but also on the interests of others. Act like Christ, who as a man, humbled Himself, becoming obedient unto death even death on a cross.

- COL 3:12–13 ~ As a child of God, reflect His mercy, kindness, humility, gentleness, and patience. Bear with one another and forgive each other of any grievances that you carry, just as the Lord forgives you.

- TIT 3:2 ~ Do not speak evil or fight with others; instead, be gentle and humble to everyone.

- HEB 12:14–15 ~ Try to be a peacemaker, and exhibit holiness, without which nobody can see the Lord. Make sure that nobody misses out on their opportunity to enjoy the grace of God. Help prevent roots of bitterness from springing up trouble among yourselves which might defile some people.

- JAM 3:13 ~ Who is wise and knowledgeable among you? Let them show it through good conversation and by good works done with the humility that comes from wisdom.

There are some who do not care about others or how their behavior affects people. They see nothing wrong with taking advantage or putting people down. They would justify such behavior by asking, "Didn't Jesus insult people?" It is true that Jesus frequently admonished sinners. He was especially critical of the Pharisees and Sadducees with their holier-than-thou attitudes. Jesus, who was without sin, called out sin so everyone would recognize sin for what it was. He made examples of people so they might change their ways and possibly influence others to likewise change. Calling someone out is not the same as insulting them; an insult is rarely the truth. A person may be a sinner, but not necessarily a hater. One who insults is a hater; one who reproves is a helper. For example, if your child misbehaves, you coach him or her; sometimes this admonishment includes punishment. But calling your kid names will not help to reprove him or her. We are children of God, and He will scold us and reprimand us when we cross the line. We are brothers and sisters and are responsible for one another, so we are obliged to admonish one another out of love and with humility. It is best not to conceal the matter or brush it off. I can assure you that God will not forget about it, unless you confess and seek His forgiveness.

- DAN 2:22 ~ God reveals deep and secret things. He knows what lies in darkness, for the light abides with Him.

- LUK 12:2–3 ~ Everything that is hidden will be revealed, everything that is concealed will be found out. Whatever you speak in darkness will be heard in the light; and that which was whispered in closets will be shouted from rooftops.

DAILY DEVOTIONAL EVENTS

- MAT 12:34–37 ~ Jesus said, "You generation of vipers, how can you who are evil speak good things? For from the heart flows the words you speak. A good person will, from the good treasures of the heart, bring forth good things; an evil person will, from the evil treasures of the heart, bring forth evil things. I assure you that everyone will give an account of every idle word they have spoken when the day of judgment comes. By your words you will be justified, and by your words you will be condemned.

We can call people out if we employ a righteous judgment. The purpose is to reason with them from the standpoint of welcoming them into the flock, not with the purpose of making a spectacle of them. They might not know what they are doing is wrong or that it is against God's will. This we should convey privately using humbleness and respect, not publicly. Granted, they may take offense anyway, in which case you should leave them be after that (MAT 10:14). Some will listen and some will not. Make sure you practice what you preach however, otherwise you might irritate someone who would otherwise listen.

- EZE 3:18–19 ~ God has said to the wicked that they will surely die. If you do not speak to them and warn the wicked to change their ways and be saved, they will die in their iniquity; but their blood will be partly on your hands. If you warn the wicked and they continue a life of wickedness, they will die in their iniquity; but you will have safeguarded your soul.
- JOH 7:24 ~ Do not judge according to appearances, so you can make a righteous judgment.
- GAL 6:1 ~ Brothers, if a person is found to be sinning, you who are spiritual should restore that person using the spirit of gentleness. But take caution that you are not tempted yourself.
- EPH 5:11–13 ~ Do not associate with the unfruitful works of darkness, but rather expose them. For it is shameful even to speak of the things they do in secret. Everything exposed by the light can be seen, because the light makes all things visible.

Freedom of speech, religion, and assembly are inalienable rights, insofar as they are endowed by God and not society or government. But there are restrictions. You cannot instigate an emergency where there is none, like yelling fire in a theater for amusement. You cannot feign a peaceful protest in order to incite rioting, looting and burning of private and public property. You cannot assault or murder people who do not share your belief system or worldview, even if directed to do so by your holy book or spiritual leader. Simply put, you cannot turn the exercise of liberty into a pernicious act. It is impossible to apply your civil rights if you are violating the civil rights of another. If your intentions are evil the result will be sin. The government does not outlaw every sin; but within your conscience you will know if it is against God's Law. Any motivation of the heart that runs contrary to God's will is sin. And don't forget, sin is not only an action but also can be a word or a thought (JAM 1:15).

Have you ever been called, or called someone else, a sinner? Well, that is what we are, sinners, every last one of us. But I rarely hear the "S" word except in church. In particular, the media avoids that word like the plague. This is because the majority of media outlets are complicit with the craziness going on about the globe. It is a fact that the word "sin" fits the person using that word when describing others. But we should warn others when they are becoming overcome by their vices. It is not an insult since it is the truth. The only one who is insulted is God when someone is persistent in their rebellion. God is especially offended if such insults are directed at Him (EXO 20:7). That's right, people that hate God or claim not to believe in Him are prone to blaming Him for all the evil in the world or in their life. God does not cause evil, but He calls it out. Jesus had to call certain people out who were accusing Him of being a blasphemer, liar, or seditionary. Since Christ is sinless, He is most qualified to be calling out sin. The only thing that makes followers of Christ worthy is they have accepted His righteousness in exchange for their sin, and this is good news for everybody. Yeah, Jesus called the Pharisees hypocrites, the ultimate insult in that culture; but that is what they were, believing themselves to be above others, even Christ. Jesus didn't have to put them down, they did it by exalting themselves (MAT 23:12; LUK 14:11). To this day, people put others down to make themselves feel higher; but the opposite effect ultimately will result. Thus, unseemly speech will feed into one's own psychological hang-ups.

You can call someone every name in the book using every letter in the alphabet, knowing that people will get stuck on a name or a label. We need to remember who we are, and to whom we belong. We bear the name of Christ, so any other name-calling is meaningless (well, except for birth names). I am not offended to be called a sinner, because I know that I will arrive in heaven without sin. Like St. Paul wrote, I am not swayed by the judgment of others because God is my judge. And I will be judged not guilty because I gave my sin to Jesus who left it on the cross. Jesus didn't just call out sin, He gathered every sin and dragged it to Calvary. That is why He has a name above all other names (PHP 2:9). No matter what names I am called, I am called by God to bear His name. So, it doesn't bother me personally, but it saddens me that name-calling has become a routine element of political speech.

We are obliged to call out sin when moved by the Holy Spirit to do so. If you are not sure when the Holy Spirit is calling you, He probably isn't. But it is not that hard to figure out after you examine yourself (1 CO 11:28–32). If you ponder what Jesus would do, the Holy Spirit will tell you.

Dear Heavenly Father, thank you for receiving sinners like us into your heavenly realm, giving us your name and an inheritance equal to your only Son, our Lord. Help us to learn self-control, so that we do not offend others, especially when they are eager to hear and know the truth. Let us be an example of your love so that it might spread to those around us. Let our thoughts, words, and actions speak of your love and your influence in our lives. Help us to be ready when others seek our help in getting their affairs in order, and in getting their walk with you into practice. Help us to be diligent in controlling our tongues, becoming more mindful of speech or words that should be avoided at all times. Let us improve as listeners, and refrain from talking until it is our turn and we have something worthwhile to say. And let us ever walk with Jesus, following His example to the best of our ability. In His name we pray, Amen.

February 13

Mardi Gras is a period of feasting, joviality, dancing, partying, and parading, leading up to the season of Lent. The church calendar shifts from Epiphany to Lent; in-between these solemn events people will engage in eating, drinking, and being merry which culminates on Fat Tuesday, the day before Ash Wednesday. Celebrations involve parties and pigging out, to which we assign the French term *shrove*, meaning fat. This day is highlighted in an annual festival and parade in New Orleans, LA. The same theme is eminent in other places around the world though called by different names. The objectives are the same, however: engage in all manner of earthly delights because Lent and Holy Week are coming during which you are supposed to give all that up.

Like most other church observances, there is a pagan one occurring within the same timeframe. Just like the church chose Christmastime which coincides with pagan rituals associated with the winter solstice, pagans chose all hallows eve (Halloween) to counter the Protestant Reformation (October 31) and All Saints Day (November 1). There is nothing wrong with celebrating, depending on what is done in the name of that celebration. Holy Week will involve celebrations with family and friends, to include eating, worship, singing, and merriment. It sounds similar to Mardi Gras, but much different with respect to the morality continuum.

- LEV 23:1–37 ~ God instructed Moses about seven feasts to celebrate annually. The fourteenth day of the first month is Passover, followed by seven days of Unleavened Bread with its holy convocations. First Fruits occurs during those eight days. Count seven weeks and offer a sacrifice on the fiftieth day which is Pentecost. The first day of the seventh month is the Feast of Trumpets; the tenth day of that month is the Day of Atonement. The fifteenth day will be the Feast of Tabernacles, during which sacrifices are given for seven days.

- 1 KI 8:66 ~ On the eighth day, feasting and celebrations ceased and everyone went home rejoicing.

- ECC 3:1, 4 ~ For everything there is a season, and a time for every purpose under heaven. A time to weep and a time to laugh; a time to mourn and a time to dance.

- LUK 15:11–32 ~ A young man asked his father for his share of the inheritance. The father gave his son the inheritance, and the son left for a foreign land where he squandered all his money on wine and women. Meanwhile, a great famine arose in that country. The son had to feed pigs to make a living. Even his father's servants were better off than this, he reasoned, so he returned home to confess everything to his father and apologize. His father saw him coming, ran out to meet his son, and embraced him. The son told his father that he was not worthy of being called a son and should be treated as a servant. But the father had his servants prepare a great feast of celebration, butchering a fatted calf for the occasion. The elder son became angry, refusing to enter the house. The father consoled him saying, "You are always with me and all that is mine is yours. But it is fitting to celebrate, because your brother was lost, and now he is found; he was dead to us but now he is alive."

- ROM 14:5–6 ~ One person considers a particular day more sacred than other days; another person considers each day alike. Both should be completely confident in their decision. Those who regard one day as special, do so to the Lord. Those who feast, eat to the Lord and give Him thanks. Those who fast, do so to the Lord and give Him thanks.

Heavenly Father, help us live for you, whether we are rejoicing, celebrating, feasting or fasting—let everything we do or do not do be done to glorify you. Prevent us from using a time of celebration to engage in lusts of the flesh. We live for you and we die for you, to be raised to live with Jesus, and be with you forever as your adopted children. We pray in His name, Amen.

February 14

Valentine's Day is named after Saint Valentinus, which reflects one or more Christians martyred under the tyrannical rule of Rome during the first four centuries AD. One such individual was executed for performing secret wedding ceremonies for soldiers who were prohibited by the emperor to marry, believing they would make better fighting men if they remained unattached. Legend has it that this Christian evangelist and minister possessed the gift of healing: curing a jailer's daughter of blindness. Before his death he left her a note signed, "your Valentine" and hence, the *Be My Valentine* phrase on greeting cards. Considered a man of God and an example of the love of Christ, the Feast of St. Valentine was launched by Pope Gelasius I at the end of the fifth century; this festival was the precursor to celebrations being held today. Valentine is hailed by some as the patron saint of love and miracles. Given differing versions about who, what, and how many, it is hard to separate fact from fiction, so Valentine remains a fabled figure.

Over time, the romantic love angle was added to this observance and has prevailed to this day. Celebrate today with a true love or spouse. It is a good opportunity to strengthen the bond, enhance the romance, and add passion, fidelity, and commitment. Share greeting cards with red hearts and add a handwritten note. Other relationships are celebrated also: kinfolk, classmates, and virtually anybody and everybody. All partnerships are fair game, intimate or platonic. The holiday has been commercialized to the extent it may have lost its original meaning.

This day should be about sharing love: God's love, marital love, romantic love, brotherly love, even puppy love. Love does no harm to a neighbor; therefore, love is the fulfilling of God's Law (ROM 13:10). But mostly, this will be a day to honor your soulmate with gifts, cards, flowers, candy, entertainment, and above all, authentic love. The symbol of a heart is on all of these shared moments, both literally and figuratively.

- 1 KI 8:61 ~ Let your heart be completely true to the Lord, walking in his statutes and keeping His commandments.

- PSA 37:4–5 ~ Find your delight in the Lord and He will give to you the desires of your heart. Commit yourself to the Lord and trust in Him, and He will make your desires come to pass.

- PRO 13:12 ~ Hope deferred makes the heart sick, but a desire fulfilled is a tree of life.

- PRO 27:19 ~ The heart reflects the person just like a mirror.

- ECC 11:9 ~ Rejoice in your youth and let your heart cheer you. Walk in the ways of your heart and the sight of your eyes. But remember, for all these things God will judge you.

- MAT 5:8 ~ Blessed be the pure in heart for they shall see God.

- MAT 6:21 ~ Jesus said, "Where your treasure is, there your heart will be."

- COL 2:2 ~ Let your hearts be comforted for you are bound together in love. You have received the wealth of knowledge and understanding by acknowledging the mystery of God, the Father and the Son.

- 2 TH 3:5 ~ May the Lord direct your hearts into God's love and Christ's perseverance.

- 1 PE 1:22 ~ Purify your souls by obedience to the truth and earnest love for one another.

The Bible teaches us how to love, though we are unable to love with the kind of perfect, unconditional love that God displays. We are empowered by God's love to love Him above all others and to love others as ourselves. With God's love living in our hearts, we have the power to overcome a multitude of problems, including sin.

- LUK 6:32, 35 ~ Jesus said, "If you love only those who love you, what reward will you receive? Even sinners love those who love them. Therefore, love everyone, even your enemies. Help others whenever you can, expecting nothing in return, and your reward will be great, and you will become a child of God."

- 1 CO 13:2–8, 13 ~ Even if you have the gift of prophecy, can understand mysteries, and have a faith to move mountains, you are nothing without love. Even if you give all you have to the poor, you profit nothing if you do not have love. Love is patient. Love is kind. Love is never envious or conceited. Love is not rude, self-seeking, or angered, nor does it find pleasure in sin. Love does not think of sinful things nor is it provoked by evil. Love rejoices in the truth. Love always protects, always trusts, always hopes, and always endures. Love never fails... Faith, hope, and love abide; but the greatest of these three is love.

- COL 3:14 ~ Above all, put on love, which binds all things together in perfect harmony.

- 2 TI 1:7 ~ God did not give us a spirit of fear, but of power, love and a sound mind.

- 1 JO 4:11–12, 18–19 ~ Since God loved us, we should love one another. Although nobody has seen God, if we love each other, God's love will live inside us to be perfected in us. There is no fear in love, but perfect love repels fear, because fear has torment. We love God because He loved us first; but you cannot love God and hate your neighbor. For how can you love someone you have not seen if you cannot even love someone you have seen?

When it comes to love between a man and a woman, the Bible provides a prescription for how to proceed. For example, in the Old Testament book Song of Solomon, guidelines have been provided about mutual respect, courting, falling in love, marriage, and partnership. My favorite passage from that book is repeated for good reason: Do not arouse or awaken love until it is ready. Follow God's recommendations for intimacy, relationship, teamwork, love and mutual respect, and you will have a successful and enduring marriage, and every day will be like Valentine's Day.

- GEN 2:24 ~ A man will leave his parents and cling to his wife; and they will become one flesh.

- ECC 9:9 ~ Always be happy with your spouse, and love him or her the rest of your life.

- MAL 2:14–16 ~ The Lord formed a husband and wife into one flesh. In both flesh and spirit, they belong to Him. Why is this so? Because He wishes godly offspring from them. Guard your spirit, and do not break the covenant with your wife or husband by getting divorced.

- MAT 19:6 ~ Jesus said, "Once you are joined in marriage you are no longer two separate persons, but are one flesh. Whatever God has joined together, nobody should split apart.

- 1 PE 3:1, 7 ~ Wives, obey your husbands, and teach them the Word if they do not understand it. Husbands, listen to your wives; honor your wives as the weaker sex, and as an equal. Stay together in the grace of life, and your prayers will be answered.

Father in heaven we love you because you loved us first. Help us to reflect your love so that others may see your love alive inside of us, through Jesus Christ who is the perfect example of your love. Help us to love our spouses, just like Jesus loves His church on earth. Help us to work together as a team: equal partners in sharing the workload and responsibilities, both heading in the same direction which leads to your kingdom in heaven. Let our love grow continuously; and when we grow old, let us be as much in love with each other as when we married. Help us always to be faithful to the soulmate you provided, and to be thankful, so that your name can be glorified in our matrimony. In the name of Christ, the love of our lives, we pray, Amen.

On this day this year we also will be observing Ash Wednesday (next page).

FEBRUARY

Ash Wednesday is the beginning of Lent. Though the date varies from year to year, it occurs about forty days before Palm Sunday and forty-six days before Easter. Forty is a significant number as it represents the forty years the Israelites wandered the wilderness and the forty days Christ fasted while being tempted in the wilderness. This can be a day of fasting and prayer, to emulate Christ in the wilderness. For many denominations, there is a special convocation in the church. Some people will have a cross drawn on their forehead using ash, as a sign of humility.

The placing of ashes on the forehead is a Catholic tradition that is still practiced by many. Ashes to ashes, dust to dust: this is a reference to death and the fact that our mortal bodies began from dust and end that way. Of course, in a few weeks we will be mourning the death of Jesus, who died in our place, and then celebrating His coming back to life. Ashes reflect our shame for sin, being worthy of death but being saved from it. The tradition of mourning in sackcloth and ashes goes back to Old Testament rituals of godly sorrow and humility over one's sins.

- JOB 42:6 ~ I abhor myself, and I repent in dust and ashes.

- ISA 61:1–3 ~ The Spirit of God is upon me, because He has directed me to preach His good news to the humble, to heal the broken hearted, to free the slaves, and to release those who are bound in chains and in prison; to proclaim the Lord's favor and His vengeance, to comfort all who mourn, and to tell those who mourn to exchange their ashes for beauty; to replace mourning with joy, and to don the garment of praise in exchange for the spirit of sorrow, so that they may be trees of righteousness, planted by the Lord for His glorification.

- DAN 9:3–5 ~ I placed my focus on the Lord and sought Him through prayer and supplications, with fasting, sackcloth, and ashes; and I prayed to the Lord my God, making confession, saying, "Oh Lord, great and awesome God, who keeps His covenant of mercy for those who love Him and keep His commandments; we have sinned and committed iniquity, we have done wickedly, and have rebelled by departing from your precepts and judgments."

- JOE 2:12–13 ~ The Lord says to turn to Him with all your heart, in fasting and prayer, with weeping and mourning. Rend your heart, not your garments and turn back to God. For He is gracious and merciful, slow to anger, with great kindness, and He will forgive those who repent of evil.

- HEB 9:13–14 ~ The blood of animals and the ashes sprinkled on the ceremonially unclean sanctified those who were clean on the outside but not the inside. How much more will the blood of Christ, who through the eternal Spirit offered Himself unblemished to God, cleanse our consciences from acts that lead to death, so that we may live to serve the living God!

The marking of our souls already has been performed by God, for His cross has been etched into our hearts. Therefore, whatever is left of our remains and ashes, they will be raised to produce a new body, one without sin, glorified with Jesus.

- EZE 37:3–6 ~ The Lord asked Ezekiel, "Son of man, can these bones live? Prophecy to these bones saying, "Surely, I will cause breath to enter you again so you might live; I will put muscles and flesh upon you, all covered with skin. Then you will know that I am the Lord."

Heavenly Father, we come before you with humility and sorrow for the sins we have committed, some of which we are aware and some of which we are unaware; and we confess them all before your throne of mercy, asking forgiveness once again. We ask for your Holy Spirit to be upon us, and cover our sins with the blood of Christ, replacing our mourning and regret with your comfort and grace. Help us to cling to your saving grace, not only during this season but throughout the entire year, shining your light and love. Empower us to walk in newness of life, through the life given us in Christ, who gave His life for us, that we may live and not die. In His name, Amen.

February 15

Susan B. Anthony Day recognizes a great woman of faith born on this day in 1820. She led the movement for women's suffrage, as well as other woman's rights issues including equal education and equal pay. She also supported alcohol prohibition and the prohibition of slavery of any kind. She was mentored by Frederick Douglass, and they developed a lasting friendship. She also partnered with Elizabeth Stanton, and the two championed woman's rights, such as voting and equal opportunities for women. Though not a national holiday, today is observed in several US states. Anthony never lived to see the full results of her efforts, which culminated in the passage of the Nineteenth Amendment to the Constitution in 1920, granting voting rights to women almost two decades after her death. She was the first American woman to be honored by placing her face on a US minted coin (1979–1981, 1989); this and other dollar coins have been phased out for the most part, being used mostly with machine transactions.

It takes guts taking a stand for liberty when you are surrounded by people that don't want to hear about it. They will talk over you in an effort to not listen. They will try to have you cancelled or arrested. These hazards were present for women's suffrage and women's temperance movements in the USA. But the impact of these strong women is felt to this day. Males and females were deemed equal in New Testament (GAL 3:28). Yet it has been scarcely one hundred years since women were seen equal to men in this country. There is still a long way to go when it comes to women being treated equal to men across the globe. Susan Anthony got it started; she won on the voting initiative but lost on abolishing alcohol. Men and women are equal in their right and their ability to buy, abuse, and become dependent upon alcohol or drugs.

- PSA 133:1 ~ Behold, how good and how pleasant it is for brothers and sisters of the faith to live together in unity!
- PRO 2:9 ~ You will understand righteousness, judgment, and equity; yes, every good path.
- ISA 56:5–8 ~ The righteous will be like God's sons and daughters, only better than that, with a name that will last forever. People of all walks of life will be joined together on His holy mountain to worship Him, for His house will be called a house for the righteous.
- ACT 10:34–35 ~ Peter said, "Truly, God does not show favoritism to any person. Within every nation, anyone who fears the Lord and works righteousness is accepted by Him."
- 2 CO 6:17–18 ~ Come out from among them and be separate, says the Lord. Do not touch unclean things, and I will receive you. I will be your Father and you will be my sons and daughters.
- HEB 6:10–11 ~ God is fair; He will never forget your work, and the love you showed to Him, and the help you were to His people. We want you to continue to show this same diligence until the end, in order to make your hope complete.
- 1 PE 2:17 ~ Respect all people. Love the brotherhood. Fear God. Honor the King of kings.
- 2 PE 1:5–10 ~ In diligence, add virtue to faith, knowledge to virtue, temperance to knowledge, patience to temperance, godliness to patience, kindness to godliness, and charity to kindness. If these things abound in you, you will never be barren or unfruitful in the knowledge of our Lord Jesus Christ. Those lacking these attributes are blind and short-sighted, and have forgotten that past sins were purged. Therefore, my brothers and sisters, be diligent to make your calling and election sure, for if you do these things, you will never fail.

Heavenly Father, Son, and Holy Ghost, you are the great equalizer; help people to know this truth. Help us to treat people the way we want to be treated, and may we always be free, Amen.

February 16

National Caregivers Day falls on the third Friday of the month to honor caregivers who provide physical, mental, and emotional support to people who cannot fend for themselves. This is a profession and discipline of self-sacrifice. Helpers often work long hours, since many patients require special or intensive care, and/or around the clock supervision. Take time today to show appreciation to helpers, no matter what their field. Oftentimes, they get no reward, salary, or recognition. Send them a thank you card or note, or give them a gift. If you have a loved one requiring care that you cannot provide, you know how valuable helping services are.

- LUK 6:32, 35 ~ Jesus said, "If you love only those who love you, what reward will you receive? Even sinners love those who love them. Therefore, love everyone, even your enemies. Help others whenever you can, expecting nothing in return, and your reward will be great, and you will become a child of God."

- ROM 12:20 ~ If your enemy is hungry, feed him; if he is thirsty, give him a drink. Maybe you can turn him or her around by being nice.

- 1 CO 12:27–28 ~ You are of the body of Christ and each one of you has a part in it. In the church God has appointed apostles first, prophets second, teachers third, then miracle workers, those with the gift of healing, helpers, administrators, and those who can speak in different tongues.

- 1 CO 14:12 ~ Since you are eager to have spiritual gifts, try to excel in those gifts which edify the church.

- 2 CO 1:3–4 ~ Praise to God, the Father of our Lord Jesus Christ, who comforts us in all our troubles, so we will be able to comfort others who are troubled, giving the same comfort that we ourselves have received from God.

- COL 3:24 ~ If you help others, you are really serving Christ.

- 1 TH 5:14 ~ We urge you, brothers, admonish the idle, encourage the fainthearted, help the weak, be patient with them all.

- HEB 13:1–2 ~ Let brotherly love continue. Do not forget to help strangers, for you may be ministering to angels for all you know.

- 1 JO 3:16–18 ~ We can understand the love of God because He gave His life for us; therefore, we should be willing to give our lives out of brotherly love. Those who have the means to help their fellow man and do not must not have the love of God in them. My children, let us love, not just in writing or in voice, but let us show it in action and in truth.

As a professional helper, I often would wonder what became of people I had treated. Sometimes they returned for more treatment; other times I never heard from them again. On rare occasions one would call, or send a card or letter, just to say thanks. Allowing me to know that they were helped, and were better for it, was heartwarming. This is what gets you through the day-to-day grind, one thank-you or a brief word of recognition from clients or staff. Infrequently does sufficient recognition come from upper echelons, except during holidays like Christmas.

This day is an opportunity for recognizing those who helped you; it doesn't matter what kind of help they provided or whether or not you paid for the help. Say thank you as often as someone helps you or meets your needs; make a habit of saying thanks to people and giving thanks to the Lord for their help. This habit is healthy; it will never get you into trouble. There is a term we call "burn out" in the helping professions; it's when a person has reached the pinnacle of exhaustion or frustration. It is the primary reason people leave jobs as a helper. As for me, I felt the burn several times. What kept me going is a hint from the Holy Spirit that I was where He wanted me to be. That was all the recognition I needed.

- JOS 1:9 ~ God said, "Have I not commanded you? Be strong and courageous. Do not be frightened, and do not be dismayed, for the Lord your God is with you wherever you go."

- PSA 1:1–5 ~ Blessed is the person that does not walk in the counsel of the ungodly, or stand among sinners, or sit in the seat of the scornful. Blessed is the person whose delight is in God's Law, for that person meditates on God's Law every day and night. Such a person will be like a tree planted by flowing streams of water, bearing good fruit in season, with leaves that never wither. Whatever he or she does will prosper. But the ungodly are not so; they are like the chaff that the wind blows away. Therefore, the wicked will not stand with the just, and sinners will not assemble with the righteous. For God watches over the ways of righteous people, but the ways of the wicked will perish.

- ISA 3:10 ~ Tell the righteous that all will be well with them, for they will partake of the fruit of their deeds.

- JER 17:10 ~ I, the Lord, search the heart and test the mind, that I may give to everyone according to the fruit of their deeds.

- ROM 8:28–31 ~ We know that all things work together for good to those who love God and are called according to His purpose. For God knew them in advance and predestined them to be conformed to the image of His Son, and to be among the firstborn of His brothers. Whomever He predestined, He called; and whomever He called He justified; and whomever He justified, He also glorified. Therefore, if God is with us, who can be against us?

- PHP 2:13–15 ~ For it is God who works in you both to want and to do that which pleases Him. Do this without grumbling or quarreling, so you can remain blameless and harmless children of God, without reproach, in the midst of a crooked and perverse nation where you shine as lights to the world.

- EPH 2:8–10 ~ You are saved by the grace of God because of your faith in Jesus Christ. Salvation is a gift of God, it cannot be earned through good works, so nobody should brag. We are God's workmanship, created in Jesus Christ to do good works which God prepared in advance for us to do.

- COL 3:15 ~ Let the peace of God rule in your hearts, since as members of one body you were called to peace. Be therefore, thankful. Let the Word of Christ live in you richly as you teach and admonish one another with wisdom, and as you sing psalms, hymns, and spiritual songs with gratitude in your hearts toward God.

Father God, who helps everyone who comes to you in faith, we thank you. We give thanks today for people who help people that come to them with needs and problems; further, we thank you for all who work in the helping professions, and for their endurance. We especially thank you for those who help out of the kindness in their hearts and not for personal gain or recognition. Let us be that kind of helper, one who is there for others even after completing our work and desiring rest. You have said that anything we do to help another, we do for Jesus; and whenever we fail to do something to help, we have not helped Jesus. Help us therefore, to help others as if we were helping Jesus, because indeed, we are. Let us never tire from doing good; give us stamina to continue even when we are weary. Remind us, when we feel overloaded, to bring it to Jesus and He will carry the load for us. Let us be a blessing to others as you have been to us, through your Son who is a blessing to all of humanity; in His name we pray, Amen.

February 17

Random Acts of Kindness Day is a national day to commend the gift of kindness, which is one of many spiritual gifts listed in the Bible. Kindness is a two-way street: if you are kind to people, you are more likely to be treated with kindness. But even when people are nasty, we should return kindness regardless. It gets back to what the previous lesson was about, and that is helping others for no other reason than the kindness in your heart. Maybe if you help them, they will be inclined to help someone else, and it will have a multiplicative effect. The above phrase came from Anne Herbert who had placemats made in 1982 with the inscription: Practice random kindness and senseless acts of beauty; this became the title of her book published in 2016. The Random Acts of Kindness Foundation was established in 1995 in Denver CO, where they started an initiative for an annual observance. That idea had an additive effect and is now being honored worldwide, though on different days.

Altruism is the philosophy of helping others, with time, money, or any way you can. It is about having a generous heart, which gives selflessly without expecting anything in return. But there is a reward; it is the uplift one feels in the heart after helping another. It's kind of a spiritual high. As pointed out earlier, kindness is contagious; unfortunately, so is unkindness. Goodness, kindness, and godliness are attributes of Christ; these are ways we can reflect Him as we serve others which serves God. Christ is the one who will ultimately judge whether we've been kind.

- MAT 6:2 ~ When you help the needy, do not sound your trumpet as the hypocrites do in the churches and in the streets, so that they can receive praise from others. The truth is, that is all the reward they will ever receive.

- 2 CO 6:4–6 ~ Do not give the ministry a bad reputation, but show that you are good ministers of God by demonstrating patience in time of trouble, hardship, distress, punishment, imprisonment, rioting, hard work, sleepless nights, and hunger. Be an example of purity, understanding, patience, and kindness, through the Holy Spirit, with sincere love.

- 2 CO 10:17–18 ~ When you brag, brag about the Lord. Those who commend themselves do not gain approval, but only those who God commends.

- EPH 4:1–3 ~ I Paul, a prisoner for the Lord, implore that you stay worthy of the vocation for which you are called, with humbleness, kindness, and perseverance; loving one another, staying unified in the Spirit, and bonded together in peace.

- 2 PE 1:2–8 ~ Grace and peace be multiplied to you through the knowledge of God, and of Jesus our Lord. His divine power has given us everything we need for life and righteousness through our knowledge of Him who called us by His own glory and goodness. He has given us His very great and precious promises, so that through them we may participate in the divine nature and escape the corruption of this world and its evil desires. So, add to your faith goodness, knowledge, self-control, perseverance, godliness, kindness, and love. For if you possess these qualities, you will not be unproductive or ineffective in your knowledge of our Lord Jesus Christ.

We are to bear good fruit using all of our faculties. We are given talents, abilities, and callings to match them; what a waste to use those skills and energy to bear bad fruit. God blesses all who follow Him and bear fruits of righteousness. He sometimes awards us with additional gifts and purposes to further His will through our lives. I wouldn't be surprised if everybody possesses hidden skills of which they are unaware, and possibly never discover. Thus, whenever opportunities to lend a hand present themselves, step in and help; it may come as a surprise what you are able to do when God is directing your path.

- MAT 3:7–10 ~ John was baptizing people in the Jordan River when many of the Pharisees and Sadducees came to observe. John spoke to them saying, "You snakes! Has anyone warned you of the judgement that awaits you? You had better start bearing fruit that is worthy of repentance. You say to yourselves that you have Abraham as your father. I assure you that God can produce children of Abraham from these stones. The ax is ready to strike at the roots; any tree that does not bear good fruit will be chopped down and burned in the fire."

- MAT 7:17–19 ~ A good tree bears good fruit; a corrupt tree bears evil fruit. A good tree cannot bear bad fruit and a bad tree cannot bear good fruit. Any tree that does not bear good fruit will be cut down at the roots and burned in the fire.

- JOH 15:1–10 ~ Jesus said, "I am the true vine, and my Father is the cultivator. He removes any of my branches that do not bear fruit. Those that do bear fruit, he prunes, so that they can bear even more fruit. You have been made clean through the Word which I have spoken to you. Stay in me and I will stay in you. The branch cannot bear fruit by itself; it must be connected to the vine. You cannot bear fruit unless you remain in me. I am the vine and you are the branches. Those abiding in me will bear much fruit but without me you can do nothing. If you do not abide in me, you will be removed like a dead and withered branch that is burned in the fire. If you live in me, and my words live in you, you can ask for anything and it will be done. This brings glory to my Father: that you bear much fruit and that you follow me. As the Father has loved me, so I have loved you. Continue in my love. If you keep my commandments you will remain in my love, even as I have kept my Father's commandments and remain in His love."

- 1 CO 15:58 ~ Be steadfast, firm, and fruitful in the Lord; for your efforts will not be in vain.

- GAL 5:22–23 ~ The fruits of the spirit include love, joy, peace, patience, kindness, goodness, faithfulness, gentleness, and self-control. There is no law against such things.

A little bit of kindness goes a long way. Grab some paper and list all of your spiritual gifts on the left side of the page and list your shortcomings on the right side. Line up the ones that are opposite. For example, the opposite of kindness is bitterness; the opposite of temperance is overindulgence; the opposite of gladness is depression; the opposite of peace of mind is anxiety; the opposite of loyalty is betrayal; the opposite of hope is despair. Notice how the positive attributes are greater in power; in other words, the spiritual gift on the left can overpower and defeat its negative counterpart. That's right, spiritual gifts are higher powers and they can lift you up, as well as those around you. Drawbacks have negative power and can bring you down. Tap into your higher powers for they come from the highest power who is God; and they will lift spirits just as high tide lifts all boats. Exhibit awareness and kindness and you might notice a lift.

- 1 TH 5:21–22 ~ Examine all things and hold onto the good. Abstain from all appearance of evil.

- 1 PE 3:8–9 ~ Live in harmony with one another with love, sympathy, compassion, and humility. Do not repay evil with evil or insult others, but repay with blessings. Be a blessing to others for you were called to inherit a blessing.

Our Father in heaven, help us to be spiritually minded and not materialistic or carnally minded. Help us to employ our spiritual gifts and bear fruit worthy of repentance. Let us be an example of kindness, gladness, temperance, loyalty, and hope so others can be invigorated in their spirits and experience the lift. May we spread kindness to others, and may their kindness spread, so that it creates a tidal wave of kindness flowing over our nation, continuing over the continents, and all across the planet. May the kindness of Christ be boldly proclaimed, Amen.

February 18

Two Testaments Day recognizes the importance of the Holy Bible: both testaments. Why does the Bible have two testaments? Is one testament more important than the other? Well, no, since they cross-reference each other, providing irrefutable proof that the entire Word of God is true and has one author: God.

There are two, and only two, testaments to the Holy Bible. The first was God's message to the Jews about faith, law, forgiveness, salvation, and Messiah who would come. The second was God's message to all people about faith, law, forgiveness, salvation, and Messiah who had come. The former was delivered to God's chosen via Moses and the prophets. The second was delivered to all people through Jesus Christ and the apostles. Jew or Christian, God is calling all people to Himself if only they will choose Him. If you choose God, you will believe every word proceeding from the breath of the Holy Spirit.

- ISA 9:6 ~ A child is born for us; a Son is given to us. The government will be on His shoulders. His name will be called Wonderful Counselor, Mighty God, Everlasting Father, and Prince of Peace.

- ISA 42:6 ~ I the Lord have called you (Messiah) in righteousness and will hold your hand and keep you; and give you as a covenant for my people and a light for the Gentiles.

- MAT 20:16 ~ Jesus said, "The last will be first, and the first last, for many are called, but few are chosen."

- JOH 1:17 ~ For the Law was given by Moses, but Grace and Truth came by Jesus Christ.

Our Judeo-Christian founders, framers, and leaders brought forth a novel way of self-government based on both testaments of the Bible and the sovereignty of God. The concept of three equal but separate branches of government came straight from the Holy Bible (ISA 33:22). This instruction has enabled our nation to prosper and prevail. We must not abandon the fundamentals of our faith such as love, mercy, morality, liberty, truth, and justice, else we go the way of great nations before us which is progressively downward. Beware when those in power whittle away at your liberties, scorn solid tenets of morality and spirituality, confound the borders between branches of government, and disseminate justice unevenly. To quote Alexis de Tocqueville "Liberty cannot be established without morality, nor morality without faith." Adding justice to his message, I have proposed four pillars of fate: faith, liberty, morality, and justice, which if any one falters, the whole system comes crashing down (Barber, 2016). It appears that all four pillars are cracked and wobbling, but it is not too late to reinforce and strengthen them. To quote Benjamin Franklin who was asked what was accomplished while leaving the Constitutional Convention, "A republic if you can keep it."

- ISA 33:22 ~ The Lord is our judge, the Lord is our lawgiver, the Lord is our king; He will save us.

There are sixty-six canonical books of the Holy Bible comprising the sole, faultless testimony of God who directed the authors to spread His Word (2 PE 1:16–21). Many religions and denominations have added additional references from which they derive historical, cultural, and social material to augment their belief system. At times, these traditions and rituals are elevated to doctrinal level, which is dangerous; both the Old and New Testaments warn not to add to or subtract from God's Word. If our nation strays from the path God revealed to us into any other direction, that policy will fail, we will lose our way, and the republic will slip away. Let us hold fast to the precepts of God and abandon those of humankind whenever they are unaligned with the Holy Bible.

- ISA 29:13 ~ The Lord says, "These people come near to me with their mouth and honor me with their lips, but their hearts are far from me. Their worship of me consists only of precepts taught by men."
- MAR 7:6–9, 13 ~ Jesus said, "Isaiah prophesied about you hypocrites (ISA 29:13). For you put aside the commandments of God and follow the traditions of men. By following your own traditions, you show a disregard for the Word of God."
- COL 2:8, 20–22 ~ Beware that you are not spoiled by errant philosophies or vain deceptions, originating from worldly traditions and principles and not from Christ. You are in Christ and not the world, so why submit to its rules? You are not subject to ordinances based on the doctrines and commandments of men (such as do not touch, taste, or use certain things). Those traditions are destined to die out. People may appear reasonable with their self-imposed worship, false humility, and harsh treatment of the body, but these practices lack value in restraining the sinful flesh.
- 2 TH 2:15 ~ Fellow Christians, stand fast in your faith and hold onto those traditions that you have been taught in God's Word through the prophets and apostles.

To repeat, we must be careful not to add to or subtract from the Holy Bible. No matter what your belief system, everyone knows in their heart what is right and wrong, because your conscience will acquit you or convict you (ROM 2:15). That is, God has written His laws upon our hearts, so nobody has an excuse for doing evil or opposing God (ROM 1:20–21). Morality and truth are not relative, they are absolute, since they come directly from God who is perfectly holy and absolutely true to His Word.

- DEU 4:1–2, 5–6 ~ God said, "Listen Israel to the laws and statutes I am about to teach you. Follow them so you can live and take possession of the land I am going to give to you. Do not add to my commands and do not subtract from them. Keep these laws carefully, for this will demonstrate to other nations your wisdom and understanding."
- DEU 12:32 ~ Do what God has commanded you, and do not add to it or diminish from it.
- GAL 1:8 ~ Anyone, including the angels, who preaches anything contrary to what Jesus Christ and the apostles preached are cursed.
- 1 TH 2:13 ~ We thank God that you received His Word and accepted it as the Word of God and not the word of men. The Word of God is at work in believers like you.
- 2 TI 3:16 ~ All scripture is inspired by God. God's Word provides the doctrine of truth, refutes that which is false, and instructs all people in the ways of righteousness.
- 2 PE 1:16, 21 ~ We did not follow cleverly devised fables when we told people about the power and coming of Jesus Christ, for we were eye witnesses to His majesty. No prophecy ever came from the impulse of man, but holy men spoke as they were directed by God.
- REV 22:18–19 ~ For I testify to everyone who hears the words of the prophecy of this book, that if anyone adds to these words, God will add unto that person the plagues mentioned in this book. If anyone subtracts from the words of this prophecy, God will take away their name from the Book of Life, and they will not share in the inheritance.

The central message of Judeo-Christian theology is communicated and remembered during Holy Week. The significance of this week should not be marginalized. It is not about vacations, candy, food, games, or chores; it is about the Lamb of God who takes away the sin of the world (JOH 1:20). This is represented in three important events: first, Abraham sacrificing a ram in place of his son Isaac; second, the slaying and eating of the Passover lamb which saved the firstborn of the Jews, who had painted their doorposts with the lamb's blood. Third, the fulfillment of covenants with Abraham and Moses, which foreshadowed the sacrifice of God's firstborn and only Son, slain on the cross during the celebration of Passover, thereby bringing to mind all of the Biblical prophecies of Messiah who would come and who will come again.

Jesus is the Passover Lamb. Abraham knew about Messiah and rejoiced, as testified by Christ Himself (JOH 8:56–58). Moses knew this when he declared the New Covenant to the nation of Israel (EXO 24:8), while sprinkling the blood of the sacrifice on the Book and the people. God's chosen include all who possess a faith like Abraham, which requires inviting the Holy Spirit to guide you in your walk. God is there anyway, and always; all you need to do is acknowledge Him and He will show you the best path to the way home.

- GEN 22:2–8 ~ God told Abraham to take His only legitimate son Isaac and sacrifice him on a mountain. Abraham proceeded to do as God requested. Along the way, Isaac asked his father, "Where is the lamb for sacrifice." Abraham answered, "God Himself will provide the lamb."

- EXO 24:8 ~ Moses took blood from the sacrifice and sprinkled it on the people saying, "This is the blood of the everlasting covenant revealed by the Lord in these His words."

- JOH 1:29–35 ~ John the Baptist saw Jesus coming and said, "Look, here comes the Lamb of God who takes away the sin of the world. He is the One of whom I spoke who would come after me, though He is preferred over me for He existed before me. I did not know Him intimately, but He is the reason I have been baptizing people with water. He told me that I would see the Spirit of God descending upon Him and remaining there. I saw the Spirit of God descending upon Him like a dove, and it rested upon Him. He is the same One who will baptize with the Holy Spirit. I am a witness that He is the Son of God."

- JOH 8:56–58 ~ Jesus said, "Abraham saw my day and rejoiced." The Jews replied, "You are not even fifty years old and you claim to have seen Abraham." Jesus declared, "I tell you the truth, before Abraham was, I AM."

- 1 CO 2:13 ~ We teach using words taught by the Holy Spirit, not by human wisdom. Spiritual truths can be interpreted only by people who possess the Spirit.

- HEB 9:19–22 ~ Moses sprinkled the blood of the sacrifice on the Book of the Law, the church, and the people, testifying of God's everlasting covenant. By the Law evil is purged with blood, and without blood there can be no remission of sins.

- 1 PE 1:18–19 ~ You were redeemed, not with corruptible things such as gold and silver, but with the precious blood of Christ, a Lamb without any imperfections.

It is by faith that we are saved, solely by the grace of God and the sacrifice of His Son (ISA 53; JOH 3:16; EPH 2:8–9). This free gift of salvation is the theme of the entire Bible. If you want to live forever with the Lord of the universe, believe in Him; if you refuse you will spend eternity separated from Him. God reveals Himself to anyone who seeks Him and loves Him (MAT 7:7–8). God loved us first (1 JO 4:19), and He wants us to love Him back; but He will not force anyone, it's our choice. The faith evident in Abraham and the patriarchs of the Old Testament was shown in the followers of Christ in the New Testament. Like them, we are flawed human beings, incapable of fulfilling God's Law in entirety, which is why Christ fulfilled the Law on our behalf and why our faith is founded on Him.

- GEN 22:18 ~ God told Abraham, "In your seed all the nations of the world will be blessed because you have been obedient to me."

- ISA 41:8 ~ You Israel, are God's servants, the children of Jacob whom I have chosen, and the seed of my friend Abraham.

- JOH 8:31–47 ~ Jesus spoke to those Jews who believed in Him saying, "If you continue in my Word, you are indeed my disciples, and you will know the truth and the truth will set you free." Some of the bystanders answered, "We are descendants of Abraham, and we have never been slaves to anyone; how can we possibly be set free?" Jesus replied, "Whoever sins becomes a slave to sin. A slave has no position in the family, but a son does. If the Son sets you free, you will definitely be free. I know you descended from Abraham, yet you are ready to kill me because you have no room for my Word in your heart. I have been telling you what I have seen in the Father's presence." They responded, "Abraham is our father." Jesus announced, "If you were Abraham's children you would do as he did. Instead, you plot to kill me, a man who has given you the truth directly from God; Abraham would never do such a thing. You are following the ways of your earthly father." They protested, saying, "We are not illegitimate children; God Himself is our Father." Jesus explained, "If God was your Father, you would love me, for I came from Him and here I AM; I have not come on my own but He has sent me. Why is this so hard for you to understand? Because you belong to your father the devil, and your desire is to carry out his will. He was a murderer from the start and despised the truth, for there is no truth in him. He speaks only lies whereas he is the father of lies. I speak only the truth but you refuse to listen. Can you prove me wrong; if not, why do you not believe? Whoever belongs to God listens to Him. The reason you do not understand is because you do not belong."

- ROM 4:13, 16; ROM 9:6–7 ~ For the promise that he should be an heir to the world, was not given to Abraham or to his seed through the Law, but through the righteousness of faith. Therefore, it is by grace through faith that the promise is given to all the seed; not only to those who obey the Law, but also to those who demonstrate the faith of Abraham who was the father of us all. Not everyone who is a descendant of Jacob is of the house of Israel. That is, just because someone is from the lineage of Abraham, it does not necessarily make them children or heirs.

- GAL 3:6–9, 16, 26–29 ~ Consider Abraham. He believed God and his faith was credited to him as righteousness. Understand then, that those who believe are the children of Abraham. The scriptures foresaw that God would justify the Gentiles by faith, and announced it in the Gospel to Abraham as it is written: All nations of the world will be blessed through your seed (GEN 22:18). Anyone having faith is blessed along with Abraham, a man of great faith. To Abraham and his seed, the promises were made. God did not say "seeds" meaning many people, He said "seed" meaning one person, who is Christ. You are children of God through faith in Jesus Christ, for you have been baptized unto Him and have clothed yourselves in His righteousness. There is neither Jew nor Greek, slave nor free, male nor female, for you are all one in the Lord. If you belong to Christ, then you are Abraham's seed and heirs according to God's promise.

Without faith, we cannot please God no matter how many good works we perform; however, with faith we are compelled to do good works and improve in our ability to resist sin and temptation. Belief systems presuming that being good will earn salvation are in error. There is nothing we can do to earn salvation or pay for it, since it is free and paid for in full. Religious leaders of Jesus's time were repeatedly warned about elevating works above faith. However, those exhibiting the faith of Abraham will bear good fruit worthy of repentance.

- MAT 3:7–10 ~ John was baptizing people in the Jordan River when many of the Pharisees and Sadducees came to observe. John spoke to them saying, "You snakes! Has anyone warned you of the judgement that awaits you? You had better start bearing fruit that is worthy of repentance. You say to yourselves that you have Abraham as your father. I assure you that God can produce children of Abraham from these stones. The ax is ready to strike at the roots; any tree that does not bear good fruit will be chopped down and burned in the fire."

- MAT 23:23–25 ~ Jesus said, "Woe to you scribes and Pharisees. You make tithes of your spices, yet you ignore the more important matters of the law: justice, mercy, and faith. You are like the blind guide, who would gag on a gnat but easily swallow a camel. Woe to you hypocrites, for you make the outside appear clean while the inside is full of extortion and excess."

- LUK 20:46–47 ~ Jesus said, "Beware of the Pharisees. They enjoy wearing fancy robes, being greeted in the marketplace, sitting in places of honor at church, and reserving the nicest rooms for their banquets; yet they cheat widows out of their homes, and for a show, recite long prayers. They will receive the greater damnation."

Before concluding, allow me to reiterate the importance of Holy Week to all Bible believers. From the Old Testament perspective, the week (eight days) begins and ends on a "high" Sabbath, in addition to the weekly Sabbath observed in like manner. Pivotal feasts included Unleavened Bread, Passover, and First Fruits. From the New Testament perspective, Holy Week begins and ends on a Sunday; pivotal events coinciding with those listed above are Palm Sunday, Maundy Thursday, Good Friday, and Easter Sunday. Therefore, Jews and Christians alike attend worship services multiple times for eight days, in addition to attending the weekly convocation. The many parallels between and among these sacred observances are not a coincidence. The unleavened bread represents Jesus's body which was without sin, broken on the cross where He shed His blood on the very day the Jews were celebrating Passover. Interestingly, Jesus arose from the dead Easter Sunday, after the Jews had given tithes during the Feast of First Fruits. It is illogical to conclude that these events are coincidental, since they are inseparable.

Heavenly Father, we come again before your throne of Grace, to pray for all believers, that we might remain steadfast in our faith forever. We also pray for those who are lost or faltering, that they may be lifted up by one or more of your servants, and returned to the flock. Help the world to see you in the Word and the world, and in people of faith. Help our nation to return to our roots which were planted in the Holy Bible. We were once a shining light on a hill that drew people of all races, tongues, and political views to come here and be free. But without you, nobody is free and we need to restore that notion in the minds of our citizens, children, and visitors to our land. Help us rebuild our foundation of morality, justice, liberty, and faith, the four pillars of fate, and restore unto us the unity of truth and individual responsibility that once held our people together. In Jesus's name we always pray, Amen.

February 19

Presidents Day encompasses the birthdays of arguably, our two greatest presidents: Washington (02/22) and Lincoln (02/12). The day is celebrated on the third Monday of the month, falling in-between these two birth dates, though the original federal holiday celebrated only Washington. Now we honor all the presidents who have served in the USA, but few come close to these two in stature and importance.

It appears that the office of the presidency doesn't get the same level of respect that it used to. It has become a partisan situation, where some people in the opposing party do not respect the person in office purely from an ideological position. Whether you voted for the current president or not, the office of the presidency deserves respect, particularly on this day when we venerate those who have led our country through disasters, wars, and social unrest.

Leaders in all three branches of government, executive, legislative, and judicial, must swear allegiance to the USA and vow to uphold our Constitution and Bill of Rights. They used to make this oath on the Bible but that is optional now. Too often leaders do not honor that oath of office. The government was set up to have checks and balances among the three branches. We have seen the judiciary getting involved in law making which is the job of the legislature; we have seen the president circumventing the legislature by imposing regulations through executive fiat. Perhaps this is because the legislature is too busy to pass laws while they focus on investigating their opponents; the laws they do pass are spending bills that are so filled with pork that nobody knows where the money goes because nobody keeps track of it. The lines are blurred between the three branches and this opens us up to all kinds of vulnerabilities, not the least of which are tyranny and corruption. Elections are the only recourse open to the citizenry to reset the government. Those who do not vote are shunning their civic duty.

Too bad there are many who refuse to submit to God; if we did as a country, He would select our leaders for us. The greatest presidents have been men of great faith. God picked the leaders of Israel and had them anointed by the prophets indicating His choices. If God would intervene here, we wouldn't be in the mess we're in now. I pray that He will lend His hand in all future elections. Leaders God chose pledged allegiance to Him and their nation Israel. God removed from office those who did not measure up to the standards He set (like with King Saul: 1 SA 28:1–17). We the people need to intervene by asking for God's intervention.

- EXO 18:21–22 ~ Moses's father-in-law advised him, "Select capable men who fear God, who are trustworthy, and who hate dishonest gain; appoint them as governors over thousands, hundreds, and tens. Have them serve as judges for the simple cases, so that you can decide the difficult cases."

- DEU 17:14–17 ~ After you have entered the land which the Lord has given you, and you possess it and live there, you will say, "Let us elect a king to rule over us like the other nations." You must let the Lord choose your king from among you; do not select a stranger who is not your brother. The king should not be intent on collecting wealth, livestock, or wives, for that might cause him to turn from God.

- 2 SA 23:3 ~ God, the Rock of Israel, spoke saying, "Whoever rules others must be just, ruling in the fear of God."

- NEH 9—10 ~ Nehemiah spoke a great prayer of worship and thanksgiving to God for bringing the Israelites back home. A written agreement was prepared binding the people in obedience to God and His rules. The leaders and priests affixed their seal to this agreement, and all the people swore an oath of allegiance to the Lord.

FEBRUARY

- JOB 34:17 ~ Shall someone who hates what is right govern others? Can a just person be condemned?

    If leaders would get back to being godly, placing God and country before partisan politics, we would thrive again as a nation. Until they do, this country will continue down the wrong path which leads to destruction. The best way to ensure this doesn't happen is elect people who know the Bible and revere God. The following should be included in the oath of office.

- PSA 119 (abridged and paraphrased) ~ David wrote this prayer: Blessed are they who walk in the ways of the Lord, who seek Him, and who keep His commandments. God has laid down His precepts and they are to be obeyed completely. Oh, that my ways were steadfast in obeying your decrees, Lord. I will praise you as I learn your righteous ways and obey your regulations. How can anyone keep his or her ways pure, but by living according to God's demands? Never let me stray from your commands, Lord. I will meditate upon your precepts; I will delight in your decrees; I will not neglect your Word. Open my eyes so I may see clearly the wonders of your Law. Teach me your ways and help me to understand your teaching and the meaning of your precepts. Turn me away from worthless things and preserve my life. May your unfailing love always be a comfort to me. I will walk in freedom, for I seek your wisdom and speak of your decrees. I know that your laws are righteous. Your Word is a lamp to my feet and a light to my path. If your Law had not been my delight, I would have perished in my affliction. Look upon my suffering and deliver me, for I have not forgotten your Law. How I love your Law; I meditate upon this night and day. I wait for your salvation, Lord, as I follow in your footsteps.

    Leadership is a spiritual gift, and the requirement is to lead diligently (ROM 12:6–8). I yearn for the day this becomes reality again. If our leaders veer from God's instructions or from His declaration of truth, we are obliged to obey God first.

- 2 CH 30:12 ~ Also in Judah, the hand of God was on the people giving them unity of mind to carry out the orders of their leaders in accordance with the Word of the Lord.

- PRO 12:15, 20 ~ The way of fools is true in their own eyes, but the one who listens to advice is wise. There is deceit in the hearts of those who plot evil, but to those promoting peace there is joy.

- ACT 5:22–29 ~ When the authorities commanded the apostles to stop preaching in the name of Jesus they replied, "We must obey God rather than men."

- ROM 13:1–6 ~ Everyone is subject to the higher powers, for all power comes from God; that is, all powers that exist have been ordained by God. Anyone who resists these powers are resisting the ordinance of God, and those who resist God receive damnation as punishment. Those who do what is right have no fear of the authorities, only those who do wrong are afraid of them. Do what is right and the authorities will commend you. Governments are God's servants; they are there to make sure you do what is right. But if you do what is evil, beware, for they do not carry a sword in vain, but to execute judgment on those who are evil. Submit to those who are in authority, not just because you will be punished if you do not, but also as a matter of keeping a clear conscience. This is why you should pay your taxes, because governments are God's servants who work fulltime in governing.

- 1 TI 2:1–2, 8 ~ I urge that supplications, prayers, intercessions, and thanksgiving be made to God for all people, for leaders, and for all who are in authority, so that we can lead an honest and peaceful life of godliness and truth. People should pray everywhere, lifting up holy hands, without being doubtful or angry.

- TIT 3:1 ~ Be submissive to rulers and authority, be obedient, and be ready for honest work.

- HEB 13:17 ~ Obey those who rule over you, and submit yourselves to them; for they will be watching you and will give an account, and you want them to give a good report.

- 1 PE 2:13–14 ~ Submit to every ordinance of society for the Lord's sake, whether to the king, or to his governors who are given the authority to punish evildoers and to commend those who do right.

In the Gettysburg address (1863) Lincoln closed by saying, "It is for us the living, rather, to be dedicated here to the unfinished work which they who fought here have thus far so nobly advanced. It is rather for us to be here dedicated to the great task remaining before us—that from these honored dead we take increased devotion to that cause for which they gave the last full measure of devotion—that we here highly resolve that these dead shall not have died in vain, that this nation under God shall have a new birth of freedom, and that government of the people, by the people, for the people shall not perish from the earth." We the people are supposed to be in charge, not they the government. They neither heed the will of the people nor do they heed the will of God. They do things in accordance with their personal preferences, as if they were gods. These people love themselves and want the world.

- NUM 15:38–40 ~ God commanded Moses: Put tassels on your garments, so that when you see the tassels, you will remember my commandments and obey them, and so you do not corrupt yourselves by seeking after your own hearts and your own eyes. Then you will remember and obey, and you will be consecrated unto me.

- JOS 24:15, 21–22 ~ Joshua announced, "If serving the Lord seems undesirable to you, then choose who you will serve… As for me and my household, we will serve the Lord." The people said to Joshua, "We promise to serve the Lord." Joshua replied, "You are witnesses before me and your countrymen that you have chosen the Lord, and have promised to serve him." They responded, "Yes, we are witnesses."

- 1 KI 3:9 ~ Solomon prayed to God, "Give your servant an understanding mind to govern your people and to discern between good and evil."

- JOB 31:26–28 ~ If my heart was enticed by worldly things and celestial bodies, or if I was infatuated with myself, I would be guilty of denying God and worthy of His punishment.

- PSA 7:16 ~ His mischief will return upon his own head, and his violent dealing will come down upon his own skull.

- PSA 10:4 ~ The wicked through their pride do not seek God; He is never in their thoughts.

- 2 TH 2:3–4 ~ Beware of the son of perdition who exalts himself and proclaims to be God.

Dear Father, Lord of the universe, ruler over all peoples, nations, and governments, we love you, we praise you, we glorify your holy name. You are in charge and we are your subjects. Help our leaders to remember that they work for us, are appointed by you to lead, and are responsible to you and to us. May we be resolute, and hold our leaders accountable: to you first and then to the people. Help this nation return to one nation under God, indivisible, with liberty and justice for all. Help this nation to elect a government that is by, of, and for the people. Help us to remove from office those who do not support these principles. Let us come together in unity of spirit governed by your Holy Spirit, so together we can save this republic. The majority of Americans want to keep it, but there are those who want to move us towards socialism, globalism, and other precarious directions. Let us join in one voice and declare that we are a God-fearing people, and wish to keep it that way. In the name of our King of kings and Lord of lords, Amen.

February 20

World Day of Social Justice was established by the United Nations in 2009, to highlight social causes affecting all people such as equality, peace, safety, education, and human rights. Sadly, there are people around the world who do not have the necessities for a proper existence: opportunity, work, education, home, food, healthcare, protection, and so forth. The goal is to remove barriers that impede these people from developing, succeeding, progressing, and upward mobility. Those who are not concerned about social justice problems can become indifferent, to the degree they are oblivious to the poverty and suffering in various regions of the world. The purpose is to draw attention to the plight of others who are not given equal opportunity, who are subjected to tyrannical rule, and who have no freedom to do anything about their situation.

The problem remains, however: how to execute reforms in places where governments are hostile to outside influence. They might come to the negotiating table but it will not be to develop their countries as much as to enrich themselves. We send food, money, medical supplies, and people to help others to help themselves, as well as constructing facilities. Often, these resources are abused or kept from the people. Missionaries and other professional workers are not guaranteed protection, transportation, or government assistance in many locations. Therefore, people don't get the help they need in a timely manner, if at all. That doesn't mean we do not try; we merely have to be very judicious about it.

For example, do some homework before you send your donation. Check out the charities which provide help, whether domestically or overseas, and review their balance sheet. The bottom line is this: what percent of your donation actually goes to the people in need? Nonprofits are required by law to provide accounting data; the range of proportions can be as low as five and as high as ninety-five percent. When administrative costs (including advertising) exceed one third, something is amiss. There are internet services which provide charity data for free.

- DEU 16:17 ~ Everyone should give as they are able, in accordance with the blessings which God has given them.

- PRO 22:16 ~ Those who oppress the poor to increase their own wealth and those who give to the rich eventually will become needy.

- ISA 32:6–7 ~ The vile person speaks villainy, plots evil, practices ungodliness, and deprives the needy. His instruments are evil. He devises wicked plans to destroy the poor and the just with his lies.

- ACT 2:44–45 ~ And the believers were as one, for they had everything in common. They sold their possessions and goods and gave generously to the needy.

- ACT 20:35 ~ In your labors, give to the needy, remembering the words of Jesus Christ, "It is more blessed to give than to receive."

- 2 CO 9:7 ~ Everyone should give whatever they think is fair in their heart. Giving should be done voluntarily, not out of obligation, for God loves a cheerful giver.

Father in Heaven, you are a just and fair God, and you treat every man, woman, and child as equal in your sight. You know the plight of people who are living off the bare minimum; many will die because they do not have enough. Help us to be generous, we who have everything we need, and more. Remind us to give our tithes to the church and our offerings to the poor and needy. Thank you for our many blessings, and help us to be a blessing to those less fortunate by supporting charities and organizations that are legitimate, and not only care about these people, but are leading the effort to improve their living conditions. In Jesus's name, Amen.

February 21

Marx and Engels Published Communist Manifesto on this date in 1948. This is not a commemoration, but is offered for information purposes. It is prudent to understand what communism is all about. The pamphlet was released shortly after the end of World War II, when there was unrest in Germany, communism was on the rise, and the Communist League was founded in London. Their doctrines were rejected by Germans, having had enough with the Nazis. Marx was banished and relocated to London.

We remember this day so we do not forget the consequences of communism. Let me tell you about communism. It has been around since time immemorial, particularly evident in feudalism and serfdom, but also in fallen empires of the world. It is a move to seize control by the ruling class, the elites, or the bourgeoisie as Marx called them. It is them versus the lower class, or proletariat. Notice there is no middle class, and that is the most important point. How can there be equality among people of different classes if one class has everything and the other class is allowed nothing of their own, because it all belongs to the "collective". We are equal in Christ; we do not need others to rule our lives because God rules everything and everybody. Humans are free to make our own decisions, but we need to know God to make the right decisions (JOH 15:4–5). With the elites in charge of their lives, the citizenry can do nothing without permission.

- GAL 3:28 ~ There is no such thing as Jew or Greek, slave or free, male or female, for we are equal in Jesus Christ.

- COL 3:4, 10–11 ~ When Christ appears, who is our life, all Christians will appear with Him in glory. For we have become new people, renewed in God's image by our knowledge of Him through Christ. There are no longer Jews or Greeks, circumcised or uncircumcised, civilized or uncivilized, slave or free, because Christ is all and in all.

- JAM 2:1–9 ~ Do not be partial to people just because you like the way they look or act. Do not give the rich or the famous more respect than anyone else, and do not give the poor and lowly less respect. If you abide by the royal law according to the scripture, "Love your neighbor as yourself," you are doing the right thing. But if you show favoritism to certain persons, you commit sin, and are convicted by the law as a lawbreaker.

- 2 CO 8:12–14 ~ If the willingness is there, a gift will be acceptable, whether large or small, in accordance with the degree to which one has prospered. Our desire is not that others might be relieved even when you are hard-pressed, but that there will be equality. For now, your plenty will supply the needs of others, so that in turn their plenty will supply you in times of need.

The communist manifesto was a criticism of capitalism and free enterprise, which were wrongly deemed undemocratic and unequal. It stressed division, assuming class warfare always exists between administrators and workers. All other classes of workers like mid-managers, supervisors, interns, migrants, consultants, and part-timers were irrelevant. It argued that workers are being exploited under capitalism, which is evil. The opposite is actually true: workers are exploited under socialism and communism, which are evil, because the ultimate results are tyranny and slavery. The idea of social elites ruling the populous is a globalist objective; socialism, communism, statism, fascism, collectivism, jihadism, these are forms of globalism, and all lead to totalitarianism. Their positions are antithetical to Christianity, and inherently atheistic.

- JOB 20:15 ~ Those who swallow down riches will vomit them up again, just like God rids Himself of those who relish in their riches.

- PSA 37:16 ~ Better is the little that the righteous have, than the abundance of many wicked people.

- PRO 11:4, 28 ~ Riches will not profit anyone in the day of wrath; only righteousness can save a person from death. Those who trust in their riches will fail, but those who trust in God will flourish.

- PRO 27:23–24 ~ Pay attention to your business, for riches do not endure forever, and an earthly crown does not endure to every generation.

- PRO 28:6, 22 ~ Poor people who walk in righteousness are better off than rich people who are perverse in their ways. Those who are in a hurry to become rich have an evil eye, and do not realize the poverty that will come upon them.

- ECC 5:10–12 ~ Whoever loves riches will never have enough, and whoever loves money will never be satisfied with their income. This is vanity. As goods increase, so do those that consume them. And of what benefit are belongings to the owner except the enjoyment of looking at them? The sleep of the hard worker is sweet; but the abundance of the rich prevents them from sleeping.

- 1 CO 2:14 ~ Worldly people do not receive the things of the Spirit of God, for these things are foolishness to them; neither can they know these things for they must be discerned spiritually.

- COL 2:20 ~ You are in Christ and not of this world, so why submit to its rules?

- 1 TI 6:5–10, 17 ~ Corrupt minds that are devoid of the truth will argue that godliness is a way of obtaining wealth. But godliness means being content with what you have. You brought nothing into this world, and you will take nothing out of it. People who want to get rich fall into the trap of temptation, consisting of foolish and harmful lusts that drown them in destruction and condemnation. For the love of money is the root of all evil. Those who have pursued it have strayed from the faith and brought upon themselves a multitude of sorrows. Tell those who are rich not to be miserly or greedy, trusting in their wealth for their needs. Tell them instead to trust in God who richly gives us all things to enjoy.

- TIT 2:11–12 ~ For the grace of God that brings salvation has appeared to all people. It teaches us to say no to wickedness and worldly pleasures. It teaches us to live in a self-controlled, upright manner.

- 1 JO 4:5–6 ~ They are of the world, and therefore speak of worldly things, and the world listens to them. We are of God. Those who know God will listen to His messengers, and those who are not of God will not listen. We know the difference between the Spirit of truth and the spirit of untruth.

Every country that has tried a globalist system of government has failed, and it is the citizenry that receives the brunt of their economic demolition. Politicians who are trying to push what they call "democratic-socialism" or "critical theory" are pushing Marxism. A similar philosophy was advanced by Hitler in *Mein Kompf,* and Alinsky in *Rules for Radicals*. We can see what communism has done around the world by looking at China, Russia, Cuba, and Venezuela.

- REV 6:6 ~ A ration of bread will cost a day of wages, and only the rich will be able to afford the oil and wine.

To Marxists, worker bees are akin to slaves, who must revolt to break free; this is actually an anarchist point of view. It implies superiority of the working class, but it is the ruling class that believe themselves superior. To them, the populous comprises morons who need to be controlled. Supposedly, workers gain control over their lives under socialism and communism, but lose everything with capitalism. Again, the converse is true; this is a grandiose deception, based upon false premises. Hidden beneath the hype is the subordination of the working class and a whittling away of their rights. In particular the common folk cannot own property, they are heavily taxed, they cannot inherit anything, government is centralized, and all businesses and schools are owned and run by the state. Everybody has to work hard, only to receive the bare minimum to survive. There is no incentive to excel; there is no opportunity for entrepreneurship. Because all income goes into the collective, namely, the government coffers. The government doles things out as they wish. We must remember, it is God who provides everything if we depend on Him. We certainly cannot depend on government to provide everything we need. We must remain a self-governing and self-determining people as God gifted us to be, or we will lose our freedom.

- JOB 8:13–14 ~ The destiny of those who forget God is the loss of all hope, for their trust in worldly things is a fragile one.

- JOB 31:26–28 ~ If my heart was enticed by worldly things and celestial bodies, or if I was infatuated with myself, I would be guilty of denying God, and worthy of His punishment.

- ECC 2:22–26 ~ What does a man get for all his work and striving under the sun? He gets pain and grief, and no rest at night. This is meaningless. A man can do nothing better than to eat and drink, and find satisfaction in his work. This comes from God, for without Him who can eat, drink, and find enjoyment? The man who pleases God will receive wisdom, knowledge, and happiness. But to the sinner God gives the task of gathering wealth, only to hand it over to the one who pleases God. That too is meaningless, a chasing after the wind.

- MAT 6:31–33 ~ Jesus said, "Do not worry about your worldly needs, for your heavenly Father knows what you need. Instead, seek first the kingdom of God and His righteousness, and this you will receive, as well as your worldly needs. Do not be concerned about tomorrow for it will bring its own problems; you have enough to deal with today to be worrying about the future."

- MAR 7:6–9, 13 ~ Jesus said, "Isaiah prophesied about you hypocrites. For you put aside the commandments of God and follow the traditions of men. By following your own traditions, you show a disregard for the Word of God."

- LUK 12:15–21 ~ Jesus said to them, "Beware of greed, for a person's life does not consist of the abundance of their possessions." Then He told them the parable about the rich man who had such an abundance of wealth, he decided to build bigger warehouses to store his goods. The man said to himself, "Now that you have got it made, take it easy; eat, drink, and be merry." But God said to him, "You fool! This very night your soul will be demanded from you, and then who will enjoy your prosperity?" Jesus concluded, "This is how it will be for those who store up worldly things for themselves but are not rich toward God."

- 2 TH 2:15 ~ Fellow Christians, stand fast in your faith and hold onto those traditions that you have been taught in God's Word, through the prophets and apostles.

Does communism sound like a good deal to you, giving up your liberties and having your life goals dictated to you? This country has thrived precisely because of our freedoms: freedom to choose, trade, move, own property and buy things; free to become, and to control our own destiny; to make decisions for ourselves rather than have some bureaucrat decide.

Back in the sixties and seventies, communism was tried in its truest form by "hippies" who lived together in communes. The concept was attractive in theory, all for one and one for all; everybody contributes equally using their knowledge and skills and everybody benefits equally. Why did this experiment fail? Because it only takes one person who refuses to put in the same amount of work; some people are plain lazy and freeload on the system. Then there are those who want more than their equal share; they are misers and steal or hoard goods for themselves. It is unavoidable; selfish and greedy people mess it up for everybody, which increases division and discord. In the Bible, it was taught that if you do not work you do not eat. Communism has no provision for those who do not work or cannot work, or are otherwise a drag on the system. In a capitalist country like the USA, we take care of people needing help to get going.

- PRO 6:6–9 ~ You who are lazy, consider the ant. The ant has no supervisor, guide, or ruler, yet manages to provide plenty of food. How long will you sleep, you lazy people; when are you going to wake up?

- PRO 10:4–5, 26 ~ Whoever slacks off will become poor, but the diligent will become rich. Whoever gathers during the summer is wise; whoever sleeps during the harvest is shameful. As vinegar is to the teeth and smoke to the eyes, so is a sloth to an employer.

- PRO 26:13–16 ~ The lazy person will not work, giving stupid excuses like, "There could be a lion in the street." Just like a door on its hinges, the lazy person is attached to the bed, tossing and turning. The lazy person is too tired even to lift a spoon to eat. Lazy people can convince themselves better than seven people with a good excuse.

- ECC 10:18 ~ Because of laziness and idleness the building decayed and collapsed.

- 2 TH 3:10–12 ~ When we were with you, we gave you this rule: if a man does not work, he should not eat. We have heard how some of you are lazy. They are not busy, they are busybodies. We urge these people, in the name of Christ, to settle down and to earn the bread that they eat.

- 1 TI 5:8 ~ If anyone does not provide for his relatives, especially his immediate family, he has denied the faith and is worse than an unbeliever.

Communism continuously widens the gap between the bourgeoisie and the proletariat. They take away all your privileges while adding expenditures. Do not give into this deception. Capitalism works better; it allows people to work as much as they want and progress within their environment from one economic class to another. Free people can climb the ladder of success, they can choose to stay where they are, they can move to another job, they can go freely anywhere in the country, and they can retire from work. I worked hard and made my way to the apex of the ladder in different fields; it was a nice ride. With aging I can no longer maintain that pace, neither physically or mentally. As a result, I have purposefully climbed down the ladder, into a modest lifestyle. I was lucky; I had the Lord the entire time, and for this I am grateful and happy. Even in my youth, when I had to live month to month, life was good. Diligent study and hard work paid off, just like it does for everybody who has the desire and puts in the effort. This defines capitalism, free enterprise, entrepreneurship, choices. It doesn't matter if you have more or less, but that you learn to be responsible with what you do have. There is no amount of money that can make you happy; it is a choice. But if you have more than you need, share the wealth. None of these options exist with any globalist system.

If our country continues in this direction, it will lead to our downfall. The very reason we have prospered for 250 years is because of our belief in God, and our dedication to unalienable rights given all people by God: the right to life, liberty, and pursuit of happiness; freedom of worship, speech, and assembly; right to work and own property; right to defend oneself, one's family, and one's property. Are you going to let the government steal these rights and tell you what to do, and give you what they think you deserve? No more democracy means no more choices. You will be stuck in the same rut for the rest of your life; and that rut gets narrower as the government spends all the money. Eventually, everybody ends up equally destitute.

The early Christians were able to pull this off, through their generosity, community of wealth, and equality towards everyone in their church (ACT 4:32–35). But unless everyone believes the same, and uses the same Bible, and worships as one body, it cannot endure. Why not? Because of sin. This is why we have governments, to serve and protect the people. But when they get too much power, you can forget about them serving and protecting anyone but themselves. Our forefathers foresaw this, and placed protections in our system of government like the separation of powers doctrine.

Do you want to know how the socialist-communists are able to eliminate the middle class? See if any items in this list look familiar. This is what they will do to seize power and control, and are already starting to do it.

- Create calamities that put people out of work.
- Give people a handout to make them dependent on the government.
- Provide benefits that exceed what people had when they were working.
- Levy burdensome taxes while lowering wages.
- Spend money recklessly causing out-of-control inflation.
- Take over businesses, and run others out of business.
- Centralize government by dissolving rights of citizens and states.
- Indoctrinate people, especially children.
- Threaten, arrest, or take captive people who disagree.
- Reimagine history, redefine culture, eliminate distinctions that reflect performance.
- Change the meaning of words and phrases.
- Stage events, catastrophes, and news stories.
- Lie and deceive; attack rather than debate; selective censorship.
- Take over institutions such as elections, mass media, educational, judicial, and military.
- Attack and cancel Christians, churches, families, parents, and good people.
- Cause divisions between people: age, race, sex, religion, politics, culture, ethnicity, economic status, legal status, etc.

Heavenly Father, your Word is truth and we love the truth, because the Holy Spirit is the truth. This republic was founded upon your Holy Word, employing principles of morality, justice, liberty, and equality. Please help us to get back to these tenets of our faith, which are founded on Jesus Christ, our Redeemer. Help us to thwart the efforts of those who would move us into the new world order, otherwise known as globalism. Help people to know the truth about socialism, communism, statism, fascism, collectivism, and other forms of globalism. We know that such ideologies will lead to the last world empire, when Satan and his followers attempt to grab power over everyone and everything. Help the people of the USA to rise up against this lunacy and stand firm for you, with the protection of your armor and shield, as we carry the sword of the Spirit which will cut them down by the truth that you breathed into the Bible, in order that all people could know the truth which sets us free. Let that truth have free course, so it can spread to every corner of the USA and throughout the world. In the name of Jesus, under whom all may unite, we pray, Amen.

February 22

Be Humble Day is observed around the world, though its origin remains a mystery. This is an international observance, unlike National Humility Day last month (01/03). Hopefully, our humility will be contagious, and envelop the nation, so that we can be humble before other nations, without giving up any of our sovereignty. Of course, this requires that we acknowledge the sovereignty of God in our hearts, in the world, and in the universe.

Today is another day to be unselfish rather than self-absorbed. Humility is about placing others above you, not putting anyone down, including yourself. It is about paying attention to the needs of others rather than wanting to be the center of attention. For some, this is a very difficult thing to do. As Christians, we should not boast about our achievements but about what God has done in our lives and the universe, all for humankind. God deserves the credit for everything good. Sinners, Satan, demons, and humans deserve credit for all things evil. Before you are about to brag about yourself or act arrogantly in public circles, ruminate on the following scriptures.

- PSA 12:3 ~ The Lord will silence those who speak arrogantly and with flatteries.

- PRO 16:18–19 ~ Arrogance and a proud spirit are followed by destruction. It is better to share a humble spirit with the lowly than to share the wealth of the proud.

- PRO 29:23 ~ Pride brings a person down, but honor lifts the humble in spirit.

- ISA 2:11–12 ~ The eyes of the arrogant ones will be humbled, and their pride will be torn down. The Lord alone will be exalted in that day. He has reserved a day for the proud and conceited, when these so-called exalted ones will be disgraced.

- ISA 10:15–17 ~ Should the axe boast itself as greater than the one who uses it to chop the wood? Should the saw magnify itself over the one who uses it to shape the wood? It is as if the rod could strike the one who lifts it up, or the club could lift up by itself and beat the one holding it, who is not made of wood but of flesh. Therefore, the Almighty will send a wasting disease among the great warriors; under their pomp a fire will be kindled like a blazing inferno. The Light of Israel will become a fire, and their Holy One a flame. In a single day this fire will burn away all the thorns and briers.

- ISA 10:33 ~ Those who appear to be high and mighty will be cut down, and those who are proud will be humbled.

- ISA 13:11 ~ The evil and wicked will be punished for their sins. God will cause the arrogance of the proud to cease and will make them the lowest of all.

- OBA 1:4 ~ The Lord says, "After you exalt yourself as the eagle, and build a nest among the stars, then I will knock you down."

- LUK 18:14 ~ Those who exalt themselves will later be humbled, and those who humble themselves will later be exalted.

- EPH 2:8–9 ~ You are saved by the grace of God because of your faith in Jesus Christ. Salvation is a gift of God, it cannot be earned through good works, so nobody should brag.

- 2 CO 12:6 ~ Even if I had something to brag about I would not. I do not want people to think more highly of me than they ought.

- JAM 3:5–6 ~ The tongue, although a little member, boasts great things; how great a matter a little fire can kindle. For the tongue is like fire, creating a world of sin; the tongue defiles the entire body, setting on fire the course of nature, burning with hellfire.

Humility is a righteous attitude; if you do not believe that, look at Christ. He humbled Himself before humanity, referring to Himself as a servant to all. Even though He was God, He did not walk around proudly like a king or a movie star or a Pharisee. He behaved like a man who cared about every living soul, and was willing to give His life to save those who choose to believe in Him. Christ is our example. The Bible teaches us to treat others as equal to ourselves, and vice-versa; because nobody is above or below another in the eyes of God.

- ISA 57:15 ~ God says, "I will live in the high holy place as will all people having a humble and repentant spirit, because I will revive the spirits of those who are humble."
- JER 9:23–24 ~ If you are wise, do not glory in your wisdom; if you are mighty, do not glory in your might; if you are rich, do not glory in your wealth. Whoever wants to rejoice, let them rejoice in the fact that they know God, who is loving, kind, righteous, and just.
- MAT 6:2 ~ When you help the needy, do not sound your trumpet as the hypocrites do in the churches and in the streets, so that they can receive praise from others. The truth is, that is all the reward they will ever receive.
- LUK 14:7–11 ~ Jesus told a parable to address those who sought the best seats in the house. When you are invited to a formal affair like a wedding, do not choose the seat with the highest honor, for that seat may be reserved for someone else who is more important than you. It will be embarrassing for you when you are asked to move to a seat of lesser honor. Instead, go sit at the seat with the lowest honor; if a seat of higher honor has been reserved for you, you will be shown respect by being asked to move to a seat of higher honor. The moral of the story is this: Those who exalt themselves will be humbled and those who humble themselves will be exalted.
- 2 CO 3:5 ~ We are not self-sufficient enough to claim responsibility for what we have, because all of our sufficiency comes from God.
- PHP 2:5–11 ~ Keep your thoughts on Jesus Christ who, although He was God in the flesh, did not glorify Himself but became a servant. In the form of a man, He humbled Himself, becoming obedient unto death even death on a cross. Therefore, God has exalted Him and given Him a name above all other names. Everyone should bow at the name of Jesus Christ, whether they are in heaven or on earth. Every tongue should confess that Jesus Christ is Lord, to the glory of God the Father.
- 1 PE 4:13–14 ~ Rejoice when you partake of Christ's sufferings, so that you can be filled with joy when His glory is revealed. If you are insulted because you carry the name of Christ, be happy, for the Spirit of glory and of God rests upon you. On their part He is despised, but on your part, He is glorified.

Humility is having a giving and kind heart, which is selfless and compassionate. Today is a day to cultivate that persona and lend a helping hand to others in need. Let go of your ego, and let the light of Christ shine in you and through you. We can witness Jesus simply in the way we conduct our lives. In every circumstance people will be watching, and judging your character, so watch yourself; that's right, monitor what you are doing as you monitor others. It is one thing being mindful of the behavior of others; it is yet another to be mindful of how you are coming across to them. Take a look in the mirror. Do you see Christ in you. If not, others won't either.

- PRO 11:2 ~ With pride comes shame; with humility comes wisdom.
- PRO 15:33 ~ The fear of the Lord is the instruction of wisdom, and before honor comes humility.

FEBRUARY

- PRO 22:4 ~ Through humility and the fear of God we receive riches, honor, and life.

- LUK 6:32, 35 ~ Jesus said, "If you love only those who love you, what reward will you receive? Even sinners love those who love them. So love everyone, even your enemies. Help others whenever you can, expecting nothing in return, and your reward will be great and you will become a child of God."

- ROM 12:3, 16–21 ~ Do not be conceited in your own mind, but think soberly, according to the measure of faith God has given you. Be of the same mind one toward another. Do not be high-minded, but humble yourself before others, even those of low estate. Do not pretend to be wise in your own conceit. Do not recompense evil for evil. Always be honest in all things. Live peaceably with all people. Do not seek revenge when someone has done you wrong but rather hold back your wrath. For it is written: Vengeance is mine; I will repay, says the Lord. Therefore, if your enemy is hungry, feed him; if he is thirsty, give him a drink; in doing so you will heap hot coals on his head. Do not be overcome with evil, but overcome evil with goodness.

- GAL 6:1–4 ~ Brothers, if someone is overtaken by sin, you who are spiritual need to restore that person in the spirit of humility, considering that you also can be tempted. Bear one another's burdens to fulfill the law of Christ. People who think they are something when they are nothing are deceiving themselves. But test your own actions, without comparing yourself to others, for everyone should carry their share of the load.

- 1 PE 3:8–9, 15 ~ Live in harmony with one another in love, sympathy, compassion, and humility. Do not repay evil with evil or insult others, but repay with blessings. Be a blessing to others for you were called to inherit a blessing. Sanctify the Lord in your hearts, and always be ready to give an answer, with humility and respect, to anyone who asks about the hope that is within you.

- 1 PE 5:5 ~ Show respect to your elders. Serve each other. Clothe yourselves in humility. For God resists the proud and gives grace to the humble.

- 1 JO 2:6 ~ Whoever says they are a Christian should show they are following Christ by the way they conduct their lives.

Our Father in heaven, you are the author of life and the creator of the universe; your goodness and mercy knows no bounds. Help us to show sincere appreciation for everything you do for us, by doing things for others, expecting nothing in return. Help us to be respectful at all times, no matter how people treat us. Let us support harmony and not contribute to discord. Help us to be a blessing, even as we our blessed. Remind us to be humble and not proud, giving and not selfish. Let us seek the truth and share it, without jumping to conclusions. Equip us to use our gifts to serve you and to serve others in your name, just as Jesus served us in your name, Father. In Jesus's name we pray, Abba Father, Amen.

February 23

World Understanding and Peace Day unofficially started in 1983. This observance follows Be Humble Day, and rightfully so. Today is about promoting peace and understanding, just as Jesus did throughout His ministry. Like humility, these characteristics we obtain from Jesus, who showed us who God the Father is. And as Christ ministered to humanity, Christians should be following His lead. Humanitarianism is the discipline of welfare to humanity, recognition of culture, and altruism to society and its members. Many organizations have been spawned from this spirit of peace and good will towards all peoples, cultures, and religions.

- PSA 34:14 ~ Depart from evil and do good; seek peace and pursue it.

- PRO 2:1–6 ~ My child, if you would receive my words and hold fast to my commandments, so that you listen to wisdom and desire understanding; if you seek knowledge and truth instead of worldly riches; then you will understand the fear of the Lord and you will find the knowledge of God, for only He can provide wisdom and from Him comes all knowledge and understanding.

- ISA 56:2–8 ~ Blessed are all people, and their children, if they obey God, avoid evil, keep the Sabbath, and cling to His covenant. Even those who are strangers to God's people Israel will be part of God's house if they obey Him. All the righteous will be like God's sons and daughters, only better than that, with a name that will last forever. People of all walks of life will be joined together on His holy mountain to worship Him, for His house will be called a house for the righteous.

- LUK 2:8–14 ~ There were shepherds watching their flocks that night in the hills nearby. An angel of the Lord appeared to them, and the glory of God shined all around them. The shepherds were terrified. The angel told them, "Do not be afraid, I bring you good news that will be of great joy to all people on earth. Today, in the city of David, a Savior is born who is Christ the Lord. This is a sign to you: You will find a baby wrapped in cloths and lying in a manger." Suddenly, a great multitude of angels appeared in the heavens, praising God and singing, "Glory to God in the highest, and on earth peace and good will to all people."

- JOH 14:27 ~ Jesus said, "Peace I leave you; my peace I give you; I do not give as the world gives, so never let your hearts be troubled or afraid."

- ROM 15:13 ~ May the God of hope fill you with all joy and peace in believing, so that by the power of the Holy Spirit you may abound in hope.

This day commemorates an occasion when a charitable society was inaugurated. A few businessmen gathered at the behest of Paul Harris in Chicago 02/23/1905, to establish what would become Rotary International (1922). They sought to set aside politics and religion and focus on issues affecting disadvantaged people globally. They paused operations through two world wars but have continued to provide aid ever since then for the underprivileged. They are known familiarly as the Rotary Club or Rotarians, a philanthropic organization started in the USA, and now on every continent except Antarctica. They have conducted countless projects: community and economic development; conflict intervention and peace building; water utilities, disease eradication, and sewage disposal; health, education, and literacy programs; and consultation with the United Nations on international initiatives. There are upwards of 46,000 clubs, with already a century of service behind them. Though not a religious organization per se, they definitely have done the Lord's work.

- PSA 41:1 ~ Whoever helps the poor will be blessed by God, and God will deliver them when they experience a time of trouble.

FEBRUARY

- ROM 12:20 ~ If your enemy is hungry, feed him; if he is thirsty, give him a drink. Maybe you can turn him or her around by being nice.

- EPH 6:7 ~ With good will serve others, as to the Lord and not to men.

- COL 3:24 ~ If you help others, you are really serving Christ.

People who help others without seeking a reward will be blessed because they have been a blessing to others. Acts associated with the spreading of peace and understanding through charitable and humanitarian efforts, strengthens people in body, mind, and spirit. Just as Jesus Christ strengthened us by His coming, we should likewise strengthen others who are not as fortunate as we are. Humanitarians bring peace and good will to the people they visit, as they build their economies and bolster their dreams. By doing so, humanitarians reflect Christ.

- DEU 4:1–2, 5–6 ~ God said, "Listen Israel to the laws and statutes I am about to teach you. Follow them so you can live and take possession of the land I am going to give to you. Do not add to my commands and do not subtract from them. Keep these laws carefully, for this will demonstrate to other nations your wisdom and understanding."

- JOB 28:28 ~ God declared to humanity, "The fear of the Lord is the beginning of wisdom, and to shun evil is understanding."

- PRO 14:33 ~ Wisdom abides in the minds of those with understanding, but it is not known in the minds of fools.

- ROM 2:10 ~ Glory, honor, and peace is given to all who do good, regardless of race.

- ROM 14:17–19 ~ The kingdom of God does not mean food and drink, but righteousness, peace, and joy in the Holy Spirit. Those who serve Christ with these things are acceptable to God and approved of humankind. Let us therefore seek that which results in peace and mutual uplifting.

- COL 1:9–10 ~ We have not stopped praying for you and asking God to fill you with the knowledge of His will, through all spiritual wisdom and understanding. This is so you might live your lives worthy of the Lord and may please Him in every way, bearing good fruit and growing in the knowledge of God; being strengthened with all power according to His glorious might so that you will be able to endure hardship with great patience and joyfulness.

- COL 2:2 ~ My hope is that people's hearts will be comforted, being bound together in love, and that they receive the riches of understanding and acknowledgement of the mystery of God, and of the Heavenly Father, and of Jesus Christ.

- HEB 12:14 ~ Strive for peace with everyone, and for holiness; for without these things, nobody can see the Lord.

- JAM 3:17–18 ~ The wisdom from above is pure, peace-loving, gentle, accommodating, merciful, productive, impartial, and sincere. When the fruit of righteousness is sown in peace, it generates a harvest of peace and righteousness.

- 2 JO 1:3 ~ Grace, mercy and peace be with you, from God our Father, and from Jesus Christ His Son, in truth and love.

If you are connected to Christ, you live in Him, and you will produce good fruit (JOH 15:1–16). He is the vine and we are the branches; if you become disconnected from Christ you will not bear good fruit. Examine yourself and determine if your behavior is producing good fruit or bad fruit, then respond accordingly. Those who produce bad fruit are evil and will be destroyed along with the rest of this sinful world.

DAILY DEVOTIONAL EVENTS

- MAT 7:17–19 ~ A good tree bears good fruit; a corrupt tree bears evil fruit. A good tree cannot bear bad fruit and a bad tree cannot bear good fruit. Any tree that does not bear good fruit will be cut down at the roots and burned in the fire.

- 2 CO 8:2–7 ~ Even during times of poverty, the abundance of their joy became a wellspring of generosity. They gave as much as they could, even beyond their ability. They considered it a privilege to serve, giving themselves to the Lord and to His ministers. Therefore, as you abound in everything, including faith, speech, knowledge, and earnest love, see that you also abound in the grace of giving. If the willingness is there, the gift will be acceptable, whether large or small, in accordance with the degree to which one has prospered.

- PHP 3:8–9 ~ Without a doubt, I count everything loss except the excellent knowledge of Christ Jesus my Lord, for whom I have suffered the loss of all worldly things, which to me are as garbage because of what I have gained in Christ; finding righteousness from Jesus, though not having any of my own in accordance with the law, but possessing the righteousness of God by faith in His Son.

- PHP 4:6–7 ~ Do not have anxiety about anything, but pray for everything. With thanksgiving let your requests be known to God. And the peace of God which passes all understanding will keep your heart in mind in Jesus Christ.

- EPH 5:9 ~ The fruits of the Spirit originate in goodness, righteousness, and truth.

- 2 PE 1:2–8 ~ May the Lord's grace and peace be multiplied to you, through the knowledge of God and of Jesus Christ our Lord. His divine power has given us everything we need for a life of godliness, through the knowledge of Him who called us to His glory and virtue. He has made wonderful and precious promises so that you can partake in His divine nature, and escape the corruption and sinful desires of this world. So be diligent, and become multiplied in your faith, adding to it virtue, knowledge, discipline, patience, godliness, kindness, and love. For, if these things abound in you, you will bear abundant fruit in the knowledge of our Lord Jesus Christ.

- REV 20 ~ When Christ returns, the first fruits of God's chosen people will be resurrected. The next resurrection will occur after the millennial reign. Everyone will be judged according to the fruit that they produced, and whether it was good fruit or bad fruit.

God our Father, you provide us with peace of mind, health of body, and strength of spirit, so that we may bear good fruit in accordance with the degree to which we have prospered and endeavored. Let us remain grafted to the Branch, which is your Son Jesus Christ, that our fruit will be plentiful and so we can grow in the spirit of wisdom, knowledge, and understanding which come from your Holy Spirit. Help us to be willing to bestow these gifts upon others who do not know you, who are detached from you, who are physically unhealthy, who are mentally unstable, or who are suffering in body, mind, and/or spirit. Let us use our time, talents, offerings and tithes in a way that brings your peace and understanding to those who are lacking these gifts. Help us to spread the love and joy, so that the unfortunate and hurting people can find the peace which surpasses all understanding, that their hearts and minds could be joined with you and with the body of Christ. In His name we pray, Amen.

February 24

Gregorian Calendar Introduced on this day in 1582 by Pope Gregory XIII replacing the Julian calendar, in order to better calibrate it with the solar year, which is one rotation of the earth around the sun. This change resulted in the current system of 365.2425 days per year, with one day added each leap year. The correction amounted to only one day per century, but it eliminated drifting of the vernal equinox, which was important to the Catholic church for normalizing the season of Easter. It also set the annual starting date to January 1. The change altered historic dates from the past, because the Julian calendar was behind in time; so, astronomers often use the old system. Many countries did not adopt this calendar until the 1700s to 1900s. Some countries still use other calendars, especially the lunar calendar from which we get our seven-day week. We also can thank the egotistical Roman emperors Julius and Augustus for the irregularity in the number of days allocated to months. The Gregorian calendar is not perfect; it has an error of one day every three millennia or so. There is no point in recalibrating the calendar again.

Calendars can be a convenience and an inconvenience. Everybody gets overly concerned about what day it is, what time it is, or not exceeding some expiration date. We get wrapped up in time windows to the degree we do not take time for God. In His realm, there is no time, for He is an eternal being. That means there was an eternity before the day of creation and there will be an eternity after this world is long gone. Though God exists outside of time, he can intervene into our timeline any time He wants. Oftentimes, such intervention takes the form of a miracle. Some people do not believe in miracles; they think everything can be explained with science. How can you explain the immaculate conception and resurrection of Jesus using science? Scientists cannot explain the origins of the universe, life, and reasoning, which defy the laws of physics.

Consequently, many believe science and the Bible are incompatible; but this is wrong. In fact, the book of nature from which we derive the laws of physics and mathematics, are in alignment with the book of scripture, namely the Holy Bible. Both books were authored by God so how can they be contradictory? Scientific theories, however, do not pass as fact unless they can be proven; the Bible is proven. Did you know, some great men of the Bible were scientists?

- JOB 26:6–11, 14 ~ Hell is naked before Him and destruction is left uncovered. He stretches the sky over the emptiness and suspends the earth on nothing. He brings water into clouds yet they do not burst under the weight. He divides the limitless heavens from the earth, the waters from the land, and the light from the darkness. Heaven and earth tremble at astonishment. These are only a small fraction of His mighty works. We hear but a whisper of His works, so who can possibly understand the thunder of His power?

- DAN 1:1–7 ~ King Nebuchadnezzar of Babylon conquered Israel. After the siege of Jerusalem, he searched for Israelites who were well known for their uprightness, wisdom, analytical abilities, and understanding of science. Among those who were brought before the king were Daniel, Shadrach, Meshach, and Abednego.

- MAT 2:1–16 ~ Wise men (likely astronomers) came from the east, following the Star of Bethlehem. When they found the Christ child, they were very happy. They worshipped the Christ child and presented offerings of gold and incense. They avoided King Herod for they were told in a dream that he wanted to destroy the child.

- JDE 1:10 ~ They speak evil of those things they do not understand. However, the things they know naturally by instinct only serve to corrupt them.

Scientists believe the universe began at a single instant when the arrow of time began, which is also what the Bible teaches. Scientists say the universe is made up of particles, energy, gravity and things that cannot be seen or detected; but we can see their effects and measure them. The Bible agrees, the universe was created by God from things unseen though we can see their effects.

- GEN 1:1–3 ~ In the beginning, God created the heaven and the earth. And the earth was without form, and void; and darkness was upon the face of the deep. And the Spirit of God moved upon the face of the waters. And God said, "Let there be light" and there was light.

- ROM 1:18–25 ~ The wrath of God is being revealed from heaven against the wickedness of men, who suppress the truth through unrighteousness, though the things that are known about God are clear to them because God has made these things clear. Since the creation of the world, God's invisible qualities have been obvious, including His eternal power and His divine nature. Therefore, they have no excuse; because, while they knew God, they neither glorified Him nor gave thanks to Him. Their thinking became futile and their foolish hearts were darkened. Though they claimed to be wise, they were ignorant, exchanging the glory of God for graven images. God allowed them to become depraved, who turned God's truth into a lie and worshipped and served the creature rather than the Creator who is blessed forever.

- COL 1:16–17 ~ For by God all things were created that are in heaven and earth, whether visible or invisible, including thrones, dominions, principalities, and powers. All things were created by Him and for Him. He is before all things, and because of Him all things exist.

- HEB 11:3 ~ Through faith we understand that the worlds were framed by the Word of God, such that things which are seen were made from things that do not appear.

Most of the lifeforms (phyla) that exist on our planet emerged during the same period; scientists call this the Cambrian explosion. This coincides with the Genesis account (GEN 1:11–25). The Bible is a great source of information regarding physical sciences including hydrology, geology, cosmology, meteorology, geography, biology, and medicine (Barber, 2020b).

There was no time before creation, and time will end after the resurrection. I long for a day without calendars, when we have become timeless beings (JDE 1:24–25). Eternity will start the day Christ returns, when our bodies are glorified like His; we will never die because we will be without sin like Him. Everything will be continuously new, and nothing will get old. Time makes things age and deteriorate. But without time, nothing degrades, dies, or ceases to exist. Time can be divided into years, months, weeks, days, minutes; but eternity cannot be divided, partitioned, or measured. Perhaps we won't even need science in heaven; we certainly will not need calendars.

- JOB 19:25–26 ~ I know my Redeemer lives, and He will stand upon the earth on the last day. And though my body may be destroyed by worms, yet in my flesh I will see God.

- ROM 8:17 ~ Now if we are children, then we are heirs: heirs of God and joint-heirs with Christ, if indeed we share in His suffering so that we may also share in His glory.

- PHP 3:21 ~ Christ will change our vile bodies into bodies like His glorified body.

- 1 JO 3:2 ~ Dear friends, now we are the sons of God, and what we will become is not yet known. But we do know this: when He returns for us, we will become like Him, for we shall see Him as He really is.

Father, we long to come home to be with you, where time will be meaningless, and where our lives will be more meaningful. Bring us blameless into your heavenly realm, to remain blessed forever; where there will be no calendars or clocks because the present tense will remain steadfast for eternity. We offer this prayer through Jesus Christ who is timeless throughout the ages, along with you and the Holy Spirit, now and forevermore, Amen.

February 25

Samuel Colt Patented the Revolver on this day in 1836. He began to manufacture his invention, but sales were sluggish, until the government started placing orders during the war with Mexico (1846–1848). His business grew exponentially so he expanded his operation, becoming the largest manufacturer of firearms in the world. He produced his revolver using interchangeable parts so they could be repaired without buying a new gun. When the Civil War fell upon the United States, the Colt revolver was the weapon of choice for close combat. Colt was a very rich man when he died an untimely death from rheumatism in 1862 at the age of 47.

Why do we need guns? Because there are evil people in the world seeking to do harm. Unfortunately, they have access to guns and other weapons too. But guns are not evil, nor are people who manufacture them. Getting rid of guns does not stop crime, murder, or wars; but guns can prevent those things from happening by making the consequences dire for criminals who threaten the lives of innocent people. Why is there a second amendment to the Constitution allowing people to bear arms? It is to provide a disincentive to tyranny, slavery, and other crimes. Why would radicals want to confiscate our guns? To eliminate any threats to their plan to finish democracy and introduce socialism. Consider the nuclear standoff, affectionately called mutual assured destruction (MAD). If an enemy launches a first strike, they can be assured that enough missiles are pointed in their direction. This creates a stalemate, reducing the likelihood of nuclear war. It has worked so far, but who knows how much longer? When rogue nations with crazy rulers get their hands on nukes, heaven help us. That's why some guns are against the law.

One of our inalienable rights is to protect and defend ourselves, our homes, families, and property. We also have the right to fight against governments who abandon the rights of people in attempt to control or enslave them. God gave humans rights which nobody can deny or steal. If they try to take our freedoms by force, they can expect an equally forceful response.

- JOB 4:7–8 ~ Consider this: Who among the innocent ever perished? When were the righteous ever destroyed? I have seen for myself, that those who plow evil and those who sow trouble reap the same.

- PSA 55:21 ~ His words were as smooth as butter, but war was in his heart. His words were softer than skin cream, but they were drawing their swords.

- ISA 3:9 ~ It shows on their faces that they are guilty; they declare their sin like Sodom, they do not hide it. Woe unto their souls for they have recompensed evil unto themselves.

- ISA 59:3–7 ~ Your hands are defiled with blood and sin. Your lips have spoken lies and wickedness. They conceive evil and rely on foolishness and lies. They run to evil and hasten to shed innocent blood. Desolation and destruction ride their highways.

- JER 6:14; JER 8:11, 15 ~ They kept saying "peace, peace" but there was no peace. We looked for peace but none came; we hoped for health but got trouble instead.

- EZE 13:19 ~ They will pollute me among my people for a piece of bread. They will kill people that should not have to die and save others that should not live, then lie to people about it.

- MIC 7:2–6 ~ All the godly and upright men are gone. The wicked lie in ambush for blood. They do evil with diligence. Princes and judges ask for bribes. Great men speak of and pursue the evil desires of their souls. Even the best of them is like a thorn. Their confusion and punishment await them. Nobody can be trusted; even family and friends become the enemy.

- ACT 20:30 ~ From among yourselves persons will come speaking perverse things to draw disciples after them.

- EPH 5:11–12 ~ Do not take part in their evil schemes but expose them instead. It is shameful even to speak about the evil they do in secret.

- 1 TH 5:3 ~ When they talk of peace and safety, total destruction will come.

God provides protection, like any loving parent protects their children. The followers of Jesus also were armed for protection; case in point when Judas betrayed Jesus in the garden, with a riotous mob in tow. Peter drew a blade and attacked, slicing an ear off the priest's bodyguard. Jesus picked up the ear and reattached it, healing the man. This event was recorded by all four Gospel writers (MAT 26:46–53; MAR 14:44–48; LUK 22:47–52; JOH 18:3–12). Clearly, there is a time to kill and a time to heal (ECC 3:3). Those who start wars are not always in the right, but those who protect and defend usually are. Love always protects (1 CO 13:7).

- DEU 20:1, 4 ~ When you go into battle against your enemies, and you see horses and chariots, and you realize you are outnumbered, do not be afraid. For the Lord your God is with you. He is the same one who rescued you out of Egypt. He goes with you to fight for you and to save you.

- 2 KI 6:15–17 ~ The servant awoke and found they were surrounded by the Syrians, who were coming for Elisha the prophet. He told the servant not to fear as his army was greater than theirs. Then Elisha prayed, "Lord, I pray you would open his eyes that he may see." And the Lord opened the young man's eyes and he beheld a mountain full of horses and chariots of fire surrounding the Syrian army. Then Elisha prayed, "Lord, smite these people with blindness." And the Lord did so, and they escaped.

- 2 KI 19:35; 2 CH 32:21 ~ The angel of God killed 185,000 Assyrian warriors.

- 1 CH 21:15–16 ~ God sent an angel to destroy Jerusalem, and as he was destroying it, the Lord had a change of heart and said to the angel, "That is enough." David saw the angel of the Lord standing between heaven and earth with his sword drawn.

- PSA 17:7~ Show us your wonderful loving kindness, Lord, who saved us by your right hand, those who trust in your protection.

- ISA 43:2 ~ God says, "When you pass through the waters, I will be with you; and the rivers will not overflow upon you. When you walk through the fire, you will not be burned, nor will any fire be kindled against you."

- JER 29:11 ~ I know the plans I have for you, says the Lord: plans for prosperity, protection, hope, and a bright future.

- JOE 3:9–10 ~ Go, tell the Gentiles to prepare for war. Wake up the mighty warriors and tell them to come. Beat your plowshares into swords and your pruning hooks into spears. Let the weak say, "I am strong."

- MAT 26:52–56 ~ Jesus said, "Put away your sword, for those who live by the sword will die by the sword. Do you not know, I could ask my Father to summon twelve legions of angels? But then how could the scriptures be fulfilled?" Later that hour Jesus said to the nob, "Have you come as a thief with swords and clubs to take me? I sat daily preaching in the temple and you never laid a hand on me." This was done to fulfill the scriptures. Then the disciples deserted Him and ran away.

Heavenly Father, you are the protector and defender of those who believe your words and promises. Help us defend your words and promises, and help us defend the innocent. Let us be good protectors of our children and loved ones, even as you protect us. In Jesus's name, Amen.

February 26

Amendment Limiting President to Two Terms was added to the US Constitution on this day in 1951. The Twenty-second Amendment was ratified after Franklin Roosevelt was elected four times, dominating the political field until dying after his fourth victory. The amendment limited the president to ten years. Neither constituency wanted the other party to dominate; now, power tends to sway from right to left and back. Many argue that Congress should be held to twelve years. Perhaps Supreme Court justices should likewise be limited. It makes no sense for those who govern to make a career out of it; it makes more sense that they have another profession or skillset. Those who stay in office too long get wrapped up in the establishment and become more beholding to the party and special interests than their electorate. People should hold public office to make a difference, not a living. After a decade you need new blood to keep things moving forward. If they want politics as a career, they could become a journalist, diplomat, or lobbyist.

Greed for power is contagious. This is the original sin of Satan, wanting the power and knowledge of God. Anyone, including Satan, who thinks it possible to be a god is delusional. There will forever be only one God, the Father of us all. Politicians fall into the same trap as Satan. Once they get a taste of power, they get hooked; really, it's like an addiction. If they were to be voted out of office, they would lose their gravy trains and probably their minds, given they haven't acquired the knowledge and skills to do things any other way than crooked.

Regrettably, Satan has not given up the fight, and will make a last stand for world dominance. It will not last very long, after which he will inherit an eternity of emptiness. You can bet he won't go quietly. But that is what happens to those addicted to power or money; they never get enough, like a drug addict who burns out. The demon of addiction is every bit an evil spirit as the devil himself; without another fix the addict becomes irrational, psychotic, and dangerous.

- DAN 8:23–25 ~ In the latter days, when the evil ones are fully in power, a fierce king will arise from darkness. He will be powerful and mighty, but not by his own power. He will destroy tremendously, and will prosper and increase. He will crush mighty and holy people, and with cunning, will cause deceit to flourish. He will exalt himself in his heart, and will destroy many in their prosperity. He will take a stand against the Prince of princes who will defeat him without raising a hand.

- DAN 11:18–39 ~ A prince will rise and fall; then a raiser of taxes will come lasting but a few days. A contemptible person will replace him without warning, obtaining the kingdoms through flatteries and deceit. He will overthrow armies. He will make alliances deceptively, and will plunder. He will corrupt people. He will forecast devices against his enemies. He will employ the power of forces. He will honor with money, pleasure, and luxury. He will exalt himself and speak against the Lord. He will profane the holy temple and honor those who forsake the holy covenant. He will set up in the holy place the abomination that makes desolate. He will give no heed to God or to the love of women. He will honor with riches and divide the land for a price. He will destroy many. He will prosper until the indignation is finished, but only for a short time.

- LUK 10:18–20 ~ Jesus said, "I saw the devil, like a star falling from heaven. I have given you power over that enemy; nothing can harm you. But do not rejoice because the demons submit to you, rather rejoice because your names are written in the Book of Life."

- REV 13:1–18 ~ Standing on the seashore I saw a beast rise from the sea, with seven heads and ten horns, a crown on each horn, and on each head was the name of blasphemy. And the dragon provided his power. One of the heads was wounded and healed itself. The world marveled at the beast and worshipped him, and worshipped the dragon who gave its power to the beast.

The people said, "Who is like the beast? Who can possibly oppose him?" The beast spoke blasphemy against God for 3.5 years. He waged war against anyone who was holy, and defeated them. He gained power over all races, peoples, and nations. Everyone except the righteous honored the beast. Then another beast with two horns arrived, speaking like the dragon, exercising the same power as the first, performing magic feats such as bringing fire down from heaven. He convinced everyone to worship the first beast, and make a graven image of it. And the second beast brought the image of the beast to life. He caused everyone to receive the mark of the beast on their right hand or forehead; only those with the mark could buy and sell goods. They tracked down and murdered anyone who did not receive the mark and worship the beast. The beast's number is the number of a man: 666.

- REV 16:13–14 ~ I saw three evil spirits that looked like frogs come out of the dragon, the beast, and the false prophet. These were the demons that performed magic, and coerced the kingdoms of the world to unite against God.

- REV 17:12–14 ~ Ten kings obtain power for one hour with the beast. They give their power and strength to the beast and make war with the Lamb of God, only to be defeated.

Our representative form of government works when candidates place the interests of those who elected them before their own. We have three branches of government meant to be equal in power. The executive is limited to ten years; the legislative and the judiciary should be limited, else the balance of power shift due to tenured positions in these other two branches. But the legislature would have to place term limits on itself (and the judiciary), and amend the amendment. Instead, they vote to raise their salaries. Representative government is as old as Moses; it worked then and it works now. But you have to change generals, rulers, delegates, and agents every so often. When people stay in power too long, they accumulate too much power, which corrupts.

- EXO 18:21–22 ~ Moses's father-in-law advised him, "Select capable men who fear God, are trustworthy, and hate dishonest gain; appoint them as governors over thousands, hundreds, and tens. Have them serve as judges for simple cases, so that you can decide difficult cases."

- DEU 1:13 ~ Take the wise men of understanding and notoriety, and make them rulers.

- DEU 17:14–17 ~ Having entered the land God gave to you, possessing it and living there, you will say, "Let us elect a king to rule over us like other nations." Let the Lord choose the king from among you; do not select a stranger who is not your brother. Your king should not be intent on collecting wealth, livestock, or wives, which might cause him to turn from God.

- PRO 29:12 ~ If a ruler listens to lies, his entire cabinet will be evil.

- 1 TI 1:8–9 ~ Laws are good if used lawfully. Laws are not made for the righteous, they are made for the lawless, profane, and disobedient; laws are for ungodly people and for sinners.

- 2 PE 1:10–11 ~ Therefore, my brothers, be diligent to make your calling and election sure; for if you exercise your spiritual gifts, you will never fall. And you will receive a warm welcome into the eternal kingdom of our Lord and Savior Jesus Christ.

Our Father, you are the supreme ruler; all other authorities are subject to you. Help our leaders and governors remember that they should yield to your Holy Spirit, making Him their principal advisor, and thereby serve those they represent conscientiously and honestly. Help us to elect rulers who follow and obey your laws and the laws of our great land, and who will serve long enough to make good things happen but short enough not to crave the power. In the name of Jesus we pray, Amen.

February 27

Emperor Theodosius Affirmed Christianity on this day in the year AD 380, by officially endorsing orthodox Christianity. He upheld the Nicene Creed and the divinity of Christ, rejected the philosophy of the Arians, and outlawed pagan temples of worship. After yielding some of his powers to the church, the Roman emperor clashed with church leaders on numerous occasions. Theodosius (AD 347–395) was an accomplished military strategist and tactician which elevated him to emperor, first in the east and then over the entire empire which was reunited under his reign. But the empire would split into west and east once again following his untimely death four months later, never to be reunited again. Meanwhile the Roman Catholic Church continued to grow in influence and power, while the Roman empire progressively deteriorated. Though not an emperor of great notoriety, his reign was pivotal in changing the social climate surrounding European imperialism, and in promoting Christianity.

Christianity was legalized by emperor Constantine in AD 313, who sponsored the first ecumenical council at Nicaea in AD 325; the Roman capitol was established at Constantinople in AD 330. Thus began the domination of the catholic (meaning universal) church in Europe, which was further bolstered by Theodosius during his tenure. The splitting of the empire resulted in formation of eastern orthodoxy in Constantinople and western orthodoxy in Rome. Its spread throughout the world resulted in the Catholic Church being the largest Christian organization on the planet, now with about 1.25 billion adherents; all the Protestant denominations combined comprise another 1.25 billion Christians. The Vatican is now the center of operations for one of the most powerful faith-oriented forces in the world today, not to mention the wealthiest.

The idea of separation of church and state is a misnomer. The two are supposed to work in harmony. God institutes government to take care of matters of the state, while it is the church's responsibility to address matters of religion. But these two efforts are not mutually exclusive, because obedience to the law is a matter of church and state. We are to obey God's laws, as well as laws promulgated by our government. Of course, if those laws are contradictory, we are obliged to follow God (ACT 5:29). Beware when the government or the church asks you do something that contradicts God's Word, and be ready to act accordingly.

- EXO 1:15–17 ~ The king of Egypt ordered the Hebrew midwives to kill the male babies. But the midwives feared God and did not obey the king.

- PSA 108:12; PSA 118:8 ~ Give us help from trouble, for vain is the help of man. It is better to trust the Lord than put confidence in humans.

- ISA 2:22 ~ Stop trusting in people who have but one breath in their nostrils. Who will hold them accountable?

- JER 26:11–13 ~ The priests and prophets addressed the princes and the people saying, "This man deserves death, for he has prophesied against this city which you have now heard." Then Jeremiah spoke to the princes and people saying, "The Lord sent me to prophesy against this house and against this city using all the words that you heard. Amend your ways and your actions and obey the voice of the Lord your God, and He will relent of the evil He has pronounced against you."

- DAN 6:7–27 ~ King Darius commissioned princes to be his eyes and ears throughout the kingdom. After observing Daniel's devotion to God and his status in the kingdom they sought to eliminate him. They convinced the king to sign a decree that nobody could be found praying to anyone but the king for thirty days. Daniel, being aware of the decree, conducted his daily prayers. They accosted him and brought him before the king demanding his death. Daniel was thrown into the lion's den. The king was troubled because he liked Daniel, saying to him, "The God who you serve will deliver you." Early the next morning the king hastened to the lion's den and found Daniel alive. The king threw Daniel's accusers into the lion's den, along with their wives and children; and the lions feasted upon them. Darius sent out a decree stating that the God of Daniel is the true living God whose kingdom will last forever.

- MAT 15:7–9 ~ Jesus said to the scribes and Pharisees, "You hypocrites, Isaiah prophesied about you with a word of truth from God: These people draw near to me with their mouths, and honor me with their lips, but their heart is far from me. In vain they worship me, teaching as doctrine the commandments of men."

- MAT 23:1–4 ~ Jesus spoke to the crowd and His disciples saying, "The scribes and Pharisees sit in the seat of Moses. Therefore, observe those things they tell you to observe, but do not do as they do, for they do not observe those things they are telling you. For they place heavy burdens on people while they will not lift a finger."

- LUK 20:20–26 ~ They kept an eye on Jesus and sent spies pretending to be simple men, to catch Him saying something that would justify arresting Him. They asked Him, "Master we know that your teachings are upright and show the way to God, so tell us if it is lawful to pay tribute to Caesar or not." Jesus knew they were trying to trick Him and replied, "Why then do you tempt me?" Then He obtained a penny from someone in the crowd and asked, "Who's image and inscription do you see on this coin?" They answered, "Caesar's." Jesus said, "Render unto Caesar what is Caesar's, and unto God what is God's." The spies held their peace because of the wisdom in His words.

- ROM 13:3–8 ~ Rulers are not a terror to those who do good, but to those who do evil. You should be afraid of their power if you do evil, but you will receive praise if you do good. Law enforcement is a ministry sanctioned by God for your welfare. But if you do evil beware, for they do not carry a sword in vain; because they are there to execute wrath upon those who do evil. Therefore, do good so you can avoid their wrath, and for the sake of your own conscience. Render to everyone their due, whether in taxes, customs, respect, or honor. Owe nothing to anyone except your duty to love your neighbor as the law commands.

- TIT 3:1 ~ Remind them to be subject to rulers and those in power, to obey judges, and to be ready to perform every good work.

- HEB 13:17 ~ Obey those who rule over you and submit to the authorities; for they keep watch over you and must give a report; and you want them to give a positive report not a negative report which would be bad for you.

- JAM 1:25–26 ~ Whoever looks into the perfect law of liberty and continues therein, not forgetting what they heard but actually doing it, this person will be blessed in his or her deeds. Those claiming to be religious who cannot control their tongues deceive themselves.

Dear Father, the giver and enforcer of all laws, we love your Law and we will try our best to obey your laws, as well as laws passed by the legislatures of our nation and our states. Help us to be mindful of these laws as we go about our daily lives, so we can avoid committing any violation. Help us to stay out of trouble by choosing good and doing good. If we are forced to choose between the commandments of men and your commandments, please give us the boldness and resolve to do and say as you command, without being disrespectful of the authorities. Help us to cooperate with law enforcement in any way we can, so that we will become known to them and trusted rather than being suspected by them. We pray in the name of Jesus, who perfectly fulfilled all of your commandments when we were guilty of all, Amen.

February 28

Watson and Crick Discovered Structure of DNA on this day in 1953 at Cambridge University. Known as the double-helix, this landmark discovery revealed how DNA replicates itself within two strands running in opposite directions; this configuration stores the chemical and genetic information for life. Their findings were reported two months later in the April edition of *Nature*, a top scientific journal. They would be awarded the Nobel Prize in 1962 for their body of work. There were many other scientists doing research on DNA, and the team got help through the findings of others, but they literally beat the rest to the finish line.

Of course, the world has come a long way since then, to the degree that scientists can reengineer DNA, for better or worse. There are obvious ethical issues involving tampering with DNA which we needn't get into here; suffice it to say that it is akin to playing God when creating superbugs or superhumans.

A frequently overlooked finding is this: the irreducible complexity of the double-helix proves it was designed by an intelligent being, namely God; that is to say, it is impossible for something this sophisticated to have evolved via natural processes. Reductionism is a method for tracing underlying causes back to an original cause. When it comes to creation, we are left with an uncaused first cause, which is God. God is the only cause who was not caused because He is eternal; He is the reason for His own existence, as well as ours. When scientists pose questions about what caused the universe, or life, or intelligence this cannot be answered using reductive or any other analytical processes without arriving at one answer: God.

- GEN 1:11–12, 20–28 ~ God said, "Let the earth bring forth grass, herbs, and trees yielding fruit after its kind, the seed of which is in itself." And God said, "Let the waters bring forth living creatures, and birds that fly in the heavens above." God said, "Let the earth bring forth every living creature after its kind, cattle, animals, and other beasts." God made every living thing after its own kind. Then God said, "Let us make humans in our image, after our likeness; and let them have dominion over the fish, birds, and animals." God created humans in His own image; male and female He created them both. God blessed them and told them, "Be fruitful and multiply, replenish the earth and subdue it, and have dominion over all living creatures that move upon the earth."

- COL 1:15–16 ~ Jesus Christ is the image of the invisible God, the firstborn of all creation. By Him were all things created in heaven and earth, visible and invisible, including thrones, dominions, governments, and powers; all things were created by Him and for Him.

- JOH 1:3 ~ All things were made by Him and without Him was nothing made that was made. In Him was life and the life was the light of humanity.

Within every cell of your body a unique DNA sequence exists, which is a complete blueprint of you containing enough information to fill a library. Our DNA is chemically and biologically incompatible with the DNA of all other living organisms. In other words, one kind can only reproduce within its own kind. It is unfortunate how some people are not comfortable in their own skin; they want to be someone else so they have surgery to make them look like someone else, even another gender; but their DNA remains unaltered.

- JOB 12:7–10 ~ Ask the animals, birds, or fish and they will tell you; or ask the earth to teach you. Who cannot see that in all these the hand of the Lord is evident? In His hand is the soul of every living thing, including the breath of human beings.

- 1 CO 15:38–39 ~ God has given a body to every kind of seed. All flesh is not the same flesh. There is a type for humans, a type for animals, a type for fish, and a type for birds.

Intelligent design is apparent in all life forms because their genetic coding is different and unique for each lifeform. The idea that everything burst into existence of its own volition and evolved from that point forward is ridiculous. One must believe that nothing can produce everything to adopt this position; some scientists will go to great lengths attempting to explain how this could be possible, because they cannot accept that a supreme being did it. Some have argued that aliens from outer space brought life to earth, without explaining who created them. Irreducible complexity and intelligent design have been proven empirically by scientists. The fact is, God created all of this for us; He wanted children to love, and to love Him back. It is proper for parents to love their kids and for them to love back.

- JOB 10:11–12 ~ God has clothed me with skin and flesh, and has fenced me in with bones and muscles. He granted me life and favor, and His coming has preserved my spirit.

- PSA 33:6–9; PSA 104:11–14 ~ By the word of God the heavens were made, and all its hosts from the breath of His mouth. He gathered the elements together. Let all the earth fear the Lord and let all the inhabitants of the world stand in awe of Him. For He spoke and it was done. He causes all things to grow for the service of humankind.

- ISA 45:12, 18 ~ God made the earth and created humans to live here. With His hands He stretched the heavens, and commanded all the host of heaven. The Lord who created the heavens, the earth, and everything in it formed this universe to be inhabited, for He alone is God, and there is no other.

Science can explain that which is observable and measurable. However, physicists believe that the building blocks of the universe are invisible. Sometimes they describe these undetected and unknown aspects of the universe as if they were real, however unobservable; but they cannot fathom an invisible God who is absolutely real, and whose works can be seen everywhere.

- PSA 139:14 ~ I will praise the Lord for I am fearfully and wonderfully made. Marvelous are His works, such that my soul knows this is right.

- PRO 20:12 ~ Concerning the hearing ear and the seeing eye, the Lord has made them both.

- ROM 1:20 ~ For the invisible qualities of God from the beginning of the world are clearly seen in the things He made, to include His eternal power and Godhead.

- 2 CO 4:18 ~ We look, not at things which are visible, but at the things that are not visible; for the things we can see are temporal, but the things we cannot see are eternal.

- HEB 11:1–3 ~ Faith is the assurance of things hoped for, the evidence of things not seen. For their faith our forefathers were commended. Through faith we understand that the worlds were framed by the Word of God, so that things which are seen were made from things that do not appear.

Father in heaven, you created the universe from things we cannot see; and even you are invisible to us. But we can see evidence of you in the universe and in the man Jesus Christ. Increase in us true knowledge of you and your creation; help us to trust in you by faith, and still continue to grow in our learning of you and this universe which you created for us. Help us to use science and the study of the universe to better understand you; and help us to study you from your Word to better understand our universe. Surely, both will enable us to know the truth which is the reality of your creation and the evidence of our salvation. You have made us to be special, for you love us as your children, though we be mere humans of limited understanding and reach. Help us to grow in understanding, especially the knowledge of sanctification by your Holy Spirit, to become righteous through the blood of Jesus in whose name we pray, Amen.

February 29

Leap Year Day occurs every four years to update our calendar. Set your clocks today, change your calendar tomorrow; or not. Measurements of time will never be perfectly accurate. Many things need updating; in particular, our faith needs a periodic boost and our moral compass needs periodic recalibration. Worldly distractions take our eyes off of God; we get wrapped up in the worries of life. These things will not matter when Jesus brings us home: no calendars, clocks, or deadlines in heaven. Seriously, can you tell, time is running out for this world? Our universe will pass away, says the Bible. By the way, astrophysicists believe that too; it is called the second law of thermodynamics, yet another truth which both nature and scripture confirm as absolute. Many claim there are no absolutes, so their truth is all that matters. But I've got news for them.

- MAT 5:18 ~ Jesus said, "Truly I say unto you, until heaven and earth pass away, not one bit of the Law will pass until all has been fulfilled."

- LUK 21:33 ~ Jesus said, "Heaven and earth will pass, but my words remain true forever."

- JOH 20:29 ~ Jesus said to Thomas, "You believe because you have seen me; blessed are those who have not seen and yet believe."

- 2 PE 3:3–4 ~ Do not forget that in the latter days, scoffers will come pursuing their own lusts and saying, "Where is the promise of His coming? Everything is the same as it was before."

When I hear the word "leap" I think of a long jump, not one day every 1460. Personally, the word "leap" is misleading; it is more like one extra day. You carve off enough from the other four years to get one free day. If you are paid by the hour or day, that's an additional wage you are owed today. In the latter days, a whole day's pay gets you a ration of bread; no wine or oil (REV 6:6). Imagine a big jump from prosperous to destitute. Maybe God takes us home first. In the meantime, be grateful to Him for what you have and responsible with what He gives you.

- LUK 12:36–48 ~ Be the man who awaits his master's return from the marriage feast, opening the door when he arrives. Blessed be those who the master finds awake. If the owner knew when a thief would rob his home, he would have been prepared. Be ready for the Son of man to return, for no-one knows the hour. Who is a faithful and wise servant, whom the Lord appoints to rule His household? Blessed is the one doing a good job when the Lord returns; he will become ruler over the Lord's possessions. But to the one believing the master's return is far off, who chastises others and engages in drunkenness and gluttony, for him the Lord will arrive unexpectedly. The evil servant will be punished severely; those disobeying out of ignorance will get a lesser punishment. Of those who have been given much, much will be required; of those who have been entrusted with much, more will be demanded.

- LUK 19:12–26 ~ A king gave ten shares of gold to his servants to invest during his absence. Upon returning, he gathered them together. The first servant made ten more shares. The king was pleased, giving him ten cities to govern. The second made five; he got five cities. The third stated, "Knowing you are a stern man, I hid mine in the ground to not lose it; here they are." The king said, "You could have invested the money in the bank. You called me stern; I will deal with you sternly." The king gave the unwise man's share to the man investing the wisest; he ordered the wicked servant to be thrown into the dungeon. Because, to those who have, more will be given; to those who do not have, the little they have will be taken away.

Father, Son, Holy Ghost: our time is yours, from now until eternity. Let us today take a leap of faith, no matter how weak or strong our faith; for we are sanctified by your Holy Spirit to conform into the image of Christ. Our leaps of faith bring us ever closer to you Father. Thanks Dad, in the name of Christ who is the image of you, and in who's image we were made, Amen.

March 1

Employee Appreciation Day is observed on the first Friday of the month though unofficially. The idea was hatched in 1995 by Bob Nelson and his publisher, Workman Publishing. It is an opportunity for bosses to develop teamwork and an atmosphere of cooperation and appreciation: from the top down as well as from the bottom up. Oftentimes there will be a luncheon or a get-together at the office or elsewhere. Games, contests, gift cards, decorations, prizes, trainings, activities (indoor and outdoor), recognitions and awards help to create cohesiveness among the various echelons in the business. Organizational unity is extremely important, especially in small businesses. Too often, executives and officers of a business are out of touch with what is going on at the lower levels. Workers might feel unappreciated, ignored, or manipulated, as if their opinions don't matter. This is a good time to see what's going on by opening lines of communication going up, down, and laterally. Satisfied workers will equate to productive workers, so it behooves owners and executives to find out what workers need to perform their best. There should be incentives to make workers want to stay, especially given the volatility in the workplace. The worst kind of work environments are authoritarian, hostile, and condescending.

It's a proven fact that hard work pays off. Most bosses and executives got to their lofty positions through due diligence, which can move anyone up the ladder of success. But you have to want it; if you do the bare minimum, you likely will not progress in the organization. This country was built on the hard work principle; it is the underlying foundation of capitalism. We seem to have lost the significance of honest work; in fact, the nation has become downright lazy since the pandemic. People got used to working from home, or not working at all and getting a paycheck anyway. We need to reinstate work ethics, because this is a righteous value.

- PRO 12:13–14; PRO 13:11; PRO 23:4 ~ An evil man is trapped by his sinful talk, but a righteous person escapes trouble. From the fruit of his lips a man is filled with good things as surely as the work of his hands rewards him. Wealth obtained by pride will diminish; but those who achieve by way of hard work will see their wealth increase. Do not labor to become rich, and do not concentrate on your own feeble wisdom.

- ECC 2:22–24 ~ What does a man get for all his work and striving under the sun? He gets pain and grief, and no rest at night. That is meaningless. A man can do nothing better than to eat and drink, and find satisfaction in his work. This comes from God.

- 1 CO 3:13–14 ~ Everyone's work will be seen for what it is because the light will illuminate it; it will be revealed by the fire which tries every person's work as well as his or her dedication. If that which is built endures, the builder will be rewarded. If it burns down, the builder will suffer the loss but will be saved from the flames.

- PHP 2:12–13 ~ Just as you were obedient while I was there, continue to do so, especially now that I am no longer with you. Continue to work on your salvation with fear and awe before the Lord. God works within you, making you want to do His will. Therefore, carry out what He asks without complaining or arguing.

- TIT 3:1 ~ Be submissive to rulers and authority, be obedient, and be ready for honest work.

- HEB 6:10–11 ~ God will not forget your hard work and labor of love, which you showed others in His name as you ministered to the saints. We desire that every one of you will show the same diligence until the end to make your hope secure.

- REV 14:13 ~ I heard a voice in heaven saying, "Blessed are those who die in the Lord; they will find rest from their hard work, for their actions precede them."

We not only are to work for a living, but also to do our share of the work in the harvest of God's vineyard. The work of the church involves all members; it is one of the most integrated work environments you will find. Every employee has job satisfaction because Jesus Christ is their mentor and the Holy Spirit is their boss. Every day is Employee Appreciation Day if your labor is done for Christ who will bless your work no matter what your job is. Bosses would be well-advised to acknowledge this fact: you may be the head honcho in your mind, but Jesus is the head if you are a true believer. He can guarantee success, although nobody else can.

- PSA 133:1 ~ Behold, how good and how pleasant it is for brothers and sisters of the faith to live together in unity!

- ISA 65:22–24 ~ They will not build houses for someone else to live in; they will not plant crops for others to eat; for my elect will enjoy the fruits of their labor. They will not labor in vain or produce fruit for nothing, for they are my offspring. When they call, I answer; when they speak, I hear.

- LUK 10:2–3 ~ Jesus said, "The harvest is plentiful but the laborers are few. Pray that the Lord of the harvest would send more laborers to help. Keep in mind, I am sending you out like lambs among wolves."

- ROM 4:4–5 ~ When people work, their wages are not considered a gift but an obligation. However, to those who do not work, but trust in God who justifies the sinner, their faith is credited as righteousness.

- 1 CO 3:8–9 ~ Everyone will receive their own reward according to their labor. For we are all laborers for God.

- 1 CO 15:58 ~ Brothers, be constant in your labor, unwavering, firm, and productive. For you can be assured that your labor for the Lord will not be in vain.

- EPH 4:15–16 ~ We will speak the truth out of love, and we will grow in every way in Christ, who is our head. In Christ, the whole body is joined and held together just as our bodies are joined and held together by ligaments and joints. Christ is the head of this body, in which all members work together as an integrated system; through Him the body is nurtured and grows in His love.

- EPH 6:7–8 ~ Serve wholeheartedly, as if you were serving the Lord and not people, because you know that the Lord will reward everyone for whatever good he or she does, regardless of whether slave or free.

- PHP 1:6 ~ Be confident, for He who began a good work in you will prolong it until the day Christ returns.

- 1 TH 1:3 ~ We will always remember your work of faith, your labor of love, and your patience of hope in the Lord Jesus Christ before God our Father.

Dear Father, we work for you; help us to remember that. Help us to enjoy working, and rejoice when we obtain employment. If we work hard and credit you for our success, we know we will prosper. Whatever we choose to do or not to do, let us choose it for you. If we are not sure, help us to remember that you are there and we need but ask, and we will receive the answer. No job will be too hard if we rely on your strength, Lord; therefore, we pray for vigor to make it through each day, whether tough or easy. And we pray for continued knowledge and skill, with the motivation to work hard and learn everything about our job and our employer, so that we can be a resource to everyone in the business, as well as being your witness through our employment. In the name of your Son Jesus, who worked hard for us and died doing it, Amen.

March 2

World Day of Prayer is also celebrated on the first Friday of the month. It was started by a group of Christian women beginning in 1887, promoting prayer globally, supporting evangelical mission work, advocating for international peace, and highlighting women's (and their children's) rights and responsibilities in a world where men have dominated, and still do in most places. The idea got impetus from the two world wars. Educational classes continue to be held and resources published, as well as annual conferences bringing women together from some 170 countries for fellowship, learning, and praying. Regional gatherings are organized and can be attended on this day, to encourage prayer, address women's issues, share cultural exchanges, identify disconnects in the community, and address disputes around the globe. This is an interdenominational Christian initiative exclusively organized and executed by strong, educated, and experienced women. The World Day of Prayer International Committee deliberates on Christian themes, and publishes an agenda based on current events, future concerns, and member countries in the news. They determine which country and location conferences are to be held. Local chapters also organize events and coordinate with their international partners. It behooves us, regardless of gender, age, ethnicity, socioeconomic status, etc. to pray for this organization, and the success of their mission, which is to offer earnest and fervent prayer by as many people as possible for the furtherance of the Christian faith and its foundation of love and equality.

    This day has long been observed to pray that international affairs be resolved by God; after all, it is called the World Day of Prayer. Don't just pray for world peace, pray that the love of Jesus will find people all across the planet who are eager to hear the good news of the Gospel, and connect with God and His people. Finding God will provide joy and riches in the throes of poverty.

- ACT 2:42 ~ And those who listened remained steadfast in the doctrine and fellowship of the apostles, in the breaking of bread together and in prayer.

- ACT 4:31 ~ When they finished praying, the place was shaken where they were assembled; and the Holy Ghost filled them, and they spoke the Word of God with boldness. The multitude that believed were of one heart and soul; and nobody spoke on their own behalf but for the common good.

- ACT 12:5–11 ~ Peter was imprisoned. But earnest prayer for him was made by the church. Their prayers were answered and Peter escaped with the help of an angel.

- EPH 6:18–19 ~ Pray all the time in the Spirit. Keep alert and persevere. Pray for Christians, prophets, and priests, that their words will proclaim the mystery of the Gospel.

- 2 CO 1:11 ~ You have helped us with your prayers. Many people will thank God for our ministry and for the favor God has granted us on behalf of your support and prayers.

- 2 TII 3:1 ~ Pray for Christian teachers and ministers, and pray for the freedom to openly speak God's Word.

- JAM 5:13–16 ~ Are any of you afflicted? If so, then pray. Are any of you happy? If so, then sing praises. Are any of you sick? Then ask the church to pray for you in the name of the Lord. Confess and pray for each other, and be healed. For the fervent prayer of the believer yields high returns.

    Dear God, Father of the universe and creator of all things visible and invisible, we come before you with a humble heart to pray for the heart of the world, its nations, and its peoples. Let everyone who seeks you to immediately know you are right there; help them listen to your Holy Spirit, and see your glory which appeared to the world in Jesus Christ, in whom we pray, Amen.

March 3

World Hearing Day is held annually on this date. It is about aiding the hearing impaired, introducing ways to prevent hearing loss, and enabling the deaf through education, technology, fundraising, and awareness. An agenda for the annual event is produced by the World Health Organization; their first such event was held in 2007. An important aspect regarding any environment is knowing how much noise or amplitude is too much; this has become an increasingly important safety issue in workplace studies.

There are various levels of hearing loss, and most people will experience some loss in their senior years. The main causes of deafness and hearing loss include infectious diseases, genetic propensity, long-term exposure to loud noises, organic problems, and head injuries. Deaf people have undergone considerable stigmatization over the years; fortunately, this has lessened as awareness has risen. Education has advanced tremendously, with more schools for the deaf, training and work programs, and occupational health standards; certainly, learning to read lips, sign language, and braille are part of education programs for the deaf. Prevention is gaining ground through immunizations, developmental care, rehabilitation, and genetic analysis; medical advances in detection, care, surgery, devices, and medicine have prevented and sometimes cured deafness. Of course, Jesus Christ healed the deaf with His touch; He is also the cure for death.

- LEV 19:14 ~ You should never curse a deaf person or put an obstacle before the blind, but you should fear God.

- MAR 7:37 ~ The people were astonished concerning Jesus, saying, "He has done everything well. He even makes the deaf hear and the dumb speak."

- HEB 11:7–38 ~ With faith, the great prophets were able to endure anything and performed great feats such as subduing kingdoms, escaping certain death, overcoming incredible odds, healing the sick, and even raising the dead.

Then there is the problem of people with perfectly good hearing who do not listen. Often people do not want to hear. Maybe they think they've heard it all. They disagree with an opinion before hearing it; perhaps it brings back unpleasant memories. Maybe they don't listen because they are distracted, stressed, or overloaded. Maybe you are too longwinded, they don't like your tone, they don't trust you, or they are not interested. But these reasons do not justify tuning someone out. If you do not want to listen for whatever reason, tell someone or politely excuse yourself. Whatever you do, don't open your mouth if you haven't thought it over.

- PSA 78:2 ~ David prophesied: He will speak in parables and disclose hidden truths.

- PRO 12:15 ~ The way of fools is right in their own eyes, but the one who listens to advice is wise.

- ISA 6:9–10 ~ God told Isaiah, "Go and speak to your people. They will hear but will not understand; they will see but will not perceive. For their heart is fat, and it makes their eyes heavy. They shut their eyes and ears so they cannot see or hear, and therefore they cannot understand in their heart, become converted, and be healed."

- JER 6:10 ~ Who should I speak to and warn that will hear? For their ears are closed and they cannot listen. The Word of God has become a reproach to them; they have no delight in it.

- AMO 8:11 ~ There will be a famine of the Word; people will hunger to hear the Word but they will not be filled.

- ZEC 7:11 ~ They refused to pay attention and turned away, covering their ears from hearing.

- MAT 13:10–17 ~ The disciples asked Jesus why He spoke in parables. Jesus replied, "You are able to know the mysteries of the kingdom but others are not so fortunate. I speak to them in parables because they have eyes but do not perceive and they have ears but do not listen. In them the prophecy of Isaiah is fulfilled (ISA 6:9–10): Their hearts have hardened; they hear but do not understand; they see but do not perceive. They have closed their eyes and ears so they cannot understand with their heart and become converted. You are blessed because your eyes and ears are open to me. Many people have longed to hear and see what you have heard and seen."

- MAR 4:33 ~ Jesus spoke the Word to the crowds with many parables, for the benefit of those who would listen and understand.

- JOH 5:24–25 ~ Jesus said, "Truly I tell you, whoever hears my Word and believes in Him who sent me will receive eternal life. They will not be condemned, but will pass from death into life. Truly I say that the hour is coming when the dead will hear my voice, and those who listened to me will live."

- ROM 11:7–8 ~ The Israelites did not find what they were looking for; but God's elect found it. Thus, it is written, "They have eyes that do not see and ears that do not hear."

- 2 TI 4:3–4 ~ The time will come when people will turn away from sound doctrine and pursue their own lusts, finding teachers who will tell them what they want to hear. They will turn away their ears from the truth, and turn their ears towards fables.

- JAM 1:19 ~ Be swift to listen and slow to speak; also, be slow to anger.

When wise people are speaking, it is wise to listen. Consider taking notes and discussing it; that's how we learned stuff in school at every level. What about when the Word of God is being spoken? Study, concentrate, underscore, take notes, organize your notes and thoughts, and be prepared to declare it, for that is what the great schoolmaster instructed (LUK 6:40).

- PRO 1:32–33 ~ The waywardness of simple-minded people will be their demise, and the complacency of fools will destroy them. But whoever chooses to listen will be safe and at peace, free from fear of harm.

- PRO 19:20 ~ Listen to advice and accept instruction, and you will be wise.

- PRO 22:17 ~ Incline your ear to hear the words of the wise and apply your mind to knowledge.

- PRO 23:19 ~ Hear and be wise, and direct your mind in the true way.

- MAT 13:23 ~ If the Word is received by someone who listens and understands, it will take root in his or her heart and that person will bear much fruit.

- LUK 10:16 ~ Those who listen to my disciples whom I have sent will listen to me; whoever rejects those whom I have sent reject me. And those who reject me reject Him who sent me."

- ACT 2:42 ~ Those who listened remained steadfast in the doctrine and the fellowship of the apostles, in the breaking of bread together and in prayer.

- ROM 10:10, 17 ~ Those who believe with their hearts are justified. Those who confess with their lips are saved. Faith comes by hearing and hearing by the Word of God.

Help us eternal Father to be hearers of your Word and doers of your Word. Bless the hearing impaired. Help them and all to listen with open minds and perceive your truth: whether by spoken or written word, in a manner they can understand and share. Thank you, Jesus, Amen.

March 4

Holy Experiment Day is a relatively obscure observance celebrated in the USA on this date. It commemorates a religious freedom experiment advanced by William Penn, who established the Quakers in Pennsylvania in 1681 after experiencing considerable religious persecution in England. He was given a land grant in lieu of money owed to his family by the British crown, so Penn decided to establish a colony where religious freedom would be accepted and encouraged. The colonists were a peace-loving, diverse, and tolerant people of faith, who accepted all denominations where God was the almighty creator and ruler of the universe. Like most of the settlers in the New World, they wanted a representative government that did not discriminate on the basis of religious beliefs. Penn referred to his plan as a holy experiment, where all forms of Christianity were welcome. Penn drew colonizers from across Europe to join in his experiment which was enormously successful at the start, though some of the original tenets were abandoned due to tension with natives, Dutch settlements, and secularism. The success of his experiment would come later, for Pennsylvania would be the new seat of the colonial government until 1800.

How, then should we celebrate Holy Experiment Day? Well, you might want to try an experiment of your own. For example, you could witness to someone you care about who is unsure about faith; or sponsor an event that brings people of faith together; or pray fervently to God for a spiritual gift, miracle, or intervention and get others to participate. Like any experiment, you need a goal, a method, and a means of measuring the results. If you are not overtly religious, you might try prayer, going to a Bible study, or attending a worship service. I often encouraged clients who included spiritual growth as a treatment goal to experiment with different churches until they found one representing their values and beliefs, and where the congregation treated them like family. If based on genuine love, it might be the right place; but if it does not employ both testaments of the Holy Bible, it is the wrong place.

- DEU 12:32 ~ Make sure you do what God tells you; do not add to it or take away from it.

- ISA 29:13 ~ God says, "The people honor me with their lips but have removed their heart from me; their knowledge of me is taught using the principles invented by men."

- LUK 4:12–13 ~ Jesus replied, "It also is written that you should never tempt the Lord your God" (DEU 6:16). At that, the devil gave up and left Jesus.

- JOH 6:63 ~ Jesus said, "It is the Spirit that gives life, not the flesh; the flesh profits nothing. The words that I speak are from the Spirit and give life."

- ROM 8:1–2, 8–9 ~ There is now no condemnation for those who are in Christ Jesus, who walk after the Spirit and not the flesh. For the law of the Spirit of life in Christ has made us free from the law of sin and death. Those who live in the flesh cannot please God. If you are in the spirit, it is because God's Spirit dwells within you. As for people who do not have the Spirit of Christ, Christ has no part of them or they in Him.

- ROM 14:18–19, 23 ~ He who serves Christ in these things is acceptable to God and approved of men. Let us therefore follow after the things which promote peace and edify one another. If you have any doubts, do not do it; for whatever is not of faith is of sin.

- GAL 1:8 ~ Anyone, including angels, who preaches anything contrary to what Jesus and the apostles preached is cursed.

- JDE 1:17–19 ~ Dear friends, remember what the apostles told us before, that in the latter days there would be scoffers who follow their own ungodly desires. These people have come to divide you; they follow the instincts of their flesh and do not have the Spirit within them.

There are countless Christian denominations in the world, some with a Catholic and some with a Protestant foundation. If they believe that Christ is the Son of God, conceived by the Holy Spirit, who saved the world from sin and death through His death and resurrection, this will pass as Christian. And though people may diverge with respect to specific doctrines, practices, and observances, this is not a reason for division. Diversity is a good thing, division causes conflict. Our freedom of religion, listed first in the First Amendment to the Constitution, is precisely so we can unite as a Judeo-Christian nation, and not divide over ancillary issues that are not essential to one's salvation.

- ECC 4:9–12 ~ Two are better than one because the reward of their labor is greater. If one falls, the other lifts him up. But it is unfortunate when alone, for if you fall there is nobody to lift you up. Similarly, two people lying together produce more warmth. And two are better able to defend themselves; as the saying goes, a rope of three strands is not easily broken.

- ROM 14:5–6, 18–20 ~ One person may esteem one day above another while another person esteems every day equally. Whoever regards one day as special does so for the Lord. Whoever eats or does not eat something, does so for the Lord, with thanksgiving. Let everyone be fully persuaded in his or her mind. Do not destroy the work of God for the sake of food. All things are clean, but do not allow the eating of something to be offensive to others.

- ROM 14:7–10 ~ None of us lives to himself, and none of us dies to himself. For if we live, we live unto the Lord; and if we die, we die unto the Lord. Whether we live or die, we are the Lord's. Christ died, revived, and arose so that He might be Lord over both the dead and the living. But why do you judge your brother? And why do you call him out? Because everyone will stand before the judgment seat of Christ.

- 1 CO 11:17–18 ~ I have heard that when you assemble together as a church there are divisions among you. I am telling you that such meetings do more harm than good.

- COL 2:8, 18–19 ~ Beware of those who would lead you astray with their errant philosophies and vain deceptions, following traditions fashioned by the world and not by Christ. Do not let anyone swindle you out of your reward. Beware of those who practice false humility and worship angels. They claim to have seen things, but they have filled their unspiritual and arrogant minds with silly notions.

- 1 TI 1:3–7 ~ Do not teach false doctrine, or recognize any myths or irrelevant genealogies, which only serve to raise questions, without providing any answers concerning the faith. The goal is to love with a pure heart, a right conscience, and a sincere faith. Some have wandered away from these principles and turned to meaningless jabber; desiring to be teachers of the Law yet knowing nothing about the Law or about what they purport to be true.

Dear Father, the church is in need of renewal, for evil encompasses us and multiplies as we speak. But if true Christians, regardless of denomination or persuasion, rallied together as one in Christ which we already are for He is our head, we would be a force to be reckoned with, in opposition to the wickedness and the forces of darkness in this world. Our prayer is that we will be a part of and see this renewal and revival, and rejoice together here, and again in heaven. As for those who have yet to join in the body of your elect, help them to try new things to inspire them, especially seeking your Spirit wherein they can discover their own spirituality, which will show them your love and your light which shined in Jesus, your only begotten, who is one with you and the Holy Ghost. Help people to seek you on this day, to experiment and compare what you offer to what other religions offer. Help them to find the way, the truth, and the life which will give them a new hope based on a true faith. And this will prove the evidence to be true: that you, Lord, are alive and well, living in the hearts of your people, Amen.

March 5

Boston Massacre Occurred on this day in 1770. The British imposed burdensome taxes on goods, so colonists began to boycott those goods. Clashes between colonists and British soldiers and loyalists became commonplace. Abuses by the military and the British crown stirred colonials to incite riots and harass British agents. It was inevitable that bloodshed and revolution would follow. A series of events began with the ransacking of a loyalist's store who had ignored the boycotts. An armed officer came to his defense and the two holed up in the store which was being pelted with rocks. A shot rang out of a broken window to drive them away, but instead, a boy was struck and later died. During the next couple of weeks trade workers clashed with the British soldiers repeatedly; one such soldier ended up missing and presumed dead. Finally on this date, a British soldier guarding the customs office was threatened, and retaliated against a colonist with his bayonet. The crowd began to stone him as alarms sounded, creating a larger mob of irate colonists. A loyalist summoned the British military which arrived soon thereafter; they were insulted and assaulted with sticks and stones. One soldier fired his weapon, and then more soldiers opened fire, resulting in three deaths and many wounded, two of which would also die from their wounds. This became known as the Boston Massacre.

A trial was set for nine British soldiers and four civilians who were defended by a team including John Adams himself, who had earnestly supported fair trials for everyone. All but two soldiers were acquitted and they received only minimal punishment. Clearly there was fault on both sides, but neither side agreed with the verdict. March 5 became a rallying day each year thereafter. In December 1773 the Sons of Liberty, tired of taxation without representation, instigated the Boston Tea Party; a second tea party occurred in March 1774, triggering additional "tea parties" throughout the colonies. In September of 1774 the first Continental Congress was convened which authorized the building of an American militia. The shot heard around the world occurred on 04/19/1775 at the battle of Concord; this was followed by another clash the next day killing several minutemen. The Revolutionary War had begun and would continue until the surrender of Cornwallis at Yorktown, October 19, 1781.

This nation has fought many wars in the name of liberty, and because of our faith in God, the author of liberty, we have prevailed. The same is true for people of God throughout history, who endured great hardship to be free from tyranny and oppression. God fights for the righteous, but if we turn away from Him, He will fight against us. This nation is at a crossroads, and we had better pick the right side, or we will be destroyed. We can only remain free if we preserve our principles of liberty, faith, and morality which come from God.

- EXO 23:20–23 ~ God told Moses: I will send my angel to fight with you, do not provoke him but obey him, for I am the one who sent him and he is my representative. If you do as I say, then I will be an enemy to your enemies and an adversary to your adversaries.

- DEU 20:3–4 ~ The Lord is He that goes with you to fight against your enemies, and to save you. So, there is no need to be afraid of your enemies when going into battle.

- JOS 5:13–15 ~ While Joshua was preparing to attack Jericho, he saw a man with a sword drawn, and Joshua asked, "Are you for us or against us?" The man replied, "I am the captain of the angels of the Lord." Joshua fell to his face in worship, asking the angel what he wants. The angel told Joshua to remove his shoes for he was standing on holy ground; and Joshua complied.

- 1 SA 17:45–47 ~ David told Goliath, "You have come with a sword, a spear, and a shield, but I come in the name of the Lord of hosts, the God of the armies of Israel, whom you have defied. Today the Lord will deliver you into my hand, for I will strike you down and take your head as a trophy. And everyone will know that there is a God in Israel who saves, not with a sword or spear. This battle belongs to the Lord, for He will give you to us."

- 2 CH 20:15 ~ The prophet declared: Pay attention all of Judah, inhabitants of Jerusalem and King Jehoshaphat, for the Lord says, "Do not be afraid or dismayed by the multitude gathered against you, for the battle is not yours but God's."

- PSA 27:1–2 ~ The Lord is my light and my salvation. Who should I fear? He is the strength in my life. Of whom shall I be afraid? Even if a whole encampment of my enemies is preparing war against me, I will not be afraid but confident.

- ZEP 1:17–18 ~ I will bring calamity on them; they will become disoriented, for they have sinned. Their blood will be poured out like dust and their bodies like dung. Their riches will not save them on the day of the Lord's wrath. The land will be devoured with fire. The Lord will quickly rid the land of all of them.

- HEB 11:32–40 ~ What more can I say about the power of faith? I could tell you about great judges like Gideon, Barrack, Samson, and Japhtheh, and about great kings like David and Solomon, and the great prophets. Through faith, they subdued kingdoms, administered justice, enforced treaties, shut the mouth of lions, quenched fires, and escaped certain death. They were weak but were made strong, and they fought valiantly in battle, routing even the greatest of armies. They raised the dead. They endured torture, refusing to renounce God as a condition for their release. They were mocked, beaten, chained, and imprisoned. They were stoned and beheaded. They wandered the wilderness in shaggy clothes, destitute, tormented, and afflicted. Although their life on earth was full of strife, they awaited their deliverance, as we all must do until God makes us perfect before Him.

- 2 CO 3:3, 17–18 ~ The Spirit of the living God has written His Word into our hearts; it is not written in ink or on tablets of stone. The Lord is that Spirit, and wherever that Spirit is there is liberty. All of us can see His glory when we look into the mirror, for we have been changed into His image by God's Holy Spirit.

- JAM 1:22, 25–27 ~ Do not merely listen to the Law, do what it says. Whoever considers the perfect law of liberty, and continues, focusing on doing what is right and not just hearing what is right, that person will be blessed because of their actions. If anyone among you appears to be religious but cannot control their tongue, they deceive themselves and their religion is in vain. Exercise pure religion, and be undefiled, visiting the widows and orphans in their time of need, and remaining unblemished by the world.

Father of life, and defender of your people, we pray for your protection, knowing that we must remain faithful to receive it. There is a spiritual war going on and we are caught in the middle of it. Be with us, we pray, as we face the enemy head on in battle. Send your angels among us to guard us from the evil one and his demonic army. Help us to stand strong and confident because the battle belongs to you. Remind us not to fear our adversaries but to trust in you for our safety. We have made it through countless battles, and our patriots have shed rivers of blood; do not let their sacrifices be in vain, but to your glory. For they sought no glory of their own, but to secure our unalienable rights of life and liberty. We ask that you preserve us in our faith and hope, preserve our nation and our liberties, and carry us through every conflict and engagement; and when the dust settles, let us remain standing tall in your light. Thank you for this great nation and help us to remember it is your greatness that makes us who we are, for we are children of the most-high God: Father, Son, and Holy Spirit, Amen.

March 6

Thirteen Day Siege at the Alamo Ended on this day in 1836. The Alamo was an eighteenth-century Spanish (Catholic) mission that doubled as a fort. Fewer than 200 men, including the likes of William Travis, Jim Bowie, and Davy Crockett, fended off General Santa Anna and a seasoned Mexican army numbering approximately 4000. The standoff lasted thirteen grueling days during which the Alamo was overrun the final day on the third assault, and every defender killed; a few women and children taking shelter in the mission were set free. Roughly a thousand Mexican soldiers also lost their lives.

The siege at the Alamo bought time for Sam Houston, general of the Texan army; enough to train new recruits, resupply, and strategize. Santa Ana had divided his army in order to chase after Houston and back him into a corner. However, after three weeks the Texans countered with a surprise attack and routed the Mexican encampment of about 1500 men with a force half their size. The battle lasted less than twenty minutes. Santa Ana disguised himself as a peasant to make his escape but was captured. He was brought before a wounded Houston who stated his terms of surrender to the Mexican president-general. Santa Ana returned to Mexico a broken man while Texas became an independent republic. Texas would be the twenty-eighth state to join the USA in 1845. "Remember the Alamo" was the battle cry in San Jacinto and remained so during the Mexican-American War (1846-1848).

The interesting thing about the fight for Texas independence is that it mirrors the fight for America's independence from the British. In both cases, Americans were fighting tyranny, taxation without representation, broken promises, confiscation of liberty and property, and oppression. It would appear that Providence pulled them through, as they were outmanned, outgunned, and undertrained, and yet knocked off a superior force in what would appear to be a miracle. Not unlike the many times the Israelites defeated a more formidable enemy when God fought by their side, but were on the losing end when they were on the wrong side of God. They had help from God outsmarting their enemies, which were His enemies also. Yes, God really does intervene in matters of right and wrong. Look how this nation has prospered when we were embracing God and not mammon. These days, too many people are focused on mammon.

What do you think God will do if we keep ignoring Him and allowing wickedness to get a pass? Do you think He will do the same thing to the USA that He did to Israel when they strayed? We could be on the wrong end of history if we do not return to Providence for guidance and direction. Of course, when Israel amended their ways and returned to God, He prospered them again. It stands to reason that God will heal our land if we return to Him in humility and contrition.

- DEU 30:19–20 ~ Moses said, "I have presented you with life and death, blessing versus cursing. I recommend that you choose life so that you and your descendants may live. I hope you choose to love God, obey his Law, and cling to Him; for He is your life and He is your time; and you will live in the land which He promised to you and your ancestors."

- PSA 33:12 ~ Blessed is the nation whose God is the Lord, and blessed are the people He has chosen for His own inheritance.

- ISA 66:4 ~ I will choose their delusions; I will bring their fears upon them. Because, when I called nobody answered; when I spoke, nobody listened. Instead, they were evil before my eyes, and they chose to do the things which I despise.

- JER 2:31–32; JER 14:10 ~ God says, "Why do my people say that they are free to roam? Does a maiden forget her jewelry? Does a bride forget her wedding ornaments? Yet my people have forgotten me for days without number." The Lord says this about the people: "They love to wander; they cannot keep their feet from straying. Therefore, the Lord does not accept them; He will now remember their iniquity, and punish them for their sins."

- EZE 21:24; EZE 36:22–32 ~ The Lord says, "You have caused your iniquity to be remembered because of your open rebellion, revealing your sins in everything you do; for this you will be taken captive. It is not for your sake, Israel, that I am doing this, but for the sake of my holy name which you profaned among the nations where you have been taken. I will sanctify my great name that you profaned and the heathen will know that I am Lord when I am sanctified in your eyes. For I will gather you back, cleanse you from impurity and idols, and give you a new heart and a new spirit. I will allow you to prosper once again. Then you will remember your previous evil ways and you will be ashamed of yourselves. I am doing this for your own good; I want you to feel ashamed and disgraced for your contemptible conduct."

Our nation is splitting, just like Israel split in two after the death of King Solomon. Solomon's son Rehoboam would rule the southern kingdom of Judah (two tribes), and Solomon's general Jeroboam would rule the northern kingdom of Israel (ten tribes). And what caused the split? Spiritual riches versus material riches, same as usual. We need to reoccupy the high ground, for that is where the Almighty will be. And with God on our side, we will conquer evil, just as Israel did when David defeated Goliath and the Israelites chased away the Philistines (1 SA 17).

- 1 KI 11:11–12 ~ The Lord told Solomon, "Because of your insolence and because you have not kept my covenant and statutes which I commanded, I will tear the kingdom in half, giving the greater part to your subordinates. But for the sake of your father David, this will not occur in your lifetime, but I will tear it from the hand of your son (see 1 KI 12; 2 CH 10).

History indeed repeats itself when it comes to the consequences of nations heeding God's call versus ignoring it. We learned our lesson, but now we take our prosperity for granted. If we forget God, He will forget us. And the longer we put Him off, the more dire the circumstances will become. Hopefully, we will not fall like the other great empires of the world due to our lust, greed, pride, corruption, and dishonesty. The last global empire will be the new Babylon, and it will fall to pieces just like the old Babylon. Nobody wants that to be our fate. Or do they?

- MAT 12:22 28 ~ A demon possessed man, blind and mute, was brought to Jesus and He healed him; and the man could see and speak. The multitude was amazed wondering, could this be the Son of David? The Pharisees heard this and said that Jesus was casting out devils by the power of Beelzebub, the ruler of demons. Jesus read their minds and replied, "Every kingdom divided against itself is brought down; every city or house divided against itself cannot stand. If Satan casts out Satan, he is divided against himself. How then would his kingdom stand? If I cast out demons by the power of Satan, how do your sons cast them out? Let them be your judge. If I cast out demons by the Spirit of God, surely the kingdom of God has come to you."

Oh, Father divine, we again find ourselves in a predicament and only you can get us out of it. Wake us up from this nightmare and help us to see your light shining before us. It is the light of your Son Jesus that will show us the way if we will simply open our spiritual eyes. Though the worldly distractions are many, Jesus will shine through all the darkness. Help us to return to you and your Word which is a light unto our path and a lamp unto our feet. Please reroute us off this dark path quickly, because there is danger ahead. People are becoming blind to the truth and to where they are headed. They have been deceived and tricked into thinking they have it made. Help us to get back on the path of righteousness, which leads to you and to our true home which is heaven. Help us to recenter our government upon the foundation of truth, morality, justice, and faith, before the pillars of fate crumble to pieces and we become a wasteland. We ask these things in Jesus's name, Amen.

March 7

Alexander Graham Bell Patented the Telephone on this day in 1876. Bell established the Bell Telephone Company shortly thereafter in 1877; the company is now known as AT&T. He had moved from London to Boston in the early 1870s, becoming an instructor at a school for the deaf. He had worked in the field for years with his father, and with his mother who was deaf. He married a deaf student in 1877. Bell was determined to improve the hand-operated telegraph, invented by Morse in 1843. In the fall of 1876, Bell made a call to his partner Tom Watson who was miles away. Together they had managed to convert electricity into sound and transmit it over wire. The first transcontinental phone call was again from Bell to Watson (New York to San Francisco, 1915). Bell invented a metal detector, audiometer, and more. He helped the startup of *Science* magazine, and was president of the National Geographic Society for eight years.

The telephone modernized the world, moving us forward into this era of electronic devices. Nowadays, people cannot survive without their mobile phones and tablets. Parents, test and see what happens when you take away your child's phone for not finishing homework; be prepared to wear earplugs for a while. It is wise not to get "hung up" on worldly things, as it can lead to a psychological dependency. This increases the desire for immediate self-gratification, which is worldly and not godly. Such behavior can become addictive and is akin to idolatry.

- DEU 5:8–9 ~ Never make graven images. Do not worship idols. Do not bow before any idols or worship them in any way.

- JOB 31:26–28 ~ If my heart was enticed by worldly things and celestial bodies, or if I was infatuated with myself, I would be guilty of denying God and worthy of His punishment.

- PSA 37:4 ~ Delight in the Lord and He will give you the desires of your heart.

- PSA 97:7 ~ Those who serve graven images or brag about their idols are confused. Everyone must worship God alone.

- MAT 6:31–33 ~ Jesus said, "Do not worry about your worldly needs, for your heavenly Father knows what you need. Instead, seek first the kingdom of God and His righteousness, and this you will receive, as well as your worldly needs.

- ACT 17:29 ~ Do not think of God as an idol made from wood, metal, or stone.

- 2 CO 7:10 ~ Do not regret godly sorrow which produces repentance leading to salvation. But worldly sorrow produces death.

- GAL 5:17 ~ The desires of the flesh are against the spirit, and vice-versa, for they are opposed to each other.

- 1 JO 2:15 ~ Do not love the world or worldly things. If a person loves the world, he or she cannot love God.

Kids spend so much time on electronic devices, talking, texting, emailing and sharing photos, they haven't the ability to engage in contemporaneous conversation; much less mingle amongst a crowd of people they do not know, or speak fluently in public. One of the most critical aspects of grade school is developing socialization skills. After being forced into online learning for two years, kids started losing the ability for interpersonal relationship building. You cannot learn a skill or discipline using online methods only; it must be integrated with onsite teaching and hands-on instruction. Now students are further behind in academics, not just the Bible.

- PRO 1:2–7 ~ Try to know wisdom and instruction; perceive words of understanding. Receive the instruction of wisdom, justice, judgment, and equity. Learn to give subtlety to the simple and knowledge and discretion to the young. A wise person listens and increases in learning; a person of understanding seeks wise counsel, and tries to understand a proverb and its interpretation, or the words of the wise and the hidden meaning of what they say. Remember, the fear of God is the beginning of understanding; only fools despise wisdom and instruction.

- PRO 2:2–6, 10–12 ~ Incline your ears to wisdom and apply your heart to understanding. If you cry for knowledge and ask for understanding, seeking wisdom as you would treasures, you will understand the fear of the Lord and find knowledge of Him: for He gives wisdom, knowledge, and understanding. When wisdom enters your heart and knowledge is pleasant to your soul, discretion preserves you and understanding keeps you, delivering you from evil.

- PRO 11:3, 14 ~ The integrity of the righteous guides them; the perverseness of the wicked destroys them. For lack of guidance a nation falls, but many advisors assure the victory.

- PRO 19:20 ~ Listen to advice and accept instruction, and you will be wise.

- ISA 30:1 ~ Woe to rebellious children, declares the Lord. Woe to those who carry out plans that are not mine, who form alliances but not with my Spirit, and who heap sin upon sin.

- 2 TI 3:14 ~ Continue in things you have learned and are convinced, knowing from whom you learned them.

Adults and children alike need to refrain from allowing these devices to control their lives. If you have thought about fasting, try taking time from your schedule to cease electronic communications; replace it with more face-to-face interactions. Public speaking is necessary to succeed in public life; the new age movement pulls kids away from interpersonal communications into isolation, withdrawal, possibly despair. They brainwash and indoctrinate through the mass media and the dispersion of algorithms controlling what kids see and hear. Do not let your kids adopt these habits for it will disconnect them from God, parents, peers, and society. Do not believe in the social media's feigned diversity, for it is division that these platforms are promoting. Parents need involvement in their kids' education, now more than ever. And make sure they learn the ways of God, and how His Holy Spirit works in us through faith in Jesus. Then they will be able to discriminate whether things said or shown to them are real or appropriate.

- PRO 12:15 ~ The way of fools is right in their eyes, but the one who listens to advice is wise.

- 1 CO 2:12–14 ~ We have received the Spirit of God, not the spirit of the world, so we might know the things God has given to us for free. This is why we teach in accordance with the wisdom of the Spirit, not the wisdom of the world, for you cannot compare spiritual things with worldly things. Worldly people do not receive things of the Spirit, for they are foolishness to them; neither can they know them for they must be discerned spiritually.

- TIT 2:11–12 ~ The grace of God which brings salvation has appeared to all people. It teaches us to say no to wickedness and worldly pleasures. It teaches us to live in a self-controlled, upright manner.

Omniscient Father, who dispenses knowledge at your discretion, we pray for wisdom, knowledge, and understanding of you; help us to compare all that we see and hear on television, the internet, and via electronic devices against the truth of your Word. Do not let us trust in fables, gossip, or information from questionable sources; instead, show us how to fact check everything. Especially help our children to steer clear of caustic material on various platforms, and guide them towards wisdom, learning, and truth; for in the public schools, they dismiss any teaching or mentioning of you, Lord. Help parents educate their children about your works and ways, and especially your Word of truth, which lived in Jesus Christ our Savior, Amen.

March 8

International Women's Day is an annual observance for the advancement of women and women's rights, in a world that has been dominated by men since Adam and Eve. Gender equality always existed in God's realm, given the prominence of many women in the Bible and throughout history. God sees women as equal to men in becoming His children forever (GAL 3:28). And though the sexes differ in ways designed by God, and are given brains and skills unique to their gender, they also are equal in their ability to learn and be as successful as men.

For years, women fought for equal rights, and little by little they obtained this goal in various nations of the world. The first women's recognition day occurred on 02/28/1909 in New York; it was called National Women's Day. In 1910 the first International Socialist Women's Conference was held in Copenhagen, Denmark. The women's rights movement was in full force in Europe when Soviet Russia allowed women to vote in February 1917. March 8 was designated shortly thereafter as International Women's Day. Regarded initially as a socialist movement, it quickly gained momentum in the USA. *Women's Day* magazine, which covered all things women, was launched in 1931; it included health, fitness, fashion, appearance, marriage, and homemaking. Then a new face emerged when the feminist movement hit the 1960s. The United Nations adopted this holiday in 1977; they sponsor an annual program addressing women's rights, opportunities, international programs, and sociocultural initiatives around the globe.

Women have held important positions throughout history. There were many noteworthy women in the Bible, two of whom have books named after them (refer to the lesson on 07/31)

- JDG 4—5 ~ Deborah was a prophetess and judge of Israel; she defeated the Canaanites with her cunning. She judged the people of Israel for forty years.

- RUT 1—4 ~ Ruth was a foreigner who converted to Judaism after her husband died. She followed her mother-in-law Naomi to Bethlehem, and became an ancestor of God's Messiah (MAT 1:5).

- EST 1—10 ~ Esther, a Jewess, was queen of Persia when she assisted in saving the Jews from extermination. She had help from her foster father and relative Mordecai who would become second in command to the king.

- EXO 2:1–10; EXO 15:20–21 ~ Miriam a prophetess, was the elder sister of Moses; she helped save his life as an infant and was instrumental in getting their mother to nurse him while he was reared in the pharaoh's palace. She also led a music ministry for the Israelites as they wandered the wilderness.

- LUK 1—2 ~ Mary the mother of Jesus became a significant figure throughout His ministry, beginning with the wedding at Cana (JOH 2:2–5), and ending at the foot of the cross (JOH 19:25–29).

- MAR 16:1–14; LUK 8:1–4 ~ Mary Magdalene was a prostitute who was demon possessed until she met Jesus, after which she remained part of His inner circle, and with the apostles long after His resurrection. She was the first to see Jesus on the day He arose from the dead.

Certainly, we can mention many great women from antiquity. If you gather with friends or coworkers this day, discuss some of them; name your favorites and why. Or, join one of the sponsored events and learn about the current issues with respect to women in the world today.

Father, we pray for women in positions of leadership and authority, to include those who are raising children, that they would be wise in your Word and lead with honor. We pray that women and men be treated with respect, as in heaven and in the Bible. In Jesus's name, Amen.

March 9

Battle of the Ironclads Occurred on this day in 1862; the union had the *Monitor* and the confederacy had the *Merrimack* which already had sunk one union ship and disabled another. They faced off later that year. The Monitor with its rotating turret held off the Merrimack (aka *Virginia*), but neither ship sank because cannonballs bounced off. It was the last battle for both ships after they limped away. They were the first of their kind, armored ships. Henceforth, warships have been armored. Today we have steel warships as big as aircraft carriers.

Warships have been used as far back as the fifth century BC, when galleys would ram an enemy ship to disable and/or board it; soon they were equipped with catapults. The Phoenicians were capable seamen and mass-produced galleys, though it is unclear where this design actually originated. It wasn't until the fifth century AD that ships were equipped with cannons. Ships with reloadable artillery didn't show up until the fourteenth century, when man-propelled ships were replaced with sailing ships that were larger and capable of carrying heavy artillery. In the nineteenth century, steam-propelled ships came into play, as did explosive ordnance, and ironclad wooden ships. Later that century torpedo boats were invented; they were fast and able to deliver the kill and escape. By the twentieth century, heavily armed warships had evolved into fighting machines that ran on fuel oil instead of coal. Now many are nuclear-powered.

Ships played a substantial role in the Bible, to include King Solomon's navy. Many apostles of Christ owned and operated fishing boats; their trips around the Sea of Galilee included carrying Christ Himself after commissioning them for catching men. Many voyages of Paul are recorded, who crisscrossed the Mediterranean frequently, and was shipwrecked three times.

- 1 KI 9:26–28; 1 KI 10:10–11, 22 ~ Solomon, king of Israel, was one of the first to build a large navy. He obtained the technology and knowledge after making alliances with Phoenicia, Egypt, and Sheba. He used his fleet primarily for trade purposes, as well as to extend diplomatic relations abroad. He brought back precious metals, gemstones, and other riches, making him the wealthiest man that ever lived.

- MAT 4:18–22 ~ Jesus, walking by the Sea of Galilee, saw two men, Simon called Peter and his brother Andrew casting a net into the sea, for they were fishermen. Jesus said to them, "Follow me, and I will make you catchers of men." Immediately they left their nets and followed Him. Continuing along the shore, Jesus met up with the sons of Zebedee, James and John mending nets in their boat with their father; Jesus called them and they came immediately.

- MAT 14:22–33 ~ Jesus told His disciples to take the boat across the Sea of Galilee and He dismissed the crowd. He went up the mount to pray until nighttime. He arose and saw the boat at a distance being buffeted by the wind and the waves. Just before dawn Jesus walked out to them atop the water. When they saw Him, they were frightened thinking it was a ghost as they cried out. Jesus said, "Do not worry it is I." Peter replied, "If it is you Lord, beckon me to come." "Come," Jesus said. Peter got out of the boat and started walking towards Jesus. But he was distracted by the wind, and in fear he started to sink, crying "Save me Lord!" Jesus reached out His hand and pulled him to his feet saying, "You of little faith, why did you doubt?" Once they had climbed aboard the boat, the wind stopped. Those in the boat worshipped Jesus saying, "Truly you are the Son of God."

- MAR 4:35–41~ That evening Jesus told His disciples He wanted to cross the sea. Leaving a crowd of people on the shore, the boats shoved off with Jesus. A storm arose throwing waves across the bow, filling the boat with water. Jesus was sleeping on a cushion in the stern. The men woke Him saying, "Teacher we are about to drown!" Jesus arose and rebuked the wind saying, "Quiet, be still." Immediately it was calm. He asked the disciples, "Why are you so afraid; have you no faith?" They were still shaken as they asked among themselves, "Who is this? Even the wind and waves obey Him?"

- LUK 5:1–11 ~ Jesus was standing by the sea at Gennesaret crowded by listeners. Two boats were parked by the shore with fishermen mending nets. Jesus boarded the boat owned by Simon and asked him to pull out so He could preach to the crowd from the boat. After His sermon He told Simon to drift out into deeper water and cast the nets. Simon replied, "Master, we fished all night and caught nothing; but because you say so we will do it." When they had gathered their nets there were so many fish, they had to summon their partners in another boat to help. Their nets were tearing as they loaded enough fish to fill both boats, until they started sinking. Simon fell to his knees and pleaded that the Lord leave him for he was a sinful man; everyone was amazed to include their partners James and John Zebedee. Jesus told them not to worry because henceforth they would be catching men. And they pulled their boats ashore and followed Jesus.

- ACT 27:1—ACT 28:1 ~ They decided to sail to Italy, with Paul, a centurion, and a certain Macedonian as passengers, along with prisoners that were being transported. They launched, hoping to sail along the coast of Asia, touching shore at Sidon where they took liberty. Then they sailed to Cyprus because the winds were contrary, eventually making it to a city in Lycia. There the centurion found a ship headed for Alexandria, and then Italy. They were days at sea and the wind was not favorable, passing Crete for a place called Lasea. They had wasted so much time, sailing became dangerous. Paul admonished them, saying, "The voyage will be a disaster, the ship and cargo will be damaged, and our lives will be at risk." Nevertheless, the captain, the owner, and the centurion agreed to continue on and winter at Phenice. But a south wind blew them off course, and then a tempest arose; the ship was tossed about near an island called Clauda. They had to reinforce the hull with ropes and lower an anchor to avoid getting stuck in quicksand. They started tossing things overboard to lighten the load. The third day they tossed the ship's tackle overboard using their hands. For several days the storm raged; the crew was starving and giving up hope. Paul stood up and addressed them, "Men, you should have listened to me and we would have avoided this disaster. But do not give up hope because not one of you will be lost. For an angel of God came to me telling me not to be afraid, because I am to stand trial before Caesar, and God has mercifully spared your lives. Be courageous and have faith in God. Even so, we will wreck on an island." After two weeks being driven across the Adriatic Sea, the sailors detected land; they kept checking the depth as it became shallower, so they dropped four anchors before reaching the rocks. Some of the men tried to steal the lifeboat and Paul summoned them back, else they all would perish; so, the line was cut letting the lifeboat drift away. As dawn approached, Paul encouraged them to eat something and reassured them; then they threw the rest of the food into the sea. After sunup they saw a beach and attempted to make a run for it; they cut the anchor ropes, released the rudder, and raised the foresail. The ship hit a sandbar and ran aground with the bow stuck in the sand, and the stern broken to pieces. The soldiers were going to kill the prisoners so they couldn't swim to safety, but the centurion stopped them. He ordered everyone to make it ashore; some swam and others paddled using planks, but everyone made it to land unharmed. They had arrived on the island of Malta.

Father God, you are the creator and savior of humankind and we thank you so much. We thank you for protecting and preserving us, bringing us through every squall and tempest. We pray to remain steadfastly tied to you by faith, and not be afraid when life becomes stormy and the prospects look bleak. Help us always to trust in your saving grace. In the name of your Son we pray, who died to save us and rose again so we could be raised to life eternal, Amen.

March 10

Transfiguration of Christ Sunday commemorates the day Jesus Christ was transfigured in the presence of three apostles. Christ appeared to them in shining glory joined by Moses and Elijah. Jesus had recently told His apostles of His impending death; then brought three of them up a high mountain to receive an extraordinary revelation. There, God the Father proclaimed aloud that Jesus is His Son; recall a similar statement was spoken by God at Jesus's baptism. Thus, these two occasions represent a beginning and ending, the alpha and omega. They reveal to us that our eternal life begins with a commitment to Christ witnessed in our baptism and ends with glory in the presence of Christ, Moses, Elijah, and the rest of the heavenly saints and hosts. This image represents Christ's victory over death and the glory of His resurrection (see also JOH 12:23–33).

Transfiguration Sunday ushers in the season of Lent which will vary from year to year in accordance with Passover and Easter. The actual transfiguration quite possibly occurred forty days (give or take) before the passion of Christ, we just don't know for sure. The date is determined as the Sunday preceding or beginning the Lenten season; it is celebrated much like the season of Advent prior to Christmas. Note that similar revelations of the ascending and descending of Christ can be found in the Old Testament, in the testimony of both Moses and Elijah.

- EXO 34:29–30 ~ Moses descended from mount Sinai with the two tablets of testimony (the Ten Commandments), not knowing that his face shone bright or why the people were afraid to come near him. Even Aaron hesitated until Moses called the leaders to him. Then the rest of the congregation assembled and Moses presented the commandments God had given them, though he veiled his face while he spoke.

- 2 KI 2:8–14 ~ Elijah took his cloak, rolled it together and struck the river; then he and Elisha crossed on dry land. Elijah gave Elisha one last request; Elisha asked for a double-portion of his spiritual strength. Elijah replied, "What you ask is a difficult thing, but if you see me as I am taken away, you will have it." As they were speaking a fiery chariot with horses of fire descended, parting them while taking Elijah up in a whirlwind into heaven. Elisha watched and cried to God, "My Father, behold the chariot and horsemen of Israel." He ripped his clothes in two, picked up Elijah's cloak, struck the water, and returned on dry land.

- LUK 9:28–36 ~ Jesus took Peter, James, and John to the mountaintop to pray. While Jesus prayed, His countenance changed and His clothes shined as lightning. Two men, Moses and Elijah, appeared with Jesus in glorious splendor; they were conversing about Jesus's departure from this earth which would occur upon His return to Jerusalem. The apostles had been in a deep sleep and awakened to witness this. The two prophets were preparing to leave Jesus when Peter interrupted, "Master, it is good to be here; let us build three shelters for you." Peter had no idea what he was talking about, but while he spoke, a cloud surrounded the summit and the apostles became afraid for it enveloped them. A voice spoke from the cloud saying, "This is my beloved Son; listen to Him." Then the fog cleared and Jesus stood alone with them. The apostles kept this secret until after Jesus's resurrection. (Also recorded in MAT 17:1–9; MAR 9:1–10.)

- JOH 1:1, 14 ~ In the beginning was the Word, and the Word was with God, and the Word was God. And the Word became flesh and lived among us; and we saw His glory, the glory of the Father's only Son, full of grace and truth.

- 2 PE 1:16–18 ~ We did not follow cunningly devised fables when we testified of the power and coming of our Lord Jesus Christ, for we were eyewitnesses to His majesty. He received honor directly from God the Father, when a voice from heaven announced gloriously, "This is my beloved Son in whom I am well-pleased."

Christians will behold the glory of Christ firsthand when we see Him face to face in our own glorified bodies. We will be in fine company; the last day is the quintessential all saints day.

- JOB 19:25–26 ~ I know that my Redeemer lives and that He will stand upon the earth. And although my flesh will have been destroyed, yet in my flesh I will see God.

- ISA 40:5 ~ The glory of the Lord will be revealed, and all human flesh will see it together, for the Lord has said so.

- JOH 17:22–24 ~ Jesus prayed to God, "The glory that you gave me I have given to them, so that they may be one even as we are one. Just as you are in me and I in you, may they also be in us so the world will see that you have sent me. Father, it is my wish that they also, whom you have given to me, would be with me wherever I am, so that they may behold the glory that you have given me; for you loved me before the foundation of the world."

- ROM 8:16–18, 30 ~ The Holy Spirit testifies with our spirits that we are God's children. If we are His children, then we are heirs: heirs of God, and joint-heirs with Christ, if indeed we share in His sufferings in order that we may later share in His glory. For I consider the sufferings of this present time to be nothing compared to the glory that will be revealed in us. Whomever He predestined, He called; and whomever He called He justified; and whomever He justified, He also glorified.

- 1 CO 13:12 ~ Presently, we see in a mirror dimly, but later face to face. Now I know in part, but then I will know fully, even as I am fully known.

- 1 CO 15:42–44 ~ Regarding the resurrection, the body that is sown is perishable but it is raised imperishable. It is sown in dishonor but it is raised in glory. It is sown in weakness but it is raised in power. It is sown a natural body but it is raised a spiritual body.

- 1 CO 15:51–58 ~ Here is a mystery of God: We will not all sleep (die) but we will all be changed. Upon Christ's return, in a single moment when the great trumpet sounds, Christ's own, whether alive or dead will arise into heaven to receive new, incorruptible bodies. Hence, the corruptible will have become incorruptible and the mortal will have become immortal. Then at the end, when Christ delivers the kingdom of God to the Father, He will destroy death, at which time the statement "death is swallowed up in victory" will be true. The godly will receive spiritual bodies which will never die. The flesh is of the earth, the spirit is of heaven; thus, flesh and blood will not inherit the kingdom of heaven. Therefore, be confident in your faith because your labor is not in vain.

- PHP 3:20–21 ~ Our citizenship is in heaven. We eagerly await our Savior, who using the same power that brought everything under His control, will change our vile bodies into bodies like His glorified body.

- COL 3:4 ~ When Christ appears, who is our life, you also will appear with Him in glory.

- 1 JO 3:2 ~ Now we are sons of God, and what we will become is not yet known. We do know this: when He returns for us, we will be like Him, for we shall see Him as He really is.

Heavenly Father, to whom all glory and honor belong: you sent Jesus to us to show us who you are. He glorified you in His body and you glorified Him before all the world. And the whole world will see Him again, in all His glory, when He returns for His elect. We praise and thank you, for we are rich in your blessings; we pray to always watch and wait with hope and joy for that day when Jesus will bring us with Him to your heavenly kingdom. We thank you for this wonderful blessing, and we pray that we can point the way to Jesus in our lives, reflecting His glory as was shown on the day of His transfiguration. In His name we pray, Amen.

March 11

National Johnny Appleseed Day commemorates the legendary John Chapman, sower of apple and pear seeds in numerous states and territories. This day was chosen to celebrate his legacy because it occurs during planting season, as well as coinciding with the timeframe of his death in 1845. He was born on 09/26/1774 in Massachusetts; he lost his mother at age two. His father served with the minutemen and fought at Bunker Hill. Johnny left home in 1797 and began his quest to plant seeds of faith as well as apples wherever he traveled, including Pennsylvania, West Virginia, Ohio, Indiana, Illinois, Iowa, Michigan, and Wisconsin. He didn't simply drop seeds randomly, his plantings were organized, mostly apple seed used in cider. Sometimes he bought a plot of land and planted an orchard; he would sell it later for a decent profit because there was an orchard to go with it. Other times he would plant seeds whenever someone asked him to, often without charge. He was a Christian conservationist, who gave spiritually charged sermons, sold books, and planted seeds and saplings. Orchards all over the Northeast and Midwest claim him: Leominster MA has a street named after him and marks his birthplace; the city of Springfield MA where he grew up has a park named after him; and his burial place at Ft. Wayne, IN is identified with a marker. So yes, he really did exist. In his honor, consider planting a tree today, or start an orchard. God is in the business of planting seeds as well, and so are His followers.

- ECC 3:1–2 ~ To everything there is a season, and a time to every purpose under heaven. A time to be born and a time to die; a time to plant and a time to uproot.

- JOB 4:8 ~ I observed that those who plow iniquity and sow wickedness will reap the same.

- ISA 55:10–11 ~ The rain and snow fall from heaven, but do not return, but rather water the earth, making the plants bud and bloom, which provides seeds to the sower and bread to the hungry. Likewise, God's Word proceeds from His mouth, and does not return to Him void, but rather accomplishes His will and prospers in the minds of those to whom it was sent.

- MAT 13:1–23 ~ Jesus told a parable about sowing to the Spirit: A sower of seeds left seeds by the wayside where the birds ate them. He left seeds in the rocky ground where there was insufficient soil for them to grow. He left seeds among the weeds and thorns where they were choked to death. He also left seeds on fertile ground where they grew and bore fruit. The seeds represent the Word of God. If the Word is left by the wayside, it will be snatched away by the wicked one. If the Word is given to those with a heart of stone, it will never take root in their hearts. If the Word is given to corrupt and worldly people, it will be choked out by the lusts of the flesh. But if the Word is received by someone who listens and understands, it will take root in his or her heart and that person will bear much fruit.

- 1 CO 3:7–9 ~ Neither he who plants nor he who sows is anything, but only God who makes things grow. The man who plants and the man who waters have one purpose, and each will be rewarded according to his labor. For we all are laborers with God in His plantation; and you are God's building.

- 2 CO 9:6 ~ Those who sow sparingly will reap sparingly, and those who sow bountifully will reap bountifully.

    Heavenly Father, you planted your seed, who is Christ, into the hearts of believers; let that seed grow into a tree of life that bears good fruit in our lives. Help us to likewise sow seeds of faith wherever we go; may your Holy Spirit nurture those seeds like He has in us, so they too may yield fruit leading to repentance and eternal life. We thank you for those who passed along your seed to us and nurtured us, as we developed into seasoned Christians, capable of spreading seeds of truth all of our days. In the name of Jesus, the seed of Abraham, we pray, Amen.

March 12

National Girl Scouts Day honors girl scouts around the country. On this day we commemorate the first Girl Scout meeting held in 1912 in Savannah GA by Juliette Gordon Low. She organized the girl scouts after meeting the man who first organized the boy scouts, Robert Baden-Powell. Eighteen girls attended, and now there are over 3.7 million girl scouts, and approximately fifty million total since that first meeting. The organization is run by women who want to see girls grow up to be responsible, educated, confident, and independent women. You can celebrate this day by enjoying the girl scout cookies you bought for the occasion, in order to support your local troop. You also can volunteer for or sponsor an event, fundraiser, and/or join a troop. Like boy scouts, the girls learn first aid, fire safety, camping, and survival skills; and they conduct nature conservation and community service projects. In 1965, the age structure was set as follows: Brownies (ages 8–9); Juniors (10–12), Cadettes (13–15), and Seniors (16–18), with only negligible adjustments since then. Naturally, the progressives would do away with them too.

We must cherish our young women and protect them. Girl scouting provides training and skills that will help young ladies to be vigilant and stay safe, as well as assist others with first aid comfort. It is a dangerous world out there, and girls need to learn what to do and when, in the event of an attack or a calamity. And not just the young ladies but also the young men need to learn and acquire survival skills, make contingency plans, fend off assailants and aggressors, and assist others to safety. Ensure your children know what to do in the event of an emergency, by developing your own family plans for fire, invasion, attempted abduction, and attack; include in your planning some secret codes, a communications network, and memorizing emergency contacts.

- LAM 1:18–19 ~ Virgins and young men have been taken captive. Lovers deceive each other. Priests and elders perish searching for food for the soul.

- JOE 3:3–4 ~ They gamble for my people, and trade a boy for a harlot, and sell a girl to get intoxicated. What are you doing? Are you paying me back? It all will come down upon your heads.

- AMO 8:11–13 ~ I will send a famine of the Word. They will seek the Word of God and not find it. The virgins and young men shall faint of thirst for the Word. Sundown will occur at noon; the clear day will be darkened.

- MAT 25:1–13 ~ The kingdom of heaven is like ten virgins who took their lamps with them on the way to meet the groom. Five of them were prepared and brought extra oil with them. The other five ran out of oil and their lamps went out. They asked the prepared girls for some of their oil, but they replied, "We cannot spare any oil, or we will run out of oil too." The others left to buy more oil for their lamps. Meanwhile, the groom came and everybody went into the church for the wedding. The doors were already locked when the other girls tried to enter. They asked to be admitted but the doorman replied, "I do not know you." Jesus summed up the parable saying, "Watch for my return for nobody knows the day or hour."

Father God, you are the lawmaker and enforcer; you protect us and defend us from evil people, disasters, and ourselves. Make us aware of your presence, and help us to be vigilant when we are out and about, because evil is lurking everywhere. Assist our parents, teachers, scoutmasters, and churches in educating children in the right path, and to be on the lookout for suspicious people hiding in the darkness, as they go about their routines. Protect our young girls and boys from predators, and help us to successfully prosecute and incarcerate violent offenders. Help our government to pass proper laws at the federal, state, and local levels that will protect the citizenry, providing sufficient law enforcement, and levying appropriate penalties on those who violate children and our laws. In the name of Jesus, who fulfilled every law, we pray, Amen.

March 13

National Good Samaritan Day is an annual celebration of people helping others who have fallen on hard times, or who have been attacked or injured. This date was selected because of an event that occurred in 1964 when a woman named Kitty Genovese was brutally stabbed on the streets of New York City as she was returning home from her job. Despite her screams for help, nobody came to her aid. Apparently, numerous onlookers and passersby witnessed the event or its aftermath, but they chose not to get involved; if someone had, she might have lived. When someone finally called the police, it was too late. The case became a focal point of Social Psychologists who identified a condition called "diffusion of responsibility". In group situations, the larger the number of individuals the less each person feels responsible or guilty; their personal stake in the outcome becomes more diffused as more individuals become involved. It's the same excuse when someone claims "everyone else is doing it" as if that makes it less a sin.

This observance honors selfless people who take the initiative and lend a hand, regardless of whether anyone else does. Obviously, this holiday is based on a parable of Jesus Christ, known as The Good Samaritan; in His day, Jews and Samaritans hated each other, and were often violent toward the other group. In the parable, a Samaritan rendered aid to a wounded Jew, after two Jewish clergymen went out of their way to avoid the man. Just like the Genovese case: they turned a blind eye as if there was nothing to look at or nothing they could do.

- PSA 41:1 ~ Whoever helps the poor will be blessed by God, and God will deliver them when they experience a time of trouble.

- LUK 6:36 ~ Be merciful to others even as your Father in heaven is merciful.

- LUK 10:29–37 ~ Jesus told the parable of the Good Samaritan: A man was traveling from Jerusalem to Jericho when he was ambushed by thieves who beat and robbed him, leaving him for dead. A priest passed that way later in the day, and after seeing the poor man, passed by him on the other side of the road. Likewise, a Levite saw the wounded man and went around him. Finally, a certain Samaritan saw the man and took pity on him. The Samaritan rendered first aid, set him on his beast, and took him into town. He placed the injured man at an inn, asking the innkeeper to take care of the man and he would pay the bill. Jesus then asked, "Which of these passersby was a neighbor to the man who was attacked?" The lawyer answered, "The man who was merciful." Jesus replied, "Go and do likewise."

- JOH 4:7–26 ~ A Samaritan woman came to the well for water. Jesus asked for a drink. She wondered why a Jew would be speaking to her. He answered, "If you knew the gift of God and who was speaking, you would be asking me for living water." She asked, "How can you draw water? Are you greater than our father Jacob who used this well?" Jesus told her, "Whoever drinks this water will thirst again, whoever drinks my water will never thirst, for the water I give becomes a wellspring of eternal life." She asked Jesus for some living water. He told her to fetch her husband. She said she had no husband. He said she had five ex-husbands and lived with a man not her husband. She saw Him a prophet and said how they worshipped on the mountain, while Jews worshipped in Jerusalem. Jesus replied, "The time is now when true worshippers will worship the Father in Sprit and in truth." She replied, "I know Messiah is coming; He will explain everything." Jesus replied, "I who speak am He."

- ROM 12:20 ~ If your enemy is hungry, feed him; if he is thirsty, give him a drink. Maybe you can turn him or her around by being nice.

- HEB 13:2 ~ Do not forget to help strangers, for you could be ministering to angels.

Father God, help us to help others as directed in your Word. In Jesus's name, Amen.

March 14

Scientists Day recognizes the contribution of scientists, appropriately celebrated on Albert Einstein's birthday. Scientists help make sense of our world; observing, measuring, and analyzing it. Science means knowledge (from Latin). God is the author of nature and He enables humans to examine His creation and make sense of it, making us all scientists in a way. God also provides His Word, helping us make sense of Him, nature, and things we discover. The scientific method is an approach for studying the universe and testing theories. Aspects of our world are investigated repeatedly to establish cause and effect, often through trial and error. Hypotheses are tested one at a time, for a theory is broad, with many variables to control. Scientists investigate a phenomenon repeatedly, collect data and synthesize it, perform an analysis with empiricism and statistics, interpret findings, draw conclusions, and explore how variables affect outcomes. Greek philosopher Aristotle (384–322 BC) employed such an approach. Englishman Sir Isaac Newton (1643–1727) is recognized as the father of classical physics. Among other things, Newton explained the effects of gravity and discovered calculus (see lesson on 07/05).

German born Einstein (1879–1965) moved to Switzerland as a teenager, where he graduated from polytechnical school and became a clerk in a patent office. He obtained his doctorate degree in 1914 at the University of Zurich (1905) and became a Swiss citizen; he later moved to Berlin, joining the Prussian Academy of Sciences. He taught at Berlin University and became director of the Kaiser Wilhelm Institute of Physics. He is considered the greatest scientist in modern history, known for his theory of relativity, equation of mass/energy ($E=mc^2$), and contributions to quantum mechanics. He won the Nobel Prize in Physics for his body of work in 1921. He was visiting the United States when Hitler rose to power; being Jewish he did not return to his native Germany and instead became a citizen of the USA in 1940.

Science is a gift from God, who expects us to be curious and seek understanding of Him and His creation. Scientists examine the universe and its splendor, trying to figure out how it works. To some extent, the Bible explains how it works, compelling us to admire God's creation and His works, and to seek His wisdom which can be found everywhere, especially in His Word.

- PSA 111:2 ~ The works of the Lord are great, and sought by all who take pleasure in them.

- PRO 25:2 ~ It is the glory of God to conceal a matter, but the honor of kings to search it out.

- ECC 3:11 ~ He has made everything beautiful in its time. He has set eternity in the human heart. Nobody can fathom what God has done from the beginning to the end.

- ISA 40:25–26 ~ God says, "Who can you compare with me? Who is equal to me? Look into the sky and behold: who has created these things; who brings out the stars and calls them by name from the greatness of His might? For I am strong in power."

- AMO 9:6 ~ He builds stories in the sky, and layers in the earth. He brings waters from the sea and pours it out over the land. The Lord is His name.

- COL 1:17 ~ He is before all things, and by Him all things hold together.

It has been argued that science and religion are incompatible. Nothing could be further from the truth. Newton was a devout Christian and gave God the credit for his wisdom and understanding; I would submit that Christians make the best scientists. Many scientific findings have supported the Bible, even when the investigator was attempting to refute the Bible. Given that God is the author of nature and the universe, as well as being author of the Holy Bible, it stands to reason that the book of scripture can be used to explain the book of nature and vice-versa. They both are helpful in determining knowledge and establishing truth.

- JOB 26:7–14 ~ God stretches the northern sky over an empty space and hangs the earth upon nothing. He gathers up the water in thick clouds, but the clouds do not break under the weight. He veils the face of the moon and spreads the clouds over it. He encompasses the waters with boundaries where the day and night come to an end. The pillars of heaven tremble, astonished at His reproof. He stirs the sea with His power, and by His understanding He breaks the proud. By His Spirit He has painted the heavens; His hands have twisted the crooked serpent. Even so, these are merely parts of His ways; only a small portion is heard of Him. The thunder of His power, who can understand it?

- PSA 8:3–4 ~ When I consider your heavens, Lord, the work of your fingers, the moon and stars that you have ordained, I wonder: Who is man that you are mindful of him? And the son of man that you visit him?

- PSA 19:1–2 ~ The heavens declare the glory of God and the firmament shows His handiwork. Every day they speak, revealing knowledge of Him.

- PSA 104:1–3 ~ The Lord wraps Himself in light as a garment, stretched across the heavens like a curtain. He lays the foundation under the waters and makes the clouds His chariot that glides along with the wings of the wind.

- PRO 14:15 ~ The simple man believes every word; the prudent man looks into the matter.

- ISA 40:22–23 ~ It is God who sits upon the circle of the earth; its inhabitants are as grasshoppers. He stretches the heavens as a canopy and spreads them out like a tent to live in. He brings princes to nothing and makes judges of the earth look vain.

- ROM 1:19–20 ~ What we can determine about God is plainly seen because God has revealed it. God's invisible attributes, such as His eternal power and divine nature, have clearly been perceived since the beginning of creation; so, nobody has an excuse to deny Him.

I was a scientist by trade (PhD in Psychology) and I am a Christian for life. I used the scientific method to conduct psychological research and I performed statistical analyses to interpret data for various US defense contractors. I was a professor of psychology, statistics, and religion; at the same time, I was teaching Bible classes at my church. I practiced psychotherapy and was an administrator at a psychiatric hospital; and I also wrote Christian books. I have no conflict in my brain between psychology and faith, or science and religion. Not only do I believe that science and religion are perfectly compatible, it can be proven statistically (Barber, 2020a). Plenty of scientific data exist that support the truth of the Bible. I use the keyword *HARP* to describe the plethora of confirmatory evidence: History, Authenticity, Reliability, Prophecy. Science can be used to confirm the Bible; the Bible can be used to explain science.

Compelling evidence the Bible is true is found in the accuracy of testimony from eyewitnesses. Luke was a first rate historian providing extraordinary detail in his Gospel. He named various governors and emperors to create a timeline (read LUK 2:1–2; LUK 3:1–2). At first, historians dismissed Luke because they could not verify the names; in time, all names were verified. It seems history eventually catches up with itself. The New Testament was written by apostles (Matthew, John, Paul), their colleagues (Mark, Luke), and Jesus's half-brothers (James, Judah), all who personally witnessed the divinity of Christ. Mainstream scientists and historians do not refute that Jesus lived and was crucified. Many refute the resurrection, though it was documented by multiple sources, some antagonistic to Christianity (like Josephus and Tacitus).

Heavenly Father, we thank you for science and scientists, and for giving us the intellect to understand you and your creation. Help those examining nature and the universe to find you in the process. Help all people to eagerly seek knowledge through Jesus Christ our Lord, Amen.

March 15

Assassination of Julius Caesar Occurred on this date in 44 BC, otherwise known as the ides of March. While not the official record of the incident, the history was quite eloquently presented in Shakespeare's play. Basically, the senate held a coup against the renown ruler and conqueror; over twenty stab wounds did-in the power-hungry emperor. You might call that a crime of passion; but the murderers were no better than Caesar, pretending to be gods. This kind of greed and pride did not die with him for it was passed onto his heir apparent, Augustus Caesar, and those following. The two were so proud of themselves they each stole a day out of February and had a thirty-one-day month named after them (July, August). How narcissistic can you get!

Regardless, we are stuck with this calendar system, not to honor those egotistical pagans, but out of convenience. We follow the Gregorian calendar now, so February gets one day back each leap year. Today's observance needn't be celebrated per se, but it is significant Biblically speaking. For several emperors who followed Julius would be key players, from a Roman perspective, during the history of the New Testament.

Augustus (formerly Octavian) was the adopted son of Julius; he would beat Marc Antony to the throne (6 BC—AD 14). The city of Caesarea was named after Augustus; his son Tiberius would follow him as emperor. Then came Gaius, called Caligula (AD 37); he became seriously ill and went mad. His was a short reign; then his uncle Claudius took over (AD 41). Next came Nero (AD 54), stepson of Claudius, who probably executed Paul and Peter, as reported by Clement of Rome (AD 96). Vespasian acquired the throne next (AD 68), and then Titus (AD 79).

Most of these men were carbon copies of Julius, seeing themselves as gods and treating those they subdued with disdain. It leaves no doubt the cause of the fall of the Roman empire; these emperors were tools of Satan. They persecuted Christians, God's people, and they hated God. How dare God think Himself more important than they, who were more like their father the devil. Keep in mind, the devil will return again to commandeer the final world empire, grooming an antichrist to oppose Christ. Who do you think is going to win that one?

- LUK 2:1–4 ~ Caesar Augustus decreed that a census of the entire Roman empire was necessary. It took place when Quirinius was governor of Syria. Everyone had to travel to their hometown to be counted for the tax rolls. Joseph and Mary, his betrothed who was pregnant, had to leave Galilee for Bethlehem, because they were of the lineage of David.

- LUK 3:1–3 ~ In the fifteenth year of Tiberius Caesar, Pontius Pilate was the governor of Judea, Herod was tetrarch of Galilee, his brother Philip was tetrarch of Ituraea and the region of Trachonitis, and Lysanias was tetrarch of Abilene; Annas and Caiaphas were the high priests in Jerusalem. And the Word of God came to John, son of Zacharias, in the wilderness; he left for the countryside near the Jordan River, preaching baptism for the remission of sins.

- ACT 11:27–30 ~ Prophets came from Jerusalem to Antioch. One named Agabus showed the Spirit was with him, prophesying that death would come upon the Roman empire, which it did during the reign of Claudius. The disciples sent relief to the brothers in Judea and to the elders, through Barnabas and Saul.

- ACT 18:1–3 ~ Paul left Athens and went to Corinth; there he met up with Aquilla and his wife Priscilla who had fled when emperor Claudius commanded all Jews to leave Rome. Paul and Aquilla had been fellow tentmakers, so they shared an abode.

- ACT 25:8–14 ~ Paul said that he had not violated any law, neither against the Jews nor against Caesar. Festus, willing to please the Jews, tried to persuade Paul to go to Jerusalem and be judged by him. Paul said he would stand before Caesar's judgment seat to be judged. Paul did not want to be delivered to the Jews, appealing his case to Caesar. Festus replied that he would send Paul to Rome to be judged by Caesar. Later Festus received visitors: King Agrippa and Bernice. Finally, Festus declared Paul's case to the emperor, concerning a certain man (Paul) being kept in bondage by Felix.

- 2 TI 4:6–8 ~ Paul wrote to Timothy one last time. In that epistle he said: I am now ready to be offered (sacrificed), for the time of my departure is at hand. I have fought the good fight and finished my course, having kept the faith. Now a crown of righteousness awaits me, which the Lord our righteous judge will give me on the last day; and not only to me but to all who look forward to His appearing.

Incidentally, prior to becoming emperor, Titus was the commander of a legion; he was a conqueror for the Roman empire, sacking Jerusalem and destroying the temple just as Christ warned the Jews would happen within one generation. That event occurred in AD 70, almost exactly 40 years (one generation) after Christ predicted it in AD 30.

- MAT 24:1–2; MAR 13:2; LUK 21:5–6 ~ As they left the temple, the disciples approached Jesus who said to them, "Do you see all of these buildings? I tell you the truth, there will not be one stone left upon another; all will be thrown down."

- LUK 19:43–44 ~ Jesus said, "The time is coming when your enemies will surround you, and Jerusalem will be utterly destroyed; and they will not leave one stone sitting on top of another."

There is considerable evidence from the archives of history to verify the Biblical narrative. As mentioned earlier, Luke was a topnotch historian. He authored the Gospel of Luke and the Book of Acts, where he presented the succession of Roman rulers and regional governors throughout his testimony. Luke provided ample references to the events and figureheads which were current during his writings, giving a precise chronology. Secular historians also confirmed a great deal of the New Testament, including the scriptures above penned by Luke.

First century Jewish historian Josephus (circa AD 30–100) prepared a Jewish history on behalf of the Roman government in his *Annals* and *Histories*. He identified Herod the Great as King of Judea during the reign of Augustus Caesar. In fact, the Herodians and the Caesars got along quite well after the crucifixion of Jesus. Josephus also identified Pilate as procurator over Judea during the reign of Tiberius; he covered all the emperors listed above in his history. He affirmed procurator Felix who held Paul in bondage as he awaited extradition to Rome, and Festus who replaced Felix. John the baptizer was mentioned separately along with an account of a wise man called Christus who performed miracles, and how He was executed under Pilate.

Tacitus (circa AD 56–120) was a first and second century Roman historian who was no fan of Nero, suspecting him for the fire that destroyed much of Rome in AD 64. Tacitus wrote about a sect called Christians that was tormented mercilessly by Nero. He also recorded how the leader of the sect called Christians was executed under the authority of Pontius Pilate, prefect of Judea during the reign of Tiberius Caesar. Thus, we have confirmation of Luke's testimony by a Jewish historian and a Roman historian, who were never associated with Christ or His followers.

Father, you are wise beyond our comprehension; we thank you for providing proof of your Word and its truth. Even historians that were hostile to you and your people stumbled upon the truth, validating both testaments of the Holy Bible, and more importantly, the crucifixion and resurrection of Christ. The Bible is holy because you breathed that Word into the minds of your faithful servants and to all who read their testimony. As hard as the world has tried to suppress your truth, it cannot be erased, and it is alive and well today. Praise to you, in the name of your Son Jesus who died and yet lives, Amen.

March 16

Freedom of Information Day is an annual observance occurring on James Madison's birthday (1751). Madison was the principal author of the US Constitution and the Bill of Rights; he advocated for limited and transparent government. Unfortunately, our government has a bad habit of withholding information from the public, though it is our right to know what and why. On July 4, 1966, Congress passed the Freedom of Information Act (FOIA) to provide a means of obtaining information, by submitting a formal written request identifying specific information being sought. Given that "we the people" are in charge, our leaders have an obligation to keep us informed; when government officials are secretive it makes the citizenry very suspicious. To be a self-governing people we must have access to the information our leaders have, unless that information is classified to protect our national security. Governments collect information on many things, including its citizenry, the legality of which is questionable. Anyone can submit a FOIA request and supposedly obtain the information our government has collected on you; but you cannot get information on other people. Today there are events and awards for those who champion our freedom of information: the James Madison Award, and the Eileen Cooke Awards for state and local events, which are bestowed through the American Library Association.

It has been said that information is power, and so it is. If the government is hiding information, it could be to secure their power over us. Whenever any government official refuses to share information, or they provide false information, they should be fired on election day. There is an awful lot of false information being put out by politicians, the media, and those who are greedy for power. When they deliberately mislead us, you can bet they are up to no good.

- ISA 59:13 ~ They know they are being disobedient to God; they carefully plan their lies.
- 2 TH 2:9–11 ~ Those false signs and fake miracles come from Satan. Such deceptions belong to the self-righteous who will die, for they did not believe the truth that could save them. God will let them believe their lies and perish.
- 2 TI 3:13 ~ Evil people and false teachers will get worse, deceiving many; they themselves have been deceived by Satan.
- TIT 1:11 ~ They must be silenced, those who would ruin entire households, teaching things that are wrong for the sake of ill-gotten gain.
- JDE 1:4 ~ False teachers have infiltrated the churches, claiming that once you become Christians you can do whatever you want without being punished.

We need information to make decisions; a lack of information increases the risk of a decision because of the uncertainty. The more factual information we have, the more confident we are, and the more certain what to do. God's information is always factual, for He cannot lie or mislead. God does not withhold information; He does not keep things we need to know secret.

- DAN 2:28 ~ There is a God in heaven who reveals mysteries.
- LUK 12:3 ~ Jesus said, "What we have discussed in the dark will be repeated in the light. What you have heard in closed rooms will be shouted from the rooftops."
- LUK 12:11–12 ~ Jesus said, "When they bring you before the authorities do not worry about what to say or do, for the Holy Spirit will provide the information when you need it."

Heavenly Father, thank you for revealing truth. You gave humans a mind to discern good from evil, and truth from lies. Help us to always fact check what people, especially politicians, put out as truth; help us remove from office those who lie for a living. In Jesus's name, Amen.

March 17

Saint Patrick's Day acknowledges the patron saint of Ireland. He was born in Roman Britain in the late fourth century AD, into a well-to-do family; his father was a deacon in the church and his grandfather a priest. Patrick was kidnapped at age sixteen and taken to Ireland as a slave where he tended sheep. Legend has it that he converted to Christianity, received a vision from God, and escaped to the coast, where a ship picked him up and took him back to Britain; there he entered the priesthood. He later returned to Ireland to spread the Gospel to the pagans there. Traditionally, his death in Northern Ireland was on this date (circa AD 461), which is why his life is celebrated today in countries around the world with parades and festivals. Here in the USA the holiday has become rather secularized as is the case with many holidays; now it is more about Irish things than the Gospel of Jesus Christ. Boston held the first St. Patrick's Day parade in 1737, which is still a tradition. Everyone is encouraged to wear green on this day to symbolize the shamrock (three leaves and one stem), which St. Patrick purportedly employed to teach the Holy Trinity.

With the start of the Roman Catholic Church (circa AD 590) and its first pope Gregory I, the idea of sainthood took hold. In the beginning, saints were selected on the basis of public awareness and from dialogue among the Catholic leadership. Pope John XV formalized the sainthood process 400 years later (tenth century AD). St. Patrick well could have been the first officially designated saint. But in actuality, God determines sainthood. By the way, the word "catholic" means universal, entire, or whole; the early church fathers referred to the "holy catholic church" in the creed. Many people associate the term with the Roman Catholic church, which is why Protestant denominations now say "holy Christian church" when reciting the Apostle's Creed.

The designation of saints began with the Old Testament. God separated people who sought Him diligently, from Adam to Abraham. God promised Abraham a son; in their old age, he and wife Sarah had a son who would be the father of God's chosen Israel. God led their descendants to the land He had appointed for them. Also promised to Abraham was a king from his seed; this was a reference to Christ, for He would be the "seed" that saves the world. The Jews were God's chosen; those possessing the faith of their forefathers, namely Abraham, Isaac, and Jacob (Israel), would become saints when they died. That is, they would go to heaven. God chooses all who bear His name to become saints. But we do not worship or pray to St. Patrick, though we do honor his legacy today, for bringing the good news of Jesus Christ to Ireland.

- GEN 17:19 ~ God told Abraham, "Your wife Sarah will surely bear a son and you will name him Isaac. And I will establish my everlasting covenant with him, and his descendants."

- GEN 22:18 ~ God told Abraham, "In your seed all the nations of the world will be blessed because you have been obedient to me."

- ROM 4:13–16 ~ The promise that Abraham would produce an heir for the entire world was made not only to Abraham, or to his seed according to the Law, but also was made to all people according to their faith. If heirs were made in accordance with the Law, there would be no need for faith, because the Law works wrath, and where there is no Law there is no sin. Therefore, the promise is one of faith, given by God's grace to all the seed, not only to those who are under the Law, but also to those who have the same faith Abraham displayed.

- GAL 3:6–9, 16, 26–29 ~ Consider Abraham. He believed God, and his faith was credited to him as righteousness. Understand this: those who believe are children of Abraham. The scriptures foretold that God would justify the Gentiles by faith, and announced it in the Gospel, and to Abraham as it is written: All nations of the world will be blessed through your seed (GEN 22:18). Anyone having faith is blessed along with Abraham, a man of great faith. To Abraham and his seed, the promises were made. God did not say "seeds" meaning many people, He said "seed" meaning one person who is Christ, the mediator between God and us. What then was the purpose of the Law? It was added due to sin, until the seed promised to Abraham had come. You are children of God through faith in Jesus Christ, if you have been baptized unto Him and have clothed yourselves in His righteousness. There is neither Jew nor Greek, slave nor free, male nor female, for you are all one in the Lord. If you belong to Christ, then you are Abraham's seed and heirs according to His promise.

Those who die in Christ become saints, as indicated in the New Testament. Jesus selects them precisely because they have chosen God through Him. This Judeo-Christian foundation has been the strength of our country since it became a country. We seem to be losing that footing, for people seem less respectful of the Old and New Testaments, and more respectful of ideologies, many of which are contrary to Christianity. As mentioned previously, the secularization of society results in more people choosing to leave the faith or to deny it. By rejecting Jesus, they reject God, and will have no inheritance in the kingdom of heaven. I have emphasized repeatedly, without God the USA will receive the same fate Israel did when they turned their back on Him; but if we return to God, He will take us back again just like He did when Israel returned to Him.

- DEU 7:6–9 ~ You are a holy people to the Lord your God who has chosen you to be separated from other people of the earth. The Lord did not shower His love on you or choose you because you were greater in number for you were among the fewest. But because He loved you and made an oath with your forefathers, He has brought you out with a mighty hand and redeemed you from bondage in Egypt. Know then that He is God, faithful and just, who keeps His covenants and gives mercy to those who love Him and obey His commandments.

- PSA 33:12 ~ Blessed is the nation whose God is the Lord, and blessed are the people He has chosen for His own inheritance.

- ISA 14:1 ~ The Lord will have mercy on Jacob; He will choose Israel and place them in their own land. And strangers will be joined with them who are among the house of Jacob.

- JOH 15:16–19 ~ Jesus said to His disciples, "You did not choose me, I chose you and ordained you, so that you could bear fruit that would not wither. Anything you ask of the Father in my name will be given to you. Love one another. If the world hates you, it is because it hated me first. If you were of the world, the world would love you as its own. But I have chosen you out of the world, and that is why the world hates you."

- EPH 1:4 ~ God chose us to be His own before the foundation of the world, that we should be holy and without blame as we come to Him in love.

- 2 TH 2:13 ~ We will give thanks to God always for you brothers, beloved of the Lord, because God chose you from the beginning to receive salvation through sanctification of the Spirit and belief in the truth.

- 1 PE 2:9 ~ You are a chosen generation, a royal priesthood, a holy nation, a unique people. So, praise Him who has called you out of darkness into His marvelous light.

Sainthood is not a small thing; it means you get to live in heaven as an adopted child of Almighty God. I cannot understand why anybody would decline this offer. God said He would separate His people from the rest, because we are not of the world, for our citizenship is in heaven. If you want to be numbered with the saints of heaven you need to love God and believe in His Son, Jesus Christ.

- PSA 31:23 ~ Love the Lord, all you saints. For the Lord preserves the faithful, but the proud He pays back.

- PSA 34:4, 9, 11 ~ I sought the Lord and He heard me, and delivered me from my fears. So, fear the Lord all you saints, and you will never need anything. Come to me, people, and I will teach you about the fear of the Lord.

- PSA 50:3–5 ~ God will come with a terrible fire burning all around Him. He will call everyone from heaven above to the earth below for judgment. He will gather the saints unto Himself.

- PSA 145:11–12 ~ The saints will speak of the glory of your kingdom, Lord, and tell of your power, making known to everyone your mighty deeds and the glorious splendor of your kingdom. Your kingdom is everlasting, and your dominion endures throughout all generations.

- DAN 7:18, 27 ~ The saints of the Lord will receive the kingdom, and will possess it forever. And the kingdom and the dominion, and the greatness of the kingdoms under heaven, will be given to the saints of the Lord. That kingdom will be everlasting, and all dominions will serve and obey them.

- 2 CO 5:1 ~ We know that when this temple, which is our body, is dissolved, we will have a home in heaven; not a house made by hands but one that is eternal.

- EPH 1:9–11 ~ He made known to us the mystery of His will according to His good pleasure, which He purposed in Christ to be put into effect when the times reached their fulfillment, thereby bringing all things in heaven and on earth together under one head who is Christ. In Him we were chosen, being predestined according to His plan, ensuring that everything conforms to His purpose and will.

- EPH 2:18–22 ~ Through Christ we have access by one Spirit to the Father. Thus, we are no longer strangers or foreigners, but fellow citizens with the saints in the household of God. We are built upon the foundation set by the apostles and the prophets, with Jesus Christ being the chief cornerstone. Together we comprise a well-framed building, a growing temple in the Lord. We are joined together by His Spirit into one home.

- COL 1:26–27 ~ The mystery, hidden from ages past, has now been revealed to the saints, to whom God will give the riches of His glory. It is for anyone who turns to Christ for their hope including Jews and Gentiles.

- REV 10:7 ~ When the seventh angel sounds his trumpet, the mystery of God will be finished, as He declared to the prophets and the saints.

Father in heaven, we thank you that, as Christians, we are counted with the saints. Though we are separated from this world, we must live in in this world until we are called home. Help us to be a light to others, sharing your peace and joy, so that they might find Christ through us. Help us to love you before all others and love our neighbors as ourselves. Help us to grow in our faith and hope through the power of your Holy Spirit living in us. Help us to follow Christ all the days of our lives, and all the way to heaven. Because we have chosen Christ instead of the world, you have chosen us out of the world; and we sincerely appreciate this great honor. Remind us daily where our true home lies, and of the glory we will receive because we were imputed the righteousness of Jesus when He took our sins upon Himself. In His precious name we pray, Amen.

March 18

National Supreme Sacrifice Day honors those who have made the ultimate sacrifice for the welfare of others. This observance began in 2004, and has many origins which may have contributed to its inception, though none specific to this date. Heroes come in many forms, but they have these attributes in common: courage, bravery, and unselfishness. They risk their lives, placing themselves in danger to protect and defend. Of course, people in uniform whether military, police, or firefighters risk their lives every day even when they are not on the job. You would think it takes a special person to their job, but these are ordinary people in every other respect; but ordinary people can become extraordinary in the most unlikely circumstances.

Today is an opportunity to honor someone you know that made such a sacrifice, or to honor those whose jobs routinely place them in peril. You might want to contribute to families of lost heroes, or volunteer your time and talents in service. You might want to visit a military graveyard, or a memorial, or events that honor first responders, the military, or veterans that once wore a uniform. Schools might allow classroom discussions about sacrifice and share heroic stories personal to the students and teachers.

Everybody has an iconic hero in their lives who inspired them to persevere or to make sacrifices. Often it is the unsung hero that comes to mind, who is deserving of recognition, tribute, or honor, though most heroes do not view themselves as such. When faced with dire circumstances, people you might have thought were the least likely to step up are the ones risking their lives to help others make it to safety. Who knows, maybe you are such a person but have never had an opportunity to prove it. If you do, you are doing God's work.

Certainly, Jesus Christ is the best example of someone whose entire life was one of sacrifice for humankind. And many martyrs followed His example when facing certain death for the faith. All but one of the apostles of Christ died a horrible death, and many of the early church fathers were martyred. What is the driving force within people willing to face extreme odds and certain death? It is usually the Spirit of the Lord.

- PSA 51:17 ~ The sacrifices of God are a broken spirit; a broken and contrite heart, oh God, you will not despise.

- ISA 40:29 ~ God gives power to the weak and increases strength in the weary.

- ISA 41:13 ~ I, the Lord your God, will hold your hand. I will tell you not to fear for I am the one who will help you.

- JOH 3:16–17 ~ Jesus said, "God loved the world so much that He sacrificed His only Son, so that anyone could believe in Him and not die but live forever. For God sent His only Son into the world to save it, not to condemn it."

- JOH 15:12–15 ~ Jesus said, "Love each other as I have loved you. No greater love exists than to give one's life for their friends. You are my friends if you do whatever I command of you. From now on, I will not call you servants, for a servant does not know what his master does; I call you friends because everything you know about my Father you have heard from me."

- ROM 12:1–2 ~ Let your body be a living sacrifice, acceptable to God; this is the least you can do. Do not live according to this world but according to the perfect will of God.

- 1 CO 16:13–14 ~ Always be on your guard, standing firm in your faith; be courageous and strong, and do everything in love.

- EPH 5:2 ~ Live a life of love, just as Christ loved us and gave Himself for us as a fragrant offering and sacrifice to God.
- HEB 10:10, 18 ~ We are sanctified by the offering of the body of Jesus Christ, one sacrifice for all people. No more offering for sin will ever be needed again.
- REV 2:10 ~ Jesus said, "Do not be afraid of suffering, imprisonment, and tribulation, for many will endure such hardships. Be faithful unto death and you will receive a crown of life."

There are some great examples in the Bible of bravery, often coming from unlikely sources. What a great source of inspiration is God's Word.

- 1 SA 17 ~ David, who was a teenage shepherd boy, was the only one willing to face the giant Goliath who wore a suit of armor and was armed with a sword and a spear. David trusted in the Lord to guide his actions; armed with only a sling, he defeated Goliath. This inspired the rest of the army of Israel to attack and disperse the Philistine army.
- DAN 3:12–27 ~ The king of Babylon had Shadrach, Meshach, and Abednego thrown into the fiery furnace for not worshipping his false idol. The king looked into the fire and said, "I see four men in the fire and none of them have been affected in the least. And the fourth man looks like the Son of God." The king ordered, "You men, who serve the most-high God, come out of the furnace," and the three men came out unscathed.
- 2 CO 4:8–10, 16–17 ~ Paul wrote: We are surrounded by troubles, yet we are not distressed; we are perplexed, but we are not in despair. We are persecuted, but not forsaken; beaten down, but not destroyed. We always carry in our bodies the death of Jesus Christ, so that His life will be revealed in our bodies. Therefore, we never give up, though outwardly we are worn down; yet inwardly we are renewed day after day. Our insignificant and temporary problems bring us closer to the eternal glory, and that glory far outweighs the sum of all our troubles combined.
- 2 CO 12:10 ~ Yes, I take pleasure in infirmity, reproach, necessity, persecution, and distress for Christ's sake, for in my weakness I am made strong.
- HEB 11:32–40 ~ What more can I say about the powers of faith? I could tell you about great judges like Gideon, Barrack, Samson, and Japhtheh, and about great kings like David and Solomon, and about the great prophets. Through faith, these people subdued kingdoms, administered justice, enforced treaties, shut the mouth of lions, quenched fires, and escaped certain death. They were weak but were made strong, and they fought valiantly in battle, routing even the greatest of armies. They raised the dead. They endured torture, refusing to renounce God as a condition for their release. They were mocked, beaten, chained, and imprisoned. They were stoned and beheaded. They wandered the wilderness in shaggy clothes, destitute, tormented, and afflicted. Although their life on earth was full of strife, they awaited their deliverance, as we also must do until God makes us perfect before Him.

Father in heaven and Lord of the universe, your might is unmatched, as is your love for us. We thank you for those who make the ultimate sacrifice to save others; surely, they are examples of your Son Jesus, who made the ultimate sacrifice to save the world. Help us to be living sacrifices for Him who died and rose again so that we could be made whole and live forever in your heavenly realm. Remind us to turn to you in time of trouble, to be courageous with your strength, to face the enemy without fear knowing that you are there beside us. Do not allow the enemy to overtake us, but help us to overcome, even as Christ has overcome the world on our behalf. In His name we pray this prayer, Amen.

March 19

Vernal Equinox varies from year to year, and differs depending on which hemisphere you are in. It occurs in the northern hemisphere around March 19–21, marking the beginning of spring. Those in the southern hemisphere will be experiencing the autumnal equinox. Calendars have been based on equinoxes and solstices since ancient times making them very accurate. Monuments were built; namely, Egyptian and Mayan pyramids, and Stonehenge, marking these periods with respect to the angle of the sun, when the poles are virtually equidistant from the sun. The sun will be perpendicular to earth's equator during the equinoxes, a time when the amount of day and night are relatively equal. Very little has changed in calendars except minute recalibrations. Our Gregorian calendar is accurate to about 3000 years, much better than the lunar calendar which is useful for other purposes such as determining Passover and Easter. Easter is designated the first Sunday following the first full moon after the vernal equinox.

Equinox means equal night, referring to the daylight and the nighttime being the same length of time, or approximately twelve hours. Naturally, the amount of light was important to the ancients since most people worked when there was daylight (JOH 9:4). The early harvest would occur after the onset of spring rains, and the late harvest would likewise occur after the fall rains. Pivotal events for Israel occurred around the early harvest of barley and flax; those days led to Passover, a sacred time for the Jews, and for Christians, for Passover was being celebrated the day Christ, the Lamb of God, was sacrificed on the cross. Christ arose from the dead the first Easter Sunday, which coincided with the Jewish Feast of First Fruits.

- EXO 9:23–32 ~ Moses sent a plague of hail and fire upon Egypt so Pharaoh relented, but Moses knew he would renege. The barley and flax were destroyed, except in the land of Goshen where the Israelites were spared the hail. [This was the seventh plague; Passover corresponded with the tenth plague.]

- EXO 23:15–16, 19 ~ You must keep the feast of unleavened bread (eating it for seven days) as I commanded you in the time appointed (month of Abib) for that was when you came out of Egypt. At the feast of harvest and the early gathering of the first fruits of your yield, as well as the one occurring at the end of the year, return from the fields with the best of your harvests which shall be offered to the Lord. [First Fruits is a feast celebrated during the week of Unleavened Bread which follows Passover.]

- LEV 23:10–11 ~ Tell the Israelites, when you enter the land that I am giving to you and reap your first harvest, bring to the priest a sheaf of your finest grain. On the day after the Sabbath, the priest will wave the sheaf of the grain offering before the Lord and He will accept it on your behalf.

- JOS 2:1–6 ~ Joshua sent spies to Jericho, and they were hidden in the abode of Rahab, a prostitute. She told the men to climb onto her roof where she had laid stalks of flax. Officials showed up at her door asking for the men, and she told them they already had fled the city (see JAM 2:25). [Note that Rahab was spared the destruction of Jericho, married a man from the tribe of Judah, and became an ancestor of Joseph and Mary.]

- RUT 1:11–18, 22 ~ Naomi (who had lost two sons, both married to Moabite women) said, "Turn back my daughters-in-law, why should you follow me? I will never marry again or bear more sons to marry; besides you should not have to wait to remarry. It grieves me tremendously for your sakes how the hand of the Lord took my two sons, your husbands." The widows wept. Then Orpah kissed her mother-in-law goodbye and departed. But Ruth held onto Naomi who suggested, "Your sister-in-law has returned to her people and their gods; you should go with her." Ruth replied, "Please do not ask me to leave, for I would rather follow you, and go where you go and live where you live. Your people will be my people and your God my God. Where you die, I will die and be buried with you." When Naomi saw that Ruth was determined, she kept quiet. Naomi and Ruth (the Moabitess) went to Bethlehem together, arriving at the beginning of the barley harvest. [Note that Ruth would marry Boaz, and become an ancestor of Joseph and Mary.]

- 2 CH 31:5 ~ Everyone brought in abundance the first fruits of their crops, wine, oil, honey, and all their profits.

- JER 5:23 ~ This people have a revolting and rebellious heart. They do not say in their heart, "Let us fear the Lord our God who gives rain in the former and in the latter seasons, wherein He has appointed us weeks of harvest."

- 1 CO 15:20, 23 ~ Now is Christ raised from the dead, becoming the first fruits of those who have died. The next to be raised will be Christ's own, when He returns.

- 1 CO 16:1 ~ On the first day of each week everyone should set aside something for the Lord in accordance with the degree to which they have prospered by His grace, so it will not be necessary to take a collection.

- COL 1:18 ~ Christ is the head of the body which is the church. He is the beginning and the firstborn of the dead, so that in all things He might reign supreme.

- JAM 5:7–8 ~ Brothers, wait patiently for the coming of the Lord, like the farmer who must patiently await the rain and the harvest. Be patient and take courage, for His coming is near.

Apparently, the events occurring between the start of spring and the first Easter Sunday are crucial for establishing the connection between the Old and New Testaments. The Passover and subsequent freeing of the Israelites from Egyptian bondage concurs with the crucifixion of Christ, who frees us from the bondage of sin. The offering of first fruits reflects the resurrection of Christ, the first fruits of God. It also represents the resurrection of humankind on the last day, during which Christ will bring his first fruits, the saints, into heaven and present them before God. Note that during the days of early harvest two important ancestors of Christ were mentioned, both foreign women who converted to Judaism: Rahab and Ruth.

- EPH 1:9–11 ~ He made known to us the mystery of His will according to His good pleasure, which He purposed in Christ to be put into effect when the times reached their fulfillment, thereby bringing all things in heaven and on earth together under one head who is Christ. In Him we were chosen, being predestined according to His plan, ensuring that everything conforms to His purpose and will.

Our Father, who has unveiled many mysteries in His Word so that we may understand your plan and be convinced in our hearts that your words are true, let this knowledge fuel our faith so that we never doubt you again. Let this revelation encourage us to delve into your words of truth more often and more deeply, increasing in us greater insight into you, Father, Son, and Holy Spirit, and how everything relates to our eternal salvation. We are weak and uncertain in this world of pain and inhumanity, where the only certainty we can be sure of is your unconditional love and our resurrection, after which we will receive glorified bodies that will never die. Help us to hold fast to these truths and our hope, and carry them through to the end; knowing that this earth and its sin will pass, but your words will never pass away, and neither will we. In the name of your Son, our Lord and Savior and the Passover Lamb, we pray, Amen.

March 20

International Day of Happiness was part of an initiative passed by the United Nations to develop a "balanced approach" for promoting economic growth, fighting poverty, and restoring equality, ultimately leading to happiness and wellness for disadvantaged people. A UN resolution encouraged participation in schools, businesses, and government to occur on this date every year to create dialogue on these issues, and to foster happiness building. The first observance of this day of happiness was in 2013.

Pursuit of happiness happens to be an unalienable right granted by God and listed in the Declaration of Independence. This right needs to be promoted worldwide more often than one day a year. Yet there are numerous places in the world where this God-given right is still denied. No government has the right to take away a right granted by God; at times, our own government has tried, however. Beware when basic rights are being disallowed, for this leads to suppression, subjection, and tyranny. Hopefully, the UN can use its influence in the world to bring human rights and moral values to the forefront. But we must remember that without God, there would be no right to pursue happiness.

Note that happiness must be pursued; we do not have a right to be happy. Happiness doesn't grow on trees, does it? It will not be found everywhere, and sometimes there is nothing you can do about it. But happiness is contagious, and it is facilitated by keeping a smile on your face. Certainly, helping people out of poverty, tyranny, and slavery is a good cause, and that might be something to consider as you ponder what you can do today to support happiness around the world. You also could make it your mission to cheer people up today and spread the happiness, simply by being cheerful, friendly, and kind.

- JOB 36:11–12 ~ If they obey and serve God, they will spend their days in prosperity, and their years in pleasure. But if they do not obey, they will perish by the sword, and they will die without knowledge.

- PSA 5:11 ~ Let everyone who trusts in the Lord rejoice and shout for joy, because He will defend them. Let all who love the Lord be joyful.

- PSA 34:14 ~ Depart from evil and do good; seek peace and pursue it.

- PSA 95:2 ~ Let us go before God with thanksgiving; make a joyful noise to Him with singing.

- ECC 2:26 ~ The man who pleases God will receive wisdom, knowledge, and happiness. But to the sinner God gives the task of gathering wealth, only to hand it over to the one who pleases God. That too is vanity, a vexation of spirit.

- LUK 6:22–23 ~ Jesus said, "Blessed be those who are hated and cast out for my sake. Rejoice in that day and leap for joy for your reward in heaven will be great."

- JOH 16:20–22, 33 ~ Jesus said to the apostles, "I tell you the truth, you will weep and lament but the world will rejoice. You will be sorrowful but your sorrow will turn to joy, just like when a mother in labor groans; but when her child is born her pain is replaced with happiness. I will see you again and your heart will rejoice; and nobody will ever take that joy away from you. I have told you that I will bring you peace. In the world you will have tribulation; but be happy because I have overcome the world."

- PHP 4:6–7 ~ Do not have anxiety about anything, but pray for everything. With thanksgiving let your requests be known to God. And the peace of God that surpasses all understanding will keep your heart in mind in Jesus Christ.

- 1 PE 4:13 ~ Rejoice when you are partakers of Christ's sufferings; for when His glory is revealed, you will be glad and exceedingly joyful. You will be happy for being rejected by men because you know Christ, whose Spirit rests upon you.

  In heaven you will have every right to be happy. In fact, all sorrow, tears, and pain will be extinguished. Instead, there will be celebration, singing, joyfulness, praise, and thanksgiving to our Lord, the creator of all people and all things. There is nothing on this planet to compare, because it will better than anything found here or even imagined. Try to imagine the best heaven possible, and the reality is that it will be magnitudes better than your wildest dreams.

- PSA 37:9–11 ~ Evil people will be cut off, but those who wait on the Lord will inherit the earth. In a little while the wicked will cease to be; you will search for them but they will not be found. The meek will inherit the earth and will find joy and peace in abundance.

- ISA 35:10 ~ The ransomed of the Lord will return and come to Zion with songs and everlasting joy; sorrow and sighing will be gone forever.

- ISA 51:2 ~ The Lord will comfort Zion and her wasted places. The wilderness will become like Eden; joy, gladness, thanksgiving, and singing will be found there.

- ISA 64:4 ~ Since the world began, nobody has heard, seen, or perceived, except God, the wonderful things He has prepared for those who wait for Him (quoted by Paul in 1 CO 2:9).

- ISA 65:17–19 ~ I will create new heavens and a new earth; the former heavens and earth will never be remembered or recalled. You will be glad and rejoice forever, for I will make Jerusalem a place of happiness. I will rejoice in Jerusalem for I will be happy with my people, and there will nevermore be the sound of crying among my people.

- JOE 2:32 ~ Whoever calls upon the name of the Lord will be gathered and delivered to live in mount Zion and Jerusalem.

- ZEC 8:3, 5–8 ~ I will return to Zion and I will live in Jerusalem; and Jerusalem will be called the city of truth and Zion will be called the holy mountain. Children will be playing in the streets. It will be marvelous for my people and also for me. I will save my people from the corners of the earth and bring them to Jerusalem. They will be my people and I will be their God, in truth and in righteousness.

- HEB 12:22 ~ You will come to mount Zion, and to the city of the living God, the heavenly Jerusalem, and to the innumerable company of angels.

- 2 PE 3:13 ~ We, according to God's promise, look for new heavens and a new earth, wherein dwells righteousness.

- REV 21:1–4 ~ John saw a new heaven and a new earth, for the old heaven and earth had passed away; and there was no sea. I saw the holy city of Jerusalem coming down out of heaven from God, prepared as a beautiful bride dressed for her husband. A loud voice came from the throne saying, "Look, God's dwelling place is now among the people and He will live with them. He will wipe away every tear from their eyes. There will be no more death, mourning, crying, or pain, for the old order of things will pass away."

  Father in heaven, we long to be with you in your kingdom, where there will be constant joy and happiness. Though we have to endure trials and tribulations on earth, we always will have joy in our hearts knowing that the current situation is temporal but the glory of your kingdom is eternal. Thank you, Lord, for this magnificent promise; help us to cling to that peace which surpasses all understanding found through Christ the Lord in whose name we pray, Amen.

March 21

World Poetry Day was established in Paris (1999) by the United Nations Educational, Scientific, and Cultural Organization (UNESCO). One of the objectives of UNESCO is to expand literacy worldwide, by providing education to improve reading and writing skills in impoverished parts of the world. Certain cities are designated World Book Capital or Creative Cities of Literature, where literacy initiatives will be extended within and beyond their borders. Poetry has been around since Adam; it's a creative way of speaking or writing. There is a great deal of poetry in the Bible which we sing in hymns and psalms. Poetry is a beautiful means of expressing thoughts through language, making the message more discernable and uplifting. Today we celebrate poetry, poets, songwriters, and any other form of creative speech, all of which stimulate other forms of artistic expression such as drawing, dance, drama, and music. Unlike everyday matter-of-fact interactions, there is an emotional component to poetry which adds emphasis or value to the words, as well as stimulating imagery and improving retention. Celebrate poetry today by sharing with your family and friends, attending or sponsoring a workshop, or scheduling a reading. Schools can have classroom activities in reading, reciting, composing, and discussing poems, which will stimulate interest and interaction. This is the point: to improve interpersonal communications through creative and imaginative discourse.

In olden days, the news was mostly transmitted orally, due to widespread illiteracy, not to mention the vast number of languages. Sometimes a minstrel would travel from town to town, singing and playing an instrument to convey an experience, message, or mood. The more pleasant the delivery, the more likely that the target audience will get the gist and remember.

- 1 CH 16:1–43 ~ Give thanks to the Lord; call upon His name. Make known His wondrous deeds; sing praises to Him and rejoice. Continuously seek the Lord with all your strength. Remember the great things He has done. Sing to the Lord all the earth; tell others about His salvation. Declare His glory to the nations. For great is the Lord and greatly to be praised. He is held in awe above all gods. Give the Lord His due glory, with praise and offerings. Worship the Lord in holy array; tremble before Him. Let the heavens be glad and the earth rejoice; let everyone say, "The Lord reigns." Give thanks to the Lord for He is good and His steadfast love endures forever. Ask God to deliver, gather, and save you, so that you may give eternal thanks and glory to Him. Blessed be the Lord from everlasting to everlasting.

- PSA 95:1–3; PSA 98:1 ~ Let us sing to the Lord, the rock of our salvation. Let us come before Him with thanks, praise, and psalms. For He is a great God, and a great King above all gods. Sing to the Lord a new song, for He has done marvelous things. The right hand of His holy arm has won for Him the victory.

- ACT 17:28 ~ In God we live, move, and have our being, as many of your poets have said, for we are also His offspring.

- COL 3:15–17 ~ Let the peace of God rule in your hearts, since as members of one body you were called to peace. Be therefore, thankful. Let the Word of Christ live in you richly as you teach and admonish one another with wisdom, and as you sing psalms, hymns, and spiritual songs with gratitude in your hearts to God. Remember what Christ taught you and let His words enrich your lives and make you wise. Teach His words to each other. Sing them openly and spiritually in psalms and hymns with thankful hearts. Whatever you do or say, do it in Jesus's name, and give thanks to God in Jesus's name.

- HEB 13:15 ~ Let us continually offer to God the sacrifice of praise; praise and thanks are the fruit of our lips.

- REV 15:3–4 ~ They were singing the song of God's servant Moses, the song of the Lamb. "Great and marvelous are your works, Lord God Almighty; fair and true are your ways, King of saints. Who does not fear you and glorify your name, Lord? For only you are holy, and all nations will come and worship before your throne while your judgments are pronounced."

Poets in the Bible include Moses, Job, David, Solomon, Isaiah, and Jeremiah. Musicians put melodies to some of their writings; many passages of the Bible are sung during worship. In particular, Psalms are songs written by David and others; David himself sang his songs while playing the lute. Early church fathers were musicians and poets like many current church leaders.

- EXO 15:10–11 ~ Moses led the people in a song of praise after safety crossing the Red Sea. "You blew the wind, and the sea covered them as they sank to the bottom as lead. Who is like you, oh Lord, majestic in holiness, awesome in glory, who works such great wonders?"
- 2 SA 22:1–3 ~ David sang, "The Lord is my rock, my fortress, and my deliverer. In Him I place my trust. He is my shield, the horn of my salvation, my high tower, my refuge, and my Savior. He saves me from violence."
- PSA 23:1–6 ~ The Lord is my Shepherd; He provides everything I need. He lets me graze in green pastures beside still waters. He restores my soul. He leads me in paths of righteousness for His namesake. Even when I walk through the valley of the shadow of death, I will fear no evil; His rod and staff protect and comfort me. He prepares a table before me in the presence of my enemies. He anoints my head with oil; my cup overflows. Surely goodness and mercy will follow me all of my days, and I will live in the house of the Lord forever.
- PSA 51:10–12 ~ Create in me a clean heart, Lord, and renew an upright spirit within me. Do not remove me from your presence and do not take your Holy Spirit from me. Restore to me the joy of your salvation, and uphold me with your free Spirit.
- ECC 3:1–8 ~ For everything there is a season, and a time to every purpose under heaven. A time to be born and a time to die; a time to plant and a time to uproot. A time to kill and a time to heal; a time to tear down and a time to build up. A time to weep and a time to laugh; a time to mourn and a time to dance. A time to toss away stones and a time to gather stones; a time to embrace and a time to refrain from embracing. A time to gain and a time to lose; a time to keep and a time to throw away. A time to rend and a time to sew; a time to keep silent and a time to speak. A time to love and a time to hate; a time of war and a time of peace.
- ISA 12:2–5 ~ God is my salvation; in Him I trust. I am not afraid for He is my strength and my song. With joy, the righteous draw water from the well of His salvation. Give thanks to the Lord; call upon His name. Make His name known among the nations; declare all He has done and proclaim how His name is exalted. Sing to the Lord, for He has done marvelous things; let everyone in the world know that He alone is God.
- LAM 3:21–23, 32–33 ~ When I think of my sorrows, it brings my soul down. If I am down, I remember that I will always have hope. Because of the Lord's great love, we are not consumed and His kindnesses never fail; they are new every morning. Great is His faithfulness. Though He allows grief He shows compassion, because great is His unfailing love. For God does not deliberately bring affliction or grief upon the children of men.

Thank you, heavenly Father, that we can praise you in song and with poetry. Help us to appreciate the art of writing and learn how to communicate effectively in speech and in writing. Help us to reinforce these skills in our children. Let us sing songs of praise together in worship and in our daily living. Let us to be more creative, and make up our own songs or hymns as we praise and glorify you, your Holy Spirit, and your Son Jesus, in whose name we pray, Amen.

March 22

World Water Day is a United Nations observance initiated in 1993. The primary source of drinking water resides underground, which is arguably the most precious resource known to humankind. Sadly, billions of people in the world do not have clean drinking water. This UN initiative was to help people extract clean water for drinking, irrigating, washing, and disposing of sewage in an environmentally sound manner. Groundwater settles into the fissures and caverns of the earth and into bodies of water, providing sustenance for people and other inhabitants of earth. These sources of water must be identified, preserved, protected, managed, sanitized, and conserved so they do not become polluted or run dry; this is particularly necessary as the population of the planet increases. Many infectious diseases come from water that is not potable due to contamination by chemicals, sewage, and flooding. The UN provides information and training about these objectives, particularly through their office and website: UN Water. This day can be celebrated by attending events or supporting proposals related to water conservation, by researching water maintenance projects, watching documentaries disseminated through the UN or institutions of higher learning, or participating in related classroom activities at school.

In developed nations we tend to take water for granted, and end up wasting much of it. In other parts of the world people are dying from lack of potable water, overpopulation, and water-borne diseases. Further, third world governments profit from water, yet they leak toxic chemicals into waterways, destroy wetlands and rain forests, and/or fail to invest in proper infrastructure.

- PSA 42:1 ~ As the deer pants for streams of water, so my soul pants after you, oh God.
- PRO 30:15–16 ~ There are four things that are never satisfied: the grave, the barren womb, the dry earth which thirsts for water, and fire that is unquenched.
- ISA 48:21 ~ They did not thirst while Moses led them across the desert, for Moses struck the rock and God caused water to come gushing out.
- JOE 3:18 ~ The mountains will flow with wine and the hills will flow with milk. The valleys will flow with water from a fountain in the center of the Lord's house.
- JOH 3:5–6 ~ Jesus answered Nicodemus, "I tell you the truth, unless a man is born of water and of the Spirit he cannot enter into the kingdom of heaven. That which is born of the flesh is flesh; and that which is born of the Spirit is spirit."

Water is necessary for life, everyone knows this. There is enough water to sustain life, as long as everyone participates in preserving and safeguarding it (see REV 8:7–12). There also is a special kind of water necessary for eternal life, and that living water comes from God.

- ISA 58:11 ~ The Lord will guide you continuously. He will satisfy your soul when it thirsts and He will put meat on your bones. You will be like a watered garden, and like a wellspring where the waters never fail.
- EZE 47:1–9, 12–13, 22 ~ God brought me to His house, and I saw waters flowing from the temple on either side. We waded out one thousand cubits; the water was ankle deep. After another thousand cubits it was to the knees; another thousand cubits it was to the waist. After another thousand it was deep enough to swim under. And the river went on and on, becoming a river I could not cross. Everything the water touched flourished, healing the desert and the sea. On both sides of the river grew different kinds of trees that never died, producing new fruit every month; the fruit provided food and the leaves provided medicine. God said the river bordered the land promised to the twelve tribes of Israel; it would be divided as an inheritance for God's chosen people and the strangers who lived among them.

- JOH 4:14 ~ Jesus said, "Whoever drinks the water I give them will never be thirsty again; it will be a well of water that springs up into everlasting life."
- ACT 11:15–16 ~ While Peter was speaking, the Holy Spirit came upon them, just as it came upon the apostles when their ministry began. And Peter remembered the words of Jesus when He said, "John indeed baptized with water, but you will be baptized with the Holy Spirit."
- 1 CO 12:13 ~ By one Spirit we are baptized into one body, whether Jews or Gentiles, bond or free; because we all have received water from the one true Spirit.
- 1 JO 5:4–8 ~ Whoever is born of God overcomes the world; the victory that overcomes the world is found in faith. Jesus Christ overcame the world; anyone believing in Him will also overcome the world. Christ is He who came by water and blood. The Holy Spirit is He who bears witness, because the Spirit speaks the truth. There are three who bear witness in heaven: the Father, the Word, and the Holy Spirit; these three are one. There are three who bear witness on the earth: the Spirit, the water, and the blood; and these three agree as one.
- REV 7:15–17 ~ They will live before the throne of God and serve Him day and night in the temple. They will never be hungry, thirsty, hot or cold again. The Lamb among them will feed them, will lead them to fountains of living waters, and will remove all sorrow.
- REV 22:1–2, 14, 17 ~ The Lord showed John a pure river of the water of life, crystal clear, proceeding from the throne of God and the Lamb. In the middle and on either side was the Tree of Life. It bore twelve kinds of fruit each month, and its leaves provided healing power to all nations. Blessed be those who keep God's commandments, so that they can receive the right to the Tree of Life, and to enter into the gates of heaven. And the Spirit and Christ will say, "Those who thirst may come in and freely drink the water of life."

Living water is given to all who trust in God for everything. One way to publicly demonstrate that commitment is through participation in baptism. Baptism provides forgiveness of sins through the water, which represents a spiritual washing by the Spirit, the Word of God.

- MAT 3:2, 11 ~ John preached, "Repent, for the kingdom of heaven is at hand. I baptize with water unto repentance. But One comes after me who is mightier than I, and whose shoes I am not worthy to carry. He will baptize with the Holy Spirit, and with fire."
- JOH 1:33 ~ The One who sent me to baptize with water said, "Upon whom you see the Spirit of God descending and remaining on Him, the same is He that baptizes with the Holy Spirit."
- ACT 1:4–5 ~ Jesus assembled the disciples together, commanding them not to depart from Jerusalem, but to wait for the promise of the Father: "For John truly baptized with water; but you will be baptized with the Holy Spirit several days from now."
- ACT 8:35–38 ~ Philip read the scripture which the eunuch had asked about, and preached to him how Jesus fulfilled that scripture. As they journeyed along the way, they came upon a certain body of water, and the eunuch asked, "See, here is water; what is stopping me from being baptized right here and now?" Philip replied, "If you believe with all your heart, you can be baptized." The eunuch answered, "I believe that Jesus Christ is the Son of God." Then he halted the chariot, and the two men went down into the water; and Philip baptized him.
- EPH 5:26 ~ Jesus gave Himself for His people to sanctify them through the washing of water by the Word.

Father God, thank you for giving us clean water and let us help those who do not have clean water. We especially thank you for the right to drink the water of life through Jesus, Amen.

March 23

Feast of Lots, called *Purim* in Hebrew, occurs on Adar 14 of the Jewish calendar. It is a commemoration of God sparing the Jews who were destined for extermination at the hand of a Persian king's advisor. You will find the account in the book of Esther, who became queen to Xerxes (aka Ahasuerus) during a critical era of history, after Babylon had fallen to the Medes and Persians. The Persian king banished his wife Vashti for disobeying a direct command, and sought a new queen who was young and beautiful. His servants discovered Esther (aka Hadassah) and brought her and several other maidens to the palace. She had been raised by Mordecai, a cousin, after her parents died. The king fell in love with her the moment he saw her. Haman, the king's right-hand man, plotted to eradicate all Jews from the land, which had been displaced when taken captive by Babylonian king Nebuchadnezzar. Haman especially despised Mordecai because he would not bow to Haman. Mordecai was favored by the king for previously alerting him to a conspiracy. Haman tricked the king into issuing a decree to rid the land of the Jews, not knowing that the king himself was married to a Jewess. Esther consulted Mordecai, and they developed a strategy. This involved a series of banquets during which the queen would honor the king, and endear him to her. On the third such banquet she informed Xerxes of Haman's evil plot and how the people he plotted to destroy were her people. Xerxes had Haman hanged on the gallows he built to execute Mordecai, and Mordecai replaced Haman as the king's second-in-command. Thus, the Jews were saved once again by an act of God. Why do they call it the feast of "lots"? Because Haman took a gamble (cast his lots) on promoting himself and increasing his power, at the expense of innocent Jews who had settled the land not by choice. What is an important takeaway from this story? Never bet against God.

- EST 2:1–23 ~ After the king got mad at the queen (Vashti) and evicted her, he was remembering her and his decree, and was feeling depressed. His ministers suggested that fair young virgins be brought to the king to select a replacement for Vashti. The king appointed officers in every province to gather lovely ladies and bring them to the keeper of the women. The king would select from among them the one who pleased him the most. Esther caught his eye immediately and he monitored her progress during the lengthy purification process. The king loved Esther above them all so Xerxes made her his queen. But two of the gate guards were angry about this and plotted together to assassinate the king. Mordecai found out and reported this to Esther, who told the king what Mordecai had uncovered. Discovering the information to be true, the king honored Mordecai and had the conspirators impaled on poles.

- EST 4:10–17 ~ Esther sent a message to Mordecai explaining how no man or woman was permitted to enter the king's throne room unannounced, at the penalty of death. Only when the king raised his scepter was a person permitted to enter, and she had not been called by the king for thirty days. Mordecai sent word to Esther: Do you think you will escape the evil decree because you live in the king's house? If you hold your peace at this time, then the deliverance of the Jews will fall upon another, but you and your father's house will be destroyed. And who knows, maybe you have become a royal member of the kingdom for such a time as this? She replied to Mordecai asking for the Jews to pray and fast for three days, as she and her attendants would also fast, and then she would risk her life and go to the king though it was against the law. And Mordecai approved of this plan.

- EST 8:7–14 ~ Xerxes told Mordecai and Esther that the Jews would acquire the entire estate of Haman, whom he executed along with his family. He appointed Mordecai to prepare another decree to overturn the evil decree of Haman; the decree was sent to all the provinces of the kingdom from India to Ethiopia, and in all the languages of the people. The edict granted the Jews freedom to assemble, to protect themselves, and to retaliate against anyone who attacked them, including their wives and children, and as payment acquire the property of their assailants. This edict was issued by King Xerxes on Adar 13. When Mordecai left the king's palace, he was wearing royal attire of blue and white, a purple robe, and a crown of gold. All the Jews in Susa celebrated, with feasting, joyfulness, and honor. And many others converted to Judaism for fear of the Jews.

Haman gambled and lost; he exalted himself, while Esther the queen humbled herself. This historical event typifies Jesus Christ, who humbled Himself in service to others, and who is exalted above all people. It also reflects the self-exaltation of the enemy, Satan, and the fate he can expect, as well as others who place themselves and their desires above God.

- ISA 14:12–15 ~ You have fallen from heaven and have been cut down to the ground, Lucifer, who brought down the nations. For you deceived yourself expecting to be exalted, even above God. Instead, you will be brought down into the depths of hell.

- EZE 21:26–27 ~ The Sovereign Lord says: Remove the diadem and take off the crown. Nothing will be the same as before: the lowly will be exalted and the exalted will be brought down. I will ruin, ruin, yes ruin it all; and it will not be restored until He comes to whom it rightfully belongs, and I will give it all to Him.

- EZE 28:14–19 ~ You were the anointed cherub; you lived upon the holy mountain of God. You were perfect from the day you were created until evil was found in you. Your great wealth made you violent inside and you became sinful. Therefore, you were thrown off the holy mountain, and you will be destroyed. You exalted yourself because of your beauty, thereby corrupting yourself. You defiled the sanctuaries with your abominations. You will be destroyed by the fire within you, and your terrible deeds will come to an end.

- LUK 14:7–11 ~ Jesus told a parable addressing people who sought the best seats in the house. When you are invited to a formal affair like a wedding, do not choose the seat of highest honor, for that seat may be reserved for someone more important than you. It will be embarrassing when you are asked to move to a seat of lesser honor. Instead, sit at the seat of lowest honor; if a seat of higher honor has been reserved for you, you will be shown respect by being asked to move to a seat of higher honor. The moral of the story is this: Those who exalt themselves will be humbled and those who humble themselves will be exalted.

- LUK 18:9–14 ~ Jesus told the parable of the Pharisee and the publican. Two men went to the temple to pray: a Pharisee and a publican. The Pharisee said, "Thank you Lord that I am not a sinner like other men, such as that tax collector, because I give tithes and I fast twice a week." The publican bowed low before the altar and beat on his breast saying, "God be merciful to me a sinner." Only the publican returned home justified by God. Those who exalt themselves will later be humbled, and those who humble themselves will later be exalted.

- PHP 2:5–11 ~ Jesus Christ, though equal with God, took upon Himself the nature of man, becoming a humble servant. He was obedient unto death, even a humiliating death on a cross. God has therefore exalted Him to the highest position and given Him a name that is above every other name, so that every knee should bow, whether in heaven, on earth, or under the earth, and every tongue confess that Jesus Christ is Lord to the glory of God the Father.

Glorious Father, your divine providence is apparent throughout the Bible and throughout the history of our nation. We thank you for continuously helping us, and protecting your people from enemies that would destroy us. Please remind us daily that you are in charge, and we are not; let us be humble before others and never exalt ourselves, keeping you always in the highest position of honor in our lives, in our nation, and for all time. In Jesus's name we pray, Amen.

March 24

Palm Sunday is the theme today; this Sunday service occurs exactly seven days before Easter. Palm Sunday commemorates Christ's triumphant entrance into Jerusalem, humbly riding on a young donkey that had never been ridden, as onlookers dropped palm fronds in the path and sang, "Hosannah to the son of David." The event was foretold in multiple places in the Holy Bible. Jesus knew that this would be the week of His passion, with the first Holy Communion occurring midweek, His crucifixion the day after that, and His resurrection three days later on Easter Sunday. Like the Jews, Christians observe eight days of Holy Week, including two holy convocations (worship services) in addition to the weekly service or sabbath.

- LEV 23:5–8 ~ On the fourteenth day of the first month is the Lord's Passover. On the fifteenth day will begin the Feast of Unleavened Bread lasting seven days; the first day will be a holy convocation so do not work. Present offerings by fire each day; the eighth day will be another holy convocation [These are the eight days referred to as Holy Week. Note that the Feast of Tabernacles has a similar format, beginning with a high Sabbath and ending that way; it occurs six months later.]

- PSA 118:26–27 ~ Blessed is He that comes in the name of the Lord; we have blessed you out of the house of the Lord. God is Lord who has used His light to tie the sacrifice to the altar.

- ZEC 9:9–10 ~ Rejoice, for here comes your righteous king riding on a donkey's colt. He will bring peace to all nations.

- MAT 21:1–9; MAR 11:1–10; LUK 19:29–38 ~ They were nearing Jerusalem when Jesus asked two of His disciples to go into the nearby village and find a donkey tied next to her colt. "Unloose them and bring them here, and if anyone questions you tell them the Lord needs them, and he will send them right away." This was done to fulfill the prophecy: daughter of Zion, behold your King comes sitting upon the foal of a donkey. They brought the donkey and her colt, and put their garments on the colt for Jesus to sit upon. As He entered Jerusalem, a great multitude spread their garments and branches from palm trees in His path. They went before Him chanting, "Hosanna to the son of David. Blessed is He who comes in the name of the Lord, Hosanna in the highest."

- JOH 12:12–16 ~ The next day people were gathering for the feast when they heard Jesus was coming. They took palm branches and went to greet Him shouting, Hosanna: Blessed is the King of Israel that comes in the name of the Lord. Jesus sat upon a young donkey as it was written: Fear not, daughter of Zion, behold your King comes riding on a donkey's colt. At first, the disciples did not understand the significance of this event, but when Jesus was glorified, they remembered how all these things were prophesied that happened to Him.

- REV 7:9–10, 13–14 ~ I saw a giant multitude, too many people even to count; there were people from every nation, race, and tongue standing before the throne and the Lamb who was clothed in white. They held palm branches and sang, "Salvation to our God who sits on the throne, and to the Lamb." One of the elders asked me who these people were. I replied, "Tell me sir." He said, "These are the ones who came from great tribulation; they have washed their robes and made them white with the blood of the Lamb."

Thank you, merciful Father, for sending your Son Jesus, an example of humbleness and courage for all people; help us, therefore, to follow His example of humbleness and courage as we bring the good news to others. Thank you for making His coming clear in the Old Testament, proving that Jesus is the Christ revealed in the New Testament. Both testaments proclaim His coming and the salvation He brought with Him. Let us proclaim Christ in whom we pray, Amen.

March 25

Feast of the Annunciation commemorates the announcement to Mary by the angel Gabriel that she would give birth to the Messiah of God. The Old Testament has over three hundred passages prophesying the coming of Messiah, providing an enormous amount of detail and leaving no question that Jesus is the Messiah. God came to earth as a human being to show the world who He is and how we can be saved through His Son. Celebrate this day with your family and explain its significance to your children. You may want to decorate the dinner table with red carnations and a special candle to be lit as you gather together to study God's Word and discuss this sacred occasion. A children's Bible with pictures helps to leave a lasting impression of family time together, along with photographs. Some churches (especially Catholic) may have a special service on this day. The date is arbitrary, likely selected because it is exactly nine months until the traditional celebration of Christmas, nine months being the normal gestation of a fetus.

- GEN 17:2, 7 ~ God said to Abraham: Walk in righteousness and be blameless and I will make a covenant with you. I will multiply you exceedingly, and the everlasting covenant will be with your descendants from generation to generation.

- GEN 49:10 ~ The royal scepter will not depart from Judah until the One to whom it belongs comes, who all people will obey (Joseph and Mary were descendants of Judah.)

- NUM 24:17 ~ I shall send Him, but not now. A star will rise out of Jacob (Israel), a ruler to strike down Moab and the children of Seth. (Joseph and Mary were descendants of Jacob.)

- 1 KI 1:4 ~ The king knew her not (refers to the fact that King David never had sex with the concubine that kept him warm and ministered to him in his old age). [This verse points to the fact that Joseph did not have sex with Mary until after Jesus was born (see MAT 1:24–25).]

- ISA 7:14 ~ God Himself will provide the sign: A virgin shall conceive and bear a son. His name will be called "God with us."

- ISA 11:1–2, 10 ~ From the lineage of Jesse will come a branch who will possess the spirit of wisdom, understanding, knowledge, counsel and might, and the fear of God. Jesse's root will become the symbol of God's people, including the Gentiles. (Joseph and Mary were descendants of Jesse.)

- ISA 40:3 ~ The one crying in the wilderness will prepare the way for the Lord; he will clear a straight path in the desert to be a highway for our God. [John the Baptist, son of Zachariah, and Jesus's first cousin, was that messenger (LUK 1:17).]

- MAT 1:20–25 ~ The angel of the Lord appeared to Joseph in a dream saying, "Joseph, son of David, do not be afraid to take Mary as your wife, for that which she has conceived in her is from the Holy Spirit. She will give birth to a Son and you will name Him Jesus because He will save His people from their sins." This took place to fulfill the prophecy. Behold a virgin will become pregnant and give birth to a Son, and He will be called Emmanuel, which means "God with us" (ISA 7:14). Then Joseph awoke from his sleep and did as the angel said, and married Mary. But he knew her not until after she had brought forth her firstborn child and named Him Jesus.

- LUK 1:1–20 ~ In the days of Herod, king of Judea, was a priest named Zachariah; his wife was named Elisabeth. They were righteous people, but had no children and were advanced in years. It was Zachariah's turn to burn incense in the temple, as many people had gathered outside to pray. Suddenly an angel appeared at the right side of the altar and Zechariah was afraid. The angel said to him, "Do not be afraid Zechariah, for your prayers have been heard and will be answered: your wife Elisabeth will bear a son and you will name him John. He will be a great man before the Lord. He must not drink alcohol for he will be filled with the Holy Spirit, even from his mother's womb. He will turn many people toward God, going before Him in the spirit and power of Elijah, to turn hearts back to God and make ready the coming of the Lord." Zechariah replied to the angel, "How is this possible, for we are old." The angel answered, "I am Gabriel and I stand in the presence of God who sent me here to convey this good news. And since you doubted, you will be unable to speak a word until all I have told you has come to pass."

- LUK 1:26–38 ~ Then God sent the angel Gabriel into the city of Nazareth in Galilee, to speak to a virgin named Mary, who was engaged to a man named Joseph a descendant of David. The angel came to her and said, "You are highly favored by God and He is with you; you will be blessed more than other women." Mary trembled with fear. Gabriel said, "Do not be afraid, for you are favored by God. You are going to conceive and bear a son; and you will name Him Jesus. Your son will be holy, for He will be the Son of the most high. God will give to Him the throne of his ancestor David. He will reign over the house of Jacob (Israel) forever; His kingdom will never end." Mary replied, "How can I bear a child since I have never been with a man?" Gabriel replied, "The Holy Spirit will come upon you and impregnate you. Thus, your child rightly will be called the Son of God." And behold, your relative Elisabeth has conceived a son in her old age and is in her sixth month, though people called her barren. For nothing is impossible with God." Then Mary said, "Behold, I am the handmaiden of the Lord. Let it be unto me according to your word." Then the angel departed.

- LUK 1:39–50 ~ Mary left to the hill country to visit Elisabeth. As soon as Elisabeth heard Mary's salutation, the baby in her womb leaped with joy, and Elisabeth was filled with the Holy Spirit. She spoke aloud saying, "Blessed are you among women and blessed be the fruit of your womb. Who am I that the mother of my Lord would visit me? The moment I heard your voice, the baby in my womb leaped for joy." And Mary said, "Behold, my soul does magnify the Lord, for my spirit has rejoiced in God my Savior; for He has regarded His handmaiden, a woman of low estate. And now all generations will call me blessed. Almighty God has done great things for me and holy is His name; His mercy will be on those who fear Him from generation to generation."

- LUK 2:1–4 ~ Joseph took his pregnant wife Mary from the city of Nazareth in Galilee to the city of David which is called Bethlehem, because he was a descendant of David; it was there that he and his family were to be taxed by the Romans.

- JOH 1:1, 14 ~ In the beginning was the Word, and the Word was with God, and the Word was God. And the Word became flesh, and lived on earth; and we saw His glory, the glory of the Father's only Son.

Heavenly Father, you sent your only begotten Son to earth to show us the way, for He is the only way to heaven for humankind, and all that you require of us is to remain faithful. Let it be so, and let that faith implanted in our minds by the Holy Spirit, just as He implanted Himself into the womb of the virgin Mary, be a wellspring of life and love as long as we live, which is forever. We love your Word of truth, which foresaw our Savior from ages past until He appeared in the flesh in accordance with the prophecies. It is unmistakable your majesty and glory which lived in full in Jesus Christ, and is the reason He alone can redeem us from sin; for He is the Word made flesh though He was without sin. We thank you for the salvation we obtain through the shedding of His blood, His death, and His resurrection, proving the He is God, and that we have been freed from the stench of sin and the curse of death. In the name of Jesus, who came alive in Mary's womb on this day, we pray, Amen.

March 26

Peace Treaty Signed Between Israel and Egypt in Washington DC on this day in 1979. Israel's prime minister Begin and Egypt's president Sadat met at Camp David with President Carter as witness, and forged the accord in 1978. The two men recognized each nation as sovereign and both agreed to end the constant wars. They established normal relations and trade for the first time since the 1948 Arab-Israeli war. Israel obtained free passage through the Suez Canal and other international shipping channels and in turn, removed their military presence from occupied territories gained in the Six-Day War of 1967. Both countries agreed to demilitarize, and resume the Sinai boundary created in 1949. This was the first time any Arab (Muslim) nation had recognized the free state of Israel. Sadat and Begin both were awarded the Nobel Peace Prize for this monumental achievement.

There was no love lost between Israel and Egypt after Moses negotiated their exodus at the height of the Egyptian empire. Israel would start an empire of their own, which peaked with kings David and Solomon. The kingdom split into Israel in the north and Judah in the south before succumbing to Assyria and then Babylonia who took the Jews into captivity. The demolition of Jerusalem and subsequent scattering of the Jews is referred to as diaspora. Details of this history are recorded in the Old Testament.

- DEU 4:26–28 ~ I call heaven and earth to witness against you this day, that soon you will perish from the land where you are going across the Jordan River. You will not possess it for long, but will be utterly destroyed. I will scatter you among the nations, and you will become a minority among the heathen where I shall lead you. And there you will serve other gods, the work of men's hands: wood and stone which cannot see, hear, eat, or smell.

- DEU 28:63–66 ~ Just as the Lord rejoiced over you, so He will destroy you. You will be taken from the land He gave you, and scattered from one end of the world to the other. You will never find peace or rest, and your life will hang in doubt day and night.

- 1 KI 14:15 ~ God will strike Israel down, uproot them, and scatter them abroad.

- 2 KI 17:6–8 ~ During the ninth year of Hoshea, the king of Assyria captured Samaria and carried the Israelites away. This occurred because the people of Israel had sinned against the Lord their God who brought them out of the land of Egypt from the hand of Pharaoh. But they feared other gods and adopted the customs of their neighbors who the Lord had driven out to make way for the people of Israel.

- 2 CH 36:21 ~ The captivity of the Israelites in Babylon lasted seventy years.

- NEH 9:32–33 ~ Our God is great and mighty, an awesome God who keeps His covenant of mercy. Do not think that our problems are trivial, those hardships that have come upon our nation since the Assyrians ruled. God has been fair in punishing us this way, for we have been wicked.

- HAB 1:6 ~ I am raising up the Chaldeans (Babylonians), a bitter and hasty nation who will march through the breadth of the earth to possess dwellings not their own.

- MIC 5:8 ~ The remnant of Israel will be scattered among foreigners.

- ZEC 7:14 ~ I scattered them like a tornado among nations they did not know; and the land was laid to waste behind them.

- JAM 1:1 ~ I, James, a servant of God and the Lord Jesus Christ, send greetings to the twelve tribes which are scattered abroad.

God promised that Israel would return home someday, which occurred in 1948. This was largely the reason for the war with Egypt because they didn't want Israel as a neighbor and the borders were in dispute. Thus, the land promised to Abraham was inhabited by the Israelites, then they practiced the idolatry of their neighbors and were conquered and scattered, and then God brought them back to their homeland as He promised He would.

- DEU 30:3–5 ~ The Lord will have compassion on you; He will gather you up, return you to your land, and allow you to multiply.

- ISA 11:11–12 ~ It will come to pass that the Lord will reach His hand a second time to recover the remnant of His people left in Assyria, Egypt, Cush, Babylonia, and elsewhere. He will raise a banner and gather the exiles of Israel and assemble the scattered people of Judah from the four corners of the earth.

- JER 31:10 ~ He who scattered Israel will gather them up again as a shepherd does his flock.

- EZE 20:34; EZE 36:24; EZE 37:24; EZE 39:27 ~ God will gather you from countries everywhere and bring you back to your homeland.

- ZEC 1:18–21 ~ Zechariah saw a vision of four horns that drove the Jews out of Israel, Judah, and Jerusalem; then he saw four carpenters dismantle the horns that scattered the Jews.

It seems the ancient land of Palestine was and still is a hotly contested tract of real estate. The Israelites took the land from previous inhabitants, who were evil and worshipped false gods. With Joshua as their leader, they conquered numerous tribes and drove out others. But Israel did not eliminate them as God commanded, precisely because He didn't want them to be corrupted by pagan nations. God knew if Israel did not obey, they would lose the land of promise, and so it was; but then they got it back. And they have fought wars with many of their neighbors and are still at odds with most of them. They are surrounded just as God said would happen in the latter days. And their enemies will once again try to eliminate Israel but will be destroyed trying.

- EZE 38—39 ~ Face northward, toward Magog, and prophesy: God is against you Gog. You will mobilize armies of the distant north, as well as from Africa and Asia. You will invade Israel in an attempt to obtain her wealth and conquer her, Israel who has been at peace after having returned home from all over the world. This will happen in the latter years. There will be a great earthquake. You will end up fighting yourselves in the confusion. I will send animals to eat you, death, disease, and calamities. I will destroy five-sixths of your armies. I will rain fire and brimstone upon Magog and your allies to include the islands and coastlands, and places east of the Dead Sea. It will take seven months to bury the bodies. It will be a glorious victory for Israel. I will be their Lord from that day on, and forever.

- ZEC 12:2–3, 9, 11 ~ I will make Jerusalem a menace to all the peoples surrounding them; they will lay siege to Jerusalem and Judah. On that day, when the nations are gathered against her, I will make her like a rock that cannot be moved. All who try to move it will be cut to pieces. I will destroy any nation that comes against Jerusalem. There will be great sorrow in Jerusalem as there was in the valley of Megiddo.

- LUK 21:20 ~ When you see Jerusalem surrounded by her enemies the desolation is nigh.

Father of peace and love, we praise you and adore you. You punish your people to teach them a lesson and then you forgive them; you are always giving us another chance to get right with you. Thank you for being so gracious; we truly love you, despite our infidelity toward you, and we thank you for bringing us back home. We look forward to coming home to you for the last time forevermore. In the name of your Son we pray, Amen.

March 27

World Theater Day was first observed in 1962; it was organized by the International Theatre Institute (ITI) to draw the world's attention to theatric arts as a means of entertainment. The ITI has an annual message delivered by an entertainer, reaching millions of people via radio, television, and newspapers, as well as schools and theater programs. Theater has been enjoyed since the sixth century BC, when stage performances were the rave in Athens, Greece. They were famous for festivals, rituals, sporting events, and all manner of live performances. The Romans expanded on the theme, adding more dramatics, acrobatics, magic, music, comedy, tragedy, violence, and nudity. Literary artists fed the popularity of the genre. In the Middle Ages, the stage was used for many applications such as delivering religious, political, and social content; as well as plays, characters, costumes, and scripts. Some artists made a living doing stage acts. The theatre emerged in England during the sixteenth century AD where companies of actors would tour. Certainly, Shakespeare was a catalyst, who wrote prose in the form of stage plays, often acted out in his famous Globe Theatre built in 1599. The Spaniards followed with their own version of renaissance art, which surpassed in sophistication their predecessors. Theater is still alive and well in the USA and the world. If you have never attended a live play, opera, concert, or symphony you should try it; take the kids they might like it too. Lazy people stay at home and watch television, livestreaming and ordering shows, sometimes going to the movies; they probably should get out more. Attend a theatrical show, stage presentation, or musical event. Live performances add more creativity and style than that available with studio productions.

There were live performances during Biblical times, mostly incorporating death as the attraction. For instance, gladiators, lions, massacres, and battles, were elements of entertainment desired by decadent emperors and aristocrats. Many Christians died entertaining the Romans. The renown Colosseum, completed during the reign of emperor Titus, is a tourist attraction to this day; it once held up to fifty thousand spectators. It was the precursor to stadiums, amphitheaters, and superdomes of today. Crucifixion was another type of Roman entertainment, whereby the torture and execution of major felons (and Christians) was put on public display.

- 1 CO 4:9 ~ God put us, the apostles, on display, like those who die in the arena; for we were made to be a spectacle to the world, and to angels, and to men.

The cool thing about art is that all forms are compatible. You can add pictures, songs, drama, dance, prose and poetry in any combination to spice up an act. For example, rock bands began to add lighting, costumes, makeup, and theatrics to their performances in the 1960s and 1970s; this became part of their brand, attracting people to shows that provided more than music. Such additions are commonplace in live performances today. Be advised, in the latter days, the performance of dramatic fake miracles will fool many people who otherwise might seek God.

- 2 TH 2:9–11 ~ Those false signs and fake miracles come from Satan. Such deceptions belong to the self-righteous who will die, for they did not believe the truth that could save them. God will let them believe their lies and perish.

- REV 13:5–7 ~ He spoke arrogant words and blasphemies against the Lord for forty-two months (3.5 years). He was given power to make war with the saints and overcome them. He possessed power over various peoples, nations, and tongues, deceiving them through fake miracles when in the presence of the beast, who was wounded and yet lived. He commanded the image of the beast to speak, forcing many to worship the image of the beast or be killed.

Father in heaven, help us be alert to the deceptions and lewdness of those who put on a show for attention but who aim to deliberately pervert. We know that the end times may be near; please do not let us fall into those traps, wherein they themselves will fall. In Jesus's name, Amen.

March 28

Maundy Thursday is the Christian celebration of the institution of Holy Communion, administered by Jesus to His apostles after their last Passover dinner together. Maundy means commandment; and communion means joining. Jesus commanded His apostles to repeat this holy sacrament often to remember Him. Through the wine and the bread, His body and blood were conveyed, thereby joining the apostles in spirit with Christ via His Spirit. Thus, all three persons of the Holy Trinity were present at this unprecedented event, which awarded forgiveness of sins to the partakers. It is a public commitment of faith in the atonement found in the shedding of Christ's blood from His broken body on the cross. Christians who have confirmed themselves in the true faith will receive the same forgiveness through this sacred act: receiving Christ into their physical bodies, purifying their minds (soul), as well as joining their spirits with that of God's. This is extremely powerful, my friends, and to be eligible is to believe God's promises that you receive His eternal gifts through His Son and by participating often in this sacrament. You can decline those gifts, but I would not advise it.

- MAT 26:26–28; LUK 22:19–20; 1 CO 11:24–26 ~ Jesus took bread, gave thanks, and broke the bread, giving it to His disciples saying, "Take and eat; this is my body which is given for you; do this to remember me." In like manner He took a cup of wine saying, "Drink from this cup all of you. It is the New Covenant in my blood which is poured out for you, and for many others, for the forgiveness of sins. Do this often to remember me." For whenever you eat of the bread and drink from the cup you proclaim the Lord's death until He returns.

- 1 CO 5:7 ~ Throw out the old leavened dough and become a new dough, without yeast; for that is what you have become because of the sacrifice of Christ who is the Passover Lamb.

- 1 CO 10:16–17, 21 ~ The cup of blessing that we bless, does it not represent our communion with the blood of Christ? The bread that we break, does it not represent our communion with the body of Christ? Although we are many, we have become one body for we all are partakers of that one bread. You cannot drink from the cup of the Lord and from the cup of devils.

- 1 CO 11:25–29 ~ Jesus commanded the apostles on the first Holy Communion to partake of the sacrament often to remember Him. For, as often as you eat the bread and drink the wine of Holy Communion, you proclaim the death of Christ until His return. But if you participate in this holy sacrament unworthily (without sincerely repenting of your sins and desiring a communion with Christ), you will become one of those who are found guilty of Christ's crucifixion. Examine yourself before partaking of Holy Communion, because if you partake unworthily, you will be eating and drinking damnation upon yourself.

Like Holy Baptism, Holy Communion represents a commitment to the Lord. Baptism covers the original sin that we were born with, communion covers the sins we commit ourselves. Since we cannot cease the sinning, we are obliged to partake of Holy Communion often, to remember how Christ allowed Himself to be sacrificed so that we might live. Maundy Thursday is considered a high sabbath in the Christian faith, much like the high sabbath which begins the Feast of Unleavened Bread in the Jewish faith occurring the day after Passover. This is why Jesus is referred to as the Passover Lamb, because His death saves us from eternal death. This is also why the Jews eat bread without yeast (unleavened), for it represents the body without sin. Of course, that is a reference to the body of Christ, the only sinless human.

Father, we thank you for the gift of Holy Communion, wherein we are refreshed as often as we partake, renewed in our faith through the bread and wine, receiving forgiveness of sins through the body and blood of our Lord and Savior Jesus Christ. Help us to obey this and all of your commandments. In Jesus's name we pray, Amen.

March 29

Good Friday is the day Christians commemorate the crucifixion of Christ, honoring His ultimate sacrifice for sins. A dedicated church service is held this day, when most fulltime workers have the day off. Much like the Jewish tradition of the high sabbath, it is spiritually uplifting to observe this holy day. Jesus gave His life so we might live; it doesn't get more important or personal than that. Christians observe the sacrifice of the Lamb of God, which frees us from sin and death, in the same timeframe Jews celebrate the freedom bought for them by the sacrifice of a lamb on the first Passover. This is not a coincidence; it is another wonderful part of God's plan, and evidence that both testaments of the Bible are in accord with each other.

Contrary to what you might have heard, this event is a historical fact, not just some tale told in the Bible. It is well documented, not only in the Bible, but also in reliable secular accounts, such as Hebrew historian Josephus (first century AD), and Roman historian Tacitus (late first, early second century AD).

Christ was betrayed, tried, and crucified in one day with respect to the Jewish calendar (recall, the Jewish day began at dusk). Therefore, Jesus didn't actually die on Friday, for His body already had been taken down; Friday started at sundown shortly after Jesus's body was interred. Tradition was, a crucified victim could not remain on a cross during any sabbath, so soldiers broke the legs to hasten death. Most people assume this particular sabbath was on Saturday, but it was a high sabbath (LEV 23:3–8; JOH 19:31). Jesus could not have died on Friday and arose in three days on Sunday, and we know with certainty that the resurrection was on Easter Sunday. Given that Jesus was crucified during Passover, it was likely Thursday, because Friday was the High Sabbath of Unleavened Bread, and Saturday was the weekly sabbath. Like many observances on the church calendar, this is a floating holiday, so Friday is as good a time as any to celebrate this solemn event.

- PSA 22:16–18; PSA 34:20; PSA 69:21 ~ David prophesied: Evil men circle me like a pack of wolves. They have pierced my hands and feet (ZEC 13:6). They have bruised every bone in my body. They gloat and stare. They divide my clothes by casting lots. Not a bone in my body will ever be broken (JOH 19:36). They offered me gall when I was weak, and vinegar when I was thirsty (MAT 27:34; JOH 19:28–29).

- ISA 53:4–12 ~ He took upon Himself all of our grief and sorrows; yet we treated Him as an outcast. He was tortured for our sins and punished for our peace, and through His wounds we are healed. He was slaughtered like a lamb (EXO 12:3–12). He was buried like a criminal but in a rich man's grave. He was made an offering for sin, though He never committed a single act of sin or spoke an evil word. Therefore, His days will be prolonged and His name will be made great. He will be exalted, for He emptied his soul unto death.

- MAT 26:2 ~ Jesus said, "You know that after two days will be the feast of the Passover, and the Son of man will be betrayed to be crucified."

- MAT 27:26–30 ~ The Romans released Barabbas. Then they whipped Jesus and delivered Him to be crucified. Soldiers gathered around Jesus, stripped Him, and put a scarlet robe on Him. They placed a crown of thorns on His head and a reed in His hand. They bowed before Him mocking Him, saying, "Hail, king of the Jews." They spat on Him and beat Him on the head.

- MAT 27:41–43 ~ The chief priests, scribes, and elders mocked Jesus saying, "He saved others but cannot save himself. If he is the king of Israel let him come down from the cross and we will believe him. He trusted in God to deliver him, let God deliver him now, if God even wants him; for did this man not say he was God's son?"

- JOH 18:28 ~ They led Jesus away from Caiaphas (the high priest) to the judgment hall; it was still early so the mob did not accompany Jesus into the judgment hall to avoid defiling themselves, which would preclude them from eating the Passover meal with their loved ones.

- JOH 18:37–38 ~ Pilate asked Jesus if He was a king. Jesus replied, "My kingdom is not of this world. I was born so I could give witness to the truth. Everyone who searches for truth hears my voice." Pilate then asked, "What is truth?"

- JOH 19:10–16 ~ Pilate told Jesus, "Do you not realize I have the power to crucify you or release you?" Jesus replied, "You can do nothing to me without being given the power from above. The ones who delivered me to you for crucifixion, they have committed a greater sin than you." Pilate appealed to the Jews to release Jesus but they cried for His execution; and Pilate caved to the pressure, delivering Jesus to be crucified.

- JOH 19:31–37 ~ The Jews did not want bodies of the crucified to hang on their crosses into the Sabbath for that was a holy day. So, they asked Pilate to have the soldiers break the legs of the crucified to hasten death, and be taken away for burial. The soldiers broke the legs of the first two, but when they came to Jesus, they could tell He was already dead so they did not break His legs. One of the soldiers pierced Jesus's side with a spear and out flowed blood and water, verifying that He was indeed dead. These things were done to fulfill the scriptures, "No bone of His will ever be broken," and, "They looked upon Him who was pierced."

- ACT 4:10–12 ~ Let everybody know that it was Jesus Christ, whom you crucified, but whom God raised from the dead, who has become the chief cornerstone. There can be salvation in nobody else, for there are no other names under heaven that can save us except Christ alone.

What a price Jesus paid to redeem sinners like us. The torture, the anguish, the pain, the death: all so we wouldn't have to endure the penalty of sin which is death. Yes, it was sinners like you and I who did this to Christ, and He was willing to forgive them too.

- LUK 23:33–34 ~ When they arrived at the place called Calvary, they crucified Him along with two malefactors, one on the right and the other on the left. Then Jesus prayed aloud, "Father, forgive them for they know not what they do."

- LUK 23:39–47 ~ One of the malefactors ridiculed Jesus saying, "If you are the Christ, save yourself and us." But the other rebuked him saying, "Do you not fear God, seeing how you are receiving the same sentence? We are indeed guilty, deserving the due reward for our misdeeds. But this man has done nothing wrong." Turning to Jesus he said, "Lord, remember me when you enter into your kingdom." Jesus replied to him, "Truly I say to you, this day you will be with me in paradise." It was about the sixth hour, and there was darkness over all the earth until the ninth hour. The sun was darkened, and the veil of the temple was rent in two. Then Jesus cried in a loud voice, "Father, into your hands I commend my spirit." Having said that, He gave up the ghost. After the centurion witnessed these things, he glorified God saying, "Certainly this was a righteous man."

Heavenly Father, we cannot imagine the pain Christ endured for us but we thank you and Jesus for your perfect plan of salvation. Surely, it was hard for you, but because of your grace, we now can live as an adopted child in heaven, and an equal heir with your only begotten Son. How beautiful is your Word, the Holy Spirit, who became flesh and died on a cross paying the price of sin for all who believe. We are humbled that Jesus died in our place, for He is perfect in righteousness. Thankfully, death had no hold over Him, and now death has no hold over us either. And we too will come alive when He returns, to live in your kingdom forever! Praise the Lord: Father, Son, and Holy Spirit, Amen.

March 30

National Doctors Day began in the USA on 03/30/1933 to honor Dr. C. W. Long who was the first to administer anesthesia before a procedure on this date in 1842. It finally became an official holiday in 1991 when signed off by President G. H. W. Bush the year before. Today we celebrate those in the medical profession in general and doctors in particular. Doctors sacrifice a great deal of time, money, and effort to become experts in anatomy, medical diagnosis and treatment, while also specializing in particular fields of medicine. People need to trust their doctors, and this is why they undergo intense scrutiny. Physicians work tirelessly, routinely putting in long days and weeks, improving health and saving lives, which can be mentally and physically exhausting. Their contribution to health and wellbeing is laudable, which is why doctors are highly regarded and respected among professions. Today many medical offices have a celebration or a luncheon. Individuals may want to send a gift, thank-you note, or greeting card to their favorite doctors.

Physicians have been around since Old Testament times. The first mention of physicians is in the book of Genesis, though some scholars believe the mention of physicians in the book of Job was an earlier reference. Of course, doctors are not perfect and cannot heal everyone; but God can heal everyone because He is perfect. Christians call Jesus the Great Physician because He could heal everything, including death. Without God, there would be no healing, and no life.

- GEN 50:2 ~ Joseph commanded the physicians to embalm his father Israel and so they did.

- 2 CH 16:12–13 ~ King Asa became diseased, the disease spread, and he died; for he had turned to the physicians for healing instead of God.

- JOB 13:2–5 ~ What you know, I also know; I am not inferior to you. I would rather speak to the Almighty and reason with Him, because you are proposing lies; you physicians are of no value, and I wish you would hold your peace, then you would appear wise. [Job was chastising his companions for blaming his sinfulness for his infirmities.]

- MAT 9:12; MAR 2:17 ~ Jesus said, "Those who are healthy do not need a doctor, only those who are sick. I came to call sinners, not the righteous, to repentance."

- MAR 5:25–34; LUK 8:43–48 ~ A woman had a hemorrhage for twelve years; she suffered at the hands of several physicians, making matters worse. When she heard about Jesus, she thought that merely touching His garment would make her whole; the second she touched Him she was healed. Jesus noticed power had gone from Him and asked, "Who touched me." The disciples said it could have been anyone. He asked again and then she came forward, falling to His feet. Jesus told her, "Daughter, your faith has made you whole, go in peace."

- LUK 4:22–27 ~ The Jews were amazed at the teachings of Jesus saying amongst themselves, "Is this not Jesus the carpenter's son?" Jesus replied, "You would say this proverb about me: physician, heal yourself. You say I should do in my hometown what I did in Capernaum. I tell you the truth, no prophet is accepted in their hometown. There were many widows in Israel that Elijah could have ministered to, but he chose to help a widow in the region of Sidon (Philistia). There were many lepers in Israel that needed healing but Elijah chose to heal Naaman the Syrian." These words angered the people in the synagogue, and they sought to throw Him off of a cliff, but He disappeared in the midst of them.

- COL 4:14 ~ Paul wrote to the Colossians: Luke, the beloved physician, and Demas greet you.

Dear Father, we thank you for doctors and we ask your blessings upon them. We especially thank Jesus, the Great Physician, for He healed everyone He touched. Please heal us of our infirmities, be they physical, mental, or spiritual. In Jesus's name we pray, Amen.

March 31

Easter Sunday is a time to reflect on the resurrection, because that is the pivotal event without which Christians would have no religion. It brings to mind the birth of Jesus Christ, and how we shared peace and love during the holy week of Christmas; we expressed the joy of His first coming, while looking forward to His second coming. Jesus was born for us, so that He could die for us. His birth gives us life, and His resurrection saves us from death. As we bring gifts and sing praises, let us also remember the gift of eternal life and celebrate the gift of God's Son. And let us not forget to worship the Holy Spirit who Jesus left with us to comfort us after His ascension into heaven. As we reflect, we also anticipate His return and our subsequent homecoming in the kingdom of heaven. Easter Sunday is determined to be the first Sunday after the full moon following the vernal equinox (must be later than March 20).

Holy Week is a good time to reflect on God's Covenant, which He promised to all who seek Him. A covenant is an agreement or contract; you can bet that when God makes a covenant, He will never break it. God offers people salvation for free if they will be faithful to Him; and that faith leads to eternal life. It is the greatest deal anyone will ever offer you.

In the Old Testament, God made covenants with Noah, Abraham, Isaac, Jacob, Moses, and David. Through these prophets, God also promised a New Covenant: His Messiah. The New Covenant was further confirmed through Isaiah, Jeremiah, Daniel, Zechariah, Micah, and other great prophets. The Old Covenant was based on faith in God by obedience to His Law, demonstrated by sacrificial offerings to atone for sin. The New Covenant is based on faith in God and is confirmed in the New Testament, with the sacrifice of Christ on the cross atoning for the sin of the world. God knew all along that humans were incapable of remaining obedient due to their sinful nature (ROM 3:20; ROM 7:7, 14; JAM 2:10), which is why He promised a more perfect covenant based on faith in Christ's self-sacrifice (ROM 16:25–26; GAL 3:13–23; HEB 7:15–19; HEB 8:6–13).

Jesus Christ is the Messiah, the Redeemer, our Savior, and the New Covenant (LUK 1:68–79). Christ came to earth to perfectly fulfill the Law on our behalf (MAT 5:12–19), as well as to assume the punishment for our noncompliance with the Law (ISA 53:1–12; PHP 3:11–12). His sufferings and death paid the price of sin which is death (ROM 6:23), thereby conquering sin (1 JO 2:2). His resurrection from the dead brought with it the resurrection of all people (ROM 8:11), thereby conquering death (2 TI 1:10). By redeeming our bodies from the grave and washing our souls clean, we become unblemished like Christ (1 CO 1:8), making us acceptable to live with our perfect Father in His kingdom forever (COL 1:29; HEB 10:14).

Interestingly, the Old and New Covenants have several things in common and this is not coincidental. God's plan was repeatedly announced during Holy Week and upon God's holy mountain in the City of David which is Jerusalem (meaning city of peace).

Abraham was visited by King Melchizedek, and communed with this great High Priest and King of Salem (meaning peace), sharing bread and wine, and giving tithes of all he owned to the Lord (GEN 14:18–20). Later, Abraham was sent by God to the holy mountain to sacrifice his only legitimate son Isaac (GEN 22:1–8). Isaac asked his father where the lamb was that would be offered and Abraham replied, "God Himself will provide the lamb." Of course, Isaac was spared because Abraham remained faithful; a ram was sacrificed in Isaac's place (GEN 22:9–13). This ram represents the sacrificial Lamb, God's firstborn and only Son, who was offered for the sin of the world (JOH 1:29).

God used Moses as a messenger of the Law as well as a messenger of the New Covenant (EXO 24:7–8). During the first Passover, God spared the firstborn of all who obeyed His commandment by sacrificing an unblemished lamb (EXO 12:3–13). Again, Christ is represented in that Passover Lamb (1 PE 1:19). There are numerous references to Messiah in the Old Testament; each of these examples illuminates Christ who shined the light of God for all living souls to see. If you cannot see His light, you will lose your way and remain in darkness.

God commanded His people to remember forever His great works when He freed them from the bondage of Egyptian oppression. This is the purpose of the Old Testament feasts of Passover, Unleavened Bread, and First Fruits (LEV 23:5–10), which Jews celebrate during Holy Week to this day.

During this same Holy Week, Christians celebrate the breaking of Christ's body on the cross (Feast of Unleavened Bread), the shedding of His blood unto death (Feast of Passover), and His resurrection from the tomb on Easter Sunday (Feast of First Fruits). In accordance with Christ's commandment, we commemorate these wonderful acts of God every time we partake of Holy Communion (1 CO 11:25–26), in which we share the bread and wine in a spiritual communion with God's Holy Spirit just as Abraham did so long ago. This we do to remember forever that God has freed us from the slavery and bondage of sin (LUK 22:19–20).

As we reflect on the sacrifice of Christ and His resurrection, we cannot help but be awestruck. What a great time to express our gratitude by giving to the Lord the first fruits of our increase (2 CH 31:5; PRO 3:9; 1 CO 16:2). Christ is the first fruits of those who have been raised to live forever on God's holy mountain of Zion (1 CO 15:20–23, 44). All believers will follow Christ in death, and be resurrected to live forever with Him and our heavenly Father in the New Jerusalem (EZE 34:12, 23–24; EPH 1:10–11; PHP 3:20–21). What a marvelous gift God has given us; He gave us everything, even Himself! And all He requires in return is our gratitude and love. This we show by offering our worship and gifts through faith (LEV 27:30; DEU 14:22; MAL 3:6–8). Plus, God promises that if we give Him our first fruits (tithe), He will further bless us with increased prosperity, so how can we lose (MAL 3:10; LUK 6:38)? Is there any limit to God's goodness, grace, and mercy? No, there is not (PSA 100:1–5)!

Interestingly, many significant sacrifices (all using spotless male sheep) have occurred during Holy Week. In the Old Testament era, this week included the feasts of Passover, Unleavened Bread, and First Fruits, lasting a total of eight days. Jews have celebrated these feasts annually by eating the Passover meal (also called Seder supper) of which the main course was lamb; unleavened bread and wine have been traditionally served with this meal. Based on the New Testament accounts, Christians observe Holy Week and special occasions including Palm Sunday, Maundy Thursday, Good Friday, and Easter Sunday. Christ, who is the Passover Lamb, is celebrated in like manner by Christians for eight days, often including the Seder supper.

In the Old Testament, the body of Christ is reflected in the feast of Unleavened Bread and the blood of Christ is reflected in the feast of Passover. Unleavened bread, or bread without yeast, signifies the body without sin, representing Jesus Christ. Christ purged us of our sins, making us pure like Him. In the New Testament, the body and blood of Christ were offered to the apostles during the first Holy Communion, and then offered to the world during Jesus's crucifixion the next day, just as the blood of the lamb was offered during the first Passover. Jews and Christians celebrate every anniversary of Holy Week. Unmistakably, this is God's design; it is a commemoration of the covenants made by God with His people. People who celebrate God and His Son are among His chosen; and this celebration will continue without end.

- LEV 23:5–6 ~ The feasts of the Passover and Unleavened Bread are described, during which faith offerings are to be made.

- MAT 26:26–28 ~ The Eucharist is described which occurred subsequent to the Last Supper. Jesus said, "Take and eat, this is my body; take and drink, this is my blood of the New Covenant, shed for you for the forgiveness of sins."

- JOH 6:30–35, 51–58 ~ The people said to Jesus, "Can you show us a sign to convince us that we should believe you, like when our fathers ate manna in the desert?" Jesus answered, "The manna from heaven did not come from Moses; it came from God who gives you the true bread from heaven. The bread of life comes from heaven and gives life to the world. I am the bread of life; whoever comes to me will never hunger again and whoever believes in me will never thirst again. The bread I give is my flesh, and I will give it for the life of the world. Unless you eat the body and drink the blood of the Son of man, you have no life. If you eat my body and drink my blood, you live in me and I in you; and you will have eternal life, for I will raise you up on the last day. Mine is not like the manna from heaven, for whoever eats the bread I give will live forever."

- 1 CO 5:7–8 ~ Throw out the old leavened dough and become a new dough, without yeast; for that is what you have become because of the sacrifice of Christ who is the Passover Lamb. Therefore, let us keep the feast (of Passover), not with old leaven or with the leaven of malice and wickedness, but with the unleavened bread of sincerity and truth.

- EPH 5:26 ~ We are cleansed from sin by the washing of water and the Word who is Christ.

The resurrection of Christ is reflected in the feast of First Fruits, Christ being the first fruits of those raised from the dead to abide forever with God. Christ's resurrection occurred on the first Easter, in conjunction with the feast of the First Fruits. His resurrection signifies that all believers will, like Christ, be raised from the dead to inherit eternal life in the kingdom of heaven. That makes believers the first fruits of Christ.

- LEV 23:10–12 ~ The feast of the First Fruits is described in which offerings and tithes are given. During that feast, a male lamb is sacrificed.

- JOH 11:25–26 ~ Jesus said, "I am the resurrection and the life. Those who believe in me, though they were dead, yet shall they live."

- 1 CO 15:20–23, 44 ~ Christ has been raised, the first fruits of those who have died, so that we too may obtain a new life.

- GAL 4:5–7 ~ Believers in Christ will become children of God and fellow heirs to His kingdom.

To repeat, Jesus Christ is the unblemished sacrificial lamb. He is represented by the ram sacrificed by Abraham, and He is represented by the lamb sacrificed by the Israelites during the first Passover. Instead of Abraham sacrificing his only son and heir, and instead of the Israelites sacrificing a lamb to save their first born from the angel of death, it was God's firstborn and only son, the Lamb of God, who would be sacrificed to atone for the sin of the world, saving humankind from the curse of death. Thus, multiple sacrifices in the Old Testament were a shadow of one perfect sacrifice of Jesus Christ our Passover Lamb, the decisive event in the New Testament.

- JOH 1:15, 25–29, 32–36 ~ John the Baptist preached about the coming of Christ and addressed Him as the Lamb of God.

- ACT 8:32 ~ Jesus Christ was led as a sheep to the slaughter (also ISA 53:7).

- 1 PE 1:19 ~ Peter describes Christ as a sacrificial lamb without blemish.

- REV 5–22 ~ Jesus Christ is depicted throughout the book of Revelation as the Lamb who was slain, and who now sits upon the throne of God.

In addition to being the sacrificial lamb, Jesus Christ is also the Good Shepherd who died to save His sheep. He will return to gather His sheep together. The Good Shepherd is the protector. He protects us from evil and death just like the Israelites were protected by the blood of the lamb during the first Passover (EXO 12). Note that King David was originally a shepherd, and his descendant Jesus Christ inherited David's throne and is our King and Shepherd forever.

- PSA 23 ~ The Good Shepherd is the one who always protects and cares for His sheep.
- ISA 44:28 ~ He is my appointed Shepherd and He will do everything I ask. He will build Jerusalem, and lay the foundation of the temple.
- EZE 34:5–12, 23–24 ~ The sheep were scattered because there was no shepherd. The sheep were hunted and killed. Beware you shepherds, for I will require my flock, and I will deliver them. I will find every last one of them. As a shepherd searches for His flock when they become scattered, so I will find my sheep and deliver them from danger on that dark and cloudy day. I will set one Shepherd over them and He will feed them. I will be their God and my servant David will be their prince. [This is a reference to the ancestor of David who will inherit the throne, namely Messiah.]
- ZEC 13:7 ~ They will strike down the Shepherd and the sheep will scatter. (also MAT 26:31).
- MAT 25:32, 46 ~ The Son of God will gather everyone together, and will separate them, as a shepherd separates the sheep from the goats. The sheep will inherit eternal life, but the goats will inherit eternal punishment.
- JOH 10:1–2, 7, 14–18; JOH 10:27–28 ~ Jesus described Himself to the apostles as the Good Shepherd who lays down His life for His sheep, and who comes back to find His sheep, gathering them together to live under His protection and care forever.
- HEB 13:20 ~ Jesus is the Great Shepherd who brings salvation to His sheep.

Are further sacrifices to God necessary? Not for sin. But we still are supposed to give of ourselves to others and to God, offering the first fruits of our increase to the church and sacrificing ourselves daily for the sake of Christ (ROM 12:1). Further, we still are obliged to abide by God's laws. However, we cannot be saved by doing these things; only by faith in Christ can we come to the knowledge of salvation, for which we give generously of ourselves in gratitude. (Barber, 2020a). We have assurance that our next life is coming, where we will not even think an evil thought, having been separated from sin and death. God will be separating the fallen from Himself, but we will be with Him forevermore; while this current world will be scarcely an afterthought.

- PSA 101:1–4 ~ I sing of mercy and judgment to you, oh Lord, who inspires me to sing praises. In my house I will behave wisely and perfectly. Oh when will you come to me? I will not point my eyes to any wicked thing. I despise the works of those who fall away; but it will not cling to me. A perverse heart will depart from me and I will never tolerate wickedness.

Dear Heavenly Father, without your Holy Spirit we would know nothing of you. We have been shown the light in the written Word, and the Word made flesh, who is Jesus Christ the Lord in whose name we always pray. We will thank you every day for this great gift which leads to our eternal life with you in the Kingdom of Heaven. As Jesus sacrificed Himself for us, let us likewise sacrifice ourselves to you by serving others, and by sharing the Gospel of Jesus Christ at every opportunity, proclaiming the resurrection of your Son, and the resurrection of the dead. Help us to convince others to become like sheep and be among the group selected by God to live forever under the eternal protection of the Good Shepherd. We ask this in faith for all who listen and cling to your Word, beloved Holy Trinity. Amen, and Amen!

April 1

April Fools' Day has been around for hundreds of years, but there is no exact date or year of origin, though there are numerous theories. One angle is that the equinox, which introduces seasonal changes, makes people uncertain or giddy. More likely, it is associated with the introduction of the Gregorian calendar in the sixteenth century; because the former Julian calendar began on April 1, while the revised calendar started on January 1. People certainly could have joked about forgetting that date. Apparently, eighteenth century England regularly observed the day by pulling pranks on people, like taping a sign to their backs. Over the years, the day has become an opportunity to trick people by telling tall tales and getting them believing it until they hear, "April Fools" and then they know they've been duped. Harmless pranks are still popular on this day, but malicious pranks are unlikely to be laughed off and are unadvised.

The dictionary defines the noun "fool" as a person lacking judgment or good sense; as a verb it means to dupe or trick someone. Today is about fooling people, or making fools out of them; but it is the prankster who is acting foolish. Thus, the antics may have multiple effects, none positive. Calling someone a fool is an insult, unless said in jest, but it still might hurt a person's feelings. People calling others "fool" are themselves, fools. This entire holiday is rather foolish.

- PSA 14:1 ~ Only a fool would say in his or her heart that there is no God. Such people are corrupt and have done terrible things in the eyes of the Lord.
- PSA 107:17 ~ Fools become afflicted because of their evil ways.
- PRO 10:18, 23 ~ Those who disguise their hatred with lies and those who slander another are fools. It is the sport of fools to do mischief, but a person of understanding is wise.
- PRO 12:15, 20 ~ The way of fools is right in their own eyes, but the one who listens to advice is wise. There is deceit in the hearts of those who plot evil, but for those promoting peace there is joy.
- PRO 18:7 ~ A fool's mouth is his or her destruction, and a snare to the soul.
- ECC 7:9 ~ Do not hasten to be angry, for anger belongs to fools.
- ISA 44:9–11 ~ Only fools would create their own gods and idols.
- MAT 5:21–22 ~ Jesus said, "You have heard that you must never kill or you will be in danger of the judgment, but I say that if you become angry with another person, or call a person a fool without cause, you will be in danger of the judgment."

Now take the word "foolishness" as a noun, which can mean either absurdity or stupidity, the former denoting silly and the latter denoting folly. Again, there is a big difference depending on intent. It is not so simple for the recipient of a foolish comment or action to determine intent or meaning from it. Therefore, foolishness should be avoided.

- LEV 5:4 ~ Anyone who vows to do something foolish, whether the vow is sincere or not, is guilty.
- ISA 29:13–14 ~ God says, "Those people speak of me but their hearts are far from me. Their worship of me is made of rules taught by men. Therefore, I will take vengeance upon them, and turn their wisdom into foolishness."
- EZE 13:3 ~ Woe to the foolish prophets who follow their own spirit and have seen nothing.
- MAT 12:36 ~ Jesus said, "On Judgment Day, people will have to give account for every foolish word they spoke."

- 1 CO 1:19–27, 31 ~ It is written: I will destroy the wisdom of the wise and bring to nothing the understanding of the prudent. Where is wisdom? Has God not made foolish the wisdom of this world? The world through its wisdom cannot know God. The Jews want a sign and the Gentiles want wisdom. But we preach to them about Christ's crucifixion, which to the Jews is an obstacle and to the Gentiles is foolishness. But Christ is the power and wisdom of God to all who are called, both Jews and Gentiles. The foolishness of God is wiser than the wisdom of humankind. The weakness of God is stronger than the strength of people. You can see that not many of those who are wise, mighty, and noble by earthly standards, are called by God. But God has chosen the foolish things of this world to confuse the wise, and the weak things of this world to confound the mighty. Those who glory, let them glory in the Lord only.

Next, let's look at the word "fooled" as an adjective, which means being misled or conned. Both refer to deception. If a person feels fooled, they might not take someone's comment or action as a joke. It might be funny to the instigator, but if it isn't funny to the receiver, it would be better to have refrained from the ploy. In actuality, nobody likes being fooled. Even if they are good sports about it, they probably could do without it.

- PRO 1:7 ~ The fear of God is the beginning of wisdom; only fools despise wisdom and instruction.
- PRO 14:6, 8, 16, 29, 33 ~ A scornful person seeks wisdom but does not find it; however, knowledge is easy for those who understand. The wisdom of the prudent is to understand where they are going, but the folly of fools is deceit. Wise people shy away from and depart from evil, but a fool rages on with confidence. Those who are slow to anger have great understanding, but those who are hasty produce folly. Wisdom abides in the minds of those with understanding, but it is not known in the minds of fools.
- PRO 17:27–28 ~ Those who have knowledge spare their words, and a person of understanding has an excellent spirit. Even fools, if they hold their peace, are considered wise; those who shut their mouths are considered to be people of understanding.
- ECC 7:25 ~ I directed my mind to know the truth, to investigate matters, to seek wisdom and find answers; and to know the evil of folly and the foolishness of madness.
- ISA 44:25 ~ God proves the false prophets to be liars and fools, causing their prophecies to be invalid.
- LAM 2:14 ~ Your prophets have said foolish things and seen false visions. They have not pointed out to you your sins but rather have told you that everything is fine.
- MAT 24:11 ~ Jesus said, "False prophets will come and lead many astray, performing wonders in an attempt to trick people."
- 2 CO 11:13–14 ~ They have fooled people into thinking they are Christ's apostles. But that is not surprising, for even Satan disguises himself as an angel of light.

Father, we pray for people who are taken advantage of, whether to deceive, to be funny, or to swindle. We also pray that those who selfishly take advantage of others would see their error and change their ways, or otherwise be subject to action that might compel them to rethink foolish words and actions. Deception, trickery, lying, and bearing false witness are violations of the ninth commandment. Help us to obey this commandment and refrain from staging cruel pranks or con games. Let us be wise, to listen and observe, and not assume things arbitrarily. Let us refrain from foolishness, insults, and deception. In the name of Jesus we pray, Amen.

April 2

International Children's Book Day was organized in 1967 to commemorate Hans Christian Andersen's birth in Denmark in 1805. His family-oriented books inspired a great many parents and children to read together. Reading with your kids is an educational experience for everyone involved. Most children need considerable encouragement to value reading; they think it is boring until they learn cool things that spark their imagination, or find it entertaining. Some people naturally enjoy reading and that is a gift; others would prefer to watch a video or have someone read to them. Yeah, it takes work; the best way to get the kids to work is to make it fun. This day is dedicated to children's books that teach an important message and deliver it in a fun way. International sponsors determine the annual theme, message, and host country, soliciting successful authors to deliver the keynote address. Additional local events include gatherings of aspiring authors, guest speakers, competitions, awards, book buyers, publishers, and enthusiasts.

This is a good day to read a book with your children and encourage them to read to you. Share a book that was one of your favorites at their age. Ask, about their favorite book or story, or what types of stories they prefer, or their favorite characters, heroes, or writers. Have discussions with your child often, and read about and research the things you talk about that engages and interests them. Give them book gifts when there is no special occasion. Take them to the library often and let them select a wholesome book. Encourage them to write down their ideas in a journal, or keep a diary. Reinforce all their creative instincts even if it is not one you would choose for them: any of the fine arts might stimulate them to be creative.

- DEU 4:9, 29 ~ Keep your soul diligently. Do not forget the things your eyes have seen; teach these things to your children and your children's children. If you seek the Lord with all your heart and soul you will find Him.

- DEU 6:6–7 ~ Keep God's Word in your heart and teach His ways carefully and thoughtfully to your children. Talk with your family all the time about God, every day and night, whenever you are together.

- PSA 115:13–14 ~ God will bless anyone who acknowledges Him, both great and small. He will increase you more and more, you and your children.

- MAT 13:37–42 ~ Jesus summarized His parable saying, "The field represents the world. The harvest represents the end of the world. The reapers are the angels. The good grain represents the children of God, and the evil weeds represent the children of Satan. Jesus Christ is the sower of the grain. The enemy that sows the weeds is Satan. The weeds will be gathered by the angels and burned in the fire; all things that are offensive and evil will be thrown into the furnace where there is weeping and gnashing of teeth."

- ROM 8:14–18 ~ Whoever is led by the Spirit of God becomes a child of God. They have not received a spirit of slavery or fear, but a spirit of adoption, which is why we refer to God as our Father. The Spirit of God is a witness with our spirits that we are the children of God. If we are children of God, then we are His heirs and joint heirs with Christ. So, if we suffer with Christ, we will be glorified with Him also. For the sufferings in this present time cannot be compared to the glory which will be revealed in us.

Parents, take your kids to church and get them into a good Sunday School and Vacation Bible School. The use of craftwork, illustrations, videos, cartoons, and movies enhance spiritual stories and stimulate group discussions. Dramatic portrayals can be incorporated into the actual readings and memory work, all increasing learning and retention to include furthering interactional skills. The most important textbook and primer for children of all ages is the Holy Bible. And there are many great stories to choose from that are among popular favorites depending on age group. For elementary school kids and younger try these: Abraham Enters the Promised Land; Joshua and the Fall of Jericho; David and Goliath; Daniel in the Lion's Den; Jesus Feeding Five Thousand; Jesus Raising Lazarus. For older kids, try these: Abraham and Isaac's Sacrifice; Moses and the Tablets; Sermon on the Mount; Poor Lazarus and the Rich Man; Paul's Address to the Athenians. The Bible has great stories for people everywhere: every man, woman, and child of every generation; what's more, they are true. By the way, parents should be monitoring the things their kids are watching and reading, and participate in these activities with them.

- PRO 22:6 ~ Instruct your children in the way they should go and when they mature, they will not depart from it.

- DAN 12:1–3 ~ At that time Michael will stand up, the great prince (angel) that stands for the children of God. It will be a time of trouble, unlike any before or since. You will be delivered, everyone whose name is written in the book. Some will arise to receive everlasting life and some will arise to everlasting shame and contempt. Those who are wise will shine as bright as the stars.

- LUK 18:15–17 ~ The people brought children and babies to Jesus so that He could bless them. The disciples tried to prevent them from bringing the children but Jesus told them, "You must allow the little children to come to me, and never forbid them from entering my presence. Those who can demonstrate the trust and faith of a little child will inherit the kingdom of God. I tell you the truth, unless you receive the kingdom of God like a child, you will never enter there."

- ROM 9:4–8 ~ Who are the Israelites, to whom God gave the Law and granted the adoption, and with whom God made the covenants and promises? Christ came for them and for all people. It is not as if God's Word had no effect; for they who are of Israel, are not all from Israel. Those who are of Abraham's seed are not all his children. In other words, those who are the children of the flesh are not children of God; only those who cling to God's promises are counted as children.

- GAL 3:24–29 ~ Wherefore, the Law was our schoolmaster to bring us to Christ, that we could be justified by faith. Once you have faith there is no need for a schoolmaster. You are the children of God because of your faith in Jesus Christ. Everyone who is baptized has put on Christ like a suit of armor. There is neither Jew nor Greek, slave nor free, male nor female, for we are all equal in Jesus Christ. If you belong to Christ then you are part of Abraham's chosen seed, and heirs according to God's covenant.

Our God, the Father of humanity, we know that you refer to us as your children, those who follow your Son. And we will be going home to be with you where our true family will abide forever. Regardless of age, we need you, Father; we love you dearly, though it seems harder to show it than to think it. Help us to make you proud by learning and teaching the truth, in particular, your truth conveyed by the Holy Spirit. Let your words be pleasant to our ears and hearts, as we ponder the stories in the Bible, and share them with our children and our children's children. Help us to do that often, making this part of the family's regular routine: reading, marking, digesting, and being enriched as we share your Word with one another. Remind us to talk frequently with our parents and our children, and read together, especially the Holy Bible; studying in depth the mysteries, histories, and literary excellence of the greatest and most popular book ever written—authored by the Holy Spirit and communicated to us in the written word and the Word made flesh, who is Christ our Lord and Savior, in whose name we now pray, Amen, and Amen.

April 3

Pony Express Began Operations on 04/03/1860 to reduce delivery time of mail going from east to west and back; it was the express mail of its time. Shipping mail over water required lengthy travel and weeks to get there. Stagecoaches didn't fare all that well either. The idea of a pony express was dreamed up by William Russell, William Waddell, and Alexander Majors. They proposed to purchase four hundred horses, build two hundred stations between St. Joseph MO, Sacramento CA, and San Francisco CA, and ship mail cross-country on horseback. There were relay stations every ten miles, home bases every thirty miles, eighty riders and four hundred support personnel; the mail was taken two thousand miles in ten days. These tough men faced physical challenges, rough terrain, injury, bandits, renegades, and possible death. It was a logistical masterpiece and ran relatively smoothly, but not wholly profitable; plus, after eighteen months the telegraph would connect America (October 1861). It was a pivotal period in history, connecting both sides of our vast country by land. But then the Civil War would tear us apart again from north to south and back. The idea of joining the east and west, and the contributions of the gold rush, the railroad, and the pony express all added to the mystique of the wild west. Plus, these developments emphasized the importance of intracontinental communications. The country was growing like a weed, with settlers covering the landscape from coast to coast. Information was in high demand, especially for newspapers and by the government.

Nowadays everyone demands information, and can get it with the tap of a finger. Such is the thirst for evidence, and the need to have it gratified immediately. You can do research, have a meeting, or hold a class without leaving your study or office. We pick and choose the information we seek or that suits us. Everyone can watch, listen, or read tons of fake news, garbage science, and rigged data from speculative sources. The problem is, some people cannot tell the difference. Be careful what you believe, fact check everything, and hold onto the good.

God communicates His love, truth, and laws to all people throughout the world, by way of His Holy Spirit. He speaks to our spirits directly, and He speaks to our souls by His Word, which was alive in Jesus Christ. He also speaks to us through nature, as a demonstration that He provides everything we need if we trust in Him. There are those who would prefer to do it their own way, believing they do not need God to be successful; yes, we can succeed at certain things, but we need God to live. Do not be deceived by the pleasures and treasures of this world, for they are fleeting; seek God and spiritual treasures and you will have more than you ever need, both here and in the life to come. Do it your way, without God, and you will die, leaving it all behind with nothing to look forward to. Jesus is the express mail avenue to our Father in heaven.

- DEU 31:12 ~ Gather the people together including men, women, and children, as well as the strangers among you, so that everyone can hear, learn, fear the Lord your God, and obey all the words of His Law.

- PRO 2:2 ~ Make your ear attentive to wisdom and your heart to understanding.

- PRO 8:1, 4, 21, 34–35 ~ God says, "Does wisdom not cry out, and understanding speak? I call to you people; my voice speaks to everyone. I want those who love me to inherit something of substance, for I will fill their treasure troves. Blessed is the person who listens to me, watches daily at my gates, and waits at the door. For whoever finds me finds life and obtains my bountiful favor."

- AMO 4:13 ~ He forms the mountains, He creates the wind, He communicates His thoughts to humankind, and He turns the dawn into dusk. He can be found in the high places of the earth, and the Lord God Almighty is His name.

- JOH 15:26 ~ Jesus said, "I will send the Comforter to you and He will testify about me; the Comforter is the Spirit of Truth which proceeds from the Father."

- EPH 1:4–5 ~ For He chose us before the creation of the world to be holy and blameless in His sight. In love, He predestined us to be adopted children through Jesus Christ, in accordance with His pleasure and will.

- 1 CO 2:13 ~ We teach using words taught by the Holy Spirit, not by human wisdom. Spiritual truths must be interpreted by those who possess the Spirit.

God has provided prayer, worship, and meditation as means of communicating with Him. Take time to acknowledge His presence in your life, His answers to your prayers, and His comfort in times of need or grief. Confess your sins to Him and be aware of your misdeeds. The more you remember Him in your walk, the less you will be inclined to allow the temptations of the world to entice you, and the more the Holy Spirit will guide you, protect you, and inform you. Maintain a line of communications from earth to heaven and back: your life depends on it.

- PSA 19:14 ~ David prayed, "Let the words of my mouth and the meditation of my heart be acceptable to you, oh Lord, my strength and my redeemer."

- PSA 50:15 ~ The Lord says, "Call upon me in the day of trouble, and I will deliver you, and you shall glorify me."

- MAT 6:6–7 ~ Jesus taught: When you pray, do so in private. Pray to the Father in your mind and He will know what you are thinking. Pray to Him secretly, and He will reward you openly. Do not use vain repetitions like the unbelievers do, for they think they will be heard for their many words.

- MAR 11:23–24 ~ Jesus taught: Whatever you ask in prayer, believe that you will receive it and you will. If you pray without doubting, you can make the mountain fall into the sea.

- MAR 14:38 ~ Jesus said, "Watch and pray that you do not enter into temptation."

- ROM 12:12 ~ Rejoice in hope, be patient in troubled times, be constant in prayer.

- EPH 6:18–19 ~ Pray all the time in the Spirit. Keep alert and persevere. Pray for Christians, prophets, and priests, that their words will proclaim the mystery of the Gospel.

- PHP 4:6–7 ~ Do not have anxiety about anything, but pray for everything. With thanksgiving let your requests be known to God. And the peace of God that surpasses all understanding will keep your heart and mind in Jesus Christ.

- COL 4:2 ~ Continue to pray and wait for the answer, giving thanks for the result.

- 1 TH 5:17–18 ~ Pray constantly. Give thanks in all circumstances.

- JAM 1:6 ~ Ask in faith without doubting.

- 1 JO 5:14–15 ~ If we ask Him anything according to His will, He will give it to us. If we believe that He hears us, He will hear us and He will fulfill our desires.

Heavenly Father, you are all we need; let us always trust in you for our needs. Help us to listen when you speak, to seek wisdom from your Word, and to be attentive to the presence of your Holy Spirit as often as we can think of you. Help us to offer our thanks and praise, to give you our worship and adoration, and to meditate on your words of truth day and night, teaching them to our children and to one another. Help us always to look forward, and not get stuck in the present or the past. In the name of Jesus we pray, Amen.

APRIL

April 4

National Walking Day occurs on the first Wednesday of April. Experts say that walking thirty minutes or more every day promotes health, and lessens the effects of certain ailments such as heart disease, cancer, and diabetes; this has been repeatedly proven in multiple scientific studies. This day is endorsed by the American Heart Association and the National Institutes of Health. There will be numerous walkathons that you can participate in, or just take a walk with your loved ones, classmates, or office mates; walking is a lot more fun when you have company. Have a regular walking routine until it becomes a habit that you do not want to break. Good habits help to eliminate bad habits, as well as contributing to a longer, happier, and more robust life.

Can you imagine the number of miles Jesus Christ walked during His short ministry? He basically walked everywhere, except when he rode into Jerusalem on a donkey. The Bible tells us how to walk, which is in the light of Christ; because the light shows us where to walk. Those who walk in darkness will lose their way. Those who follow the light will walk in righteousness and truth, all the way to the glory land.

- DEU 10:12–13 ~ The Lord requires you to fear Him, to walk in His ways, to love Him, to serve Him will all your heart and soul, and to obey His commandments.

- JOS 22:5 ~ Be diligent and take heed to the commandments and the law, which Moses, the servant of the Lord, commanded: love the Lord your God, walk in His ways, and keep His commandments; cleave to Him and serve Him with all your heart and soul.

- PSA 1:1 ~ Blessed is the person who does not walk in the counsel of the ungodly, or stand in the path of sinners, or sit in the seat of the scornful.

- PSA 23:4 ~ Even when I walk beneath the shadow of death, I will not be afraid because God is with me.

- PSA 84:11 ~ The Lord is our sun and shield; He will give grace and glory to all who walk in righteousness.

- PSA 86:11 ~ Teach me your ways Lord and I will walk in your truth; unite my heart to fear your name.

- PRO 28:6 ~ Poor people who walk in righteousness are better off than rich people who are perverse in their ways.

- ISA 2:3 ~ People will say, "Come, let us go to the mountain of the Lord to the house of the God of Jacob, and He will teach us His ways and we will walk in His paths. For out of Zion will come the Law; and out of Jerusalem will come the Word."

- ISA 26:7–8 ~ Lord, you make the path of righteousness a smooth one. Yes Lord, walking in the way of your laws we wait for you. Your name and majesty are the desires of our hearts.

- ISA 30:21 ~ Whether you veer to the left or to the right, your ears will hear a word behind you saying, "This is the way, walk in it."

- ISA 40:30–31 ~ Even youths faint and become weary, and young men stumble and fall. But those who trust the Lord will be renewed in their strength; they will soar on wings like eagles. They will run and not grow weary; they will walk and not feel faint.

- MIC 4:5 ~ The nations will follow after their own gods, but we will walk after the Lord our God forever.

DAILY DEVOTIONAL EVENTS

- MAT 9:2–8 ~ They brought a man stricken with palsy lying on a bed. Seeing their faith, Jesus said to the man, "Be of good cheer, your sins are forgiven." The scribes mumbled to themselves saying, "This man blasphemes." Jesus, knowing their thoughts said, "Why do you think evil in your minds? Which is easier, to say to this man your sins are forgiven or to say arise and walk? But so that you might know that the Son of man has power on earth to forgive sins…" Then Jesus turned to the man and said, "Arise, pick up your bed, and go home." The man got up, took his bedding, and walked away. When the crowd saw this, they marveled, and glorified God who had given such power to men.

- JOH 8:12 ~ Jesus said, "I am the light of the world. Whoever follows me will not walk in darkness but will have the light of life."

- JOH 12:35 ~ Jesus said, "The light will be with you a little longer. Walk while you have the light, before the darkness overtakes you; those who walk in darkness do not know where they are going."

- ACT 3:12, 16 ~ Peter answered them, "Men of Israel, why do you marvel at this, and look with earnest upon us, as if by our own power we enabled this lame man to walk. By faith in the name of Jesus was this man healed, a man whom you have seen and known. Yes, it was faith in Christ which made him whole in your presence."

- ROM 8:1–6 ~ There is no condemnation for those who are in Jesus Christ, because they walk after the Spirit not the flesh. For the law of the Spirit of life in Christ has made us free from the law of sin and death. The righteous requirement of the Law is fulfilled in those who walk according to the Spirit and not according to the flesh. Those who walk according to the flesh set their minds on things of the flesh, and those who walk according to the Spirit set their minds on things of the Spirit. To be carnally minded means death, but to be spiritually minded means life and peace.

- 2 CO 5:7 ~ We walk by faith, and not by sight.

- GAL 5:16–18 ~ Walk in the Spirit not in the flesh. For the Spirit and the flesh oppose one another. If you are led by the Spirit, you are not under the Law.

- EPH 2:2 ~ In the past, you walked according to the course of this world, according to the prince of the power of the air, the same spirit that works in the children of disobedience.

- 1 JO 1:7 ~ If we walk in the light as He is in the light, we have fellowship with one another; and the blood of Jesus Christ, God's Son, will cleanse us from all sin.

Today is a good day for a long walk. Even if you do not have company, you actually have God walking with you: simply invite Him to come along. And you can have a conversation with Him as you think of things to say in your mind. And when you finish a thought, pause and listen very carefully within your soul. Tell God in your mind what you think. Yes, God already knows what you are thinking, He just wants you to talk to Him since He is there. After your walk with the Holy Spirit, jot down your thoughts and what you imagined God is saying to you. Make this exercise part of your everyday routine and see how much your faith and knowledge grow.

Heavenly Father, we love that you are here with us; help us to think this thought often and to listen intently to what you think. Help us to walk in your ways and your light, so that we will know your thoughts and your plans, and so we can walk proudly, knowing that we are your sons and daughters and we can come to you anytime. We have loved ones and we tell them our thoughts, feelings, and plans; but we need to walk with you more often and have these intimate conversations with you. Let this be so in accordance with your will, in Jesus's name, Amen.

April 5

Gold Star Spouses Day is an annual acknowledgement and appreciation for spouses of fallen or maimed military heroes. Nobody can know how these families feel unless they have experienced this themselves. But everybody can show their gratitude and indebtedness to military spouses and families. This follows a tradition that began with World War I, when families hung flags with a star for each family member who had gone to war; when one of them was killed, the blue star was replaced by a gold one. Spouses and mothers of those serving overseas were called Blue Star Wives and Blue Star Moms; if they had lost someone in the war, they were Gold Star Wives and Moms. Gold Star Mothers' Day began in 1936 (last Sunday in September). The Gold Star Wives Association was promoted by Eleanor Roosevelt (and others) near the end of World War II. In 1947, Gold Star lapel buttons were given to spouses and families who had lost a loved one in war. The first Gold Star Wives Day was observed in 2010; it is now called Spouses Day since fallen heroes are not limited to men. Attend ceremonies and events on military installations to remember with dignity our fallen heroes and their families today.

Caring about and helping widows and orphans has always been a commandment of God. They have lost their husbands and fathers at no fault of their own, and are often neglected and ignored. But not so in the USA, where we care about and take care of families left without their head of household. Of course, that can involve any single-parent home. This memorial can be extended to include those who lost their wives and mothers through honorable military service.

- DEU 26:12–13 ~ After you have tithed during the third year, which is the year of tithing, and you have given your tithes to the Levites, strangers, orphans, widows, and the hungry, then declare this to the Lord.

- EXO 22:22 ~ You must never mistreat a widow or fatherless child.

- PSA 68:5 ~ Father of the fatherless and protector of widows is God in His holy habitation.

- PSA 146:9 ~ The Lord watches over the travelers; He upholds the widows and the fatherless. But the way of the wicked He brings to ruin.

- ZEC 7:9–10 ~ God says, "Render true judgments; show kindness and mercy to one another. Do not to oppress the widow, fatherless, traveler, or poor; never devise evil in your heart."

- MAL 3:5 ~ He will execute swift and permanent judgment against the sorcerers, adulterers, perjurers, cheaters, oppressors of widows and the fatherless, abusers of human rights, and people who refuse to fear God.

- MAT 23:14 ~ Woe to you hypocritical scribes and Pharisees, who confiscate widows' houses and speak long prayers for show; you will receive the greater damnation.

- JAM 1:22–26 ~ Do not just listen to the Word, but do what it says. Whoever listens but does not act is like a person who looks in the mirror and later forgets what they look like. But those who look intently into the perfect law of liberty, and who act on this, they will be blessed in all they do. Those who consider themselves to be religious, but do not control their tongue, deceive themselves and their religion is worthless.

- 1 TI 5:5 ~ The true widow who is left alone has set her hope on God, and continues in prayers and supplications night and day.

Father, we thank you for the sacrifices of those who must endure after losing their loved one in war. Please comfort them with the love and comfort of your Holy Spirit. Help them to overcome their hardship, even as Jesus Christ overcame the world for us all. In His name, Amen.

April 6

USA Entered World War I on this day in 1917, about three years into the war. Though President Wilson wanted to remain neutral, he did manage to support the war effort with supplies and money. In 1915 a German submarine took out the passenger ship *Lusitania* killing over a thousand people of which ten percent were Americans. Further, Germany was pushing for an alliance with Mexico to keep the USA at bay, while we tracked down raider Poncho Villa at the border in 1916. Wilson was reelected largely for keeping us out of war, while many Americans joined the French Foreign Legion and other outfits to fight the Germans. A German submarine sank yet another passenger ship with Americans on board after promising not to attack defenseless ships without warning. Wilson broke ties with Germany; they commenced attacking and sinking US merchant ships, after which Congress had no choice but declare war. Shortly thereafter, the Selective Service Act was passed to reinstate the draft. This, combined with a surge in enlistments, grew the US military by approximately five million service members. By the end of the war in 1918, the US had lost over fifty thousand troops at the Western Front.

Christ told us when we hear of wars and rumors of wars the beginning of the end will be nigh. This prophecy is difficult to decipher: wars have been around since ancient Mesopotamia. Many of these wars escalated into a full-scale world war, with a power-hungry regime succeeding in controlling the majority of the world as it existed then. This gave rise to the great empires: Egyptian, Assyrian, Babylonian, Media-Persian, Greek, and Roman. The Nazis also were globalists, intending to rule the world; they were giving it a go until the USA entered World War I. The US under Eisenhower took the lead in World War II resulting in the second defeat of the Nazi regime in 1945. The Bible indicates the next globalist takeover will be the last, and it will be over faster than the fall of the Third Reich.

- DAN 7:14–25 ~ Four beasts represent four kings who will come (see REV 17). The fourth beast, representing the fourth kingdom that will come, is different, exceedingly terrible. The ten horns represent ten kings; three will fall being overtaken by one. This one will speak bold things against God and will make war with the saints, defeating them. He will change the times and the rules. He will reign for a time, times, and half a time (3.5 years).

- DAN 9:26 ~ The followers of the evil prince will destroy the city and the sanctuary. The end will come like a flood; the wars will continue until the desolations have run their course.

- MAT 24; MAR 13; LUK 21 (introduction) ~ Do not be deceived; many will claim to be the Messiah or a prophet from God. They will perform magic tricks and will fool many people. There will be wars and rumors of wars. There will be earthquakes in different places. Nation will rise against nation and kingdom against kingdom. There will be famines, afflictions, and pestilence. The righteous will be persecuted, interrogated, imprisoned, and crucified. People will betray one another and wickedness will abound. It will be like the days of Noah and Lot, only worse; the philosophy will be: eat, drink, and be merry. You will be hated for following me. This is the beginning of the time of sorrows; the beginning of the end. A time of great tribulation will come, worse than the world has ever known before or will ever know again.

- REV 17 (synopsis) ~ The beast's whore is described which sits on seven mountains and governs many waters, nations, tongues. There are seven kings. Five have fallen, one is now (sixth), and one is coming (seventh) having a short reign. The beast is number eight and also one of the previous seven. Ten kings reign with the beast for one hour and make war with the Lamb who will overwhelm them, for He is Lord of lords and King of kings.

We've been at war somewhere in the world, including here at home, since day one. Yes, there have been intermittent periods of peace, but evil keeps trying to take it away by force. The deceivers will clash again with the godly, which have prevailed thus far thanks to God. But those who turn away from God and become greedy power-hungry globalists, will not have God to protect or fight with them. We must remain a sovereign nation able to protect our way of life, our borders, and our citizenry. We must not make friends with the avarice of global power. The way to win this war is with God on our side; like Christ said, you are either with us or against us.

- NUM 14:9 ~ Joshua said, "Do not rebel against God, and do not be afraid of your enemies; for the Lord is with us, and their assaults against us will have no effect."

- JOS 5:13–15 ~ While Joshua was preparing to attack Jericho, he saw a man with a sword drawn, so Joshua asked, "Are you for us or against us?" The man replied, "I am the captain of the angels of the Lord. Remove your shoes for you are standing on holy ground."

- MAR 9:38–40 ~ John spoke, "Master, we saw a man casting out devils in your name, and he is not one of us." Jesus replied, "Do not stop him; no man performing miracles in my name can be speaking evil against me at the same time. For he that is not against us is on our side."

- ROM 8:31, 38–39 ~ If God is for us, who can be against us? Neither death nor life, nor angels, principalities, or powers, nor things present or future, nor any creature can separate us from the love of God which is in Jesus Christ our Lord.

The principal cause of war starts with the conflict within oneself, between the flesh and the spirit. The flesh wants to fulfill its worldly desires which are often against God's Law. The spirit seeks to do God's will and wants to fulfill heavenly desires like abiding with God our Father. Therefore, world wars usually have a spiritual and moral component: evil versus good, tyranny versus liberty, socialism versus capitalism, wrong versus right. We must be right, else we lose the war for being wrong. We have the truth, and need only to believe it to be right.

- MIC 3:2–5 ~ They hate good and love evil. They skin people and eat their flesh. They chop their bodies into pieces. They will cry out to the Lord but He will not hear them, for their behavior has been detestable. They talk of peace but make war.

- 2 CO 10:3–5 ~ Although we are human flesh and blood, we do not make war with flesh and blood. For the weapons we use are not of this world, because we have the Spirit on our side to bring down the strongholds of the enemy. We break down the arguments and the influences of those high and mighty people who stand against God; we take captive human thoughts, making them obedient to Jesus Christ.

- 2 TI 2:3–4 ~ Endure hardship like a good Christian soldier. Those who fight wars need not get caught up with the affairs of this life, but rather should concern themselves with the affairs of Jesus Christ who chose them to be a soldier.

- JAM 4:1 ~ Where do arguments and wars come from? From the lusts that battle inside you.

- 1 PE 2:11 ~ Abstain from lusts of the flesh which wage war against your soul.

Father God, bless America that we never fall on the wrong side of you! We know the end could begin in our lifetime and that we need to be vigilant; let it be so even as you have written it, and let us always fight on the side of goodness. Let ours be your battle, as they all are; help us defeat the temptations that war against our spirits and the soul of our nation. Help our nation to turn away from the globalists and deceivers that would suck us into another world war; in the meantime, help us to defend our democracy and our republic from enemies of the state, and anarchy from within. We pray that you will fight for us if we enter a war to preserve the moral foundation of our country and its citizenry. Help us to remember that we are sojourners here, for our citizenship is in heaven. This we pray in the name of the Father, Son, and Holy Spirit, Amen.

April 7

World Health Day coincides with the day the World Health Organization (WHO) was founded in 1945. This holiday was first observed in July 1949, after which the date was moved to match up with the start of WHO. On this day we promote physical and mental wellness in the world. Every year, a particular application of healthcare is examined, discussed, and presented by the WHO in terms of improving worldwide wellness. The holiday was established to draw awareness of the WHO by promoting what they do, garnering support, and recruiting nations to join and contribute financially. The USA contributes roughly a billion annually to the WHO, representing about twenty percent of their budget. Whether or not we get our money worth from that investment is debatable. But world health is important which is why anyone can give a donation to a reputable organization that actually provides hands-on help domestically or in foreign countries. Check with your favorite church because many of them support missionary work providing physical, mental, and spiritual health services abroad. You can find dozens of charities and check their budgets on the internet; some spend over ninety percent of their donations on direct services to people in need. Maybe you are inclined to volunteer your services, or become a missionary yourself, for such is the work of the Lord.

All too often, when you hear talk of wellness and healthcare, they limit the discussion to physical and mental health, ignoring the most important component of health which is spiritual. The holistic health paradigm suggests we need to be healthy body, mind, and spirit to be wholly complete. Therefore, it is necessary to exercise and nurture all three. Missionaries who go into dangerous places to help people are often sponsored by Christian foundations which address the three components of wellness.

- PSA 107:17 ~ Fools become afflicted because of their evil ways.

- PRO 3:5–8 ~ Trust in the Lord with all your heart; do not rely on your own understanding. Acknowledge God in everything you do, and He will direct your ways. Do not consider yourself wise, but fear the Lord, refrain from evil, and you will be healthy and strong.

- PRO 12:18 ~ Words can pierce like a sword but the words of the wise brings health.

- PRO 16:24 ~ Pleasant words are sweet to the soul and health to the body.

- JER 30:15 ~ Why bother crying over your afflictions? There is no cure for your sorrow because you have done evil things. Bad things happened to you because of your wickedness.

- MAT 14:35–36 ~ When the people recognized Jesus, word spread rapidly, and everyone brought their sick to Him. They begged Jesus just to touch His garment, because everyone that did was made perfectly healthy.

- MAT 22:37 ~ And Jesus said to him, "You shall love the Lord your God with all your heart and with all your soul and with all your mind."

- ROM 12:2 ~ Do not be conformed to this world but be transformed by the renewal of your mind; by testing, you may discern the will of God: what is good and acceptable and perfect.

- 1 CO 12:27–28 ~ You are of the body of Christ and each one of you has a part in it. In the church God has appointed apostles first, prophets second, teachers third, then miracle workers, those with the gift of healing, helpers, administrators, and those who can speak in different tongues.

Spiritual health is most important because if you have that, you are more likely to be healthy physically and mentally. As you ponder about what to do in celebration of World Health

APRIL

Day, consider that most of the planet is not healthy spiritually. The Holy Spirit empowers us to live, love, feel, decide, and act in the most beneficial way for us and for the greater good, as long as we open our hearts and let the Holy Spirit in. Next, we must pour out our hearts and share the Spirit with those who are spiritually ill. Jesus asked for laborers to work in His harvest, and that is what Christian missionaries and ministers do wherever the Lord calls them.

- 2 CH 20:9 ~ If evil comes upon us, like the sword, judgment, pestilence, or famine, and we stand before God's house and in His presence (for His name is spoken there), and we cry to the Lord in our affliction, He will hear us and help us.

- EZE 22:26–27 ~ Their priests have violated my laws and profaned the holy things. They do not know the difference between holy and unholy, or clean versus unclean. They have ignored my sabbaths and dishonored my name. Their rulers are like wolves tearing apart their prey; they shed blood and destroy people for dishonest gain.

- MAT 4:24 ~ Jesus's fame spread all over the country; the afflicted (diseased, tormented, crazy, lame, and possessed) were brought before Him and He healed them all.

- MAT 9:35–38 ~ Jesus healed every illness and disease wherever He went. As He traveled about, Jesus was moved with compassion for the multitudes, because they were weary and scattered about like sheep with no shepherd. Jesus said, "The harvest is plentiful but the laborers are few. Pray, therefore, that the Lord will send laborers into the harvest."

- MAR 2:17 ~ Jesus said, "Those who are healthy do not need a doctor, but those who are sick do. I came to call sinners, not the righteous, to repentance."

- LUK 9:1–6 ~ Jesus called His twelve disciples together, giving them authority over demons and the power to cure diseases. He sent them to preach the kingdom of God and heal the sick. Jesus said to them, "Take nothing for your journey: no food, no luggage, no money, no extra clothes. When you enter a house, stay there until you leave that town. If a town does not welcome you, shake the dust from your feet when you leave, as a testimony against them." And the disciples departed, and went through the towns preaching the Gospel and healing people everywhere.

- ACT 5:11–16 ~ The apostles healed the sick and possessed.

- 2 CO 4:16 ~ We do not lose heart. Though our outer self is wasting away, our inner self is being renewed day by day.

- EPH 4:22–24 ~ Put off your old self, which belongs to your former manner of life and is corrupt through deceitful desires. Be renewed in the spirit of your minds, by putting on the new self, created after the likeness of God in true righteousness and holiness.

- 1 TH 5:23 ~ Now, may the God of peace Himself sanctify you completely, and may your whole spirit, soul, and body be kept blameless at the coming of our Lord Jesus Christ.

  We praise you, Heavenly Father, healer of the nations; who sent His Son into the world to heal all manner of disease, illness, injury, and affliction of the body and mind, as well as the sin that afflicts our souls and degrades our spiritual health. Thank you for the gift of health; we pray that you sustain us in our health, physically, mentally, and spiritually. Help us to be ministers of your grace and prepare us to minister to others in whichever skills and knowledges that we possess or pursue. Prepare helpers and missionaries to be equipped to address the holistic health of those they serve, so they can be well within their soul and have a healthy relationship with your Holy Spirit, through your Son Jesus Christ in whose name we pray, Amen.

April 8

National Library Week occurs the second full week of April and is sponsored by the American Library Association; its first official observance was in 1958. On this day, libraries across the nation have events to promote reading, books, and local public libraries; activities include music, art, theater, meetings, classes, forums, contests, socializing, fundraisers, and more. Each year has a different theme, and days of the week have a different focus as well: America's Libraries Report, Library Workers Day, Outreach Day, Take Action Day, and Bookmobile Day. Other countries have followed suit and adopted their own library week.

Libraries of today offer much more than just books; you can check out movies, videos, audiobooks, and use a computer to do research. If you haven't been to your local library in a while you might want to check it out; get your kids accustomed to visiting the library so they'll know how necessary they are, especially during college. Reading and writing are essential skills, yet many American kids are left behind, especially in the inner city and impoverished areas. In some areas of the world, kids are deprived of education and learning resources completely.

The most popular book of all time is the Holy Bible. There are sixty-six books in that one book: thirty-nine in the Old Testament and twenty-seven in the New Testament. Though written by men, God is the author of these books of scripture. God also is the author of the book of nature since He created the universe; everything that exists is open for us to examine, observe, and study such that all knowledge gleaned from nature (e.g., science) is a gift from God. To ensure that the Bible was not altered or suppressed, God authorized tens of thousands of manuscripts of the Bible, including the writings of early church fathers, and the translation of the Bible into hundreds of languages, thereby preserving His Word. Case in point, the Dead Sea Scrolls which date to the time of Christ and earlier, and included all Old Testament books except Esther. The scroll of Isaiah was found perfectly intact, identical to the current Hebrew version; other scrolls documented the apparent arrival of Messiah. Countless manuscripts, scrolls, and fragments have been found over the years. One fragment, dated to the first century AD, was from the book of Mark. It is recommended that you research the manuscript evidence of the Bible, it is very fascinating. You might consider checking out a book from the library on this topic.

- MAT 24:35 ~ Jesus said, "Heaven and earth will pass away, but my words will remain forever."

- 1 TH 2:13 ~ We thank God that you received His Word and accepted it as the Word of God and not the word of men. The Word of God is at work in believers like you.

- 2 TI 2:24–26 ~ The servant of the Lord must not be argumentative, but gentle to all people, able to teach with patience and meekness, instructing those who oppose the truth. For perhaps God will allow them to repent and acknowledge the truth; and come to their senses, thereby escaping the devil's traps who would take them captive to his will.

- 2 PE 1:16, 21 ~ We did not follow cleverly devised fables when we told people about the power and coming of Jesus Christ, for we were eye witnesses to His majesty. No prophecy ever came from the impulse of man, but holy men spoke as they were directed by God.

God also wrote the Book of the Law and the Book of Life. These books will be opened on Judgment Day. If you have exhibited the faith of Abraham and you die believing in Christ, you will be judged not guilty (justified) under the Law, because Christ has obliterated your sins from the record. Plus, your name will be written in the Book of Life, which is your passport to heaven. If your name is not written in the Book of Life, you will be judged by the Law and found guilty; in which case, you will not be given life since the penalty for sin is death.

APRIL

- PSA 69:27–28 ~ By adding more sin upon sin, people can never know righteousness. Let their names be obliterated from the Book of Life.

- DAN 7:10 ~ A stream of fire flowed before Him. Millions ministered to Him. Billions stood before Him. The judgment was set and the books were opened.

- DAN 12:2 ~ God's elect will be delivered, all whose names are written in the Book of Life.

- LUK 10:18–20 ~ Jesus said, "I saw the devil, like a star falling from heaven. I have given you power over that enemy, so nothing can harm you. But do not rejoice because the demons submit to you; rather rejoice because your names are written in the Book of Life."

- ROM 2:12–13 ~ All who sin apart from the Law will perish apart from the Law. All who sin under the Law will be judged according to the Law. Hearing the Law does not make you righteous in God's eyes; you must obey the Law to be declared righteous.

- ROM 3:23–24 ~ All people have sinned and come short of God's glory, and all people are justified freely by His grace through the redemption that is in Jesus Christ.

- ROM 10:10 ~ Those who believe with their hearts are justified. Those who confess with their lips are saved.

- GAL 3:11, 24–26 ~ No man is justified before God by the Law, but those who are righteous live by faith. Before faith came, we were under the Law. The Law was in effect until Christ came, so we could be justified by faith. In Christ we become children of God through faith.

- EPH 2:8–9 ~ You are saved by the grace of God because of your faith in Jesus Christ. Salvation is a gift of God, it cannot be earned through good works, so nobody should brag.

- JAM 2:17–22 ~ Faith without works is dead. Was Abraham justified by works when he offered his son Isaac? Faith was active before that and was completed by the works.

- REV 3:5 ~ Jesus said, "Those who overcome will be clothed in white raiment. Their names will never be blotted out of the Book of Life, for I will acknowledge them before our Heavenly Father and His angels."

- REV 20:12, 15 ~ John saw the dead, both small and great, standing before God. The books were opened, along with another book called the Book of Life. And everyone was judged according to the things written in the books about their actions during their lifetimes. Whoever's name was not found in the Book of Life was thrown into the lake of fire.

- REV 22:18–20 ~ For I testify to everyone who hears the words of the prophecy of this book, that if anyone adds to these words, God will add unto that person the plagues mentioned in this book. If anyone subtracts from the words of this prophecy, God will take away their name from the Book of Life, and they will not share in the inheritance. He who testifies of these things says, "Behold, I come quickly." Amen, even so, come Lord Jesus.

Dearest Father, we know the truth because you have given us your Word, the Holy Bible, conveyed to our hearts and minds by your Holy Spirit. We thank you for books and the ability to read and learn, especially to know the truth directly from you in the Holy Bible, where we see your plan of salvation unveiled for all who study it intently. Father, we know we will live forever because you have given your Son to take our place in death, and all you require is that we place our faith and trust in Him. Thank you for your Son who is the Lamb of God given for us so that we can be forgiven and freed. Thank you for justifying us by faith, for we know it is impossible to be justified by works alone. We love you Holy Trinity and pray in your name, Amen.

April 9

US Civil War Ended when General Lee of the Confederate Army surrendered to General Grant of the Union Army, on this day in 1865 at the courthouse in Appomattox, VA. Of course, we mean "civil" war in terms of social or political, for it certainly wasn't civil with respect to politeness. Over 600,000 American soldiers died fighting each other, not counting civilian deaths. There are causes one could point to which triggered this war between the states, but we all know it boiled down to slavery, which was immoral from the start. The framers knew this, but words to that effect were taken out of the original Declaration of Independence penned by Thomas Jefferson in order that all thirteen colonies approve it. These were mostly southern states which exploited slaves to tend crops, though all states participated to some degree. I expect Jefferson and others might have anticipated an eventual war over this; having owned slaves themselves, it was politically expedient for them to put it off. But the union had to be mended and lives were spent to do it; and now we are among the least racist nations on the planet. We are indebted to those who fought in that war. Nowadays, most modern countries disallow slavery, but not all.

In the Bible, slavery was common. There are two types of slavery mentioned in the Bible, the first is actual slavery, with bondage, subjection, capturing, incarcerating, and abuse. This was a common outcome of warfare, with conquerors taking humans prisoner: the victors' spoils. The clearest Biblical examples of actual slavery are twofold. In the Old Testament is the record of the captivity of the Israelites who were in bondage to the Egyptians over four hundred years. In the New Testament, Christ taught how everybody is in bondage, for we are slaves to sin.

The Israelites were prosperous and powerful when they kept God's laws. When they were unfaithful to God and His laws, conquerors took them captive. The Egyptians enslaved Israel after they lived peacefully among them in Joseph's time; a subsequent pharaoh did not recognize Joseph and confined the entire nation of Israel. Israel had been warned by God in advance; they finally repented, so God appointed Moses to guide them to the promised land. But they strayed again. So, God let the Assyrians capture the northern kingdom (Israel); next, the Babylonians sacked Assyria and took the southern kingdom (Judah) including Jerusalem. The Jews were waylaid, to be scattered across the globe, persecuted wherever they went. In 1948, God let them return to their homeland. Is this not a clear example how God will prosper people who are faithful, and let the world deal with people who turn their backs on Him? It should also be clear that the USA must unite in God as a nation and never turn away, else we start another civil war.

- GEN 15:13–14 ~ God told Abraham his seed would be enslaved four hundred years.

- DEU 7:6–9 ~ You are a holy people to God, for He has chosen you to be a special people to Him, above all people on the earth. God did not choose you and love you because you were greater in number than the others, for you were actually fewer in number. He loves you, and He keeps His holy covenant with you; He brings you out with His mighty hand and redeems you from slavery. Know then that He is God, faithful and just, who keeps His covenants and gives mercy to those who love Him and obey His commandments.

- DEU 28:1, 15–16, 47–48 ~ God said, "If you listen diligently to the voice of the Lord, and observe His commandments, I will place you high above all nations of the earth. But if you do not listen to the Lord and you do not observe His commandments and statutes that I have commanded you to follow, curses will come upon you and overtake you; you will be cursed in the city and in the field. The Lord will do these things because you did not serve Him joyfully and thankfully in response to the abundance that He gave to you. Therefore, you will be thirsty, hungry, naked, and needy. You will end up serving a nation which will come against you from afar speaking an unknown language; you will be enslaved and destroyed."

APRIL

- HOS 10:10 ~ When it pleases God, He will punish them; nations will gather against them and enslave them because they betrayed the Lord.

  Being a slave to sin is more serious than being enslaved by people, because sin enslaves you for life: not only this life but also the next, unless you repent, confess, and turn your life over to Christ. If you belong to Him, you have been freed from sin and death. Live your life in servitude to the Lord, and receive an inheritance in His kingdom. Be an indentured servant in bondage to Christ: bound to Him by faith, and in death, to be bound to Him for life eternal.

- GAL 4:6–9; GAL 4:22–23, 28, 31~ Because you are children, God has sent the Spirit of His Son into your hearts. Thus, you are no longer servants but children of God, and as children, heirs with Christ. Why then, when you did not know God, did you serve beings who were not gods, and now that you have known God you choose bondage again? Abraham had two sons, one born in bondage after the flesh and one born in freedom after the promise. My brothers, like Isaac we are born under the promise. We are not born in bondage but are born free.

- EPH 6:19–20 ~ Paul wrote: Pray that God will give me the right words so that I may boldly proclaim the mystery of the Gospel, for which I am His ambassador in bondage.

- HEB 13:3 ~ Remember those in bondage as if you were bound with them; remember those who suffer as if you were suffering with them, because you are fellow members of the body.

  The second type of slavery in the Bible was civil, since it was an agreement: one became an indentured servant to make payment for certain debts or damages. These "slaves" actually lived with the families, not in bondage but through employment. The Jewish law required they be set free after six years; the seventh was the year of jubilee, when the terms of service were completed. In many cases, the slave could elect to become a member of the household by having his or her ear pierced and corked; that person was allowed to continue working, and be cared for in kind. Obviously, an indentured servant is not a slave. Do not be confused by the word "slave" in the Bible; if you read the entire context, you can tell what kind of a slave is implied.

- EXO 21:5–6 ~ If a servant is granted his freedom, but the servant declares, "I love my master, his wife and children, and I prefer not to go free," then his master will bring him before the judges and pierce his ear, and he will be a servant for life.

- DEU 15:12–17 ~ If your Hebrew brother or sister is indebted to you and serves you for six years, he or she must be set free the seventh year, the year of jubilee. And when you release them, do not send them away empty-handed, but give them ample supplies from your stock. Give generously as God has given to you, remembering how you were slaves in Egypt before God redeemed you. But if your servant does not wish to leave because he loves you, and if your family is blessed by that servant, pierce the earlobe and he will serve you for life.

- ACT 20:22–24 ~ Paul wrote: I go forward to Jerusalem, bound in the Spirit, not knowing what will happen except that the Holy Spirit is witnessed in every city, and that bondage and affliction go with me. But these things do not move me, neither do I count my life dear to myself, in order that I can finish my course with joy, and complete the ministry which I have received from the Lord Jesus Christ to testify concerning the Gospel of the grace of God.

- ROM 8:14–15 ~ Those led by the Spirit of God become His children. They have not received a spirit of bondage and fear, but of adoption whereby we cry, "Abba, Father".

  Abba, Father, we are happy to be called your children; it is our prayer that we may serve you now and forever. We have been freed from sin and we wish to remain with you for eternity. Mark us as your indentured servants with the blood of your Son, in whose name we pray, Amen.

April 10

National Siblings Day was conceived by Claudia Evart in 1995 in memory of her brother and sister who died when they were young; she chose this date because it was her sister's birthday. She established a Siblings Day Foundation to gain support for this holiday. Give your siblings a call or a hug today. If you do not like your siblings, you should begin a dialogue, because you may need them someday. Yes, sibling rivalry can be a problem, especially if a parent shows favoritism; siblings should not show or encourage favoritism. Regardless, when your parents are gone, your siblings will be all that remain of the family you grew up with. Siblings are a blessing, ask any only child and most will say they wish they had at least one brother or sister.

- PRO 24:23 ~ A word to the wise: partiality in judgment is not good.

- ACT 10:34–35 ~ Peter said, "Truly, God does not show favoritism for any person. Within every nation, anyone who fears the Lord and endeavors to be righteous is accepted by Him."

- ROM 2:10 ~ Glory, honor, and peace is given to all who do good, regardless of race.

- JAM 2:1–9 ~ Do not be partial to people just because you like the way they look or act. Do not give the rich or the famous more respect than anyone else, and do not give the poor and lowly less respect. If you abide by the royal law according to the scripture, "Love your neighbor as yourself," you are doing the right thing. But if you show favoritism to certain persons, you commit sin and are convicted of the law as a lawbreaker.

Did you know that Jesus had siblings? I've heard some say no, but they obviously do not know their Bible very well. Jesus's siblings are mentioned on multiple occasions in the New Testament. Of course, they were half-siblings because Jesus was the progeny of the Holy Spirit and their mother, while His siblings were the progeny of Joseph. Jesus was obviously the first born and the eldest child in the family. I wonder what it was like for His siblings, growing up with Jesus. They may not have known who He was when they were young, but they did after He appeared to them alive, having been crucified the week before. Jesus's Holy Spirit inspired two of His brothers to author books in the New Testament: James and Jude (aka Judah).

- MAT 13:53–56; MAR 6:1–3 ~ After Jesus had finished sharing parables He departed into His own country. He taught in the synagogue, and the people were astonished saying, "Where does He get such wisdom, and the power for such mighty works? Is He not the carpenter's son, and is His mother not Mary? Are his brothers not James, Joseph, Simon, and Judah, and are His sisters not also with us? And many Jews were offended of Him.

- ACT 1:12–14 ~ They returned to Jerusalem from the Mount of Olives, a sabbath day's walk from the city. After arriving, they went to the place where they were staying. Those present included Peter, James, John, Andrew, Philip, Thomas, Bartholomew, Matthew, James Alphaeus, Simon Zelotes, and Judas (aka Judah) the brother of James. Together they prayed constantly, along with the women, including Mary the mother of Jesus, and His brothers.

- GAL 1:15–19; GAL 2:9 ~ God, singled me out since birth and called me by His grace, pleased to reveal His Son to me so I might preach about Him to the heathen. Immediately, without consulting anybody, and without going to Jerusalem to meet the apostles, I went into Arabia, and returned to Damascus. Finally, after three years I went to Jerusalem to meet Peter, and stayed with him fifteen days. But I did not see any of the other apostles except James, the Lord's brother. And when James, Cephas (meaning "rock" in Hebrew; namely Peter which is *Petra* in Greek), and John, pillars of the Christian church, saw the grace given to me, they offered to me and Barnabas the right hand of fellowship. It was agreed that we would preach to the Gentiles and the other disciples would preach to the Jews.

APRIL

- JAM 1:1–4 ~ Greetings from James, a servant of God and of the Lord Jesus Christ, to the twelve tribes which are scattered abroad. My brothers, count it all joy when you fall into different temptations, for the trying of your faith produces patience. But let patience have her perfect work so that you may be complete, and want for nothing.

- JDE 1:1–2 ~ From Jude (aka Judah or Judas), the servant of Jesus Christ and brother of James, to those who are sanctified by God the Father, preserved in Jesus Christ and called to be His disciples: Mercy to you; peace and love be multiplied unto you.

Alas, siblings do not always get along, though it is the Lord's wish that they would. Sibling rivalry can cause dysfunction in families, runaways, fights, or worse. Case in point, the first family in which the first two sons born to Adam clashed. When presenting their offerings to God, Abel's sacrifice from his herd was accepted by God, but Cain's sacrifice of his crop was not. The rule of sacrificial offerings given as first fruits to God was that they be the best of one's increase, without blemish or disease. Apparently, Cain's was deficient, and God chastised him for it, after which Cain became jealous and angry with his brother Abel and murdered him.

- GEN 4:3–12 ~ The time came to bring offerings to the Lord. Cain brought some of his harvest and Abel brought the first fruits of his flock, and of the fat thereof. The Lord respected Abel's offering but not Cain's. Cain became angry and frowned. And God said to Cain, "Why are you angry and why has your countenance fallen? If you do what is right, will you not be accepted? But if you do what is wrong, sin will be crouching at your door." Cain went to talk with Abel and ended up killing him in the field. Then God said to Cain, "Where is your brother Abel?" Cain replied, "Am I my brother's keeper; how would I know?" God said, "What have you done? The voice of your brother cries to me from the ground. Now you are cursed from the earth, which has received your brother by your hand. Henceforth, when you till the ground, it will not yield. You will be a fugitive and a vagabond."

- GAL 5:19–21 ~ Works of the flesh include adultery, fornication, perversion, lust, witchcraft, idolatry, hatred, quarreling, rivalry, dissension, rage, fighting, sedition, heresy, jealousy, murder, drunkenness, orgies, and the like. Those engaging in such activities will not inherit the kingdom of God.

- PHP 1:15 ~ Some actually preach Christ out of envy and rivalry; others preach out of good will.

- HEB 11:4 ~ By faith, Abel offered to God a more excellent sacrifice than Cain, showing a more righteous motivation.

- 1 JO 3:11–12 ~ You have heard from the beginning to love one another. Do not be wicked like Cain, who killed his brother; because his works were evil and Abel's were righteous.

- JDE 1:10–11 ~ Woe to false teachers who pervert the grace of God and deny the sovereignty of Jesus Christ. For they have gone the way of Cain (GEN 4); they have run towards the greed of Balaam (NUM 24), they have perished with the rebellion of Korah (NUM 16).

Thank you, Father, for our siblings; not only those born into our family but also those born again into the body of Christ. Bless them and keep them steadfast in the faith which leads to eternal life, wherein we will live together as brothers and sisters of Christ, adopted by you, Heavenly Father, into your family, to be your own and live under you in your kingdom. Let us always give you the best of our increase, serving you first before serving ourselves. How we look forward to that day when time will cease to be, and a moment will last forever; let that joy never leave our hearts regardless of the setbacks and hardships we endure on earth. In Jesus's name we pray, who is not ashamed to call us His brothers and sisters, Amen.

April 11

National Pet Day was the brainchild of animal welfare advocate Colleen Paige in 2006. Her intent was to raise awareness of the suffering of animals in shelters, and to support adoption in lieu of extermination. Her motto was, "Do not shop, adopt!" This holiday is supported by the Humane Society of the United States and the American Society for the Prevention of Cruelty to Animals (ASPCA). This popular day has spread throughout the world. Who doesn't love pets? Many are particular about their pets; they want the best breed and more. Breeding animals is a very lucrative industry, often corrupted by greed; some engage in inbreeding and they provide substandard conditions for the animals. There is poor regulation and enforcement outside of the ASPCA, though anyone can report abuse of animals anonymously and usually get a proactive response. Normally, both an adopted pet and the so-called purebred pet will be a good companion if the owner is caring and nurturing; but too much inbreeding produces retarded and handicapped animals; this practice will pass for to cruelty to animals.

Animals can learn many things, but the first thing they notice is the attitude of their master; people need to endear themselves to their pets and love these animals. Some animals excel in intelligence and can be trained to perform special functions like farm or ranch animals which work alongside owners, or service dogs that alert and ground people with PTSD, or emotional support animals for the depressed and lonely. God loves all creatures, and He gave us dominion over them; He expects us to care for and protect them, not eliminate them. That doesn't mean we avoid preventive measures like having pets neutered when appropriate. Truly, we love God because He loved us first; likewise, an animal will love you if you love it first.

- PSA 97:10 ~ Those who love the Lord hate evil.

- LUK 6:31–32 ~ Jesus said, "Treat others as you would like to be treated. If you love only those who love you, what reward will you receive? Even sinners love those who love them."

- JOH 13:34–35 ~ Jesus said, "I am giving you a new commandment, to love one another as I have loved you. This is how people will be able to tell that you are my disciples."

- COL 3:14 ~ Above all put on love, which binds all things together in perfect harmony.

- 1 JO 4:19 ~ We love because God loved us first. You cannot say you love God and hate your brother without being a liar,

Today, like every day, is a time to celebrate your pets. It is healthy to have a pet, for they give us an incentive to exercise which improves our physical health; their companionship, watchfulness, protection, and love improve our behavioral health. They also may contribute to our spiritual health, though this has not been studied extensively. But it stands to reason that their unconditional love would most certainly lift one's spirit. Initially, an animal that is new to you might be afraid; this is normal for an animal for their biggest predator is the human.

There have been pets since God charged Adam with naming the animals, right after God had given humans dominion over every creature on earth (GEN 1:28). You can view images of cats carved or painted on walls in Egyptian ruins; or look at pictures of cave paintings featuring livestock and wild animals from prehistoric times. Pets have been popular since the beginning and will be with us till the end, and maybe even in heaven. Pets can do many things, some better than humans. So yes, choose animals that can be useful, helpful, lovable, and loyal; generally speaking, a wild animal will be unable to meet those requirements. Most important, we are not to abuse any animal, wild or domesticated. And though we are able to use them as food, indiscriminate killing of any of God's creatures is wrong. The animal is not there for you to hunt and kill unless you are hungry and intend to eat it.

APRIL

- GEN 9:2 ~ The fear and dread of you will be upon every beast, bird, land animal, and fish.

- 2 SA 12:1–10 ~ God sent Nathan the prophet to David relating this story to the king. Two men lived in a city, one rich and the other poor. The rich man had flocks and herds. The poor man had only a little ewe lamb, which he had bought and nurtured; the lamb grew up with his kids and sat in his lap. A traveler visited the rich man, who was so greedy he didn't want to spare any of his livestock. So, he seized the man's lamb and butchered it. David was irate and told Nathan that the rich man must die, after restoring the lamb fourfold. Nathan told David, "You are that man," explaining how David had committed adultery with another man's wife, then sent her husband into battle to be killed, and keep her as his own wife. A curse was put on David that the sword would never leave his house. [That evil would cost David four sons.]

- JOB 30:1 ~ The younger men mock me, whose fathers I would put with the dogs who tend my livestock.

- JOB 41:1–6 ~ Can you fish leviathan out of the sea with a hook? Can you make it a pet like a bird or give it to your daughters to play with? Will it pray with you and speak softly to you? Will it make a bargain with you to be your servant forever? Will your companions make a banquet of it, or chop it up and distribute it among the merchants? [Leviathan was a large sea serpent or reptile (see PSA 74:14; ISA 27:1).]

- PSA 50:10 ~ God says, "Every animal in the forest, all the cattle in the hills, all the birds in the mountains, indeed everything that moves, is mine."

- PRO 12:10 ~ A righteous man is concerned for the life of his animal; but tender mercies of the wicked are cruel.

- ISA 11:6 ~ The wolf will lie down with the lamb; the leopard will lie down with the goat. The calf will be with the lion and together a little child will lead them.

- ISA 56:8–11 ~ God, who gathered the outcasts of Israel says, "I will gather others to dwell there instead. Listen, beasts of the forest and the field, come devour them. For his watchmen are blind; they are ignorant like dumb dogs without a bark, lying down and slumbering. They are greedy dogs, which never have enough; shepherds that cannot find their way."

- MAT 15:26–28 ~ Jesus told the Canaanite woman, "It is not right to take the children's food and throw it to the dogs." She replied, "That is true, Lord, but the dogs eat the crumbs which fall from the master's table." Jesus answered her, "Woman, your faith is great. You may have what you asked." And her daughter was healed that very hour.

- JAM 3:7–8 ~ Every kind of animal, bird, reptile, or fish can be tamed by humankind. But nobody can tame the tongue, which can be unruly and poisonous.

Dear Father, what an honor it is to call you that, for you are holy; we love that you have made us whole so we can appear before you righteous, with the covering Christ laid on us when He took our sins upon Himself. You have dominion over all things; and you have given us dominion over things associated with this planet, like the plants and animals, the water and the air, the natural resources and our civilizations. It is an honor to be given this responsibility, and we pray that we care for this your creation as faithful stewards, to protect and nurture it; let us cultivate the environment and not destroy it. Help us be kind to the animals so they needn't fear us. Thank you for the creatures, for they give us sustenance, companionship, and love, as well as helping us maintain the ecology of the environment. Help us to treat everything that moves with respect and concern; help us to be able guardians of all that you leave in our care. In Jesus's name, Amen.

April 12

International Day of Human Space Flight is a United Nations observance which began this day in 2011. The date was chosen because on 04/12/1961 Russia sent the first man into space to orbit the earth. The value of space exploration has been tremendous in explaining our universe, solar system, and planet. The technological advancements are awe inspiring: we can put people on the moon, emplace powerful telescopes above the atmosphere, send spacecrafts into places we cannot go and receive real-time data from them, and build an international space station enabling continuous scientific research. We have yet to reach the level of *Star Trek*, but we are getting there fast when you consider the USA put men on the moon in 1969, scarcely eight years after the first manned space flight. The first unmanned deep space exploration vehicle was launched in 1977 and there have been countless more. Consider the breakthroughs since space exploration became common knowledge. We are able to see the edge of the universe, view the rings of Saturn up close, examine the violence of the sun, and spot anything on the surface of the earth with triangulated precision. We have international space missions, we have private industry involved in space exploration, and we have a new race to land someone on Mars.

Today, all the nations of the world celebrate space exploration. We also celebrate the joint operation of the international space station which has been visited by astronauts mostly from the USA and Russia, followed by Japan, Italy, Canada, Germany, and France. Space technology has resulted in major developments in science and technology; unfortunately, there also have been advances in weaponry and targeting, so it behooves nations not to share, else they use a nations' secrets against them. Therefore, it is unlikely there will be a successful accord among nations, much less a global society. This was tried in ancient Mesopotamia, but God confused the languages when humanity had begun to build a tower to the sky. Collectively, their power had gone to their heads, so God intervened and every tribe formed their own language.

- GEN 10:8–10 ~ The city of Babel was founded by Nimrod, son of Cush, who was the son of Ham, who was the son of Noah.

- GEN 11:1–9 ~ People spoke one language when civilization spread north to Shinar, where the people decided to build a temple to heaven. It started with bricks and tar to form a solid base, and upon it they began building a tower. The Lord looked down from heaven and said, "Behold, the people have united, unrestrained in their imagination; nothing will be impossible for them. Let us go down and confound their language, so they cannot understand each other." The people left the tower unfinished and went separate ways across the face of the earth. This is why the city was named Babel, because it was where the Lord confused the languages.

The Bible speaks of three principal atmospheres or heavens: the air we breathe within our atmosphere, the space beyond our atmosphere which comprises the cosmos, and God's realm, the kingdom of heaven which is located outside this universe. God placed a layering of the atmospheres surrounding our planet by separating elements ("waters") into stories like a skyscraper. We look up into the sky through our immediate layer of atmosphere, and we can see through several other layers into outer space to view planets, stars, and galaxies. But God's domain lies beyond, though He sees all that goes on here and everywhere because He is omnipresent. God also can invoke Himself into our realm, as in the case of Jesus Christ.

- GEN 1:6–8 ~ And God said, "Let there be a firmament in the midst of the waters and let it divide the waters from other waters. And God made the firmament, and let it divide the waters which were under the firmament and above the firmament. And God called the firmament heaven. And the evening and the morning were the second day."

APRIL

- DEU 10:14 ~ Behold, the heaven and the heaven of heavens is the Lord's, and the earth also, including everything in it.

- 1 KI 8:27 ~ Will God dwell on earth? Behold the heaven and the highest heaven cannot contain Him.

- JOB 22:14 ~ Thick clouds are a covering to Him so He cannot be seen as He walks in the circuit of heaven.

- JOB 37:18 ~ Were you with God when He stretched out the sky, which is as strong as a mirror forged from metal?

- PSA 148:4 ~ Praise Him you highest heavens and waters above the skies.

- AMO 9:6 ~ He builds the stories in heaven, and places a foundation on the earth. He commands the waters in the sea to pour out over the dry land. The Lord is His name.

- 2 CO 12:2–4 ~ I knew a man in Christ over fourteen years ago (whether in the body or out of the body I know not, but God knows). This man was taken up to the third heaven, and I knew him. How he was caught up into paradise to hear unspeakable words I am not free to explain.

God came down to earth and performed miracles and He also has sent angels to do His bidding. How do we know when a miracle has occurred? Because it defies the laws of nature and physics. For example, when Jesus instantaneously turned water into wine, it was a miracle because there is no physical or natural process that can do this. There is no such power in nature or humanity, for that power comes only from God who is omnipotent. Scientists call such events singularities because they only happen once. The creation of the universe, the immaculate conception, Jesus Christ raising Himself from the dead, these are singularities; they can happen only by an intervention from God. The resurrection of humankind will be the last singularity for this world; it will happen only once for everybody, after which God will separate those judged not guilty who claimed the blood of Christ, and those judged guilty in accordance with the Law. There will be a new heaven and a new earth which provide for eternal life in the new universe. The old heaven and earth will pass away; eternal death will occur in concert with the old universe dying.

- JOH 9:14–16 ~ It was on the Sabbath Day when Jesus made clay and opened the beggar's eyes. The Pharisees asked the man how he had received his sight and the man replied, "Jesus put clay upon my eyes, and I washed, and now I can see." Some of the Pharisees complained about Jesus, "This man is not of God because he does not keep the Sabbath." Others said, "How can a sinful man perform miracles?" And there was division among them.

- JOH 10:17–18 ~ Jesus said, "Therefore, my Father loves me, because I lay down my life so that I may take it back again. Nobody takes it from me but I lay it down of my own free will. I have power to lay it down and I have power to take it back again. This commandment I have received from my Father."

- 2 PE 3:13 ~ We, according to God's promise, look for new heavens and a new earth, wherein dwells righteousness.

Dear Father, we look forward to being with you in the highest heaven, when you create everything new. We gaze into the sky and realize that the universe is astounding; and we look around the planet as we travel to exotic places and we are mystified by the beauty. Everything on earth and in heaven proclaim your magnificence. Help others who cannot see to discover that we have an awesome God who has promised us amazing things. Let them know you have reserved a place for them in heaven where everything will pale in comparison to what we experience in this life. What a wonderful pleasure, to live with you and our brother Jesus, in whom we pray, Amen.

April 13

International Plant Appreciation Day is an unofficial holiday of unknown origin, though it has been observed for about two decades. Today we acknowledge the importance of plants, without which we could not survive. We exhale carbon dioxide which is deadly to humans but necessary for plants, whereas the plants emit oxygen which humans cannot live without. Plants provide food, seasoning, protection, medicine, shade, and aesthetic value; they reduce pollution, noise, winds, flooding, and stress. Plant something today whether indoors or outdoors: vegetables, flowers, ferns, fruit trees, houseplants. Teach your kids how to plant and tend a garden, create a compost pit, graft plants together, conserve water, and expose them to sunlight. Plants make great gifts, especially when you can't think of what to get somebody who already "has everything". Plants are alive, and they are useful; like animals they should be treated with respect which was the lesson two days ago. We should eat plants, prune them, love and sing to them, and weed out the bad or poisonous ones. It is smart to learn about plants, especially in the area where you live; most of the time plants can be left alone, other times they should be removed.

God likens us to a vineyard in the Bible; He nurtures us, prunes us, waters and cultivates the ground around us so that we can bear good fruit. But those who bear bad fruit, or no fruit, are chopped down and burned in the fire. Jesus is the Branch to which we are joined; apart from Him we can do nothing but wither and die.

- PSA 80:14–19 ~ Return to us Almighty God! Look down from heaven and see! Watch over this vineyard that your right hand has planted, and the Branch you have raised up for yourself. The vine has been cut down and burned in the fire; at your rebuke your people perish. Let your hand rest on the man at your right, the Son of man who you have raised for yourself. Do this so we will not turn our backs on you. Revive us so we can call on your name. Turn us back, Lord of hosts, and let your face shine on us so we can be saved.

- ISA 5:1–13 ~ Isaiah compared the house of Israel to a vineyard: My most beloved has a vineyard on a hill with good soil. He fenced it, landscaped it, and planted the choicest vine. However, it bore wild grapes, despite the care that was taken. Therefore, the vineyard will be trampled down, and weeds and briers will grow; the rain will cease and the vineyard will wither. This vineyard belongs to the Lord of hosts, and the vineyard represents the house of Israel and those who have fallen from God's grace.

- JER 2:21 ~ God planted a noble vine, a wholly perfect seed. Why then, have you grown into a degenerate plant from a strange vine?

- MAR 12:1–9 ~ Jesus told the parable of a vineyard owner: The owner of a vineyard traveled to a far country and leased his vineyard to others. At harvest time, the owner sent a servant to collect profits from the vineyard. The servant was beaten and sent away. The owner sent other servants that either were beaten or killed. Then the owner sent his only beloved son, thinking the tenants would treat him with respect. The tenants killed the son, figuring if they killed the only heir, they would inherit the vineyard. What do you think the owner will do to the tenants? He will destroy them and lease the vineyard to others. This parable reveals the meaning of prophecy, "The stone they rejected became the chief cornerstone" (PSA 118:22).

- JOH 15:1–6 ~ Jesus said, "I am the true vine, and my Father is the cultivator. He removes any of my branches that do not bear fruit. Those that bear fruit, he prunes, so they can bear even more fruit. You have been made clean through the Word which I have spoken to you. Stay in me and I will stay in you. The branch cannot bear fruit by itself; it must be connected to the vine. You cannot bear fruit unless you remain in me. I am the vine and you are the branches.

APRIL

Those abiding in me will bear much fruit but without me you can do nothing. If you do not abide in me, you will be removed like a dead and withered branch that is burned in the fire."

- ROM 11:20–24 ~ Branches can be broken off due to unbelief, and branches can be grafted in because of faith. If God did not spare the natural branches that were broken off, He will not spare you either. God was stern with those that fell, but He will be kind to you if you continue in Him; if you do you not will be cut off as well. Anyone that refrains from disbelief will be grafted in. You were wild olive branches that, contrary to nature, were grafted into a cultivated olive tree.

One of the ways we can serve God is by planting seeds of faith. All good fruit has seeds, which produce more plants. When the plant dies, it replenishes the earth thereby providing nutrients to the soil, strengthening its progeny. Such is the cycle of life which all living things have in common. But as humans, more is expected for we have something other creatures do not, a soul: a discerning mind, an imagination, the ability to reason. This is not the same as the spirit which gives life to the flesh (JOH 6:63); spirits of the dead return to God (ECC 12:7). Human spirits are not destroyed in hell, only the bodies and souls of the fallen (MAT 10:28). Angels are spiritual beings, and they also have a soul; all evil spirits will lose their souls in the lake of fire.

- JOB 4:8 ~ I have seen for myself: those who plow evil and those who sow trouble reap the same.

- ISA 55:10–11 ~ The rain and snow fall from heaven, but do not return, but rather water the earth, making the plants bud and bloom, which provides seeds to the sower and bread to the hungry. Likewise, God's Word proceeds from His mouth, and does not return to Him void, but rather accomplishes His will and prospers in the minds of those to whom it was sent.

- MAT 13:1–23 ~ Jesus told a parable about sowing to the Spirit: A sower of seeds left seeds by the wayside where the birds ate them. He left seeds in the rocky ground where there was insufficient soil for them to grow. He left seeds among the weeds and thorns where they were choked to death. He also left seeds on fertile ground where they grew and bore fruit. The seeds represent the Word of God. If the Word is left by the wayside, it will be snatched away by the wicked one. If the Word is given to those with a heart of stone, it will never take root in their hearts. If the Word is given to corrupt and worldly people, it will be choked out by the lusts of the flesh. But if the Word is received by someone who listens and understands, it will take root in his or her heart and that person will bear much fruit.

- MAT 13:37–42 ~ Jesus summarized His parable saying, "The field represents the world. The harvest represents the end of the world. The reapers are the angels. The good grain represents the children of God, and the evil weeds represent the children of Satan. Jesus Christ is the sower of the grain. The enemy that sows the weeds is Satan. The weeds will be gathered by the angels and burned in the fire; all things that are offensive and evil will be thrown into the furnace where there is weeping and gnashing of teeth."

- GAL 6:8 ~ Those who sow to the flesh will reap corruption to their flesh; those who sow to the Spirit will from the Spirit reap eternal life.

- 2 CO 9:6 ~ Those who sow sparingly will reap sparingly, and those who sow bountifully will reap bountifully.

Heavenly Father, let us bear good fruit, sowing seeds of faith so that others can grow in their faith. Help us to plant ourselves in the Holy Bible which is our handbook for harvesting souls. Let us cultivate your garden of souls, enriching them with your Word, so they can be grafted to the Branch, your Son and our Deliverer, in whose name we pray, Amen.

April 14

World Art Day has been observed on April 15 since 2012, which coincides with Leonardo da Vinci's birth in 1452. The holiday was recognized in 2019 by UNESCO, a branch of the United Nations. There also is National Art Day on January 31, and International Artist Day on October 25. This is one of many UN holidays on the calendar emphasizing diversity, unity, connection, and expression. Schools and colleges often have exhibits, competitions, classes, and events. There are numerous forms of art from painting, sculpture, printmaking, photography, ceramics, and jewelry, to film, music, singing, theater, literature, video, and comedy. Art can be considered creativity as a means of expression, and applied to different disciplines. When we think of da Vinci we often think of paintings like the *Last Supper*, a mural in the Sistine Chapel; but he also was a scientist, inventor, and philosopher. Da Vinci was an artist in every sense of the word.

Unfortunately, too much passes for art these days. The National Endowment for the Arts (NEA) was established by Congress in 1965, under President L. B. Johnson. The NEA gets enormous amounts of money from taxpayers, but how much of their funding and donations go towards real art? For example, a plastic crucifix placed in a glass of urine won an award for visual arts in a 1987 competition sponsored by the NEA. Do you think $300 billion given by the US to the NEA annually is wise? What a far cry from the *Last Supper* by da Vinci. I wonder if there were other pieces of art in that exhibit depicting Christ. I have no problem with World Art Day, but I do have a problem with certain things deemed "art". As an artist, I believe in a more conventional definition of the term, though some might find my works offensive since it depicts Jesus Christ in a positive light. But I digress. I suppose art should be in the eye of the beholder.

One of the principal components of art is design. When I critique a work of art, I often apply what I learned in art school regarding design: composition, movement, color, contrast, balance, perspective, and so on. Consider the architecture of ancient buildings; much thought and work went into the design. They built things to last, that's for sure. Take the capstone of an arch: though it goes on top, it actually holds the entire arch together. Christ often was referred to in the Bible as the capstone of the arch (our head) or the cornerstone of the foundation (the church).

- PSA 118:22 ~ The stone rejected by the builders has become the capstone (see ZEC 4:7).

- ISA 28:16 ~ The Lord says, "Behold, I lay in Zion a foundation stone, a tried, true and precious cornerstone, a sure foundation; and those who believe will never be dismayed."

- MAT 21:42 ~ Jesus said, "Have you read in the scriptures: The stone which the builders rejected has become the chief cornerstone? This is the Lord's doing; is it not marvelous?"

- ACT 4:10–12 ~ Let everybody know that it was Jesus Christ, whom you crucified but whom God raised from the dead, who has become the chief cornerstone. There can be salvation in nobody else, for there are no other names under heaven that can save us except Christ alone.

- EPH 2:19–20 ~ You are no longer foreigners but fellow citizens with God's people and members of His household, for you are built upon the foundation of the apostles and prophets, Jesus Christ Himself being the chief cornerstone. In Him the whole building is held together and rises to become a holy temple to the Lord.

- 1 PE 2:6–7 ~ It is written: God has laid a chief cornerstone in Zion; those who trust in Him will never be ashamed. To believers, this stone is precious. But let this be a warning to unbelievers: that stone will be an obstacle which causes you to stumble and fall.

Father, we thank you for a faith founded on Jesus Christ who is our head and the foundation of your church on earth. He is the Savior of the world! In His name we pray, Amen.

April 15

Patriots' Day is held on the third Monday of the month. It started in 1894 in Massachusetts to commemorate the battles of Lexington and Concord; the shot heard around the world was on 04/19/1775 in Concord. Reenactments of these battles and of Paul Revere's midnight ride take place in Massachusetts. The Boston marathon also runs during this timeframe. Other states have different ways of celebrating the holiday and some states do not celebrate at all, as yet. This day is not to be confused with Remembrance Day (09/11/2001), sometimes called Patriot Day.

Patriotism is loyalty to one's country. Imagine the dedication of our founders who faced enormous hardship. They were up against the most formidable military of their time and were greatly outnumbered, but being on the side of righteousness, defeated the enemy. Theirs was a worthy cause, because they were fighting for the right to worship God in their own way, the right to have representative government, the right to speak their minds without repercussions, and the right to pursue happiness as they envisioned it. These rights were given by God but denied by the British government, leading to the Revolutionary War.

Most people love living the American dream, and dreamers still come here from every region of the planet for the same reason. Oftentimes, those who immigrated to our shores love this country more than natural born citizens. How is it that many of our fellow citizens want to reimagine our laws and founding documents? They tear down statues, promote socialism, throw words around like racism, radicalism, equity, inclusion, and revolution but do not know the meaning of these words. They are deniers, delusional, and ignorant, making themselves vulnerable to the fake prophets of our time, who are nothing but powermongers and globalists who want to control everything. It starts with eliminating freedoms one by one. We need more patriots, people who love our country, our Constitution, and our Bill of Rights, to take a stand, run for office, and lead us into the future.

- DEU 13:1–5 ~ A prophet may emerge from among you claiming to be a dreamer and declaring miraculous signs or wonders. And these signs may even come true sometimes. But if he says, "Let us follow other gods," do not listen to him. God could be testing you to see if you are loyal to Him, and to see if you love God with all your heart and soul. Such false prophets should be put to death in order to remove this evil from your midst.

- JER 23:25–32 ~ God says, "I have heard those who prophesy lies in my name, claiming that they have dreamed great dreams. How much longer will these lying prophets share the delusions of their own minds? They think their visions will cause people to forget my name, like their forefathers did when they worshipped Baal. Let a prophet who has a dream tell it to others, and let those who know my Word speak it faithfully. For what is the chaff to the wheat? Is my Word not like a hammer that can break a rock into pieces? I am against those false prophets that steal words from each other and say they come from me. I despise those that wag their tongues and declare that I gave them their falsehoods and contrived dreams. Their lies lead people into sin. I did not send them and they have nothing important to say."

- JER 29:8 ~ God says, "Do not let those prophets and diviners among you deceive you, and do not pay attention to their dreams which they themselves caused to be dreamt."

- JDE 1:6–8 ~ The angels who lost their positions are kept in everlasting chains and darkness until that great day of judgment. Like Sodom, Gomorrah, and the adjacent towns who gave themselves over to fornication and perversion, they will be made examples of the suffering and vengeance of eternal fire. This will be the inheritance of filthy dreamers who defile the flesh, despise authority, and speak evil of dignitaries.

Above all, we need the citizenry to return to our Judeo-Christian roots. Let us defer to God and godly people to be in control of government, who are loyal to this great nation, and who honor the will of the people. Those who hate our country and its heritage, or despise people with a different opinion and ideology, or would alter our moral standards of behavior, law and order—well they probably hate God as well. Those who love God, His laws, and His ways are patriots of the kingdom of heaven, and will be loyal to the people of the United States.

- JOB 34:17 ~ Should a person who hates what is right govern others? Would anyone condemn a person who is honest and fair?

- PSA 33:12 ~ Blessed is the nation who makes God their Lord, for they will be the people God chooses for His own inheritance.

- PRO 8:13, 36 ~ To fear God is to hate evil, pride, arrogance, wickedness, and perverse speech. Those who sin against God harm their own souls, and all who hate God love death.

- PRO 19:16 ~ Those who keep the commandments will be saved; but those who hate God's ways will die.

- ISA 5:20–24 ~ Woe to those who call evil good and good evil, who put darkness for light and light for darkness, who put bitter for sweet and sweet for bitter. Woe to those who consider themselves wise and prudent, who are mighty in their ability to drink alcohol, who justify and reward the wicked, and who take away righteousness from the righteous. Just as fire devours stubble and chaff, so will their roots become rotten and their blossoms wither; for they have thrown away God's laws and despised the Word of the Holy One of Israel.

- ISA 29:13 ~ The Lord says, "These people come near to me with their mouth and honor me with their lips, but their hearts are far from me. They worship me in accordance with rules invented by men."

- LUK 16:10–13 ~ The moral is this: Those who are faithful in a little will be faithful in much, and those who are dishonest in a little will be dishonest in much. If you have trusted in worldly wealth, who can trust you with true riches? If you cannot be faithful with another person's wealth, who will give you wealth of your own? Nobody can serve two masters; they will be loyal to one and despise the other. You cannot serve God and money."

- LUK 17:21 ~ Jesus said, "They cannot say, behold, here it is or there it is, because the kingdom of God is within you."

- JOH 3:17–21 ~ Jesus said, "Those who believe in God's Son are not condemned, but those who do not believe are condemned already. God sent His light into the world, but people loved the darkness rather than the light because they were evil. Everyone who follows evil hates the light, so they avoid the light because it will uncover their evil deeds. Everyone who follows the truth will come to the light, and the light will show that their ways are godly."

- EPH 2:19 ~ You are no longer strangers or foreigners, but fellow citizens with the saints in the household of God.

Merciful Father, we come to you with a heavy heart on behalf of our nation, which is backsliding and losing its way. Please help us to get back on the path of righteousness; help us to return to the faith of the patriarchs and the patriots, who believed that you are sovereign and who trusted in you for guidance and wisdom. Silence the mouths of the self-righteous and arrogant deceivers, whose visions for this country are contrary to your will and your laws. Help us to replace them with men and women who are loyal to you first and our nation second, so that we do not go the way of the greedy globalists. In the name of Christ our Lord we pray, Amen.

April 16

National Tax Day is actually observed on April 15; it is the last day to get your taxes filed. If postmarked after midnight you will be delinquent and the government will fine you, unless you were approved for an extension. Lots of people lose hair over this, and some end up going to jail. It is stressful for many, but mostly just an annual hassle. They have convoluted the tax code to such a degree, you have to hire a specialist rather than risk being off the slightest amount. When I was a college student and barely making it, the IRS audited me and found a twenty-dollar discrepancy years before; they charged me an extra twenty bucks for being late. I thought, man, loan sharks don't even charge 100% interest, only the US government. Anyway, if you haven't filed your taxes by today, expect a nasty letter from the IRS. Certainly, this is not a day to celebrate unless you have filed your taxes and are expecting a substantial refund.

Tax collectors were a despised people in Jesus's time, often for good reason, for they were known to be crooked; Jews even stole from fellow Jews. But we know of at least two Jewish taxmen who repented and gave back to the people and more: Matthew the apostle and Gospel writer who was martyred, and Zacchaeus who climbed a tree to see Jesus, and later gave away much of his wealth. Let this be a lesson to the taxman, you know. The IRS is not impartial when it comes to who they go after and who they leave alone; further, government officials have used the IRS to harass rivals, which is unlawful. We need leaders who will respect the will of the people in all branches of government, and who respect the laws of the land; and we need to remove those who are insanely greedy for power and riches. If the integrity of our leaders and associated government bodies fades further, pursuing the ways of evil, lawlessness, excessive taxation, and globalism, economic collapse will follow and so will our posterity before God.

- NEH 5:4–5 ~ Some were saying they had to mortgage their fields, vineyards, and homes to buy food; others had to borrow money against their property to pay the king's taxes.

- EZE 22:29 ~ The people have used oppression, robbery, and swindling, so I will recompense it upon their heads and consume them with the fire of my wrath.

- MAT 22:17–21 ~ The Pharisees asked Christ, "What do you think? Is it lawful to give tribute to Caesar, or not?" Taking a coin, Jesus asked whose image was imprinted. Then He stated, "Render unto Caesar the things that are Caesar's, and unto God the things that are God's."

- LUK 2:1, 4–5 ~ In those days, a decree went out from Caesar Augustus that the entire Roman empire should be registered (for taxation purposes). Joseph took his pregnant wife Mary from the city of Nazareth in Galilee to the city of David which is called Bethlehem, because he was a descendant of David; it was there that he and his family were to be counted and taxed by the Romans.

- LUK 19:1–9 ~ Zacchaeus was the chief publican (tax collector), and very rich. He wanted to see Jesus so he climbed a sycamore tree for he was a short man. Jesus called him down and told him He would visit his house. Some murmured to themselves about how Jesus was going to the house of a sinful man. Zacchaeus accepted Jesus Christ as Lord, saying, "Lord, I will give half my wealth to the poor, and if I have cheated anybody, I will repay them four times." Jesus replied, "Today, salvation has come to this house, of the lineage of Abraham."

- LUK 20:46–47 ~ Jesus said, "Beware of the Pharisees. They enjoy wearing fancy robes, being greeted in the marketplace, sitting in the places of honor in church, and reserving the nicest rooms for their banquets; yet they cheat widows out of their homes, and for a show, say long prayers. They will receive the greater damnation." (also MAT 23:14)

- ROM 13:5–7 ~ Submit to the authorities, not just because you will be punished if you do not, but as a matter of keeping a clear conscience. Pay your taxes, because governments are God's servants who work fulltime in governing. Render to everyone their dues, paying tribute when it is owed. If you owe money pay it, and if you owe respect, give it.
- TIT 1:11 ~ They must be silenced, those who would ruin entire households, teaching things that are wrong for the sake of ill-gotten gain.

The Bible teaches that it is right to pay tribute to the government for they exist to protect and punish. We also need to pay tribute to God who has given us life and love; He will protect and punish too. How do we pay our taxes to God? By using our time, talents, and treasures to His glory and in service to others. Part of our giving should include one-tenth of our increase; this was a commandment of God in the Old Testament. While not obligatory, it is wise to follow the tradition of tithing, because God's promise of a return on your investment is still in effect.

- GEN 14:19–20 ~ Melchizedek (God's high priest) blessed Abraham, and Abraham gave Melchizedek tithes of everything he had.
- EXO 23:19 ~ As you reap, offer to God the choicest sample of the first of your harvest (i.e., the first fruits).
- LEV 27:30 ~ Tithe of all your increase to the Lord, for He considers that portion to be holy.
- NUM 18:26 ~ Moses told the Israelites they were commanded by God to give tithes to the Levites for their support, and for the Levites to offer a tenth (tithe) to God of those tithes.
- DEU 26:12–13 ~ After you have tithed during the third year, which is the year of tithing, and you have given your tithes to the Levites (who ran the church), as well as strangers, orphans, widows, and the hungry, then declare this to the Lord.
- MAL 3:6–10 ~ God says, "I am the Lord, I never change. But you have not kept my commandments. Return to me and I will return to you. Will you rob God? Yet you have robbed me. You ask how you have robbed me? You have robbed me by not presenting your tithes and offerings. Bring tithes of all your income to the storage room so that there will be plenty in my house, and prove to yourself how I will open the windows of heaven and pour upon you so many blessings that you will not have room for them."
- LUK 6:38 ~ Give and it shall be given to you in abundance, overflowing; for the same measure that you give is returned to you.
- 1 CO 16:1 ~ On the first day of each week everyone should set aside something for the Lord in accordance with the degree to which they have prospered by His grace, so it will not be necessary to take a collection.

Father in Heaven, it is right to pay our taxes on time; help us to do so honestly and without fail, else we bring the government upon us. Let us especially remember that we owe tribute to you for all that you have done for us. You have promised to open the windows of heaven and bless us with more than we can receive, merely by providing ten percent, the first fruits of our income, to the church, and by offering our time and talents to the ministry. Help us to give often and generously with respect to the degree to which you have prospered us, and to do so cheerfully and sincerely. You have sacrificed more than we can imagine by giving your only Son in death so that we could receive newness of life. And because He lives, we will live also, hallelujah! The least we can do is give ourselves back to you. Use us, Lord, to work diligently in the harvest of your vineyard in whatever capacity we can, for we in turn will become the first fruits of your Son Jesus Christ, in whose name we pray, Amen.

April 17

Spain Commissioned Columbus to explore a route to Asia on this day in 1492. The objective was to locate a sea passage to the other side of the world, because it was burdensome, costly, and time consuming to move goods over land. Although Columbus failed to find a route to Asia, his serendipitous discovery was the Americas on 10/12/1492. Noted, Columbus was not the first to sail to the Americas, but he was the first to gather its treasures and return to Europe, not once but four times. Fellow seaman Amerigo Vespucci sailed the same route and proclaimed that Columbus had stumbled upon a continent, after which it was named America. The discovery sparked an exodus of European explorers, followed by freedom seekers which still come to this day. People everywhere leave their homeland for the land of the free and the home of the brave.

Many settlements were founded, including one by Columbus; unfortunately, small pox also arrived in the new world and killed large numbers of natives. Natives were enslaved and mistreated by numerous European conquerors and invaders, who sought fortune and fame. When Columbus landed in the new world, he thought he was in India and that is why the natives were called Indians; now we call them Indigenous People or Native Americans. We observe Columbus Day on October 12, though many prefer to call it Indigenous People's Day because of earlier maltreatment of the natives; some have spouted disdain for Columbus as if all the blame should fall on him. He actually engaged the natives to convert them to Christianity, and many did. People who would dismiss Columbus as a racist or cancel him from their calendar are misinformed. Maybe Columbus was a jerk, who knows? What we do know is that he was an Italian who sailed for Spain since he couldn't get his own government to fund the expedition. It would be Spain who would send explorers and conquistadores to expand their holdings here. There is no reason to forget that it was Columbus who started the mass exodus from Europe to America. He may have been poor at human relations but he was one heck of a navigator. Must we disavow great people and forget their achievements, because jerks do not deserve to be recognized? Should we tear down statues erected in their honor? History cannot be cancelled, but it can be forgotten or rewritten to suit an ideology based on selective facts and partial truths.

It's a good thing God doesn't cancel sinners, which includes everyone. Therefore, nobody should judge another, else they be judged by the same standards they apply.

- PRO 2:6–9 ~ The Lord gives wisdom; from His mouth come knowledge and understanding. God stores up sound wisdom for the righteous and is a shield to those with integrity. He guards the paths of justice and preserves the way of the saints. Thus, you will understand righteousness, justice, equity, and every good path.

- MAT 7:1–2 ~ Do not judge others or you will be judged. And you will be judged according to the same standards by which you judge others.

- ROM 2:1 ~ It is inexcusable to judge another person, for by judging another you condemn yourself, because you are guilty of the same things.

- 1 CO 4:3 ~ To be judged by another person is insignificant to me. In fact, I do not even judge myself because I do not know me as well as the Lord does.

- JAM 2:13 ~ Whoever shows judgment without mercy will receive no mercy. Whoever shows mercy will receive mercy, because mercy prevails against judgment.

Heavenly Father, who does not show favoritism but loves everyone equally, we love you. Help us to judge nobody, not their heart or their soul. When we make judgments, let them be based on the right thing to do, after listening to your voice. Let us trust that your judgment is wise, impartial, and true, for through Christ we will be judged not guilty. Thank you in His name, Amen.

April 18

World Heritage Day, also called International Monuments and Sites Day, originated in 1982 from the International Council of Monuments and Sites (ICOMOS); the holiday was adopted by UNESCO the following year. The mission of ICOMOS is to preserve and maintain natural and manmade historic places, structures, and buildings which highlight antiquity, cultural diversity, achievement, and heritage. It is a celebration of the human race, by preserving ancient edifices and lost civilizations which must be preserved for future generations to learn about and cherish. To date, over a thousand worthy sites have been catalogued for conservation, preservation, protection, and restoration. The organization has expanded into 150 countries, with close to 10,000 members from various disciplines such as archaeology, engineering, geography, and academia. Some of the places designated by ICOMOS as either culturally or naturally significant and requiring preservation included: the Great Barrier Reef, Australia; the Acropolis, Greece; the Great Wall, China; the Mayan city, Mexico; the Taj Mahal, India; and Yellowstone, USA.

There are preserved locations associated with the Bible, which might not be as familiar as those listed above. Take for example, Susa. It was called Shushan in the Hebrew (Old Testament). The city was the primary capital of Persian king Xerxes, the husband of Esther. There is a shrine in Susa, reportedly the gravesite of Esther and Mordecai. The tomb of Daniel is also claimed in Susa. We know that Daniel was carried away to Babylon and served the kings there until it was conquered by the Medes and Persians. Daniel also served their kings until his death; so perhaps they did entomb Daniel in Susa for it was a hub of the Media-Persian empire.

- EST 1:1–3 ~ It was during the reign of Ahasuerus (Xerxes in the Greek), when he ruled the land from India to Ethiopia. His throne sat in the palace in Shushan (Susa). The third year he had a feast for the princes, nobles, and servants of Persia and Media.

- EST 1—10 ~ Esther, a Jewess, was queen of Persia when she assisted in saving the Jews from extermination by the evil Haman. She had help from her foster father and relative Mordecai who would become second in command to the king after Haman was hanged.

- DAN 5 ~ Belshazzar, the son of Nebuchadnezzar, asked Daniel to employ his unique gift to interpret his vision of a hand writing on the wall. Daniel revealed the secret message which the king saw written on the wall by the hand of God. Daniel told him how his father had defied God and was punished; but his father finally repented. Daniel continued that he had not humbled himself before God as his father did. He told Belshazzar that his days were numbered, for Babylon would fall to the Medes and Persians. That very night, Belshazzar was assassinated, and Darius the Mede seized power. [Darius was relieved after he was tricked into sending Daniel into the lions' den, because Daniel came out unscathed the next morning (DAN 6). Daniel also served a Persian king named Cyrus (DAN 10).]

- DAN 9 ~ During the first year of the reign of a Persian king named Darius, son of Ahasuerus (Xerxes), Daniel had a prophetic dream. He was given the interpretation of Jeremiah's revelation of the seventy years (JER 25) and its relationship to seventy weeks. Once again, Daniel foresaw the abomination of desolation and the tribulations to come at the end of days.

Another example of interesting historic locations listed by ICOMOS are the mounds of Megiddo, Hazor, and Beersheba in the land of Israel. High mounds were strategic outposts for military defense emplacements, especially Megiddo in the Jezreel valley, where many battles were fought. Megiddo also will be the location of the last battle, in the latter days. It is called Armageddon meaning hill of Megiddo. These lessons in history provide historical and supportive evidence of events, places, and people in the Holy Bible. Many of these events, sites and characters are corroborated in secular historical archives.

APRIL

- JDG 5:19 ~ Zebulun and Naphtali risked their lives in the high places of the field. The kings came and fought the Canaanite kings by the waters of Megiddo, but not for monetary gain.

- 2 KI 9:25–27 ~ King Jehu told his captain that he would avenge the blood of a man named Naboth from Jezreel, who was murdered by King Ahab (and wife Jezebel). Ahab's son Ahaziah, king of Judah, got word of this and fled. Jehu caught up with him and told his commander to slay him as he rode his chariot; Ahaziah made it to Megiddo where he died.

- 2 KI 23:29–30; 2 CH 35:22–23 ~ During the reign of King Josiah of Judah, King Necho of Egypt sought to join up with the king of Assyria at the Euphrates River. Josiah attacked the Egyptian pharaoh at Megiddo, after being warned against doing it. Josiah was fatally wounded by an arrow and carried home to die.

- REV 16:12–17 ~ The Euphrates River dried up, creating a path for the army (kings) from the east. Three evil spirits came from the dragon, the beast, and the false prophet; they went throughout the earth gathering armies to battle against God Almighty. They assembled their armies together at a place called Armageddon near the mountain of Megiddo. Then the seventh angel poured out his vial of wrath, and a voice from heaven said, "It is over."

Hazor was one of the fortified kingdoms defeated by Joshua when Israel conquered the land of promise on the other side of the Jordan River. In time, the kingdom would split into Israel in the north and Judah in the south, after which the Assyrians came to power.

- JOS 11:10 ~ Joshua turned back and took Hazor and killed their king with the sword; he was the ruler over several kingdoms in the region.

- 2 KI 15:29 ~ During the reign of Pekah, king of Israel, the Assyrian king Tiglath Pileser took Hazor and many other cities in the land of Naphtali in the northern kingdom of Israel.

Beersheba was a very important landmark in the Old Testament. It was the location of a water well that Abraham himself dug and laid claim to, which was agreed upon by King Abimelech of Egypt. This well would be a welcome site to travelers from Egypt to Jerusalem.

- GEN 21:27–31 ~ Abraham made a deal with Philistine king Abimelech. Abraham gave him seven lambs to witness his well that he dug at Beersheba (meaning well of seven).

- 1 SA 8:1–2 ~ When he was old, Samuel made his sons judges over Israel at Beersheba. But his sons were evil, and took bribes, and perverted judgment. The elders of Israel came to Samuel and told him that his sons were evil and they wanted a king instead. This troubled Samuel who prayed. Though it displeased the Lord, He granted their wish, for the Israelites had rejected Him as their king. [This move would backfire on the Israelites, for the kings and the people would turn their backs on God, leading to their eventual fall after the heyday of Kings David and Solomon.]

- 1 KI 19:1–8 ~ King Ahab told his wife Jezebel how the prophet Elijah had slain the prophets of Baal. Jezebel made it her life's goal to make Elijah pay, so he fled to Beersheba in the land of Judah where he left his servant and continued his journey another day through the wilderness. He was distraught, pleading with God to take him. The Lord sent him an angel to bring him back to health, after which Elijah traveled to mount Horeb (also called Sinai).

Omniscient Father, we thank you for providing proof that your holy Word is true. You know all things but we know very little; but you give us insight when we doubt, and knowledge when we do not understand. Thank you for helping us recognize and preserve important sites which validate relevant Biblical events occurring there. We love your Word of truth, and the wisdom of saving grace shown to us through your Son Jesus, in whose name we pray, Amen.

April 19

Humorous Day is observed today to introduce humor and laughter into your home, workplace, or wherever you might find yourself. It is a day to liven up the place, with a smile and a joke or funny story. April was declared Humor Month in 1976 by the director of the Carmel Institute of Humor, Larry Wilde, largely because we kick off the month with April Fools' Day. It has been said that laughter is the best medicine; actually, this has an element of truth, since it releases endorphins within your body which help in healing and fitness. Anybody that lacks a sense of humor needs to laugh today, since this is also good for your mental soundness. Think of what you can do to spread a little happiness today. It is important to remember that we laugh with people and not at them; practical or dirty jokes are not fun for everyone so it is recommended that you avoid this kind of amusement.

- GEN 17:15–20; GEN 18:10–14 ~ God said to Abraham that his wife Sarai will be called Sarah, and He will bless her with a child, and she will be the mother of nations. Abraham fell down laughing, saying in his heart, "Will a hundred-year-old man and his ninety-year-old wife bear a child?" God said, "Sarah will surely bear a son and you will call his name Isaac (meaning he who laughs), and I will establish my covenant with him and his seed after him." Sarah was listening at the tent door and she laughed as well, saying to herself, "After I am stricken with age, will I have this pleasure?" God said to Abraham, "Sarah also laughed to herself. Is anything too hard for the Lord? When the time is right, I will return, and Sarah will have a son."

- GEN 21:6 ~ Sarah said, "God has brought me laughter, so that all who hear will laugh with me."

- PSA 126:2 ~ Our mouths were filled with laughter and our tongues with singing. It was proclaimed among the nations, "The Lord has done great things for them."

- PRO 17:22 ~ A merry heart is good medicine, but a broken spirit dries up the bones.

- ECC 3:1, 4 ~ For everything there is a season, and a time for every purpose under heaven. A time to weep and a time to laugh; a time to mourn and a time to dance.

- ECC 7:6 ~ Like crackling of thorns under the pot, so is the laughter of fools. This is vanity.

- MAT 9:18–19, 23–26 ~ A certain ruler approached, worshipping Jesus saying, "My daughter has died, but if you lay your hand on her she will live." Jesus arose and followed him and with His disciples. When they arrived at the ruler's house, there were minstrels and other people making noise. Jesus said to them, "Make way, she is not dead but sleeping." And they laughed scornfully at Him. Then Jesus went inside, took her by the hand and lifted her to her feet. And His fame spread throughout the land.

- LUK 6:21–25 ~ Jesus said, "Blessed be those who hunger now, for they will be filled. Blessed be those who weep now, for they will laugh. Blessed be those who are hated, separated, criticized, and banished for the Son of man's sake. Rejoice in that day and leap for joy, for your reward in heaven will be great. But woe unto those who are rich, for they have received their consolation. Woe unto those who are full, for they will be hungry. Woe to those who laugh, for they will mourn and weep.

Father, we thank you for laughter; but let us never laugh at the misfortune of others. Let us laugh with people and not at them, and let us mourn with those who are hurting. May we be merry and sing joyfully at the knowledge of you, the truth of your Word, and the salvation of your Son, in whose name we pray, Amen.

April 20

Husband Appreciation Day is observed on the third Saturday of the month. It is a worldwide celebration of husbands, their love, protection, hard work, and service to their wives and children. Regrettably, marriage is no longer honored in the tradition of the Bible, and the word "husband" has been distorted to mean many things other than a man with a wife. The wife and husband are one in flesh, and equal partners under God whose Spirit becomes part of their union during nuptials. Our bodies are temples of the Holy Spirit, and when joined in matrimony, the couple becomes one in Christ. Just as Christ is the head of the church, the house of God on earth, the husband is the head of the household. How should we observe this day? I leave it to you wives and kids out there to think of creative ways to celebrate your husband and father.

- GEN 2:24 ~ A man shall leave his parents and cling to his wife; and they shall become one flesh.

- PRO 31:10–31 ~ When a man finds a virtuous woman for a wife, he will have something more valuable than rubies. She will do her husband good all of her life. She will work hard and give herself to the household. She will be generous and complimentary to others. Her husband will be well known and powerful. She will be clothed in strength and honor. She will be wise and kind. She will not be lazy and her husband and children will praise her for it. Although favor can be deceitful and beauty can be vain, faith in God will always yield His praise.

- MAL 2:14–16 ~ The Lord has formed a husband and wife into one flesh. In flesh and spirit, they belong to God. But why is this so? Because God wishes godly offspring from them. So, guard your spirit and do not break the covenant with your wife or husband by getting divorced.

- 1 CO 7:1–10, 28, 39 ~ It is fine if you never touch a member of the opposite sex. But to avoid the sin of fornication, let a man have his own wife and let a woman have her own husband. The husband and wife should regard conjugal rights, because the husband does not have power over his own body and neither does the wife. Do not deprive your spouse unless you have agreed to fast and pray for a period of time. It is fine to remain single, but if you cannot contain your emotions then marry, for it is better to marry than to burn with passion. If you marry you must be charitable to your spouse. Do not lie to your spouse, and do not ever split apart. It is not a sin to marry, but married people will have problems associated with their sinful and weak nature. Once married, you are bound to each other until one of you dies.

- 2 CO 11:2 ~ God has a godly jealousy toward the church, for He promised you to one husband, so that He can present you unto His Son as a chaste virgin.

- EPH 5:21–25, 28, 33 ~ Submit to one another. Wives, submit to your husbands because the husband is the head of the wife just like Christ is the head of the church. Thus, the wife is subject to the husband at all times. Husbands, love and protect your wives even as Christ loved the Church and gave Himself for it. Husbands, you must love your wives as much as you love yourselves, so that your wife will respect her husband.

- COL 3:18–19 ~ Wives, submit to your husbands, as long as it is within the Law. Husbands, love your wives and do not be bitter with them.

- 1 TI 3:1–5 ~ Becoming a bishop is a noble and worthy cause. He must be above reproach, the husband of one wife, vigilant, sober, and of good behavior, hospitable and able to teach. He should not be inclined to drink, nor to violence, not quarrelsome, and not a lover of money. If he manages his family well, his children will obey him and he will be worthy of their respect. If he cannot control his own household, how will he be able to manage the church?

- 1 TI 5:14 ~ It is good for a young woman to marry, bear children, and guide the household. It is not good for a wife to be contrary, or to speak blamefully or rashly.

- TIT 2:1–12 ~ Here is sound doctrine about how to conduct oneself: older men should be sober, calm, moderate, faithful, charitable, and patient. Wives, be temperate, and love your husbands and your children. Be discreet, chaste, good homemakers, and obedient to your husbands, so the Word of God will not be blasphemed. Young men, be restrained, upright, and not corrupt, serious and sincere, speaking good things about others and faithful to God.

- 1 PE 3:1, 7 ~ Wives, obey your husbands, and teach them the Word if they do not understand it. Husbands, listen to your wives; honor your wives as the weaker sex and as an equal. Stay together in the grace of life, and your prayers will be answered.

The Bible is very thorough in telling husbands and wives how to behave in a marriage. There should be love and respect, an equal amount of give and take, and they should make a good team in a way that fill each other's gaps. Above all, the marriage should be between one man and one woman, united by God in holy matrimony, to remain faithful to each other and to God. With this formula, they will always be happy and will not be inclined to be unfaithful.

- LEV 21:7, 13 ~ Do not take a prostitute for a wife, or a profane woman, or a divorced woman.

- EZR 10:11–12 ~ Confess unto the Lord God of your fathers, and do what pleases Him. Separate yourselves from the people of the land, and from strange wives. Then all of the congregation said with a loud voice, "As you have said, thus we must do."

- MAT 5:27–28 ~ Jesus said, "You have heard that it was said long ago that you must not commit adultery. But I say unto you, that to lust after someone with your eyes is to commit adultery in your heart."

- MAT 19:6, 19 ~ Jesus said, "Once joined in marriage, the two spouses become one flesh. People must not split apart something that God has joined together. Anyone who gets a divorce, except for infidelity, and then marries another, is guilty of adultery."

- 1 CO 7:14–16 ~ The unbelieving husband can be sanctified by the believing wife, and vice-versa; otherwise, your children would be unclean instead of holy. If the unbelieving spouse departs, let them go; a brother or sister is not bound under such circumstances. But, how would you know, you wives and husbands, whether or not you might be able to save your spouse?

- 2 CO 6:14–15 ~ Do not be unequally yoked with unbelievers, for what fellowship has righteousness with unrighteousness, and what communion has light with darkness? And what accord can Christ have with the devil, or what does a believer have in common with an infidel?

Father in heaven, you instituted marriage from the start by creating humans, male and female, as well as animals and plants. You commanded humankind to be fruitful and multiply, and raise children in the fear and admonition of the Lord. Because you wanted godly children from us, help us to obey this commandment and raise our children in the way they should go, so that when they mature, they will not depart from your Word and your path. Help us to remain faithful to our spouses, until death do us part. Help married couples to love and cherish their spouses for better or worse, for richer or poorer, in sickness and in health. Let us honor all vows made at the altar of the Lord. Help husbands and fathers to be there for their families, and not abandon them. We have an epidemic of absent fathers in our country and the world; help men of all cultures to correct this problem by being faithful husbands and fathers for the duration of their lives. Let us ever be faithful to our spouses, and to you heavenly Father, until we can come home to be with you eternally, when you present us as the chaste bride of Christ, your Son. In the name of Jesus we pray, Amen.

April 21

World Creativity and Innovation Day was established by the United Nations, first observed in 2018, focusing on human and individual development. This day is about exchanging ideas in economic enhancement, job creation, entrepreneurship, technology innovation, industrial growth, poverty reduction, social and financial opportunity, and global stability. Creativity, invention, and innovation are ways to meet goals, solve problems, and advance communications between various professions, disciplines, and nations. The objective is to improve and enhance the lives of everyone everywhere by creating conditions for positive growth. But if proposed changes are not in accordance with God's will, they will be detrimental to those purported to be helped.

- JOB 32:8 ~ It is the spirit in a man, the breath of the Almighty, that makes him understand.

- PRO 2:2–6, 10–13 ~ Make your ear attentive to wisdom; incline your heart to understanding. Seek it like silver and search for it as hidden treasures. For the Lord gives wisdom; from his mouth come knowledge and understanding. When wisdom comes into your heart, and knowledge is pleasant to your soul, discretion will preserve you, and understanding will keep you, to deliver you from the ways of evil, and people who speak perverse things.

- ECC 7:24–25 ~ That which has been is far off, and deep, very deep; who can find it out? I turned my heart to know and to search it out; to seek wisdom and the scheme of things, and to know the wickedness of folly and the foolishness that is madness.

- ECC 9:10 ~ Whatever your hand finds to do, do it with all your might; for there is neither working nor planning nor knowledge nor wisdom in the grave where you are going.

- JER 29:11 ~ For I know the plans I have for you, declares the Lord, plans for welfare and not for evil, to give you a future and a hope.

- HAB 2:2–3 ~ And the Lord answered me, "Write the vision; make it plain on tablets, so he may run who carries it. For still the vision awaits its appointed time; it hastens to the end; it will not lie. If it seems slow, wait for it; it will surely come without delay."

- 1 CO 12:31 ~ If you eagerly desire the greater gifts, I will show you the most excellent way.

- JAM 3:17 ~ But the wisdom from above is first pure, then peaceable, gentle, open to reason, full of mercy and good fruit, impartial and sincere.

It helps to have a vision of what progress and hope look like. Get a picture of it in your mind, imagining what it looks like to you. Then diagram, illustrate, and/or write a narrative describing your vision. I often used this technique in group therapy; it was very well received and gave people a glimmer of hope so I know it works. If you can imagine it and put it on paper, the dream becomes real. Work out a plan for making the dream come true and it becomes doable.

- JOB 33:14–17 ~ God will speak once, maybe twice, but people do not perceive. He speaks in a vision, at night, when we are asleep. He may speak into a person's ears and alert them with warnings to turn them from sin and pride, in order to keep their souls from the pit.

- JOE 2:28 ~ I will pour out my Spirit upon all people. Your sons and daughters will prophesy, your old men will dream dreams, and your young men will see visions.

Help us Father, that our visions of hope and peace be from you, and that our plans for the future are in accordance with your will. If we trust in you, we know that you will show us what to do and where to go. Let our faith be strong throughout the trials we must face. Let our love for you be continuous and never-ending. Let your Holy Spirit guide our thoughts and decisions, enabling us to reflect your love. In the name of Jesus in whom our faith and love are founded, Amen.

April 22

Earth Day occurs this day every year to boost the preservation and conservation of the planet, nature, and natural resources. The first commemoration was spearheaded by Senator Nelson (WI) in 1970, who ran with the idea after it was proposed in a 1969 UNESCO conference. April 22 was selected to be a day for teaching people, especially college students, about how we can protect the planet. Nelson would later receive the Medal of Freedom from President Clinton for his work and dedication to make Earth Day an annual event. The first year, millions of people supported the movement gathering in their hometowns and attending trainings, in small and large groups, to learn about oil spills, industrial waste, plants and factories polluting air and water, the irresponsible use of pesticides, endangered species, deforestation, and assorted environmental issues. Air, water, and nature conservation was a big deal in the 70s, and has been ever since.

Today is a day to connect with nature, and nature lovers; to educate and become educated of potential risks to our planet and potential solutions such as clean energy, environmental protection, safeguarding natural treasures, emission control, etc. The holiday has become popular worldwide, as hundreds of countries and cities observe this important event. Advocates maintain that every day should be earth day, insofar as we should be mindful, kinder, and more respectful to our planet continuously. There are things that everybody can do to help, like not throwing garbage out the window, in a waterway, or anywhere but a receptacle; not letting the faucet run while doing other things; being conservative with energy use, and the list goes on.

- 1 CO 4:2 ~ It is required of stewards that they be proven trustworthy.

    God created the earth and told humankind to take dominion over it and all living creatures. For starters, God entrusted Adam with the upkeep of the Garden of Eden. To this day, it is our responsibility to take care of God's creation. He gave it to us for our sustenance and we have no right to destroy it. After all, if we lose our natural resources, it'll be our fault, and then how are we to survive here? So let us agree, at least on this one issue, regardless of political persuasion: the earth is home to everyone and everyone has equal responsibility to use it; but those who abuse this responsibility and the human rights that go with it, need to pay a fine and do some community service, with a penalty that fits the egregiousness of the infraction.

- GEN 1:26–30 ~ God said, "Let us make humans in our image, after our likeness. And let them have dominion over the fish of the sea, over the fowl of the air, over the cattle, and over all the earth and everything that creeps upon the earth." So, God created humankind in His own image; in the image of God, He created us all, males and females alike. God blessed the man and woman and told them to be fruitful, multiply, replenish the earth, and subdue it; to have dominion over the fish, fowl and every living thing that moves upon the earth. God said, "I have given to humankind every seed-bearing plant on the face of the entire earth, and every tree that has fruit and seed in it. They will be yours for food. And I have given to you every green plant, the beasts of the earth, the birds in the sky, and all creatures that move on the ground: everything that has breath and life in it."

- GEN 2:15 ~ God took the man and put him in the Garden of Eden to take care of it.

- DEU 20:19 ~ When you besiege a city continually until you take it, do not destroy the trees which produce edible fruit. If you cut them down, you cut down a man that is useful to your war.

- JOB 12:7–10~ Ask the animals, birds, or fish and they will tell you; or ask the earth to teach you. Who cannot see that in all these the hand of the Lord is evident? In His hand is the soul of every living thing, including the breath of human beings.

APRIL

- PSA 8:4–9 ~ Who are humans, that you would be mindful of them, and the offspring of humans that you would care for them? You made man only a little lower than the angels and crowned him with glory and honor. You made him ruler over your creations, and put everything on earth below him, including the animals, birds, and fish. Oh Lord, how majestic is your name in all the earth!

- ISA 55:10–12 ~ The rain and snow that fall from heaven do not return to heaven but water the earth, causing the plants to bud and to seed and providing food. So also, God's Word does not return to Him void, but accomplishes what He wishes, and prospers wherever He sends it. We joyfully go out, being led in peace. The mountains and hills sing before you and the trees clap their hands; all the world will rejoice around you. Instead of a thorn bush, a tree will grow. And the name of the Lord will be magnified as an everlasting sign of the nurturing He provides.

- JER 2:7 ~ I brought you into a plentiful country to eat the fruit and enjoy its goodness; but when you arrived you defiled the land, and made my heritage an abomination.

- JOH 15:1–2 ~ Jesus said, "I am the true vine, and my Father is the cultivator. He removes any of my branches that do not bear fruit. Those that do bear fruit, he prunes, so that they can bear even more fruit.

- 1 CO 3:7 ~ Those who plant and those who water are nothing by themselves, because it is God that provides the increase.

In the beginning God created the heavens and the earth (GEN1:1). This is followed by the six days of creation where God formed the cosmos in such a way as to make earth inhabitable for plants, animals, and particularly humans. That's right, He did all of this for humanity. And how do we show our gratitude? By ransacking the place, exploiting it for personal gain, wasting resources, killing for the sport of it, leveling hills and forests, and polluting it with toxic chemicals, trash, and waste. Hey, I'll be the first to admit that I am guilty as charged. But I've repented and changed when it comes to cherishing God's creations, and respecting others' rights to finding everything to be in as good or better shape than I found it.

We are not to place our esteem for the planet above God, however. Loving God and others (in that order) are the two most important commandments (MAT 22:37–40). God has revealed Himself through His book of nature and His book of truth: the Holy Bible. When these two sources converge, we get a glimpse of absolute truth. Keep in mind that God gives us all things to use, but not to abuse or to idolize. Those who do are a disgrace to the race.

- JOB 31:24–28 ~ If I placed my hope and confidence in wealth, and I rejoiced in how much of it I had attained, or if I was enticed by the beauty of the sun and moon, or even myself, such that they became an object of my affection, I would be guilty of disregarding God.

- 1 JO 2:15 ~ Do not love the world or the things in the world. If anyone loves the world, the love of the Father is not in him.

Dear Heavenly Father, who has created this beautiful universe and made us the center of it all, we thank and praise you for the breath of life and for bringing us into this lovely place. It is our desire that we be good stewards of your creation as you have commanded us, and not treat the earth like a possession, because it provides sustenance for every person and lifeform. Those who exploit, damage, or disregard this planet are ruining it for everybody; and not only humans but all inhabitants, without which the synergy of life would collapse. Awaken those who carelessly abuse this world and the things in it; instead of trashing the place, enable them to see the beauty in it all and conserve it. Let everyone experience the beauty and be reminded of your beauty, Father, and the beauty of your Son Jesus Christ, Amen.

April 23

Feast of Passover (*Pesach*) occurs in the Jewish calendar on Nisan 14. Passover begins at dusk on the first full moon following the vernal equinox (March-April timeframe). This day commemorates the first Passover when the firstborn of Egypt, whether man or beast, died; unless the front door posts were painted with the blood of a lamb. Only the Hebrew slaves followed this command of God. It was the last of ten plagues sent upon Egypt by God to persuade Pharaoh to free the Israelites. The next morning, the Jews exited the land of Goshen for the Red Sea which Moses parted, allowing the Israelites to cross over dry land. The charioteers and soldiers of Egypt chased after them but were drowned in the sea when the waters swelled. Jews still celebrate Passover with a feast which include the Seder supper, unleavened bread, and wine. Many Christians celebrate Passover as well, because we believe this was a foreshadowing of the coming of Messiah, the Lamb of God, which is Jesus Christ who takes away the sin of the world. The lamb's blood shed on the first Passover represents the blood of Jesus, shed for us all.

- EXO 24:8 ~ Moses took blood from the sacrifice and sprinkled it on the people saying, "This is the blood of the everlasting covenant revealed by the Lord in these His words."

- LEV 17:11 ~ The life of the flesh is in the blood, and I have given you the opportunity to offer this upon the altar for atonement of your souls; because it is through the blood that atonement is provided.

- JOH 1:29 ~ The next day John saw Jesus coming towards him and declared, "Behold, the Lamb of God who takes away the sin of the world. This is who I said will come after me though He was preferred before me, for He existed before me."

- MAT 3:11 ~ The blood of Christ represents the refiner's fire that purifies one's very soul.

- 1 CO 5:7 ~ Throw out the old leavened dough and become a new dough, without yeast; for that is what you have become because of the sacrifice of Christ who is the Passover Lamb.

- HEB 9:22 ~ Almost everything under the Law can be purged with blood, and there can be no remission without the shedding of blood.

- 1 PE 1:18–19 ~ You were redeemed, not with corruptible things such as gold and silver, but with the precious blood of Christ, a Lamb without any imperfections.

Passover initiated eight days of unleavened bread; the day after Passover was a high sabbath. The Feast of First Fruits occurred on Nisan 16; the week of unleavened bread ended on another high sabbath. This same week is celebrated by Christians for eight days which also includes two high sabbaths (Maundy Thursday and Good Friday); Palm Sunday begins the eight-day observance, which ends on Easter Sunday, represented in the Feast of First Fruits.

Although there are variations between the Jewish lunar calendar and the Gregorian calendar, the meaning of Holy Week remains unaltered and often coincides with the Christian Holy Week. Such was the case in AD 30, when the death of Christ fell on the day of Passover. Jesus's birth was likely in late 5 BC, prior to the death of Herod around the early harvest of 4 BC; thus, Jesus would have died at the age of 33.5. A little research and you will find in AD 30, Holy Week on the Jewish calendar matched up with the eight days of our Christian Holy Week.

Father God, how amazing are your ways and your Word; you gave us both testaments of the Holy Bible for cross-validation, in order to make your plan of salvation known to all people. All Biblical truth in prophecy and history has been repeatedly proven in both testaments of the Holy Bible. We thank you for the foretold truth that sets all people free from sin and death, through the sacrifice of your Son this day almost 2000 years ago, Amen.

April 24

Feast of Unleavened Bread (*Matzah*) occurs in the Jewish calendar on Nisan 15; today is a holy day, considered a high sabbath in which a worship service is mandatory and work is disallowed. A church service is called a holy convocation in the Bible. Recall, Christians also have an eight-day Holy Week around the same time period, which will vary year to year because of different calendars. You can expect this week to occur in the March-April timeframe right after Passover.

- EXO 13:6 ~ God instructed Moses that for seven days the people would eat unleavened bread, beginning with the celebration of the Passover feast.

- LEV 23:3–8 ~ Six days shall work be done, but the seventh day is the Sabbath of rest, a holy convocation. You will do no work because it is the Lord's Sabbath in all your dwellings. There are feasts of the Lord, also holy convocations, which you will observe in their seasons. The fourteenth day of the first month (Nisan) is the Lord's Passover. The fifteenth day of Nisan begins the feast of Unleavened Bread; seven days you must eat unleavened bread. The first day of that period will be a holy convocation: you will do no work on that day. You will present burnt offerings to the Lord throughout the celebration. The seventh day will be another holy convocation: you will do no work on that day.

- DEU 16:8 ~ Eat unleavened bread six days and then rejoice and thank God the seventh day with a solemn assembly; do not work that day.

- JOH 6:26–35, 51–58 ~ Jesus pronounced, "Truly I tell you, the reason you follow me is not for the miracles, but because you have partaken of the bread and are filled. Labor not for meat that perishes but for meat (bread) which endures unto everlasting life. This is the Son of man, the one who carries the seal of God the Father." The people answered, "What should we do to perform the works of God?" Jesus replied, "God's work is to believe in Him whom He sent." They asked Jesus, "Can you show us a sign to convince us that we should believe you, like when our fathers ate manna in the desert?" Jesus answered, "The manna from heaven did not come from Moses; it came from God who gives you the true bread from heaven. The bread of life comes from heaven and gives life to the world. I am the bread of life; whoever comes to me will never hunger again and whoever believes in me will never thirst again. The bread I give is my flesh, which I give for the life of the world. Unless you eat the body and drink the blood of the Son of man, you have no life. If you eat my body and drink my blood, you live in me and I in you; and you will have eternal life, for I will raise you up the last day. Mine is not like the manna from heaven, for whoever eats the bread I give will live forever."

- 1 CO 5:7 ~ Throw out the old leavened dough and become a new dough, without yeast; for that is what you have become because of the sacrifice of Christ who is the Passover Lamb.

Unleavened bread is prepared without yeast; yeast represents the body without sin. Christ alone has a body without sin, until we are brought to heaven with our sins removed, after which we will have bodies without sin too. His body was broken on the cross, reflected in His breaking unleavened bread the night before with His apostles. Christ purifies us if we partake of Him in Holy Communion.

- MAT 26:26–28; LUK 22:19–20; 1 CO 11:24–26 ~ Jesus took the bread, gave thanks, and broke the bread, giving it to His disciples and saying, "Take and eat; this is my body which is given for you; do this to remember me." In like manner He took the cup of wine saying, "Drink from this cup all of you. It is the New Covenant in my blood which is poured out for you, and for many others, for the forgiveness of sins. Do this often to remember me." For whenever you eat of this bread and drink from this cup you proclaim the Lord's death until He returns.

- 1 CO 10:16–19 ~ The cup of blessing that we bless, does it not represent our communion with the blood of Christ? The bread that we break, does it not represent our communion with the body of Christ? Although we are many, we have become one body for we all are partakers of that one bread. And He is the head of the body, the church, who is the beginning, the firstborn of the dead, that in all things He might have preeminence. For it pleased the Father that in Him all His fullness would dwell.

- COL 1:19–22 ~ God was pleased to have His fullness living in Christ, so that through Him, everything on earth and in heaven could be reconciled to Himself, by the peace that came through the shedding of Christ's blood on the cross. Before, you were separated from God; you were His enemies because of your sinful minds and evil deeds. But now, God has reconciled you by the body of Christ through His death, to be presented holy, blameless, and pure in the sight of God.

Since Christ ascended into heaven, the body of Christ has become synonymous with Christians around the world, who have given their lives to Him just as He did for us. Christ is the head of the body which is His church on earth. Members are among the resurrected who go immediately to heaven upon death; for they have invited the Holy Spirit of Christ and His righteousness into themselves, which He imputed when He took our sins upon Himself. But since He was without sin, death had no hold over Him; He has therefore conquered sin for the entirety of humankind, and the only requirement of you is that you accept this free gift. You can decline it through disbelief, in which case you probably do not want to spend eternity alive with God; for you will have chosen death and eternal separation from Him instead.

- ROM 12:4–6 ~ Just as we have many members in our body, and all members have the same purpose, so we, being many, are one body in Christ, and members of one another. We all have different gifts according to the grace God has given us.

- EPH 3:6 ~ The Gentiles will be fellow heirs, members of the same body, and partakers of God's promise through Christ.

- COL 3:15–17 ~ Let the peace of God rule in your hearts, since as members of one body you were called to peace. Be therefore, thankful. Let the Word of Christ live in you richly as you teach and admonish one another with wisdom, and as you sing psalms, hymns, and spiritual songs with gratitude in your hearts to God. Remember what Christ taught you and let His words enrich your lives and make you wise. Teach His words to each other. Sing them openly and spiritually in psalms and hymns with thankful hearts. Whatever you do or say, do it in Jesus's name, and give thanks to God in Jesus's name.

- HEB 13:3 ~ Remember those who are in bondage as if you were bound with them, and remember those who suffer adversity as if you were suffering with them, because you are fellow members of the body.

Gracious Father, Son, and Holy Spirit: what a marvelous God you are for appointing us to be the recipients of such a blessing by giving yourself for us so that death will never harm us. We cannot thank you enough, but the day will come when we will be thanking you for eternity as soon as we arrive home. Help us to be steadfast in awaiting that glorious day, as we struggle through these days on earth; without losing hope or faith, but always being replenished through your Word, sacraments, and ever-present Spirit. On this day we remember the commandments to your people, and the broken bread without yeast, and Christ's broken body on the cross, and His spilled blood which atoned for our sin. And we readily receive your body and blood, infused into ours through the Eucharist and your Holy Spirit conveyed to us. Let us always be ready to listen to you, Father, and to die in your Son Jesus, in whom we pray, Amen.

April 25

Feast of First Fruits (*Omer*) occurs in the Jewish calendar on Nisan 16. It generally coincides with the early harvest, after which the first of the crops and flocks were given to the Lord. The Jewish calendar begins with Nisan; a lot happens during this month as you can see. Some would argue it is the most important period of the year, in recognition of the most important period in the history of humankind. For without the death and resurrection of Jesus Christ nobody would ever overcome death. But everybody will, because He conquered sin with His death, and conquered death with His resurrection. The key is knowing where you will go after that and for how long.

- EXO 23:19 ~ The choicest part of the first fruits of your harvests shall be given to God.
- RUT 1:22 ~ Naomi and Ruth (the Moabitess) went to Bethlehem together, arriving at the beginning of the barley harvest. [Ruth and Boaz would become ancestors of Christ, through the lineage of David, whose hometown also was Bethlehem.]
- 2 CH 31:5 ~ Everyone brought in abundance the first fruits of their crops, wine, oil, honey, and all their profits.
- PRO 3:9 ~ Honor the Lord with the first fruits of all your income.
- JER 2:3 ~ Israel was holy to the Lord and represented the first fruits of His increase. Those who try to destroy God's elect will have evil come upon them.
- JAM 5:7–8 ~ Brothers, wait patiently for the coming of the Lord, like the farmer who must patiently await the rain and the harvest. Be patient and take courage, for His coming is near.

Just as the first fruits from the early and late harvests belonged to God, we also give to Him the first fruits of our income in our tithes and offerings. We have been claimed by Christ, the first fruits of God the Father. Since we belong to Christ, we are His first fruits which He will present blameless before our Father in heaven, having already provided for our atonement. At the resurrection we will be judged not guilty (justified), for Christ has erased our iniquities from the record and recorded our names in the Book of Life.

- ROM 8:22–23 ~ We know that the whole creation groans in pain, as if in labor, up until the present. And not only that, for we ourselves are the first fruits of the Spirit. Yes, even we groan, waiting for the adoption and the redemption of our bodies.
- 1 CO 15:20–24~ Now is Christ raised from the dead, becoming the first fruits of those who have died. Since by man came death, by the godman came the resurrection of the dead. Just as Adam died, all die; in Christ all will be made alive, each in their own time and order, with Christ the first fruits, and after that those who belong to Him. So, the next to be raised will be Christ's own, when He returns. Then comes the end, when He delivers His kingdom to God the Father, having brought down all other dominions, powers, and rulers.
- 1 TH 4:1–17 ~ The Lord Himself will descend from heaven with a shout, the voice of the archangel, and the trumpet of God. And the dead in Christ will rise first; next, those who are alive in Christ will meet in the air with Him to be forever with the Lord.
- JAM 1:18 ~ God chose to give us birth through the Word of truth, to be a type of first fruits of all He created.
- REV 14:3–4 ~ The 144,000 sang a new song; nobody could learn the song except them. They were the ones who were undefiled by women, virgins who follow the Lamb wherever He went. They were redeemed from humankind as the first fruits of God and the Lamb.

The feast of first fruits is all about the resurrection: first, the resurrection of Christ, the first fruits of the Father; and second the resurrection of humans, the first fruits of Jesus, when it is our turn. Believe in Him if you want to be among the chosen. Every soul will be raised and stand before God. Those who accepted Christ as Savior will be raised into eternal life with Him; those who did not will be raised for judgment. Christians automatically are justified, because Christ our advocate will declare us as His, when He presents His Church to the Father, pure and holy.

- PSA 5:11 ~ Let everyone who trusts in the Lord rejoice and shout for joy, because He will defend them. Let all who love the Lord be joyful.

- PSA 37:18 ~ God knows those who are blameless, and their inheritance will be forever.

- PSA 106:4–5 ~ Remember me with favor, Lord. Bring your salvation to me, so that I may rejoice in the gladness of your people, and glory in your inheritance.

- ISA 53:10–11 ~ It pleased the Lord to bruise Him (Messiah) and to make Him suffer. His life was given as an offering for sin; but God will see His Son and prolong His days whereas the will of God will flourish in Him. After His soul has suffered enough, He will be able to look back with satisfaction. By knowledge of Him many will become justified, for He took their sins upon Himself.

- 1 CO 1:5–8 ~ You are enriched by Christ in everything you say and everything you know. Even as the testimony of Christ was confirmed among you who wait for the day of His return, so He will confirm you until the end, ensuring that you receive all your spiritual needs, and be found blameless upon that day.

- EPH 1:3–8 ~ Praise to God, the Father of our Lord Jesus Christ, who has chosen us before the foundation of the world to be holy and blameless before Him in love. We were destined to be God's adopted children, in accordance with His good will and grace, through Jesus Christ, in whom we have redemption and forgiveness through His blood, wherein He lavished upon us with all wisdom and insight.

- COL 1:19–22 ~ God was pleased to have His fullness living in Christ, so that through Him, everything on earth and in heaven could be reconciled unto Himself, by the peace that came through the shedding of Christ's blood on the cross. Before, you were separated from God; you were His enemies because of your sinful minds and evil deeds. But now, God has reconciled you by the body of Christ through His death, to be presented holy, blameless, and pure in the sight of God.

- 1 TH 5:23 ~ May the God of peace sanctify you wholly, so that your entire spirit, soul, and body can be preserved blameless until the coming of our Lord Jesus Christ.

- JDE 1:24–25 ~ To Him that is able to keep you from falling, and to bring you blameless into His glorious presence with endless joy, to the only God our Savior be glory, majesty, power, and authority, through Jesus Christ our Lord, timeless throughout the ages, now and forevermore, Amen.

Heavenly Father, Christ is your first fruits and we are His first fruits, and we couldn't be happier belonging to Him. Thank you that we mean so much to you, and help us to keep you, Father, number one in our lives, along with your Son Jesus Christ, together with the Holy Spirit. Let us be fruitful with our faith, and give the first fruits of our increase to you in service with thanksgiving. For all that we have is yours, especially the best of our portion. Help us to wait patiently and joyfully, knowing what lies in store, which is to meet Christ in the air to follow Him home and be with you forever, Amen.

April 26

Arbor Day is observed by countries across the globe. Mass plantings of trees throughout the ages have been celebrated on days like this. It became an event in the USA when J. S. Morton of Nebraska proposed to the state board of agriculture a celebration to be held on 04/10/1872 for the planting of about one million trees. This prompted other states to follow their lead, and by the 1920s most US states had adopted their own version of Arbor Day. President Teddy Roosevelt gave the holiday a boost by suggesting schools across the country plant trees. It became official in 1970 under President Nixon; it is now held on the last Friday of the month in most states, but the date can vary depending on the best time of the year to plant trees which are indigenous to a particular state.

What better day to plant a tree than today? If you want to get involved in tree planting, try contacting the Arbor Day Foundation (established 1972). They can help you decide what trees to plant in your location. If you have the urge, fruit trees are always a good choice. It is the perfect time of year to get a sapling in the ground. If you plant seeds, you might want to start earlier in the year depending on where you live. Trees are a valuable commodity, not just for the wood, but for their contributions toward protecting the earth, its people, animals, and birds, from pollution, high winds, thunderstorms, catastrophes, and changes in climate.

- GEN 1:29 ~ God said, "I have given to humankind every seed-bearing plant on the face of the entire earth, and every tree that has fruit and seed in it. They will be yours for food.

- EXO 15:27; NUM 32:9 ~ There were twelve fountains and seventy palm trees at the encampment of the Israelites. [There also were twelve tribes of Israel and seventy elders of the Jewish synagogue.]

- ISA 55:12–13 ~ The mountains and hills sing and the trees clap their hands; the world rejoices around you. Instead of a thorn bush, a tree will grow. And the name of the Lord will be magnified as an everlasting sign of the nurturing He provides.

- JOE 1:19–20 ~ I will cry to the Lord, for fire has burned the pastures and the trees of the field. The animals cry, for the rivers are dried up and there is no grass in the wilderness (see REV 8 below).

- REV 8:7 ~ The first angel sounded and hail mixed with blood fell to earth; one third of the trees and all the grass were burned.

The Bible has a lot to say about trees; however, references to trees are not always about actual trees. For example, trees can represent people and the fruit they bear.

- PSA 1:2–3 ~ Blessed is the person whose delight is in God's Law, for that person meditates on God's Law every day and night. Such a person will be like a tree planted by flowing streams of water, bearing good fruit in season, with leaves that never wither. Whatever he or she does will prosper.

- PSA 52:4–8 ~ Surely God will bring you down into everlasting ruin; He will uproot you from the land of the living. The righteous will see and fear. They will laugh, saying, "Here is the man that did not make God his strength, but instead placed his trust in the abundance of his riches and found strength in wickedness. But I am like a green olive tree, flourishing in the house of God, trusting in His mercy forevermore.

- PRO 11:30 ~ The fruit of righteousness is a tree of life, and those who win souls for God are wise.

- PRO 15:2–4 ~ The tongue of the wise will employ knowledge properly; but the tongue of fools pours out foolishness. The eyes of the Lord are everywhere, noticing the evil and the good. A wholesome tongue is a tree of life, but a perverse tongue breaks the spirit.

- ISA 61:3 ~ People of God are referred to as trees of righteousness.

- JER 11:19–23 ~ I was taken like a lamb to the slaughter. They had plotted against me, saying, "Let us destroy the tree that bears the fruit; let us cut Him down so that He will not be remembered." But they will be the ones who are destroyed and forgotten.

- EZE 31:16 ~ God made the nations shake at the sound of Egypt's fall, when He cast Pharaoh down to hell with the others who descend into the pit. Meanwhile, the trees of Eden, and all that drink water, will be comforted throughout the earth.

- ZEC 4:1–3, 11–14 ~ The angel woke Zechariah and asked him what he saw. He replied that he saw a golden candlestick with a large bowl on top; there were seven lamps that were fed by seven pipes from the large bowl. There were two olive trees on either side of the bowl. Zechariah asked the angel what they were, and why they emptied golden olive oil into the bowl. The angel said they represented the two anointed ones who stand before the Lord over the earth.

- MAT 3:7–10 ~ John was baptizing people in the Jordan River when many of the Pharisees and Sadducees came to observe. John spoke to them saying, "You snakes! Has anyone warned you of the judgement that awaits you? You had better start bearing fruit that is worthy of repentance. You say to yourselves that you have Abraham as your father. I assure you that God can produce children of Abraham from these stones. The ax is ready to strike at the roots; any tree that does not bear good fruit will be chopped down and burned in the fire."

- MAT 7:17–19 ~ Jesus said, "A good tree bears good fruit; a corrupt tree bears evil fruit. A good tree cannot bear bad fruit and a bad tree cannot bear good fruit. Any tree that does not bear good fruit will be cut down at the roots and burned in the fire."

- MAR 11:12–14, 20–24 ~ Upon entering Bethany Jesus was hungry. He spotted a fig tree from afar with leaves, so He went to see if it had fruit, but it was too early in the season. Jesus proclaimed that nobody will ever again eat fruit from that tree. The next morning, they passed that way again and the tree was withered from the roots up. Peter remembered the morning before and said, "Master, behold the fig tree that you cursed; it has withered away." Jesus answered him, "Truly I tell you that anyone can tell this mountain to be removed and be thrown into the sea, without doubting but believing, and it will happen; you can have everything you ask. Whatever you desire, pray for it, believing that you will receive it, and you will."

- REV 11:3–6 ~ I will give power to my two witnesses (see ZEC 4 above). These are the two olive trees and the two candlesticks. They have the power to breathe fire, to stop the rain, to turn water into blood, and to send plagues.

Trees also are depicted to illustrate the end of days, the kingdom of heaven, and its Tree of Life, as well as the Tree of Knowledge of good and evil. In the Garden of Eden were the Tree of Knowledge and the Tree of Life. Adam and Eve ate of the forbidden fruit from the Tree of Knowledge and brought sin and death upon humanity. They were driven from the garden to prevent them from eating of the Tree of Life; angels with a flaming sword guarded the garden to avert entry by sinful people. This is analogous to the kingdom of heaven where only those whose sin has been removed can enter and partake of the Tree of Life.

APRIL

- GEN 2:9, 16–17 ~ God allowed every tree that is pleasant to the sight and good for food to grow out of the ground. This included the Tree of Life which was in the middle of the garden, and the Tree of Knowledge of good and evil. And God issued a commandment to man saying "You may eat from any tree in the garden except the Tree of Knowledge; for if you eat from it, you will surely die."

- GEN 3:1–7 ~ The serpent was cleverer than the other animals. One day he tricked Eve into trying some fruit from the Tree of Knowledge, even though she knew it was forbidden by God. The serpent lied, telling her that whoever ate the fruit would not die but would become like a god, knowing good and evil. When Eve saw that the fruit looked good and pleasant, she ate; then she gave some to Adam who was with her, and he also ate. And their eyes were opened, and they saw themselves naked so they sewed fig leaves together to make aprons.

- GEN 3:24 ~ God drove Adam and Eve out of the Garden of Eden. He placed cherubim with a flaming sword at the east end of the garden to guard the Tree of Life.

- PRO 3:13–14, 18 ~ Happy are those who find wisdom and gain understanding. For this is worth much more than gold and silver. She is a tree of life to those who grasp it, and happy are those who keep it.

- EZE 47:1–12 ~ Later, God brought me again to His house in heaven, and I saw waters flowing out from it which formed a river that I could not pass over. Everything the water touched flourished. On both sides of the river grew all kinds of trees that never died. The trees produced new fruit every month; the fruit of the trees provided food and the leaves provided medicine (see REV 22 below).

- MAT 13:31–32 ~ Jesus told a parable about sowing to the Spirit: The kingdom of heaven is like the mustard seed. It is one of the smallest of seeds yet it grows into one of the largest of trees. Then the birds come and make homes in its branches.

- REV 2:7 ~ Jesus said to the churches, "To those who overcome evil, I will allow them to eat from the Tree of Life, which is in the paradise of God."

- REV 22:1–2, 14 ~ In John's vision of heaven he saw a pure river of the water of life, clear as crystal, proceeding from the throne of God and the Lamb. The river nourished the Tree of Life which bore twelve different kinds of fruit each month, with leaves that provided enough medicine to heal all nations. Blessed be those who keep God's commandments, so that they can obtain the right to the Tree of Life, and to enter into the gates of heaven (EZE 47).

Trees reflect life. In the Bible trees represent life on earth and life in heaven. Life on earth is reflected in the Tree of Knowledge; that is, the knowledge of good and evil and our sinfulness. The tree itself does not connote sinfulness; but the knowledge of sin is conveyed whenever we give into temptation. The Tree of Life is evidence of righteousness, which anyone can receive from Christ in exchange for their sins. Without this cleansing, you will not be allowed to partake of the Tree of Life, which represents everlasting life with God in paradise.

Our Father in heaven, paradise is your domain; it also is the ultimate destination for all who praise your holy name and confess the atonement of Christ your precious Son. We thank you that we have been chosen by you to be your children, because we have chosen Christ to be our Lord and Savior. You will be our God now and forever. Please have your Holy Spirit remind us of this every time we see a beautiful tree: that we will eat of the Tree of Life and drink of the River of Life in heaven, as equal heirs to the kingdom. Let us be healthy trees that bear good fruit abundantly and eternally. We offer these petitions in the name of your Son Jesus, Amen.

April 27

Morse Code Day honors Samuel Morse who was born on this day in 1791. He invented his coding scheme in 1836 to transmit information over telegraph wire. Morse and his colleagues Joseph Henry and Alfred Vail together had developed the electrical telegraph machine as well as the coding scheme. Electric impulses representing letters of the alphabet were transmitted via short and long clicks; the translator made dot and dash marks on paper tape at the other end; spaces between words and sentences were based on a timed pause. Commercial use of this technique began in 1844. Shortly thereafter the code could be sent audibly using radio waves via dits (dots) and dahs (dashes). Initially, only the English language was coded, but soon other languages were encoded using the method. This coding scheme became very helpful in World War II on ships and planes to send messages long range via sound or light. Morse code is still used; for example, the universal distress signal is "SOS" (dit dit dit, dah dah dah, dit dit dit).

Speaking of distress signals, we can bring our problems, trials, and tribulations to the Lord and He will respond in ways that bring us closer to Him. We can always call upon Him in times of trouble, knowing that He will give us comfort and hope. His Spirit, the great Comforter, is with us at all times; and the times will become all the more distressing as we approach the end.

- DEU 4:29–31 ~ If you seek God with all your heart and soul you will find Him. If you are distressed, even in the latter times, turn to God and obey His commandments. God is merciful and He will never abandon you or destroy you; He will never forget the covenant He made with your forefathers.

- ZEP 1:15–18 ~ A great day of wrath, distress and anguish, ruin and devastation, darkness and gloom is coming. Their blood will be poured out like dust and their flesh like dung. Their riches will do them no good then. All the earth will be consumed at once.

- MAT 11:28 ~ Jesus said, "Come to me all of you who labor and are heavy laden and I will give you rest."

- JOH 14:16, 26; JOH 15:26–27; JOH 16:7, 13 ~ Jesus said, "I will ask the Father and He will give you another Comforter to abide with you forever. The Comforter that the Father is sending in my name, which is the Holy Spirit, will teach you all things and will remind you of everything I have said to you. When the Comforter, the Spirit of Truth comes, whom I will send to you from the Father and who proceeds from the Father, He will testify about me. And you also must testify, for you have been with me from the beginning. It is good for me to go, because until I am gone, the Comforter cannot come to you; but I will send Him to you when I leave. When the Spirit of truth comes, He will guide you into all truth. He will speak the words of God and He will show you what is yet to come."

- JOH 16:33 ~ After the last supper on the night Jesus was betrayed, Jesus was about to leave for the Garden of Gethsemane to pray. Jesus said, "The reason I told to you these things is so you could have peace. In the world you will have distress, but be cheerful for I have overcome the world."

- ROM 5:3; ROM 8:35–39 ~ We also rejoice in our tribulations, because we know that tribulation produces patience, and patience produces character, and character produces hope. And hope will not disappoint us, because God has poured out His love into our hearts by His Holy Spirit. What can separate us from the love of Christ: tribulation, distress, persecution, famine, nakedness, peril, or sword? As it is written, for your sake we face death on a daily basis; we are sent as sheep to the slaughter. But we have conquered these things through Him who loved us. For I am convinced that neither death nor life, neither angels nor demons, neither the present nor the future, nor any powers, neither height nor depth, nor anything in all creation can separate us from the love of God that is in Jesus Christ our Lord.

- 2 CO 1:3–7 ~ Paul wrote: Praise God, the Father of our Lord Jesus Christ, the Father of compassion and the God of all comfort. He comforts us in all our tribulations, so that we can comfort others who are troubled, using the same comfort we ourselves have received from God. Just as the sufferings of Christ flow over into our lives, so also through Him our comfort overflows. If we are distressed, it is for your comfort and salvation. If we are comforted, it is for your comfort as well, which produces in you the patience to endure the same sufferings we suffer. And our hope for you is firm, because we know that just as you share in our sufferings, so also you share in our comfort.

- 2 CO 4:8–10, 16–17 ~ We are surrounded by troubles, yet we are not distressed; we are perplexed, but we are not in despair. We are persecuted, but not forsaken; beaten down, but not destroyed. We always carry in our bodies the death of Jesus Christ, so that His life will also be revealed in our bodies. Therefore, we never give up; though outwardly we are worn down, yet inwardly we are renewed day after day. Our insignificant and temporary problems bring us closer to eternal glory, which far outweighs the sum of all of our troubles combined.

- 2 CO 6:3–10 ~ We do not place obstacles in anyone's way because we do not want the ministry to be discredited. Rather, as servants of God we commend ourselves in every way, through much endurance, trouble, hardship, and distress; through abuse, imprisonment, and rioting; through hard work, hunger, and sleepless nights; in purity, understanding, endurance, and kindness; in the Holy Spirit and in sincere love; in truth and in the power of God; carrying weapons of righteousness in each hand; through times of glory and dishonor, favor and rejection. We are genuine yet regarded as imposters; known yet regarded as strangers; dying yet still alive; beaten down but not defeated; sorrowful but always rejoicing; poor yet spreading wealth; having nothing yet possessing everything.

- 2 CO 12:7–10 ~ So that I would not exalt myself by the many revelations God showed to me, I was given a thorn in the flesh, a messenger of Satan to buffet me. I prayed to the Lord thrice, that it might depart from me. He replied to me, "My grace is sufficient for you because my strength is made perfect in weakness." Therefore, I will gladly revel in my infirmities, so that the power of Christ may rest upon me. That is, I take pleasure in illness, reproach, hunger, persecution, and distress for Christ's sake; for when I am weak, then I become strong.

- 2 TI 3:1–7 ~ Know this, that perilous times will come in the last days. People will love only themselves. They will be covetous, boasters, blasphemers, arrogant, disobedient to parents, unthankful and ungodly, void of natural affection. They will be promise breakers, false accusers, undisciplined, fierce despisers of goodness; traitors, reckless, conceited, lovers of worldly pleasures more than God; displaying a form of godliness, but denying the power thereof. Stay away from people like this. For they attempt to sneak into houses and coax weak-minded women swayed by lustful pleasures.

Dear Father, we thank you for your Holy Spirit who comforts us when we are in distress; for you are always with us in Spirit and in Truth, and we have nothing to fear from the world. Help us to share with others the love, peace, and comfort which you have showered upon us, so they too can be comforted by your Holy Spirit as we are. Prepare us to receive your strength when we feel weak and in despair, receiving the hope that we own by faith in Jesus Christ. Jesus said that we can come to Him whenever we are beaten down or carrying a heavy load; let us remember that we can lay our troubles at the foot of the cross and Jesus will take them off our shoulders. It is in His name that we pray this prayer, Amen.

April 28

International Workers Memorial Day recognizes lost or maimed loved ones who were gravely injured, disabled, made seriously ill, or perished on the job. In recent decades, efforts have improved workplace safety by addressing health hazards and safety issues with appropriate training, labeling, engineering, and documentation. Certainly, some occupations come with known dangers such as fire fighters, police, military, and other first responders. In the USA, the AFL-CIO labor union observed this date as Worker's Memorial Day in 1989. The International Confederation of Free Trade held a candlelight vigil drawing attention to unsafe work places and practices. This date is the anniversary of the passing of a law in 1970, which instituted the Occupational Safety and Health Association (OSHA), America's business and industry watchdog.

If you know of a family who has been affected by workplace accidents that caused loss of life or limb, or perhaps you or a loved one meets that description, reach out today and show you care. You also can get involved in health, safety, and risk assessment at your place of employment or at your school or university. There will be various events and trainings available to the public as well, in case you want to learn more. Visit the OSHA website if you have the inclination to get involved or to learn about recommendations that could affect you or others.

When it comes to the workplace being hazardous to your health, consider what Jesus and the apostles had to go through, not to mention the early church fathers. Almost all of these men were martyred. Even today, being a Christian is risky business, for we are a most abused and hated of people. But then, Christ warned us this would be the case.

- LEV 19:17–18 ~ Never hate your brother in your heart; confront him openly with your grievance so that you do not fall into the same sin as he. Never bear a grudge or seek revenge against one another. Instead, love one another as much as you love yourself.

- MAT 5:43–44 ~ Jesus said, "You have heard that you should love your neighbor as yourself, but you can hate your enemy. I tell you to love your enemies, and pray for those who persecute you or take advantage of you."

- MAT 10:26–27 ~ Jesus said, "Do not fear those who hate you, for everything that is hidden now will be revealed later; everything that is unknown will become known. What I tell you in darkness, you will speak in the light. Things you have heard will be shouted from the rooftops."

- LUK 21:17–19 ~ Jesus said, "People will hate you because of me; but be patient and you will keep your soul."

- JOH 15:18–19, 23–25 ~ Jesus said, "The world hates you because it hated me first. If you were of the world, the world would love you as its own. But you are not of the world since I have chosen you out of it, and that is why the world hates you. Those who hate me hate the Father. This is the fulfillment of the prophecy: They hated me without cause."

- JOH 16:33 ~ Jesus said to the apostles, "I have told you these things that you might have peace, because in the world you will have tribulation. But be of good cheer for I have overcome the world."

- ACT 14:22 ~ Paul informed the disciples they would endure considerable tribulation before entering the kingdom of God.

- 1 CO 4:1, 11–12 ~ We are ministers of Christ and stewards of the mysteries of God. We are hungry and thirsty, we are naked and beaten, and we have no home. We work hard using our abilities. We bless those who mistreat us; we endure the persecutions of others and carry on.

APRIL

- 2 TI 3:11–13 ~ Although I endured much hardship, persecution, and affliction, God always delivered me. All righteous people will suffer persecution. Evil people will get perpetually worse.

- HEB 11:35–40 ~ People of faith raised the dead. They endured torture, refusing to renounce God as a condition for their release. They were mocked, beaten, chained, and imprisoned. They were stoned and beheaded. They wandered the wilderness in shaggy clothes, destitute, tormented, and afflicted. Although their lives on earth were full of strife, they awaited their deliverance, as we also must do until God makes us perfect before Him.

- JAM 5:10–11 ~ Remember the prophets as examples of patience in the face of suffering. We consider those who have persevered to be blessed by God.

- 1 PE 2:19–21; 1 PE 4:12–13, 16–17 ~ It is commendable if a man suffers unjustly because he is conscious of God. If you suffer for doing good and you endure it, you are favored by God. This is one reason you are called, because Christ suffered for you, giving you an example to follow. Do not consider it strange, the fiery trial that you must endure, but rejoice when you partake of the sufferings of Christ; when His glory is revealed you will be exceedingly glad. If you suffer for being a Christian do not be ashamed, but glorify God in the process; for judgment will begin with God's house. And if it begins with us first, what will be the end of those who do not obey the Gospel of the Lord?

- REV 2:10 ~ Jesus said, "Do not be afraid of the things you must suffer. Satan will throw some of you into prison to be tried; you will endure tribulation for ten days. Be faithful unto death and I will give you a crown of life."

The apostles of Christ were tormented, persecuted, and executed; St. John was the only one to live a full life. The following are accounts of the demise of the apostles, where they ministered and how they died; only one death is recorded in the Bible (from Barber, 2020a).

Apostle	Ministry	Demise
Andrew	Russia; Ukraine	Crucified in Patras Greece on an X-shaped cross
Bartholomew	Armenia	Beheaded in Armenia
James A.	Palestine	Beat and cut to pieces in Jerusalem
James Z.	Palestine	Beheaded by Herod Agrippa I (MAT 14:1–13)
John	Asia Minor	Died a natural death in Ephesus after his exile
Matthew	Ethiopia	Impaled with swords in Ethiopia
Paul	Asia Minor; Rome	Executed in Rome by Emperor Nero
Peter	Babylon; Rome	Crucified upside-down in Rome
Philip	Asia Minor	Executed in Asia Minor
Simon	Arabia	Beaten to death by an angry mob in Arabia
Thaddaeus	Assyria; Persia	Shot with arrows in Babylonia
Thomas	Persia; India	Impaled with a spear in India

Heavenly Father, help us to be brave Christian soldiers as we face the enemy in battle every day of our lives. With your Holy Spirit by our side, we have nothing to fear; let us remember this when we feel overwhelmed, fatigued, or in pain. Embolden us to tell the truth of your Word, no matter the cost, even as the apostles spread the Word to hostile nations, knowing that many would not receive it but would be offended, yet they continued to be witnesses unto death, without fear or hesitation. We are proud to die with Jesus, knowing that if we join Him in death, we also will join Him in life. In His name we pray, Amen.

April 29

International Dance Day was established by the International Theatre Institute (ITI) in 1982 in partnership with UNESCO. Today is the birth date of J. G. Noverre (1727) considered to be the first pioneer of modern ballet (as opposed to classical ballet). Every year is a presentation by a famous dancer, along with classes and projects featured from the dance community. It is a celebration of dance and choreography as forms of art which enrich the lives of everyone. It is not necessary to be a good dancer to dance, and nobody should judge you for it. Every country has a cultural element in which folkloric dance has been a part. It is interesting to watch ensembles perform original dances in the traditional costumes. Dancing is actually healthy as it is good exercise and releases endorphins, the body's natural healing hormone.

Though some religions are against dancing of any kind, other religions incorporate dance into their worship. There is considerable dancing in the Bible, all kinds actually. It depends on what form of dancing, for some of it is outright vulgar. Other times it is romantic, a ritual for dating or married couples. Dancing can be done with or without a partner as well as with large groups of people. It is fun to dance and it is fun to watch others dancing, particularly skilled troupes dancing in traditional garb to folkloric music.

- ECC 3:1, 4 ~ For everything there is a season, and a time for every purpose under heaven. A time to weep and a time to laugh; a time to mourn and a time to dance.

    There is a time to dance and to laugh. There also is a time to mourn and to weep, which is not the time to be dancing and laughing. There is a time to refrain from partying because there is other business to attend to. You wouldn't want to be caught off guard, get fired, or flunk a test!

- EXO 32:1–8 ~ Moses had gone up into Sinai to visit with the Lord; he was a long time on the mountain. The people below got impatient. They persuaded Aaron to make them a calf of gold; he did what they asked collecting all their golden jewelry, melting it and forming it into the shape of a calf. He also built an altar for the idol, telling the people there would be a party in the morning. They got up early to eat, drink, and play; they even sacrificed to their idol. And the Lord told Moses to go back down the mountain, for Israel had sinned after God had brought them out of Egypt.

- JDG 21:17–24 ~ There was an annual feast to the Lord in Shiloh near Bethel. To restore the tribe of Benjamin from being lost from Israel, the men went to the festival. They were lying in wait for the dancing girls to come out in order to make wives of them.

- 1 SA 30:13–20 ~ David forced a servant of the Amalekites to lead him to their encampment in the valley, where there was eating, drinking, and dancing in celebration of the tribute they had taken from the lands of the Philistines and of Judah. David attacked at twilight into the next day, and not a man escaped. David retrieved the stolen goods and his two wives which had been kidnapped; he also took the rest of their spoils which became his.

- LAM 5:11 ~ They ravished the women of Zion and the maids in Judah. They hanged princes by their hands, and dishonored the elders. They captured young men to be grinders, and the children to haul wood. The elders no longer stood at the gate and the young men had refrained from their music. The joy in their hearts had ceased, and dancing had turned to mourning. [They were lamenting the invasion and captivity by Babylon.]

- MAT 14:6–11; MAR 6:22–28 ~ For Herod's birthday party, the daughter of his partner, who was his brother's wife, danced for him and his guests. He was so pleased he swore she could have anything to the half of his kingdom. Her mother Herodias instructed her to ask for the head of John the Baptist on a platter. To avoid embarrassment, Herod capitulated.

APRIL

Dancing was a joyful expression of good tidings and fortune in the Bible; this has been true for the duration of man. It's not like the people of the Bible didn't know how to throw a party. Sometimes there were festivities associated with the act of worship.

- EXO 15:19–21 ~ There was singing and dancing after God buried the horsemen of Pharaoh in the Red Sea. Miriam a prophetess and sister of Aaron took a tambourine, along with other women with timbrels, and danced and sang to the Lord about His great triumph over the Egyptians.

- 2 SA 6:12–14; 1 CH 15:25–28 ~ David was pleased that Obededom had taken good care of the Ark of the Covenant, and now the king could return it to Jerusalem. David, the elders and the captains, followed by thousands more came up the main street. They sacrificed to the Lord seven bulls and seven rams. David was dressed in his royal linen, dancing and shouting using all his might, with the sound of trumpets, singers, cymbals, lyres and harps.

- PSA 149:1–7 ~ Praise the Lord! Sing to the Lord a new song; praise Him, congregation of the saints. Let Israel rejoice in the Lord who made them; let the children of Zion be joyful in their King. Praise His name with dance; sing praises with tambourines and harps. For the Lord takes pleasure in His people, beautifying the humble with salvation. Let the saints be joyful in glory, let them sing aloud upon their beds. Let the high praises of God be in their mouths, and a double-edged sword in their hand, to execute vengeance upon the heathen, and punishment on the wicked people.

- PSA 150:1–6 ~ Praise the Lord! Praise God in His sanctuary. Praise Him from on high. For His acts are mighty and His greatness excellent. Praise Him with the trumpet, lyre, and harp. Praise Him with tambourines and dancing; praise Him with stringed instruments, pipes, and cymbals. Let everything that has breath praise the Lord!

- JER 31:3–4 ~ The Lord had appeared to me once before, saying how He had loved Israel with an everlasting love; with loving kindness He had chosen us. Again, He will build you, oh virgin of Israel. You will take tambourines, dance and make merry.

- LUK 15:21–32 ~ When the prodigal son returned home, he told his father that he was not worthy of being called a son and should be treated as a servant. But the father had his servants prepare a great feast to celebrate. The elder son arrived from the field and found music and dancing inside the house; he asked a servant about it, who said his brother had returned. The elder brother became angry and refused to go inside. The father consoled him saying, "You are always with me and all that is mine is yours. But it is fitting to celebrate, because your brother was lost, but now he is found; he was dead but now he is alive again."

Our Father in heaven, we praise you and we worship you. We will make a joyful noise to you with thanksgiving and psalms including music, dancing, and singing your praises here on earth, along with the hosts of heaven. We do this because we look forward to the wedding feast and celebration of the Lamb. You will give Him your church who is the bride and we will belong to Him forever as He rules at your right hand. He is our judge and has sanctified us with your Holy Spirit, to be presented to you as adopted sons and daughters. We will be one big happy family eternally, and we can hardly wait. Let us be patient and continue the work you have given us here, always taking take time every week to worship you and to celebrate your Son, in whose name we pray, Amen.

April 30

Honesty Day was the brainchild of M. H. Goldberg, author of the 1991 book: *The Book of Lies*, which was about scams, fakes, frauds, and such. Thirty years later, it seems those problems have progressively gotten worse. Our politicians cannot be trusted to tell the truth, unless it's either convenient or it's not embarrassing for them; many of them tell lies for a living. Our kids are being taught lies about history, sexuality, and socialism. The mass media is packed full of fake news; they put out false narratives before the facts are in, to project their ideology, but do not retract after they are proven wrong. Truth in advertising has gone out the window, but you never see any legal action for false advertising. Certain business executives circumvent the facts when it comes to reporting to the government, their shareholders, or subordinates. Personal relationships, marriages, friends, and coworkers are found to be untrustworthy, unfaithful, or backstabbing. People will lie under oath, because they are expecting little or no consequences; or cheat on their taxes figuring they can hide from the IRS. Worst of all, the truth is being stifled because it exposes the underhanded, self-aggrandizing, and destructive motives of the elites in power. And to top that off, liars come to believe their own lies; they can't even be honest with themselves!

- LEV 19:16 ~ Do not go around spreading gossip or rumors.
- PRO 15:28 ~ The righteous heart studies the situation before giving an answer; however, a wicked mouth pours out evil words.
- PRO 17:4 ~ An evildoer gives heed to false lips; and a liar gives ear to a filthy tongue.
- ISA 59:13 ~ They know they are being disobedient to God; they carefully plan their lies.
- MIC 2:1 ~ Woe to those who plot evil and think of sinful things to do, and then carry out their evil plans just because they think they can get away with it.
- ZEC 8:16–17 ~ Always tell the truth to your neighbor; always execute judgments of truth and peace. Do not imagine evil in your hearts against another.
- MAT 15:14 ~ Stay away from false teachers, for they are like the blind leading the blind. And when the blind lead the blind, both fall into the ditch.
- EPH 4:25 ~ Do not lie, but tell the truth to people; for we are members of one another.
- EPH 5:6 ~ Let nobody deceive you with vain words, for because of these things God's wrath comes upon the children of disobedience.
- False prophets will come bringing damnable heresies, denying the Lord and deceiving many. They will exploit you with false words and entice you with lusts of the flesh. They have eyes full of adultery, insatiable for sin. Their hearts are greedy, and they gain through dishonesty. They promise freedom but are themselves slaves to corruption, and are condemned. They will get perpetually worse.
- REV 18:23 ~ The businessmen were the most powerful men on earth, and through their cunning they deceived the nations.

The purpose of this holiday is to honor people who are trustworthy, faithful, honest, and upright, and above all, who tell the truth. We begin the month of April making fools out of each other, and offset that by ending the month making up for it. Does this make sense? All things considered, the truth makes fools out of more people than practical jokes do. Besides, those telling lies will be found out eventually, because it is impossible to keep track of lies after they pile up. But the truth is easy to remember, because it is greater and more powerful than the lie.

APRIL

Clearly, dishonesty has a deleterious effect on individuals, families, the nation and the world. Take for example the Covid pandemic; that whole affair consisted of a series of lies: they were not conducting gain of function research on viruses, the virus was not transmissible to humans, the origin of the virus was a wet market and not a biolab, the vaccines were able to prevent people from getting the disease and passing it onto others, therapeutic medications were of no avail, and the list goes on. Had we been given accurate information it might have prevented millions of deaths from that evil virus and those responsible for it. God will judge them for what they did. Ben Franklin once wrote, "honesty is the best policy" (*Poor Richard's Almanac*). God would agree with that, having made it clear in His Holy Word.

- PSA 24:4 ~ Those who have a pure heart, a truthful soul, and do not swear deceitfully will receive the Lord's blessing, and salvation for their souls.

- PSA 145:18 ~ The Lord comes to all who call upon Him in truth.

- PRO 12:19 ~ The lips of truth will be established forever, but a lying tongue is just for the moment.

- PRO 24:28 ~ Do not testify against your neighbor without just cause, and do not use your lips to deceive.

- JOH 8:31–36 ~ Jesus spoke to those Jews who believed in Him saying, "If you continue in my Word, you are indeed my disciples, and you will know the truth and the truth will set you free." Some of the bystanders answered, "We are descendants of Abraham, and we have never been slaves to anyone; how can we possibly be set free?" Jesus replied, "Whoever sins becomes a slave to sin. A slave has no position in the family, but a son does. If the Son sets you free, you will really be free."

Deceit and dishonesty seem to be pervasive in this world; truthfully it always has been. This comes as no surprise because Satan is the father of lies and he isn't going to stop telling lies, and many people are not going to stop believing those lies. Those choosing to believe lies when the truth is staring them in the face will deny Jesus and experience not one, but two deaths. After the second death, it will be over for those who chose the death option, for they will have denied the Lord's truth and chosen to believe the lie of Satan.

- JER 23:28 ~ God says, "Whoever has my Word should speak that Word faithfully so others might hear it."

- JOH 8:37–47 ~ Jesus said to the Jews who did not believe, "I know you descended from Abraham, yet you are ready to kill me because you have no room for my Word in your heart. I have been telling you about things I have seen in the Father's presence." They responded, "Abraham is our father." Jesus announced, "If you were Abraham's children you would do as he did. Instead, you plot to kill me, a man who has given you the truth directly from God; Abraham would never do such a thing. You are following the ways of your earthly father." They protested, saying, "We are not illegitimate children; God Himself is our Father." Jesus explained, "If God was your Father, you would love me, for I came from Him and here I AM; I have not come on my own because He has sent me. Why is this so hard for you to understand? I will tell you why, because you belong to your father the devil, and your desire is to carry out his will. He was a murderer from the start and despised the truth, for there is no truth in him. He speaks only lies whereas he is the father of lies. I speak only the truth but you refuse to listen. Can you prove me wrong; if not, why do you not believe? Whoever belongs to God listens to Him. The reason you do not understand is because you do not belong to God."

- JOH 18:36–38 ~ Jesus told Pilate that His kingdom was not of this world. Pilate asked Jesus if He was a king. Jesus replied, "You have said it. I was born into this world so I could bear witness to the truth. Everyone who searches for truth hears my voice." Pilate asked, "What is truth?" and then left the room. Upon returning, Pilate declared to the crowd, "I find no fault in this man."

- EPH 4:14–15 ~ We will no longer be helpless as children, swayed by false teachings and influenced by the trickery of deceitful schemes. Instead, we will speak the truth out of love, and we will grow in every way through Christ, who is our head.

- JAM 4:17 ~ To anyone who knows to do good and does not do it, that for them is sin.

- REV 20:6–15 ~ John wrote: Blessed and holy are those who take part in the first resurrection for they will not experience the second death. Instead, they will be priests of God and of Christ and will reign with Him a thousand years. After that, Satan was unloosed and waged war against God, deceiving the nations, God and Magog; the devil gathered his armies but they were devoured by fire from heaven. He was cast into the lake of fire where the beast and false prophet were, to be tormented day and night forever. I saw a white throne and Him who sat on it, whose face the world turned away from though there was no place for them to go. And I saw the dead, great and small, standing before God; and the books were opened, and so was the Book of Life. The dead were judged according to what was written in the books, in accordance with their works. The sea gave up its dead, and death and hell delivered up their dead, and all were judged according to what they had done. Ultimately, death and hell were cast into the lake of fire; this is the second death. Whoever's name was not written in the Book of Life inherited the lake of fire.

Well, there are consequences for living a lie after all; and those consequences are grave, figuratively and literally. It doesn't pay to be dishonest, not in the long run. But greedy eyes will focus on what they want right now, though they have no vision for what it might become later in their lives. What does it profit a person who wins the world but loses his or her soul (MAR 8:36–37); is there anything on this planet worth the price of your soul?

Honesty Day is something we should practice every day. Although this is probably impossible for sinful man, there is much room for improvement and everyone is capable of doing better. It takes a lot of practice, however. Those who practice telling lies will find it easier to tell the lie than the truth, even when the truth is not embarrassing or threatening. Sure, people make good money telling lies; the pay is great. But the payment is horrendous, for the price is your soul. Think carefully before you speak, and you will know the truth before you tell the lie. This is the greatest lie, the one we tell ourselves, especially when we begin to believe it. Be advised, disbelief in the truth that has been given to us by the Holy Spirit is the only unpardonable sin, for it is a sin unto death.

Heavenly Father of all truth, teach us to be wise in your Word and to tell the truth as your Holy Spirit has shown us through the Bible and through Christ the living Word. Truth is the most valuable commodity on earth; help us Father to remember this. Let us hesitate and ponder the value of truth, before we open our mouths and spew lies from our hearts, thinking it will give us some advantage. We know this is a deception from the devil, and that we must seek your love and truth which will drive away the devil; for he can't stand the truth. Let our faith be as a rock, built on the salvation of Jesus Christ, so that we do not doubt; and on the occasions that we do, help us overcome our unbelief with the wisdom of your Word. We pray in the name of Jesus Christ who spoke only the truth, Amen.

May 1

Law Day began on this date in 1958 when President Eisenhower declared it. The idea was first proposed in 1957 by C. S. Rhyne of the American Bar Association (ABA); he was a legal advisor to Eisenhower. Law Day became official when Congress passed a bill designating May 1 in 1961. Today we celebrate the law and our legal system, which is unique from other countries largely because our philosophy proclaims a person innocent until proven guilty in a court of law. This system has worked quite well thus far. The fact is, we are a nation of laws and it is our government's responsibility to make and enforce these laws.

Law Day is mostly observed by attorneys and law firms who sponsor luncheons, fundraisers, and conferences. A national conference is held by the ABA at a different city each year, with a specified theme. A speaker who is an expert in law gives the keynote address. Workshops, presentations, dinners, and classes are provided for professionals in the field of law and students of law who are in attendance. Events also are available in schools, courts, and other venues; check with your local bar association for details.

In the USA, all three branches of government have a role in creating laws: the legislature debates and passes the laws, the executive branch signs off on laws and enforces them, and the judiciary upholds and interprets the laws and administers judgment in courts of law. The people also have a role because they elect those who serve at the top levels of government, as well as in local and state courts. The elected president appoints and the senate approves judges for federal courts and the Supreme Court. Our founders developed this system of government and the framers put it into writing. Founding documents include the Declaration of Independence, the Constitution of the United States, and the Bill of Rights.

Amending the Constitution requires two thirds of both houses of Congress to pass, as well as the signature of the president. If the president declines to sign it for ten days it becomes law; if the president vetoes it, Congress can override the veto with two-thirds of each house. Another way to propose an amendment is with a Convention of States whereby two thirds of the state legislatures call for a convention to debate and vote on suggested amendments or laws; this process does not require the president's signature. Either way, three fourths of all the states have to ratify the amendment to change the Constitution. To date, the USA has not called for a Convention of States.

In Biblical times, rulers were tyrants; there were no legislative bodies per se. However, prior to the era of the kings, Israel was led by judges (ACT 13:20), and the land was mostly at peace. God's Law was handed down to the Israelites through Moses the prophet. This began with the Ten Commandments, followed by hundreds more statutes and edicts, and the associated penalties for violations, which are outlined in the books of Leviticus, Numbers, and Deuteronomy, all written by Moses as directed by God.

- EXO 18:21–22 ~ Moses's father-in-law advised him, "Select capable men who fear God, who are trustworthy, and who hate dishonest gain, and appoint them as governors over thousands, hundreds, and tens. Have them serve as judges for the simple cases, so that you can decide the difficult cases." If you will do this, and God wills it, you will endure and the people will come and go in peace. So Moses listened to and followed his wise counsel.

- EXO 20:3–17 ~ The Ten Commandments: 1) Do not place any other gods before God Almighty. 2) Do not make or worship graven images or practice idolatry. 3) Do not take God's name in vain or swear false oaths. 4) Keep the Sabbath a holy day. 5) Respect, honor, and obey your parents. 6) Do not murder. 7) Do not commit adultery. 8) Do not steal. 9) Do not falsely accuse anyone or commit perjury. 10) Do not covet anything that belongs to someone else including their possessions and spouses.

After the reigns of Saul, David, and Solomon, Israel split in two, with Judah in the south. This era consisted of a series of good and bad kings; corruption resulted in their ruin beginning with Israel in the north, then Judah. The Jews were taken captive again and dispersed about the nations. The empires before and after fell due to corruption and lawlessness. The fall of the last great empire in the final days of earth also will be caused by corruption and lawlessness. The government will be a party to this lawlessness and destruction, for the leaders will be ignoring God and His Law and perverting the laws of the land.

- 2 SA 23:3 ~ God, the Rock of Israel, spoke saying, "Whoever rules others must be just, ruling in the fear of God."

- EZR 7:25 ~ Ezra, since you have the wisdom of God, you will select magistrates and judges to govern those beyond the river. They must know the laws of your God, and if they do not, you must teach them.

- PRO 3:1–2 ~ Do not forget God's Law. Keep His commandments and He will give you peace and a long life.

- JER 31:33 ~ This is the covenant that I will make with my people. I will place my Law into their minds and write it upon their hearts. And I will be their God and they will be my people.

- MIC 7:2–6 ~ All the godly and upright men are gone. The wicked lie in ambush for blood. They do evil with diligence. Princes and judges ask for bribes. Great men speak of and pursue the evil desires of their souls. Even the best of them is like a thorn. Their confusion and punishment await them. Nobody can be trusted; even family and friends become the enemy.

- HAB 1:4 ~ Law and judgment are loosened, for the wicked encompass the righteous. Therefore, wrong judgment proceeds.

- LUK 21:11 ~ Jesus said, "They will capture you, persecute you, and bring you before their judges to be tried."

- ROM 8:6–7 ~ To have a carnal mind is death; to have a spiritual mind is life and peace. The carnal mind hates God; it disregards God's Law for it is in complete opposition to it.

- ROM 13:10 ~ Love creates no ill will towards another; therefore, love is the fulfillment of the Law.

- 1 TI 1:8–9 ~ Laws are good if they are used lawfully. Laws are not made for the righteous, they are made for the lawless, profane, and disobedient; laws are for ungodly people and for sinners.

- 2 TI 3:12–13 ~ Righteous people will suffer persecution. Evil people get perpetually worse.

- JAM 4:11 ~ Do not speak evil about someone else. Whoever speaks evil of another or judges them unfairly judges the Law. If you judge the Law, you cannot be adhering to the Law.

- 1 JO 3:4 ~ Whoever commits sin disobeys the Law, for that is how sin is defined.

Father God, we love your Law and we pray that we remain obedient to you and to your will concerning our lives, church, and country. Help our legislators to write and pass laws in accordance with your laws and your justice; help them to enforce those laws so we can remain free and faithful to you and to one another. Enable us to respond to your Holy Spirit, especially when we are uncertain about the correct action or path we should take. Write your laws upon our hearts; let us meditate on them in our minds. May we develop good habits that operate automatically, preventing influences that detract from our purpose. In the name of Jesus we pray, Amen.

May 2

National Day of Prayer is a call for prayer from people of all faiths, that our nation and our leaders be guided by the one true God. On this day, people assemble in locations all across the USA, to lift their prayers up to God and sing hymns of praise as a cooperative body. These gatherings may include musicians and choirs, food and refreshment, celebrity artists, and assorted activities. Usually an evening convocation is held, conducted much like a church service where many prayers are offered to the Lord. This tradition originated in 1775 by the Continental Congress, to guide our founding fathers as they sought to establish a new nation. It became a tradition for each standing president to propose an agenda that supported our nation's unity, and declare a day of coming together to bring those petitions to God. President Lincoln revived the idea in 1863 declaring a day of prayer as the Civil War was raging. An official Day of Prayer was signed into law by President Truman in 1952 at the end of the Korean War. The law was amended under President Reagan in 1988, changing the date to the first Thursday in May. The agenda is set by a task force formed back in 1972 called the National Prayer Committee.

People can gather on this day, either in public or at home, to offer their prayers in unison, regardless of culture, ethnicity, or faith. Such prayers generate added power, as more persons join the prayer chain. How often does our nation do anything as a collective whole? I can think of nothing more important than uniting as a nation under a banner of faith, as we collectively appeal to God to provide guidance to our leaders, security for our country, and free and respectful communication among our citizens. Regardless of what different individuals or groups are thinking about and praying for, the Holy Spirit will hear, interpret, and answer in a way that provides the most benefit. This day is not to be confused with the World Day of Prayer which occurs globally among women of faith on the first Friday of March.

- DEU 26:7 ~ When we cried to the Lord, He heard us and looked into our affliction, burden, and oppression.

- 2 CH 7:14 ~ God says, "If my people, who are called by my name, humble themselves, pray and seek my face, and turn from their wicked ways, I will hear them, and I will forgive their sins and heal their land."

- PSA 37:3–8 ~ Trust in the Lord and do good and you will have security. Take delight in the Lord and you will receive the delights of your heart. Commit yourself to the Lord and He will vindicate you. Wait patiently for the Lord and do not worry. Refrain from anger.

- MAT 18:19–20 ~ Jesus said, "If any two of you agree about what to ask of my Father in heaven, He will give it to you. For where two or more of you are gathered in my name, I am there in the midst of them."

- ROM 8:26 ~ The Holy Spirit intercedes for us when we pray. We do not know what we should pray for all the time. But through the act of prayer, God analyzes our needs and answers our prayers in the best possible way.

- 1 TI 2:1–2, 8 ~ I urge that supplications, prayers, intercessions, and thanksgiving be made to God for all people, for leaders, and for all who are in authority, so that we can lead an honest and peaceful life of godliness and truth. People should pray everywhere, lifting up holy hands, without being doubtful or angry.

Nationalism and patriotism are evidence of unity and cooperation among people with diverse points of view. There is no reason to divide over points of view. This is a good day to pray for a citizenry of patriots; undivided and unambiguous in their love for this land, our flag, and our freedom. People who pledge allegiance to God and country, do so because their beliefs are founded on love, truth, and freedom. Lift up your prayers to God that we remain a free constitutional republic where all rights as human beings are protected and defended, where there is equal justice under the law, and where there is representative government of, by, and for the people.

- ACT 17:26–27 ~ God has made out of one blood all nations of people to dwell on the face of the earth, and has determined the appointed times and the boundaries of their borders. They should be seeking the Lord; if they happily seek Him, they will find Him, though He is not far from any of us.

- PSA 33:12 ~ Blessed is the nation who makes God their Lord, for they will be the people God chooses for His own inheritance.

- GAL 3:28 ~ There is neither Jew nor Greek, slave nor free, male nor female, for we are all equal in Jesus Christ.

- 1 PE 2:9 ~ You are a unique, chosen generation, a priesthood and holy nation, because you praise Him who called you from darkness into His marvelous light.

- TIT 3:1–4 ~ Be submissive to rulers and authority, be obedient, and be ready for honest work. Do not speak evil of others; do not be brawlers but be gentle and meek to all people. We too were sometimes foolish, disobedient, deceived, lustful, envious, malicious, and hateful. Then we discovered the love of God through our Savior Jesus Christ.

You cannot have diversity in a country where there is division; the two are incompatible. We see divisions being created to deliberately cause chaos and conflict between genders, age groups, ethnicities, economic status, religion, and every category mentioned in the Civil Rights Act of 1964. Every time an attempt has been made in this country to segregate or isolate a group of people because of their attributes or beliefs, it has caused extreme societal problems if not civil war. United we stand, divided we fall; but if we are to stand united, we will need equal representation for every individual, demographic, and segment of society. If the union cannot be reunited, we will be vulnerable to foreigners that hate us. Without a strong and secure country, our enemies will take advantage. To be able to fend them off we will need to end these internal wars between ideologies.

- ECC 10:4–6 ~ If the spirit of a ruler rises up against you, do not give up your place, for yielding sometimes enables great offenses. There is an evil to be found under the sun, when error proceeds from a ruler. Fools are placed in high positions and the rich in the lower positions.

- JOH 7:41–44 ~ Some people said, "He is the Christ," while others said, "Will the Christ come from Galilee?" Others replied, "Did the scriptures not tell us that God's Messiah would be a descendant of David and be born in Bethlehem, the city of David?" So, there was division among them concerning Jesus. There were those that wanted to seize Him, but nobody dared lay a hand on Him.

Father in heaven, you have led us through many conflicts and catastrophes; you have fought on our side when we held the moral high ground. You made us a free society, but now it seems our freedoms are being challenged if not stolen. These freedoms were given to humanity by you, Lord; we pray that those who would take them away be the ones to lose their freedom. Help citizens to be brave and take a stand when foolish rulers attempt to change our laws, traditions, and founding documents; help us to have them removed either by election or by edict. May we elect leaders that will unify the nation, enforce the laws, uphold the Constitution, and govern your people in accordance with your will and your Law. In the name of Jesus we ask, Amen.

May 3

National Space Day was introduced in 1997 by Lockheed Martin, a defense contractor; they discussed technology and careers in aerospace to garner interest. It was a big hit, later evolving into International Space Day in 2001 with the backing of former astronaut, Senator John Glenn. There were intermittent "space days" before that, not the least of which was the USA putting Neil Armstrong and Buzz Aldrin on the moon (06/20/1969). I remember watching it being televised on national TV. Every eye was glued to the tube; it sure gave the space program a huge boost, and swayed public opinion in favor of its continuation.

Today's date is not to be confused with International Day of Human Space Flight (established in 2011) which is observed on April 12. On that date in 1961 the Russians became the first to orbit the earth. But the first Friday of May remains a national observance in the USA when we applaud our own space program. An enormous amount of science and physics, technology and engineering, interagency coordination, not to mention taxpayer dollars, have gone into the space race: the next destination on the minds of aerospace engineers is Mars. The USA is poised to arrive there first. But who knows, for many more countries have joined the race?

Celebrate today by making space the topic of the day wherever you may be. What lies beyond the stars? We barely have scratched the surface. Try doing some research on astrophysics and cosmology; check out websites on NASA, the Hubble telescope, or the International Space Station. Watch movies or documentaries about space, and talk about the advances with your kids or your classmates. Bring up the subject at work, you might discover several who have this interest in common. Buy a telescope as a gift and teach your kids about the cosmos, and how God formed the universe.

Another activity for today is to discover some facts for yourself or with your family and friends. Simply search the worldwide web for what the Bible says about space. It will be an amazing journey, as inspiring as space itself. A short introduction will be provided in this lesson.

The Bible speaks frequently about space, how its mysteries are revealed, observed, measured, and analyzed. In fact, a great many Old and New Testament books provide details about the universe: its beginnings, expansion, and atmospheres; the planets, sun, stars and constellations; forces holding things together, invisible building blocks; fine-tuning, the vastness of the universe, and entropy. Many of these observations were confirmed scientifically within the last two hundred years (this is like yesterday, cosmologically speaking). Conduct a Bible study on your own or with family and friends; it will corroborate what science has proven from the list above. You can start by reading the following scriptures for a general discussion of cosmology.

GEN 1:6–15   DEU 10:14   JOB 9:4–9   JOB 26:7–10   JOB 38:18–38   PSA 148:4–5
ISA 40:21–26   ISA 51:6   JER 31:35   JER 51:15–16   AMO 9:6   MAR 10:6–8
ROM 1:20   1 CO 15:40–41   HEB 11:3

We know that, in time, this heaven and earth will pass away; it is inevitable according to the second law of thermodynamics: heat death. Universal expansion means celestial bodies will become increasingly farther away from other bodies, unless of course they collide. When the end of time nears there will be unusual occurrences in the sky, which may be an indication that the universe is dying. Before the end of the present universe there will be a fiery melting of the earth. God will create a new heaven and a new earth which will not resemble the old heaven and earth. Perhaps this suggests an entirely new universe that God will provide for those who are saved from this aging and deteriorating universe.

- PSA 102:25–27 ~ From days of old God laid the foundation of the earth, and the heavens were the work of His hands. But these will perish; they will not endure. They wax old like a worn garment; and like clothing, God will change them. But you, oh God, will never change and your years have no end.

- ISA 65:17 ~ God will create new heavens and a new earth; the former heaven and earth will never be remembered or recalled.

- ISA 66:22 ~ The new heavens and the new earth which I will make will remain before me, says the Lord, and so will your seed and your name remain.

- JOE 2:2, 10, 30–31 ~ The day of great darkness, cloudiness, and gloom is coming. The earth will quake and the heavens will tremble. The sun and moon will be dark and the stars will cease to shine. There will be wonders in the sky and on the earth: blood, smoke, and fire. The sun will become dark and the moon will become like blood, before the great and terrible day of the Lord comes.

- MAT 24:29, 35 ~ Jesus said, "Immediately after the time of tribulation, the sun will become dark, the moon will be shrouded in gloom, and stars will fall from the sky. Heaven and earth will pass away, but my words will remain forever."

- ACT 2:19 ~ I will show wonders in heaven above and the earth below: blood, fire, and smoke. The sun will turn dark and the moon into blood, before the great and notable day of the Lord comes.

- 2 PE 3:7, 12–13 ~ The heavens and earth which we see now are kept in store, reserved for fire on the day of judgment and the perdition of the ungodly. Watch, for the day of God is coming fast; the heavens will be dissolved with fire, and the elements will melt from the heat. We, according to God's promise, look for new heavens and a new earth, wherein dwells righteousness.

- REV 6:12–13 ~ There was a great earthquake; the sun became black and the moon became like blood. The stars fell from the sky.

- REV 21:1, 5 ~ I saw a new heaven and a new earth, for the old heaven and earth had passed away. He that sat on the throne said, "Behold I make all things new." God told me to write these words which are true and trustworthy.

As beautiful as this universe, our planet, and solar system are, they will die; for they too have been corrupted by the sin of man. But God knew this was going to happen which is why He did not create this universe to last; it was like a scientific experiment to see who finds God and loves Him and who does not. Those who do not will die along with this universe, both of which are destined to burn out. If you think the old universe was amazing, wait until you see the new one; it will be like nothing you have ever imagined, magnitudes more beautiful and amazing than this one. You can try to imagine it but you will not come close (ISA 64:4; 1 CO 2:9).

Heavenly Father, we are excited about the new heavens and the new earth. Help us to remain faithful until the end, despite all the calamities and tribulations that will come. With the help of your Holy Spirit, we can endure anything; so please let us be strong in the power of your might, donning the armor of God so that we can stand against the wiles of the devil and deflect the fiery darts of evil that he flings at us. Help us to search for truth in your creation and in your Word; do not let us be conned by the false teachings of those who would dismiss your truth, for it is evident every time we look upwards into the night sky. In the name of Jesus, who will carry us into the next dimension of space where time is irrelevant, we pray, Amen.

May 4

International Firefighters Day is observed today to honor the profession in general and firefighters in particular, especially those who died or were injured protecting their communities and surrounding areas. In addition to fighting fires, professionals and volunteers serve in many other ways, requiring them to have communication, social, first aid, and helping skills. Firefighting is a noble calling, which requires strength, endurance, courage, and dedication.

The idea got momentum in Australia after five firemen perished in 1998; later, a ranking fireman named J. J. Edmondson suggested in a massive email release to establish a national day for mourning. This would become an annual event in the first international observance the following year. Eventually, the date was moved to May 4 because it overlaps the Feast of St. Florian, patron saint of firefighters in the Roman Catholic and Eastern Orthodox Churches. Florian was a chief firefighter in AD 300. Thus, acknowledging firefighters this time of year has been a tradition in many places for centuries; but it has undergone a revival in recent decades.

Many will honk their horns at twelve noon today in remembrance of the sacrifices that have been made by firefighters around the world. It is also a practice to hang red and blue ribbons, or place one on the lapel; for these are the colors of fire and water. The essential elements listed in the Bible are air, earth, fire, water. It seems appropriate to celebrate them all. They are equally destructive when uncontrolled and they are more powerful when combined. For example, you need earth (fuel) and air (oxygen) to make fire, but you can put out a fire with air, earth, water, and yes fire. John the Baptist baptized with water, but Jesus Christ baptizes with fire (MAT 3:11; LUK 3:16). Both convey the Holy Spirit. In Christ, we all fight fire with fire.

- PSA 83:14–16 ~ As fire consumes the forest, and the flame puts the mountains ablaze, so God will pursue your enemies with a tempest, and terrify them as a hurricane. Oh Lord, fill them with shame so they will seek you.

- PSA 104:4 ~ God makes His angels spirits, His ministers a flaming fire.

- ISA 43:2 ~ When you pass through the waters and the rivers you will not be overwhelmed; when you walk through the fire you will not be burned or consumed.

- DAN 3:12–27 ~ The king of Babylon had Shadrach, Meshach, and Abednego thrown into the fiery furnace for not worshipping his false idol. The king looked into the fire and said, "I see four men in the fire and none of them have been affected, and the fourth man looks like the Son of God." The king ordered, "You men, who serve the most-high God, come out of the furnace," and three men emerged unscathed.

- JOE 2:3 ~ A fire devours everything in its path, leaving a wasteland. The land is like the garden before them, but behind them is a desolate wilderness where nothing can escape.

- MAT 7:24–27 ~ Jesus said, "A wise man builds his house upon a rock, not upon the sand. A house built upon a rock will stand against the elements, but one built upon the sand will not."

- EPH 6:16 ~ The shield of faith will consume the fiery darts of the devil.

- 2 PE 3:7, 12 ~ Watch, for the day of God is coming fast; the heavens will be dissolved with fire, and the elements will melt from the heat.

- JDE 1:22–23 ~ Have compassion and make a difference. Save them by pulling them out of the fire, showing mercy with fear; despising even their garment which is defiled by the flesh.

Heavenly Father, your Holy Spirit is like a consuming fire, purifying us as refined gold. Thank you for making us clean and pure with the blood of your Son Jesus. In His name, Amen.

May 5

World Laughter Day is celebrated on the first Sunday of the month so the date is arbitrary. They say laughter is the best medicine and so it is for some things (PRO 17:22); however, there is a time to weep and time to laugh (ECC 3:1, 4). Whatever the circumstances, cheerful exchanges can be uplifting (keep it clean folks). Who doesn't like a great joke that they've never heard? Laughing releases chemicals in the brain that promote physical and mental wellness, so it is a good diversion much of the time, while other times we can even laugh at ourselves. But there is a time not to laugh, and you might want to consider that before trying to make someone laugh.

The first world laughter day was in Mumbai India in 1998, when thousands of members of local and international laughter clubs had a collective laugh, with celebrations and dining. The idea spread to Copenhagen Denmark in the year 2000, where ten thousand gathered at the town square. The original objective was to spread laughter in the interest of world peace. More countries are marking their calendars for this holiday, the date floating around the same week as the first observance (May 10). This day is not to be confused with Humorous Day (April 19), although humor and laughter go together well.

There is a time to laugh and make merry.

- JOB 5:21–22 ~ You will be hidden from the scourge of the tongue; you will not be afraid of destruction when it comes. You will laugh at destruction and famine; you will not be afraid of the beasts on earth. You will be at peace.

- JOB 8:20–21 ~ God will neither cast out the righteous man nor help the evil doers. He will yet fill your mouth with laughter and your lips with rejoicing.

- ECC 3:1, 4 ~ For everything there is a season, and a time for every purpose under heaven. A time to weep and a time to laugh; a time to mourn and a time to dance.

- LUK 6:21 ~ Blessed be those who hunger now, for you will be filled. Blessed be those who weep now, for you will laugh.

- JAM 5:3 ~ If you are in trouble, pray. If you are happy, sing praises.

There are circumstances when it is not a laughing matter

- PSA 22:7–8 ~ They that look upon me laugh at me and scorn me. Shaking their heads, they say, "He trusted in the Lord for deliverance, let the Lord save him" (see MAT 27:41–43).

- PRO 14:12–13 ~ There is a wrong way that seems right but it leads to death. Even in laughter, the heart is sorrowful; and the end of that is grief.

- ECC 10:18–19 ~ Through laziness the building decays; because of idle hands the house falls. A feast is made for laughter, and wine to make merry, where money answers everything.

- JER 50:4–5 ~ In those days, the children of Israel will come weeping, seeking the Lord. They will ask the way to Zion saying, "Let us join with the Lord in a perpetual covenant that will not be forgotten."

- MAT 25:30 ~ He will cast the cynical people into outer darkness where there is weeping and gnashing of teeth.

- ROM 12:15 ~ Rejoice with those who are rejoicing; mourn with those who are mourning.

Father, we pray for those who mourn; let us mourn with them. Remind us never to laugh at someone's misfortune but comfort them, and rejoice with them. In Jesus's name, Amen.

May 6

Knowing that You Know Day is a day for self-examination. Do you believe in Jesus Christ? Do you believe in the infallibility of God's Word? How do you know that Christ is real and His truth can be known? How do we know that we know? I mean, how can we be sure, given the myriad of speculations being advanced as truth? To the secularists all truth is relative to their own vantage point, but not necessarily to anybody else's; but truth, by definition, must be the same for everybody. There cannot be multiple truths for a single reality. To the atheists and nihilists, they deny the truth because they do not believe they will be held accountable by a supreme being. They believe that death is the end. For them it will be, when they are held accountable at the second death. In the interest of space, I will forgo calling out other false doctrines and errant belief systems which do not trust in the truth of God's Word and the salvation of His Son Jesus Christ (see MAT 16:13–16).

Perhaps an equally poignant question is how do we know that we don't know? Well, my friends, that is a far easier question to answer. For example, we don't know when we will die, or when Christ will return, or if there is profound meaning to be gleaned from random events, dreams, or life's curves and stop signs. There are plenty of theories about the relevance of such things, but they are unproven or ambiguous. And never trust in partial truths; truth must be impartial, complete, and incontrovertible. If you keep researching, eventually you will find knowledge and you also will discover how much knowledge you lack.

To be absolutely sure necessitates verification and validation. To illustrate, our judicial system is not supposed to convict someone of a capital crime when there is reasonable doubt. But to be utterly assured of justice one would require zero doubt. That alternative implies truth and certainty, which are absolute. But only God's justice is absolute. The aforementioned skeptics cannot accept absolutes, even if true. As such, they must be absolutely wrong because truth can be verified when it comports with reality. However, truth can change when reality changes. That you are alive today may not be true tomorrow; whereas you cannot be alive and dead at the same time. But is it possible to die and live again? Yes, if you believe God.

- GEN 27:2 ~ Isaac said, "Now I am old, and I know not the day of my death."

- DEU 18:20–22 ~ If a prophet presumes to speak on my behalf when I have not directed them to do so, or speaks in the name of other gods, he or she will die. If people wonder how they will know if a prophecy comes from the Lord, they can observe whether the words spoken by the prophet come true or not. Do not be afraid of a prophet who speaks presumptuously.

- MAT 24:35–36 ~ Jesus said, "Heaven and earth will pass away but my words will remain true forever. Truly I say to you, nobody knows that day and hour, not the angels in heaven, but my Father only."

- 1 CO 13:12 ~ For now we see a dim image as if looking into a cloudy mirror; but someday we will see clearly, face to face. Now I know in part; but then I will know in full, even as I am known.

The most sought-after truth is whether God exists. Interestingly, when you ponder it carefully it becomes intuitively obvious that He does. Then there is the question of the truthfulness of God's Word. It is unscholarly to outright dismiss the vast evidence demonstrating the reliability and validity of the Holy Bible, especially in the case of Biblical prophecy which comes true to the finest detail. There is no other explanation but God. How often does it happen when all of the evidence points in one direction? You see, everyone gets to examine the proof of God, because He is everywhere and so is the proof. Even the demons believe there is a God and it scares the daylights out of them, for they know they have double-crossed Him and are doomed. When Christ cast out demons they evacuated posthaste; they feared Him and acknowledged publicly that He was God's Son (MAR 5:1–16).

- EXO 18:10–11 ~ Jethro (Moses's father-in-law) said to Moses, "Now I know that the Lord is greater than all other gods because of the things He did to Pharaoh and the Egyptians on behalf of Israel."

- JOB 42:1–2 ~ Job said to the Lord, "I know that you can do everything, and that no thought can be hidden from you."

- PSA 135:5–6 ~ I know that the Lord is great, and that He is above all gods. Whatever pleased the Lord, that is what He did both in heaven and on earth, including the seas and the depths.

- MAR 1:23–25; LUK 4:33–35 ~ A man possessed by a demon came out from the synagogue yelling, "Leave us alone; what do want with us Jesus of Nazareth? Have you come to destroy us? I know who you are, the Holy One of God." Jesus told him, "Be quiet," and ordered the demon, "Come out of him." And the demon threw the man to the ground and came out, leaving the man unharmed.

- 1 JO 5:19–20 ~ We know that we are of God, and that the whole world is wicked. We also know that the Son of God has come giving us understanding, so that we may know Him who is true. And we abide in God who is true, including His Son Jesus Christ who is truly God and the way to eternal life.

As was the case with Israel, the USA has seen the providence of God working throughout our history. Our forefathers spoke of this often. It defies the laws of probability the number of calamities our nation dodged, the adversity that we overcame, and the odds that we beat to make it this far. As a former research psychologist and statistician, I find this amazing and convincing. Then there is the magnificence of God's creation itself with its countless intricacies, calibration, and beauty. How can one deny that it is beyond anything humankind has ever invented, produced, or imagined? The mystery is how did God create all of this from things that we cannot see, perceive, or observe? There are no scientific explanations except an uncaused first cause.

To be sure, there is power in truth for the Holy Spirit is Truth (JOH 14:26; JOH 16:13–15). And He doesn't only breathe life into every soul, but the Word (*Logos*) itself is God-breathed. That the Word gives life must certainly be true because Jesus Christ, who was the Word made flesh, was revived by the Holy Spirit after being tortured to death. Thank God for that miracle, because it makes the promise of the resurrection secure for all who believe. Those clinging to that truth rejoice and have hope, despite life's hindrances. Regarding God's chosen who make it out alive and into His kingdom, it will be the last they taste of death; for the rest it will be the last they taste of life.

- JOS 2:9 ~ Rahab said to the men, "I know that the Lord has given to you this land, and your terror is coming upon us; all the inhabitants of Jericho will faint because of you."

- PSA 119:160 ~ God's Word is true from the very beginning; every one of His righteous judgments endure forever.

- ECC 3:14–15 ~ I know whatever God does, it will endure forever; nothing can be added to it or subtracted from it. God does this so people will fear Him. That which is, already has been; and that which is yet to come, also has been; and that which has passed will be brought to account.

MAY

- ROM 8:26–28 ~ God's Spirit helps us in our weakness, and intercedes for us when we pray. The mind of the Spirit contends for the saints according to God's will. We know all things work together for good to those who love God and are called according to His purpose.

- 2 TI 3:16 ~ All scripture is inspired by God. God's Word provides the doctrine of truth, refutes that which is false, and instructs all people in the ways of righteousness.

- HEB 10:30 ~ We know the Lord who has said, "Vengeance belongs to me, I will recompense." And again, "The Lord will judge His people."

Consider the sophistication of every inhabitant on the planet. Unquestionably, human beings are among the most complicated of God's creations. And He has given us dominion over this planet and other creatures. What did we do to deserve this? Not a thing, only that God loves us like His own sons and daughters. He wants our respect and trust, as a perfect father deserves. Isn't respect what you want from your kids, or from your parents? It makes more sense to put your faith and hope in God than in someone else. Not that people can never trust one another, but not absolutely; even so, we should respect others whether we trust them completely or not.

- JOB 19:25–26 ~ I know that my Redeemer lives and that He will stand upon the earth. And although my flesh will have been destroyed, yet in my flesh I will see God. I will see Him with my own eyes and I yearn for that day.

- PSA 144:3 ~ Oh Lord, what are humans that you are mindful of us? Or our children that you also would think of them?

- 1 JO 3:2 ~ Dear friends, now we are the children of God, and what we will become is not yet known. But we do know this: when He returns for us, we will become like Him, for we shall see Him as He really is.

God provides all we need to sustain our bodies and lives, not to mention the wisdom and understanding to know Him: His laws, His truth, and His ways. He began dispensing this knowledge to the Jews via Moses and the prophets, and then turned to educating the world through His own Son and the apostles of Christ. People of all walks are discovering the truth and following Jesus. God has revealed essential knowledge in His Holy Word; and it is still spreading like wildfire. Everyone can come to God in prayer and ask Him anything, and He will answer. I recommend that the first thing you ask for is forgiveness through His Son. Then you can commence to bring others to faith and everlasting life, enabling truth to proliferate further.

- PRO 2:1–6 ~ My child, if you would receive my words and hold fast to my commandments, if you listen to wisdom and desire understanding; if you seek knowledge and truth instead of worldly riches; then you will understand the fear of the Lord and find the knowledge of God, for He alone provides wisdom and from Him comes all knowledge and understanding.

- JOH 3:2 ~ A Pharisee named Nicodemus came to Jesus by night and said, "Rabbi, we know you are a teacher who has come from God, because no man can perform the miracles that you have done unless God is in Him."

- JOH 4:25–26 ~ The Samaritan woman at the well told Jesus, "I know when Messiah comes who is called Christ, that He will teach us all things." Jesus replied, "I who speaks am He."

- JOH 11:24–26 ~ Martha told Jesus, "I know that my brother Lazarus will rise again at the resurrection on the last day." Jesus replied, "I AM the resurrection and the life. Those who believe in me, though they were dead, yet shall they live. Whoever believes in me will never die."

- JAM 1:5 ~ If any of you lack wisdom, ask God who gives generously to all people.

    One thing that sets people apart from other living creatures is our realization of morality. Everybody has a conscience and inherently knows right from wrong. It is spelled out in God's Law which is the foundation of other laws and standards of decency. Even those who deny God still manage to obey man's laws, fully understanding the consequences if they don't. Listen to your inner spirit, where God has implanted into your heart the truth, the freedom to choose, and the knowhow to obey Him. God selects those who choose Him to be His people, though everybody is equally special and loved by Him, even the ones that don't make it. It follows that we should treat one another as special and worthy of our love.

- ECC 8:12 ~ Though a sinner does evil and lives a long life, I know it will be better for those who fear God and worship Him.

- ISA 59:12 ~ Our transgressions are innumerable and they testify against us. Our sins follow us all of our lives for we know what we have done.

- JER 11:18 ~ The Lord warned me about certain people and told me what they were doing.

- ROM 7:14 ~ We know that the law is spiritual; but I am carnal, sold to sin.

- ROM 7:18 ~ I know that nothing about my flesh can be good; though I want to do good I cannot seem to do it.

- ROM 8:22–23 ~ We know that the whole creation groans in pain, as if in labor, up until the present. And not only that, for we ourselves are the first fruits of the Spirit. Yes, even we groan, waiting for the adoption and the redemption of our bodies.

- 1 TI 1:8–10 ~ We know that the law is good, as long as it is used lawfully. Know this, that the law does not exist for the righteous, but for the lawless and disobedient; the ungodly and profane; the murderers and slayers; the whoremongers, adulterers, and defilers; liars and perjurers; and anything that goes contrary to sound doctrine.

- 1 JO 2:3–4 ~ We know that we can know God if we keep His commandments. Whoever says, "I know Him," but does not keep His commandments is a liar, and the truth is not in him.

- 1 JO 3:24 ~ Those who keep God's commandments live in Him, and He lives in them. We know that He lives in us by the Spirit which He has given us.

    So then, the best way to know that you know is to listen to the Holy Spirit who knows all things. He has revealed much in the Holy Bible and through His only begotten Son Jesus Christ. If you seek truth, you should start with the Holy Trinity: Father, Son, and Holy Spirit. Remember, His truth is conclusive, so anything that does not agree can never be true. Faith is required since the Holy Spirit is what enables us to grasp God's complex truth and acquire pieces of His wisdom which transcend the whole of humanity.

    Thus, the primary source for validating truth is to ensure it agrees with the Holy Bible. If it comes from the mouth of God, believe it. Science is a secondary means of verifying facts by examining God's other major work, the Book of Nature. The examination of the universe, its reality, enormity, and regularity can produce truth, and the way we can be sure is when it agrees with the Bible. In other words, when the Bible and science converge upon a single truth, we can know that we know. For instance, in the last century scientists figured out that the universe (including the earth) had a beginning, just like every lifeform which has lived on this orb. The Bible presented this truth from the start of Genesis, thousands of years ago. We also know from science that the universe will fade away through a process called entropy; this agrees with the

Bible which clearly states that heaven and earth will pass away (MAT 24:35; MAT 28:18–20; REV 21:1). Similarly, living beings will live for a while and then they will pass away; both science and the Bible are in perfect agreement on these matters.

What science cannot establish is that the dead will come alive again to face judgment (ISA 26:19; REV 20:5–15), after which those judged not guilty will live forevermore while the guilty will die a second death (DAN 12:2; JOH 5:28–29). Such wisdom only can be grasped by trusting the Bible, where God has promised eternal life via the sacrifice of His Son and His subsequent resurrection. Science will not be able to corroborate the resurrection of humankind since it has not happened yet, though the resurrection of Christ has been confirmed. Science cannot confirm the resurrection of humankind as true or untrue since this event cannot be observed, predicted, or measured scientifically. Actually, there are a great many true and factual things which science has yet to explain, such as how the universe could have come into existence from "nothing" or more accurately, from "things unseen" (2 CO 4:18; HEB 11:3). Anyone who knows God knows that He created all things whether visible or invisible, with one exception: Himself, for God is not a created being; God has always been and always will be (MAL 3:8; HEB 10–11; HEB 13:8; JAM 1:17). One could suppose that God is the reason for His own existence. God certainly and without a doubt is the reason for our existence, and science cannot dispute this fact though many scientists and atheists will try. Not me, for I am convinced beyond all possible doubt: a standard seldom achieved through science where reasonable doubt is usually set at five percent. How can you know that you know? Answer: when there is absolutely zero doubt. If you are reading this, you are not dead, yet. Is there any doubt in your mind about that? If so, you might want to consult a psychiatrist.

People who do not know, have closed their minds to God. They use the same excuses, such as science prevents them, or other fallacies in logic. They would prefer not to know so they can continue to engage in willful sin. This is why the globalists want control over the people and the world: they wish to legalize their abhorrent lifestyles. God's wrath will pour out upon the power mongers, globalists, perverts, and the final kingdom of the beast (REV 16:1–14).

- JOB 20:4–5 ~ You have known from days of old, ever since man was placed upon the earth, that the triumph of the wicked is short and the joy of the hypocrite lasts only a moment.

- ISA 11:4 ~ With righteousness He will judge the poor and reprove with equity the meek on this earth. He will beat the earth with the rod of His mouth, and with the breath of His lips He will slay the wicked.

- ISA 14:29–32 ~ Do not rejoice Palestine (i.e., Philistia), that the rod which beat you is broken; for from the root of that snake will emerge an abominable monster, a fiery, flying serpent. The firstborn of the poor will eat and sleep in safety. But I will kill that root with famine and slay your remnant. Scream at your gates and cry in your city, for Palestine will be dissolved. From the north will come smoke, and an army of eager fighters. What will the messenger report of this nation? The Lord has founded Zion, and in her gates the afflicted of His people will find refuge.

- ISA 33:1 ~ Woe to you who plunder but were not plundered; who dealt treacherously though you were not treated in this manner. When you cease to plunder you will be plundered; when you stop dealing treacherously, you will be dealt treachery.

- JER 34:17 ~ The Lord says, "Since you have disobeyed me by not supporting the freedoms of your own people, I will proclaim a new kind of freedom unto you: freedom to be destroyed by war, disease, and famine. I will make you an example that will make all nations cringe.

- JER 51:13–14 ~ To you who live by many waters (Babylon), rich in treasure: it is over, your destruction has come. The Lord has sworn it. You will be overrun with warriors, like locusts, shouting victory.

In conclusion, what is your answer to this question, "Do you know that you are saved?" Do not reply with another question such as, "How do I know that I know?" If you are not sure, examine yourself. You know the rules: love God first and love everyone second including yourself. Also, cling to that which is good and reject that which is evil (ROM 12:9). I mean, doesn't wickedness and malevolence repulse you? Doesn't love and kindness uplift you? Exercise the fruits of the Spirit, such as kindness, joyfulness, faithfulness, patience, humbleness, peacefulness, self-control (GAL 5:22–23; PHP 4:6–8; 2 PE 1:5–10). In short, do you act like a Christian? Are you proud to be a child of the living God? Do you confess your faith in Christ and let your light shine? As for me, I know that my Redeemer lives, and I will see God in my flesh when Christ returns (JOB 19:25–26).

- PSA 119:59 ~ When I think about my ways, I return to your words, oh Lord.
- LAM 3:40 ~ Search and test your ways, and turn back to the Lord.
- 2 CO 13:5 ~ Examine yourself, whether you are in the faith; prove it to yourself. Do you not know that Jesus Christ is in you? If not, you are probably a reprobate. (See also 1 CO 11:27–29 about examining yourself.)
- EPH 1:4–5 ~ For He chose us before the creation of the world to be holy and blameless in His sight. In love, He predestined us to be adopted children through Jesus Christ, in accordance with His pleasure and will.
- 2 PE 1:10 ~ Be diligent in making your calling and election sure. If you exercise your spiritual gifts, you will not fail.
- 1 JO 3:19–25 ~ This is how we know that we are of the truth, and assured in our hearts before God. If your heart condemns you, remember that God is greater than your heart and knows all things. Who is a liar if not the one denying Jesus Christ? A person is an antichrist who denies the Father and the Son. Those who deny the Son deny the Father; those who acknowledge the Son acknowledge the Father. Let that knowledge abide in your heart, which you have heard from the beginning. If this remains in you and you continue in the Son, you are in the Father, and you will receive the promise of eternal life.
- REV 2:5 ~ Jesus said, "Remember how far you have fallen. Repent and return to the things you did in the beginning of your walk. If you do not, I will come to remove your lampstand" (you will lose the light and fall into darkness).

Most merciful Father, thank you for the knowledge of truth, without which we would know nothing. Thank you for the knowledge of salvation through Jesus Christ, which we can obtain merely by believing in Him and cherishing your Word. Thank you, Holy Spirit, for conveying this knowledge to us and making it understandable. Thank you, Triune God, for faith, by which we can be certain that your truth is absolute and our redemption is secure. Let us always cling to these truths and not be confused by the wisdom of the world. For the world will pass away, but your words will remain true forever. Jesus loves us, this we know, for the Bible tells us so. In Jesus's name we pray, Amen.

May 7

National Tourism Day occurs on this date during the first full week of May which is National Travel and Tourism Week, initially celebrated in 1983 under President Reagan. Many other countries have their own tourism day, since tourist seasons differ. World Tourism Day was established on 09/27/1997 by the UN World Tourism Organization, designating a different host country each year. Tourism is a major part of income or GDP for most countries. Tourism here in the states has always been popular since there are so many things to do and see.

The week will be celebrated with advertisements, offers, and packages to plan your next vacation: national parks, restaurants, airlines, travel agencies, and popular vacation spots. This national observance is to encourage travel within the USA. Our great land has so many beautiful sites and cities, it would be illogical if not inconceivable to stay home all the time. Many such excursions can be undertaken in a single day or weekend, and are quite affordable. Depending on your budget and timeframe, you are guaranteed to find something interesting, whether close by or far away; simply investigate and you'll find countless possible destinations. Take a vacation, you earned it! Go touring in your car; take a bus, train, plane, or take a walk around town.

- ECC 3:13 ~ Everyone should eat and drink and take pleasure in all their labor. This is a gift from God.

- MAR 6:30–32 ~ Jesus gathered the apostles and they exchanged information. He told them, "Take some time off by yourselves and go to a remote place and rest awhile," for they had been coming and going, with no leisure time, even to eat. So, they departed by ship for a private place in the desert.

- COL 2:16 ~ Let nobody judge you in matters of food and drink, or regarding a holiday, new moon, or sabbath days.

A change in environment can be quite therapeutic for anyone who is feeling bored, tired, or stressed. Even if you cannot travel a great distance take a look around your area and I bet you can find things to do and places to go of which you were previously unaware. Naturally, there will be some joy mixed with melancholy, especially when you must depart from the scenery and return to your life. But if you have enough excursions mixed with the humdrum of everyday business, you will be left with intermittent memories of hope and pictures of light.

The more people travel, the more they want to see; and many are eager to return to it. People save up so they can travel upon retirement. And for good reason: it feeds the soul. Traveling can be fun, and it can be expensive; it is wise to have a budget before you go. There is much to look forward to while here on earth; by seeking you will find it, here and in eternity. So don't forget, you have advance tickets to a better life that lasts forever in a spectacular universe that you cannot even perceive, but you will have eternity to tour it (ISA 64:4).

- PSA 18:36 ~ You have widened my steps, that my feet would not slip.

- PSA 19:105 ~ God's Word is a lamp unto my feet and a light unto my path.

- PSA 121:7–8 ~ The Lord will preserve you from all evil. The Lord will preserve your going out and your coming in from this time forward even forevermore.

- PRO 16:9 ~ In the heart we choose our way, but the Lord directs our steps.

- MAT 24:31 ~ Jesus said, "At the great sound of the trumpet, God will send His angels to gather His elect together from the four winds and one from end of heaven to the other."

- LUK 10:38–39 ~ As they traveled along, Jesus entered a village where Martha welcomed Him into her home. And her sister Mary sat at His feet while He spoke.
- LUK 17:20–21 ~ Jesus said, "The kingdom of heaven will not appear while you are looking around for it, because the kingdom of heaven is with you."
- JOH 14:2 ~ Jesus said, "In my Father's house are many mansions; I will be going ahead to prepare one for you."

As we journey through life, we take the Spirit of truth with us, sharing that truth with whomever will listen. This is the calling of Christ, to make disciples of every nation. Just as the apostles spread the Gospel to their world, we should be sharing God in ours, to include our travel to various destinations and worlds.

- GEN 50:2, 10 ~ Joseph commanded the physicians to embalm his father. They journeyed to Atad, which is beyond the Jordan River, and there they mourned for seven days.
- 1 KI 19:8 ~ Elijah journeyed forty days and nights to Mt. Horeb (mountains include Sinai).
- ISA 43:10–12, 15 ~ There are no gods before Him or after Him. God says, "You are witnesses to what I have said. My servant whom I have chosen is also sent to be a witness, so that you can know me and believe; and even so, I am He. I am the Lord and there is no other savior besides me. I have declared myself to you and I have saved you whenever you have forsaken all other gods for me. You are witnesses that I am God, the Holy One, the creator of Israel, and your King."
- LUK 9:1–6 ~ Jesus called His twelve disciples together, and gave them authority over demons, and power to cure diseases. He sent them to preach the kingdom of God and heal the sick. Jesus said to them, "Take nothing for your journey: no food, no luggage, no money, no extra clothes. When you enter a house, stay there until you leave that town. If a town does not welcome you, shake the dust from your feet when you leave as a testimony against them." And the disciples departed, and went through the towns preaching the Gospel and healing people everywhere.
- JOH 20:21 ~ Jesus said to the apostles, "Peace be unto you. As my Father has sent me, even now I am sending you."
- ACT 1:8 ~ Jesus told His disciples, "You will receive power once the Holy Spirit has come upon you. And you will be witnesses all across the land, and into the most remote corners of the earth."
- ACT 7:35–36 ~ When their freedom was gained, Moses showed he possessed the power of the Holy Spirit by the many miracles he performed, as the Israelites roamed the wilderness those forty years.
- ROM 10:20 ~ Just as Isaiah boldly proclaimed: I (God) was found by those who were not even looking for me.

Heavenly Father, we love to travel around this beautiful orb; thank you for this fantastic gift. We also thank you that we are free to move about, and pray for those whose right of free movement is repressed. We look forward to our final trip away from this earth: how stupendous it will be. This is our hope and joy when life weighs us down. We pray that we remain watchful and waiting for that day, without presumption but with commitment. We know your promises are true; renew us in that belief so our faith will be revealed in our actions wherever our journeys take us. And let us always walk with Jesus, even as your Holy Spirit walks with us, Amen.

May 8

World Red Cross Day is celebrated on the birthdate of J. H. Dunant of Geneva, 1828; he was founder of the Red Cross and the International Committee of the Red Cross. He was awarded the Nobel Peace Prize in 1901 for humanitarian efforts helping people wounded in battle. After World War II, the International Federation of the Red Cross and the Red Crescent were established. The first observance of Red Cross Day was in 1948; it is also referred to as World Red Cross and Red Crescent Day: Red Cross has Christian sponsorship and Red Crescent is the equivalent for Muslim sponsors (since 1906). The Red Cross is known for its compassionate efforts here and abroad, rendering emergency medical services, disaster readiness, and social services to areas hit with catastrophes and war. They also provide trainings and recruit volunteers from countries around the globe, through cooperative Red Cross societies in various nations.

Speaking of emergency treatment and aid, a great deal of medical knowledge can be gleaned from the Holy Bible. This includes instruction on tending wounds, washing when exposed to possible contamination, quarantine outside of the city, contagious and bloodborne diseases, hazardous mold, and other ailments and wounds and how to treat them.

- LEV 13:1–59 ~ When a man or woman whose skin is rising, or there is a scab or bright spot, it might be the plague of leprosy. They must be brought to the priest to be examined to see if the hair has turned white and the skin anomaly is more than skin deep; if so, it is leprosy. The leper must tear off his clothes, shave his head, put a covering on his mouth, and cry "unclean, unclean". He is defiled and unclean and must live in a camp outside the town. The priest will examine the garment for seven days to see if the plague spreads. If it has spread it is unclean and the garment will be burned; if not the priest will examine it for seven more days before pronouncing it clean or unclean.

- LEV 14:34–48 ~ When you enter the land of Canaan which I am giving you and come upon a house with spreading mold, declare this to the priest. If the walls have greenish or reddish depressions that are lower than the surface, there is mold. The moldy surfaces, stones, and timbers will be torn out and taken to an unclean place outside of the city; the walls will be scraped and the scrapings taken out as well. They will be replaced with new stones, timbers, and plaster.

- LEV 15:2–13 ~ If a person has a discharge that runs or blocks them up, he or she is unclean. The bed and everything on it will be unclean. Anyone who has touched the bed will need to bathe and wash their clothes, as well as anyone who sat in the same place. Everyone who has come into contact will wash; all the vessels in the abode will be washed thoroughly. After the discharge is gone the individual will remain unclean for seven days and bathe and wash their clothes again.

- LEV 17:12–13 ~ Nobody will eat blood. After hunting for game, the blood will be poured out on the ground and covered with dirt.

- NUM 19:14–22 ~ If someone dies in his tent, everyone who enters the tent will be unclean for seven days. All open and uncovered vessels will be unclean. Nobody is to touch a dead body on the battleground or in the fields, not even a bone or a grave, or they will be unclean for seven days. Take hyssop, dip it in water, and sprinkle it on the tent, the vessels, or on the person who touched any part of a dead body or a grave. On the seventh day he or she will bathe and wash their clothes. If a person is unclean and does not follow these instructions they will be banned. Whatever an unclean person touches will be unclean and so will anyone who touches it will be unclean until evening.

- 2 KI 20:7 ~ Isaiah instructed to cover Hezekiah's boils with an ointment made from figs, and he was healed.
- PRO 31:6–7 ~ Give strong drink to one who is dying, and wine to those who are sorely depressed. Let them drink and forget their misery for a while.
- LUK 10:34 ~ He poured oil and wine on the man's wounds and bandaged him, placed him on his own beast, and took care of him.
- 1 TI 5:23 ~ Do not just drink water, but try a little wine for your stomach and your frequent infirmities.

Apparently, in Old Testament times, priests were trained in medicine and contagious diseases, similar to doctors. Probably the most famous doctor in the Bible was Luke (COL 4:14). Of course, Christ is the great physician who heals all injuries, diseases, illnesses, deformities, and even death. Christ endows His gifts onto disciples to perform greater feats than these.

- JOH 14:12–13 ~ Jesus said, "Truly I tell you that anyone who believes in me, the works that I do he or she also will do, and greater works than these will they do because I go unto my Father. Whatever you ask in my name I will do, so my Father can be glorified in the Son."
- ACT 3:12, 16 ~ Peter answered them, "Men of Israel, why do you marvel at this, and look with earnest upon us as if, by our own power, we enabled this lame man to walk. It was by faith in the name of Jesus that was this man healed, a man whom you have seen and known. Yes, it was faith in Christ which made him whole in the presence of you all."
- JAM 5:13–16 ~ Are any of you afflicted? If so, then pray. Are you happy? Then sing praises. Are you sick? Then ask the church to pray for you in the name of the Lord. Confess and pray for each other, and be healed. For the fervent prayer of the believer yields high returns.

There will be no sickness, death, sadness, pain, or sin in the new heaven and earth.

- ISA 51:11 ~ Those redeemed by the Lord will return singing praises; they will have everlasting joy, and all sorrow and grief will be gone forever.
- ISA 65:17–19 ~ I will create new heavens and a new earth; the former heaven and earth will never be remembered or recalled. You will be glad and rejoice forever, for I will make Jerusalem a place of happiness. I will rejoice in Jerusalem for I will be happy with my people, and there will nevermore be the sound of crying among my people.
- EZE 47:12~ On both sides of the river grew all kinds of trees that never died. They produced new fruit every month; the fruit of the trees provided food and the leaves provided medicine.
- REV 21:1, 4 ~ I saw a new heaven and a new earth, for the old heaven and earth had passed away. There was no more crying, sorrow, pain, or death, for these things had passed away.
- REV 22:1–2 ~ In John's vision of heaven he saw a pure river of the water of life, clear as crystal, proceeding from the throne of God and the Lamb. The river nourished the Tree of Life which bore twelve different kinds of fruit each month, with leaves that provided enough medicine to heal all nations.

Dear Father, Son, and Holy Spirit, we thank you for healing us body, mind, and spirit. We thank you for those who have heeded the call to minister to others, to heal, to mend their wounds, and to care for them. We thank you for those who go to foreign lands and into the face of war to minister to the wounded and diseased; truly this is a high calling. We pray that you protect them and keep them safe from harm and danger. In Jesus's name we pray, Amen.

May 9

Ascension of Christ Day is celebrated by counting forty days after Easter Sunday; so, it will always fall on a Thursday, though a special service is often conducted the Sunday after. Easter varies from year to year based loosely on the vernal equinox; Holy Week, Ascension Day, and associated Jewish feasts occur during this liturgical season. We know that Jesus continued to minister for forty days and nights following His resurrection, then ascended into heaven while His followers watched. He took His place in heaven at the right hand of God where He sits in judgment. When He departed earth, Jesus left His Holy Spirit behind to comfort those who follow Him.

- MAR 16:19; LUK 24:50–53 ~ Jesus led them to Bethany where He lifted up His hands and blessed them. While He spoke, He arose into heaven. They worshipped Him and returned to Jerusalem with joy.

- ACT 1:9–11~ While He spoke these things, Jesus ascended above the clouds. As they stared into heaven two angels appeared with them and said, "Men of Galilee, why do you gaze into heaven. Jesus, who you just saw ascend into heaven, will return the very same way."

Forty is a common theme in the Bible; for instance, forty years represents a generation. Jesus was in the wilderness forty days where He was tempted by Satan, and He was on the earth after His resurrection forty days prior to His ascension. Thus, Christ began His ministry fasting forty days in the wilderness after his baptism, and ended it forty days after His resurrection in His glorified body. The Israelites wandered the wilderness for forty years, which was one year for each day they sinned while Moses was on Mt. Sinai. These are but a few references illustrating the importance of the number forty.

- GEN 7:4–17 ~ God made it rain for forty days and nights after Noah loaded the ark.

- GEN 50:1, 3 ~ Joseph was deeply saddened when his father Jacob died. He mourned for forty days, because the custom was to allow the embalmed body to rest in state forty days.

- EXO 24:18; EXO 34:28; NUM 14:33–34; NUM 32:13; DEU 2:7; DEU 9:18; DEU 10:10 ~ The Lord's anger against Israel was provoked for worshipping the golden calf. God made them wander the wilderness for forty years, until the adults from that generation which committed evil before the Lord had died. They spent one year for each day they sinned while Moses was on the mountain.

- JOS 5:6 ~ The children of Israel wandered forty years in the wilderness, until all the men of war which came out of Egypt were consumed, because they disobeyed the voice of the Lord. For the Lord had warned them that He would not show them the land flowing with milk and honey promised to their fathers.

- LUK 4:1–2 ~ Jesus was filled with the Holy Spirit who led Him into the wilderness. He was tempted during the forty days He fasted there.

- ACT 1:3 ~ Jesus Christ showed Himself alive for forty days, after being crucified to death, speaking about the kingdom of God. He proved to us many times that He had unquestionably risen from the dead.

When Jesus ascended into heaven, He resumed His position at God's right hand. Jesus is the instrument of God's hand on earth. And He will judge every human being with respect to their conduct and faith (PSA 96:13; PSA 98:9; JOH 5:22; ACT 10:42). Christ will return to earth and bring His faithful up to heaven with Him, after which He will judge the rest of humanity who remain under the Law, because they rejected His Grace.

- PSA 16:10–11 ~ God will not leave my soul in hell, and He will not allow His Holy One to be corrupted. He will show me the path of life. In His presence will be fullness of joy; with His right hand there are pleasures forevermore.

- PSA 80:14–19 ~ Return to us Almighty God! Look down from heaven and see! Watch over this vineyard that your right hand has planted, and the Branch you have raised up for yourself. The vine has been cut down and burned in the fire; at your rebuke your people perish. Let your hand rest on the man at your right, the Son of man who you raised. Do this so we will not turn our backs on you. Revive us so we can call upon your name. Turn us back, Lord of hosts, and let your face shine upon us so we can be saved.

- PSA 110:1, 4 ~ The Lord said to my Lord, "Sit at my right hand and I will make your enemies your footstool." He is priest forever, after the order of Melchizedek.

- PSA 118:15–16 ~ The Lord is my strength and song; He has become my salvation. The voice of rejoicing and salvation are in the tabernacles of the righteous, announcing the right hand of the Lord who goes valiantly before us. The right hand of God is exalted.

- ISA 48:12–13 ~ God said, "Listen to me oh Jacob, Israel who I have called; I AM He. I AM the first and the last. My hand laid the foundation of the earth, and my right hand spans the heavens. When I call, all will stand up in unison."

- MAR 14:61–62 ~ The high priest asked Jesus, "Are you the Christ?" Jesus replied, "I AM. And you will see the Son of man sitting at the right hand of power, and coming in the clouds of heaven."

- ACT 5:30–32 ~ God exalted Jesus as Prince and Savior with His own right hand, so that He might give repentance and forgiveness to Israel. We are witnesses to these things, and so is the Holy Spirit whom God has given to those who obey Him."

- ACT 7:55–56 ~ Stephen, being enthralled by the Holy Spirit, gazed into heaven and saw the glory of God, and Jesus standing at His right hand. And Stephen proclaimed, "Behold, I see an opening in the heavens and the Son of man standing at God's right hand."

- ROM 8:34 ~ Who is He, who condemns? It is Christ who died, and more than that, who rose from the dead and now sits at the right hand of God, and who also intercedes for us.

- EPH 1:20–21 ~ God set Jesus at His right hand, with power greater than all principalities, powers, and dominions. His name is above every other name in this world and the world to come.

- HEB 1:3; HEB 8:1–2 ~ The Son is the radiance of God's glory and the exact representation of His being, sustaining all things by His powerful Word. After He had provided purification for sins, He sat down at the right hand of His Majesty in heaven. To summarize, we have a High Priest, who sits at the right hand of God's throne in heaven and who serves in the sanctuary, the true tabernacle, set up by the Lord and not by man.

- REV 1:18 ~ When I saw Him, I fell before His feet as dead. And He laid His right hand upon me and said, "Do not fear. I AM the first and the last. I AM He, who lives though He was dead; and here, I AM alive forevermore, Amen. I hold the keys to hell and death. Write down the things you have seen, and the things which are, and the things which will be hereafter."

At His ascension, Jesus left His Spirit behind to comfort us. The Bible speaks of the Holy Spirit as our Comforter. It is He who stays with us at all times to show us the way to go, giving us the words to speak, and protecting us as we minister for the true Word, which is Christ.

MAY

- PSA 23:3–4 ~ The Lord restores my soul. He leads me in paths of righteousness for His namesake. Even when I walk through the valley of the shadow of death, I will fear no evil, for His rod and staff protect and comfort me.

- ECC 4:1 ~ I saw oppression occurring under the sun; I saw the tears of the down and out, and noticed that they had no comforter. Even though they had power, they had no comforter.

- ISA 61:1–3 ~ The Spirit of God is upon me, because He has directed me to preach His good news to the humble, to heal the broken hearted, to free the slaves, and to release those who are bound in chains and in prison; to proclaim the Lord's favor and His vengeance, to comfort all who mourn, and to tell those who mourn to exchange their ashes for beauty; to replace mourning with joy, and to don the garment of praise in exchange for the spirit of sorrow, so that they may be trees of righteousness, planted by the Lord for His glorification.

- ZEC 1:16–17 ~ I will return to Jerusalem with mercy, and I will rebuild my house there. My cities will prosper again; I will again comfort Zion, and I will again choose Jerusalem.

- LUK 4:16–20 ~ Jesus came to Nazareth and stood in the synagogue on the Sabbath day. He was handed the book of Isaiah to read aloud (ISA 61 above). After reading it, He closed the book and sat down, while everyone stared at Him. Then He proclaimed, "That scripture was fulfilled as you were hearing it."

- JOH 14:26 ~ Jesus said, "God will send the Comforter in my name, which is the Holy Spirit. He will teach you everything, and will help you remember all the things I have taught you."

- JOH 15:26 ~ Jesus said, "I will send the Comforter from the Father, which is the Spirit of truth that proceeds from the Father to testify about me."

- JOH 16:7, 13 ~ It is good for me to go, because until I am gone, the Comforter cannot come; but I will send Him to you when I leave. When the Spirit of truth comes, He will guide you into all truth. He will speak the words of God and will show you what is yet to come."

- 2 CO 1:3–5 ~ Blessed is God the Father of our Lord Jesus Christ, the Father of mercies and the God of comfort who comforts us in our tribulations, so that we may comfort others who are troubled, with the same comfort God has given to us. Whereas our sufferings in Christ are many, so also our consolation in Christ is abundant.

It is interesting how Jesus arrived on this planet by the Holy Spirit coming down to impregnate the virgin, Mary. And when Jesus ascended into heaven, His Spirit came down again to stay with us, as Jesus was ascending to sit beside His Father and rule at His right hand.

- ISA 7:14 ~ God Himself will provide the sign: A virgin shall conceive and bear a son. His name will be called "God with us."

- MAT 1:18, 20, 24–25 ~ Mary, before she had come together with Joseph, became pregnant by the Holy Spirit. God made this fact known to Joseph in a dream. Joseph took Mary to be his wife, but did not consummate their marriage until after Jesus was born.

- LUK 1:35 ~ The angel told Mary, "The Holy Spirit will come upon you. Therefore, your child will be called the Son of God."

Heavenly Father, how great are your works and your plan of salvation. Though there are many pieces to the grand scheme, they all come together for us in the Holy Bible. This is why we are compelled to take the time to read it, study it, digest it, and teach it. Thank you for making your Word clear for anyone who seeks the truth; let us always stand for the truth and speak the truth, as a testimony to our Lord and Savior Jesus Christ, in whose name we pray, Amen.

May 10

Clean Up Your Room Day is an unofficial observance, but reflects an age-old tradition called Spring cleaning. Many cultures have a cleaning day this time of year. Whatever day you select to clean your home, it is a necessary chore that everyone can participate in. If the entire household pitches in together, you can get it all done in one day, after which you can celebrate it being finished as you look over your clean house. Spring cleaning adds many benefits to your living environment: healthier, less clutter, nicer appearance, increased comfort and convenience.

Gather stuff you no longer use and dispose of it or give it to charity. Redecorate and rearrange the rooms, and maybe add some paint. Add music, song, laughter, games, and dancing while you're at it. Make it fun and interesting and the time will go fast; and you will be pleased with the outcome, and that will be good for your overall health as well. Do this to bring glory to God for all He has abundantly provided; it is a form of praise and worship when you invite God.

While it is important to keep your house clean and free of germs and vermin, it is vastly more important that you clean up your act. If you have a habitual sin that you cannot seem to shake off, you need to be cleansed by the blood of Christ so that the Holy Spirit can live inside you (1 CO 3:16–17). Your body is a temple of the Lord and it is not to be defiled (1 CO 6:15–20); instead, you should nurture your body and mind. You need to be cleaned on the inside, like your house. The blood of Christ will clean your heart; it is akin to laundry soap for the soul (MAL 3:1–5).

- EXO 24:7–8 ~ Moses preached about the everlasting covenant which God was going to make with all believers. After the peace offerings and burnt offerings were sacrificed, Moses sprinkled the blood of the offering on the alter and on the people, to signify that their sins would be cleansed by the blood of the New Covenant (i.e., the Lamb of God).

- PSA 51:10 ~ Create in me a clean heart, Lord, and renew an upright spirit within me.

- ISA 64:6 ~ All of us have become unclean, and our acts of righteousness are as filthy rags. We shrivel like a leaf, and like the wind, our sins sweep us away.

- JER 13:27 ~ God says, "I have seen your adultery, your lewdness, and your abominations. Woe to you, Jerusalem. Will you ever become clean again?"

- EZE 36:24–28 ~ I will remove you from among the heathen, gather you out of all countries, and bring you into your own land. Then I will sprinkle clean water upon you, and you will be clean of all filth; from your idols I will cleanse you. A new heart I will give you; and a new spirit I will put inside you. I will take away the heart of stone and place my spirit within you. And you will walk in my statutes and keep my judgments. You will live in the land I gave to your fathers; and you will be my people and I will be your God.

- MAT 3:11 ~ The blood of Christ represents the refiner's fire that purifies one's very soul.

- MAT 23:25 ~ Jesus said, "Woe to you hypocritical scribes and Pharisees, for you make the outside appear clean while the inside is full of extortion and excess."

- MAR 7:14–19 ~ Jesus said, "Can you see that nothing entering a person from the outside can make him or her unclean? It is what comes out of the person that makes them unclean. Something entering from the outside goes into the stomach (not the heart) and then out of the body. If something evil comes from the heart, it will make that person unclean."

- LUK 3:16 ~ John answered them, "I baptize you with water. But One comes after me whose shoelaces I am unworthy to loosen. He will baptize you with the Holy Spirit and with fire."

- JOH 15:1–5 ~ Jesus said, "I am the true vine, and my Father is the cultivator. He removes any of my branches that do not bear fruit. Those that do bear fruit, he prunes, so that they can bear even more fruit. You have been made clean through the Word which I have spoken to you. Stay in me and I will stay in you, but without me, you can do nothing."

- EPH 5:26 ~ Jesus Christ gave Himself for His people so He could sanctify them through a spiritual washing by the Word.

- COL 3:5 ~ Repress those who practice or promote fornication, uncleanness, promiscuity, unnatural desires, and avarice, which is idolatry.

- HEB 9:13–14 ~ If the blood of animals could sanctify those who are unclean, how much more will the blood of Christ, who offered Himself unblemished to God, cleanse our consciences from sin that leads to death so that we may serve the living God.

- HEB 10:10–18 ~ Jesus's sacrifice is the last sacrifice that will need to be made to atone for sin. Under the Old Covenant, sacrificial offerings were made as an atonement for sin. Under the New Covenant, we are made clean by the blood of Christ in one final sacrificial offering. This sacrifice will stand for all time, so there is no longer any need for sin offerings or sacrifices.

- JAM 4:8 ~ Draw nigh unto God and He will draw nigh unto you. Cleanse your hands you sinners and purify your hearts you who are double minded.

- 1 PE 3:21 ~ Baptism will also save us through the resurrection of Jesus Christ. Baptism does not mean washing a dirty body, but rather establishing a clean conscience toward God.

- 1 JO 1:8–9 ~ If we say we do not sin we deceive ourselves and we are liars. If we confess our sins, God is faithful and just to forgive our sins and cleanse us from all unrighteousness.

- REV 1:5 ~ Jesus Christ is the faithful witness, and the firstborn of those who have died. He is the prince, who is above all the kings of the earth. He loved us and cleansed us of all sin by His own blood.

Though we were dead in our sins, we have been revived through the shedding of Christ's blood on the cross. In the Old Testament, blood offerings provided temporary atonement for sin. In the New Testament, Christ's blood, offered on the cross for forgiveness of sins, provides permanent atonement for every sin for all time. One must believe that their own sins have been removed, and make an effort to do better, in order to receive the atonement that leads to salvation of the soul. That is, we must have faith, and that faith should be apparent by the way we act.

If we engage in habitual sin without confession, repentance, and belief in the atonement of Christ, we are not saved. If that is your situation, you need to clean up your act and have a change of heart. Then your heart can be cleansed of unrighteousness by the Holy Spirit and your soul can be purified, making you ready and acceptable to stand before God Almighty and be ushered into His Kingdom.

Almighty Father, who gave His Son to atone for our sins, thank you for the precious gift of Christ's atonement, and we thank you Holy Spirit for sanctifying us day by day, as we become conformed into the image of Christ who is the image of you, Father. We choose you to be our God forevermore, and we are happy to be chosen by you to be your sons and daughters. Help us to clean up our act if we are living in sin that leads to death; let us commit our lives as a living sacrifice to you while we serve and witness in this life through our faith and our actions. May we correct behaviors that require changing, and adopt replacement behaviors that emulate Christ. We praise you Father for adopting us into your family, where we can live with you forever, and your Son who is not ashamed to call us His brothers and sisters. We pray in His name, Amen.

May 11

American Bible Society Was Founded on this day in 1816 to advance the translation, production, and distribution of the Holy Bible throughout the world. Many of our founding fathers were a part of this initiative to include Elias Boudinot, John Jay, John Quincy Adams, Francis Scott Key and others. The American Bible Society (ABS) started distributing copies of the King James Version of the Bible to hotels and organizations. In four years, they had distributed over 100,000 Bibles, and by 1831 that number rose above one million; to date they have distributed over six billion partial or complete Bibles. They translated the Bible into the language of the Delaware natives in 1818. ABS soon began producing Bibles in Italian, Swedish, Danish, German, French, and Spanish; they also obtained Bibles in many other languages for distribution. They produced pocket-size Bibles for soldiers during the Civil War. In 1843, they produced the first Bible for the blind using a raised letter system. In 1934 they produced scriptures in Chinese for missionaries to distribute in China. In 1946 they established United Bible Societies, a global organization for promoting and distributing God's Word to every corner of the earth and in every language. In 1966 they produced the widely popular New Testament translation *Good News for Modern Man*. In 2012 they set up a digital library, making numerous translations available in digital format. In 2019 they produced a video of the Bible using American sign language. ABS is supported by mainstream Protestant denominations, military chaplains, and several past US presidents and evangelists. ABS has collected tens of thousands of complete and partial manuscripts, representing numerous languages, and dating back to the Gutenberg Bible (fifteenth century AD). They have been involved in the translation of scripture into over 1800 languages. Their goal is to have a Bible translated into every language on the planet by 2033. Today we can thank God for people and organizations which pass the Word.

Translation of the Bible requires accurate interpretation of scripture; and this requires one to interpret scriptures in light of the rest of scripture. Many themes are repeated throughout the Bible precisely because they are meant to stand out, and collectively point to truths that are indisputable, providing additional clarification each time the theme is repeated. Such contextual translation is a fundamental rule of Biblical hermeneutics (Barber, 2020a).

- ISA 44:24–26 ~ The Lord, your redeemer who formed you from the womb, says, "I AM the Lord who creates all things, who stretches the heavens and spreads out the earth; who frustrates the signs of the fake prophets, and drives diviners crazy; who turns the wisdom of the wise around, and makes their knowledge foolish; who confirms the words of His servants and fulfills the proclamations of His messengers; who says to Jerusalem, you will be inhabited, and to the cities of Judah, all will be rebuilt for I will restore it from ruins."

- 1 CO 2:13–14 ~ We teach using words taught by the Holy Spirit, not by human wisdom. Spiritual truths must be interpreted by those who possess the Spirit. Worldly people do not receive the things of the Spirit of God, for these things are foolishness to them; neither can they know these things for they must be discerned spiritually.

- GAL 1:6–8, 11–12 ~ It amazes me how you can turn away so suddenly from the one who called you into the grace of Christ, to a different gospel of which there is only one. People are misleading you with their perversion of the gospel of Christ. If a person or an angel preaches a different gospel than that which we preached to you, they are cursed. Let it be known, brothers and sisters, the gospel we preach is not of human origin, neither did I receive it from any man, nor was I taught it, but it was given to me by a revelation from Jesus Christ.

- GAL 3:23–24 ~ Before faith came, we were under the Law; faith was yet to be revealed. The Law was our teacher to bring us to Christ so we could be justified by faith.

MAY

- 2 TI 3:14–16 ~ Continue in the things you have learned and are convinced, knowing from whom you have learned them. From a child you have known the holy scriptures, which are able to make you wise unto salvation through faith in Jesus Christ. All scripture is given by inspiration of God and is effective for doctrine, guidance, correction, and instruction in righteousness.

- 2 TI 4:3–4 ~ People will seek teachers who conform to their own likes and dislikes; they will turn away from the truth and wander into myths.

- JDE 1:4 ~ False teachers have infiltrated the churches, claiming that once you become Christians you can do whatever you want without being punished.

A perfect example of a valid interpretation of the Bible is when Old Testament (OT) prophecy is fulfilled in the New Testament (NT). This prophecy comes true to the utmost degree to ensure there is no confusion about the meaning. There are over three hundred OT prophecies about Messiah alone, all of which come true through Jesus Christ in the NT. The statistical likelihood of that many predictions coming true in one man is infinitesimally small (one over ten followed by over a thousand zeroes). Furthermore, the OT is quoted over three hundred times by Christ and the apostles, as well as other writers of the NT. This adds additional proof that the OT validates the NT and vice-versa. The following is a sample of such cross-validation.

- LUK 4:1–13 ~ Jesus was filled with the Holy Spirit who led Him into the wilderness. There He was tempted during the forty days He fasted there. He was very weak and hungry when the devil came to Him. The devil said, "If you are hungry, command those stones to become bread." Jesus replied, "It is written that man will not live by bread alone, but by the Word of God" (DEU 8:3). Next, the devil brought Jesus into a high mountain and showed Him all the kingdoms of the world in a single moment of time. The devil said, "All the power and glory associated with these kingdoms I will give to you if you will worship me." Jesus replied, "Get behind me, Satan, for it is written that you must worship the Lord your God and serve only Him" (DEU 6:13–15). Next, the devil brought Jesus to Jerusalem where they sat at the pinnacle of the temple. The devil said, "Jump down, and the angels will catch you, since it is written that God gives His angels charge over you to keep you always from harm and danger" (PSA 91:11). Jesus replied, "It also is written that you should never tempt the Lord your God" (DEU 6:16). At that, the devil gave up and left Jesus.

- ROM 12:19 ~ Do not seek revenge and give way to wrath, for it is written: "Vengeance is mine. I will repay, says the Lord" (DEU 32:35).

- 1 CO 2:9 ~ It is written: Nobody has ever heard or seen, or even imagined, the wonderful things God has prepared for those who love Him (ISA 64:4).

- HEB 8:10 ~ This is the covenant that I will make with the house of Israel, says the Lord. I will put my laws into their minds and write them upon their hearts. And I will be their God and they will be my people (JER 31:33–34).

- 1 PE 2:6–7 ~ It is written (ISA 28:16): Behold, I lay in Zion a chief cornerstone, and anyone who trusts in Him will never be ashamed. To those who believe, this stone is precious. But let this be a warning to those who do not believe: the stone which the builders rejected has become the chief cornerstone, and that stone will be an obstacle which causes the unbelievers to stumble and fall.

Father, we praise you for making your Word clear, and providing proof within the Holy Bible itself. Thank you for organizations like the American Bible Society who translate and distribute Bibles all over the world in the reader's native language. Thank you, Jesus, Amen.

May 12

Mother's Day was started by Anna Jarvis who began the movement when her mother died. Jarvis had been involved in a ministry in the aftermath of the Civil War, helping war veterans from both sides, and fostering harmony and peace. Two years later in 1907 she organized a memorial service at her church in West Virginia to unite and celebrate mothers. Her hope was to create a national holiday to honor mothers since they have the greatest impact on the lives of everyone; and she was successful; churches all over the US began to observe Mother's Day. In 1914 President Wilson signed a declaration designating the second Sunday of May as Mother's Day in the USA. It didn't take long before the whole world started celebrating Mother's Day. This day is based upon the sacrifices, nurturing, and mending provided by mothers.

Today is a day to honor our mothers, showering them with love, praise, hugs, cards, and gifts. Mothers are the epitome of human love; not only does that love help to unify families it also is the magnet that can bring families back together. This is a day to spend together as a family, and thank mothers for the nurturing and supervision they provide. In addition to individuals honoring their mothers, this day has become a reason to honor motherhood in general, for theirs is a very high calling. Oftentimes, mothers end up the breadwinner, cook, cleaning lady, caregiver, nurse, taxi, and more; even in the animal world we find mothers doing the lions' share of the work. Yes, there are dedicated fathers that do all of these things. But there are fewer single fathers raising kids then there are single mothers.

- EXO 20:12 ~ Honor your father and your mother, that your days may be long upon the land where God places you.

- EPH 6:1–4 ~ Children, obey your parents, for God has given them authority over you. Honor your father and mother as commanded by God in His Ten Commandments. This is the first commandment that brings a promise: If you honor your parents your life will be long and happy. Parents, do not provoke your children to anger and frustration. Instead, raise them in the nurture and discipline of righteousness, as instructed by God in the Bible.

Mothers have that special touch and smile which can soothe the soul. They are the emotional support system of the children, husband, and home. Let us review some things that the Bible has to say about godly mothers and wives.

- GEN 3:16 ~ God said to Eve, I will multiply your suffering during childbirth, and with painful labor you will deliver your children. Your desire will be for your husband, and he will rule over you.

- RUT 1:16–18, 22 ~ Ruth told her mother-in-law, "Please do not ask me to leave, for I would rather follow you, and go where you go and live where you live. Your people will be my people and your God my God. Where you die, I will die and be buried with you." When Naomi saw that Ruth was determined, she kept quiet. So, Naomi and Ruth traveled from Moab to Bethlehem together, arriving at the beginning of the barley harvest.

- PRO 31:10–31 ~ Whoever finds a virtuous woman for a wife will have something more valuable than rubies. She will do her husband good all of her life. She will work hard and give herself to the household. She will be generous and complimentary to others. Her husband will be well known and powerful. She will be clothed in strength and honor. She will be wise and kind. She will not be lazy and her husband and children will praise her for it. Although favor can be deceitful and beauty can be vain, faith in God will always yield His praise.

- LUK 1:39–50, 56 ~ When Mary was pregnant with Jesus, she travelled to visit her cousin Elisabeth who also was with child. When Elisabeth heard her salutation, the baby leaped in her womb; and Elisabeth was filled with the Holy Spirit, saying aloud, "Blessed are you among women and blessed is the fruit of your womb; for the moment I heard your voice the baby in my womb jumped for joy." She was blessed for her faith, being a part of great things told to her by the Lord. Mary replied, "My soul magnifies the Lord and my spirit has rejoiced in God my Savior. He has regarded me, a woman of low estate, to be His handmaiden, and henceforth all generations will call me blessed; for God has done mighty things and holy is His name. His mercy is upon those who fear Him from generation to generation." And Mary stayed with her of about six months before returning home.

- TIT 2:3–8 ~ Women (mothers) should conduct themselves in a godly manner, teaching what is good. Women should not be gossipers or false accusers, nor should they drink a lot. Mothers should teach their daughters to be thoughtful and obedient homemakers, and to love their husbands and their children. Daughters should be taught to be chaste and discreet. Sons should be taught to be sober, helpful, sincere, and incorruptible. Sons should be taught to be calm and collected in their speech and actions; they should be taught not to say evil things about others.

Mom deserves her special day. Motherhood is a cherished responsibility, one which most women would like to experience at least once in their lifetimes. These days, fewer women are interested in having children in lieu of a career; others are perfectly capable and willing to juggle both duties. Many choose to raise their children without a father figure. But the Bible makes it clear that a two-parent system of a loving wife and husband is the best environment in which to raise kids. Honor the woman who toiled for years to raise you, nurture you, and teach you; most likely, she will continue to love and nurture you until she is gone. Celebrate the one who was a mother to you more than anybody else, in case it was not your biological mother.

- PRO 14:1 ~ The wise woman builds her house up; the foolish woman tears it down.

- PRO 18:22 ~ He who finds a good wife has a great blessing and obtains favor from the Lord.

- ISA 66:13 ~ God says, "As the child is comforted by his or her mother, so will I comfort you."

- 1 CO 13:4–8 ~ Love is always patient and kind, without envy or arrogance. Love does not behave rudely or selfishly, and is not easily provoked or irritated. Love thinks of no evil, nor does it rejoice in sin; love rejoices in the truth. Love bears all things believes all things, hopes all things, and endures all things. Love never fails…

Most gracious and merciful Father, we thank you today for mothers: including our own mothers and mothers across the globe. They sacrificed much to bring us into the world, as well as providing nurturing, guidance, encouragement, understanding, and love. Mothers are examples of your love, and they teach us how to love. Help us to love them back, no matter what their faults. You loved us despite our faults and for this we love you back. Protect mothers and defend them against evil people. Especially help mothers who have been abandoned by their husbands or the fathers of their children. Despite many hardships, they persevere, raising and protecting their little ones. We ask that you please assign your angels to the little ones, especially those who are being abused, abandoned, or stolen; let them grow in knowledge and truth, and discover that they have a Father in heaven who loves them, even more than their own mothers. Help all children to be taught about God's patient and enduring love, and to learn respect and honesty, so they might show respect, honesty, and love to their mothers and fathers, and possibly become God-fearing and dedicated parents. Through mother Mary, all mothers have an example of humbleness and love to her child; and through her love for Jesus Christ and His love for all people, everybody has an example of humbleness and love. Help us to follow and become an example of love, obedience, humility, and compassion for all of our days. In the name of your only begotten child Jesus Christ our Lord, we ask you Father, Amen.

May 13

International Nurses' Day is actually celebrated on May 12 in commemoration of the birth of Florence Nightingale on 05/12/1820; she was a pioneer in nursing during the Crimean War with Russia. Of British descent, she was named Florence because she was born in Florence Italy. She was affectionately dubbed "the lady with the lamp" for her many visits to the wounded after dark. She authored many treatises and manuals on nursing practices which she influenced if not instituted, backing up her information with statistics and data charts. She established a nursing school in 1860, which is now part of King's College, London. She introduced sanitation procedures, environmental and hygiene requirements, and protective gear such as the nurse's cap and gown.

The International Council of Nurses (ICN) began the annual observance in 1965; the May 12 date became official in the USA in 1974. Every year the ICN disseminates information and training materials for nurses everywhere: the latest in technology, best practices, critical care and triage, and modernization of facilities are among topics that will be shared by professionals in what has become a very wide field of diverse specialties.

Nurses are a special breed of helper; with dedication and sacrifice they endure tedious work and long hours. They ensure the wounded and ill are comfortable, while providing everything required for patients to make a full recovery. This is where we get the phrase, "nursing someone back to health" because that is precisely their prime objective. Although doctors perform highly skilled procedures and surgeries, they need the assistance of nurses to complete them. Plus, nurses do everything the doctors do not do up until the patient is discharged, and sometimes after that. So, thank a nurse or two today and give them some love. Thank God for nurses, for they are saving lives, caring for patients before and after the doctor arrives, whether on the road or in medical facilities, and at all hours of the day and night.

Nurses have always been with us, long before nursing programs were invented. It is and always has been a very noble occupation. In olden days, direct care was a role best suited for women, especially with respect to caring for small children and other women. Some moms had assistants to help with the nurturing, direct care, and comforting of children, the elderly, and their loved ones who were in poor health. This may be why women dominated the nursing field for years: women were the first nurses largely because they were mothers. When you were a child, who did you run to when you skinned your knee?

Nurses in the Bible were generally midwives who delivered babies; some nurses served as nannies or wet nurses. Numerous references to nurses in the Bible relate to breast feeding and wet nurses (EXO 2:5–10; RUT 4:16; 2 KI 11:2; ISA 60:4; 1 TH 2:7). But there were women in Old and New Testament times who performed care for the young and old, the injured and ill; and many of them made this their profession.

- GEN 24:59; GEN 35:8 ~ Rebekah (Isaac's wife) had a personal nurse named Deborah, who remained her assistant until the day she died.

- 2 SA 4:4 ~ King Saul's son Jonathan had a son who was five years old when he became a paraplegic because his nurse picked him up in haste and dropped him. His name was Mephibosheth. [King David would save the lame boy making him part of his family, in tribute to his best friend Jonathan whose family line had been wiped out by the Philistines.]

- 1 KI 1:2–4 ~ King David become an old and decrepit man. His servants found a young virgin girl to be his personal nurse and to keep him warm at night. But the king did not have sex with her. [The words "he knew her not" was a reference to Mary who would remain a virgin until after Jesus was born; Joseph did not consummate their marriage until Mary was renewed.]

- MAT 25:37–40 ~ Jesus said the righteous group will ask, "Lord, when did we see you hungry and fed you, or thirsty and gave you drink, or a stranger and took you in, or naked and clothed you, or sick or in prison and we visited you." The King will answer, "Truly I tell you, if you did something to help one of the least of these my people, you did it also to me."

- ROM 12:13 ~ Distribute care to meet the needs of the saints, and be inclined to being hospitable.

- ROM 15:1 ~ We who are strong ought to bear the infirmities of the weak, and not only please ourselves.

- ROM 16:1 ~ I (Paul) entrust to you our sister Phebe (also Phoebe), a servant of the church at Cenchrea. Receive her as you would a fellow saint and assist her in her business. She has been a minister to many people, myself included. [Theologians believe Phebe had the skills of a nurse, and she also may have served as deaconess in the early church.]

Midwives were women who were trained and experienced with childbirth and associated complications. Doctors were in short supply, so each community had a cadre of midwives to help deliver babies.

- GEN 35:16–18 ~ After leaving Bethel for Ephrath, Rachel was in travail with a difficult pregnancy. When she was in hard labor, the midwife told Rachel not to fear for she would have a son. Rachel died giving birth to her son whom Jacob named Benjamin.

- GEN 38:27–30 ~ When Tamar, Judah's daughter in law, was in labor it was apparent that there were twins in her womb. One of the babies put out his hand and the midwife tied a scarlet thread around his wrist; but he withdrew his hand and his brother came out. Since his hand came out first, he was called Pharez (also Perez), meaning breach. And his brother was named Zerah (meaning sun). [Note that Perez was Judah's son and was an ancestor of King David, and Jesus the King of kings.]

- EXO 1:15–22 ~ The king of Egypt summoned the chief Hebrew midwives, named Shiphrah and Puah; he ordered them to kill the baby boys but not the girls. However, the midwives feared God and did not obey the king, who became angry with them and summoned them back. They told the king that Hebrew women give birth too quickly to stop the male babies from being born. And the Hebrew slaves multiplied even more. Pharoah again ordered the male babies to be killed but not the females. [This decree resulted in the infant Moses being floated down the Nile River to spare him; Moses was rescued from the river by Pharoah's daughter who raised him in the king's palace (EXO 2:1–10).]

There is not a single soul alive or dead that has not been helped by a nurse. In many cases, they would not have survived if not for the intervention of a nurse or other emergency health worker. Tell your nurses how much you appreciate their help from this day forward. Take time to remember how you were blessed to have a gracious and caring nurse minister to you or a loved one. Drop them a line or send them a card; and don't forget to pray on their behalf.

Heavenly Father, we thank you for nurses and other healthcare workers and we appreciate the sacrifices they make to ease the suffering of others. We pray that they be given all due respect and honor. Give them strength to endure the workload and the hours, for they must keep a cool head as they toil in a very tedious and often chaotic environment. Hold them up with your right hand who is Jesus Christ our Lord the Great Physician. In His name we pray, Amen.

May 14

National Police Week is celebrated every year in the middle of May. Today we honor the men and women in blue, who stand between law abiding citizens and criminals. In 1962, Peace Officers Memorial Day was inaugurated under President Kennedy to be observed on May 15, in remembrance of police officers who had died in the line of duty. A memorial service has been conducted in Washington DC since 1982, attended by survivors and supporters of our fallen men and women who enforce the law. During this week, upwards of 50,000 people will flock to DC to attend daily events, memorial services, candlelight vigils, and to honor and thank the police. Support your police and tell them the truth; allow and enable them to do their jobs. The police have one of the most thankless jobs in the world, while placing their lives on the line daily to protect us. Police have been particularly unappreciated in recent years by people suggesting we don't need them; but those idealogues have been proven wrong with the rising crime rates in areas where funding of police forces has been withdrawn. Cops are there for a reason; we owe it to society to uphold them and provide necessary resources. Sack bureaucrats who defund cops.

- AMO 5:15 ~ Hate evil, love goodness, and establish justice.

- JOH 15:12–13 ~ Jesus said, "Love each other as I have loved you. No greater love exists than to give one's life for their friends."

- ROM 1:32 ~ People commit evil acts, knowing full well that their acts are worthy of the death penalty. Yet they continue to be evil and to find pleasure in others who do the same.

- ROM 2:12–13 ~ All who sin apart from the Law will perish apart from the Law. All who sin under the Law will be judged according to the Law. Hearing the Law does not make you righteous in God's eyes; you must obey the Law to be declared righteous.

- ROM 13:1–10 ~ Everyone is subject to higher powers. All power comes from God; powers that exist are ordained by God. Anyone resisting these powers are resisting the ordinance of God, and those who resist God receive damnation as punishment. Those who do right have no fear of authorities, only those who do wrong. Do the right thing and the authorities will commend you. Governments are God's servants; they make sure you do what is right. But if you do what is evil, beware, for they do not carry a sword (gun) in vain, but to execute judgment on those who do evil. Submit to those who are in authority, not only because you will be punished if you do not, but also as a matter of keeping a clear conscience. This is why you should pay your taxes, because governments are God's servants who work fulltime in governing. Give them their dues, paying when payment is due, obeying the customs and laws of the people, and rendering fear and honor to their position. Do not owe anyone, except to love them. Obey the commandment to love your neighbor, and you fulfill all laws.

- 1 TI 2:2 ~ Pray for your leaders and all who are in authority.

- HEB 13:17 ~ Obey those who rule over you, and submit yourselves to them; for they will be watching you and will give an account, and you want them to give a good report.

- JAM 4:11 ~ Do not speak evil about someone else. Whoever speaks evil of another or judges them unfairly judges the Law. If you judge the Law, you cannot be adhering to the Law.

- 1 PE 2:13–14 ~ Submit to every ordinance of society for the Lord's sake, whether to the king or his governors, who have authority to punish evildoers and commend those who do right.

Father, we thank you for the police; help us to thank them personally when we have the opportunity. Help them to enforce the law properly, honestly, and bravely for this has been their legacy; let it continue to be so in our land of the free. In Jesus's name who set us free, Amen.

May 15

International Day of Families was introduced through a 1993 UN resolution, establishing this date for recognizing the necessity of solid family structures in all societies and cultures. The UN also proclaimed 1994 to be the International Year of Families. The Economic and Social Council of the UN had been examining the economic and social needs of families in various cultures since the 1980s, and this initiative brought more visibility to their efforts. There are different functions, events, and seminars that will occur within the UN and in various political arenas on this day. The objective is to develop and promote social policies that promote families everywhere. The nucleus of the family and its benefits far exceed alternative living situations.

Certainly, families deserve a day, since we have mothers', fathers', children's, and grandparents' day. So, take a day for the immediate family to be together and have some fun with it. As a therapist, I recommended the family choose a day every week for a special activity they could do together, to maintain the spiritual togetherness; I also suggested that each member take turns deciding what to do on family day. The unity in a family begins when a man and a woman are joined in matrimony; they make a vow before man and before God to stay together. Children should be trained about God's view of marriage and the family, and the importance of staying together. Upholding family unity is a godly endeavor wherein all members have a say and are loved equally; this emulates the love between God the Father and the Son, through the Holy Spirit. This is the best formula for a functioning and thriving family.

- GEN 2:24 ~ A man shall leave his parents and cling to his wife; and they shall become one flesh.

- DEU 6:2–7 ~ Fear the Lord and keep His commandments and laws. Ensure that your children, and your children's children, obey God. Do this and you will prosper and your life will be prolonged. Love God with all your heart, soul, and might. Keep God's Word in your heart and teach His ways carefully and thoughtfully to your children. Talk with your family all the time about God, every day and night, whenever you are together.

- PSA 127:3–5 ~ Children are a heritage from the Lord; the fruit of the womb is a reward. Like arrows in the hand of a warrior are the children of our youth. Blessed is the man who fills his quiver with them. He will not be put to shame when he faces his enemies at the gate.

- PRO 5:18 ~ Rejoice with the wife of your youth.

- ECC 9:9 ~ Always be happy with your spouse, and love him or her the rest of your life.

- JER 29:6 ~ Get married and have children. Encourage your children to do the same so that your family can increase and not diminish.

- MAL 2:14–16 ~ The Lord has formed a husband and wife into one flesh. In both flesh and spirit, they belong to Him. But why is this so? Because He wishes godly offspring from them. Guard your spirit, and do not break the covenant with your wife or husband by getting divorced.

- ROM 17:6 ~ Grandchildren are the pride of their grandparents and the glory of their parents.

- 1 CO 7:2, 10–11 ~ Nevertheless, let every man have his own wife, and let every woman have her own husband. God requires that a wife must not leave her husband and the husband must not divorce his wife.

- EPH 6:4 ~ Parents, do not provoke your children to anger and frustration. Instead, raise them in the nurture and discipline of righteousness.

- 1 TI 3:4 ~ If a man manages his family well, his children will obey him and he will be worthy of their respect.

In addition to our immediate family, we have a family in Christ. Take your family to church and Sunday school; make this your family day so that after church you can discuss what everyone saw and heard and have a nice meal or picnic in the process. Quality family time is very important. A good church will have family events and activities after church and on special occasions. This is a great opportunity to spend quality time with your church family. The church is a good place to make friends, both for children and for adults. Festivals and feasts have always been a part of worship, both in the Jewish faith and the Christian faith.

- DEU 31:12 ~ Gather the people together including men, women, and children, as well as the strangers among you, so that everyone can hear, learn, fear the Lord your God, and obey all the words of His Law.

- PSA 133:1 ~ Behold, how good and how pleasant it is for brothers and sisters of the faith to live together in unity!

- LUK 21:16–18 ~ Jesus said, "You will be betrayed by parents, siblings, relatives, and friends; and some of you will be put to death. You will be hated for my namesake. But not a hair on your head will perish."

- 1 CO 1:10 ~ I urge you, my brothers, in the name of our Lord Jesus Christ, to be in agreement with one another so that there will be no divisions among you. Be perfectly joined together in mind and thought.

- GAL 6:1–2, 10 ~ Brothers, if someone is overtaken by sin, you who are spiritual need to restore that person in the spirit of humility, considering that you also can be tempted. Bear one another's burdens to fulfill the law of Christ. Whenever the opportunity arises, do something nice for someone, especially your brothers and sisters in the faith.

- COL 3:12–16 ~ As God's elect, holy and blessed, we should be merciful, kind, humble, meek, and patient. Hold back your anger towards others and forgive them. If you have a disagreement, forgive each other as Christ forgave you. Above all, put on love, which binds all things together in perfect harmony. Let the peace of Christ rule in your hearts; for this you were called into one body. Let the Word of Christ abide in you richly in all wisdom. Teach and admonish one another in psalms, hymns, and spiritual songs, singing to God with grace in your hearts.

- 1 TH 5:11 ~ Comfort each other and edify one another just as you have been doing.

- HEB 10:24–25 ~ Let us encourage one another to promote love and good works. Let us never cease to fellowship with one another in God's house as others have the habit of doing.

- 1 PE 1:22 ~ You have purified your souls by obeying the truth that the Holy Spirit has shown to you; so fervently love your brothers and sisters with a pure heart.

Our Father, we thank you for giving us the gift of families; humankind would never have made it without them. Especially we thank you for our family in Christ, who serve as a surrogate family when our own family is far away. If we do not get to visit with our immediate family very often, our church family is always there for us; and for this we are indeed blessed. And regarding our church family, we pray that we will not allow divisiveness to enter in and destroy our unity in the faith and the brotherhood of our congregation. Thank you for our loved ones; we pray for your blessing upon them. Thank you for the family of saints, who will have a reunion in your kingdom as brothers and sisters, having received the inheritance of Jesus Christ, in whom we pray, Amen.

May 16

National Biographer's Day is an annual observance celebrating biographers and biographies. This date was selected because it is the anniversary of a meeting in London (1763) between Samuel Johnson and James Boswell. Johnson was a renowned poet, essayist, journalist, editor, literary critic, and biographer. Boswell was a lawyer, writer, journalist, and biographer. The two became great friends, and Boswell would eventually write Johnson's biography (1791), which received high acclaim. Boswell's personal autobiography can be gleaned from his extensive journaling. It is unclear when this unofficial holiday started, but it has caught on and is now observed worldwide to some degree. Biographies and autobiographies provide information about people who we revere, so their legacy can be preserved; biographies also can be about people we must not imitate.

If you get bored today, start working on your own biography, or the biography of a close friend or relative. Research your ancestry to find out biographical information regarding your lineage. Biographies are the most popular form of nonfiction. If you are interested in reading a biography to celebrate this occasion, visit your public library. Sometimes you can find several biographies written about a single person; when selecting any one biography you might want to consider Samuel Johnson's rule: friends make the best biographers.

There have been famous biographies throughout the ages, dating back to ancient Greece and Rome. But the oldest biography is the one God Himself wrote about the history of the universe, humankind, and most notably, the biography of His only Son, Jesus Christ. This is the greatest and most popular biography of all time, which provides a complete and integrated picture of God's plan of salvation for those who follow His Son. The biography of Christ begins in Genesis and continues through Revelation. Essentially, every book of the Bible contributes to declaring and explaining God's Messiah, our Redeemer.

- GEN 3:14–15 ~ You (Satan) and your offspring will hate the woman (Eve) and her offspring (Messiah). He will crush your head and you will strike His heel.

- GEN 12:3 ~ Through the seed of Abraham (Christ) all nations will be blessed (GAL 3:6–29).

- GEN 28:12 ~ Jacob dreamed about a ladder that stood on earth and reached into heaven, and the angels of God were ascending and descending the ladder. (Jesus Christ is the ladder; He is the way to heaven: see JOH 1:51).

- 2 SA 7:12–16 ~ God said to David, "I will make one of your descendants a strong king who will rule forever. I will be His Father and He will be my Son." (Jesus was a descendant of David: see MAT 1:6; LUK 2:4; REV 5:5).

- PSA 22:16–18 ~ David prophesied: Evil men circle me like a wolf pack. They have pierced my hands and feet (also ZEC 13:6). They have bruised every bone in my body. They gloat and stare. They divide my clothes by casting lots (see MAT 27:35; JOH 19:37).

- ISA 7:14 ~ God Himself will provide a sign: A son will be born of a virgin (see MAT 1:22–23; LUK 1:26–35); He will be called "God with us."

- ISA 9:1–2, 6–7 ~ In the future, this land (Galilee to Jerusalem: MAT 4:12–16; ACT 5:31) will behold the glory of God, the light of life. For a Son will be born and the government will be upon His shoulders. He will be called Wonderful Counselor, Mighty God, Everlasting Father, and Prince of Peace. His eternal reign will bring truth and justice to all nations.

- ISA 11:1–2 ~ A descendant of Jesse will come, and the Spirit of the Lord will be upon Him, the spirit of wisdom and understanding, the spirit of counsel and might, the spirit of knowledge, and the fear of the Lord.

- ISA 49:7; ISA 60:6 ~ Kings and princes will see the sign and will come to worship. They come with caravans of camels from Midian, Ephah, and Sheba, bringing gold and incense and praising God (MAT 2:1–2, 11).

- ISA 50:6 ~ I gave my back to be whipped; I gave my face to be mocked and spat upon.

- ISA 53:4–12 ~ He took upon Himself all of our grief and sorrows; yet we treated Him as an outcast. He was tortured for our sins and punished for our peace, and through His wounds we are healed. He was slaughtered like a lamb. He was buried like a criminal but in a rich man's grave. He was made an offering for sin, although He never committed a single act of sin or spoke an evil word. Therefore, His days will be prolonged and His name will be made great. He will be exalted, for He emptied his soul unto death.

- DAN 7:13–14 ~ From the clouds of heaven there came one like the Son of man (ACT 1:9–11), and to Him was given all dominion, glory and kingdom, so that all people, nations and languages should serve Him.

- MIC 5:2–4 ~ Oh Bethlehem, you are such a small village but will be the birthplace of my King, who has been foretold from time eternal. God will forget Israel until the time has come for the chosen woman to bear the child; then the children of Israel will return. The Son will stand for and feed off the Lord, and will share His majesty. The children shall live in Him who is great, even to every corner of the earth. (see MAT 2:5–6; JOH 7:42)

- ZEC 3:8–9 ~ I will bring forth my servant, the Branch. He will be the foundation stone; He will remove the sins of the world in a single day.

- ZEC 9:9–10 ~ Rejoice, for here comes your righteous king riding on a donkey's colt (MAT 21:7; JOH 12:14–15). He will bring peace to all nations.

- ZEC 11:12–13 ~ His price was thirty pieces of silver, thrown down in the house of the Lord, and used to buy the potter's field (MAT 27:6–10; ACT 1:17–19).

- MAT 1:1–16; LUK 3:23–38 ~ The genealogies of Joseph and Mary are provided.

- MAT 1:21–25 ~ God told Joseph that Mary would bear a son to be named Jesus (meaning Savior), for He would save His people from their sins. This took place to fulfill the prophecy that a virgin would bear a son who would be called Emmanuel (ISA 7:14), meaning "God with us."

- MAT 2:1–6, 9–11, 16–18 ~ Jesus was born in Bethlehem of Judea in the days of Herod the king. Wise men came from the east to Jerusalem asking Herod, "Where is He who is born king of the Jews? From the east we have seen His star and we have come to worship Him." Herod gathered together the chief priests and scribes, demanding to know where the Messiah would be born. They replied that it would be Bethlehem of Judea, for it was written: Bethlehem is not insignificant among the cities of Judea, for from there will come a governor who will rule my people, Israel. After leaving Herod they followed the star. Finally, they stood directly under the star. They found the young Christ child with Mary, His mother, and worshipped Him. They opened their treasures and presented to Him gifts of gold, frankincense, and myrrh. Attempting to kill Jesus, Herod ordered the deaths of all babies in Bethlehem two years old and younger. This fulfilled the prophecy of Jeremiah (JER 31:15): In Ramah was heard the bitter weeping and mourning over the children who were killed.

- MAT 4:12–16 ~ Jesus lived and preached in the land of Capernaum, which is along the seacoast between Zebulun and Naphtali, thereby fulfilling the prophecy of Isaiah (ISA 9:1–2, 6–7).

- MAT 27:3–10 ~ Judas who had betrayed Jesus, after recognizing he had reviled himself, relented and returned the thirty silver coins to the chief priests and elders saying, "I have sinned because I betrayed an innocent man." They replied, "Do you think we care?" Judas threw the money on the floor of the temple, and left to hang himself. The chief priests took the money, declaring that it was unlawful to place blood money into the treasury, so they decided to buy a field owned by a potter, and use the field as a graveyard for strangers. The graveyard was known thereafter as the field of blood. Thus, the Old Testament prophecy (ZEC 11:12–13) was fulfilled which stated, "They took the thirty silver coins, the price of Him that was valued, and bought the potter's field."

- LUK 2:4–5 ~ Joseph took his pregnant wife Mary from the city of Nazareth in Galilee to the city of David which is called Bethlehem, because he was a descendant of David; it was there that he and his family were to be taxed by the Romans.

- LUK 24:46–48 ~ Jesus taught, "It was written that Messiah would suffer, but would rise from the dead in three days. It was written that He would preach repentance and forgiveness of sins among all nations, beginning with Jerusalem. You are witnesses of these things."

- JOH 1:51 ~ Jesus said, "Truly I tell you, from now on you will see the angels of God ascending and descending upon the Son of man." (see GEN 28:12)

- JOH 7:41–43 ~ Some people said, "He is the Christ," while others said, "Will the Christ come from Galilee?" Others replied, "Did the scriptures not tell us that God's Messiah would be a descendant of David and be born in Bethlehem, the city of David?" So, there was division among them concerning Jesus.

- JOH 12:14–15 ~ Jesus sat on the young donkey just as it was written: Fear not daughter of Zion, for here comes your king, riding on a donkey's colt (ZEC 9:9–10).

- ACT 1:9–11~ While He spoke these things, Jesus ascended above the clouds. As they stared into heaven two angels appeared with them and said, "Men of Galilee, why do you gaze into heaven. Jesus, who you just saw ascend into heaven, will return the very same way."

- ACT 1:16–20 ~ Peter told the people, "The scriptures written by David had to be fulfilled concerning Judas who betrayed Jesus. Judas was with us and was part of this ministry. The reward for his sin was used to buy a field, and that field is called the Field of Blood. In Psalms it was written that his place in this ministry would become vacant and would have to be filled by another." (see PSA 41:9–10; ZEC 11:12–13)

- GAL 3:16 ~ God made His promises concerning Christ to Abraham and his descendants.

- REV 5:5 ~ One of the elders said, "Look, the Lion from the tribe of Judah the descendant of David; He has prevailed to open the book and loosen the seven seals which bind it."

This is the abridged version of Messiah's biography. The Old and the New Testaments proclaim His birth, life, death, and resurrection leaving no doubt that Jesus Christ came and will come again in glory to bring believers with Him into heaven. He is the alpha and omega (REV 1:8), the beginning and the end, who we worship and praise with the Father and the Holy Spirit.

Heavenly Father, we thank you for Jesus and we thank you for living proof that He is the Christ, Messiah, Savior, Redeemer, King of kings, and Lord of lords. Let all who seek Messiah find Him through the truth of your Word. You have given us the biography of your only begotten Son in the New Testament, and the history of your people and the prophecy of Christ's coming validates it all in the Old Testament. He lived the Word because He is the Word, and your Holy Spirit has communicated it to the whole of humanity. Thus, in the name of Christ, we pray, Amen.

May 17

Dinosaur Day is an unofficial holiday for celebrating reptiles that roamed the earth during the Mesozoic era of geologic history (Triassic, Jurassic, and Cretaceous periods). This holiday is repeated on June 1, so you have two dinosaur days to choose from. Dinosaur bones are found all across the globe, though the earliest discoveries were merely three to four hundred years ago. Before then, few would have recognized a dinosaur bone. Now people are hunting bones for profit like prospectors searching for gold; some collections and excavations fetch a pretty penny. Enough bones from a Tyrannosaurus Rex can make a person a millionaire. Though paleontology is a fairly recent science, hundreds of different dinosaurs have been unearthed. Fossils are generally petrified impressions of bones; but some animal bones, mostly from the Cenozoic period like the woolly mammoth, have yielded traces of DNA. When determining the dates of various geologic columns, the science is speculative, because they are determined by the types of fossils found. This is an inaccurate way of dating prehistoric relics and fossils, especially given the varying speeds at which layers of sediment can be deposited. I will leave it to the reader to study this further, rather than get into the nuts and bolts of paleontology and geology. One thing we know, there were no known animal species until the Cambrian era when occurred an explosion of phyla. Lifeforms from the Precambrian era, which represents over three-fourths of geologic time, were microscopic organisms, some multicellular.

To celebrate Dinosaur Day, you might take your family to the library and borrow some books on dinosaurs, or go to a museum. There are national parks and dinosaur parks in various locations if you like to travel and hike. Or just watch dinosaur movies all night. Who is not fascinated by dinosaurs? I had a formidable toy dinosaur collection as a child, as well as quite a number of fossils that I found in southwest Texas and New Mexico.

What do dinosaurs have to do with the Bible? Is there any evidence of dinosaurs in the Bible? The answers to these questions can be found in the Old Testament, where unique reptilian animal types are described; oftentimes these humongous lizards are referred to as dragons. The Bible speaks of a sea monster called leviathan and a land monster called behemoth. The prophet Job described both of these beasts in great detail. One is described as having scales and breathing fire. These accounts are often dismissed as mythical, but the amount of detail is compelling.

- JOB 40:15–24 ~ Behold the behemoth that I made along with humans; it eats grass like an ox. But there is strength in its loins and power in its belly. Its tail swings like a cedar tree; the sinews of its thighs are wrapped tightly. Its bones are hard as brass with limbs like iron. It ranks among the great works of God. Who but God can approach it with a sword? It lies under shady trees in the marsh, concealed among the reeds and ferns. Watch it drink up a river; it could draw the Jordan into its mouth. It can neither be subdued by its eyes nor snared by its nose.

- JOB 41:1–34 ~ Can you snag leviathan with a hook, or catch its tongue on a line? Can you run a rope through its nose or pierce its jaw with a hook? Will it plead for mercy or speak softly to you? Will it make a bargain with you to be your servant for life? Can you make it a pet like a bird, or give it to your daughters to play with? Will your companions make a banquet of it, or chop it up and distribute it among the merchants? Can you pierce its skin with harpoons or its head with fishing spears? If you lay a hand on it, you will not forget the battle, and you will never try it again. Any hope of overcoming it is false. You will be overwhelmed at the sight of it. Nobody is so fierce that they dare stir it. Who can remove its outer coat or penetrate its double armor? Who can open its mouth with terrible teeth all around? The rows of scales on its back are its pride, shut tightly together as a seal so that no air can come between them; they are stuck so tightly they cannot be parted. It snorts out burning lights; sparks of fire shoot from its mouth while smoke pours out of its nostrils, like a boiling pot steaming over burning reeds.

Its breath kindles coals when the flame comes out of its mouth. Its neck is strong and fear goes before it. The folds of its flesh are joined together and cannot be moved. Its belly is as hard as a millstone. When it rises up, the mighty are afraid; because of its thrashings, they flee. Though a sword reaches it, this avails nothing; nor does a spear, dart, or javelin. It breaks iron like straw, and bronze like rotting wood. An arrow does not scare it, nor slingshots or darts; it laughs at javelins. Its belly is like ceramic, leaving a trail in the mire and causing the deep to boil like a pot, turning the sea into a cauldron of ointment, and leaving a glimmering wake behind. One would think the deep had white hair. On earth there is nothing like it, a creature without fear. It puts down the proud for it reigns over them.

- PSA 74:12–14 ~ God is my King of the ages, bringing salvation to the earth. You divided the sea with your strength and broke the heads of the dragons in the waters. You smashed the head of leviathan into pieces, and gave his meat to the creatures of the wilderness.

- ISA 27:1 ~ On that day, the Lord with His mighty sword will punish leviathan the wicked serpent, and He will kill the dragon that lives in the sea.

- JER 51:34, 37 ~ Nebuchadnezzar, king of Babylon has devoured me (Israel); he has crushed me like a broken jar. He has swallowed me up like a dragon, filling his belly with our delicacies and then vomiting us out. Babylon will become a heap of ruins, where only dragons can dwell; an astonishment, a place of derision.

- MIC 1:6–8 ~ God will make Samaria a heap of ruins because of their idols. Their land will be desolate. It will wail and howl as a madman running naked, like the howling of dragons and the mourning of owls.

- MAL 1:3 ~ I hated Esau, and laid waste his mountains and heritage and gave it to the dragons of the wilderness.

Okay, so the Bible does talk about giant reptiles on land and in the water. Were these dinosaurs? Well, gigantic animals with scales, armor, and a tail as big as a tree trunk—yeah, that sounds like a dinosaur. People that refute this argument often say that the word dinosaur does not appear in the Bible, which is true, because they weren't called dinosaurs (translated as "terrible lizard") until the 1800s; they were called dragons in the Bible and in ancient literature. So, if there were dinosaurs in the Bible what happened to them? Did they die in the flood or just starve to death? You will not find that answer in the Bible; however, science would suggest that they were destroyed by a cataclysmic event, maybe a meteor strike, or they starved, or both.

The devil and his demons are also referred to as dragons in many passages in the Old Testament (DEU 32:33; PSA 44:19–20; JER 9:11; JER 10:22; JER 49:33; JER 51:37); in fact, all occurrences of the word "dragon" in the New Testament are found in Revelation and refer to Satan, who is also called a serpent or snake throughout the Bible. I guess this is an appropriate analogy, to compare Satan to a terrible cold-blooded monstrosity.

- JER 9:11 ~ I will turn Jerusalem into ruins, and a den of dragons; all the cities of Judah will be desolate and uninhabited.

Heavenly Father, we thank you for uncovering mysteries in the Bible, as well as answers to many dilemmas, if we simply would search your Word. Help us to intently seek the truth in your book of scripture and your book of nature. We know if we seek your truth we will find it, as long as we are persistent in our search; lead us to the right passages wherein we will find answers, truth, and wisdom. Show us where to search to verify the truth. Especially, lead us so we can show others the truth that sets people free. May we all believe and know the truth; implant it into our hearts, through faith in Christ who is our Lord. In His name we pray, Amen.

May 18

Armed Forces Day was inaugurated in 1949 to consolidate existing commemorative days for the Army, Navy, and Air Force. On the third Saturday in May, a full week of admiration for those who serve in the military begins: Army, Air Force, Navy, Marine Corps, and Coast Guard. Not only do we honor these institutions but also the men and women who honor us through their military service. The USA needs a strong military if we are to deter rogue nations from attacking us or our allies. Service members get the best training and equipment, and that equates to winning wars. This is the philosophy of peace through strength held by previous presidents. The strategy worked, since nobody wanted to mess with the USA. When our foes detect weakness, this is when they strike. We must be ready to strike back hard and fast at any given time.

- NUM 1:3, 18–22; NUM 26:2–4 ~ Men past the age of twenty were eligible for going to war. Each of the twelve tribes were separated into divisions, and had marching orders by clan whenever the Israelites traveled.

- DEU 20:1, 4 ~ When you go into battle against your enemies, and you see horses and chariots, and you realize you are outnumbered, do not be afraid. For the Lord your God is with you. He is the same one who rescued you out of Egypt. He goes with you to fight for you and to save you.

- PSA 27:3 ~ Though an army encamps against me, my heart will not fear; though war rises against me, I will remain confident.

- PRO 21:31 ~ The horse is prepared for the day of battle, but safety is from the Lord.

- ECC 3:8 ~ There is a time to love and a time to hate; a time for war and a time for peace.

- JOE 3:9–10, 14 ~ Go, tell the Gentiles to prepare for war. Wake the mighty warriors and tell them to come. Beat your plowshares into swords and your pruning hooks into spears. Let the weak say, "I am strong." Multitudes are gathered in the valley of decision, for the day of the Lord is approaching.

Today's holiday is celebrated with parades, picnics, festivals, speakers, and often equipment demonstrations at various military installations. Depending on the type of specialty, an installation may sponsor all kinds of displays and booths, with service members willing to answer questions and give presentations. I used to go with my friends and we would take our kids to the local army post where there was a lot to see and do; the kids loved it. It is useful to learn about the armed forces and their missions.

The Bible is an excellent source of military history. In fact, some of the tactics employed during Old Testament times have been utilized in recent wars and battles. Here are some of the great military strategists and victories in the Bible: Deborah outsmarted and defeated the Canaanite commanders (JDG 4—5); with an inferior army, Gideon confused and defeated the Midianites (JDG 6—8); Joshua drove various pagan tribes and kings out of Palestine (JOS 5—12); David tricked and outmaneuvered the Philistines for decades (1 SA; 2 SA).

- PSA 144:1–2 ~ Blessed is the Lord my strength, who teaches my hands to make war and my fingers to fight. He is my goodness and my fortress; my high tower and my deliverer; my shield in whom I trust; who subdues the people before me.

- HEB 11:32–40 ~ What more can I say about the powers of faith? I could tell you about great judges like Gideon, Barrack, Samson, and Jephthah, and about great kings like David and Solomon, and about the prophets. Through faith, these people subdued kingdoms, administered justice, enforced treaties, shut the mouth of lions, quenched fires, and escaped certain death.

They were weak but were made strong, and they fought valiantly in battle, routing even the greatest of armies. They raised the dead. They endured torture, refusing to renounce God as a condition for their release. They were mocked, beaten, chained, and imprisoned. They were stoned and beheaded. They wandered the wilderness in shaggy clothes, destitute, tormented, and afflicted. Although their life on earth was full of strife, they awaited their deliverance, as we also must do until God makes us perfect in His sight.

It is a dreadful thing to fight conventional wars between nations. Obviously, a lot of planning goes into such engagements. It is quite another thing to engage in a spiritual war. The tactics and doctrine are entirely different, as is the enemy and their tactics. To fight such a war requires considerable training, equipment, and preparation, to include donning the armor of God and carrying the shield of faith as defense systems, and wielding the sword of the Spirit as an offensive weapon. To be a Christian soldier you will need to know your enemy and your equipment; you will need to know the strategy and the objective. To prepare for duty, study God's Word which is your training manual and your mission field manual.

- ISA 59:17 ~ He put on righteousness as a breastplate, and a helmet of salvation on his head; he put on garments of vengeance for clothing, and wrapped himself in zeal as a cloak.

- 2 CO 10:3–5 ~ Although we are human flesh and blood, we do not make war with flesh and blood. For the weapons we use are not of this world, because we have the Spirit on our side to bring down the strongholds of the enemy. We break down the arguments and the influences of those high and mighty people who stand against God; we take captive human thoughts, making them obedient to Jesus Christ.

- EPH 6:10–17 ~ Be strong in the Lord and in the power of his might. Put on the whole armor of God so that you will be prepared to stand against the trickery of Satan. For we are not wrestling against flesh and blood, but against principalities, powers, rulers of darkness in this world, and wickedness in high places. Wear this armor so that you can withstand that day of evil, and remain standing when it is over. Gird your loins with truth and put on the breastplate of righteousness. Put on the shoes of the gospel of peace; and take with you the shield of faith which will repel the fiery darts of the wicked. Don the helmet of salvation and arm yourself with the sword of the Spirit which is the Word of God.

Lord God in Heaven, we pray for our armed forces, that they may be strong and smart whenever they are deployed, and ready for every contingency. Let them especially be strong in the power of your Spirit. Whenever they are called to war, let it be for a worthy cause, one that will be fought with your angels alongside them and your Spirit guiding them. Please bestow integrity, diplomacy, and resolve upon our leaders, ensuring they do not prompt a war or enter a conflict for the wrong reasons. If we stay connected to you Lord, we will know the right thing to do when the time comes; help our military and their leaders to remember that. Let them not act too hastily or too hesitantly, always seeking your counsel before choosing a course of action. And if it is necessary for us to go to war, help us to have a plan to win and leave, and not allow the conflict to drag on for years. If we need to move into the battlefield and face the enemy, let us dispatch the enemy expediently and then get out the same way. Additionally, Lord you know we fight the forces of evil in the world every day, and they are not always human. Help people of God to be well-trained in the art of spiritual warfare, so that we can meet the enemies of darkness, and crush them; and after the dust settles to remain standing on solid ground. These things we humbly ask of you as soldiers of Christ, in whose name we pray, Amen.

May 19

Pentecost Sunday commemorates the day the apostles preached the Gospel in foreign tongues, a week after Jesus had ascended into heaven. The event represents an anointing by the Holy Spirit. After his sermon on Pentecost Sunday, Peter and the apostles baptized everyone who wanted to receive the Holy Spirit; over three thousand souls were baptized. Pentecost Sunday is a Christian observance which occurs the seventh Sunday after Easter.

Jewish Pentecost (*Shavuot*) is the Feast of Weeks and occurs in the month of Sivan on the sixth and seventh days. It is fifty days after the feast of Passover: seven sabbaths plus one day. The Jewish harvest season would begin around Passover. Then they would give an offering on the Feast of First Fruits, and close the season around Pentecost, when another offering was given. Both the Jewish and Christian Pentecost seasons occur around the same time.

- EXO 34:22 ~ You will celebrate the Feast of Weeks, that is the first fruits of the wheat harvest, and the Feast of Ingathering at the end of the year.

- LEV 23:10–16 ~ The fourteenth day of the first month is Passover, followed by seven days of Unleavened Bread. Count seven weeks and offer a sacrifice on the fiftieth day which is Pentecost.

- NUM 28:26–31 ~ You will do no work, you will have a holy convocation, and you will sacrifice a new burnt offering of animals and grain.

- DEU 16:10 ~ Celebrate the Feast of Weeks to the Lord your God with a tribute, a freewill offering from your hand, given to the Lord in accordance with how He has blessed you.

- JOE 2:28–32 ~ I will pour out my Spirit on humankind. Your sons and daughters will prophesy and see visions; your old men will dream dreams. There will be wonders in the sky and on earth: blood, fire, and columns of smoke.

- JOH 14:26 ~ Jesus said, "The Comforter, the Holy Spirit, whom the Father will send in my name, will remind you of all the things I have taught you."

- ACT 1:8 ~ Jesus said, "You will receive power when the Holy Spirit comes upon you, and you will be my witnesses in Jerusalem, Judea, Samaria, and all the ends of the earth."

- ACT 2:1–6, 16 ~ And when the day of Pentecost had come, they were joined with one accord in one place. Suddenly a rushing noise came from heaven sounding like a mighty wind; it filled the house where they were sitting. Next appeared cloven tongues of fire, sitting upon each of the evangelists' heads. They were filled with the Holy Spirit and began to speak in other languages, as the Spirit directed them. There were many Jews living in Jerusalem, devout men from every nation. When the news spread, they came to see and were amazed, because everyone heard the Word being spoken in his or her native tongue. This event was spoken of by the prophet Joel.

- ACT 2:38–41 ~ Peter said, "Repent and be baptized every one of you, in the name of Jesus Christ for the remission of sins, and you will receive the gift of the Holy Spirit. This promise pertains to you, to your children, and to people everywhere: to whomever the Lord calls." Those who gladly listened to Peter's testimony were baptized, numbering about three thousand souls.

Father, we pray for the anointing by your Holy Spirit; let us be filled so that we can serve you and humankind with our gifts. Help us to share the truth and speak the truth which you have shown to us through your Word by your Spirit and your Son, in whose name we pray, Amen.

May 20

Flower Day is an unofficial holiday celebrated annually with flowers. May 20 is among many different dates in which Flower Day is observed; it depends on the city, state, and country, but most are during springtime when flowers are in full bloom (SOS 2:10–13). Flowers have many uses aside from their beauty and their sweet aroma; they are used in medicine, as food or in tea, to decorate a church or home, to bring a smile to a loved one, and to augment certain ceremonies like weddings and funerals. They take considerable care to grow and nurture, even after they have been clipped for display. Indeed, everything that lives on God's earth needs love and nurturing.

Oftentimes, a flower is compared to a person in the Bible. It sprouts, grows, flourishes, and then either withers or is cut down. The number of days it lasts is unknown; and once gone, it does not return. And the place it once stood becomes empty. Sometimes the word flower is used to imply innocence or virginity, and other times it refers to menstruation.

- JOB 14:1–2 ~ Man, who is born of a woman, has few days that are full of trouble. He shoots forth like a flower and is cut down; he runs as a shadow that ceases to continue.

- PSA 103:15–16 ~ Regarding man, his days are as grass; like a flower in the field, he flourishes. But when the wind blows over it, it is gone; and the place where it grew is unknown.

- ISA 40:5–8 ~ The glory of the Lord will be revealed, and all flesh will see it together; for the Lord has spoken it. A voice said, "Cry out." I said, "About what?" "All people are as grass, and faithfulness as a flower in the field. The grass withers and the flower fades, because the Spirit of the Lord blows upon it. Surely the people are grass. Grass withers and flowers fade, but the Word of God stands forever."

- MAT 6:25–34 ~ Jesus taught, "Do not worry about your life, what you will eat or drink, or what you will wear. Is there not more to life than food and clothing? Look at the birds; they do not sow or reap, or gather food into the barn, yet our heavenly Father feeds them. Are people not more important than birds? Consider the lilies of the field, they grow just fine yet they do not work; however, King Solomon in all his glory was not clothed in such beauty. If God cares for the birds and the flowers, will He not care for you even more? Therefore, do not worry about things such as food and clothing, for your heavenly Father knows you need these things. Instead, seek first the kingdom of God and His righteousness, and everything else you need will be yours. Do not be anxious about tomorrow, because tomorrow will take care of itself. Each day has enough problems to face without adding more."

- JAM 1:10–11 ~ The rich are made low, as the flower in the grass passes away. As soon as the sun has risen with its burning heat, the grass withers and the flower falls; and the grace of its presence dies with it. So will a rich man fade away with his ways.

- 1 PE 1:24–25 ~ All flesh is as grass, and the glory of man is as a flower. The grass withers and the flower falls. But the Word of the Lord endures forever, and this is the Word which by the Gospel is preached to you.

Heavenly Father, you nurture us and care for us, and we rarely show our appreciation. We thank you sincerely, for without you we would perish; we would wilt and fade away like a beautiful flower. But you promised if we seek you, your righteousness, and your kingdom, we would not only receive everything we need to sustain our bodies and lives, we also would receive an inheritance in your kingdom. Again, we thank you Father. And we thank you, Holy Spirit for preserving us in faith and truth. Thank you, Jesus, for without you we would die and wither away, never to live again. We pray in your name that we may bloom as flowers, Amen.

May 21

World Meditation Day is another unofficial holiday observed on this day because it has received a lot of attention from various organizations which promote mindfulness through meditation. Meditation has been proven to be effective in reducing anxiety and stress; it also can facilitate concentration with fewer distractions. This day competes with a similar observance on New Years' Eve known as World Peace Meditation Day; if you are not the partying type, you might try meditation instead. Meditation is mostly a mental exercise, although it also can be applied in the spiritual sense. For example, read a piece of scripture and study it in light of similar scriptures, and then go to a quiet place, get comfortable, and meditate on those scriptures in prayerful communion with God. The daily devotions provided in this book are an opportunity to meditate on God's Word, followed by prayer, which is essentially another form of meditation. Both activities are spiritually uplifting and mentally engaging.

If you investigate meditation, you will find sources suggesting it was introduced to the western world via eastern philosophies such as Hinduism and Buddhism. Actually, all religions have a meditative component to them, but not all have a spiritual component to them. Thus, there are different types of meditation depending on your religious foundation and the reasons why you meditate. Certainly, in a deep state of concentration, conceptualizing an eternal and loving God can help you reach a spiritual connection. Any spiritual connection which is not of God can become an invitation to the demonic realm.

Meditation is mentioned many times in the Bible, mostly concerning God's words, laws, will, and wonders. David spoke of meditation often in the book of Psalms. Meditate on these scriptures and discover what the authors of the Bible were meditating and praying about.

- GEN 24:63 ~ At evening, Isaac went out to meditate in the field. When he looked up, he saw camels coming. When Rebekah looked up, she saw Isaac, and she dismounted her camel. [This is when Isaac and Rebekah met for the first time.]

- JOS 1:7–8 ~ God said, "Be strong and courageous, so that you are able to observe the laws which Moses commanded of you. Do not turn to the right or to the left, and you will prosper wherever you go. This book of the Law must not depart from your speech, and you must meditate on my words every day and night, and live according to all that is written therein. Then I will make you prosperous and you will be successful."

- PSA 1:1–5 ~ Blessed is the person that does not walk in the counsel of the ungodly, or stand among sinners, or sit in the seat of the scornful. Blessed is the person whose delight is in God's Law, for that person meditates on God's Law every day and night. Such a person will be like a tree planted by flowing streams of water, bearing good fruit in season, with leaves that never wither. Whatever he or she does will prosper. But the ungodly are not so; they are like the chaff that the wind blows away. Therefore, the wicked will not stand with the just, and sinners will not assemble with the righteous. For God watches over the ways of righteous people, but the ways of the wicked will perish.

- PSA 5:1–2 ~ Listen to my words oh Lord, and consider my meditation. Respond to my voice when I cry, my King and my God, for only to you do I pray.

- PSA 19:13–14 ~ Keep your servant from shameless sins; do not let them have dominion over me. Then I will be upright, and innocent of the great transgression. Let the words of my mouth and the meditation of my heart be acceptable to you oh Lord.

- PSA 49:3 ~ My mouth will speak wisdom and the meditation of my heart will be for understanding.

- PSA 77:6, 12, 14 ~ I remember my song during the night when I commune with my own heart, and my spirit searches diligently. I will meditate on your works and speak of them. You are the God who does wondrous things; you have declared your strength among the people.

- PSA 104:33–34 ~ I will sing to the Lord as long as I live; I will sing praises to Him every day. My meditation of Him will be sweet, and I will be glad in the Lord.

- PSA 119:15, 18, 27, 33 ~ I will meditate on your precepts, and respect your ways. Open my eyes so I can see wondrous things from your Law. Make me understand the way of your precepts and I will speak of your wondrous works. Teach me your statutes and I will keep them until the end.

- PSA 119:97–99 ~ How I love your Law; I meditate on it daily. Through your commandments I have been made wiser than my enemies who follow me wherever I go. I have more understanding than my teachers, for your testimonies are what I meditate on.

- LUK 21:14–15 ~ Jesus said, "You will not need to meditate before answering, for I will give you the words and the wisdom, which your opponents will not be able to contradict or resist."

- ACT 1:14 ~ All of them continued with one accord in prayer and meditation.

- 1 TI 4:14–15 ~ Do not neglect the gift within you which was given to you by prophecy and the laying of hands by the elders. Meditate on these things, and submit entirely to them, so your progress will be evident to everybody.

Clearly, David meditated on God's Law often, largely because he had been guilty of some heinous crimes, to include adultery and murder. But God forgave David, and the famous king cleaned up his act, which anybody can, if they put sufficient effort into godly changes that work. But we still need the salvation of Christ, no matter how hard we work at being righteous. Consider meditating on the righteousness of Jesus, and you will see what a fantastic gift He gives us in exchange for our sins, at the moment He said, "It is finished" (JOH 19:28–30).

As I mentioned previously, meditation can improve your emotional state of mind. Meditation is a proven stress reliever. I often taught clients how to meditate using progressive relaxation to calm the anxiety, breathing exercises to slow the system down which affords additional relaxation, and suggested imagery to conjure visual, auditory and other sensory experiences in order to escape the outside world and explore inside the mind. Where a person goes inside their mind is up to them. Try to progressively delve deeper into your unconscious database as you search your memory banks with greater concentration. There is a lot of powerful knowledge there. The above techniques can be self-taught (Barber, 2020b), but it helps to have a guide. Your counselor or coach will walk you through the process to get you started. Where you journey from there will be in accordance with your personal needs and spiritual objectives. Meditation is a means of gaining control over thoughts, which is the essence of mindfulness. Treatment plans in the behavioral health field should include mindfulness as a goal of therapy.

Father, you taught us right from wrong by placing a conscience into our soul, so we might know in advance when we are about to disobey you; yet we cannot seem to stop. But we have to try, for faith without action is no faith at all. Bolster our faith, we pray, that we may fight the temptation more vigorously, rather than let it have its way. We know our salvation will not be earned by anything we could ever do, but we still want to do better, and with your Holy Spirit reminding us, we can be mindful of what we are about to say or do. Thank you that we can come to you in prayer and ask these things, and meditate with you about your will and your laws, finding our path which you will reveal if we stay focused on Jesus Christ. In His name, Amen.

May 22

National Maritime Day was declared by Congress in 1933, dedicating this day to the contributions of the maritime industry to our national prosperity. This day commemorates the crossing from the USA to England on the steamship *Savannah* in 1819. People tend to forget that merchant marines served in World Wars I and II. Some 250,000 mariners assisted in the second world war alone; thousands died, hundreds were taken captive, and over eight hundred merchant ships were sunk by the enemy. The sinking of merchant and passenger vessels was a major consideration when the US entered the first world war. They shipped supplies, personnel, and munitions into battle zones, returning for more at great peril to themselves and their ships. These heroes were an important arm of our military interventions in Europe. In times of peace, the demand for import and export support services never lets up, and for many it is a job that takes them to numerous international ports of call. Many such ports will have events, demonstrations, and entertainment on this day. Things to do in recognition of the merchant marines and the maritime industry include touring ships from a century ago, or going to a maritime museum. Maybe take the family on a boat ride, or a boat tour around the nearest port. Take time to learn about the merchant marines; it is a vocation that preceded the use of ships as weapons of war.

During Biblical times, merchants mostly transported goods cross-country on camels (GEN 37:25). Shipping items by sea became vastly important as it was faster and more economical. Shipping channels were understood by the ancients, whereby safe passage across certain sea lanes had been established. The Phoenicians were builders of ships and their port cities of Tyre and Sidon were booming. Ships sailing through the straits of Gibraltar (e.g., Tarshish) were filled with exports of their goods. King Solomon capitalized on the shipping of goods by sea (1 KI 9:26–28; 1 KI 10:10–11, 22). Solomon commissioned king Hiram of Tyre to build his navy and soon he had a fleet of ships, establishing trade and alliances with foreign governments. During the peak of his empire, Solomon received a bounty of 666 talents of gold every year, not including profits from merchants and traders (1 KI 10:14; 2 CH 9:13).

- GEN 49:13 ~ Zebulun (one of the twelve tribes of Israel) will settle along the seashore bordering Sidon, and become a safe haven for shipping.

- 2 SA 22:16; PSA 18:15 ~ The channels of the sea appeared and the foundations of the world were uncovered at the rebuke of the Lord and with a blast of breath from His nostrils.

- 1 KI 10:11–12; 2 CH 9:10–11 ~ The navy of Hiram brought gold from Ophir, as well as plenty of hardwood trees and precious stones.

- PSA 8:6–8; PSA 77:19 ~ God gave humankind dominion over the works of His hand, including the beasts of the field, the fowl in the air, and the fish of the sea and everything that passes through the paths of the seas. His path led across the sea through the pathways of mighty waters, though His footprints could not be seen.

- PSA 107:22–24 ~ Let them offer sacrifices of thanksgiving and declare the works of the Lord with rejoicing, those who go down to the sea in ships and do business on the great waters. They get to see the works of the Lord and the wonders of the deep.

- PRO 30:18–19 ~ There are four things that are amazing: the flight of an eagle, the slithering of a snake, the sailing of a ship, and the love between a young man and woman.

- PRO 31:14 ~ A good wife is like merchant ships bringing food from afar.

- ISA 23:1–3 ~ Isaiah prophesied against the port cities of Phoenicia (Tyre and Sidon): Tyre is destroyed. The ships of Tarshish moan, for there is no port or harbor. From the island of Cyprus

MAY

word has spread. Remain silent, inhabitants of the islands and merchants of Sidon, who once was the marketplace of nations.

- EZE 27:1–3, 12, 25–27, 36 ~ Ezekiel prophesied against Tyre: Tarshish did much business with you because of your great abundance of goods, exchanging precious metals for your merchandise. The ships of Tarshish carried your goods and were filled with your heavy cargo; you were once the glory of the seas. Your oarsmen will take you out to the high seas and the east wind will break you into pieces, and everything and everyone on board will be lost. The merchants among the people will sneer at you, and your horrible end.

- REV 18:10–11 ~ They will stand afar off for fear of her torment, when that great and mighty city of Babylon falls; for in one hour your judgment will come. And the merchants of the earth will weep and mourn over her, for nobody will buy their merchandise again.

The Bible teaches that we never mix business with our church life. For example, no work was to be done on the Sabbath as it was dedicated to God's work, and not our own work. This is not to say that we cannot sell our goods to the church, but that we do not turn our church into a profit seeking business. Churches enjoy nonprofit status to avoid the tax. God's church on earth regards profit as souls being won for Christ, reaping spiritual profits versus material. Jesus regarded material things expendable, especially when compared to spiritual riches.

- MAT 13:45–48 ~ Jesus told a parable about the kingdom of heaven: The kingdom of heaven can be compared to a great pearl for which the merchant sold everything he had to purchase it. The kingdom of heaven is like a big net that catches all varieties of fish. The good fish are saved and the bad fish are thrown in the trash.

- JOH 2:14–22 ~ Jesus drove the merchants out of the temple. The Jews asked Jesus to show them a sign to verify that He had the authority to disrupt the temple merchants. Jesus replied, "Destroy this temple and I will raise it in three days." They exclaimed, "It took forty-six years to build this temple, how can you rebuild it in three days?" But Jesus was talking about the temple of His body. The disciples remembered this when Jesus's own prophecy had become fulfilled, proving that the scriptures and the words of Jesus were true.

- REV 18:2–3 ~ With a mighty voice the angel shouted, "Babylon the great has fallen, fallen. It has become the habitation of devils and every foul spirit, like a cage for unclean and hateful birds. All nations have drunk the wine of the wrath of her fornication, kings of the earth have committed fornication with her, and merchants have become rich through the excess of her luxuries."

Clearly, maritime trafficking of merchandise has been around since man learned to build boats. And who was the greatest boat builder ever? Well, Noah of course (read GEN 6—8). He built the largest known wooden ship ever, with three levels, built in accordance with God's exact specifications. Anything larger in length, width, or height likely would not have been seaworthy. The size of the ark was 300 x 50 x 30 cubits; that would be 450 x 75 x 45 feet (the estimated length of a cubit was eighteen inches, the distance from the elbow to the tip of the middle finger). Imagine the amount of cargo Noah's ship held, in addition to the animals and his family. Noah was five hundred years old when he began building the ark which took one hundred years to finish. He lived three hundred more years, dying at age nine hundred fifty (GEN 9:28–29).

Father, your creations are amazing. You have gifted us with the knowledge and ability to subdue this earth, including its mighty oceans and seas. Thank you for mariners and their contributions to our nation which are often taken for granted; protect them, their ships, and their cargo. We pray for continued prosperity and godliness in our nation. In Jesus's name, Amen.

May 23

Bank Robbers Bonnie and Clyde Met Their Doom at the hands of Texas Ranger Mike Hamer and his police posse. Rarely referred to by their surnames Parker and Barrow, these bank robbers went on a killing spree until finally cornered in Louisiana. The couple became Great Depression folk heroes as they eluded law enforcement from 1932–1934, leaving over a dozen dead cops and civilians. They were one of many gangs that haunted the government and private citizenry with their violence and crooked dealings. The gangsters violated as many commandments as they could in a single day, which is basically the epitome of pure evil. You might compare them to the cartels of our day, who traffic humans, sex slaves, drugs, terrorism, and all forms of vice. Humans have contended with these subhuman fools throughout our history, beginning with the first family, when out of jealousy, Cain murdered his brother Abel.

Today's observance is not meant for celebrating any friends of Satan or comparing career criminals to heroes. Theirs is a dark and dreary path, a downhill highway to fire and brimstone. Societies have law enforcement precisely because of people like that, as recognized by God Himself to be a basic human need for government (ROM 13:3–5). But when government becomes the stealers, killers, fornicators, liars, and coveters, then we are really in trouble. Such is the fate of communism and all other forms of tyranny and subjugation. This is what the evil ones live for; this is why they must be denied all public access via death or dungeon.

If you do anything today to observe this historical event, it might be to thank the men and women who have the guts to face this kind of evil and remove it, people like Mike Hamer. With out-of-control crime occurring here and worldwide, it makes you wonder who will stand up to the corruption in government, the media, big business, and many of our institutions. Lord knows whatever earthly delights these maniacs derive from of their debauchery and human abuse, it will be short lived, after which is permanent fire.

Consider the corruption of Jesus's time. First, they had a tyrannical and brutal empire pushing them around, and second, they had equally corrupt Jewish leadership. Jesus and His cousin John likened them to snakes and hypocrites, calling them out to their faces. Elders of the church were behaving like gangsters. They were the spokespersons for Jewish Law, the Torah and Talmud; they became controlling political figures, persecuting people, even seeking the execution of those who spoke contrary to their narrative. Among those targeted were Jesus, John the baptizer, James, and Lazarus. Sound familiar? Not all Pharisees were bad however, because Nicodemus, Joseph of Arimathea, and the apostle Paul also had been members of the Jewish Sanhedrin.

- MAT 3:7–10; LUK 7:30 ~ John was baptizing people in the Jordan River when many of the Pharisees and Sadducees came to observe. John chastised them saying, "You snakes! Has anyone warned you of the judgement that awaits? You had better start bearing fruit worthy of repentance. You say to yourselves you have Abraham as your father. I assure you: God can produce children of Abraham from these stones. The ax is ready to strike at the roots; any tree that does not bear good fruit will be chopped down and burned in the fire." But the Pharisees rejected God's counsel and refused to be baptized.

- MAT 15:13–14 ~ Jesus said, "Every plant that has not been planted by my heavenly Father will be pulled up by the roots. Stay away from them, for they are like the blind leading the blind; and when the blind lead the blind, both fall into the ditch.

- MAT 23:1–9 ~ Jesus said, "The scribes and Pharisees tell you to do this and observe that; it is all right to obey them but do not imitate them, for they do not practice what they preach. They place heavy burdens on the people, but they themselves are not willing to lift a finger to help. Everything they do is for others to see. They love to be greeted in public. But do not call them

Teacher or Master, for you have but one Teacher and Master, Christ the Lord. And do not call them Father, because God in heaven is your Father."

- MAT 23:23–25 ~ Jesus said, "Woe to you teachers of the Law and Pharisees, all hypocrites. You tithe yet you neglect the more important matters of the law such as justice, mercy, and faith. You should have practiced the latter without neglecting the former. You are blind guides, who would strain at a gnat but swallow a camel. Woe to you hypocrites, for you make the outside appear clean while the inside is full of extortion and excess."

- MAT 27:62–66 ~ After the day of preparation, the chief priests and Pharisees came together appealing to Pilate, "Sir, we remember that deceiver said He was going to rise again in three days. Please command that the sepulcher be made secure until the third day, so his disciples cannot come by night and steal him away, and say to the people he arose from the dead. If that happens, the last error will be worse than the first." Pilate assured them, "You have your watch, now go your way; see that the sepulcher is made secure to your satisfaction." They left for the cemetery, and made the tomb secure by sealing the stone and posting a guard.

- LUK 18:14 ~ Those who exalt themselves will later be humbled, and those who humble themselves will later be exalted.

- LUK 20:46–47 ~ Jesus said, "Beware of the Pharisees. They enjoy wearing fancy robes, being greeted in the marketplace, sitting in the places of honor in church, and reserving the nicest rooms for their banquets. Yet they cheat widows out of their homes, and for a show, say long prayers. They will receive the greater damnation."

- JOH 11:43–53 ~ Jesus called Lazarus to come forth from the grave after being dead four days. And he came out alive, still wrapped in bandages. Many were astonished and believed; others left to tell the Pharisees. The chief priests and Pharisees met in private to discuss how to deal with this miracle worker, supposing they should do something before the Romans did. The high priest named Caiaphas spoke, "You know nothing at all; consider how expedient, if one man was to die for the people, in order that we keep our places and our nation." He was suggesting Jesus should die for them. From that day they plotted to have Him put to death.

- JOH 12:10–11 ~ Many of the Jews came to see Jesus and also Lazarus, whom He raised from the dead. Then the chief priests plotted to have Lazarus put to death as well, because Jesus was able to convert many Jews.

Aside from the corruption in the church, the Jews had one of the most ruthless and vicious empires of the world riding them all the time. The people prayed for their deliverer to come, and He did, but the Jews rejected Him because they were looking for someone to get the Romans off their backs. Few would realize that it was their sin keeping them in bondage, not the Romans; and it was Jesus who was setting them free. Many chose not to believe and remained subjects of Rome. They couldn't see what Jesus meant by being "truly free" (JOH 8:31–36).

Thank you, Father, for setting us free. We know you allow authorities to govern, and for good reason. We pray you would protect us from leaders and governments who abuse that authority, particularly those interested only in continuing their corrupt and evil ways to placate their warped personal whims and pleasures. Bless us with God-fearing leaders and officials who will respect their offices and the people they serve, with humbleness and uprightness. Help us to nominate spiritually strong men and women who will govern with integrity, enforce all laws, keep us safe, and ensure the security of our nation. Do not allow political operatives to punish people who are protecting us, while exalting the criminals as if they were victims. In Jesus's name, in whom our hope is secure, Amen.

May 24

John Wesley Established Methodism on this day in 1738 in a conference at Aldersgate Street England, when he experienced a revelation concerning the doctrine of grace through faith. During several discussions with men of God about the writings of Luther and other reformers, this doctrine became clear to Wesley, and so did his mission to spread the truth about the importance of faith. His views were dismissed by the Church of England so he decided to witness to people that had no church affiliation. He became a traveling evangelist, preaching in fields to crowds, converting many to this new branch of Protestantism. Wesley, an ordained Anglican priest, published his treatise on Methodist societies in 1743. He would continue to buck the Church of England, who denied his right to preach Methodism. Perhaps a more liberal form of intellectualism, the essential doctrines of the Christian faith were never abandoned and remain the core beliefs of the Methodist church. This denomination fared better across the Atlantic than it did in England. Wesley was the last in a long line of major Protestant reformers.

Perhaps the first reformer to make a difference in England was John Wycliffe, a Catholic priest who translated much of the Bible into English. He felt that anyone able to read could find answers for themselves in the Holy Bible, which is God's highest authority on Christianity. He began to take a stand against Catholic practices that were not supported in scripture, preaching his reformed views until his death in 1384.

Martin Luther, another Catholic priest, got Protestantism rolling when he tagged the church door at Wittenberg Germany on 10/31/1517 with his ninety-five theses disputing Roman Catholic positions. He became enemy number one to the Catholic leadership who tried to silence him and even eliminate him. But Luther escaped them and continued preaching; against his will, his followers began calling themselves Lutherans as his theology spread throughout Germany. Zwingli broke from Luther and took his reformed approach to Switzerland (1519); others veered away from his stance on baptism and formed the Anabaptists. Tyndale, like his predecessor Wycliffe, was a reformer and translator of the Bible into English from the original Hebrew and Greek. He was executed for heresy by the king of England in 1536. John Calvin took his reformed view to France, publishing his theological treatise on Calvinism in 1536. John Knox broke from the Catholic church and introduced Presbyterianism to his native Scotland in 1557.

To this day Protestants and Catholics still disagree about a few doctrines and traditions. But the essentials handed down in the early Christian church and at the Council of Nicaea are still followed by both factions. Anyone holding to these essential tenets are considered Christian, since they acknowledge the sixty-six canonical books of the Holy Bible. You might ask, what are the essential doctrines that all Christian denominations agree upon? If you understand them and believe, you are on your way to heaven (from Barber, 2020a)

Seek God and you will find Him everywhere: in the scriptures, in the creation, and in humanity for we are made in the likeness of God. The Bible is God's Word conveyed by the Holy Spirit; that Word became flesh and lived among us through Christ the Lord who is the very image of God in human form. Christians believe that the Bible is God-breathed, and that is why we call it holy. The Holy Bible is truth, and is therefore free of contradictions, because truth never changes just as God never changes. His words will remain true forever.

- DEU 4:29–31 ~ If you seek God with all your heart and soul you will find Him. If you are distressed, even in the latter times, turn to God and obey His commandments. God is merciful and He will never abandon you or destroy you; He will never forget the covenant He made with your forefathers.

- ISA 55:6–7 ~ Seek the Lord while He may be found; call upon Him while He is near. Let the wicked forsake their evil ways and their unrighteous thoughts, and return to the Lord; and He will have mercy on them and will pardon them abundantly.

- MAT 7:7 ~ Jesus taught: Ask and you will receive. Seek and you will find. Knock and the door will be opened.

- 2 TI 3:16 ~ All scripture is inspired by God. God's Word provides the doctrine of truth, refutes that which is false, and instructs all people in the ways of righteousness.

God expects us to do our best to obey His laws and to do His will as proof of our faith. We are saved by faith alone, though it should be evident in our actions. By faith we receive the grace of God, which is His undeserved favor given freely to everyone believing in His Son and trusting in His Word. Because God has given us a chance to have a personal relationship with Him, we should respond with prayer, worship, giving to others, and self-sacrifice. That is, we give ourselves to Him because He gave Himself for us; and because He loved us first, we are honored to love Him back and we are obliged to make a sincere attempt to be obedient by loving all people.

- EXO 20:3–17 ~ The Ten Commandments were given to Moses on our behalf by God Himself. 1. Do not worship or honor any gods but the Lord God Almighty; 2. Do not make graven images and do not bow down to or serve idols; 3. Do not take God's name in vain; 4. Remember the Sabbath and keep it holy (i.e., reserved for worshipping God); 5. Honor your father and mother; 6. Do not kill; 7. Do not commit adultery; 8. Do not steal; 9. Do not commit perjury or falsely accuse anyone; 10. Do not be envious or jealous of someone else, desiring what belongs to them (including their home, spouse, belongings, etc.).

- MAT 6:9–13 ~ Jesus taught us to pray: Our Father in heaven, your name is holy. Bring us to your kingdom. Let your will be done on earth as it is in heaven. Provide us our daily needs. Forgive our sins, as we forgive others who sin against us. Lead us away from temptation and deliver us from evil. For the kingdom, power, and glory are yours forever, Amen.

- MAT 22:37–40 ~ Jesus said, "Love the Lord your God with all your heart, mind, and soul: this is the first and greatest commandment. The second is like unto the first: Love your neighbor as yourself. All the laws and the prophets depend on these two commandments."

- ROM 8:4–6 ~ Live, not according to the flesh but according to the spirit. Those who live according to the flesh set their minds on evil, but those who live according to the spirit set their minds on God. To set the mind on flesh results in death, but to set the mind on God results in peace and life.

- 1 JO 4:11–12, 18–19 ~ Since God loved us, we should love one another. Although nobody has seen God, if we love each other God's love will live inside us and become perfected in us. There is no fear in love, but perfect love repels fear, because fear has torment. We love God because He loved us first; but you cannot love God and hate your neighbor. For how can you love someone you have not seen if you cannot love someone you have seen?

Salvation is a free gift through the atonement of Christ on the cross. He paid the price for our sin in full, and gives us His righteousness in return by simply accepting this gift. We cannot earn salvation by doing good deeds, only by the work Christ performed at Calvary. After the resurrection of Jesus, we will be brought back alive to a new life in paradise, with an inheritance that lasts forever. Without having our souls purified by the blood of Jesus we would never be allowed into heaven. But by faith we are justified, and by the Spirit we are sanctified, so we can enter into the kingdom of heaven pure, holy, and blameless with a glorified body free from sin.

- ISA 53:10–12 ~ God was pleased to bruise and grieve His Son, making His soul an offering for sin. God will prolong His days and God's pleasure will prosper in His hands. He will see the travail of His soul and be satisfied, and through knowledge of God's righteous servant many will be justified, for He will bear their iniquities. God will render to Him a position of greatness and the best of the spoils, because He poured out His soul unto death. Though numbered with the transgressors, He bore their sins, interceding for them.

- JOH 3:16–17 ~ Jesus said, "God loved the world so much that He sacrificed His only Son, so that anyone could believe in Him and not die, but live forever. For God sent His only Son into the world to save it not to condemn it."

- ROM 3:23; ROM 6:23 ~ Everyone has sinned and come short of God's glory. The risk of sin is death. But God's gift of eternal life is available to all through Jesus Christ our Lord.

- 1 PE 1:18–22 ~ You are not redeemed with corruptible things like gold or silver, you are redeemed with the precious blood of Christ, who was like a lamb without blemish or spots. He, who was ordained before the foundation of the world, was made manifest in these past days just for you. Believe in Him who God raised from the dead and gave glory, so that your faith and hope can remain in God. Your souls will be purified by obeying the truth that the Holy Spirit has shown you; so fervently love your brothers and sisters with a pure heart.

The Holy Trinity is essential because we believe in one infinite God who exists in three persons: Father, Son, and Holy Spirit, equal in power, authority, majesty, and deity. All three persons play a role in our salvation, sanctification, and justification. This is why we pray in the Spirit, to our Father in heaven, in the name of Jesus Christ.

- ISA 11:1–2 ~ A descendant of Jesse called "The Branch" will be born. The Spirit of God will be upon Him: the Spirit of wisdom, understanding, counsel and might; the Spirit of knowledge and the fear of God.

- ISA 48:16 ~ Come and listen. I have not spoken in secret since the beginning. I (Christ) was there all along, and now, the Lord God and His Spirit have sent me.

- MAT 28:18–20 ~ Jesus said to His apostles just before leaving them, "All power in heaven and earth is given to me. Go and teach all nations the things I have taught you, baptizing them in the name of the Father, Son, and Holy Spirit. And remember, I will be with you always, even until the end of time."

- JOH 1:1, 14 ~ In the beginning was the Word, and the Word was with God, and the Word was God. And the Word became flesh and lived among us; and we saw His glory, the glory of the Father's only Son, full of grace and truth.

- 1 JO 5:7 ~ There are three in heaven who reveal themselves to us: the Father, the Word (Christ), and the Holy Spirit; and these three are one.

Thank you, Father, for making it so easy to love you, trust in you, and depend on you. Thank you for sending messengers of your truth so we can learn the truth and compare everything we see and hear to this same truth, verifying what is right and dismissing what is wrong or false. Help us always to be eager to hear your Word, and teach it to our children, and share it with the world. Help all evangelical churches to never veer from the truth or the essential doctrines of our Christian faith, for there are many counterfeit saviors in our midst that know nothing of your Word. Remind us to search the scriptures diligently so we can identify and call out false prophets and errant religions, using your Word as proof. We pray in the name of Jesus who is that Word, the living truth of your presence in our lives, Amen.

May 25

National Missing Children's Day was announced by President Reagan to occur on this date in 1983. It was in remembrance of a six-year-old boy who disappeared in New York city on his way to school in 1979. Today's observance became the International Missing Children's Day in 2001. The Department of Justice holds an annual commemoration to recognize people and agencies fighting for these missing children and against the sinister abductors responsible for their disappearance. Law enforcement organizations as well as the National Center for Missing and Exploited Children (NCMEC) will provide trainings and seminars to educate parents and children about dangers, techniques used by abductors, escape and evasion measures, and what families can do proactively to reduce the threat. Every family should have safety plans and coded messages to prevent their children from falling into the hands of predators.

One thing that everybody can do for the missing children is pray constantly for their deliverance. You also can get involved by reporting child abuse, keeping apprised of Amber Alerts in your area, and partnering with local law enforcement. You might sponsor an event in your city, enlist guest speakers, and distribute flyers and materials. For more information on reporting a missing or exploited child, or holding a local event, contact the NCMEC at 800-843-5678 (*www.missingkids.org*). Note that cartels are exploiting children and women, selling some as sex slaves. The government is allowing these atrocities to continue via open border policies which violate immigration laws. Help the innocent by supporting enforcement of our borders and prosecution of human traffickers.

- EXO 21:16; DEU 24:7 ~ Kidnappers must be put to death, whether they are in possession of victims or have sold them as slaves. You must purge the evil from among you.

- PSA 127:3 ~ Children are a heritage to the Lord; the fruit of the womb is His reward

- ISA 2:6, 11, 19 ~ These people practice divination and fortunetelling. They please themselves with the children of strangers. The pride of man will be humbled, and the Lord alone will be exalted on that day. Those people will try to hide from the terror of the Lord when He comes.

- LAM 4:6, 10, 13 ~ Their punishment will be greater than that of Sodom. Women have boiled their children. Prophets and priests shed innocent blood.

- EZE 16:20–21 ~ You have taken your sons and daughters, who you bore unto me (God), and sacrificed them. If you think this is a small matter you are mistaken.

- MAT 18:3–6; MAR 9:42; LUK 17:2 ~ Jesus said, "Unless you become converted and receive God as a little child, you will never enter the kingdom of heaven. Those who humble themselves like a child can become the greatest in God's kingdom. Whoever receives a child in my name receives me. But anyone committing an offense with a child who believes in me, they would have been better off being tossed into the sea with a millstone tied to their neck."

Christians are children of God and will live with our Father in heaven for eternity. For He has adopted us to be His own, and live under Him in His kingdom as members of His household. Those who have not accepted Christ are lost; they are missing and need to be found alive, else they end up in hell.

- ISA 41:8 ~ You Israel, are my servants, the children of Jacob whom I have chosen, and the seed of my friend Abraham.

- ISA 65:1 ~ I revealed myself to those who did not ask about me and I was found by those who did not seek me. To the nation that did not call on my name, I said, "Here I AM."

- HOS 2:23 ~ I will bring them to me and have mercy on those who had not received mercy. I will say to them who were not my people that they are my people, and they will say, "You are my God."

- HOS 4:6 ~ My people are destroyed from lack of knowledge. Because you rejected knowledge, I will reject you, and you will not serve as my priests. Since you have ignored God's Law, I will ignore your children.

- MIC 5:4 ~ The Son will stand for and feed off the Lord, and will share His majesty. The children shall live in Him who is great, even to every corner of the earth.

- JOH 1:12 ~ To all who have received Christ, and believed in His name, He has given the privilege to become children of God.

- ROM 8:16–18 ~ The Holy Spirit testifies with our spirits that we are God's children. If we are His children, then we are heirs: heirs of God, and joint-heirs with Christ, if indeed we share in His sufferings in order that we may later share in His glory. For I consider the sufferings of this present time to be nothing compared to the glory that will be revealed in us.

- ROM 9:4–8 ~ Who are the Israelites, to whom God gave the Law and granted the adoption, and with whom God made the covenants and promises? Christ came for them and for all people. It is not as if God's Word had no effect, for they who are of Israel are not all from Israel. Those who are of Abraham's seed are not all his children. In other words, those who are the children of the flesh are not children of God; only those who cling to God's promises are counted as children.

- ROM 9:25–26; ROM 10:20 ~ God spoke through Hosea (HOS 2:23) saying, "I will call them my people who were not my people, and I will call them beloved who were not my beloved. And at that place (Israel) where I told them they were not my people, others (Gentiles) will be called the children of the living God." God also spoke through Isaiah (ISA 65:1) saying, "I was found by those who did not seek me; I revealed myself to those who did not ask for me."

- GAL 3:6–7, 26, 29 ~ Just as Abraham believed God, and it was accounted to him as righteousness, so also are those who have the same faith, children of Abraham. You are the children of God because of your faith in Jesus Christ. If you belong to Christ then you are part of Abraham's chosen seed, and heirs according to God's covenant.

- GAL 4:4–7 ~ When the time was right, God sent His Son, who was born of a woman under the Old Covenant of the Law, to redeem those who were under the Law. He did this so that everyone could receive the honor of becoming adopted children of God. If you are a child of God, you are no longer His servant, but a fellow heir of God through Christ.

- EPH 1:3–7 ~ Praise to God, the Father of our Lord Jesus Christ, who has chosen us before the foundation of the world to be holy and blameless before Him in love. We were destined to be God's adopted children, in accordance with His good will and grace, through Jesus Christ, in whom we have redemption and forgiveness in His blood.

- HEB 2:10–11 ~ In bringing many children to glory, it was appropriate that God would make the author of their salvation perfect through His suffering. Both the One who makes us holy and those who are made holy are of the same family. Therefore, Jesus is not ashamed to call us His brothers and sisters.

- 1 JO 3:1–2 ~ How great is the love our Father has for us, to be called His children. The world does not know us since it did not know Him. We are His children, but we do not know what we will be; we do know, however, we will be like Him, for we will see Him as He really is.

- 1 JO 4:4 ~ You are from God my children, and have overcome the world; because greater is He that is in you (Christ) than he that is in the world (Satan).

- REV 21:7 ~ Those who overcome will inherit all things, and I will be their God and they will be my children.

There are times when it is not okay to tolerate someone crossing the line. Everybody has a personal line they won't cross, even when it comes to sin. For example, when a temptation flashes before you, you may think about it, but you could never do it. It is difficult being mindful all the time about what we should and should not do; no matter how saintly, we all mess up. But when it comes to kidnapping, molesting, assaulting, or whatever to a child, that action is way over the line for sane people. For monsters who think it is fun, where would you draw the line when it comes to their punishment? Can such a sin be forgiven? Jesus said all sins can be forgiven except the sin of disbelief, otherwise known as blasphemy against the Holy Spirit who is the messenger of truth: whether found in God's Word, or breathed from the very mouth of God to the prophets and patriarchs, or spoken by His Son Jesus Christ while He walked the earth. Keep in mind that being forgiven does not absolve us of the natural consequences of sin. However, being forgiven by the atonement of Christ and via the sacraments does mean we need not fear death.

Societies have laws and they draw all kinds of lines and borders, some of which should never be crossed; but unless the law is applied evenly, there is no justice. God's justice for any violation of His Law is death. Then who can be saved? Only those claiming the blood atonement of Christ. As for our justice system, it is flawed because the line of equal representation is not being followed. Some offenders get off light and others get the book thrown at them, for doing the same things! Some want open borders and some say let anyone come. But they would never permit those persons to cross the threshold of their front door. Some will say their line is more accurate than yours, or their truth is all there is no matter what anyone else says, including God. But it is the line drawn by God Himself that matters, which is clear to all people of conscience.

- JOB 26:7–14 ~ God marks the horizon over the waters for a boundary between darkness and light.

- MAT 7:7 ~ Jesus taught: Ask and receive. Seek and find. Knock and the door will be opened.

- LUK 12:36 ~ Be like the man who awaits his master to come home from the marriage feast, so that he may open the door when he arrives.

- LUK 16:25–31 ~ Abraham reminded the rich man how thoughtless and unmerciful he had been to the poor man. Abraham also told him that nobody could pass through the chasm separating Hades, where he was, and Abraham's bosom where Lazarus was. The rich man implored that his family be warned, to prevent them from the same fate. Abraham informed the rich man that they would have to rely on the Word of God like everybody else; if they did not, even a visit from the dead would not persuade them to change their ways.

- REV 3:7–8, 20 ~ To the church in Philadelphia John wrote: He who is holy and true says, He has the key of David, and whatever door He opens no person can shut, and every door He shuts, nobody can open. I have set before you an open door that nobody can shut. To the church in Laodicea John wrote: Behold, I stand at the door and knock. Everyone who hears my voice and opens the door, I will come in and commune with them, and they with me.

Father, we pray for children who are missing at this time, and for their safe return to their homes or at least a safe environment. We pray for justice against those who violate children. We pray that people can see eye to eye about what your Law reveals and what is not allowed. We pray that our nation would return to you and listen to the truth. In Jesus's name, Amen.

May 26

Holy Trinity Sunday occurs the first week after Pentecost Sunday on the liturgical calendar. The Holy Trinity is a major tenet of the Christian faith. Simply put, it recognizes one God in three persons: God the Father, Jesus Christ the Son, and the Holy Spirit. This triad was explained by Theophilus of Antioch (circa AD 180) as follows: God, His Word, and His Wisdom. Though somewhat imprecise, one can extrapolate: God is our Father, Jesus is the Word made flesh, and the Holy Spirit is the messenger of God's wisdom and truth. This early church father also accurately explained man as consisting of three similar components in which we reflect the image of God. In modern terms, we have a physical component or body like Christ, a mental component or mind like God, and a spiritual component through which the Holy Spirit can communicate truth to the depths of our inner being. The trinity was clarified more succinctly at the first ecumenical Council of Nicaea (AD 325): God exists eternally in three distinct persons: Father, Son, and Holy Spirit. Each person is fully God and there is only one God.

Though the word "trinity" was introduced to explain this mystery, people will argue that there is no such doctrine for the very reason the term is not found in the Bible. This evasion is one reason for the many distortions of Christianity such as Mormonism and Jehovah Witnesses who do not accept the doctrine of the trinity or the deity of Christ. But these doctrines are spelled out in the Bible quite succinctly. Many passages refer to all three persons of God in a single instance, such as the ones listed below.

- GEN 18:1–3, 1 ~ The Lord appeared to Abraham in the plains of Mamre where he sat at the door of his tent. Abraham looked up and saw three men standing, so he arose and ran to greet them, bowing before them. Abraham said, "My Lord, if I have found favor in your sight, I pray that you would never leave your servant." And they said to him, "Your wife Sarah will have a son; and Sarah laughed at the thought of bearing a child in her old age.

- ISA 6:3 ~ They seraphim shouted, "Holy, Holy, Holy is the Lord of hosts; the whole earth is full of His glory."

- ISA 11:2 ~ The Spirit of the Lord shall rest upon the Messiah: the Spirit of wisdom, understanding, counsel, might, knowledge, and the fear of the Lord.

- ISA 48:16 ~ Come and listen. I have not spoken in secret since the beginning. I (Christ) was there all along; and now the Lord God and His Spirit have sent me. (see JOH 1:1–14)

- ISA 49:7 ~ The Lord, the Redeemer of Israel, and His Holy One that humankind hates say, "Kings and princes will see and come worship, for the Lord is faithful as is His Holy One."

- MAT 3:16–17; MAR 1:10–11 ~ Jesus, after He was baptized by John, emerged from the water, and the heavens were opened, and John saw the Spirit of God descending like a dove and resting upon Jesus. Then a voice from heaven said, "This is my beloved Son who pleases me very much."

- MAT 28:18–20 ~ Jesus said, "All authority in heaven and earth is given to me. Go and teach everyone what I have taught you; baptize them in the name of the Father, Son, and Holy Spirit."

- JOH 1:1–4, 14 ~ In the beginning was the Word, and the Word was with God, and the Word was God. All things were made by Him. In Him was life, and that life was the light of humankind. The Word was made flesh and lived among us; and we saw His glory, like the glory of the only Son of the Father, full of grace and truth.

- 2 CO 13:14 ~ May the grace of Jesus Christ, the love of God, and the communication of the Holy Spirit be with you.

MAY

- COL 2:2 ~ My hope is that their hearts will be comforted, being bound together in love, and that they receive the riches of understanding and acknowledgment of the mystery of God, and of the Heavenly Father, and of Jesus Christ.

- 1 TI 3:16 ~ Without question, the mystery of God is great. For God has appeared in the flesh and He is justified in the Spirit. He is worshipped by angels, is preached to the nations, is believed all over the world, and is glorified above all others.

- 1 PE 1:1–2 ~ Peter, an apostle of Jesus Christ, was elected according to the prior knowledge of God the Father, through sanctification by the Spirit, unto obedience and cleansing by the blood of Christ.

- 1 JO 5:6–8, 20 ~ There are three who are recorded in heaven: the Father, the Word, and the Holy Spirit. These three are one. The same three bear witness: the Spirit, the Water, and the Blood. The Spirit is the witness, because the Spirit bears the truth. We know Jesus Christ who is true so that we may know God who is true. We live in Him who has shown us His Son, the source of eternal life.

- REV 4:8 ~ The four beasts (seraphim) had six wings and were filled with eyes; they never slept, repeating, "Holy, Holy, Holy Lord God Almighty, who was, who is, and who is to come."

God the Father is one with the Son and the Holy Spirit. There is one God, whose Spirit is conveyed through both the Father and the Son, for the Spirit bears the truth. God reveals the truth through His Holy Spirit in His Holy Word the Bible, and the words of Christ who was conceived by the Holy Spirit in the virgin Mary. Therefore, God walked on the earth in the flesh, making Jesus fully God and fully man.

- DEU 6:4 ~ The Lord your God is one Lord.

- ISA 43:10; ISA 44:6 ~ There are no gods before Him or after Him. He is the first and last; there is only one God.

- LUK 4:1 ~ Jesus was filled with the Holy Spirit.

- JOH 4:24 ~ God is Spirit and should be worshipped in spirit and in truth.

- JOH 14:26; JOH 15:26 ~ Jesus informed the apostles, "The Comforter, the Holy Spirit, who the Father will send in my name..." and, "I will send the Comforter, the Holy Spirit."

- ROM 3:29–30 ~ There is only one God, and He is the God of the Jews as well as the Gentiles. God will justify the circumcised according to their faith, and the uncircumcised according to their faith.

- 1 CO 12:4–5 ~ There are a variety of spiritual gifts, but only one Spirit. There are different ways of administering but only one Lord.

- GAL 3:20 ~ Although an intermediary (Christ) implies more than one, God is still only one being.

- EPH 4:5–6 ~ There is one Lord, one faith, one baptism, one God and Father of us all, who is above all, through all, and in all.

- 1 TI 2:5 ~ There is only one God, and the only mediator between Him and humanity is Jesus Christ.

- HEB 1:3 ~ The Son is the image of the Father, having His radiance and sharing His glory.

- JAM 2:19 ~ If you believe in one God you are smart. Even the demons believe, and tremble.

Jesus Christ is God. Many religions regard Jesus as a mere prophet, including Islam and Bahai. Those who do not believe that Jesus is God are not true Christians. Who but God could give His life and then take it back again (JOH 10:18), or turn water into wine (JOH 2:1–11), or walk atop a raging sea (MAT 14:22–23), or raise the dead (JOH 11:1–44)? These are actual miracles because they cannot be explained through physics or nature. Such events require intervention from a deity unconstrained by the laws of physics and nature, characterizing them as supernatural, with power that exists outside of this universe in which humans are confined but God is not.

- PSA 2:6–7, 11–12 ~ God says, "I have set my King on the holy mountain Zion. I will declare to the world that you are my Son for this day I have begotten you. Serve the Son with fear and joy. Kiss the Son, because you will die if you get in the way of His wrath."

- ISA 7:14 ~ God Himself will provide the sign: A virgin shall conceive and bear a son. His name will be called Immanuel ("God with us").

- ISA 9:6 ~ A child is born for us; a Son is given. The government will be on His shoulders. His name will be called Wonderful Counselor, Mighty God, Everlasting Father, Prince of Peace.

- ISA 43:10–12 ~ There are no gods before God or after Him. God says, "You are witnesses to what I have said. My servant whom I have chosen is also sent to be a witness so that you can know me and believe; and even so, I am He. I am the Lord and there is no other savior besides me. I have declared myself to you and I have saved you whenever you have forsaken all other gods for me."

- ISA 44:6 ~ God and His Redeemer the Lord of hosts say, "I am the first and last; there are no other gods besides me."

- JOH 8:19, 42, 58 ~ Jesus said, "If you know me you know the Father, since I came from the Father. I tell you the truth, before Abraham was, I AM."

- JOH 10:30 ~ Jesus said, "The Father and I are one."

- JOH 14:6, 9–11 ~ Jesus said, "I am the way, the truth, and the life; nobody comes to the Father but by me. If you have seen me, you have seen the Father, because the Father lives in me and I in Him."

- COL 2:9 ~ In Jesus Christ the whole deity of God lives.

- 1 JO 2:23 ~ Whoever denies the Son denies the Father. Whoever acknowledges the Son acknowledges the Father.

There are three components of man: the physical (body, flesh); the mental (mind, soul, intellect, will, emotions, self), and the spiritual (conscience, moral compass, heart). We are made in the image of God who also has a body (Christ), mind (Father), and spirit (Holy Spirit). God has given us a discerning mind (soul), to know right and wrong, unlike other inhabitants of planet earth. God can speak to our spirit and connect His words with our soul. The three persons of God are inseparable, unlike the three components of man (MAT 10:28; HEB 4:12).

- GEN 1:26–27; GEN 3:22 ~ God said, "Let us make humans in our image, after our likeness. And let them have dominion over the fish of the sea, over the fowl of the air, over the cattle, and over all the earth and everything that creeps upon the earth." So, God created humankind in His own image; in the image of God, He created us all, males and females alike. God said, "Behold, man has become like us, able to discern good and evil. But so he cannot reach out his hand and take from the Tree of Life and live forever, he must be removed from the Garden of Eden, and will till the soil from which he was taken."

MAY

- DEU 6:5 ~ You should love the Lord with all your heart, soul, and might.

- DEU 10:12–13 ~ The Lord requires you to fear Him, to walk in His ways, to love Him, to serve Him will all your heart and soul, and to obey His commandments (also JOS 22:5).

- 1 KI 8:48–49 ~ If they repent with all their minds and hearts, I will hear their prayers.

- 1 CH 28:9 ~ Know your God and serve Him with a whole heart and a willing mind. For the Lord searches all hearts and understands every thought and plan.

- MAT 22:37 ~ Jesus said, "You must love the Lord with all your heart, soul, and mind."

- ROM 8:4–6 ~ Walk, not according to the flesh, but according to the spirit.

- 1 CO 14:15 ~ I will pray and I will sing, with the mind and with the spirit.

- COL 3:10 ~ Put on the new person, which is renewed in knowledge after the image of God who created you.

- HEB 8:10, 16 ~ God says, "This is the covenant that I will make with the house of Israel after those days: I will put my laws into their minds, and write them in their hearts; and I will be their God, and they will be my people." (see JER 31:31–34)

- 1 JO 3:8 ~ Whoever commits sin is of the devil, who sinned from the very beginning. The Son of God was manifested to destroy the works of the devil.

Receive the Holy Spirit and live forever. Jesus gave His Spirit when He left the earth, to be our comforter, advisor, and partner. Consequently, He still abides with us who believe; and He will come back to get us. And we will abide with our Father, Christ, and the Holy Spirit forever.

- JOH 7:37–39 ~ On the last day, that great day of the feast, Jesus cried aloud, "If anyone thirsts, let them come to me and drink. Those who believe on me, as the scripture says, from the inside will flow rivers of living water. This Jesus spoke in the Spirit, which believers would receive; though the Holy Spirit was not given quite yet, for Jesus was not yet glorified.

- JOH 14:16–19 ~ Jesus said, "I will pray to the Father, and He will give you another helper, so He can be with you forever: He is the Spirit of truth. But the world cannot receive Him because people can neither see Him or know Him, though you know Him, for He lives in you and will abide with you. I will not leave you as orphans; I will return for you. A little while longer and the world will see me no more; but you will see me, and because I live, you will live also."

Holy, Holy, Holy is our great God, one God in three persons: Father, Son, and Holy Spirit. When we pray to you, Lord, we pray to all three. And though we don't always know what to pray for, we know your Holy Spirit will intercede for us and that you, Father, will answer our prayers in the way that benefits us most. Thank you for this privilege. We pray today for increased knowledge and understanding of your mysteries such as the Holy Trinity. Thank you for your Word which explains this phenomenon in a way that we can grasp it and believe. Open our spiritual eyes and ears so we can know the truth even as the world tries to hide or deny it. Help us to continue our search for truths and mysteries in the scriptures explaining your works and your ways. There is so much to glean from the Bible it would take a lifetime, and even then, we will not be able to unravel all the intricacies of your Word. We look forward to the opportunity to bring our questions before you face-to-face, Lord. When that day comes, we will have an eternity to learn from you, constantly growing in understanding, hearing the Word directly from you. How we long for that day when we can approach you, Father, and ask or request anything at all without fear, and receive love, truth, and grace immediately and constantly. Help us to always find comfort and joy in that assurance. As always, we ask you in the name of your Son Jesus, Amen, Amen, and Amen.

May 27

Memorial Day is a federal holiday that recognizes those who fell in battle fighting for our freedom, rights, and sovereignty. This tradition dates back to the end of the Civil War, which claimed about 620,000 lives. A number of groups including mothers, former slaves, veterans' advocates, and churches started holding services and ceremonies, specifically memorializing our fallen dead. It was a means of reconciling relatives and friends, as the nation honored combatants who perished in our deadliest war. After World War II, the popularity of the holiday grew substantially. It became official in 1971, when the last Monday in May was designated the date to memorialize our heroes lost in war. Nowadays a moment of remembrance lasting two minutes occurs at 1500 hours (EST). During this long weekend Americans travel to visit national cemeteries and memorials, relatives and veterans; especially sites in the DC area, most notably, Arlington National Cemetery directly across the Potomac River in Virginia. Traditionally, the president (or an appointee) hangs a wreath next to the Tomb of the Unknown Soldier. This is an occasion when patriots of all parties can be united under a single ideology, which ensures the USA is the place to be, where we welcome everyone with a heart for this land of the free, who come here legally.

If you happen to be vacationing in the DC area, take a trip to Arlington cemetery, observe the guards at the tomb, see the sights and take it all in; it is very inspiring and touching. Visit the monuments to the founding fathers and those who fought in the various wars. Yes, there are a great many things to see and do in DC but these are a must.

Take time today to attend a service or ceremony, watch a parade, have a barbeque with friends, go to a military cemetery; and don't forget to say a prayer for families and friends who have lost loved ones in foreign wars or through acts of terrorism. We need to defeat terrorists and warmongers wherever they may be found, eradicating them from the face of the earth. It seems the United States sheds more of our own blood than any other country fighting wars on foreign soil; I guess it beats fighting those wars here. Even if you are not mourning a fallen hero, you can mourn for and with those who mourn. And after that you can rejoice along with them as they celebrate and honor the lives of those who gave the last full measure.

- PSA 3:18–19 ~ The Lord visits those with a broken heart, and saves those with a contrite heart. Many are the afflictions of the righteous; but the Lord delivers them all.

- PRO 10:7 ~ The memory of the just is blessed; but the name of the wicked will rot away.

- ECC 3:1, 4 ~ For everything there is a season, and a time for every purpose under heaven. A time to weep and a time to laugh; a time to mourn and a time to dance.

- ISA 61:1–3 ~ The Spirit of God is upon me, because He has directed me to preach His good news to the humble, to heal the broken hearted, to free the slaves, and to release those who are bound in chains and in prison; to proclaim the Lord's favor and His vengeance, to comfort all who mourn, and to tell those who mourn to exchange their ashes for beauty; to replace mourning with joy, and to don the garment of praise in exchange for the spirit of sorrow, so that they may be trees of righteousness, planted by the Lord for His glorification.

- JOH 15:12–13 ~ Jesus said, "Love each other as I have loved you. No greater love exists than to give one's life for their friends."

- REV 2:10 ~ Jesus said, "Do not fear those things that you must suffer; behold, the devil will cast some of you into prison to be tried; you will have tribulation ten days. Be faithful unto death and I will give you a crown of life."

MAY

    Men and women who served and didn't come back, or came back maimed and handicapped deserve more than just your prayers. God commands us to be charitable, and give a tithe to the church in addition to our offerings. If you are inclined to donate money to worthy causes, consider helping the widows and orphans of these brave individuals. Their families are often left destitute; others are barely making ends meet, forced to leave their homes. There are some great charities out there who help these families financially; check their financials (which are reported by law). Give generously, because God loves a cheerful giver. If you do not have the money, consider donating your time to one of these worthwhile nonprofit organizations.

- DEU 16:17 ~ Everyone should give as they are able, in accordance with the blessings which God has given them.
- MAL 3:10 ~ The Lord says, "Bring tithes of all your income to the storage room so that there will be plenty in my house, and prove to yourself how I will open the windows of heaven and pour upon you so many blessings that you will not have room for them."
- MAT 25:40, 45 ~ Jesus said, "Whenever you have done something to help another person, you have done it to me as well; whenever you have not done something to help another person, you have not done it to me."
- LUK 6:38 ~ Give and it shall be given to you in abundance, overflowing; for the same measure that you give is returned unto you.
- LUK 12:48 ~ Jesus said, "To whomever much is given, much will be required. To those who have committed much, of them more will be asked."
- ROM 12:14–15 ~ Bless those who persecute you; do not curse them. Rejoice with those who are rejoicing, and mourn with those who are mourning.
- 2 CO 9:7 ~ Everyone should give whatever they think is fair in their heart. Giving should be done voluntarily, not out of obligation, for God loves a cheerful giver.
- ROM 12:6–8 ~ We have different gifts, given to each in accordance with the grace God has given everyone. If you have the gift of prophecy, do so in proportion to your faith. If you have the gift of giving, do so generously. If you have the gift of governing, do so with diligence. If you have the gift of mercy, show it cheerfully.
- 1 TI 6:7, 9 ~ We brought nothing into this world and we can bring nothing out of it. The rich fall into temptation, and a trap, and they succumb to many foolish and harmful lusts, which can drown a person in destruction and damnation.

    Lord of the universe and Father of humankind, we give thanks for those who have died for freedom, in particular your only begotten Son, Jesus Christ. We pray for precious loved ones of our fallen heroes, who are left to fend without them: that they be assisted as needed, protected and defended. We appreciate our fallen heroes and their sacrifice, for they emulate Christ. We pray for servicemen and women who are deployed oversees and for their wellbeing, safety, and security; we pray that they return to their families safe and sound. And we raise those up to you who never came home. Help us to generously give to charities and Christian organizations that support these causes, to show our appreciation, and as a memorial to courageous and honorable lives well spent. Let this be a day of reverence to them and to your Son, all of whom made the ultimate sacrifice. And we pray that those who follow in their footsteps will be following Christ along the way, until they are called home. Help us all to be faithful soldiers in the army of the Lord, fighting the good fight of faith the rest of our days. Until that day when we can speak to you in person, we pray in Jesus's name, Amen.

May 28

Nothing to Fear Day is actually observed on May 27 (yesterday); it coincides with the day in 1941 when President F. D. Roosevelt spoke these renown words, "We have nothing to fear but fear itself." It was during the Great Depression, and the economy was in shambles, and people were concerned about how they were going to make ends meet. World War II was also underway and that created considerable fear around the world; real fear was further magnified by false fear.

Today in the USA and abroad, people are experiencing their own crises, mostly economic, while war looms again. But I doubt FDR's statement would bring any comfort unless one's trust was in God. FDR was right in this regard: You should be afraid of ungodly fear, for it leads to death and evil. Fear is the tool of Satan, who wants people to think he is powerful like God, but he doesn't come close. If you fear God with a godly fear, you literally will have nothing to fear, including Satan. If you have God's Spirit living in you, the devils in the world will fear you. And make no mistake, you will become a target for some who loathe Christians and/or God.

We worry endlessly, becoming stressed, anxious, and depressed; but these episodes pass. Sometimes we look back and wonder what all the fuss was about. Examine the things that you fear about life, and you will find that what you thought was going to happen is not inevitable and when it does happen it is not permanent. The only permanency is death; but you needn't fear death either when you believe that you are saved unto life eternal. For those people who are not committed to Christ there is plenty to fear, because their end is dreadful.

The ways of the world and the demonic is death, no escape. This is why the most common fear is the curse of death. It is also why we fear God, for the world is His and He created it for us; the only thing from this world to fear is our own sin which leads to death. The devil employs ungodly fear to trick and terrify us into sin and submission, using crafty and deceitful methods; he teaches these ways to people who allow evil to seep into their thoughts. Evil keeps coming back to trip us up, but we can rebuke the devil himself and he will leave (JAM 4:7), seeing how the demons are no match for the Holy Spirit who lives in our hearts. Fear has torment and that is what the demons and all of those who do not fear the Lord are going to get. The Bible verses that follow discuss common human fears. Not that it is easy to dismiss these things because it isn't; unless you change your focus back to Christ after which you might not feel quite as worried.

- EXO 14:13, 31 ~ Moses told the people, "Do not be afraid of the Egyptians. Stand and watch, and you will see the salvation of the Lord; for after this day you will never see the Egyptians again." And the people saw what the Lord did to the Egyptians (drowning them in the Red Sea); and the people feared the Lord and believed in God and His servant Moses.

- DEU 1:17 ~ You must not discriminate against others in judgment; permit the testimony of the lowly as well as the great. You should not be afraid when facing man's judgment for judgment belongs to God. If you have a cause that is too difficult for you, bring it to God and He will hear it.

- PSA 34:4 ~ I sought the Lord and He heard me, and delivered me from my fears.

- PRO 3:25 ~ Do not be afraid of sudden fear or of the desolation of the wicked when it comes.

- PRO 29:25 ~ The fear of humanity brings a snare; but those who put their trust in God will be safe.

- ISA 8:12–13 ~ Do not join in any conspiracies or alliances with people who are afraid; do not fear the things that they fear; do not be afraid at all. Sanctify the Lord of hosts, and let Him be your fear.

MAY

- ISA 33:14 ~ Sinners are afraid; fear surprises the hypocrites. Who among you will live in the devouring fire and burn?

- ISA 35:4 ~ Tell those who are afraid not to fear, because God will come with a vengeance and will save them.

- ISA 51:7 ~ God says, "Look for me, you who know righteousness and you who hold my laws in your hearts. Do not be afraid of the accusations of others or their verbal abuse."

- MAT 6:31–34 ~ Jesus said, "Do not worry about what you will eat or drink, or what you will wear; for your heavenly Father knows that you need these things. Instead, seek first the kingdom of God and His righteousness, and He will provide everything you need in addition."

- MAT 10:19–20, 26–28 ~ Jesus said, "When you are captured, do not worry about how to act or what to say, for the proper words will be given to you even as you speak them. It will not be you, but the Holy Spirit doing the talking. Do not fear those who hate you, for everything that is hidden now will be revealed later; everything that is unknown will become known. What I tell you in darkness, you will speak in the light. What you hear in private will be preached from the rooftops. Do not worry about those who can kill your body, but cannot reach your soul. Instead, fear Him who is able to destroy both your body and soul in hell."

- LUK 5:26 ~ Everyone was amazed at Jesus when He cured the man who was stricken with palsy. They were filled with fear, saying, "We have seen strange things today."

- LUK 12:32 ~ Jesus said, "Fear not, little flock, for it is your Father's good pleasure to give to you the kingdom."

- ACTS 2:22–38 ~ Peter, accompanied by the apostles, preached to the crowd on Pentecost. "Men of Israel, listen to me. Jesus of Nazareth, a man attested of God through miracles, wonders, and signs done in your presence, as you well know—was sent to fulfill God's purpose and with His foreknowledge, to be taken by lawless hands and crucified to death, only to be raised from the dead by God, having avoided the pain of death because it was impossible for death to hold Him. This was in accordance with the words of David who wrote that he foresaw the Lord sitting at the right hand of God; he rejoiced and was glad, for he knew his flesh would rest in hope, assured that his soul would not be left in Hades, neither would His Holy One see corruption. This is the same David who died and whose tomb lies here, who prophesied that God would raise up Messiah to sit on his throne, thereby foreseeing His resurrection from the dead, which we ourselves witnessed, and who is now exalted at the right hand of God. Whereby we received the promise of the Father that the Holy Spirit would be poured out, which you now are witnessing and hearing. For David did not ascend into heaven, but said of himself, "The Lord said to my Lord, sit at my right hand until I make your enemies your footstool." Therefore, the entire house of Israel can know with certainty that God has made this man Jesus, whom you crucified, both Lord and Messiah." When they heard this, they were cut to the heart, asking Peter and the apostles what they should do. Peter replied, "Repent and be baptized, every one of you, in the name of Jesus Christ for the remission of your sins, and you will receive the free gift of the Holy Spirit."

- ROM 13:4 ~ If you do what is evil, be afraid, for God's minister will not bear the sword in vain, because he is sent to execute wrath upon those who do evil.

- PHP 4:6 ~ Do not worry about anything, but pray for everything with thanksgiving, humbleness, and eagerness.

- JAM 2:19 ~ If you believe in one God you are smart. Even the demons believe, and tremble.

- 1 JO 4:2–6 ~ Every spirit that confesses that Jesus Christ is God in the flesh is of God. Those spirits that do not confess are not of God, but are spirits of the antichrist, which you have heard about and are in the world. You belong to God and have overcome these spirits of malice. For greater is He that is within you than he that is in the world.

- 1 JO 4:18 ~ There is no fear in love, but perfect love casts out fear, because fear has torment. Those who fear are not made perfect in love.

- REV 2:10 ~ Jesus said, "Do not be afraid of any of the things you may suffer. The devil will throw some of you into prison to be tried; you will have tribulation for ten days. Be faithful unto death and I will give you a crown of life."

- REV 15:4 ~ Who will not fear you, Lord, and glorify your name? For only you are holy; all nations will come to worship you, for your judgments are clearly obvious.

- REV 21:8 ~ The fearful, the unbelieving, the murderers, prostitutes, sorcerers, idolaters, and liars will take part in the lake of fire which is the second death.

Basically, ungodly fear is being afraid for no good reason, and this is the weapon of Satan, the father of lies. But godly fear is incompatible with ungodly fear. What exactly is godly fear? We fear God because He is an awesome God. We fear God because it reminds us of the penalty for disbelief and disobedience. To those who harbor resentment, seek revenge, or hold animosity in their hearts: there is much to fear. Cleanse your heart with the blood of Jesus, forgive others, and you will have that weight lifted from your heart, and you will be, and also feel, cleaner and stronger on the inside, and less fearful of the world.

- DEU 5:29 ~ God said, "I wish the people had such a heart that they would fear me and keep my commandments always, so they and their children would be well."

- DEU 31:6 ~ Be strong and take courage; do not be afraid, for the Lord goes with you. He neither will fail you nor forsake you.

- JOS 24:14 ~ Fear the Lord and serve Him in sincerity and truth. Put away false gods.

- 1 SA 12:24 ~ Fear only the Lord and serve Him in truth with all your heart. Consider the wonderful things He has done for you.

- 1 CH 16:24–25 ~ Declare God's glory to the infidels and His marvelous works among the nations. Great is the Lord; He is greatly to be praised. He is to be feared above all gods.

- JOB 4:6 ~ Is the fear of God not your confidence, hope, and righteousness?

- JOB 5:21–22 ~ You will be hidden from the scourge of the tongue; you will not be afraid of destruction when it comes. You will laugh at destruction and famine; you will not be afraid of the beasts on earth. You will be at peace.

- JOB 13:11 ~ Does God's excellency not make you afraid?

- JOB 28:28 ~ The fear of the Lord is wisdom; to depart from evil is understanding.

- PSA 23:3–4 ~ He restores my soul; He leads me in the paths of righteousness for His namesake. Although I walk through the dark valley of death, I fear no evil, for you oh Lord, are with me; your rod and staff are a comfort to me.

- PSA 27:1–2 ~ The Lord is my light and my salvation. Who should I fear? He is the strength in my life. Of whom shall I be afraid? Even if a whole encampment of my enemies is preparing war against me, I will not be afraid, but confident.

- PSA 33:8, 18 ~ Let all the earth fear the Lord; let inhabitants stand in awe of Him. The eye of the Lord is upon those who fear Him and hope in His mercy.

- PSA 37:7 ~ Find solace in the Lord and wait patiently for Him. Do not worry about evil people who prosper.

- PSA 56:3–4 ~ If I am afraid, I will praise God's Word and put my trust in Him. I will not be afraid of what flesh can do to me.

- PSA 119:120 ~ My flesh trembles with fear at the Lord for I am afraid of His judgments.

- PRO 1:7, 33 ~ The fear of the Lord is the beginning of knowledge; but fools despise knowledge and wisdom. Those who seek God will be safe and sound from the fear of evil.

- PRO 8:13 ~ To fear the Lord is to hate evil, pride, conceit, sin, and verbal abuse.

- PRO 16:6 ~ By mercy and truth, sin is purged; by the fear of the Lord, people can depart from evil.

- ISA 41:10 ~ God says, "Fear not, for I am with you. Do not be dismayed, for I am your God. I will strengthen and help you. I will hold you up with the right hand of righteousness."

- MAT 10:28 ~ Jesus said, "Do not be afraid of those who can kill the body but not the soul. Fear only Him who can destroy both your body and soul in hell."

- MAR 7:14–19 ~ Jesus said, "Can you see that nothing entering a person from the outside can make him or her unclean? It is what comes out of the person that makes them unclean. Something entering from the outside goes into the stomach (not the heart) and then out of the body. If something evil comes from the heart, it will make that person unclean."

- JOH 14:27 ~ Jesus said, "Peace I leave you; my peace I give you; I do not give as the world gives, so never let your hearts be troubled or afraid."

- PHP 1:14 ~ Brothers in Christ are bold enough to speak the Word without fear.

- 2 TI 1:7 ~ God has not given us the spirit of fear, but of power, love, and a sound mind.

- HEB 5:7 ~ When you offer prayers and humble requests to God, He will hear you because you fear Him.

- HEB 12:28–29 ~ Since we will receive a kingdom which cannot fall, let us have grace to willingly serve God with reverence and awe, for He is a consuming fire.

- REV 14:6–7 ~ I saw another angel fly through heaven with the everlasting gospel, to preach to those who live on earth, and to every nation, kindred, tongue, and people; saying with a loud voice, "Fear God and give Him the glory; for the hour of His judgment has come. Worship Him who made heaven and earth, the sea and the fountains of water."

Oh Father, awesome God, you are gracious and merciful, giving us everything we need, so that we need not fear or worry, for you are always with us. We thank and praise you for our lives and livelihood, provisions and prosperity, and for our salvation which we did nothing to deserve. And all that you ask is that we love you. And we do love you, dearly, though we often are not very good at showing it. Help us to show our love for you more sincerely, and help us to love one another more authentically. For you are love, and that great love was shown to us by your Son who loved us so much He gave Himself for us so that we might live. In His glorious name we pray, Amen.

May 29

Constantinople Fell to the Turks on this date in 1453, led by the young sultan Mehmed II. The assault was from land and sea, with cannon barrages. Though the fortifications were formidable there was an insufficient fighting force inside the fortress and none of their allies came to their aid in time. This was largely due to unrest and division between Eastern and Western Roman Catholic orthodoxies. The subsequent invasion of Europe by Muslims was a jihad in opposition to Christianity in general. This event marked the end of the Byzantine Empire which had long been the objective of the Ottoman Turks. The famous cathedral Hagia Sophia became a mosque and, henceforth, the city became recognized as Istanbul. The governance of Suleiman would soon follow during the peak of the Ottomans, which would begin to decline after his death in 1566. But for six hundred years the Ottomans occupied Palestine and the Mediterranean coast, much of the Middle East, lands between Turkey and Greece and as far north as Hungary and Moldovia. Curiously, the fall of Constantinople also marked the transition from the Middle Ages to the Renaissance period.

The vast Ottoman empire would eventually shrink into the nation we now call Turkey which officially became a republic in 1923. The lengthy campaign was an attempt to create a global theocracy of Islam, but they ran into a dead end in their attempt to capture more of Europe. To this day, many of the lands occupied during the Ottoman Empire remain Muslim; and their global initiative has not diminished. If the Sunni and Shia Muslim factions ever joined forces, they could easily reestablish domination in the region and be a force to be reckoned with. But Biblical prophecy would indicate that this too will be unsuccessful.

- EZE 38—39 (summarized) ~ Face northward, toward Magog, and prophesy: God is against you Gog. You will mobilize armies of the distant north, as well as from Africa and Asia. You will invade Israel in an attempt to obtain her wealth and conquer her, Israel who has been at peace after having returned home from all over the world. This will happen in the latter years. There will be a great earthquake. You will end up fighting yourselves in the confusion. I will send animals to eat you, death, disease, and calamities. I will destroy five-sixths of your armies. I will rain fire and brimstone upon Magog and your allies. I will present Gog a graveyard in Israel, along the eastern passage by the sea. It will be called the Valley of Hamongog. And Israel will be burying the bodies for seven months to cleanse the land. It will be a glorious victory for Israel. I will be their Lord from that day on, and forever.

- JOE 3:1–2, 9–14 ~ Judah and Jerusalem will again become captives in those days. I will gather all nations together at the valley of Jehoshaphat, where I will plead with them on behalf of my people and my heritage Israel whom they have scattered throughout the world. Tell the Gentiles to prepare for war. Wake up the warriors; beat your tools into weapons of war. Let the weak say, "I am strong." Multitudes are gathering in the valley of decision, for the day of the Lord is coming when He will judge the pagans.

- MAT 24:15–20; LUK 21:20–21 ~ Jesus said, "When you see Jerusalem surrounded by its enemies the abomination of desolation is nigh. Flee into the mountains; do not turn back for anything. Hope it is not in winter; it especially will be difficult for those with small children."

- REV 18:21–24 ~ A mighty angel picked up a gigantic stone and cast it into the sea saying, "With such violence Babylon will be thrown down and disappear. There will be no music or art, no craft or trade. The lights will have gone out, and the bride and groom will have departed. Their vendors and businesses had once comprised the most powerful people on earth, and through their cunning they deceived the nations. Now the only thing remaining is the blood of prophets, saints, and the slain."

The Islamic jihad is alive and well in many countries, even though their dictatorial rule is unpopular among their own citizenry. But these extremists are determined to wipe out Jews and Christians in what they believe to be a holy war. They will cite passages from the Koran to justify their violence (Surah 3:151; Surah 8:39–60; Surah 9:1, 123), but there also are passages in the Koran suggesting that violence is necessary only in response to violence (Surah 2:190; Surah 4:90–91). There are contradictions; likewise, there are peaceful Muslims and violent Muslims. Interestingly, a growing membership of recent converts to Christianity were former Muslims.

Islam arose from a desire to be counted as God's chosen, much like Israel was in the Old Testament. So, they produced a holy book that would identify themselves as the chosen, claiming the birthright must have gone to Ishmael (Abraham's first son with his wife's servant Hagar) and not Isaac (Abraham's second son with Sarah, the son of promise, and father of Jacob who was renamed Israel). The Koran actually cites many Old Testament passages, often incorrectly. Further, Islam accepts the Bible ("the book") and recalls many of the events and persons in both the Old and New Testaments. Islam, Judaism, and Christianity share common beliefs, such as monotheism, heaven and hell, forgiveness and salvation. But there are numerous irreconcilable differences between the Bible and the Koran (from Barber, 2020a).

- The original Biblical text repeats the lineage of "Abraham, Isaac, and Jacob" but the Koran reads "Abraham, Ishmael, and Isaac" (Surah 2:133). Muslims presume that the promise to Abraham was through Ishmael, though the Bible explicitly states that Isaac was chosen by God to carry the "seed" of Abraham, meaning that Messiah would descend from Abraham and Isaac.
- The Koran denies the crucifixion and resurrection of Christ (Surah 41:147–148) asserting an imposter was crucified instead of Jesus (Surah 4:157).
- In the Koran, Jesus is a created being like Adam (Surah 3:59). He is considered a lesser prophet to Muhammad.
- The Koran describes paradise as a place where men are adorned with jewels and dressed in fine robes, relaxing on luxurious couches, drinking wine continuously without getting drunk, and enjoying the services from virgins created exclusively for man's enjoyment (Surah 52:14–20; Surah 55:52–68; Surah 56:7–48; Surah 83:22–25). It does not mention clearly what paradise will be like for women or even if they go to the same paradise as men.
- Women are treated as second class citizens in the Koran; they do not possess the rights and benefits of men (Surah 2:187; Surah 4:10–12; Surah 4:129–130; Surah 16:72; Surah 33:57). Women receive but a fraction of the inheritance of a husband; the same is true for siblings.
- The Christian concept of the trinity is misrepresented in the Koran as follows: God, Mary the mother of Jesus, and Jesus (Surah 5:116). The Koran states it would be perverse that God would have a son (Surah 10:68); they vehemently reject the deity of Christ.
- The Koran teaches that good works must outweigh bad ones to be saved (Surah 5:9; Surah 8:29; Surah 33:70–71; Surah 49:14). The Bible teaches that works do not save anyone, but for the work of Christ and our faith in Him.

Father, we ask for your protection from those who hate your people and make war with them. We also pray that those who follow counterfeit gods will find you through the power of the faith they possess. We pray for those who seek you in the wrong places, that they would find you anyway, for it is written: seek the Lord with all your heart and you will show yourself to them. We pray for those who are subjected to tyranny or are treated as second class citizens in their own country. Help us to boldly proclaim your name and witness the truth to all who ask about the love, peace, hope and joy that we possess through Christ, in whose name we pray, Amen.

May 30

Joan of Arc Was Burned at the Stake in Rouen France on this date in 1431. During the Hundred Years War between England and France, this teenager was declared a heretic because she claimed receiving visual and auditory messages from God at an early age via angels and saints; one such message was to join the war for freedom against the British. The peasant girl became a military leader committed to liberating France; her first victory was at the siege of Orleans. She continued to lead armies to more victories before her capture by the Burgundians. She was jailed, and charged with witchcraft and for dressing as a man, ignoring the fact that she was, in fact, an effective adversary. She rightfully identified herself as a wounded warrior, dressing like a man because she was always around men; but being a woman, she was abused and molested by the British and their allies. The French repelled the English invasion twenty years later, inspired by her martyrdom. She was canonized a saint by Pope Benedict XV (1920). Her feast day was declared May 30 in observance of her lawless execution; it is a national holiday in France.

France and England had long been adversaries, fighting over who should be sovereign in Europe. The century-long war had transpired off and on for eighty years when Joan of Arc arrived on the scene. She was influential in turning the tide of the war, and in the coronation of King Charles in 1429, thereby preventing England from installing their choice of ruler. This rivalry would continue sparking dissent in both countries, and increasing the exodus of residents seeking freedom in the New World which was discovered later that century (1492). The French Revolution erupted centuries later, during a reign of terror against suspected insurrectionists. The entire population of France became needy, disgruntled, and divided from the economic failures of various regimes responsible for destroying the nation's equity, economy, and stability.

When nations allow themselves to be ruled by despots and tyrants, the governments become fragile relatively quickly and revolutions often ensue. The uncertainty created in the populace adds further to the instability, as the ruler attempts to gain control over everything while taxing the people into submission. Due to greed, the collection of power goes to the dictator's head, thus becoming an adversary of God and the public. When rulers are corrupt, the citizenry becomes corrupted. When the citizenry is corrupt, the government becomes corrupt. In essence, corruption breeds more corruption. We need to steer clear of corrupt bureaucrats.

- PSA 12:8 ~ The wicked are all around when vile men are exalted.
- PSA 62:10 ~ Do not use oppression or robbery to obtain wealth; and if you are fortunate to become wealthy, do not set your heart on your wealth.
- PRO 1:18–19 ~ Those who are greedy for riches and oppress others to obtain riches are ambushing their own lives and will succeed in destroying themselves.
- PRO 16:12 ~ It is an abomination for kings to commit wickedness, for their throne is established in righteousness.
- PRO 28:15 ~ Like a roaring lion or a raging bear, so is a wicked ruler to the poor people.
- PRO 29:2 ~ When the righteous are in authority, the people rejoice.
- PRO 29:12 ~ If a ruler listens to lies, his entire cabinet will be evil.
- HAB 1:4 ~ The law becomes loose and justice is not served, for the wicked encompass the righteous and wrong judgment proceeds.

As the era of judges waned, the elders of the church in Israel insisted on having a king like the other countries around them. God was displeased, for He had been sovereign in Israel and was their King; God did not want His people to give their full allegiance to any man. Kings, despots, and tyrants have an awful track-record, because they turn into greedy control freaks. There have been dictators throughout history and the nations they ruled always collapsed from greed, pride, and lust. Such is the fate of totalitarianism when leaders strive for total control and power.

- 1 SA 8:4–22; 1 SA 10:1 ~ The elders of Israel gathered together and went to see Samuel at Ramah; lacking confidence in Samuel, they requested a king to judge them instead. Other nations had kings and they wanted one. Samuel was displeased; but the Lord allowed Samuel to affirm their demand, for it was not Samuel they were rejecting, but the sovereignty of God Himself. Samuel warned the people with the words of the Lord: The king they would get would steal their sons for his chariots, horses and runners, making them all instruments of war; this king would steal their daughters to serve his palaces, officers, and staff; he would take the best of the fields, employees, and livelihoods for his own use; when Israel eventually cries to the Lord, He will not hear. Nevertheless, the elders did not obey the voice of Samuel and again demanded a king to lead them and judge them. The Lord told Samuel to move forward with their plan. Later, Samuel took a vial of oil and poured it over the head of Saul, kissed him, and said this was the Lord's anointing as king over His inheritance.

- 1 SA 15:20–28 ~ Saul explained to Samuel how he had obeyed God and defeated the Amalekites. But the people took the spoils which God forbade them from doing. Samuel said to King Saul, "Does the Lord appreciate burnt offerings and sacrifices as much as He does obedience? To obey is better than to sacrifice, and to listen is more important than the flesh of rams. Rebellion is as bad as witchcraft, and pride is as evil as idolatry. Since you have rejected the command of the Lord, He has rejected you as king." Saul asked for forgiveness. Samuel was turning away when Saul took hold of his sleeve, tearing it. Samuel said, "The Lord has torn the kingdom of Israel from you and given it to another who is better than you."

- 1 SA 28:7–20 ~ After Samuel the prophet had died, Saul sought an audience with him, and decided to consult a spiritual medium. Wearing a disguise, Saul went to the witch of Endor, herself possessed by a demon. She summoned Samuel, had a vision, and cried out. Both assumed it was Samuel, especially when they heard the entity ask, "Why have you summoned me?" Saul asked about her vision, and she told him she saw an old man wearing a robe and spirits rising from the ground. Saul asked for guidance against the Philistines. The entity told him he and his sons would suffer defeat at the hands of the Philistines, for the kingdom had been torn away from him and given to his neighbor David. Saul dropped to the ground in fear and despair.

- PSA 22:28 ~ The kingdom belongs to the Lord; He is the governor of all the nations.

Our constitutional republic has succeeded precisely because of the separation of powers doctrine. The executive or president must neither have full sovereignty nor authorization to enact unilateral commands. The legislative branch makes the laws; the executive enforces the laws. Our judiciary interprets the application of law and passes judgment on the constitutionality of laws. These checks and balances prevent any one branch from presiding over the other two. We must not lose this balance in government else we lose our freedoms guaranteed under the Constitution, and/or bestowed by God, the divine lawmaker; His Law trumps all other laws.

Father, we pray that you would bless our native land and enable us to keep our republic from the greedy powermongers. Likewise, help the citizens of foreign lands where the people are oppressed at the hand of tyrants and dictators to be set free by the blood of Jesus. We ask this in Jesus's name which means Savior; for He is the King of kings whose name is above all other names, Amen.

May 31

Worst Flash Flood in US History occurred on this day in Johnstown, PA in 1889. Approximately 2200 souls were lost when the South Fork Dam broke; spillways were clogged up and unable to drain the heavy rainfall. The people downstream had no idea what was coming. Flooding is one of many natural disasters occurring annually whether by flash flood or sustained hurricanes. When it comes to hurricanes, the US record goes to Galveston TX (1900) when a category four flooded the island and coastlands, killing over 8000 people.

When God created the earth, it was flooded in entirety, until the waters separated and dry land emerged. Due to the proliferation of wickedness, God destroyed the earth by flood; there were only eight survivors, which were Noah and his family. God has been known to use floods and other natural disasters to punish wickedness.

- GEN 1:6 ~ God said, "Let there be an expanse in the midst of the waters, to divide the waters from other waters."

- GEN 6:5–8, 13–14 ~ God was appalled by the proliferation of evil on earth. It grieved God to His heart. But Noah found grace in the Lord. God told Noah He would destroy the world and its wickedness with a flood. Then God instructed Noah to build an ark.

- GEN 7:4, 17 ~ It rained continuously for forty days and nights causing a great flood.

- GEN 19:24–25 ~ God rained fire and brimstone upon Sodom and Gomorrah. He destroyed those cities, the plains, the inhabitants, and everything that was alive or growing.

- DEU 28:21–28, 59 ~ God will send diseases, plagues, and war to destroy you. The heavens and earth will be unyielding as iron; a blight will destroy your crops. The land will become dry as dust from lack of rain; dust storms will destroy you. You will be defeated by your enemies. If you do not observe God's Law or revere His glorious and awesome name, He will send horrible plagues, harsh and prolonged disasters, and severe and lingering illnesses upon you and your descendants.

- EZE 5:17 ~ I will send famine, evil beasts, pestilence and the sword upon you.

During the end of times there will be a series of catastrophes, which are signs of Christ's return. There will be floods, earthquakes, famines, pestilences, wars, fire and brimstone. The earth will be destroyed with fire (2 PE 3:10) and the unfaithful will inherit the lake of fire.

- LUK 17:16–30 ~ As it was in the days of Noah, so it will be when the Son of man returns. The people ate, drank, and married until Noah and his family entered the ark, the flood came, and the rest drowned. Likewise, it will be as the days of Lot; they ate, drank, bought, sold, planted and built, until Lot and his family departed; then it rained fire and brimstone destroying them all. Accordingly, perilous times will draw closer in the last days.

- REV 6:8 ~ I saw a pale horse, and riding upon it was Death, and Hell followed him. And power was given to them to kill one quarter of the earth via the sword, hunger, death, and wild beasts.

- REV 21:8 ~ The fearful, unbelieving, abominable, murderous, promiscuous, idolatrous, lying, and ungodly will have their part in the lake that burns with fire and brimstone; this is the second death.

Father in heaven, we pray for forgiveness and protection. Help us to be ready for Jesus to return, and prepare us to face the calamities that will precede His coming. Let us be faithful until the end, individually and as a nation, with the courage of our forefathers. In Jesus's name, Amen.

June 1

National Pen Pal Day is dedicated to people who enjoy writing letters to others and receiving letters from them, to include total strangers. The idea was promoted in 1917 by Rosie Throll, an American who had many pen pals of her own, and even traveled abroad to visit some of them. She also was cofounder of Pen Pals United. There was a time when letter writing was the only way to communicate with loved ones who lived far away. Interest in having pen pals that are not known to one another began in the early 1900s. In 1936 the Student Letter Exchange was formed which provided a service connecting people from across the globe. They could commence exchanging letters by mail with someone who shared similar interests, dispositions, and desires. It is still a fun fad, but most people have turned to electronic communications, particularly social media which makes keeping in touch less personal and more regulated.

Making friends with people in other parts of the world can be enlightening and educational. So today, you might consider finding a pen pal, especially if you are short on friends, want to make more friends, or seek a diversion. You will be able to learn their culture, habits, religion, or whatever the two of you like or dislike. Share memories, photographs, and things unique to your respective cultures. After you get to know them, you might want to follow them on social media. But social media is not a reliable way to begin friendships, in fact it can be downright risky. For example, studies show that online dating is chancy; the probability of a breakup or divorce from such relationships is significantly higher than with traditional dating. People are losing their ability to speak to others spontaneously and extemporaneously, especially students who are spending more time on the computer and less in the classroom or at school. Writing letters helps to build communication skills that will be useful in other settings.

Letters were valuable in preserving Biblical history. Writers in the Old and New Testaments used durable material such as animal hide, papyrus, and copper, which was the case with the Dead Sea Scrolls. Those scrolls, dating from the fourth century BC to the second century AD, were found preserved in clay jars in caves near Qumran, Israel from 1946-1956. The entire Old Testament was represented, minus the book of Esther. The complete book of Isaiah was found intact; the current Hebrew version of Isaiah does not differ appreciably from the one found at Qumran. One might entertain the possibility that God directed these scrolls to be preserved and discovered, providing evidence for the skeptics that God's truth never changes. Also found were writings from the New Testament with references to Messiah. One fragment had the words "Son of the Most High" a phrase found in the book of Luke.

Most New Testament books were written as letters, called epistles; the only exceptions were the four Gospels (Matthew, Mark, Luke, and John). Acts of the Apostles was written by Luke and addressed to Theophilus. Revelation was written by John and addressed to the seven principal Christian churches in Asia Minor. Thirteen epistles were written by Paul, and seven were written by apostles or brothers of Jesus: Peter (1 & 2), John (1, 2, & 3), James, and Jude. Hebrews was likely written by Paul or one of his companions (indicated in HEB 13 below, where the letter writer mentions Timothy and the fact that Paul was writing from Rome, Italy).

- 1 CO 7:1–4 ~ Regarding the matters you wrote to me (Paul) about: It is good when a man does not touch a woman intimately. Avoid fornication; let each man have sex with his own wife and each woman with her own husband. The husband should fulfill his marital duty to his wife and likewise the wife to her husband. The wife does not have exclusive power over her body but makes herself available to her husband. In the same way, the husband does not deprive his wife.

- 2 CO 3:1–3 ~ Should we start by commending ourselves? Or do we need, as others do, epistles of commendation to you or from you? You are an epistle written inside our hearts, known and read of all men, inasmuch as you are manifestly declared to be the epistle of Christ, ministered by us: not written with ink but with the Spirit of the living God; not in tablets of stone but in the fleshy tablets of the heart.

- 1 TI 3:14 ~ These things I (Paul) write to you with the hope of visiting you soon.

- HEB 13:18–25 ~ Pray for us, for we hope that we are in good conscience, willing to live honestly in all things, and can return to you soon. May the God of peace who brought Jesus back to life, the great Shepherd of the flock, through the blood of the everlasting covenant make you prosper in every good work to obey His will, doing that which pleases God through Jesus Christ in whom is the glory forever and ever, Amen. I ask you brothers, endure my word of exhortation which I have written to you in these few words. Know that your brother Timothy has been freed, with whom I will see you if he can get here soon. Say hello to your leaders and all the saints. Those in Italy salute you. Grace be unto you all, Amen.

- 1 JO 2:12–13, 21–22 ~ I write to you children because your sins are forgiven for Jesus's sake. I write to you fathers because you have known the Lord from the beginning. I write to you young men because you have overcome the wicked one. I write to you little children because you have known the Father. I do not write because you are ignorant of the truth, but because you know it; you are able to tell when a lie is not the truth. The liar is the one who denies Jesus as the Christ; that person is an antichrist who denies the Father and the Son.

- REV 1:4–6 ~ John greeted the seven churches saying, "Grace and peace be to you from the One who is, was, and is to come, and from the seven spirits before His throne, and from Jesus Christ the faithful witness, the firstborn of the dead, and the ruler over all earthly kings. Unto Him who loved us and washed away our sins in His own blood and has made us kings and priests to God and His Father, to Him be glory and dominion forever and ever."

- REV 2:1–7 ~ To the angel of the church of Ephesus John wrote: He who holds the seven stars in His right hand and walks in the midst of the seven golden candlesticks says, "I know your works, your labor, and your patience, and how you cannot tolerate evil people who claim to be apostles, knowing they are lying. You have endured with patience for my name's sake without growing weary. Nevertheless, I have a complaint about you losing the kind of love you had in the beginning. Consider how far you have fallen and repent, and return to your original ways, or I will come quickly and remove your candlestick from its place. To your credit, you have rejected the false teachings of the Nicolaitans which I also despise. Listen to what the Spirit of the churches says: to those who overcome I will allow them to eat of the tree of life in the paradise of God."

- REV 2:8–11 ~ To the angel of the church of Smyrna John wrote: These things are said to you from He who was dead and yet lives, the first and the last, "I know your works, tribulations, and poverty (though you are rich); and I know the blasphemy of those calling themselves Jews who are not, for they are from the synagogue of Satan. Do not fear the things you must suffer, for the devil will throw some of you into prison to be tried. You will have tribulation ten days, but be faithful unto death and I will give you a crown of life. Listen to what the Spirit of the churches says: those who overcome will not be affected by the second death."

- REV 2:12–17 ~ To the angel of the church of Pergamos John wrote: He who holds the sharp double-edged sword says, "I know your works and where you live, where Satan also has his throne; I know you hold tightly to my name and have not denied your faith in me, even when my faithful witness Antipas was executed in your city where Satan resides. Nevertheless, I have a few complaints, for some among you follow Balaam who taught Balak to throw an obstacle before the Israelites, eating things sacrificed to idols and committing fornication. You also have followed the teachings of the Nicolaitans who I despise. Repent or I will come quickly and will fight against them with the sword of my mouth. Listen to what the Spirit of the churches says: to those who overcome I will give them the hidden manna to eat, and I will give each one a white stone upon which their name will be written, which nobody can see but they who receive it."

- REV 2:18–29 ~ To the angel of the church of Thyatira John wrote: The Son of God whose eyes are like flames of fire and feet are like polished brass says, "I know your works, charity, service, faith, and patience; you have increased in good works since the start. Nevertheless, I have complaints: you tolerate that woman Jezebel, who calls herself a prophetess, seducing you into fornication and eating things sacrificed to idols. I gave her a chance to repent of her fornication but she did not. Therefore, I will throw her along with those committing fornication with her into a bed of tribulation, unless they repent. I will slay her children unto death so all the churches will know that I am He who searches hearts and minds, repaying everyone according to their works. To the rest of you in Thyatira who do not follow her or listen to her Satanic secrets, I will not burden you, just hold onto what you already have. To those who overcome and keep my ways until the end, I will give power over nations to rule with an iron scepter and shatter them as pottery, just as I have received power from my Father. I will give them the morning star. Listen to what the Spirit says to the churches."

- REV 3:1–6 ~ To the angel of the church of Sardis John wrote: He who holds the seven Spirits of God and the seven stars says, "I know your works, and your belief that you are alive, but you are dead. You need to wake up and strengthen what remains before it dies, for I have not found your works to be right in the sight of God. Remember what you have received and heard, hold onto it, and repent. If you are not watchful, I will come as a thief at an hour when you least expect it. There are some of you in Sardis who have not defiled their clothing, and walk with me in white; they are worthy. Those who overcome will be clothed in white, and their names will not be erased from the Book of Life, for I will vouch for them before my Father and His angels. Listen to what the Spirit says to the churches."

- REV 3:7–13 ~ To the angel of the church of Philadelphia John wrote: He that is holy and true, and holds the key of David says, "Whatever I open, nobody can shut; and whatever I shut, nobody can open. I know your works and I have opened a door to you, and nobody can shut it. For you have just a little strength, keeping my Word without denying my name. I will make those liars who are of the synagogue of Satan, calling themselves Jews which they are not, to fall down at my feet, and know that I have loved you. Because you followed my directions and persevere, I will keep you from the hour of temptation which will come upon the entire world, to try the souls of those who live on the earth. For I will come quickly, so keep hold of the faith so that nobody can steal your crown. Whoever overcomes, I will make them a pillar in the temple of God; and there they will stay. I will write the name of God upon them and the name of His city, the new Jerusalem which comes down from heaven, and I will give them all a new name. Listen to what the Spirit says to the churches."

- REV 3:14–22 ~ To the church of Laodicea John wrote: Listen to what the Amen, the faithful and true witness from the beginning of creation says, "I know your works; you are neither cold nor hot; I would rather you were one or the other. Because you are lukewarm, I will spit you out of my mouth. You say you are rich, with an abundance of goods, lacking nothing; but you do not realize that you are wretched, miserable, poor, blind, and naked. I suggest you buy from me gold refined in the fire and become truly rich, with white clothes to cover your shame and nakedness; and salve to put in your eyes so you can see. Those who I love I will rebuke and chastise; be excited and repent. Behold, I stand at the door and knock. Whoever hears my voice and opens the door, I will come in and dine with them and they with me. To those who overcome I will allow to sit with me in the throne room, even as I overcame and am sitting with my Father beside His throne. Listen to what the Spirit says to the churches."

We exchange countless emails, texts, and phone calls for spontaneous conversations with people we know, forgetting most of it shortly thereafter. Rarely do we correspond in letters and cards, unless it is a close friend or family member. We tend to be leery corresponding with perfect strangers, especially on electronic media where there is a high degree of deception and exploitation. In fact, if your kids are engaging in such communications, you should monitor them because predators are becoming a greater threat with the expansion of internet applications and capabilities, anonymity, and artificial intelligence. Sending letters and cards with a message is safer, and more discreet, intriguing, and satisfying, because the persons have taken their time preparing and refining the content. It is private because it is in writing and sealed in an envelope. Thus, the content cannot be cancelled by an algorithm, or the political correctness police; neither is it easily monitored by the government, media trackers, or hackers. So, if you want your communication to remain confidential, mail it; of course, that doesn't guarantee it won't be intercepted by your spouse, parent, or child. Anyway, the personal touch makes quite a difference, making pen pal correspondence more personal than everyday communications. Besides, pen pals do not have to be strangers; they merely need to enjoy writing to one another.

- PRO 2:11–12 ~ Discretion will protect you and understanding will guard you, to deliver you from the way of evil and those who speak perverse things.

- PRO 8:12 ~ Wisdom goes with forethought, wherein lies knowledge and discretion.

- PRO 15:2 ~ The tongue of the wise applies knowledge prudently, but the mouth of fools pours out foolishness.

- PRO 25:9–10 ~ Argue your case with your neighbor personally, and do not betray their confidence, so if others hear it they will not shame you or ruin your reputation.

Father, you have written your Word into our hearts; help us to forward that message as good stewards of your grace. Let us respect the privacy of others, and to be discreet and prudent in our communications. Never let us be gossipers, presumptuous, or to denigrate people behind their backs, especially when the sources of our opinions or evidence are questionable. When it comes to your Word of truth, help us to be outspoken and honest; and hopefully, folks will listen and repent, and be blessed, as we ourselves are blessed. Let all who shun the sacrifice of Jesus take notice and turn from their disbelief and sinful ways, and open the door when He knocks, which is often; in His name we pray, Amen.

June 2

Indian Citizenship Act Became Law, signed by President Coolidge on this date in 1924, granting US citizenship to all native Americans. This was basically an addendum to the Fourteenth Amendment of the Constitution which had not explicitly stated that indigenous people could be considered citizens by birth. Since they avoided taxation because of their tribal affiliation, they were not considered citizens in certain courts of law prior to this bill being passed. Many native tribes were not interested in citizenship for fear of losing their sovereignty and land, and for good reason. The Indian Reorganization Act of 1934 resulted in the return of Indian lands, and also provided for education, healthcare, and infrastructure to improve the quality of life on the reservations. A few states continued inhibiting natives from voting; those practices were outlawed and the laws enforced after the passage of the Civil Rights Act of 1964.

Our Bible-based foundation has not stopped racists and politicians from discriminating against minorities, women, and indigenous people. The truth of God's Word is not accepted by the unbelievers who would make or change our rules and laws. Previous efforts to subvert the Constitution have failed; but once again, our nation is faced with ungodly people trying to force their unpopular and unrighteous will upon the rest of us. Christians need to stand up against those who do not believe in equality and opportunity for others, and remove derelicts from office and positions of authority. They have forfeited the right to govern by showing favoritism to their funding sources, certain individuals, groups, businesses, and foreigners. In God's eyes we are equally loved with equal opportunity to become citizens of His kingdom by believing His Word, accepting the free gift of Christ's salvation, and proving our commitment with an active faith.

- HOS 2:23 ~ I will call them my people who were not my people, and I will call them beloved who were not my beloved.

- ROM 9:4–5 ~ Who are the Israelites, to whom God gave the Law and granted the adoption, and with whom God made covenants and promises? Christ came for them and for all people.

- 1 CO 1:24 ~ To those whom God has called, both Jews and Gentiles (non-Jews) alike, Christ is the power of God and the wisdom of God.

- EPH 2:18–21 ~ In Christ we have access to our Father in heaven via the Holy Spirit. Therefore, God's people are no longer strangers or foreigners; they are fellow citizens with the saints and the household of God. God's house is built upon the foundation laid by the apostles and prophets, Christ Himself being the chief cornerstone. Upon Him the entire church is built, and in Him the entire church is held together to be a holy temple of the Lord.

- GAL 3:28 ~ There is no such thing as Jew or Greek, slave or free, male or female, for we are equal in Jesus Christ.

- PHP 3:20 ~ Our citizenship is in heaven where we also look to our Savior, the Lord Jesus.

- COL 3:15 ~ Let the peace of God rule in your hearts, since as members of one body you were called to peace. Therefore, be thankful.

- HEB 13:14 ~ Here on earth we have no city, but we are looking for the city to come.

- 1 PE 1:3–4 ~ Praise be to God the Father of our Lord Jesus, who according to His abundant mercy we are reborn into a living hope through the resurrection of Christ from the dead, to obtain an inheritance that is incorruptible, undefiled, and eternal, reserved in heaven for you.

Father, we thank and praise you for our inheritance in heaven through Jesus Christ. We pray that all people would come to know you and your Son in whose name we pray, Amen

June 3

National Love Conquers All Day is an annual celebration of love and loved ones. The phrase was coined by Virgil, a Roman poet from the first century BC, who wrote (in Latin) "Love conquers all, so let us yield to love." Today is an unofficial holiday of unknown origin but it is definitely a good idea. The Bible teaches that God is love, so it stands to reason that He conquers every form of evil that comes against love. God's is the only kind of love that conquers all, although brotherly love for fellow human beings can conquer a multitude of sins.

- LEV 19:18 ~ Do not take revenge or bear a grudge but love your neighbor as yourself.
- PRO 10:12 ~ Hatred stirs up strife, but love covers all sins.
- AMO 5:15 ~ Hate evil, love goodness, and establish justice.
- JAM 5:19–20 ~ If a person strays from the truth, and another person converts him or her, the person who converted the sinner from the error will save a soul from death, and will cover a multitude of sins.
- 1 PE 4:8 ~ Love one another fervently, for love will cover a multitude of sins.

The Greeks have several words for love. Physical love, often associated with passion and sex is *eros*; Eros was the Greek god of love. Then there is playful or casual love (*ludus*), romantic love or commitment (*pragma*), obsessive love (*mania*), and familial love (*storge*). Next is brotherly love (*philia*); the city of brotherly love (Philadelphia) is named from this Latin word. The most powerful and perfect kind of love is *agape*, which is ascribed to God alone, for only He is perfect. Consider the power of pure love, for it is the most powerful force in this universe. Perfect love destroys evil, conquers fear, and overcomes the world.

- JOH 3:16 ~ Jesus said, "God loved the world so much that He gave His only begotten Son, so that anyone who believed in Him would never die but would live forever."
- ROM 8:35–39 ~ What can separate us from the love of Christ: tribulation, distress, persecution, famine, nakedness, peril, or sword? As it is written, for your sake we face death on a daily basis; we are sent as sheep to the slaughter. But we have conquered these things through Him who loved us. For I am convinced that neither death nor life, neither angels nor demons, neither the present nor the future, nor any powers, neither height nor depth, nor anything in all creation can separate us from the love of God that is in Jesus Christ our Lord.
- 1 JO 4:7–12, 16–21 ~ Let us love one another, for love is from God, and those who love are born of God and know Him. If you do not love God, you cannot know Him because God is love. The love of God was manifested among us through His only Son, so we might live through Him. If God loves us so much, we should love one another; if we love one another, God lives in us and His love is perfected in us. If you abide in love you abide in God, and God abides in you. This perfect love gives us confidence on the day of judgment, because there is no fear in love but perfect love destroys fear, because fear brings torment. We love because God loved us first. You cannot say you love God and hate your brother without being a liar, because you cannot hate someone you have seen and still love God who you have never seen. So, you should love God and your brother (neighbor).
- 2 TI 1:7 ~ God has not given us the spirit of fear but of power, love, and a sound mind.

Perhaps the most powerful type of love which humanity can muster, outside of one's family perhaps, is brotherly love: loving your neighbor as yourself; loving all people, for we all are made in the image of God. We are supposed to love them, but oftentimes we don't like them. Therefore, such love is not altogether unconditional like God's love is. Humans are incapable of expressing perfect love continuously due to our sinfulness. But we will possess perfect love when we receive glorified bodies in heaven, where we will be surrounded by love, enveloped with love, and filled with love, having been purified by the love of Christ, perfected in the love of God the Father, and saturated with the love of the Holy Spirit.

- DEU 6:5 ~ You must love the Lord your God with all your heart, soul, and might.

- MAT 22:37–40 ~ Jesus said, "Love the Lord your God with all your heart, mind, and soul: this is the first and greatest commandment. The second is like unto the first: Love your neighbor as yourself. All the laws and the prophets depend on these two commandments."

- LUK 6:32, 35 ~ Jesus said, "If you love only those who love you, what reward do you receive? Even sinners love those who love them. Love everyone, even your enemies. Help others whenever you can, expecting nothing in return, and your reward will be great, and you will be a child of God."

- JOH 13:34–35 ~ Jesus said, "I am giving you a new commandment, that you love one another as I have loved you. This is how people will be able to tell that you are my disciples."

- JOH 15:12–13 ~ Jesus said, "Love each other as I have loved you. No greater love exists than to give one's life for their friends."

- ROM 13:10 ~ Love does no wrong to a neighbor; therefore, love is the fulfilling of the Law.

- 1 CO 13:2–8, 13 ~ Even if you have the gift of prophecy, can understand mysteries, and have a faith to move mountains, you are nothing without love. Even if you give all you have to the poor, you profit nothing if you do not have love. Love is patient. Love is kind. Love is never envious or conceited. Love is not rude, self-seeking, or angered, nor does it find pleasure in sin. Love does not think of sinful things nor is it provoked by evil. Love rejoices in the truth. Love always protects, always trusts, always hopes, and always endures. Love never fails. Faith, hope, and love abide; but the greatest of these three is love.

- COL 3:14 ~ Above all put on love, which binds all things together in perfect harmony.

- HEB 13:1–2 ~ Let brotherly love continue. Do not forget to help strangers, for you may be ministering to angels for all you know.

- 1 PE 1:22 ~ Purify your souls by obedience to the truth and earnest love for one another.

- 1 JO 3:16–22 ~ We can understand the love of God because He gave His life for us; therefore, we should be willing to give our lives out of brotherly love. Those who have the means to help their fellow man and do not help must not have the love of God in them. My children, let us not love just in writing or in voice, let us show it in action and in truth. This is how we are sure that we belong to the truth and why our hearts are at rest in the Lord's presence. If our hearts condemn us, we know that God is greater than our hearts and that He is all-knowing. Dear friends, our hearts do not condemn us because we have confidence before God, receiving from Him anything we ask, as long as we keep His commandments and do what pleases Him.

Father, your power is love, and you have bestowed that love upon us. Thank you for giving us the power to repel and defeat evil in our midst using the love we possess, bestowed upon us through faith in Christ. Help us to cling to that love and willingly express it to all people, loving them as ourselves as you have commanded. Above all, help us to love you first and foremost, with all of our might, body, soul, and spirit. In the name of Jesus, by whose loving act of sacrifice we are saved, Amen.

June 4

Audacity to Hope Day is another unofficial holiday which makes sense. Today we are reminded that there is hope; there always is no matter how bad our circumstances may seem. It is appropriate that hope day follows love day. Because love gives us faith, and faith builds hope; the three come as a package. It has been said that the last thing ever lost is hope (another ancient Latin proverb), because the absence of hope leaves us with hopelessness and despair; hopeless people are more likely to take desperate measures. No matter what the world throws at us, hope is an option, because we know bad luck will pass in time. In fact, everything bad and evil occurring in this world will someday pass; and the world itself will someday pass (MAT 24:35). If you possess godly hope, you realize that evil, fear, sadness, and deceit cannot exist in heaven: where Bible-believing people who have put God first in their life will be headed for a new life. Since we know the truth and therefore trust in God's promises, we can begin to walk in newness of life today (ROM 6:4). Hope supports faith, because it acknowledges truth; faith is the proof that what we hope for already exists. Those who do not believe in God's guarantee have no hope of an afterlife in paradise, and that reflects the epitome of despair. Today, take a chance on hope. In the lesson yesterday we read: love, faith, and hope abide but the greatest of these is love (1 CO 13:13). The next is faith and then hope. Faith is greater, because if you do not believe there is no hope. Similarly, if you hope but do not believe, you will not trust in it. Our belief in Jesus Christ provides the hope of salvation; that faith proves we are trusting in Him alone.

- JOB 8:13–14 ~ The destiny of those who forget God is the loss of hope, for their trust in worldly things is a fragile one.

- JOB 11:18, 20 ~ You will be confident because there is hope; you will be protected, so take rest in your safety. But the wicked will not escape; their hope will be like taking their last breath.

- PSA 31:24 ~ Be strong and let your heart take courage, you who hope in the Lord.

- PSA 130:5 ~ I wait for the Lord, my soul waits; and in His words will I hope.

- PRO 10:28 ~ The hope of the righteous ends in gladness, but the expectation of the wicked comes to nothing.

- LAM 3:21–22 ~ I have hope because the steadfast love of the Lord never ceases and His mercies never end.

- ACT 2:26–27 ~ My heart is glad and my tongue rejoices; my body abides in hope. For the Lord will not destroy my soul in hell.

- ROM 5:2–5 ~ Through Jesus we have obtained access to His grace in which we stand, and we rejoice in our hope of sharing the glory of God. We rejoice in our sufferings knowing that they produce endurance, which produces character, which produces hope. And hope does not disappoint us, because God's love has been poured into our hearts through the Holy Spirit.

- ROM 8:19–20, 24–25 ~ All creation waits eagerly for the revealing of the children of God. For the creation was subjected to futility, not of its own will, but by the will of Him who subjected it in hope. With this hope we were saved. However, hope that is seen is not really hope; for who hopes for what one has? But if we hope for what we cannot see, we must wait for it patiently.

- ROM 15:13 ~ May the God of hope fill you with all joy and peace in believing, so that by the power of the Holy Spirit you may abound in hope.

JUNE

- GAL 5:5–6 ~ Through the Spirit, by faith, we wait for the hope of righteousness. Circumcision is of no avail; instead, it is faith working through love.

- COL 1:23, 27 ~ Continue steadfast in the faith, not shifting from the hope of the Gospel proclaimed to all of creation under heaven. The riches of the wonder of God's mystery, which is Christ in you, is the hope of glory made known to the Gentiles.

- 1 TH 5:8 ~ Let us be sober, and put on the breastplate of faith and love, and for a helmet, the hope of salvation.

- HEB 11:1, 3, 6 ~ Faith is the assurance of things hoped for, the evidence of things not seen. By faith we understand that the world was created by the Word of God, such that things we see were made from things which do not appear. Without faith, it is impossible to please God, for whoever would wish to come to Him must believe He exists and that He rewards those who seek Him.

- 1 PE 1:18–22 ~ You are not redeemed with corruptible things like gold or silver, you are redeemed with the precious blood of Christ, who was like a lamb without blemish or spots. He, who was ordained before the foundations of the world, was made manifest in these past days just for you. Believe in Him who God raised from the dead and gave glory, so that your faith and hope can remain in God. Your souls will be purified for obeying the truth that the Holy Spirit has shown us; therefore, you must fervently love each other with a pure heart.

The name of this holiday was taken from President Obama's book *The Audacity of Hope: Thoughts on Reclaiming the American Dream* (2006). The statement is a bit of a misnomer because hope does not require one to be audacious, bold or daring; it requires that we be humble and persevere with patience. I would argue that faith requires audacity, since one has to have guts to share their faith in a world where people of faith are persecuted. Certainly, hope and the American Dream are related, insofar as the hope of everyone who lives in America or immigrates to America will at some point consider this as an opportunity to live out their dreams.

- PRO 24:14 ~ Wisdom is sweet to the soul; find it and you find hope that cannot be removed.

- ROM 12:12 ~ Rejoice in hope, be patient in tribulation, and be constant in prayer.

- COL 1:26–27 ~ The mystery, hidden from ages past, has now been revealed to the saints, to whom God will give the riches of His glory. It is for anyone who turns to Christ for their hope including the Gentiles.

- 1 TI 6:17 ~ Tell the rich people in the world not to act so proud or to set their hopes on uncertain earthly riches. Tell them to set their hope and trust in God, who furnishes everything in this world for us to enjoy.

- TIT 2:11–14 ~ The grace of God that brings salvation has appeared to all people. It teaches us to refrain from ungodliness and worldly passions, and to live our lives in an upright, godly, and self-controlled manner. This we do as we await the blessed hope for the glorious appearing of our great God and Savior Jesus Christ, who gave Himself for us to redeem us from sin and to purify His people for Himself.

- TIT 3:7 ~ Justified by God's grace, we are made heirs according to the hope of eternal life.

- 1 PE 3:15 ~ Sanctify the Lord in your hearts, and always be ready to give an answer, with humility and respect, to anyone who asks about the hope that is within you.

Father, we thank you for our hope which is based on the blessed assurance of eternal life, through faith in Christ our Savior, whose love lives in us along with your Holy Spirit, Amen.

DAILY DEVOTIONAL EVENTS

June 5

World Environment Day is one of many holidays introduced by the United Nations. Today is about protecting and preserving the environment, including the climate, habitat, air, water, natural resources, etc. This holiday was spawned in 1972 at the close of the UN *Conference of the Human Environment*, in Stockholm Sweden. The international holiday falls in the first week of June with a UN conference and theme in a different world metropolis each year. Obviously, all people on earth should be involved in conserving the planet, ensuring we do not destroy it, our life support, and the creatures that live here. The problem is, while people may care, not all governments do. The USA does, by far, the most to protect the planet in terms of innovations, investments, reducing emissions, and production regulations. This is not the case in other parts of the world such as India and China who have the highest populations, and also are the greatest polluters on earth. Whether or not the relative differences between the carbon footprints of nations are important to the overall life of this planet is debatable. Science indicates the percent of impact on climate change is negligible given all of our recent efforts and costs. Unless all nations invest the same amount of effort, enforce the same regulations, and honor the treaties equally, there will be no improvements, whereas resource conservation is critical to all nations.

- GEN 1:26 ~ God said, "Let us make humans in our image, after our likeness. And let them have dominion over the fish of the sea, over the fowl of the air, over the cattle, and over all the earth and everything that creeps upon the earth."

- GEN 2:15 ~ God took the man and placed him in the Garden of Eden to dress it and keep it.

- PSA 8:4–9 ~ Who are humans, that you would be mindful of them, and the offspring of humans that you would care for them? You made man only a little lower than the angels and crowned him with glory and honor. You made him ruler over your creations, and put everything on earth below him, including the animals, birds, and fish. Oh Lord, how majestic is your name in all the earth!

- PSA 104:23–24, 27 ~ A man goes to work and labors until evening. Oh Lord, how numerous are your works. In wisdom, you have made us all and filled the earth with your riches. The creatures wait on you to feed them; they gather at your hand and are filled.

- 1 CO 4:1–2 ~ Regard evangelists as servants of Christ, entrusted with the mysteries that God has revealed. It is required that those who have been given a trust prove faithful in it.

UN environmental initiatives and this holiday are supported by governments, businesses, and private entities, establishing a platform to publicize views on environmental issues, and obtain funds to address those issues. Given the wide range of possible topics it's hard to pick any one. It is up to each and every citizen to choose a cause that is meaningful to them and try to make a difference in their arena or surroundings. Many cities will have group gatherings on the various themes for the day, and this would be worthwhile attending if you want to learn about becoming involved by donating your money and/or your time.

We as stewards of the planet have been appointed by God. We must be conscious of our own actions towards the environment, be they negative or positive. Caring about the planet is a commandment of God, and is part of one's maturity as a human being, by doing a better job than in the past. So, think twice about tossing that piece of garbage out the window; if you don't have a trash bin in your car, get one. If your yard looks like a pigsty, tidy it up, for it degrades the entire neighborhood; if your office is a mess, organize it for it degrades the entire business. If your city is a litter box, you could help clean that up too. These are things you can do to celebrate World Environment Day, starting with your own environment and working outward from there.

JUNE

There are everyday things people can do to make our planet cleaner. We are all responsible for the planet and for each other. Stewardship is a way of acting on your faith in God; He has entrusted the world to us and we must follow through. We should be good stewards of the planet as well as good stewards of God's love, grace, and mercy. We must take care of this beautiful habitat that God has given to us to thrive.

- NUM 35:33 ~ You must not pollute the land where you are; blood defiles the land and it cannot be cleansed except by the blood of him who shed it. Therefore, do not defile the land that you inhabit or in which you live. For I the Lord will be dwelling there among my children Israel.

- PRO 10:16 ~ The labor of the righteous brings life; the labor of the wicked brings sin.

- JER 2:7 ~ I brought you into a land of plenty to enjoy its fruits and goods. But when you came you defiled my land and turned my heritage into an abomination.

- MAT 5:13–16 ~ Jesus said, "You are the salt of the earth, but if the salt has lost its flavor, how can it be made salty again? It is no longer good for anything, except to be thrown out and trampled down. You are the light of the world. A city built on a hill cannot be hidden. People do not light a lamp and then cover it; instead, they put it on a stand so it will provide light to everyone in the room. In the same manner, let your light shine before others so they can see your good deeds and praise your Father in heaven."

- MAT 25:40, 45 ~ Jesus said, "Whenever you have done something to help another person, you have done it to me as well; whenever you have not done something to help another person, you have not done it to me."

- LUK 10:2–3 ~ Jesus said, "The harvest is plentiful but the laborers are few. Pray that the Lord of the harvest would send more laborers to help. Keep in mind, I am sending you out like lambs among wolves."

- 1 CO 3:8–9 ~ Everyone will receive their own reward according to their labor. For we are all laborers for God.

- 1 CO 12:7 ~ The manifestation of the Spirit is given to everyone for the common good.

- 2 CO 9:8 ~ God is able to bless you abundantly, that in all things and at all times you have what you need, so you can abound in good works.

- PHP 2:2 ~ Make my joy complete by being like-minded, having the same love and being one in spirit and in purpose.

- 1 JO 2:6 ~ Whoever says they are a Christian should show they are following Christ by the way they conduct their lives.

- 1 PE 4:10–11 ~ Whoever has received the gift of salvation in Christ should share that gift with others, as a steward of God's eternal grace. If you preach, do so as a messenger of God. If you minister, do so with the ability God gives you. Do this to glorify God through His Son Jesus Christ.

Heavenly Father, you have made us overseers of your creation; help us to be faithful to that task as good stewards to you, one another, and the planet. Let us be diligent in preserving and protecting the earth, its resources, and its inhabitants. Help the nations of the world come together and agree on measures that will protect the earth rather than exploit it or pollute it in the cause of material gain. Thank you, Holy Spirit for preserving us in the true faith, and help us to share that faith as good stewards of your Word. In the name of Jesus, who is the Word, Amen.

June 6

National Higher Education Day recognizes the importance of a good education to our success in life. Many institutions of higher education will be holding seminars, displaying information, distributing packets, and recruiting students; providing information on academics, financial aid, degree plans, and career paths. This celebration of learning got an enormous boost at the passage of the Higher Education Act of 1965. It made higher education more available, particularly for minorities and those of low income, using federal funds to assist participating organizations. In turn, this motivated a large number of young people to investigate higher education and seek professional jobs, who otherwise might have pursued a trade or a less skilled vocation. Consequently, college became popular and baby boomers started enrolling more than ever before. For decades, it was almost a given that a high school graduate should go to college. But government grants were not as available for certain brackets, especially if the student lived with their parents, since eligibility for certain grants was based on their parents' income, not their own.

Meanwhile, institutions continued to raise tuition while receiving more tax dollars. Then they turned to watering down the curricula so people could enter a field they weren't qualified for, or major in something that wasn't going to prepare them sufficiently for jobs that interested them. Now the cost of tuition has become astronomical, and the nation is back to where we started, with the cost-effectiveness of higher education diminishing and more students looking into skilled trades and specializations. So, we have come full-circle. Maybe the government should have kept out of it, who knows? I know that what I spent on my undergraduate degree is pittance compared to what it cost to put my child through the same university. Having been a professor in several undergraduate and graduate programs, I expect I got a lot more bang for my bucks when I was a college student. So be advised, those who major in basket weaving are getting a useless degree and will not learn much except how to party more economically. Imagine, being stuck with a bunch of student loan debt, holding a useless piece of paper in your hand, and wondering what you are going to do next. Will you still pursue higher education or a psychiatrist at that point?

Certainly, everyone needs at least a high school education. But higher education or additional training is to be expected, whether specializing in a trade, becoming an associate or an apprentice, or entering an occupation requiring college-level coursework. For many other occupations, a master degree, doctorate degree, or medical degree is required. Thus, ambition has a lot do with choosing higher education, especially if it is a necessary step to fulfilling one's career goals. Experience also counts towards higher education in some cases. Parents should help their kids perform educational planning while they are in high school, and not depend on school teachers or counselors to steer them in the right direction.

- EXO 31:3–4 ~ I have filled him with the Spirit of God, with talent and intelligence, with knowledge and abilities, to create works in gold, silver, and brass.

- PRO 1:2–7 ~ Try to know wisdom and instruction; to perceive the words of understanding; to receive the instruction of wisdom, justice, judgment, and equity; to give subtlety to the simple; to give knowledge and discretion to the young. A wise person will listen and will increase in learning; a person of understanding will seek wise counsel, and will try to understand a proverb and its interpretation, or the words of the wise and the hidden meaning of what they say. Remember, the fear of God is the beginning of understanding; only fools despise wisdom and instruction.

- PRO 2:2–6, 10–12 ~ Incline your ears to wisdom and apply your heart to understanding. If you cry for knowledge and ask for understanding, if you seek wisdom as you would for treasures, then you will understand the fear of the Lord and find knowledge of God. For God gives wisdom, knowledge, and understanding. When wisdom enters your heart and knowledge is pleasant to your soul, discretion will preserve you and understanding will keep you to deliver you from evil.

- PRO 13:11 ~ Wealth obtained by pride will diminish; but those who achieve by way of hard work will see their wealth increase.

- PRO 21:5 ~ The plans of the diligent person will lead to prosperity, but those who are in a hurry to get rich will find poverty.

- PRO 22:29 ~ Do you know someone who is diligent in business matters? That person will serve kings, and will be able to avoid obnoxious people.

- PRO 23:4 ~ Do not labor to become rich, and do not concentrate on your own feeble wisdom.

- PRO 24:30–34 ~ I visited the field of the slothful man and the vineyard of the ignorant man and all I found were thorn bushes, weeds, and broken fences. And I learned from what I had seen. Just a little sleep, a little slumber, a little folding of the hands to rest, and poverty will come upon you like a thief, and neediness like an armed robber.

- ECC 5:12 ~ The sleep of the hard worker is sweet; but the abundance of the rich prevents them from sleeping.

- ECC 12:14 ~ God will judge every work, including works done in secret, whether they be good or evil.

- 1 CO 12:7–10, 28 ~ The manifestation of the Holy Spirit is given to everyone, and is exhibited in unique abilities and attributes including wisdom, faith, healing, miracles, prophesy, discerning spirits, interpreting tongues; and evangelizing, teaching, governing, helping, and speaking multiple languages.

- 2 TI 3:14 ~ Continue in the things you have learned and are convinced of, knowing from whom you have learned them.

- JAM 1:25 ~ Those who study the perfect law of liberty and continue therein, not forgetting but continuing to do the work, these persons will be blessed for their deeds.

Actually, no matter what level you are at with your education, you can always go higher. Today would be a good day for everyone to decide what to study next. Even when you get old there are things worth learning, and you need to exercise your mind anyway else you lose it faster. So, I recommend higher education for everybody at every age, and continue adding to it for the duration of your life. Higher education gave me many paths to choose from, and I sampled quite a few. And even if a course wasn't always directly pertinent to what I was after, it still came in handy, every tidbit. If you run out of things to study you should turn to the Bible; if you haven't run out of things to study you should still turn to the Bible. To this day I have not picked it up without learning something, which is the reason I write Christian books, to share what I have learned from God's Word. If you are interested in higher learning, you cannot get any higher than God, for His Word is always true wherein He reveals things you never dreamed.

- DEU 31:12 ~ Gather the people together including men, women, and children, as well as the strangers among you, so that everyone can hear, learn, fear the Lord your God, and obey all the words of His Law.

- PSA 32:8 ~ I will instruct you and teach you in the way you should go. I will guide you with my eye.

- ISA 40:13–14 ~ Who can understand the mind of God, and who can instruct Him? Did God have to consult anyone to enlighten Him, to teach Him the right way, or to show Him the path of understanding?

- JER 10:2–3 ~ Do not learn the ways of unbelievers or be dismayed by signs in the heavens, for the customs of the people are false.

- MAT 11:28–30 ~ Jesus said, "Come to me all who are weary and burdened and I will give you rest. Take my yoke upon you and learn from me, for I am gentle and humble in heart; and you will find rest for your souls. For my yoke is easy and my burden is light."

- ROM 11:33–35 ~ Oh how deep are the riches of the wisdom and knowledge of God. How unsearchable are His judgments; how untraceable are His steps. For who knows the mind of the Lord, and who has been His counselor? Who has ever sacrificed to God, that God should repay them?

- COL 3:16 ~ Remember what Christ taught you and let His words enrich your lives and make you wise. Teach His words to each other. Sing them openly and spiritually in psalms and hymns with thankful hearts.

- 2 TI 3:16 ~ All scripture is inspired by God and is effective for teaching, for reprimanding, for correcting, and for instruction in the ways of righteousness.

- 2 PE 1:3–11 ~ God's divine power has given us everything we need for life and righteousness through our knowledge of Him who called us by His own glory and loving kindness. He has given us wonderful and precious promises, so that through them you may participate in the divine nature and escape the corruption of the world caused by evil desires. For this reason, be diligent in your faith, adding to your faith virtue, and to virtue knowledge, and to knowledge self-control, and to self-control perseverance, and to perseverance godliness, and to godliness brotherly kindness, and to brotherly kindness love. For if these things abide in you and abound, they will keep you from being ineffective and unproductive in the knowledge of our Lord Jesus Christ. But those who lack such things are blind, they cannot see the long-term benefits, and have forgotten that they were purged of old sins. Therefore, brothers and sisters, be even more conscientious and sure in your calling, for if you do these things, you will never fail and you will receive a hearty welcome into the eternal kingdom of our Lord and Savior Jesus Christ.

Dear heavenly and divine Father, you are the source of all truth, wisdom, knowledge, and understanding. Thank you for giving us the ability to learn and to grow, with skills, talents, and experiences that enable us to become successful professionals, tradespersons, and entrepreneurs. Help us never lose our desire to learn new things, and to exercise our bodies, minds and spirits. We especially thank you for your Word which teaches us everything we need to know about you, your works, your ways, your laws, and your will. The Holy Bible is so deep and broad, we continue to learn every time we pick it up and read it with an open mind and heart. We are immensely thankful because we love your Word, and your Holy Spirit who has conveyed your thoughts to us in the Bible, and who lived in full in your Son Jesus Christ our Lord. Oh Lord, yours is the highest education, and for the knowledge and wisdom of your plan of salvation, we are and will be eternally grateful. In your holy name we pray, Amen.

D-Day—The invasion of Normandy (Operation Overlord) began this date in 1944, which turned the tide towards victory in Europe during World War II. Today should be recognized with solemnity, in remembrance of the lives of Americans and allies sacrificed for freedom. We thank God for these brave men, their leaders, and our resounding defeat of Nazi Germany: lest we forget!

June 7

Daniel Boone Day recognizes the day in 1769 when he became the first American, outside of native Americans, to view Kentucky. The famous frontiersman made several trips there and established the town of Boonesborough near the Kentucky River. He crossed the Cumberland Gap on what was named the Wilderness Road, when he and thirty associates carved a path through the Appalachian Mountains. This route has been an interstate gateway to the west ever since. The Kentucky Historical Society established this observance in the 1800s about 150 years ago and is a happening event every year.

Boone's career as a hunter and pioneer began in Pennsylvania where he became friendly with the natives, before his family relocated to North Carolina. He was not formally educated but learned a lot by reading books, especially the Holy Bible. He married and had ten children; he also helped raise several of his deceased relatives' children, whose fathers died fighting in the Indian wars. Boone became a warrior from various bouts with Indians that were not friendly. He made several hunting and trapping trips exploring a great deal of Kentucky and surrounding areas, often through Indian territory. He was a member of the Carolina militia and fought in the Revolutionary War against the British and their Indian allies. He later resigned his commission to remain and protect Kentuckians from hostile natives and criminals. He became a surveyor and merchant for a while before losing his money in land speculation. He left his beloved Kentucky and resettled in Missouri with his kids and grandkids. He was a legend in his own time, with many books written, not all factual; but there is plenty of truth about Boone to make him a genuine icon. Boone was the quintessential wilderness man. He spent years away from home, for long stretches at a time. He tamed the land, the animals, the natives, and himself out in the wild.

Wilderness people of the Bible started with the Israelites and Moses. Israel would be enslaved by Egypt after settling there when Joseph was second to Pharaoh. Moses was sent by God to free them. And yet they betrayed God again in the desert wilderness of Sinai, where they would pay dearly, wandering the wasteland until the adults of their generation had passed; only Caleb and Joshua would step foot in the promised land from that generation. Unfortunately, the desire for kings and idols would cause the Israelites to once again lose the promised land and be enslaved. However, from that wilderness would grow a rose, the Messiah of the Lord.

- EXO 32; DEU 8 ~ The Lord's anger against Israel was provoked by their worshipping of the golden calf. God made them wander in the wilderness for forty years, until the adults from that generation which committed evil before the Lord had died.

- LEV 16:8–10 ~ Aaron the priest shall present two goats and randomly select one to be the Lord's and the other to be the scapegoat. The first will be sacrificed and the second will be presented alive before the Lord for atonement, sending it into the wilderness to be a scapegoat for sin.

- NUM 14:29–30 ~ Because of their sin at Sinai and their doubting of the Lord's promises, everyone past the age of twenty had to wander the wilderness until their death. Only Joshua and Caleb were spared of those who were older than twenty when the Lord punished Israel.

- JOS 5:6 ~ The children of Israel wandered forty years in the wilderness, until all the men of war that came out of Egypt were consumed, because they disobeyed the voice of the Lord. For the Lord had warned them He would not show them the land flowing with milk and honey promised to their fathers, for not trusting in His promise.

- SOS 2:1 ~ I AM the rose of Sharon among the lilies of the valleys. Like a lily among thorns is my beloved among the daughters.

- ISA 35:1 ~ The wilderness and its arid land will be glad; the desert will rejoice and blossom as a rose.

    Before Messiah would arrive, a forerunner prophesied by Isaiah was coming to clear a path for Him, and this would be John the Baptist, who declared it himself; the prophecy of a man crying in the wilderness and making way for Messiah was fulfilled in John. He was another quintessential wilderness man. John baptized people in the Jordan River, the very river the Israelites had crossed to exit the wilderness and enter the promised land with Joshua at the lead. The name Joshua being a type and shadow of Jesus (Jeshua).

- ISA 40:3 ~ The one crying in the wilderness will prepare the way for the Lord; he will clear a straight path in the desert to be a highway for our God.

- ISA 51:2 ~ The Lord will comfort Zion and her wasted places. The wilderness will become like Eden; joy, gladness, thanksgiving, and singing will be found there.

- JOE 1:18–20 ~ The beasts groan and the herds are confused; because they have no pasture, in fact the flocks have been desolated. I cry to the Lord, for fire has burned the pastures of the wilderness and the trees of the field. The animals cry, for the rivers are dried up and there is no grass in the wilderness.

- MAL 3:1–4 ~ Behold, I will send my messenger and he will prepare the way before me. And the Lord whom you seek will come suddenly into His temple, that messenger of the covenant in whom you delight. He is coming says the Lord of hosts. But who can endure the day of His coming? Who can stand when He appears? For He will be like a refiner's fire or a launderer's soap. He will refine and purify like silver; He will purify the Levites and refine them as gold so they may present to the Lord an offering in righteousness. Then will the offering of Judah and Jerusalem be pleasant to the Lord as in the days of old and in former times.

- MAT 3:1–3, 11 ~ John the Baptist came preaching in the wilderness of Judea, saying, "Repent for the kingdom of heaven is near." This is the person spoken of by Isaiah who said, "The voice of the one crying in the wilderness will prepare the way for the Lord, making straight a pathway to Him." John told the people, "Indeed, I baptize you with water unto repentance. But He who comes after me is mightier than I; I am not even worthy of untying His shoes. He will baptize you with the Holy Spirit, and with fire."

- MAR 1:4 ~ John baptized in the wilderness and preached the baptism of repentance for the remission of sins.

    John had been welcoming people to come to repentance, when Christ Himself showed up to be baptized. Immediately afterwards, Jesus crossed the Jordon into the wilderness where He fasted forty days, as many years as the Israelites sojourned there for sinning, even as Moses was receiving the Ten Commandments from God on the mountain. There are wilderness men, and then there is Jesus, the superlative wilderness man. Satan tried to tempt the Messiah of God in that wilderness. Christ rebuked Satan, returned back across the Jordan, and began His ministry. Then John announced Jesus as the Lamb of God, reminding us of His coming. This event fulfilled several Messianic prophecies.

- LUK 4:1–13 ~ Jesus was filled with the Holy Spirit who led Him into the wilderness. There He was tempted during the forty days He fasted there. He was very weak and hungry when the devil came to Him. The devil said, "If you are hungry, command those stones to become bread." Jesus replied, "It is written that man will not live by bread alone, but by the Word of God." Next, the devil brought Jesus into a high mountain and showed Him all the kingdoms of the world in a single moment of time. The devil said, "All the power and glory associated with these kingdoms I will give to you if you will worship me." Jesus replied, "Get behind me, Satan, for it is written that you must worship the Lord God and serve only Him." Next, the devil brought Jesus to Jerusalem where they sat at the pinnacle of the temple. The devil said, "Jump down, and the angels will catch you, since it is written that God gives His angels charge over you to keep you from harm and danger." Jesus replied, "It also is written that you should never tempt the Lord your God." At that, the devil gave up and left Jesus.

- JOH 1:29–35 ~ John the Baptist saw Jesus coming and said, "Look, here comes the Lamb of God who takes away the sin of the world. He is the One of whom I spoke, who would come after me, though He is preferred over me, for He existed before me. I did not know Him intimately, but He is the reason I have been baptizing people with water. He told me that I would see the Spirit of God descending upon Him and remaining there. I saw the Spirit of God descending upon Him like a dove, and it rested upon Him. He is the same One who will baptize with the Holy Spirit. I am a witness that He is the Son of God."

- HEB 11:1–3, 6, 32–40 ~ Faith is the assurance of things hoped for, the evidence of things not seen; for by faith, the elders obtained good standing with God. By faith we understand that the world was created by the Word of God, such that things we see were made from things which do not appear. Without faith, it is impossible to please God, for whoever would wish to come to Him must believe He exists and that He rewards those who seek Him. Consider great men of faith in the Bible. Some were treated cruelly and mocked, bound and imprisoned. They wandered the wilderness in shaggy clothes, destitute, tormented, and afflicted. Although their life on earth was full of strife, they awaited their deliverance, as we also must do until God makes us perfect before Him.

- REV 12:13–14 ~ The dragon persecuted the woman and the child, so she was given wings of an eagle to fly away into the wilderness, where she was nourished for 3.5 years, far from the face of the serpent. The serpent spewed water from its mouth to carry her away like a flood but the earth swallowed up the water which came out of the mouth of the dragon. The dragon hated the woman and made war with the remnant of her seed, those who keep the commandments of God and have the testimony of Jesus Christ.

A wilderness can be thick forests or a desolate desert, depending on where it is located. And that place can be a place of comfort or a place of violence. But those who know the lay of the land and the inhabitants thereof, can conquer it and turn it into a land of beauty and prosperity. This is what Daniel Boone had in mind, converting the land in a way that benefited good people regardless of tribe or culture. This also was the intention of wilderness men like Moses, Joshua, John, and Jesus, opening paths and freeways into the promised land of God wherein we pass through the wilderness, cross the river, and end up in the presence of the Lord.

Thank you, Father, for giving us leaders to show us the path to paradise. Thank you for pioneers who paved the way for our nation, connecting the east and the west, making the entire USA accessible. Similarly, we thank the prophets that you sent to show us the path through the wilderness of sin, violence, and pain, and find the Way to heaven who is Jesus Christ: He is the Truth and the Life, and one with you and the Holy Spirit. We have a roadmap of the route that was mapped out from ages past, showing us where to go and where not to go, so that we do not get lost, but are found by Christ who gathers all of His sheep into the fold and brings them to you, Father, into your kingdom of paradise. Praise be to God! Amen.

June 8

National Best Friend's Day is all about friends and the importance of friendship. This holiday was the brainstorm of the US Congress, which in 1935 announced this date to celebrate best friends; it was not an act of Congress, just a suggestion that caught on. It is not to be confused with National Friendship Day celebrated in August. Many other countries observe this day and it continues to spread, thanks to social media. For most people, this will be a good day to take some time to visit with friends face-to-face in a personal way, or at least write to them in a card or letter, or arrange a phone call at a convenient time to catch up and possibly facetime with them. If you have lost friends or had a falling out, make new friends, whether at your place of work, school, church, or most anyplace where your proximity is itself proof that you have something in common. There is never a bad time to make good friends, but you must be patient because solid friendships develop over a long period of time. Be prepared to invest quality time.

Normally, a best friend is a friend for life; most people can count the number of top friends on one hand. These are the ones who are there for you through thick and thin. A true friend is someone you can trust, plain and simple. They will never sacrifice the friendship over money or disagreement. They will never compromise your sense of decency or integrity, test your loyalty, or insult your faith or belief system.

You might argue with friends from time to time without creating bad blood. When bad blood does emerge, it might be time to let go. A great example of bad blood can be found in the betrayal of Christ by a close friend. Anyone following Jesus was and will be susceptible to treachery. Guard your friends, and sort them out if need be.

- DEU 23:19 ~ Do not lend money or anything else at extreme interest rates to your friends and relatives.

- JOB 2:13 ~ Job mourned with his friends, without speaking for seven days and nights.

- PSA 41:9–10 ~ The trusted friend with whom I ate bread has betrayed me. Have mercy on me. Raise me up so that I can rebuke them.

- MIC 7:2–6 ~ The godly and upright men are gone. The wicked lie in ambush for blood. They do evil with diligence. Princes and judges ask for bribes. Great men speak of and pursue the evil desires of their souls. Even the best of them is like a thorn. Their confusion and punishment await them. Nobody can be trusted; even family and friends become the enemy.

- ZEC 11:12–13 ~ His price was thirty pieces of silver, thrown down in the house of the Lord, and used to buy the potter's field (MAT 27:6–10; ACT 1:17–19).

- ZEC 13:6 ~ Someone will say, "What are these wounds on your hands?" He will reply, "Wounds I received in the house of my friends" (MAT 27:1, 11–12, 37; JOH 18:12, 31).

- LUK 16:8–13 ~ Jesus summarized His parable about the dishonest bookkeeper: The rich man commended the dishonest bookkeeper's shrewd tactics. He thought it was wise how his employee made friends through greed and deceit, a crafty way to prepare for retirement. He would have some means of external support when his job ended. That type of behavior will be considered wisdom to this evil generation. In fact, the evil children in that wicked generation will be craftier than the children of light. Those who are faithful in a little will be faithful in a lot, and those who are dishonest in a little will be dishonest in a lot. If you are not faithful in worldly things, who will trust you with true riches? Especially when that which you were unfaithful with was not even yours. Nobody can serve two masters; they will be loyal to only one, honoring the one and despising the other. In other words, you cannot serve God and money (mammon) at the same time.

- JDE 1:17–19 ~ Dear friends, remember what the apostles told us. They said that in the latter days there would be scoffers who follow their own ungodly desires. These people have come to divide you; they follow the instincts of their flesh and do not have the Spirit within them.

Give your friends a call or send them a greeting this week, indicating how you value their friendship; a simple text message won't do. I don't know about you, but when someone texts "happy birthday" to me, I feel nothing. I think: what, are they too busy to call or send a card with a personal note? Ensure they know you care, whether it is today or any other day of the year which is not their birthday or Christmas. If you do not have a friend whom you can call when you are down and out, I am very sorry about that. Everybody needs someone they can talk to in addition to their spouse, which should be their very best friend if they have a good marriage.

- SOS 5:16 ~ The maiden's opinion of her man: His mouth is sweet and he is altogether lovely. He is my beloved and he is my friend; listen you daughters of Jerusalem.

Some things you cannot talk over with your spouse, especially if you are having a spat; in which case the two spouses might want to cool off, or speak to someone else who is in your corner and will not get emotionally charged, but will console. Although your dog might be your best friend, the dog is incapable of giving you advice, though fully capable of sensing when you are down and fully able to console. Take your dog for a walk and you could make a new friend at the dog park. There are many places to find good friends, and there are many places to find bad people who are willing to become your friend. Give it time before you commit to a friendship. Be aware of alarms going off in your head, such as asking for money or sketchy favors. Many a friendship is lost over material riches; it is also the principal reason couples get divorced.

- PSA 133:1 ~ Behold, how good and how pleasant it is for brothers and sisters of the faith to live together in unity!

- PRO 22:24–25 ~ Do not make friends with an angry person or associate with someone who has a quick temper, for you risk learning their ways and falling into the same trap.

- ECC 4:9–12 ~ Two are better than one because the reward of their labor is greater. If one falls, the other lifts him up. But it is unfortunate when alone, for if you fall there is nobody to lift you up. Similarly, two people lying together produce more warmth. And two are better able to defend themselves; as the saying goes, a rope of three strands is not easily broken.

- JER 32:39 ~ I will give them one heart, and one way, so that they will fear me forever for their own good, and for the good of their children after them.

- 1 CO 5:11, 13 ~ Do not associate with someone who claims to be a Christian but who is sexually promiscuous, greedy, idolatrous, slanderous, a drunkard, or a swindler; do not even eat at the same table with such a person. You must expel the wicked from among you.

- JAM 1:8 ~ A double-minded person is unstable in all their ways.

God makes friends with people on earth who seek Him and love Him. It is good for your soul when you make friends with Jesus, and when you have friends who share that friendship, for they also are good for your soul and your mental health. It is a choice to make friends with those not sharing your faith; but in time, it may cause division if not irreconcilable differences. It is good to love all people, but that doesn't mean you should become their friends; associating with some people can be harmful to your mental and spiritual health. Most of the time, you will be able to discern rather quickly whether they are a person of good character, and/or a believer.

- ISA 41:8 ~ You Israel, are my servants, the children of Jacob whom I have chosen, and the seed of my friend Abraham.

- JOH 11:18–45 ~ Jesus heard of the death of His friend Lazarus. He already had planned to raise Lazarus from the dead, and did not mourn at that time. But when He arrived and felt all the pain and sorrow of Lazarus's sisters and friends, Jesus sobbed with them. Then He raised Lazarus after being dead four days. Many Jews who had come to be with his sisters Mary and Martha, also friends of Jesus, were converted that day.

- JOH 15:12–13 ~ Jesus said, "Love each other as I have loved you. No greater love exists than to give one's life for friends."

- JOH 20:22–23 ~ Jesus appeared to His friends after His resurrection and said, "Receive the Holy Spirit. Anyone's sins that you forgive, they will be forgiven. Anyone's sins that you retain, they will be retained."

- ACT 1:14 ~ All of them continued with one accord in prayer and meditation.

- ACT 2:47 ~ And the believers were as one, for they had everything in common.

- PHP 2:2 ~ Make my joy complete by being like-minded, having the same love and being one in spirit and in purpose.

- 2 TH 3:14–15 ~ If there are people among you who fail to conform to the Word as we have taught it to you, make note of them and stay away from them, so that they will feel ashamed of their behavior. However, do not consider them as an enemy, but admonish them as you would a brother or sister.

- 1 TI 6:5 ~ Those who teach that material wealth is godly have perverse minds, devoid of the truth. They would exploit the truth to gain riches. Stay away from them.

- 2 TI 3:1–13 ~ Know this, that perilous times will come in the last days. People will love only themselves. They will be covetous, boasters, blasphemers, arrogant, disobedient to parents, unthankful and ungodly, void of natural affection. They will be breakers of promises, false accusers, undisciplined, fierce, despisers of goodness; traitors, reckless, conceited, lovers of worldly pleasures more than God; displaying a form of godliness, but denying the power thereof. Stay away from people like this.

- JAM 4:4 ~ You are an adulterous people. Do you not know that friendship with the world results in hatred towards God?

- 1 JO 5:20–21 ~ Remain in Christ who is true. Stay away from anything or anyone who would distort God's truth or attempt to take God's place in your heart.

Father God, what a great friend we have in Jesus; and because He is our friend, then you and the Holy Spirit will always be there for us as well, because you are one God. Let our friendship with Christ spawn many more between us and your people; and let those friendships and our commitment pervade the body of Christ. Help us to avoid friendships that are bad for us, and still love those people from afar as we ought. Let us always be humble and friendly regardless of the places and people, and not be swayed by circumstances. As we carry your promise to the world, let us be confident to share this with our friends when occasions arise, and let us be part of groups of friends sharing the good news with others. Let your Word spread through the hand of friendship in our lives, whether in our hometowns, or wherever we may travel or visit. It is our hope that we will see the growth of your kingdom here on earth, and that we will see our faithful friends and relatives in heaven. In Jesus's name, Amen.

June 9

Inoculate Against Sin Day is to remind us that we are vulnerable, not only to diseases old and new, but also to sin. Therefore, we are dying a slow death due to physical maladies as well as spiritual maladies, both of which lead to death, physical and spiritual respectively. There is the death of the body and there is a death of the soul. As for the spirit, it belongs to God.

The principal disease among humans is sin. It is the one contagion that is always fatal. Everyone has been infected by sin, and sin affects every aspect of one's life and health. The holistic health paradigm is central in the healthcare field, and purports that one needs to be healthy in body, mind, and spirit to be completely whole. Sin can destroy all three components of holistic health, with the final outcome of sin being eternal death of body and soul (MAT 10:28).

- ROM 6:23 ~ The wages of sin is death, but God's gift of eternal life is available through Jesus Christ our Lord.

God told Adam not to eat the forbidden fruit or he would surely die (GEN 2:16–17). Satan lied to Eve claiming they would not die if they ate the fruit but would be like God, able to know good and evil (GEN 3:1–5). Both Adam and Eve violated God's command and became cursed, because they did the very thing they were told not to do; and they were expelled from the Garden of Eden (GEN 3:7–24). This original sin was passed onto their offspring, and has continued to be passed onto every generation since then. Everyone is compelled to do what is prohibited; and to a sinner, the attractiveness of something seems to increase the more that it is forbidden or otherwise bad for us.

- PSA 51:5 ~ I was formed in sin and in sin I was conceived.

- ROM 5:12–13, 18–19 ~ Sin entered the world by one man, resulting in universal death. Sin was in the world before the Law, but nothing can be attributed to sin where there is no Law. So, sin and death have been passed onto all people, for all have sinned. Consequently, just as the result of one sin condemned all people, so also the result of one act of righteousness brought justification to all people. Through the disobedience of Adam, we all became sinners; through the obedience of Christ, we all can become righteous.

- 1 JO 1:8–9 ~ If we say we do not sin we deceive ourselves and we are liars. If we confess our sins, God, who is faithful and just, will forgive our sins and cleanse us of all unrighteousness.

Physically, sin causes natural maladies in the body, though it is initiated in our minds via evil thoughts; sinning therefore causes maladies in the body and mind. You cannot separate the physical and the mental, else you die. You cannot separate the spirit either, for it is the spirit that gives life; and sin darkens the spirit, making us unwilling to see the light or to shine the light.

Knowledge of consequences, and the law of cause and effect, are available to all people. For example, we learn quickly not to place our hand on a hot surface; it only takes once to learn that lesson. Another example in which people learn the hard way is through promiscuous sex. It is well established that such behavior leads to disease, divorce, even death. When you play around with the laws of nature, you are likely to endure natural consequences, not to mention punishment from God, for there are spiritual repercussions as well. Sexual intercourse outside of marriage is unnatural and against God's Law. If you engage in adultery, incest, bestiality, or homosexuality, be prepared for dire outcomes (LEV 18:6–18; LEV 18:20; LEV 18:22; LEV 18:23). These are sins against one's own body, soul, and spirit, not to mention God's will. Our sinful behavior can have a negative impact on other people and disrupt their walk through life, because sin has a chain reaction effect. The sin of each one of us contributes to the rest, building towards chaos, which the world is destined to experience. This reality gets increasingly darker and bleaker; and we see it happening faster as well. The degradation and deterioration of the body, mind, and spirit has become more commonplace. Many will self-destruct. All people will need help, but fewer will lend a hand.

Mentally, sin can cause behavioral and psychological problems. Sometimes we become preoccupied with things that we feel and know are wrong. This may develop into bad habits such as addiction which destroys lives, both yours and possibly others. Bad habits can be substance related, behavior related, or thought related. In the case of drugs or alcohol, the substance can cause permanent brain damage resulting in physical and mental dysfunction, birth defects, and substance-induced psychosis. When it comes to behavioral problems, the habit can land a person in jail or worse. With respect to thought problems, the habit can drive a person crazy. Case in point, people who frequently choose to believe lies over the truth tend to speak and act insane; that is, they become delusional because they have convinced themselves of a lie (JER 23:25–32; ROM 1:18–32; 2 TH 2:3–12).

Spiritually, sin separates us from God who wants us to seek, trust, and love Him. Striving for worldly things is contrary to striving for spiritual things, because you cannot love the world and God at the same time (MAT 6:22–25; LUK 16:8–13). The sin of Adam brought death upon him, but it was spiritual death that he was facing, not merely physical; that is, he did not die right then and there though death was always imminent. We all are facing a spiritual death if we do not rely on Jesus Christ to save us. The problem with spiritual death is that it lasts for eternity. God takes your spirit away from you and destroys your body and soul in hell (MAT 10:28)

- ISA 59:2 ~ Your iniquities have separated you from God; your sins have caused Him to hide His face from you, until He will not listen.
- GAL 5:4 ~ Christ becomes of no effect to those who have justified themselves under the law, for they have fallen from grace.
- EPH 2:1, 5–6 ~ You will be brought back to life, who were once dead in trespasses and sins. God has raised us up together, and allowed us to sit in heavenly places with Jesus Christ.
- 2 TH 1:9 ~ They will be punished with everlasting destruction, far from the presence of the Lord and from the glory of His power.
- 1 JO 5:12 ~ Those who have the Son have life; those who do not have the Son do not.

Sin leads to death no matter what kind of sin it is. But there is life through forgiveness of sins, which is why Christ died. Sin resulted in His death, and it will result in your death as well if you do not believe in the salvation bought for you on a cross at Calvary. Anyone who believes that Christ died in their place will be forgiven. This knowledge will compel people to change their thinking, speech, and behavior. When a believer dies, he or she will be raised to eternal life.

The world is experiencing an explosion of evil and sin, resulting in errant behavior, maniacal thinking, deathly diseases, and the rejection of morality and religion. Yes, this planet and its intelligent inhabitants are dying body, mind, and spirit, due to corruption from the sins of humanity. If this backsliding continues to escalate, a terrible end will come sooner than later. Are you prepared? If not, cry out to God and beg for forgiveness, not just for you and your family, but also for your country and the world. Do not be caught off guard, because when Christ returns it will be too late. The choices are clear: life or death. This is the easiest and most critical decision you will ever make. Jesus warned of perilous times ahead (MAT 24; MAR 13; LUK 21). Theologians believe the last days have begun, given the signs of Christ's return appear to be ensuing: floods, earthquakes, famine, disease, pestilence, war, conflict, persecution, deceit and trickery. It is prudent to be watchful, prepared, and eager for Christ's coming (REV 22:20).

- MAT 24:4–42 ~ Jesus said the last days will begin with wars, famine, pestilences, and earthquakes, followed by persecution of Christians, betrayal, hatred, and a proliferation of false prophets. He urged that we be watchful and prepared

- 2 TI 3:1–4, 12–13 ~ In the last days, perilous times will come. People will be self-centered, proud, boastful, envious, blasphemous, disobedient to parents, unthankful, and ungodly; people will be perverted, peace breakers, false accusers, unrestrained, vicious, and despisers of those who are good; they will be traitors, violent, arrogant, and lovers of pleasure rather than of lovers of God. Those who live a godly life in Christ will be persecuted. Evil people and impostors will progress from bad to worse, as will the deceivers and the deceived.

- REV 3:2–3 ~ Jesus said, "Be watchful and strengthen each other in the truth, for I have found imperfection on the earth. Remember everything you heard, hold fast to it, and repent. If you are not watchful, I will surprise you like a thief, for you never know when I might come."

The world, society, government, and business are wrought with corruption and dishonesty. You may have heard cries for unity and peace, but those advocating peace are often themselves cruel, selfish, treacherous, abusive, and dishonest. This is Satan's deception, to replace God's truth with lies. The evil that they are perpetuating is ascribed to others, the classic projection: convince people that the innocent are guilty and vice-versa. Lately it has become dangerous to profess the truth, confess Christ, or take a stand for morality. The silent majority are compelled to remain so, else they face recrimination and retaliation. But we must not fear the enemy, for God is with us; He will fight with the righteous when the enemy comes against them.

- 2 CH 20:17 ~ You will not need to fight this battle; hold back and be still, and you will see the salvation of the Lord who is with you. Fear not, Judah and Jerusalem; do not be dismayed. Tomorrow you may go out against them for the Lord will be with you.

- PRO 21:31 ~ The horse is prepared for the day of battle, but safety is from the Lord.

- EPH 6:12 ~ We must fight, not against flesh and blood, but against principalities, powers, rulers of earthly darkness, and spiritual wickedness in high places.

- 1 TI 6:12 ~ Fight the good fight of faith and grab hold of eternal life, to which you have been called and have ably professed before many witnesses.

- 2 TI 4:7 ~ I have fought the good fight and I have finished my course, having kept the faith.

- 1 JO 4:4 ~ If you belong to God, and He lives in you, you have the power to overcome evil spirits, because He (Christ) living in you is greater than the he (Satan) who is in the world.

Our Father in heaven above, we need your love, mercy, and peace now more than ever. Evil is surrounding us; sin and indecency are rampant. Temptations are frequent; in fact, we are being overwhelmed with decadent sensory inputs being thrown at us, as if it was normal or acceptable to be doing it or displaying it. In addition, wicked people are trying to indoctrinate our children and youth, to defile them. We pray for justice and protection, especially since these same circles of wickedness are attempting to corrupt if not eliminate law and order. Make us immune from these hellions and their filth, by inoculating us with your Holy Spirit. Drive out the demons, reprobates, and perverts from among us, just as Jesus did when he cast a legion of them into a herd of swine. Let your Spirit be a force field that protects us, as we don the armor of God each day, and carry the shield of faith to repel all of the fiery arrows of evil. Help us remember to invoke the name of Jesus to defeat the demonic in our midst; in His name we pray, Amen.

June 10

Alcoholics Anonymous Was Founded on this day in 1935 by stockbroker Bill Wilson and surgeon Robert Smith, (Dr. Bob); both were recovering alcoholics who had tried different types of interventions and therapies. They were experienced with addiction and treatment; they had worked with alcoholics, conducted research, and interviewed subject matter experts to see what helped. The impetus of their methodology was a twelve-step program that addressed key issues facing alcoholics. The main feature was belief in a higher power, which would be God for most people. Within five years there were over 6000 members. The first AA convention was held in 1950. With the growth of membership came an expansion of services and supporting agencies. By 1955 it became necessary to turn the operation over to the Fellowship. Today there are over 60,000 local chapters in the USA; millions of people participate in meetings every week throughout the world. The success of the twelve-step model has been applied to other addictions, through Narcotics Anonymous and Gamblers Anonymous as well as other applications.

What was the secret to their success? First, we must turn back the clock to 1931, when a heavy drinker named Rowland Hazard sought help from the famous Swiss Psychiatrist Carl Jung, who recommended a Christian organization called the Oxford Group. Their spiritual approach to recovery emphasized giving one's life to God, confessing sins with fellow alcoholics, making amends to people they had wronged, and listening to God's voice which would reveal a path forward. The Oxford Group helped Hazard quit the habit, so he referred people to the program, who referred others including Bill Wilson who had been in and out of rehab. Bill consulted Dr. William Silkworth, who had treated him before, and who helped Bill with his book, *Alcoholics Anonymous* (AA). Bill collaborated with Dr. Bob, who relapsed and nearly died; Bill took care of him, nursing him back to health and sobriety. The first day of Dr. Bob's sobriety was this day in 1935. And the rest, they say, is history.

Wilson consulted with Carl Jung, in an interchange that would form the philosophy of AA. Jung had proposed three paths to recovery: God's grace, edification/support, and education about the disease and its consequences. These principles were incorporated into AA and the twelve-step program. [Rather than spend the entire lesson on this excellent program, I invite the reader to look into it, especially if you are grappling with a bad habit that you cannot shake. Read up on the twelve steps and the twelve traditions of AA. Fellowship with former and recovering addicts and attend meetings for edification, support, and educational resources.]

The most important of the twelve steps is number three: connecting with God (your higher power) and relinquishing control to Him. Spirituality was integral to Jung's philosophy; he likened the spirits of alcohol to an evil spirit that was in opposition to the Holy Spirit of God.

- PSA 37:4 ~ Delight yourself in the Lord and He will give you the desires of your heart.
- PRO 15:33 ~ The fear of the Lord is the instruction of wisdom, and before honor comes humility.
- PRO 28:25 ~ People with proud hearts serve only to create conflict, but those who trust in God will prosper.
- ISA 57:15 ~ God says, "I will live in the high holy place as will all people having a humble and repentant spirit, because I will revive the spirits of those who are humble."
- MAT 26:41 ~ The spirit indeed is willing, but the flesh is weak.
- GAL 5:17 ~ The desires of the flesh are against the spirit, and vice-versa, for they are opposed to each other, preventing you from doing what you ought.

JUNE

- 1 PE 2:11 ~ Abstain from the passions of the flesh which wage war against your soul.
- 1 JO 3:8 ~ Whoever commits sin is of the devil, who sinned from the very beginning. The Son of God was manifested to destroy the works of the devil.

Given that addicts are out of control, they need to ask God for help controlling their thoughts, behaviors, emotions, and attitude. All worldly addictions can be defeated with the Holy Spirit who represents the highest power. Invite God to lead your recovery support system; admit that you are addicted, confess and repent of your sins, and ask God for His grace. This proved successful at the Oxford House. Similarly, the first pathway to recovery: God's grace.

- PRO 23:21 ~ The drunkard and the glutton will come to poverty.
- ISA 5:20–24 ~ Woe to those who call evil good and good evil, who put darkness for light and light for darkness, who put bitter for sweet and sweet for bitter. Woe to those who consider themselves wise and prudent, who are mighty in their ability to drink alcohol, who justify and reward the wicked, and who take away righteousness from the righteous. Just as fire devours stubble and chaff, so will their roots become rotten and their blossoms wither; for they have thrown away God's laws and despised the Word of the Holy One of Israel.
- JER 51:7 ~ Babylon got the world drunk with her wine, and they became crazy like her.
- 1 CO 6:9–11 ~ Do you realize that the wicked will not inherit the kingdom of God? Do not be deceived, for sinners, fornicators, idolaters, adulterers, homosexuals, perverts, thieves, greedy people, drunkards, slanderers, and swindlers will not inherit the kingdom. And many of us were sinners just like them. But we have been washed clean, sanctified, and justified in the name of our Lord Jesus Christ, by the Spirit of our God.

Addiction is overindulgence or gluttony. It is considered a deadly sin for good reason: because it allows the flesh to rule the thoughts, the mind, the soul. God made everything for us to use for our sustenance and enjoyment; but He has warned us not to abuse it, else it takes His place in our lives. The Bible teaches moderation in all things and this is excellent advice.

- GEN 1:29 ~ God said, "Behold, I have given you every plant that yields seed on the face of all the earth, and every tree with seed in its fruit."
- 2 SA 22:22–24 ~ Within each of us is the power to obey God.
- PRO 3:5–8 ~ Trust in the Lord with all your heart; do not rely on your own understanding. Acknowledge God in everything you do, and He will direct your ways. Do not consider yourself wise, but fear the Lord, refrain from evil, and you will be healthy and strong.
- PRO 16:3 ~ Commit your acts to God and He will establish your thoughts.
- ECC 7:16–18 ~ Do not try to be too righteous or wise, too wicked or foolish. It is good to hold onto the one and not let go of the other. Those who fear God will avoid all extremes.
- LUK 21:34–35 ~ Jesus said, "Be careful. Do not let overindulgence, drunkenness, and the worries of life get the better of you, so when that fateful day comes you will not be caught by surprise. It will be like a snare that catches the whole earth in its trap."
- ROM 13:13–14 ~ Be honest, as in the daylight; do not engage in rioting, drunkenness, overindulgence, promiscuity, fighting, and jealousy. Build your life around Jesus Christ, do not indulge in the lusts of the flesh.
- 1 CO 3:16–17 ~ Do you know that you are the temple of God, and His Spirit lives in you? If you defile this temple, you will be destroyed. God's temple is holy and you are that temple.

- 1 CO 6:12; 1 CO 10:23 ~ Something that is permissible is not necessarily beneficial or constructive. It is all right to enjoy something but I will not let it control me.

- 1 CO 6:19–20 ~ Your body is the temple of the Holy Spirit who lives in you, so your body does not belong to you. You were bought with a great price. Therefore, glorify God in your body, and in your spirit, both of which belong to God.

- EPH 5:18, 29 ~ Do not get drunk, which is excess; instead, fill yourself with the Holy Spirit. Nobody hates their own bodies; instead, they nourish and cherish their bodies, just as Christ nourishes and cherishes the church.

To be completely whole, one needs to be healthy mind, body, and spirit. Thus, all three need to be exercised and nourished. An essential element of any effective rehabilitation program is an action plan. This includes corresponding modifications individuals must make in their environments to reduce temptations and eliminate bad influences: meaning changes in people, places, things, events, and use of time (Barber, 2020b). Additionally, people need outlets for processing, expressing, or venting emotional material: spiritually (church, prayer, Bible study, service, sponsorship), mentally (journaling, letter writing, crafts, creativity, group meetings), and physically (fitness, running, weight lifting, housework, yardwork, manual labor). The key is to stay meaningfully busy, fighting the disease with all aspects of your being.

- HAG 1:9 ~ "You expected much, but see, it turned out to be little. What you brought home I blew away," declares the Lord Almighty. "Why? Because my house remains in shambles while each of you is too busy with your own house."

- ROM 8:26–28 ~ The Holy Spirit helps us with our problems. We really do not know what we should pray for, so the Spirit intercedes for us in ways that words could never express. God, who searches the hearts of everyone, knows the mind of the Spirit, because the Spirit intercedes for God's people according to God's will. We can be sure that God will provide good things to those who love Him, and are called according to His purpose.

- EPH 5:11 ~ Do not associate with the evil works of darkness, but rather express your disapproval.

- PHP 1:6 ~ Be confident of this: He who began a good work in you will carry it to completion until the day Christ returns.

- PHP 4:5 ~ Let your moderation be an example to others.

- 1 PE 4:1–3 ~ Even though Christ has done away with sin, you must not continue to sin as you have in the past when you engaged in sexual sin, lust, drunkenness, overindulgence, orgies, and idolatry.

Heavenly Father, we pray for those who are struggling with addiction, that they would find solace in your Holy Spirit, who will lead them back to you. They have lost control over their lives, allowing worldly lusts of the flesh to dominate their thoughts. What they need is the proverbial wake-up call, alerting them to the destruction that awaits them if they continue down the path they are on. Help them to find their way through Jesus Christ who is the Way. Help them to exchange the lies they are telling themselves with the truth of your Word, through your Holy Spirit who is ever-present. Help them to confess their sins and repent before you, so they can let go of the emotional baggage and give it to Jesus, who will give them His righteousness in exchange for their sin. Help us all to be addicted solely to your love. In Jesus's name, Amen.

June 11

Beware the Second Death Day is a warning of the consequences of sin, which is death. But not only death of the body, but also death of the soul. You see, living a life of sin without repentance will result in your body and your soul being destroyed in hell. The Holy Bible speaks of death, life after death, and the second death. We all live, die, and are revived at the last day to receive judgment. Some will inherit eternal life, and the rest will die again, a second time, for the last time. The former group will live in a new heaven and earth, but the latter group will die out with the old heaven and earth. A fundamental of physics is the phenomenon of entropy, heat death, the end of the universe. The Bible also informs that heaven and earth will pass away. It seems science and scripture are in agreement regarding the passing of heaven and earth. For the chosen however, all will become new; scientists will never be able to explain that.

- REV 20:14–15 ~ Death and hell were thrown into the lake of fire: this is the second death. Anyone not found written in the Book of Life was thrown into the lake of fire.

- REV 21:1, 6, 8 ~ And I saw a new heaven and a new earth, for the first heaven and earth had passed away... The fearful, unbelieving and abominable; murderers, whoremongers and sorcerers; idolaters and liars—they all will have a part of the lake of fire that burns with fire and brimstone, which is the second death.

- REV 21:10, 23–27 ~ God carried me away in the spirit to a large and high mountain, and showed me the great city, a holy Jerusalem, descending out of heaven from God... The city had no need of the sun or the moon to shine in it, for the glory of God illuminated it and the Lamb is its lamp. The nations which are saved will walk in the light of it; kings of the earth will bring their honor and glory into it. Its gates will never be locked, for there will be no night. Access will be denied to all things which could defile, or work abomination, or create a lie. Access is given only to those people who are written in the Lamb's Book of Life.

Here it is: one group lives the other dies. In which group are you? Be assured, if you are not sure, you are in the second group and will experience the second death. If you are in the first group, you should know; because you have accepted the atonement of Christ, cleansed by the blood of the Lamb. Be aware of the wrath of God which awaits the unrepentant sinner; do not be indifferent about Christ. It is surprising the mere numbers of people who are in denial of God's judgment or have rejected His salvation. They have much to be afraid of, especially death; fear only God and have nothing to be afraid of, especially death (PSA 23).

- MAT 10:28 ~ Jesus said, "Do not fear those who kill the body but cannot kill the soul. Rather, fear Him who can destroy both soul and body in hell."

- REV 20:1–13 ~ The devil who deceived them was thrown into the lake of fire and brimstone, where the beast and false prophet are, to be tormented day and night forever and ever. And I saw a great white throne and Him who sat upon it, from whose face the earth and heaven fled away; and there was found no place for them. The dead, small and great, stood before God; and the books were opened, and another book was opened: the Book of Life. The dead were judged from the things written in the books, in accordance with their works. The sea gave up the dead that were in it, and death and hell delivered up their dead as well; and they were judged according to their works.

Understand this: if you try to be saved by your own works you will be judged by those works; nobody can save themselves regardless of the abundance of their good works. That is why believers rely on the perfect work of Christ. You can be judged by works or by faith, but as you can see, the only works that count were those of Jesus Christ. Your works mean nothing, except those done in obedience to God, which is by faith. Simply put, your good works will never earn salvation because it's free; however, being saved will lead you into works of obedience, in which case you will be judged by the righteousness of Christ.

- JDE 1:4–8 ~ Certain men have secretly crept in, who were ordained for condemnation; ungodly men, who turned the grace of God into lasciviousness, denying the only true God and our Lord Jesus Christ. I remind you that you know this, how the Lord saved the people out the land of Egypt but afterwards destroyed them when they ceased to believe. Also, angels who did not keep their first estate (in heaven) but left their habitation are reserved in everlasting chains under darkness until the great day of judgment. Same as Sodom and Gomorrah and nearby cities which gave into fornication and deviant sex, they are an example of the ones suffering the vengeance of eternal fire. Also included are those filthy dreamers who defile their bodies, despise authority, and speak evil of the righteous.

- JDE 1:11–13 ~ These people speak evil of that which they know nothing about; but by what they know instinctively, as animals, they corrupt themselves. Woe unto them, for they have taken the wayward path of Cain, consumed by greed for an earthly reward like Balaam, only to perish in their rebellion as with Core. These people tarnish your charitable feasts, while they engorge themselves without concern. They are clouds without water carried away by the wind, trees without fruit that wither away—twice dead, plucked up by the roots. They are as raging waves foaming with shame, or wandering stars which are resigned to blackness forever.

- REV 2:10–11 ~ Jesus said, "Do not fear the things that you will suffer, for the devil will throw you into prison to be tried, and you will have tribulation ten days. But be faithful unto death and I will give you a crown of life. Those with and ear let them hear what the Spirit says to the churches: Whoever overcomes will not be hurt by the second death."

Who doesn't wonder if we are in the last times? Well, those who don't care. It is written: you cannot love God and mammon (MAT 6:19–24; LUK 16:1–13). What is mammon? It encompasses worldly wealth and possessions. In other words, you can choose to love things of the world or to love God (JAM 4:4; 1 JO 4:6–8). If you love the world you die with it; if you love God you live with Him. Either way, it's forever. I pray for those who do not care; I hope they will see the light and discover the truth. For many, they don't want to know the truth, they don't desire God, and they choose to do everything their way; but that way will take them down.

- DEU 7:9–10 ~ Know this, that the Lord your God is a faithful God who keeps His covenant of love and mercy to a thousand generations, with those who love Him and keep His commandments. He will repay those who hate Him to their face, and will destroy them; He will give them no slack.

- JOB 14:14 ~ If a person dies, can he or she live again? All the days of my appointed time I will wait, until my change comes.

- 1 JO 2:15–17 ~ Do not love the world or the things in it. If anybody loves the world, the love of the Father is not in them. All that is in the world, the lust of the flesh, the greed of the eyes, and the pride of life is not of the Father but of the world. And the world passes away; but those who do the will of God will abide forever.

Jesus said that in the last days things are going to get progressively worse, even worse than the times of Lot and the destruction of Sodom and Gomorrah, and Noah and the destruction of the world's population. Note there were few survivors when God brought wrath down upon humankind during these two occasions. What do you think lies in store for those who behave so immorally that it will be the worst of times? Remember, you are either of God or of the world

(JOH 15:18–19); you either serve God or mammon (MAT 6:24). In the end, the world will be in such tribulation, God may save His people out of it (JER 30:7; MAT 24:21–22); then again, there may be some who must endure it (REV 2:10).

Dreadful times are coming (2 TI 3:1). It is possible the Antichrist has arrived. Could this be the beginning of the end, the beginning of sorrows (MAT 24)? I'm sure generations before have thought this. Notice how all of God's Ten Commandments are being violated left and right already. Is this era worse than ever before? In my observation, everything appears to be going haywire.

1. Placing the world or worldly things before God is in violation of the first commandment.
2. Idolizing or worshipping other gods, people, or self violates the second.
3. Rejecting the Holy Spirit in favor of a life of disobedience violates the third.
4. Defaming God's truth and His Holy Word blasphemes His name, in violation of the fourth.
5. Dishonor and disrespect of those God placed in charge of children violates the fifth.
6. Taking a life indiscriminately, regardless of age, is murder.
7. Having sex outside of wedlock (between one husband and one wife) is adultery.
8. Taking something by force that is not yours is stealing.
9. Lying, deceit, and nonfactual testimony are bearing false witness.
10. Desiring something or someone forbidden to you is covetousness.

Okay, maybe we have violated all ten at least once in our lives, but nowadays people are violating them all continuously. Naturally, it only takes one sin to be outside of God's Law, which is why everyone needs to be saved from themselves. The smart ones are choosing Christ and therefore, life. People and governments trying to eliminate your freedom, livelihood, and choices are among the latter group choosing death; you know, the ones loving mammon. But they'll never be satisfied, always wanting more, trying to control everything and everyone. In simple terms, they are globalists, though known by many other names (e.g., communists, socialists, fascists, statists, anarchists, jihadists, new world order, and the list goes on). It is tyranny, any way you look at it: people dictating to you that which you must do or else. Sound familiar? They will grab it all and squander it like preceding empires which fell due to massive corruption, with the last global empire already screaming down the road to hell (REV 17:10–11). This is the very scenario our nation's founders fought against and warned it could happen again. It is happening now, by the look of it. That is why God's Word needs to reach the world; for the clock is ticking and the countdown impending.

- PSA 63:1 ~ Oh God, you are my God; I will seek you every morning. My soul thirsts for you, my flesh longs for you in a dry and thirsty land where there is no water.

- AMO 8:11–12 ~ Behold, the days are coming, says the Lord God, when I will send a famine in the land; not a famine of bread or a thirst for water, but of hearing the words of the Lord. People will wander from coast to coast, from the north to the east, running to-and-fro seeking the Word of the Lord, but will not find it.

- MAT 5:6 ~ Jesus said, "Blessed be those who hunger and thirst after righteousness, for they shall be filled."

- MAT 24:14 ~ Jesus said, "The gospel of the kingdom will be preached throughout the world as a witness to every nation; then the end will come."

- MAR 16:15 ~ Jesus said, "Go into the world and preach the gospel to everyone. Those who believe will be saved, and those who do not will be damned."

- JOH 6:35 ~ Jesus said, "I am the bread of life; those who come to me will never hunger, and those who believe me will never thirst."

   People often brag about how they intend to live life to the fullest. Rarely are they talking about life after death; they are usually referring to this life and this world. It reminds me of a parable Jesus taught (LUK 12:16–21) about the guy who had it made and decided to "eat, drink, and be merry." Then God said to him, "Fool, tonight your soul will be required from you." Jesus stated that this would be the fate of people who collect earthly treasures for themselves but are not rich towards God. Yeah, you can gather riches and party until you drop or until they turn out the lights; either way, that is how it ends. But in heaven, the celebration never ends and the light is never switched off.

   It is easier to live life to the fullest on this planet if you have the Holy Spirit guiding you. A godly person does not have to forfeit pleasure, success, happiness, or desire; all these can be had in accordance with God's will. Those believing sin is fun are misguided, because you can have fun without sinning, whereas sin results in penalties, natural and spiritual. One can be fulfilled in this life and in the next, and that would be living life to the fullest. If you constantly indulge the evil desires of your mind and body or make this life a continuous blast, you will go down in flames when time runs out. The self-indulgent appease only themselves; they do not intend to please God, because they would rather be their own god, make their own rules, and have their own way (JDE 1:18–19). To them, God, faith, and obedience are a huge burden. And since they do not want God, they will get their wish, permanently banned from His presence.

- PSA 68:1–2 ~ Let God arise, let His enemies be scattered; let them who hate God flee before Him. As smoke is driven away, so drive them away; as wax melts before the fire, let the wicked perish at the presence of God. But let the righteous be glad; let them rejoice before God exceedingly.

- JER 23:36–40 ~ The burden of the Lord will be mentioned no more, since every man's word will be his own burden. For you have perverted the words of the living God, the Lord of hosts. Say to the prophet, "How has the Lord answered you, and what did God say?" But you said, "The burden of the Lord" after God told you not to say that. Therefore, I will utterly forget you, and I will forsake you and the city I gave to you and your fathers, and I will cast you out of my presence. I will bring an everlasting reproach upon you, with perpetual shame that will not be forgotten.

   Thank you, dearest Father, that your children will not experience the second death. We fear you because you are awesome; therefore, we do not fear death because we know it results in our passage into eternity with you oh Father, and with Jesus our brother. We pray for those who do not care, and we hope they will see the light and discover the truth. Help us to recall the joy of salvation when we are down and out, always looking forward to the prize that awaits us. Help us to not dwell on our mistakes but to correct them; help us to not desire sin but let our desire be you, for we know that you will fulfill every desire of our hearts if we stay focused on Christ. Help everyone to see Jesus in us by allowing us to shine brightly with His light, Amen.

June 12

Feast of Weeks (*Shavuot*) occurs on the Jewish calendar in the month of Sivan 6–7. The day will vary from year to year between 05/15–06/14 on the Gregorian calendar. The feast occurred seven weeks after Passover, coinciding with the harvest of wheat. Also called Pentecost, it is associated with the bestowing of the Holy Spirit, commemorating the handing down of the Law (Torah) to Moses on Mt. Sinai. The feast is celebrated throughout the night and day, often with readings from the book of Ruth, with a holy convocation and no work.

The book of Ruth in the Bible was set during this season, when Ruth gleaned wheat left by the harvesters in the field of Boaz. They would later marry, for Boaz was in line to take the role of her kinsman redeemer. The tradition was that a Jewess who was widowed would marry a close relative of the deceased so that her children would not lose their inheritance. Ruth had converted to Judaism and her husband was deceased. Boaz accepted the role as kinsman and married Ruth. They would have a son named Obed, who would be an ancestor of both Joseph and Mary. Jesus would become the kinsman who would redeem all the Jews who trusted Him.

- EXO 34:21–22; LEV 23:16; DEU 16:9–10 ~ After six days of work, you will rest the seventh even during the harvest. Then celebrate the Feast of Weeks, offering the first fruits of the wheat. The morning after the seventh sabbath will number fifty days, and you will present a grain offering to the Lord. Count seven weeks from the corn harvest, and the next day observe the Feast of Weeks to the Lord with a freewill tribute offering from your hand, given to the Lord in proportion with how much He has blessed you.

- RUT 1:11–18, 22 ~ Naomi had lost two sons married to Moabite women. She said to the widows, "Turn back my daughters-in-law, why should you follow me? I will never marry again or bear more sons to marry; you should not wait to remarry. It grieves me for your sakes how the hand of the Lord took my two sons, your husbands." The widows wept. Then Orpah kissed her mother-in-law goodbye and departed. But Ruth held onto Naomi who said, "Your sister-in-law has returned to her people and their gods; you should go with her." Ruth replied, "Please do not ask me to go, for I would rather follow you, and go where you go and live where you live. Your people will be my people and your God my God. Where you die, I will die and be buried with you." When Naomi saw that Ruth was determined, she kept quiet. So, Naomi and Ruth went to Bethlehem together, arriving at the beginning of the harvest.

- ISA 43:13–15; ISA 44:6; ISA 49:7 ~ Yes, before there was day, I AM He. Nobody can be delivered out of my hand. When I do something, it cannot be undone. This is what the Lord, your Redeemer, the Holy One of Israel says: For your sake I will take down Babylon. I AM the Lord, your Holy One, the creator of Israel, and your King. This is what God and His Redeemer the Lord of hosts say: I AM the first and last; there are no other gods besides me. The Lord, the Redeemer of Israel, and His Holy One that humankind hates say: Kings and princes will see, come, and worship, because the Lord is faithful as is His Holy One.

- ACT 2:1–6 ~ When the day of Pentecost came, they were joined with one accord in one place. Suddenly a sound from heaven was heard like a mighty rushing wind, filling the house where they were sitting. Next appeared cloven tongues of fire sitting atop the head of each evangelist. They were filled with the Holy Spirit and began to speak in other languages, as the Holy Spirit directed them. While the news spread, people came to see, including many devout Jews. All were amazed for everyone heard the Word spoken in their native tongue.

We thank you Father, and Jesus who is the kinsman redeemer of the world, Jews and Christians alike. We celebrate His first coming and look forward to His second, when He comes to harvest His own, and bring us to a place where the celebration will continue forever, Amen.

June 13

Supreme Court Ruled in Favor of Miranda Rights on this day in 1966 in a landmark case, Miranda vs. Arizona. In a 5-4 decision, the court made it mandatory for police to inform a person of their Constitutional rights before being questioned or arrested. No doubt you have heard a version of this on every cop show: You have the right to remain silent and the right to an attorney; anything you say can be used in court. This ruling made it improper to force someone into confessing without telling them their rights to remain silent, to not self-incriminate (Fifth Amendment), and not be questioned without an attorney present (Sixth Amendment). The decision required these rights to be read to a suspect or person of interest prior to questioning or while arresting them, otherwise all statements made would be inadmissible during trial. Many a case has been thrown out as a result of neglecting to "mirandize" suspects, including Miranda himself who received a new trial and was found guilty anyway; now his name is well known.

It is likely that most people are unaware of their rights granted in the US Constitution and Bill of Rights. It would behoove all people to read these documents, which would take a few hours at most. I keep a pocketsize booklet handy; it is a whole thirty pages long. I would advise everyone to know what it says; it is very educational. I also would advise everyone who is brought for questioning by police never to waive their rights, especially if they are a suspect. However, if you can help in an investigation, you should, but you still might consider having counsel present. Even innocent people have been known to confess things after hours of intensive interrogation, thinking the police will lay off if they give in. Either way, police are immune from damages as of 1983. Our system of justice works, if everyone stays within the law.

When Jesus was being interrogated, He remained silent, for the most part. It would have been pointless to tell His accusers who He was until the time was right. Jesus knew it wouldn't matter because their minds were made up. And try as he would, Pontius Pilate still gave Christ over to be executed, after publicly declaring Him innocent three times. All four Gospel writers describe Jesus's trial, each providing additional details, proving that they did not collaborate on their stories but testified independently, making them credible and their testimony reliable.

- MAT 26:57–67 ~ They took hold of Jesus and brought Him before Caiaphas, the high priest, with elders and scribes. Peter followed from afar inside the gates and sat with the servants. The Jewish leaders tried to find witnesses to testify against Jesus for crimes worthy of the death penalty; since they couldn't find any, they produced two witnesses to testify falsely. One testified, "He said he could destroy the temple and rebuild it in three days." The high priest stood and asked Jesus, "Have you no answer to this accusation?" Jesus remained silent. The high priest said, "I demand in the name of the living God that you tell us whether you are the Christ, the Son of God." Jesus answered, "You have said it. Nevertheless, I say to you that hereafter you will see the Son of man sitting at the right hand of power, and coming in the clouds of heaven." The high priest ripped his garment saying, "He has spoken blasphemy. What do the rest of you think?" They answered, "He is guilty and worthy of death." Then they proceeded to mock Jesus, spitting on Him, beating Him, and slapping Him.

- MAT 27:12–13, 24–25 ~ The Jewish priests and elders took Jesus before Pontius Pilate and made accusations against Him, but Jesus remained silent without responding to a single charge. Pilate asked Jesus, "Do you hear what they are accusing you of?" But Jesus did not answer. When Pilate saw he was getting nowhere and a riot was brewing, he took water, washed his hands, and declared, "I am innocent of this man's blood." The people answered, "Let his blood be on us and our children."

JUNE

- MAR 15:9–13 ~ Pilate answered the people, "Do you want me to release unto you the king of the Jews?" For Pilate knew that the chief priests were envious of Jesus. The chief priests encouraged the mob to ask Pilate to release Barabbas instead of Jesus. Pilate asked them what they wanted to do with Jesus and the crowd cried again loudly, "Crucify him."

- LUK 23:3–24 ~ Pilate asked Jesus, "Are you the king of the Jews?" Jesus answered, "Whatever you say." Then Pilate announced to the chief priests and to the people, "I see no fault in this man." Discovering that Jesus was from Galilee, Pilate sent Jesus to Herod to be tried since he was the authority in Galilee. Herod mocked Jesus, toyed with Him, asking Him stupid questions but Jesus remained silent the entire time. Then Herod sent Jesus back to Pilate. That same day Herod and Pilate became friends having previously been enemies. Pilate gathered the Jewish priests and rulers before the crowd and announced, "I have examined this man and found no fault in Him concerning your accusations; neither did Herod disclose any evidence worthy of His death. Therefore, I will chastise Him and let Him go." It was customary to release one prisoner during the Passover, but the people demanded to put Jesus away and release Barabbas, a man convicted of sedition and murder. Pilate again offered to release Jesus, but the crowd yelled, "Crucify him". A third time Pilate appealed to them asking what evil had He done, and explaining the he had found no crime worthy of death, but would punish Jesus and turn Him loose. The chief priests and their followers again called for His execution and Pilate gave them what they wanted.

- JOH 18:33–38 ~ Pilate asked Jesus, "Are you a king?" Jesus answered, "Are you saying this yourself or because others have said it?" Pilate replied, "Am I a Jew? Your own people and priests have brought you here. Tell me, what have you done?" Jesus answered, "My kingdom is not of this world, if it was, my servants would fight to keep me from being delivered to you. But my kingdom has yet to come." Pilate said, "Then you are a king." Jesus answered, "You have said that I am a king. The reason I was born into this world was to testify to the truth. Everyone who is interested in the truth will listen to me." Pilate asked, "What is truth?" Pilate abruptly left but returned, stood before the Jews, and stated, "I find no fault in him."

Notice how none of the accusers of Jesus had any interest in the truth, which is why Jesus said nothing. He only responded when they asked Him directly for the truth, but when He told them, they couldn't stand to hear it making them angrier and more determined to kill Him. Even Pilate, who knew Jesus was innocent, turned his back after asking Jesus, "What is truth." Having already declared His innocence, Pilate sentenced Jesus to death anyway, refusing to accept responsibility, even though he was the only authority in the region authorized to sentence someone to death. Jesus showed by example how to respond in a crisis. You would be smart to remain silent when you know nobody will believe or accept what you have to say. But if you are sent by God to testify, He will tell you what to say and when, so no worries. There is a time to speak and a time to hold your tongue. The conscience within your soul connects you to the Holy Spirit; listen carefully to the spirit within you, and you will know the truth, and when it needs telling. You will be a true witness for Jesus, not one responsible for His blood.

- MAT 10:19–20 ~ When they capture you, do not worry about what to say, for the words will be given to you by the Holy Spirit. Thus, it will not be you speaking, but the Almighty Father speaking through you.

Almighty Father, Spirit of all truth, which lived fully in Jesus Christ who spoke only the truth, for He is God and is uncapable of lying—grant that we may know and tell the truth at all times and in all places when it is exactly the right time for us to tell it. Help us to listen to the Word inside of us and speak it whenever someone asks about the truth of your Word which sets people free. May they listen to and obey it. In the name of Truth, our Triune God, Amen.

June 14

National Flag Day recognizes this day in 1777 when the Second Continental Congress put aside writing the Articles of Confederation and discussed the need for a flag. They agreed on the stars and stripes, thirteen of each to represent the thirteen colonies; they also chose the colors of white stars on a blue background, with red and white horizontal stripes. But today wasn't declared a national holiday until 1916 when President Wilson decreed this day to be celebrated henceforth. However, many had started to commemorate the date as early as 1885, when a Wisconsin school teacher named Bernard Cigrand celebrated it at his school, later suggesting in a mainstream newspaper that it be celebrated across the country every year. Other movements were organized in various states until it became official. What do we do on flag day? Raise the flag high. Fly the flag outside your home if you have one, maybe display one in your office or classroom if allowed. Wear a flag pin if you are prohibited from doing anything else.

Flags have been a symbol of patriotism since there were independent nations, armies, and settlements. Flags, banners, standards, and other objects were used to denote identity since there were walls, forts, and borders being protected. Israel had its own flag and each tribe had their own banner to identify themselves. The enemies of Israel also used banners and standards. The same signs and banners are used in modern armies whether in battle or during training, so units and posts can be identified by those who need to understand its meaning or significance.

- NUM 1:52; NUM 2:2, 34 ~ The sons of Israel will camp, each army designated by their standard, with the banners of each father's household marking each encampment around the tent of meeting. The sons of Israel did as the Lord commanded Moses, camping near their standards; and they set out, every one by family household.

- PSA 20:5 ~ We will rejoice in your salvation, and in the name of our God we will set up banners saying: May the Lord fulfill your petitions.

- PSA 60:4–5 ~ You have given a banner to those who fear you, to display in the name of truth. Save us with your right hand and deliver those you love.

- ISA 31:8–9 ~ The Assyrian will fall in battle, but not by mean or mighty man. Their stronghold will crumble from terror when they see the battle standard approaching, says the Lord, whose fire is in Zion and His furnace in Jerusalem.

- JER 4:6 ~ Lift up a standard toward Zion! Seek refuge; do not hesitate, for I am bringing evil and great destruction from the north.

- JER 4:20–21 ~ Disaster follows disaster; the whole land lies in ruins. In an instant our homes are destroyed. How long must we see the battle standard and hear the sound of the trumpet?

God uses signs to indicate certain events. When we see them, it raises flags inside our minds alerting us to His message. Some are red flags, warning us to stay away, and others are flags inviting us to come. We are given signs of things that are happening and signs of things that will happen. For example, there are literally hundreds of signs of the first coming of Messiah as well as His second coming. At the second coming, we will see the banner and hear the trumpet, inviting us to be members of the new Jerusalem on the mount Zion of heaven.

- PSA 74:2–4 ~ Lord, remember your congregation which you purchased a long time ago; the rod of your inheritance who you redeemed from this mount Zion where you have lived. Stomp your feet upon the perpetual desolations, which the enemy has done wickedly in the sanctuary. Your enemies roar in the middle of meeting places and set up their own standards as signs.

JUNE

- ISA 11:10–12 ~ In that day a rod of Jesse will stand as a signal to the people, and the Gentiles will seek it and find glorious rest. The Lord will lift His hand a second time to recover the remnant of His people from the nations. He will set up a flag for the nations and assemble those who were scattered, and gather them from the four corners of the earth.

- ISA 18:3 ~ You inhabitants of the world and all who dwell on the earth, watch for a standard raised on the mountain, and listen for the trumpet when it is blown.

- ISA 49:22 ~ The Lord says, "Behold, I will lift my hand to the nations and set up my standard to the people. They will come with their sons and daughters."

Until Christ returns for us, we will continue to fight the good fight of faith, carrying His standard as we go into battle. For Christians, our standard of behavior is Jesus, and the standard we carry is the cross of Christ on our hearts, with His name written on our foreheads.

- DEU 20:1, 4 ~ When you go into battle against your enemies, and you see horses and chariots, and you realize you are outnumbered, do not be afraid. For the Lord your God is with you. He is the same one who rescued you out of Egypt. He goes with you to fight for you and save you.

- EZE 9:4–5 ~ God said to the angel, "Set a mark on the foreheads of all who sigh and cry over the abominations they have witnessed; strike the others down by the sword, without pity."

- JOE 3:9–10, 14 ~ Go, tell the Gentiles to prepare for war. Wake the mighty warriors and tell them to come. Beat your plowshares into swords and your pruning hooks into spears. Let the weak say, "I am strong." Multitudes are gathered in the valley of decision, for the day of the Lord is nearing.

- MAT 10:34, 38–39 ~ Jesus said, "Do not think I came to send peace to the earth, because I am sending a sword. You must take up your cross and follow me if you want to be counted worthy. Those who wish to keep their lives will lose their lives; but those who lose their lives for my sake will be given back their lives."

- 2 CO 10:3–5 ~ Although we are human flesh and blood, we do not make war with flesh and blood. For the weapons we use are not of this world, because we have the Spirit on our side to bring down the strongholds of the enemy. We break down the arguments and the influences of those high and mighty people who stand against God; we take captive human thoughts, making them obedient to Jesus Christ.

- 1 TI 6:12–13 ~ Fight the good fight of faith. Keep a firm grasp on eternal life, for this is why you were called, and why you testified before many witnesses and before God.

- 2 TI 2:3–4 ~ Endure hardship like a good Christian soldier. Those who fight wars need not get caught up with the affairs of this life, but rather should concern themselves with the affairs of Jesus Christ who chose them to be a soldier.

- REV 22:3–4 ~ The curse was gone forever. Everyone served the Lamb, and His name was on their foreheads.

Father God, we are standard bearers for your Son Jesus. Please, Holy Spirit, equip us as we carry His banner into battle against enemies we can see, as well as enemies we cannot see, knowing that you go with us to fight and to save us. Let us be soldiers in your army, using our knowledge and skills to defeat evil forces in this world, and free those who are captive to sin, and uplift those who are destined for the grave. Help us to regain control over our land, and replace godless leaders with spiritually enlightened leaders. In the name of Christ our Savior, Amen.

June 15

King John Signed the Magna Carta on this day in 1215, a document which outlined the laws and rights of free people. It became the basis of our laws, justice system, free elections, and founding documents during the birth of the USA. The king of England placed his seal on it to avert civil war, and avoid a rebellion by the French over tyranny, whether from royalty or the church. The various parties agreed on the Articles of Barons on this date, which would become known as the Magna Carta. It was modified several times but remained a representation of common law and due process, as well as a testimonial against oppression and feudalism. It established a constitutional form of government, which was emulated in part in the Constitution of the United States. An important clause of the Magna Carta concerned *Habeas Corpus*, which states that citizens cannot be imprisoned or deprived of their property without due process of the law. Interestingly, this very statute was violated by imprisoning people without due process who were "associated" with a riot near the Capitol building on 01/06/2021. Amazingly, the riots, looting, and arson which took place the summer before were permitted with no reprisals. Clearly the application of the law has become a political tool to thwart the opposing party.

- EXO 22:6 ~ If a fire breaks out and spreads into the bushes, consuming the grain or the fields, the one who started the fire must make restitution.

- PRO 28:7 ~ Whoever keeps the Law is a wise child; but riotous children embarrass their parents.

- PRO 29:24 ~ The partner of a thief is his own worst enemy; he is called to testify but admits nothing.

- MAL 2:10 ~ Do we not have one father? Has God not created us? Why do we deal treacherously each man against his brother, profaning the covenant God made with our fathers?

- MAT 26:47 ~ As Jesus was trying to awaken His apostles, Judas showed up with a riotous mob, carrying swords and clubs; they had been sent by the chief priests and elders of the church. The one who betrayed Jesus said he would identify Jesus by kissing Him on the cheek, and after Judas kissed Him, Jesus asked, "Friend, why have you come?" Then they grabbed Jesus and took Him away.

- MAR 15:11–13 ~ The chief priests and elders stirred up the crowd, inducing them to ask Pilate to release Barabbas and crucify Jesus.

- LUK 4:28–30 ~ After speaking in the synagogue, a mob of observers became angry and rose up to grab Jesus and take Him out of the city to throw Him off a cliff. But Jesus passed unnoticed through the midst of them.

- ACT 5:11–13; ACT 7:58–59 ~ Some of the men in the crowed claimed Stephen was a heretic and stirred up a mob which seized Stephen and brought him before the Sanhedrin. And they produced false witnesses to testify against him. The angry mob took Stephen outside the city and stoned him to death in the presence of Saul (who later became the apostle Paul).

- ROM 13:13 ~ Be honest, as in the daylight; do not engage in rioting, drunkenness, overindulgence, promiscuity, fighting, and jealousy.

As mentioned previously, everyone should know their rights, and learn the normal balance of powers succinctly explained in the Constitution. Among many other things guaranteed in the Fifth Amendment, a person cannot be "deprived of life, liberty, or property without due process of law". Further, the Tenth Amendment states that all powers not specifically ascribed to the federal government nor denied to the states "are reserved to the states respectively, or to the people". The greatest power of this land belongs to the people, who choose those who represent us in Congress and the White House; they have pledged to ensure powers delegated to the federal and state governments are lawfully exercised and the rights and powers of citizens are not denied or circumvented. Unfortunately, the people we elect do not always follow the rules, and violate federal or state laws. Lawlessness is becoming more rampant; due process of law occurs rather infrequently, with those in power using the system to go after opponents and dissidents vigorously.

- PSA 103:19 ~ The Lord has prepared His throne in heaven and His kingdom rules over all.

- PRO 29:12 ~ If a ruler listens to lies, his entire cabinet will be evil.

- ISA 9:1–2, 6–7 ~ There will be no more gloom for those in distress. In the past God humbled the land of Zebulun and Naphtali, but in the future, the land of Galilee will be honored from the sea to the Jordan. People walking in darkness will see a great light of life; to those living in a land of darkness their light will be dawning. For unto us a Son is born and the government will be upon His shoulders. He will be called Wonderful Counselor, Mighty God, Everlasting Father, and Prince of Peace. Of the increase in His government and of His peace there will be no end. From the throne of David, He will reign over His kingdom, establishing it and upholding it in justice and judgment, henceforth and forever. The zeal of the Lord of hosts will ensure this.

- MAT 23:25 ~ Jesus said, "Woe to you hypocrites, for you make the outside appear clean, while the inside is full of extortion and excess."

- 2 PE 2:9–10 ~ The Lord knows how to deliver the godly from temptation, and to reserve the wicked for the day of judgment to be punished. This includes those who seek the lusts of the unclean, who despise government, who are shameless, self-gratifying, and openly despise dignity.

- 1 JO 3:4 ~ Whoever commits sin transgresses the law, for sin is the transgression of the law.

In this week's lessons we have talked about rights and how due process of the law is needed to guarantee them. But human rights are stolen by corrupt governments and their officials, and the citizenry should beware; for such is the road to totalitarianism, reflected in tyranny, communism, socialism, and globalism, which cannot exist in a constitutional republic. This is the very reason the Magna Carta became law back in the thirteenth century. The US Constitution is like a contract between the people and our government, so those representing us who break that contract and skirt the law are lawbreakers. God makes contracts too, called covenants; though humans are fickle and have broken those covenants, God never has and never will. God's promises are firm and sure; and His justice is complete, final, and unchallengeable.

- LEV 26:14–2 ~ If you do not listen to my commands, and reject my statutes and disregard my ordinances, failing to carry out my will, and thus breaking the covenant, I will bring sudden terror upon you, with wasting diseases and fever which will destroy your sight and sap your strength. I will turn my face from you, allowing your enemies to defeat you; those who hate you will rule over you. And you will run away even though nobody is chasing you.

- JDG 2:20–23 ~ The anger of the Lord was hot against Israel. He said, "Because this people have broken the covenant that I made with their fathers and have not listened to my voice, I will drive them out by the hand of the nations that Joshua spared, so that through them, Israel will be tested to see whether they keep the ways of the Lord as their fathers did, or not."

- ISA 24:5 ~ The earth is polluted by its inhabitants, for they transgressed the laws, violated statutes, and broke the everlasting covenant.

- JER 31:31–34 ~ I will make a New Covenant with my people. It will not be like the covenant I made when I brought my people out of Egypt, which they broke. The New Covenant will be this: Instead of writing my laws on stone, I will write my laws into their minds and upon their hearts. I will be their God and they will be my people; they will know me from the least to the greatest, because I will forgive them and forget their sins.

- DAN 8:23–25 ~ In the latter days, when the evil ones are fully in power, a fierce king will arise from darkness. He will be powerful and mighty, but not by his own power. He will destroy tremendously, and will prosper; routing mighty and holy people, and causing deceit to flourish. He will exalt himself, and through the guise of peace he will kill many. He will take a stand against the Prince of peace, but the Prince will defeat him without raising a hand.

- REV 17:12–14 ~ Ten kings will obtain power for one hour with the beast. They will give their power and strength to the beast and make war with the Lamb, only to be defeated.

Consider the case of Christ. On Passover He had His last supper with the apostles. Next, He went to pray at the Garden of Gethsemane with three of them. Around midnight Jesus was accosted by a riotous mob hired by the chief priests to arrest Him. They dragged Jesus before the priests, elders, and witnesses who mocked, abused, accused, and denounced Him as a heretic. They dragged Jesus before the governor, falsely accusing Him of crimes against Rome. Jesus was questioned, found innocent, whipped and executed. Before sundown, Jesus was dead. Their due process was completed in less than one day (midnight to sundown). Here is a classic violation of habeas corpus, and every other human right stolen from Christ. If globalists get their way, you can wave goodbye to these same rights which already have been repeatedly infringed in the USA.

A sequence of events will occur if we lose our constitutional republic: we will lose our freedoms, rights, privileges, property, liberty, and life, in that order. Beware when you see a whittling away of your freedoms and rights. Beware when you see a deprivation of privileges, a confiscation of property, prohibiting of free movement, the imprisoning of people without due process. You also will notice countless unfortunate deaths at the hands of people who are never punished.

- ECC 12:14 ~ God will judge every work, and things done in secret, whether good or evil.

- ISA 59:3–7 ~ Your hands are defiled with blood and sin. Your lips have spoken lies and wickedness. They conceive evil and rely on foolishness and lies. They run to evil and hasten to shed innocent blood. Desolation and destruction ride their highways.

- HAB 1:4, 11 ~ The law has been slackened and sound judgment cannot be found; for the wicked have encompassed the righteous causing wrong judgment to proceed. They are blown with the wind and pass on, those guilty men who relish their own power as their god.

- LUK 16:8 ~ People are commended for being dishonest. The dishonest people of this evil generation are shrewder than the honest people.

- 2 TI 3:13 ~ Evil people and impostors will progress from bad to worse, as will the deceivers and the deceived.

Heavenly Father, you have made a contract with humanity to give us an inheritance in your kingdom, and all we have to do in return is listen to you and obey; and even though we are unable to fulfill the letter of the law, you will accept our faith as righteousness when Jesus comes to take us home. We will be eternally grateful for your mercy. Help us Father to uphold rights and laws common to all people, and given by you in your Law. May we be ready to show mercy, as you have shown to us. Praise be to you oh Lord, thanks be to you oh God; in the name of Jesus, Amen.

June 16

Father's Day was not recognized as a national holiday until 1972 when President Nixon signed a proclamation making it official. Inspired by Mother's Day, its roots extend back to 1908 when several men who died in a coal mine disaster in West Virginia were honored. The idea gradually caught on despite resistance from some men who considered the celebration to detract from their manliness. The third Sunday in June is the day we celebrate fatherhood with gifts and festivities in honor of the traditional head of the household.

Every father should consult our Heavenly Father for tips about how to be a good dad. Did you know, if you love God above all, He is proud when you to call Him "Dad"? If you have kids, are they proud to call you "Dad"? Well, if you show them genuine love and attention, they will trust you. So, you dads out there, listen up. Do not ever give up on your kids, and be there when they need their dad most of all; that's what God does. Consider the love of our Heavenly Father in the following verses.

- ISA 12:6 ~ Shout with joy you inhabitants of Zion, for great is the Holy One of Israel who will be with you.

- ISA 56:2–8 ~ Blessed are all people, and their children, if they obey God, avoid evil, keep the Sabbath, and cling to His covenant. Even those who are strangers to God's people Israel will be part of God's house if they obey Him. The righteous will become as God's sons and daughters, only better than that, with a name that will last forever. People of all walks of life will be joined together on His holy mountain to worship Him, for His house will be called a house for the righteous.

- LUK 15 ~ The parables of the lost sheep and the prodigal son are great examples of how our Father in heaven desires for us to return to Him and live with Him forever. The father welcomed back the prodigal son after he squandered his inheritance on lustful pleasures. The father rejoiced and had a banquet for his wayward son, who had been lost and then was found. Similarly, the shepherd left the ninety-nine sheep as he searched for the one that was lost, rejoicing when it was returned to the flock. Both examples reveal the love our heavenly Father has for His sheep; He loves them whether they are good or bad, and rejoices when they return to the fold.

- JOH 1:12 ~ To all who have received Christ, and believed in His name, He has given the privilege to become children of God.

- ROM 8:15–18 ~ You have not received the spirit of bondage to be afraid; you have received the Spirit of adoption, whereby we cry, Abba, Father. The Holy Spirit testifies with our spirits that we are God's children. If we are His children, then we are heirs: heirs of God, and joint-heirs with Christ, if indeed we share in His sufferings in order that we may later share in His glory. For I consider the sufferings of this present time to be nothing compared to the glory that will be revealed in us.

- ROM 9:4–8 ~ Who are the Israelites, to whom God gave the Law and granted the adoption, and with whom God made covenants and promises? Christ came for them and for all people. It's not as if God's Word had no effect, for they who are of Israel are not all from Israel. Those who are of Abraham's seed are not all his children. In other words, those who are children of the flesh are not children of God; those who cling to God's promises, they are counted as children.

- GAL 3:26–29 ~ You are the children of God because of your faith in Jesus Christ. Everyone who is baptized has put on Christ like a suit of armor. There is neither Jew nor Greek, slave nor free, male nor female, for we are all equal in Jesus Christ. If you belong to Christ then you are part of Abraham's chosen seed, and heirs according to God's covenant.

- EPH 2:18–19 ~ In Christ we have access through the Holy Spirit to our Father in heaven. Therefore, God's people are no longer strangers or foreigners, they are fellow citizens with the saints and the household of God.

- HEB 12:9 ~ The fathers of our mortal flesh corrected us, and we gave them reverence. Should we not we be in subjection to the Father of spirits even more, and live?

- 1 JO 3:1–2 ~ How great is the love that God the Father has for us, that we should be called His children. The world does not know us because it did not know Him. We are His children, but we do not know yet what we will be; we do know, however, that we will be like Him, for we will see Him as He really is.

One of the greatest societal problems of our time is absent fathers. Kids without a hands-on dad are more prone to crime, dropping out, drugs, and immorality. The Bible teaches that the father should be the spiritual leader of the home; he needs to be there to teach the children the ways of God and the works of Christ. Without a solid moral foundation, kids will stray too far and they will get hurt, or worse. The absent dad problem is the tip of the iceberg, as it creates a myriad of difficulties, especially for kids. Broken homes, dysfunctional families, deadbeat dads: this causes moral decline, not only in the home, but in the nation, and the world.

- PSA 78:6–8 ~ God established a testimony in Jacob and appointed a law in Israel, which He commanded our fathers to obey and make known to the children. Each generation will be taught these precepts; children born to you will declare them to their children. This is so they would set their hopes on God, never forget His works, and keep His commandments; and so they would not be like their fathers, a stubborn and rebellious generation, whose heart was not right with God and whose spirit did not hold steadfast to Him.

- PRO 22:6 ~ Instruct your children in the way they should go and when they mature, they will not depart from it.

- DAN 2:23 ~ I thank and praise you God of my fathers, who has given me wisdom and power, and has told me what you want me to know and to do.

- 1 CO 11:3 ~ I want you to know that the head of every man is Christ; and the head of the woman is the man; and the head of Christ is God.

- EPH 5:23, 25, 28 ~ The husband is the head of the wife even as Christ is the head of the church. Husbands, love and protect your wives even as Christ loved the Church and gave Himself for it. You must love your wife as much as you love yourself.

- EPH 6:4 ~ Fathers, do not provoke your children to anger but bring them up in the nurture and discipline of the Lord.

Our Father in heaven. Your name is Holy. Let your kingdom come to us. Let your will be done here on earth as in heaven. Provide to us our daily needs. Forgive us our sins, as we are to forgive others who sin against us. Defend us from temptation and evil. For the kingdom, power, and glory are yours forever. Send your Holy Spirit into the hearts of fathers, that they do not shun their responsibilities. Honor and dignity belong to the man who loves his wife and kids, and they will honor him for it. Please, Lord, if ever we needed a heads up in this country, it is to return the head of the household to his family, and correct the absent dad problem. Let it be so in accordance with your will. Praise be to you Father in the name of Jesus, Amen.

June 17

Supreme Court Banned Prayer, Bible in School on this day in 1963. It was argued that such behavior was unconstitutional with respect to the First Amendment, maintaining it violated the clause forbidding the government's establishment of a religion; but that clause also states that the government cannot prohibit the free exercise of religion by citizens. While the action targeted two states in particular, its application was broader in interpretation. The ruling applied to public schools everywhere in the USA. Private schools already had existed, mostly with curricula including religious education. Those schools, which also were privately funded, got a tax break because they were not supported with tax money, so only tax supported schools were affected by this decision. Private schools have yet to be prohibited from claiming nonprofit status, but it is just a matter of time when religious schools will be targeted for teaching the Bible.

The fact is, this country began with a religious framework, with religious freedom being listed first in the First Amendment, which also covered freedom of speech, listed second. Individuals and groups have a right to exercise these two personal freedoms: saying prayers and reading the Holy Bible. This does not preclude the right to pray and read the Bible in public, unless it is a public school, according to the Supreme Court. Public schools might be operated by local governments, but they are not funded by the government, they are funded by the people through taxation. The school boards and districts waste that tax money as bad as the government does. And the things they are teaching in public schools will not prepare a student for college or business. What happened to reading, writing, and arithmetic? Parents could be better teachers too, you know.

- ISA 59:13 ~ They know they are being disobedient to God; they carefully plan their lies.

- ACT 20:30 ~ From among yourselves will come those speaking perverse things to gain followers.

- 2 TI 3:13 ~ Evil people and false teachers will get worse, deceiving many; they themselves have been deceived by Satan.

- 2 TI 4:3–4 ~ People will seek teachers who conform to their own likes and dislikes; they will turn away from the truth and wander into myths.

- TIT 1:11 ~ They must be silenced, those who would ruin entire households, teaching things that are wrong for the sake of ill-gotten gain.

- JDE 1:4 ~ False teachers have infiltrated the churches, claiming that once you become Christians you can do whatever you want without being punished. They deny the Lord and turn God's grace into lust.

A 1980 ruling required removal of the Ten Commandments from public schools. In 1983 a moment of silence was considered prayer or meditation and therefore disallowed. In 1992 the Supreme Court ruled that a member of the clergy cannot give an invocation at the beginning or a benediction at the end of a graduation commencement. In 1995 the court ruled that sporting events are school related, disallowing religious speech there. It is baffling, because recently, one school was allowed to let children chant a Moslem song. Several districts started allowing boys to use the girls' restroom and dressing room. Some schools have been teaching secular humanism which is religiously dogmatic, thereby violating their own law banning such speech. Meanwhile, decision makers have vacated the teaching of morality and the disciplining of unruly pupils. Many classrooms have become free-for-alls endangering teachers who get fired if they intervene; as a result, many are quitting. These things have occurred because God is not welcome in public schools, so there is no standard of decency and no corrective action. School administrations and boards are becoming yet another political entity that pushes irreligious principles and rules.

- JOB 5:17 ~ Happy is the person that God corrects; therefore, do not despise being chastised by the Almighty.

- PRO 3:11–12 ~ Do not despise the Lord's discipline and do not resent His correction, for the Lord corrects those He loves just as any father who delights in his child.

- PRO 13:1, 18 ~ A wise son listens to his father's instructions, but those who reject wise counsel hear nothing. Poverty and shame are the rewards for those who refuse instruction, but those who respectfully listen when being scolded will be honored.

- PRO 29:15–17 ~ Punishment provides wisdom; but children left to themselves shame their parents. When the wicked are multiplied, transgression increases, but the righteous will see their fall. Correct your children when they are wrong, and you will be able to rest at night, and they will be your pride and joy.

- ISA 1:18–19 ~ Come now, and let us reason together, says the Lord. Though your sins be as scarlet they will be white as snow; though they be red like crimson, they will be as wool. If you are willing and obedient, you will eat the good of the land.

- 1 CO 9:25–27 ~ Whoever strives to master a task must discipline themselves. For example, athletes strive for an earthly, corruptible crown. But I pursue an incorruptible, heavenly crown. I run my race and fight my battles with confidence. I discipline my body. I practice what I preach so that I will not be found to be a hypocrite.

- EPH 6:4 ~ Do not provoke your children to anger but raise your children in the nurture and discipline of the Lord.

- 2 TI 3:16 ~ All scripture is given by inspiration of God and is effective for doctrine, for guidance, for correction, and for instruction in righteousness.

Our founders felt that religious education from the Holy Bible was an essential part of the curricula; now it is quite the opposite. Is it any wonder that reading grade level is so low, a great number of kids cannot do algebra, and the graduation rate in public schools has plummeted? Research found that college entrance exam scores were significantly higher for private school graduates than for public school graduates; the graduation rate was much higher as well. Maybe all schools should be turned over to the private sector, for the amount of tax money public school districts blow is not worth the value of the education they provide. If you want your children to be successful, check out the available schools first; if you can afford it, check out the private schools too. Odds are, your kids will get a better education at a private, religious, or charter school.

- MAT 13:52 ~ Jesus said, "Every teacher who has been instructed about the kingdom of heaven is like a homeowner who has a treasure chest of things both old and new."

Heavenly Father, we pray for your wisdom and truth to come upon us, especially decision makers who are in charge of educating our children. We also pray that leaders in the field of education and schools at all levels would get an education in your words, works, and ways. If the school teachers and administrators do not know your will and your laws, help them to be taught the truth and knowledge found in the Holy Bible, so they will know how to proceed and decide. Help parents to elect school board members and other politicians who will consider the morality of their decisions more carefully, and realize that forcing immoral rules and introducing harmful teachings to students will result in harsh judgment upon them. There is division in this country about what is acceptable, proper, and honorable; help us to unite on principles and methods from your holy Word. Help leaders, teachers, and boards to see the perspective of Jesus Christ, who is the best model of excellence known to humankind. In His name we pray, Amen.

June 18

Napoleon Was Defeated at Waterloo on this day in 1815, by the Duke of Wellington, ending his imperialistic pursuits. A renown military general, Napoleon became the ruler of France. He widened his empire, incorporating large sections of Europe, but ran into the British and Prussians in Belgium at the town of Waterloo near Brussels, and it would be his last stand. This was not his first defeat, for he already had invaded Europe once and was eventually pushed back by the Russians and the Spaniards. He also abdicated the throne for a second time, and fled France in disgrace. The Brits caught up with him and exiled him to the island of St. Helena, Africa where he died six years later at age fifty-one. His body was returned to Paris and buried with honors.

Apparently, Napoleon tried to bite off more than he could chew. His lust for power and his greed to expand his empire were squashed twice. You would think he'd learned his lesson the first time. He was practically handed the title of emperor and gave it back after being vanquished. Acclaimed as one of the great conquerors in history and held in high esteem by France, his cause was global not honorable. His end was to be banished and die relatively young.

- PSA 39:6 ~ People put on a vain show all the time, and they become troubled in vain. People try to heap up riches not knowing who will gather them in the end.

- PRO 1:18–19 ~ Those who are greedy for riches and oppress others to obtain riches are ambushing their own lives and will succeed in destroying themselves.

- PRO 11:4, 28 ~ Riches will not profit anyone in the day of wrath; only righteousness can save a person from death. Those who trust in their riches will fail, but those who trust in God will flourish.

- PRO 23:5 ~ Do not set your eyes on something that is not there, because riches will certainly find wings and fly away like an eagle.

- JER 9:23–24 ~ If you are wise, do not glory in your wisdom; if you are mighty, do not glory in your might; if you are rich, do not glory in your wealth. Whoever wants to rejoice, let them rejoice in the fact that they know God who is loving, kind, righteous, and just.

- MAT 16:26 ~ Jesus said, "What does it profit a person who gains the world but loses his soul. What can a person give in return for his soul?"

- MAR 4:19 ~ Jesus said, "Earthly desires, the deceitfulness of wealth, and other lusts of this world choke the Word, and it becomes useless to those who are enticed by these things."

- JAM 5:1–3 ~ Go cry and moan, you rich people, for the miseries that will come upon you. Your riches are corrupted and your clothes are worn out. Your disintegrating wealth will eat at you in the same fashion. You have heaped up riches for the last time.

- 1 PE 2:11 ~ Abstain from the passions of the flesh which wage war against your soul.

The powermongers of today are no different. Their addiction to power cannot be quenched, and when they are defeated at the polls, they go ballistic. They become like an alcohol or heroin addict going through delirium tremens (DTs). Napoleon's famous defeat has become a cliché; when people meet their match or end, they have "met their Waterloo". Everybody has setbacks, but those who know the Lord will bounce back, for they do not pursue a worldly crown but a heavenly crown. Napoleon had more than a few defeats; but he never learned from them. His desire for power and control was not unlike other dictators before him, and after him. It seems the primary motivation has been to fulfill desires of the flesh without recognizing the power of the Holy Spirit in the world or their lives.

- DEU 28:21–29 ~ You will go to battle in glory but will run from your enemies in seven different directions, and you will be scattered all across the earth. Your dead bodies will become food for wild animals. God will send boils, tumors, and various diseases to crush you. You will become mad, blind, and confused. You will grope at noon as a blind man, in darkness. You will not prosper; you will be oppressed and despoiled forever, and nobody will save you.

- DAN 8:23–25 ~ In the latter days, when the evil ones are fully in power, a fierce king will arise from darkness. He will be powerful and mighty, but not by his own power. He will destroy tremendously, and will prosper. He will destroy the mighty and holy people. He will cause deceit to flourish. He will exalt himself, and through the guise of peace he will destroy many. He will even stand against the Prince of peace, but the Prince will defeat him without raising a hand.

- GAL 5:17; GAL 6:8 ~ For the flesh is against the Spirit and the Spirit is against the flesh, because they are contrary to one another, wherefore you end up doing the things you do not want to do. Those who sow to the flesh will reap corruption, but those who sow to the Spirit will reap eternal life.

- REV 17:12–14 ~ Ten kings obtain power for one hour with the beast. They will give their power and strength to the beast and make war with the Lamb of God, only to be defeated.

- REV 20:9–15 ~ The devil waged war against God and was defeated a final time. Then he was cast into the lake of fire where the beast and the false prophet were, to be tormented day and night forever. Death and hell were thrown into the lake of fire. Whoever's name was not found written in the Book of Life was thrown into the lake of fire. This is the second death.

A similar scenario will unfold during the latter days, with powermongers trying to gain the world but losing their lives and souls in the process. You would think history has made it clear the outcome of such global strivings. But they cannot see the truth which is clouded by their visions of conquest and dominion. They have no interest in what God and the Bible have to say, because they do not choose to believe, though the evidence is overwhelming. Their belief is in vain for they see themselves as gods, and will go the way of all earthly gods and Satan who deceived them: the lake of fire.

- PRO 24:19–20 ~ Do not fret over the evil ones and do not be jealous of the wicked. Evil has no future. Their light will be extinguished.

- ISA 14:20 ~ The evil doers will nevermore be named.

- ISA 26:14 ~ All memory of them will be wiped out.

- REV 19:19–20 ~ And I saw the beast, the kings of the earth, and their armies, gathered for battle against the King of kings. The beast was taken, and with him the false prophet that worked miracles in his sight and deceived those who had the mark of the beast and worshipped its image; all were thrown into the lake of fire.

Heavenly Father, we know that you are in control, and the entire universe is yours; and we worship you and adore you for you alone are sovereign, King of kings and Lord of lords. We pray that you would thwart the efforts of those who would sell out our country and their own souls for a taste of global power. Save our republic from the globalists and their new world order. Fight with us against the tyrants; lift up all nations who follow Jesus Christ. Help your people on earth to prevail over the powermongers; help the USA to retain our status as one nation, under God, indivisible, with liberty and justice for all. In the name of Jesus, to whom this world really belongs, Amen.

June 19

Juneteenth is observed this day, when in 1865 Union soldiers marched into Galveston TX to assert martial law and emancipate the slaves there. Slavery had been abolished and the Civil War had ended. It was time to enforce the law granting freedom to people of color throughout the land, with the rights of citizenship belonging to all natural born Americans. The slaves had been freed nationwide by President Lincoln in 1863 and the southern states had surrendered in April of 1865, but the remotely located Texans had been the last holdouts, which ended on Juneteenth. Later that year, the Thirteenth Amendment was ratified, granting blacks the right to vote. Interestingly, slave owner President Jefferson signed a law in 1803 banning the enslavement and importation of blacks from Africa, but it was poorly enforced. This day has been recognized annually, but became a federal holiday in 2021 when signed into law by President Biden.

- EXO 21:16; DEU 24:7 ~ Kidnappers must be put to death, whether they are in possession of victims or have sold them as slaves. You must purge the evil from among you.

- PRO 22:16 ~ Those who oppress the poor to gain wealth and who give to the rich will surely become needy themselves.

- PSA 62:10 ~ Do not use oppression or robbery to obtain wealth; and if you do become wealthy, do not set your heart on your wealth.

- ISA 3:5, 9, 11 ~ The people will oppress each other. Youth will be insolent to their elders. They proclaim their sin like Sodom, they do not hide it. Woe to them. What they have done to others will be done to them.

- EZE 11:21 ~ To those whose hearts seek detestable things and abominations, I will recompense it back upon their own heads.

- EZE 22:29 ~ The people have used oppression, robbery, and swindling, so I will recompense it upon their heads and consume them with the fire of my wrath.

- JOE 3:4 ~ God will return recompense upon your head.

Today is celebrated as the last day of slavery in the USA. It became a holiday in Texas in 1980 and other states followed, so the federalizing of the holiday in 2021 was a mere formality. Even foreign nations had been celebrating the end of slavery in the USA. The country has come a long way since then, though many who are unaware of the history of slavery believe that blacks and other people of color are still being subjected in this land. News flash: everybody in the USA has the same rights, and though some politicians would like to keep oppressing people, it is because they are racists and bigots. The status of minorities in this country has improved since Juneteenth, and all Americans equally enjoy our liberties. But those who continue to push individuals and groups down and keep them down will themselves be thrown down.

- PSA 12:2 ~ They speak vainly about their neighbors; with flattering lips and two faces they speak.

- PSA 36:1–2 ~ The sins of the wicked show God that they do not fear Him. The wicked people flatter themselves, ignoring the fact that they are evil and sinful.

- ISA 30:1 ~ Woe to the rebellious children, declares the Lord. Woe to those who carry out plans that are not mine, who form alliances but not with my Spirit, and who heap sin upon sin.

- JER 8:12 ~ They were not ashamed when they committed their abominations. They will be among those who fall; at the time of their judgment, they will be cast down.

- 1 JO 2:9–11; 1 JO 3:15; 1 JO 4:20 ~ Those who say they are in the light, yet hate their brother, are still in darkness. Those who love their brother live in the light, and therefore they can see where they are going without stumbling. Those who hate their brother walk in darkness and they cannot see where they are going because the darkness has blinded them. Whoever hates their brother is a murderer, and murderers cannot inherit eternal life. Anyone who says they love God and hate their brother is a liar. How can you hate someone you have seen and still love God who you have not seen?

Kidnapping, enslavement, and the selling of slaves has not ended, however, because the trafficking of these victims continues by the cartels due to the demand among evil and depraved oligarchs, the demented, and the decadent: all people devoid of decency, morality, and spirituality. But they are slaves to sin and will be paying the price, receiving a greater damnation for their deeds when they face the judgment of God. Do not trust people who play the race card repeatedly; they oppress and subject the very people they claim to be advocating for.

- EZE 7:3 ~ God will judge everyone according to their ways, and will recompense the abominations of the wicked back upon them.
- OBA 1:15 ~ The day of the Lord is near for the wicked. As they have done, so shall it be done to them; it will come back upon their heads.
- MAT 18:6 ~ Jesus said, "Whoever would cause a little child that believes in me to sin, it would be better for him if a millstone was hung around his neck and he was drowned in the depths of the sea."
- MAT 23:14 ~ Woe to you hypocritical scribes and Pharisees, who confiscate widows' houses and speak long prayers as a ploy; you will receive the greater damnation.
- JOH 19:10–11 ~ Pilate told Jesus, "Do you not realize I have the power to crucify you or release you?" Jesus replied, "You can do nothing to me without being given the power by God. The ones who delivered me to you for crucifixion, they have committed a greater sin than you."
- ROM 2:5–9, 11 ~ Because of stubbornness and an unrepentant heart, they are storing up vengeance against themselves until the day God unleashes His wrath, when His righteous judgment is revealed. God will give back to each person according to what he or she has done. To those who patiently continued to do right, seeking God's glory, honor, and immortality: theirs will be eternal life. To those evil doers who were contentious, and did not obey the truth, but pursued unrighteousness, indignation, and wrath: theirs will be tribulation and anguish, regardless of whether they were Jews or Gentiles. There is no partiality with God.
- REV 21:8 ~ The fearful, the unbelieving, the murderers, prostitutes, sorcerers, idolaters, and liars will take part in the lake of fire which is the second death.

We are tremendously grateful, Father, that we are born free in the USA. And though freedom is a right that you gave to all human beings, this right is being denied to certain groups everywhere in the world. In particular, the rights to life, liberty, and the pursuit of happiness are being violated, even here in America, by people who think they are superior to others. But they are superior only in their minds and will be brought down with the fallen. We pray for protection from these criminals and their criminal enterprises; we pray also for those who are being kidnapped, violated, exploited, and enslaved as they yearn for the freedoms and protections they came here seeking. Revoke from these evil cartels, gangs, and syndicates the very freedoms they subvert; cause them to lose their rights to life, liberty, and pursuit of happiness before they can harm another living soul. We pray in the name of Jesus who gives us true freedom, Amen.

June 20

Summer Solstice Day marks the first day of summer, astronomically speaking, since the sun is at its highest point in the sky. Solstice is Latin for the "sun stops", at the axis of the earth which is tilting towards El Sol. The date falls on either 06/20, 21, or 22, due to inexactness which results in a leap year every four years. Today is noted as the longest day of the year and the shortest night in the northern hemisphere; the sunlight is more direct making it warmer. The longest day in the southern hemisphere occurs on 12/20, 21, or 22. Obviously, the dates for the longest day will vary depending on your distance from the equator, and which side of it you are on. Regardless, sunrise and sunset will seem to drift northward or southward from your hemispheric vantage point.

Stonehenge (England) was built to mark the solstices, like many other ancient structures such as the pyramids and sphynx of Khafre (Egypt), the Machu Piccu stone (Peru), and the Chichen Itza pyramid (Mexico). Naturally, the solstices and the equinoxes were very important to the ancients.

Ancient cultures like those mentioned above worshipped the sun god; to them, the sun represented life. The Bible associates God with light and life as well; in fact, the Bible itself reflects the light of God. The big difference is, these other religions were polytheistic, that is, they had multiple gods and goddesses; whereas Christianity is monotheistic, meaning one God. The God of the Bible is the only true God with three distinct persons, Father, Son, and Holy Spirit, all of whom shine the light of life.

- ISA 60:1–2 ~ Arise and shine, for your light has come; yes, the glory of God has come to you. Darkness covers the earth and great darkness covers its people. But the Lord will arise and come to you, and you will see His glory. And the Gentiles will come to His light, and kings will come to the brightness of His rising.

- MAT 5:16 ~ Let your light shine before others, so they may see your good works and glorify your Father who is in heaven.

- LUK 1:79 ~ The baby Jesus was born to give light to those who sit in darkness and in the shadow of death, and to guide their feet into the way of peace.

- JOH 1:7–9 ~ John came to be a witness of the light so that others might believe in Christ. This was the true light that brings light to everyone born in this world.

- JOH 6:63 ~ Jesus said, "It is the Spirit that gives life, not the flesh; the flesh profits nothing. The words that I speak are from the Spirit and give life."

- JOH 8:12 ~ Jesus said, "I am the light of the world; those who follow me will not walk in darkness, but will have the light of life."

- JOH 10:10 ~ Jesus said, "I came that you might have life, and have it more abundantly."

- JOH 11:25 ~ Jesus said, "I am the resurrection and the life; whoever believes in me, though they were dead, yet shall they live."

- JOH 12:35 ~ Jesus said, "The light will be with you a little longer. Walk while you have the light, before the darkness overtakes you; those who walk in darkness do not know where they are going."

- 2 CO 3:5–6 ~ We owe everything we are to God who has made us ministers of the New Testament. We do not tell people that they must adhere to the very letter of the Law, but to the Spirit; for the Law kills but the Spirit gives life.

- JAM 1:17 ~ Every good thing comes from God; every perfect gift comes from above, from the Father of lights. God never varies, and in Him there is no darkness, not even a shadow.

- 1 PE 2:9 ~ You are a unique, chosen generation, a priesthood and holy nation, because you praise Him who called you from darkness into His marvelous light.

- 1 JO 1:5 ~ God is light; in Him is no darkness at all.

Those who have the light of life will never live in darkness. Those who live in darkness do not have the light and are lost, for they cannot find their way. If they could find Jesus, they would know the way, and He would give them eternal life in heaven. But they have to look for Him, and that means they must move towards the light if they want to live. It is interesting how people with near death experiences are always beckoned to go towards the light. It is wise to follow the light before you die, else you end up in darkness forever.

- ISA 5:20 ~ Woe to those who call evil good and good evil, who put darkness for light and light for darkness, who put bitter for sweet and sweet for bitter.

- MAT 6:22–23; LUK 11:34–36 ~ Jesus said, "The eye is the lamp of the body. If your eye is sound, your whole body will be full of light. If your eye is not sound, your whole body will be full of darkness. So, if the light in you is darkness, how great is that darkness. Be careful, so that the light in you does not become darkness. If your whole body is full of light and has no darkness, it will be wholly bright as when a lamp with its rays gives light."

- JOH 3:19 ~ The light came into the world, but men loved darkness rather than light, because their deeds were evil.

- ROM 13:12 ~ The night is gone and the day is at hand. Let us cast away the works of darkness and put on the armor of light.

- 1 CO 4:5 ~ Judge nothing before the Lord returns, for He will bring to light all that is hidden in darkness, and will reveal the motivations of the heart. Then everyone will praise God.

- 2 CO 4:6 ~ God commanded light to shine out of darkness. This same light shines in our hearts and radiates that light through knowledge of Jesus Christ.

- EPH 5:8–14 ~ You were once in darkness, but now you are in the light of the Lord. Live as children of light and discover what pleases the Lord, for the fruit of the light consists of goodness, righteousness, and truth. Have nothing to do with the fruitless deeds of darkness, but rather expose them. For it is shameful even to mention what the disobedient do in secret. But everything exposed by the light becomes visible for all to see, for it is light that makes things visible. This is what is meant by the saying, "Wake up you sleepers; rise from the dead and Christ will shine on you."

- 1 JO 2.10–11 ~ Those who love others abide in the light and will not stumble. Those who hate others abide in darkness and do not know where they are going because the darkness has blinded their eyes.

Father of light, it is easy to find you because your light shines during the day and during the night; and nobody can hide from you for you see all things, including the works of darkness. Help us to see you through your Son Jesus Christ, and to be reminded that He represents you, for He is our light, and our life, and our time. May His light forever shine in us and through us by the indwelling of your Holy Spirit. Let us as a nation become that beacon on a hill once again, shining the light of freedom to the world, which is an unalienable right given to all people by you, dear Father. In Jesus's name we pray, Amen.

June 21

World Music Day began when a French director of Art and Culture and a French composer collaborated in 1981. The first observance was on this date in 1982 in Paris. The idea caught on quickly, and became a worldwide phenomenon. I mean, who doesn't like music in some form? Personally, there are but a few genres that I can barely stand but everything else I like it or love it. I am a musician and songwriter myself; I have a special appreciation, because music day is practically every day in my house. Research suggests that as much as fifty percent of people can play an instrument to some degree. Then again, all of us did when we were toddlers: banging on our play piano, rattling the shaker and beating it on the toybox, cranking the jack-in-the-box repeatedly, or crying "goo bah" with pitch or tonality.

The original music day in Paris was launched to encourage beginners and professionals to play, perform, and organize, exhibiting their musical art whenever and wherever possible. Annual concerts started being held, showcasing all types of music, with varying levels of competence, to provide an occasion for interested persons to perform before a live audience. Over a hundred countries have events and concerts today including many cites in the USA; check it out if you want to make plans to attend. Otherwise, gather with friends and play, sing, listen to tunes, have contests—use your musical imagination. Everybody should be able to sing without being criticized, unless the circumstances are grossly inappropriate. Anybody can clap, or snap their fingers, sing along, take turns doing karaoke, and have fun doing it. I have heard people say they won't even sing in church; but I bet they have sung in the shower.

God doesn't care if you sing like an angel, He just loves to hear the sound of your voice, like any loving father or mother. Sing praises to the Lord for it is music to His ears. Psalms of David and others were actually put to music and sung. Write a poem, put a tune to it, and sing it; it really is not as hard as it sounds. But when played it sounds original and creative, and God will appreciate it if nobody else does.

- PSA 9:1–2; PSA 30:4, 12 ~ I will praise you Lord with all my heart; I will show your marvelous works. I will be glad and rejoice. I will sing praises to your holy name. Sing to the Lord and give Him thanks forever.

- PSA 40:3; PSA 98:1 ~ He has put a new song in my mouth, a hymn of praise for our God. Many will notice, and will fear and trust in the Lord. Oh, sing to the Lord a new song, for He has done marvelous things. His right hand, which is His holy arm, has won for Him the victory.

- PSA 95:2; PSA 147:1 ~ Let us go before God with thanksgiving; make a joyful noise to Him with singing. It is good to sing praises to God for this is pleasant and beautiful.

This is a day that can be appreciated by all; brainstorm with your colleagues, friends, or family and do something musical at your location. Music is best enjoyed with others, although it is very entertaining when you want to be alone. Music is good for the soul and the spirit. All living things can be influenced by rhythmic sound waves. Research has proven that animals and plants thrive on soft or classical music; your pets can get into what you are listening to as well, sometimes as much as you do. We live longer and happier with music, and it can be soothing when one feels down and out. I often used music therapy in groups of all ages; they had different diagnoses but had a common interest in music.

Music livens things up which is why singing, chanting, and playing instruments are an integral part of worshipping in most churches. Christmastime is my favorite time of year. I love hearing and singing the Christmas carols, and listening to the choir. How about you? If you have not experienced this phenomenon, give it a try. You'll find that church does not have to be boring.

- 2 CH 5:13–14 ~ As the orchestra and choir joined in musical harmony to thank and praise God, the church was filled with a cloud, for the glory of God had encompassed the church.

- JER 20:13 ~ Sing to the Lord and praise Him, for He has delivered the souls of the poor from the wicked.

- COL 3:16–17 ~ Remember what Christ taught you and let His words enrich your lives and make you wise. Teach His words to each other. Sing them openly and spiritually in psalms and hymns with thankful hearts. Whatever you do or say, do it in Jesus's name, and give thanks to God in Jesus's name.

- HEB 13:15 ~ Let us continually offer to God the sacrifice of praise; praise and thanks are the fruits of our lips.

One's favorite music identifies them to a large extent: age, experiences, heritage, even gender. There is certainly more to music than merely sounds; there is the physical stimulation, there is psychological relevance, and there is a strong spiritual component. Music is present in most religious ceremonies and gatherings, as well as social and cultural events. It is a medium that has unlimited potential for artistry and creativity, for it evolves into many different genres every generation. I grew up with old time rock and roll and saw it progress into dozens of varieties. Music is a wonderful gift of God, meant to bring us joy and peace. By the way, everyone will be singing praises and making music in heaven, alongside the choirs of angels who sing continuously.

- ISA 35:10; ISA 51:11 ~ The ransomed of the Lord will return to Zion singing songs of praise and everlasting joy. They will have joy and gladness, while sorrow, sighing, and grief will be gone forever.

- ZEC 8:3, 5–6 ~ I (God) will return to Zion and I will live in Jerusalem; and Jerusalem will be called the city of truth and Zion will be called the holy mountain. Children will be playing in the streets. It will be marvelous for my people and also for me.

- REV 4:6–8 ~ John had a vision of four beasts surrounding Christ's throne. They had eyes all around them, and they had six wings (likely seraphim). Each had a different face: lion, ox, eagle, or human. They sang praises to God all day and night.

- REV 5:11–12 ~ Then I looked and saw a multitude of angels, numbering thousands upon thousands, literally millions of angels encircling the throne. And they sang aloud with one voice, "Worthy is Christ the Lamb who was slain, to receive power and wealth, and wisdom and strength, and honor, glory and praise."

- REV 7:9, 14 ~ I saw a gigantic choir in white robes; they were from various nations, kindreds, and tongues, and had come from great tribulation. They had washed their robes in the blood of Christ.

- REV 14:3–4 ~ The 144,000 sang a new song; nobody could learn the song except them. They were the ones who were undefiled by women, virgins who followed the Lamb wherever He went. They were redeemed from humankind as the first fruits of God and the Lamb.

We praise you, Father, and we will sing your praises now and forevermore. How glorious it will be to sing with the heavenly hosts, in your magnificent presence. Let us make joyful noises to you, oh Lord, as often as we think of it, especially at our places of worship where we honor you, Holy Trinity. Help us to be vigilant in recognizing music that is evil in its lyrics and sound, and steer our children clear of music and musicians who stir up evil mages and thoughts, for music should be a gift, not a curse. In Jesus's name, Amen.

June 22

GI Bill of Rights Became Law, signed by President F. D. Roosevelt on this date in 1944. The idea started after World War I, with many returning veterans unable to find employment or housing. So, Congress passed the Bonus Act of 1924 to help them with a stipend based on their length of service. But it was the dawn of a collapsing economy and they didn't get their money for two decades, when World War II was already nearing an end; for many it was too little too late. The Servicemen's Readjustment Act of 1944 was passed to further help veterans who were returning from World War II. It was renamed the GI Bill. Both men and women who served were eligible for assistance in college or vocational school, along with a cost-of-living bonus or unemployment compensation if they chose to work rather than pursue higher education; also included were low interest mortgage rates. In just a few years, half of college admissions were veterans. The GI Bill has been revisited and upgraded periodically since its inception. Of all the things our government has spent money on which were reckless at best, this was one cause worthy of the investment, for the lives of veterans have been vastly improved through this type of assistance, and the country has reaped the benefits.

- PRO 3:13–14 ~ Happy is the individual who finds wisdom and understanding, for these are more precious than fine silver and the gain is more valuable than fine gold.

- PRO 4:5–7, 13 ~ Obtain wisdom and understanding; do not avoid it. Listen to what I say. Do not forsake wisdom and she will protect you; love her and she will watch over you. Wisdom is the most important thing; get wisdom and with it will come understanding. Take hold of instruction, do not let go. Guard her, for she is your life.

- PRO 10:4 ~ Lazy hands lead a person to poverty, but diligent hands bring a person wealth.

- PRO 11:3, 14 ~ The integrity of righteous people can guide them, but the perverseness of wicked people will destroy them. For lack of guidance a nation falls, but many advisors assure the victory.

- PRO 21:5 ~ The plans of the diligent person will lead to prosperity, but the ones who are in a hurry to get rich will find poverty.

- ECC 9:18 ~ Wisdom is better than weapons of war; but one sinner destroys much good.

- LUK 12:48 ~ Jesus said, "To whomever much is given, much will be required. To those who have committed much, of them more will be asked."

- PHP 4:13 ~ I can do all things through Christ who strengthens me.

I must say, had it not been for the GI Bill, I probably would not have attended college. My parents were unable to cover the expenses, and it would have been too difficult for me to begin working fulltime while trying to tackle college. The military skills I had were not transferrable to the civilian workplace, so I started at the bottom of the ladder. But the GI Bill, though it did not cover all of my tuition and expenses, was enough for me to get by working odd jobs and going to school. I will be forever grateful for that opportunity. I came to value education very much; I ended up with twenty-four years of schooling, not counting workshops, seminars, and classes that I taught. To this day, I continue to read, study the Bible, and learn. The learning never ends as long as you have breath, unless you do not value learning, which itself must be learned. Like all types of learning, it takes patience to grasp the fullness of it.

- PRO 2:10–13 ~ When wisdom enters your heart and knowledge is pleasant to your soul, discretion will preserve you and understanding will keep you, to deliver you from evil and from those who speak evil.

- PRO 9:9–10 ~ Give instruction to a wise man and he will become wiser. Teach an honest man and he will increase in learning. The fear of the Lord is the beginning of wisdom, and the knowledge of the righteous is understanding.

- PRO 22:24–25 ~ Do not make friends with an angry person or associate with someone who has a quick temper, for you risk learning their ways and falling into the same trap.

- ROM 5:3–4 ~ We can glory in our tribulations because through them we obtain patience, through patience, experience, and through experience, hope.

- 1 CO 1:19–25 ~ It is written: I will destroy the wisdom of the wise, and I will bring to nothing the understanding of the prudent. Where is the wise person? Where is the scholar? Where is the philosopher of this world? Has God not made foolish the wisdom of this world? The world through its wisdom did not know God, but through simple preaching, God enabled people who would believe to be saved. The Jews required signs and miracles and the Greeks searched for wisdom and truth. We preach about the crucified Christ, which to the Jews is an obstacle and to the Gentiles is foolishness. But to those whom God has called, both Jews and non-Jews, Christ is the power of God and the wisdom of God. For the foolishness of God is wiser than the wisdom of humanity, and the weaknesses of God are stronger than the might of men.

- 2 TH 3:5 ~ May the Lord direct your hearts into God's love and Christ's perseverance.

- HEB 6:12 ~ Do not be lazy, but follow those who, through faith and patience, inherit the promise.

- HEB 12:1 ~ Since we are being watched by numerous spectators, let us discard everything that hinders us such as the sin that trips us up, and run the race that has been set before us with perseverance.

- JAM 1:2–4 ~ Brothers, count it as joy when you fall into various trials, knowing that the testing of your faith produces patience. Let patience have her perfect work, so that you may be complete, wanting nothing.

- JAM 3:17–18 ~ The wisdom from above is first pure, peaceable, gentle, easily approachable, full of mercy and good deeds, impartial, and never hypocritical. The harvest of righteousness is sown in peace by those who make peace.

The military is not for everyone, but had I not learned the discipline it taught me, I would not have been prepared for college. I learned self-control and patience, things I was severely lacking. I learned to fight, not only with weapons of war, but with a presence of forethought. I entered the army an impulsive and foolhardy teenager, but I learned moderation and endurance. These attributes were not taught to me in college; quite the contrary, I could have obtained a degree without trying very hard. But I wanted to learn the material, and I did. As a professor, I met plenty of students that did the bare minimum to get by; some merely collected their financial aid and stopped attending classes. None of those students were veterans. Just saying, you know?

Dear Father, you are very generous with your love and gifts. Today we thank you for opportunities and assistance that propelled us forward, which might not have occurred otherwise. Let us never take such support for granted, but to make good use of it so that we can be there someday to support someone else who otherwise would not be given opportunities or assistance. Let us be generous with our love and gifts, reflecting Christ in the way we conduct ourselves and communicate with others. Help us to exhibit self-control, perseverance, patience, and discipline so people might learn these valuable lessons from us. In the name of Jesus, who is the epitome of these qualities, Amen.

June 23

Public Service Day was introduced by the United Nations in a resolution designating UN Public Service Day to begin on this date in 2003; included in the celebration were presentations of public service awards. Like most UN holidays, there is an annual event in a host city, attended by policy and decision makers from across the world, with guest speakers, exhibits, demonstrations, and focused discussions. Governments are established to protect and serve the public; this is the primary responsibility of public servants in general and the annual conference in particular.

Today we acknowledge public servants in the community, nation, and world. This includes everyone from the mayor to the garbage collector. Thank people you see who provide a service; get to know them if they can spare the time. I always make it a goal to become acquainted with a new mailperson; you might be surprised at the many ways he or she is willing to assist you. Of course, public servants are not created equal; that is, some are proud to serve, but to others it is just a job or a chore. If you thank them, showing appreciation for their service, they just might like the job more, and you will get better service, and you could make a new friend.

Everybody can serve the public, whether you work in a service field or not. For example, you can serve the public at your church, or volunteer at your kids' school, or a local hospital, or a scout troop, or a park, or whatever you might enjoy; the number of available places that could use your service is unlimited. If you do not have time, donate some money to nonprofit public service agencies such as a homeless shelter or an animal shelter. There are countless ways you can serve others, and this will glorify the Lord in the process.

- PSA 41:1 ~ Whoever helps the poor will be blessed by God, and God will deliver them when they experience a time of trouble.

- ROM 12:20 ~ If your enemy is hungry, feed him; if he is thirsty, give him a drink. Maybe you can turn him or her around by being nice.

- 2 CO 4:5 ~ What we preach is not about ourselves but Jesus Christ our Lord. We are your servants for His sake.

- COL 3:24 ~ If you help others, you are really serving Christ.

- EPH 6:5–7 ~ Servants should be obedient to their masters even as to Christ. Do this not for show or to impress those you serve, but from the heart as unto the Lord, with good will. Knowing that whatever good a person does, the same will they receive from the Lord, whether as a laborer or a volunteer.

- HEB 13:1–2 ~ Let brotherly love continue. Do not forget to help strangers, for you may be ministering to angels for all you know.

In addition to serving the public, we are obliged to serve God. Certainly, serving others is serving God, and there are gifts and abilities that God has given us to serve Him and the body of Christ which is His church on earth. You can serve simply by telling people about the great things God has done for you, your family, your church, and humanity as a whole. People who work in churches are public servants who are funded by people and synods not the taxpayers.

- JOS 24:15, 21–22 ~ Joshua announced, "If serving the Lord seems undesirable to you, then choose who you will serve… As for me and my household, we will serve the Lord." The people said to Joshua, "We promise to serve the Lord." Joshua replied, "You are witnesses before me and your countrymen that you have chosen the Lord, and have promised to serve Him." They responded, "Yes, we are witnesses."

- MAT 6:2 ~ Jesus said, "When you help the needy, do not sound your trumpet as the hypocrites do in the churches and in the streets, so that they can receive praise from others. The truth is, that is all the reward they will ever receive."

- MAT 25:20 ~ Jesus said, "Whenever you serve others you are serving me."

- ROM 6:17–18 ~ Thank God that we, who were servants of sin, have obeyed in our hearts the doctrine that delivers us, being made free from sin, and now serving righteousness instead.

- ROM 12:6–8 ~ Use those gifts God has given to you. If you have the gift of prophecy, exercise that gift according to the proportion of your faith. If your gift is ministry, then minister; if it is teaching, then teach; if it is encouraging, then encourage; if it is giving to the needy, then give generously; if it is leadership, then lead diligently; if it is showing mercy, then do so cheerfully.

- 1 CO 12:4–12 ~ There are a variety of spiritual gifts, but only one Spirit. There are different ways of administering but only one Lord. There are different operations, but the same God who works through them. The Spirit is manifested in some way for everyone to use productively. Some people have received wisdom, some knowledge, some faith, all from the same Spirit. Some people have the ability to heal, others to work miracles, others to prophesy, others to discern spirits, others to speak foreign tongues. But all of them are working with the same Spirit, who divides power among His people as He chooses. Just as one body has many members so is Christ one body with many members.

- EPH 4:11–13 ~ God gave some the abilities of apostles, prophets, evangelists, pastors and/or teachers for the work of the ministry, the edifying of the saints, the perfecting of the body of Christ, and the unity of faith. Each can impart the knowledge of the Son of God, who was a perfect man, so that we could take on the characteristics of Christ.

- 1 TI 6:7 ~ We brought nothing into this world and we can bring nothing out of it.

- HEB 12:28 ~ Since God has given us the kingdom, let us please Him by serving Him with thankful hearts, with holy fear, and with awe.

Sometimes a particular service is better handled by a private entity or person; the government is less effective doing these things and at greater cost. Big government is not your friend when it continues to raise taxes to take on roles that are better performed by the citizenry. Government roles, responsibilities, and limitations are spelled out in the Constitution. They should not be in charge of all public services because they are not the experts. For example, do you want the government to tell you what surgery, medicine, or therapy you need, or would you prefer your doctor or other healthcare professional to advise you on these decisions. There is nothing in the Constitution allowing the government to control and execute public services from Washington DC. The Tenth Amendment states explicitly that powers not delegated to the federal or state governments belong to the people. Government has no business being involved in your healthcare choices, or what you put into or remove from your own body. They have no business circumventing the rights of parents to raise their children, or forcing schools to teach things that violate the moral code or religion of students and their parents. Numerous government departments, agencies, and boards should be disbanded; they do not serve us, they take from us.

Merciful Father, equip us to serve you, our church, our neighbors, and our communities using the talents that you have richly bestowed upon us. Help us to be willing to learn more skills and practices so that we can serve in areas we didn't know we could. May we always follow the example of your Son, whose entire life was dedicated to serving humanity. In His name we pray, Amen.

June 24

Roe Vs. Wade Was Ruled Unconstitutional by the Supreme Court on this day in 2022. The original decision was in error because the original ruling by the Supreme Court concerning abortion was itself unconstitutional. The court is not allowed to pass legislation; that role is given to Congress or state legislatures. This reversal merely sent the establishing of abortion laws back to the state legislatures where it belongs. People elect state legislators, so it stands to reason they will pass laws in accordance with the will of their constituents. The federal government has no authority to determine abortion rights unless Congress passes a bill and the president signs it; otherwise, the court is prohibited from interpreting laws that do not exist. The Supreme Court should reverse their decision allowing gay marriages as well, because it is not within their purview to make that call either. It is up to the states, unless Congress wants to take it to the floor. If one state disallows certain things, a person can always travel or move to a state that allows them.

The abortion rights activists were livid over this ruling, and used the mass media as a pulpit, preaching that abortion is an unalienable right. It is not. Unalienable rights are those granted by God, not people or governments. I assure you that God is not in favor of abortion or gay marriage. Both of these subjects are covered in the Bible in great length, leaving no question as to where God stands on them. When there is a conflict between God's Law and man's, we are obliged to go with God on that one. Which rights are more important: the unborn child's God-given right to life, liberty, and pursuit of happiness, or the right of the mother to forcibly remove the unborn child from her womb in pursuit of what makes her happy? And does the father have no rights in a pregnancy? We must first look at what the Bible says to answer these questions.

- PSA 139:13–16 ~ The Lord controlled my very being, even when I was in my mother's womb. I will praise God for we are fearfully and wonderfully made; marvelous are His works and any soul knows that is right. My essence was never concealed from God, for He knew me even as I was being secretly made, developing inside my mother. He saw me when I was still imperfect, and in His book were written all the members of my body while they were being formed and were yet undeveloped.

- ISA 44:2, 24; ISA 49:5 ~ The Lord made you and formed you in the womb. The Lord formed Isaiah from the womb to be His servant.

- ISA 46:3–4 ~ God says, "Listen all of you in the house of Jacob and the remnants of Israel, for you were mine since you were conceived and lived in the womb; when you are old and gray, I still will be the one who keeps you. I made you, I sustain you, and I will deliver you."

- JER 1:5 ~ God said to Jeremiah, "I knew you before I formed you in your mother's womb; I sanctified you before you were delivered from your mother's womb. I ordained you to be a prophet to all nations."

- LUK 1:13–15, 44 ~ God told Zachariah that his wife Elisabeth would bear a son, and to call him John. That son would be filled with the Holy Spirit, even from his mother's womb. Elisabeth said to Mary, "The moment you said hello, the baby in my womb leaped with joy."

There is a hierarchy in rights depending on who grants them: God, government, state and local, neighborhood, or personal choice. And we often debate the personal choices because what is okay for you is not always okay with me, and vice-versa. For example: life, liberty, and pursuit of happiness are God-given rights. To deprive someone of their life is a capital crime, it has been and always will be; murder is covered in the sixth commandment. Freedom of religion is a government-given right, otherwise the majority could decide and Christianity would be the law of the land. God would be pleased if we all joined the body of Christ; but of course, He allows everyone to make a personal choice. States will let you buy and smoke marijuana; however, one can assume that another state might prosecute you for bringing it across their border. Local governments also have their statutes and penalties, like jaywalking; even neighborhoods grant rights under their homeowners' associations. Ultimately, each one of us is left with the final decision of what we do, and we must be ready to give an account whether it was right or wrong. This accounting is required at all levels of the law, and was promulgated by God, who allows governments to evenly enforce laws and defend the rights of people regardless of demographics.

- GEN 9:6 ~ Whoever sheds the blood of another human being will have their blood shed as well; for everyone was made in the image of God.

- LEV 18:21 ~ Never let any of your offspring be sacrificed to Molech (pagan Ammonite god).

- JOB 31:15 ~ Did He who formed me in the womb not make others the same way? Was it not the same God who formed every one of us within our mother's womb?

- PSA 22:10 ~ The Lord called me in the womb, and I have been His since I was born.

- PSA 100:3 ~ The Lord is God. He is the One who made us, not we ourselves...

- 1 CO 7:4 ~ Neither the wife nor the husband has exclusive power over their bodies.

God's Law trumps all other laws. There is an inherent hierarchy in laws, rights, and penalties. Clearly, murder is worse than stealing, and draws a greater punishment; or at least that is the way the law is supposed to work. Thinking of evil is not as bad as doing it in man's law; but it is in God's law. Society will not bring charges for thinking you want someone to die, but if you tell someone you want them dead it is a crime; and if you take their life, you can expect a worse sentence. If someone violates your right to property, will you not want them tried for robbery? If your loved one is murdered, will you not attend every court hearing and decision until you get justice? Is the right to decide what you put into or take out of your body above the right to another human being's life? People get away with heinous crimes all the time due to government agencies and officials neglecting their duty to serve, protect, and enforce. Be assured, God will not look the other way, and His punishment will be far more severe than that of governments or societies.

- ISA 28:15, 18–19 ~ You brag about entering into a covenant with death and making an agreement with the grave. Do you think you will escape the overwhelming scourge by making a lie your refuge and a falsehood your hiding place? Your covenant with death and your agreement with hell will be null and void. You will be beaten down by the scourge. Then you will understand this message and it will bring sheer terror to you.

- ROM 13:4 ~ If you do what is evil, be afraid, for God's minister will not bear the sword in vain, because he is sent to execute wrath upon those who do evil.

- HEB 10:28–29 ~ Those who violated the laws handed down by Moses were put to death on the testimony of two or three witnesses. How much greater punishment do you suppose will befall those who trample on the Son of God, treating the blood covenant with disdain and insulting the Spirit of grace?

Father of life, you breathed into us your Spirit and man became alive. Your Holy Spirit gives life, and your Son Jesus Christ saves life, and you Father bestow eternal life on every living person who believes these things to be true. How endless is your merciful kindness and your amazing grace. We praise you and thank you; we commit our lives to you even as your only Son committed His life to us. Help us to show all due respect to life, especially human life, for we are all made in your very image. Thank you, Jesus, Amen and Amen.

June 25

Melanchthon Presented Augsburg Confessions on this day in 1530. A colleague of Martin Luther, he represented Lutheran Protestantism in his confessions of the faith presented in Augsburg Germany to the Catholic authorities who were backed by Charles V. Luther had faced-off with the Roman Catholic church himself a decade earlier at the Diet in Worms (1521), but was still in hiding since they tried to assassinate him more than once. Like other reformers, Melanchthon questioned the authority of the Roman Catholic Church which had been teaching unscriptural doctrines, like taking money in the selling of forgiveness or penance. Catholic theologians disputed many of the articles of confession in a rebuttal, which Melanchthon countered with his Apology (defense) of the Augsburg Confession (1531). Melanchthon's articles are summarized below, reflected in Luther's confessions and the ninety-five theses he posted on the castle church door at Wittenberg (1517). They also relate to the Apostles', Nicene, and Athanasian creeds. The Catholic church agreed to most of these principles, but not all.

- Affirmation of the Holy Trinity
- Affirmation of original sin passed onto all people since Adam
- The nature of Christ as true God and true man; affirmation of His immaculate conception, crucifixion, and resurrection, leaving the Holy Spirit with us upon His ascension
- Justification by faith and the imputation of Christ's righteousness in exchange for sin
- The ministry, administering the sacraments, and the importance of and the means of grace
- Obedience of bearing good fruit as proof of faith, not to obtain merit
- The congregation of saints and the unity of the church (body of Christ)
- The sanctity of the church and sacraments despite the presence of evil members and leaders
- Baptism offered to all people including children
- Both the bread and wine are to be administered during the Eucharist
- Presence of the Lord's body and blood in the bread and wine of the Eucharist
- The sacraments themselves do not justify, but a true faith behind them does
- Enumeration of every sin at confession is unnecessary and impossible
- Repentance involves contrition and faith, leading to forgiveness and deliverance
- Rejection of the ecclesiastical order requiring one to be called in order to teach
- Traditions and holidays are not to be elevated as doctrine or as a means of grace
- Christians have the right and freedom to enter public office or service
- Christ will return in judgment; condemnation leads to eternal punishment
- Free will to receive the Holy Spirit, or reject Him who is the source of our faith
- Sin is not created by God but by people
- Holiday observances, pilgrimages, fasts, honoring saints, rosaries, and monasticism are not counted as good works; they are not conjoined with faith to assume them equally important
- New ceremonies, orders, holy days, and seasons are not doctrinal and do not convey grace or demonstrate faith; people cannot be compelled to participate in them
- Saints can be remembered or emulated but are not to be worshipped or prayed to; we pray only to God Himself in the name of Jesus Christ
- The church service or mass is an important part of worship and obedience, and should be performed in like manner during weekly services and special services (sabbaths)

- The power of the keys is given to the clergy who properly deliver the Word and the Holy Sacraments, and for bestowing forgiveness of sins on behalf of Christ
- The ecclesiastical power of the church and the pope is not warranted; the power of the keys does not authorize leaders to place burdens on people; they are not the government and are not enforcers of the law; they have no civil authority
- There is no requirement in the Bible preventing priests from getting married
- Monastic vows were never meant to ensnare people and do not represent the forgiveness provided in the sacraments; monasteries are supposed to be schools of theology; unscriptural commandments given by leaders are not required to be followed

The Biblical justifications for these confessions are provided in the scriptures that follow. Most of these passages were quoted by Melanchthon himself in his presentation at Augsburg.

- GEN 2:18 ~ God said, "It is not good for man to be alone so I will make a helper for him."
- PSA 19:12–13 ~ Who can understand their own errors? Cleanse me from secret thoughts. Keep your servant from improper sins; do not let them have dominion over me, so I can be upright and innocent of the great transgression.
- PSA 51:5 ~ I was formed in sin and in sin I was conceived.
- ISA 48:16 ~ Come and listen. I have not spoken in secret since the beginning. I was there all along, and now, the Lord God and His Spirit have sent me.
- HAB 2:4 ~ The soul which is lifted up is not upright, but the just will live by faith.
- MAT 15:8–9 ~ These people come near to me with their mouth and honor me with their lips but their hearts are far from me. In vain they worship me, teaching doctrines which come from the commandments of men.
- MAT 15:14 ~ Stay away from false teachers, for they are like the blind leading the blind. And when the blind lead the blind, both fall into the ditch.
- MAT 23:1–3 ~ Jesus said, "The scribes and Pharisees tell you to do this and observe that; it is okay to obey them but do not imitate them, for they do not practice what they preach.
- MAR 7:6–9, 13 ~ Jesus said, "Isaiah prophesied about you hypocrites (ISA 29:13). For you put aside the commandments of God and follow the traditions of men. By following your own traditions, you show a disregard for the Word of God."
- JOH 5:22 ~ The Father judges no man but has committed all judgement to the Son.
- JOH 7:39 ~ Jesus spoke of the Spirit and preached that those believing in Him would receive the Holy Ghost, whom they had yet to receive because Jesus was not yet glorified.
- JOH 10:17–18 ~ Jesus said, "Therefore, my Father loves me because I lay down my life so that I might take it back again. Nobody takes it from me but I lay it down of my own free will. I have power to lay it down and I have power to take it back again. This commandment I received from my Father."
- JOH 14:6, 9–11 ~ Jesus said, "I am the way, the truth, and the life; nobody comes to the Father but by me. If you have seen me, you have seen the Father, because the Father lives in me and I in Him."
- JOH 15:26 ~ Jesus said, "I will send the Comforter to you and He will testify about me; the Comforter is the Spirit of truth which proceeds from the Father."

JUNE

- JOH 16:33 ~ Jesus said, "I have spoken to you so that you may have peace. In the world you will have tribulation; but cheer up for I have overcome the world."
- ACT 2:38–39 ~ Peter told the crowd, "Repent and be baptized every one of you for the remission of sins, and you will receive the gift of the Holy Spirit. This promise is for you, your children, and people everywhere: to whomever the Lord calls."
- ACT 4:10–12 ~ Let everybody know that it was Jesus Christ, whom you crucified, but whom God raised from the dead, who has become the chief cornerstone. There can be salvation in nobody else, for there are no other names under heaven that can save us except Christ alone.
- ROM 1:16–17 ~ I am not ashamed of the Gospel of Christ, for it is the power of God unto salvation given to everyone who believes; to the Jew first and also the Gentile. Therein is the righteousness of God revealed from faith to faith as it is written: the just will live by faith.
- ROM 5:1–2 ~ Being justified by faith, we have peace with God through Jesus Christ, by whom we have access to His grace wherein we stand, rejoicing in hope of the glory of God.
- ROM 10:9 ~ If you confess with your mouth that Jesus is Lord and believe in your heart that God raised him from the dead, you will be saved.
- 1 CO 2:14 ~ Worldly people do not receive things of the Spirit of God, for these things are foolishness to them; neither can they know them for they must be discerned spiritually.
- 1 CO 7:2–3, 8–9, 28, 39 ~ To avoid fornication get married and love your spouse. It is fine to stay single, but if you cannot control your emotions get married, for it is better to marry than to burn with passion. It is not a sin to marry, but married people will have problems due to their sinful nature. Once married, you are bound to your spouse until one of you dies.
- 1 CO 11:23–26 ~ Jesus commanded the apostles on the first Holy Communion to partake of the sacrament often to remember Him. Thus, as often as you eat the bread and drink the wine of Holy Communion, you proclaim the death of Christ until His return.
- 1 CO 14:40 ~ Let all things be done (in church) in a decent and orderly manner.
- 2 CO 5:19–21 ~ God was in Christ, and reconciled the world to Himself. He has not imputed our sins upon us, but rather has given us the message of reconciliation. So now we have become ambassadors for Christ, as though God was speaking His message through us, so that you too may be reconciled to Him. For He gave us His Son Jesus Christ, who knew no sin, to bear our sins, so that we could receive the righteousness of God that was in Him.
- 2 CO 13:8 ~ We can do nothing against the truth, but only for the truth.
- GAL 2:16; GAL 5:4 ~ A man is not justified by the works of the Law but by faith in Christ. We too have placed our faith in Jesus Christ and do not depend on works of the Law, because nobody can be justified by observing the Law. If you are attempting to be justified through works of the Law, you have separated yourselves from Christ and have fallen from grace.
- EPH 2:8–9 ~ You are saved by the grace of God because of your faith in Jesus Christ. Salvation is a gift of God, it cannot be earned through good works, so nobody should brag.
- EPH 4:3–6, 11–13, 16 ~ Keep the unity of the Spirit through the bond of peace. There is one body, one Spirit, even as you are called into one hope. There is only one Lord, one faith, one baptism, one God and Father of us all, who is above all, through all, and in all. Remember, Christ assigned some of you to be apostles, some prophets, some evangelists, some pastors, and some teachers, to prepare God's people for works of service. This He did so that the body

of Christ can grow, until all reach a oneness of the Spirit and unity in the knowledge of the Son of God, and become mature in the faith attaining the whole measure of the fullness of Christ. In Christ, the entire body is fitly joined and held together by every supporting ligament, and grows and builds itself up in love as each component performs its function.

- PHP 2:5–11 ~ Keep your thoughts on Jesus Christ who, although He was God in the flesh, did not glorify Himself but became a servant. In the form of a man, He humbled Himself, becoming obedient unto death, even death on a cross. Therefore, God has exalted Him and given Him a name above all other names. Everyone should bow at the name of Jesus Christ, whether they are in heaven or on the earth. Every tongue should confess that Jesus Christ is Lord, to the glory of God the Father.

- PHP 3:20–21 ~ We look to heaven as our home, the home of our Savior Christ the Lord, who will change our vile bodies into glorious bodies like His own.

- COL 2:16 ~ Do not let anyone judge you according to what you eat or drink, or with respect to a holy day or sabbath.

- 1 TI 2:5 ~ There is one God, and one mediator between Him and us, who is Jesus Christ.

- 1 TI 3:2, 12 ~ The directions Paul gave to Timothy about pastors, deacons, and elders included that they must be the husband of only one wife. (also TIT 1:6)

- TIT 1:14 ~ Pay no attention to Jewish fables and the commandments of men that turn people from the truth.

- HEB 10:10, 18 ~ We are sanctified by the offering of the body of Jesus Christ, one sacrifice for all people. No more offering for sin will ever be needed again.

- 1 PE 2:4–8 ~ He is a living stone, rejected by men, but chosen by God and precious to Him. He is the stone of offense that makes men stumble and fall. You are also like living stones, built into a spiritual house to be a holy priesthood.

- 1 PE 5:2–4 ~ Be shepherds of God's flock, serve them and be an example to them; and when the Chief Shepherd appears you will receive a crown of glory that will never fade away.

- 2 PE 1:5–8 ~ Be diligent in all things. Add to your faith: virtue, knowledge, self-control (temperance), patience, righteousness, kindness, and brotherly love. If these attributes abound in you, you will bear good fruit.

- 1 JO 2:1–2 ~ If anyone sins, we have an advocate with the Father: Jesus Christ the righteous who abolished the sin of the whole world.

- 1 JO 3:4 ~ Whoever commits sin transgresses the law, for sin is the transgression of the law.

- 1 JO 5:6–8, 20 ~ There are three who are recorded in heaven: the Father, the Word, and the Holy Spirit. These three are one. The same three bear witness: the Spirit, the Water, and the Blood. The Spirit is the witness, because the Spirit bears the truth. We know Jesus Christ who is true so that we may know God who is true. We live in Him who has shown us His Son, the source of eternal life.

Father God, we confess that you, along with Jesus Christ and the Holy Spirit are one Lord. We are sincerely sorry for our sins, and we hereby repent and confess them before you this day. Remind us of the salvation that brings everlasting joy through the atoning sacrifice of your Son, as we proclaim our faith to you and to others, in obedience to the great commission of Christ to make disciples. In the name of Christ whose name is above all others we pray, Amen.

June 26

Day Against Drug Abuse and Trafficking was established by the UN General Assembly to be observed internationally on this day starting in 1988. Given that the trafficking and abuse of drugs is an international malady, it was proper to bring worldwide attention to this scourge on society. The challenge to law enforcement, behavioral health, and medical personnel is enormous, considering the lives lost and ruined by illicit drugs and the cartels who push them. This problem has been exacerbated in recent years by deliberate government policies and actions restricting law enforcement, overburdening hospitals and clinics, and squandering money on programs and people who do nothing to address the root causes. Every year, the UN Office on Drugs and Crime issues a report providing current statistics and data to help decision makers adjust their focus to the problems at hand. Unfortunately, the problems have only gotten worse, particularly during and after the lockdowns associated with the Covid pandemic. Participants and profiteers associated with the drug trade, whether directly or indirectly, will face calamity and destruction.

- PRO 1:18–19 ~ Those who are greedy for riches and oppress others to obtain riches are ambushing their own lives and will succeed in destroying themselves.

- PRO 10:2 ~ Wealth gained by wickedness will not be profitable, for only righteousness can deliver one from death.

- PRO 11:4, 28 ~ Riches will not profit anyone in the day of wrath; only righteousness can save them from death. Those trusting in riches will fail; those trusting in God will flourish.

- PRO 13:11 ~ Wealth gained in a hurry will dwindle, but those who gather it little by little will see an increase.

- PRO 15:27 ~ Those who are greedy for unrighteous gain will bring trouble on their own house; but those who reject bribes will live.

- PRO 22:16 ~ Those who oppress the poor to increase their own wealth and those who give to the rich eventually will become needy.

- JER 17:11 ~ Like the partridge that gathers a brood she did not hatch, so is the person who gets rich illegally. In the middle of their days, they will lose all, leaving them as fools.

- EZE 7:19 ~ They throw their money around like it is trash; but their riches will not deliver them when the wrath of the Lord is unleashed. It will not satisfy their hunger or fill their stomachs, for it will become the stumbling block of their iniquity.

- MIC 2:1–3 ~ Woe to those who plan iniquity, who plot evil as they lie in bed! In the morning they carry it out because it is within their power to do it. They covet what does not belong to them, such as fields and houses. They defraud people of their homes and rob people of their inheritance. The Lord says, "I am planning disaster against them, from which they cannot save themselves; they will nevermore walk proudly, for it will be their turn for calamity."

- MAT 6:19–20 ~ Jesus said, "Do not accumulate earthy treasures that can be corrupted by insects or rust or that can be stolen by thieves. Instead, accumulate heavenly treasures, that cannot be corrupted or stolen."

- 1 TI 6:10 ~ The love of money is the root of all evil; through the craving for worldly riches many have wandered away from the faith and pierced their hearts.

- JAM 5:1–3 ~ Go cry and moan you rich people, because misery will come upon you. Your riches are corrupted and your clothes are worn out. Your disintegrating wealth will eat at you in the same fashion. You have heaped up riches for the last time.

When I directed an addiction rehabilitation program, I conducted extensive research continuously to stay abreast of the statistics, the new drugs being circulated, and the effects on individuals and society. I was alarmed to find that only twenty percent of those receiving inpatient treatment would be drug-free after two years. Despite the programs, resources, and money that have been poured into this problem, the statistics have not improved. In fact, with the introduction of synthetic opiates (namely Fentanyl), the casualty rate has dramatically increased. People who are not drug users end up dying when they buy the cheaper alternatives found on the street to ease their pain or anxiety, since they cannot afford the doctors and medications. These deaths are not suicides or overdoses, they are murders. The guilty parties are manufacturers and governments where the drugs are being made (e.g., China), the cartels who mix lethal dosages into the pills they push, governments who support them (e.g., Mexico), and the syndicates in the USA which distribute this poison on the streets. How can we stop it when law enforcement is outnumbered and outgunned, when treatment availability is restricted to people with insurance or money, and when practitioners lack training, resources, and community support needed to house and treat addicts? Success in recovery is correlated with two important factors: the intensity of treatment and the longevity of treatment. The most intense environment is inpatient and the minimum effective length of stay is four weeks. Many of my patients detoxed, got prescriptions from the doctor, and discharged themselves against medical advice. You can see how cost-prohibitive this is, to keep a hospital bed occupied for weeks, with a full staff of doctors, nurses, therapists, and others trained and dedicated to the program. We need to put the brakes on the nations involved in the trafficking of drugs, and provide more effective long-term treatment facilities, personnel, and programs where addicts are motivated to complete an inpatient program and continue treatment as an outpatient. Addiction is like cancer: if you are in remission for at least five years, your chances of having a long and fulfilling life are significantly improved.

- PRO 28:13 ~ Whoever conceals their transgressions will not prosper; but those who confess and forsake their sins will obtain mercy.

- ISA 5:11 ~ Woe to those who arise early to begin drinking alcohol, and who continue late into the evening as the alcohol inflames them.

- MAR 4:19 ~ Jesus said, "Earthly desires, the deceitfulness of wealth, and other lusts of this world choke the Word, and it becomes useless to those who are enticed by these things."

- ROM 2:5–6 ~ Because of stubbornness and an unrepentant heart, they are storing up vengeance against themselves until the day God unleashes His wrath, and His righteous judgment is revealed. God will give back to everyone according to what they have done.

- 1 CO 10:13 ~ No temptation has overtaken you that is not common to humankind. God is faithful, however, and will not let you be tempted beyond your ability, but with the temptation He will provide a means of escape so you can overcome it.

- 1 CO 15:33 ~ Do not be deceived, for evil company corrupts good character.

- JAM 1:12 ~ Blessed is the person who endures when faced with trials, for when they pass the test, they will receive a crown of life which God promises to those who love Him.

Father, we pray that those plagued by addiction will find escape through Christ; help them to find a solid twelve-step inpatient treatment program that includes spiritual growth. We pray that money allocated for treatment is spent wisely in this manner. We pray that those responsible for facilitating the drug racket will be brought to justice. Help law enforcement to take down the cartels, pushers, and dealers, especially those exploiting children to do their dirty work. We ask these things in Jesus's name, whose love is the cure, Amen.

June 27

Helen Keller Day celebrates an extraordinary woman who was stricken blind and deaf as a toddler from a debilitating infection. Yet she overcame her disabilities to become a scholar and educator, and famous writer and speaker. Today we also celebrate the woman who trained her named Anne Sullivan, herself partially blind. She helped Helen learn the alphabet, sign language and braille by stimulating her sense of touch. Helen later learned to speak and read lips as a teenager, before entering Radcliffe College at the age of twenty, and graduating with honors in 1904. In turn, Helen dedicated her life to serving the handicapped and raising funds to assist foundations and schools; she also advocated for women's rights. We honor Helen Keller who was born on this date in 1880, as well as her relationship with Anne Sullivan, which was memorialized in the award-winning film, *The Miracle Worker* (1962). Though her birthday has been observed since her death, this holiday became an official observance by proclamation from President Carter in 1980, the hundredth anniversary of her birth.

Everybody has potential for success and greatness; that is what I often taught in workshops at a psychiatric hospital. Every handicap or obstacle can be overcome with the power of Christ on your side. With Him all things are possible; without Him, nothing is.

- MAR 9:17–27 ~ A man asked Jesus to cast the demon out of his child. Jesus told the man, "All things are possible to those who believe." The man replied, "I believe, Lord; help me overcome my unbelief." Then Jesus ordered the demon to leave the child.

- JOH 16:33 ~ Jesus said to the apostles, "I have told you these things so that you might have peace, because in the world you will have tribulation. But be of good cheer for I have overcome the world."

- ROM 12:17–21 ~ Do not return evil for evil. Behave decently in the sight of God. If possible, to the degree that you can, live peaceably with all people. Do not take vengeance but rather hold you anger; for it is written: Vengeance is mine and I will repay, says the Lord. Therefore, if your enemy is hungry, feed him; if he is thirsty give him a drink. For by doing so you will heap hot coals upon his head. Do not be overcome with evil but overcome evil with goodness.

- EPH 6:11, 13 ~ Be strong in the Lord and in the power of His might. Take with you the whole armor of God, so that you can stand against evil and overcome it.

- 1 JO 4:2–6 ~ Every spirit confessing that Jesus Christ is God in the flesh is of God. Those spirits that do not confess are not of God, but are spirits of antichrist, which you have heard about and already is in the world. You belong to God and have overcome these spirits of malice. For greater is He that is within you than he that is in the world. They are of the world, and therefore speak of worldly things, and the world listens to them. We are of God. Those who know God will listen to His messengers, and those who are not of God will not listen. We know the difference between the Spirit of truth and the spirit of untruth.

- 1 JO 5:4–6 ~ Whoever is born of God overcomes the world; the victory that overcomes the world is found in faith. Jesus Christ overcame the world; anyone believing in Him will also overcome the world.

- REV 2:7, 11, 17; REV 3:5, 21 ~ Jesus said, "Listen to what the Holy Spirit has to say to the churches: Those who overcome will eat from the Tree of Life which is in the paradise of God. Those who overcome will not be hurt by the second death. I will give the heavenly food to those who overcome. I will give each one of them a white stone, and on the stone their new name will be engraved. Those who overcome will be clothed in white gowns and their names will be recorded in the Book of Life, and I will confess their names before my Father and the angels. Those who overcome will sit with me on my throne, even as I also overcame and am now sitting by my Father at His right hand."

- REV 21:7 ~ God says, "Those who overcome will inherit all things, and I will be their God and they will be my children."

Is there an obstacle in your path that has got you stuck? Have you been down so long you cannot tell which way is up? There is a way out, just follow the light of Christ and He will show you the way out; and that comes with the promise of hope, that God will provide and make good on His guarantee of eternal life with Him.

- ECC 8:6–7 ~ For every purpose under heaven there is a season, a time designated by God, although misery and trials may continue to occur. Since we do not know what that purpose is, who but God will be able to tell us when?

- ROM 5:1–5 ~ Being justified by faith we achieve peace with God through Christ, in whom we have access by that faith to the grace in which we stand, rejoicing in the hope of glory. Therefore, we rejoice in time of tribulation, knowing that it teaches us patience, it strengthens our hope, and we gain experience. And hope does not disappoint us, because God's love has been poured into our hearts through the Holy Spirit.

- ROM 8:24–25 ~ We are saved because we hope. But hope that is seen is not hope, for who hopes for things they can see? However, if we hope for what we cannot see, we must be patient.

- ROM 12:12 ~ Rejoice in your hope, be patient in tribulation, and be constant in prayer.

- ROM 15:13 ~ May the God of hope fill you with all joy and peace in believing, so that by the power of the Holy Spirit you may abound in hope.

- ROM 16:17 ~ I urge you, my brothers, identify those who cause divisions among you, and who place obstacles in your way that are contrary to the doctrine you have learned. Avoid them completely.

- 2 CO 6:3–10 ~ We do not place obstacles in anyone's way because we do not want the ministry to be discredited. Rather, as servants of God we commend ourselves in every way, through much endurance, trouble, hardship, and distress; through abuse, imprisonment, and rioting; through hard work, hunger, and sleepless nights; in purity, understanding, endurance, and kindness; in the Holy Spirit and in sincere love; in truth and in the power of God; carrying weapons of righteousness in each hand; through times of glory and dishonor, favor and rejection. We are genuine yet regarded as imposters; known yet regarded as strangers; dying yet still alive; beaten down but not defeated; sorrowful but always rejoicing; poor yet spreading wealth; having nothing yet possessing everything.

- COL 1:27 ~ The riches of the wonder of His mystery, which is Christ in you, is the hope of glory.

Heavenly Father, we know that all things are possible for those who believe. We pray for people all over the world who are disabled, handicapped, maimed, or hindered, that they would be given assistance and opportunity in the manner given by Ann Sullivan to Helen Keller. Help people who are stuck, or facing trials, or who are disadvantaged in any way, to believe in the hope that you alone can provide, which is the hope of glory. Help people see that there is always a way out of their trouble, a way over the mountain they face, a way to overcome their disability or hardship, and a way home to you. Through Jesus Christ who is the way, the truth, and the life, we pray this prayer, Amen.

June 28

Early Church Father Irenaeus Died on this day in the year AD 195. He was one of the earliest of the first evangelists to take the New Testament of Jesus Christ to the world. He was a student of Polycarp who was mentored by St. John the apostle. Polycarp was born in the latter half of the first century and was part of the first wave of evangelists who followed in the steps of Jesus and His apostles. Irenaeus was born around AD 125; he lived in Smyrna which was Polycarp's hometown. Though the writings of Polycarp have been lost to antiquity, Irenaeus wrote about Polycarp, and how his mentor was instructed in his youth by actual apostles of Christ. Polycarp lived to a ripe old age before being burned at the stake for refusing to renounce Christ. Irenaeus carried the baton from there and was one of many early church fathers to quote Polycarp often; another was Ignatius. Irenaeus became a productive writer, teacher, and Christian apologist. His mission was to establish and preserve the canon of scripture. He also was a vocal opponent of the Gnosticism of his time.

A second generation of Christian leaders emerged, taught by the apostles of Christ and disciples from His inner circle. They kept the scriptures alive and distributed them around the world, and were followed by third and fourth generation apologists. Who, in their right mind, would suffer such sorrow, punishment, imprisonment, torture, and death for something they knew to be a lie or a hoax? And not just the apostles but the early evangelists. The following list includes some of these men, many of whom were martyred or banished for their faith between AD 100–400: Polycarp, Papias, Clement, Ignatius, Justin Martyr, Irenaeus, Clement, Tertullian, Hippolytus, Origen, Cyprian, Athanasius, Eusebius, Ambrose, Jerome, Augustine.

An important aspect of this process was the secure chain of custody of the scriptures. God ensured honorable, dedicated, and determined believers would carry the torch and safeguard His Word, much like the process which law enforcement uses to prevent evidence from being tainted. Jesus commissioned us to take the Gospel to all the nations. It behooves us to learn the Holy Bible and to be conversant in it. Otherwise, how are we to teach others among us who need to know?

God commands us to study His Word. God commands us to spread His Word.

- JOS 1:7–8 ~ God said, "Be strong and courageous, so that you are able to observe the laws which Moses commanded of you. Do not turn to the right or to the left, and you will prosper wherever you go. This book of the Law must not depart from your speech, but you must meditate on my words every day and night, and live according to all that is written there. Then I will make you prosperous and you will be successful. This book of the Law will never leave your mouth, and you will meditate on it day and night, so that you can act in accordance with all that is written therein. Then your ways will be prosperous and you will enjoy success."

- ISA 55:10–13 ~ The rain and snow that fall from heaven do not return to heaven but water the earth, causing the plants to bud and to seed and providing food. So also, God's Word does not return to Him void, but accomplishes what He wishes, and prospers wherever He sends it. We joyfully go out, being led in peace. The mountains and hills sing before you and the trees clap their hands; all the world will rejoice around you. Instead of a thorn bush, a tree will grow; and this will magnify the name of the Lord as an everlasting sign.

- MAT 28:19–20 ~ Jesus told His disciples, "Go into every nation and teach the people everything I have taught you. Baptize them in the name of the Father, Son, and Holy Spirit. Remember, I will always be with you, even until the end of time."

- ACT 15:7–9 ~ After much disputing, Peter arose and spoke, "Men and brothers, you know a good while ago God chose some of us to take the Gospel message to the Gentiles so they would hear and believe. God, who knows all hearts, bore witness, giving them the Holy Spirit just like He did with us. There is no difference between us and them regarding the purifying of hearts through faith.

- ACT 17:10–12 ~ They sent Paul and Silas, who were noble in that they received the Word with all readiness of mind, and searched the scriptures daily to prove things that were true. And many believed, including numerous honorable Greek men and women.

- ROM 8:16–17 ~ The Holy Spirit is a witness with our spirits that we are the children of God, Now, if we are children, then we are heirs: heirs of God and joint-heirs with Christ, if indeed we share in His suffering so that we may also share in His glory.

- ROM 15:1–7 ~ We who are strong ought to bear with the failings of the weak. When we do the right thing, it should not be to please ourselves, but to please others and to build them up in the Lord. Even Christ did not please Himself, but as it is written of Him, "The insults of those who would insult you have fallen on me." Everything that was written in the past was for our instruction, so that through endurance and the encouragement of the scriptures we might have hope. May the God who gives endurance, encouragement, and hope give you a spirit of unity as you follow Christ. Give glory to God the Father of our Lord Jesus Christ with one voice and one heart. Accept each other as Christ accepted you, so that God may be praised.

- PHP 2:10–11 ~ Everyone should bow at the name of Jesus Christ, whether they are in heaven or on earth. Every tongue should confess that Jesus Christ is Lord, to the glory of God the Father.

- EPH 6:17 ~ Take with you the helmet of salvation, and the sword of the Spirit which is the Word of God.

- 2 TI 2:2, 15, 24–26 ~ The things you have heard of me and many witnesses, the same shall you share with faithful men, who also are able to teach others. Study hard to show yourself approved of God, a workman that is not ashamed, properly describing the word of truth. The servant of the Lord must not be argumentative, but gentle to all people, able to teach with patience and meekness, instructing those who oppose the truth. For perhaps God will allow them to repent and acknowledge the truth; and come to their senses, thereby escaping the devil's traps who would take them captive to his will.

- 1 PE 4:7–11 ~ The end is coming, so be sober, watchful, and prayerful. Above all have fervent love among yourselves, for love covers a multitude of sins. Be hospitable to each other, without complaining. Whoever has received the gift of salvation in Christ should share that gift with others, as a steward of God's eternal grace. If you preach, do so as a messenger of God. If you minister, do so with the ability God gives you. Do this to glorify God through His Son Jesus Christ.

Dear Father in heaven, just as you sent Jesus into this world to testify of you, and He sent His apostles and others into the world to testify of Him, and they instructed and sent the early church fathers to spread the good news, we pray that you would send us into the world to likewise testify. Jesus left the Holy Spirit behind to be our comforter, counselor, and companion, empowering us to employ our gifts for spreading your Word, and equipping us with even greater abilities, so that we can have confidence as we carry on your mission work. Help us to diligently prepare to teach and serve, by studying the Bible, praying in the Spirit, and witnessing to anyone who shows interest in hearing your Word and learning about Jesus, so that they will eagerly seek you and serve, knowing that they will receive eternal life through Jesus Christ, and join the community of saints. We lift up our prayers through Him, Amen.

June 29

National Camera Day is an annual observance for camera buffs out there, and in this age of cell phones, everybody is a camera buff. People are taking pictures of everything, posting them on social media, and sending them to relatives. The digital revolution enabled us to take and send photographs instantaneously. Some people have thousands of photos on their phone, making it difficult to find any single one. Personally, I would rather have a glossy print to put into a photo album, but I suppose that is old-fashioned; besides, I can send pictures to my email, download it on my desktop computer, photoshop it, save it, and print it out myself.

The history of cameras goes back to the fourth century BC, when a Chinese sage named Mozi posed his idea of *camera obscura*, which is Latin for "dark room". He experimented with light passing through a small hole in a wall into a dark room; the light source from the opposite field of view would appear upside-down on the back wall. Aristotle (also fourth century BC) used a similar technique with a shadow box and small hole through which he could view solar eclipses. Over centuries, the physics of the camera were further determined and explained. One noteworthy physicist from Arabia named Ibn al-Haytham (circa 1020), provided geometrical solutions to the dynamics involved and demonstrated it in a dark room. An Italian scientist named Cardano proposed using a convex optical lens to sharpen the image (1550). A French inventor named Niepce (1816) began to refine the use of photographic paper coated in silver chloride to produce an image, though it faded fast. Next, he tried a mixture of bitumen and oil on tin or copper which worked better, employing an acid wash that would etch the image onto the metal plate. He consulted with a colleague named Daguerre (1828), who continued where Niepce left off.

Daguerre managed to take long-exposure still-life photos which did not fade. Some of these photo etchings have survived to this day. He used copper coated with a solution of silver and iodine, exposing the plate to light for varying lengths of time. In a dark room, he preserved the photos with various solutions including heated saltwater, leaving a positive mirror image. His reusable and functional camera box enabled him to experiment with different techniques. Many more inventors jumped on the bandwagon to improve the process. Maxwell and Sutton produced the first color photograph. The development of the gelatin dry plate by Maddox (1871) was revolutionary. But George Eastman produced the first photographic film which could record multiple exposures; he incorporated it into his Kodak camera, which was marketed in 1888. He began to mass produce the device, and it evolved into the single-shot camera and other variations and improvements. From there the technology rapidly evolved. By the twenty-first century the digital age had arrived and film became unnecessary, except for some professional photographers who still develop their own negatives. So, who really invented the camera? One could say it was a work in progress.

The earliest actual photograph was taken by God Himself. Two millennia ago, Jesus arose from the dead and left a three-dimensional negative image on His burial cloth. Known as the Shroud of Turin, scientists have been baffled concerning the source of this image. But it cannot be explained scientifically since it was an unnatural event, or singularity. In physics a singularity is something that only happens once, like the immaculate conception of Christ, or the "big bang" when the universe exploded into existence, both of which occurred outside the realm of nature and physics and were therefore, miracles. It was asserted that carbon dating proved the shroud to be too recent, until it was discovered that the tested portion had been repaired with interweaving. Eventually, another sample of the shroud was tested and found to be closer in time to the death of Jesus. Scientists also were able to identify pollen and other biomaterial in the shroud which were indigenous to ancient Palestine.

The imprint on the shroud itself provided irrefutable proof, because light had passed through the shroud in a dark tomb, creating the negative image of a man crucified, showing the very wounds Jesus suffered: puncture marks around the crown of the head, welts on the back from repeated flogging, puncture holes in the hands and feet that went all the way through, and a wound in the side the size of a spearhead. Additional proof was the headcloth known as the Sudarium of Oviedo, which had the same blood flow and spatter as the shroud when the images were overlayed. The exact match proved the two burial cloths came from the same victim.

- MAT 27:59–60~ Joseph of Arimathea took the body of Jesus and wrapped it in clean linen and laid it in his own freshly cut tomb. He had a great rock rolled across the entrance to close the tomb.

- MAR 16:43–47 ~ Joseph of Arimathea, an honorable counselor who also looked forward to the kingdom of God, came to Pilate pleading for the body of Jesus. Pilate was surprised that Jesus was already dead so he called the centurion who verified that Jesus had been dead for some time. Pilate released the body to Joseph, who wrapped Jesus's body in linen and laid Him in a sepulcher which was cut out of rock; then he rolled a stone to cover the entrance. And Mary Magdalene who was with them took notice of the location of the tomb.

- LUK 23:50–51 ~ There was a man named Joseph of Arimathea who was a member of the council (Sanhedrin); he was a good and righteous man who had not agreed to decisions and actions of the council. He was among those who looked forward to the kingdom of God.

- JOH 19:38–42 ~ A disciple of Jesus named Joseph of Arimathea secretly met with Pilate and asked for the body of Jesus, and his request was granted. He took the body of Jesus, along with Nicodemus (another member of the council) who had once visited Jesus secretly by night (see JOH 3:1–21), and who had brought myrrh and aloes to embalm the body. They wrapped His body in linen cloths with the spices, in accordance with Jewish tradition. They laid Him in a newly cut sepulcher close to where Jesus was crucified.

- JOH 20:1–18 ~ The first day of the week, Mary Magdalene came to the sepulcher early while it was still dark, and saw that the stone had been rolled away from the entrance to the tomb. She ran to tell Peter and John that someone had taken the body of the Lord. The men ran all the way to the tomb, with John arriving first; while waiting outside, John looked inside and saw the linen cloths lying there. Peter arrived and immediately went inside; he saw the linens, and the napkin used as a headcloth, folded and off to the side. John followed Peter inside and looked around; and John believed, remembering that Jesus said He would rise from the dead. The men departed but Mary stayed there weeping. Stooping down to look into the tomb she saw two angels one near the head and the other by the feet where Jesus had lain. They asked, "Woman, why do you weep?" She replied, "Because they have taken my Lord away and I do not know where they laid Him." Then she turned around and saw a man behind her. Thinking it was the gardener she asked where Jesus's body had been taken. Jesus turned and said, "Mary." She faced Him and said, "Teacher." Jesus told her not to touch Him, but to return to His disciples and tell them He would be ascending to His Father and their Father. She left to tell the disciples that she had spoken with Jesus.

So now we know how God created the first photograph: He used the embalming ointment soaked into a linen shroud to capture a negative image when the light of Christ illuminated the tomb the very moment He arose from the dead. Before He exited the tomb, Jesus folded the linens and the headcloth, placing them where they were discovered by Peter and John. The matching linens had an imprint of His body, both front and back, as well as His head, which revealed every spot where He was wounded and bled. The image was in three dimensions because the body had been wrapped tightly enough for the covering to conform to His body. All of this can be explained using physics, with the exception of how Jesus arose from the dead very much alive, leaving the tomb open and empty.

God has left ample proof of His miracles for people to discover and understand. But nobody has yet to understand how miracles are performed, though God has incorporated them into our universe, defying all natural laws; and since Christ performed miracles, it proves that He was God in the flesh. The passages that follow provide a sampling of miracles God performed in His role as Father and in His role as Son (for more on miracles see Barber, 2020b). Do miracles still occur today? I would say yes. And since Christ left the Holy Spirit behind to be our comforter and guide, these miracles can be performed by God the Holy Spirit as well.

- EXO 14:21–23 ~ Moses stretched out his hand over the sea, and the Lord caused a powerful wind from the east to blow all night, dividing the sea and leaving a path of dry land. And the children of Israel crossed on dry land with a wall of water on either side of them. When the Egyptians pursued them, the sea returned and drowned all of Pharaoh's chariots, horses, and horsemen.

- NUM 22:20–38; ~ God spoke to Balaam during the night telling him to meet with the men who called for him, and to tell them what God wanted him to say. Balaam got up the next morning, saddled his donkey, and set off for Moab. God knew he had not listened, so He sent an angel to stand on the road and stop Balaam, who was riding his donkey accompanied by two servants. The donkey saw the angel with a sword in his hand and turned aside into a field; and Balaam struck the donkey. The angel again stood in their path blocking the way, and the donkey turned aside, and Balaam struck the donkey again. As they continued, the road narrowed; the angel blocked the way and the donkey stopped; this time Balaam struck the donkey with his staff. Then the Lord opened the donkey's mouth who said, "What have I done to you that you would strike me three times?" Balaam replied to the donkey, "Because you mocked me; you are lucky I did not have my sword with me." The donkey spoke again, "Am I not your donkey which you have ridden since I was with you? Have I ever crossed you before?" Balaam said no. Then God opened his eyes and he saw the angel standing in the path with his sword drawn. And Balaam fell down and bowed before the angel. The angel asked, "Why did you strike your donkey three times? The Lord sent me to stop you because you are doing the opposite of what He told you to do. The donkey saw me and turned away three times, saving your life; for I would have slain you with this sword." Balaam admitted to having sinned, saying he did not know the angel was there and he would do as the Lord commanded. The angel reminded Balaam to speak the words of the Lord. Balaam proceeded to meet with the princes of Balak, who came out to meet him near the border of Moab by the coast. Balak said, "Did I not summon you? Why did you delay? Am I not able to promote you to a place of honor?" Balaam said, "I am here now, but I can only say what the Lord wills." [Balak wanted Balaam to prophesy against Israel, but Balaam blessed Israel as God commanded, angering Balak. Balaam told the king that he could not curse what God had not cursed. Balak asked him to curse Israel again and again; all three times Balaam blessed Israel as God told him. Balaam prophesied and then he left the beleaguered king. (NUM 23—24)]

- 1 KI 17:17–24 ~ The woman's son became ill and died. She said to Elijah, "What have you against me, that you would come into my house and bring death to my son?" Elijah told her to bring her son; he carried him upstairs. Elijah cried to God, then he stretched himself over the boy three times, asking God to spare him. The Lord heard Elijah's cry and revived the boy who was fully healed. Elijah took the boy to the widow and said, "See, your son lives." And the woman said, "Surely you are a man of God and the word in your mouth is true."

- 2 KI 6:4–7 ~ Elisha went with them to the Jordan, where they cut some wood. As one man was chopping the beam, the axe-head flew off into the water. The man was distraught saying, "Oh no, I borrowed this axe from my employer." Elisha asked the man to show him where the axe-head landed. Then Elisha took a stick and threw it into the water, and the axe-head floated to the surface. The man reached out and fetched it from the water.

- DAN 3:12–27 ~ The king of Babylon had Shadrach, Meshach, and Abednego thrown into the fiery furnace for not worshipping his pagan idol. The king looked into the fire and said, "I see four men in the fire and none of them have been affected in the least. And the fourth man looks like the Son of God." The king ordered, "You men, who serve the most-high God, come out of the furnace," and three men came out unscathed. [Note: the servants tending the furnace were burned to death because the king ordered them to make it seven times hotter.]

- JOH 2:1–11 ~ Jesus attended the wedding at Cana; His mother Mary was a hostess. When they ran out of wine, she asked Jesus to help. He said His time had not come. Mary told the servants to do whatever Jesus asked. He told them to fill large vessels with water, and they filled them to the brim. Then Jesus told a servant to dip a cup into a vessel, and take it to the master of ceremonies. The man did not know where the wine came from but the servants knew. He called the groom aside saying, "Usually the best wine is brought out first, but you have saved the best for last." This was the first of many miracles that Jesus would perform.

- JOH 6:1–15 ~ Jesus fed the multitude (over 5000 men not counting women and children) with a little boy's lunch, consisting of five barley loaves and two small fish. After everyone was fed, the disciples gathered the scraps and filled twelve baskets. The people who witnessed this miracle were amazed saying, "Surely, this man is a prophet who has come into the world." They wanted to make Him a king so Jesus withdrew alone into the mountain.

- JOH 9:1–15 ~ Jesus passed a man born blind. His disciples asked, "Who sinned that this man should be born blind, him or his parents?" Jesus answered, "Neither he nor his parents sinned, but so the works of God would be revealed through him. For I will do the work of Him who sent me while it is daylight, until the night comes when nobody can work. As long as I am in the world, I will be the light of the world." Then Jesus spat on the ground, made clay with the mud, and placed it on the man's eyes. Jesus told him, "Go wash in the pool of Siloam." He left, washed in the pool, and returned seeing. Everyone was asking, "Is this not the blind beggar, how is it that he can see?" He told them that Jesus had given him his sight.

- JOH 10:17–18 ~ Jesus said, "Therefore, my Father loves me, because I lay down my life so that I might take it back again. Nobody takes it from me but I lay it down of my own free will. I have power to lay it down and I have power to take it back again. This commandment I have received from my Father."

There are dozens of other miracles recorded in the Bible both in the Old and the New Testaments. Jesus performed miracles every day of His ministry on earth, from calming the storm (MAT 8:23–27), to walking on water (MAT 14:23–33), to paying the tax using a coin fetched from the mouth of a fish (MAT 17:24–27). These can be considered singularities because they never had happened before and they never will happen again.

Father, we thank you for miracles, and for leaving behind evidence, so that we can be certain and believe. We know you can intervene in this world at any time and any place, and this gives us assurance that you are sovereign and that our hope is secure. We have seen miracles in our own lives and this gives us confidence in our faith. Help us to depend on you for all things, for we know you will provide. Especially, we thank you for the miracle and proof of Jesus's resurrection as we pray in His name, Amen.

June 30

Don't Worry Day is hereby introduced for dedicating time to our mental health, by not worrying for an entire day. No doubt, you have experienced a catastrophe, illness, loss, problem, or dilemma and somebody told you, "Don't worry." Right? You probably cannot count the number of times this has happened. Maybe you replied to them, "That's easy for you to say." Well, that is exactly what God has said multiple times in His Word, and if you believe Him and trust in His promises, you have nothing to fear. In other words, don't worry, because God is in control. Acknowledge this, even when it seems the entire world is out of control, and you will find comfort in the face of adversity.

- GEN 15:1 ~ God told Abraham, "Do not be afraid, because I will be your shield, and I will reward you for your faith."

- DEU 31:6 ~ Be strong and courageous, do not worry or be afraid; for the Lord your God is with you. He will never fail you or forsake you.

- PSA 31:19 ~ How great is your goodness, Lord, which you have given to those who fear you and trust in you before all others.

- PSA 37:7 ~ Find solace in the Lord and wait patiently for Him. Do not worry about evil people who prosper.

- MAT 6:25–34 ~ Jesus taught, "Do not worry about your life, what you will eat or drink, or what you will wear. Is there not more to life than food and clothing? Look at the birds; they do not sow or reap, or gather food into the barn, yet our heavenly Father feeds them. Are people not more important than birds? Consider the lilies of the field, they grow just fine yet they do not work; however, King Solomon in his glory was not clothed in such beauty. If God cares for the birds and the flowers, will He not care for you even more? Therefore, do not worry about things such as food and clothing, for your heavenly Father knows you need these things. Instead, seek first the kingdom of God and His righteousness, and everything else you need will be yours. Do not be anxious about tomorrow, because tomorrow will take care of itself. Each day has enough problems to face without adding more."

- MAT 11:28 ~ Jesus said, "Come to me all of you who labor or are heavy laden and I will give you rest."

- LUK 12:11–12 ~ Jesus said, "When they bring you before the authorities do not worry about what to say or do, for the Holy Spirit will provide the information when you need it."

- PHP 4:6–8 ~ Do not worry about anything, but pray for everything with thanksgiving, humbleness, and eagerness. Focus your mind on things that are true, honest, just, pure, lovely, admirable, virtuous, and praiseworthy.

- 2 TI 1:7 ~ God has not given us the spirit of fear, but of power, love, and a sound mind.

Those who do not believe in God or trust in His promises have much to fear. And this kind of fear will dominate their lives. They will suffer from anxiety, depression, paranoia, and other mental problems; they may take numerous medications to offset their suffering but it will not go away until they bring their troubles to the Lord. If they do not come to the Lord for guidance, their problems might become compounded.

- PSA 5:11 ~ Let all who trust in God rejoice and sing for joy, for God will defend them; and those that love God will exalt in Him.

- PSA 23:4 ~ Even when I walk through the valley of the shadow of death, I will not be afraid of any evil, for God will be with me to comfort me.

- PSA 37:4–5 ~ Find your delight in the Lord and He will give to you the desires of your heart. Commit yourself to the Lord and trust in Him, and He will make your desires come to pass.

- PRO 1:7, 33 ~ The fear of the Lord is the beginning of knowledge; but fools despise knowledge and wisdom. Those who seek God will be safe and sound from the fear of evil.

- PRO 3:5–8 ~ Trust in the Lord with all your heart; do not rely on your own understanding. Acknowledge God in everything you do, and He will direct you in your ways. Do not consider yourself wise, but fear the Lord, refrain from evil, and you will be healthy and strong.

- PRO 29:25 ~ The fear of man is a trap; but those who trust in the Lord will be safe.

- ISA 33:14 ~ Sinners are afraid; fear surprises the hypocrites. Who among you will live in the devouring fire and burn?

- MAT 10:28 ~ Jesus said, "Do not fear those who can kill the body but cannot kill the soul. Rather, fear Him who can destroy both your body and soul in hell."

- ROM 13:4 ~ If you do what is evil, be afraid, for God's minister will not bear the sword in vain, because he is sent to execute wrath upon those who do evil.

- EPH 1:5, 11, 13–14, 18 ~ We were predestined to become adopted children of God by Jesus Christ, according to His marvelous will. In Christ we obtain an inheritance in heaven, because we listen to the truth and trust in Him for our redemption and salvation. I hope your eyes will be opened and you will become enlightened, and you will feel the hope of His promise, and experience the glory of the inheritance of the saints.

Worry and anxiety are incompatible with peace and joy, which can defeat the worry and anxiety. Simply put, the positive thought overpowers the negative thought. If you focus on the world, you will observe a great deal of negativity. If you focus on Jesus Christ, you will observe positive and uplifting things. It is your choice, what you think, say, and do and whether they are positive or negative. Stay connected to the Holy Spirit and He will continuously calibrate your moral compass pointing you in a direction that leads to the Kingdom of God.

We must act on our faith and trust in the Lord; and we will be compelled to respond to His correctly to commandments. For example, if you trust that God will forgive you, you must try to quit whatever you are doing that is offending Him. If you do not try to improve, then you cannot be sincere in your belief or your repentance. Further, if you know the truth that sets people free, you should be willing to tell the truth so others can be freed, especially from their sin. Above all, love others and be kind, generous, and unselfish with that love, for love fulfills all laws (ROM 13:10). Yes, we will have our doubts from time to time, but this should be a reminder that God is with us and His Spirit is willing to comfort and sustain us until the end.

- DEU 28:9–10, 58–59, 66 ~ God will establish a holy people unto Himself, just like He promised, as long as you keep His commandments and walk in His ways. And all people on earth will see that you are called by the name of the Lord, and they will be afraid of you. If you do not observe all the words in the Bible and fear only God, then He will send plagues and sickness upon you continuously. And your life will hang in doubt, and you will be afraid night and day, having no assurance concerning your life.

- JOB 8:13–14 ~ The destiny of those who forget God is the loss of all hope, for their trust in worldly things is a fragile one.

JUNE

- PSA 27:1–2 ~ The Lord is my light and my salvation. Who should I fear? He is the strength in my life. Of whom shall I be afraid? Even if a whole encampment of my enemies is preparing war against me, I will not be afraid, but confident.

- PSA 34:4, 9, 11 ~ I sought the Lord and He heard me, and delivered me from my fears. So, fear the Lord all you saints, and you will never need anything. Come to me people, and I will teach you about the fear of the Lord.

- PSA 40:4 ~ Blessed be those who trust in the Lord rather than giving their respect to the proud and deceitful.

- PSA 56:3–4 ~ If I am afraid, I will praise God's Word and put my trust in Him. I will not be afraid of what flesh can do to me.

- PRO 28:25 ~ People with proud hearts serve only to create conflict, but those who trust in God will prosper.

- ISA 26:3 ~ Those whose minds are set on God and trust in Him will be kept in perfect peace.

- ISA 41:10 ~ God says, "Fear not, for I am with you. Do not be dismayed, for I am your God. I will strengthen and help you. I will hold you up with the right hand of righteousness."

- 1 TI 6:17 ~ Tell the rich people in the world not to act so proud or to set their hopes on uncertain earthly riches. Tell them to set their hope and trust in God, who furnishes everything in this world for us to enjoy.

- HEB 12:28–29 ~ Since we will inherit a kingdom which cannot fall, let us have grace to willingly serve God with reverence and awe, for He is a consuming fire.

- 1 JO 4:18 ~ There is no fear in love, but perfect love casts out fear, because fear has torment. Those who fear are not made perfect in love.

People who refuse to acknowledge God and His sovereignty in this universe are heading in the wrong direction, and it leads them along a path that goes continuously down. Do not let secular society or governmental activists influence you with promises they cannot fulfill, or riches they did not earn, or safety they cannot provide.

- ISA 8:12–13 ~ Do not join in any conspiracies or alliances with people who are afraid; do not fear the things that they fear; do not be afraid at all. Sanctify the Lord of hosts, and let Him be your fear.

- MAT 15:14 ~ Stay away from false teachers, for they are like the blind leading the blind. And when the blind lead the blind, both fall into the ditch.

- ACT 17:23–34 ~ Paul addressed the men of Athens saying, "As I walked through the city, I observed your objects of worship and one caught my eye with its inscription: To the unknown God. Today I proclaim to you this God, who made heaven and earth and everything in it. The Lord of heaven and earth does not live in temples made by man, nor is He served by human hands as if He needed anything, since He gives all things to humankind: life, breath, and all we have. From one blood, God made all the nations to dwell upon the earth. He determined the appointed times, boundaries, and dwelling places beforehand. So that people would seek the Lord if they feel His presence, and find Him; though He is not far from every one of us. In Him we move and have our being, as sure as your poets have said, for we are His offspring. Therefore, we must not think of God as like unto an idol made by man. God ignores such things; He would rather that we repent. For He has appointed a day when He will judge the world in righteousness by the chosen man who He ordained, giving reassurance to all people that God has raised Him from the dead. When they heard of the resurrection of the dead, some mocked and others showed an interest to hear more about this. Then Paul departed; and many of them believed and became followers of Paul.

- 2 TH 3:14–15 ~ If there are people among you who fail to conform to the Word as we have taught it to you, make note of them and stay away from them, so that they will feel ashamed of their behavior. However, do not consider them as an enemy, but admonish them as you would a brother or sister.

- 2 TI 3:1–5 ~ Know this, that perilous times will come in the last days. People will love only themselves. They will be covetous, boasters, blasphemers, arrogant, disobedient to parents, unthankful and ungodly, void of natural affection. They will be promise breakers, false accusers, undisciplined, fierce despisers of goodness; traitors, reckless, conceited, lovers of worldly pleasures more than God; displaying a form of godliness, but denying the power thereof. Stay away from people like this.

We face countless decisions and challenges every single day. The outcome of our choices will depend on our attitude, outlook, and beliefs. Do not allow trials and confrontations to cause worry or anxiety, but face them with confidence as you seek the counsel of the Holy Spirit. If we trust in God's love and mercy we will triumph; we will overcome obstacles and temptations for Christ has overcome the world on our behalf. It comes down to where you place your faith and trust: the world which will pass away, or the Lord who is eternal. Side with the Lord and you will overcome the world.

- JER 8:11–12 ~ To heal your pain they came saying "peace, peace" but there was no peace. Were they ashamed of their atrocities? Not in the least; they did not even blush. But they will join the fallen. When the Lord comes, they will be cast down.

- 1 JO 4:2–6 ~ Every spirit that confesses that Jesus Christ is God in the flesh is of God. Those spirits that do not confess are not of God, but are spirits of the antichrist, which you have heard about and are in the world. You belong to God and have overcome these spirits of malice. For greater is He that is within you than he that is in the world. They are of the world, and therefore speak of worldly things, and the world listens to them. We are of God. Those who know God will listen to His messengers, and those who are not of God will not listen. We know the difference between the Spirit of truth and the spirit of untruth.

- HEB 11:7–38 ~ Because of their great faith, men of God were able to endure anything and performed remarkable feats, such as subduing kingdoms, escaping certain death, overcoming incredible odds, healing the sick, and even raising the dead.

Thank you, Father, that we have overcome the world through Christ, who overcame the world, its sin, and its death, so that we might live. You have guaranteed that we will receive all we need if we seek your face and follow your Son; so we really don't have anything to worry about. Since worrying will not add anything worthwhile to our lives, build in us complete trust and confidence in you, which will dispel the doubt and strengthen our faith. We thank you for your guidance, protection, and deliverance, oh Heavenly Father, along with your Holy Spirit, and your Son Jesus Christ in whose name we always pray, Amen.

July 1

Devotion to Duty Day has been observed on this day for only a few years. It is primarily associated with the military, but one can apply it to any occupation or responsibility. It is our duty to obey God, fulfill our obligations to family, do the work required by our teachers and employers, help one another in need, and any other assignments we have assumed. We also have a patriotic duty to our country to obey the laws and respect the rights and liberties of others. Though an unofficial holiday, it seems a worthy cause that we devote ourselves to those who depend on us. Today you may reflect on your priorities and who you are dutiful towards. I would think God would be at the top of the list, then family, employer or school, pets, whatever: you fill in the blanks. Are you a good Christian, spouse, parent, student, employee, patriot, or helper? You are when you've devoted yourself to roles you chose or were given, committing yourself to completing the tasks efficiently and effectively, in order to honor God. It may take longer than you expected to do it right the first time, but it is time well spent. By the way, you will perform better if you call it a day when it is quitting time, rather than pushing the limits and creating more work or problems.

God wants us to make Him first in our lives, followed by all human beings. If you are devoted to Him and others, you will be dutiful in every aspect of your life, and that equates to success. Do not tackle too much too quickly, but build on the number of things you can juggle.

- DEU 4:29–31 ~ If you seek God with all your heart and soul you will find Him. If you are distressed, even in the latter times, turn to God and obey His commandments. God is merciful and He will never abandon you or destroy you; He will never forget the covenant He made with your forefathers.

- PSA 9:1–2 ~ I will praise you, Lord, with all my heart. I will speak of all your wonders. I will be glad and rejoice. I will sing praises to your name.

- MAT 22:37–40 ~ Jesus said, "Love the Lord your God with all your heart, mind, and soul: this is the first and greatest commandment. The second is like unto the first: Love your neighbor as yourself. All the laws and the prophets depend on these two commandments."

- ROM 8:4–6 ~ Live, not according to the flesh but according to the spirit. Those who live according to the flesh set their minds on evil, but those who live according to the spirit set their minds on God. To set the mind on flesh results in death, but to set the mind on God results in peace and life.

The followers of Christ were devoted to Him, and willing to die for Him. In fact, all of His apostles died a horrible and untimely death spreading the Gospel, except John. We too are supposed to devote ourselves to Christ, and be willing to give our lives for the faith.

- ECC 12:12 ~ The conclusion of the whole matter is this: fear God and keep His commandments. This is the entire duty of humankind.

- JOH 6:29 ~ Jesus answered them saying, "This is the work of God: that you believe Him whom He has sent."

- ROM 12:1 ~ Give yourselves to God. Let yourself be a living sacrifice. After all He has done for you, is that too much to ask?

- 1 CO 7:35, 37 ~ I tell you this for your benefit, not to put a restraint on you but to encourage you: it is appropriate that you be devoted to the Lord without distraction.

- 2 CO 11:3 ~ Even as the serpent deceived Eve by his cunning, so Satan will attempt to lead you astray from devotion to the true Christ.

- 1 TI 4:12–16 ~ Paul wrote to Timothy: Do not let anyone put you down because you are young, but set an example for the believers through your speech, life, love, faith, and purity. Devote yourself to the public reading of scripture, and to preaching and teaching. Never neglect your gift, which was given to you in a prophetic message when the elders laid their hands upon you. Be diligent in these matters, and give yourself completely to them, so that everyone may see your progress. Keep a close watch on your life and your doctrine and persevere in them, for you will prove yourself as well as those who will listen.

We have a duty to others to serve them and to witness Christ if they will listen. This is God's work no matter what your vocation or career path.

- 1 CH 16:12, 24–25 ~ Remember God's marvelous works, His wonders, and His judgments. Declare His glory among the heathen, and His amazing works among all nations. For the Lord is great, and He is worthy of our praise.

- ROM 15:1–7 ~ We who are strong ought to bear with the failings of the weak. When we do the right thing, it should not be to please ourselves, but to please others and to build them up in the Lord. Even Christ did not please Himself, but as it is written of Him, "The insults of those who would insult you have fallen on me." Everything that was written in the past was for our instruction, so that through endurance and the encouragement of the scriptures we might have hope. May the God who gives endurance, encouragement, and hope give you a spirit of unity as you follow Christ. Give glory to God the Father of our Lord Jesus Christ with one voice and one heart. Accept each other as Christ accepted you, so that God may be praised.

- 1 CO 12:7 ~ The manifestation of the Spirit is given to everyone for the common good.

- 1 CO 14:12 ~ Since you are eager to have spiritual gifts, try to excel in those gifts which edify the church.

- 1 TH 5:11–14 ~ Comfort each other and edify one another just as you are doing. We implore of you to know those who work among you, and who are over you in the Lord to admonish you. Esteem them very highly in love for the sake of their work. Warn the lazy, encourage the timid, help the weak, and be patient with everyone.

- HEB 6:10 ~ God is not unfair, and will not dismiss your labor of love which you gave for others in His name, because you have ministered to the saints and continue to do so.

- JAM 1:25 ~ Those who study the perfect law of liberty and continue therein, not forgetting but continuing to do the work, these persons will be blessed for their deeds.

- 1 PE 4:10–11 ~ As everyone has received the gift, even so minister the same to one another, as good stewards of the manifold grace of God.

Part of our devotion to God is to study His Word. This is the reason I wrote this book, to encourage people to read the Bible daily. Every holiday in this devotional guide can be related to the Bible, or more accurately, the Bible can be related to every day. Whether we celebrate or work, this day belongs to the Lord, and that alone is reason to rejoice. Daily devotions are part of our walk with the Lord so we can know the truth and share it with confidence.

Dear Father, help us to be devoted to you and your Word; help us to serve others with the gifts you have bestowed upon us. Equip us to be dedicated and loyal, and to shine your light during the performance of all our duties to our immediate family, our church family, our employers, teachers, authorities, and society. Let us be successful in our endeavors, as we spread the good news of Jesus Christ in every arena in which we are called to serve, ever dutiful to Him in whose name we pray, Amen.

July 2

World UFO Day is dedicated to the search, identification, and awareness of unidentified flying objects. This day marks the anniversary of the incident on 07/02/1947 when an unknown airborne object crashed outside of Roswell NM. The government prohibited anyone from entering the search area, and later claimed it was only a weather balloon.

There is much debate about the existence of unidentified objects that soar in the air, and even below the sea. Some say these are alien spacecraft inhabited by extraterrestrial beings; others say they are top secret experimental vehicles being built by the USA or a foreign nation. As a research psychologist observing by night a military operation in a remote area of the country over two decades ago, my driver and I both saw an aerial object flying high above the jet stream as we lay upon the hood of our truck awaited a convoy. It flew as a discus creating a bright arc, appearing and disappearing three times, while traversing about ninety degrees of space in less than a minute (estimated at least Mach 3). Certainly, there are spacecraft that can fly ten times that, such as during a launch at Cape Canaveral. Of course, when it comes to military secrets, what they have is far more advanced than what the general population knows about. Even top-secret things that I was privy to as a military scientist were nothing compared to stuff classified at higher levels (e.g., compartmentalized). A very selected few will ever have a "need to know" about what is really going on in the highest echelons of government.

Suffice it to say that there is enough evidence to suggest that UFOs exist (aka unidentified aerial phenomenon). The question remains as to the origin of those occurrences which cannot be explained by scientists or the government. Despite the countless theories being suggested, rarely if ever is it postulated that these appearances might be portents from God, or His messengers (angels). Similarly, false portents sometimes are sent by Satan and his horde of demons. A case can be made that these sightings are spiritual phenomena, which are becoming more frequent as the end of days nears.

- JOE 2:30–32; ACT 2:19–21 ~ The Lord will show wonders in heaven above and the earth below: blood, fire, and smoke. The sun will turn into darkness and the moon into blood before the day of the Lord occurs. Whomever calls on the name of the Lord will be saved.

- LUK 21:25–27 ~ Jesus said there will be signs in the sun, moon, stars, and on the earth that will distress the nations, with the sea and the waves also roaring. People's hearts will fail them when they see these things, for the powers of heaven will be shaken. Next, we will see the Son of man arriving with power in a cloud of great glory.

- 2 TH 2:9–11 ~ Those false signs and fake miracles come from Satan. Such deceptions belong to the self-righteous who will die, for they did not believe the truth that could save them. God will let them believe their lies and perish.

- REV 6:12–15 ~ There was a great earthquake; the sun became black and the moon became like blood. The stars fell from the sky. The heaven departed as a scroll being rolled together. People tried to hide and take cover, especially the rich and powerful.

- REV 12:1–2 ~ In heaven there appeared a great wonder, a woman clothed in the sun and the moon under her feet, and upon her head were twelve stars. (More from this scripture below.)

- REV 15:1 ~ I saw another marvelous sign in heaven: seven angels bringing the seven last plagues, filled with the wrath of God.

- REV 16:13–17 ~ I saw three evil spirits leaping like frogs out of the dragon, the beast, and the false prophet; they are spirits of the devil working false miracles throughout the earth, gathering armies for battle against God Almighty. They assembled their armies at a place called Armageddon near the mountain of Megiddo. Then the seventh angel poured out his vial, and a voice from heaven said, "It is over."

There are instances in the Bible when prophets saw visions of objects flying in the sky with peculiar shapes and dynamics. Since human flight was yet to be discovered, they described these events in terms familiar to them, such as winged angels, chariots of fire, or a flying scroll. No doubt, there is symbolism attached to these events, not to mention meaning to be derived by looking at the content and the scriptures that surround these passages, as well as their connections elsewhere in the Bible. When you see many passages grouped together it is easier to see the power of God in them, and also the meaning.

- 2 KI 2:9–12 ~ Elijah brought Elisha with him, and the two prophets crossed the river after Elijah had parted it with his cloak. Elijah granted Elisha a wish, and Elisha responded he would like to have twice the prophetic power of his mentor. Elijah responded that his request would be granted if he was allowed to view Elijah's departure from this earth. About that time a chariot of fire with horses of fire came between the two men, and swept Elijah into heaven like a whirlwind. Elisha cried unto God while Elijah disappeared.

- 2 KI 6–17 ~ The Syrian army had surrounded Elisha and his servant in order to capture Elisha. The servant was very afraid. So, Elisha prayed that God might open his eyes. Quickly he could see what Elijah saw: that the Syrian army were themselves surrounded by angels with chariots and horses of fire. Then Elisha prayed to God to blind their enemies so they could escape, and God granted his request.

- EZE 1:4—EZE 2:3 ~ Ezekiel saw a fiery whirlwind coming down from the sky, with bright yellow color emerging from the center. Then emerged four living creatures that looked like men, but each had four faces and four wings. Their wings were joined together and remained so wherever they went. Each had one face of a man; to the right the face of a lion to left the face of an ox; the fourth face was of an eagle. Two wings covered their bodies, and two wings were joined with angels on each side. And they followed the spirit, these creatures which shined as burning coals or lamps; and out of the fire within them came bolts of lightning. As Ezekiel observed this phenomenon there appeared wheels, and they worked like a wheel within a wheel. The rings of each wheel were ominous, with eyes all around them. And the wheels went wherever the creatures went, as they followed the spirit, for the spirit of each creature was in the wheels. A loud noise like many waterfalls could be heard as they maneuvered. When they stood firm, they let down their wings. And a voice came from the heavens, and above that firmament was a throne like sapphire stone, and on the throne sat a man; and fire surrounded the throne and the man, creating the appearance of an emanating rainbow. This was the manifestation of the glory of the Lord. When Ezekiel saw it, he fell on his face hearing a voice speak to him saying, "Son of man, stand up and listen to me carefully. I am sending you to the children of Israel, a rebellious nation where their fathers have transgressed up to this very day."

- ZEC 5:1–4 ~ Zechariah looked up and saw a flying scroll some twenty cubits long (thirty feet) and ten cubits wide (fifteen feet). And the angel said, "This is the curse that will go forth over the face of the entire earth; for everyone who steals or swears falsely by my name will be cut off."

- REV 12:12–17 ~ Once the dragon (devil) was cast down, a curse fell upon all the earth. He arrived with great anger knowing he had but a short time. And the dragon persecuted the woman who had brought forth a male child. But the woman was given two wings like that of an eagle so she could fly away into the wilderness, to be nourished for a time, times, and half a time (assumed to be 3.5 years, or 1+2+.5). Next, the serpent tried to wipe her out with a flood, but the earth swallowed up the water, making the dragon even more furious with the woman. He left to make war with her seed who keep the commandments and adhere to the testimony of Jesus Christ.

This is not to say that UFO sightings are acts of God or acts of Satan, because many of them could be acts of humans tinkering with advanced technology, possessing secret knowledge, or equipped with artificial intelligence. The least likely explanation is that of space aliens or invaders, unless you consider an angel to be an alien from outer space. Case in point, the Roswell episode, which was written-off by the government as a weather balloon that crash landed. Certainly, that much secrecy and cleanup would not have been necessary for a weather balloon unless it was carrying something top secret. More likely, this was a ruse perpetrated by our government to keep us in the dark about what really happened. Given the proximity of the area to Holloman Air Force Base, NM (the stealth fighter base) perhaps the military was experimenting with composite (radar-reflective) materials on a drone aircraft that went down. Such knowledge could have instigated a first strike from the USSR if they thought the USA could fly into their airspace carrying a nuclear weapon without being detected by radar. Thus, there are logical and alternative explanations that are every bit as difficult to prove as the farfetched ones.

By the way, God also operates on a "need to know" basis sometimes. Consider the knowledge imparted to St. John and St. Paul, when they saw things that they were directed not to report further.

- 2 CO 12:2–4 ~ I knew a man in Christ over fourteen years ago (whether in the body or out of the body, I cannot tell, but God knows). This man was caught up to the third heaven, and I knew this man, how he was caught up into paradise to hear unspeakable words that I am not free to explain.

- REV 10:1–6 ~ I saw another mighty angel descend from heaven in a cloud. He had a rainbow over his head, his face shown like the sun, and his feet were as flaming fire. In his hand was a small, opened book. The angel stepped his right foot upon the sea and the left upon the earth. He cried aloud like a roaring lion; after he spoke, seven thunders uttered their voices. I was about to write when a voice from heaven told me, "Seal up those things which the seven thunders uttered and do not write them down."

Furthermore, we do not know when Christ will return, and for good reason. If we did, we could wait until the last minute to get our house in order, whereas God wants us to be prepared now and always. So, we do not have a need to know about this, and a great many other things.

- MAT 24:36, 44, 50 ~ Nobody knows the day and hour, not even the angels; not even the Son of man knows, but only the Father in heaven. For the Son of man will come when you least expect Him.

- MAT 25:13 ~ Watch therefore, because you know neither the day nor the hour.

- 2 PE 3:10 ~ The day of the Lord will come as a thief in the night.

- REV 3:11 ~ Jesus said, "Behold, I come quickly. Hold fast to what you have so that nobody can take your crown away from you." (See also REV 22:20.)

When there is something essential that everyone needs to know, God spells it out clearly in His Word, so there will be no mistake in interpreting its meaning or purpose. Consider this when you seek knowledge and truth, but are unable to find absolute answers.

- DAN 2:28 ~ There is a God in heaven who reveals mysteries (as opposed to hiding them).

- MAT 10:26–27; LUK 12:3 ~ Jesus said, "Do not fear those who hate you, for everything that is hidden now will be revealed later; everything that is unknown will become known. What I tell you in darkness you will speak in the light. What you hear in private will be proclaimed from the rooftops."

- MAT 13:35 ~ It was prophesied that Christ would talk in parables and would explain secrets that were hidden since the beginning of time (as opposed to keeping them secret).

- JOH 18:20 ~ Jesus said, "What I teach is widely known; I have preached it openly and often in church. Everyone, including the Jewish leaders, has heard what I teach. I teach nothing in private that I have not said in public."

- ROM 16:25–26 ~ Christ has the power to save you according to the revelation of God's mystery, which was kept secret since the world began, but which is now evident by the scriptures. According to God's will, the mystery is made known to all nations on earth for the obedience of faith.

There are things that we are sure of because God has revealed them. There are some things that we can verify as true by conducting extensive research or experimentation. There are things that we do not know because the answer is deliberately hidden from us by God or by the government. And there are things that we will never know before our Lord returns, and possibly even after we have entered the promised land. Oftentimes, our need to know is based upon our readiness to know, or our capability to understand, not to mention our need to be protected. But when it comes to keeping secrets from one another, it seems that we are always found out in the end. Therefore, it is wise to tell the truth at all times and in all places. If someone needs to be protected from the truth, there should be an explanation, or a good reason why.

When you see unusual occurrences in the sky, you might contemplate Christ's return. UFOs may or may not be portents, but they should remind us of who is in control, and it is not the government, or a foreign nation, or space aliens, or the globalists who seek to possess the world. God is sovereign and always will be, so there is no need to fear such things. It is interesting to wonder, however. I wonder what it will be like to live in the presence of Almighty God for eternity. The mere thought of this enables me to reclaim my joy, knowing that I will see Him face to face.

- JOB 19:25–26 ~ I know that my Redeemer lives, and that He will stand over the earth on the last day. And though worms will have destroyed my body in the grave, yet in my flesh I will see God.

- ISA 40:5 ~ The glory of the Lord will be revealed, and all human flesh will see it together, for the Lord has said so.

- ACT 1:7 ~ Jesus said, "It is not for you to know the times or the seasons fixed by God."

- 1 JO 3:1–2 ~ How great is the love that God the Father has for us, that we should be called His children. The world does not know us because it did not know Him. We are His children, but we do not know yet what we will be; we do know, however, that we will be like Him, for we will see Him as He really is.

- REV 1:7 ~ Behold, the Lord comes in the clouds, and everyone will see Him, including those who pierced Him. And all races of people will groan.

Heavenly Father, we ask that you would purify our thoughts and make clear your will for our lives. We also pray that our minds would not be polluted by things of this world or by otherworldly fantasies. Cleanse our minds with the purity of truth and obedience to your Word. May we know what we need to know, when we need to know it. In the name of Jesus, Amen.

July 3

North Defeated South at Gettysburg on this day in 1863; over 51,000 lives were lost in three days. After defeating the Army of the Potomac in the battle of Chancellorsville, General Lee continued his offensive. However, Lee's objective to invade and subdue the North would never be realized, after going all-in with a losing hand at Cemetery Ridge. The Union were dug-in making Pickett's ill-advised assault a disaster. General Longstreet tried to stop Lee; he wanted to faceoff with General Grant who had invaded the South. Some argue that Longstreet might have given a half-hearted effort in the invasion due to his disagreement with Lee. Meanwhile, General Grant managed to capture Vicksburg the next day (07/04/1863), so maybe Longstreet was right. We will never know for sure. We do know it was the turning point of the Civil War, with the Confederacy losing two key battles and over a third of their fighting force in a single week. Lee offered his resignation to Jefferson Davis who refused to accept it. Disheartened, Lee plodded onward with his campaign, perhaps with hesitation. Sadly, the war would drag on another two years, essentially ending with Lee's surrender at Appomattox on 04/09/1865. Over half a million Americans died in four years, in the bloodiest war throughout the history of the United States.

Scholars may differ in their analysis of this battle, but the bottom line is this: God abhors slavery and wants it to end. But it won't end until Christ returns; in fact, slavery is likely to get worse as the coming of Christ nears. And whatever one's moral stance at the beginning of the Civil War, Americans fought and died to preserve liberty, which was the foundation of this nation from the start. The South was doomed from the beginning, because their cause was not on the side of righteousness. Somehow, this seemed to weigh heavy on the heart of General Lee who was against secession but loyal to Virginia, his home. Lee had resigned his commission in the US Army, becoming commander of the army of Virginia. He made some questionable tactical decisions during the war which might indicate an eagerness to get it over with.

In our lesson two days ago (07/01) the topic was duty and devotion. One could assert that Lee had a sense of duty to the Confederacy but his devotion was to Virginia. Grant, on the other hand, who also wanted to end the war quickly, maintained his devotion and duty to the Union and President Lincoln. Who was the better general? That's debatable. Who won? That's not debatable. Why did the North win? Because it was God's will. Providence has guided this nation since day one, although I'm not sure if God is happy with the direction this nation is heading now. Recall that God let Israel lose their land after they had forsaken Him for worldly gods and idols, fraternizing with their enemies. The South, in spite of religion, were prepared to secede and fight to keep their moneymakers: the slaves, who were not free and were forced to work for free. It's not that the North held the moral high ground; it is that the South held the moral low ground.

- GEN 3:22 ~ God said, "Man is like us, able to discern good and evil. He knows not to eat the forbidden fruit."

- DEU 7:7–10 ~ The Lord did not pour His love upon Israel, or choose you because you were greater in number than other people, for you were the fewest of all people. But because the Lord loved you, and in order to keep the promise that He made with your fathers, He brought you out with a mighty hand, and redeemed you from bondage in the land of Egypt. Know therefore that the Lord is your God; He is faithful and keeps the covenant, and bestows mercy on those who love Him and keep His commandments. But He repays those to their face who hate Him, and utterly destroys them for everyone to see.

- JDG 10:13–14 ~ You have forgotten me and served other gods; therefore, I will deliver you no more. Go and cry to the false gods that you have chosen; see if they will deliver you in the time of your tribulation.

- PRO 1:28–33 ~ They will call me but I will not answer; they will look for me but not find me. They hated knowledge and chose not to fear the Lord, ignoring my advice and spurning my reprimand. Since they did not take heed, they will eat the fruit of their ways and be full of the fruit of their schemes. The waywardness of simple-minded people will be their demise, and the complacency of fools will destroy them. But whoever chooses to listen will be safe and at peace, free from fear of harm.

- JER 29:11–13 ~ God says, "I know the thoughts that I think towards you: thoughts of peace and not evil, so that you will have a future of hope. Then you will call on me and I will listen; you will look for me and you will find me, as long as you search with all your heart."

- ROM 12:2 ~ Do not conform to the ways of the world but be transformed by the renewing of your mind, so you can discern the good, acceptable, and perfect will of God.

- 1 CO 2:14 ~ Worldly people do not receive the things of the Spirit of God, for these things are foolishness to them; neither can they know these things for they must be discerned spiritually.

- PHP 1:6, 9 ~ Be confident of this: He who began a good work in you will carry it to completion until the day Christ returns. And this is my prayer: that your love will abound more and more in knowledge, depth, and insight, so that you will be able to discern what is best, and can remain pure and blameless until Christ comes.

- HEB 4:12 ~ The Word of God is alive and powerful. It is sharper than any double-edged sword, piercing deep, so as to divide the very soul and spirit. It can discern the thoughts and intents of the heart.

We will prevail if we place our confidence in the Lord. Those whose confidence is in earthly and selfish motives will not prevail, for their trust is misplaced. We need leaders who also place their trust and confidence in God and not the world, or they will make decisions that are not in the best interest of the nation. Governments that are corrupt end up corrupting the people; and people who are corrupt end up corrupting the government. Let us abandon the ways of the world and look for guidance from God, who already knows the outcome of our mortal strivings.

- 1 KI 3:9 ~ Give your servant an understanding mind to govern your people and to discern between good and evil.

- PSA 71:5 ~ For you have been my hope, oh Sovereign Lord, and my confidence since my youth.

- PSA 139:1–6 ~ Lord, you have searched me and you know everything about me. You discern my thoughts, and are familiar with all my ways. I could never attain such knowledge. Even before I speak, you know what I will say.

- PRO 3:26, 27 ~ The Lord will be your confidence, keeping your foot from being snared. Do not withhold goodness from those to which it is due, if it is within your power to do it.

- JER 17:7 ~ Blessed is the person who trusts in the Lord, whose confidence is in Him.

- HEB 10:35 ~ Do not throw away your confidence, for it will be richly rewarded.

Father, we place our confidence in your Word, for your promises are true and your wisdom never fails. Help us to lean on you at all times, following your guidance in our lives, and with respect to national and world affairs. Let us not enter into wars we cannot win, or pick battles for the wrong reasons. Help us to avoid being on the wrong side of you, and to maintain the moral high ground in times of conflict. Enable us to be victorious when evil comes against us because of our allegiance to you. In Jesus's name, Amen.

July 4

Independence Day, otherwise referred to as the Fourth of July, reveres the adoption of our Declaration of Independence in 1776, which affirmed our separation from England and its domination over the original thirteen colonies. It is a time of national solidarity and patriotism, complete with festivals, great food, sporting events, parades, and fireworks. It is a time to remember the birth of our nation, the integrity of our founding fathers, and the resolve of those who sacrificed much to secure our liberties. It is a time for sincere devotion towards our founding documents and the sacred beliefs upon which this nation stands.

Interestingly, Jefferson and Adams, the primary contributors to the Declaration of Independence, as well as the celebration of this event on an annual basis, both died on July 4, 1826, the fiftieth anniversary of Independence Day. Though these two presidents were formidable adversaries in the political arena, they never ceased conversing with one another during those fifty years. Monroe, another president and founding father, died exactly five years later on July fourth.

We are beholden to the founders of our nation and the framers of our founding documents; they all served this great nation with honor, integrity, and decency. Whatever their faults, these men arguably assembled the greatest think tank in human history. Shame on those antagonists who want to change the meaning, the words, or the actual documents, as if the edicts and principles are no longer relevant. They most certainly are relevant and always will be if we have any hope of continuing this great experiment in freedom and democracy. Beware, when leaders in your government attempt to nullify our founding documents or alter them in order to invalidate them. They are the ones who should be nullified by defeating them at the polls or impeaching them, for they swore an oath to uphold and enforce our Constitution and our laws, but violated that oath.

- PSA 33:12 ~ Blessed is the nation whose God is the Lord, and blessed are the people He has chosen for His own inheritance.

- PSA 119:44–46 ~ I will obey God's laws continuously and forevermore; I will walk in freedom, for I have sought His rules.

- 2 CO 3:17 ~ The Lord is Spirit; and where the Spirit of the Lord is, there is liberty.

- GAL 5:1, 13 ~ Stand fast in the liberty with which Christ made us free, and do not get entangled again with the yoke of bondage. Brothers, you have been called into liberty; but do not use that freedom as a reason to indulge the flesh, but love and serve one another.

- 1 PE 2:13–17 ~ Submit to the laws of the land, for it is God's will that you are lawful and upright, thereby silencing those ignorant people who would talk behind your back. Be free, but do not use your freedom to conceal evil. Instead, you must serve the Lord, respect all people, love your fellow Christians, fear God, and honor those in authority.

Freedom is not free; it comes at a heavy price. Our fight for freedom resulted in a great deal of bloodshed. Assuredly, most wars are fought over freedom, and the cost is blood. The freedom bought for us by Jesus Christ cost His blood; the sacrifices made as a sin atonement by God's people before Christ also required blood offerings. Those carrying Christianity to the world also bled, and many died. Why so much blood? Well, to be free indeed, means being free from the slavery of sin. This requires that your soul be cleansed of sin; for the payment is death. Those dying for freedom, whether Christ or our nation's freedom fighters, were willing to make the ultimate sacrifice so others can live free. People subjected to slavery will fight to be free; they would rather die than forfeit liberty. Who wouldn't want to be free of evil tyrants, that are careless with their sinning and enslave the innocent? Tyrants eventually lose their freedom if not their lives, because their causes and desires cannot be paid for with the blood of patriots.

- EXO 24:6–8 ~ Moses put half of the blood into bowls and sprinkled the other half on the altar. Then he took the Book of the Covenant and read to the people, who responded, "We will do everything the Lord has commanded, and we will obey Him." Then Moses took the rest of the blood and sprinkled it on the people, saying, "This is the blood of the covenant that the Lord has made with you in accordance with these words."

- LEV 17:11 ~ The life of all flesh resides in the blood, and I have given it to you upon the altar to make atonement for your souls, for it is the blood that makes atonement for the soul.

- DEU 18:18–19 ~ Moses sprinkled blood of the sacrifice on the Book of Law and the people, saying "This is the blood of the everlasting covenant made by God through this His Word."

- MIC 6:6–7 ~ How am I to appear before God? Shall I come before Him with offerings and sacrifices? Will He be pleased with thousands and thousands of sacrifices? Shall I sacrifice my firstborn, the fruit of my body, to atone for the sin of my soul?

- JOH 5:22, 24 ~ Jesus said, "The Father judges nobody but has entrusted judgment to the Son. Truthfully, whoever hears my Word and believes Him who sent me has eternal life and will not be condemned, but will cross over from death into life.

- HEB 9:13–28 ~ The blood of animals and the ashes sprinkled on the ceremonially unclean sanctified those who were only outwardly clean. How much more will the blood of Christ, who through the eternal Spirit offered Himself unblemished to God, cleanse our consciences from acts that lead to death, so that we may live to serve the living God! This is why Christ is the mediator of a new covenant, so that those who are called may receive the promise of an eternal inheritance. Now Christ has died as a ransom, freeing us from our sins committed under the first covenant of the Law. As is the case with a will, it is necessary to prove that the person who wrote the will is dead, since a will can only be enforced after someone has died. This is why the first covenant also could not be put into effect without blood. When Moses had proclaimed the commandments to the people from the Book of the Law, he took the blood of the sacrifice and sprinkled it on the scroll and the people saying, "This is the blood of the covenant that God has commanded for you to keep." In the same manner, Moses sprinkled blood on the tabernacle and the ceremonial utensils. In fact, the Law requires that nearly everything be cleansed with blood, for without the shedding of blood there can be no forgiveness. Christ did not enter heaven to offer Himself again and again, like the high priest did by presenting offerings year after year using blood that was not his own. If that were the case, Christ would have to suffer many times. But He appeared only once, for all people and for all the ages, to remove sin through the sacrifice of Himself. As humankind is destined to die once and then face judgment, so Christ was sacrificed once, to take away the sins of many people. And He will appear a second time, not to bear our sins, but to bring salvation to those who await His return.

Our Father in heaven, who gave His Son for us so that we could be freed from sin and death, thereby becoming acceptable in your sight: we thank you, we praise you, we worship you, we adore you. Thank you for redeeming our souls, and giving us eternal independence from sin and absolute freedom from death; how glorious it will be to live forever with you in a glorified state. Thank you for all the blood that has been shed in the name of true freedom. Let us never take this for granted. And if called upon, help us to be prepared to give our lives for Christ, knowing that death is but a momentary state, after which eternity will be ours. Help us to have the courage to give our lives for others, when their eternal salvation is at stake, knowing that ours is not in question. As Jesus sacrificed Himself for us, let our lives be a living sacrifice for Him and for His church on earth. In the name of Jesus we pray, Amen.

July 5

Sir Isaac Newton Published *Principia* on this day in 1687; the full title in English is *The Mathematical Principles of Natural Philosophy*. By far his most important work, it was a landmark treatise on classical physics. Today we honor Newton and his accomplishments. He explained the laws of interplanetary motion, and the forces acting upon celestial bodies such as gravity, which he believed to be operating in the centripetal and centrifugal forces, that is, the way bodies push and pull on each other through the law of attraction, causing irregular planetary orbits, changing of the tides, as well as keeping bodies from flying off into the atmosphere. Although he arrived at his equations and conclusions from the impetus of his colleagues Halley, Wren, and Hooke, he was the first to layout the mathematical proof of these theories.

Another thing that set Newton apart was his devotion to Christianity. Other famous scientists and physicists who were devout Christians were Boyle, Faraday, Maxwell, Pascal, Kelvin, Heisenberg, and many others. These men are bona fide examples of how science and religion are absolutely compatible. Scientists who follow the religion of atheism would disagree, even though they are examples of science being compatible with their religion (macroevolution). Either way it takes faith, whether you believe there is a God or you believe there is no god. Even agnostics must consider this question, but since they cannot prove it to their own satisfaction, they will not commit one way or another. The question remains, however, how is it that science and the Bible converge on so many truths? Because the book of nature also was written by God; so, it stands to reason that those studying our world and our universe would eventually learn its laws, its order, and its predictability. Similarly, the Bible spells out God's laws, and the natural order which He deliberately put into place to enable us to learn, analyze, define, and prove such laws as planetary motion, thermodynamics, invisible particles, and universal expansion. Interestingly, you can find hints of these phenomena in the Holy Bible.

- GEN 1:14 ~ God said, "Let there be lights in the heavens to divide the day and night, and to be signs and seasons, days and years."

- JOB 26:7 ~ God stretches the north over an empty place and hangs the earth on nothing.

- JOB 38:31 ~ Can you bind the interactions of the Pleiades, or loosen the belt of Orion?

- AMO 5:8 ~ Seek Him who made the Pleiades and Orion, who turns darkness into morning; who brings water from the sea and pours it on the face of the earth. The Lord is His name.

- AMO 9:6 ~ God builds up stories in the heavens and sets the foundation of the earth below…

- ISA 51:6 ~ Lift your eyes to the heavens and look down to the earth, for the heavens will vanish and the earth will wear out like a garment. Those dwelling here will likewise die out. But the salvation of the Lord is forever.

- ROM 1:20 ~ For the invisible qualities of God from the beginning of the world are clearly seen in the things He made, to include His eternal power and Godhead.

- 1 CO 15:40–41 ~ There are celestial bodies and there are terrestrial bodies, and the majesty of one is different than the majesty of the other. Then there is the majesty of the sun, moon, and stars; and each star differs from all the other stars.

- HEB 11:3 ~ Through faith we understand that the worlds were framed by the Word of God, such that things which are seen were made from things that do not appear.

Father, thank you for the means of describing your creation from your Holy Word and from the universe itself, both of which specify rules and laws to follow. In Jesus's name, Amen.

July 6

Sir Thomas More Was Executed for Treason on this day in 1535. He was an educated man: a lawyer, philosopher, Catholic apologist, and a close advisor and companion to King Henry VIII. More was accused of high crimes and executed for not giving his blessing to the king who wanted to exchange his wife for a younger woman. Apparently, corrupt kings and Catholicism did not mix; of course, neither did Catholicism and Protestantism, a battle that More himself was involved in. Should any man of conscience tell a tyrant he is living in sin? This is where we get the ridiculous doctrine against mixing matters of the church with matters of the state. The unsupported tenet is not from any founding document, but it was briefly mentioned in a letter from President Jefferson to a Baptist association, ensuring the freedom to practice their religion in Connecticut, since the "wall of separation between church and state," namely the First Amendment, would forbid the government from interfering with that right.

If you want an example of a bad marriage between church and state, the Thomas More affair is as bad as it gets. Frequently, the result is the death of the person doing the right thing, like when Cain killed his brother Abel. The same happened between John the Baptist and Herod Antipas (MAT 14:1–12). The wicked king was afraid of John who publicly called out the king's adultery and the fact that it was with the wife of his own brother. That evil king of debauchery had the brother's sexy daughter dance for him and his drunken pals for the price of half his kingdom. But her mother wanted John's head instead and told her daughter to ask for that; to avoid embarrassment, Herod gave it to her on a silver platter.

This is what happens when you disallow faith in God to be inserted into important decisions and matters of state. When God is excluded, the kingdom falls; without spiritual guidance, materialism dominates. Remember, you cannot love the world or things of the world and still love God at the same time (LUK 16:13). Likewise, you cannot govern justly and honestly if you are disobeying the will and laws of God.

- JAM 4:4 ~ You are an adulterous people. Do you not know that friendship with the world results in hatred towards God?

- ROM 8:6–8 ~ To set the mind on the flesh results in death, but to set the mind on the Spirit results in life and peace. Because, the carnal mind is enmity against God and will not submit to God's laws, indeed it cannot. Those who are pleasing the flesh cannot please God.

- 1 JO 2:15–16 ~ Do not love the world or worldly things. If a person loves the world, he or she cannot love God. All that is in the world, the lust of the flesh, the greed of the eyes, and the pride of humanity, do not come from the Father but are of this world alone.

The founders knew these things; they allowed prayers, Bible readings, and religious observances to be included into their general order of business, within all three branches of the government. The Ten Commandments still adorns the Supreme Court building, even though they ruled in 2005 that a Kentucky court had to remove them. The exclusion of God from matters of the state means you are getting what the state wants you to have, thereby preventing you from getting what God wants you to have. The best solution is to elect men and women who are not ashamed to proclaim their faith in God, and who will prove it by their decisions and actions.

- EXO 18:21–22 ~ Moses's father-in-law advised him, "Select capable men who fear God, who are trustworthy, and who hate dishonest gain, and appoint them as governors over thousands, hundreds, and tens. Have them serve as judges for the simple cases, so that you can decide the difficult cases."

JULY

- DEU 1:13 ~ Choose wise and respected men of understanding from among you and I will approve them to govern.
- DEU 17:15 ~ You must let the Lord choose your king from among you; do not select an individual who is not your brother in the faith.
- EZR 7:25 ~ Ezra, since you have the wisdom of God, you will select magistrates and judges to govern those beyond the river. They must know the laws of your God, and if they do not, you must teach them.
- JOB 34:17 ~ Shall someone who hates what is right govern others? Can a just person be condemned?
- PRO 29:26–27 ~ Many people seek favor from their rulers, but all judgment comes from God. An unjust person is disgusting to a just person; an upright person is disgusting to an evil person.
- 1 TI 2:2 ~ Pray for your leaders and all who are in authority.
- JAM 4:11 ~ Do not speak evil about someone else. Whoever speaks evil of another or judges them unfairly judges the Law. If you judge the Law, you cannot be adhering to the Law.

If you are a devout Christian, you may be called to witness, and you might not have a choice in the matter. You must tell the truth, knowing some people won't like hearing it; for the worst enemy of a corrupt government is an honest and godly patriot. It was honest Christian patriots that won our independence; despite their flaws, they trusted in the providence of God. Have you observed the increasing number of politicians professing their faith in God to garner votes, but when elected they push agendas that are clearly unrighteous? For example, the Supreme Court's ruling allowing gay marriage goes against God's Law and is not even within their purview to decide. Like abortion, it is the right of states to legislate such things. God does not hate or discriminate against homosexuals, and Christians don't either. But God instituted marriage to join one man and one woman, and for raising godly children. Sex outside of marriage is adultery.

- PSA 12:8 ~ The wicked are all around when vile men are exalted.
- PRO 29:12 ~ If a ruler listens to lies, his entire cabinet will be evil.
- MAT 10:19–20 ~ When they capture you, do not worry about what to say, for the words will be given to you by the Holy Spirit. Thus, it will not be you speaking, but the Almighty Father speaking through you.
- ACT 5:22–29 ~ When the authorities commanded the apostles to stop preaching in the name of Jesus they replied, "We must obey God rather than men."
- REV 2:10 ~ Jesus said, "Do not be afraid of suffering and tribulation, for the devil will throw some of you into prison to test your faith, and you will be tormented for ten days. Be faithful, even unto death, and I will give you a crown of life."

Heavenly Father, help us to be faithful unto death, always looking forward to a time when death will not exist. Lord, help us never to deny you, but to confess you no matter the consequences. Help us to elect people into office who will obey your laws and the laws of the land; help those leaders to appoint people who likewise are obedient to God and accurately interpret and execute the law. Help our government to be honest about the separation of church and state and how it is not smart to separate God from anything, including who should govern and how it must be done; for there is no contrary doctrine spelled out in any of our laws or founding documents. We cherish our right to worship in any manner that does not violate the rights of others. Please do not allow those in power to misinterpret the laws or alter any of our rights. In Jesus's name, Amen.

July 7

International Forgiveness Day is recognized annually to pardon someone who hurt you. Actually, we should be forgiving people as often as they offend us. Forgiveness is an act of kindness whereby we let go of resentment and move on with life; forgiveness is a gift, and as such, requires nothing in return. While forgiveness does not absolve anyone from guilt or consequences, it allows us to leave judgment and punishment to God and/or the legal system. It is not our place to judge as we ourselves are guilty (see MAT 7:1–2; MAT 6:14–15; COL 3:12–13). Hence, forgiveness is a process that heals, especially the forgiver. Almost all world religions practice forgiveness as an act of faith and contrition, so the international sentiment of a global day for forgiveness is appealing as it can advance peace and harmony across cultures.

Today we set aside our differences and establish a new beginning. Dump the emotional baggage to include hatred, anger, bitterness, and grudges. Did you know that scientific evidence confirms that people who forgive are happier, more well-adjusted, and heathier mentally and physically? Conversely, people that hang onto the negativity are less healthy and happy. This is because they get stuck on the memory of the event or person, making it difficult to think positive or move forward, because the intrusive thought keeps interfering with their progress. If you let go of the resentment it will lighten the load enabling you to progress more rapidly. Forgiveness enables you to dispose of the emotional baggage and lighten the load; so, regardless of whether the person cares that you have forgiven them or not, you will feel better.

- MIC 7:18 ~ Who is like you, God, who pardons sin and ignores the evil done by your people? God does not stay angry forever, but finds pleasure in giving mercy.
- MAT 6:14–15; MAR 11:25–26 ~ Jesus said, "If you forgive others, your heavenly Father will forgive you. If you do not forgive others, your heavenly Father will not forgive you."
- MAT 18:18, 21–22 ~ Jesus said, "Whatever you tie on earth will be tied in heaven, and whatever you untie on earth will be untied in heaven." Then Peter asked Jesus, "How many times should I forgive someone who has done wrong to me? Seven times?" Jesus answered, "Not seven times, but seventy-seven times."
- ACT 13:38 ~ Through Jesus Christ all people can receive the forgiveness of sins.
- JAM 5:9 ~ Do not grumble against one another, brothers, so you will not be judged; behold, the Judge is standing at the door.

Resentment is a process that begins with an event, perceived as an offense but oftentimes, was not deliberate. But when the hurtful thoughts enter the mind, it manages to seep into the heart; this destroys peace of mind and hardens the heart. Understand that the precipitating event and the people involved are not what is causing the resentment; it is the individual's belief about the event. That belief is usually based on incomplete information and truly could be wrong. People get wrapped up in their own issues and are seldom acting out because of others; they are acting out because of what is going on inside of them. Maybe they are just having a bad day and you happened to be a convenient target for their emotions. But once it becomes personal for someone, they get stuck; they are unable to forget about it. Instead, they seethe, and anger swells, which could lead to greater evils like hatred or the desire for revenge. But you never get even by lashing out in these circumstances; all you do is tip the scales in your direction. The only way you'll ever get even is to let go, which evens the score (Barber, 2016). Let go of the past and enjoy the present.

- LEV 19:18 ~ You shall not take vengeance or bear a grudge against the sons of your own people, but you shall love your neighbor as yourself, for I am the Lord.

JULY

- JOB 9:20 ~ If I justify myself, my own mouth will have condemned me. If I say I am perfect, then I have proven myself to be perverse.

- PRO 14:17 ~ A man of quick temper acts foolishly, and a man of evil devices is hated.

- PRO 15:1, 18 ~ A soft answer turns away wrath, but a harsh word stirs up anger… A hot-tempered man stirs up strife, but he who is slow to anger quiets contention.

- PRO 26:24–28 ~ The hater disguises himself with his lips but harbors deceit in his heart; if he speaks graciously, do not believe him, for there are seven abominations in his heart. Though his hatred may be covered with deception, his wickedness will be exposed to the assembly.

- ECC 7:9 ~ Do not hasten in your spirit to become angry, for anger lodges in the heart of fools.

- MAT 6:14–15 ~ Jesus said, "For if you forgive others their trespasses, your heavenly Father will also forgive you, but if you do not forgive others their trespasses, neither will your Father forgive your trespasses."

- EPH 4:26–27 ~ When angry, do not sin; do not let the sun go down on your anger. Give no opportunity to the devil.

Forgiveness also is a process; it's not like you snap your fingers and the resentment is gone. The first step is to challenge your belief that someone offended you on purpose or that the event was otherwise personal. Chances are, it was none of those things. But even if someone did purposefully offend you, it's not going to kill you; and offending them back will only turn you into them: offensive. Everyone is guilty of sin, and therefore, guilty of offending others. It is not our place to judge their heart, but to examine our own heart. After some analysis you may realize it was not that big a deal, certainly not a reason to let it ruin your whole day, or worse. An assessment enables you to entertain other reasons for their behavior: stuff happens, it wasn't on purpose, or it wasn't a catastrophe. This results in a change of mind; instead of going down the path of resentment you reverse course and head down the path of forgiveness. You have a choice as to how big or small you choose to make it. Eventually, you reach acceptance after which you can let go and get going. Time will tell if reconciliation is possible, if you even know the person to whom your resentment was directed. Get into the habit of challenging beliefs and you might find them to be untenable. Incidentally, it is okay and necessary to forgive yourself.

- PSA 130:3–4 ~ If you, Oh Lord, should mark iniquities, O Lord, who could stand? But with you there is forgiveness, that you may be feared.

- LUK 6:37 ~ Jesus said, "If you do not judge others, you will not be judged. If you do not condemn others, you will not be condemned."

- LUK 17:3–4 ~ Jesus said, "If someone sins against you, reprimand them. If they repent, forgive them. If they sin against you seven times in one day, and repent each time, then forgive them seven times."

- EPH 4:32 ~ Be kind to each other, tenderhearted, and forgiving, even as God for Christ's sake has forgiven you.

Gracious and forgiving Father, teach us to forgive others and let go of all resentment. On this day and every day, let us end the day with forgiveness so we can wake up refreshed. And whenever we feel offended, help us to remember that people were offended by Jesus also; and we have Jesus in our hearts so we can expect people to be offended at us for speaking the truth and professing our faith. Remind us that we are yours as we deflect offenses and forgive, even as Jesus forgave those who nailed Him to the cross. In His precious name we pray, Amen.

July 8

American Psychological Association Formed on this day in 1892 when a few dozen professionals met at Clark University at the behest of its President, Professor Stanley Hall, the first American to earn a PhD in psychology. The field of psychology was fairly new but rapidly grew, branching out into many disciplines. The word psychology comes from the Greek word *psyche*, meaning soul; it is literally, the study of the soul or mind. I became interested in psychology as an art student needing to fulfill a requirement in the humanities; a friend and I took *Abnormal Psychology*, not knowing anything about it. It was difficult, but I liked it anyway, so after my art degree I pursued a master degree in educational psychology, eventually obtaining a PhD in psychology. I became a research psychologist; a professor of psychology, counseling, and religion; a psychotherapist in private practice; and a clinician and administrator at a psychiatric hospital. Needless to say, I made a career of it, which is why this topic is of particular interest to me. Considered a "hard" science, there are many in the field of psychology who are atheists or otherwise reject religion of any kind. I would call them hard-headed. I have found psychology and Christianity to be quite compatible. I mean, how can you separate the soul from the spirit? Only God can do that; and if that happens to you, it means you are dead.

- PSA 86:4, 13 ~ Gladden my soul, oh Lord, for to you I lift up my soul. For great is your steadfast love toward me; you have delivered my soul from the depths of hell.

- ECC 12:7 ~ Upon death, the spirit returns to God who gave it.

- MAT 16:26 ~ Jesus said, "What does it profit a person who gains the world but loses his soul. What can a person give in return for his soul?"

- JOH 6:63 ~ Jesus said, "It is the spirit that gives life, not the flesh."

- HEB 4:12 ~ The Word of God is quick and powerful. It is sharper than any double-edged sword, piercing deep, even to divide the soul and spirit, and the joints and marrow. The Word discerns the thoughts and intents of the heart.

- HEB 6:19 ~ We have Jesus as a sure and steadfast anchor for our souls.

The holistic health paradigm proposes that one must be healthy in body, mind, and spirit to be complete or whole. Psychologists deal primarily with the mental component, often ignoring the importance of spiritual health, which can be linked to mental health problems as much as physical ailments are. Consider love: spiritual, mental, and physical love are quite different but spiritual love (*agape*) is the most powerful. The Spirit of God living in us is manifested through His love. The power of darkness and the demonic is fear. There is no fear in love, because love is magnitudes more powerful than fear. Anxiety and worry are types of fear. The Holy Spirit of love conquers that fear, and teaches us to listen to our conscience rather than the world.

- 1 JO 4:18 ~ There is no fear in love, but perfect love casts out fear, because fear has torment. Those who fear are not made perfect in love.

What does a hopeless person need more than hope? What does a doubting person need more than faith? What does an anxious person need more than peace? What does a depressed person need more than joy? These feelings can be considered mental and spiritual, for they are felt in the spirit and experienced in the soul. The negative things listed above can be conquered by the positive ones, which are opposite in feeling and in thought. Thus, the ones which bring you up (hope, peace, love, joy) are more powerful than the ones which drag you down (despair, worry, fear, depression). Higher powers such as these come from the highest power: God. Each one of us can choose to receive this power and grow, or let the opposing power take us down.

Getting your higher power in control of your thoughts is a major step in twelve step programs such as treatment for alcoholism, as well as most psychological problems. Not that you cannot make progress and succeed without God, just that it is done more expediently with Him. We need the spirit inside us to dominate our thoughts and not allow desires of the flesh to win, for they are at odds. One is of the world; one is of God. Follow the world and you lose your soul; follow God and you keep it, and live in an incorruptible glorified body that will never see death.

- MAT 10:28 ~ Jesus said, "Do not fear anyone who can kill your body but not your soul; fear the One who can destroy both your body and your soul in hell."

- LUK 21:17–19 ~ Jesus said, "People will hate you because of me, but be patient and you will keep your soul."

- 1 CO 15:42–44, 50–54 ~ This is the resurrection: a corrupt body was sown, but an incorruptible body is raised. It was sown in dishonor but raised in honor. It was sown a physical body but raised a spiritual body. Flesh and blood cannot inherit the kingdom of God; neither can corruption inherit incorruption. A mystery is revealed: we will not all die but all will be changed. Upon His return, in a single moment as the great trumpet sounds, Christ's own whether alive or dead will arise into heaven to receive new, incorruptible bodies. The corruptible must become incorruptible before the mortal can become immortal. Then the statement "death is swallowed up in victory" will be true.

- 1 PE 1:22–23 ~ You have purified your soul by obeying the truth through the Spirit, and by fervently loving one another with a pure heart. You have been born again, not of corruptible seed but of incorruptible, by the Word of God which lives and abides forever.

The higher powers listed above are referred to in the Bible as spiritual gifts, or fruits of the spirit. Tap into these powers, for you have been given them by God and need only to accept them as gifts. Once connected with the Holy Spirit, you will know how to act. Psychological problems are often the result of imbalances in homeostasis or brain chemistry. Consequently, not being wholly healthy in body, mind, and/or spirit can lower your level of functioning overall.

- ISA 1:18–19 ~ Come now, and let us reason together, says the Lord. Though your sins be as scarlet they will be white as snow; though they be red like crimson, they will be as wool. If you are willing and obedient, you will eat the good of the land.

- GAL 5:18, 22–23 ~ If you are led by the Spirit, you are not under the Law. The fruits of the Spirit include love, joy, peace, patience, kindness, gentleness, goodness, self-control, and faith. Against these things, there is no law

- EPH 4:32 ~ Be kind to each other, tender-hearted, and forgiving, even as God for Christ's sake has forgiven you.

- EPH 5:8–12 ~ You were once in darkness, but now you are in the light of the Lord. Live as children of light and discover what pleases the Lord, for the fruit of the light consists of goodness, righteousness, and truth. Have nothing to do with the fruitless deeds of darkness, but rather expose them. For it is shameful to even mention what the disobedient do in secret.

Father, we pray that we may be healthy body, mind, and spirit; let us be diligent in exercising all three so we can better serve you and function at our highest level. Help us to tap into the higher power within us, which is your Word living in our hearts, to do your will and to perform our best, and to overpower the negativity with positive energy. Empower us with your Holy Spirit, enlighten us with His truth, and save us in the name of Jesus, your only Son, Amen.

July 9

Avoid the Occult Day is to give fair warning from God that occultist activity is akin to idolatry and violates the first two of the Ten Commandments. The word occult means different things to different people, so we will go with the dictionary definition. As a verb it means to occlude, hide, or block out; and in the case of the occult, it is God being blocked out and evil being unmasked. As a noun, it means the practice of the supernatural, to include wizardry, sorcery, astrology, witchcraft, voodoo, spiritism, and the like. What it does not include is worship of God Almighty. All occultist practices are an invitation to demonic spirits of darkness. Beware of games, toys, objects, idols, websites, and people when there is a suggestion or hint of an underlying evil.

- LEV 19:31 ~ Do not confide in mediums or wizards, or be defiled by them.

- DEU 18:10–12 ~ Do not sacrifice your children. Do not practice fortunetelling, divination, calling upon the dead, or sorcery. Do not be a medium, charmer, or wizard. Whoever does these things will be condemned by God.

- ISA 8:19 ~ When others suggest that you seek those with familiar spirits [fallen angels or demons] reply, "Should we not seek God and the living instead of the dead?"

- ISA 47:10–14 ~ You felt secure in your wickedness. But evil shall come upon you and disaster will befall you. So, stand fast in your enchantments, sorceries, and counsels. Let them save you, those who gaze at the stars, divide the heavens, and predict what will happen to you according to the new moon. Fire will consume them and you.

- 2 CO 11:3, 12–15 ~ Even as the serpent deceived Eve by his cunning, so he will attempt to lead you astray from devotion to the true Christ. I will try to undermine those who claim and boast that theirs is a mission of God like ours. They are false prophets, deceitful workers, disguising themselves as apostles of Christ. No wonder, because Satan also disguises himself as an angel of light, so it is not strange that his servants disguise themselves as servants of righteousness. Their end will correspond to their deeds.

- EPH 6:10–12 ~ Put on the armor of the Lord to stand against the wiles of the devil. For we are not contending against flesh and blood, but against principalities, powers, rulers of darkness, and evil spirits.

The Bible speaks of false prophets in both testaments of the Holy Bible. In the latter days, there will be a proliferation of them. After Samuel the prophet died, King Saul was lost, so he consulted a medium hoping to conger the spirit of Samuel, but all he got was a curse from a demon instead (1 SA 16:14–23). Those telling lies in the name of spirituality and truth are themselves working for the devil. They are known as antichrists because their truth is false and their doctrine works against Jesus Christ. Anyone who claims to speak for God and denies the truth of the Bible is a false teacher; do not listen to them, but consult God and His Word to prove if their claims are supported or not. People who purport to know the future because God told them in a revelation are mistaken; because God's revelation about the future already exists in His Word, telling us what to expect; any prophecy going beyond that will be proven false in time.

- DEU 18:20–22 ~ If a prophet presumes to speak on my behalf when I have not directed them to do so, or speaks in the name of other gods, he or she will die. If people wonder how they will know if a prophecy comes from the Lord, they simply can observe if the words spoken by the prophet come true or not. Do not be afraid of a prophet who speaks presumptuously.

- ISA 44:25 ~ God proves the false prophets to be liars and fools, causing their prophecies to be invalid.

JULY

- JER 14:14 ~ False prophets tell lies in my name; I did not send them, command them, or speak to them. They receive false visions and make false predictions from the deceit of their lying hearts.

- LAM 2:14 ~ Your prophets have said foolish things and seen false visions. They have not pointed out to you your sins but rather have told you that everything is fine.

- MAT 7:15, 21–23 ~ Jesus said, "Beware of false prophets; they are like wolves disguised as sheep. Not everyone who acts righteous or appears to be so, is righteous."

- ACT 20:30 ~ From among yourselves will come those speaking perverse things to gain followers.

- COL 2:8, 18–19 ~ Beware of those who would lead you astray with their errant philosophies and vain deceptions, following traditions fashioned by the world and not Christ. Do not let anyone swindle you out of your reward. Beware of those who practice false humility and worship angels. They claim to have seen things, but they have filled their unspiritual and arrogant minds with silly notions.

- 2 TH 2:9–11 ~ Those false signs and fake miracles come from Satan. Such deceptions belong to the self-righteous who will die, for they did not believe the truth that could save them. God will let them believe their lies and perish.

- 1 TI 4:1 ~ Some will depart from the faith by recognizing evil spirits and demons.

- 2 TI 3:13 ~ Evil people and false teachers will get worse, deceiving many; they themselves have been deceived by Satan.

- 2 PE 2:1–3, 14, 18–20 ~ False prophets come bringing damnable heresies, denying the Lord, and deceiving many. They will exploit you with false words and attract you with lusts of the flesh. They have eyes full of adultery, insatiable for sin. Their hearts are greedy, and they gain through dishonesty. They promise freedom but are themselves slaves to corruption, and are condemned. They will get perpetually worse.

- 1 JO 2:18 ~ You have heard that the antichrist comes, and many will.

- 1 JO 4:1–3 ~ Do not believe every spirit, but test them to determine if they are really of God; for many false prophets have gone out into the world. Every spirit that confesses that Jesus Christ is God in the flesh is of God. Those who do not confess that Jesus is of God are not of God; they are spirits of the antichrist, who you heard is coming and is already here.

- JDE 1:4 ~ False teachers have infiltrated the churches, claiming that once you become Christians you can do whatever you want without being punished. They deny the Lord and turn God's grace into lust.

Idolatry, simply put, is the worship of idols or false gods. God alone is worthy of your worship. Other forms of idolatry include self-worship, idolizing famous people or characters as if divine, revering graven images or material possessions, praying or bowing to a person or a thing regardless of who they claim to represent. Only Jesus represents God on earth, and His Holy Spirit who is always with us. Why pray to or worship anyone but God, for can a mortal human, an animal, or a thing save you? Remember what happened to the Israelites who worshipped the golden calf? They all died in the desert, except children under twenty, and Joshua and Caleb (EXO 32—34).

- EXO 20:4–7 ~ Do not make graven images or idols resembling animals or any other creatures. Never bow to an idol or image, or worship it in any way, for God is a jealous God and will not tolerate false gods, punishing those who hate Him for generations, but showing love for a

DAILY DEVOTIONAL EVENTS

thousand generations to those who love Him and keep His commandments. Never use the name of God in vain or swear a falsehood in His name, or you will be found guilty.

- DEU 5:8–9 ~ Never make graven images. Do not worship idols. Do not bow before any idols or worship them in any way.

- JOB 31:26–28 ~ If my heart was enticed by worldly things and celestial bodies, or if I was infatuated with myself, I would be guilty of denying God and worthy of His punishment.

- PSA 16:4 ~ Sorrows will be multiplied for those who hurry after another god. I do not offer the things that they offer; I do not even speak their names.

- PSA 97:7 ~ Those who serve graven images or brag about their idols are confused. Everyone must worship God alone.

- ISA 44:9–11 ~ Only fools would create their own gods and idols.

- ACT 17:29 ~ Do not think of God as an idol made from wood, metal, or stone.

Whenever secrecy or exclusion is introduced into a gathering of people with the purpose of engaging in a spiritual ritual or activity, turn away and do not look back. Christians worship God openly and publicly. God does not keep secrets, He reveals them. Everything we need to know about God and His works, promises, and truth can be found in His Word. If a spiritual truth is not found in the Bible it is because we do not have a need to know, at least not now.

- DAN 2:28 ~ There is a God in heaven who reveals mysteries.

- MAT 10:26–27; LUK 12:3 ~ Jesus said, "Do not fear those who hate you, for everything that is hidden now will be revealed later; everything that is unknown will become known. What I tell you in darkness you will speak in the light. What you hear in private will be proclaimed from the rooftops."

- MAT 13:35 ~ It was prophesied that Christ would talk in parables and would explain secrets that were hidden since the beginning of time.

- JOH 18:20 ~ Jesus said, "What I teach is widely known; I have preached it openly and often in church. Everyone, including the Jewish leaders, has heard what I teach. I teach nothing in private that I have not said in public."

- ROM 16:25–26 ~ Christ has the power to save you according to the revelation of God's mystery, which was kept secret since the world began, but which is now evident by the scriptures. According to God's will, the mystery is made known to all nations on earth for the obedience of faith.

- 2 CO 4:2 ~ We apostles have renounced hidden and shameful ways; we do not engage in deception and we do not distort the Word of God. We appeal to those who have a conscience in the sight of God.

- EPH 5:12 ~ It is shameful to even speak about the evil they do in secret.

Blessed Father, we pray for truth, wisdom, and understanding of your words, works, and ways; help us to use that knowledge to uncover lies, expose charlatans, and undermine works of Satan, demons, and occultists. Only you, Lord has all the answers to our questions, reveals mysteries that were hidden, and unveils the truth whenever we search diligently for it through prayer and Bible study. We love you we adore you; we worship you we believe you; we praise you and only you, Father, Son, and Holy Spirit. In the name of Jesus, Amen.

July 10

Be Still My Soul Day is proposed this day for finding your inner peace. We all experience turmoil in our lives, sometimes for days on end. How can we face these troubles and still maintain the peace which surpasses all understanding?

- PHP 4:6–7 ~ Do not have anxiety about anything, but pray for everything. With thanksgiving let your requests be known to God. And the peace of God which surpasses all understanding will keep your heart in mind in Jesus Christ.

Have you been restless inside where you can't sit still? Have you felt overwhelmed with current or future events, or maybe hung-up on past ones? Do you wake up at night worrying about stuff that you can't do anything about until morning? Do your thoughts race through your head like it's the Indianapolis 500? Yeah, me too. We all get agitated and impatient sometimes. This also was the case for many Biblical figures. Take David, a man after God's own heart (ACT 13:22), who was often unsettled within his heart and soul. The anointed king spent a great part of his life on the run from his enemies. When he was disquieted in his soul, he turned to the only source of solace available, the Lord God. This uneasiness is evident in many of his psalms when he sought the loving arms of His Father in heaven.

- PSA 4:4 ~ Stand in awe, and sin not. Commune with your own heart upon your bed, and be still. Offer the sacrifices of righteousness, and put your trust in the Lord.

- PSA 42:11; PSA 43:5 ~ Why are you cast down, oh my soul? Why are you unsettled within me? Hope in God, and praise Him. He is my God, the health of my soul.

- PSA 46:1–2, 8–10 ~ God is our refuge and strength, a very present help in trouble. Therefore, we will not fear, though the earth be removed or the mountains be thrown into the midst of the sea. Come, behold the works of the Lord, what desolations He has made in the earth. He makes wars to cease, He breaks the bow and the spear in two, and burns the chariot in the fire. Be still, and know that I am God. I will be exalted among the heathen; I will be exalted in the earth.

- PSA 107:27–30 ~ They reel to-and-fro, staggering like a drunkard, and at their wit's end. Then they cry to the Lord in their trouble and He brings them out of their distress. He calms the storm and makes the waves still. Then they are happy because they are quiet, while He brings them into their desired haven.

- PSA 131:1–3 ~ Lord, my heart is not arrogant nor my eyes lofty; neither do I exercise myself in grandiose matters or in things too high for me. I have behaved and quieted myself, as a child weaned by his mother; my soul is like a weaned child. Let Israel hope in the Lord from henceforth, even forevermore.

Don't you feel troubled in your heart at times, even to your very soul? Who doesn't? We have challenges and setbacks and we want to get them over with. But they will pass soon enough so why do we worry endlessly? Does worrying do anyone any good? Apparently not according to Jesus (MAT 6:34). But anxiety and stress seem to be a frequent state of mind for the whole of humanity. However, God is always there to comfort us (2 CO 1:3; HEB 13:5). And no matter what happens, we are guaranteed salvation of our souls, as we look forward to our inheritance of eternal bliss and peace. While our minds are restless, we can find rest in the Lord, and He will calm our nerves and give us peace of mind (MAT 11:28).

- JOB 21:22–26 ~ Will anyone teach God knowledge seeing how He judges at the highest level? One man dies in his full strength, being wholly quiet and at ease; his body is nourished and his bones strong. Another man dies in bitterness of soul, and never eats with enjoyment. They will both lie down in the dust, covered by worms.

- PRO 1:33 ~ Whoever calls to me will live safely, and will be quiet from fear of evil.
- ISA 30:15 ~ The sovereign Lord of host says, "In repentance and rest you will be saved; in quietness and trust you will find strength. But you refused it."
- ISA 32:17–18 ~ The effect of righteousness will be peace, and the result of righteousness, calmness and assurance forever. My people will abide in a peaceful habitation, in secure dwellings, and in quiet resting places.

Remember when Jesus calmed the storm? His disciples were wrought with fear by the raging storm and violent waves, while Jesus slept. They roused Him out of His slumber believing they were about to die. And with an authoritative voice Jesus said, "Peace, be still." Immediately there was calm (MAR 4:39). The disciples were even more afraid of Jesus, saying amongst themselves, "What manner of man is this, that even the wind and the waves obey Him?" (MAR 4:41). Well, at least they got it right as to whom they should fear, and it certainly was not natural events or persons (MAT 10:28).

Our focus should be on Jesus, not the raging storm. It is relatedly important to look to the inward self and not dwell on external situations or appearances. What is going on outside of you is not as significant as what is going on inside of you. That is, you are responsible for how you think, feel, and react which need not be unduly influenced by others or by circumstances. Such is life, but how we respond should be spiritually focused; it is counterproductive to have the emotional or physical reaction dominating our thoughts. We have the power of the Holy Spirit living inside of us, so what can the world throw at us that we should be afraid? Does God not promise to give us everything we need (PSA 23)?

- 1 TH 4:11–12 ~ Study to be quiet and to mind your own business, and to work with your own hands as we have told you, so that you may gain the respect of others while depending on nobody.
- 1 TI 2:1–2 ~ I encourage you to offer supplications, prayers, intercessions, and giving of thanks for all people, including rulers and all who are in authority, so that you can live a quiet and undisturbed life in godliness and honesty.
- 1 PE 3:4 ~ Tap into your inner self, where resides the beautiful heart of a humble and quiet spirit, which is of great value in the eyes of God.

The soul is your inner self, which knows what is right, recognizes truth, and will be cleansed of sin by the blood of Christ, if you want (PSA 103:1–5). God will bless your soul by purifying it, and in that state it will remain, once you begin trusting in Him. When we are troubled into the depths of our souls, we are letting the world get in the way of the Way of God, obscuring the path to righteousness. Everything in the world will pass (REV 21:1–5), and none of it is too complicated for God to turn into good. Your distress is in vain; pain, anxiety, and sorrow will be done away with, because the price is already paid and your future is guaranteed.

You must look beyond the hurdles to see the finish line. No matter how long it takes for you to complete the race, you can be comforted in the knowledge that a crown awaits. There is only one first prize: all who choose Christ will receive a crown of life. This is a spiritual crown, where the heads of God's faithful are adorned by the righteousness of Christ; meanwhile, all worldly crowns will be thrown down at His feet (PSA 72:11; REV 4:10–11). Persevere with the intention of winning that crown of life; dispense with pursuing worldly crowns that distract you.

- PSA 146:1–2 ~ Praise the Lord oh my soul. As long as I live, I will praise the Lord for the duration of my being.

- 2 TI 4:7–8 ~ I have fought the good fight, finished my course, and kept the faith. Henceforth, a crown of righteousness awaits, which the Lord the righteous judge will present to me. And not only to me but also to anyone who loves His appearing.

Many renditions can be found for the famous hymn, "Be Still My Soul" which translated into modern English explains how we should believe God in order to receive the rest and peace He promises. He is our shield, our strength, and our comforter; His Holy Spirit abides with us always (MAT 18:20). Isn't it curious how we know the peace that surpasses all understanding but are quickly sidetracked by incidents, people, and society? How nice it would be to see the hoard of angels protecting us, if not the Spirit of God Himself; in which case it would be very hard to become preoccupied with the physical world. But you must look with your spirit to visualize it. We get preoccupied with worldly tests every day, not remaining mindful that God is right here.

- 2 KI 6:17 ~ Elisha prayed, "Lord, open my friend's eyes." And the man saw that the mountain was covered with horses and chariots of fire all around them.

- PSA 34:7 ~ The angel of the Lord encamps with those who fear God, and will deliver them.

- HEB 1:14; HEB 13:2 ~ Are there not ministering angels sent forth to assist those who are heirs of salvation? Do not forget to be hospitable to others, for you might be entertaining angels unawares.

I worked in the field of behavioral health for decades. It is obvious that anxiety and depression are the most prevailing symptoms. These are, of course, states of mind. Unlike personality traits that are quite resistant to change, emotional states are temporal; they come and they go. For some, those feelings may linger, developing into mental problems that necessitate therapy and medication. Of course, a spoonful of God's love works better than any clinical intervention, which is why I incorporated spirituality into my practice. Not surprisingly, clients got better faster when they agreed to spiritual goals being included in the treatment plan. In short, the more mindful we are of God's presence in our lives, the lower our stress level; that is, the stress occurs less often and is less severe. This is not rocket science, but it is scriptural. Do not lose heart (PRO 4:23; LUK 18:18), for someday you will see God (JOB 19:26; MAT 5:8).

- PSA 55:22 ~ Cast your burden on the Lord for He will sustain the righteous; He will never let them down.

- PSA 94:19 ~ Among the troubling thoughts within my soul, I find delight in your comfort.

- ISA 41:10 ~ Do not fear for I am with you; do not be dismayed. I am your God and I will strengthen you; yes, I will help you and uphold you with the right hand of my righteousness.

- MAT 6:34 ~ Take no thought of tomorrow for it will take care of itself. Sufficient to every day is the evil therein.

- JOH 14:27~ Jesus said, "Peace I leave you, my peace I give you. I do not give as the world gives so let not your heart be troubled neither let it be afraid."

- 2 CO 4:15–18 ~ Everything is for your sake, that the abundant grace of God through our giving of thanks might rebound, reflecting His glory. For such a cause we do not faint or lose heart; while outwardly we are inundated, inwardly we are renewed daily. Our menial troubles are building an eternal fortune in glory. We do not look upon things that are seen but that which is not seen; things you can see are temporal but those you cannot see are eternal.

- 1 PE 5:6–7 ~ Humble yourselves under the mighty hand of God, so He might exalt you in due time. Cast your cares upon Him, for He cares mightily about you.

It all boils down to patience, waiting until the right time; because God's timing is perfect. We either want it now when we are not ready, or we want to put it off when it is already in front of us. If we try to force the issue or if we try to avoid it, it will not go away until it's the right time; and when it has passed and no longer a threat, we wonder why we worried so much about it in the first place, especially since it is seldom what we expected. So, wait and see what happens and you probably will be pleasantly surprised; either way, you will be less disappointed.

- PSA 37:7–10 ~ Rest in the Lord and wait patiently for Him. Do not fret about people who prosper in wickedness. Refrain from anger and forsake your rage. Do not succumb to evil of any kind. For evildoers will be cut off. But those who wait upon the Lord will inherit the world. In a little while the wicked will no longer exist; you will not find them anywhere.
- PSA 130:5–6 ~ I wait for the Lord, my soul waits; and in His Word I will hope. My soul waits for the Lord more than those who watch for the morning.
- LAM 3:26 ~ It is good for one to hope quietly and wait patiently for the Lord's salvation.
- ISA 40:31 ~ Those who wait upon the Lord will renew their strength. They will mount up with wings like eagles. They will run and not grow weary; they will walk and never faint.
- ROM 8:25 ~ If we hope for what we do not have we must patiently wait for it.
- ROM 12:12 ~ Rejoice in hope, be patient in tribulation, be constant in prayer.

Did you recognize the spiritual gifts mentioned in this lesson which will help you overcome thoughts like despair, depression, disappointment, and dejection? Spiritual treasures are readily available to everybody, provided free via the Holy Spirit. Here are the aforementioned gifts listed alphabetically so as not to imply that any one is less important or necessary: calmness, comfort, faith, godliness, godly fear, honesty, hope, humility, joy, love, mindfulness, patience, peacefulness, praise, prayer, quietness, rejoicing, repentance, restfulness, righteousness, stillness, trust. If you want to feel at ease within your soul tap into your higher powers, all of which you already possess, you merely have to employ them. They will conquer the negativity and replace it with positivity because they come from God and are greater in power than their opposite; for example, peace conquers anxiety and mindfulness conquers uncertainty.

Simply put, think positive. How do we do that? Think on the spiritual fruit itemized above (PHP 4:8). Do not dwell on things that can bring you down; focus on things which can lift you up, because they are true. Place truth at the top of your list of uplifting things, whereas anything that does not comport with it will result in adversity. And what is truth if not the Holy Spirit Himself (JOH 14:16–17; JOH 16:13)? So, walk in it (PSA 86:11), and do not let the world obscure your vision of the path to heaven (JOH 14:6). Do not fear the truth, embrace it.

Dear Father, please give us peace of mind. Though the world might be filled with trials, turmoil, and tragedy, let us use these opportunities to praise and thank you, and invite your Holy Spirit the Comforter, to comfort our souls and lead us through these dark and dreary episodes of life. Make us mindful of the truth and open our eyes to the right decision. Jesus said, "My peace I leave you, my peace I give you; not as the world gives do I give. Let not your heart be troubled, neither let it be afraid." Help us to keep these words close to our hearts so that we can have peace and calm on the inside when everything outside of us appears to be in chaos. By the power of the Holy Spirit and in the name of Jesus we pray, Amen.

July 11

Cheer Up the Lonely Day has become an international phenomenon, though the origin of this observance is uncertain. Today is for spreading hope and joy to people who are alone, stranded, shut-in, hospitalized, having a rough time, or just a new face experiencing a new place. Those especially needing our tender loving care are the elderly, for they are the most neglected of any group of people. Take time today to cheer someone up, with a letter, greeting card, phone call, or personal visit; an email or text is not personal enough to convey the attention they need. Invite them to your house or for an outing; take them for a scenic drive; walk with them; or sit with them and peruse photo albums. Share yourself with them, for there will come a time when you are lonely and would appreciate a familiar face or a loving smile. Remember people who have remembered you in your time of despair or loneliness. Loneliness is one of the primary causes of depression in the world, not to mention fear and worry. If you are lonely, talk to someone who cares enough to be trusted with your feelings. The best cure for loneliness is companionship.

- PRO 18:24 ~ A person who has friends should act friendly; and there is a type of friend who is like a brother.

    The top companion anyone can have for every day and age is the Holy Spirit. Just as Jesus is our Immanuel, meaning God with us, so also is the Holy Spirit always with us now and forever. I often have thought how amazing it must have been to be a companion of Jesus, but there was a substantial price to pay for that honor. Since we have the companionship of the Holy Spirit, there may be a weighty price for acknowledging Him as well (MAT 24:9). For the world is in enmity against God (JAM 4:4); and since we are not of the world, because God has chosen us out of the world, the world will hate us too (MAT 10:22; JOH 15:18).

- DEU 31:6–8 ~ Be strong and of good courage; do not fear or be dismayed. For the Lord God goes with you; He will never fail you or forsake you. Moses told Joshua in front of the nation of Israel that God would be leading them into the promised land, and that God would always be with Joshua to secure their inheritance. The Lord will go before you and with you; He will never fail or forsake you, so do not be dismayed.

- 1 SA 12:22 ~ God will not forsake His people for His great namesake, because it has pleased the Lord to make you His own people.

- JOS 1:9 ~ God said, "Did I not command you to be strong and have courage, and not to be afraid or dismayed? For I am with you wherever you go."

- PSA 23:4 ~ Even when I walk through the valley of the shadow of death, I will not be afraid of any evil, for God will be with me to comfort me.

- PSA 27:1–2, 10 ~ The Lord is my light and my salvation. Who should I fear? He is the strength in my life. Of whom shall I be afraid? Even if a whole encampment of my enemies is preparing war against me, I will not be afraid, but confident. Even if my parents abandon me, the Lord will hold me up.

- ISA 41:10 ~ God says, "Fear not, for I am with you. Do not be dismayed, for I am your God. I will strengthen and help you. I will hold you up with the right hand of righteousness."

- MAT 28:20 ~ Jesus said, "I am with you always, even until the end of time."

- JOH 14:18, 27 ~ I will not leave you without a comforter, for I will come to you. I leave you with peace; my peace I give to you. Not as the world gives do I give, so do not let your heart be troubled or afraid.

- ROM 8:35–39 ~ Who is able to separate us from the love of Christ? Can tribulation, distress, persecution, famine, nakedness, peril, or war separate us from His love? No, in all these things we are more than conquerors through Him who loved us. Thus, I am convinced that neither death nor life, neither angels nor demons, neither the present nor the future, nor any powers, neither height nor depth, nor anything else in all creation can separate us from the love of God that is in Christ our Lord.

- 1 PE 5:7 ~ Cast all of your fears on Him for He cares for you.

- 1 JO 4:13 ~ Know that we live in Him and He lives in us, because He has given us His Spirit.

    The most valuable human companions are those who share our Christian faith. They are better equipped to show genuine love and respect for all people, and without judgment. Everybody needs companionship, for we are social creatures. We are drawn to people that have the same things in common, like our spouse and our friends. Christians also fellowship with one another for we have the body of Christ in common, as well as belief in the truth of God's Word.

- GEN 2:18 ~ God said, "It is not good for man to be alone so I will make a helper for him."

- PSA 55:14 ~ We shared sweet fellowship and walked into the house of God together.

- EZE 47:22 ~ The land will be divided as an inheritance for the house of Israel as well as the strangers who lived among them and had children among them. Thus, the land will be shared by the twelve tribes as well as their companions.

- 1 CO 5:11 ~ Do not keep company with people who are fornicators, greedy, idolatrous, flirtatious, extortionists, and drunkards.

- EPH 5:11 ~ Do not be a companion to the unfruitful works of darkness, but rather disclose them and rebuke them.

- HEB 12:22–23 ~ You have come to Zion, to the city of the living God, the heavenly Jerusalem. You have come to the company of innumerable angels, to the general assembly and church of the firstborn, all of whom are written in heaven. You have come to live with God, the judge of all, and with the spirits of all honest people made perfect, and to Jesus Christ the mediator of the New Covenant.

- 1 JO 1:3 ~ What we have seen and heard we declare to you, so you can be in fellowship with us; for truly our fellowship is with the Father and His Son Jesus Christ.

    Satan and his minions draw people into the occult and tempt them with lusts of the flesh because the devil wants companions too; he is looking for people to bring down with him into hell. That's how much Satan hates humanity; he wants us to burn with him.

- 1 PE 5:8–9 ~ Be sober and vigilant; because your adversary the devil, like a roaring lion walks about seeking whom he may devour.

    Father, your Holy Spirit is our constant companion, and for this we give thanks. He comforts us whenever we are down, depressed, or lonely. Help us to be there for others who are lonely or in despair, to cheer people up who are down, and to visit those who are lost, lonely, or abandoned. What a friend we have in Jesus, who would never abandon us or betray us; let us be a friend like Jesus, trustworthy, loyal, friendly, nurturing. Let us never forget the elderly or abandon the needy, but visit with them and love them. Help us to keep a smile on our face and have a cheerful demeanor, so people will be drawn to us, and we will be able to share with them the reason for our joy. In the name of Jesus we pray, Amen.

July 12

National Simplicity Day is about living the simple life, which was the inspiration of Henry David Thoreau, born on this day in 1817. He was an author, naturalist, philosopher, and he practiced civil disobedience and transcendental meditation. He believed that people can transcend the worries of life using their intellect, and that a retreat to the simple can help us to examine the complex. He advocated getting in touch with one's feelings through introspection and meditation, thereby escaping the external influences of the outside world and its commotion and uncertainty. On this day we celebrate the simple life that he treasured in his sanctuary at Walden Pond. He realized that one can live with less stuff, for life is not weighed with respect to the accumulation of one's possessions. Most material things are expendable if not unnecessary.

Thoreau became disenchanted with organized religion, and its rules and expectations, largely due to the controlling aspects of the church at the time in his native Massachusetts. He proposed that the eternal God is within us, a proposition that would be correct if he was referring to the Holy Spirit. He found his inner peace through transcendentalism and connected with God through nature. Unfortunately, his concept of God did not appear to include Christ, having left Christianity because he didn't like what the church and its leaders were doing. Certainly, there are religions and churches run by tyrants. If you do not agree with what your church or its leaders are doing or saying, find another church. The best way of knowing if a church is right is knowing the Holy Bible. It will teach you how to find that inner peace through the Holy Spirit.

- NUM 6:24–26 ~ The Lord bless you and keep you, the Lord make His face shine upon you and be gracious unto you; the Lord lift up His countenance upon you, and give you His peace.

- PSA 37:37 ~ Take notice of those who are blameless and upright, for they will find a peaceful end.

- PRO 12:19–20 ~ The words of truth are established forever, but the lying tongue is but for a moment. Deceit is in the heart of those who imagine evil things; but for the counselors of peace there is joy.

- ISA 26:3 ~ Those whose minds are set on God and trust in Him will be kept in perfect peace.

- MAL 2:5 ~ The Lord's covenant was one of life and peace...

- LUK 1:79 ~ Jesus came to give light to those who are in darkness or in the shadow of death, and to guide everyone in the way of peace.

- ROM 2:10 ~ Glory, honor, and peace is given to all who do good, regardless of race.

- ROM 8:6 ~ To set the mind on the flesh results in death, but to set the mind on the Spirit results in life and peace.

- 1 CO 14:33 ~ God is not a God of confusion; He is a God of peace.

- EPH 4:3 ~ Maintain unity of the Spirit in the bond of peace.

- PHP 4:6–9 ~ Do not be anxious about anything but pray for everything. With thanksgiving let your requests be known to God. And the peace of God that surpasses all understanding will keep your hearts and minds in Jesus Christ.

- COL 1:19–20 ~ God was pleased to have His fullness living in Christ, so that through Him, everything on earth and in heaven could be reconciled to Himself, by the peace that came through the shedding of Christ's blood on the cross.

- 2 TH 3:16 ~ May the Lord of peace Himself give you His peace at all times and in all ways.

So how does one celebrate this holiday? Clean out some of your junk; give the stuff you don't use to the poor. Organize the clutter in your house and pack it away where you can find it if you need it; if you don't need it dispose of it. Maybe take an inventory of your life, and reassess your priorities. Be content with what you have and not discontented over what you don't have. Or, take a trip and change the environment for a while. Of course, this would be a lot easier if you had a place like Walden Pond where you could escape; but if you don't, you can retreat to a safe and calm place in your mind. Explore different things and discover those which make you happy or give you peace. Create some memories with your loved ones. Find ways to escape the chaos. I once taught the use of visual imagery to escape into the mind. Try this: when you are in a noisy place waiting for an appointment, go to your favorite place in your mind and see, hear, feel, and smell it; when they call your name you will be alerted to finish your business.

Thoreau found a way to evade the commotion with meditation in a serene location. You can find that happy place in your mind, and shut out the world for a moment of peace, even when the outside world seems hectic. Thoreau wrote, "What lies behind us and what lies ahead of us are tiny matters compared to what lives within us," and, "There is only one path to heaven; on earth, we call it love". I would agree. Yes, there is something to meditation as a means of finding your inner self. By doing so, one can connect to the subconscious domain, and possibly find a spiritual connection to God, or tap into the conscience which is your moral compass. But this is no substitute for prayer, nor does it edify like Bible study and worship. If you want to simplify your life, start with Christ. Believe in Him and God's promises. Try to let go of sins that are complicating your life. And invite the Holy Spirit as often as you think of it.

- PSA 46:1 ~ God is our refuge and strength, an ever-present help in trouble
- PRO 1:4 ~ Give prudence to the simple; give knowledge and discretion to the young.
- PRO 6:3 ~ Commit your works to the Lord and He will establish your thoughts.
- ISA 55:6 ~ Seek the Lord while He may be found; call on Him while He is near.
- MAT 11:28 ~ Jesus said, "Come to me when weary and burdened and I will give you rest."
- PHP 4:8 ~ Whatever is true, honest, fair, pure, lovely, uplifting, virtuous, and praiseworthy—think on these things.
- 2 CO 1:12 ~ We rejoice in this, the conversation of our conscience, that in simplicity and godly sincerity, and not with the wisdom of this world but by the grace of God, we have given our testimony to the world, and more abundantly toward you.

It is true that you can find God in nature and the universe (JOB 12:7–10; PSA 19:1; ROM 1:20). You also can find Him within yourself as Thoreau proposed (DEU 4:29; PRO 8:17; JER 29:13). But if you want to know God and His will for your life, it behooves you to read the Holy Bible (PSA 119:105; JOH 1:1; JOH 17:3; PHP 3:10; 2 TI 3:16), for God's Word is truth and it is comforting when you realize it.

Heavenly Father, let us be content with what we have and responsible with what you give us. Help us to live a simple life of Christian prayer, worship, and fellowship, and not complicate our priorities dabbling in the vices of this wicked world which constantly compel us. Let us not be double-minded; do not allow our minds to pursue desires of the flesh when we are out and about, but instead, let us be a witness to the cross of Christ. We invite your Spirit to indwell us as we face the world. Help us to mediate on your Word with your Spirit beside us when we feel overburdened with life or temptations. As we pray, we lift up our troubles to you through Jesus Christ who took them and nailed them to the cross, Amen.

July 13

International Rock Day has been celebrated for years but its origin is unknown. This observance is not to be confused with Old Rock Day on 01/07, or with rock-and-roll music. Yes, it is all about rocks; because they are important, we cannot live without them. The universe is made out of rocks, among other things. We live on a giant rock, and our physical composition came from the elements found on this rock that we call Earth. Given all the rocky planets in the universe, ours appears to be fine-tuned for life. We need many of the elements and minerals to continue living, though some of them can be harmful if used improperly. We are basically carbon-based organisms, which require rocks to survive. Think of and list the many ways rocks help us; just a ten-minute exercise should fill a page. How else can you celebrate rocks? Go hunting for rocks, fossils, and artifacts. Buy a pretty rock for a friend or spouse. Learn about rocks and their categories: igneous, metamorphic, and sedimentary. Learn about geology, rock formation, and mountain formations like fault-blocks, folds, and igneous intrusions. You may be surprised how interesting rocks can be.

The Bible speaks of rocks, both literally and metaphorically. God is portrayed as solid rock, the foundation of our faith, unmovable, unchangeable, indestructible; powerful, strong, steadfast, and enduring. The following passages provide characteristics of this rock, which represents God the rock of our salvation and Christ the chief cornerstone in the foundation of our faith and His church on earth.

- DEU 32:3–4 ~ I will publish the name of the Lord and ascribe greatness unto our God. God is the rock: perfect, just, righteous and true. He is without fault, the rock of our salvation.

- PSA 89:26; PSA 95:1–3 ~ Lead me and guide me, for my soul waits for you, Father God, the rock of my salvation. Let us sing to the Lord, the rock of our salvation. Let us come before Him with thanks, praise, and psalms. For He is a great God, and a great King above all gods.

- PSA 118:22 ~ The stone rejected by the builders has become the chief cornerstone.

- ISA 17:10–11 ~ You, who have forgotten about the rock of your strength, will sow your seeds and they will flourish, but you will reap only grief and sorrow.

- ISA 28:16 ~ God says, "I have placed in Zion a tested and precious cornerstone to ensure a sure foundation."

- DAN 2:34–35 ~ A stone was cut but not by human hands, and it struck the statue in Nebuchadnezzar's dream on the feet of iron and clay and broke them into pieces. And all the kingdoms of the earth became like chaff on the summer threshing floor, blown by the wind.

- MAT 7:24–27 ~ Jesus said, "A wise man builds his house upon a rock, not upon the sand. A house built upon a rock will stand against the elements, but one built upon the sand will fall."

- LUK 20:17–19 ~ After quoting Isaiah (ISA 28:16 above) Jesus said to the crowd, "Is it not marvelous? But whoever falls on that stone will be broken, and whoever that stone falls on will be pulverized." The chief priests and scribes perceived that Jesus was referring to them; they wanted to arrest Him, but they feared the people.

- ACT 4:10–12 ~ Let everybody know that it was Jesus Christ, whom you crucified, but whom God raised from the dead, who has become the chief cornerstone. There can be salvation in nobody else, for there are no other names under heaven that can save us except Christ alone.

- ROM 9:33 ~ Behold, I am placing in Zion a stone that will make men stumble and fall. Those who believe in Him will never be put to shame.

- EPH 2:18–21 ~ We have access through Jesus Christ to God the Father. We are not foreigners, but fellow citizens with the saints in the household of God. His house is built upon the foundation placed by the apostles and prophets, with Jesus Christ being the chief cornerstone of that foundation.

- 1 PE 2:4–8 ~ He is a living stone, rejected by men, but chosen by God and precious to Him. This is the stone of offense that makes men stumble and fall. You are also like living stones, built into a spiritual house to be a holy priesthood.

God wrote His Law on stone with Moses on Mt. Sinai (EXO 31:18; EXO 34:1–4), to present to the Israelites who were sinning below. Likewise, our faith is firmly founded on the Rock of Ages. So also, will the names of the saints be etched in stone (REV 2:17), when the free gift of eternal life is granted to believers. The Israelites became thirsty in the Sinai desert so Moses pleaded with God for water. As instructed, Moses struck the rock and from it came fresh water. In the final pleading for water, God told Moses to speak to the rock; but he struck the rock twice with his staff. Though water came out, God was displeased, telling Moses he would not enter the promised land (NUM 10–13). This water represented living water that Christ provides (JOH 4:7–14), and eternal life which is the reward for our faith in Christ.

- EXO 17:6 ~ God told Moses, "I will stand before you upon the rock in Horeb, and you will strike the rock, and from it will flow pure water so that the people may drink. And the elders of Israel witnessed this.

- NUM 20:8–11 ~ God empowered Moses to bring water from a rock. That water flowed in abundance, sufficiently quenching the thirst of the Israelites in the desert.

- 2 SA 23:3 ~ God, the Rock of Israel, spoke saying, "Whoever rules others must be just, ruling in the fear of God."

- PSA 105:41; PSA 114:8 ~ God opened the rock and the water gushed out, creating a fountain of water which poured out over the dry land.

- ISA 2:10, 19, 21 ~ Hide in the rocks for fear of the Lord and for the glory of His majesty. For He has risen to shake the earth.

- ISA 48:21–22 ~ They did not thirst while Moses led them across the desert, for Moses struck the rock and God caused water to come gushing out. There will be no peace for the wicked, says the Lord.

- MAT 16:18; JOH 1:42 ~ Jesus told Simon, "You are Peter [from the Greek word *petra* meaning rock], and upon this rock I will build my church. And the gates of hell will not prevail against it." Jesus named Simon Peter *Cephas*, meaning a stone (in Hebrew).

- 1 CO 10:1 6 ~ You should know that our forefathers drank of the same spiritual drink, which came from the same spiritual rock, and that Rock is Jesus Christ. But God was not pleased with many of them, which is why they were overthrown in the wilderness. These events were examples, intended to show us not to lust after evil things like they did.

Almighty Father, you are the solid rock upon which we stand with respect to our confidence and faith. Let that faith be rock solid, just as our foundation in Christ is the solid rock upon which we have built His church on earth. Help us to be steady and true to the rock of our salvation, and represent a formidable force in the world, united as the molecules in a rock even as the church is united with Christ, and He is united with you Father, and the Holy Spirit. We ask this in the name of the cornerstone of our religion, Jesus Christ, Amen.

July 14

Bastille Day is in remembrance of the day French citizens stormed the Bastille in 1789. The Bastille was a well-guarded stone military fortress and prison in Paris. The tyrant Louis XVI drove the economy into the ground as did his predecessor, through extravagant living and wasteful spending. Add drought and famine to this predicament, and the French commoners were suffering terribly. Rioting, looting, and arson were rampant, causing many soldiers to flee from the city. Protesters had gathered outside the castle while some men penetrated the building and let down the drawbridge. The mob stormed into the courtyard, and about one hundred were killed, while many others were wounded. Part of the military who were sympathetic to the commoners opened fire on the castle with cannons, until the occupants waved the white flag to surrender. The king was dragged off and beheaded at city hall, and later also, his queen Marie Antoinette. This marked the beginning of the French Revolution. This day has been celebrated annually in France ever since, officially becoming a national holiday in 1880. It is recognized worldwide like America's Independence Day.

There were commonalities between the American and French revolutions. Similarities included the timeframe, and the desire for freedom from tyranny, injustice, taxation without representation, and the greed of monarchs and their rich associates. There were a number of dissimilarities as well, pointed out by French diplomat, philosopher, and historian Alexis de Tocqueville. While the American revolution sparked the French revolution in a way, the outcomes were quite different. In particular, Europeans observed how their dreams of economic stability, democracy, equality, and individualism could be realized, proven by America's new republic. The spirit of revolution and the motivation for reforms was equivalent, but the American's achieved these things while the French did not, until much later. While he praised American democracy, Tocqueville warned of the tyranny of the majority (*Democracy in America*, 1835). How prophetic, given the recent state of affairs with the ruling party trying to dominate politics, media, education, and the justice system.

People of the Bible were concerned with the same issues, and sought freedom from government imposition. Take taxation without representation, for example. During Jesus's time, this was a major issue. The Romans imposed burdensome taxes, and if that wasn't enough, the tax collectors (called publicans) were dishonest and often cheated people; especially heinous were Jewish tax collectors who swindled their own people. The publicans were considered the lowest form of slime, but Jesus had mercy on them as He did all people. We know of at least two tax collectors who converted to Christianity: Matthew the apostle (MAT 9:7–11), and Zacchaeus who climbed a tree to see Jesus (LUK 19:2–8).

- MAT 5:46 ~ Jesus said, "If you love only those who love you, what reward will you have? Even tax collectors do the same thing."

- MAT 21:31–32 ~ Jesus came to preach in the temple in the presence of the chief priests and elders, who would frequently try to trick or trap Him. Jesus said to them, "Truthfully I tell you that the tax collectors and prostitutes will enter the kingdom of God ahead of you, for they came to righteousness through John whom you refused to believe and repent."

- MAR 2:14–17 ~ Jesus passed by a tax collector from the tribe of Levi and said to him, "Follow me," and he arose and followed Jesus. They went to his (Matthew) house where a dinner was prepared for many guests, including tax collectors and other sinners. The scribes and Pharisees asked the disciples, "Why does your master eat and drink with such people." Jesus knew what they were saying and answered them, "Those who are healthy do not need a physician, only those who are sick. I did not come to call righteous people to repentance, but sinners."

- LUK 2:1–5 ~ Caesar Augustus ordered a census to be taken in all the land for taxation. Joseph and Mary (who was pregnant) had to travel from Nazareth in Galilee to Bethlehem in Judea, because he was a descendant of David, to be counted and taxed by the Romans.

- LUK 3:12–13 ~ Some tax collectors came to be baptized by John. They asked him, "Teacher, what must we do?" John said, "Do not collect more money than you are supposed to collect."

- LUK 18:9–14 ~ Jesus told the parable of the Pharisee and the publican. Two men went to the temple to pray: a Pharisee and a publican. The Pharisee said, "Thank you Lord that I am not a sinner like other men, such as that tax collector, because I give tithes and I fast twice a week." The publican bowed low before the altar and beat on his breast saying, "God be merciful to me a sinner." Only the publican returned home justified by God. Those who exalt themselves will later be humbled, and those who humble themselves will later be exalted.

Among the many injustices forced on the Jewish people were corrupt courts, and not only the Roman but also the Jewish justice systems. The best example was the trial of Jesus. He was detained by a riotous mob commissioned by the Jewish leaders; then He was taken to the temple, accused by false witnesses who were paid-off, and declared guilty of blasphemy. Next, He was dragged before Herod the tetrarch to be abused and mocked, then taken before the Roman governor, who found Him innocent but had him flogged and executed anyway. This happened within the span of less than twenty-four hours (MAT 27; MAR 14; LUK 23; JOH 18).

Ever since the era of the kings in the Old Testament, there have been corrupt, evil, greedy and oppressive governments and monarchs. God warned the Israelites about transitioning from judges to kings (1 SA 8:4–22). There would be a string of evil kings which would cause the kingdom to split in two: one kingdom in the north (Israel) and one in the south (Judah). Both would be conquered by their enemies. The Hebrews would end up losing their land which God promised them, because they adopted the ways of their enemies. They were subjected, abused, and enslaved by the Assyrians, Babylonians, and Romans. All of these kingdoms and empires of the world would fall due to evil and greedy tyrants wanting to control, if not own, the world.

- JOB 24:22, 24; JOB 27:13 ~ He takes down the mighty with His power, and rises up so that nobody feels safe. They are exalted for a little while, then they are removed as all the others, and cut off like the top of an ear of corn. This is the portion that wicked people will receive from God; it is the heritage of oppressors.

- ISA 13:11 ~ I will punish the world for its evil, and the wicked for iniquity. I will cause the arrogancy of the proud to cease, and will bring down the haughtiness of tyrants.

- ISA 49:24–26 ~ Will the prey be freed from the mighty, or the lawful who are taken captive delivered? The Lord says, "The captives of the mighty will be rescued; the prey of tyrants will be delivered. I will contend with those who contend with you, to save my children. I will feed oppressors their own flesh and they will be drunk with their own blood. And all people will know that I am the Lord, your Savior and Redeemer, the mighty one of Jacob."

- MAT 20:25–28 ~ Jesus called the disciples together and said, "You know that the rulers who oppress you are unbelievers and tyrants. Do not be like them, for whomever would be great among you will be ministering to you, and whomever would be chief among you will be your servants; even as the Son of man came to serve, not to be served, and to pay the ransom for many."

Father, we long to be your favored people; free us from tyranny and oppression. Let all Christians come together in your service and stand against those who subject people to extend their empires. Bring them down as in times past; may we be free of them. In Jesus's name, Amen.

July 15

First Crusade Reclaimed Jerusalem in the name of Christianity on this day in 1099. The week-long siege was waged to remove Islamic influence and dominion over the holy city and surrounding lands. Once this miraculous feat was accomplished, the first crusade was over and most of the knights returned home. Their leaders, Godfrey and others, remained behind to defend the stronghold and the region. Godfrey soon supported the archbishop to lead the city. But after Godfrey's untimely death, his brother Baldwin became king in Jerusalem. Prior attempts had been made to drive away the Muslims to no avail. After the success of the first crusade, the territory controlled by Europeans continued to expand. However, a reversal would take place almost a century later, when Jerusalem and its surrounding lands would be recaptured by Muslim conqueror Saladin in 1187. This fueled the expansion of Muslim controlled lands, giving rise to the Ottoman empire which would occupy the holy land for six hundred years. All subsequent crusades and attempts to drive Muslims out of the territory were dismal failures until 1920.

God warned Israel they would lose their land if they defied the Lord, and would be scattered among the nations of their enemies. And that is exactly what transpired.

- DEU 4:23–27; DEU 28:64; LEV 26:33 ~ God warned Israel to take heed that they do not forget the covenant of the Lord, or make graven images, or worship other gods, for God is a consuming fire, and a jealous God. He told them, "You will have children and grandchildren and remain long in the land, but if you corrupt yourselves with idols or do evil in my sight, you will provoke my anger. I call heaven and earth as a witness that you will utterly perish from the land you possessed after crossing the Jordan River. And the Lord will scatter you among the nations, and you will be a minority among the heathen. The Lord will scatter you among all people from one end of the earth to the other, where you will serve false gods of stone and wood, which your fathers never knew. I will scatter you and draw a sword after you; your land will be desolate and your cities laid to waste."

- NEH 1:8 ~ Remember, I implore you, the word commanded by God through Moses saying, if you transgress, you will be scattered abroad among the nations.

- PSA 44:11 ~ God gave us up to be devoured like sheep and scattered us among the nations.

- JER 9:16 ~ I will scatter them among the heathen, whom neither they or their fathers have known; I will send a sword after them until they have been consumed.

- EZE 12:15; EZE 20:23; EZE 22:15 ~ They will know that I am the Lord when I scatter them among the nations and disperse them across the earth. I warned them in the wilderness that I would scatter them and disperse them to drive the filth out of them.

God promised the Jews that they would return someday and reclaim their homeland, which finally occurred in 1948.

- ISA 11:11–12; ISA 43:5–6 ~ It will come to pass that the Lord will reach His hand a second time to recover the remnant of His people left in Assyria, Egypt, Cush, Babylonia, and elsewhere. He will raise a banner and gather the exiles of Israel and assemble the scattered people of Judah from the four corners of the earth. I will gather your people from the east and from the west, from the north and the south.

- JER 16:15; JER 31:7 ~ The Lord lives, who brings the children of Israel out of the lands where He has driven them, to bring them again into the land of their fathers. Sing and rejoice for Jacob, shout among the nations and praise the Lord for saving the remnant of His people Israel.

- EZE 28:25; EZE 36:22–23 ~ God says, when He has gathered the house of Israel from the nations where they were scattered, and sanctified them in the sight of the heathen, then they will live in their land that I gave to my servant Jacob. Tell the house of Israel that I do not do this for their sakes, but for my holy namesake, which you profaned among the heathen where I sent you.

  God also said that Israel would again be under siege in the latter days, surrounded by their enemies which would be defeated. So far, the first two prophecies have been fulfilled, and the third—well it has yet to happen but it might not be far off.

- EZE 38—39 ~ Face northward, toward Magog, and prophesy: God is against you Gog. You will mobilize armies of the distant north, as well as from Africa and Asia. You will invade Israel in an attempt to obtain her wealth and conquer her, Israel who has been at peace after having returned home from all over the world. This will happen in the latter years. There will be a great earthquake. You will end up fighting yourselves in the confusion. I will send animals to eat you, death, disease, and calamities. I will destroy five sixths of your armies. I will rain fire and brimstone upon Magog and your allies to include the islands and coastlands, and places east of the Dead Sea. It will take seven months to bury the bodies. It will be a glorious victory for Israel. I will be their Lord from that day on, and forever.

- MAT 24:15–20; LUK 21:20–21 ~ Jesus said, "When you see Jerusalem surrounded by its enemies the abomination of desolation is nigh. Flee into the mountains; do not go back for anything. Hope it is not in winter; it especially will be difficult for those with small children."

- REV 20:7–9 ~ After the thousand years Satan will be unloosed, and will go about to deceive the nations in every corner of the earth, Gog and Magog, gathering them for battle against the Lord with an army that cannot be counted. They will encompass the earth and surround the encampment of saints and the beloved city. Fire will come from heaven and destroy them all.

  Israel was given the promised land, lost it and got it back again. This is what all nations can expect. If they follow the Lord, they will inherit the kingdom. If they return again to their wicked ways, they will lose their inheritance. If they repent and return to God, they will gain it back again. And if they stand strong in the Lord, no nation on earth will be able to come against them. This is a lesson for all nations to heed, as well as each and every one of us.

- HEB 10:26–29 ~ If we sin willingly, after having received the knowledge of the truth, there can be no further sacrifice for sins, but only the expectation of judgment and raging fire. A worse punishment awaits those who think themselves worthy, yet have walked over the Son of God, insulted the Spirit of Grace, and treated as unholy the blood of the covenant that sanctified them.

- 2 PE 2:20–21 ~ If, after a person has escaped the wickedness of this world through the knowledge of our Lord and Savior Jesus Christ, they allow themselves again to be entangled and overcome by the world, their end will be worse than their beginning. For it would have been better for them not to have known the ways of righteousness, than to have understood and yet turned away from the holy commandments given to them.

  Holy Father, we have followed you as a nation in the past but we seem to be slipping away, following false gods, and worshipping idols just as Israel did. Help us to stop our backsliding ways and return to you now, before we lose our republic which you have so richly blessed. Please protect us from enemies foreign and domestic, and cause them to fail in their evil strivings to take us in the wrong direction, away from you and towards a new world order. We pray this in the name of your Son, who forever will remain our fortress and shield, Amen.

July 16

First Detonation of Atomic Bomb occurred on this day in 1945 at Trinity Site, near Alamogordo, New Mexico. Known as the Manhattan project, this was the first ever successful test of a plutonium implosion; it used nuclear fission to cause the giant explosion which occurred by splitting atoms apart, thereby causing a chain reaction (unlike the hydrogen bomb which uses the fusion of atoms together, creating an even greater explosion). Though many top scientists paved the way for this weapon of mass destruction, those creating the actual bomb were Oppenheimer, Bethe, Teller, and Fermi. If they had not been successful, World War II might have had a completely different outcome. Fortunately, the birth of the atomic bomb brought a rapid end to the war, at the expense of obliterating Hiroshima and Nagasaki a few weeks later. The Trinity Site became a national historic landmark in 1965.

Nowadays, many advanced countries have nuclear weapons, including the USA, Russia, China, United Kingdom, France, India, Pakistan, Israel, and there are many other countries that are anxious to complete the process. There is a total of approximately 14,500 nuclear warheads, a fraction of the all-time high back in the 1980s, though more than enough to wipe out the planet several times over. If there ever is a nuclear war, it will probably be the end of planet Earth. When St. Peter wrote about the earth being destroyed by fire, maybe that is what he meant (2 PE 3:10).

Meanwhile, we will continue fighting a spiritual war, using weapons unlike any other, and fighting an enemy that we cannot even see. This enemy is pure evil and their leader is Satan. This war will continue to heat up as the coming of Christ approaches.

- JOE 3:9–10, 14 ~ Go, tell the Gentiles to prepare for war. Wake up the mighty warriors and tell them to come along. Beat your plowshares into swords and your pruning hooks into spears. Let the weak say, "I am strong." Multitudes are gathered in the valley of decision, for the day of the Lord is nearing.

- ISA 59:17 ~ He has put on righteousness as a breastplate and salvation for a helmet. His clothing consists of the garments of vengeance and zeal is his cloak.

- EZE 32:27–29 ~ The fallen of the untrue have gone to hell with their weapons of war. They were the terror of the mighty in the land of the living, but now they join with those who go down into the pit.

- EZE 32:17–20, 32 ~ The word of the Lord came to Ezekiel. Son of man, wail for Egypt and the rest who are thrown into the pit of the uncircumcised. They will fall with the others, slain by the sword. Though I allowed him to spread terror in the land of the living, Pharoah and all his multitude will be laid among the uncircumcised and those killed by the sword.

- MAT 10:34, 38–39 ~ Jesus said, "Do not think I came to send peace to the earth, because I am sending a sword instead. You must take up your cross and follow me if you want to be counted worthy. Those who wish to keep their lives will lose their lives; but those who lose their lives for my sake will be given back their lives."

- EPH 6:11–17 ~ Put on the whole armor of God so that you will be prepared to stand against the trickery of Satan. For we do not wrestle against flesh and blood, but against principalities, powers, rulers of darkness in this world, and wickedness in high places. Wear this armor so that you can withstand the day of evil, and remain standing when it is over. Gird your loins with truth and put on the breastplate of righteousness. Put on the shoes of the Gospel of peace; and take the shield of faith which will repel the fiery darts of the wicked one. Don the helmet of salvation and arm yourself with the sword of the Spirit which is the Word of God.

- HEB 4:12 ~ The Word of God is living and active, sharper than any double-edged sword, dividing the soul and spirit, and discerning the thoughts and intentions of the heart.

How does one contend with demons? What kinds of warfare, weapons, tactics, and doctrine are needed to fight spirits of darkness? The Bible is our field manual and addresses all of these things. As we learned in the above passages, we have defensive armor, and we have a weapon of war: the sword of the Spirit which can slice asunder the soul and spirit of a human, and a demon. That sword is the Word of God. When Satan tempted Jesus in the wilderness, he quoted scripture to trick Jesus, who responded with scripture rebutting Satan's misrepresentation of scripture. After three attempts to deceive Jesus who was weak from forty days of fasting, Satan left defeated. Thus, the Word which is the Holy Bible, is the best way to defeat a demon, because they can't stand the truth, for they know it spells doom for them.

The truth provides us with the confidence to challenge evil without fear, which is the primary weapon used by the demonic. We are given the right, the responsibility, and the authority in Christ to speak on His behalf. When we do, we must be humble and respectful, showing genuine love, which will defeat the fear, for there is no fear in love because the love of Christ casts out fear (1 JO 4:18). Similarly, the love and truth of Christ casts out demons.

- DEU 14:2 ~ You are a holy people to the Lord, for He has chosen you to be a peculiar people unto Himself, above all the nations that are upon the earth.

- ROM 8:16–17 ~ The Spirit Himself bears witness with our spirits that we are children of God; and if children then heirs of God, and equal heirs with Christ, provided we suffer with Him that we also may be glorified with Him.

- 2 CO 10:3–5 ~ Although we abide in this world, we do not fight its wars. For our weapons are not of a physical nature, yet they are far more powerful, able to demolish the strongholds of the enemy. We destroy the arguments and pretensions which are raised against the knowledge of God, and bring captive every thought into the obedience of Christ.

- 1 PE 2:5–9 ~ You are living stones, built into a spiritual house; a holy priesthood, to offer spiritual sacrifices acceptable to God through Jesus Christ. You are a chosen generation, a royal priesthood, a holy nation, a special people; for you have been selected to give praise to Him who called you out of darkness into His marvelous light.

- 1 TI 2:4 ~ God wants all people to come and be saved, and receive the knowledge of the truth.

- 2 TI 1:9–10 ~ He has saved us and summoned us with a holy calling, not according to our works but according to His own purpose and grace, given us by Christ before the world began. Now, God is made manifest by the appearing of our Savior Jesus Christ who has abolished death, bringing life and immortality to light through His Gospel.

Heavenly Father, you have empowered us with your Word and your Spirit, to face evil head-on in battle, and emerge victorious. The weapons of evil nations and people are powerless against the Spirit of truth, which will pierce them to their souls, to be cast into hell. Help us with confidence to fight the good fight of faith, and persevere us until the end, when you will gather all the armies of evil and throw them into the lake of fire, along with Satan and the rest of the demons. Let your Word enrich our lives, make us wise, and make us strong; let the light of Jesus shine through us reflecting His love and His power, so that the forces of evil will fear you Father, and Jesus who lives in us through His Holy Spirit. For we have a suit of armor and a shield to repel the advances of the wicked coming against us, and we possess your powerful Word which will cut them into, before they fall into the pit. In the name of Jesus we pray, who is that Word, and whose power is in the sword we bear to defeat malevolence and Satan, Amen.

July 17

International Justice Day arose from a treaty promoted by the United Nations at a conference in Rome on this day in 1998, to establish an International Criminal Court (ICC). Inspired by the Nuremberg and Tokyo trials of Nazi and Japanese war criminals from World War II, the objective was to bring to justice those who commit genocide, sexual violence, and hate crimes against humanity. Seven member nations voted against it including the US, China, Israel, Iraq, Libya, Yemen, and Qatar; 120 countries voted for it. The ICC was formally created in 2002 and resides at the Hague, Netherlands. Today's observance became official in 2010 during a UN review conference held in Kampala Uganda. Many times, the victims of such crimes get no justice in the courts, so this court is supposed to provide another wall of defense for victims. But only member nations agreeing to the treaty accept the jurisdiction of the ICC; the US continues to deny their authority, warning against interference with judicial actions here. To date, the ICC has a questionable record when it comes to cases, convictions, and places or occasions where they have or have not interceded. Maybe they will get around to the genocide occurring in China and the war crimes being committed by Russia against the Ukrainians.

Is international justice a good thing? Of course, it is. But this could be another global initiative advanced by the UN to increase their power, and promote globalism. The UN picks the judges and when and where to intervene, so it isn't exactly a system of equal representation under the law. God's international court of law is always just, and is always applied equally.

- ISA 28:5–6 ~ In that day the Lord of Hosts will be a crown of glory, a garland of beauty to the remnant of His people. He will be a Spirit of justice, sitting in judgment: a source of strength to those that turn the battle back from the gate.

- JER 10:23–25 ~ Lord, I know a man's life is not his own; it is not for man to direct his own steps. Correct me Lord, in your justice not in your anger, else you reduce me to nothing. Pour your wrath upon nations which do not accept you, and people who do not call on your name.

- JER 23:5; JER 33:15 ~ A righteous descendant of David will become King and will reign and prosper. He will execute judgment and justice on the earth.

- AMO 5:14–15 ~ Seek the good and avoid the evil, so you can live with the Lord. Hate evil and love goodness. Maintain justice in your courts, and maybe God will have mercy on you.

- HAB 1:4 ~ The law becomes loose and justice is not served, for the wicked encompass the righteous and wrong judgment proceeds.

- ZEC 9:9 ~ Rejoice all of Jerusalem and Zion, for your King comes bringing justice and salvation; He appears lowly, riding on a donkey's colt.

- MAT 23:23 ~ Jesus said, "Woe to you hypocritical scribes and Pharisees. You make tithes of your goods, yet you ignore the more important matters of the law: justice, mercy, and faith. You should have done these things and not left the other undone."

- ROM 2:12–13 ~ All who sin apart from the Law will perish apart from the Law. All who sin under the Law will be judged according to the Law. Hearing the Law does not make you righteous in God's eyes; you must obey the Law to be declared righteous.

Father, we know your law is pure and your justice is true. Help us to be doers of the law and not just hearers of the law. Let your commandments and precepts be the example of all legal systems on earth, equally applied and enforced, so that there can be justice in the world. May all nations value justice to ensure the guilty are brought to trial and the innocent are set free. In the name of Jesus who will judge fairly every human soul, Amen.

July 18

Rome Burned Under Emperor Nero for over a week beginning on this day in AD 64, razing over two-thirds of the city. A strong wind blew the fire across town where the shops were tinderboxes. Nero was supposedly out of town; he blamed the Christians, according to Roman historian Tacitus. Nero was an evil man, possibly insane. He tormented, tortured, and sacrificed Christians for entertainment. Maybe he didn't have a hand in the fire, but I wouldn't put it past him. He sure had a hand in exterminating devotees to Jesus, including Paul, and probably Peter.

Tacitus researched and reported on the history of Roman emperors and noteworthy events, including Nero's death in AD 68. He knew all about Nero's persecution of the sect known as Christians. He recorded the account of a crucifixion during the governorship of Pontius Pilate of a man called Christos, and the rapid growth of his cult of followers. Josephus, a Jewish historian from the same period, provided additional details of this messianic figure and his alleged resurrection. Roman historian Suetonius was another source. These secular historians provided independent verification of the life, death, and resurrection of Jesus.

When it came to opposing God, Nero was a violent man who played with fire. Fire is the ultimate end for all who hate God and persecute His people.

- DEU 6:14–15; DEU 32:22–25 ~ Never follow other gods; there is only one Lord and He is a jealous God; His anger will burn against you and He will destroy you if you follow false gods. A fire will burn in the lowest depths of hell. The inhabitants will be burned with hunger, devoured with burning heat, and destroyed by wild beasts, poisonous snakes, and the sword, and from the terror within…

- 2 KI 22:17 ~ God says, "Since they have forsaken me, worshipped other gods, and angered me by their evil works, my wrath will burn against them and that fire will never be extinguished."

- ISA 10:17; ISA 33:14 ~ The Light of Israel will become a fire, and their Holy One a flame. In a single day this fire will burn away all the thorns and briers. The sinners in Zion are afraid; fear has surprised the hypocrites. Who among us will live with the devouring fire? Who among us will burn forever?

- MAL 4:1 ~ All the evildoers will burn, leaving no roots or branches.

- LUK 3:15–17 ~ The people were expecting Messiah, and some considered it might be John the Baptist, who answered them saying, "I baptize you with water. But One comes after me whose shoelaces I am unworthy to loosen. He will baptize you with the Holy Spirit and with fire. He has the winnowing fork in hand, ready to clear the threshing floor. He will gather the wheat into the barn, and He will burn up the chaff with unquenchable fire."

- REV 20:10, 15; REV 21:8 ~ The devil that deceived them was thrown into the lake of fire where the beast and false prophet were. They were tormented day and night forever. Those whose names were not written in the Book of Life were thrown into the lake of fire. The fearful, unbelieving, abominable, murderous, lecherous, sorcerers, idolaters, and liars will be thrown into the lake of fire which is the second death.

Father, please save us from the fires of hell through the indwelling of your Holy Spirit. Strengthen our faith every day so our shield can deflect the fiery darts of Satan and fend off the forces of evil. Help humankind to see the fiery fate awaiting everyone denying Christ as their personal Savior; let them see the error in their denial of Him and not be blinded to His light. Embolden Christians to warn those who are unaware of your blessings and the curse of sin. May we never deny Jesus under any circumstances. In His name we pray, Amen.

July 19

Five Women Were Hanged for Witchcraft in Salem, MA on this day in 1692. A witch hunt was underway when a few young ladies started making accusations, after which several women were rounded up. All but one of the accused denied everything; that woman proudly admitted to being a servant of Satan and named others. Soon, hundreds of women were charged with witchcraft as the infamous trials began, twenty of whom were executed. Testimony involved evil spirits and specters, Satan and black magic, and demon possession. Ghost stories were told to children to influence them, and some reportedly began acting crazy. Fear was permeating the land, causing mass panic, whether warranted or not. The hanging on this particular day was one of many conducted in Salem. Europe started these witch hunts over the previous century. There was great controversy regarding the guilt or innocence of those eliminated. A memorial was erected at the site of mass hangings on this date in 2017, in tribute to the innocents they falsely accused.

There may be other explanations for people acting weird or crazy, such as mental illness, organic brain damage, epilepsy, or hysteria. The problem is, in the seventeenth century they knew little to nothing about mental illness, or spiritual illness for that matter. Though judges and clergymen protested this rush to judgment, they were ignored. I guess they didn't have exorcists to evacuate the demons, though anyone receiving Jesus Christ into their heart could have cast them out in His name, by the power of the Holy Spirit, with the authority of God the Father.

Demon possession and witchcraft do exist, since Old Testament times. For example, Balaam was a sorcerer (NUM 24:1), King Saul consulted the witch of Endor, herself possessed by a demon (1 SA 28:7–19. Jezebel, wife of King Ahab, was a sorceress who practiced witchcraft (2 KI 9:22). In the New Testament there is the story of Simon the sorcerer, who wanted to buy the power of the Holy Spirit (ACT 8:17–20). The Bible warns about messing around with evil spirits and practices like witchcraft and sorcery.

- LEV 19:26–28, 31 ~ Do not eat blood; do not cast spells or observe times. Do not round the corners of your heads or beards. Do not cut or tattoo your flesh. Do not consult familiar spirits; do not practice witchcraft or fortunetelling. Do not confide in mediums or wizards and become defiled by them. I am the Lord your God!

- DEU 18:10–12 ~ Do not sacrifice your children. Do not practice fortunetelling, divination, calling upon the dead, or sorcery. Do not be a medium, charmer, or wizard. Whoever does these things is an abomination to God.

- 1 SA 15:23 ~ Samuel told King Saul, "Rebellion is as bad as witchcraft, and pride is as evil as idolatry. Since you have rejected the command of the Lord, He has rejected you as king."

- ISA 8:19 ~ If anyone suggests consulting familiar spirits (demons), or listening to sorcerers who search for paranormal visions and murmurings, answer them saying, "Should we not be consulting with the Lord God; should we not be seeking the living instead of the dead?"

- EZE 13:6–7 ~ They have seen vain visions and perform lying divinations; the Lord did not send them.

- DAN 4:7–8 ~ King Nebuchadnezzar consulted magicians, astrologers, and fortunetellers but none of them could interpret his dream.

- MIC 5:12–15 ~ All the sorcerers and fortune-tellers will be cut off. Their cities will be destroyed. I will execute vengeance on people that do not obey.

We know that one third of the angels joined Lucifer in mutiny and were cast out of heaven to earth. The number of demons has not increased or decreased; the evil spirits that fell to earth way back then are still here now. People who summon the dead, or play with the occult, or practice witchcraft, are inviting demons; if they keep doing these things, demons will come. There are numerous examples of demon possession in the New Testament. Jesus Christ, and those whom He anointed with the Holy Spirit, had the power to cast out demons.

- MAT 12:45 ~ Jesus talked about casting out devils, and how, when one is cast out it may find seven spirits more wicked than itself to join it, returning to the individual and making him or her worse off than before. Jesus was referring to an evil generation that would come.

- MAR 5:19 ~ Jesus told the man who He had cleansed of demon possession, "Go home to your friends and tell them what great things the Lord has done for you, and the compassion He has shown."

- LUK 8:26–33 ~ Jesus confronted the evil spirits inhabiting one possessed man. Jesus spoke to the demons and asked for its name, who answered, "Legion, for we are many." Jesus sent the demons into a herd of swine; the entire herd ran off a steep cliff and drowned in the sea below. [Note that a Roman legion was about six thousand men.)

- 2 CO 11:14 ~ Do not be tricked by Satan who disguises himself as an angel of light.

- EPH 6:12 ~ We must fight, not against flesh and blood, but against principalities, powers, rulers of earthly darkness, and spiritual wickedness in high places.

- JAM 2:19 ~ If you believe that there is one God you do well; even the devils believe and they tremble from it.

- REV 16:13–14 ~ I saw three unclean spirits of devils leap out of the dragon's mouth, and the mouth of the beast (antichrist), and the mouth of the false prophet. These spirits of devils, which work miracles, will go before the kings and the world, to gather them for battle on that great day of the Lord God Almighty.

In the latter days, Satan will possess a human being, empowering that person to seize control over governments and the world.

- 2 TH 2:3–4, 8–9 ~ Beware of false prophets who will try to deceive you, because people will fall away from God before the evil one, the son of Satan (literally, the son of perdition or hell), is revealed. He is the one who opposes God and exalts himself, pretending to be God. The evil one will be consumed by the Spirit of God and will be destroyed by the brightness of His coming. The evil son of Satan is the one possessed by Satan himself, and performs magic tricks and false miracles.

- 1 TI 4:1–2 ~ The Spirit expressly states how in the latter days, some will depart from the faith and give into seducing spirits and doctrines of devils. They will speak lies of hypocrisy having their consciences seared with a hot iron.

Heavenly Father, we need your Spirit more than ever, since it is proclaimed in your Word that wickedness will get worse as the day of our Lord nears. Strengthen us to prepare for His coming by keeping the Bible close and studying it often, especially with our youth. Help parents to keep a careful watch over their children to ensure they do not dabble in the occult. Help the kids to know your Son, oh Father, and empower them with your Holy Spirit as you have empowered us: let them know to resist evil in the world and anything demonic or occultist. Equip us and train us in the use of the sword of the Spirit to fend off the advances of evil powers, blocking the fiery arrows of Satan and his minions with the shield of faith. Remind us that we can invoke the name of Jesus and expel demons from among us. We ask this in the name of Jesus, Amen.

July 20

Apollo 11 Crew Landed on the Moon on this day in 1969. Mission commander Neil Armstrong was the first human to set foot on the moon when he said those famous words, "That is one small step for man, one giant leap for mankind." Buzz Aldrin promptly joined him in the Sea of Tranquility where the lunar module *Eagle* had landed; their colleague Michael Collins remained at the controls of the command module. They raised the American flag, took samples, explored the surface, and all of this was broadcast in near real time over television. The moon has always been quite the celebrity, especially on this occasion. Some civilizations worshipped the moon, which plays a major role in the end times also. It seems the gloomy end coincides with a blood moon, which is basically a full lunar eclipse (the earth coming between the moon and sun). The rusty tint comes from the sunrays illuminating the moon which lies in the shadow of the earth.

- ISA 13:10 ~ The stars in heaven will not give light, and the sun and moon will be darkened.

- EZE 32:7–8 ~ I will cover the heavens and make the stars dark; I will cover the sun with a cloud, and the moon will not shine.

- JOE 2:2, 10, 30–31 ~ The day of great darkness and gloom is coming. The earth will quake and the heavens will tremble. There will be wonders in the sky and on the earth: blood, smoke, and fire. The sun will become dark and the moon will become like blood.

- AMO 8:9 ~ On that day, I will make the sun set at noon and I will darken the world in broad daylight.

- ZEP 1:14–15 ~ The day of the Lord is coming quickly, the day when the mighty ones will cry. It is a day of darkness, gloom and destruction.

- MAT 24:29 ~ Jesus said, "Immediately after the time of tribulation, the sun will become dark, the moon will be shrouded in gloom, and stars will fall from the sky."

- REV 6:12–15 ~ There was a great earthquake; the sun became black and the moon became like blood. Stars fell from the sky. Everyone tried to hide and take cover, even the rich and mighty ones.

    I have been a space nut since an early age. I still enjoy reading and learning about space: there certainly is plenty of it to go around. I am particularly struck by the unfathomable fine-tuning in the universe. It proves that earth was made for humankind to thrive, and that we are very special to God among all His creation. Everything about our planet, solar system, galaxy, and universe is made to support life on earth. There are literally hundreds of factors that must be tweaked to the nth degree. If any one factor came out of tolerance by a miniscule amount, we would be no more. The complexity, synchronicity, interactivity, distances, masses, composition, synergy, and ecology prove that an intelligence far beyond the whole of humanity designed it all.

- 1 CH 29:11 ~ Yours, oh Lord, is all greatness, power, glory, victory, and majesty. Everything in heaven and earth is yours, including the everlasting kingdom. You are exalted as head above all creatures.

- JOB 5:9 ~ God performs wonders that cannot be fathomed and miracles that cannot be counted.

- DAN 7:13–14 ~ I saw visions in the night, and One like the Son of man came in the clouds of heaven before the Ancient of Days. And there was given to Him dominion, and glory, and a kingdom, that all people, nations, and languages, should serve Him. His dominion is everlasting and will never pass away, and His kingdom will never be destroyed.

- AMO 4:13 ~ He forms the mountains, He creates the wind, He communicates His thoughts to humankind, and He turns the dawn into dusk. He can be found in the high places of the earth, and the Lord God Almighty is His name.
- ROM 1:18–20 ~ The invisible qualities of God are clearly seen since the creation of the world, for through His many creations one can understand God, even His power and divine nature, so nobody has an excuse.
- 2 CO 5:17 ~ If you are in Christ, you become a new creature. Old things pass away and everything becomes new.
- EPH 1:4–6 ~ For He chose us before the creation of the world to be holy and blameless in His sight. In love, God predestined us to be adopted children through Jesus Christ, in accordance with His pleasure and will, to the praise of His glorious grace which He has freely given to us in the Son He loves.

Cosmologists suggest that time, space, matter, and energy were released at a single moment of time, and the universe has continued expanding rapidly from that point. This would be consistent with the creation account when God said, "Let there be light." The universe has continued to expand ever since, and will continue until it runs out of gas; this is called entropy or heat death. The Bible provides evidence for entropy as well. In fact, with all the fine-tuning, there is a narrow window (cosmologically speaking) for humans to survive here. After that, the earth will be uninhabitable. But God's people will be living in another universe by then.

- GEN 1:1–4 ~ In the beginning God created the heavens and the earth and the earth was without form and void, and darkness was over the face of the deep. And the Spirit moved across the face of the waters. And God said, "Let there be light." and there was light. God said the light was good and separated the light from the darkness.
- ISA 65:17–19 ~ I will create new heavens and a new earth; the former heaven and earth will never be remembered or recalled. You will be glad and rejoice forever, for I will make Jerusalem a place of happiness. I will rejoice in Jerusalem for I will be happy with my people, and there will nevermore be the sound of crying among my people.
- MAT 5:18 ~ Jesus said, "Not one rule or statute of the Law will be removed, until earth and heaven pass away and all things have been fulfilled."
- LUK 21:33 ~ Jesus said, "Heaven and earth will pass away, but my words will remain true forever."
- 2 PE 3:13 ~ We, according to God's promise, look for new heavens and a new earth, wherein dwells righteousness.
- 1 JO 2:17 ~ The world will pass away along with its sinfulness; but whoever does the will of God will live forever.
- REV 21:1, 4 ~ I saw a new heaven and a new earth, for the old heaven and earth had passed away. There was no more crying, sorrow, pain, or death, for these things had passed away.

Dear Father, we are so special to you; help us to feel special and loved and not just take your grace for granted. Help us to love others and treat them as special; for we all are created in your image. Let all people know that they have potential for greatness, for a relationship with you, and for eternal life. Let them see the value of living in a new heaven and earth, so they do not get infatuated with this universe; for we are going to a better place with no sorrow, pain, or suffering. We yearn for that day, meeting our Redeemer in person. In His name we pray, Amen.

July 21

Scopes Convicted of Teaching Evolution on this day in 1925. It was against the law in Tennessee to teach Darwinian evolution, because it contradicted the creation account in the Bible. One famous lawyer named William Jennings Bryan argued against allowing the scientific theory of evolution to be taught; another famous lawyer named Clarence Darrow argued that the Tennessee law violated the religious freedom clause in the First Amendment. Darrow introduced some theatrics to sway the jurors. But Judge Raulston had made up his mind, because the issue was whether Scopes violated state law, which he already had confessed. That law, called the Butler Act, was repealed in 1967, starting a cascade of states lifting bans on the teaching of evolution. The Scopes trial was the beginning of a lengthy debate between evolution and creation, intended to discredit the Bible. The debate itself has evolved into a war of ideologies.

Charles Darwin had proposed that changes in a species can occur via natural selection and survival of the fittest (1859). He observed birds whose beaks changed in size with changes in climatic conditions. This we call microevolution: changes within an animal type or phylum while adapting to the environment. He also postulated that one phylum could change into another given sufficient time. He suggested this possibility would be proven or disproven as more fossil evidence was uncovered. Contrary fossil evidence showed a proliferation of phyla emerging rather quickly, geologically speaking, known as the Cambrian explosion. No fossils have ever demonstrated one kind or type of animal evolving into another kind of animal, called macroevolution.

- GEN 1:11–12, 20–21, 24–25 ~ God said, "Let the earth bring forth seed bearing plants within their own kind, where the seed is within itself. Let the waters bring forth creatures of their own kind, and let there be fowl that fly in the sky above the earth. And let the earth bring forth animals according to their kinds." God made many different kinds of animals and saw that it was good.

- GEN 6:19–20; GEN 8:19 ~ Noah brought one male and one female animal of every kind into the ark: birds after their kind, cattle after their kind, animals that creep on the surface of the earth after their kind: two of each kind, male and female. After the flood withdrew, every living animal came out of the ark with their kinds.

- 1 TI 6:20–21 ~ Guard things entrusted to your care. Avoid profane and futile gibberish, and propositions falsely called science. Those professing such things have strayed from the faith.

- JDE 1:10 ~ People speak against things they do not understand, while the things they know instinctively will destroy them.

Animals evolve, adapt, and procreate within their own kind. The diagram of a tree with connecting branches, each representing a different kind of animal, was bogus. Every animal type has its own tree of life. When people introduce or argue evolution, ask them how they define the term. Microevolution occurs within kinds from adaptation and natural selection; macroevolution does not occur (one kind does not become another kind). Natural processes cannot alter the DNA or RNA of any phylum. However, gain of function engineering was found in the coronavirus making it more transmissible and lethal; though the "kind" did not change, its genetic material was modified by man to produce a superbug (Quay & Muller, 2021). So-called experts at the NIH were warned in 01/2020 that the virus was likely concocted in a laboratory; the warning was ignored and a coverup began. We are being hit with chemical and biological agents, my friends.

Father, we know your Word is true, and truths proven via science cannot disagree. Please protect us from mad scientists who engineer new weapons of mass destruction. Please silence pseudo-scientists who purport things to be true that are not. In Jesus's name we pray, Amen.

July 22

World Brain Day was created by the World Federation of Neurology, founded on this date in Belgium, 1957. The foundation performs research on the brain, the central nervous system, and associated neurological networks. The foundation publishes studies in scientific journals and provides education and training for regional professional associations, to promote brain health and to provide current information on brain disorders and treatment.

There are things everyone can do to promote positive brain health. To begin with, sleep is essential, particularly REM or dream sleep; poor sleep and dreaming increase risk of neurological degeneration, as in the cases of Alzheimer's and Parkinson's. Regular sleep habits will help maintain the balance of chemistry in the brain. Second, all head injuries should be taken seriously, from modest to repeated blows on the head. Head protection is advised for any activity in which the head is vulnerable, be it sports, riding bikes or motorcycles, or construction jobs. Exercise is good for physical and mental health. For example, sustained aerobic exercises release endorphins in the brain promoting brain health and functioning; the key is to raise and sustain heartrate for twenty to thirty minutes. Exercising the brain is also necessary. Learning new subjects, social interaction, working puzzles, reading books, memory challenges, and games of strategy will exercise the brain. While true for all ages, exercise is recommended for the elderly, in moderation. Further, occupational and recreational therapy are beneficial, to include creating art, writing in a journal, listening to music, or anything wholesome that captures active attention.

- PRO 14:30 ~ A sound mind gives life to the flesh.
- PRO 15:28 ~ The mind of the righteous ponders how to answer, but the mouth of the wicked pours out evil.
- PRO 16:23 ~ The mind of a wise person makes speech judicious, and adds persuasiveness to words.
- COL 1:18 ~ Christ is the head of the body which is the church. He is the beginning and the firstborn of the dead, so that in all things He might reign supreme.
- ROM 12:2 ~ Do not conform to the world but be transformed by the renewal of your mind to do the perfect will of God.

There are a couple of examples in the Bible illustrating the seriousness of brain trauma. First there is the story of David and Goliath (1 SA 41–51). David was armed with nothing but a slingshot. Goliath had a suit of armor, shield, sword, and spear. But David had two advantages: he had more maneuverability, and he had God on his side. David slung a rock that hit Goliath between the eyes, knocking him out. While he was unconscious, David took the Philistine giant's own sword and hacked off his head. Second is the story of the son of David's friend Jonathan whose name was Mephibosheth. He was five years old when his nurse, while in her haste to flee the house, after the death of Saul, Jonathan, and their entire family at the hand of the Philistines, she dropped the lad; he became disabled never to walk again (2 SA 4:4;). David was anointed king and defeated the Philistines once and for all (2 SA 5:17–25). David took Jonathan's crippled son into his house to protect him and to honor a promise he made to his friend (2 SA 9:1–13).

Father, help us to respect and protect our physical and mental health. Please don't let us become lazy, neglecting to exercise mind, body, and spirit. Remind us to use protective gear when appropriate, and not take unnecessary chances with our health. Help us to put on the helmet of salvation to protect our minds from entry by evil thoughts and temptations coming from the world or within our own selves. Thank you for protecting and defending us; help us to be victorious over evil thoughts and evil people that come against us to harm us. In Jesus's name, Amen.

July 23

Give God the Glory Day is a new observance that should be practiced every day, insofar as God deserves the glory for everything good, for our personal achievements, and because He deserves to be worshipped and glorified for giving us life and freedom. He created the universe and everything in it, and all of it belongs to Him. God is great, God is good, God is omnipotent, omniscient, and omnipresent. Who else should get the glory but God alone? Since Jesus is God incarnate, He also is to be glorified, along with the Father and the Holy Spirit.

- EXO 15:11 ~ Who among the gods is like you oh Lord? Who is majestic, holy, glorious, and wonderful like you?

- 1 CH 29:11 ~ Yours, oh Lord, is the greatness, the power, the glory, the victory, and the majesty; for all that is in heaven and on earth is yours. Yours is the kingdom, Lord, and you are to be exalted as head above all.

- PSA 86:12 ~ I will praise you, oh Lord my God, with all my heart, and I will glorify your name forevermore.

- ISA 6:3 ~ The angels cried to one another, saying, "Holy, Holy, Holy is the Lord of hosts; the whole earth is full of His glory."

- ISA 42:8 ~ I am the Lord, that is my name. I will not permit my glory to be given to another or my praise given to idols.

- MAT 25:31–32 ~ Jesus said, "When the Son of man comes in glory, and the holy angels with Him, He will sit upon the throne of His glory. And all nations will be gathered before Him. And He will separate them like a shepherd divides the sheep from the goats."

- JOH 1:14 ~ And the Word became flesh and lived among us. And we witnessed His glory, the glory of the Father's only Son, full of grace and truth.

- JOH 12:23, 27–28 ~ Jesus answered them, saying, "The hour is near for the Son of man to be glorified. My soul is troubled, but what can I say, Father, save me from this hour? Father, glorify your name!" Then a voice came from heaven, saying, "I have glorified it, and I will glorify it again."

- GAL 6:14 ~ God forbid that I should glory, except in the cross of our Lord Jesus Christ, by whom the world is crucified unto me, and I unto the world.

- PHP 2:10–11 ~ Everyone should bow at the name of Jesus Christ, whether they are in heaven or on earth. Every tongue should confess that Jesus Christ is Lord, to the glory of God the Father.

- HEB 1:3 ~ Christ is the brightness of God's glory and the image of God in the flesh. He upholds all things by the power of His Word, purges us of our sins, and now sits at the right hand of God.

- 1 PE 1:18–22 ~ You are not redeemed with corruptible things like gold or silver, you are redeemed with the precious blood of Christ, who was like a lamb without blemish or spots. He, who was ordained before the foundation of the world, was revealed in these past days just for you. Believe in Him who God raised from the dead and gave glory, so that your faith and hope can remain in God. Your souls will be purified for obeying the truth that the Holy Spirit has shown to us. Therefore, fervently love your brothers with a pure heart.

- REV 4:11 ~ You are worthy, oh Lord, to receive glory, honor, and power; for you have created all things, and for your pleasure they were and are created.

- REV 5:11–12 ~ I heard the multitude of angels and saints saying, "The Lamb who was slain is worthy to receive all the power, riches, wisdom, strength, honor, glory, and blessing."

Those who give glory to worldly things or people are misguided. Yes, we can appreciate a great performance, a good sporting event or player, a good speaker or orator; and while we can strive to do the same, these people should not be idolized or adored. If you want to idolize someone or become like them, let Jesus be your hero and standard of excellence. That way, you always will have room for improvement. Of course, you must love your spouse and treat him or her as an equal; do not put them on a pedestal and do not put them down. There is no single member of a team who deserves all the credit, and nobody can be a one-person team. Give credit where credit is due, remembering that, ultimately, all credit belongs to God.

- 1 CH 16:29 ~ Give to the Lord the glory due His name. Bring an offering and come before Him. Worship the Lord in the beauty of holiness.

- ISA 2:11–12 ~ The eyes of the arrogant ones will be humbled, and their pride will be torn down. The Lord alone will be exalted in that day. He has reserved a day for the proud and conceited ones; and those so-called exalted ones will be disgraced.

- ISA 10:15–16 ~ Should the axe boast itself as greater than the one who uses it to chop the wood? Should the saw magnify itself over the one who uses it to shape the wood? It is as if the rod could strike the one that that lifts it up, or the club could lift up by itself and beat the one holding it, who is not made of wood but of flesh. Therefore, the Almighty will send a wasting disease among the great warriors; under their pomp a fire will be kindled like a blazing inferno.

- OBA 1:4 ~ The Lord says, "After you exalt yourself as the eagle, and build a nest among the stars, then I will knock you down."

- JOH 14:13 ~ Jesus said, "Whatever you ask in my name, I will do, so that the Father may be glorified in the Son."

- 1 CO 1:31; 1 CO 3:21; 1 CO 10:31 ~ Whoever would offer praise, let them offer it to the Lord. Therefore, do not glorify men, because God has given all things to you. Whether you eat, drink, or whatever you do, do it to the glory of God.

- 1 PE 4:13–14 ~ Rejoice when you partake of Christ's sufferings, so that you can be filled with joy when His glory is revealed. If you are insulted because you carry the name of Christ, be happy, for the Spirit of glory and of God rests upon you. On their part He is despised, but on your part, He is glorified.

Once a person has accepted Jesus into their heart, they will be empowered by the Holy Spirit. This gives us confidence, endurance, and resolve to exercise our gifts to the glory of God. We do this, not for our own glory, but for His. Without Him, we could do nothing; but with Him nothing is impossible.

- ISA 60:1–2 ~ Arise and shine, for your light has come; yes, the glory of God has come to you. Darkness covers the earth and great darkness covers its people. But the Lord will arise and come to you, and you will see His glory. And the Gentiles will come to His light, and kings will come to the brightness of His rising.

- JER 9:23–24 ~ God says, "The wise man must not glory in his wisdom, neither the mighty man glory in his might, nor the rich man glory in his riches. But let him that glorifies, glory in

JULY

this: that he understands and knows me, that I am the Lord who exercises loving kindness, judgment, and righteousness on the earth, for in these things I delight."

- MAT 5:16 ~ Let your light shine before others, so they may see your good works and glorify your Father who is in heaven.

- 1 CO 2:6–7 ~ We speak a message of wisdom among the mature, but not using the wisdom of this age or of its rulers who will come to nothing. No, we speak of God's secret wisdom that was previously hidden, which God destined for glory before the world began.

- 1 CO 6:19–20 ~ Do you not realize that your body is the temple of God's Holy Spirit which He has given to you? Your body no longer belongs to you for you were bought with a great price. Therefore, glorify God in your body and in your spirit, both of which belong to God.

- 2 CO 4:6–10, 17 ~ For God, who commanded the light to shine out of darkness, has shined in our hearts to give the light of the knowledge of the glory of God in the face of Jesus Christ. We hold this treasure in clay jars to show how this all-encompassing power is from God and not from us. We are surrounded by troubles, yet we are not distressed; we are perplexed, but we are not in despair. Our insignificant and temporary problems bring us closer to the eternal glory, and that glory far outweighs the sum of all of our troubles combined.

- EPH 1:17 ~ I pray that the God of our Lord Jesus Christ, the Father of glory, may give you the Spirit of wisdom and revelation, so that you may know Him more completely.

- 1 TH 2:6 ~ We did not seek praise from you or anybody else. As apostles of Christ, we could have been a burden to you, but we chose to be gentle and caring like a mother is with her children.

- 2 PE 1:2–4 ~ Grace and peace be multiplied to you through the knowledge of God, and of Jesus our Lord. His divine power has given us everything we need for life and righteousness through our knowledge of Him who called us by His own glory and goodness. He has given us His very great and precious promises, so that through them we may participate in the divine nature and escape the corruption of this world and its evil desires.

- JDE 1:24–25 ~ To Him that is able to keep you from falling, and to bring you blameless into His glorious presence with endless joy, to the only God our Savior be glory, majesty, power, and authority, through Jesus Christ our Lord, timeless throughout the ages, now and forevermore, Amen.

Having dedicated our lives to God through faith in Christ, we are made perfect in God's sight, to receive an inheritance in His kingdom. For He has sanctified us by His Holy Spirit, purifying our souls so that we can appear blameless before Him. Therefore, we will receive a glorified body that will never die, living forever in heaven, where we too will be glorified in the presence of God's Son and our brother, as an equal heir.

- DEU 28:58–59 ~ If you do not observe God's Law or revere His glorious and awesome name, He will send horrible plagues, harsh and prolonged disasters, and severe and lingering illnesses upon you and your descendants.

- PSA 8:4–5 ~ Who are humans that you keep us in your thoughts, and their offspring that you would visit them? For you made humans a little lower than angels, and have crowned us with glory and honor.

- PSA 50:23 ~ God says that whoever offers Him praise, glorifies Him. To those who do this, He will show His salvation.

DAILY DEVOTIONAL EVENTS

- ISA 40:5 ~ The glory of God will be revealed and humankind will see this together.

- MAT 24:29–31~ Jesus said, "After the tribulation there will be darkness over the world. Then a sign will appear in heaven, and everyone on earth will mourn, and they will see the Son of God coming in the clouds with all His power and glory. And He will send His angels at the sound of the great trumpet, and they will gather His elect from the four winds, and from one end of heaven to the other."

- JOH 12:23, 26–33 ~ Jesus said, "The hour has come for the Son of man to be glorified. Anyone who serves me follows me, so that where I am there they will be; those who serve me will be honored by my Father. My soul is troubled, but what can I say? Should I ask the Father to save me from this hour? This is the reason I have come to this hour. Father, glorify your name." Then a voice from heaven stated, "I have glorified it and I will glorify it again."

- JOH 17:4–5, 22–24 ~ Jesus prayed, "Father, I have glorified you here on earth and I have finished the work you gave me to do. And now, oh Father, glorify me in your presence with the glory I had with you before the world began. The glory that you gave me I have given to them, so they may be one even as we are one. Just as you are in me and I in you, may they also be in us so that the world will see that you have sent me. Father, it is my wish that they also, whom you have given to me, would be with me wherever I am, so that they may behold the glory that you have given me; for you loved me before the foundation of the world."

- ROM 8:16–18 ~ The Holy Spirit testifies with our spirits that we are God's children. If we are His children, then we are heirs: heirs of God, and joint-heirs with Christ, if indeed we share in His sufferings in order that we may later share in His glory. For I consider the sufferings of this present time to be nothing compared to the glory that will be revealed in us.

- 1 CO 2:7 ~ We speak the hidden wisdom of God in a mystery, the mystery that brings us glory which He ordained before the world was made.

- 1 CO 15:42–46 ~ This is the way it will be with the resurrection of the dead. It is sown in corruption it is raised in incorruption. It is sown in dishonor it is raised in glory. It is sown in weakness it is raised in power. It is sown a natural body it is raised a spiritual body. The spiritual did not come first; the natural came first and then the spiritual. Flesh and blood cannot inherit the kingdom, and neither can corruption inherit perfection.

- 2 CO 3:18 ~ But we, as if looking in a mirror and seeing the glory of the Lord, are changed into the same image from glory to glory, by the Spirit of the Lord.

- 1 TH 1:8–9 ~ He will inflict vengeance upon those who do not know and obey God and the Gospel of Jesus Christ. They shall suffer the punishment of eternal destruction, and exclusion from the glory of God.

- 2 TH 2.14 ~ God called believers by the Gospel to obtain the glory of our Lord Jesus Christ.

Holy Father, you are everything to us and we are nothing without you. We praise you and adore you, and we thank you for our lives, talents, accomplishments, and salvation. Help us to share the Gospel of Jesus Christ and the truth of your Word to anyone who will listen. Let us show your love by being an example of Christ, who though He was God came to earth as a man, humbling Himself, so that others might find you through Him. Let Jesus be our example and our standard of excellence; help us to emulate Him and to speak His words to the fullest extent possible. Glory be to the Father, Son, and Holy Spirit; as it was in the beginning, is now and forever shall be, world without end, Amen.

July 24

National Cousins Day occurs annually, though its origin is unknown. Obviously, it is about celebrating cousins, who oftentimes are closer to us than our immediate family. If you have been to a family reunion, you possibly spent more time with your cousins than with your own family. If you have not been in touch with your cousins, today is a good day to acknowledge them in a greeting card or phone call. Maybe you can make plans to reunite at a convenient time and place. There are holidays for every other member of the family so why not cousins, right? You probably have cousins that you are not even aware of, given that the children of your cousins are called second cousins, and their children are third cousins. Then there are cousins who are "removed" by a generation; for example, the cousin of your parent is a first cousin once removed. So, after you add up the first, second, and third cousins and cousins removed by one or more generations, you discover your family was larger than you thought, and it consists mostly of cousins. I always found it aggravating figuring out which is which so I call them all "cuz".

There were a number of famous cousins in the Bible. The most significant pair of cousins were Jesus Christ and John the Baptist. The angel of the Lord appeared to Zacharias telling him that God had answered his prayer, and his wife Elisabeth would bear a son to be named John. He would be filled with the spirit of Elijah the prophet. Zacharias doubted, thinking it impossible, for he and his wife were advanced in years. The angel, identifying himself as Gabriel, told Zacharias he would be stricken dumb until the boy was delivered. Everything Gabriel said came to pass (LUK 1:11–25). Next, Gabriel came to Mary to tell her that she would bear a child while a virgin, because the Holy Spirit would impregnate her. She was told to name Him Jesus meaning "savior" for He would save His people from their sins (LUK 1:26–35).

- LUK 1:36–46 ~ Then Gabriel told Mary, "Behold, your cousin Elisabeth who they called barren also has conceived a son in her old age; she has been with child for six months. For with God, nothing is impossible. Mary replied, "I am the maid servant of the Lord." Mary decided to pay a visit to Elisabeth. As she entered the house of Zacharias she greeted Elisabeth, who acknowledged, "Blessed are you among women, and the fruit of your womb. How is it that the mother of my Lord has come to me? For as soon as I heard your voice, my baby leaped for joy inside me." Mary replied, "My soul does magnify the Lord."

- LUK 1:56–58 ~ Mary stayed almost three months with Elisabeth and then returned home. Elisabeth had a son, and her neighbors and cousins came to rejoice with her.

Note that these two passages are the only times the word "cousin" appears in the King James Version of the Bible. It likely means Elisabeth and Mary were first cousins; the cousins mentioned in the second passage could have been first cousins, second cousins, etc. There is no mention that Mary was present when Elisabeth gave birth; Mary was three months pregnant by then. Who would have been closer to Jesus by bond and blood than His cousin John, perhaps closer than His brothers and sisters, and certainly closer in age (MAT 12:46–48; MAT 13:54–56)? John would be the forerunner of Christ, introducing Him to the world as the Lamb of God who takes away the sin of the world (JOH 1:26–30). Imagine growing up in that family!

A famous set of cousins in the Old Testament were Jacob, with Leah and Rachel. Their father Laban was the brother of Rebekah, Jacob's mother (possibly her half-brother). Jacob married his two first cousins. While there were Jewish regulations against marrying family members, it did not include cousins (LEV 18:1–18). It is still illegal to marry first cousins in some US states, though I doubt if it is rigorously enforced. One can arrive at their own conclusion as to whether one should marry a first cousin. However, the Bible does mention this: a man is not to take a wife's sister to become a rival wife, nor to have sex with her sister while the wife is living

(LEV 18:18). But this is exactly what happened. And there was definitely a rivalry between the two sisters over who would produce the most sons. Leah bore four sons, and gave her maid to have more; Rachel bore two sons and gave her maid to have more. Altogether, the sons of Jacob numbered twelve, which became the tribes of Israel. This was obviously God's plan, which included a promise to inherit the land of Canaan. Imagine growing up in that family!

- GEN 28:1–5 ~ Isaac called Jacob, blessed him, and told him to leave his home and go to the house of Laban, his mother Rebekah's brother, for he did not want Jacob to marry any daughter of Canaan. Isaac assured his son that God would bless him, and he would prosper there, and his family would grow into a multitude of people. He trusted Jacob to bless his children with the blessing of his grandfather Abraham, to ensure they receive the inheritance God promised. And Jacob left, arrived at Padanaram, and went to the house of Laban, son of Bethuel the Syrian, the brother of Rebekah the mother of Jacob and Esau.

Another Old Testament set of cousins were Esther and Mordecai. Mordecai was a Benjamite whose forefathers were taken captive by Babylonian conqueror Nebuchadnezzar (EST 2:1–6). That empire would fall, to be replaced by Media-Persia. This was the time period when Mordecai's cousin Esther would become queen of Persia. She was selected to replace the queen, who had shamed King Ahasuerus (Xerxes, in Greek) (EST 1:1–22; EST 2:1–6). Esther became queen, and would save the Jews from extermination. Her cousin Mordecai became second to the king having proved himself a worthy confidant on multiple occasions.

- EST 2:7–9 ~ Mordecai brought up Esther (aka Hadassah). She was his uncle's daughter. Her parents had died so Mordecai raised her. She was beautiful. And when the king ordered lovely virgins from his kingdom be brought to the palace, Esther was among them. The king immediately chose her above the others, and had the women prepare her for marriage.

Then there is the Old Testament cousins Elimelech and Boaz. There was a Jewish tradition, that when a woman was left with no heirs, a relative would marry her so that the inheritance of their family name would not be lost. Elimelech was the husband of Naomi; they had settled in Moab where he owned property. They had two sons who married Moabite women. Elimelech would die leaving Naomi with their two sons, both of whom died with no children. She had no recourse but return to Israel. She was sending away her daughters-in-law, when the one named Ruth wished to go with her, live with her, and worship her God. So, the two went to Bethlehem, the hometown of Naomi's deceased husband; she encouraged Ruth to glean wheat from the field of Boaz (RUT 1—3). Boaz saw the two women were destitute and offered to be their kinsman redeemer. But there was another man in line, so Boaz asked if he was willing to be the kinsman redeemer, but he was unable. Being next in line, Boaz agreed to marry Ruth so the house of Elimelech would have a kinsman redeemer (RUT 4). Since Boaz was not first in line, he probably was not a sibling of Elimelech; more likely he would have been a cousin at some level ("kinsman" generally referred to relatives not identified as part of the core family).

- RUT 4:3–14, 22 ~ Boaz told his fellow kinsman about Naomi's return, and her intention to sell a parcel of land belonging to Elimelech. Boaz offered to buy it and marry Ruth who was without husband or heir, only if a closer kinsman could not. After he declined, Boaz agreed to buy the parcel and marry Ruth. The two men settled it, so Boaz explained his intention to the elders, who approved the arrangement. In time, Ruth would have a son, thereby providing an heir. The women blessed Naomi and Ruth, and her son who was named Obed. He would be the father of Jesse and grandfather of David. [All ancestors of Jesus's parents.]

Father, we thank you that we have a kinsman Redeemer, who is Jesus Christ your Son. Christ has redeemed us, so we can never lose our inheritance in heaven. In His name, Amen.

July 25

Learn How to Win Day means exactly what it says. It is one thing to be victorious in personal endeavors and quite another to win at life. If you have Christ, you win at life; if not, you lose everything, including your life. It seems the number one priority in the world today is to win no matter what. It has become so important that cheating is rampant in sports, politics, business, education, contests, you name it. Never mind the value of competition, performance, teamwork, training, perseverance, courage, enthusiasm, and especially effort as the means to attaining first place. Nowadays, it is not about how you play the game—it is about whether you win or lose. When winning is unreachable or inequitable, it is downplayed so that everybody gets the same trophy, prize, or acknowledgement. There is no losing when the worst-case scenario is a draw. A word to the wise: if the only way you can win is by cheating, you will lose. "What have I (or you) got to lose?" I frequently hear this, I'm sure everyone has. Well for starters you can lose your integrity, honor, and reputation, if not your soul.

- JOB 27:8 ~ What hope does the hypocrite have, who gained something worldly, when God takes away his soul?

- ECC 3:1, 6 ~ For everything there is a season, a time for every purpose under heaven. A time to gain, and a time to lose; a time to keep, and a time to throw out.

Ill-gotten gain brings a curse, not a reward. One may bask in the limelight, enjoy an unwarranted victory, or spend all the prize money but it will be for a short time, after which there will be less reveling and more reviling coming their way. Even if payback doesn't befall the scammers sooner, it certainly will later, and maybe for a long time after that, if not forever.

- LEV 6:1–5 ~ These rules were given Moses by the Lord. If someone sins and is unfaithful to God because he or she has deliberately deceived another who trusted them, has cheated or stolen from someone, has found property lost by another and lied about it, has sworn an oath falsely, or committed other sins common to humankind—when they have sinned and are found guilty, they will return what was taken, or entrusted, or concealed. Full restitution must be made to the injured party plus twenty percent interest, as well as a guilt offering presented to the Lord.

- JOB 31:38–40 ~ Job concluded, "If my land cries against me or my fields complain that I have eaten its fruits without paying, or I have caused the owners to lose their livelihood—let thistles grow instead of wheat and weeds instead of barley."

- ISA 33:15–16 ~ Those who walk righteously and speak uprightly, who despise gain by extortion, who withdraw from shaking hands of those holding bribes, who refrain from listening to people plotting bloodshed, and who turn away from evil activities—they will live in high fortresses surrounded by rocks and they will have ample food and water.

- EZE 22:12–13 ~ You have taken bribes to shed blood, engaged in usury and extortion, and pursued ill-gotten gain; you have forsaken the Lord your God. I will smite these people with my hand for the dishonest gain they have collected and for the blood they have shed.

What happens when people take what they want by force rather than earning it? Their victories become defeats and their wins become losses. Take for example the siege brought upon the Kingdom of Judah by the Assyrians who sought to gain more territory and broaden their empire: God brought massive death upon them (2 CH 32:1–23). This was the beginning of the end for Assyria; Babylon would conquer the world beginning with Assyria and then Judah. How is it that God allowed Babylon to prevail? This was foretold extensively by Isaiah (ISA 23; ISA 47), Jeremiah (JER 40—50), and others. King Nebuchadnezzar had been gearing up for this takeover and planned it well. I have written about this era of history at length so I won't elaborate here. Suffice it to say that Babylon in all her glory would be short-lived, falling to the Medes and Persians, followed by the Greeks, then the Romans. This prophecy foretold events that were centuries in the future, as reported with precise detail by the prophet Daniel (DAN 2; DAN 4). That scenario is a precursor to the final empire, which will be a globalist oligarchy that takes everything by force, including property, livelihood, and freedom; it is referred to as the "new" Babylon by the prophet John (REV 14—18). This power grab will be defeated in short-order by Jesus Christ when He returns to bring His people home. What will happen to the rest of the souls? The same fate as those global regimes cited above: defeat, destruction, and death.

- EZE 34:4, 16 ~ You have not strengthened the diseased, or healed the sick, or fixed the broken, or brought back the strays, or sought what was lost; but with force and cruelty you have ruled. I will find the lost, bring home the strays, fix what was broken, and heal the sick; but I will destroy the gluttons and power-mongers, and I will feed them judgment.

What motivates people and organizations to force the win in a competition, election, or event using money, power, deception, and influence? Easy answer: greed and pride. They figure they can afford it and they deserve it because they are smart and others are ignorant. Those who force the situation are desperate to claim and maintain power. Once they get a taste of it, they cannot bear to be without it because it is addicting. Like most addictions, it is never satisfied. What a blow to their egos and pride, to ever relinquish power and control. Note that greed and pride are cousins, just as fear and deceit. Add this up and it equates to pure evil. Does that bring anyone to mind? Yes, it does—Satan. Those striving to dominate others are following in Satan's footsteps, down a path that gets progressively darker. It is yet another example of people pretending to be gods. In fact, winning is the only thing in which they place their undivided faith. They want to gain the world; but even that will not satisfy. Eventually they lose everything including their souls.

- PRO 15:27 ~ People greedy for gain bring trouble upon their own houses, but those who hate ill-gotten gain will thrive.

- ISA 56:11 ~ Yes, they are ravenous dogs that can never have enough, they are shepherds that do not understand. They all follow their own way for the sake of personal gain.

- LAM 1:9–10 ~ Her filthiness clings to her skirt; she does consider how this will end. She will have a great fall with no comfort available. Behold my suffering, oh Lord, for the enemy is winning. They are grabbing all the treasures. Pagans have entered the sanctuary after being forbidden to do so.

- 1 TI 6:3–6 ~ Beware of their false doctrines and teachings which are incongruent with sound instruction. They are arrogant and lack understanding, causing trouble and discord with their words which are filled with envy, strife, condemnation, and suspicion. Such are the perverse arguments of corrupt minds which are destitute of the truth, supposing that monetary gain is associated with godliness. Stay away from these people, remembering that godliness with contentment yields a greater gain.

If you want to be a winner, you must side with God, not His adversary; if you are following Satan, you too are God's adversary. Those who are working for God are winning, and will gain for themselves an eternal inheritance and position with His company in His kingdom. The globalists will call God a tyrant, but He is only gathering His flock. Yes, He could take it all by force, but He will let it play out instead, while the world self-destructs. When they make their final assault against God, He will flick a symbolic finger and they will plunge into the lake of fire like a herd of pigs jumping off a cliff.

- JOB 14:14 ~ If a person dies, can he or she live again? All the days of my appointed time I will wait, until my change comes.

- MAT 6:33 ~ Jesus said, "Seek first the kingdom of God, and His righteousness, and all your needs will be added unto you."

- MAT 10:39; MAT 16:25–26; MAR 8:35–36; JOH 12:25 ~ Jesus said, "Those who find their life will lose it; and those who lose their life for my sake will find it. If you love your life you will lose it, and if you hate your life in this world you will keep it unto life eternal. What does it profit anyone who gains the whole world but loses their own soul? What can a person give in exchange for their soul?"

- MAT 19:30; MAT 20:16; MAR 10:31 ~ Jesus said, "Many who are first will be last; and the last will be first. For many are called, but few are chosen."

- PHP 1:21 ~ For to me to live is Christ, and to die is gain.

- PHP 3:7–9 ~ Those things which I had gained I now consider loss for Christ's sake. Without a doubt, I count everything loss except the excellent knowledge of Christ Jesus my Lord, for whom I have suffered the loss of all worldly things, which to me are as garbage because of what I have gained in Christ; finding righteousness from Jesus, though not having any of my own in accordance with the law, but possessing the righteousness of God by faith in His Son.

We are God's because we place Him first in our lives; and we will be His first fruits which He will collect on the last day. So, if you want to be in first place, give yourself and your first fruits to God (ROM 12:1–3). This is a winning strategy for sure, for what you gain is your own soul (LUK 21:19). Or would you rather win the world and lose your soul (MAT 16:26; MAR 8:36)?

- EXO 22:29; EXO 23:19; EXO 34:26 ~ Do not delay to offer the first of your ripe fruits, and your liquors, and the firstborn of your sons.

- NUM 15:20 ~ Offer a cake from the first of your dough...

- DEU 18:4 ~ Offer the first of your corn, wine, oil, and fleece...

- DEU 26:2 ~ You must take the first of all your increase from the land that God gave to you, put it in a basket, and bring it to your place of worship.

To win the race you need to learn, train, press, overcome, and continue. This requires that you read the Bible which is your training manual, consult with the Holy Spirit who is your coach, follow Christ who leads you to victory, and persevere in your faith, never doubting because your trust is in God alone. He is the source of your knowledge, abilities, strength, and skill. And you will give the performance of a lifetime, if you've given yourself to God and put Him first in your life, enduring until the end. That is how you win first place, and the trophy is a crown of life (ISA 28:5; JAM 1:12; REV 2:10).

- PRO 3:13–14 ~ Happy are those who find wisdom and gain understanding. For its value is greater than silver, and the gain is greater than pure gold.

- JOH 20:24–29 ~ Thomas was not with the other disciples when Jesus had appeared to them, so they told him about Jesus's visit. Thomas replied, "I will not believe until I myself have seen the nail prints in His hands and feet and touched His wounded hands and side." After eight days Jesus returned to His disciples, and this time Thomas was with them. Jesus said, "Peace to all of you." Then He turned to Thomas and said, "Look at me, see and touch my wounds, so that you might not be without faith but believe." Thomas answered, "My Lord and my God." Jesus replied, "Thomas, you have believed because you have seen; blessed are those who have not seen and still have believed."

- 1 CO 9:24 ~ Do you understand that there are many competitors in a race but only one will receive first prize? Therefore, run with the intention of winning that prize.

- HEB 12:1–3 ~ We are encompassed by a great cloud of witnesses; let us lay aside every burden and sin that so easily beset us, and run with patience the race set before us. We must fix our eyes on Jesus, the author and perfecter of our faith, who for the joy set before Him endured the cross, scorning its shame, and who now sits on His throne at the right hand of God. Remember Him, who endured great opposition from sinful men, so that you will not grow faint and lose heart.

The bottom line is this: care enough to try hard and exert continuous effort; play by the rules of the game, especially God's rules; learn the ropes, climb the ladder, and pay your dues. It will pay off in abundance. After all, isn't that what everyone is pursuing: beneficial outcomes. Doing it the other way, which is the worldly one, will lead to negative outcomes in the long run even when they look pleasant at first. Remember, you must exercise the body, the mind, and the spirit for each will contribute to your success, as well as to your overall health. Concentrate on the spiritual above all, for the Holy Spirit will be able to connect with your mind and lead you to glory. You will grow stronger, perform better, and persevere in the face of interference, obstacles, adversaries, and your own worries—as long as Jesus is your team leader.

Dear Heavenly Father, thank you for your Son who won the victory for us. Thank you for your Holy Spirit who guides us, trains us, and strengthens our faith, enabling us to endure the pace and win the race. You have said through your prophet that those who wait upon the Lord will have their strength renewed; and we will mount up with wings as eagles. We will run and not get weary; we will keep on going and not grow faint. Help us always to trust in these your words, as we continue to do our part in conditioning or bodies, minds, and spirits to compete in the human race and win. And help us to remember that you deserve the glory for all that we achieve in this life. To you we give all glory, praise, and honor as we pray again in Jesus's name, Amen.

July 26

National Aunt and Uncle Day is obviously to celebrate aunts and uncles. We already celebrated cousins a couple of days ago, so why not their parents, right? This is another holiday with unknown origin designed to bring families together. Maybe you can celebrate cousins, aunts, and uncles together this week during summer vacation. Generally, relationships with cousins usually develop when your parents and their siblings are together. The more siblings that mom and dad have, the more aunts and uncles you should have to enrich your life, unless they don't get along which would be unfortunate. But when the parents and their siblings get older, you will be spending more time with your own siblings and cousins. Sometimes aunts and uncles are like surrogate parents; there are things you might feel more comfortable talking about with them which you are not ready to talk about with your parents. Aunts and uncles are a wealth of information if you want to learn more about your parents, family history, and other relatives. Take time to call and visit with them; I bet it will make their day.

One of the famous nephews in the Bible was Lot, the nephew of Abraham. The story begins with Abraham's father Terah leaving Ur of the Chaldees for Haran, which was in the north. Terah was accompanied by his son Abram (before becoming Abraham) and his wife Sarai (before becoming Sarah), who were the uncle and aunt of Lot. Terah died in Heran. Shortly thereafter, Abram was called by God to depart for a land He would give to Abram and Sarai's descendants (GEN 11:32). They followed the fertile crescent toward the southwest, settling in Shechem. During a famine, they resided in Egypt. But they ran into trouble when Pharaoh became infatuated with Abram's wife Sarai. Abram told the emperor that she was his sister, which was half true because she was his half-sister, but she also was his wife. Abram failed to mention that detail and it would become a problem, because Pharaoh took her into his harem. God sent plagues on Egypt, until Pharaoh found out why, after which he sent them away and they returned to Canaan (GEN 11—12). They settled in Bethel where they prospered, to the degree that it was necessary for Abram and Lot to divide their flocks and herds and part ways. Abram let Lot choose the greener land in the Jordan valley and Abram stayed in the hill country. God told Abram to look in all directions, for the entire territory of Canaan would become the property of his offspring. Abram moved to the trees of Mamre at Hebron, and built an altar to the Lord (GEN 13). Lot faced predicaments after settling in the Jordan valley, where there was war, conflict, sin and evil; Abram had to rescue Lot who was taken captive (GEN 14). Lot would resettle in Sodom, and everybody knows what eventually happened there, when Lot, his wife, and their two daughters had to flee in a hurry. Fire and brimstone destroyed Sodom, Gomorrah, and other towns; Lot's wife didn't make it because she turned to look back.

- GEN 12:1–7 ~ The Lord called Abram and told him to leave from his father's house for a land He would show him, promising to make Abram a great nation and a blessing to others. Abram took his wife, and nephew Lot with them to the land of Canaan which was already populated. So, they passed through and stopped at Shechem. And the Lord told Abram that this was the land of promise, an inheritance for his offspring. And Abram built an alter to the Lord on that site.

- GEN 15:1–7 ~ Again, the Lord came to visit Abram in a vision telling him not to fear for he would be rewarded for his faith and patience. Abram replied that he still had no children or heir. God again promised him an heir from his own seed. God told Abram to look up and try to count the number the stars, for his seed would multiply like the stars in the sky and could not be numbered. Abram believed that God was going to give him a son and the land, even in his old age.

Time passed and still no children, so Sarai offered her maid Hagar to Abram to fulfill God's promise, and Hagar bore Ishmael. Sarai became jealous and drove Hagar and Ishmael away. God looked after Hagar and Ishmael and blessed them in the desert; later, God told them to return home (GEN 16). God reminded Abram that his wife would bear the son of promise.

- GEN 17:1–27 ~ When Abram was in his nineties, the Lord appeared again asking Abram to walk in His ways and be right with God. And God made a covenant with Abram, to make him a father of nations; and God changed his name to Abraham. The covenant would be with his seed, who would possess the land of Canaan. To seal the deal Abraham needed to be circumcised, as well as every male in his company from that time forward, whether his seed or the seed of his companions. And God changed Sarai's name to Sarah and assured him that she would be the one to bear the son promised to Abraham. Abraham laughed, since he was ninety-nine and his wife was ninety. God told him they would have a child and he would be named Isaac (meaning laughter), and the covenant would be with him and his offspring. And all the males were circumcised including Abraham and Ishmael.

This is the beginning of the story of Abraham and Lot (read GEN 18—22). Rest assured, Isaac was born and circumcised after eight days in accordance with God's instructions. And Isaac would become the father of Esau and Jacob. There were many other uncles and aunts in the Bible. For example, we already discussed Laban and his nephew Jacob who married Laban's two daughters, his first cousins, whose aunt and uncle would have been Isaac and Rebekah.

It deserves mentioning another uncle and nephew team from the New Testament. A companion of Paul named Barnabas had a nephew named Mark (aka Marcus or John Mark). They were companions of Paul for some time before going their separate ways.

- ACT 13:13–52 ~ When Paul was released from Paphos they traveled to Perga, along with John (Mark). They came to Antioch and entered the synagogue on the Sabbath and sat down. After reading the law and prophecy, the rulers permitted Paul to speak. He stood up and addressed those men of Israel who feared God and were eager to listen. Paul provided a history lesson about the judges and kings. He concluded telling them about the lineage of David and the Savior named Jesus who would come from that line, after the preaching of John the Baptist. Paul proceeded to teach them about Christ, His crucifixion and resurrection, and the salvation which comes through faith in Him and not by works of the Law. And many Jews and proselytes followed Paul and Barnabas. Plus, many Gentiles were converted. But many other Jews despised them and their teaching and wanted to be done with them.

- ACT 15:35 ~ Having traveled to Antioch, Paul and Barnabas taught and preached the Word of the Lord. After many days Paul suggested to Barnabas that they make the rounds again visiting the cities where they had preached to see how they were progressing. Barnabas wanted to bring John Mark, but Paul did not trust the nephew because he had left them once before. The disagreement led to a falling out, and Barnabas took Mark with him to Cyprus instead. Paul chose Silas who was recommended to him, and they preached through Syria and Cilicia, confirming the churches there.

- COL 4:10 ~ Paul wrote: Aristarchus my fellow prisoner gives his regards, and Marcus, the son of Barnabas's sister. If he comes to you receive him, for he is one of us.

Thank you, Father, for our family and close relatives who bring us love and joy; thank you for our family in Christ who also bring us love and joy. Help us to spread the love and joy to others, inviting them into the membership of faith in Jesus. Let us be living examples of the love of Jesus and the faith of Abraham and Paul as we go about our daily routines. In the name of Jesus, your Son, our Lord who is the author and finisher of our faith, Amen.

July 27

National Day of the Cowboy is the fourth Saturday in July. It was started in 2005 by an organization in Wyoming appropriately called, National Day of the Cowboy. The idea was taken to the Wyoming legislature and they passed a bill proclaiming this holiday; numerous other states have joined them since then. It seems a worthy cause to keep this element of our heritage alive. Most western states had cowboys and ranches before becoming states. There are still cowboys doing their thing out west: riding horses, roping cattle, branding them, driving herds to feeding grounds or the market. This is hard work for meager wages, but worth the experience of the great outdoors for those who are dedicated to it.

If you have never attended a rodeo, you probably can find one this time of year. Cowboying has become a popular spectator sport; they make a decent living, at least until their bodies can't take it anymore. Wild west shows are interesting if you want to watch cowboys roping, shooting, and wrestling cows. Some places rent horses to ride if you haven't tried that. They still make movies about this lifestyle. And who doesn't like a good western? There are great museums, and events where people dress up western style. I grew up in the southwest and I still wear cowboy boots. As a boy, I had a cap gun and holster and pretended I was the sheriff. Those days are long gone; you can't even have a cap gun because some fool will say it looks too much like a real gun. I feel sorry for little kids today; though they have video games and electronics, they seldom play outside and invent their own fun, largely because it isn't safe.

Since the beginning of humankind there have been people tending herds of cattle and sheep. In fact, Abel was a herdsman who tended sheep, until he was murdered by his brother Cain (GEN 4). The cowboys of the American West turned that job into an art form. The theaters glamorized it, and to this day, it is still entertaining to watch. The shepherds of old had many of the same skills as cowboys; they had to be strong, fight off wolves, drive herds across the land, round up strays, and work long days. The big difference, they had to do it without a skilled horse. Horses were used for chariots and farming; their value for ranching had yet to be realized.

- GEN 13:7–12 ~ There were arguments between Abram's herdsmen and Lot's, for their flocks and herds were massive; plus, there were local people using the land. So, Abram and Lot, to avoid any strife between themselves, agreed to part company. Lot selected the plain near the Jordan River because it had water and looked like a garden; he pitched his tent near Sodom. Abram remained in the land of Canaan.

- NUM 32:1–11 ~ The children of Reuben and the children of Gad both had a large number of cattle; they saw that the lands they had passed were good for cattle. They wanted to settle there and build their ranches instead of crossing over the Jordan with their countrymen. Moses chastised them, asking why their brothers should go to war while they stayed behind. God was angry and declared that nobody over age twenty would see the land that He promised Abraham, because they followed their own ways and not His.

- 1 KI 4:26; 1 KI 10:28 ~ Solomon had four thousand stables for chariot horses and twelve thousand horses in total. His horses were imported mostly from Egypt.

- JOE 1:18–19 ~ The beasts groan, the herds of cattle are confused, the flocks of sheep are dying, because there is no pasture. For fire has consumed the pastures of the wilderness and burned all the trees (see REV 8:7).

Father, we thank you for those who do the difficult jobs making our lives easier. Help them to be safe and to prosper, those who work hard, and appreciate what they have, keeping you first in their lives, and teaching their children the truth of your Word in Jesus Christ, Amen.

July 28

National Parents Day is the fourth Sunday in July. It was signed into law by President Clinton in 1994 to support parents in the process of raising children. Who is more important to anybody's life than their parents, well next to God that is? Unfortunately, some parents do not accept their responsibility leaving a lot of single parents behind. Kids with less than a two-parent home consisting of a mom and dad who exhibit genuine love will be at a disadvantage. No other family constellation works better or produces superior results regarding the morality and success of the child. Clearly, God's recipe for an excellent family requires both biological parents to be available for every child they raise, until adulthood. By their twenties they should be prepared to get married and start a family of their own, which is the way God intended.

Where would we be without our parents? We wouldn't. Children should be honoring and respecting their parents for the duration of their lives, unless of course your parents were absent, dead, or abandoned you, in which case, celebrate the person or persons who were there for you and still are. Your true parents are not always your blood and that is okay. Regardless, your heavenly Father is available at all times, in all places, and in every situation; you can't go wrong honoring God today, tomorrow, and forever. You can find Parents Day programs, honorees, and committees if you wish to pursue a social interest in this holiday. At the very least, however, get in touch with the figure you most admired growing up and tell them they are appreciated. If they are nearby, take them to lunch or have a cookout at home.

- EXO 20:12 ~ Honor your father and your mother, that your days may be long on the earth which the Lord has given to you.

- LEV 19:2–3 ~ Be holy like your Father in heaven is holy. Everyone must respect their father and mother, and obey God.

- PRO 3:5–6, 11–12 ~ Trust in the Lord with all you heart and do not depend on your own understanding. In all you do acknowledge Him and He will direct you in the way you should go. Do not despise the Lord's discipline and do not resent His correction, for the Lord corrects those He loves just as any father who delights in his child.

- ROM 17:6 ~ Grandchildren are the pride of their grandparents and the glory of their parents.

- EPH 6:1–4 ~ Children, obey your parents, for God has given them authority over you. Honor your parents as commanded in the Ten Commandments. This is the first commandment that brings a promise: If you honor your parents your life will be long and happy. Parents, do not provoke your children to anger and frustration. Instead, raise them in the nurture and discipline of righteousness, as instructed by God in the Bible.

- 2 CO 12:14–15 ~ Parents save up for their children, children do not save up for their parents.

- COL 3:20–21 ~ Children, obey your parents. Parents, do not get mad at your children or they will become discouraged.

Parental guidance helps for many reasons, not the least of which is admonishment. For what parent does not want to correct their children when they are wrong, in danger, or in trouble? It is a duty. Sometimes, it may include punishment, but this is a last resort, when reinforcement ceases to work. In the long run, the kids will thank their parents for encouragement, patience, discipline, and correction.

- DEU 4:8–10 ~ Is there any other nation so great that has laws and judgments as righteous as these laws I have set before you this day? Do not forget what God has done for you. May His works have a lasting impression on your lives. Teach your children and grandchildren about

His glorious miracles. Especially remind your children of God's instructions given to Moses at Sinai about reverencing Him and about teaching His laws from generation to generation.

- DEU 6:2–7 ~ Fear the Lord and keep all His commandments and laws. Ensure that your children and your children's children obey God. Do this and you will prosper and your life will be prolonged. Love God with all your heart, soul, and might. Keep God's Word in your heart and teach His ways carefully and thoughtfully to your children. Talk with your family all the time about God, every day and night, whenever you are together.

- JOB 5:17 ~ Happy is the person that God corrects; therefore, do not despise being chastised by the Almighty.

- PRO 1:7–10 ~ The fear of God is the beginning of wisdom; only fools despise wisdom and instruction. Children, listen to the instruction of your parents; if sinners entice you, do not give in.

There is a penalty for those who do not honor their parents or obey them. They will be more likely to land in jail, to have their lives shortened, to take unnecessary risks, to lose their money as quickly as it is earned, to use drugs and to overdose. The same is true for those who do not honor God or obey our heavenly Father.

- PRO 13:1, 18, 20, 24 ~ A wise son listens to his father's instructions, but those who reject wise counsel hear nothing. Poverty and shame are the rewards for those who refuse instruction, but those who respectfully listen when being scolded will be honored. Those who associate with wise people will become wise; but a companion of fools will find destruction. Parents that do not discipline their children must hate them, for a loving parent has to punish their children sometimes.

- PRO 28:7 ~ Whoever keeps the Law is a wise child; but a riotous child embarrasses the parents.

- PRO 29:15, 17 ~ Punishment provides wisdom; but children left to themselves shame their parents. Correct your children when they are wrong, and you will be able to rest at night, and they will be your pride and joy.

- PRO 30:11–14 ~ There is a proud and arrogant generation that thinks they are pure and guiltless, yet they curse their parents and they take advantage of those less fortunate.

- HEB 12:7–11 ~ If you endure punishment, God treats you as His own child, for what child is never disciplined by their parents? But if you are never punished then you have no parents and you are nobody's child. If we have natural parents correcting us, and if we respect them, should we not subject ourselves even more to the Father of all spirits, and live? For our parents punish us sometimes to make themselves feel better, but God punishes us so that we will profit from it, by sharing in His righteousness. Being punished may make one feel sorrowful, but later it yields the peaceful fruit of righteousness.

Father in heaven, you are the best parent ever. Help parents to follow your instructions about how children should be raised, and to work together as a team to ensure they are on the same page with your Word. The guidebook for parenting is the Holy Bible; remind young parents to teach it to their kids, to take their kids to church, and to pray every day with them. Let all who plan on becoming a parent learn your wisdom concerning parenting, emulating you, dear Father, as best they can. Help children learn about and emulate Jesus Christ, so they can know how to be an obedient child: one who brings honor to your home and family. Above all, help parents to love their children and each other like you love your Son and like He loves the church. In Jesus's name we pray, Amen.

July 29

Revelation Day is nominated to raise awareness of the countless revelations found in the Holy Bible. God reveals Himself, His Law, His works and ways, His instructions and will, His nature, His Messiah, His Holy Spirit, the beginning and the end and points in-between. Everything you need to know about God is found in His Word, disclosing but a glimpse of His attributes and majesty. Today is a good day to start delving into God's Word if you haven't already. Almost every time I pick up the Bible, I learn something new. The Bible validates itself, interprets itself, and stands alone among all written works, especially with respect to divine revelation. God reveals answers, reveals mysteries, and reveals future events. This wealth of knowledge and wisdom cannot be found anywhere else. The more you read the Bible, the more knowledge you gain, and the more evidence and facts you can bring to bear, which enhance spiritual power.

How does God reveal things? Well, His Holy Spirit is the truth (1 JO 5:1–12). That truth is spoken through the written Word, and the Word made flesh who is Christ the Lord (JOH 1:1–14). Those who speak the truth of God's Word are also speaking by the power of the Holy Spirit working through them (MAT 10:19–20).

- DAN 2:28 ~ There is a God in heaven who reveals mysteries...

- ROM 8:16–18 ~ The Holy Spirit testifies with our spirits that we are God's children. If we are His children, then we are heirs: heirs of God, and joint-heirs with Christ, if indeed we share in His sufferings in order that we may later share in His glory. For I consider the sufferings of this present time to be nothing compared to the glory that will be revealed in us.

- 1 CO 2:10–13 ~ God reveals His mysteries to us through His Spirit, for the Spirit searches all things, even the deepest things of God. Nobody can know the deepest thoughts of another, only the spirit within that person can know them. Similarly, nobody can know the deepest thoughts of God except His Holy Spirit. We have received the Spirit of God, not the spirit of the world, so that we might know the things that God has given to us for free. This is why we teach in accordance with the wisdom of the Spirit, not the wisdom of this world, for you cannot compare spiritual things with worldly things.

- EPH 1:17 ~ I pray that the God of our Lord Jesus Christ, the Father of glory, may give you the Spirit of wisdom and revelation, so that you may know Him more completely.

- EPH 3:3–6, 9–11 ~ In a revelation, God showed me the mystery of Christ, and I must share that mystery with the world. It is a mystery that was hidden but is now revealed through His apostles and prophets by the Holy Spirit. For the Gentiles will be fellow heirs with the Jews, and will partake of the promise that came true through Christ by the Gospel. All people can know the mystery which God kept hidden from the beginning of the world, and the eternal purpose for which Jesus Christ our Lord has come.

God reveals Himself to people even when they are not seeking Him. But when they realize it is God trying to get their attention, people will normally listen. Then there are those who hear God, but refuse to listen.

- NUM 24 ~ God revealed a vision to the evil sorcerer Balaam, who was ordered by King Balak to prophesy against Israel. Instead, Balaam blessed Israel and prophesied against Balak's people, in accordance with God's revelation.

- ISA 40:5 ~ The glory of God will be revealed and humankind will see this together.

- ISA 65:1 ~ I revealed myself to those who did not ask about me and I was found by those who did not seek me. To the nation that did not call on my name, I said, "Here I AM."

JULY

- ROM 1:18–20 ~ God's wrath is revealed from heaven against the sinfulness of people, who know the truth of unrighteousness, because God has made it known to them. The invisible qualities of God are clearly seen from the creation of the world, for through His many creations one can understand God, even His power and divine nature, so nobody has an excuse.

- ROM 9:25–26 ~ God spoke through Hosea saying, "I will call them my people who were not my people, and I will call them beloved who were not my beloved. And at that place where I told them they were not my people—others will be called the children of the living God."

- TIT 2:11 ~ The grace of God that brings salvation has appeared to all people.

- 1 JO 5:7 ~ There are three in heaven who reveal themselves to us: the Father, the Word (Christ), and the Holy Spirit; and these three are one.

In the Old Testament, God handed down His laws and statutes, including the Ten Commandments; everybody has heard of these commandments though many cannot list them in order. Throughout the Old Testament, God revealed His Law and His will to His chosen people, Israel. And most of those laws still apply (MAT 5:18), with the notable exception being that blood offerings have ceased since Jesus made the perfect offering for sin, for all people and for all time (HEB 10:1–18).

- EXO 24:8 ~ Moses took blood from the sacrifice and sprinkled it on the people saying, "This is the blood of the everlasting covenant revealed by the Lord in these His words."

- ROM 7:7, 14 ~ The Law told me what not to do, thereby revealing sin to me. So, is the Law sin? No, it is the opposite of sin. For the Law is spiritual, but I am carnal because I sin.

- GAL 3:8–13, 21–24 ~ The scriptures foretold that God would justify sinners through faith, announcing the Gospel in advance to Abraham, and promising him many descendants, one of whom would be a blessing to all nations. Those who live by faith will be blessed as Abraham was. But nobody is justified in God's sight by works of the Law, for it is written that the just will live by faith. Christ has redeemed us from the curse of the Law, being made a curse in our place, for it is written that cursed is he who is crucified on a cross. Is the Law, therefore, in opposition to God's promise? Absolutely not! For no law was given that could bring life. The scriptures tell us that the world is a slave to sin, and that the promise of life is given to all believers in Jesus Christ. Before faith in Christ came, everyone was a prisoner to the Law, kept there until faith was revealed in Christ. Hence, the Law is our teacher to bring us to faith in Christ, so that we might be justified by that faith.

God reveals the path of righteousness which leads to salvation through Jesus Christ. Yes, we are to obey God and His commandments; but that will not earn us a spot in heaven since we are unable to fulfill the Law perfectly. Only Christ was able to do that, which is why trust in His sacrifice for sins is the only way to obtain a position in heaven. The Old Testament revealed the Law which points us to Messiah; and the New Testament revealed Grace, by which we are saved through the death and resurrection of Jesus Christ who fulfilled the Law. Grace is undeserved favor, which is free to all who receive Christ as their personal Savior. He is our Messiah, foretold throughout the Old Testament, to be the one who would save all people from sin and death that choose to believe in Him and in His Word.

- DAN 9:1–27 ~ Daniel prayed a great prayer of confession and repentance to the Lord regarding the sinfulness of the people. He recognized that disaster had befallen the Israelites because of their disobedience to God. Daniel pleaded with God to turn away His vengeance and forgive them. And God immediately answered Daniel's prayer by sending to him the angel Gabriel, who revealed the coming of the Anointed One (Messiah).

- ROM 1:17–18 ~ The righteousness of God has been revealed from faith to faith in the Gospel of Christ. As it is written: The just shall live by faith. For the wrath of God is revealed from heaven against unrighteousness.

- GAL 1:7–12 ~ Some would pervert the Gospel of Christ. If anyone preaches another Gospel not preached by Jesus Christ and His apostles, that person is cursed by God. The Gospel of Christ does not come from the thoughts of man, or from the teachings of man, but rather from the revelation of Jesus Christ.

- COL 1:26–27 ~ The mystery, hidden from ages past, has now been revealed to the saints, to whom God will give the riches of His glory. It is for anyone who turns to Christ for their hope including the Gentiles.

- 1 PE 1:5, 18–21 ~ You are kept by the power of God through faith unto salvation, ready to be revealed in the last time. You are not redeemed with corruptible things like gold or silver, you are redeemed with the precious blood of Christ, who was like a lamb without blemish or spots. He, who was ordained before the foundation of the world, was revealed in these past days just for you. Believe in Him who God raised from the dead and gave glory, so that your faith and hope remain in God.

- 1 PE 4:13 ~ Rejoice, because you are partakers of Christ's suffering. When His glory is revealed, you may be glad and exceedingly joyful.

- 1 JO 1:1–3 ~ That which was from the beginning, the very Word of life, we heard, we saw, and we touched. For life was revealed, and we have seen it, and bear witness, and show you that eternal life, which was with the Father, visited us. That which we have seen and heard we declare to you, so that you can become one of us; for truly our fellowship is with the Father, and with His Son Jesus Christ.

God has revealed many things about the end of days. It is not a checklist that you can keep track of, it is a collection of general revelations, signs, and wonders to watch for, so that you can be reminded of His coming and be prepared for it. For He will come when you are not expecting Him, unless you stay focused on His Word and the signs, in which case you will be ready and joyful on that day.

- ISA 40:5 ~ The glory of the Lord will be revealed, and all human flesh will see it together, for the Lord has said so.

- 1 CO 3:13 ~ Everyone's works will be revealed and will be tested by the fire to determine what sort of works they really are.

- 1 CO 15:42–44, 50–56 ~ This is the resurrection: a corrupt body was sown, but an incorruptible body is raised. It was sown in dishonor but raised in honor. It was sown a physical body but raised a spiritual body. Flesh and blood cannot inherit the kingdom of God; neither can corruption inherit incorruption. A mystery is revealed: we will not all die but all will be changed. Upon His return, in a single moment as the great trumpet sounds, Christ's own whether alive or dead will arise into heaven to receive new, incorruptible bodies. The corruptible must become incorruptible before the mortal can become immortal. Then the statement "death is swallowed up in victory" will be true. Finally, when Christ delivers the kingdom of God to the Father, He will destroy death. Death, where is your sting, and Hell where is your victory? The sting of death is sin, and its strength is the Law.

- 2 TH 2:3–4, 8–12 ~ Do not let anyone deceive you, for there will be a falling away prior to the revealing of the son of perdition who opposes God and exalts himself above all others including

God. Pretending to be a god he sits at the temple in his pompous arrogance. The evil one, who will be revealed in the latter times, will be consumed by the Spirit of God and the brightness of His coming. The evil one does the work of Satan, with false signs and fake miracles, with deceitfulness and unrighteousness in those that perish, who did not love the truth. So God sent them a strong delusion allowing them to believe the lie. Those who follow false teaching, find pleasure in unrighteousness, and do not believe the truth will be damned.

- 1 PE 1:2–5 ~ Christians are chosen by God in advance through sanctification of the Spirit, to be obedient to Christ and cleansed by His blood. Blessed be God the Father of our Lord Jesus Christ. According to His abundant mercy, He recreated in us the living hope, brought by the resurrection of Christ from the dead, to receive an incorruptible and undefiled inheritance reserved in heaven and lasting forever. Through faith, He has shielded us by His power until the coming of our salvation which is ready to be revealed on the last day.

- REV 1:1–4 ~ The revelation from Jesus Christ, which God gave to Him to show His servants what would come to pass, was given to John by His angel. John testified to everything he saw and heard through the testimony of Jesus Christ. Blessed be those who read these words of prophecy, and who listen carefully and take it to heart, because the time is coming soon. John sent this revelation message to the seven churches of Asia.

There are things God reveals and makes clear, and there are things that God does not reveal. The essential things we can learn and understand; but some things we are not ready to learn, because we cannot understand them; but all things will be revealed when Christ returns.

- DEU 29:29 ~ The secret things belong to the Lord, but those things that He reveals belong to us and to our children forever, so that we may follow the words of His Law.

- MAT 10:26–27; LUK 12:3 ~ Jesus said, "Do not fear those who hate you, for everything that is hidden now will be revealed later; everything that is unknown will become known. What I tell you in darkness you will speak in the light. What you hear in private will be proclaimed from the rooftops."

- REV 10:4 ~ When the seven thunders uttered their voices I was about to write when I heard a voice from heaven saying, "Seal those things uttered by the seven thunders; do not write them down."

Father in heaven, whose divine revelation is available to all people, we praise and thank you for your wisdom and truth; because your words bring peace, joy, and life through faith in Christ, your only begotten Son. Help us to stay constant in our faith and conscientious in the study of your Word, so that we may grow in wisdom and remain steadfast in the true knowledge of you and your plan of salvation. Prepare us to be ready to give an answer to anyone who asks about the peace, joy, and hope that we have through Jesus Christ, with answers that reveal the divine truth that you have revealed to all who wish to understand it. And though we can never grasp the entirety of the insight available in the Holy Bible, let that not be an excuse for us to cease searching to know and discern more, or to set the Bible aside; but let it make us more determined to explore, examine, and learn. In the name of Christ, who will be revealed in His glory on the last day when He takes us home to heaven, we pray, Amen.

July 30

In God We Trust Became the National Motto of the United States on this day in 1956, when a joint resolution of Congress was signed by President Eisenhower. The slogan began to appear on our currency prior to that and has to this day. It was popular from the start, since God had always been the guiding light of our nation. It was used to boost morale in the Revolutionary War, and by the Union army during the Civil War. Though still revered by the majority of Americans, there are outspoken activists who dislike any mention of God anywhere; they want to remove it from our currency and everywhere else, as if it was a violation of the First Amendment, which it is not since no specific religion is being promoted. This date is not to be confused with another date in April which people have unofficially proclaimed as the day to celebrate our motto.

Anyone who trusts in the Lord will have peace, joy, and safety; those who fear God are not afraid of the world. Those who place their faith in Him will have everything they need. Faith and trust go hand-in-hand; if you have one you have the other. If you trust in God and place your faith in Jesus, this will be counted as righteousness before God apart from your good works.

- PSA 5:11 ~ Let all who trust in God rejoice and sing for joy, for God will defend them; and those that love God will exalt Him.

- PSA 37:3–8 ~ Trust in the Lord and do good and you will have security. Take delight in the Lord and you will receive the delights of your heart. Commit yourself to the Lord and He will vindicate you. Wait patiently for the Lord and do not worry. Do not act out of anger.

- PSA 62:8, 10 ~ Trust in God always and pour out your heart to Him. He is your refuge. Do not trust in extortion; do not hope in robbery. Do not set your heart on earthly riches even if they are abundant.

- PRO 29:25 ~ The fear of humankind is a trap, but those who trust in God will be safe.

- MAT 6:32–34 ~ Jesus taught: Seek first the kingdom of God and His righteousness, and everything else will be yours. Do not be anxious about tomorrow; each day has enough new challenges to confront. Trust in God to provide your needs. Who knows your needs better?

- JOH 14:1–3, 27 ~ Jesus said, "Do not let your heart be troubled. Trust in God, and trust in me. There are many mansions in my Father's house, and I am going there to prepare one for you. And I will come back for you and take you there, so that where I am you can be also. Peace I leave with you, my peace I give to you; I do not give as the world gives. So do not let your heart be troubled, neither let it be afraid."

- ROM 4:5 ~ Trust God who justifies sinners, and your faith will be credited as righteousness.

- 1 TI 6:17 ~ Tell the rich people in the world not to act so proud or to set their hopes on uncertain earthly riches. Tell them to set their hope and trust in God, who furnishes everything in this world for us to enjoy.

Those who trust in the Lord will be like a fortress against evil. Those who trust in God will know what to do next; they will be given instructions and directions. Those who trust in God will be prosperous and productive. If our nation trusts in God, He will do all these things for our nation. It is critical that we remain one nation under God in whom we trust.

- JOB 8:13–14 ~ The destiny of those who forget God is the loss of hope, for their trust in worldly things is a fragile one.

- PSA 33:8–11 ~ Let all the earth fear the Lord; let all the inhabitants of the world stand in awe of Him. For God spoke and it happened; He commanded and it stood. God thwarts the plans of the nations and the purposes of the people. But His plans stand forever and His purposes continue for all generations.

- PSA 56:3–4 ~ Whenever I am afraid, I trust in God. If I trust in God without fear, what can humankind do to me?
- PSA 125:1 ~ Those who trust in the Lord will be like mount Zion, which cannot be removed, but abides forever.
- PRO 3:5–6 ~ Trust in God with all your heart and do not depend on your own understanding. In all your ways acknowledge God and He will direct you in the way to go.
- PRO 11:4, 28 ~ Riches will not profit anyone in the day of wrath; only righteousness can save a person from death. Those who trust in their riches will fail, but those who trust in God will flourish.
- ISA 26:3–4 ~ God will keep you in perfect peace if you keep your mind on God and trust in Him forever, for in the Lord Jehovah you will find everlasting strength.
- ROM 4:16 ~ The fulfillment of God's promises in your life depends entirely on trusting Him and His ways, and embracing Him and His works. His promises are given purely as a gift. That is the only way everyone can have a chance, including those who recognize religious traditions and those who are unaware of them.

People who trust in the world or others, but do not trust in God, have no guarantees, and they risk losing their souls. Nations which follow the ways of the world will likewise fall. This is foretold to occur in a big way towards the end of days. Remember, there are people we can trust and people we can never trust; but all people can be brought to Christ and change their status. Though our allies can be trusted to a degree, there are nations we can never trust. Therefore, only trust in God is sure, and only truth will work.

- PSA 40:4 ~ Blessed be those who trust in the Lord rather than giving their respect to the proud and deceitful.
- PSA 41:9–10 ~ The trusted friend with whom I ate bread has betrayed me. Have mercy on me. Raise me up so that I can rebuke them.
- PSA 49:6–8 ~ They trust in their wealth, and brag about their riches; but none of them have the means to redeem anyone, or to give a ransom for another. The ransom is extremely costly, and no amount of money will ever be enough.
- PSA 52:4–8 ~ Surely God will bring you down into everlasting ruin; He will uproot you from the land of the living. The righteous will see and fear. They will laugh, saying, "Here is the man that did not make God his strength, but instead placed his trust in the abundance of his riches and found strength in wickedness. But I am like a green olive tree, flourishing in the house of God, and I will trust in His mercy forevermore.
- PRO 3:5–6 ~ Trust in the Lord with all you heart and do not depend on your own understanding. In all you do acknowledge Him and He will direct your paths.
- PRO 28:25 ~ People with proud hearts serve only to create conflict, but those who trust in God will prosper.
- ISA 28:15–19 ~ All covenants of death and agreements with hell will be null and void. Those who trusted in these lies will be trampled by the overwhelming scourge that passes through.

- ISA 47:10–15 ~ You trusted in your wickedness, thinking that nobody sees you; but your wisdom and knowledge have perverted you. You told yourself that your power was superior and you needed no other. But disaster will befall you; you will not see it coming and you cannot put it off. Utter desolation will be swift and unexpected. Stand by your enchantments, charms, and visions, which you practiced since your youth for profit and advantage. You will become weary of your astrologers and their monthly forecasts. Let us see if they can save you. They will burn as stubble in the fire; nobody will come to deliver them from the powerful flame. This is not a fire for providing warmth or to gather around. But it is the only thing they gave you ever since childhood, those you promoted and depended on. All of you have erred and wandered into the fire together, with nobody to pull you out.

- JER 49:4, 13, 17 ~ There is the faithless daughter who trusted in her treasures. Her cities will become a horrible disaster, a wasteland, a curse like Sodom and Gomorrah.

- EZE 16:15–20 ~ You trusted in your beauty and fornicated with anybody and everybody. You played the harlot more than ever before or ever again. You made images of men and played the harlot with them. You sacrificed your sons and daughters.

- EZE 33:13 ~ When God tells the righteous man that he will surely live, but then he begins to trust in his own righteousness and does what is evil, all his righteousness will be forgotten, and because of his sin he will die.

- MIC 7:2–6 ~ All the godly and upright men are gone. The wicked lie in ambush for blood. They do evil with diligence. Princes and judges ask for bribes. Great men speak of and pursue the evil desires of their souls. Even the best of them is like a thorn. Their confusion and punishment await them. Nobody can be trusted; even family and friends become the enemy (see LUK 21:16–18).

- MAT 27:41–43 ~ The chief priests, scribes, and elders mocked Jesus saying, "He saved others but cannot save himself. If he is the king of Israel let him come down from the cross and we will believe him. He trusted in God to deliver him, let God deliver him now; that is, if God wants him. For did he not say he was God's son?"

- JOH 5:22–24, 30 ~ Jesus said, "The Father judges nobody but has entrusted judgment to the Son, so that everyone may honor the Son as they honor the Father. Those who do not honor the Son do not honor the Father who sent Him. Truthfully, whoever hears my Word and believes Him who sent me has eternal life and will not be condemned, but will cross over from death into life. My judgment is fair, because I seek the Father's will and not my own."

- EPH 1:11–14~ In Christ we obtain an inheritance in heaven, because we listen to the truth and trust in Him for our redemption and salvation. I hope your eyes will be opened and you will become enlightened, and you will feel the hope of His promise, and experience the glory of the inheritance of the saints.

   Heavenly Father, we place all of our trust, faith, and hope in Jesus Christ your only Son. You know what we need and we thank you for providing everything; let us give thanks to you every day for preserving us, protecting us, and prospering us. Help us always to trust that you will guard us and keep us from evil; help us refrain from constantly lusting after worldly powers and pleasures. We have nothing to fear from the world because we fear you Father, almighty in power, knowledge, and presence, knowing you always are watching over us and defending us. Strengthen us daily with your Holy Spirit so that our faith and trust do not waver, but rather grow into a tree of life that continues to spread its branches and bear good fruit for eternity. May our nation remember and acknowledge that in God we trust. We pray in Jesus's name, Amen.

July 31

Women in Ministry Day is presented as a time to recognize and applaud women of faith who had a significant influence on the world from the standpoint of godly faith and service. There has long been debate among leaders of different evangelical denominations about the role of women in ministry. Apparently, theologians are equally divided (almost 50-50) on the topic of ordaining women to be pastors or priests. Specifically, the disagreement centers around a passage where the apostle Paul instructed Timothy concerning women leaders in the church: Do not allow a woman to teach or have authority over a man; she must be silent (1 CO 14:35; 1 TI 2:11–12). It is an extension of the idea that the man was to be head of the household and of the wife, and that women were to submit to men (EPH 5:22; 1 CO 11:3; 1 PE 3:6–7). This is the substance of the position that men should be the leaders of churches. However, Paul also wrote that a woman can be a prophetess (1 CO 11:5) and Peter wrote that a woman should take charge of the spiritual education in the home if the man is not knowledgeable in the ways of the Lord (1 PE 3:1).

We cannot discount the applicability of this policy to the era in which the New Testament was written and the hermeneutics associated with that scripture. No doubt, women were subordinate to men to the extent that they were not permitted to testify in court or be leaders in the temple. Further, Paul had encountered churches where women were injecting themselves into the dialogue and interrupting the general order. It follows that the guidance was specific to a perceived problem at a particular time, generic to their culture. Thus, there may be reasons that Paul wrote this guidance to Timothy and in other epistles.

But does that direction apply today? Obviously, women played major and critical roles throughout the Old and New Testaments. It seems unreasonable to suggest that such a policy must be enforced in the church today. I mean, it's not as if God will condemn all churches and their congregations which employ women for leadership roles especially given shortages in the clergy, and seeing how these churches are filled with faithful Christians. There are many traditions being practiced to this day by certain denominations, which is all well and good as long as these traditions of men are not treated equally with key doctrines of the true faith.

- COL 2:8, 20–22 ~ Beware that you are not spoiled by errant philosophies or vain deceptions, originating from worldly traditions or principles and not from Christ. You are in Christ and not the world, so why submit to its rules? You are not subject to ordinances that are the doctrines and commandments of men (such as do not touch, taste, or use). Those traditions are destined to die out. People may appear reasonable with their self-imposed worship, false humility, and harsh treatment of the body, but these lack value in restraining the sinful flesh.

- 2 TH 2:15 ~ Fellow Christians, stand fast in your faith and hold onto those traditions that you have been taught in God's Word, through the prophets and apostles.

While the ordination of women is still a subject of controversy, there is no reason for the church at large to allow this idea to divide the body of Christ. There are a great many ancillary issues that are debated among evangelicals such as how to conduct baptism, the legality of birth control, and the rules of tithing; these issues need not create dissent or division. Yes, let us discuss and debate such things in light of scripture, with humility and respect. But some practices are not essential to the faith since they do not affect one's salvation. Like Paul wrote: All things are lawful for me, but all things are not expedient; all things are lawful for me, but all things do not edify (1 CO 10:20–31).

God bestows spiritual gifts with which we can serve. Clearly, God is not preferential about whom He calls, whether Jew or Gentile, slave or free, male or female (GAL3:28), for we all are one in Christ! Jesus said, "Many are called but few are chosen" (MAT 22:14). Everyone is called to faith and service, but one must be motivated to serve in order to receive a commission directly from the Holy Spirit, in which case He will equip that person with the knowledge, skills, and spiritual gifts to ensure his or her success. Since people vary in their gifts, we should endeavor to discover them and cultivate them. God also gives us free will to choose our vocation, and even if it does not exercise an intrinsic gift or talent, we can diligently learn the skills and obtain the knowledge, and God will guide our path and secure our victory. It stands to reason that any and all gifts are fair game, available to anyone dedicated to pursuing and nurturing them in service to the Good Shepherd and His flock.

- 1 CO 12:4–12, 26 ~ There are a variety of spiritual gifts, but only one Spirit. There are different ways of administering but only one Lord. There are different operations, but the same God who works through them. The Spirit is manifested in some way for everyone to use productively. Some people have received wisdom, some knowledge, some faith, all from the same Spirit. Some people have the ability to heal, others to work miracles, others to prophesy, others to discern spirits, others to speak foreign tongues. But all of them are working with the same Spirit, who divides power among His people as He chooses. Just as one body has many members so is Christ one body with many members. When one member suffers, all suffer; when one member is honored, all are honored.

- EPH 4:11–13 ~ God gave some the abilities of apostles, prophets, evangelists, pastors and/or teachers for the work of the ministry, the edifying of the saints, the perfecting of the body of Christ, and the unity of faith. Each can impart the knowledge of the Son of God, who was a perfect man, so that we could take on the characteristics of Christ.

Obviously, women of the Bible have been integral in the communication of God's will, purposes, and law, not to mention being leaders, judges, prophets, and teachers. God calls us and directs His people, men and women alike. For example, the prophet Joel proclaimed that both sons and daughters would prophesy (JOE 2:28). Next are listed some of the great women who prophesied in the Bible or who were chosen by God to be leaders.

Deborah was a prophetess and judge over the nation of Israel (JDG 4:4) during the era of the judges (JDG 4—5), prior to the period of the kings. She was quite a formidable military tactician as well, instrumental in the defeat of Sisera and his Canaanite army. Esther was the queen of Persia and favored wife of Xerxes. While her foster father and close relative Mordecai was the strategist, Esther became the mechanism. A very significant message from Mordecai should be heeded by everyone when he said to Esther, "Who knows whether you have come into this kingdom for such a time as this" (EST 4:14). Esther took charge and prevented the eradication of Jews by Haman, the king's second in command. Xerxes had Haman hanged on the gallows he had built for Mordecai who became second to the king. This was a pivotal event in Jewish history, celebrated to this day during *Purim* (EST 9:20–32).

Many prophetesses in the Old Testament deserve mentioning. Miriam was a prophetess (EXO 15:20); she was the elder sister of Moses and Aaron. She intervened with the daughter of Pharoah to provide a Hebrew midwife, who just happened to be their mother, to nurse her baby brother. She also led a music ministry with the Israelites in the Sinai desert (EXO 15:20–21). Hannah was barren, but because of her faith she became the mother of Samuel the prophet, who she dedicated to the church to honor God for giving her a son in her old age (1 SA 1:1–28). Abigail was a widow that David married before becoming king; she predicted that David would rule over Israel (1 SA 25:28–31). Huldah was a prophetess who foretold the desolation of Jerusalem (2 KI 22:14–20).

Notable women from the Old Testament played a crucial part in God's plan by virtue of the fact that they were among the ancestors of Christ. First, we have Tamar, the daughter-in-law of Judah; she disguised herself as a prostitute and seduced him after being denied an heir when her husband died. This incestuous affair led to a pregnancy and the birth of one of Jesus's progenitors (GEN 38). Next is Rahab, a harlot from the city of Jericho who hid two spies in her home and was spared when the city was sacked (JOS 2). She married an Israelite and they had a son named Boaz who would marry a widow from Moab named Ruth (RUT 2—4). Ruth bore a son named Obed, grandfather of King David. David would have an adulterous affair with Bathsheba, and would murder her husband to take her as his wife. Their second son was Solomon, another king and forefather of Jesus. Clearly, God employs women to fulfill His purpose, even if the situation involves incest, prostitution, adultery, murder, or a foreigner. Because they were women of faith, they became God's vessels regardless of their past or gender.

Turning to the New Testament, we find the prophetess and temple servant Anna who acknowledged Jesus as the Messiah at His circumcision (LUK 2:36–38). Dorcas was a charitable woman of God whom Peter raised from the dead (ACT 9:36–43). Phebe was a deaconess at the church in Cenchrea near Corinth (ROM 16:1–2). Priscilla, with her husband Aquila, were mentored by the apostle Paul. They were very influential in the early Christian church, and held services in their home (1 CO 16:19). The couple instructed Apollos who later became a close companion of Paul during his travels (ACT 18:28). Philip the evangelist had four daughters who were prophetesses (ACT 21:8–9).

Certainly, we mustn't forget the women who were witnesses to Christ's glory. Funny how the custom of the time was to disallow women to testify or hold office, yet the first to behold and announce the resurrection of Jesus were exclusively women. Let us start with the women at the cross during Christ's crucifixion. Note that only one of the apostles are mentioned as being in attendance: John. But there were at least four women present: Mary Magdalene, Mary the wife of Cleophas, Salome the mother of James and John, and Jesus's mother Mary (MAT 27:55–56; MAR 15:40; JOH 19:25). Mary Magdalene was the first to see the risen Lord (MAR 16:9). She had been joined that morning by Mary the mother of James (the lesser), Joanna, and Salome, and possibly other women who went to the tomb to anoint Jesus's corpse with sweet spices; but they found the tomb empty (MAR 16:1; LUK 24:1–10). Thus, the apostles were notified by female witnesses who had been spreading this great news all over town before the men had breakfast.

Jesus's mother Mary was very influential as a leader in the early church and during His ministry. She was among the first to recognize Christ publicly, when she told servants at the wedding of Cana to do whatever Jesus told them (JOH 2:2–5); after which His ministry gained traction when He turned water into wine. Surely, Mary was well aware of who Jesus was from the moment the angel Gabriel announced to her that she would be impregnated by the Holy Spirit and give birth to the Son of God (LUK 1:26–38). No doubt, Mary was a witness throughout her adult life which continued until her death, and carries on to this day.

It makes no sense to set limitations concerning who can serve, for that would be up to the Holy Spirit. If a person, male or female, receives His call, he or she is obliged to heed that call if they are sincerely committed. I have been to churches with female pastors and female teachers and got to know quite a few; they received the same education as male pastors and teachers. Certainly, every leader has a cadre of people to assist with church operations, be they elders, trustees, stewards, or instructors. It would be difficult for a church to succeed if they were compelled to hire only males for these positions. But should we draw the line when it comes to pastors or executives? Maybe there are roles better suited for men or women, but serving God in whatever capacity would be fitting and right for anybody called by God. If a person has received sufficient training for the job, and knows the Bible backwards and forwards, and possesses the indwelling of the Holy Spirit, who else would you want to teach, preach, or be in charge?

As a psychotherapist and instructor by trade, I have mentored plenty of interns and students in my time and found no difference between the sexes in their capability, integrity, and enthusiasm. Many of them have progressed to positions of leadership and authority, and quite deservedly. I proudly endorsed some of them, males and females, and they have excelled and helped countless people to grapple with their mental issues. Sometimes they thanked me for my coaching, and I would point them to the Lord who commissioned me. I am especially thankful for those who later received and managed such a commission themselves.

- ROM 2:21–22 ~ If you teach others, do you not teach yourself also? Do you not practice what you preach?

- COL 3:16 ~ Remember what Christ taught to you and let His words enrich your lives and make you wise. Teach His words to one another. Sing them openly and spiritually in psalms and hymns with thankful hearts.

- HEB 5:12–13 ~ Before you are ready to be teachers you need someone to teach you the principles of the oracles of God. Then you will be ready for milk but not solid food. You will be like babes who must mature until fully grown before applying your knowledge of right and wrong.

- 2 TH 2:15 ~ Stand strong and hold onto the traditions you have been taught whether by word of mouth or by epistle.

- 2 TI 2:2 ~ Regarding things you have learned from me, commit those things to faithful followers who will then be equipped to teach others.

Heavenly Father, we give thanks to you this day for women who serve responsibly and selflessly now and in the past. We pray that you would bless the ministries of men and women alike, so that your Word of peace and love would spread to every region of the planet. For those who are eager to serve you, equip them with the necessary skills, abilities, and demeanor, enabling them to be successful even in places where women are scorned. We understand that there are peoples and religions which subordinate women; perhaps what they need is a woman to set them straight. If it be your will, give your servants, whether male or female, boldness and courage to share the good news of Jesus Christ to people who are lost or have closed their minds to you and your Word. For those who excel in true knowledge of you, make them teachers, pastors, and leaders in accordance with your will. With the power of your Holy Spirit, penetrate egotistical defenses with the power of truth, so that those who listen can see the light, find you, and follow Jesus Christ all the way home. In His name we pray, Amen.

August 1

Worldwide Web Day celebrates the internet and all of the resources, applications, and information now available at the speed of a click. Tim Berners-Lee (England) promoted the idea in 1989 and Robert Cailliau (Belgium) helped to develop hypertext transfer protocol (HTTP) software, which is the format most commonly used in websites for publishing content. By 1992, the internet was available mostly to governments, educational institutions, and businesses; quickly, its utility spread into personal and social media applications. From there it went off like gangbusters, and is now accessible to a billion people around the world. Every computer, phone, tablet and notepad device can access the worldwide web for a small fee. Anybody can connect with anybody, as long as they both have internet access, making international communications fast and cheap. You can share text, audio, and video; you can share personal information or confidential information protected with encryption. You can provide opinions, conduct research, hold conferences, get the news, learn about stuff, buy stuff, pay your bills, and the list goes on. See also the lesson on 10/30.

So how is one to celebrate this holiday? Well, since most people are on the internet every day, then you can do what you always do: search the web. Ensure you review multiple sources and fact check everything given the abundance of false information intermingled with truth. Of course, you need to take precautions about downloading things from the worldwide web given the propagation of malware out there. Hopefully, you have software on your device to protect it from unwanted contamination or hacking of your system. It is wise not to disclose personal information on insecure sites; a secure site is indicated with an "s" (e.g., https means secure).

- JAM 3:13 ~ Whoever is wise among you should show it with good conversation and meekness. But if you are bitter and envious, do not glory in this, and do not tell lies.

The ability to communicate is a great feature of the internet. Few people write letters anymore when they can email or text someone. The only person you cannot communicate with on the worldwide web is God. We communicate with God through prayer, and He communicates with us via the Holy Spirit through His Word, divine revelation, and the sacraments.

- EXO 25:22 ~ The Lord said to Moses, "I will commune with you from heaven, from between the two cherubim that are on the Ark of the Covenant. I will tell you all the commandments that I have for Israel."

- AMO 4:13 ~ He forms the mountains, He creates the wind, He communicates His thoughts to humankind, and He turns the dawn into dusk. He can be found in the high places of the earth, and the Lord God Almighty is His name.

- MAT 6:6–7 ~ Jesus taught: When you pray, do so in private. Pray to the Father in your mind and He will know what you are thinking. Pray to Him secretly, and He will reward you openly. Do not use vain repetitions like the unbelievers do, for they think they will be heard for their many words.

- LUK 10:16 ~ Those who listen to my disciples whom I have sent will listen to me; whoever rejects those who I have sent reject me. And those who reject me reject Him who sent me."

- ROM 8:26 ~ The Holy Spirit intercedes for us when we pray. We do not know what we should pray for all the time. But through the act of prayer, the Spirit analyzes our needs and answers our prayers in the best possible way.

- 2 CO 13:14 ~ The grace of the Lord Jesus Christ, the love of God, and the communion of the Holy Spirit be with you.

- EPH 6:18 ~ Pray all the time in the Spirit. Keep alert and persevere.

Information is power, or so they say. Information is power when it comes from God, that is for certain. If what is being disseminated is not true, it is not informative unless you can prove it false. Knowledge of the truth and the will of God make us wise unto salvation. Such intelligence is not available from a machine, since the machine is programmed by a person. There are different levels of intelligence, but God's Word is the most reliable source of all. Unfortunately, artificial intelligence is the least reliable source for information, especially when the creator of the "robot" inserts his or her own sinful proclivities. You can teach computers to learn routines, but none are flawless because all humans are flawed. Enable yourself to be sure before believing that which is presented as truth, taking into account the source.

- EXO 31:3 ~ I have filled Him with the Spirit of God, with talent and intelligence, with knowledge and abilities.

- PRO 30:5–6 ~ Every word of God is true; do not attempt to add to God's words or He will rebuke you and you will be proven false.

- ISA 45:21 ~ How do you know the truth? Who has told it to you all along? Has it not been I the Lord? There is no God but me, a fair God and a Savior; there are no others besides me.

- LUK 12:11–12 ~ Jesus said, "When they bring you before the authorities do not worry about what to say or do, for the Holy Spirit will provide the information when you need it."

- JOH 16:12–14 ~ Jesus informed them, "I have many things to tell you but you are not ready for them yet. Nevertheless, the Spirit of Truth comes; He will guide you into all truth. He does not draw attention to Himself but to me. He hears and He speaks, and He will show you things to come."

- ROM 1:16–19 ~ God's wrath is revealed from heaven against the sinfulness of people, who know the truth of unrighteousness, because God has made it known to them.

- 1 TH 5:16–22 ~ Rejoice every day. Pray without ceasing. In everything give thanks, for this is the will of God in Christ concerning you. Never quench the Spirit; do not despise prophecy. Prove all things and hold onto the good. Abstain from all appearance of evil.

- 1 TI 2:1–6 ~ I urge that supplications, prayers, intercessions, and thanksgiving be made to God for all people, for leaders, and for all who are in authority, so that we can lead an honest and peaceful life of godliness and truth. For this is good and acceptable in the sight of God our Savior. God wants all people to be saved and to come to know the truth. For there is one God, and one mediator between God and people: the person Jesus Christ.

- 2 PE 1:21 ~ No prophecy ever came from the impulses of men, but holy men spoke as they were directed by the Holy Spirit.

Heavenly Father, remind us to test everything we hear and read against your Holy Word, which is the final arbiter of truth. Help us to be sure before we claim that something is true. Let your truth guide us in all of our studies and endeavors as we seek the truth and expose that which is untrue. Silence those who purport to know the truth but are spreading lies and misinformation. Illuminate the truth for those who do not believe, so they can see the light and let go of the lies and false information they have been fed. Do not let the enemy convince people of things that come from the hearts of wayward people and not from you, beloved Father. Remove those people from positions of authority and power who tell lies for personal gain. Help those in power to speak truth to power, so that your name may be exalted in all the earth. Thank you for the truth which sets us free through the knowledge of redemption that only can be found in Christ, in whose name we pray, Amen.

August 2

Rejoice in the Lord Day is hereby designated to praise God's holy name all day long. We should give Him praise every day, but we are constantly too busy to think of Him, though He is always thinking of us. Do not be ashamed to declare His name and reply to people with a friendly "Praise be to God" whenever it is fitting. In certain circles you will get no complaints, but be discreet in other places, showing respect at all times to all people regardless of religious persuasion. Bringing glory to the Lord garners respect on its own. When we heap praises on our God, He elevates us to the highest heaven, where we will be able to continue singing His praises with complete joy for the duration of eternity.

- 1 CH 23:30 ~ Thank and praise the Lord every morning and every evening.

- PSA 9:1–2; PSA 50:23 ~ I will praise you Lord with all my heart; I will show your marvelous works. I will be glad and rejoice. I will sing praises to your holy name. God says that whoever offers Him praise, glorifies Him. To those who do this, He will show His salvation.

- PSA 29:4; PSA 96:6; PSA 103:2–4; PSA 104:1 ~ The voice of the Lord is powerful and majestic. Splendor and grandeur are before Him; strength and glory are His sanctuary. Praise the Lord, oh my soul, let everything in me praise Him who forgives sins, heals diseases, and redeems my life from destruction. He crowns me with love and tender mercy. He is awesome; He is clothed in brilliance and majesty.

- PSA 150:2, 6 ~ Praise God for His mighty acts and excellent greatness. Let everything that breathes praise the Lord.

- ISA 12:4–6 ~~ Praise the Lord, call on His name, declare His works to all people; mention that His name is exalted. Sing to the Lord, for He has done marvelous things, which are known in all the earth. Shout with joy you inhabitants of Zion, for great is the Holy One of Israel who will be with you.

- ISA 61:10 ~ I will greatly rejoice in the Lord; my soul will be joyful in my God. For He has clothed me with the garments of salvation, he has covered me with the robe of righteousness, just like the groom is adorned with ornaments and the bride is adorned with jewels. Blessed be those whose sins are not counted against them.

- JER 20:13 ~ Sing to the Lord and praise Him, for He has delivered the souls of the poor from the wicked.

- DAN 2:23 ~ I thank and praise you God of my fathers, who has given me wisdom and power, and has told me what you want me to know and to do.

- MAT 5:15–17 ~ Jesus said, "You do not light a candle and then put it out, because it is supposed to give light. Let the light inside you shine before others; let people see in your actions that you live to glorify your Father in heaven. Do not think that I came to destroy the law or the prophets, but to fulfil them."

- ROM 5:1–5 ~ Being justified by faith we achieve peace with God through Christ, in whom we have access by that faith to the grace in which we stand, rejoicing in the hope of glory. Therefore, we rejoice in time of tribulation, knowing that it teaches us patience, it strengthens our hope, and we gain experience.

- REV 19:5–10 ~ A voice came from out of the throne saying, "Praise our God all of you servants and all who fear Him, both small and great." And I heard the sound of a great multitude, as the rushing of many waters, with a thundering of voices singing "Alleluia, for the omnipotent Lord

God reigns. Let us be glad and rejoice, and give honor to Him; for the marriage of the Lamb has come, and His wife has made herself ready." The bride was dressed in fine linen, clean and white, representing the righteousness of the saints. Then the angel told me to write, "Blessed are those who are invited to the marriage feast of the Lamb," continuing, "These are the true words of God." And I fell to his feet to worship him and he said not to, for he was a fellow servant, and part of the brotherhood that testifies of Jesus, who worship God and affirm that the testimony of Jesus is the true spirit of prophecy.

It is wise to give thanks and praise to the Lord, because everything we have, and everything we are, come from Him. He regards our worship and adoration more than money or other offerings and sacrifices (1 SA 15:22; PRO 21:3; MIC 6:6–7). Do not hesitate to confess Christ and witness to others, for those who acknowledge Him will be acknowledged by Him before the Father. Even when it is inappropriate to bring up the subject of faith and Christ, you still can shine His light, be respectful, and display a joyful heart to people that you meet. There are rewards in heaven for all who follow Christ and rejoice in His name.

- PSA 45:7 ~ If you love righteousness and hate wickedness God will shower His joy upon you, and elevate you above others.

- ISA 65:18–19 ~ Be glad and rejoice forever in that which I the Lord create; I will establish Jerusalem for rejoicing and her people will be a joy unto me. Yes, I will rejoice in Jerusalem and be joyful with my people, where there will be no sound of weeping or crying.

- HAB 3:18 ~ I will rejoice in the Lord and find joy in the God of my salvation.

- MAT 10:32–33 ~ Jesus said, "Anybody who confesses me before others, I will confess them before my Father in heaven. Anybody who denies me to others, I will deny them before my Father in heaven."

- JOH 16:20–22 ~ Jesus said to the apostles, "I tell you the truth, you will weep and lament but the world will rejoice. You will be sorrowful but your sorrow will turn to joy, just like when a mother in labor groans; but when her child is born her pain is replaced with happiness. I will see you again and your heart will rejoice; and nobody will ever take that joy away from you."

- ROM 12:14–15 ~ Bless those who curse you; bless, but do not curse. Rejoice with those who are rejoicing and mourn with those who are mourning.

- ROM 15:13 ~ May the God of hope fill you with all joy and peace in believing, so that by the power of the Holy Spirit you may abound in hope.

- REV 5:11–12 ~ Then I looked and saw a multitude of angels, numbering thousands upon thousands, literally millions of angels encircling the throne. And they sang aloud with one voice, "Worthy is Christ the Lamb who was slain, to receive power and wealth, and wisdom and strength, and honor, glory and praise."

Father in heaven, we praise your holy name and we rejoice in the salvation of Christ. Help us to raise a joyful noise unto the Lord at every opportunity; help us to be ready and willing to explain why we appear joyful regardless of the circumstances. Even if we are unable to make personal sacrifices or weekly offerings, we always can offer praise and thanks from our hearts to you, and publicly witness our faith and hope at our church and other places of worship. This is the least we can do to show appreciation for all you have done for us. Let your Holy Spirit fill our minds and bodies with life and joy, as we share the truth of your Son and His love living in us. Especially enable us to be available to those who are hurting or sorrowful. In the name of Jesus who gave Himself for us so that we can live to serve you, now and forever, Amen.

August 3

Jesse Owens Won First of Four Gold Medals on this day in 1936 during the Olympics which were held in Berlin. Owens was cheered by spectators when he outpaced the field in the 100-meter to win gold. He would go on to win gold in the long jump, the 200-meter, and the 100-meter four-man relay. Imagine the embarrassment of the Nazis, Aryans, and other white supremacists when a black man came out on top, with world record gold. Sadly, Owens was snubbed by President Franklin Roosevelt who didn't even send a congratulatory telegram, said Owens; in fact, none of the black Olympians were invited to the White House. Though he experienced considerable discrimination and was denied many opportunities, Owens managed to succeed as a motivational speaker and promoter of sports. In 1976, Owens was awarded the Medal of Freedom by President Ford for his accomplishments and goodwill. He was truly a class act, a world celebrity, a man of integrity, and an ambassador for freedom and athletics. Considered to be top ten of all-time American athletes, he was rebuffed in his native land for most of his life.

Owens was a winner and a patriot. He overcame obstacles and prejudice, never giving up. His determination and focus scored him many medals, both in athletics and as a humanitarian. Most of the time when we run a race, there is a finish line. But when you contend in the human race, the finish line is either heaven or hell. Those who end up in heaven will have stayed on track and kept a moderate pace; they are all winners and receive a crown of life. Those going to the other place are either in a hurry to get there, or they get sidetracked easily; regardless, they will lose no matter how long, how hard, or how far they run, since it is in the wrong direction.

- JOS 1:7–8 ~ God said, "Be strong and courageous, so that you are able to observe the laws which Moses commanded of you. Do not turn to the right or to the left, and you will prosper wherever you go. This book of the Law must not depart from your speech, but you must meditate on my words every day and night, and live according to all that is written there. Then God will make you prosperous and you will be successful. Meditate on the book of the Law every day and night, so that you can act in accordance with all that is written therein. Then your ways will be prosperous and you will enjoy success."

- PRO 1:18–19 ~ Those who are greedy for riches and oppress others to obtain riches are ambushing their own lives and will succeed in destroying themselves.

- 1 CO 9:24–27 ~ Do you understand, there are many competitors in a race but only one receives first prize? Run with the intention of winning that prize. Those striving to master a task must train hard and discipline themselves. They do so to obtain an earthly crown that will not last; but we strive for a crown which lasts forever. I run like a man with a purpose. I do not fight like a boxer beating the air. Instead, I beat my body into shape, making it serve God's purpose, so that my preaching will not cause me to be disqualified for the prize.

- REV 2:10 ~ Jesus said, "Do not be afraid of suffering, imprisonment, and tribulation; many will endure such hardships. Be faithful unto death and you will receive a crown of life."

- REV 20:10 ~ The devil that deceived them was thrown into the lake of fire where the beast and false prophet were. There they were tormented day and night forever.

Our Father in heaven, help us to stay on track and keep the pace, reaching the finish line before time is called. We thank you in advance for the crown of life you have promised if we finish the race with our faith intact. Help people who are charging fast, but on the wrong track, to find their way. We can see the path which is Jesus, but the finish line is not yet in view. Help us to keep running until we reach the entrance to your kingdom, by staying loyal to Jesus and the team, which is His church on earth. In His name we pray, Amen.

August 4

Don't Lose Your Mind Day is a warning not to give into the carnal temptations of the physical world. Remember, there is a battle going on between your flesh and spirit. And the winner wields control over your mind. Those who focus on the flesh risk developing a reprobate mind (ROM 8:7–13). Those who follow the spirit seek God and His righteousness, and develop a mind like that of Christ (ROM 8:1–4; 1 CO 2:16).

Reprobate refers to a person who is without principles or morality: a twisted, vile, degenerate individual. Biblically speaking, this is someone who is destined for damnation because they deliberately have chosen to disregard God and His commandments, willfully thinking and acting in an unruly or unrighteous fashion. They neither seek forgiveness nor confess or repent their sins. A reprobate mind is inherently evil, opposing all that is of God; in fact, sometimes that person is demon possessed.

- PRO 6:16–19 ~ Seven things the Lord hates because they are an abomination to Him: a proud look, a lying tongue, hands that shed innocent blood, a heart that devises wicked imaginations, feet that run swiftly into mischief, a false witness speaking lies, and people who sow discord in their community.

- ROM 1:28–32 ~ Since they did not want to retain God in their knowledge, God gave them over to a reprobate mind, to do despicable things, being filled with all manner of unrighteousness: fornication, wickedness, covetousness, maliciousness, envy, murder, contentious, deceitful, spiteful, gossipers, backstabbers, hateful, arrogant, boasters, connivers, disobedient, promise breakers, unmerciful, ruthless, without natural affection, and without spiritual understanding. They committed these things knowing God's judgment is death, continuing to engage in such behavior and finding pleasure in others doing the same.

- 1 TI 4:1–2 ~ The Spirit expressly states that in the latter times some will depart from the faith, giving heed to seducing spirits and doctrines of devils; hypocrites speaking lies, having their conscience seared with a hot iron.

- TIT 1:15–16 ~ To the pure all things are pure; but to the defiled and unbelieving, nothing is pure. Even their minds and consciences are defiled. They profess to know God but their deeds deny Him with abominable, disobedient, and reprobate ways.

Consider people who defy God, asserting that the Bible is nothing but lies or fairy tales. Some proclaim themselves atheists, knowing full well they will be held accountable by God. Many see themselves as gods, free to say and do anything they please and avoid consequences and accountability; and choosing not to listen to their conscience, wherein the Spirit of truth has conferred upon all people the knowledge of right and wrong. Many openly claim to be depraved, ignoring God precisely because they have no intention of amending their decadent ways.

Reprobates hate God and love evil, and therefore will receive due recompense and condemnation; but they do not care for they place no value on the soul which they will gladly forfeit to continue their self-indulgent lifestyle. They do not want any part of God, so God will mercifully let them have their way and spend eternity divorced from Him and people who follow Christ. Reprobates eventually fall into the one unpardonable sin, blasphemy against the Holy Spirit: calling God a liar and refusing His Word until death separates them from God forever (MAT 12:31–32; MAR 3:9). It is an eternal sin which cannot be forgiven.

- DEU 28:15–29 ~ But if you do not listen to the Lord and you do not observe His commandments and statutes that I have commanded you to follow, these curses will come upon you and overtake you; you will be cursed in the city and in the country. Your basket and kneading trough will be cursed. Cursed will be your offspring, the fruit of your land, and your herds and flocks. You will be cursed coming in and going out. The Lord will send curses, confusion, rebuke, and destruction upon you if you forsake Him. He will send diseases, drought, and plagues upon you. You will become mad, blind, and disoriented. You will be unsuccessful at everything. You will be oppressed and robbed but nobody will help you.

- PRO 1:24–28 ~ God says, "I called and you refused; I stretched out my hand and you paid no attention; you neglected my counsel and my reproof. Therefore, I will laugh at your calamity and I will mock when your dread comes and fear approaches with desolation. When anguish and distress befall you, only then will you call upon me, but I will not answer. Many will seek but not find me; for they hated knowledge and chose not to fear the Lord. They ignored my counsel and despised my reproof. They will eat the fruit of their own ways, and be filled with their own devices. The folly of the simple-minded will slay them and the prosperity of fools will destroy them. But whoever listens to me will dwell safely and be calm from the fear of evil."

- ROM 8:5–7, 13 ~ Those who pursue things of the flesh belong to the flesh; those who pursue things of the spirit belong to the Spirit. To have a carnal mind is death; to have a spiritual mind is life and peace. The carnal mind hates God; it disregards God's Law for it is in complete opposition to it. If you live for the flesh you will die. If you live for the Spirit, you can control the flesh, and you will live.

- 2 CO 13:5–8 ~ Examine yourselves, whether you abide in the faith; prove this to yourselves. Do you not know within yourselves, how Jesus Christ abides in you, lest you become reprobates? I trust that you know how we have proven ourselves. We pray to God that you will refrain from evil, not in order to receive our approval, but that you be honest, even if you believe we have failed the test. For we can do nothing against the truth but only for the truth.

It grieves the Holy Spirit when a person falls into sin and continues in that sin without godly sorrow and repentance. Does it do us any good to seek forgiveness when we refuse to amend our ways? Sincere repentance comes from a contrite heart, without which there can be no forgiveness. Those who adamantly refuse the atonement of Christ commit a sin unto death; it is of no avail praying for such a person who has refused to change (1 JO 5:16–17). God might purge them from the world to extinguish their sin and prevent it from spreading to others (JER 7:16–18; ACT 5:1–10).

- ISA 63:10 ~ They rebelled and grieved the Holy Spirit. Therefore, He turned away from them and became their enemy, fighting against them.

- EPH 4:30–31 ~ Do not grieve the Holy Spirit by whom you were sealed for the day of redemption. Let all bitterness, rage, anger, fighting, evil speak, and every form of malice be put away from you.

- 1 TH 5:19–22 ~ Do not stifle the Holy Spirit. Do not treat prophecies with contempt, but test them all. Hold onto that which is good and reject evil of any kind.

- HEB 10:39 ~ Christians are not among those who draw back into perdition, but are with those who believe, to the saving of their souls.

The reprobate mind can become irreversible, insofar as the person has hardened his or her heart against God. They configure their brains to block God's messages of truth, honor, and justice, for these are painful to them. They program themselves to ignore or repress feelings of guilt, shame, or blame in their wrongdoing, though it takes considerable effort to do so. They assert that God does not exist, while deep down they know this to be untrue; but they deceive themselves in order to do as they please. When a person clings to lies they come to believe them, and this equates to the sin of disbelief, with the penalties being death and loss of the soul.

- EXO 9:12 ~ The Lord hardened Pharaoh's heart, for he would not listen to the words God gave him through Moses.
- JER 18:12 ~ They said, "There is no hope so we will walk after our own devices, and every one of us will follow the imagination of an evil heart."
- ROM 2:5 ~ The hard and impenitent heart stores up wrath, until the day of God's wrath and the revelation of His righteous judgment.
- EPH 4:18 ~ Their understanding has been darkened due to the ignorance of their blind hearts, alienated from the life God gives.

It is unhealthy to ignore guilt; this is a signal from your inner spirit that your moral compass is out of whack. Earned guilt is healthy since it reminds us to stop, make amends, and modify our conduct; this will resolve inner turmoil and remove the associated guilt. Unresolved guilt is an unhealthy detriment to one's mental stability, and ultimately the soul. In fact, a person may experience mental, physical and spiritual discomfort due to sin, guilt, and unforgiveness. Confess and repent of your sin and God will forgive you and remove the guilt, for Christ took the guilt of the world upon Himself and nailed it to the cross (COL 2:14).

- EZR 9:6 ~ I said, "Oh my God, I am ashamed and embarrassed to lift up my face to you, for our iniquities have risen above our heads and our guilt has grown even to the heavens."
- PSA 32:5 ~ I acknowledged my sin to you Lord, and my iniquity I did not hide. I said, "I will confess my transgressions to the Lord." And you forgave the guilt of my sin. Amen.
- ISA 55:7 ~ Let the wicked forsake their ways and the unrighteous their thoughts, and let them return to the Lord and He will have mercy on them, for our God pardons abundantly.
- 2 CO 7:9–10 ~ I rejoice, not because I made you feel sorry but because you were sorry unto repentance. For you felt sorry in a godly manner, not from a worldly perspective. Godly sorrow brings repentance leading to salvation, without regrets; but the sorrow of the world leads to death.
- 1 JO 1:9 ~ If we confess our sins, God is faithful and just to forgive our sins and cleanse us of all unrighteousness.

Problem is, the reprobates are on a power trip, hungry for clout and control to placate their narcissistic and hedonistic desires. Everything is about them, whereas others do not matter. They are working for Satan, who is always in pursuit of power, wanting to control others and bring them down into perdition where he knows he is going. Is it possible for a reprobate to repent and be saved? Well, with the Lord anything is possible, but without Him nothing is. Since they are not with or for the Lord it is unlikely that they will seek Him until it is too late.

As for Satan, he is a "lost and condemned creature" (wrote Martin Luther) because he has made his choice to compete against God. This is why Satan hates humans so terribly, because they can repent and inherit the kingdom, and ultimately be placed above the angels (1 CO 6:1–3); but Satan and his army of demons cannot repent and be forgiven, and therefore cannot be saved. Although angels were given free will, their choice to follow God or to follow Satan was final and fatal; thus, all the demons who were cast out of heaven have fallen for good and cannot go home (MAT 8:28–29; MAT 25:41; JDE 1:6;). Sadly, there are individuals who are likewise destined for destruction, holding a one-way ticket to hell.

AUGUST

- PSA 10:3–4 ~ The wicked brag about their heart's desires and bless covetous people whom the Lord abhors. Through the pride of covetousness, they ignore God, since the thought of God never crosses their minds.

- ISA 14:12–15 ~ How you have fallen from heaven, oh Lucifer, son of the morning! How you have been cast down to the earth to undermine the nations! You said in your heart, "I will ascend to heaven and exalt my throne above the stars of God. I will sit atop the mount over the congregation. I will ascend above the clouds and be like the Most High." But you will be brought down to hell, to the depths of the pit.

- JAM 3:13–17 ~ Who among you is wise and endowed with knowledge? Let them demonstrate this by way of good conversation and acts done with the humility of wisdom. But if you foster bitter envy and selfish ambition in your hearts, you must not boast of it or speak lies against the truth. Such knowledge does not descend from above but is earthly, sensual, and devilish. For where there is envy and strife, there is confusion and evil. But heavenly wisdom is above all pure, then peaceable, gentle, and easily grasped; full of mercy and bearing good fruit, without partiality and without hypocrisy.

- 2 PE 2:1–4, 9 ~ There were false prophets among God's people just as there will be false teachers among you. They will cunningly introduce damnable heresies, even denying the sovereign Lord who brought them out of bondage, bringing upon themselves swift destruction. Many will follow their pernicious ways, speaking evil about the truth. Through covetousness and insincere words, they will exploit others; their judgment approaches quickly for their damnation never sleeps. Remember, God did not spare the angels when they sinned but sent them to hell and placed them in chains of darkness to be held for judgment. The Lord knows how to deliver the godly out of temptations and to reserve the unjust until the day of judgment for punishment.

Beware, because those going the way of evil will get perpetually worse. (2 TI 3:13). This is yet another sign of the end times. Do not associate with reprobates because you could become one of them. They probably will not listen to the truth anyway. But it is not you who are separating from them, it is they who have separated from you; for they are humanistic and materialistic and do not possess the Spirit (JDE 1:19). They have lost their minds; consequently, their souls will be destroyed in hell. So do not lose your mind or you might not find it after that. If you were to die in that condition you would lose your body and your soul, in which case your spirit will be ceded back to God to whom it belongs.

Heavenly Father, thank you for being a forgiving Father. We come before your throne of Grace asking forgiveness for all the sins committed because of what we have thought, said, and done, or left undone, whether sins of commission or sins of omission, including sins we are aware of or remember, and those we do not. Help us to listen to your voice telling us within our souls to do or not do something. Speak to us through our sense of uprightness, so that we will be conscious about what we are about to do or say. Help us to dismiss the temptations that pop into our heads before giving them further thought or consideration, so that we do not give into them or act upon them. Instead, help us dispel them, putting up our shield of faith and donning our helmet of salvation, so they cannot dominate or even penetrate our thought processes. If we remember you, we will immediately be aware of your presence, for your Holy Spirit is always here. When we are weak, help us to lean on you so that we can be strong, as we battle the evil in our midst and in our world. Give us the mind of Christ so we can defeat evil, whether human or demonic. In Christ we pray, Amen.

August 5

God's Law Day is introduced in recognition of who we serve and whose law should prevail. For example, in our republic, federal laws trump state laws, which trump city laws. But God's laws trump them all (ACT 5:22–29). Our freedom of religion means government cannot compel us to do something that goes against our faith or our conscience. Consider one of the great conscientious objectors, Desmond Doss, who served his country admirably, saving dozens of lives as an Army medic (seventy-five in one day); but never did he carry a weapon and he always observed the Sabbath. God also commands us to obey the laws of the land, for He appoints governments to lead us and to enforce the law (JAM 1:22, 25; 1 PE 2:13–17).

In the past decade we have seen a rapid escalation of anarchy, rebellion, and tyranny in the USA. This has gotten worse since the Covid pandemic. Let us first take a look at anarchy, which is a deliberate attempt to overthrow government and promote lawlessness. We saw it sponsored by the far left resulting in cities being burned and looted, with innocent people and police being beaten and murdered. Was anything done to bring these perpetrators to justice? No, quite the contrary; they were usually set free or not prosecuted. We also saw anarchy coming from the far right when peaceful protesters were incited by rogue insurgents to storm the capitol building. Was justice served in this case? Not really, only one has been charged with sedition and a handful have been charged with assault or vandalism; others have been incarcerated under squalid and unhealthy conditions, without bail, for mere misdemeanors, in direct violation of habeas corpus and due process. Anarchists want chaos, not government; they are not fighting for a right-wing or left-wing cause, they are fighting because lawlessness is their drug or high, and government is their antagonist. No political position or ideology justifies such behavior.

Furthermore, rebellion, sedition, and subversion are becoming more commonplace, even within our government. These problems were documented in the Holy Bible. For example, in the New Testament the man Barabbas, who was spared from crucifixion instead of Jesus Christ, was awaiting execution for sedition and for a murder committed during an insurrection (MAR 15:7; LUK 23:13–24). Yet a riotous mob pleaded with Pilate to crucify Jesus for sedition, and release Barabbas who was a bona fide seditionary, and Pilate complied. Were the temple leaders and the rioters they instigated interested in truth and justice? Hardly. The priests and elders saw Jesus as a threat to their power, so they produced false witnesses to testify, and incited rioters in Jerusalem to scream "crucify him" (LUK 23:18–24). Similarly, high priests falsely accused St. Paul of sedition and insurrection against the Jewish state (ACT 18:12–13; ACT 24:1–6). In the Old Testament, the rebuilding of Jerusalem was delayed due to accusations of insurrection and sedition levied against Jewish loyalists (EZR 4:15–21). Thus, Jesus, apostles, Jews, and Christians were falsely accused, persecuted, and imprisoned back then, and still are in this day and age.

It seems the ones accusing others of high crimes are often the ones who actually are guilty of them. And in the above instances, it was God's people who were being targeted. The real rebels were the ones who were defying God and His laws! Here is but one of many examples of the "projection" of one's attributes or behavior onto another, something we constantly witness by our government and assorted officials who are doing the very things which they are charging and indicting others for doing.

- PSA 64:1–2 ~ Hear my prayer, oh Lord! Preserve my life from fear of the enemy. Hide me from the secret counsel of the wicked, and from the insurrection of the workers of iniquity.

- PRO 28:7 ~ Those who keep the law are wise; the riotous son shames his father.

- ROM 13:13 ~ Let us walk honestly, as in the daylight; not in rioting and drunkenness, not in sexual immorality and lasciviousness; not in strife or envying.

AUGUST

- 1 TI 1:8–10 ~ We know that the law is good, as long as it is used lawfully. Know this, that the law does not exist for the righteous, but for the lawless and disobedient; the ungodly and profane; the murderers and slayers; the whoremongers, adulterers, and defilers; liars and perjurers; and anything that goes contrary to sound doctrine.

- TIT 1:10–11; TIT 3:9–11 ~ There are many unruly and vain talkers and deceivers, especially among proponents of the circumcision (see also ACT 15:24). Their mouths must be shut, those who subvert entire houses, teaching things that are false for ill-gotten gain. Avoid foolish questions, genealogies, contentions and strivings that go against the law, for such things are unprofitable and vain. A proven heretic must be rejected; such a man is subverted, condemning himself with his sinful words and actions.

Lately, we see politicians and the mass media loosely throwing around words such as insurrection, sedition, and treason. For example, the invaders of the capitol building in January 2021 repeatedly were called armed insurrectionists though not a single weapons charge was levied. The majority of those charged were guilty of nothing more than trespassing. A number of people actually guilty of subversion and insurrection were instigators planted amongst the protesters, but were never charged. The plan was orchestrated in advance by criminals who have yet to be identified much less arrested. Those who removed barriers and prompted the crowd to storm the capitol were truly seditious. Most people who were arrested for entering that restricted area would not have known it was restricted since the barriers were removed prior to the completion of the president's speech and subsequent march to the capitol. This scheme was the working of deviant minds, as further evidenced by harassment from law enforcement of unsuspecting visitors to DC while overlooking serious criminal acts conducted that day, such as the murder of an unarmed veteran. In short, it was a setup. If it could be proven that government officials or their representatives were involved, this would pass as treasonous and seditionary.

Additionally, we hear constant chants to reduce, defund, and chastise the police; to decriminalize subversive behavior and lessen sentences for major crimes; to allow repeat offenders to go free without bail or jail time. The entirety of our justice system is being hijacked in the name of equity, impartiality, inclusion, and antiracism. Even parents are being labeled domestic terrorists simply because they want a say about what their kids are being taught, as if they are too stupid to know what is best for their own children. These aforementioned atrocities fit the very definitions of subversion, authoritarianism, oppression, and tyranny. Such is a betrayal of the laws of the land outlined in our Constitution, Bill of Rights, and Declaration of Independence. This is a threat to the civil rights of the populace and the stability of our republic. It comes as no surprise the dramatic escalation of violent crimes here and abroad, by demented, perhaps demon-possessed maniacs, as if this was the fault of the police and not government.

- ECC 5:8 ~ If you see the oppression of the poor, the perversion of judgment and justice in certain provinces, do not marvel about the matter. For one high official is supervised by a higher one, and there are others higher than they. [Corruption goes all the way to the top.]

- 2 PE 2:17–19 ~ They are wells without water, clouds blown by the wind, for whom is reserved the greatest darkness forever. When they speak grandiose words of vanity they appeal to lusts of the flesh, enticing people who would otherwise escape those living in error. Though they promise liberty they are themselves servants of corruption, because they become a slave when they are overcome by it. If they escape the pollutions of the world through the knowledge of our Lord and Savior Jesus Christ, and again become entangled and overcome by it, the end is worse than the beginning; for it would have been better for them never to had known the way of righteousness, than to have turned from it after having received the holy commandment delivered to them.

The basis of our laws and moral values is the Holy Bible. To defy these values and our founding documents is rebellion, not just against the USA but against God. Consider Saul, who was anointed king of Israel by Samuel the prophet and later rejected by him for defying God. King Saul disobeyed the command of God and did not comply with the counsel of Samuel (1 SA 15:19–28). The moral of the story is this: leaders who dismiss the Word of God are themselves in rebellion, and likewise should be rejected by the people. When you see your government slacken the laws and free the lawbreakers, while incarcerating the innocent and persecuting the faithful, whose side do you suppose they are on? If they are not against you, they are for you (MAR 9:38–40; LUK 9:49–50); and if they are not for you, they will work against you because you belong to Christ. But they are very tricky about it. Like Judas, they will betray you with a kiss; that is to say, they sugarcoat their treachery and lies.

- DEU 28:47–48 ~ Because you did not serve the Lord your God with joyfulness and gladness of heart, for the abundance of all things, you will serve your enemies which the Lord will send against you: in hunger, thirst, nakedness, and poverty. You will have a yoke around your neck until you have been destroyed.

- PSA 66:7 ~ God rules by His power forever; His eyes can see all nations. Let not the rebellious exalt themselves.

- ISA 1:23 ~ Your princes are rebellious; their companions are thieves. They love bribes and seek self-aggrandizement. They do not care about widows and orphans.

- ISA 30:1 ~ The Lord says, "Woe to the rebellious children who take counsel from others but not me, who are covered but not by my Spirit, that they may multiply their sins."

- MAR 14:21 ~ Surely the Son of man must depart, as was written. But woe to the man by whom He is betrayed; it would be better for that man had he never been born.

- LUK 21:16–18 ~ Jesus said, "You will be betrayed by parents, siblings, relatives, and friends; and some of you will be put to death. You will be hated for my namesake. But not a hair on your head will perish."

- JOH 15:16–25 ~ Jesus commanded His chosen to bear good fruit, which is demonstrated by loving one another. He warned His followers that people would hate and persecute them, because they hated and persecuted Jesus, and therefore they also hate God. Thank God that all believers are chosen to leave this hateful world.

Nihilism is the current craze: total rejection of religion and morality; rendering life meaningless in order to placate hedonists. These are the modern mutineers, traitors to their country, because their crimes are treasonous and rebellious. It matters not if they lean to the left or to the right when they have subverted decency, honor, and integrity to satisfy their lust, greed, pride, and covetousness. Money and power enable their decadent lifestyles and protect them from prosecution. They feign fairness and equal representation, but quash all dissent.

The precept of equality can be achieved only when people hold themselves accountable and are likewise accountable to one another; this is how our system of government has worked for 240 years. Most importantly we are accountable to the one true God, whom the mutineers will deny until they stand before Him in judgment at the last day, after which they will pay dearly. Ultimately, there will be an accounting and the cost will be their souls; this is the second death (REV 20:14; REV 21:8). By force they aim to grab power and seize control for a time, though they are surrendering their lives forever. Their deceptions and their delusions were given to them by Satan, though most of them probably do not realize that they are the ones being played.

AUGUST

- ROM 3:19–28 ~ Now we know that whatever the Law says, it speaks to those who are under the Law, so that every mouth may be silenced and the whole world held accountable to God. Therefore, nobody will be declared righteous in His sight by observing the Law; rather, through the Law we become conscious of sin. But now righteousness of God apart from the Law has been made known, to which the Law and the prophets testify. This righteousness is available to all believers through faith in Jesus Christ. There is no difference between Jews and Gentiles, for all have sinned and fallen short of God's glory, and all can be justified freely by His grace through the redemption that came by Christ. God presented His Son as an atoning sacrifice, received through faith in His blood. He did this to demonstrate His justice. He restrained Himself from executing punishment for the sins committed beforehand so that He could show His justice now, in order to be fair in justifying those who have faith in Jesus.

- 1 CO 7:22 ~ Those who were servants when called by Christ have become free, and those who were free when called by Christ have become servants. You were bought with a great price, so do not become a slave to humankind, but remain responsible to God and the purpose for which He called you.

- JDE 1:10–12 ~ These men speak abusively against things they do not understand; and whatever things they do understand by instinct, like unreasoning animals—these are the very things that destroy them. Woe to them! They have taken the way of Cain; they have rushed for profit into Balaam's error; they have been destroyed in Korah's rebellion. They are blemishes in your love feasts, eating your food without the slightest qualm—shepherds who feed only themselves. They are clouds without rain, blown about by the wind; autumn trees without fruit and uprooted—twice dead. (NIV translation)

Nihilists, globalists, statists, fascists, Marxists, jihadists, and anarchists refuse to accept liability. They choose themselves to be their god and engage in self-worship; they will never acquiesce to the people, the Constitution, or God Almighty. They are essentially lawless antichrists, for they are serving Satan completely unawares or perhaps deliberately, becoming allies of evil in rebellion against the Lord God. Their hate for Christians and Jews has prevailed from Old and New Testament times to this day, and will continue until all worldly empires have collapsed and lie prostrate before the King of kings.

- DAN 2:43–44 ~ The iron mixed with miry clay represents their comingling with the seed of men. But they will not cleave one to another, even as iron and clay do not mix. During the time of those kings, the God of heaven will set up His kingdom which will never be destroyed. His kingdom will not be left to others, but it will break into pieces and consume all prior kingdoms, and will stand forever.

- 1 JO 4:1–3 ~ Do not believe every spirit, but test them to determine if they are really of God; for many false prophets are in the world. Every spirit that confesses that Jesus Christ is God in the flesh is of God. Those who do not confess that Jesus is of God are themselves not of God; they are spirits of the antichrist, who you heard is coming and is already here.

- REV 16:13–14 ~ I saw three evil spirits that looked like frogs come out of the dragon, the beast, and the false prophet. These were the demons that performed miracles, and coerced the kingdoms of the world to unite against God.

- REV 17:12–14 ~ Ten kings will obtain power for one hour with the beast. They are of one mind and will give their power and strength to the beast to make war with the Lamb of God, only to be eliminated. For He is Lord of lords and King of kings; and those with Him are called, chosen, and faithful.

So, what is really going on here? It is the control game (otherwise known as tyranny), whereby they steal your liberties to dominate you. You no longer can make your own decisions because they will decide for you; and they will tell you what you must believe because faith in God is their greatest obstacle. Do what you are told or else, even though this standard does not apply to them. If they can change the rules, they can rig the game; which is why they would abandon the Constitution, reimagine our system of government, and forsake the ways and words of the Lord. But they have a weakness: morbid dread of losing power. This ungodly fear can be exploited. Anyone bearing the Holy Spirit has the power to defeat evil, for God is all powerful (JOH 16:33). This power is love, which casts out fears that torment the mind (1 JO 4:18). This is what the Bible refers to as a strong delusion: believing their own lies in order to dismiss God (see the lesson for 11/25).

- JER 8:11–12 ~ To heal your pain they came saying "peace, peace" but there was no peace. Were they ashamed of their atrocities? Not in the least; they did not even blush. But they will join the fallen. When the Lord comes, they will be cast down.

- ROM 5:3; ROM 8:35–39 ~ We also rejoice in our tribulations, because we know that tribulation produces patience, and patience produces character, and character produces hope. And hope will not disappoint us, because God has poured out His love into our hearts by His Holy Spirit. What can separate us from the love of Christ: tribulation, distress, persecution, famine, nakedness, peril, or sword? As it is written, for your sake we face death on a daily basis; we are sent as sheep to the slaughter. But we have conquered these things through Him who loved us. For I am convinced that neither death nor life, neither angels nor demons, neither the present nor the future, nor any powers, neither height nor depth, nor anything in all creation can separate us from the love of God that is in Jesus Christ our Lord.

Heavenly Father, we love your Law and we love your Word. Please help us to elect and appoint leaders and administrators who likewise love you and your laws. Our system of government and our laws were built on your laws and your words. We desperately need to get back to that foundation, and return to being one nation, under God, indivisible, with liberty and justice for all. Help us to remove from office and leadership those who place themselves first, believing themselves to be above all others and above the law. Help us to expel the power mongers that are dragging this country down. We need to replace these people with God-fearing, Constitution-abiding, Bible-believing men and women. We need governors who are motivated by love for you and country, and rid the land of those who love themselves even above the countrymen they purport to represent. Help us to restore law and order, and especially justice, whereby the guilty are prosecuted and punished, and the innocent are exonerated and freed. Let it be so if this be your will, in the name of Jesus, Amen.

August 6

Angels of the Lord Day is proposed to recognize angels which God sends to help us, protect us, inform us, and other tasks God assigns to them. Angels are not to be confused with demons, also called fallen angels, familiar spirits, and foul spirits. One third of the angels committed mutiny in heaven along with Lucifer who was a high-ranking angel; they were thrown out of heaven and now reside on planet Earth. But today is for celebrating the two-thirds of the angels who have remained loyal to God, and to humanity; whereas Lucifer and his demons despise humans.

Probably the best-known angel in the Holy Bible is Gabriel, though his name is mentioned only five times (DAN 8:16; DAN 12:21, 28; LUK 1:19, 26). He appeared to Daniel relating future events, such as the succession of empires and their eventual fall, the time of tribulation before the end, and the eternal kingdom to come. Gabriel appeared to Zechariah, to relate the birth of his son John, the baptizer. He appeared to Mary, and to Joseph in a dream (MAT 1:19–21), delivering good news about the coming of Messiah from Mary's womb. Gabriel is God's messenger to the world; on many occasions God sent a divine message through Gabriel.

- DAN 8:1, 16–25 ~ During the reign of Belshazzar, king of Babylon, I received a vision. I was by the banks of a river when I heard a man call saying, "Gabriel, help this servant understand the vision." The angel showed me things to come, including the fall of Media-Persia. Then I saw a male goat coming from the west who was mighty and strong. The goat represented Greece and the great horn represented the first king. The broken horn represented four kingdoms that would arise from the one. When the latter days come, iniquity will be rampant, and a fierce king of darkness will arise; he will be mighty but not of his own power. He will be a master of deception, destroying nations and mighty and holy people in the name of peace. He will set up the abomination that makes desolate. Considering himself great, he will challenge the Prince of princes who will defeat him without raising a hand.

- DAN 9:1–5, 21–27 ~ During the reign of Darius, king of Media, I came to understand the prophecy of Jeremiah (JER 25) concerning the seventy years leading up to the destruction of Jerusalem, and its relationship to seventy weeks (seventy times seven). I was praying for Jerusalem and the holy mountain, asking God to forgive His people and turn away His anger. As I prayed, the angel Gabriel came to help me understand this prophecy. He said it would take seventy weeks for the transgressions to end. Then reconciliation will occur, everlasting righteousness will come, and the Holy One will be anointed king. From the restoration of Jerusalem until the coming of the Messiah would be seven weeks. The rebuilding of streets and walls, even in perilous times, would take sixty-two weeks. Then Messiah would be cut off, and the evil ones would destroy the city and the sanctuary. This would be followed by a flood, war, and desolation. Then God will confirm His covenant in one week, after which offerings and sacrifices cease, and the abomination of desolation is destroyed and consumed.

- LUK 1:11–20, 26–35 ~ The angel told Zacharias that he and his wife would have a son. And he would be filled with the Holy Spirit and the power of Elijah, to prepare the way for the coming of the Lord. Zacharias doubted, and the angel, identifying himself as Gabriel, struck him dumb until his son was born. Later, God sent Gabriel to Galilee to see the virgin, Mary. She was going to conceive and bear a son, and name Him Jesus. He would be the Son of the Most High. Mary replied, "How can I bear a child since I have never been with a man?" Gabriel replied, "The Holy Spirit will come upon you and impregnate you. Thus, your child rightly will be called the Son of God."

Michael is a powerful angel referred to as the archangel. He also is mentioned by name only five times in the Bible (DAN 10:13, 21; DAN 12:1; JDE 1:9; REV 12:7). Michael is the protector and defender of God's people (DAN 3:12–27); he is the captain of the angels (JOS 5) and very likely carries a flaming sword (GEN 3; 2 KI 19; 2 CH 21).

- GEN 3:24 ~ God drove them out of the Garden of Eden. He placed two cherubim with a flaming sword at the east end of the garden to guard the Tree of Life.

- JOS 5:13–15 ~ While Joshua was preparing to attack Jericho, he saw a man with a sword drawn, so Joshua asked, "Are you for us or against us?" The man replied, "I am the captain of the angels of the Lord. Remove your shoes for you are standing on holy ground."

- 2 KI 19:35; 2 CH 32:21 ~ In one night, the angel of God killed 185,000 Assyrians by sword.

- DAN 10:1–7, 11–21 ~ During the reign of Cyrus, king of Persia, I received a revelation. I had been in mourning and fasting for three weeks. I was by the great river when I saw the angel Gabriel once again; the men with me did not see the vision and were scared away when the ground started quaking. I felt weak and ill, and I fell to the ground; but the angel lifted me to my knees. He had been contending with the kingdom of Persia which delayed him, but Michael, a chief among the angels came to help out. Then Gabriel related to Daniel about contending with the kingdom of Greece, and the fact that Michael would support that effort.

- DAN 12:1, 11 ~ Michael the great prince who protects your people will come. There will be a time of trouble such as never before, but the righteous whose names are written in the book will be delivered. From the time the daily offering will cease, and the abomination that causes desolation is set up, will be 1290 days (3.5 years).

- JDE 1:9 ~ The archangel Michael contended with Satan for the body of Moses, and rebuked Satan rather than passing judgment.

- REV 12:7–9 ~ Michael and his angels defeated the dragon, and Satan and his angels were thrown out of heaven.

The Bible speaks of cherubim and seraphim. Apparently, cherubim do God's bidding on earth, and seraphim do His bidding in heaven. Apparently, Michael and Gabriel are cherubim. Lucifer was a cherub too, before he got kicked out of heaven (ISA 14:12–15; EZE 28:14–19). Four cherubim and four seraphim are mentioned in the Holy Bible. But the total number of angels working for the Lord are innumerable (JOB 21:33; DAN 7:10; HEB 12:22; REV 5:11).

- EZE 1:5–14; EZE 10:1–22 ~ Ezekiel had a vision of four cherubim. Each had four faces (lion, ox, eagle, human), four wings, and human hands. They glowed with radiance and moved like lightning.

- DAN 7:3, 6 ~ Daniel had a vision of four beasts; one had four wings and four heads.

- ISA 6:2–3, 8 ~ Isaiah had a vision of six-winged seraphim, two wings covered the face, two covered the feet, and two were used to fly. One cried, "Holy, holy, holy is the Lord of hosts; the earth is full of His glory." The Lord asked, "Whom shall I send?" Isaiah said, "Send me."

- REV 4:6–8 ~ John had a vision of four beasts surrounding Christ's throne. They had eyes all around them, and they had six wings. Each had a different face: lion, ox, eagle, or human. They sang praises to God continuously.

Father, we thank you for angels who watch over us, protect us, and relay messages to us. When they do, we are not aware, but we know they are there because your holy Word does not lie. Help us to be kind to strangers and minister to them, for we could be assisting angels. Empower us to discern good spirits from evil ones. Never let us give into Satan or his demons. Imprint your seal upon our heads showing to all spirits that we are yours in Jesus Christ, Amen.

August 7

National Purple Heart Day celebrates our wounded warriors, who have sacrificed everything for our freedom. General Washington established the Badge of Military Merit on this date in 1782 for acts of valor. The badge was reinstated in 1932 by General MacArthur with a new design and renamed the Purple Heart. Interestingly, MacArthur himself became the first recipient of the Purple Heart for being wounded and for meritorious service in combat. The criteria were changed to include army soldiers and airmen wounded or killed in combat; in 1942 the medal was extended to all military service branches. Today there will be commemorations in various American cities sponsored by veterans, the armed services, and other patriots. Many purple heart recipients will be in attendance if you want to thank them personally. In certain venues, military institutions, and television networks you might observe a moment of silence or salutation to those heroes, alive and dead.

People who fight for the faith are not unlike those who fight for their country: they endure much hardship, they are beaten, tortured, and killed. Christ was illegally tortured and executed; even Pilate said He was innocent. All of Jesus's apostles were wounded and killed, except John who was exiled. Thousands of Christians in the early church were wounded, killed, and exiled. To this day, Christians around the world are being persecuted, tormented, tortured, and killed. It is risky business being a soldier for Christ, just as it is being a warrior representing America.

- DEU 20:1 ~ When you go into battle against your enemies, and you see horses and chariots, and you realize you are outnumbered, do not be afraid. For the Lord your God is with you.

- JOS 14:10–11 ~ Caleb said to Joshua and the tribes of Israel, "I lived to see God's promises come to pass. I feel as strong as before and I am still ready to go to war for the Lord."

- ISA 53:4–5 ~ Surely, He bore our grief and carried our sorrows. Yet we treated Him as an outcast, as if stricken, smitten, and afflicted by God. But He was tortured and bruised because of our sins. The punishment given to Him brought us peace, and through His wounds we have been healed.

- 2 CO 6:3–10 ~ We do not place obstacles in anyone's way because we do not want the ministry to be discredited. Rather, as servants of God we commend ourselves, through much endurance, trouble, hardship, and distress; through abuse, imprisonment, and rioting; through hard work, hunger, and sleepless nights; in purity, understanding, endurance, and kindness; in the Holy Spirit and in sincere love; in truth and in the power of God; carrying weapons of righteousness in each hand; through times of glory and dishonor, favor and rejection. We are genuine yet regarded as imposters; known yet regarded as strangers; dying yet still alive; beaten down but not defeated; sorrowful but always rejoicing; poor yet spreading wealth; having nothing yet possessing everything.

- 1 TI 6:12–13 ~ Fight the good fight of faith. Keep a firm grasp on eternal life, for this is why you were called, and why you testified before many witnesses and before God.

- 2 TI 2:3 ~ Being a good Christian soldier means you must endure much hardship.

- JAM 5:10 ~ Remember the prophets as examples of those who patiently endured suffering and affliction for speaking on behalf of the Lord.

- 1 PE 2:19 ~ Be thankful if you must unfairly endure grief or suffering because you maintain an upright conscience toward God.

Father, we thank you for those who fight for us in battle, defending freedom or defending the faith. Protect those who risk their lives for the welfare of your flock. In Jesus's name, Amen.

August 8

International Infinity Day occurs on the eighth day of the eighth month, illustrated by the symbol for infinity (∞). The first observance of this day was in 1988; it was proposed the previous year by sidewalk philosopher J. J. Fenyo, who offered free advice on the streets of New York City. The infinity symbol represents a number in mathematics that cannot be calculated, or which otherwise continues indefinitely. The idea of infinity can be applied widely to philosophical questions in many disciplines. In particular, people often relate it to time, the universe, and God. Of those three, the only one that is truly infinite is God. Time will end when Christ returns; plus, those who go to heaven with Him will become timeless beings like He is. Our universe will pass away through entropy, eventually fading into obscurity. The new heavens and earth will be different, primarily because the new universe will be in God's infinite domain.

God's will and the purpose of His Son's death is to give people a chance at everlasting life. That means there is life after death, for those who believe God and trust in the atonement of Christ. That new life, in a new body, will last infinitely, the second Christ comes for us.

- 1 CH 16:35–36 ~ Ask God to deliver, gather, and save you, so that you may give eternal thanks and glory to Him. Blessed be the Lord, from everlasting to everlasting.

- PSA 16:10–11 ~ God will not leave my soul in hell, and He will not allow His Holy One to be corrupted. He will show me the path of life. In His presence is fullness of joy; with His right hand there are pleasures forevermore.

- ISA 35:10 ~ The ransomed of the Lord will return singing songs of everlasting joy; they will have joy and gladness, but sorrow and sighing will be gone forever.

- DAN 7:14 ~ And there was given to Him dominion, and glory, and a kingdom, so that all people, nations, and languages, should serve Him. His dominion is everlasting which will never pass away, and His kingdom will never be destroyed.

- JOH 3:16 ~ For God loved the world so much He gave His only begotten Son, so that anyone could believe in Him and never die, but would receive eternal life.

- JOH 5:24 ~ Jesus said, "Truly I say, anyone who hears my words and believes that I was sent by God will have eternal life. They will not be condemned, but will pass from death into life."

People who reject the free gift of life which God is offering, will not be forced to live forever with Him in paradise. But they will be choosing everlasting death, entropy, nothingness, and emptiness. For them, time will have run out and their memory extinguished.

- ISA 24:4–6 ~ The earth is defiled and withers; the exalted of the earth decline. The earth is defiled by its people for they have disobeyed the laws, violated the statutes, and broken the everlasting covenant. Therefore, a curse consumes the earth; its people must bear their guilt. Earth's inhabitants are being burned up and very few are left.

- DAN 12:2 ~ Some will arise to receive everlasting life and some will arise to everlasting shame and contempt.

- MAT 25:32, 46 ~ The Son of God will gather everyone together, and will separate them, as a shepherd separates the sheep from the goats. The sheep will inherit eternal life, but the goats will inherit eternal punishment.

- ROM 6:23 ~ The wages of sin is death. But the gift of eternal life is available to everyone through Jesus Christ our Lord.

AUGUST

- REV 1:18 ~ Jesus said, "I am He who lives, having once been dead, and I live forevermore, Amen. I hold the keys to death and hell."
- REV 20:14; REV 21:8 ~ Death and hell will be thrown into the lake of fire, along with the cowardly, the unbelievers, the corrupt, the murderers, the immoral, the occultists, the idolaters, and the liars. Their place will be the eternal lake of fire which is the second death.

Philosophical questions such as these are often the topics of interest being debated on Infinity Day. It is a time to speculate, imagine, create, and research things that imply forever, or possibly never. The basic definition of infinity is limitlessness; no boundaries, no end, no constraints. Regarding our Father in heaven, His Son, and the Holy Spirit, we are talking infinity in all directions, in every attribute, to every extent; all-powerful, all-knowing, always present, always right; always superior, sovereign, and supreme. God is perfect in love, truth, life, righteousness, holiness, and grace. His kingdom is a place of everlasting joy, bliss, learning, knowledge, power, and glory. Given your choice between that and hell, the right choice practically jumps off the page.

- 1 CH 29:11 ~ Yours, oh Lord, is all greatness, power, glory, victory, and majesty. Everything in heaven and earth is yours, including the everlasting kingdom. You are exalted as head above all creatures.
- ISA 51:11 ~ Those redeemed by the Lord will return singing praises; they will have everlasting joy, and all sorrow and grief will be gone forever.
- EPH 1:9–11 ~ He made known to us the mystery of His will according to His good pleasure, which He purposed in Christ to be put into effect when the times reached their fulfillment, thereby bringing all things in heaven and on earth together under one head who is Christ. In Him we were chosen, being predestined according to His plan, ensuring that everything conforms to His purpose and will.
- COL 1:12–20 ~ Christ established an everlasting peace through His blood which was shed on the cross, thereby causing all things on earth and in heaven to exist together in harmony with Him.
- 1 TH 4:16–17 ~ The Lord will descend from heaven with a shout, with the voice of the archangel, and with a blast from the trumpet of God. Then the dead in Christ will rise first. Those who remain alive in Christ will rise to join the others in the clouds, meeting the Lord in the sky. Those chosen by Christ will live with Him forevermore.
- 1 TI 1:15–17 ~ The truth is, Jesus Christ came to earth to save sinners, of whom I am the worst. But for that very reason I was shown mercy, so that in me, the worst of sinners, Christ could reveal His unlimited patience as an example for everyone who would believe in Him and receive everlasting life. To the eternal, invisible, and immortal King, the only God, be all honor and glory forever and ever, Amen!
- JDE 1:25 ~ To the only wise God our Savior, be glory and majesty, dominion and power, now and forevermore, Amen.

Can you imagine infinite knowledge, growth, life, experience? This should motivate you to be all you can be in godliness and obedience; your reward for behaving and controlling yourself will be prosperity and honor. Additionally, the reward for your faith and trust in Christ will be to pass from death into life in paradise. You cannot simply be a good person to be heaven-bound; you have to receive the gift by faith. Once you receive Jesus into your heart, the Holy Spirit will be your infinite friend, always accessible in this life and the next. He will tell you the truth, what to do about it, and when it is the right time to speak it or perform it. Therefore, you need to be faithful and good; faith comes first and it yields good works.

- ISA 57:15 ~ The eternal and holy Lord God says that anyone who comes before Him with a contrite and humble spirit will be revived from death.

- MAT 7:14 ~ Straight and narrow is the gate that leads to eternal life.

- JOH 5:28–29 ~ The time is coming when all who are in the grave will hear His voice and come forth. Those who have been faithful and good will arise to everlasting life, and those who have been unfaithful and evil will arise to receive everlasting condemnation.

- TIT 1:2 ~ Our faith and knowledge rests on the hope of eternal life which God, who cannot lie, promised before the beginning of time.

- TIT 3:5–8 ~ He did not save us because of our deeds done in righteousness, but because of His mercy given us through the regeneration and renewal in the Holy Spirit by Jesus Christ, so we can be justified by faith and become heirs in hope of eternal life. Those who have believed will apply themselves to perform good deeds.

Generally, things that have a beginning have an end. God had no beginning; He existed for infinity past and future, and all points in-between, to the greatest height, breadth, and depth. Believers had a beginning, but they will not have an end, since we will live forever with the Lord our God. I like that idea a lot more than being forever dead, where everything you experienced in your entire life will be gone forever and so will you. God is the only infinite, but we can choose everlasting life with Him from this point forward and forever.

- ISA 65:17–19 ~ I will create new heavens and a new earth; the former heaven and earth will never be remembered or recalled. You will be glad and rejoice forever, for I will make Jerusalem a place of happiness. And I will rejoice with Jerusalem for I will be happy with my people, and there will nevermore be the sound of crying among my people.

- EPH 2:2–4 ~ In the past you walked according to the ways of the world, along with the prince of the power of the air, the spirit that works in those who are disobedient to God. We too engaged in lusts of the flesh, fulfilling the desires of our bodies and minds. Though we were dead in our sins, God in His infinite mercy and love has made us alive in Christ, and by His grace we are saved.

- HEB 9:11–12 ~ Christ has come, the high priest of all good things, into a perfect temple; not a temple made with hands like a building. He entered the sanctuary, not by the blood sacrifice of animals, but through the perfect sacrifice of His own blood. He obtained, not temporary forgiveness for us, but eternal redemption.

Infinite Father, your grace, mercy and goodness are unlimited; your love, peace, and truth are unfathomable. And you give these things to us for free; we praise you for this and we thank you, and we will be eternally grateful when we come home to you Father, in the company of the saints and the angels. Though we cannot imagine eternity we will experience it; and though we cannot understand immortality we will become it. And though we are currently flawed sinners, we will be made perfect in righteousness, innocence, and blessedness, even as your Son is perfect in love and has made us holy through sanctification by His Holy Spirit. We know of peace, joy, faith, truth, and hope but they are fleeting; please continue to restore us every day in these gifts as we look forward to the coming of Christ. Help us to share the truth of your Word as we continue to study it meticulously, so that your kingdom can multiply. In the name of Jesus Christ our Savior, whose death earned for us life everlasting, Amen.

August 9

National Book Lovers Day is rather self-explanatory; we love books we like books, but I guess some people hate books. I disliked textbooks when I was young, but I liked Mark Twain, Jack London, and John Donne, eventually learning that books can be cool. These days I read mostly nonfiction and scientific literature; and of course, the Holy Bible. I also write and publish books, so I can relate to this holiday. It remains a mystery the origin of this holiday, but it is growing in acceptance. There are many other days in the year when books are celebrated so take your pick. You might celebrate this observance by dropping by the library and checking out some books.

Books have been around since ancient times. In olden days they used durable materials to write upon like stone, animal skin, and parchment, often preserving the book or scroll with leather or wooden covers. It must have been quite the challenge authoring a book, imagine publishing one. They had to recopy the entire manuscript when it aged, or was being distributed, until Gutenberg invented the movable type printing press in 1456. Now it's easy to publish, reproduce, and distribute books; the computer age opened the door for many independent writers and publishers.

The Holy Bible is the most famous, most read, most sold, and most factual book. It has stood the test of time, and is still being translated and circulated. Because the author is God who inspired faithful devotees to write down His words and the visions they were shown. The Lord oversaw the preserving of original words, recopying them for distribution, and translating them into hundreds of languages. God personally wrote His first book on two stone tablets containing ten commandments (twice). God led Moses to write the first five books of the Bible (namely, the Pentateuch, or Torah). All sixty-six books were authored at God's direction by godly men.

- PRO 30:5–6 ~ Every word of God is true. Do not attempt to add to His words or He will rebuke you and you will be proven false.

- 1 CO 2:13 ~ We teach using words taught by the Holy Spirit, not by human wisdom. Spiritual truths can be interpreted only by people who possess the Spirit.

- 1 TH 2:13 ~ We thank God that you received His Word and accepted it as the Word of God and not the word of men. The Word of God is at work in believers like you.

- 1 JO 5:20–21 ~ Remain in Christ who is true. Stay away from anything or anyone who would distort God's truth or attempt to take God's place in your heart.

- 2 PE 1:21 ~ No prophecy ever came from the impulse of man, but holy men spoke as they were directed by God.

The Bible happens to be the book I love the most, and the one I have read the most. For many, reading the Bible is hard work. It was for me too, at first. It took several readings to get the big picture. There is nothing boring about truth, but sometimes it is difficult to hear or bear.

- PSA 119:49–50 ~ I remember your words for they give me hope; this is my comfort when I am hurting, for your Word revives me.

- PSA 119:96–99~ I am imperfect but your commandments are unbound. How I love your Law; I meditate upon it, night and day. Your precepts are always with me and they make me wiser than my enemies. I have more insight than the teachers for I meditate on your statutes.

- PSA 119:105, 140, 167 ~ Your Word is a lamp unto my feet, and a light unto my path. It is very pure, that is why I love it. My soul keeps your testimonies, for I love them exceedingly.

Father, we thank you for the Bible, the arbiter of truth. We love you and we love your Word. Let us never hesitate to study it and listen with our heart and soul. In Jesus's name, Amen.

August 10

Waiting for Heaven Day is presented to remember that the Good Shepherd is coming for His sheep, and we must wait patiently for His return. We mustn't be in a hurry to die and go to our heavenly home, thinking we are useless or feeling unappreciated where we are. We are here for a reason, every one of us, no matter our age, job, physical and mental condition, or socioeconomic status. God has a plan and if you are still here, you are not finished. In the words of Yogi Berra, "It ain't over till it's over." Many people who purport to have experienced a near-death or out-of-body occurrence believe they spent a period of time in heaven (or hell). Sometimes they say God was calling them and they wanted to go with Him, but God sent them back and restored them to health to carry on the mission. While it may be true that God restored them, there is no Biblical basis for witnessing firsthand the glory of God's kingdom in this mortal and corrupted body. Certainly, we all have had visions of heaven and hell and religious experiences. Similarly, we are constantly bombarded with words and imagery every day, which might be why people have a similar understanding of life after death, heaven and hell, and eternal bliss versus torment. But how does one determine if their visions or dreams are real, or merely a figment of the imagination? This is a good time for a deep and lengthy, heart-to-heart talk with God.

Definitely, many books have been written and many movies have been produced about near-death and out-of-body experiences, as well as visiting heaven or hell, along with detailed descriptions of events, people and places they supposedly encountered. In general, heaven is described as a pleasant place with good people and hell is just the opposite. However, this information has been available since days of old. Well, did these people really see heaven or hell, to include deceased relatives and other conditions described from their visions? As always, we need to look into God's Word. If there is disagreement among witnesses, we know the Bible will be the most credible witness.

There is only one clear example in the Bible when someone got a view of heaven, and that event is reported by the apostle Paul (2 CO 12:2–4). Paul spoke of a man who was "caught up to the third heaven" meaning God's domain; ordinarily, the first heaven is associated with sky (atmosphere) and the second heaven with outer space (cosmos). Whatever was seen and heard during that occasion, Paul was not permitted to reveal it. Paul goes on to say that his job was to tell the truth, not to exalt himself or to be exalted by others. To ensure this, Paul was given a "thorn in the flesh" which Satan used to pummel Paul, lest he be exalted (2 CO 12:5–7). Perhaps the guy who was "caught up" into heaven was Paul himself, but this is unclear. Either way, Paul was prohibited from providing further details about the experience and who experienced it.

- 2 CO 12:2–4 ~ I knew a man in Christ over fourteen years ago (whether in the body or out of the body, I cannot tell, but God knows). This man was caught up to the third heaven, and I knew this man. How he was caught up into paradise to hear unspeakable words which I am not free to explain.

Paul's episode is similar to one described by the apostle John (REV 10:1–6), in that both experienced a supernatural phenomenon but were commanded by God to exclude some things they had seen or heard. John observed an angel speaking, followed by thundering voices proclaiming things which John was not allowed to record. John was then directed by that same angel to "prophesy before many peoples, nations, tongues, and kings." By the way, this angel, and the seventh angel sounding the final trumpet announcing Jesus's return, are likely one in the same (1 CO 15:51–52). John only reported the second half of the angel's message which referred to the completion of time (REV 10:7–11). Whatever Paul and John witnessed, it wasn't for public consumption; in both cases, a portion of their testimony was withheld at God's command.

- REV 10:1–6 ~ I saw another mighty angel descend from heaven in a cloud. He had a rainbow over his head, his face shown like the sun, and his feet were as flaming fire. In his hand was a small, opened book. The angel stepped his right foot upon the sea and the left upon the earth. He cried aloud like a roaring lion; after he spoke, seven thunders uttered their voices. I was about to write when a voice from heaven told me, "Seal up those things which the seven thunders uttered and do not write them down."

Another similarity between Paul's and John's vison reflects an inheritance available in heaven, as well as the inheritance awaiting those going to the other place. The prophets have declared that nobody has seen or heard what God has prepared for the next life (ISA 64:4; 1 CO 2:9); but people sure get enough of a glimpse in scripture to make up their minds about both destinations. The two visions described above have a third thing in common: the prophets lived to bear witness; that is, Paul and John would carry on, and not die until their assigned tasks were accomplished. And they knew they were not done as explained in their testimony; and you are not done either, at least not yet.

Doubtless, Paul likely had numerous near-death experiences, which he chose not to dwell upon (ACT 14:19; 2 CO 6:3, 9). He surely suffered more than most; but miraculously, he'd be up and back on the road posthaste continuing to proselytize until his death (ACT 14:20). Obviously, "near death" doesn't have much in common with dead. And when people are brought back from the dead, they are not "nearly" dead, but fully alive body, mind and spirit. Notice how those who had their lives extended by God to minister and testify, such as Lazarus, left no reports concerning their familiarity with the other side. So, how can we be sure? Well, if it was written in the Bible, it is because God wanted it recorded, and the reason it is not is because God did not want it recorded. People purporting to think they know through personal experience about the afterlife, and then make a spectacle of themselves, would appear to be violating a basic principle outlined above. They exhibit self-exaltation and hence, their testimony is untrustworthy.

- ACT 14:19–22 ~ Some Jews from Antioch and Iconium came, persuading the people to stone Paul. They dragged him out of the city figuring he was dead. The disciples gathered him up and took his body back into the city. The next day, Paul and Barnabas left for Derbe where they preached the good news and won many disciples. Next, they left for Lystra, then on to Iconium and Antioch. And many more disciples were confirmed, in the knowledge of the trials and tribulations associated with faith.

I guess everyone gets a premonition of heaven and hell. Likewise, the consequences and circumstances determining which route one should take in life are readily available to everybody reaching the age of accountability (NUM 14:29–31; ISA 15:18; 2 PE 3:9). The mass media also provide images and scenarios which have proliferated over the years and stimulate these visions. It stands to reason that an end-of-life or out-of-body experience would produce similar pictures or perceptions for most everyone. Indeed, it does to some degree, in that consolidation of the available literature on the subject displays many consistencies, even with scripture. Anyone can see the contrast of heaven and hell, light and darkness, and good and evil everywhere and any time. Who wouldn't contemplate such things if they figured they were about to die? Who wouldn't give prayer a chance when encountering the threshold of demise? Well, the answer to these questions is, far too many human beings really don't care, because they don't believe God.

Keep in mind there also are noteworthy dissimilarities among the various testimonials regarding alleged visits to the other side. And that poses a reliability problem, statistically speaking. The similarities are what you would expect but the differences tend to contradict scripture. How do you weed out the false testimony from the truthful? You compare it to the Word of God, whether it is in agreement. But even if the descriptions are in agreement with scripture, this is not evidence that the testifier experienced the other side. Because nobody has seen or heard, remember?

- JOH 16:12–14 ~ Jesus informed them, "I have many things to tell you but you are not ready for them yet. Nevertheless, the Spirit of Truth comes; He will guide you into all truth. He does not draw attention to Himself but to me. He hears and He speaks, and He will show you things to come."

- REV 4:1–5 ~ Next I looked and beheld a door opening in heaven, and a familiar voice spoke to me as a trumpet saying, "Come up here, and I will show you things that will occur in the future." Immediately, I was in the spirit and beheld a throne in heaven and one sitting there. And He that sat on the throne appeared as jasper and ruby, and a rainbow shining like an emerald encircled the throne. Around the throne were seated twenty-four crowned elders. From the throne proceeded lightning and thunder, and voices. And seven lamps were burning before the throne which were the seven Spirits of God.

What would motivate one to testify that they went to heaven or hell? How could that possibly be verified by the dreamer or anyone else? Well, look out; because many are telling their stories for attention, profit, self-aggrandizement, or whatever. That is why critical elements of their stories do not agree; these people really didn't go anywhere outside of their own minds. When the spirit and the soul have departed, the body is dead as can be; and the deceased has already thought their last thought on the earth. Even if these people believed what they saw and boldly declared it, who can confirm their vision? Maybe they dreamt it, maybe God provided a revelation, maybe they made it up. The nice thing about the Holy Bible is this: the testimony of the prophets and apostles can be verified using additional reliable sources. But the single testimony of one person, however convincing, will always be suspect. That doesn't mean they are lying; it merely means they could be mistaken. Or, maybe they are lying, to get the attention.

Like Paul said: He didn't know if the experience was in the body or out of the body. Neither does anybody else know, and neither can the experience be measured, observed, or objectified. That such visionaries repeat the same things others do, which are revealed in the literature as well as the Bible, should not raise anyone's eyebrows. This is more commonplace than people may think. When in limbo, people may remember things long suppressed, and they may see faces of people long passed; and they might even be able to possess some awareness of things happening in the physical world although they do not appear to be conscious or responsive. And certain details may be confirmed by their relatives; but this is not evidence of an actual visit to heaven or hell. Some of these scenes could be dormant memories. What these witnesses cannot relate is that which God has forbidden from being revealed until Christ returns.

Many scriptures suggest that nobody gets to visit the other side, until death. Which means nobody can return as a disembodied spirit (Barber, 2020a). You die, and then that's it for this life (JOB 7:9–10; ECC 9:5–6; PSA 6:5; HEB 9:27); you don't go to heaven or hell and come back to tell everyone about it (1 TH 4:13–17). On rare occasions noted in scripture people were brought back from the dead. Like Paul, they probably didn't dwell on the afterlife but on the promise of eternal life. No doubt, they lived their extended life looking forward, not backward.

- JOH 3:13 ~ Nobody has ascended into heaven except He who descended from heaven, the Son of man.

- 1 CO 13:12 ~ Presently, we see in a mirror dimly, but later face to face. Now I know in part, but then I will know fully, even as I am fully known.

Anyone saying they went to heaven and were in the presence of God in their degenerate state are misguided. That doesn't mean people will never be visited by angels or Jesus Christ through a vision or a dream (JOE 2:28). Certainly, Paul was visited during his conversion and John when he received and wrote the Revelation of Jesus Christ. God came down from heaven to speak to the prophets; but they did not go up to speak with Him and return later to brag about knowing things God keeps to Himself. God obviously holds things back until we are ready.

- EXO 33:17–20 ~ Moses asked God to reveal His glory. God replied, "Nobody can see my face and live… But before my glory passes by you, I will place you inside the cliff and cover your face with my hand; when I take away my hand you will see only my back in departing."

- JOH 1:18 ~ No man has seen God at any time. It is the Son of man, who is in the bosom of the Father, that declares Him.

- REV 21:27 ~ By no means will anyone enter into heaven who is defiled, does abominable things, or invents lies; only those who are written in the Lamb's Book of Life will enter there.

It makes perfect sense that someone teetering on death may invite Jesus to visit, or ask Him to forgive and bless them (LUK 23:39–43); and I expect He would do just that because He has promised (MAT 7:7; ROM 10:12–13). Those who have never beckoned Jesus to call on them are likely to perceive something more remorseful during a death-defying experience. Many have come to Christ as the result of such a vision, recurring dream, or near-death episode; such incidents have been related by converts from Islam, Buddhism, and previous followers of other counterfeit religions. The Holy Spirit arouses them into faith and they are saved as a result of the encounter, whether by vision or revelation.

When a person doesn't know Christ, he or she will be more easily fooled by a figure of light; because malevolent spirits often disguise themselves as benevolent ones (2 CO 11:14–17). This is likely the case for such mystics as Buddha and Mohammed; both fasted for weeks before purportedly receiving a vision of a spirit of light. Since their correspondence contradicts the Holy Bible, it seems they were listening to the wrong spirit. Perhaps they were deliberately attempting to deceive, as is the case for many tale-tellers proclaiming experiences in heaven and hell or face-to-face conversations with God. How can a person tell the difference between a vision from God verses one from Satan without the Spirit of Christ guiding them? Perhaps that's why hoards are leaving other world religions in a quest for truth, and end up joining Christendom.

Just before he died, Stephen saw heaven and Jesus sitting at the right hand of God; then Stephen called to Jesus to take him home (ACT 7:55–60). Paul was actually a party to Stephen's last stand (ACT 7:58); this was prior to Paul's conversion from Saul (ACT 9:1–17). Stephen knew exactly where he was going prior to his death. His was not a near-death experience for he was alive and ready to be taken to paradise upon his impending demise. True Christians know what Stephen knew and will not be caught by surprise; and they will know in their heart their next destination. They may even see a vision of it in their mind as they lay dying. If you are not sure about your beliefs, visions, or sources, you might not have your house in order; and time is running out folks.

I recommend taking afterlife stories with a grain of salt. Yes, they can be inspirational and interesting, but not necessarily factual. Like the Bible says, "Test what the spirits and seers put out against what the Bible says" (2 CO 11:13; 1 TH 5:21; 1 JO 4:1–13). Likewise, test what is being placed into a book or a movie in light of what the Bible says. Those who are less educated or otherwise ignorant of God's Word produce deviations from the "normal" view of heaven and hell. While there is a common thread in many of the various presentations, there also is divergence regarding critical aspects of Christian theology. Therefore, before believing these stories, it helps to know the scriptures; better yet, it is best to believe the scriptures. Surely, embellishment is a tricky if not risky business when the things being portrayed are in discord with Biblical truth; naturally, one should expect this from an imposter or a spirit of darkness.

Remember this, experience is not the quintessential avenue to enlightenment, but the Bible is. Gleaning truth and enlightenment from the Bible will require intense study. There is no easy road to salvation (MAT 7:14). You cannot drop acid, have a "religious" experience, and decide you can see, hear, or feel God in this manner. Hint: It was a hallucination, duh. That's why people take illicit drugs, they are motivated to experience something unusual, abnormal, or supernatural.

Another thing to consider is this: a person in a physically incapacitated, mentally delirious, or heavily medicated state are subject to hallucinations and delusions; that is, it is normal to experience psychotic features producing sounds and sights that are fantastical or unreal under these conditions. Further, to a person suffering from psychosis, such as paranoid schizophrenia, the hallucinations and delusions seem real; and I'm sure people remembering near-death experiences might say the same thing. But the event is just as unreal as it would be if the person happened to be under the influence of drugs, medication, evil entities, delirium, or otherwise was mentally, medically, and/or spiritually vulnerable or weakened. That is, distortions to reality are likely during altered states of consciousness, medical emergencies, or medicated stupor, no matter what the cause or circumstances. This alone makes such testimony admissible only in the court of opinion.

Invite the Holy Spirit to come in, and you will never be persuaded by the superstitions of others. You will know in your heart when a revelation is real or contrived if you are well versed in the Bible, because such disclosures will be backed up by scripture. And this will illuminate the path in which the Lord is leading you. These experiences are supposed to be personal, not something that needs to be publicized. By making them public it draws attention to oneself; but God wants us to draw attention to Him.

Where and when your path ends, God only knows. Death is always forthcoming, my friends. Every moment can be considered a near-death moment from now on, until the time Christ returns, after which you will remain forever in either the lost or the found column. For some, it may be the last thing they think before drawing a complete blank.

Heavenly Father, please give us patience as we await the coming of your Son; let us not be in a frenzy wanting to be absent from this body and present with you in heaven. Help us to rely exclusively on your truth and your words; help us also to compare what we see and hear with what is written in the Holy Bible. We know that the final arbiter of truth is your Holy Spirit who testifies to the truth. Encourage us to be diligent in the study of your Word so we will have a source with which to contrast what we see and hear in the news, in the mass media, and from people who talk a good talk and say marvelous things that do not comport with what the Holy Spirit says. Remind us that we should fact check anything that contradicts what our conscience says within us. Help us to be constant in prayer and Biblical study so that we remain connected to the absolute source of all truth, your Holy Spirit who speaks truth to us in your Word, and the Word made flesh who is Christ in whose name we now pray, Amen.

August 11

Mountain Day is held annually in Japan to celebrate their mountains which formed the islands, both of which were sacred from ancient times among the Japanese people. Their polytheistic philosophy, a mix of Shintoism and Buddhism, included adulation of those mountains. It would be like Mt. Sinai which was holy to the Jews in the Old Testament, where the Lord spoke to Moses from the burning bush and where Moses later received the Ten Commandments (EXO 19, 20, 24, 32). Sinai was a holy mountain then, and still is for many. Not that we should worship mountains, but consider their significance throughout history beginning with Noah's ark coming to rest in the mountains of Ararat (GEN 8:4), and ending with the final battle between good and evil in the mountains of Megiddo (REV 16:12–17). Mountains can be a stronghold, a place of refuge and rest, an escape for privacy and prayer, or a place of death and destruction.

- 1 KI 18:20–40 ~ King Ahab alerted the citizens and prophets of Israel to gather at mount Carmel. Elijah spoke to the crowd asking them how long they would continue to be double-minded, following God and following Baal. Elijah was the only prophet of God remaining, while the prophets of Baal numbered about four hundred fifty. Elijah challenged the prophets of Baal, to see who was more powerful: Elijah's God or Baal. He challenged the false prophets to bring fire down from heaven and consume their sacrifice; but after several tries, to include yelling and cutting themselves, they were unsuccessful. Elijah built an altar of stone, and commanded servants to drench the altar, the sacrifice, and the ground with water three times. Then Elijah prayed to God to reveal Himself, and He responded by bringing fire down from heaven destroying the altar, the sacrifice, and drying up all the water in the moat around it. When the people saw this, they fell on their faces, proclaiming the one true God. Then Elijah ordered the prophets of Baal to be captured and brought to him for execution.

- LUK 6:12–16 ~ One day Jesus went up into a mountain to pray, and continued all night in prayer to God. When morning came, He called His disciples together, and He chose twelve whom He named apostles.

- LUK 9:28–31 ~ Eight days later Jesus took Peter, James, and John to the mountaintop to pray. While Jesus prayed, His countenance changed and His clothes shined as lightning. Two men, Moses and Elijah, appeared with Jesus in glorious splendor. They were conversing about Jesus's departure from this earth which would occur after returning to Jerusalem.

- MAT 24:15–16; MAR 13:14, 19, 22; LUK 17:31 ~ Jesus said, "When the abomination that brings desolation, of which the prophet Daniel spoke, is standing in the holiest place, flee Judea into the mountains and do not turn back. There will be tribulation such as the world has never seen before or ever will again. False prophets and false messiahs will arise and perform magic. Many will be led astray."

- REV 6:15–17 ~ The wicked tried to hide in the rocks and caves, praying that the mountain would fall on them, for the great day of God's wrath had come upon them.

Consider Mount Zion and its many applications in the Bible. For starters, it can represent the old Jerusalem and the new Jerusalem. The old is found on earth, the new in heaven. There will be a new Jerusalem, a new earth and new heavens, and the saved will have new bodies that never die. The old will pass away and not be remembered.

- 2 SA 5:7 ~ David took the stronghold of Zion which is called the City of David.

- PSA 76:2 ~ In Salem (meaning city of peace) is God's tabernacle; in Zion is His home.

- PSA 137:1, 8; JER 50:13, 23–24, 28, 46; ZEC 2:6–7 ~ We sat down by the rivers of Babylon and cried when we remembered Zion. Oh, daughter of Babylon, you will be destroyed; happy are we who will see you rewarded as you have done to us. Babylon will be destroyed; everyone who goes there will be astonished at the plagues and destruction. Babylon will become a desolation. They were not aware that God would catch them and punish them for continuing to sin. Flee from Babylon as the vengeance of the Lord is declared in Zion. The earth will be shaken, for the cry of Babylon's fall will be heard around the world. Escape from the north to Zion, those who dwell with the daughter of Babylon.

- ISA 60:14 ~ Those who afflicted you and despised you will bow down to you; they will call you the city of the Lord, Zion, the Holy One of Israel.

- MIC 3:11–12 ~ Their leaders judge for a bribe, their priests teach for a price, and their prophets tell fortunes for money. Yet they claim to lean on the Lord as if God is with them and nothing can harm them. But because of them, Zion will be plowed as a field and Jerusalem will become a pile of rubble; and the temple mound will be overgrown.

Both the Old and New Testaments speak of Mount Zion where the Lord lives. The Jews had their Zion, representing the promised land and their holy city Jerusalem. Christians look forward to Mount Zion in heaven, as elucidated in both testaments of the Bible. Only true believers will be allowed to worship on the new Zion in the new Jerusalem.

- ISA 2:2–3; ISA 4:2 ~ During the latter days the mountain of the Lord's house will be established at the top of all the mountains, above all the hills where the nations flow together. People will say, "Let us go up to the mountains of the Lord, to the house of Jacob, and God will teach us His ways and we will walk in His paths." For out of Zion will come the Law; and from Jerusalem will come the Word. Those who remain in Zion and Jerusalem will be called holy, including everyone who is written among the living.

- ISA 33:14; ISA 35:10 ~ The sinners in Zion are afraid; fear has surprised the hypocrites. Who among us will live with the devouring fire? Who among us will burn forever? The ransomed of the Lord will return and come to Zion with songs and everlasting joy; sorrow and sighing will be gone forever.

- JER 50:4–5 ~ The children of Israel will come weeping, seeking the Lord. They will ask the way to Zion saying, "Let us join with the Lord in a perpetual covenant that will never be forgotten."

- JOE 2:32; JOE 3:18 ~ Whoever calls upon the name of the Lord will be gathered and delivered to live in mount Zion and Jerusalem. The mountains will flow with wine and the hills will flow with milk. The valleys will flow with water from a fountain in the center of the Lord's house.

- ZEC 1:16–17; ZEC 8:3, 5–8 ~ I will return to Jerusalem with mercy, and I will rebuild my house there. My cities will prosper again. I will again comfort Zion, and I will again choose Jerusalem. I will return to Zion and I will live in Jerusalem; and Jerusalem will be called the city of truth and Zion will be called the holy mountain. Children will be playing in the streets. It will be marvelous for my people and also for me. I will save my people from the corners of the earth and bring them to Jerusalem. They will be my people and I will be their God, in truth and in righteousness.

- HEB 12:22–23 ~ You have come to Zion, to the city of the living God, the heavenly Jerusalem. You have come to the company of innumerable angels, to the general assembly and church of the firstborn, all of whom are written in heaven. You have come to live with God, the judge of

AUGUST

all, and with the spirits of all honest people made perfect, and to Jesus Christ the mediator of the New Covenant.

- REV 14:1 ~ I saw the Lamb standing on mount Zion, and with Him were 144,000 bearing His Father's name on their foreheads.

Zion is symbolized in Christ, the Prince of Peace. The old city of peace (Jerusalem), which was destroyed and their land given to other nations, represents Christ who is killed, rises from the dead, and leads all who trust in His atonement, to enter a new Jerusalem in heaven which will never be destroyed.

- PSA 2:6–7, 11–12; PSA 48:2 ~ God says, "I have set my King on the holy mountain Zion. I will declare to the world that you are my Son, for this day I have begotten you. Serve the Son with fear and joy. Kiss the Son, because you will die if you get in the way of His wrath. The joy of the whole earth is mount Zion, the city of the great King."

- PSA 125:1 ~ Those who trust in the Lord will be like mount Zion, which cannot be removed, but abides forever.

- ISA 28:16; ISA 65:9 ~ God says, "I have placed in Zion a tested and precious cornerstone to ensure a sure foundation." I will bring forth a seed from Jacob and Judah; then my elect will inherit the mountains of the Holy Land.

- JOH 12:14–15 ~ Jesus sat on the young donkey just as it was written: Fear not daughter of Zion, for here comes your king, sitting on a donkey's colt.

- ROM 9:33 ~ Behold, I am placing in Zion a stone that will make men stumble and fall. Those who believe in Him will never be put to shame.

Mountains can be seen as hurdles or obstacles in our way, which the forces of evil in the world throw into our path to trip us up or knock us off track. If you want to make it to the mountaintop, you must follow Christ, for there is no other way to get there.

- PSA 36:7 ~ How precious is your everlasting love, oh God, where we can take refuge in the shadow of your wings.

- MAT 17:20; MAR 11:23–24~ Jesus said, "If you had faith the size of a mustard seed you could command the mountain to fall into the sea; nothing would be impossible. Through prayer, you can move mountains. All you have to do is believe and you will receive what you ask for."

- 1 CO 13:2 ~ Even if you have the gift of prophecy, can understand mysteries, and have a faith to move mountains, you are nothing without love.

Since other nations have adopted our holidays, I propose that the USA adopts Mountain Day to be observed from this year onward. Mountains are essential to life, for they produce rivers from the runoff of melting snow. The land would be uninhabitable without mountains. By the way, this holiday should not be confused with International Mountain Day, a December observance proposed by the UN which has very little to do with actual mountains.

Father in heaven, your temple sits on Mount Zion, and we are very thankful to be joining the angels there to worship you and carry out your plans. In the meantime, help us to bring our problems up the mountain of Calvary, and leave our troubles at the foot of the cross of Christ. Give us the strength to climb every mountain and remove every barrier that the devil uses to obscure our view of the path ahead and our destination at the new Jerusalem. Let us ever walk with Jesus and follow His example of purity and truth. In His precious name we pray, Amen.

August 12

IBM Introduced the Personal Computer in 1981, having made computers affordable and relatively easy to learn and operate. The package consisted of a compact processing unit, keyboard, color or monochrome monitor, sound card, floppy disk drive, and ports for other peripheral devices. This configuration has been emulated ever since, with progressively more add-ons, connectivity, applications, interfaces, compactness, and speed. IBM (International Business Machines) had produced computer systems for use in business and industry. But the microcomputer changed everything, ending up in every home and office in the modern world. It was a growing experience for my generation, and the learning curve was varied. But all future generations grew up with computers and assorted electronic devices to the degree they could teach their parents how to use them. I worked in a field where I spent hours writing research and technical reports on the computer, but it sure beat pounding out documents on a typewriter. If you have an affinity for your PC, you might do a cleanup on the hardware and software, in observance of the anniversary of this milestone event.

I have imagined a world without computers; it looks quite bleak. What if an enemy was to attack our power grids, or cyber-attacked our computer systems, or used electromagnetic pulse warfare to disable our electronic devices? You couldn't drive, email, phone, or buy and sell anything. That scenario actually has a fair possibility of happening. We know a time is coming in the next world order when people will not be able to buy and sell without receiving the mark of the beast. This is indicated in Revelation by the third horse of the apocalypse, with a rider carrying scales; the scales are tipped creating a higher and a lower, but no in-between. Thus, the middle class will disappear first. Eventually everybody ends up broke, when economic collapse takes down the rich as well; they will end up destitute like the poor souls they fleeced.

- EZE 13:19 ~ They will pollute me among my people for a piece of bread. They will kill people that should not have to die and save others that should not live, and lie about it.

- ZEC 6:1–7 ~ Zechariah had a vision of four chariots emerging from between two mountains of brass. The first chariot was driven by red horses, the second by black horses, the third by white horses, and the fourth by brown and gray (or pale) horses. The chariots represented the four spirits of heaven which stand before the Lord of the earth. The black horses will go north, and the white horses will follow them. The pale horses will go south. The red horses will go back and forth across the earth.

- REV 6:2–8 ~ John had a vision of four horsemen. The first had a bow and rode a white horse; he received a crown and went forth conquering. The second had a sword and rode a red horse; he received power to wage war and destroy peace. The third carried balances in his hand and rode a black horse; and the price of bread became a day's wages. The fourth rider was called Death and rode a pale horse; he was followed by Hell. They were given power to kill one-fourth of the earth's inhabitants by the four judgments: sword, famine, disease, and wild beasts.

- REV 13:15–18 ~ And the second beast brought the image of the first beast to life. He made everyone receive the mark of the beast on their right hand or forehead; only those with the mark could buy and sell goods. They tracked down and murdered anyone who did not receive the mark and worship the beast. The beast's number is the number of a man: 666.

If any of us are around when this tribulation happens, we will have to learn to live off the land. Survival skills will be essential; it wouldn't hurt to brush up on this just in case. Unless you want to join the club and get their stamp on you, in which case you'll be scraping a living off the bare minimum, whenever they decide you should have it. They will promise much but will not

AUGUST

deliver anything. Stay in Christ and you will receive God's mark, separating you from those receiving the mark of the beast. Remember, the Lord will provide everything you need.

- EZE 9:4–6 ~ God commanded His servant to set a mark on the foreheads of those who grieved because of the wickedness around them. The others were to be slain by the sword; all were to be slain except those with God's mark.

- EPH 1:13; EPH 4:30 ~ You were included with Christ when you listened to the words of truth and believed the good news of salvation, being marked by the Holy Spirit who has guaranteed your inheritance in God's kingdom. Do not grieve the Holy Spirit of God, who has sealed you for the day of redemption.

- REV 7:2–4 ~ The angel called to four other angels, commanding them to hurt the earth and the sea, but not those with God's seal. Before they were released, they had to seal God's people by putting His mark on their foreheads. There were 144,000 from the tribes of Israel that were sealed.

What does all this have to do with computers? Well, are you dependent on your computer; can you live without it? How exactly would you pull that off without a lot of help? It would be lot harder than learning how to use a microcomputer in the eighties. You would have to start from scratch as to how to scrounge for your daily bread. There will be a varied learning curve on that one too. They will try to take over your life, and do it by making you dependent on the global administration. But if you are dependent on God, you will find a way to live without the new age establishment and their offering of things they do not possess.

- PSA 5:11 ~ Let everyone who trusts in the Lord rejoice and shout for joy, because He will defend them. Let all who love the Lord be joyful.

- PRO 11:4, 28; PRO 22:16 ~ Riches will not profit anyone in the day of wrath; only righteousness can save a person from death. Those who trust in their riches will fail, but those who trust in God will flourish. Those who oppress the poor to increase their own wealth and those who give to the rich eventually will become needy.

- 1 CO 2:12 ~ We have received the Spirit of God, not the spirit of the world, so that we might know the things which God has given to us for free.

- 1 TI 6:17 ~ Tell those who are rich not to be miserly or greedy, trusting in their wealth for their needs. Tell them instead to trust in God who richly gives us all things to enjoy.

- 2 PE 1:3–4 ~ God's divine power provides us everything we need for life and righteousness through our knowledge of Him who called us in His glory and goodness. In these He has given us great and precious promises to participate in His divine nature and escape the corruption of the world caused by evil desires.

Father God, remind us that we need not depend on the world to fulfill our needs, for you alone can guarantee and fulfill. Let us never become totally dependent on things or people, except Christ and your Holy Spirit. Help us to count our spiritual blessings; when we compare those to worldly items, we realize the former will last forever but the latter will run out. If we are faced with economic disaster, help us to be adequately prepared to continue your work knowing that you will provide what we need to survive as we continue conducting your business. Seal us with the mark of your Holy Spirit upon our heads, which will repel the evil ones from trying to put their mark on us. Above all, we ask that you restore and defend our freedom, given to us for free by your Son, who freely gave Himself for us, liberating us from the bondage of sin and the curse of death. In the name of Jesus we pray, Amen.

August 13

Construction Began on Berlin Wall this day in 1961; from that day free travel between the two Germanies did not commence until 11/9/1989. For twenty-eight years this barrier separated East Berlin and West Berlin, and East from West Germany. Many defectors died trying to escape to freedom in the west. The historic city actually was divided into four sectors after World War II, occupied by the US, UK, and France (west side); and the Soviet Union who were aligned with East Germany (east side). The Soviets commenced to establish a coalition of eastern bloc nations in opposition to the NATO alliance. In 1948, limitations were imposed on entry by land into the Soviet zone resulting in the Berlin airlift; needed supplies were distributed to the east by airdrop. The USSR increased its grasp on the eastern sector, and the reformed German Democratic Republic (GDR). Here was a classic collision between capitalism and socialism. Thus started the so-called cold war between the west and east, which evolved into a standoff between the USA and USSR. Eventually, the eastern bloc nations sought independence in determining their economic future. Plus, more citizens, especially those with technical skills, were leaving East Germany. Barbed wire barriers were erected and a new rail line was built; then came the concrete wall. These measures literally shut down the border, covering almost one hundred miles when completed. In 1962 an inner barrier was added to the eastern side. Improvements to the Berlin Wall continued over the years to keep people from leaving, resulting in increasingly greater hardship for East Germans. Finally, minimum restricted visits from the west were authorized, but not the other way around until just prior to the wall coming down. The rise of communism dropped rather quickly, and along with it, the number of nations supporting it. Premier Gorbachev and President Reagan defended this breakup because the Soviet Union was overextended. Once the rumors got out, people began to storm the barrier on both sides, taking pieces as souvenirs. Finally, in 1990, East and West Germany reunified into a single free nation.

A clash of ideals is the major factor when people divide from one another; this is because of incompatibility, otherwise known as irreconcilable differences. But the only differences that are truly irreconcilable, are those between right and wrong. This division has been evident ever since Lucifer waged war on God because he wanted what God had. Call it pride, envy, greed, lust—it boils down to evil versus good; and since God is the only one who is absolutely good, it does no good to oppose Him. Whatever the conflict: good versus evil, right or wrong, God versus Satan, sin or righteousness, spirituality versus materialism, heaven or hell, truth versus lies, we all must pick a side.

This very same conflict resides inside everyone: the flesh versus the spirit, and the winner gets to control the mind, or soul. It is written: you cannot love God and money, for you will end up loving the one and despising the other; also, the love of money is the root of all evil. In short, you cannot love the world and God at the same time, for the world is temporal but God is eternal. The world ends with you in it if you are not on the side of God where life never ends.

- MAT 6:24 ~ Nobody can serve two masters, for they will end up loving one and despising the other. You cannot serve God and money at the same time.

- ROM 8:4–6 ~ Live, not according to the flesh, but according to the spirit. Those who live according to the flesh set their minds on evil, but those who live according to the spirit set their minds on God. To set the mind on flesh results in death, but to set the mind on God results in peace and life.

- 2 CO 10:4–5 ~ We fight with spiritual weapons to break down the barriers of sin. We destroy the arguments and pretensions that oppose God's truth, and we take prisoner all thoughts so they may be obedient to God.

AUGUST

- GAL 5:17 ~ The desires of the flesh are against the spirit, and vice-versa, for they are opposed to each other, preventing you from doing what you ought.
- GAL 6:8 ~ Those who sow to the flesh will reap corruption to their flesh; those who sow to the Spirit will from the Spirit reap eternal life.
- 1 TI 6:10–11 ~ The love of money is the root of all evil; through the craving for worldly riches many have wandered away from the faith and pierced their hearts. Strive for righteousness, godliness, faith, love, steadfastness, and gentleness.
- JAM 4:4 ~ You are an adulterous people. Do you not know that friendship with the world results in hatred towards God?
- 1 PE 2:11 ~ Dear ones, I implore you as strangers and pilgrims to refrain from lusts of the flesh which war against your soul.

We have this same conflict going on inside our country and dividing our people; it's not merely conservatism versus liberalism, or the Republicans versus the Democrats. This fight is over who possesses the truth, the moral high ground, the right to be in control. Are you kidding me? Is it not clear to all people what is true, right, just, and moral? Truth requires absolute conformance with reality; right requires righteousness; morality requires justice for the innocent and the guilty. How did these lines get blurred in anyone's mind? Maybe they have been deceived, or they are afraid of the truth, or they love sin and material things too much. They surely do not love God, they do not care, and they do not want to be held responsible. Or simply put, they want to be their own gods, the original sin of Lucifer, and Adam. Consequently, they have to lie to themselves. But how does one go about believing their own lies when they know in advance it is untrue? This must take considerable determination, causing constant cognitive dissonance, a lot more than simply doing the right thing I would think. Of course, doing the right thing isn't always easy either, but it yields a lot better results.

- PSA 1:1–5 ~ Blessed is the person that does not walk in the counsel of the ungodly, or stand among sinners, or sit in the seat of the scornful. Blessed is the person whose delight is in God's Law, for that person meditates on God's Law every day and night. Such a person will be like a tree planted by flowing streams of water, bearing good fruit in season, with leaves that never wither. Whatever he or she does will prosper. But the ungodly are not so; they are like the chaff that the wind blows away. Therefore, the wicked will not stand with the just, and sinners will not assemble with the righteous. For God watches over the ways of righteous people, but the ways of the wicked will perish.
- PRO 2:10–13 ~ When wisdom enters your heart and knowledge is pleasant to your soul, discretion will preserve you and understanding will keep you, to deliver you from evil and from those who speak evil.
- PRO 3:5–7 ~ Trust in the Lord with all your heart and do not rely on your own insight. In all your ways acknowledge Him and He will make your paths straight.
- ECC 10:2 ~ A wise heart inclines a person to do what is right.
- ROM 16:17 ~ Take notice of those who cause divisions and take offense to the doctrine you have learned, and avoid them.

Heavenly Father, help us reunite under the umbrella of your love, for love is the fulfilling of the Law. Help us to love you above all others, and love our neighbor as ourselves. Regarding those who have abandoned wisdom and truth, please give them a wakeup call. For those who do not care, help them to know that you care. Help us to care like Jesus cares, and to show it, Amen.

August 14

Social Security Act Signed into Law on this day in 1935 by President Franklin Roosevelt, to provide retirement benefits for people who could no longer work for a living. This bill provided financial assistance for the elderly, handicapped, unemployed, and single mothers raising children. The country was in the middle of the Great Depression and families were struggling to make ends meet. Workers received a social security number and card which identified them for the purposes of withholding payroll taxes from their wages. That money was collected to help subsidize the plan. The government ultimately depleted the funds which were supposed to be kept in a reserve account, designed specifically to pay benefits to those who earned them. Since then, the government has invented creative ways to distribute benefits by taking money from other projects, like stealing from Peter to pay Paul. They also have been raising the retirement age, now up to age seventy; you can qualify for benefits by retiring earlier if you can afford to receive a smaller amount until your death. There is a break-even point where the amount you get and your expected longevity come together at an optimal age, which for me was sixty-six.

It is difficult for a married couple to live on social security alone, especially in times of high inflation and reckless government spending. To be safe, you should have other sources of income like savings, annuities, investments, employer or individual retirement funds, etc. It is advisable to consult retirement experts and begin saving money at a young age, taking into consideration the state of the economy and the forecast for people your age.

- PRO 13:11; PRO 23:4 ~ Wealth obtained by pride will diminish; but those who achieve through hard work will see their wealth increase. Do not labor to become rich, and do not concentrate on your own feeble wisdom.

- ISA 46:4 ~ Even in your old age with your gray hair, I am He who carries you. I created you, I sustain you, and I will deliver you.

- LUK 10:2 ~ Jesus said, "The harvest is plentiful but the laborers are few. Pray that the Lord of the harvest would send more laborers to help."

- JOH 5:17 ~ Jesus said, "My Father has been at work all the while, and I work too."

- ACT 20:35 ~ In your labors, give to the needy, remembering the words of Jesus Christ, "It is more blessed to give than to receive."

- 1 CO 3:8–9, 13–14 ~ The one who plants and the one who waters is the same; everyone receives a yield commensurate with their labor. We are laborers working together with God. You are the mission field; you are God's building. Everyone's work will be seen for what it is because the light will illuminate it; it will be revealed by the fire which tries every person's work as well as his or her dedication.

- 1 CO 15:58 ~ Brothers, be constant in your labor, unwavering, firm, and productive. For you can be assured that your labor for the Lord will not be in vain.

- 2 TH 3:11–12 ~ We heard that some of you are lazy. They are not busy, they are busybodies. We urge these people, in the name of Christ, to settle down and earn the bread they eat.

- REV 14:13 ~ Blessed be those who die in the Lord henceforth, for they will rest from their labors which will follow them.

Heavenly Father, let our labor be conducted with love and dedication, so we will not be unproductive in our occupation and in our works of love done out of faith. Remind us that we are obliged to work hard and earn our keep, just as you and Christ work hard for us, Amen.

August 15

National Relaxation Day is designed to help people destress. Yesterday, the lesson was about hard work, but today it is about taking a break once in a while. Take care of your mind and body by creating a diversion; change the scenery or your routine. A common syndrome, detrimental to one's mental and physical health, is getting into a rut; and it can get progressively deeper if you do not re-energize. Rest and relaxation are good remedies; this can be enhanced by reconfiguring the environment. Or, consider taking a road trip, maybe go camping. Schedule relaxation time into your calendar as it will improve your mood and increase your productivity. Many businesses have incorporated fifteen-minute breaks in the morning and afternoon, plus a lunch break; research has proven that these interludes increase productivity. They give the conscious mind a breather, allowing the subconscious brain to synthesize and organize information needed next.

The Bible defined hard work as six days on, and one day off for rest and worship. Those who follow this precept will flourish, both spiritually and materially. The patriarchs put God first and were trusted with His wisdom and truth. They were healthier in mind, body, and spirit; they lived longer, and prospered financially by being thrifty. God's prophets had a tough job; some were cast out, beaten and murdered, others were priests and kings. We all get where we are by the grace of God, in spite of the fact we are guilty of crimes against Him in thought, word, and deed. God gave Himself as an example for us to follow: six days are ours and the seventh is His.

- GEN 1:24–27; EXO 20:11; EXO 31:16–18 ~ In six days God created the physical world as we know it. On day six God created human beings. God blessed the seventh day as the Sabbath, a day for reverencing Him and thanking Him for His many blessings. The children of Israel were to keep the Sabbath for all generations as a lasting covenant. Participation was a sign between God and His people forever. For in six days God made heaven and earth, and the seventh day He rested and was refreshed.

- LEV 23:3–4 ~ Six days shall work be done, but the seventh day is the Sabbath of rest, a holy convocation. You will do no work because it is the Lord's Sabbath in all your dwellings. There are feasts of the Lord, also holy convocations, which you will observe in their seasons.

- JOH 9:4 ~ Jesus declared, "We will do the work of Him who sent me while it is day, for the night approaches when nobody can work."

During my career I worked forty to sixty hours, five days a week, with time off; back in Biblical times they worked an average of ten to twelve hours, six days a week. Nowadays, people can get by working part time (less than thirty-two hours). Then there are those who abuse the system to get out of doing work. The problem with all of these workload conditions is the tendency to skip God that one day per week, regardless of how hard or easy the previous week was. Remember the Sabbath day and keep it holy; that is the fourth commandment (EXO 20:8–11). A holy convocation is basically public worship; go to church, unless there is a reasonable excuse like an illness. In which case, worship and study the Bible at home; for where two or more are gathered in the name of the Lord, His Spirit is there in the midst of them (MAT 18:20). Many evangelicals observe the Sabbath on Sunday in commemoration of Jesus's resurrection on Easter Sunday. Some Christian denominations worship on Saturday, as do Jews (ROM 14:5–8).

- 1 CH 23:30–31 ~ Thank and praise the Lord every morning and every evening. Regularly offer burnt sacrifices to Him every Sabbath, at the beginning of each month, and during the appointed festivals and feasts, in accordance with God's command.

- ISA 56:2–8 ~ Blessed are all people and their children if they obey God, avoid evil, keep the Sabbath, and cling to His covenant. Even those who are strangers to God's people Israel will be part of God's house if they obey Him. The righteous will be like God's sons and daughters, only better than that, with a name that will last forever. People of all walks of life will be joined together on His holy mountain to worship Him, for His house will be called a house for the righteous.

- MAR 2:27–28 ~ Jesus announced, "The Sabbath was made for man, not man for the Sabbath. Therefore, the Son of man is Lord even of the Sabbath."

When you have put in a full day, additional work will not be effective and quite possibly detrimental. After you get home from work, unwind; try some relaxation exercises. You can use a progressive relaxation method called systematic desensitization, which gradually makes you calmer and less aroused. Another excellent method is controlled breathing. After a few long, deep breaths, gradually slow your breathing; your heartrate likewise slows and you become more relaxed and less anxious. A third method is controlled imagery; it is a form of meditation where you envision a happy or favorite place in your mind. I used all of these methods in my practice, and found that every client could attain relaxation with one or more of them. I prefer imagery, for it enables me to escape the outside world and explore the world within. Going to a place in your conscious mind will distract you long enough to access the unconscious mind. Remember, worriment leads to stress, which leads to anxiety, which leads to depression So, try to relax!.

- DEU 31:6 ~ Be strong and courageous, do not worry or be afraid; for the Lord your God is with you. He will never fail you or forsake you.

- PSA 94:19 ~ Oh Lord, when I was overcome with anxiety, your comfort brought joy to my soul.

- MAT 6:25–34 ~ Jesus taught, "Do not worry about your life, what you will eat or drink, or what you will wear. Is there not more to life than food and clothing? Look at the birds; they do not sow or reap, or gather food into the barn, yet our heavenly Father feeds them. Are you not more important than birds? Consider the lilies of the field, they grow just fine yet they do not toil or spin; however, King Solomon in his glory was not clothed in such beauty. If God cares for the birds and the flowers, will He not care for you even more? Therefore, do not worry about things such as food and clothing, because your heavenly Father knows you need these things. Instead, seek first the kingdom of God and His righteousness, and everything else you need will be yours. Do not be anxious about tomorrow, because tomorrow will take care of itself. Each day has enough problems to face without adding more."

- LUK 21:34–35 ~ Jesus said, "Be careful. Do not let overindulgence, drunkenness, and the worries of life get the better of you, so when that fateful day comes you will not be caught by surprise. That day will be like a snare that catches the whole earth in its trap."

- PHP 4:6 ~ Do not worry about anything, but in everything, through praise and thanksgiving, make your needs known to God.

Holy Father, we thank you for giving us yourself as an example to follow. You showed us what hard work can yield, when followed by a day of rest and worship. We worship you and your Son, who gave us an example to follow in life and in death. We owe you at least one day each week where our focus is not on our works but on yours. Help us to remember how public worship and fellowship edifies, not only us but also everyone present. Let us be your servants by serving others before serving ourselves, even as Jesus became a humble servant to humankind. Remind us to take time to relax, reflect, and recuperate. Surely, meditating on your works and your Word, and inviting your Holy Spirit to join us, will always be a good place to start. Let it be so in Jesus's name, Amen.

August 16

National Airborne Day was declared a national holiday under President George W. Bush in 2002, to commemorate the first successful airborne jump on this day in 1940. Today we celebrate airborne troops and their contributions to victory, particularly during World War II. They were first deployed in North Africa, and later played a crucial role in the invasion of Normandy (06/06/1944) where airborne soldiers landed behind enemy lines and wreaked havoc. Since then, there have been numerous deployments, including Korea and Vietnam, further proving the strategic advantage of dropping fighting men into a battle zone.

The two major airborne divisions are the 82nd at Ft. Bragg, NC who wear the All American (AA) patch. Then there is the 173rd at Ft. Campbell, KY, which includes the 101st airborne/airmobile assault division; these two wear the Screaming Eagle patch. Prior to this were the 11th, 13th and 17th divisions. Additional airborne-qualified personnel are Army special forces and rangers, as well as other service specialties like the Navy seals. The idea of rapidly emplacing soldiers into critical areas of the battle zone came from Ben Franklin who proposed using hot air balloons to deploy soldiers. The idea was revived in 1940 by General Mitchell resulting in the first successful test on this day at Ft. Benning GA, which remains the primary Army airborne training post.

If you would like to participate in celebrating this observance, check your local US Army post or airborne association for events. Sometimes there are demonstrations you can attend; in particular, the Golden Knights parachute team is well worth watching. Or you might try skydiving with an expert to get the sensation of being aloft with only a parachute. But this experience will not be remotely similar to a jump made by a combat soldier carrying a full load of gear, dropping at considerably lower altitude into a hot drop zone, where they land quickly and hit the ground running to secure an area, setup a perimeter, or execute an offensive. This holiday is special to me because I was a paratrooper with the 82nd during 1971 and 1972.

If you want to know how it feels to fly, try parachuting or paragliding. Of course, when we make it to heaven, we will be able to soar like the angels. We may have wings, or possibly a more advanced means of propulsion. Imagine being able to move like lightning. Actually, that is a logical inference considering the speed of light negates the relevance of time, and we will become timeless beings, even as our brother Jesus is timeless throughout the ages.

- PSA 8:5 ~ For God made humans a little lower than angels, and has crowned us with glory and honor.

- EZE 1:5–14; EZE 10:1–22 ~ Ezekiel had a vision of four cherubim. Each had four faces (lion, ox, eagle, human), four wings, and human hands. They glowed with radiance and moved like lightning.

- MAT 22:30; MAR 12:25 ~ After the resurrection, the saints will not marry, but will be like the angels in heaven.

- LUK 20:36 ~ Those accounted worthy will become like angels, and will never die.

- REV 12:4, 9 ~ His (Lucifer's) tail swept the third part of the stars (angels) of heaven, which fell to the earth.

- REV 5:11 ~ Thousands upon thousands of angels were praising Jesus in heaven.

In heaven, we will be praising God along with the angels. And though we were created slightly lower than the angels, we will be judging them when we get to heaven. Those mutineers who joined Lucifer in the fall have been found guilty and will be condemned to the lake of fire.

Incidentally, God's authority living in us through Christ already allows us to give commands to fallen angels (i.e., demons) on earth, and they must obey whether they like it or not (LUK 10:18–20; JAM 4:7). God also has appointed guardian angels to protect us from harm and danger.

- PSA 91:11–12 ~ God will appoint angels to take charge over you to protect you in all your ways, lest you dash your foot on a stone.

- ISA 14:12–15 ~ You have fallen from heaven and have been cut down to the ground, Lucifer, who brought down the nations. For you deceived yourself, wanting to be exalted, even above God. Instead, you will be brought down into the depths of hell.

- MAT 25:31–32 ~ Jesus said, "When the Son of man comes in glory, and the holy angels with Him, He will sit upon the throne of His glory.

- LUK 10:18–20 ~ Jesus said, "I saw the devil fall like lightning from heaven. I have given you power over that enemy, so nothing can harm you. But do not rejoice because the demons submit to you; rather rejoice because your names are written in the Book of Life."

- COL 2:18–19 ~ Do not let anyone swindle you out of your reward, including those who practice false humility and worship angels. They claim to have seen things, but they have filled their unspiritual and arrogant minds with silly notions.

- HEB 12:22–24 ~ You have come to the joyful assembly of millions of angels to the church of the firstborn, whose names are written in heaven. You have come before God, the judge of the entire human race, among the spirits of the righteous who have been made perfect by Jesus Christ, the mediator of the New Covenant.

- HEB 13:1–2 ~ Let brotherly love continue. Do not forget to help strangers, for you may be ministering to angels for all you know.

- 2 PE 2:4; JDE 1:6 ~ God did not spare the angels that sinned, but sent them to hell, imprisoning them in chains of darkness to be held for judgment.

- JDE 1:24–25 ~ To Him that is able to keep you from falling, and to bring you blameless into His glorious presence with endless joy; to the only God our Savior be glory, majesty, power, and authority, through Jesus Christ our Lord, timeless throughout the ages, now and forevermore, Amen.

There may be a hierarchy in heaven, kind of like the army, where there are echelons with designated authority; thus, angelic beings appear to be organized hierarchically, according to power and purpose. Michael the archangel is probably the captain of the angels mentioned by the prophet Joshua (JOS 5:13–15). Michael is of the class of cherubim, and his partner Gabriel is likely a cherub of high rank as well. Lucifer was a cherub, once. But he got busted in rank and placed on house arrest on earth, which is his path to the lake of fire. The devil's only purpose, along with his subordinate devils, is to bring down humans, whom the demons despise because we are above them; some of these fallen angels already have been incarcerated (2 PE 2:4)

Heavenly Father, whose angels have been charged to look after us, we thank you for your merciful kindness. How proud we are to be counted as children, and to be accepted as brothers and sisters by your Son Jesus Christ. Let your light shine in us through the Holy Spirit who indwells our hearts and minds. Empower us, therefore, to call out and defeat the demonic in our midst, and never let them get a foothold in our lives. Dress us in your armor, Lord, and equip us with your shield, which is our faith in Christ, so we might deflect the advances of the army of evil. Arm us with your sword, the Holy Bible, so we can cut them in two, removing their spirits from the living, and condemning their souls to the fire. In the name of Jesus we pray, Amen.

August 17

National Nonprofit Day recognizes the signing of the Tariff Act on this day in 1894. This law was a tax on businesses, but allowed charitable organizations to avoid being taxed, including places of worship, and other nonprofit organizations which use donations strictly to provide humanitarian help, aid, and services to people in need of medical, material, economic, educational, and spiritual aid. The idea was spawned by S. J. Herring in 2017, to bring attention to the needs of others and to support organizations which meet those needs but do not profit financially from their services. There are over a million nonprofits operating in the USA; unfortunately, a large percentage of those are fronts for money laundering and self-aggrandizement. Most charities can cover administrative expenses with ten percent of their donations; if it is considerably higher than that, money is being wasted on too much advertising, inflated salaries, travel and expenses, costly fundraisers, assorted foundation leaders and administrators. You can check out most nonprofits on the internet to determine how much of your donation actually goes to people in need. I have seen charities where that number is a mere five percent, meaning the other ninety-five percent is being stolen and misused. It is advisable to check out a charity before you give, so you are not enriching frauds or those who already have become rich through dirty dealings.

You can celebrate this occasion by donating your time, talent, or treasure to a charity or church. America is the most charitable nation on earth, because we follow a traditional Judeo-Christian practice of giving tithes to our church and offerings to charities and the poor. It is the right thing to do, sharing your wealth and giving generously, especially to organizations and foundations that reflect Christ in their mission statement, with faithfulness as their motivation. Incidentally, all financial contributions to nonprofits are tax-deductible (at least for now).

- LEV 27:30 ~ Tithe of all your increase to the Lord, for He considers that portion to be holy.

- DEU 16:17 ~ Everyone should give as they are able, in accordance with the blessings which God has given them.

- MAL 3:6–8 ~ God says, "I am the Lord, I never change. But you have not kept my commandments. Return to me and I will return to you. Will you rob God? Yet you have robbed me. You ask how you have robbed me? You have robbed me by not presenting your tithes and offerings."

- 1 CO 16:2 ~ On the first day of the week, everyone should set aside some money in accordance with the degree to which God has prospered them and give it to the church so that a collection will not be necessary.

- 2 CO 8:2–14 ~ Even during times of poverty, the abundance of their joy became a wellspring of generosity. They gave as much as they could, even beyond their ability. They considered it a privilege to serve, giving themselves to the Lord and to His ministers. Therefore, as you abound in everything, including faith, speech, knowledge, and earnest love, see that you also abound in the grace of giving. If the willingness is there, the gift will be acceptable, whether large or small, in accordance with the degree to which you have prospered. Our desire is not that others might be relieved even when you are hard-pressed, but that there will be equality. For now, your plenty will supply the needs of others, so that in turn their plenty will supply you in times of need.

- 2 CO 9:7 ~ Everyone should give whatever they think is fair in their heart. Giving should be done voluntarily, not out of obligation, for God loves a cheerful giver.

- COL 1:9–10 ~ We have not stopped praying for you and asking God to fill you with the knowledge of His will, through all spiritual wisdom and understanding. This is so you might live your lives worthy of the Lord and may please Him in every way, bearing good fruit and growing in the knowledge of God; being strengthened with all power according to his glorious might so that you will be able to endure hardship with great patience and joyfulness.

 Most of us work for money in order to buy everything we need; we also save money for retirement, emergencies, and vacations. Some of that income belongs to God, however. If we hold back, we will be less prosperous than if we give our tithes and offerings. In other words, we usually do not need more than we have, unless we are not giving back to God. It is unwise to be in a hurry to get rich, or to expect something in return for your generosity. We are to give in secrecy and the Lord will prosper us openly, with more than we can store. All of God's work should be not-for-profit, notwithstanding paid employees of the church. If you volunteered your time at church or at a charity, you would not expect to be paid for it would you? Absolutely not, because it is a gift; it is our way of giving back to God.

- DEU 11:26–28 ~ Behold, I set before you a blessing and a curse: a blessing if you obey the commandments of the Lord your God; a curse if you disobey and turn away from the way I have commanded you this day, to never go after other gods which you have not known.

- PRO 3:9–10 ~ Honor the Lord with your profits, and with the first fruits of your income, and your barns be filled and your winepresses will burst with new wine.

- PRO 10:2; PRO 11:4, 28 ~ The treasures of the wicked will not profit them anything on the day of their death, but the righteous will be delivered from death. Riches will not profit anyone on the day of wrath. Those who trust in their riches will fail, but those who trust in God will flourish.

- MAT 6:1–4 ~ Jesus said, "Remember that you should not give to the poor just so others can see you do it; otherwise, you will receive no reward from your Father in heaven. In other words, do not put on a display when you give, like the hypocrites do, who do it only so that others will see them and praise them for it. Truly, this is the only reward they will ever receive for their good deeds. Give generously, but do so in secret; and your Father in heaven will see it and He will reward you openly."

- JOH 6:63–64 ~ Jesus said, "It is the Spirit that gives life, not the flesh; for the flesh profits nothing. The words that I speak are from the Spirit and give life. But there are some of you that do not believe." For Jesus knew in advance who did not believe in Him as well as who would betray Him.

- ROM 12:1 ~ I implore you brothers and sisters, by the mercies of God, that you present yourselves as living sacrifices, holy and acceptable to Him; this is your reasonable service.

- 1 CO 13:3 ~ Even if you give all you have to the poor, you profit nothing if you do not have love.

 Help us Father, to be generous in our giving, for you have been more than generous to us. Remind us to support our local churches, and to help those we encounter who are destitute or suffering. We often hesitate when we see a beggar or a homeless person because some of them are dangerous. Guide us in our wisdom to help those who truly need it, whether physically, mentally, or spiritually. Likewise, help us to call out frauds and expose scams, and show these wayward people the way to you, Father, who is merciful to everyone who seeks you. Help us to prosper in everything we do, for we place you first in our lives and depend on you for everything. Therefore, enable us to do everything with love, even as your Son did with all people regardless of age, gender, ethnicity, and socioeconomic status. We pray that we can follow Christ's example as long as we live, so that everyone will know that we belong to you. We pray in His name, Amen.

August 18

Never Give Up Day was established to encourage perseverance in people who are trying to achieve personal goals, greater wellness, elevated performance, social objectives, and so forth. Every goal worth pursuing requires desire, effort, teamwork, and determination which usually involves overcoming obstacles, difficulties, setbacks, financial issues, and possibly starting over. The purpose is to engender positive motivation, careful planning, setting milestones and timelines, and executing each step in a reasonable plan in order to meet a specified goal. This observance started in 2019, but didn't catch on until 2021 when several city mayors in Canada adopted this initiative, while many more in the USA and overseas joined in.

The best way to celebrate this day is to identify a goal that you have been putting off, create a gameplan that includes the objectives, tasks, and steps that will get you there; then set a realistic timeline for attaining each segment of the plan so you can track your progress. Begin by starting on step one of task one and you will be on your way. If you can't get motivated, read a book or attend a lecture on how to motivate yourself. The best way to turn your dreams into reality is to believe that you can; remember, with God you can achieve anything. You can become things without asking for God's help but you are more likely to succeed with His help.

Your motivation will often be determined by your immediate needs. You may be familiar with Maslow's hierarchy of needs (listed from the bottom up): health and sustenance; safety and security; love and belonging; self-esteem and recognition; reasoning and learning; understanding and order; beauty and aesthetics; self-actualization, which is becoming all you can be. Examine where you are in this hierarchy and establish smart goals to meet those needs (Barber, 2016).

- PSA 145:14–16 ~ The Lord raises those who fall and lifts those who are down. The eyes of all wait for Him and he gives them what they need when they need it. He opens His hand and satisfies the desires of every living thing.

- PRO 2:10–11 ~ When wisdom enters your heart and knowledge is pleasant to your soul, discretion will preserve you and understanding will protect you.

- PRO 19:21 ~ People develop their own plans, but it is the Lord's purpose that will prevail.

- JOB 14:14 ~ If a person dies, can he or she live again? All the days of my appointed time I will wait, until my change comes.

- MAT 6:31–32 ~ Jesus said, "Do not worry about your worldly needs; your Father in heaven knows what you need. Instead, seek first the kingdom of heaven and the righteousness of God, and this you will receive, as well as your earthly needs."

- PHP 3:13–16 ~ Brothers and sisters, I have yet to take hold of the prize, but I have forgotten the past and focused on what lies ahead. I continue to press onward toward the goal for which God has called me heavenward through Jesus Christ. Those of us who are mature in the faith should share this viewpoint. And if you have a different opinion, God will clarify it for you.

Have you ever heard of the process of developing smart goals? SMART is an acronym that stands for simple, measurable, achievable, relevant, and timed. Do not make the goal so complex that there are multiple goals in one statement, otherwise you will not be able to measure your progress or identify what worked and what didn't. Break down one realistic goal at a time, related to your ultimate destination, which is stated simply (noun, verb, direct object) so that you can track progress in accordance with your timeframe. You also need to identify resources, equipment, personnel, and other requirements needed to be successful, ensuring that you identify God as the most important resource available to you. After each success a new goal might emerge.

Perseverance and patience will pay off in the long run if you do not give up. It may take longer than you planned but that is not a reason to quit; you may need to adjust your calendar however. Believe in God and yourself; it is one thing to believe and another to take action on that belief. Before taking action, do your homework; determine what has worked in the past as you research your objective. Then be diligent in your pursuit of knowledge, skill, and performance.

- PSA 46:1 ~ God is our refuge and strength, an ever-present help in trouble
- PRO 11:27 ~ People who diligently seek good will find favor, but people who seek mischief will have mischief come to them.
- PRO 13:11 ~ Wealth obtained by pride will diminish; but those who achieve by way of hard work will see their wealth increase.
- 1 CO 15:58 ~ Be steadfast, immovable, and fruitful in the Lord; for your efforts will not be in vain.
- HEB 11:1 ~ Faith is the assurance of things hoped for, the evidence of things not seen.
- JAM 1:2–4 ~ My brothers, count it all joy when you fall into different temptations, for the trying of your faith produces patience. But let patience have her perfect work so that you may be complete, and never wanting.
- JAM 2:17 ~ Faith without works is useless.

When a person gives up, it is because he or she has lost hope; but there is always hope if you believe.

- ROM 5:1–11 ~ Being justified by faith we achieve peace with God through Christ, in whom we have access by that faith to the grace in which we stand, rejoicing in the hope of glory. Therefore, we rejoice in time of tribulation, knowing that it teaches us patience, it strengthens our hope, and we gain experience. For when we were weak, Christ died for the ungodly. Most people would scarcely give their life, even for a righteous person; but God consigned His love to us, for while we were yet sinners, Christ died for us. Now, being justified by His blood, we can be saved from God's wrath through Christ. For, if when we were enemies, we were reconciled to God by the death of His Son, much more now, having been reconciled, we are saved by His life. And not only this, but we also find immense joy in God through our Lord Jesus Christ, by whom we now have received the atonement.
- ROM 8:24–25 ~ We are saved because we hope. But hope that is seen is not hope, for who hopes for things they can see? However, if we hope for what we cannot see, we must be patient.
- ROM 12:12 ~ Rejoice in hope, be patient in tribulation, and be constant in prayer.
- 2 CO 4:16 ~ Therefore, we never give up, though outwardly we are worn down; yet inwardly we are renewed day after day.

Loving Father, you have given us your Holy Spirit who is the source of our faith, and you have given us your Son who is the source of our hope. You provide all of our needs when we keep you first in our lives, by seeking the righteousness of Christ. We thank you and we praise you for considering humans and blessing us with these gifts which lead to life eternal with you, gracious Father. Help us to develop goals which are in accordance with your will, knowing that our plans and efforts will not be in vain because you will communicate to us our purpose, and you will empower us to achieve it. Let us never give up on you, or our goals, or our loved ones; instead give us hope, peace of mind, and perseverance, to attain the highest levels of achievement in pursuit of the highest good. In the name of Jesus, we ask these things, Amen.

August 19

World Humanitarian Day was established by the United Nations in 2003 to renounce terrorism and to foster charitable, benevolent, and altruistic behavior. This date was designated to support humanitarian efforts in areas with the greatest need, to act as ambassadors of peace throughout the world, to increase awareness of what is going on about the globe where people are suffering, and provide guidance as to how helpers can become involved and pitch in. We are commanded by God to serve others, help those in need, and give of ourselves—talent, treasure, and time. This holiday is not to be confused with Make a Difference Day which is observed primarily in the USA and highlights what we as individuals can do with respect to our sphere of influence. Today is focused more on global initiatives and charities.

People are in crisis every hour of the day somewhere in the world. When an immediate need arises, there should be an adequate and timely response. There are agencies, volunteer groups, and missionaries that go into disaster areas, sometimes in remote locations, providing shelter, food, clean water, healthcare, security, and so on. Each year certain target areas are highlighted through social media and internet sites enabling humanitarian aid workers, funding sources, and certain professionals that partnership to meet the most urgent needs. They have the same courage as first responders, but are often treated like outsiders among various radical groups and militias. Nevertheless, these volunteers go into danger zones and many do not come back due to disease, injury, or gunfire. This day recognizes those who have made the ultimate sacrifice to protect, feed, aid, build things, and medically treat unfortunate people of the world.

- DEU 15:11 ~ There will never cease to be poor in the land. Therefore, open wide your hand to your brother, the needy, and the poor.

- 2 CH 20:9 ~ If evil comes upon us, like the sword, judgment, pestilence, or famine, and we stand before God's house and in His presence (for His name is spoken there), and we cry to the Lord in our affliction, He will hear us and help us.

- PSA 56:3–4 ~ If I am afraid, I will praise God's Word and put my trust in Him. I will not be afraid of what flesh can do to me.

- ECC 9:5–6 ~ For the living know that they will die, but the dead know nothing; they receive no reward and their memory is forgotten. Their love, their hate, and their jealousy vanished a long time ago; never again will they take part in anything that happens under the sun.

- JOS 1:9 ~ God said, "Did I not command you to be strong and have courage, and not to be afraid or dismayed? For I am with you wherever you go."

- ISA 41:10 ~ God says, "Fear not, for I am with you. Do not be dismayed, for I am your God. I will strengthen and help you. I will hold you up with the right hand of righteousness."

- MAT 6:4 ~ Give generously, but do so in secret; and your Father in heaven will see it and He will reward you openly.

- JOH 15:12–14 ~ Jesus said, "Love each other as I have loved you. No greater expression of love exists than to give one's life for their friends. You are my friends if you obey my commandments."

- ROM 12:6–8 ~ Use those gifts God has given you. If you have the gift of prophecy, exercise that gift according to the proportion of your faith. If your gift is ministry, then minister; if it is teaching, teach; if it is encouraging, then encourage; if it is giving to the needy, give generously; if it is leadership, lead diligently; if it is showing mercy, do so cheerfully.

- ROM 14:7–9 ~ Nobody can live for themselves or die for themselves; whether we live or die it is for the Lord because we belong to Him. Christ died and rose from the dead to be the Lord of the living and the dead.

- 1 PE 2:19 ~ Be thankful if you must unfairly endure grief or suffering because you maintain an upright conscience toward God.

Giving is an essential part of being a Christian. Yes, we must have faith; but we also must act on that faith (JAM 2:17–26). Use your talents, donate money, employ your professional skills. Naturally, not everyone has what it takes to go to foreign countries, into zones where there is unrest, disaster, or bloodshed. Sometimes, these heroes do not know where they safely can go or who to trust, or who is in charge, or who needs immediate help; but that does not stop them from trying. If you cannot give your time or you are in no position to sacrifice your livelihood or life, you still can give of your wealth, and you can volunteer some of your free time in your area.

- PRO 19:17 ~ Those who show compassion to others are lending to the Lord, and that which was given will be paid back.

- MAT 5:15–16 ~ Jesus said, "You do not light a candle and then cover it, because it is supposed to give light. So, let the light inside you shine before others; let people see in your actions that you live to glorify your Father in heaven."

- LUK 6:38 ~ Give and it shall be given to you in abundance, overflowing; for the same measure that you give is returned unto you.

- 1 CO 12:4–12, 26–27 ~ There are a variety of spiritual gifts, but only one Spirit. There are different ways of administering but only one Lord. There are different operations, but the same God who works through them. The Spirit is manifested in some way for everyone to use productively. Some people have received wisdom, some knowledge, some faith, all from the same Spirit. Some people have the ability to heal, others to work miracles, others to prophesy, others to discern spirits, others to speak foreign tongues. But all of them are working with the same Spirit, who divides power among His people as He chooses. Just as one body has many members so is Christ one body with many members. When one member suffers, all suffer; when one member is honored, all are honored. Now you are the body of Christ, and members each one of you.

- GAL 6:2–3 ~ Carry one another's burdens, thereby fulfilling the law of Christ. For if a man thinks more highly of himself than he ought, he deceives himself and he is nothing.

- 2 TI 2:12 ~ If we suffer with Him, we will reign with Him; if we deny Him, He will deny us.

- HEB 13:16 ~ Do not forget to do good and communicate love, for God is pleased with self-sacrifice.

Heavenly Father, you have provided the ultimate sacrifice so that we can be free and live forever. Bless those who are doing your work in dangerous places, under extreme hardship conditions, with no concern about themselves but for those you have sent them to serve. Protect, defend, and lead them to safety, we pray; we also pray for the loved ones of those who lose their lives or limbs doing what it takes to shed your grace upon the oppressed, lost, and forgotten people. Thank you for these men and women who place others before themselves, to the greatest extent possible. Let them feel your presence as they daily face disaster, disease, and death faithfully and courageously, just like Jesus did as well as His apostles and friends as they traveled into hostile zones to spread the good news. May we be among the elite who willingly face danger and peril in the name of Jesus in whom we pray, Amen.

August 20

National Radio Day celebrates the contributions of the radio to civilization. The invention of the radio is attributed to Tesla and Marconi, but they capitalized on the work of many important names in science and technology such as Faraday, Maxwell, Hertz, Lodge, and Bose. These men discovered radio waves, electromagnetism, transmission, and conductivity before the radio was actually born. But it was Lee de Forest who was the first to broadcast music over public radio in 1910. This was followed by the regular broadcasting of news out of Madison WI beginning on this day in 1920. Soon, people could tune into radio shows involving commentary, drama, comedy, religion, and history. Despite advances in television, computers, internet, and digitization, the radio has not been replaced. In fact, the radio is gaining popularity with the addition of thousands of satellite stations, as well as local stations which you can listen to in your car while on the road. Radio remains the mainstay of emergency broadcast systems in remote locations where there are no cell towers or televisions. Nowadays, radio frequency technology is used for radar, sonar, walkie-talkies, remote control devices, space research, global positioning systems, tomography, sonograms, security systems, microwave ovens, cell phones, and the list goes on. Radios have been celebrated on this day since the 1990s but it got a boost in 2011 when National Public Radio began endorsing it.

I wonder what it was like before radio. There was no way of reaching a lot of people at once except through a public address in the town square or in church. The only other way was to mass produce a letter or flyer by hand, multiplied by the number of recipients, and pass it around or display it in strategic locations. When it came to Old Testament scripture, scholars had to recopy the scrolls frequently, word for word, without error. In the event of a mistake, the copier had to start over from the beginning.

Imagine the difficulty distributing God's Word to the masses in the first century AD. Since a small percentage of people could actually read, it was transmitted orally from person to person. Fortunately, apostles and other disciples could read and write, so they preached and they wrote. Their writings began to circulate within a few years after Christ's ascension into heaven. These manuscripts were further distributed by the early church fathers who also wrote and copied. Before the close of the second century, the New Testament had been translated into several languages and recopied and circulated throughout the Roman empire and further.

Now, the entirety of the Holy Bible is available in almost every language of the world. God made sure that His Word would spread to the world, as stated repeatedly in the Bible. Once a person has read and digested God's Word of truth, he or she should share this knowledge with others, spreading the good news to anyone who will listen. The oral tradition is still an excellent way to teach the Gospel of Jesus Christ, anywhere and everywhere, and it is enabled via radio.

- PSA 96:3–4 ~ Declare God's glory among the nations, tell of His wonderous works to all people. For the Lord is great, and He is worthy to be praised; He is to be feared above all gods.

- MAT 24:14 ~ The gospel of the kingdom will be preached in all the world as a witness to the nations, before the end comes.

- MAT 28:19–20; MAR 16:15–16 ~ Jesus told His disciples, "Go into every nation and teach the people everything I have taught you. Baptize them in the name of the Father, Son, and Holy Spirit. Remember, I will always be with you, even until the end of time."

- ACT 2:1–4 ~ And when the day of Pentecost had come, they were joined with one accord in one place. Suddenly a sound from heaven was heard like a rushing mighty wind; it filled the house where they were sitting. Next appeared cloven tongues of fire, sitting upon each of the evangelists' heads. They were filled with the Holy Spirit and began to speak in other languages, as the Spirit directed them.

- ACT 10:42–43 ~ Peter preached, "Christ commanded us to preach to the people and to testify that it was He who was ordained by God to be the judge of the living and the dead. All the prophets have been witnesses, instructing that faith in Christ provides remission of sins."

- ROM 10:14–20 ~ How can people call on Him whom they have not believed? How can they believe in Him whom they have not heard? How can they hear about Him without a preacher? And how can they preach unless they have been sent? As it is written: How beautiful are the feet of those who preach the gospel of peace, and bring glad tidings of good news to the world. But not all who have heard have believed and obeyed the gospel. Like Isaiah wrote: Lord, who has believed our message? For faith comes by hearing the truth, and the truth comes from the Word of God. Have they not heard? Yes, for it is written: Their words will reach the far corners of the world. I ask you: Did Israel not understand? Moses wrote: I will provoke you into jealousy of those who are not your people, I will make you angry at a nation that did not understand. Just as Isaiah boldly proclaimed: I was found by those who were not looking for me, and I revealed myself to those who did not ask.

- 2 TI 4:2–5; 2 TI 2:2 ~ Preach the word in every season; reprove, rebuke, and encourage with patience and sound doctrine. For the time is coming when people will not listen to sound doctrine, but will follow their own lusts, gathering teachers who tell them what their itching ears want to hear. They will turn away from the truth and towards myths. So, keep your head in all situations, enduring hardship as an evangelist executing the duties of the ministry. Those things you heard me preach to many witnesses, entrust the same to faithful people who also are able to teach.

- REV 14:6–7 ~ I saw another angel fly through heaven with the everlasting gospel, to preach to those who live on earth, and to every nation, kindred, tongue, and people; saying with a loud voice, "Fear God and give Him the glory; for the hour of His judgment has come. Worship Him who made heaven and earth, the sea and the fountains of water."

The radio has been very influential in bringing the Word of God to people in secluded areas of the nation and the world. Since many countries prohibit citizens from practicing Christianity or reading the Holy Bible, the radio is all they have to hear the Word being taught. They have to huddle in enclosed places and turn the volume down low to avoid getting caught, which could mean death. Radio programs with a wide broadcast range can reach those people with the Word spoken in their native language. There are organizations which translate the Bible into new languages and distribute those Bibles where the language is spoken. There are organizations which produce the Bible in foreign languages on audio discs, tapes, and electronic devices and distribute those items within various countries. If you are pondering ways to celebrate today's observance, you might consider donating to groups who bring the Gospel of Jesus Christ to distant corners of the globe, often at great peril to themselves.

Father in heaven, we thank you that we are free to worship you and study your Word, and we pray for those who are not allowed those freedoms. We pray that your Word will have free course to reach people who are denied access to churches, Bibles, and Christian leaders. Assist organizations and missionaries who take the truth to unstable countries. Protect these messengers as they preach and teach to people who have not heard about or have not understood the wonders of your works, the power in your words, and the sweetness of your salvation. Help each and every one us to do our part in donating our prayers, time, and money to distribute to foreign lands the Gospel of Jesus Christ our Lord, in whom we confess, teach, worship, and pray, Amen.

August 21

Senior Citizens Day was introduced by President Reagan in 1988, to be an annual recognition of our population of seniors. Reagan himself was pushing seventy by the time he was sworn into office. Generally, people reaching sixty have an average of one-fourth of their life remaining. They put in one quarter of their lives learning what to do, then spend half of it working their tails off doing it. Many will retire after that, but some will continue working if it suits them. Either way, most of them have paid their debt to society, having put in forty-plus years contributing to the growth of the nation. The trend to continue being productive through retirement is associated with longevity; if you keep exercising your physical, mental, and spiritual faculties you will keep them longer, and you can continue to employ them to the glory of God.

- 1 KI 3:11–13 ~ God replied to Solomon, "Since you have asked for wisdom and not for riches, a long life, death to your enemies, or any other selfish thing, I will not only make you wise, but also I will give you riches and honor."

- PRO 3:1–2 ~ Do not forget God's Law. Keep His commandments and He will give you peace and a long life.

- PRO 10:27 ~ The fear of the Lord will prolong your days; but the years of the wicked will be shortened.

- ISA 46:4 ~ God said: Even in your old age with your gray hair, I am He who carries you. I created you, I sustain you, and I will deliver you.

Most cultures have a special veneration for their wise elders and forefathers. This is a good day to thank those who have mentored you, whom you still revere and have not kept in touch with often enough. Contact several people who were an inspiration, like a grandparent, parent, teacher, pastor, coworker, whatever. I bet you can think of five people who you should catch up with. Take your aunt or uncle out to lunch; send a thank you note to an adviser. Volunteer at a senior center or nursing home; visit older people in the hospital. I'm sure there are events, activities, and get-togethers available today in your area if you want to socialize at a party or gala. Salute the seniors you come across in your business or during recreation time today. Don't forget to remind people what this day honors, especially your elders.

- NUM 11:16, 24–25 ~ God said to Moses, "Gather seventy of the elders of Israel and bring them to the tabernacle." Moses told the people what the Lord said, and gathered the seventy elders in the tabernacle. Then the Lord came in a cloud and spoke to Moses, and gave His Spirit to the seventy elders; and when the elders received the Holy Spirit, they prophesied without ceasing.

- 1 PE 5:1–5 ~ Peter wrote to the elders as a fellow elder and witness of Christ's sufferings: Be shepherds to the flock that God has placed under your care, serving as overseers. Do this, not because you must or for money, but because you want to, as God desires. Be eager to serve, not lording over those God has entrusted to you, but as an example to the flock. And when the Chief Shepherd appears, you will receive a crown of glory that will never fade. Show respect to your elders. Serve each other. Clothe yourselves in humility. For God resists the proud and gives grace to the humble.

- REV 4:4, 10–11 ~ Surrounding the throne were twenty-four seats of honor, and upon the seats sat twenty-four elders clothed in white raiment; and they had crowns of gold on their heads. The elders fell down before Him who sat on the throne, and worshipped Him who abides forever and ever; and they cast their crowns of gold before the throne saying, "You alone are worthy, oh Lord, to receive glory, honor, and power; for you have created all things and for your pleasure all things that exist were created.

- REV 5:5 ~ One of the elders said, "Look, the Lion from the tribe of Judah the descendant of David; He has prevailed to open the book and loosen the seven seals which bind it."

The patriarchs in the Bible lived longer from the start, literally hundreds of years; Methuselah lived 969 years (GEN 5:27). After Noah, the average length of life dropped significantly and progressively, falling below age fifty. But there has been quite an upswing in the last few hundred years, thanks to medical advances, healthy living, and keeping nimble and occupied. As lifetime goes up, the more one should work; keep contributing to the extent you are able. The worst thing a senior can do is become lazy or idle; for the mind will soon follow.

- EXO 3:2–14 ~ The angel of the Lord appeared to Moses in the burning bush. God called to Moses from the bush saying, "I am the God of your father, and of Abraham, Isaac, and Jacob. I will deliver the Israelites from the Egyptians and give them the promised land. You will lead them there." Moses replied, "Who am I to do such a great thing?" God said, "I will be with you to help you." Moses asked, "When I tell the Israelites this, who am I going to say spoke to me?" God replied, "I AM that I AM. Tell them I AM has sent you."

- LEV 26:40–44 ~ Repent and confess, and God will remember the covenant He made with your forefathers.

- DEU 8:18 ~ Remember God, for it is He who gives you the power to prosper, thereby confirming His covenant which he swore to your forefathers, and which still applies to this day.

- DEU 30:19–20 ~ I call heaven and earth as witnesses that I have set before you both life and death, blessings and curses. I recommend that you choose life so that you and your children may live, and so you may love the Lord your God, listen to Him, and cling to Him. Because He is your life; and He will bless you with many years of prosperity in the land He promised your forefathers, Abraham, Isaac, and Jacob.

- ACT 3:11–16 ~ After Peter healed the lame man the people marveled. And when Peter saw this, he responded, "Men of Israel, why does this amaze you? Why do you look at us as if, because of our own holiness or power, we were able to make this man walk? The God of Abraham, Isaac, and Jacob, yes, the God of our fathers has glorified His Son Jesus, the same man you delivered to Pilate to be crucified. It was by the name of Jesus Christ, and through faith in His name, that this man became strong. Faith in Christ has healed this man before your very eyes."

- 1 CO 10:1–4 ~ You should know that our forefathers drank of the same spiritual drink, which came from the same spiritual Rock, and that Rock is Jesus Christ.

- 2 TI 1:3 ~ Paul wrote to Timothy: I thank God, whom I serve with a pure conscience as my forefathers did; for night and day I remember you as you are constantly in my prayers.

Eternal Father, Lord of life, you have blessed us all of our days with your wisdom and truth. Help us to continue serving you until you decide to bring us home, no matter how long we live. Help us to take care of our bodies and minds that we may serve you better, continuously learning and increasing in the wisdom of your Word to be a resource to the generations after us, just like our forefathers were before us. Let us be counselors and mentors in our senior years, giving freely of our experience and education to our children, to their children, and in service to our church, congregation, and community. In the name of Jesus we pray, Amen.

August 22

First Geneva Convention was held on this day in 1864 to provide for the protection, treatment, and retrieval of wounded on the battlefield. The USA was experiencing the agony of the Civil War. Europe was experiencing frequent conflicts and endless wars. Originally, twelve nations signed the treaty, followed by eight more which included the USA in 1882. The second Geneva Convention (1906) added provisions for noncombatant organizations to be admitted into war zones to treat and extract the wounded and ill. The third convention (1929) provided for the humane treatment of prisoners of war (POW) and recognized the International Red Cross as neutral aid workers. It was expanded further in 1949 to include admission of noncombatant medical personnel, chaplains, and medical equipment. It also prohibited the use of torture, and it required POW camps to provide adequate shelter and food. An update in 1977 provided protection for journalists, and banned the use of certain types of weapons producing terrible suffering such as chemical and biological. It also prohibited terrorism, slavery, rape, taking hostages, humiliation, pillaging, and collective punishment. Currently, close to two hundred countries have signed off on most if not all of these rules of warfare. However, the rules have been violated on numerous occasions and by several countries. Obviously, any of the abovementioned neutral persons taking up arms would be considered a hostile act; further, combatants often disguise themselves to penetrate enemy perimeters. Such confusion leads to uncertainty which increases risk; and war is a risky business to begin with. The Red Cross has appeared in multiple war zones over the years, at significant risk to aid workers, for they are more easily recognized and attested.

- JER 6:14~ They kept saying "peace, peace" but there was no peace.
- MIC 3:2, 5 ~ You hate good and love evil. You talk of peace but make war.
- MAT 24:6 ~ Jesus said, "You will hear of wars and rumors of wars, but the end is yet to come."
- 1 TH 5:3 ~ When they talk of peace and safety, total destruction will come.

Yes, the Geneva Convention suggested the right thing to do, but it is unenforceable at the forward edge of the battle area and beyond. Besides, even those on the right side of a war do deplorable things which go against what is right. But that is what wars are fought over: both sides thinking they are right and the other wrong. However, only the one siding with God is on the right side, and sometimes neither side has God. In either case, God will choose the outcome and use it as a lesson to everyone: for example, two wrongs do not make a right. God will fight for you if you are beholding to Him; but if you turn against Him, He will fight for the other side.

- 2 CH 25:8 ~ God has the power to help people, and the power to cast them down into hell.
- ISA 31:8 ~ The Assyrian will fall by the sword, only not of man, and his army will be overthrown.
- EZE 16:15–38 ~ [Oh Jerusalem], you trusted in your beauty and played the harlot for which you became famous, and poured out fornications upon everyone passing by. You adorned yourselves with colorful garments in the high places where you engaged in prostitution. Such things are not supposed to happen. You made jewelry out of my gold, silver, and stones, then fashioned them into idols with which you also had sex. And you clothed them in embroidered garments and offered my oil, incense and food to them, as you would a sweet sacrifice to the Lord your God. Moreover, you took the sons and daughters born to me and sacrificed them. Do you think this is a small matter? You murdered my children, allowing them to pass through the fire! Do you remember in your youth, how you were naked, bare, and bathed in blood? Consider the extent of your wickedness ("Woe, woe unto you," says the Lord). You built shrines on every street corner and declared your beauty, which became abhorrent. You had sex

with anyone and everyone, including your neighbors the Egyptians, and provoked me to anger. Behold, I have stretched out my hand towards you and snatched your resources, and delivered you to your enemies the daughters of the Philistines who were embarrassed by your lewdness. You fooled around with the Assyrians, Canaanites, and Chaldeans, for your lust was insatiable. You must be weak-minded, committing such despicable acts. You are like an adulterous wife who sleeps with any man but her husband. Prostitutes charge a fee but instead you showered them with expensive gifts to coax them into your houses. Because of your utter filthiness, whoremongering, idolatry, and murdering of your children, I will gather those you have played with and those you have fought against, and uncover your nakedness before them. You will be judged as an adulteress and a murderer, with wrath and blood.

- EZE 38:1–23 ~ Son of man, set your face against Gog of the land of Magog, the chief prince of Meshech and Tubal, and prophesy this against him. The Lord says, "I am against you Gog. I will turn you around, put hooks into your jaws, and drag you out with your entire army, horses, horsemen, and armored warriors. That includes Persia, Ethiopia, and Libya; Gomer and his soldiers; the house of Togarmah in the north and his soldiers; and the others with you. Prepare yourselves and those assembled with you, and take command; after many days you will be called into action (by God). In the latter years you will invade a land that has laid down the sword, gathered around the mountains of Israel which has long been harsh terrain." You will say, "I will invade that land of unwalled villages, those who live in peace and without walls, gates, and fortifications. I will plunder their goods, cattle, gold and silver, and overrun their settlements." Sheba, Dedan, and merchants of Tarshish will ask, "Have you come to plunder and take lives?" Therefore, son of man, prophesy to Gog the words of the Lord, "In that day when my people Israel live safely and in peace, will you not notice? Yes, in the latter days you will invade from the north and many nations with you, advancing like a cloud that covers the land. I will bring you down upon my people so that all the world will know who I am, for I will reveal my holiness through you." This has been spoken of since ancient times by the prophets: a future time when Gog will attack Israel, and God's wrath will be poured out in retaliation. The earth will quake, and there will be trembling and fear. Their armies will be fighting amongst themselves while cliffs and walls crumble around them. "I will send plagues and swords upon them, with rainstorms of hail, fire and brimstone. The world will behold my greatness," says the Lord, "and realize that I alone am God."

- EZE 39:11–13 ~ The Lord says, "It will come to pass in that day when I will present Gog a graveyard in Israel, along the eastern passage by the sea. It will be called the Valley of Hamongog. And Israel will be burying the bodies for seven months to cleanse the land. Indeed, all the people in the land will help bury them; it will be a day of remembrance, and I will be glorified."

As you can see, God establishes the rules of war, and He chooses the victor. In the case of Israel, God made them conquerors because they chose Him. When Israel adopted the decadent ways of their neighbors, God allowed them to be destroyed by those neighbors. But God promised they would return to their homeland someday, and they did; and they have been independent and free ever since. In the latter days, their enemies will surround them, with the intention of upsetting their peaceful existence by invading and annihilating them. But God will arrange for the armies of the invaders to be destroyed.

- PSA 97:10 ~ Those who love God hate evil.
- REV 17:14 ~ The devil's own will make war with the Lamb, but the Lamb will overcome them, for He is Lord of lords and King of kings. Those who are with the Lamb are those who were called, chosen, and faithful.

AUGUST

General Sherman of the Union army is credited with the saying "War is hell," which he said in so many words on more than one occasion. His unorthodox methods included attacking civilians and burning cities. Sherman also said (in so many words), what is done in the name of war is ugly and horrible, and basically inevitable, and most people don't have the stomach for it. When in the throes of battle amidst the gore, crying, and suffering, one cannot help but agree with the famed general. Witnesses of such horrors tend to become unhinged, especially when their comrades are the ones being mauled, dismembered, or tortured. When they act out on their rage, they often do things they regret. This is a frequent issue with veterans suffering from PTSD (Post Traumatic Stress Disorder), also called PTS. I have treated this syndrome extensively and found that they served their country with honor. But many lost focus in a moment of rage, and acted out with hate; and they ended up hating themselves, finding it hard to forgive or let go.

- LEV 19:17–18 ~ Do not hate anyone in your heart; do not scold or sin against your neighbor. Do not take revenge or bear a grudge, but love your neighbor as you love yourself.

- JOB 34:17 ~ Should a person who hates what is right govern others? Would anyone condemn a person who is honest and fair?

- PRO 8:13, 36 ~ To fear God is to hate evil; God hates pride, conceit, evil ways, and perverse speech. Whoever sins against God hurts their own soul, and all who hate God love death.

- PRO 14:17 ~ Those who are easily angered do stupid things, and those who do hateful things are themselves hated.

- ISA 3:11 ~ What they have done to others will be done to them.

- EZE 32:27–29 ~ The fallen of the untrue have gone to hell with their weapons of war. They were the terror of the mighty in the land of the living, but now they join with those who go down to the pit.

- 1 JO 2:11 ~ Someone who hates another is walking in darkness; they cannot see where they are going because the darkness has blinded them.

- 1 JO 3:15 ~ Whosoever hates another is a murderer, and murderers do not receive eternal life

Trauma, fear, and hate are what war does to people; it can get so extreme one forgets why they are there, or if they are on the wrong side of right. Fighting for right might get obscured because of the utter darkness of hate, war, and hell. It is a dilemma for anyone of conscience knowing they must kill to achieve their mission. How difficult it is to forgive their enemies; but harder still, forgiving themselves for actions done during war, supposedly conducted in the name of peace. As for the wounded warriors, scarred and maimed physically and mentally, forgiving themselves is the only way to freedom. Freedom is what they were fighting for in the first place. If you don't think fighting against evil is a worthy way to die, have a talk with Jesus Christ.

- PSA 130:3–4 ~ If you, Lord, counted our sins against us, who would be able to stand? But there is forgiveness with you that you may be feared.

- ACT 13:38 ~ Through Jesus Christ all people can receive the forgiveness of sins.

- 1 JO 1:9 ~ If we confess our sins, He is faithful and just to forgive our sins and cleanse us from all unrighteousness.

Father, we pray to never leave your light; help us to stay in that light forever. When we have been ugly and hateful remind us that we need to confess and repent in order to be forgiven. Help us to likewise forgive others, and to forgive ourselves, letting go of the shame and guilt, which Christ took upon Himself so we could live. In His name we pray, Amen.

August 23

Children of Abraham Day is a new celebration which I propose for today, since other observances for this date are basically duplicates of other so-called holidays. Numerous holidays and celebrations will show up on the calendar multiple times anyway. Today's topic, children of Abraham, is seldom explained sufficiently. I selected this topic, because it is close to my heart. This is a lesson about the Jews who descended from Abraham in the Old Testament, as well as the New Testament Christians, who also are children of Abraham, insofar as they possess the same degree of faith. Both testaments of the Bible declare how we are justified by faith (GEN 15:6; HAB 2:4; ROM 1:17; ROM 5:1; GAL 2:16). Abraham is an example of saving faith. He believed God's promises, and exhibited this in a big way when he was willing to sacrifice his son Isaac to please the Lord. This action was based on Abraham's belief that God would make a great nation through Isaac. Abraham never doubted it, for he was ready to take his son's life to prove it. But of course, that is not what God wanted. God permitted this test of Abraham's faith to highlight his willingness to offer Isaac, as a foreshadowing of what God had planned from the very beginning of time. This same example is represented in the lamb during the first Passover.

- GEN 17:19 ~ God told Abraham, "Your wife Sarah will surely bear a son and you will name him Isaac. And I will establish my everlasting covenant with him, and his descendants."

- GEN 22:2–13 ~ God told Abraham to take His only legitimate son Isaac, and sacrifice him on a mountain. Abraham proceeded to do as God requested. Along the way, Isaac asked his father, "Where is the lamb for the sacrifice." Abraham answered, "God will provide the lamb Himself." Abraham was about to offer Isaac when an angel of God called from heaven. Abraham responded, "Here I am." The angel replied, "Do not harm your son, for it is obvious that you fear and honor God since you were willing to sacrifice your only son as God asked." Abraham found a ram caught in the bushes and offered it instead, as a sacrifice to God.

- EXO 12:3–13 ~ God renewed the covenant with Moses and the Israelites. The Israelites were commanded by God to sacrifice an unblemished male lamb and sprinkle the lamb's blood on the door. This act of faith spared the first born of Israel from God's curse on the Egyptians. The lamb's blood signified that God would protect the homes of the righteous from the angel of death on this the first Passover.

- JOH 1:29 ~ John the Baptist saw Jesus coming when He said, "Look, here comes the Lamb of God who takes away the sin of the world."

- 1 CO 5:7 ~ Throw out the old leavened dough and become a new dough, without yeast; for that is what you have become because of the sacrifice of Christ who is the Passover Lamb.

- HEB 10:10–18 ~ Jesus's sacrifice is the last sacrifice that will need to be made to atone for sin. Under the Old Covenant, sacrificial offerings were made as an atonement for sin. Under the New Covenant, we are made clean by the blood of Christ in one final sacrificial offering. This sacrifice will stand for all time, so sin offerings and sacrifices are no longer needed.

Jesus Christ is the image of God in human form. The sacrificial lamb symbolizes the blood offering for sin that is necessary for atonement. The same is exemplified in the Old Covenant of the Law and the New Covenant of Grace. Under the Mosaic law, sacrifices were made routinely, as an act of faith in God to forgive sins and to provide temporary atonement. In the New Testament, Christ provides forgiveness and atonement through the sacrifice of Himself for the sin of the entire world, providing a permanent offering that would stand forever. Sacrifices made in accordance with the Old Testament of the Law represented Christ, the New Covenant, whose sacrifice is sufficient and final.

- EXO 24:6–8 ~ Moses put half of the blood into bowls and sprinkled the other half on the altar. Then he took the Book of the Covenant and read to the people, who responded, "We will do everything the Lord has commanded, and we will obey Him." Then Moses took the rest of the blood and sprinkled it on the people, saying, "This is the blood of the covenant that the Lord has made with you in accordance with these His words."

- LEV 17:11 ~ The life of all flesh resides in the blood, and I have given it to you upon the altar to make atonement for your souls, for it is the blood that makes atonement for the soul.

- MIC 6:6–7 ~ How am I to appear before God? Shall I come before Him with offerings and sacrifices? Will He be pleased with thousands and thousands of sacrifices? Shall I sacrifice my firstborn, the fruit of my body, to atone for the sin of my soul?

- MAT 26:26–28 ~ Jesus took bread, blessed it, broke it into pieces, and distributed it to the apostles saying, "Take this bread and eat it, for this is my body." Then He took a cup of wine, thanked God, and passed the cup to the apostles saying, "Each of you drink from this cup of wine, for this is my blood of the New Covenant, shed for you and for many for the remission of sins."

- 2 CO 5:17, 21 ~ If we believe in the atonement provided in the blood of Christ, we are saved from sin and death and we are transformed into a new creation.

- HEB 9:1–18 ~ The first covenant included rules concerning service to the Lord and the operation of a sanctuary for worship and prayer. This was a facility made by man. Part of the covenant provided for the offering of gifts and sacrifices. But such sacrifices were insufficient to make the offerer's conscience perfect before God. This is why Christ the High Priest came. He was a divine and perfect sanctuary, not a sanctuary made by man but by the Holy Spirit. Christ obtained eternal redemption for us, not by the blood of sacrificial offerings but by His own blood. If the blood of sacrifices could sanctify and purify, in accordance with the Old Covenant, how much more the blood of Christ can purify and sanctify! Christ, who was without blemish offered Himself, to purge our consciences from dead works to serve the living God. Therefore, He is the mediator of the New Covenant; for by His death, the redemption and inheritance promised in the Old Covenant is realized. The Old Covenant also was dedicated with blood, for when Moses had finished reading from the Book of the Law, he took the blood of the sacrifice and sprinkled it on the book, the altar, and the people saying, "This is the blood of the everlasting covenant which God has prescribed for all people." Almost everything under the Law can be purged with blood, and without the shedding of blood there can be no remission. Christ must have suffered often since the beginning of time, but now He has abolished sin once and for all through His self-sacrifice. Just as it is necessary for all to die and then to be judged, so is it possible to be saved because Christ has taken our sins upon Himself. For the Law, which pointed to the good things that were to come, could never with its continuous sacrifices make the offerer perfect before God; otherwise, the people would have been able to cease the offerings. The blood of such sacrifices could not cleanse the entire soul. God did away with the first covenant so He could establish the second, which provides for the sanctification of all people for all time, through the offering of the body of Jesus Christ. Christ offered one sacrifice for sins that would last forever, and now He sits at the right hand of God. Through that one offering, He has made eternally perfect those He has sanctified. The Holy Spirit has been a witness of this fact in both covenants. This is the meaning of the scripture, "This is the covenant I will make with my people after those days: I will put my laws in their hearts and write them in their minds, and I will remember their sins no longer." Priests repeatedly offered the same sacrifices which alone could never take away sins. Therefore, God set aside the first covenant to establish the second, through which we are made holy by the sacrifice of the body of Jesus Christ. Never again will a sacrificial offering need to be made to atone for sin, for Christ paid the price of sin for all humankind that will last for all time.

Everyone who possesses the faith of Abraham will be saved. God revealed to Abraham the coming of Messiah, and Abraham believed (GEN 14:18–20; JOH 8:56–58; HEB 7:1–7). Throughout the Old Testament, there are references to God's Messiah, which make it clear that God would be sending His Son Jesus Christ to make atonement. Therefore, God was essentially sending Himself in human form to make good on His promises. Christians know Christ to be that Messiah, who will return again to bring us home. Those who believe in Messiah possess the faith of Abraham. The seed of Abraham comprises all believers, who by faith are saved through the atonement of Christ, the chosen and prophesied Messiah.

- GEN 15:5 ~ And God brought Abraham outside and said, "Look up to the heavens, and count the stars, if indeed you can. So will your offspring be."

- GEN 22:18 ~ God told Abraham, "In your seed all the nations of the world will be blessed because you have been obedient to me."

- GEN 26:24 ~ God appeared to Isaac and said, "I am the God of your father Abraham. Do not be afraid for I am with you and I will bless you. I will multiply your seed for the sake of your father Abraham."

- ISA 41:8 ~ You Israel, are my servants, the children of Jacob whom I have chosen, and the seed of my friend Abraham.

- ROM 4:13, 16 ~ For the promise that he should be the heir of the world, was not to Abraham or to his seed through the Law, but through the righteousness of faith. Therefore, it is by grace through faith that the promise is given to all the seed; not only to those who obey the Law, but also to those who demonstrate the faith of Abraham who was the father of us all.

- ROM 9:4–8 ~ Who are the Israelites, to whom God gave the Law and granted the adoption, and with whom God made covenants and promises? Christ came for them and for all people. It is not as if God's Word had no effect, for they who are of Israel are not all from Israel. Those who are of Abraham's seed are not all his children. In other words, those who are children of the flesh are not children of God; those who cling to God's promises, they are counted as children.

- GAL 3:6–29 ~ Abraham believed God and his faith was credited to him as righteousness. Understand then, that those who believe are the children of Abraham. The scriptures foresaw that God would justify the Gentiles by faith, and announced it in the Gospel to Abraham as it is written: All nations of the world will be blessed through your seed. Anyone having faith is blessed along with Abraham, a man of great faith. No man is justified before God by the Law, because those who are righteous live by faith. To Abraham and his seed, the promises were made. God did not say "seeds" meaning many people, He said "seed" meaning one person, who is Christ the mediator between God and us. What then was the purpose of the Law? It was added due to sin, until the seed promised to Abraham had come. The Law was in effect until Christ came, so we could be justified by faith. In Christ we become children of God through faith. You are all children of God through faith in Jesus Christ, for you have been baptized unto Him and have clothed yourselves in His righteousness. There is neither Jew nor Greek, slave nor free, male nor female, for we are all one in the Lord. If you belong to Christ, you are Abraham's seed and heirs according to His promise.

- GAL 4:4–7 ~ When the time was right, God sent His Son, who was born of a woman under the Old Covenant of the Law, to redeem those who were under the Law. He did this so that everyone could receive the honor of becoming adopted children of God. If you are a child of God, you are no longer a servant, but a fellow heir of God through Christ.

The Old Testament (OT) and the New Testament (NT) cross-reference each other, making it clear that we need both testaments to see the elaborate plan of salvation God prepared before the creation of the world and humanity. There are hundreds of prophecies in the OT pointing to Messiah, which are fulfilled in the NT. Further, Christ and His followers who wrote the NT quoted the OT on hundreds of occasions. If you want to understand a particular concept, lesson, or prophecy, you need both testaments to fully comprehend it. Words of truth that are repeated in the OT continue to be repeated in the NT to ensure the reader grasps the significance. This is the hermeneutical rule called the progressive mention principle. We see this principle at work with the concepts of the Seed of Abraham and the Lamb of God. We see the comparative mention principle in the faith of Abraham who looked forward to the coming of Messiah, and our faith in Christ who is that Messiah, who came once and will come again for His people, whether alive or dead.

There is no book since the history of humankind providing this degree of self-explanatory validation, with internal consistency and reliability. Yes, the Holy Bible is deep, broad, complex, and mysterious, but it all fits together like a jigsaw puzzle. The more you study it, the greater will be your knowing, for the Word of God exhibits His wisdom which is available to everyone who wishes to expand their knowledge and envision the big picture. And though we receive tidbits at every reading, with clarity, we will never grasp its entirety; well, not until God brings us home, when the big picture becomes reality. In heaven, learning and wisdom will be never ending as we continue to grow and to know exponentially under God's divine guidance and love.

- PRO 8:1, 14, 22–23 ~ Wisdom and understanding are calling you. Counsel and sound judgment are mine; I understand all things and I have great power. The Lord possessed me in the beginning of His way, before His works of old. I was set up from everlasting, before the earth existed.

- ISA 48:16 ~ Come and listen. I (Messiah) have not spoken in secret since the beginning. I was there all along; and now the Lord God and His Spirit have sent me.

- ROM 16:25–26 ~ By the power of God you have received the Gospel of Jesus Christ and the revelation of His mystery which was kept secret since the world began. This mystery has now become a reality through Christ, according to the scriptures and the commandment of the everlasting God, and is sent to every nation for all to understand the obedience of faith.

- 2 CO 4:6 ~ God, who commanded the light to shine out of darkness, has shined in our hearts to give the light of the knowledge of the glory of God in the face of Jesus Christ.

Heavenly Father, how extraordinary is your Word; it is a wellspring of wisdom that never stops. We thank you that you have revealed yourself to us since the beginning of time, so that all people could come to the knowledge of the truth that sets us free from death, which is the curse of sin. Give us the faith of Abraham so we will never doubt, willing to sacrifice ourselves for the faith; prepare us to share that faith with anyone at any time. Let us continue in our pursuit of understanding you, your works, and your words. For they convince us beyond a shadow of a doubt that you alone are God, along with your Holy Spirit, and Jesus Christ the Lord who is the promised seed of Abraham, and in whose name we pray, Amen.

August 24

First Printing of the Gutenberg Bible was completed on this day in 1456. Never before had there been a system to mass produce large documents with moveable metal type. The apparatus allowed the Bible to be reproduced and disseminated in mass quantities. Over a hundred copies of the forty-two lines per-page manuscript, from the Latin Vulgate version of the Bible, was printed in Mainz Germany. This monumental invention kicked off a new industry in printed books and newspapers, and led to typesetting and typewriters. Printing presses were used for half a millennium before computerization made them virtually obsolete.

Bibles were produced by hand in Biblical times, with repeated scroll copying and dissemination. Fragments, pages, full scrolls, and complete copies of the New Testament date back to the first century when they were first transmitted by the followers of Jesus. And their followers became early church fathers who were prolific in writing things down, rapidly getting the written Word into more and more hands. The availability of the complete Bible began to multiply into new languages, from the original Hebrew and Greek into Latin, Coptic, Syriac, Armenian, Slavonic, Ethiopic, and Arabic. This rapid reproduction made it impossible to fake the truth or circulate a false rendition, because it could be compared easily to the plethora of versions converging on the known truth. Try as the secularists would, the Bible could not be stifled.

- ISA 55:10–11 ~ The rain and snow that falls from heaven does not return to heaven but waters the earth, causing the plants to bud and seed, and providing food. So also, God's Word does not return to Him void, but accomplishes what He wishes and prospers where He sends it.

- MAT 24:25 ~ Jesus said, "Heaven and earth will pass away but my words will never pass away."

- LUK 2:15–18 ~ When the angels left, the shepherds said to each other, "Let us go to Bethlehem and see this great miracle which the Lord has made known to us." They hurried to Bethlehem and found Mary and Joseph, and the baby Jesus lying in a manger. Afterwards, they spread the word to everyone they met concerning the marvelous things they had seen and experienced. And everyone who heard it was amazed at what the shepherds said.

- 2 TH 3:1 ~ Pray for teachers of the true faith, and pray that the Word of God will be spoken freely and understood, like it was for you.

The printing press was a very timely event for the Reformation which would begin with Martin Luther nailing his ninety-five theses on the Wittenberg church door in 1517. Luther would later translate the Latin Bible into German, finishing the New Testament in 1522 and the Old Testament in 1534. Melanchthon was a close confidant and worked with Luther on the texts, as well as taking it on the road while Luther was in hiding. Luther was determined to get the Word into the hands of the people, so they would not rely exclusively on the Catholic clergy to interpret it for them, but rather could rely on God's Word itself. In like manner, everybody can read God's Word and the Holy Spirit will expand their wisdom into a tree of life.

- MAT 22:31–33 ~ Jesus instructed the crowd: Regarding the resurrection of the dead, have you not read the Word of the Lord who said, "I AM the God of Abraham, Isaac, and Jacob?" God is not a God of the dead; He is a God of the living. When the multitude heard this, they were astonished at His doctrine.

- JOH 20:21–23 ~ Jesus said to the apostles, "Peace be unto you. As my Father has sent me, even now I am sending you." After saying this, He breathed on them saying, "Receive the Holy Spirit. Those whose sins you forgive they are forgiven; those whose sins you retain, they are retained."

AUGUST

- JAM 1:25 ~ Those who study the perfect law of liberty and continue therein, not forgetting but continuing to do the work, these persons will be blessed for their deeds.

- 1 PE 4:10 ~ Whoever has received the gift of salvation in Christ should share that gift with others, as a steward of God's eternal grace.

- REV 2—3 ~ St. John disseminated copies of the Revelation of Jesus Christ to seven principal churches in Asia Minor, including Ephesus, Smyrna, Pergamos, Thyatira, Sardis, Philadelphia, and Laodicea.

The duty of every Christian is to distribute the truth of God's Word through confession, public witness, written and oral means, whatever it takes. This is the great commission: make disciples. Everybody should do what they can with the abilities God gave them. People like Gutenberg, Luther, and Melanchthon got the Word circulating in Germany. Tyndale was doing the same thing in England until he was executed by the Catholic leadership, who also tried to eliminate Luther, unsuccessfully. This blot on Roman Catholicism was equal to that of the Inquisition that came before and again after the Reformation movement. The church's power was never meant to be for profit or power; when used in this manner, the damage has been irreversible. Hence, the splitting-off of the Protestants from Roman Catholicism was inevitable.

- HEB 2:3–4 ~ How can we escape, if we neglect such a great salvation? This salvation, which was announced by Christ the Lord, was confirmed to us by those who heard Him. God also testified to it by signs, wonders, various miracles, and gifts of the Holy Spirit distributed according to His will.

God meant for us to read the Word on our own. This does not discount the worthiness of public worship, group Bible study, and prayer. It helps to know the Word yourself so you can contribute to discussions of the Word when studied together. Read the Bible individually and collectively, as well as listen to the Word preached and taught in the sanctuary and the school. Prepare to defend the truth, by equipping yourself with a thorough understanding of it.

- ROM 15:4 ~ Whatever was written before was for us to learn patiently, finding comfort in the scriptures and giving us hope. May that patience and consolation grant you unity with one another through Jesus Christ.

- PHP 1:15–18 ~ Some indeed preach Christ out of envy and rivalry; others preach out of good will. One preaches Christ in order to be controversial, insincerely pretending to be an authority to draw attention to themselves. Another preaches out of love, the way I preach in defense of the Gospel. But whether in pretention or in truth, Christ is being preached, and for this I rejoice.

- 2 TI 2:15 ~ Study diligently to show yourself approved of God; and you will never be ashamed, for you will be accurately sharing the truth.

- 2 TI 3:14–15 ~ Continue in the things you have learned and are convinced of, knowing from whom you have learned them. From a child you have known the Holy Scriptures, which are able to make you wise unto salvation through faith in Jesus Christ.

Father, how intricate are you plans, how magnificent are your deeds, and how amazing is your grace. When we look at how everything is synchronized and organized in accordance with your will, one can only marvel at the completeness it brings to our lives. You have made your truth known to the world from the start, and it continues to spread even to this day. Help us to be equipped with your Word and know it backwards and forwards; help us to be part of the dissemination of your truth to anyone and everyone, by possessing a comprehensive grasp of what we are sharing. In the name of your Son, the Word, whose name saves, we pray, Amen.

August 25

Council of Nicaea Affirmed Essential Doctrines in AD 325; the monthlong conference concluded on this day. It was the first of several ecumenical councils held under the auspices of the early Church, this one hosted by Emperor Constantine. One purpose was to settle disputes of what constitutes scripture: the original twenty-seven books of the New Testament were officially canonized. Another topic of debate was over Arianism, which held that Jesus was a created being; that theology was summarily rejected. The deity of Christ was essential to the true faith and was not to be compromised. The doctrine of the Holy Trinity was firmly established and explained, and remains a fundamental doctrine of the Christian faith. The council rejected lunar calendars, though Easter Sunday would still follow shortly after the equinox. Another important result was the declaration of the Nicene Creed, which provided clarification and expansion of the Apostles' Creed. Both creeds are used in Christian churches around the world today. Another creed which expanded this statement of faith would later be developed by the up-and-comer Athanasius, a scholar who was in attendance at this very council. Below is the Nicene Creed (scriptural references for all clauses in the creed can be found in Barber, 2020a).

I believe in one God, the Father Almighty, Maker of heaven and earth and of all things visible and invisible. And in one Lord Jesus Christ the only-begotten Son of God, begotten of His Father before all worlds, God of God, Light of Light, Very God of Very God, Begotten, not made. Being of one substance with the Father, By whom all things were made; Who for us men and for our salvation came down from heaven And was incarnate by the Holy Ghost of the Virgin Mary And was made man; And was crucified also for us under Pontius Pilate. He suffered and was buried; And the third day He rose again according to the Scriptures; And ascended into heaven, And sits at the right hand of the Father; And He shall come again with glory to judge both the living and the dead; Whose kingdom shall have no end. And I believe in the Holy Ghost, The Lord and Giver of Life, Who proceeds from the Father and the Son, Who with the Father and the Son together is worshipped and glorified, Who spoke by the Prophets. And I believe one holy Christian and Apostolic Church. I acknowledge one Baptism for the remission of sins, And I look for the resurrection of the dead, And the life of the world to come. Amen.

Our confession acknowledges before God our Father that we need a Savior who is Christ the Messiah to remove our sins and purify us through sanctification by the Holy Spirit. Additionally, we affirm this confession of faith as a public witness before the church as well as to others we encounter in our Christian walk with Jesus.

- ISA 57:15 ~ The eternal and holy Lord God says that anyone who comes before Him with a contrite and humble spirit will be revived from death.

- MAT 10:32–33 ~ Jesus said, "Anybody who confesses me before others, I will confess them before my Father in heaven. Anybody who denies me to others, I will deny them before my Father in heaven."

- ROM 10:9–10 ~ If you confess the Lord Jesus with your mouth, and believe in your heart that God raised Him from the dead, you will be saved. For with the heart, we believe unto righteousness; and with the mouth confession is made unto salvation.

- 1 JO 1:9 ~ If we confess our sins, God is faithful and just to forgive us our sins and cleanse us from all unrighteousness.

Father, we confess our sins to you in humble contrition. We ask for your forgiveness and your guidance, that we may refrain from such behavior. Sanctify us by your Spirit, and empower us to boldly confess Jesus to others, that they might believe on His name, Amen.

August 26

Women's Equality Day celebrates a women's right to vote which was granted in the Nineteenth Amendment to the Constitution, ratified on this day in 1920. In 1866, Elizabeth Stanton and Susan B. Anthony created the American Equal Rights Association for woman of all ethnicities to campaign for women's suffrage. In 1916, Alice Paul and Lucy Burns created the National Women's Party to press the cause of women's suffrage via civil disobedience. Though women finally obtained their right to vote, they had yet to attain true equality in education and opportunity, often hindered by a male-dominated world, including in America.

On 08/26/1971 women marched to the Statue of Liberty to demand gender equality. Meanwhile New York congresswoman Bella Abzug had introduced a resolution to recognize Woman's Equality Day as an annual observance. A proclamation to that effect was issued by President Nixon in 1972 making the holiday official. Abzug, a civil rights attorney who took her cause to the US House of Representatives, joined Gloria Steinem, Shirley Chisholm, and Betty Friedan to found the National Women's Political Caucus; she continued the fight for women's rights and equality for twenty more years.

Here in the twenty-first century, we see women in key roles, though they still tend to make less money than men for the same job. But they have come a long way from the days when they were not even allowed to own property. Most people are unaware of the plight of women in the USA, so this is a good day to discover what they went through and how they won their rights when they took a stand for justice and equality. Unfortunately, many other countries still subordinate women, often treating them as second-class citizens. Religions such as Islam make women subservient to men; women in these countries are prohibited from educational and vocational opportunities, with fewer rights and privileges, and enduring subjection and abuse.

Though women were subordinated by men in the Bible, it is clearly stated in the Bible that they are equal to men. However, God made men and women different for a reason, since each sex excels in abilities that the other sex lacks. Many women in the Bible occupied positions of great authority, and women were instrumental in the ministry of Jesus Christ. For more information on this topic reread the lesson about women in ministry (July 31).

- GEN 1:27 ~ God created humans in His own image, both male and female.

- DEU 10:17 ~ The Lord your God is God of gods and Lord of lords; He is great, mighty, and awesome, He is impartial and does not accept bribes.

- JOH 8:23–24 ~ Jesus, told the unbelieving Jews, "You are from below and I am from above. You are of this world; I am not of this world. I told you that you will die in your sins; because if you do not believe that I AM He, you will die in your sins."

- ROM 2:11 ~ God does not show favoritism.

- GAL 3:28 ~ There is neither Jew nor Greek, slave nor free, male nor female, for we are all equal in Jesus Christ.

- 1 PE 3:1, 7 ~ Wives, obey your husbands, and teach them the Word if they do not understand it. Husbands, listen to your wives; honor your wives as the weaker sex and as an equal. Stay together in the grace of life, and your prayers will be answered.

Heavenly Father, you love all people the same; help us to do likewise. Let us never treat another person as beneath us; guide us in public elections to choose people who refuse to show favoritism. Help nations and religions which subordinate women to correct the error of their ways. In Jesus's name, whose inner circle included men and women preaching the Word, Amen.

August 27

Krakatoa Volcano Erupted in Indonesia on this day in 1883, the second worst volcano in world history. It triggered a devastating tsunami that collectively killed over 35,000 people. The worst volcano in history also occurred in Indonesia when Tambora erupted in 1815; after the dust settled a great famine ensued, eventually leaving approximately 85,000 people dead.

Clearly, our planet is constantly in flux, it never rests. Volcanos are mild compared to some natural disasters. For example, China's Yellow River and Yangtze Rivers flooded (1887, 1931) resulting in a combined total of five million deaths. A cyclone that hit Bangladesh (1970) killed about a million people. Earthquakes have taken their toll, and like volcanos, they produce tsunamis that take additional toll on the lives of people. Hurricanes and tornadoes hit the USA every year, sometimes destroying entire towns, and causing widespread flooding and wreckage. Then there are wildfires, meteorite impacts, blizzards, plagues, and famines.

Do you ever wonder if God is punishing us with such disasters? I mean, He used natural disasters to punish people in the Bible (GEN 7—12). Israel knew it was God bringing wrath upon them after they had turned their backs on Him, engaging in the wickedness of other nations and following strange gods. This is exactly what God told them would happen, as written.

- GEN 6:5–7, 12–13 ~ God was appalled by the wickedness that abounded on earth. There was evil and violence everywhere. God told Noah He would destroy this wicked world with a great flood. It rained continuously for forty days. The entirety of civilization was wiped out, save Noah and his family (eight people).

- GEN 19:24–25 ~ God destroyed Sodom and Gomorrah for the same reason that He sent the great flood: wickedness and evil. The only survivors were Lot and his two daughters.

- DEU 28:21–28, 58–59 ~ God will send diseases, plagues, and war to destroy you. The heavens and earth will be unyielding as iron; a blight will destroy your crops. The land will become dry as dust from lack of rain; dust storms will destroy you. You will be defeated by your enemies. You will go into battle in glory but will run from your enemies in seven different directions, and you will become scattered across the earth. Your dead bodies will become food for wild animals. God will send boils, tumors, and various diseases to destroy you. You will become mad, blind, and confused. If you do not observe God's Law or revere His glorious and awesome name, He will send horrible plagues, harsh and prolonged disasters, and severe and lingering illnesses upon you and your descendants.

- DEU 31:16–17 ~ The Lord told Moses, "After you have fallen asleep with your fathers, this nation will become unfaithful to me, pursuing the false gods of others; they will forsake the covenant that I made with them. My anger will be kindled against them and I will forsake them. I will hide my face from them and they will be devoured; many evils and hardships will befall them. They will ask themselves if these evils have come upon them because God has left them."

- ISA 47:10–11 ~ You trusted in your wickedness, thinking that nobody sees you; but your wisdom and knowledge have perverted you. You told yourself that your power was superior and you needed no other. But disaster will come upon you; you will not see it coming and you cannot put it off. Utter desolation will be swift and unexpected.

God warns us that the same will happen in the end times, because of the wickedness of humanity. In fact, it will be worse than that which befell the people of Noah's time when a flood destroyed the world, or Lot's time when fire and brimstone destroyed Sodom, Gomorrah, and neighboring towns.

AUGUST

- EZE 5:17 ~ I will send famine, evil beasts, pestilence and the sword upon you.

- JOE 2:2–3, 10, 30–31 ~ The day of great darkness and gloom is coming. A fire devours everything in its path, leaving behind a wasteland. Nobody can escape. The earth will quake and the heavens will tremble. There will be wonders in the sky and on the earth: blood, smoke, and fire. The sun will become dark and the moon will be like blood.

- ZEP 1:14–15 ~ The great day of the Lord is coming quickly, when mighty men will cry. It is a day of wrath, trouble, and distress, of destruction and desolation, gloom, clouds, and darkness.

- MAT 24:4–12, 21; MAR 13:6–8, 19~ Do not be deceived, for many will claim to be a messiah or a prophet from God. They will perform magic tricks and will fool many people. There will be wars and rumors of wars. Nations will rise up against other nations. There will be earthquakes in different places. There will be famines, afflictions, and pestilence. This is only the beginning of sorrows, the beginning of the end. False prophets will be everywhere. Iniquity will abound and the love of many will grow cold. The righteous will be persecuted, interrogated, imprisoned, and crucified. People will betray one another and wickedness will abound. You will be hated for following me. It will be like the days of Lot, only worse; the philosophy will be eat, drink, and be merry. A time of great tribulation will come, worse than the world has ever known before or will ever know again.

- LUK 17:26–33~ As it was in the days of Noah, so it will be when the Son of man returns. The people ate, drank, and married until Noah and his family entered the ark, the flood came, and the rest drowned. Likewise, it will be as the days of Lot; they ate, drank, bought, sold, planted and built, until Lot and his family departed; then it rained fire and brimstone destroying the cities. It will be like this when the Son of man comes. In that day, the one on the housetop will not have a chance to gather his things in the house; and the one in the field will not be able to return to the house. Remember what happened to Lot's wife. Whoever would seek to save their own life will lose it; and whoever would lose their life for my sake will preserve it.

- LUK 21:34 ~ That generation will not pass away until all these things have happened.

- 2 TI 3:12–13 ~ All the righteous people will suffer persecution. The evil people will get perpetually worse, deceiving many and being deceived.

- REV 6:12–17 ~ There was a great earthquake; the sun became black and the moon became like blood. The stars fell from the sky. Everyone tried to hide and take cover, even the rich and mighty ones. They cried to the rocks to fall on them as they hid in caves deep within the mountains; for they could not face Him who sits on the throne, or the wrath of the Lamb. For when that great day comes, who can withstand it?

Almighty Father, we have been a nation loyal to you and your Word, but we are becoming like other nations who are abandoning you by committing evil, sexual immorality, and violence. Let us not follow their backsliding ways but return to you quickly, before it is too late. Do not allow the powermongers, the self-worshippers, and their decadent followers to gain a foothold here. Instead, help your people to rally together as one in Christ, and soundly disperse them. Even though the end may be near, let us remain faithful; and even if the lying and deceitful people of darkness gain momentum, protect your people from them and give us shelter under the umbrella of your love, and give us the sword of your Spirit which is the Word, to fend them off and cut them down. If it be your will, Father, we pray this in the name of your Son Jesus, who will bring wrath upon the wicked ones when He comes, Amen.

DAILY DEVOTIONAL EVENTS

August 28

I Have a Dream Speech by Martin Luther King was presented in Washington DC in front of the Lincoln Memorial on this day in 1963 before a crowd of about one quarter of a million people. It was the peak of the human rights movement in the sixties, which divided certain groups of people, though all groups of people were represented in the audience. The Baptist pastor said, "Even though we face the difficulties of today and tomorrow, I still have a dream. It is a dream deeply rooted in the American dream. I have a dream that one day this nation will rise up and live out the true meaning of its creed: We hold these truths to be self-evident, that all men are created equal." He continued, "I have a dream that my four little children will one day live in a nation where they will not be judged by the color of their skin but by the content of their character." He concluded, "When we let freedom ring, when we let it ring from every tenement and every hamlet, from every state and every city, we will be able to speed up that day when all of God's children, black men and white men, Jews and Gentiles, Protestants and Catholics, will be able to join hands and sing in the words of the old spiritual—Free at last, free at last. Thank God Almighty we are free at last."

Some would argue that there is more racism today than ever before, but that is not the case; but then most of these skeptics were not alive in 1963. Surely, the times leading up to Dr. King's murder were worse, not to mention the days before, during, and after the Civil War. The fact that a man of color was elected president is proof that everybody has opportunity to be all they can be in the USA. However, politicians still propose policies that subjugate or inhibit minorities; they are akin to the segregationists, racists, and murderers of the past. They marginalize people of color to keep them dependent on the government. But people of color are not falling for that rubbish anymore, because they too have a dream which King called the American Dream. It is okay to dream big like King did, because there are opportunities for everyone willing to put in honest hard work; and if you love God, He will bless your work.

We can dream when are awake or asleep. Let me tell you about sleeping dreams. The unconscious mind is an incredible processor; when we dream, the brain is capable of parallel processing, meaning we can process numerous clusters of information simultaneously, something we cannot do at the conscious level. This is why dreams appear so bizarre when we awaken, because many neural pathways are open at the same time (Barber, 2020b). Dreams are necessary for restful sleep, and for organizing the vast amount of information gathered every day; otherwise, we would experience serious information overload. Dreams also can be informative; they can provide clues to the future, understanding of the past, and solutions for the present. But be careful about trying to read too much into a dream; some dreams will not make sense and that is okay. The brain is doing its job categorizing data and storing it. The Bible talks about dreams and visions quite a bit (see also the lesson on 01/13).

- GEN 28:12, 16 17 ~ Jacob dreamed about a ladder set on earth and reaching into heaven. He saw angels of God ascending and descending upon it. Jacob awoke and declared, "Surely the Lord abides in this place and I was unaware. How awesome is this place for it is the very house of God and the gate to heaven." (The ladder in Jacob's dream was Jesus: JOH 1:51.)

- NUM 12:6 ~ The Lord said, "If there is a prophet among you, I will make myself known to him in a vision and will speak to him in a dream."

- 1 SA 3 ~ God called Samuel three times as he slept; Samuel thought it was Eli the priest. But Eli told him it was the Lord and to listen to what God had to say. Samuel went back to sleep and God told him he would be a prophet and revealed what would happen to the house of Eli.

AUGUST

- JOB 33:14–18 ~ God will speak once, maybe twice, but people do not perceive. He speaks in a vision, at night, when we are asleep. He may speak into our ears, and terrify us with warnings, to turn us from sin and pride, and to preserve our souls from hell to save our lives.

- JOE 2:28 ~ I will pour out my Spirit on humankind. Your sons and daughters will prophesy and will see visions; your old men will dream dreams.

- DAN 5:12 ~ Daniel had an excellent spirit, with the knowledge and understanding to interpret dreams, explain riddles, and solve problems.

- JER 29:8 ~ God says, "Do not let those prophets and diviners among you deceive you, and do not pay attention to their dreams which they themselves caused to be dreamt."

- COL 2:8, 18–19 ~ Beware of those who would lead you astray with their errant philosophies and vain deceptions, following traditions fashioned by the world and not Christ. Do not let anyone swindle you out of your reward. Beware of those who practice false humility and worship angels. They claim to have seen things, but they have filled their unspiritual and arrogant minds with silly notions.

In the Old Testament were prophetic dreamers who could interpret dreams; it was a special gift from God. Among them were Joseph and Daniel; and they always gave God credit for the interpretation of a dream (GEN 40:8; DAN 2:28).

- GEN 37 ~ Joseph's dreams about the sheaves and the sun, moon, and stars indicated that someday he would rule over his brothers and parents.

- GEN 40 ~ Joseph accurately interpreted the dreams of fellow prisoners, after he was betrayed by his brothers into slavery, and again by his master's wife to be imprisoned.

- GEN 41 ~ Joseph accurately interpreted Pharoah's dreams about seven years of plenty followed by seven years of famine. Pharoah made Joseph his second in command to manage the grain, ensuring there was enough to feed everyone in the region for those fourteen years.

- DAN 2 ~ Daniel interpreted Nebuchadnezzar's dream about the empires which would follow Babylon; these empires would fall prostrate before the everlasting kingdom of the Lord.

- DAN 5 ~ Daniel interpreted Belshazzar's dream about the writing on the wall and the fact that Babylon would fall to the Medes and Persians; Belshazzar was assassinated that night.

- DAN 7 ~ Daniel dreamed of the final four great empires before the Son of man would come down from heaven and claim His kingdom.

As you can see, God can communicate with us while we sleep and dream, and sometimes He communicates to us in visions while awake. But do not expect this to happen frequently if at all. When God places a thought into our minds through His Holy Spirit, it will not be like a normal conversation between two people; it will be God speaking words into one's heart or inner sanctum. If you see a vision from an angel, keep in mind that Satan disguises himself as an angel of light (2 CO 11:14). You are not likely to receive messages directly from God or His angels if you have not sufficiently prepared yourself for ministry by being conversant in His Word.

Dear Father in heaven, who spoke to the prophets in visions and dreams, speak to us through your Holy Spirit so that our plans are in alignment with your purpose. Help us to hear your voice when you call and to heed that call. We know that the Holy Spirit gives us knowledge of your will and tells us what is true and right; help us, oh Lord, to hear, listen, and digest these communications, and act on them in accordance with your wishes for our lives and for our nation. We pray in the name of Jesus, Amen.

August 29

Armor of God Day is proposed to encourage the reader to try on the armor of God, which Christians should do every morning when they awaken. The armor includes a good defense system, as well as a formidable weapon: the sword of the Spirit. We will need these tools to fight the evil in this world coming against us; this is the good fight of faith, which is our shield. Don the armor to combat evil entities, malevolent people, the myriad of temptations in this world, and the weapons of evil sent to vex your spirit. The enemy is not just bad people, it includes forces of evil in this earthly realm which are not human. We're talking spiritual warfare. Indeed, there are people who are inherently evil, because they have given into the powers of darkness. They do not have a clue about the armor of God; but if they come up against someone who possesses this armor and who wields the sword of the Spirit, they will be caught by surprise and summarily expunged.

- ISA 59:17 ~ He has put on righteousness as a breastplate and salvation for a helmet. His clothing consists of the garments of vengeance and zeal is his cloak.

- EPH 6:11–17 ~ Put on the whole armor of God so that you will be prepared to stand against the trickery of Satan. For we do not wrestle against flesh and blood, but against principalities, powers, rulers of darkness in this world, and wickedness in high places. Wear this armor so that you can withstand the day of evil, and remain standing when it is over. Gird your loins with truth and put on the breastplate of righteousness. Put on the shoes of the Gospel of peace; and take with you the shield of faith which will repel the fiery darts of the wicked. Don the helmet of salvation and arm yourself with the sword of the Spirit which is the Word of God.

- HEB 4:12 ~ The Word of God is living and active, sharper than any double-edged sword, dividing the soul and spirit, and discerning the thoughts and intentions of the heart.

Vexation of one's spirit is a direct attack against the spirit inside a person, usually from someone or something outside that person to include demons, evil people, temptations of the flesh, etc. Vexation brings trouble, affliction, distress, possibly death. Addiction is an invitation to greater evil, and is an example of vexation coming against one's spirit. There are a great many sins that can become habit forming which are dangerous, and will vex one's spirit. If the evil heart refuses to turn to God, He will vex that spirit to death.

Nowadays, the prevalence of evil is everywhere, as is the presence of demons and the numbers of humans capitulating to them. One needs only a cell phone or computer to connect to all kinds of evil, from hardcore pornography, to making drug deals, engaging in adulterous affairs, viewing and posting violence, conspiracy to commit murder, rip-off scams, and the list goes on. Many social media applications actually promote such behavior.

Remember this: the flesh and the spirit are at war. And what are they fighting over? Answer: control. Control over what? Answer: your soul. Your soul encompasses your mind, will, thoughts, and emotions. The more important question to ask is, which is controlling your thoughts: your flesh or your spirit? You'll want the spirit within you to be in charge.

Your soul is what makes you unique from everyone else as well as from other earthly creatures; and it makes you particularly valuable to God. Protect your soul from the influence of evil by tapping into your higher power, which is your connection to God, the highest power. That connection is a spiritual one between your spirit and God's Holy Spirit. God gave everyone the spirit of life (JOH 6:63); upon death that spirit returns to Him (ECC 12:7). Everything and everyone beholding to the physical/material world will be destroyed by it and with it (ISA 51:6; MAT 24:35; REV 21:1), including the lost souls condemned to the lake of fire.

- JOB 33:4 ~ The Spirit of God has made me; the breath of the Almighty has given me life.

AUGUST

- ROM 8:5–6 ~ Those who follow the flesh are mindful of things concerning the flesh; those who follow the spirit keep in mind spiritual things. To be carnally minded is death; to be spiritually minded is life and peace.

- GAL 5:13–21 ~ Brothers, you have been called to be free men, but do not use that freedom as an excuse to engage in lusts of the flesh, but in love serve one another. For all the Law is fulfilled by loving your neighbor as yourself. So, walk in the Spirit not in the flesh, because the spirit and the flesh oppose one another. If you are led by God's Spirit you are not under the Law.

- GAL 5:19–21 ~ The works of the flesh include adultery, fornication, perversion, lust, idolatry, witchcraft, hatred, quarreling, rivalry, dissension, rage, fighting, sedition, heresy, jealousy, murder, drunkenness, orgies, and the like. Those who engage in such activities will not inherit the kingdom.

- GAL 5:22–23 ~ Fruits of the Spirit include love, joy, peace, patience, kindness, goodness, faithfulness, gentleness, and self-control. There is no law against those things.

The verb "vex" means to make someone annoyed, worried, frustrated, defiant, deviant, and/or fearful. Vexation is a form of harassment or maltreatment, and is often an attempt to get someone to do something that goes against their better judgment or moral compass—unless it comes from God in the form of vengeance (DEU 32:35, 41; PSA 7:16; ISA 26:14; ROM 1:32).

- EXO 22:21–22 ~ Do not vex or oppress a stranger; remember, you were once strangers in the land of Egypt. You shall not afflict a widow or a child.

- NUM 25:16–18; NUM 33:55–56 ~ The Lord said to Moses, "Vex the Midianites, and kill them; for they vex you with their tricks with which they have beguiled you… If you do not drive out the inhabitants of the land from before you, those who remain will be like a stick in your eye and a thorn in your side, and you will be vexed living in that land. Moreover, I will do to you as I wanted done to them."

- 2 CH 15:5–6 ~ In those times there was no peace for anyone going out or coming in, but great vexations were upon all the inhabitants. A nation was destroyed by another nation, and a city by another city; for God vexed them with all adversity.

- JOB 19:2 ~ Job asked, "How long will you men vex my soul, to break me into pieces with your malicious words?"

- ECC 1:14–15; ECC 2:17; ECC 4:6; ECC 6:9 ~ I have seen all the works committed under the sun, and behold, all is vanity and vexation of spirit. That which is crooked cannot be made straight. Therefore, I hated life because of the works done under the sun, for it grieved me; because all is vanity and vexation of spirit. Better is a handful of quietness than two hands filled with travail and vexation of spirit. Better is the sight of the eyes than the wandering of desire, which also is vanity and vexation of spirit.

- ISA 65:14 ~ Behold, God's servants will sing for joy of heart; but the others will cry for sorrow, and will howl from vexation of spirit.

Vexation can be a temptation that keeps plaguing one's mind or soul. Note that it is one thing to be tempted but another to give into temptation. Everyone has a choice either to dismiss the temptation or to succumb. Being tempted is not a sin; many things tempt us in this natural world, not to mention Satan and other evil spirits. Once a person gives the temptation further consideration, he or she has sinned in thought. Once a person acts out on that thought, he or she has sinned in deed. The Bible warns us to be careful what we think and do. The most difficult part is to remain mindful at all times about what you are thinking; for example, entertaining lust is akin to adultery (MAT 5:28), entertaining hate is akin to murder (1 JO 3:15).

- ISA 28:18–19 ~ Those who have made a contract with death and hell will find their agreements to be null and void. They will be trampled into the dust when the scourge passes through. From that time forward the scourge will take people away; it will be a vexation just to hear this message.

- EPH 2:3–4 ~ In times past we also engaged in lusts of the flesh, fulfilling desires of the body and of the mind; we were by nature children of wrath, just like the rest. But because of God's great love for us we were made alive in Christ, even when we were dead in our sins. It is by that grace that you also can be saved.

- JAM 1:15 ~ When lust is conceived it brings forth sin; and sin, when finished, brings forth death.

Consider the frequency of lone-wolf murderers, whether by gun, knife, car, shoving someone into train, or whatever. Or what about the random unprovoked beatings going on every day in certain cities here and abroad? Then there are the arsonists, looters, robbers, vandals, and assorted anarchists menacing the country. These people most certainly are vexed in spirit. Are they mentally deranged? Well, yeah. Are they possessed by a demon(s)? Hmm, quite possibly. Most are repeat offenders who have been in and out of jail, let loose on low or no bond, not prosecuted to the fullest extent, or simply ignored by law enforcement both before and after their crimes. Maybe the enablers are vexed in spirit as well. Citizens become reluctant to get involved, or report suspicious activity, or call 9-1-1 for fear of retaliation.

You know, fear can vex the spirit too. What is the cure for fear? Answer: perfect love (1 JO:18). Keep watch over your soul and trust in the Lord to protect you; listen to His guidance before you follow through with your plans. Put on the armor of God which is the power of the Holy Spirit who is battling the evil alongside you.

- DEU 4:9–10 ~ Keep your soul diligently. Do not forget the things your eyes have seen; never let them slip away. Teach these things to your children and your children's children.

- EZE 22:26–27 ~ Their priests have violated my laws and profaned the holy things. They do not know the difference between holy and unholy, or clean versus unclean. They have ignored my sabbaths and dishonored my name. Their rulers are like wolves tearing apart their prey; they shed blood and destroy people for dishonest gain.

- PRO 4:23 ~ Guard your heart with all diligence, for from it flows the issues of life.

- ROM 12:2 ~ Do not conform to the world but be transformed by the renewal of your mind, to do the will of God.

- COL 3:2 ~ Set your mind on things above, not earthly things.

Out of control people who strive to control others are neither in their right mind nor a right spirit. How can anyone be trusted to run our government, institutions, and lives when they are focused on power, riches, and lasciviousness? Incidentally, research has shown these three to be the top three motives for murder and other capital crimes. Leaders who are hedonists, power mongers, and control freaks become tyrannical; history has shown them to be the greatest mass murderers of all time: Mao, Stalin, Hitler, and many more. People addicted to power go bonkers without it; to be sure, they already were crazy for power before seizing it, and become crazier the longer they possess it.

- ECC 8:8 ~ Nobody has the power to retain the spirit when they die, and nobody has authority over death.

- ISA 29:20 ~ The ruthless will come to nothing and the scoffers will cease. All who watch evil and do evil will be cut off.

- JER 18:12 ~ They acted according to the abominations of an evil heart.

- MIC 7:2 ~ All the godly and upright men are gone. The wicked lie in ambush for blood. They do evil with diligence.

- HAB 1:4 ~ Law and judgment are loosened, for the wicked encompass the righteous. Therefore, wrong judgment proceeds.

Tyranny is once again at our doorstep. Americans had to fight it off twice during our beginnings. Who knows, maybe we'll have to fight it off again. That's why the framers put the Second Amendment in the Constitution in the first place. What is the motivation of certain politicians who would take away your right to protect yourself, your family, and your property? They would remove guns from our possession, yet are actually multiplying the number of guns, because more Americans feel responsible to personally prepare, protect and defend. Notice how the lions' share of violent crimes occur in areas where this right is suppressed. The criminals pursue soft targets such as the weak, innocent, unarmed, and unprotected. They avoid locations with high probability of the presence of law enforcement or others inclined to fight back (namely, hard targets).

Violent people are the ones who are weak-minded cowards. The USA needs to get back to the philosophy of "peace through faith" not only for leaders but also for the citizenry. By faith we are made strong in the Lord (2 CO 12:10). Faith is our shield. And the sword of the Spirit is our weapon of war, which is far more powerful than a firearm. We do not have to submit to tyranny; indeed, we must resist it. Among many noteworthy sayings from the statesman Patrick Henry (paraphrased): Slavery is not a reasonable price to pay for peace.

God is all powerful. What did God do with that power? Well for starters, He created the universe and He sent Jesus Christ to the earth to save us from sin (JOH 3:16–17). What did Jesus do with that power? He humbled Himself in service to humanity. Note that Satan has considerable power as well. What does he do with that power? He seeks to destroy humankind. God gives us power too, and we should use that power in the same manner as Christ: in service to others and to vanquish Satan and his demon army. Those using their power to subjugate others are abusing that power; they are as out of control as a drug addict. They should never be in a position of leadership or authority since they have lost their way and cannot find a pathway back to the light. They are using their power to benefit Satan, not God and country. If you do not have the Spirit of Christ, you are susceptible to the spirit of antichrist (1 JO 4:3–4).

- DAN 8:24 ~ The evil one's power is mighty but not by his own power. He will destroy awfully, and will prosper; he will destroy mighty and holy people.

- PHP 2:10–11 ~ Everyone should bow at the name of Jesus Christ, whether they are in heaven or on earth. Every tongue should confess that Jesus Christ is Lord, to the glory of God the Father.

To conclude this lesson, let us return to the basics: right versus wrong; good versus evil. Everyone has to pick: the former or the latter. Adam and Eve learned this immediately, as will every human being. That means we all know to do what is right though we struggle trying to be principled people. Then there are those who dismiss all of God's laws because they love sin.

Consider the first ten laws God handed down to Moses listed below; a plain hierarchy is implied. The first five are spiritual duties to God; the second five are how we treat others. If you get into the habit of disobeying any of these laws, your spirit is likely vexed. If you do not discontinue the bad behavior, you leave yourselves open to fallen devils. Yes, all sins can be forgiven if sincerely confessed and repented with true godly sorrow; this will compel you to want to quit the bad habit, and make it a habit to let your conscience or higher power guide your thoughts and behavior.

1. Love God above all others
2. Never practice idolatry
3. Never take the Lord's name in vain.
4. Honor the Sabbath by dedicating a day of worship to God
5. Honor your parents.
6. Never murder anyone.
7. Never commit adultery.
8. Never steal.
9. Never lie.
10. Never covet.

- PSA 97:10 ~ Those who love the Lord hate evil.
- AMO 5:15 ~ Hate evil, love goodness, and establish justice.
- MIC 3:2–5 ~ You hate good and love evil. You skin people and eat their flesh. You chop their bodies into pieces. You talk of peace but make war. When you cry to the Lord He will not listen; He will hide His face from those engaging in such behavior.
- 1 TI 6:10–11 ~ The love of money is the root of all evil; through the craving for worldly riches many have wandered away from the faith and pierced their hearts. Strive for righteousness, godliness, faith, love, steadfastness, and gentleness.
- 1 JO 3:8 ~ Whoever commits sin is of the devil, who sinned from the very beginning. The Son of God was manifested to destroy the works of the devil.

Our Father in heaven, we thank you for our preservation, protection, and security; help us always to rely on you to keep us safe from harm and danger. Help us also to do our part to combat evil in this world, by donning the armor that you have provided to us as we face rulers of darkness and wickedness in high places. Bring to mind the power of the shield of faith that we hold onto as we fight the good fight, so we may deflect the fiery arrows of the wicked adversary. Instruct us how to wield the sword of the Spirit which is your Holy Word, and cut down the strongholds of the evil ones, the demons, and their leader Satan, and remain standing when the battle is finished. In Jesus's name we pray, Amen.

August 30

Titus of Rome Destroyed Second Temple in Jerusalem on this day in AD 70. He was the son of Vespasian and would later become emperor, but at this point in his career he was a Roman commander, who had set his sights on sacking Jerusalem, a thorn in Rome's behind for much too long. Under Titus, the army desecrated the second temple and burned it to the ground. After leaving Jerusalem in ruins, they sacked the Herodian outpost, and later managed to build a ramp using Jewish slaves to ascend upon Masada, hoping to destroy the fortress and finish them off. But the occupants committed suicide to avoid being captured and interrogated. Given their link to Qumran, they may have known the location of hidden scrolls which they did not want to divulge. God protected the books, through the Essenes and others. Those scrolls became known as the Dead Sea Scrolls, and would validate the canon of scripture from two thousand years ago.

Jesus prophesied these events before His death in AD 30 when He said a generation would not pass before the temple and surrounding buildings would come down and not one stone would be left upon another. Given that a generation was considered forty years, that adds up to AD 70. Jesus had His prophecy down to the exact number of years. The arch of Titus can be found in Rome, built by emperor Domitian in AD 81, to commemorate his brother's conquest of Judea and destruction of Jerusalem. That second temple was authorized to be built by King Cyrus of Persia (2 CH 36:22–23). You may recall that the empire of Babylon, who had taken captive the Israelites, was replaced by the Medes and Persians. Most of the Israeli exiles were far from home, while a remnant had returned to restore that temple.

- DAN 9:26 ~ After sixty-two weeks, Messiah will be cut off; then the great prince and his army will come to destroy the city and the sanctuary. The end will come as a flood and there will be war until all is desolated.

- MAT 24:1–2, 33–34; MAR 13:2, 30; LUK 21:5–6, 32 ~ As they left the temple the disciples approached Jesus and He said to them, "Do you see all of these buildings? I tell you the truth, there will not be one stone left upon another; all will be thrown down." After telling the disciples about the end times Jesus concluded, "When you see these things happen, you will know that the end is near. Truly I tell you, this generation will not pass until all the things I told you have been fulfilled."

- LUK 19:43–44 ~ Jesus said, "The time is coming when your enemies will surround you, and Jerusalem will be flattened to the ground; and they will not leave one stone sitting on top of another, because they did not recognize my coming."

The first temple was destroyed along with the holy city of Jerusalem by the Babylonian conqueror Nebuchadnezzar. It was destroyed for the same reason the second temple was destroyed and the city demolished: Israel had turned away from God. Regarding the second temple, the Jews had turned away from Christ and sought His death when He prophesied its destruction. They had forgotten about God once again. Note that the first temple was built under King Solomon (1 KI 8:17–18; 1 CH 28:2–3; 1 CH 22:9–10; 2 CH 2:1).

- 1 KI 9:8–9 ~ This house will become a heap of ruins. Everyone passing by will be astonished, hissing, "Why has the Lord done this to the land and this house?" They will answer, "Because they rejected the Lord their God who brought them out of Egypt by following false gods."

- 2 KI 25:8–12 ~ During the reign of King Nebuchadnezzar of Babylon, the commander laid siege to Jerusalem and burned down the temple, the king's palace, and all the houses in Jerusalem. Then they tore down the walls surrounding the city. The survivors were carried off to Babylon, but the poor people were left to tend their farms.

- EZR 5:12 ~ Since our fathers provoked the God of heaven, He gave them into the hand of Nebuchadnezzar, king of Babylon, who destroyed the temple and took the people captive.

There is a prophecy that a third temple will be built in Jerusalem. This is not to be confused with the eternal temple in the kingdom of heaven. It is unclear who builds the third temple and when. Regardless, it will be desecrated by the beast, the son of perdition, also referred to as the abomination of desolation. This will occur during the latter days, when evil pervades the earth. Satan will adopt a human to be his possession, in complete opposition to God's Son Jesus Christ, which is why we call him the antichrist (instead of *an* antichrist). It is this son of hell who will desecrate the third temple. It might be a temple built upon the old site, or it might be a reference to the Mosque of Omar that presently sits over the ancient site called the Dome of the Rock. Nevertheless, the abomination is the desecration of a once holy place by blood sacrifices, and the desolation will be the obliteration of wicked souls in the once holy city.

- EZE 8:9–10, 17 ~ In Ezekiel's vision he observed many abominations occurring in God's holy temple. Particularly loathsome was the abominable image of jealousy. And God said to him, "Did you see this, son of man? Is it a trivial thing for them to commit such abominations in the house of Judah? They have provoked me to anger. I will deal with them in fury without pity; though they cry out I will not hear them."

- DAN 9:27; DAN 11:31; DAN 12:11–12 ~ During the last half of the week the abomination that causes desolation will continue, until the terrible end that awaits is poured out upon them. They will profane the temple and the fortress. They will take away the burnt offering and set up the abomination that makes desolate for 3.5 years.

- MAT 24:15–16; MAR 13:14; LUK 21:20 ~ Jesus said, "When the abomination that brings desolation which the prophet Daniel spoke of is standing in the holiest place, flee Judea into the mountains."

- REV 11:2–3 ~ I was given a measuring rod and told to measure the temple of God and the altar, and those who worshipped there; but I was told not to measure the court outside the temple for it would be given over to the nations; they will trample the holy city forty-two months (3.5 years).

This is a terrifying finale to civilization and the earth; hopefully we will be spared from it, either by rapture, death, or victory. Nevertheless, when it's over, that's it. No more chances to confess, repent, receive the gift, or give thanks. You either go up or down. I for one, will choose God, and that means up. All other choices go down. Choose now, before time runs out.

Father in heaven, we pray for your deliverance from the scourge that will overrun the nations. Help us to be aware and know when and where to act, in order to avoid getting run over. For we know this by trusting in your grace with faith in your plans and promises. Let us be lights to a world shrouded in darkness, so many more can find their way into the light. If it comes to all-out warfare, you will be on our side; sustain us mentally, physically, and spiritually, empowered by your Holy Spirit to tell the truth. Father, your Word which is the truth, is our sword, and Christ who is the Word made flesh, is our shield of faith. We proudly bear the armor of God in our fight against evil. In the beloved name of Jesus we pray, Amen and Amen.

August 31

Jack the Ripper's Murderous Spree in London occurred in 1888, resulting in at least five women linked to the same mass murderer; many more murders during the timeframe could have been copycats. We don't know for sure because he was never caught; it is one of those unsolved mysteries. The first body was found on today's date, but this is not a day of remembrance. It is a day to recognize that random heinous crimes are occurring a lot more often than ever before. Insane psychopaths get a physical rush from hacking up humans; many of them start with animals and graduate to humans. The point is, we must be vigilant and cautious of evil and its apparent escalation. The degree of myth added to the legend of Jack is of no consequence. Monsters pervade every society, civilized or uncivilized. Note that there is a fine line between pure evil and clinical psychopathology. Be assured: people are not born that way. They might be possessed whether mentally, spiritually, or both. Demon possession still exists, it always has; devils seek to control the victim's mind and actions. Channeling familiar spirits is asking to be influenced by them; this is very unhealthy for the soul, and belongs to those joining the fallen in hell. God wants every soul to live, but grants free will, allowing people to choose a side.

- LEV 19:31 ~ Stay away from people with familiar spirits, and do not seek sorcerers to be defiled by them, for I am the Lord your God.

- JOH 8:44 ~ Jesus said to the unbelievers, "You belong to your father the devil, and the evil of your father you will do. He was a murderer and a liar from the start. He never tells the truth. In fact, he is the father of lies."

- 1 CO 10:21 ~ You cannot drink the cup of the Lord and the cup of devils; you cannot partake at the Lord's table and the table of devils.

- 1 TI 4:1–2 ~ The Holy Spirit explicitly states that in the latter days some will depart from the faith, conferring with seducing spirits and following the doctrine of devils; speaking lies of hypocrisy, and possessing a conscience seared by a hot iron.

The day of reckoning is right around the corner for people who take pleasure in evil. They will be punished, either in this life, the next life, or probably both. Either way, their lot in life is death and their destiny is the lake of fire.

- PSA 52:5 ~ God will destroy the evil ones forever. He will uproot them from the living.

- PRO 1:18 ~ They lay in wait for their own blood. They will ambush their own lives.

- PRO 24:20 ~ Evil people have no future. Their light will be extinguished.

- ISA 29:20 ~ The ruthless will come to nothing and the scoffers will cease. All who watch evil and do evil will be cut off.

- 2 PE 2:2–9 ~ The Lord knows how to deliver the godly out of temptations, and to set aside the unjust until the day of judgment to be punished.

- REV 21:8 ~ The fearful, unbelieving, abominable, murderous, lecherous, sorcerers, idolaters, and liars will be thrown into the lake of fire which is the second death.

There is a spiritual void in people who love evil, meaning they have rejected the Holy Spirit. This makes them vulnerable to evil spirits. Whether they are possessed or not, they choose evil voluntarily. They have no hope of forgiveness; they believe there is no way out. So, they commit their souls to hell, while their crimes progress from bad to worse. There is always a way out: Jesus Christ who forgives all sin. But the sin that will condemn them is their disbelief, which is the only unpardonable sin since it is a rejection of the truth given all people by the Holy Spirit.

- PSA 130:3–4 ~ If you, Lord, counted our sins against us, who would be able to stand? But there is forgiveness with you that you may be feared.

- MAT 12:31–32 ~ Jesus said, "All manner of sin and blasphemy will be forgiven by God, except blasphemy against the Holy Spirit. Whoever speaks against the Son of man can be forgiven. But whoever speaks against the Holy Spirit will not be forgiven, neither in this world nor in the world to come."

- MAR 5:19 ~ Jesus told the man who had been cleansed of demon possession, "Go home to your friends and tell them what great things the Lord has done for you, and the compassion He has shown."

- MAR 9:17–27 ~ A man brought his son who was demon possessed to Jesus hoping He would cast the demon out. Jesus asked the man, "If you have faith, all things are possible to those who believe." The man replied, "I believe Lord; help me in my unbelief." Then Jesus cast the demon out of the child.

- ROM 6:12 ~ Do not let sin rule in your mortal body, obeying the lusts therein. Do not use your body as an instrument of unrighteousness unto sin. Yield yourselves to God, as those who are alive from the dead, and use your body as an instrument of righteousness unto God.

The atrocities being perpetrated in our cities are escalating partly due to the degradation of law enforcement, where police departments are losing funding, prosecutors are downgrading crimes, politicians are supporting cashless bail, and authorities are letting people out of prison when they haven't even served half of their time. Plus, we see the department of justice and the federal government going after private citizens who are innocent, tossing them into jail and throwing away the key, merely to make a statement or support an idealistic narrative. We are a nation of law and order but we are becoming a nation of lawlessness and disorder. Do you think peaceful protests should include vandalism, rioting, and arson? Dr. King would be appalled to see what became of the American Dream which he wanted for his children and his country.

- ISA 3:9 ~ It shows on their faces that they are guilty; they declare their sin like Sodom, they do not hide it. Woe unto their souls for they have recompensed evil unto themselves.

- ISA 59:3–7 ~ Your hands are defiled with blood and sin. Your lips have spoken lies and wickedness. They conceive evil and rely on foolishness and lies. They run to evil and hasten to shed innocent blood. Desolation and destruction ride their highways.

- JER 8:12 ~ They were not ashamed when they committed their abominations. They will be among those who fall; at the time of their judgment, they will be cast down.

- EPH 5:11–12 ~ Do not take part in their evil schemes but expose them instead. It is shameful to even speak about the evil that they do in secret.

- 2 TH 2:3–4, 9–12 ~ The man of lawlessness comes, who is the son of perdition. He exalts himself to be a god or an object of worship, taking the seat in the temple of God. He brings about the acts of Satan through deception and magic. People will deceive themselves, and will be condemned for not believing the truth.

Father God, we are becoming a backsliding nation falling for Satan's schemes; please help us to get back on the path of righteousness before it is too late. Cast out the evil which has infiltrated our government, institutions, and citizenry; help God-fearing people to defeat them in elections, courts, and public discourse. Enable us to remove godless leaders, corrupt judges, and illicit prosecutors, replacing them with people who will uphold and enforce the law. Please help us to return to equal justice and opportunity for all Americans. In Jesus's name we pray, Amen.

September 1

Billy Graham Crusade Attracted Two Million people during a sixteen-week event in New York City which ended on this day in 1957; some estimates were up to 2.4 million attended over the duration of the revival. The rallies started on May 15 in Madison Square Garden and ended on September 1 when 100,000 people packed Yankee Stadium. The streets were crowded with additional onlookers. It was reported that over 60,000 people gave their lives to Jesus in four months. Like his predecessors, Graham had an altar call after each sermon, during which thousands would come forward with a change of heart. Graham was an ordained Southern Baptist minister who started these massive rallies in 1947 until his retirement in 2005. His revivals were aired on radio and television, and he had his own radio show, as well as periodic television guest appearances. Some of his sermons are still being televised. It is unlikely that anyone will break the records that he made with respect to people reached and people converted, outside of Jesus Christ and the apostles. Interestingly, Graham himself converted to Christianity at a Mordecai Ham revival meeting in 1934. He was the third of a string of evangelists that really drew the crowds for over a century: D L Murphy (1832-1899); Billy Sunday (1862-1935); Billy Graham (1918-2018).

This is what we need in the USA and the world: a major Christian revival. Christians still hold the majority here, in Europe, and in most of the Americas. If we came together as a united front, it would have an impact that could reverberate worldwide. The radicals and progressives seem to have the loudest voice but they do not represent the majority, yet. Christians need to raise our voices, become more visible, and stand up for Jesus, else we become the minority.

- ISA 6:8 ~ When God asked who to send as His messenger, Isaiah replied, "Here I am, Lord, send me."

- ISA 12:4 ~ Praise the Lord, call on His name, declare His works to all people; mention that His name is exalted.

- MAT 9:36–38 ~ When Jesus saw the multitudes He was moved with compassion, because they were weak and scattered abroad with no shepherd. Then Jesus said to His disciples, "The harvest is plentiful but the laborers are few. Pray, therefore, that the Lord will send laborers into the harvest."

- JOH 8:23–24 ~ Jesus, told the unbelieving Jews, "You are from below and I am from above. You are of this world; I am not of this world. I told you that you will die in your sins; because if you do not believe that I AM He, you will die in your sins."

- ROM 12:4–5 ~ Just as we have many members in our body, and all members have the same purpose, so we, being many, are one body in Christ and members of one another.

- ROM 15:1–7 ~ We who are strong ought to bear with the failings of the weak. When we do the right thing, it should not be to please ourselves, but to please others and to build them up in the Lord. Even Christ did not please Himself, but as it is written of Him, "The insults of those who would insult you have fallen on me." Everything that was written in the past was for our instruction, so that through endurance and the encouragement of the scriptures we might have hope. May the God who gives endurance, encouragement, and hope give you a spirit of unity as you follow Christ. Give glory to God the Father of our Lord Jesus Christ with one voice and one heart. Accept each other as Christ accepted you, so that God may be praised.

- 1 CO 1:10 ~ By the name of Christ, be united in one mind and be of one opinion.

- 2 CO 5:19–21 ~ God was in Christ, and reconciled the world to Himself. He has not imputed our sins upon us, but rather has given us the message of reconciliation. So now we have become ambassadors for Christ, as though God was speaking His message through us, so that you too may be reconciled to Him. For He gave us His Son Jesus Christ, who knew no sin, to bear our sins, so that we could receive the righteousness of God that was in Him.

- EPH 4:2 ~ Be humble, gentle, and patient, holding up each other in love. Try earnestly to stay united in the Spirit through the bond of peace.

- EPH 4:11–13 ~ God gave some the abilities of apostles, prophets, evangelists, pastors and/or teachers for the work of the ministry, the edifying of the saints, the perfecting of the body of Christ, and the unity of faith. They impart the knowledge of the Son of God who was a perfect man, so that we could take on the characteristics of Christ.

- 2 TI 4:5 ~ Always be watchful, willing to endure afflictions, doing the work of the evangelist, doing what is necessary for the ministry.

- 1 PE 5:2–3 ~ Feed God's flock which is among you; be overseers of the kingdom. Do this, not out of obligation but willingly; do this not for ill-gotten gain but with a clear conscience. Do not act like lords over God's heritage but set an example to the flock.

- REV 5:11–12 ~ Then I looked and saw a multitude of angels, numbering thousands upon thousands, literally millions of angels encircling the throne. And they sang aloud with one voice, "Worthy is Christ the Lamb who was slain, to receive power and wealth, and wisdom and strength, and honor, glory and praise."

It can't be easy being an evangelist, what with the long hours, constant travel, being crowded and bombarded. It is very impressive what the evangelists of old had to endure and they just kept going, kind of like St. Paul: beaten down but not staying down. The TV evangelists have it a lot easier, except for the ones who are mostly on the road. This is what Jesus told His apostles to expect when He sent them out into the world to get the Word out.

- MAT 10:7–12 ~ Jesus told the twelve, "As you go preaching, saying that the kingdom of heaven is at hand, heal the sick, cleanse the diseased, raise the dead, and cast out devils. Freely you have received and freely you must give. You will not need to bring any money, or a script, or extra clothing, or a staff, for the worker is worth his accommodations. When you enter a town, find out who is interested and stay with them, blessing the home."

- MAT 10:16–20 ~ Jesus continued, "I am sending you as sheep among the wolves, so be wise like serpents and harmless as doves. Beware of men who would drag you before their councils, and scourge you in their synagogues. You will be brought before governors and kings for my sake, so give testimony to them and the Gentiles. When they deliver you up, do not worry about what to say for it will be given to you; it will not be you speaking but the Holy Ghost speaking through you."

Gracious Father, you have given us the gift of your Holy Spirit through Jesus Christ our Lord. Help us to share that free gift, openly and without reservation to anyone who shows curiosity in knowing the truth and the way to eternal life. Let us remind people that the kingdom of heaven is at hand and time is running out. Reveal the power of your Spirit through us as we speak, heal, and witness to others, not only to the lost sheep but also to everyday acquaintances, as well people in positions of leadership and government. Empower us to execute your plan and boldly spread your Word without fear of retaliation or retribution. Help us to endure hardship and suffering. Let us not fall into the hands of evil people who mean to do us harm, but help us to elude them whenever possible. Thank you for your Son Jesus Christ in whose name we confess, witness, and pray, Amen.

September 2

Labor Day became a federal holiday in 1894; it is observed on the first Monday in September. Labor Day was advanced by labor unions to elevate the American worker and the contributions that labor has made to our growth as a nation and in securing our way of life. It is a day to reflect on personal achievements, to plan for the future, and to thank God for the blessing of gainful employment. Hard working citizens deserve a breather, to enjoy a day off and celebrate the opportunities and possibilities available to those who eagerly and vigorously pursue their vision of the American Dream.

This country was built on hard work, and it will continue if we work hard all of our days. This doesn't mean one should never retire from their job, it means that God's work never ends. And this nation has stood tall because we were doing God's work in addition to our own. Do not let deluded pundits convince you that you will be taken care of, so you needn't bother developing a hard work ethic. Because it is that ethic which has prospered us. God will be our shield and protection if we continue on the right path; and that will require labor, and for some, heavy lifting. As far as those deluded pundits, who talk without stopping or taking pause, in order to dodge doing any work or answer any questions; they are lazy and expect you to support them because they think they are more important, which is why they think they should be calling the shots for you.

God is calling the shots, and He is sorely displeased with sloth: one of seven deadly sins in the Catholic church. Sloth opens the door to many more grievous sins: substance dependency; hate and resentment; conspiracy; sexual immorality; capital crimes in general; and sins that lead to death. And as far as the government, we the people are supposed to be calling the shots.

- PRO 6:6–9 ~ You who are lazy, consider the ant. The ant has no supervisor, guide, or ruler yet manages to provide plenty of food. How long will you sleep, lazy people; when are you going to wake up?

- PRO 10:4–5, 26 ~ Whoever slacks off will become poor, but the diligent will become rich. Whoever gathers during the summer is wise; whoever sleeps during the harvest is shameful. As vinegar is to the teeth and smoke to the eyes, so is a sloth to an employer.

- PRO 12:24 ~ The diligent person will be in charge, and the lazy ones will be slaves.

- PRO 13:4 ~ The lazy person desires many things and has nothing; but the soul of the diligent person will be fully satisfied.

- PRO 14:23 ~ In all of your labor there is profit; but idle talk trends only towards poverty.

- PRO 20:4 ~ The slothful person will not plow when it is cold and will end up begging during the harvest, and have nothing.

- PRO 21:25 ~ The desires of the slothful lead to death; for his hands refuse to work.

- PRO 24:30–32, 34 ~ I visited the field of the slothful man and the vineyard of the ignorant man and all I found were thorn bushes and broken fences. And I learned from the experience. People like that will receive poverty like hard labor, and neediness like an armed robber.

- PRO 26:13–16 ~ The lazy person will not work, giving stupid excuses like, "There could be a lion in the street." Just like a door on its hinges, the lazy person is attached to the bed, tossing and turning. The lazy person is too tired even to lift a spoon to eat. Lazy people can convince themselves better than seven people with a good excuse.

- 2 TH 3:10–12 ~ When we were with you, we gave you this rule: if a man does not work, he should not eat. We have heard that some of you are lazy. They are not busy, they are just busybodies. We urge these people, in the name of Christ, to settle down and to earn the bread that they eat.

- 1 TI 5:8 ~ If anyone does not provide for his relatives, especially his immediate family, he has denied the faith and is worse than an unbeliever.

God will bless your work if you do it His way; and you will prosper and so will those you work for whether business, family, or community. Those who work hard are happier and have higher self-esteem, especially when they trust in God to provide direction, thereby contributing to the greater good and the glory of God. Yes, work can be tiring, boring, or unpleasant; but the payoff far outweighs the fact that the job may be difficult, time consuming, and exhausting.

- PSA 90:17 ~ Let the beauty of the Lord our God be upon us and establish the work of our hands; yes Lord, establish the work of our hands.

- PRO 16:3 ~ Commit your acts to God and He will establish your thoughts.

- ECC 9:10–11 ~ Whatever your hand finds to do, do it with your might; for there is no work, device, knowledge, or wisdom in the grave where you are going. I returned, and realized that the race does not belong to the swift, nor the battle to the strong, nor sustenance to the wise, nor riches to the intelligent, nor favor to the skilled, but time and circumstance happen to everyone.

- PHP 2:14–15 ~ Conduct your business without arguing or complaining, so that you remain blameless and harmless, as sons of God; without rebuke in the midst of a crooked and perverse nation where you shine as lights in the world.

- PHP 4:13 ~ I can do all things through Christ who strengthens me.

Remember to take a day each week to rest, worship, and be refreshed. There is such a thing as working too much. Workaholics end up wasting time with unproductive work, if not counterproductive. When it's break time, take five; when it's quitting time, go home. Sometimes you may have to work overtime, but it won't kill you. Keep this in mind, the world has many deadlines, but God has the same deadlines for every human: death, and the second coming. Make sure you listen to the Holy Spirit and stay on a path illuminated by the love of Christ; and you'll qualify for a great job in heaven, working for God with the best benefits package ever, and lasting for eternity.

- PRO 11:18 ~ The wicked work deceitfully; but for those who sow righteousness there will be a sure reward.

- ECC 12:14 ~ God will judge every work, including works done in secret, whether good or evil.

- ISA 65:17–25 ~ I am creating new heavens and a new earth. The former will be remembered no more; it will not even come to mind. Be glad and rejoice forever in that which I the Lord create; I will create Jerusalem for rejoicing and her people will be a joy unto me. They will be heard for all of their days; while the sinners, though their days may be many, will be accursed. My people will build houses and inhabit them; they will plant vineyards and eat the fruit thereof. They will not build a house for another to inhabit, or plant a vineyard for another to consume. My people will enjoy the works of their hands, for their labor will not be in vain nor will it cause them trouble. For they represent the blessed seed of the Lord, as well as their offspring with them. Before they call, I will answer; and while they speak, I will hear. The wolf and the lamb will feed together, and the lion will eat straw like the ox; but dust will be the serpent's supper. The Lord says, "Nobody will harm or destroy those who abide on my holy mountain."

SEPTEMBER

- JOH 9:4 ~ Jesus declared, "While it is day, we will do the work of Him who sent me, for the night approaches when nobody can work."

- JOH 14:12 ~ Jesus promised, "Truly I tell you, those believing in me will do the works that I do; and greater works than these shall they do, when I have gone to be with my Father."

- 1 CO 3:13–14 ~ Everyone's work will be seen for what it is because the light will illuminate it; it will be revealed by the fire which tries every person's work as well as his or her dedication. If that which is built endures, the builder will be rewarded. If it burns down, the builder will suffer the loss but will be saved from the flames.

- PHP 1:6 ~ Be confident, for He who began a good work in you will prolong it until the day Christ returns.

- JAM 1:4 ~ Let patience have her perfect work, that you may be complete and want for nothing.

Labor is a good thing. Not only because it is a command of God, but it is His way. It's not like God, Jesus, and the Holy Spirit do not work very hard on our behalf. They are at work night and day, every day; for an eternity past, present, and future. And we will work too, doing things one cannot imagine; and God will bless all of our work done in the light. We have bosses on earth; most of them have earned that authority. They have bosses, and their bosses have bosses, but the one who is sovereign is God. We work for Him to receive an eternal inheritance; and He works fulltime for us, to provide our heritage which is already kept secure in paradise.

- HAB 1:5 ~ Take note, you heathen; regard and wonder marvelously, for I will work a work in your days which you will not believe, though you were told.

- JOH 4:33–34 ~ After His disciples implored Him to eat, Jesus informed them, "My nourishment is doing the will of Him that sent me, and to finish His work."

- JOH 5:15–17 ~ The Jews were annoyed by Jesus healing others on the Sabbath. Jesus answered them, "My Father has been at work all the while, and I work too."

- 1 TH 4:11–12 ~ Be studious and hold your tongue; mind your own business. Do the work of your hands as you have been commanded, so you can walk honestly towards those who are without, and that you may lack nothing.

Dear heavenly, omnipotent Father, let us never forget that you are the boss. Bless our labor that it will glorify you and contribute to the greater good. Help us to remember, we do it all for Christ, and it never will be boring, tiresome, or unhelpful when we remember your Holy Spirit is present to watch and guide. If things get tough, dangerous, or taxing, remind us that in our weakness we become strong, because your Spirit is pulling us through, reenergizing us along the way. Help us always to shine your light in the workplace by being honest, ethical, helpful, considerate, thoughtful, thorough, loyal, and conscientious, knowing that this will be noticed by you, Lord, as well as the people we work with and work for. We give you the glory for everything we have accomplished; help us remember to be humble, and give you the credit whenever someone praises our efforts. And let us not be hesitant to give credit to our family, friends, coworkers, neighbors, and students, with added encouragement included. In Jesus's name, whose work on the cross paid for everything, Amen.

September 3

Territories Added to the Union with Treaty of Paris on this day in 1783. The Revolutionary War was officially over and peace was negotiated with England. Leading the negotiations were Ben Franklin, John Adams, and John Jay. Our independence was declared and the northwest territories held by the British crown were ceded as were the original thirteen colonies. The Union doubled in size, with borders extended into present-day Ohio, Michigan, Indiana, Illinois, Wisconsin, and Minnesota. Trade was resumed and relations were normalized, until the British attacked us again, starting another war in 1812; they were dispatched relatively quickly under General Jackson. The next major purchase was sale of Florida by Spain in 1819. In 1823, President Monroe declared all territories in the western hemisphere off limits for European expansion. This philosophy became known as Manifest Destiny: it was our destiny to explore, tame, and occupy this land from sea to shining sea. US expansions continued over the decades following. In 1803 President Jefferson bought the Louisiana Purchase from France for fifteen million dollars, adding present-day Louisiana, Arkansas, Missouri, Iowa, Oklahoma, Nebraska, South and North Dakota, and most of Kansas, Colorado, Wyoming, and Montana. Texas won independence from Mexico in 1836 and accepted statehood in 1846. Conflict with Mexico was far from over, but after a brief war, the Treaty of Hidalgo with Mexico was negotiated in 1848, adding California, Nevada, Utah, parts of Arizona and New Mexico, and outstanding regions of Oklahoma, Kansas, Colorado, and Wyoming. Mexico also recognized the Rio Grande as the official border with Texas. In the Gadsden Purchase of 1854, southernmost parts of Arizona and New Mexico were added to make way for the railroad. Western expansion continued until the entire contiguous US border was drawn. An ingenious purchase from Russia was Alaska in 1867 for seven million. Hawaii, our fiftieth state, was annexed in 1900, gaining statehood in 1959.

Clearly, God had a hand in the establishment and growth of the new world. The reason God blessed the USA is because of our faith in Him, which is reflected in all of our founding documents. This is the same reason God blessed Israel. When Israel abandoned God, their land was decimated. Guess what will happen if the USA abandons God.

- LEV 20:24 ~ You will inherit their land for I will give it to you to possess it, a land flowing with milk and honey. I am the Lord your God, and I have separated you from other people.

- DEU 6:17–19 ~ Do not test God, and ensure that you continue to keep His commandments. Do what is good and right so everything may go well with you, and you will take the land that has been promised and drive away your enemies.

- 2 CH 7:19 ~ If you turn away from me, and forsake the statutes and commandments I set before you, and serve other gods and worship them, I will uproot Israel from the land I have given them, and I will reject this temple I consecrated for my name. Israel will be a byword and an object of ridicule among all nations.

- PSA 105:42–45 ~ God remembered His holy promise, and Abraham His servant. And God brought His people forth with joy, and His chosen with gladness, and gave them the lands of the heathen. And His chosen inherited the labor of those people, so that they might observe His statutes, and keep His laws. Praise be to the Lord!

- JER 18:8, 10 ~ God says, "If a nation who I have pronounced my wrath against will turn from their evil ways, I will relent of the wrath I was planning against them. If a nation turns to evil and does not obey me, I will relent of the good I was planning for them."

Father, remind us that you chose us because we chose you; keep us in your loving hands lest we stray. Please do not let the people of this nation forsake you. In Jesus's name, Amen.

September 4

National Wildlife Day occurs twice every year, on this day and on February 22. This day was proposed by animal behaviorist and author Coleen Paige in 2005. The objective of this observance is to protect one of our most valuable natural resources: wildlife, which covers every living creature that has breath, and moves by land, sea, and/or air. Particular attention is placed on endangered species. The second observance was added to double efforts spreading awareness and advocacy for wildlife. That day also honored animal behaviorist and television celebrity Steve Irwin whose birthday was 02/22/1962; it just so happens that Irwin died on today's date 09/04/2006 from a stingray attack. Thus, the two holidays represent his birth and his death. You can get involved in this celebration by contributing time and money to animal and habitat preservation, water and land conservation, animal abuse prevention, and/or law enforcement of illegal activities such as poaching, and hunting or fishing without a license. Learn about wildlife conservation, endangered species, and collaborative efforts to protect our wildlife.

God created hundreds of kinds of animals and each was made to be male or female, including humans. Note: angels can appear as humans or animals (EZE 1:5–14; EZE 10:1–22).

- GEN 1:21–30 ~ God made each animal after its own kind: beasts, cattle, creeping things, whales, fish, and fowl. And God blessed all the animals saying, "Be fruitful and multiply in accordance with each kind." God said, "Let us make man in our image, after our likeness; and let him have dominion over all the other creatures on the earth". And God made humans, male and female, in His own image. God blessed the man and woman and told them to be fruitful, multiply, and replenish the earth. God said, "I have given to humankind every seed-bearing plant on the face of the entire earth, and every tree that has fruit and seed in it. They will be yours for food. And I have given to you every plant, the beasts of the earth, the birds in the sky, and all creatures that move on the ground: everything that has breath and life."

- GEN 2:19–28 ~ From the ground the Lord God formed every beast of the field and every fowl of the air, and brought them before Adam to give them names; and whatever he called each living creature, that was its name. Adam gave names to all of the cattle, beasts of the field, and fowl of the air. But Adam had no mate to help him. So, God caused Adam to go into a deep sleep and took a rib from man to make woman. Adam said, "This woman is bone of my bones and flesh of my flesh; she will be called woman for she was taken out of man."

- GEN 6:19–20 ~ God instructed Noah to collect a male and female of each kind of animal and bird and bring them into the ark so that they could replenish the earth.

- PSA 8:6–7 ~ God placed humans to be ruler over His creations, and put everything on the earth below them, including animals, birds, and fish.

- JOE 1:19–20 ~ I will cry to the Lord, for fire has burned the pastures and the trees of the field. The animals cry, for the rivers are dried up and there is no grass in the wilderness.

Father God, creator of humankind and all other life forms on this planet, we are honored to be given such a high position in your creation. You have given us dominion over all other living creatures on our beautiful planet. Help us to be good stewards of every type of wildlife sharing the land, sea, and sky with us. Equip us to preserve that which must be preserved: human life, wildlife, the planet, the water and the air. Let there be justice for those who preserve our plentiful resources; likewise, let there be justice for those who destroy them. Thank you for your Holy Spirit who sanctifies, sustains, and preserves us. Let us be dutiful protectors of our wildlife. Thank you, Father, for your Son whose death give us life eternal, and your Holy Spirit who preserves us even now. In His name we pray, Amen.

September 5

International Day of Charity was proposed by Hungary in 2011 and adopted by the United Nations in 2012 making it an international observance. The purpose was to recognize charitable people, mobilize helping organizations, and promote giving worldwide for the underprivileged and impoverished. This day was chosen to honor the life of Mother Teresa who died on this day in 1997. She became a missionary in Ireland after learning English; then she moved to India and became a citizen and a Catholic nun. She started establishing orphanages, hospices, and homes for lepers. She developed quite a following in India, which branched into several organizations around the globe, providing assistance to the poor. For half a century her quest was to fight poverty, illness, crises, and unhealthy living conditions, until her death at age eighty-seven. She received the Nobel Peace Prize in 1979 for her humanitarian work, in addition to many other awards and honors over the years. Her name became synonymous with self-sacrifice.

In recognition of her lifetime of charity and giving, consider making a contribution to a fund or charity, volunteering your services at a charitable organization, or doing humanitarian work yourself. There will be charity and fundraising events in many cities and countries if you want to participate. Remember, by helping others you are ministering to Jesus Christ. Integral to the work of Mother Teresa was the influence of Christ in her life, whom she emulated in her service and love toward others, by helping the poor, sick, and needy. When we give of ourselves, we reflect Jesus; and that is what she did her entire life.

- DEU 16:17 ~ Everyone should give as they are able, in accordance with the blessings which God has given to them.

- 1 SA 15:22 ~ Samuel said to King Saul, "Does the Lord appreciate burnt offerings and sacrifices as much as He does obedience? To obey is better than to sacrifice, and to listen is more important than the flesh of rams.

- PRO 21:3 ~ To do what is fair and proper is more acceptable to God than sacrifice.

- HOS 6:6 ~ I desire mercy, not sacrifice, and acknowledgement more than burnt offerings.

- MIC 4:7 ~ I will make a remnant from the handicapped and a great nation from the outcasts. The Lord will rule over them in mount Zion henceforth, even forevermore.

- MAT 9:9–12; MAR 2:14–17; LUK 5:27–31 ~ Jesus called Matthew from his tax collecting booth saying, "Follow me." Matthew immediately got up and followed Jesus. They went to dine at Matthew's house where many publicans and sinners had assembled. The Pharisees asked Jesus's disciples why He associated with such people. Jesus heard what they were saying and replied, "Those who are well do not need a physician, but those who are sick do. You need to learn what this means: I desire mercy not sacrifice, for I came to call sinners to repentance not the righteous."

- MAR 12:33 ~ It is more important to love God and to love others, than to offer different kinds of sacrifices on the alter.

- LUK 14:16–23 ~ Jesus told the parable of the wedding of the king's son and how the invited guests had lousy excuses not to come. Then the master told the servants to gather the poor, handicapped, lame, and blind, and to search the highways and alleys inviting everyone to come to the wedding feast, "so that my house may be filled." Those who were on the original guest list were no longer welcome.

- ACT 20:35 ~ In your labors give to the needy, remembering the words of Jesus Christ, "It is more blessed to give than to receive."

SEPTEMBER

- ROM 12:1, 6–8 ~ Give yourselves to God. Let yourself be a living sacrifice; this is your reasonable service. After all He has done for you, is that too much to ask? Use those gifts God has given to you. If you have the gift of prophecy, exercise that gift according to the proportion of your faith. If your gift is ministry, then minister; if it is teaching, then teach; if it is encouraging, then encourage; if it is giving to the needy, then give generously; if it is leadership, then lead diligently; if it is showing mercy, then do so cheerfully.

- 2 CO 9:7 ~ Everyone should give whatever they think is fair in their heart. Giving should be done voluntarily, not out of necessity, for God loves a cheerful giver.

This is a rare phenomenon: when someone dedicates his or her entire life to helping other people less fortunate. It is hard work and long hours. It is not a way to make a living, because the people in need cannot pay. But God provides; He repays people for their dedication to others. Since those who serve others are serving God and reflect the love of Christ, they will prosper.

- MAT 25:40, 45 ~ Jesus said, "Whenever you have done something to help another person, you have done it to me; whenever you have not done something to help another person, you have not done it to me."

- LUK 9:3 ~ Jesus told them, "Take nothing for your journey, no staff, bag, bread or money."

- LUK 10:29–37 ~ A man was traveling from Jerusalem to Jericho when he was ambushed by thieves; they beat and robbed him, leaving him for dead. A priest came across him, and after seeing the poor man, passed him on the other side of the road. Likewise, a Levite saw the poor man and went around him. Finally, a certain Samaritan saw the man and took pity on him. He rendered first aid, set him on his beast, and took him to town. He placed the injured man at an inn, asking the innkeeper to take care of the man and he would pay the bill. Jesus then asked, "Which of these passersby was a neighbor to the man who was mugged?" The lawyer answered, "The man who was merciful." Jesus replied, "Go and do likewise."

- LUK 14:14 ~ If you help others who cannot repay you, you will be blessed, and you will be repaid at the resurrection of the just.

- 1 CO 3:13 ~ Everyone's work will be seen for what it is because the light will illuminate it; it will be revealed by the fire which tries every person's work as well as his or her dedication. If that which is built endures, the builder will be rewarded.

- 2 CO 5:15 ~ Since Jesus Christ died for all, we should dedicate our entire lives to Him who died and rose again.

- 2 PE 1:5–8 ~ In diligence, add virtue to your faith, knowledge to your virtue, temperance to your knowledge, patience to your temperance, godliness to your patience, kindness to your godliness, and charity to your kindness. If these things abound in you, you will never be barren or unfruitful in the knowledge of our Lord Jesus Christ.

Our Father in heaven, you love all people of the world. We who are well-off should share our time and treasure with those who are struggling. Help us to be servants and ministers even as Jesus served and ministered to the lowly and downtrodden. Let us be willing at all times to use our gifts and abilities as helpers, to the glory of your holy name. Do not allow us to turn a blind eye to someone who needs our assistance; do not let us invent excuses why we cannot lend a hand. Instead, may we be eager to make ourselves available to people when it is appropriate to do so. And as we minister to the needy, let our example be a witness of Christ, uplifting others spiritually with renewed faith and hope in you, so they will remember when they were in trouble and be ready and willing to help another in need. In the name of Jesus we pray, Amen.

September 6

Reconciliation Day is a new holiday celebrating our reconciliation with God our Father. God wants all people to be saved, and all they have to do is choose Christ as their Savior. Those who believe in and follow Christ will be reconciled with our Father in heaven on the last day, when Jesus comes to bring us home. Christians regard home as heaven, not earth, because our time here is short, especially when compared to eternity in God's heavenly realm. People who confess and repent of their sins, trusting in the atonement achieved by Christ on the cross, will be saved to receive an inheritance in the paradise of God as an adopted child. A great example of reconciliation is found in the parable of the prodigal son.

- LUK 15:11–32 ~ Jesus told the parable of the prodigal son, who asked his father for his share of the inheritance. The father gave the son his inheritance, and the son left for a foreign land where he squandered all his money on wine and women. Meanwhile, a great famine arose in that country. The son had to feed pigs to make a living. He thought, even his father's servants were better off than this, so he returned home to confess everything to his father, and apologize. His father saw him coming, ran out to meet the son, and embraced him. The son told his father that he was not worthy of being called a son and should be treated as a servant. But the father had his servants prepare a great feast to celebrate. The elder son learned of this and became angry, refusing to enter the house. The father consoled him saying, "You are always with me and all that is mine is yours. But it is fitting to celebrate, because your brother was lost, but now he is found; he was dead but now he is alive again."

God accepts us as we are, no matter what we have done, as long as we confess and repent. If you believe in God's Son your sins have been removed and your soul cleansed by His blood. We are forgiven if we believe we are forgiven, because of our faith in the sacrificial offering of the Lamb of God. True contrition and godly sorrow enable us to be restored in our relationship with God the Father. Our faithful response is repentance, worship, Bible study, prayer, and participation in the Holy Sacraments.

Reconciliation is like repairing a broken marriage and accepting the spouse despite their peculiarities. However, it is expected that one would make a serious effort to change certain behaviors that were destructive to the marriage, such as adultery or addiction. God forgives us if we sincerely repent, which means we try very hard to cease habitual sins that lead to death. If we ask to be forgiven and keep doing the same thing, then our intentions are not sincere and our confession is empty. Yes, we will keep messing up; but with faith, not nearly as often. The Holy Spirit is perfect in righteousness. He cannot dwell inside of us if we are unclean; but if our souls have been purified by the blood of Jesus, the Holy Spirit will come. Without Christ, our evil nature would not enable us to be reconciled with God who is holy.

- GEN 50:19–20 ~ Joseph told his elder brothers that what they had done to him was evil, but God used it for good in order to save them from the famine and to reunite their family.

- DAN 9:24 ~ The angel said it will take seventy weeks for the transgressions to end. Then reconciliation will occur, everlasting righteousness will come, and the Holy One will be anointed King.

- LUK 15:3–7 ~ Jesus told them a parable. Suppose a shepherd is charged with watching one hundred sheep and one gets lost. Does he not leave the ninety-nine and search until he finds the lost sheep, and return it to the flock? When he finds it, he rejoices with his friends. Jesus concluded, "I assure you that there will be more rejoicing in heaven for one lost sinner who repents, than for ninety-nine righteous people."

SEPTEMBER

- ROM 5:8–11 ~ God showed His great love for us, for although we were sinners, Christ died for us. Therefore, we are justified by the blood of Christ, saved from God's wrath through Him. We were reconciled to God by the death of His Son and we were saved by His life. We find great joy in God through our Lord Jesus Christ by whom we now have received the atonement.

- 2 CO 5:19–21 ~ God was in Christ, who reconciled the world to Himself. He has not imputed our sins upon us; instead, He has given us the message of reconciliation. So now we have become ambassadors for Christ, as though God was speaking His message through us, so that you too may be reconciled to God. For He made Christ, who knew no sin, to bear our sins so that we could receive the righteousness of God which was in Him.

- COL 1:19–22 ~ God was pleased to have His fullness living in Christ, so that through Christ, everything on earth and in heaven could be reconciled to Himself, by the peace that came through the shedding of Christ's blood on the cross. Before, you were separated from God; you were His enemies because of your sinful minds and evil deeds. But now, God has reconciled you by the body of Christ through His death, to be presented holy, blameless, and pure in the sight of God.

It comes down to how serious you are about your faith and the practice of your religion. Remember, faith without works is useless (JAM 2:14–17). So, if you think your faith is sufficient, examine your actions. If you are not sure whether you are saved, you probably aren't. If you have the Holy Spirit, you are saved and you know it. That does not mean we will never doubt, because we are feeble creatures who know we are doomed without Jesus. But if you sin, your conscience will either convict you or acquit you. If you feel guilty, ashamed, and sorrowful, you are in the right state of mind to confess and repent. Further, through contrition we become equipped with the power to forgive others as Christ has forgiven us.

- PSA 16:10–11 ~ For you will not leave my soul in hell; neither will you allow your Holy One to be corrupted. You will show me the path of life; and in your presence I will find fullness of joy. At your right hand are pleasures forevermore.

- JOH 20:21–23 ~ Jesus addressed them once again, "Peace be unto you. As my Father has sent me, now I am sending you." After saying this, He breathed on them, and announced, "Receive the Holy Ghost. Those who's sins you remit, they are remitted; and those who's sins you retain, they are retained."

- ACT 3:19 ~ Repent and be converted, so your sins can be blotted out; and times of refreshing will come to you from the Lord.

- ROM 2:14–15 ~ When the Gentiles, who were not given the law, do by nature the things required of the law, though they have not the law they are a law unto themselves. They exhibit the work of the law written upon their hearts, their conscience also bearing witness; because their thoughts either accuse them or excuse them for things they say and do.

We thank you, dearest Father, that you have given us the message of reconciliation in your Holy Word, that through the offering of your Son Jesus we might be made blameless in your sight, and accepted into your kingdom with the righteousness He imputed upon us. What a lovely and precious gift is life, and you have given us eternal life in heaven as adopted children, with an inheritance equal to that of your only begotten Son. Remind us of this every day, so that we will know the true meaning of life and our purpose on this earth, which is to glorify you and show others how they can receive an inheritance in the world to come, through faith in Jesus Christ and sanctification by the Holy Spirit. In the name of Jesus we pray, Amen.

September 7

International Day of Clean Air for Blue Skies is an observance established in 2019 by the UN to combat air pollution, reduce carbon emissions, slow global warming, and other initiatives. The UN has a global agenda to unite nations on these issues, but many nations do not adhere to the same regulations or preventive measures. For example, the US has reduced carbon emissions significantly, while in other nations emissions have increased, cancelling us out. In China, they still depend on coal for most of their heating and electricity; so, no matter what the US does, the overall climatic conditions will not improve because other nations cannot afford to or are unwilling to make sacrifices. One other point that deserves mentioning is the disagreement among experts on the science of climate change, and the assumed trend towards global warming which is negligible; many scientists say there is no discernable trend. Either way, the planet has gone through periods of sweltering heat as well as an ice age. Granted, air pollution is a problem; solving that problem will make the skies a lot bluer. I am personally in favor of improving the air quality and any technology that will improve it without causing unnecessary burdens on people.

Air conservation and water conservation have been around since the 1960s. So has pollution. A great deal has been done about this, especially in the USA. The amount of emission from a new car that runs on gasoline is minimal. Further, electric cars provide no answer; in fact, in the long run, electric batteries in cars will present a greater environmental hazard than cars running on fossil fuels. The mere mining of the materials used in electric car batteries emits enormous amounts of carbon into the air. Besides, the maximum distance for a battery before recharge is 250 miles; this is impractical in many US states. Then there are other sources of fuel that have almost zero emissions such as natural gas and nuclear. Of course, with nuclear there is still the matter of disposing of spent fuel cells. I do believe that clean air and blue skies are great, and will gladly celebrate air conservation today and every day. Sometimes, that means taking a drive out into the country if you live in the city. Note: nature has the knack for purifying itself.

The time is coming, maybe sooner maybe later, when the entire sky will be darkened and that will be very close to the end. Chances are, our air will last until then, but who knows? God may take us home before that episode occurs.

- GEN 1:28~ Noah saved a pair of each kind of beast that "breathed air" to replenish the earth.
- JOE 2:2–3, 10, 30–31 ~ The day of great darkness and gloom is coming. A fire devours everything in its path, leaving behind a wasteland. Nobody can escape. The earth will quake and the heavens will tremble. There will be wonders in the sky and on the earth: blood, smoke, and fire. The sun will become dark and the moon will be like blood.
- MAT 24:29 ~ Jesus said, "Immediately after the time of tribulation, the sun will become dark, the moon will be shrouded in gloom, and stars will fall from the sky."
- REV 6:12–15 ~ There was a great earthquake; the sun became black and the moon like blood. Stars fell from the sky. Everyone tried to hide, even the rich and mighty ones.
- REV 9:1–2 ~ The fifth angel blew a trumpet and I saw a star fall from heaven to the earth, and to him was given the key to the bottomless pit. And there arose smoke from the pit, and the sun and air were darkened. And from the smoke came locusts who were given power to sting like scorpions.

Father, help us to be conscious of things that cause air pollution, and to take appropriate measures to clean our skies. You breathed into us the breath of life, and as long as we keep breathing, we will be alive; let us dedicate every breath we take to you. Help us to leave a clean planet for the next generation and the next. In the name of Jesus, who is our life, Amen.

September 8

National Grandparents Day became an official holiday when President Carter signed it into law in 1978, establishing the first Sunday after Labor Day to be the day we celebrate grandparents. This holiday was suggested many times to different presidents; it makes one wonder why it took so long. It is unclear why Congress chose this particular date. Perhaps this holiday should have been scheduled during summer vacation to enable everyone to make plans to be with grandparents for this occasion.

Grandparents are among the most loved persons in the world. Time with our grandparents is usually quality time and valued time. I learned things from my grandparents that my parents never told me. I wish we could have lived closer together, but we wrote letters frequently (long distance phone calls were quite expensive back then). Spend time with your grandparents or grandchildren today if you can; do something special together. The more generations you can assemble the better. Family reunions are a great way to celebrate grandparents. Grandparents also love phone calls, greeting cards, handmade arts and crafts, and pampering their grandkids.

- DEU 4:9 ~ Do not forget what God has done for you. May His works have a lasting impression on your lives. Teach your children and grandchildren about His glorious miracles.

- PSA 71:9 ~ Do not forget me in my old age; do not forsake me when my strength is spent.

- PSA 73:26 ~ Though my flesh and my heart may fail, God will remain the strength in my heart, and my portion forever.

- PSA 103:17 ~ The mercy of the Lord is from everlasting to everlasting upon those who fear Him, and share His righteousness with their children and grandchildren.

- PSA 128:5–6 ~ The Lord will bless you out of Zion, and you will see the good in Jerusalem all of your days; you will see your grandchildren live in peace in Israel.

- PRO 17:6 ~ Children's children are a crown to the elderly, and parents are the pride of their children.

- PRO 13:22 ~ A good man leaves an inheritance to his grandchildren; but the wealth of the sinner is saved for the just.

- ISA 59:20–21 ~ God says the Redeemer will come to Zion, unto everyone who turns from sin in Israel. This is my covenant with you. My Spirit is upon you and my words will never depart from your mouth, or the mouth of your offspring, forever.

- ISA 46:4 ~ God said: Even in your old age with your gray hair, I am He who carries you. I created you, I sustain you, and I will deliver you.

- ROM 17:6 ~ Grandchildren are the pride of their grandparents and the glory of their parents.

Grandparents played important roles in the Bible. Imagine having as a grandparent Noah, Abraham, Joshua, Ruth, Esther, or Mary. They were people of great moral strength, patience, endurance, and godly faith. I was fortunate to have a few patriarchs and matriarchs who had these qualities (2 TI 1:5; 2 TI 3:14–15). I grew up in the faith and God has stayed with me all this time, even when I strayed. If you have elders in your family who have kept you in the faith, thank them on this day of celebration or remembrance.

- GEN 5:27–3 ~ Methuselah was Noah's grandfather. He lived the longest of any known person: 969 years. His son Lamech was Noah's father. Noah had three sons: Shem, Ham, and Japheth.

- GEN 48:9 ~ Joseph told his father, "Here are the sons that the Lord has given to me." Jacob replied, "Bring them here so I may bless them."
- RUT 4:13–15 ~ Boaz took Ruth to be his wife, and she conceived and bore a son. The women said to her mother-in-law Naomi, "Blessed be the Lord who has not left you without an heir, for the boy's name will be well known in Israel. He will restore your heritage and will nurture you in your old age. And your daughter-in-law who bore your grandson will be more valuable to you than seven sons."
- MAT 1:5 ~ The parents of Boaz were Salmon and Rahab. Boaz and Ruth had a son named Obed, who was the father of Jesse, who was the father of David the king. David had a son named Solomon with the former wife of Urias (e.g., Bathsheba). Solomon inherited the throne of David. [These were all ancestors of Joseph and Mary, the earthly parents of Jesus.]
- ACT 3:13 ~ The God of Abraham, Isaac, and Jacob, yes, the God of our fathers, has glorified His Son Jesus, the same man you denied before Pilate who was ready release Him.

Grandchildren are a blessing for grandparents; they should never be denied access. Some states have laws entitling grandparents certain rights regarding their grandchildren. The little ones need to know and interact with their grandparents for their wisdom will generally surpass that of the parents.

- DEU 1:13 ~ Take the wise men of understanding and notoriety, and make them rulers.
- JOB 12:12–13 ~ With age comes wisdom and understanding. With God is wisdom and strength, counsel and understanding.
- PRO 4:7–9 ~ Wisdom is the principal thing; therefore, seek wisdom, and with it receive understanding. Make this your priority, for with wisdom comes honor. And you will obtain a garland of grace, and a crown of glory.
- PRO 11:13 ~ A gossip betrays a confidence, but a wise person does not.
- PRO 15:1, 18 ~ A gentle answer repels anger but a harsh answer provokes it. An angry person creates conflict, but a calm person creates peace.
- PRO 15:32 ~ The fear of God is the instruction of wisdom; and before honor comes humility.
- PRO 16:23; PRO 19:11 ~ A wise person is patient, and to his or her credit, overlooks an offense. The mind of a wise person makes speech judicious, and adds learning to his or her words.
- PRO 22:17 ~ Incline your ear to hear the words of the wise and apply your mind to knowledge.
- JAM 3:13, 17 ~ Whoever is wise among you should show it with good conversation and meekness. Wisdom from heaven is pure, merciful, gentle, peaceful, and easily obtained. It always produces positive results that are impartial, straightforward, and sincere.

All of my elders have long passed, but the one I miss the most was my maternal grandfather. I could tell him anything, things I couldn't even tell my parents. He was a meek and mild man of God. I hope you have been lucky to have a person like that in your life. He emulated Jesus. This should be the goal of all grandparents.

Father, thank you for grandparents who lead their families towards you. Thank you for our elders who have guided us in the true faith. Help us to become wiser as we age and not onerous. Help us to listen and to pass on the wisdom of your Word, through Jesus Christ, Amen.

September 9

First Settlement in St. Augustine FL was established on 09/08/1565. Florida was explored and claimed for Spain by Ponce de Leon in 1513; he became governor of Puerto Rico, but his whimsical search for the "fountain of youth" would lead to his demise. Meanwhile, the French had established bases near present day Jacksonville and in South Carolina. Spanish conquistador Menendez took refuge in the St. Augustine area in 1565 to engage the French, but he discovered the French fleet was far superior to his and retreated. As luck or providence would have it, a tropical storm blew the French fleet out to sea where they disappeared; otherwise, Florida surely would have fallen to the French. Menendez named the settlement St. Augustine because the day of his arrival coincided with the feast of St. Augustine (San Agustin), patron saint of his hometown Avilez. To solidify their claim, Menendez attacked and routed the French stronghold at Ft. Caroline. St. Augustine became a major Spanish port and stronghold. The city was attacked many times by the British, most notably by Sir Francis Drake who burned the city in attempt to extend their empire. The settlement was rebuilt in 1672 to include erecting the Castillo de San Marcos, a Spanish fortification that stands to this day and is the oldest fortress in America. Additional attempts by the British to take the fort were unsuccessful. In 1763 a long, dragged-out war between the Spanish and the British was settled, wherein Spain relinquished Florida and St. Augustine in exchange for Havana and Cuba. St. Augustine has the distinct honor of being the oldest city in the continental United States.

The Spanish conquerors had mixed objectives: they wanted to find land and gold, and they wanted to convert indigenous peoples to Catholicism. They were equipped with state-of-the-art weaponry and armor. Apparently, the former goal took precedent, because they were savage warriors more than missionaries. They treated the natives atrociously and often wiped them out along with their villages. Notable conquistadors included Cortez who explored Mexico and eradicated the Aztecs; Almagro explored Mexico and destroyed the Mayans; Pizarro went to Peru and crushed the Incas; Balboa made it to the Pacific Ocean and conquered natives in California; Coronado explored the southwest discovering the Grand Canyon, while murdering natives along the way. Some of the conquerors were accused of war crimes and failed to return to Spain; others died in battle or from disease. The ones who returned were very rich men, largely due to the gold they confiscated from American Indians.

It would appear that many who survived the Spanish conquest of the Americas adopted Catholicism, while also incorporating some of their own theology such as Santeria, Voodoo, Spiritism, and the religions of the ancients (Aztec, Mayan, Incan). Unfortunately, the incompatibilities made for an unorthodox system of beliefs that were not exactly Biblical. Here is evidence that trying to proselytize people by force is ineffective. The Bible says to use humility and respect when sharing the faith (1 PE 3:15). It is counterproductive attempting to share the Gospel if gathering riches is your priority. It's easy to see how the conquistadors were given and acceded to conflicting directives, seeing how spirituality and materialism don't mix.

- PSA 49:6–8, 15 ~ Those who trust in their wealth and brag about their riches will never be able to redeem the life of another nor provide a ransom for them. For the redemption of their soul is precious; no worldly payment will ever be enough. But God will redeem my soul from the power of the grave.

- EZE 22:12–13 ~ You have taken bribes to shed blood, engaged in usury and extortion, and pursued ill-gotten gain; you have forsaken the Lord your God. I will smite these people with my hand for the dishonest gain they have collected and for the blood they have shed.

- MAT 6:19–20 ~ Jesus said, "Do not accumulate a lot of earthy treasures that can be corrupted by insects or rust or that can be stolen by thieves. Instead, accumulate heavenly treasures that cannot be corrupted or stolen. For where your treasure is, there your heart will be."

- MAT 6:24 ~ Nobody can serve two masters, for they will end up loving one and despising the other. You cannot serve God and money at the same time.

- MAT 23:1–3 ~ Jesus said, "The scribes and Pharisees tell you to do this and observe that; it is all right to obey them but do not imitate them, for they do not practice what they preach.

- ACT 8:17–20 ~ The apostles laid their hands on the converts, and they received the Holy Spirit. And when Simon the sorcerer saw how through the laying of hands the Holy Spirit was bestowed, he offered money saying, "Give me this power, so I can lay hands on others and bestow the Spirit." Peter admonished him, "Your money will perish with you because you think the gift of God can be purchased."

- 1 CO 9:25–27 ~ Whoever strives to master a task must discipline themselves. For example, athletes strive for an earthly, corruptible crown, but I pursue an incorruptible, heavenly crown. I run my race and fight my battles with confidence. I discipline my body; I practice what I preach so that I will not be found to be a hypocrite.

- 1 TI 6:10 ~ The love of money is the root of all evil; through the craving for worldly riches many have wandered away from the faith and pierced their hearts.

- 2 TI 2:24–26 ~ A servant of the Lord does not waste time arguing, but is gentle to everyone, able to teach, and not resentful. Such disciples gently instruct those who are in opposition to them, hoping that God will grant repentance for acknowledging His truth, so that they may escape the devil's traps who would otherwise capture them for his own purpose.

- 2 TI 4:5 ~ Always be watchful and willing to endure afflictions, doing the work of the evangelist, doing what is necessary for the ministry.

- 1 PE 4:10–11 ~ Whoever has received the gift of salvation in Christ should share that gift with others, as a steward of God's eternal grace. If you preach, do so as a messenger of God. If you minister, do so with the ability God gives you. Do this to glorify God through His Son Jesus Christ.

- 1 PE 5:1– ~ I urge the elders among you, which I am also an elder and a witness to the sufferings of Christ, and a partaker of the glory that will be revealed in Him, that you feed God's flock which is among you; be overseers of the kingdom. Do this, not out of obligation but willingly; do this not for ill-gotten gain but with a clear conscience. Do not act like lords over God's heritage but set an example to the flock. When the chief Shepherd appears, you will receive a crown of glory that never fades. Therefore, humble yourselves under the mighty hand of God, so you may be exalted in due time; casting all of your cares upon Him who cares for you.

Beloved Father, Son, and Holy Spirit, we humbly ask you to help us keep our priorities in order with you being first, our neighbors next, and ourselves last. We know that serving others serves you, but not so much serving ourselves. Let our service be without conflict or distractions, especially from worldly riches, for our treasures reside with you in your kingdom. Let us always cling to your promise to provide everything we need, and not worry about our lives, but to seek you first and your righteousness. Your gifts of salvation, freedom, and eternal life are free, so help us to share these gifts freely, without expecting anything in return. Because we know that our reward will come in the next life. In your name we pray, Amen.

September 10

World Suicide Prevention Day began in 2003 when the International Association for Suicide Prevention (IASP) and the World Health Organization (WHO) joined together to promote an observance that addresses the tragedy, trauma, and stigma of suicide. The objectives were to conduct research, educate professionals and families, raise awareness, create outreach facilities, identify preventative measures, provide mental health resources and interventions, and bring down the suicide rate globally. There are conferences every year to address these concerns, examine progress, and establish policies and programs.

The most common denominator in suicide attempts is major depression, characterized by extreme despair. This can be a byproduct of loneliness, isolation, helplessness, losing a loved one through death or divorce, nagging shame and guilt, dramatic loss of physical functioning, and feelings of worthlessness. Suicidal ideation is a state of mind; such emotional states usually come and go, but they can become pervasive. Keeping the person engaged often helps them process the self-destructive thoughts. Certain medications also help to quell these reactions, by balancing the chemistry in the brain. An immediate intervention that can reduce the prevailing symptoms is introducing spiritual countermeasures. For example, if the person is lonely, they need companionship (especially the Holy Spirit). If they feel hopeless, they need hope; if they are isolating, they need to get out more; if they feel worthless, they need uplifting. If they need professional help, call 9-1-1. Mental illness is common among people who attempt to take their own lives. Any concerned party can request an emergency detention for a suicidal person in a facility where they will be safe and will receive an examination by a psychiatrist within twenty-four hours.

- PSA 130:5 ~ I wait for the Lord, my soul waits; and in his Word I have hope.

- 1 PE 1:2–5 ~ Christians are chosen by God in advance through sanctification of the Spirit, to be obedient to Christ and cleansed by His blood. Blessed be God the Father of our Lord Jesus Christ. According to His abundant mercy, He recreated in us the living hope, brought by the resurrection of Christ from the dead, to receive an incorruptible and undefiled inheritance reserved in heaven and lasting forever. Through faith, He has shielded us by His power until the coming of our salvation which is ready to be revealed on the last day.

Oftentimes, people who consider taking their own lives have committed a terrible sin and cannot forgive themselves; they think there is no hope for them. But with God there always is hope; without God there is no hope. Below are five suicides recorded in the Bible. Note that all of these men were evil, having committed such sins as betrayal, murder, and sorcery. And they took the cowardly way out rather than turning to God or Christ in godly sorrow and contrition.

- 1 SA 31:1–6; 1 CH 10:13 ~ King Saul was wounded in battle and ordered his armor bearer to run him through, but he could not. So, Saul fell on his own sword to avoid the shame of being killed or captured by the Philistines. When he saw the king fall on his sword, the armor bearer killed himself too. Saul died for sins committed against the Lord, for not keeping God's commandments, and for seeking counsel from a witch possessed by an evil spirit.

- 2 SA 16—17 ~ When King David's son Absalom rebelled, he took his father's advisor Ahithophel with him. But his counsel was ignored, so Ahithophel settled his affairs and hanged himself.

- 1 KI 16 ~ Zimri tried to seize the throne by murdering the king of Tirzah and most of his family. Omri, the commander of the army was encamped nearby. He was immediately declared king and he came after Zimri, who burned down the palace, with himself in it.

- MAT 26:20–25; MAT 27:1–10 ~ Jesus told the disciples that one of them would betray Him and they were very worried. He said it would have been better for that man had he never been born. When Judas asked if it was him, Jesus affirmed it... After selling out the Lord, Judas Iscariot realized he had betrayed an innocent man, and returned the blood money to the elders of the temple. Instead of repenting or seeking Jesus, he went away and hanged himself. If he had truly known Jesus, he would have known there was forgiveness with Jesus, but he chose to take his own life rather than bear his shame.

Some religions believe that persons who die by their own hand are not saved. What does the Bible say? The Bible says there is only one unpardonable sin, and suicide isn't it; suicide violates the sixth commandment, however: murder (EXO 20:13; NUM 35:16–31). Blasphemy against the Holy Spirit is the only unpardonable sin, which is rejecting God and His salvation. Some people want to be their own gods and make their own decisions; they are people who do not want or need God. They prefer to choose their destiny and how they will die. Ultimately, they choose separation from God and that is what they will get for the rest of eternity.

What happens if suicide victims were believers who were not right in their minds? If they had a heart for Jesus, do you think God would condemn them to hell? Not if they had chosen Christ before they experienced their breakdown. Keep reminding suicidal people about faith, hope, and salvation; have a conversation about Christ and they might reconsider. Keeping them engaged is crucial. This is why suicide hot lines are effective; the phone operators are gifted at connecting with suicidal people and delaying their action. Again, time is the best remedy because emotional states of mind often fade. Talking about loved ones who will mourn them also helps.

- ECC 7:20 ~ Surely there is not a righteous man on earth who does good and never sins.
- MAT 12:31–32 ~ Jesus said, "All manner of sin and blasphemy will be forgiven, except blasphemy against the Holy Spirit. Whoever speaks against the Holy Spirit will not be forgiven, neither in this world nor in the world to come."
- ROM 5:19 ~ For by one man's disobedience (Adam) many were made sinners, and by one man's obedience (Jesus) many will be made righteous.
- ROM 6:23 ~ The wages of sin is death; but the free gift of God is eternal life through Christ the Lord.
- EPH 1:5, 11, 13–14, 18 ~ We were predestined to become adopted children of God by Jesus Christ, according to His marvelous will. In Christ we obtain an inheritance in heaven, because we listen to the truth and trust in Him for our redemption and salvation. I hope your eyes will be opened and you will become enlightened, and you will feel the hope of His promise, and experience the glory of the inheritance of the saints.

Most suicide victims give warning signs: they appear withdrawn, they seem infatuated with death, they verbalize things like "I wish I was dead" or "You would be better off if I was not around." They generally have low self-esteem and/or they plainly hate themselves. Sometimes they will destroy prized possessions or memorabilia; they will quit their jobs, school, or enjoyable activities; they will withdraw from friends and family; they will not sleep, eat, or take care of their hygiene. Abrupt changes in behavior or personality indicate something is wrong. Loved ones should be aware of these signs and take suicidal threats seriously.

Father of life, be with those who are in despair, feel worthless, and wish that their life would end. Help those who need help to seek it and help those who seek help to find you. Let us be alert and aware of suicidal warning signs so we can notify authorities and keep the individual engaged in conversation about the gift of eternal life through Jesus Christ, Amen.

September 11

National Day of Service and Remembrance, also called Patriot Day, is a solemn day of reflection and prayer as we bring to mind the suicide bombings of the World Trade Center twin towers in New York and the Pentagon near Arlington VA on 09/11/2001. Four planes were hijacked that day; three hit targets, but a fourth plane destined for DC went down in a Pennsylvania field when the passengers fought the hijackers. President George Bush, who was in office at the time, proclaimed a national observance to be held annually on this day.

Today we pause to remember those who lost their lives, and the brave first responders who saved lives, many of whom perished in the process. Almost three thousand citizens and visitors to our country died that day from a cowardly act of terrorism. Flags will be flown today at half-staff, and a nationwide moment of silence will occur about ten minutes till nine, eastern time. The entire week preceding 9/11 is considered a period of mourning.

Terrorists generally pick soft targets where they are unlikely to be challenged with force. They do not handle fear well, and do not like it when people fight back. But fighting back is the only way to gain an edge, using the element of surprise and a diversion if possible. Terrorists will experience terror themselves, worse than they can ever imagine. Maybe they think they are heroes if they die for jihad, but it is not a holy war, they will die in vain, and they will inherit the lake of fire. When they discover Christians who are not afraid, they will fail in their evil mission in an attempt to instill their personal fears upon us.

- ISA 28:15, 18–19 ~ You brag about entering into a covenant with death and making an agreement with the grave. Do you think you will escape the overwhelming scourge by making a lie your refuge and a falsehood your hiding place? Your covenant with death and your agreement with hell will be null and void. You will be beaten down by the scourge. Then you will understand this message and it will bring sheer terror to you.

- ISA 59:3–7 ~ Your hands are defiled with blood and sin. Your lips have spoken lies and wickedness. They conceive evil and rely on foolishness and lies. They run to evil and hasten to shed innocent blood. Desolation and destruction ride their highways.

- EZE 26:20–21 ~ God says, "You will go down into the pit, into the lowest parts of the earth, in old and desolate places, but I will set glory in the land of the living. And I will make you a terror, and then you will be no more; you will be sought but never found again."

- EZE 32:25–29 ~ They have set the harlot in the middle of those who were slain; her graves surround those who were uncircumcised, slain by the sword. Though their terror was caused in the land of the living, they have taken their shame with them who go down into the pit. The fallen of the untrue have gone to hell with their weapons of war. They were the terror of the mighty in the land of the living, but now they join with those who go down into the pit.

- MAT 25:30, 41 ~ Jesus said, "God will cast the worthless people into outer darkness where there is weeping and gnashing of teeth. They will depart into the eternal fire prepared for the devil and his angels."

- 2 TH 1:8–9 ~ God will inflict vengeance upon those who do not know Him and who do not obey the Gospel of Jesus Christ. They will suffer the punishment of eternal destruction and exclusion from the glory of the Lord.

Terrorism is a fear-based tactic. Like demons who follow Satan, terrorists depend mostly on the powers of fear and deceit. If they are doing it for their religion, then they are basically satanists. They do not fear God as they should; therefore, they are the ones who have much to fear.

They want others to be fearful too, just like devils want company in promoting the demise of humankind. Demons shivered at the sight of Christ. In like manner, terrorists fear being terrified, which is why they do not fight fair, picking innocent people as targets or shields. It is the ultimate exhibition of cowardice, because terrorists cannot appear brave in the face of fear. Fear is of the flesh, not the spirit. Terrorists have lived with it all of their lives. Fortunately, some are leaving that philosophy and finding Christ when they realize terror is a losing proposition. They find answers in love, and they witness the love in Christ, and they know it is the love of God.

- DEU 10:12 ~ God wants people to fear Him, walk in His ways, love Him, and serve Him with all their heart and soul.

- JOS 24:14 ~ Fear the Lord and serve Him in sincerity and truth. Put away false gods.

- 1 CH 16:25 ~ Great is the Lord; He is greatly to be praised. He is to be feared above all gods.

- JOB 4:6; JOB 13:11; JOB 28:28 ~ Is the fear of God not your confidence, hope, and righteousness? Does His excellency not make you afraid? The fear of the Lord is wisdom and to depart from evil is understanding.

- PSA 33:8, 18; PSA 119:120 ~ Let all the earth fear the Lord; let inhabitants stand in awe of Him. The eye of the Lord is upon those who fear Him and hope in His mercy. My flesh trembles with fear at the Lord for I am afraid of His judgments.

- PRO 1:7, 33; PRO 10:27 ~ The fear of God is the beginning of knowledge; but fools despise knowledge and wisdom. Those seeking the Lord will be safe and sound from the fear of evil. The fear of the Lord will prolong your days; but the years of the wicked will be shortened.

- ISA 8:12–13 ~ Do not join any conspiracies or alliances with people who are afraid; do not fear the things they fear. Do not be afraid at all. Sanctify the Lord of hosts, and let Him be your fear.

- JOE 2:1, 15 ~ Blow the trumpet and sound the alarm; let everyone tremble, for the day of the Lord is at hand.

- LUK 8:26–33 ~ Jesus confronted evil spirits inhabiting a possessed man. Jesus asked the name of the demons, who answered, "Legion, for we are many." Jesus cast the demons into a herd of swine; the entire herd ran over a steep cliff and drowned in the sea below.

- JAM 2:19 ~ If you believe in one God you are smart. Even the demons believe, and tremble.

- 1 JO 3:8 ~ Whoever commits sin is of the devil, who sinned from the very beginning. The Son of God was manifested to destroy the works of the devil.

- 1 JO 4:18 ~ There is no fear in love, but perfect love casts out fear, because fear has torment. Those who fear are not made perfect in love.

Notice how godly fear is the path to freedom. The fear of evil is the path to destruction. God is love, which defeats fear; and we are on the side of love because we are His. There is nothing the evil ones can do to us that can change who we are. They hate that; and they hate us because we love Christ. When demons see that power in us, they are afraid and flee (JAM 4:7).

Heavenly Father, let us never fear anything of the flesh or from the natural world, for you are greater in majesty, your mercy is overpowering, and your love is constant. Let your love rain upon us continually, and help us absorb it deep into our roots, growing stronger in our love daily. Empower us to employ our love in defeating evil, both human and demon, without fear but with fire in our eyes. For love casts out fear since it is far greater in power. In Jesus's name, Amen.

September 12

National Day of Encouragement was the brainchild of the National Encouragement Project at Harding University in Searcy AR. The mayor of Searcy got behind the idea, followed by the governor of Arkansas. President Bush became involved and officially proclaimed it a national holiday in 2007. The purpose was to follow up yesterday's somber lament with a day of heartening encouragement. These two observances provide a contrast which illustrates that feeling down or disheartened is a reversible condition. As I have pointed out repeatedly, the best way to overcome a negative emotion or state of mind is to choose the opposite. A positive emotion that lifts us up will be incompatible with the negative feeling that brings us down; and the former can overcome the latter because it is greater in power and truth. A positive spiritual force can defeat the destructive forces of evil. When people speak of their higher power it is a reference to a spiritual feeling or force, which not only neutralizes the negativity, but reverses it, resulting in a positive feeling such as hope, joy, or fulfillment.

Encouragement is something we all need, some more than others; it should be given often. For example, whenever an achievement at the office occurs it should be recognized publicly; whenever a child is struggling a parent should be there reassuring him or her; whenever a student wins a merit scholarship it should be announced; whenever a person is ill, aging, or suffering they need comforting; whenever someone lends a hand or helps with contributions or time, they should be thanked and appreciated. Recognition, reassurance, comfort, appreciation, and thankfulness, all are forms of encouragement. Anything that is uplifting will have a positive effect, including all the spiritual fruits mentioned in the Holy Bible and the previous lesson.

- PRO 11:30 ~ The fruit of righteousness is a tree of life, and those who win souls for God are wise.

- ISA 1:18–19 ~ Come now, and let us reason together, says the Lord. Though your sins be as scarlet they will be white as snow; though they be red like crimson, they will be as wool. If you are willing and obedient, you will eat the good of the land.

- ISA 4:2 ~ Isaiah spoke of a Branch from the Lord (Christ), beautiful and glorious, bearing excellent fruit of the Spirit.

- JOH 15:1–10, 16 ~ Jesus said, "I am the true vine, and my Father is the cultivator. He removes any of my branches that do not bear fruit. Those that do bear fruit, he prunes, so that they can bear even more fruit. You have been made clean through the Word which I have spoken to you. Stay in me and I will stay in you; without me, you can do nothing. The branch cannot bear fruit by itself; it must be connected to the vine. You cannot bear fruit unless you remain in me. I am the vine and you are the branches. Those abiding in me will bear much fruit but without me you can do nothing. If you do not abide in me, you will be removed like a dead and withered branch that is burned in the fire. If you live in me, and my words live in you, you can ask for anything and it will be done. This brings glory to my Father: that you bear much fruit and that you follow me. As the Father has loved me so I have loved you. Continue in my love. If you keep my commandments you will remain in my love, even as I have kept my Father's commandments and remain in His love. You did not choose me I chose you and ordained you, so you could go out into the world and bring forth fruit, that your fruit should continue, and that whatever you ask of the Father in my name, He may give it to you."

- ROM 12:6–8 ~ Use those gifts God has given you. If you have the gift of prophecy, exercise that gift according to the proportion of your faith. If your gift is ministry, then minister; if it is teaching, then teach; if it is encouraging, then encourage; if it is giving to the needy, then give generously; if it is leadership, then lead diligently; if it is showing mercy, then do so cheerfully.

- GAL 5:22–23 ~ The fruits of the Spirit include love, joy, peace, patience, gentleness, goodness, faith, kindness, and self-control. There is no law against these things.

- EPH 5:9 ~ The fruits of the Spirit originate in goodness, righteousness, and truth.

Encouragement is in short supply. It is discouraging when people who deserve praise and recognition do not receive it, while people who do not deserve it are the ones receiving it. All too often, bosses, managers, or directors take credit for the hard work of their subordinates; they are the ones getting bonuses, raises, and awards. But the productivity of any business or office comes from the worker bees; and if you want your business to thrive, give them encouragement, praise, and recognition and you will see a rise in your bottom line. By the way, such encouragement also should come with incentives, such as a gift card, or some other monetary reward. Give people a reason to work hard and to love their jobs, rather than making them feel as if going to work is an unpleasant chore, I had jobs that provided incentives and jobs that didn't: which of them do you think I preferred, or possibly enjoyed?

- JOB 4:8 ~ I have observed that those who plow iniquity and sow wickedness reap the same.

- PRO 13:11 ~ Wealth obtained by pride will diminish; but those who achieve through hard work will see their wealth increase.

- ECC 5:12 ~ The sleep of the hard worker is sweet; but the abundance of the rich prevents them from sleeping.

- 1 CO 12:4–7 ~ There are a variety of spiritual gifts, but only one Spirit. There are different ways of administering but only one Lord. There are different operations, but the same God who works through them. The Spirit is manifested in some way in everyone to use productively.

- 1 TH 5:11–15 ~ Continue to encourage one another and edify each other just as you are doing. We ask you brothers to know those who labor among you and are over you in the Lord to admonish you, to esteem them very highly in love for their work's sake, and be at peace among yourselves. We encourage you to warn those who are unruly, comfort the feeble minded, support the weak, and be patient towards everyone. Make sure that nobody renders evil for evil unto any person, but always follow that which is good among yourselves and with others.

- 2 TI 4:2 ~ Preach the Word; always be prepared to correct, rebuke, and encourage with patience and sound doctrine.

- JAM 3:17–18 ~ The wisdom from above is pure, peace-loving, gentle, accommodating, merciful, productive, impartial, and sincere. When the fruit of righteousness is sown in peace, it generates a harvest of peace and righteousness.

- REV 14:13 ~ I heard a voice in heaven saying, "Blessed are those who die in the Lord; they will find rest from their hard work, for their actions precede them."

Our Father, if not for your encouragement we would get nowhere in life. You give us freedom to choose our own way, knowing your way is the only way, and every other way the wrong way. Remind us which path we are on, showing us the fork to take. May we be sure we are choosing appropriate, worthwhile, and positive causes and paths. May we encourage others who cannot find their way, or have lost their bearings. Your Word is a lamp to our feet and a light to our paths; let us shine for others so they can see that pathway illuminated by your Son, a road continuing forever. Thanks Jesus, for showing us the way, the truth, the life. Help everyone connect to your spiritual vine, by which a Christian bears fruit worthy of repentance; becoming trees of life that never die, and produce beautiful fruit continuously. In Jesus's name, Amen.

September 13

International Chocolate Day was introduced by the US National Confectioners Association to commemorate the birth of Milton Hershey (09/13/1857); his is the most famous name in chocolate in the USA ever since introducing Hershey bars in 1900. Chocolate comes from cocoa beans (categorized as a fruit), which were discovered by Spanish conquistadors exploring Mexico in the sixteenth century. The Aztecs used the beans as currency: cocoa was a delicacy, and producing it was a tedious and time-consuming process. Chocolate had spread from Spain throughout Europe and the US by the end of the seventeenth century, especially after the Dutch developed a means of extracting cocoa powder more efficiently. This made cocoa easier and cheaper to produce, and before long the world began to love its byproducts. This day is not to be confused with World Chocolate Day on July 7 which is mostly observed in Europe, or the myriad of chocolate days celebrated in other countries around the world.

Dark chocolate is an antioxidant and it also releases endorphins; thus, it has positive health benefits that are not afforded with milk chocolate or chocolate fudge. Nevertheless, too much chocolate can be bad for you; it is advisable to refrain from overindulging in it. Actually, overdoing it with any substance is bad for you and can become addicting. But the sugar added to most chocolate products is very unhealthy in large quantity.

- GEN 1:29 ~ God said, "I have given to humankind every seed-bearing plant on the face of the entire earth, and every tree that has fruit and seed in it."
- PRO 16:24 ~ Pleasant words are sweet to the soul and health to the body.
- PRO 24:14 ~ Wisdom is sweet to the soul, and if you find it you will have hope, and that hope will not be removed.
- 1 CO 6:12; 1 CO 10:23 ~ Something that is permissible is not necessarily beneficial or constructive. It is all right to enjoy something but I will not let it control me.
- PHP 3:17–19 ~ Follow Christ with me and do not stray from the path of righteousness like others who have left the faith; this causes me great despair. Their end is destruction for their god is their stomach; their glory is their shame, for their minds focus only on earthly things.
- PHP 4:5 ~ Let your moderation be an example to others.

The Bible teaches us to practice moderation. Everything on earth was given to us by God to use, as long as we do not overindulge. The sin of gluttony is considered a deadly sin because it focuses the individual's attention on worldly pleasures or indulgences above spiritual ones. You cannot love worldly things and love God, for one will eventually dominate. Enjoy chocolate today with friends or family, remembering that too much will give you a bellyache, or worse.

- PRO 23:21 ~ The drunkard and the glutton will come to poverty.
- LUK 16:13 ~ Jesus said, "You cannot serve God and mammon."
- ROM 13:13–14 ~ Be honest, as in the daylight; do not engage in rioting, drunkenness, overindulgence, promiscuity, fighting, and jealousy. Build your life around Jesus Christ, do not indulge in the lusts of the flesh.

Dear heavenly Father, let us not allow pleasures of the flesh to dominate our thoughts; help us to keep you in our thoughts through your Holy Spirit who is always there to guide us. Enable us to hear His words directly in our minds so we will have the wherewithal to say no when it is in our best interest. May we enjoy in moderation earthly pleasures you have provided, and never overdo it. We ask this in the name of Jesus whose example we follow, Amen.

September 14

Handel's Masterpiece *Messiah* Was Completed, a musical score that told the story of Jesus Christ based on the King James Version of the Holy Bible. It is largely an operatic composition complete with chorale accompaniment. Handel worked tirelessly on this piece for almost a month, driven by the inspiration of the Holy Spirit. Like most of Handel's musical works, there is a Christian focus, because he was a man of great faith and used his talents to glorify God. It has been a mainstay for Christmas, especially the finale called the *Hallelujah Chorus*. Born in Germany, Handel spent his formidable years in England; he debuted *Messiah* in Dublin in 1742.

Most of the classical composers of the Baroque period and following were devout Christians. Bach (Lutheran), Haydn (Catholic), and Mozart (Catholic) integrated spirituality and Christianity into their compositions. Composers who publicly affirmed their faith in God also included Liszt, Brahms, Mendelsohn, Wagner and others. Thus, music was a major component of worship in those days, as it always has been from Old Testament days until now. In fact, even before the creation of man it is commonly asserted that Lucifer led the singing of hymns in heaven before the revolt that expelled fallen angels to earth; we refer to them as demons, devils, and foul spirits, who have lost their standing to be called angels.

David was the quintessential musician; he played the harp (e.g., lyre) and sang songs. He also composed music; in fact, many of the Psalms are songs of praise that he wrote and arranged. While king, he incorporated music as an integral element of worship, to include singing accompanied by string, wind, and percussion instruments. A parade of singers, musicians, and dancers would follow with other members of the congregation on their way to the synagogue.

- 1 SA 16:14–23 ~ The Spirit of the Lord departed from King Saul, and an evil spirit came to trouble him. The servants told Saul, behold an evil spirit is troubling you. Let us find someone who is skilled at playing the harp, and maybe the music will help calm you; Saul agreed. They told him about a man from Bethlehem, the son of Jesse who could play the harp, was valiant in battle, prudent in thought, nice looking, and the Lord was with him. So, the servants went to Jesse and asked for his son David who was tending sheep. Jesse took his donkey and loaded him up with bread, wine, and a young goat and sent David to the king. Saul immediately liked David and made him his armor bearer. Saul replied to Jesse asking that David stay because he was highly favored by the king. It just so happens that when David played the harp, Saul was refreshed, and the evil spirits left him.

- 2 SA 6:5 ~ David and the house of Israel celebrated before the Lord with instruments such as lyres, harps, tambourines, castanets, and cymbals.

- 1 CH 15:16 ~ David spoke to the Levite leaders to appoint singers, musicians, instruments, harps and cymbals in order to raise a united voice of resounding joy to the Lord.

- 1 CH 25:1–31 ~ Twenty-four people from each of the twelve tribes of Israel (288 people) were assigned to the music ministry for the church.

- PSA 71:23; PSA 101:1 ~ My lips will shout for joy when I sing praises to you oh Lord who has delivered me.

- PSA 90:1–6 ~ Sing to the Lord a new song, for He has done marvelous things. His right hand (Christ) and holy arm have worked salvation for Him. He remembered His love and faithfulness to Israel; all the ends of the earth have seen the salvation of our God. Shout for joy to the Lord; let all the earth burst into jubilant song and music. Make music to the Lord with harp and singing, and with trumpets and the blast of the ram's horn. Shout for joy before the Lord our King.

SEPTEMBER

- PSA 95:1 ~ Come let us sing for joy to the Lord; let us shout aloud to the Rock of our salvation.
- PSA 150:3–5 ~ Praise Him with the sound of the trumpet, harp, and lyre. Praise Him with the tambourine and dancing, praise Him with the strings and pipe, praise Him with the clash of cymbals.

As you can see, worship included orchestras and vocalists in Old and New Testament times. The Lord requests singing and music, so if you go to church today and nobody is singing hymns of praise, there might be a problem.

- EXO 15:1 ~ Moses and the Israelites sang this song to the Lord: "I will sing to the Lord, for He is highly exalted."
- 1 CH 9:33 ~ Singers from the homes of the Levites lived in the temple chambers, as this was their sole responsibility.
- 2 CH 5:13–14 ~ As the orchestra and choir joined in musical harmony to thank and praise God, the church was filled with a cloud, for the glory of God had encompassed the church.
- LUK 2:8–14 ~ There were shepherds watching their flocks that night in the hills nearby. An angel of the Lord appeared to them, and the glory of God shined all around them. The shepherds were terrified. The angel told them, "Do not be afraid, I bring you good news that will be of great joy to all people on earth. Today, in the city of David, a Savior is born who is Christ the Lord. This is a sign to you: You will find a baby wrapped in cloths and lying in a manger." Suddenly, a great multitude of angels appeared in the heavens, praising God and singing, "Glory to God in the highest, and on earth peace and good will to all people."
- EPH 5:19 ~ Speak to one another with psalms, hymns, and songs from the Spirit. Sing and make music from your heart to the Lord.
- COL 3:16 ~ Let the message of Christ live richly among you as you teach and admonish one another with all wisdom, through psalms, hymns, and songs from the Spirit, singing to God with gratitude in your hearts.
- JAM 5:13–15 ~ Is anyone among you ill? Let him pray. Is anyone merry? Let him sing psalms. Is anyone sick among you? Let him call the elders of the church to pray over him, anointing his head with oil in the name of the Lord. And the prayer of faith will save the sick, and the Lord will raise him up; and if he has sinned, he will be forgiven.

Many of the great reformers, priests, and pastors were talented musicians, singers, and songwriters. Martin Luther composed dozens of hymns that are still sung in churches regularly. Some of my personal favorites include, *A Mighty Fortress Is Our God, From Heaven Above to Earth I Come, Lord Keep Us Steadfast in Thy Word*. Other great clergymen who were prolific hymn composers were Wesley (*Hark the Herald Angels Sing*), Lowry (*Shall We Gather at the River*), Newton (*How Sweet the Name of Jesus Sounds*), and Watts (*When I Survey the Wonderous Cross*).

Dear Heavenly Father, we thank you for the music and the musicians that have graced our worship services for centuries, and in our churches today. Certainly, this music is calming to our souls, and the lyrics are strengthening to our faith; to be sure, the music inspires the spirit within us, inviting your Holy Spirit to lift us up. It is a blessed gift being able to play, sing, and compose music. Help people to use these and all their gifts to the glory of your holy name. Even if we sing like a frog, we still can raise a joyful noise unto the Lord. Let us never tire of singing praises to you, and let that be forever and ever, in Jesus's name, Amen.

September 15

International Day of Democracy was established by the United Nations in 2007 to be observed annually. The emphasis was on the freedoms of speech and the press. These two are among our freedoms listed first in the Bill of Rights. There are many countries in the world where there is no such freedom, like China and Iran. The goal of the UN has been to promote a free press, the free-flow of information-sharing without censorship, and the enforcement of laws and policies intended to protect the press and facilitate the dissemination of valuable data in a timely fashion. They also provide guidance to governments in establishing and maintaining principles of democracy, and allowing the citizenry access to unbiased information.

Everyone is entitled to their opinion and should have the right to express that opinion without retaliation. But some speech should be regulated: yelling fire in a theater as a prank; showing pornography to children; false advertising; verbally assaulting and abusing individuals or groups; claiming to being an unbiased news outlet that offers only one side of an argument or dismisses truth. There are laws against a great deal of speech, including terroristic threats or malicious slander. But nowadays the press gets away with saying anything they want, presenting opinions as news or facts; this was never the intention of the framers regarding a free press.

An international UN conference is held annually on this day with a different theme each year. Past themes have included political tolerance; defining free speech avenues; teaching democracy to youth; encouraging participation in the democratic process; increasing civility among people and nations; political conflict resolution; enabling universal human rights, etc.

Certainly, the freedoms of speech and the press do not include the deliberate censoring of discourse; it does not include the right to promote violence, incite a riot, or spread false rumors. It does not allow for terrorists, bullies, or evil people to harass and threaten others. Yet more news outlets seem to abuse the First Amendment by lying and spreading misinformation; stifling important news, such as health updates or scientific findings; and blatant historical inaccuracy. Freedom of the press was not codified to give a platform to professional liars and spreaders of disinformation; it does not allow for the invention of nonexistent data or facts, or the purposeful misrepresentation of research findings and statistics.

- PRO 12:19 ~ The lips of truth last forever, but a lying tongue lasts but a moment.
- PRO 15:28 ~ The righteous heart studies the situation before giving an answer; however, a wicked mouth pours out evil words.
- PRO 16:23 ~ The mind of a wise person makes speech judicious, and adds persuasiveness to words.
- ECC 5:1–2 ~ Trod carefully when you enter God's house. Listen intently rather than offering the sacrifice of fools who do not realize their error. Do not hasten to speak, and when you do let your words be few. Much dreaming and many words are meaningless.
- MIC 6:12 ~ The rich men are full of violence and lies.
- ZEC 8:16–17 ~ Always tell the truth to your neighbor; always execute judgments of truth and peace. Do not imagine evil in your hearts against another.
- MAT 12:37 ~ Jesus said, "You are justified and condemned by the words you speak."
- PHP 2:14 ~ Conduct your business without arguing or complaining.
- 2 TH 3:1 ~ Pray for Christian teachers and ministers, and pray for the freedom to openly speak God's Word.

- JAM 1:22–26 ~ Do not just listen to the Word, but do what it says. Whoever listens but does not act is like a person who looks in the mirror and later forgets what they look like. But those who look intently into the perfect law of liberty and who act on this will be blessed in all they do. Those who consider themselves to be religious, but do not control their tongue, deceive themselves and their religion is worthless.

- 1 PE 2:17 ~ Serve the Lord, respect all people, love your fellow Christians, fear God, and honor those in authority.

- 2 PE 2:18–19 ~ They will exploit with false words and attract you with lusts of the flesh. They have eyes full of adultery, insatiable for sin. Their hearts are trained in greed, and they gain through wrongdoing. They promise freedom but are themselves slaves to corruption, and are condemned. They will get perpetually worse.

- REV 18:23 ~ The businessmen were the most powerful men on earth, and through their cunning they deceived the nations.

The amount of information accessible in the world today is massive, whether via the internet, social media platforms, news media outlets, periodicals, all in the palm of your hand. Unfortunately, access to additional sources has not improved the reliability of the information; quite the contrary, it has increased the volume of mis- and disinformation being circulated. In addition, truthful, empirically-based, scientifically-derived information has been stifled if not dismissed or discredited. The proliferation of untrustworthy information sources has only served to multiply the uncertainty and confusion regarding what is truthful and fact-based, versus what is fabricated, rumored, or innuendo. It takes great patience and meticulous investigation to weed out the false narratives being endorsed. We must keep the Holy Bible as the final arbiter of truth; if it doesn't comport with God's Word, it is false.

- ISA 29:13 ~ The people honor me with their lips but have removed their heart from me; their knowledge of me is taught using principles invented by men.

- ACT 20:30 ~ From among yourselves will come those speaking perverse things to gain followers.

- ROM 16:17 ~ Take notice of those who cause divisions or take offense to the doctrine you have learned, and avoid them.

- 1 TI 6:5 ~ They are corrupt and have no knowledge of the truth. They think it is moral to exploit others for money.

This holiday has particular significance in a world of artificial intelligence and the worldwide web. Once, it was easy to research the net and get corroborative information. But now, readily available information does not equate to accuracy. One must page down past the ads and the monetarily supported positions at the top of a search list to get to the real data. As a research scientist, I learned how to recognize sound scientific methodology, identify fabricated studies or data, detect the misinterpretation of findings or statistics, and discover investigative and experimental bias. If you want to become an informed consumer of information, consider taking a few classes in data analysis, critical thinking, fallacies in logic, even statistics, and/or learn how to discriminate between truth and fiction in research and reportage. To begin with, anyone can check the source if it is provided; if it is unknown then you cannot be sure the source is valid.

- EXO 18:20–21 ~ Moses's father-in-law advised Moses to teach the people God's laws and doctrines, and tell them the way to live and what duties to perform. He further advised Moses to select capable men to help him govern the people: men who feared God and were trustworthy and honest.

- LUK 16:8–10 ~ Jesus summarized the parable saying, "The rich man commended the dishonest bookkeeper's shrewd tactics. He thought it was wise that his employee had made friends through greed and deceit. He thought it was shrewd how he prepared for his retirement, so he would have some means of external support when his job ended. That type of behavior will be considered wisdom to this evil generation. In fact, the evil children in that wicked generation will be shrewder than the children of light. Those who are faithful in a little will be faithful in a lot, and those who are dishonest in a little will be dishonest in a lot.
- PHP 4:8 ~ Focus your mind on things that are true, honest, just, pure, lovely, admirable, virtuous, and praiseworthy.

We have seen political censorship on social media platforms; public shaming and threatening of invited speakers; widespread distribution of false data; claiming of findings that are patently false; denial of facts that prove the opposite position; mass media news outlets supporting single political entities, people, and candidates; suppression of newsworthy stories; spreading propaganda; and supporting initiatives that are counterproductive to free speech and the free exchange of ideas. As an American, I find it appalling that our country is moving away from truth-to-power in favor of pushing socialist, Marxist, immoral, and globalist agendas, all of which are antithetical to democracy, capitalism, and freedom. Honest government is what many freedom seekers hoped to find when they arrived here; how appalling this must be to them. But those in power are plucking away our freedoms, redefining them, or making them unenforceable.

- PSA 51:6 ~ God desires truth inwardly, for inside my heart He will give me wisdom.
- PSA 119:44–47 ~ I will obey God's laws continuously and forevermore; I will walk in freedom, for I have sought His rules. I will boldly testify before kings, and I will delight in God's commandments that I have loved.
- ROM 1:18 ~ God's wrath is revealed from heaven against the sinfulness of people who suppress the truth through unrighteousness, though God has made these things clear to them.
- GAL 5:13 ~ Brothers, you have been called to be free men, but do not use that freedom as an excuse to engage in lusts of the flesh, but in love serve one another.
- 2 TH 3:1 ~ Pray for Christian teachers and ministers, and pray for the freedom to openly speak God's Word.

Father, we pray that you appoint leaders for us who are truthful and will fulfill their promises; who will be transparent and who will put the country first on their agendas. We pray that the citizenry will strive to become informed and critical of information and information sources, and not rely on a single platform or news outlet for their information. We pray that the freedoms of speech and the press will not be exploited to indoctrinate, reeducate, mislead, or brainwash our youth, and that the country will not elect leaders and governors who repeatedly lie to the people they are supposed to be serving. Please help us to unite in the name of freedom and faith, and reclaim our liberties; while weeding out those who are antagonistic to our democratic and capitalist philosophy or the laws and principles of our constitutional republic. In the name of Jesus, who always spoke truth-to-power, we pray, Amen.

September 16

Wife Appreciation Day occurs the third Sunday of the month, and honors wives; the day of the week will vary from year to year. The history of this holiday is vague, though the year 2006 is commonly cited. Today is the woman's turn just as husbands have their day. Husbands should talk with their wives about how to celebrate; let the wife choose where to go to dinner, or what piece of jewelry to pick out, or some destination to investigate. Husbands, you can pick the card and flowers. Being a wife is as important as being a mother, for marriage represents the union between Christ and His church on earth. Thus, marriage is a Biblical concept and a privilege, which was ordained by God and is not to be redefined. Motherhood should be within marriage, for the couple has become one flesh, and the child is flesh of their flesh; this was commanded by God for us to follow (GEN:1:28; GEN 9:1).

- GEN 2:24 ~ A man shall leave his parents and cling to his wife; and they shall become one flesh.

- LEV 21:7 ~ Do not take a prostitute for a wife, or a profane woman, or a divorced woman.

- DEU 17:17 ~ The king should not be intent on collecting wealth, cattle, or wives, for that might cause him to turn from God.

- EZR 10:11 ~ Confess unto the Lord God of your fathers, and do what pleases Him. Separate yourselves from the people of the land, and from strange wives.

- EPH 5:21–25, 28–29, 33 ~ Submit to one another. Wives, submit to your husbands, because the husband is the head of the wife just like Christ is the head of the church. Thus, the wife is subject to the husband at all times. Husbands, love and protect your wives, even as Christ loved the Church and gave Himself for it. For no man ever hated his own flesh, but nourishes and cherishes it, even as the Lord does with His church. You must love your spouse as much as you love yourselves.

- COL 3:18–19 ~ Wives, submit to your husbands, as long as it is within the Law. Husbands, love your wives and do not be bitter with them.

- 1 TI 5:14 ~ It is good for a young woman to marry, bear children, and guide the household. It is not good for a wife to be contrary, or to speak blamefully or rashly.

There are roles meant for women and roles meant for men. The Bible spells this out in detail. The woman and the man share responsibilities equally, they plan their lives together, and they work hard together as a team, making a good life and raising a godly family. They may have other occupations, but their primary loyalty is to their spouse and children, and of course, God.

- PRO 18:22 ~ Whoever finds a virtuous wife finds a good thing and obtains favor from God.

- PRO 19:13–14 ~ A quarrelsome wife is a continuous drag upon a marriage, but a prudent wife is from God.

- MAT 19:6, 9 ~ Jesus said, "Once you are joined in marriage you are no longer two separate persons, but have become one flesh. Whatever God has joined together, nobody should split apart. You cannot divorce your spouse unless he or she has committed adultery against you. If you divorce your spouse and marry another you are guilty of adultery. If you marry someone who is divorced you are guilty of adultery."

- 1 CO 7:4 ~ The wife does not have exclusive power over her body, neither does the husband have exclusive power over his body.

- TIT 2:4–5 ~ Wives, be sober, and love your husbands and your children. Be discreet, chaste, good homemakers, and obedient to your husbands, so the Word of God will not be blasphemed. Young men, be sober, upright and not corrupt; be serious and sincere, speaking good things about others.

- 1 PE 3:1, 7 ~ Wives, obey your husbands, and teach them the Word if they do not understand it. Husbands, listen to your wives; honor your wives as the weaker sex and as an equal. Stay together in the grace of life, and your prayers will be answered.

The wife in a marriage represents the bride of Christ who is the head of the Christian church. There will be a celebration and banquet in heaven, when Jesus collects His bride for the marriage feast of the Lamb of God. We will be His forever, in love and service, which is exactly what the wife on this earth represents to her husband. The wife and husband are to remain married until death parts them. But Jesus will love us with His perfect love forever, and there will be no death to separate us from Him.

- ISA 61:10 ~ I will greatly rejoice in the Lord; my soul will be joyful in my God. For He has clothed me with the garments of salvation, he has covered me with the robe of righteousness, just like the groom is adorned with ornaments and the bride is adorned with jewels. Blessed be those whose sins are not counted against them.

- ISA 62:5 ~ As the groom rejoices over the bride, so God rejoices over His people.

- MAT 25:1–13 ~ The kingdom of heaven is like ten virgins who took their lamps with them on the way to meet the groom. Five of them were smart and brought extra oil with them. The other five ran out of oil and their lamps went out. They asked the smart ones for some of their oil, but they replied, "We cannot for we do not want to run out of oil too." The others left to buy more oil for their lamps. Meanwhile, the groom came and everybody went into the church for the wedding. The doors were already locked when the other girls tried to enter. They asked to be admitted but the doorman replied, "I do not know you." Jesus summed up the parable saying, "Therefore, watch and prepare for my return for nobody knows the day or the hour."

- REV 19:6–9 ~ I heard the sound of a great multitude, as the rushing of many waters, with a thundering of voices singing "Alleluia, for the omnipotent Lord God reigns. Let us be glad and rejoice, and give honor to Him; for the marriage of the Lamb has come, and His wife has made herself ready." The bride was dressed in fine linen, clean and white, representing the righteousness of the saints. Then the angel told me to write, "Blessed are those who are invited to the marriage feast of the Lamb," continuing, "These are the true words of God."

Father God, we belong to you and you have given to us your Son. This union will be consummated when we are brought to heaven as the bride before Christ who is the groom. He loves us unconditionally and died in our place, just as a faithful husband would do for his wife. Father, please help husbands to love and protect their wives, every day and always. The husband is the head of the wife just as Christ is the head of the church. Help wives everywhere to honor and respect their husbands as we honor and respect Jesus, and help husbands to cherish and serve their wives as Jesus cherishes and serves His church. Thank you for godly wives and mothers, who teach virtue, respect, fidelity, and duty to their children. Thank you for godly wives who bring honor to their husbands, and husbands who openly respect their wives. Teach the world the true meaning of marriage, as defined by your Word, so that this sacred religious ritual is not defiled by immoral people. Help married Christians to be an example of faithfulness and teamwork, evenly yoked in all their affairs. In the name of Jesus Christ, who is our head, our life, and our deliverer, Amen.

September 17

Constitution Day (aka Citizenship Day) is a national observance commemorating the day in 1787 that Constitutional Convention delegates signed the US Constitution. It was celebrated as early as 1917 by the Sons of the American Revolution which included such notables as Calvin Coolidge, J. D. Rockefeller, and General John Pershing. Later, Citizenship Day (aka "I am an American" day) was created in 1941 and celebrated in May, before being combined with Constitution Day through an act of Congress in 2004. When this date falls on a weekend it is observed on a weekday so schools, government agencies, and other institutions can recognize and celebrate it. We are blessed to be citizens of the United States and we are blessed even more to be citizens of the Kingdom of Heaven.

- PSA 22:28 ~ The kingdom belongs to the Lord; He is the governor of all the nations.

- JER 31:33 ~ This is the covenant that I will make with my people. I will place my Law into their minds and write it upon their hearts. And I will be their God and they will be my people.

- EPH 2:18–19 ~ We have access through Jesus Christ to God the Father. We are not foreigners, but fellow citizens with the saints in the household of God.

- 2 TH 2:13 ~ Give thanks always to God for choosing you from the beginning to be saved through sanctification of the spirit and belief in the truth.

- 2 PE 1:3–4 ~ By God's divine power we have received all things pertaining to life and godliness, because we know Him who called all people to righteousness and glory. We cling to His precious promise, that His people will receive an exalted nature, and escape the corruption and lust of the world.

- ACT 10:34–35 ~ Peter said, "Truly, God does not show favoritism to any person. Within every nation, anyone who fears the Lord and works towards righteousness is accepted."

- 1 JO 3:1–2 ~ How great is the love that God the Father has for us, that we should be called His children. Thus, the world does not know us because it did not know Him. We are His children, but we do not know yet what we will be; we do know, however, that we will be like Him, for we will see Him as He really is.

Today we honor the Constitution framed by the founders of our country to establish a self-governing republic. Today we also celebrate those who came here and became citizens because they wanted to be a part of this society and enjoy the freedoms granted all Americans. Surprisingly, many immigrants who have sought freedom here know the Constitution better than many natural born citizens. It behooves all citizens to read and study the US Constitution, the Bill of Rights, and the Declaration of Independence, all of which used to be required reading for people seeking citizenship. Recently, the Biden administration simplified the citizenship exam in attempt to make citizens out of the millions of immigrants already here including those they have allowed to cross our borders without scrutiny.

- JDG 21:25 ~ In those days there was no king in Israel; every man did that which was right in his own eyes.

- PRO 4:27 ~ Do not turn to the right or to the left until you remove your foot from evil.

- ISA 30:21 ~ Your ears will hear a word behind you saying, "This is the way, you are to walk in it whether you turn to the right or to the left."

- ACT 5:29 ~ Peter and the apostles with him said, "We ought to obey God rather than men."

Everyone should at least know this about the Constitution: Article I sets up the legislative branch, Article II sets up the executive branch, and Article III sets up the judicial branch. Each separate but equal branch of the federal government is meant to be a check on the other two so that no single branch dominates. Article IV recognizes rights and privileges of individual states, and Article V allows for the Constitution to be amended. There are twenty-six amendments to the Constitution with the first ten constituting the Bill of Rights.

- 1 KI 3:9 ~ Give your servant an understanding mind to govern your people and to discern between good and evil.

- JER 10:23–25 ~ Lord, I know a man's life is not his own; it is not for man to direct his own steps. Correct me Lord, in your justice not in your anger, else you reduce me to nothing. Pour your wrath upon nations which do not accept you, and people who do not call on your name.

- EZE 18:21 ~ If the wicked would turn from their sins and keep God's commandments, doing what is lawful and right, they would surely live and would not have to die.

- 1 TI 1:8–9 ~ Laws are good if they are used lawfully. Laws are not made for the righteous, but for the lawless, profane, and disobedient; laws are for ungodly people and for sinners.

- 1 PE 2:13–17 ~ Submit to the laws of the land, for it is God's will that you are lawful and upright, thereby silencing those ignorant people who would talk behind your back. Be free, but do not use your freedom to conceal evil. Instead, you must serve the Lord, respect all people, love your fellow Christians, fear God, and honor those in authority.

The framers were principally men of God, who regarded the Holy Bible with high esteem. Their Judeo-Christian values were incorporated into our founding documents. All other laws in our land derive from two primary sources: the Old and New Testaments. This is partly true for nations practicing other religions requiring a consistent moral stance. Countries where the governments shun the free practice of religion or faith are led by dictators, despots, and self-centered narcissists. Not all of their citizens refrain from practicing religion, though it is often done in secret. Inwardly, people know what is right, and everyone wants freedom from totalitarianism. But not everyone wants God, and that is their prerogative, and a big mistake.

- DEU 26:7 ~ When we cried to the Lord, He heard us and looked into our affliction, burden, and oppression.

- PRO 2:9 ~ You will understand righteousness, judgment, and equity; yes, every good path.

- ISA 55:7 ~ Let evil and wicked people everywhere change their evil ways, forsake their immoral thoughts, and turn to the Lord, and He will have mercy on them; for the Lord will abundantly pardon those who seek Him.

- EZE 22:29 ~ The people have used oppression, robbery, and swindling, so I will recompense it upon their heads and consume them with the fire of my wrath.

- 1 JO 3:4 ~ Whoever commits sin transgresses the law, for sin is the transgression of the law.

Heavenly Father, who reigns supreme over all kingdoms, governments, nations, and peoples, we pray that you remain the standard for all who are given authority in our land. We pray that our constitutional way of government of, by, and for the people will never dissolve. Be with our leaders and our nation and direct them into paths of righteousness, whether they seek you or not. Please, do not let them destroy or rewrite our founding documents. Help us individually and collectively to always consider your will before taking action, knowing that we will prosper wherever you guide our steps as we follow Jesus to the promised land. Amen.

September 18

National First Love Day is an annual celebration dating back to around 2015. Who does not remember their first love? We all have salient memories which are more available than most memories; they include firsts, lasts, eventful or impactful things, and things experienced frequently. We remember our first love, first kiss, first date, or our last love, kiss or date. Some people are fortunate to have their first love-interest to spend this and every day with. Otherwise, spend the day with your current love connection; no doubt, they also had a first love that wasn't you. Either way, generate some memorable occasions as you celebrate this occasion. Discuss memories with your mate like your first kiss or most recent kiss. How do they compare to the best kiss? This is a day for romantic love. The following passages are indicative of the wisdom of King Solomon and express attractiveness, love, intimacy, and sharing as God meant it to be.

- PRO 5:18 ~ Rejoice with the wife of your youth.

- PRO 10:7 ~ The memory of the just is blessed; but the name of the wicked will rot away.

- SOS 1—8 ~ Song of Solomon is a book about love and attraction. The first chapter covers the magnetism between the man and woman and shows how their love begins to grow. Notice that the maiden is attracted to the king's reputation, not his power, glory, or money. She exclaims that his name is pleasant, and that is why all the maidens in the king's domain adore him (SOS 1:3–4). Notice that the primary characteristic that the king admires in the maiden is her dedication and sense of duty, as opposed to her physical attractiveness. He overlooks the fact that her skin has been darkened by the sun from laboring in the fields where she tends flocks that are not her own (SOS 1:5–9). Further, the shepherdess is a woman of virtue, a virgin, undefiled and flawless (SOS 1:7; SOS 4:12; SOS 5:2), not flirtatious, flippant, or provocative. In the second chapter the king begins to court the young maiden. He entertains her through a ritual similar to what we call dating or wooing. Their love continues to grow, without becoming sidetracked by premarital sex or any "fooling around." Instead, they yearn for the time when they can experience greater intimacy as a result of being joined by God in marriage. Chapters three through five tell how they marry, are intimate, and consummate their marriage. Sex within marriage is revealed to be a beautiful experience (SOS 4:16—SOS 5:1). Notice that they are not only lovers, but friends (SOS 5:16). They became friends as they were courting and as their love grew; perhaps they were lovers all along, but they waited to "make love" until the time was right and they were man and wife. In chapters six and seven we see their love and commitment continue to increase and flourish, as they share the gifts of life, love, and companionship. In fact, sharing seems to be the principal theme of these chapters. Keep in mind that marriages which do not include much sharing are usually doomed; spouses should want to share everything and always. In the final chapter, the major theme is loyalty; for a marriage to last a lifetime, the devotion should never fade. Another theme of this chapter is the power of lasting love: it is stronger than death, unyielding as the grave, unquenchable as an inferno, and as permanent as a rock that cannot be eroded or washed away (SOS 8:6–7).

- SOS 2:7; SOS 3:5; SOS 8:4 ~ Do not arouse or awaken love until it is ready.

We tend to remember certain moments better than others. Some memories are stored as a complete scene with visual and auditory, possibly kinesthetic or olfactory sensations. Like a snapshot in time, they are known as flashbulb memories, psychologically speaking. For example, people can remember where they were during the 09/11 attack. Similarly, people can bring to mind details about their great dates, maybe when they got to make-out in the back seat or at the drive-in movie. Most other memories will not be stored as a whole but rather become fragmented over time, as the brain assigns data elements to templates or files containing similar information.

- PSA 119:11 ~ Your Word I have guarded in my heart so I would not sin against you.

- ISA 46:9–10 ~ Remember the former things of old, for I am God and there is none like me. I declare the end from the beginning, and from ancient times the things that have yet to happen. My counsel will stand and I will do as I please.

- JAM 2:1–9 ~ Do not be partial to people just because you like the way they look or act. Do not give the rich or the famous more respect than anyone else, and do not give the poor and lowly less respect. If you abide by the royal law according to the scripture, "Love your neighbor as yourself," you are doing the right thing. But if you show favoritism to certain persons, you commit sin, and are convicted of the law as a lawbreaker.

How does one classify a first love anyway? I played house with a girl I knew at church, and I think I loved her because I kissed her on the cheek one day and she blushed. Perhaps that was a wee bit forward of me, given I was only about ten at the time and she was nine. Does puppy love count as your first love? Or is the first love the one you were going steady with in high school or college? Was your first love the one you gave your heart, or a promise, or a ring? Are you still together? If so, you are blessed indeed. I have two friends who have been together since their first kiss over fifty years ago. Is the love in the above scenarios different? They all illustrate the power of love which comes from God. And since God is love, then *agape* love is the most powerful force in the universe. Expressing love is a command of God (MAT 22:36–40).

There are degrees of love. Physical love is enchanting, mental love is stimulating, and spiritual love is outstanding. If you have a soulmate for life, you are connected in all three of these ways. Then there is God's love which is unfathomable. God's Son instills the best of our love which will be with us from the beginning until the end, and after forever.

- PSA 85:8, 10 ~ Let me listen to what the Lord has to say, for He speaks peace to His people, to His saints, and to all who turn their hearts to Him. Steadfast love and truth will meet; righteousness and peace will kiss each other.

- ISA 41:4 ~ Who has done this, calling every generation from the beginning? It is I, the Lord; from the first through the last, I AM He.

- HEB 13:8 ~ Jesus Christ is the same yesterday, today, and forever.

- 1 JO 4:7–8, 11, 19 ~ Let us love one another, for love is from God, and those who love are born of God and know Him. If you do not love God, you cannot know Him because God is love. If God loved us so much, we also should love one another. We love because God loved us first.

- REV 1:8 ~ Jesus said, "I am the alpha and omega, the beginning and the end; who was, is, and is to come—the Almighty."

- REV 2:4–5 ~ I have something against you, because you have left your first love. Remember from where you have fallen, and repent; do what you did before or I will come and remove your candlestick from its place.

Father, we love you because you loved us first. You are our first love. In like manner we love your Son Jesus, for He is our example of perfect love on earth; help us to love like He loves, by putting others before ourselves. We love your Holy Spirit who speaks the truth to us and shows us where to go, what to do, and what to say. Help us to remember that you are always present and your love will never fail us; let it become deeper and stronger within us. In Jesus's name we pray, Amen.

September 19

Steadfastness Day is proposed so we remain true to the fundamentals of the faith in general, and faithfulness to Christ in particular. It is one thing to believe, it is yet another to be active and vocal about it. Not that we want to force-feed anyone what the Bible says, because the message of Christ must be delivered with patience and humility (1 PE 3:15). If you believe in Jesus, you are a child of the living God; if this is so, it should show in your face, your actions, and your love. If you are sure in your heart that Christ is the Messiah, you should proclaim Him to the world; that is, if you truly believe, it will show and people will know. [Note that excerpts of this lesson were taken from an earlier work (Barber, 2020a).]

- ROM 10:9–10 ~ If you confess the Lord Jesus with your mouth, and believe in your heart that God raised Him from the dead, you will be saved. For with the heart, we believe unto righteousness; and with the mouth, confession is made unto salvation.

    Perseverence requires courage (DEU 31:6–8; 1 CO 16:13), commitment (PSA 37:5; 1 JO 2:6), patience (PSA 37:7; JAM 1:3), endurance (1 CO 10:13), service (PSA 41:1; MAT 25:40–45), and generosity (DEU 16:17; LUK 6:38). These are lifelong duties, done in response to what God has done for us since He has given us everything we have.

    A person can believe but not have faith; belief and faith are different. The Bible says we are created in the image of God; I know this to be true for His Word is true. I believe wholeheartedly in the salvation of Jesus Christ and I am compelled to proclaim this by faith. I also believe that a great many will reject Christ as Savior and will be condemned. But I do not place my faith in the latter statement but in the former, though I believe them both to be true.

    Can you gain salvation and lose it? This has long been debated, and a case can be made that you can lose your salvation insofar as you never fully received God's Holy Spirit (2 PE 2:20–22; ACT 19:16). A case also can be made that you cannot lose your salvation, insofar as once you are sealed by God, you are sealed forever (2 CO 1:22; ROM 8:28–39). But the point is this, if you never lose your faith you will keep your soul (LUK 21:19). The things required of you is to love God first and love your neighbor as yourself second; you can keep the faith by acting on it which is demonstrated by obeying these two commandments. People who do not agree with you, who are disappointed in you, or otherwise do not accept the truth God gave to you, will separate from you for they do not possess the Spirit and you do (JDE 1:17–19).

- EZE 18:24 ~ When a righteous person turns away from righteousness, commits sin, and is motivated by evil, can that person live? All the righteousness that occurred beforehand will never be remembered, but because of their sin he or she will die.

- MAT 7:21–23 ~ Jesus informed the people that not everyone who says to Him, "Lord, Lord," will enter the kingdom of heaven, but only those who do the will of our heavenly Father. Many will say to Him, "Have we not prophesied and done mighty works in your name?" Jesus will reply to them, "I never knew you; depart from me you who work iniquity."

- MAT 13:3–23 ~ Jesus told the parable of the sower of seeds. He explained that some people will receive the Word with joy; it will begin to grow but it will not take root (because the seed was sown in rocky places). Tribulations and persecutions associated with being a follower of Christ will offend many people and many will let the Word die in their hearts.

- HEB 6:4–6 ~ It is impossible for those who were once enlightened, who tasted of the heavenly gift and were made partakers of the Holy Spirit, who understood the good Word of God and the powers of the world to come, to be renewed unto repentance if they should fall away. They crucify the Son of God all over again and put Him to open shame.

God chooses people who choose Him. For this we thank God every day from the beginning of our conversion through the end of time. Those who are sanctified eventually will be glorified (ROM 8:30); it is a process that ends when Christ brings you home to our Father in heaven. Like steadfastness, sanctification is a lifelong process, whereby we remain committed because God remains committed; He will never leave us or forsake us.

- PHP 1:3–6 ~ Paul wrote: I thank God every time I think of you, and pray to Him with joy for your fellowship in the Gospel, from the very first day until now; being confident that He who began a good work in you will bring it to completion when Jesus Christ returns.

- 2 TH 2:13–14 ~ Give thanks always to God for choosing you from the beginning to be saved through sanctification of the Spirit and belief in the truth. He called you by His Gospel to share in the glory of our Lord Jesus Christ.

- 1 PE 1:2–5 ~ Christians are chosen by God in advance through sanctification of the Spirit, to be obedient to Christ and cleansed by His blood. Blessed be God the Father of our Lord Jesus Christ. According to His abundant mercy, He recreated in us the living hope, brought by the resurrection of Christ from the dead, to receive an incorruptible and undefiled inheritance reserved in heaven and lasting forever. Through faith, He has shielded us by His power until the coming of our salvation which is ready to be revealed on the last day.

Steadfastness means consistently reaching out to the Holy Spirit to guide, direct, embolden, and protect. With the love of Christ in your heart, you are changed from the inside-out. Your motivation will be to obtain a heavenly reward, not a worldly one. Your service will be to God, to your church, and to the lost sheep. By loving God first and everyone else second (you are part of the second group), you will have met the requirements of the Law and the Gospel.

- ROM 6:6–18 ~ If we have been planted together in the likeness of His death, we also will be raised together in the likeness of His resurrection; knowing that our old self was crucified with Him, so that the body of sin might be destroyed, and henceforth we would serve sin nevermore. For the dead in Christ are freed from sin. We who have died with Christ believe that we also will live with Him; knowing that Christ who was raised from the dead cannot die again, since death has no power over Him. Jesus died once unto sin, but He lives forever unto God. Likewise, you must die unto sin, but will live forever unto God through Jesus Christ our Lord. Do not let sin rule in your mortal body, or give into the lusts thereof. Neither employ your members as instruments of unrighteousness unto sin, but yield to God as a person alive in Christ, and use your members as instruments of righteousness unto God. Then sin will have no dominion over you; for you are not under the law but under grace. What then? Can we sin because we are not under the law, but under grace? Absolutely not! Do you not realize that a slave must obey the master? Will you be a slave to sin unto death, or obedient to God unto righteousness? Thank God! Though you once served sin, you now serve the doctrine of deliverance. Being made free from sin, you became servants of righteousness.

- PHP 2:13–15 ~ For it is God who works in you both to want and to do that which pleases Him. Do this without grumbling or quarreling, so you can remain blameless and harmless children of God, without reproach, in the midst of a crooked and perverse nation where you shine as lights to the world.

- PHP 3:8–14 ~ Without a doubt, I count everything loss except the excellent knowledge of Christ Jesus my Lord, for whom I have suffered the loss of all worldly things, which to me are as garbage because of what I have gained in Christ; finding righteousness from Jesus, though not having any of my own in accordance with the law, but possessing the righteousness of God by faith in His Son. So that I may know Him, and the power of His resurrection, and the fellowship of His sufferings, becoming like Him in death so I might attain the resurrection of the dead. I have not yet attained it however; it is not like I am already perfect. But I continue forward, that I may hold onto the promise for which Christ holds onto me. Brothers, I have not obtained it as yet, though I have let go of the past, forgetting those things which are behind and reaching for those things which are to come. Pressing onward toward the goal of receiving the prize of eternal life for which God has called me on behalf of Jesus Christ.

If you want a great example of steadfastness, consider Job. Most everyone knows the story of Job, and how God allowed the devil to try Job's faith (JOB 1—2). Satan figured he could break Job while God knew that Job's faith would not falter. Satan threw everything he had at Job, to include deaths, losses, hardship, and disease. Job was reaching his breaking point, exhausted from the suffering, to the point he questioned God's motive. God responded to Job by explaining the intricacy of the universe and the forming of the cosmos; the wonders of nature and its processes; the variety of lifeforms, and the wisdom of human beings. These miraculous accomplishments could only be performed by the one true God who created this splendid world in its entirety (JOB 38—39). Then God asked Job, "Can anyone instruct Almighty God? Let him who accuses God provide an answer" (JOB 40:1–2). Job replied, "I am unworthy to answer, so I must cover my mouth with my hand. I have spoken time and again, but now I have nothing to say" (JOB 40:3–5). Then God told Job, "Prepare yourself like a man, for I will question you further and you will answer me. Would you doubt my justice? Would you condemn my works to elevate yourself? Do you have the reach of my arm or the thunder of my voice? If so, then clothe yourself with majesty and excellency, and array yourself with beauty and glory. Unleash your wrath upon the proud and bring them down; humble them and crush the wicked. Hide them in the dust and cover them in the grave. Then I will agree that you have the ability to save yourself by the power of your own right hand" (JOB 40:6–14). God spoke of the behemoth and the leviathan: intimidating giants that roamed the earth and the sea. They were powerful and not easily subdued; yet marvelous in their stature, though menacing in their appearance (JOB 40:15–41:34). Job responded, "I know that you can do anything and that you know everything. You spoke of people who obscure your counsel and are lacking in knowledge (JOB 38:1–2), and you asked me to give an answer. I have heard about you, but now I have seen who you are. And I detest myself, and I repent in dust and ashes" (JOB 42:1–6). Therefore, God blessed the latter part of Job's life more than the former, with a double portion (JOB 42:10–16). God also chastised Job's friends Eliphaz, Bildad, and Zophar for being among those who spoke of things they knew nothing about. God commanded them to humble themselves, repent, and offer sacrifices (JOB 42:7–9).

To conclude this lesson, let us aggregate the many facets of steadfastness. First, we need to stay strong in our faith, cling to our hope, surround ourselves with fellow believers, and pray for Christians all around the world. Second, we must keep the commandments of God and follow the teachings of Jesus to the best of our ability; passing these along to our children so that they will pass them along to their children. Third, we must be constantly on the alert, fully aware, and very cautious, so that we do not fall into social and political traps, follow or join others who are heading in the wrong direction, or give into worldly temptations which defile the flesh and darken the spirit. Fourth, we must use our love, time, gifts, abilities, and knowledge to further God's kingdom throughout our lives with courage; living confidently for Jesus who died for us, and forever striving to be more like Him by continuously eliminating previous immoral tendencies.

- JOB 11:14–16 ~ If iniquity is in your hand, put it far away; do not let wickedness dwell in your tents. And you will raise your face without spot; yes, you will be steadfast and never afraid. Because you will forget your misery, and remember it as waters that flow away.

- PSA 78:6–8 ~ God established a testimony in Jacob and appointed a law in Israel, which He commanded our fathers to obey and make known to their children. Each generation will be taught them; those children born to you will declare them to their children. So that they might set their hope on God, never forget His works, and keep His commandments; not like their fathers, a stubborn and rebellious generation, whose heart was not right with God and whose spirit did not hold steadfast to Him.
- ACT 2:42 ~ And those who listened remained steadfast in the doctrine and fellowship of the apostles, in the breaking of bread together and in prayer.
- 1 CO 15:58 ~ Therefore my beloved brothers, be steadfast, unmovable, and abounding in the work of the Lord, insofar as you know your labor is not in vain.
- HEB 3:14 ~ We are made partakers of Christ, if we hold the beginning of our confidence steadfast unto the end.
- HEB 6:19 ~ We have hope as an anchor to the soul; it is sure and steadfast, and penetrates into the depths of our being.
- 1 PE 5:8–9 ~ Be sober and vigilant, because your enemy the devil roams about like a lion searching for someone to devour. He will attempt to consume anyone who is not steadfast in their faith.
- 2 PE 3:17 ~ Beloved, now that you know these things, beware that you are not led astray by the error of the wicked, and thus fail in your steadfastness.

Repeat the following prayers of David about properly carrying out God's assignments. Remember, you are saved by the blood of Jesus not by your steadfastness; but steadfastness does help to keep you on track.

- PSA 51:10–12 ~ Create in me a clean heart, Lord, and renew an upright spirit within me. Do not remove me from your presence and do not take your Holy Spirit from me. Restore to me the joy of your salvation, and uphold me with your free Spirit.
- PSA 141:1–5, 8–10 ~ Lord I cry out to you; hear my prayer. I offer it as incense and lift it up with my hands toward you. Please warn me before I open my mouth. Let me not be inclined toward any evil thing, or associate with those who work wickedness, or be enticed by their luxuries. If I am admonished by righteous men, it will be a blessing to be reproved by them, and I bid your blessing upon them. My eyes are fixed upon you, Lord God, in you I will trust to never leave my soul destitute. Keep me from snares being laid for me and protect me from traps set by workers of iniquity. Let the wicked fall into their own nets, that I may escape.

Father, your steadfast love is what keeps us going. Help us to respond to that love by loving you back, and loving all people as ourselves. Help us to be steadfast in our faith and love so that we are not influenced to follow the ways of the world. May we always return to you when we become lost or get sidetracked. Let us grow in our knowledge of you so that we become more convinced of the truth, thereby preparing us to share the truth of your Word with confidence and conviction to anyone you assign to us. Cover us with the blood of Christ and comfort us with the blanket of the Holy Spirit, to remain steadfast until the end, when Jesus returns to bring us blameless before you, Father. In Jesus's name we pray, Amen

September 20

War Was Declared Against Terrorism before a joint session of Congress and President Bush Jr. on this day in 2001. This was in direct response to the terrorist bombing on 09/11/01. The initial target of the declaration was Islamic terror cells in countries around the world, and the governments that protect them. Given that some Muslim nations were sponsoring, harboring, and financing terrorists, they also were named in this war. Immediately, certain networks were targeted such as al-Qaeda and Taliban, and attacks commenced upon terrorist training camps in Afghanistan. In 2003 began the war in Iraq, when it was discovered that Saddam Hussein was harboring terrorists and engaged in the production of biochemical weapons; the evil dictator and his two sons were dispatched rather swiftly. Ten years after the bombing of the World Trade Center, the architect of the bombing, Osama bin Laden was killed in a secret raid on his compound in Pakistan ordered by President Obama. President Trump ordered similar kills during his administration..

Though the wars in Iraq and Afghanistan have ended, the war on terror is far from over. Unfortunately, some administrations are softer on terror than others, so there is inconsistency in how the global war on terror is prosecuted. In recent cases, our leaders appeared to be in league with sponsors of terrorism such as Iran and Afghanistan; additionally, they appear to be against Israel, our greatest ally fighting terrorism in the Mideast. Further, the problem has spilled over within our own borders, and is likely to get worse given the substantial illegal entries of bad actors across our borders, not to mention the slacking of the laws in certain states, and the ineptness of certain law enforcement agencies. So, one can expect more terrorism.

They call it a holy war, these jihadists who commit acts of terrorism. And that includes homegrown terrorists looking for an excuse to kill people. But terrorists are working for Satan, and will be annihilated when God pours out His wrath upon the earth, bringing terror upon them.

- PRO 29:25 ~ The fear of humankind is a trap, but those who trust in God will be safe.

- ISA 2:11–12, 17–19 ~ The pride of men will be humbled, and the Lord alone will be exalted on that day. The day of the Lord of hosts will be upon the proud and arrogant; and those who lift themselves up will be brought down. The Lord will be exalted on that day; He will destroy all the idols. People will hide in the rocks and caves in terror of the Lord and the glory of His majesty when He rises up to shake the earth.

- ISA 28:19 ~ You will be beaten down by the overwhelming scourge. Then you will understand this message and it will bring sheer terror unto you.

- ISA 31:9 ~ Their stronghold will crumble from terror when they see the battle standard approaching.

- JER 49:15–16 ~ You will be diminished and despised. Your terrorism and pride deceived you, who abide among the cliffs and in the heights. You built your nest as high as the eagle, but you will be brought down to the dirt.

- ZEP 1:14 ~ The great day of the Lord is coming quickly, when mighty men will cry.

- 2 TI 3:1, 13 ~ In the last days, perilous times will come. The evil ones will get continuously worse.

- REV 6:15–17 ~ They tried to hide in the rocks and caves, praying that the mountain would fall on them, for the great day of God's wrath had come upon them.

Heavenly Father, we ask that you protect the innocent from acts of terror, and we pray that you will help us to eliminate those servants of Satan. In the name of Jesus we pray, Amen.

September 21

International Day of Peace was established in 1981 by the United Nations to combat war, civil unrest, racism, violence, and hatred. The UN changed the observance to 09/21 starting in 2002, petitioning all nations of the world engaged in unrest, civil war, and regional conflicts to order a ceasefire and maintain a cessation of violence for twenty-four hours.

Global peace is something that resonates with everybody, except people who aren't interested in peace, like warmongers and terrorists pretending they are in favor of peace. Many nations and certain groups make a lot of money promoting violence; sometimes they use it as an excuse to test their weapons, tactics, and readiness. There is always a fight or war happening on the planet, so attaining global peace is highly unlikely because of the sinfulness of humankind.

In recognition of this day of peace, it will be up to individuals to promote peace and resolve conflicts in their own arena. The UN can provide a setting but leaders, policymakers, and individuals are the ones who can make a difference. Some will stand up; some will cower.

- PSA 34:14 ~ Depart from evil and do good; seek peace and pursue it.
- PRO 3:1–2 ~ Do not forget God's Law. Keep His commandments and He will give you peace and a long life.
- ISA 9:6 ~ A child is born for us; a Son is given to us. The government will be upon His shoulders. His name will be called Wonderful Counselor, Mighty God, Everlasting Father, and Prince of Peace.
- ISA 45:5, 7 ~ God says, "I am the Lord; there are no other gods besides me. I created the light and the dark; I created peace and despair."
- ISA 54:10 ~ The mountains and hills may be removed, but God's steadfast love will never depart, and His covenant of peace will be forever.
- ZEC 9:9–10 ~ Rejoice, for here comes your righteous king riding on a donkey's colt. He will bring peace to all nations.
- JOH 14:27 ~ Jesus said, "Peace I leave you; my peace I give you; I do not give as the world gives, so never let your hearts be troubled or afraid."
- ACT 10:36 ~ The Word that God sent to Israel is Jesus Christ; in Him God's peace can be found.
- ROM 15:13 ~ May the God of hope fill you with all joy and peace in believing, so that by the power of the Holy Spirit you may abound in hope.
- COL 3:15 ~ Let the peace of Christ rule in your hearts, since by members of one body you were called to peace.
- 1 TH 5:23 ~ May the God of peace sanctify you wholly, so that your entire spirit, soul, and body can be preserved blameless until the coming of our Lord Jesus Christ.
- 2 TH 3:16 ~ May the Lord of peace Himself give you His peace at all times and in all ways.
- 2 PE 1:2–3 ~ Grace and peace be multiplied to you through the knowledge of God, and of Jesus our Lord. His divine power has given us everything we need for life and righteousness through our knowledge of Him who called us by His own glory and goodness.
- 2 JO 1:3 ~ Grace, mercy and peace be with you, from God our Father, and from Jesus Christ His Son, in truth and love.

SEPTEMBER

- JDE 1:1–2 ~ From Jude, the servant of Jesus Christ and brother of James, to those who are sanctified by God the Father, preserved in Jesus Christ, and called to be His disciples: Mercy unto you; let peace and love be multiplied unto you.

    It is days like these when a moment of prayer is in order. We need people of all nations to come before the throne of Grace at the same time, and pray for peace in their land and in the world. A minute of silence around noontime has been suggested, but this should be a moment of prayer and it should last all day. Fervent prayer yields results (JAM 5:16). Everyone everywhere could be part of a collective pleading before God for twenty-four hours. But how many would actually comply? The UN will have a conference on this day, plus events in various places around the world, possibly in your city. These gatherings provide a venue where people of different walks can exchange ideas and develop a dialogue. The key is to continue the discourse after the conclusion of the meetings. It would help immensely to invite God to attend and guide the process. The best way to obtain tangible outcomes is to tap into the peace of God that surpasses all understanding.

- PSA 50:15 ~ The Lord says, "Call upon me in the day of trouble, and I will deliver you, and you will glorify me."

- PSA 122:6–7 ~ Pray for peace; may those prosper who love God. Peace be within your walls and security within your towers.

- ISA 65:24 ~ God says, "I will answer you before you even call; I will hear you before you even speak."

- ROM 2:10 ~ Glory, honor, and peace is given to all who do good, regardless of race.

- ROM 5:1–5 ~ Being justified by faith we achieve peace with God through Christ, in whom we have access by that faith to the grace in which we stand, rejoicing in the hope of glory. Therefore, we rejoice in time of tribulation, knowing that it teaches us patience, it strengthens our hope, and we gain experience.

- ROM 8:26 ~ The Holy Spirit intercedes for us when we pray. We do not know what we should pray for all the time. But through the act of prayer, God analyzes our needs and answers our prayers in the best possible way.

- ROM 12:12 ~ Rejoice in hope, be patient in troubled times, be constant in prayer.

- ROM 14:17, 19 ~ The kingdom of God does not mean food and drink, but righteousness, peace, and joy in the Holy Spirit. Let us therefore seek that which results in peace and mutual uplifting.

- PHP 4:6–8 ~ Do not have anxiety about anything, but pray for everything. With thanksgiving let your requests be known to God. And the peace of God which surpasses all understanding will keep your heart in mind in Jesus Christ. Focus your mind on things that are true, honest, just, pure, lovely, admirable, virtuous, and praiseworthy.

- 2 CO 13:11 ~ Finally, brothers, farewell. Be perfect, be comforted, be of one mind, and live in peace; and the God of love and peace shall be with you always.

    We need leaders and authorities who exhibit an upright character and a godly demeanor to promote peace in their locality and on the world stage. It is easy to give lip service to the cause of peace, but that needs to be backed-up with actions, through policies and laws which produce results. Those declaring that they stand for peace and seek to resolve differences are not always sincere; especially when they stir up conflict, wage war, and endorse terrorism. It is easy to tell by one's actions whether their words have potency, and if they have the gumption to follow through.

DAILY DEVOTIONAL EVENTS

- PRO 12:20 ~ Deceit is in the heart of those who imagine evil things; but for the counselors of peace is joy.

- ISA 32:17 ~ The results of righteousness are peace and trust forever.

- JER 6:14; JER 8:11, 15 ~ They kept saying "peace, peace" but there was no peace. We looked for peace but none came; we hoped for health but got trouble instead.

- JER 23:17 ~ They say to those who despise God that He will give you peace and no harm will come upon you, including all who follow the imaginations of their own hearts.

- MIC 3:2–5 ~ You hate good and love evil. You skin people and eat their flesh. You chop their bodies into pieces. You talk of peace but make war.

- ROM 8:4–6 ~ Live, not according to the flesh, but according to the spirit. Those who live according to the flesh set their minds on evil, but those who live according to the spirit set their minds on God. To set the mind on flesh results in death, but to set the mind on God results in peace and life.

- ROM 12:3, 16–18 ~ Do not be conceited in your own mind, but think soberly, according to the measure of faith God has given you. Live in harmony with one another. Be humble, not proud or arrogant. Never return evil for evil. Always be honest with everybody. Live in peace with all of God's creation.

- 1 TI 2:1–2, 8 ~ I urge that supplications, prayers, intercessions, and thanksgiving be made to God for all people, for leaders, and for all who are in authority, so that we can lead an honest and peaceful life of godliness and truth. People should pray everywhere, lifting up holy hands, without being doubtful or angry.

- JAM 3:18 ~ The harvest of righteousness is sown in peace by those who make peace.

Is peace possible in this world? Yes, if what you seek is inner peace, which is available through Christ the Lord. Is world peace possible? No, because it only takes one arrogant, greedy, and/or selfish leader or group to mess it up for everyone else. The United Nations, despite being a place where people of different cultures can meet and dialogue together, can do very little to change the dynamics of the world. The security council of the UN is composed of fifteen member nations, five of which are permanent members: US, UK, France, Russia, and China. How can there be an accord among these nations which have such diverse governments, objectives, and philosophies? The push for a global society, economy, and governance is a last-ditch effort to control global power under the guise of socialism, which will not stand because it works against God. Do not be deceived by those who proclaim this to be a pathway to peace.

Heavenly Father, we thank you for your steadfast love which is the only thing in our life that we can always count on. We thank you that we have Jesus Christ, the Prince of Peace who gives us confidence, hope, and inner peace. We thank you for your Holy Spirit who gives us comfort, guidance, and steadfastness. Let us be ambassadors to our community, nation, and the world, promoting your peace which surpasses all understanding. Help all nations and their leaders to seek counsel from you via your Holy Spirit, so they can be strong in the power of your might, which is unconditional love. Show the nations the way through your Son, so they can pave a path for their people to go, to thrive, to love, and to make peace with other peoples and nations. For there is only one way to achieve global peace, and this is through the body of Christ which is your church on earth. The more people who will join with us in godly faith, the better the chances of finding peace, even in a world of violence, hate, and despair. Glory be to God in the highest, and on earth, peace and goodwill towards all people. In Jesus's name, Amen.

September 22

Autumnal Equinox marks the beginning of autumn. It is one of two days in the year when the amount of daylight and darkness are practically equal; the term equinox means equal night. While we are experiencing the fall equinox in the northern hemisphere, those in the southern hemisphere are experiencing the spring equinox. Thus, the days on which the equinoxes fall will differ depending on which side of the equator you are on. This is a time of harvest which is why the full moon nearest the equinox is called the harvest moon. The next full moon is called the hunter's moon. These were important seasons in all generations, given that farming and hunting have been common means of employment and survival since Adam and Eve were expelled from Eden. Incidentally, in the Bible, Cain was a farmer; Esau was a hunter.

- EXO 23:19 ~ The first fruits of your harvests shall be given to God.

- DEU 14:22 ~ You should give tithes of all your crops (i.e., income).

- 2 CH 31:5 ~ Everyone brought in abundance the first fruits of their crops, wine, oil, honey, and all their profits.

- LUK 3:16–17 ~ John the Baptist answered them saying, "I baptize you with water. But One comes after me whose shoelaces I am unworthy to untie. He will baptize you with the Holy Spirit and with fire. He has the winnowing fork in hand, ready to clear the threshing floor. He will gather the wheat into the barn, and He will burn up the chaff with unquenchable fire."

- LUK 10:2–3 ~ Jesus said, "The harvest is plentiful but the laborers are few. Pray that the Lord of the harvest would send more laborers to help. Keep in mind, I am sending you out like lambs among wolves."

- JAM 5:7–9 ~ Brothers, wait patiently for the coming of the Lord, like the farmer who must patiently await the rain and the harvest. Be patient and take courage, for His coming is near. Do not carry a grudge against another, for behold, the judge stands at the door.

Many religious rites and observances are associated with the equinoxes. The fall equinox and the harvest moon have been celebrated for millennia. For example, Yom Kippur is a Jewish observance occurring in the September-October timeframe; this was considered the time period when Moses was receiving the Ten Commandments on Mt. Sinai. It is the holiest day of the year for Jews, when atonement has been traditionally sought; the day is celebrated in like manner as the weekly sabbath. The Jewish feast of Rosh Hashanah continues for ten days preceding Yom Kippur, and is a time for reflecting on one's sins until the celebration of God's atonement.

- GEN 17—22 ~ Abraham was prepared to atone for his sinfulness by sacrificing his son Isaac. Abraham's act of faith, demonstrated by his willingness to please God at the cost of his own son, was sufficient for God to bless Abraham and Isaac, and to make a covenant with them.

- LEV 1—5 ~ Atonement was made for sin by offering sacrifices in accordance with God's laws given to Moses. Thus, the first covenant was the Law.

- LEV 17:11 ~ The life of all flesh resides in the blood, and I have given it to you upon the altar to make atonement for your souls; for it is the blood that makes atonement for the soul.

- MIC 6:6–7 ~ How am I to appear before God? Shall I come before Him with offerings and sacrifices? Will He be pleased with thousands and thousands of sacrifices? Shall I sacrifice my firstborn, the fruit of my body, to atone for the sin of my soul?

- ROM 5:8–11 ~ God showed His great love for us, for although we were sinners, Christ died for us. Therefore, we are justified by the blood of Christ, saved from God's wrath through Him.

We were reconciled to God by the death of His Son and we were saved by His life. We find great joy in God through our Lord Jesus Christ by whom we now have received the atonement.

- HEB 10:10–18 ~ Jesus's sacrifice is the last sacrifice that will ever need to be made to atone for sin. Under the Old Covenant, sacrificial offerings were made as an atonement for sin. Under the New Covenant, we are made clean by the blood of Christ in one final sacrificial offering. This sacrifice will stand for all time, so there is no longer any need for sin offerings or atonement sacrifices.

- 1 JO 2:1–2 ~ My little children, I am writing these things to you so you will not sin. But if anyone does sin, we have an advocate with the Father who will speak in our defense: Jesus Christ the Righteous One. He is the atoning sacrifice for our sins, and not only for our sins, but also for the sins of the entire world.

Other historical festivals associated with the fall equinox and harvest moon were held by the Druids (England), Mayans (Mexico), Japanese and Chinese. Ancient cultures worshipped different gods associated with the harvest. In the Old Testament, one such false god was Baal, the fertility god who brought rain to raise crops from the fertile ground. Baal worship was the reason God wanted the eradication of the Canaanites, to prevent such idolatry from sneaking into Israel, but it did, because they did not eliminate that threat. The female counterpart to Baal was Ashtoreth, goddess of fertility. Baal was the producer of crops and Ashtoreth the producer of babies. Sometimes the heathen nations sacrificed their firstborn babies to these gods, especially Molech the pagan god of the Ammonites; such practices have always been of the devil.

- LEV 18:21 ~ Never let any of your offspring be sacrificed to Molech.

- 1 KI 18:31–39 ~ Elijah had the pagan priests drench the sacrifice, the altar, and the wood three times. At the time of the evening sacrifice, the prophet Elijah came forward and prayed, "Oh Lord, God of Abraham, Isaac, and Israel, let it be known today that you are God and that I am your servant doing the things you have commanded me to do. Answer my prayer so that these people will know that you alone are God, and how your desire for them is to turn their hearts back towards you." Then fire fell from heaven and consumed the sacrifice, the wood, the stones, the soil, and all the water in the trench. When the people saw this, they dropped prostrate on the ground and cried, "The Lord is God!"

- JER 23:25–32 ~ God says, "I have heard those who prophesy lies in my name, claiming that they have dreamed great dreams. How much longer will these lying prophets share the delusions of their own minds? They think their visions will cause people to forget my name, like their forefathers did when they worshipped Baal.

If you want to celebrate this season, concentrate on the atonement provided to you by Christ, who paid your debt for sin, thereby purifying your soul with His blood. This act prohibited further sacrificial offerings to be made in accordance with the Mosaic Law. No blood offerings will ever be required because Christ made the atonement that would stand for all time.

Father, we thank you for the atonement of Christ, offered on Passover to take the place of the sacrificial lamb. No longer will any blood offerings be required because the Lamb of God paid the debt of the world's sin in full, for anyone who has accepted His free gifts of atonement and salvation. Thank you again, Father, for your Son who conquered the grave by rising from the dead, without which nobody would be brought back to life. Now we can be assured of the resurrection and our eternal freedom. We will always have hope as we look forward to the ascension of all your chosen people, whether alive or dead. In Jesus's name, Amen.

September 23

Obedience to God Day is something we should strive for every day. But on this new observance, try to remain mindful of God's presence the entire day, and see if you can stay obedient to Him for one whole day. I challenge you to try this, but be advised, it may be impossible due to our sinful nature. But the more you try, and the more you recognize that God's Spirit is there with you, the more likely you will hear His voice when you are tempted. Being tempted is not a sin, but taking it to the next level, which is considering it, is a sin; and the level after that is doing it either in word or deed, and that becomes a sin that can lead to death.

Are you keeping the law or breaking it? When it comes to God's Law, all humans are lawbreakers, every one of us. But if you have confessed and repented of your sins and received the forgiveness that only Christ can provide, you are probably doing a better job obeying laws of God and man. Be careful, however, not to slide back into your old ways. Habitually breaking any law is a sure way to lose your soul. Nobody has an excuse who engages in habitual sin, because everybody has knowledge of morality, whether they believe in God's truth or not.

- PSA 111:10 ~ The fear of the Lord is the beginning of wisdom; understanding is found in obeying His commandments.

- PRO 3:7 ~ Do not be wise in your own eyes but fear God and you will depart from evil.

- JER 31:33 ~ This is the covenant that I will make with the house of Israel. After those days, says the Lord, I will put my law in their minds and write it on their hearts. And I will be their God and they will be my people. (also HEB 8:6–13)

- ACT 10:34–35 ~ Peter said, "Truly, God does not show favoritism for any person. Within every nation, anyone who fears the Lord and endeavors to be righteous is accepted by Him."

- ROM 1:18–20 ~ God's wrath is revealed from heaven against the sinfulness of people, who know the truth of unrighteousness, because God has made it known to them. The invisible qualities of God are clearly seen from the creation of the world, for through His many creations one can understand God, even His power and divine nature, so nobody has an excuse for being evil.

- ROM 2:14–15 ~ When the Gentiles, who were not given the law, do by nature the things required of the law, though they have not the Law they are a law unto themselves. They exhibit the work of the Law written upon their hearts, their conscience also bearing witness; because their thoughts either accuse them or excuse them for things they say and do.

- 1 CO 6:9–11 ~ Do you realize that the wicked will not inherit the kingdom of God? Do not be deceived, for sinners, fornicators, idolaters, adulterers, homosexuals, perverts, thieves, greedy people, drunkards, slanderers, and swindlers will not inherit the kingdom. And many of us were sinners just like them. But we have been washed clean, sanctified, and justified in the name of our Lord Jesus Christ, by the Spirit of our God.

- HEB 8:10 ~ According to His covenant, the Lord will put His laws into our minds and write them upon our hearts (JER 31:33).

- JAM 2:1–10 ~ Be faithful like our Lord Jesus Christ, and do not show favoritism. Will you show more respect for a rich person than a poor person? Do you judge another with respect to their appearance, wealth, or status? If so, you are committing sin. If you follow the Law and love your neighbor as yourself you are doing right. However, whoever keeps the Law but violates it in one area, they are guilty of all.

- JAM 4:7–12 ~ Submit to God; resist Satan and he will flee from you. Draw nigh unto God and He will draw nigh unto you. Cleanse your hands you sinners and purify your hearts you who are double minded. Be hospitable to others without reservation. Humble yourselves before God and He will exalt you. Do not speak evil of one another or judge one another, for you will be guilty of speaking evil of the Law and of judging the Law. If you judge the Law, you cannot be a doer of the Law. There is only one lawgiver, who is able to save and to destroy.

- 2 PE 2:20–22 ~ For if, after they have escaped the pollution of the world through the knowledge of the Lord and Savior Jesus Christ, they are again entangled therein and overcome, the latter end is worse for them than the beginning. For it would have been better for them not to have known the way of righteousness, than after they had known it, to turn from the holy commandment delivered to them. What will happen to them is like a true proverb: The dog has returned to his vomit, and the pig that was washed is again wallowing in the mire.

What are we to do when God's Law is in discord with society's laws? Clearly, the will of God trumps the will of humans at all times and in all circumstances. That does not mean we can disobey the laws of the land or take the law into our own hands, for even the laws promulgated by governments are to be heeded. Exceptions to this rule are when governments and leaders dictate to the populace what they are to believe, force them to act against their consciences, or worse, expect them to pay imposing taxes for services, whether rendered or not. Our founders knew this when they declared "Congress shall make no law respecting the establishment of religion, or prohibiting the free exercise thereof..."

- DAN 3 ~ Shadrach, Meshach, and Abednego refused to worship the king, and were sentenced to death. God spared these men from the flames of the fiery furnace because they adhered to a higher authority, namely God.

- DAN 8 ~ Daniel was spared from death in the lion's den after he was caught praying to the Lord. The king was pleased to see that he was spared and sent Daniel's accusers and their families into the lion's den to be executed.

- ACT 5:22–29 ~ When the authorities commanded the apostles to stop preaching in the name of Jesus they replied, "We must obey God rather than men."

- 1 JO 5:1–12 ~ Whoever believes in Jesus Christ is born of God; whoever loves God, loves His Son. We know we are God's children, because we love God and obey His commandments, which are not that difficult to follow. Everyone who is born of God overcomes the world. This is the victory, that by faith we can overcome the world. So, who can overcome the world? Anyone who believes that Jesus Christ is the Son of God can overcome. Christ is the One who came by *water* and by *blood*. It is His Holy Spirit who testifies for the Spirit is the truth. There are three that testify in heaven, the Father, the Word, and the Holy Spirit, and these three are one. Likewise, there are three that testify on earth, the spirit, the water, and the blood. If we are willing to accept the testimony of men, then we should accept the testimony of God even more, and He has testified about His Son. People who believe in God's Son will have His testimony in their hearts. People who do not believe are essentially calling God a liar, because they do not believe the truth about Christ, even though it comes directly from God. The testimony that God has given us concerns eternal life, and this life is God's Son, Jesus Christ. Those who do not have the Son do not have life.

- ROM 13:1–2 ~ Everyone is subject to the higher powers, for all power comes from God; that is, all powers that exist have been ordained by God. Anyone who resists these powers are resisting the ordinance of God, and those who resist God receive damnation as punishment.

Clearly, modern societies allow behaviors that Christians believe are contrary to God's Law. All three branches of our government have passed and supported rules and regulations that go against our morals and the guidance of the Holy Spirit. Governments are often too permissive on the one hand and too dictatorial on the other. We need to be vigilant, because evil people have infiltrated all areas of our society in an attempt to change the culture, brainwash our kids, disseminate lies, and control our lives. This is the very environment that forced our forefathers to fight tyranny, which is an attempt to replace God with government. Tyrants and dictators are behaving in the same manner as the evil kings and kingdoms during Daniel's day, and the king and government of England when our country's founders declared independence from them.

One can look back and see how the providence of God was behind people who stood with Him, and how goodness and honor prevailed when the odds were against His people. This is because, when evil and good are at odds, it becomes God's battle. And God will fight with the upright just as He did when David took a stand against Goliath and the Philistines. As David prevailed time and again facing the Philistines, so can we prevail against Satan and evil, if we remain steadfast in our adherence to God's will for our lives and our country. If we stick with God, we will prevail over sin in the end.

- DEU 20:1, 4 ~ When you go into battle against your enemies, and you see horses and chariots, and you realize you are outnumbered, do not fear. For the Lord your God is with you. He is the same one who rescued you out of Egypt. He goes with you to fight for you and to save you.

- DEU 31:6 ~ Be strong and of good courage; do not fear or be dismayed. For the Lord God goes with you; he will never fail you or forsake you.

- JOS 1:9 ~ God said, "Did I not command you to be strong and have courage, and not to be afraid or dismayed? For I am with you wherever you go."

- ISA 41:10 ~ God says, "Fear not, for I am with you. Do not be dismayed, for I am your God. I will strengthen and help you. I will hold you up with the right hand of righteousness."

- ROM 7:21–25 ~ I am aware of a law within me compelling me to do good, while evil is also present in my mind. I delight in the Law of God placed there for my edification, but I see another law in my body waging war against God's Law and making me a captive to the law of sin. What a wretched person I am! Who will deliver me from this body of death? Thank God through Jesus Christ our Lord! Although in my mind I serve the Law of God, in my flesh I am a slave to sin.

- 2 CO 10:3–5 ~ Although we are human flesh and blood, we do not make war with flesh and blood. For the weapons we use are not of this world, because we have the Spirit on our side to bring down the strongholds of the enemy. We break down the arguments and the influences of those high and mighty people who stand against God; we take captive human thoughts, making them obedient to Jesus Christ.

Heavenly Father, we know that we cannot earn salvation through good works, because we are saved by faith in Christ, who was obedient unto death. And though we are saved because we believe, we are compelled to do a better job at obeying your rules and laws. Help us to continuously raise the bar with respect to our subservience to you. Our faith gives us a good reason to keep trying to be good, and not get complacent in life. Encourage us, Father, to be mindful of these objectives for our lives. Sanctify us with your Holy Spirit as we gradually become an example of godliness in the world. Since Christ is our example, help us to be more like Him, so others can see that He is our guide, our mentor, and our hero. Let the light of Jesus Christ shine more brilliantly both in us and in the world. In His name we pray, Amen.

September 24

Harvard College Held First Graduation on this day in Cambridge MA, 1642. This was the first commencement ceremony in English America, proving to the world that the US would be able to compete with more advanced countries. Harvard started with a Puritan influence, producing magistrates, clergymen, and statesmen characterized as the *First Fruits* of American higher education, a term used in the Bible about dedicating the first of our increase to the Lord. Sadly, the Christian roots of Harvard faded, and they are now one of the leaders in educating future secularists. Most of our original universities were Christ-centered, and founded on the Holy Bible. But they have flipped to a position contrary to Christianity, with few exceptions.

- EXO 23:19 ~ Moses instructed the Israelites to give to God the first fruits of their labor.
- PRO 1:5–7 ~ A wise person will listen and will increase in learning; a person of understanding will seek wise counsel, and will try to understand a proverb and its interpretation, or the words of the wise and the hidden meaning of what they say. Remember, the fear of God is the beginning of understanding; only fools despise wisdom and instruction.
- PRO 19:20 ~ Listen to sound advice and accept proper instruction, and you will be wise.
- PSA 32:8 ~ I will instruct you, teaching you the way to go, and guiding you with my eye.
- MAT 13:52 ~ Jesus said, "Every teacher who has been instructed about the kingdom of heaven is like a homeowner who has a treasure chest of things both old and new."

Universities of today are failing their students, offering worthless degrees, meaningless classes, and watered-down coursework which is deliberately biased towards humanism and socialism. I noticed it back when I was an undergrad, instructors endorsing a political ideology. I also noticed this as a professor and academician, that liberal politics and unchristian philosophies were being propagated. But now it is permeating all aspects of academia and most public institutions; in the name of equity they are loosening entry requirements, becoming less strict on grading, and integrating dogma into the curricula that mimics fascism, statism, and collectivism.

- ACT 20:29–30 ~ Paul said, "After I leave, vicious wolves will infiltrate among you, not sparing the flock. From among your own people, they will come speaking perverse things to draw disciples after them."
- 2 TI 4:3–4 ~ People will seek teachers who conform to their own likes and dislikes; they will turn away from the truth and wander into myths.
- 2 PE 3:17 ~ Dear friends, you have been forewarned; be on your guard so you are not led astray by the error of the wicked, and depart from your devotion.
- JDE 1:4 ~ False teachers have infiltrated the churches, claiming that once you become Christians you can do whatever you want without being punished.

Father, help our schools and colleges to clean up their curricula, returning to the basics and the truth. We pray that lazy administrators and biased instructors be replaced with faculty, staff, and leadership that will tighten the rules of admission, grading, expectations, coursework, and degree plans, so that students get a first-rate education regardless of the location, and the cost of tuition and fees. Let us as a country raise the bar on our academics lest we drop further below the rest of the world. May we be competitive in our schools like we were in our beginnings, when Christian institutions were turning out highly educated and skilled graduates that could match those in more advanced countries. Influence our educational systems to advance wise, ethical, and worthy students fully prepared for their occupation and your service. Amen.

September 25

Peace at Augsburg with Lutherans and Catholics was reached on this day in 1555. After the division between Protestantism and Catholicism had been triggered by Martin Luther, the two prevailing churches in Germany decided to coexist in harmony. Still, the long battle between the Roman Catholic church and the numerous Protestant denominations would continue for centuries. Though the two factions of Christianity disagree on certain positions, they reached an agreement in 1999 on the doctrine of justification by faith and not by works of the Law. We are saved through a faith that motivates us to do good.

- EZE 33:13 ~ Those who are righteous will surely live. But if you trust in righteousness and continue to sin, none of your righteous deeds will be remembered; and the sin will cause you to die.

- HAB 2:4 ~ Those whose souls are not upright will fail; but the just will live by faith.

- ROM 3:21–22 ~ The righteousness of God is apart from the Law, although the Law and the prophets bear witness to it. Righteousness from God exists through faith in Jesus Christ.

- ROM 10:10, 17 ~ Those who believe with their hearts are justified. Those who confess with their lips are saved. Faith comes by hearing and hearing by the Word of God.

- GAL 2:16, 20–21 ~ Nobody is justified by works of the Law, but by faith in Jesus Christ. I have been crucified with Christ; thus, it is no longer I who live but Christ who lives in me. And the life I live in the flesh I live by faith in the Son of God who gave His life for me. I do not discount God's grace, for if righteousness came by the Law, then Christ died in vain.

- GAL 3:11, 24, 26 ~ No man is justified before God by the Law, but those who are righteous through faith shall live. The Law was in effect until Christ came, that we might be justified by faith. In Christ we can become children of God through faith.

- EPH 2:8–9 ~ You are saved by the grace of God because of your faith in Jesus Christ. Salvation is a gift of God, it cannot be earned through good works, so nobody should brag.

- 2 TI 1:9 ~ God saved us and called us, not by virtue of our works, but by virtue of His own purpose and the grace He gave us through Jesus Christ ages ago.

- TIT 3:5–8 ~ He did not save us because of our deeds done in righteousness, but because of His mercy given us through the regeneration and renewal in the Holy Spirit by Jesus Christ, so we can be justified by faith and become heirs in hope of eternal life. Those who have believed will apply themselves to perform good deeds.

- JAM 2:17–26 ~ Faith without works is dead. Was Abraham justified by works when he offered his son Isaac? Faith was active before that and was completed by the works. So, a person is justified also by works and not by faith alone. Just as a body apart from the spirit is dead, so is faith apart from works.

- 1 PE 1:3–4, 9–10 ~ Through God's mercy we have been born anew to a living hope by the resurrection of Jesus Christ, to receive an inheritance which is imperishable, undefiled, and unfading, kept in heaven for all believers. The outcome of faith in Jesus is salvation of the soul. A salvation of which was inquired and searched diligently, who spoke of the grace that should come to you.

There is still disagreement regarding Catholic practices of praying to saints, paying indulgences, incarceration in purgatory, and mandatory penance. These were among the ninety-five theses Luther posted in 1517. These concepts were derived from traditions of men and go against the Word of God as illustrated in the following verses.

- PSA 49:6–8, 15 ~ Those who trust in their wealth and brag about their riches will never be able to redeem the life of another nor provide a ransom for them. For the redemption of their soul is precious; no worldly payment will ever be enough. But God will redeem my soul from the power of the grave.

- ISA 53:5 ~ He was wounded and bruised for our sins, His punishment bought our peace, and His wounds healed us.

- MAR 10:45 ~ Jesus said, "Even the Son of man did not come to be served but to serve, and to give His life as a ransom for many."

- JOH 14:6, 9–11, 13 ~ Jesus said, "I am the way, the truth, and the life; nobody comes to the Father but by me. If you have seen me, you have seen the Father, because the Father lives in me and I in Him. Whatever you pray for in my name, the Father will do, so He may be glorified in the Son."

- JOH 16:23 ~ Jesus said, "If you ask the Father anything in my name, He will give it to you."

- PHP 2:9–11 ~ God exalted Him to the highest position and gave Him a name that is above every other name, so that at the name of Jesus Christ every knee should bow, whether in heaven, on earth, or under the earth, and every tongue confess that Jesus Christ is Lord to the glory of God the Father.

- 1 CO 6:20 ~ You were bought with a great price, so glorify God in your bodies and your spirits, for you belong to Him.

- 2 CO 5:1, 6–8 ~ We know that when this temple, which is our body, is dissolved, we will have a home in heaven; not a house made by hands but one that is eternal. This gives us the confidence we need, for we are living here in the flesh and absent from the Lord. We must walk by faith not by sight. I am not afraid; indeed, I yearn to be absent from this body and present with the Lord.

- 2 CO 5:21 ~ Christ, who never sinned, became sin for us so we could receive the righteousness of God that was in Him.

- COL 2:13–14 ~ You, being dead in your sins and your sinful flesh, have been brought alive with Him, who has forgiven you all of your trespasses, blotting out your debt from the record and nailing it to the cross.

- 1 TI 2:5 ~ There is one God, and one mediator between Him and us, who is Jesus Christ.

- HEB 10:10–18 ~ Jesus's sacrifice is the last sacrifice that will ever need to be made to atone for sin. Under the Old Covenant, sacrificial offerings were made as an atonement for sin. Under the New Covenant, we are made clean by the blood of Christ in one final sacrificial offering. This sacrifice will stand for all time, so there is no longer any need for sin offerings or sacrifices.

Given that evangelicals agree on the essential doctrines of the faith, it seems unnecessary to have these persistent debates among denominations of the Christian faith on ancillary issues that will never be resolved, or cannot be known, much less proven scripturally. For example, there is no need to divide over such things as the age of the universe, baptism, confirmation, or tithing; but there is a need to unite over such things as marriage, abortion, liberty, and law.

SEPTEMBER

- EZE 11:19–20 ~ I will give them an undivided heart, and place a new spirit within them. I will remove their heart of stone and replace it with a heart of flesh. Then they will follow my decrees and carefully obey my commandments. They will be my people and I will be their God.

- HOS 10:2 ~ Their heart is divided; they have been found guilty. God will break down their altars and destroy their graven images.

- ROM 16:17 ~ Take notice of those who cause divisions and take offense to the doctrine you have learned, and avoid them.

- 1 CO 1:10 ~ By the name of Christ, be united in one mind and be of one opinion.

- 1 CO 11:17–18 ~ I have heard that when you assemble together as a church there are divisions among you. I am telling you that such meetings do more harm than good.

- 1 CO 12:25–26 ~ There should be no division in the body of Christ, but all members should have equal concern for one another. If one member suffers, everyone should suffer; and if one member is honored, all the members rejoice.

- EPH 4:2–3 ~ Be humble, gentle, and patient, holding up each other in love. Try earnestly to stay united in the Spirit through the bond of peace. Maintain unity of the Spirit in the bond of peace.

- JDE 1:17–19 ~ Dear friends, remember what the apostles told us. They said that in the latter days there would be scoffers who follow their own ungodly desires. These people have come to divide you; they follow the instincts of their flesh and do not have the Spirit within them.

The peace among congregations and denominations has been rejuvenated somewhat in recent decades. There was a time when you would not find official representatives from several denominations collaborating on public initiatives such as giving, serving, charity fundraising, and ministry in the Gospel of Jesus Christ. Serving, helping, and witnessing to people in need is something that all Christians can unite over, and this is becoming more commonplace with teams of mixed denominations.

- EPH 4:12–13 ~ We are to prepare God's people for works of service, so that the body of Christ may be edified, until we reach unity in the faith and in the knowledge of the Son of God, and become mature, attaining the whole measure of the fullness of Christ.

- 1 PE 3:8–9 ~ Live in harmony with one another with love, sympathy, compassion, and humility. Do not repay evil with evil or insult others, but repay with blessings, so you may inherit a blessing.

- ROM 15:5–7 ~ May the God who gives endurance, encouragement, and hope give you a spirit of unity as you follow Christ. Give glory to God the Father of our Lord Jesus Christ with one voice and one heart. Accept each other as Christ accepted you, so that God may be praised.

Father, help all who worship you, your Son, and your Spirit to come together in unity of spirit under the canopy of your grace, so we can be a positive force on the earth to drive out evil in our government, institutions, and churches. Let your church on earth become more involved in the direction of our nation and the world. Fight with us against those who would infiltrate your church, our schools, our government, and or our nation to destroy or divide it. Help the Christian church to always be a refuge for anyone who seeks truth, freedom, and peace. In the name of Jesus whose blood sets us free to be people of your kingdom, Amen.

September 26

National Situational Awareness Day was established in 2016 as a reminder to be alert, vigilant, and observant at all times. This requires that we do our homework and prepare for upcoming events; have an escape plan, safety plan, or contingency plan; be cognizant of any possible threats in the environment or on the way; or whatever the circumstances dictate. This holiday was the brainchild of Beth Warford who averted an attack on herself and her children the year before. She credited it to being situationally aware of her surroundings and the predator. This inspired her to found *Pretty Loaded LLC*, an organization that disseminates information about situational awareness, provides trainings and presentations, and advocates for gun ownership and safety. Her proposal for this holiday was accepted by the National Day Calendar association. This date was chosen as it was the birthday of Dru Sjodin, a woman who was stalked and murdered by a repeat offender in 2003; the felon was later sentenced to death. This case received national attention when President Bush signed the Adam Walsh Child Protection and Safety Act in 2006, and renamed the sex offender registry as the Dru Sjodin National Sex Offender Public Website (NSOPW).

- PRO 22:24–25 ~ Do not make friends with an angry person or associate with someone who has a quick temper, for you risk learning their ways and falling into the same trap.

- ISA 30:1 ~ Woe to the rebellious children, declares the Lord. Woe to those who carry out plans that are not mine, form alliances but not with my Spirit, and who heap sin upon sin.

- JER 18:11–12 ~ God warned that He was going to destroy them unless they turned from their evil ways. But they said, "It is hopeless. Let us continue with our own plans. We will follow the imaginations of our evil hearts."

- MIC 2:1 ~ Woe to those who plot evil and think of sinful things to do, and then carry out their evil plans just because they think they can get away with it.

- 2 TI 3:12–13 ~ All the righteous people will suffer persecution. The evil people will get perpetually worse.

- 1 PE 5:8–9 ~ Be sober and vigilant, because your enemy the devil roams about like a lion searching for someone to devour. He will attempt to consume anyone who is not steadfast in their faith.

Every family should have a situational awareness plan of their own. Create rules and procedures with your children, complete with secret codes, short list of contact names and phone numbers, instructions on when to scream and run, how to pay attention to changes in the environment, possibly even how to shoot a firearm or employ available weapons. As your children age, these plans need to be updated including additional roles, responsibilities, and situations. Mom and Dad need their plans and codes as well. It is almost like a military operation, with strategies, tactics, doctrine, threat analyses, contingency plans, maps, and diagrams. If organized properly, this can be a fun and beneficial way to spend quality time with those you love or live with. In these days of uncertainty and violence it is an essential precaution. Even if not feeling threatened, it is a good policy to practice vigilance, which might come in handy someday.

- DEU 4:9 ~ Be careful and keep close watch over your soul, so you do not forget the things that you have witnessed, or let them slip away from your heart. Teach these things to your children and your children's children.

- ISA 55:3 ~ Listen up and come to me, pay attention so your soul might live. I will make an everlasting covenant with you, to give you all the faithful love and mercies I showed my servant David.

SEPTEMBER

- LUK 21:36 ~ Jesus taught, "Watch for the signs and pray that you have the strength to escape the terrible things that will take place, then to stand before the Son of man."
- ACT 20:28 ~ Keep watch over yourselves and the flock of which the Holy Spirit has made you overseers. Feed the church of God which He purchased with His own blood.

When out and about, keep a watchful eye and ear covering 360 degrees, maintaining a visual representation as the situational environment changes. Know the neighborhood, buildings, parking lots, and alleyways on your route if you are walking, and your map if you are riding. Identify unordinary things, events, and people; beware of situations that can become emergencies and detect sudden changes in the surroundings. Watch for hazards, unsafe circumstances, movement in your direction, and vulnerabilities. Beware of artificial intelligence that can mimic the voice of your loved ones; check in regularly. Report suspicious behavior to the authorities.

- PRO 15:28 ~ The righteous heart studies the situation before giving an answer; however, a wicked mouth pours out evil words.
- PRO 21:31 ~ The horse is prepared for the day of battle, but safety is from the Lord.
- ROM 6:23 ~ The risk of sin is death. But God's gift of eternal life is available to everyone through Jesus Christ our Lord.

Does every circumstance require situational awareness; can't you relax sometimes? The answer is yes and yes. There are places where you can feel safe most of the time, but it is wise not to let your guard down. More importantly, when it comes to your situation with Christ you have to be alert and aware at all times because He could return today.

- MAT 24:36, 44, 50 ~ Nobody knows the day and hour, not even the angels; not even the Son of man knows, but only the Father in heaven. For the Son of man will come when you least expect Him.
- MAT 25:13 ~ Watch therefore, because you know neither the day nor the hour.
- MAR 13:35–37 ~ Jesus taught, "Watch for the Master, for you do not know if He will come in the evening, at midnight, or at dawn. Do not let Him catch you sleeping on your watch."
- LUK 12:37–46 ~ Jesus said, "Blessed are those who the Lord finds watching for Him when He returns; like a waiter, He will seat them at the table and serve them a banquet. If He comes at the second watch, or the third, and finds them alert they will be blessed. Know this, if the good man of the house was aware a thief was coming, he would have watched and protected his house from being burglarized. So be ready, for the Son of man comes when you least expect Him."
- HEB 3:12, 19; HEB 4:6 ~ Brothers beware, in case any of you have an evil heart of unbelief that strays from the living God; for they will not enter the kingdom because of their unbelief.
- 2 PE 3:10 ~ The day of the Lord will come as a thief in the night.
- REV 3:2–3 ~ Jesus said, "Be watchful and strengthen each other in the truth, for I have found imperfection on earth. Remember everything you have heard, hold fast to it, and repent. If you are not watchful, I will surprise you like a thief, for you never know when I might come."

Father in heaven, help us to be vigilant, prepared, and ready for the return of our Lord. Help us also to be diligent in maintaining safety and security in our homes, offices, and churches, so that the evil plans of predators and malefactors are thwarted. Remind parents to review safety precautions with their children regularly so they can memorize them. In Jesus's name, Amen.

September 27

Ford Motor Company Assembled First Model T on this day in Detroit, 1908. Many others were developing motorcars but they were very expensive to build and market. Henry Ford's Model T was an affordable, reliable, durable, and maintainable form of transportation. The "Tin Lizzy" had a twenty-horsepower engine with a top speed of forty-five miles per hour; it got about fifteen miles to a gallon of gasoline. Ford had no idea how quickly his car would become the rave. He sold almost ten thousand the first year. He demonstrated remarkable ingenuity when he invented the assembly line five years later for mass production of his cars. Other industries followed suit. The car did more to connect the east and west than the railroad. Highway systems began to be built as the number of drivers increased.

Throughout the Bible, land transportation was limited to horses, donkeys, oxen, and camels, sometimes pulling wagons, carts, and plows. But the basic components of the car were there: wheels, axles, carriage, wagon bed, horsepower. They also had learned how to smelt metal. Many inventions in the Old Testament were war machines, such as chariots, war towers, catapults, and battering rams. We have come a long way. But devices in the latter days will be far more advanced than what we see now, when the evil one gains a stronghold prior to the end.

- EXO 14:28 ~ And the waters of the Red Sea returned and covered the chariots and the horsemen, and they all drowned.
- 2 CH 26:14–16 ~ Uzziah fabricated shields, spears, helmets, armor, bows, and slings for the entire army. In Jerusalem he produced machines devised by creative men to place on towers and defensive walls, and also catapults to hurl giant stones and arrows. Uzziah helped tremendously, becoming famous and powerful, but pride was his downfall.
- JOB 28:1–2 ~ Surely there is a mine for silver and a place to refine gold. Iron is taken out of the earth and copper is melted from ore.
- ECC 1:10 ~ Is there anything that can be called new which has not been around for ages?
- DAN 11:21–24 ~ In his place will arise a contemptible person, without warning, and obtain the kingdoms by flattery and deceit. He will overthrow armies, make alliances deceptively, and plunder. He will forecast devices against his enemies; he will employ the power of forces.

St. Paul was possibly the most traveled person in the Bible whether by foot, beast, or ship. He covered some ten thousand miles by land and ten thousand more by sea on boats, unprotected from the elements. He spent half of his missionary life traveling to take the Gospel to the Gentile nations. Evangelists today put in a lot more travel over longer distances but in shorter time. Imagine having to pound the dust for months to get from one place to another.

- ACT 22–21~ Paul said that after the blood of the martyr Stephen was shed, where he stood consenting to his death and guarding the coats of those who stoned him, God told him to depart far away unto the Gentiles.
- 2 COR 11:24–26 ~ Paul said he received thirty-nine lashes five times, was beaten with rods three times, stoned once, shipwrecked three times, and spent a night and a day in the deep sea. He journeyed often, facing perils in the seas, robbers, even his own countrymen; in foreign lands, in the city, in the wilderness, and among false believers.

Father, help us use our ingenuity and apply it to tasks you have assigned us. Help us to be willing to take your Word of truth to the world, wherever you call us and whenever you need us, even as Paul spent his formidable years as a traveling evangelist up until his death. In Jesus's name, whose Word travels fast, we pray, Amen.

September 28

National Good Neighbor Day was officially established by President Carter in 1978 to promote communications and goodwill among neighbors. Today is a good day to celebrate with others who live in your neighborhood, or work in your office building, or even people you meet on the street. Everybody is your neighbor when you are sharing the same space. Take an opportunity to get acquainted with those you have seen but not met.

Good neighbors make for safer and friendlier neighborhoods, and help build thriving and stable communities. What are the qualities of a good neighbor? The Bible has the answer, which is always love. What kind of love should we portray?

- LUK 10:36–37 ~ After telling the parable of the Good Samaritan, Jesus asked, "Which of these passersby was a neighbor to the man who was attacked?" The lawyer answered, "The man who was merciful." Jesus replied, "Go and do likewise."

- 1 CO 13:2–8, 13 ~ Even if you have the gift of prophecy, can understand mysteries, and have a faith to move mountains, you are nothing without love. Even if you give all you have to the poor, you profit nothing if you do not have love. Love is patient. Love is kind. Love is never envious or conceited. Love is not rude, self-seeking, or angered, nor does it find pleasure in sin. Love does not think of sinful things nor is it provoked by evil. Love rejoices in the truth. Love always protects, always trusts, always hopes, and always endures. Love never fails... Faith, hope, and love abide; but the greatest of these three is love.

If your neighbor is confused as to why you are interested in becoming friends, tell them about National Good Neighbor Day. Explain to them the commandment of God to love your neighbor as yourself. This may break the ice or it may turn them completely off. If they want to know more about where you are coming from, share the Word of God with them.

- LEV 19:17–18 ~ Do not hate anyone in your heart; do not scold or sin against your neighbor. Do not take revenge or bear a grudge, but love your neighbor as you love yourself.

- PSA 12:2 ~ They speak vainly about their neighbors; with flattering lips and two faces they speak.

- PRO 11:9, 12 ~ A hypocrite can destroy his neighbor with his mouth, but through knowledge the just will be delivered. Those who are void of wisdom despise their neighbors, but a person of wisdom holds his peace.

- PRO 24:28–29 ~ Do not testify against your neighbor without just cause, and do not use your lips to deceive. Do not say, "I will do to him as he has done to me, or I will render unto the man according to his work."

- ZEC 8:16–17 ~ Always tell the truth to your neighbor; always execute judgments of truth and peace. Do not imagine evil in your hearts against another.

- MAT 5:21–26 ~ Jesus said, "You have heard that you must never kill or you will be in danger of the judgment, but I say that if you become angry with another person, or call a person a fool without cause, you will be in danger of the judgment. Do not carry a grudge or any animosity towards another, but reconcile with your neighbor before bringing your offerings to the altar."

- MAT 18:21–22 ~ Peter asked Jesus, "How many times should someone forgive a person? Up to seven times?" Jesus replied, "Not seven times, but seventy times seven (or seventy-seven)."

- MAT 22:37–40; MAR 12:30–31 ~ Jesus said, "Love the Lord your God with all your heart, mind, and soul: this is the first and greatest commandment. The second is like unto the first:

Love your neighbor as yourself. All the laws and the prophets depend on these two commandments."

- LUK 6:31–36 ~ Do unto others as you would like them to do unto you. For if you love those who love you, what thanks do you have, for even sinners love those who love them? And if you do good to them who do good to you, what have you gained, for sinners to the same. And if you lend to them from whom you hope to receive, what have you gained, because sinners lend to other sinners for the same reason. Love your enemies, and do good, and lend, expecting nothing in return, and your reward will be great; and you will be children of the Most High. For He is kind to the unthankful and to the sinner. So be merciful, even as your Father is also merciful.

- ROM 13:10 ~ Love does no wrong to a neighbor; therefore, love is the fulfilling of the Law.

- GAL 5:13–18 ~ Brothers, you have been called to be free men, but do not use that freedom as an excuse to engage in lusts of the flesh, but in love serve one another. For all the Law is fulfilled by loving your neighbor as yourself. So, walk in the Spirit not in the flesh. For the Spirit and the flesh oppose one another. If you are led by the Spirit, you are not under the Law.

- JAM 2:1–9 ~ Do not be partial to people just because you like the way they look or act. Do not give the rich or the famous more respect than anyone else, and do not give the poor and lowly less respect. If you abide by the royal law according to the scripture, "Love your neighbor as yourself," you are doing the right thing. But if you show favoritism to certain people. you commit sin, and are convicted of the law for being a lawbreaker.

- 1 JO 4:19–21 ~ We love God because He loved us first. If someone says they love God but hate their neighbor they lie. For how can you love someone you have not seen if you cannot even love someone you have seen? God has commanded that we love Him and love our brothers (neighbors) also.

The more difficult task is for nations to love their neighbors. I mean, some countries are downright unfriendly and ungodly. Our nation started out as a Bible believing people, which is nothing to be embarrassed about. Regrettably, many citizens want to remove God completely from the dialogue. But if we do this, we will become like other ungodly nations. Either way, some countries do not want to be neighborly because they hate the USA; maybe they are jealous of our freedoms. But some self-centered souls in this country would remove our freedoms so they can control us. I doubt if these people love our country, much less God, or their neighbors.

- MAT 5:38–48 ~ Jesus said, "It is written: an eye for an eye and a tooth for a tooth; but I say that if someone strikes you on the cheek, turn to him the other cheek. If someone would sue you under the law for your coat, give him your overcoat too. If a person compels you to walk with them one mile, walk with them an additional mile. You have heard: love your neighbor and hate your enemy. But I am telling you to love your enemies; bless those who curse you, do good to those who hate you, and pray for those who take advantage of you and abuse you. What reward do you receive if you love only those who love you? Even sinners love those who love them. Strive to be perfect like your Father in heaven."

Father in heaven, help us to love you first, and love others as ourselves as you have commanded. Help us promote leaders and government authorities who know you and who love you and your Word, and intend to abide by your Law and the laws of the land. Help us as a nation to be a good neighbor to other countries, demonstrating strength in love and peace, as well as in might. Help us not to shy away from opportunities to make friends individually and as a nation. In the name of our best friend Jesus, Amen.

September 29

World Heart Day is an annual observance highlighting the dangers of cardiovascular disease. It was introduced by the World Heart Federation and first celebrated on 09/04/2000. The date was changed to 09/29 in 2011. Heart disease is the number one cause of death, so it is advisable to learn how to best protect and preserve your heart. This day millions of people from dozens of countries will be presented information, instruction, seminars, broadcasts, fundraisers, and localized gatherings to discuss heart health and current science in cardiovascular medicine and practice. The American Heart Association will be recognizing this observance with different themes and goals as well.

Take control of your heart and you will live longer, if not forever. We have a physical heart and we have a spiritual heart. Both need nurturing. Take care of your cardiovascular needs and you live longer on this horizontal plane; take care of your spiritual needs and you live forever on the vertical plane.

- DEU 10:12–13 ~ The Lord requires you to fear Him, to walk in His ways, to love Him, to serve Him will all your heart and soul, and to obey His commandments.

- 1 KI 8:48–49, 61 ~ If they repent with all their minds and hearts, I will hear their prayers. Let your heart be true to the Lord, walking in his statutes and keeping His commandments.

- PSA 10:17; PSA 34:18; PSA 147:3 ~ Lord, you know the needs of the afflicted; you hear them and give encouragement to their hearts. The Lord is near to those with a broken heart; He saves those with a contrite spirit. God heals the broken hearted and binds their wounds.

- PSA 31:24; PSA 37:4 ~ Be strong and let your heart take courage, you who hope in the Lord. Make the Lord your delight and He will give you the desires of your heart.

- PSA 51:10–12, 17 ~ Create in me a clean heart, Lord, and renew an upright spirit within me. Do not remove me from your presence and do not take your Holy Spirit from me. Restore to me the joy of your salvation, and uphold me with your free Spirit. Sacrifices to God represent a broken spirit; God will not despise a broken and contrite heart.

- PRO 2:10–13 ~ When wisdom enters your heart and knowledge is pleasant to your soul, discretion will preserve you and understanding will keep you, to deliver you from evil and from those who speak evil.

- PRO 3:5–7 ~ Trust in the Lord with all your heart; do not rely on your own understanding. In all your ways acknowledge Him and He will make your paths straight.

- PRO 15:4, 13 ~ A perverse tongue breaks the spirit. A sorrowful heart breaks the spirit.

- PRO 27:19 ~ The heart reflects the man just like a mirror.

- ECC 10:2 ~ A wise heart inclines one to do what is right.

- EZE 11:21 ~ To those whose hearts seek detestable things and abominations, I will recompense it back upon their own heads.

- MAT 5:8 ~ Blessed be the pure in heart for they shall see God.

- MAT 15:18–19 ~ What comes out of the mouth proceeds from the heart and defiles the person. For out of the heart come evil thoughts and sinful acts.

- JOH 14:1 ~ Jesus said, "Do not let your heart be troubled. Trust in God, and trust in me."

- JOH 16:22 ~ Jesus said, "You may have sorrow now, but I will see you again and your heart will rejoice, and nobody can take that joy from you."

- ACT 8:22 ~ Pray that the intent of your heart may be forgiven.

- ROM 1:21 ~ They knew God but did not glorify Him, nor were they thankful; they became futile in their thinking and their foolish hearts were darkened.

- ROM 5:5 ~ Hope does not disappoint us, because God's love has been poured into our hearts through the Holy Spirit.

- ROM 10:10 ~ Those who believe with their hearts are justified. Those who confess with their lips are saved.

- 2 CO 4:16–18 ~ Therefore we do not lose heart. Though outwardly we continue to deteriorate, yet inwardly we are constantly renewed. For our momentary and minor troubles are achieving for us an eternal glory that far outweighs them all. We do not focus on the things we can see, but on the things that we cannot see; for the things that we can see are temporal, but the things that we cannot see are eternal.

- HEB 4:12 ~ The Word of God is living and active, sharper than any double-edged sword, dividing the soul and spirit, and discerning the thoughts and intentions of the heart.

The heart represents the person's physical health. A healthy heart requires exercise and a proper diet. The mind represents the person's soul: will, emotions, thoughts, desires. The spirit represents the conscience, morality, and truth. We reflect the image of God in all three areas.

- DEU 11:16 ~ Guard your heart from deceptions that would cause you to turn aside and serve other gods and worship them.

- PSA 73:26 ~ My flesh and my heart may fail, but God is the strength of my heart and my portion forever.

- PRO 4:23 ~ Keep your heart with diligence, for from it flows the springs of life.

- PRO 17:22 ~ A cheerful heart is good medicine.

- MAT 10:28 ~ Jesus said, "Do not fear those who can kill the body but not the soul. Rather fear God who can destroy both your body and soul in hell."

- MAT 22:37 ~ Jesus said, "Love the Lord with all your heart, soul, and mind" (see DEU 6:5).

- COL 3:15 ~ Let the peace of God rule in your heart.

- 1 TH 5:23 ~ May the God of peace sanctify you wholly, so that your entire spirit, soul, and body can be preserved blameless until the coming of our Lord Jesus Christ.

- 1 TI 4:8 ~ Physical training helps the body, but godliness has value in all things, holding promise for the present life and the life to come.

Eternal Father, help us to guard our hearts physically and spiritually, so we can live our lives for Christ, and so we can live forever with you. Remind us to exercise and train physically, mentally, and spiritually so we can be healthy and whole, and fit for duty. Give us endurance in all these areas as we combat the evil in this world, and denounce the sin in our own lives. Let us be confident and persevere in our faith in Jesus, crowned in His righteousness until the day we pass from this life into the next, when we ourselves will stand righteous before you. In the name of your Son, who gave us the righteousness that was in Him, we pray, Amen.

September 30

Gold Star Mother's and Family's Day is celebrated on the last Sunday of the month in honor of the mothers and families who have lost loved ones as a consequence of war. There are countries that hate us and refuse to be good neighbors to the USA or our allies. They push the limits until we have no recourse but to fight. If feeble humans were actually capable of loving their neighbor as themselves there would be no wars. But Christians are compelled to try.

The gold star tradition began with World War I, to distinguish the sacrifice of those left hurting for our fallen heroes. Service flags being flown outside homes had a blue star signifying their loved one was deployed to the battle zone; if they perished, the blue star was changed to a gold star. Thus began the Gold Star Mothers association in 1928. Their objective was to bond together with other mothers through love, support, and patriotism as they grieved and upheld one another; group edification always assists in the process of mourning. Congress approved this observance in 1936 as Gold Star Mother's Day. Then the Gold Star Wives got a boost in 1945 with the help of Eleanor Roosevelt. In 1947, Gold Star lapel buttons were given to spouses and families who had lost a loved one from war. In 2011, President Obama combined families and mothers who mourn their fallen dead into one holiday to separate it from Spouses Day (April 5). Now, any family member losing a loved one in a fight for our country's freedom is authorized to fly a service flag with a gold star. Those losing loved ones can register their family member in the National Gold Star Family Registry (2010) which provides a database of fallen heroes.

- JOB 16:6 ~ If I speak, my pain is not quieted, and if I refrain, how much of it leaves me?

- ISA 61:1–3 ~ The Spirit of God is upon me, because He has directed me to preach His good news to the humble, to heal the broken hearted, to free the slaves, and to release those who are bound in chains and in prison; to proclaim the Lord's favor and His vengeance, to comfort all who mourn, and to tell those who mourn to exchange their ashes for beauty; to replace mourning with joy, and to don the garment of praise in exchange for the spirit of sorrow, so that they may be trees of righteousness, planted by the Lord for His glorification.

- JER 45:3 ~ You said, "Woe is me! For God added sorrow to my pain. I am weary with my groaning, and I find no rest."

- LAM 3:31–33 ~ The Lord will not remove forever, Though He causes grief, He will have compassion according to the multitude of His mercies; for He does not afflict from His heart to deliberately grieve the children of anyone.

- ROM 12:15, 21 ~ Rejoice with those who are rejoicing and mourn with those who are mourning. Do not be overcome by evil but overcome evil with goodness.

- ROM 14:18–19 ~ He who serves Christ in these things is acceptable to God and approved of others. Let us therefore follow after the things which promote peace and edify one another.

- MAT 24:30 ~ Then a sign in heaven will appear; the entire earth will be in mourning when the Son of God returns in a cloud, with all His power and glory.

- 1 TH 5:11 ~ Comfort each other and edify one another just as you are doing.

Father, we pray for the mothers and the families of our fallen heroes and wish your abundant mercy and peace upon them. We pray for protection of our loved ones going to war that they would return home safe and sound; and we pray for their loved ones who are feeling disheartened or grieved knowing they are going into the danger zone. We thank you Jesus for going to your death, and winning the war over sin and death, so we can live free forever, Amen.

October 1

International Day of Older Persons recognizes the challenges of the elderly and addresses issues associated with aging. This UN observance was proffered by the General Assembly in 1990, to be held annually on this date. The old age demographic has widened due to increases in life expectancy; in twenty-five years the number of retirement-aged people is projected to hit 1.5 billion worldwide. Discrimination against older people in the workplace is a violation of the Age Discrimination in Employment Act of 1967. Most senior citizens are perfectly capable of gainful employment and taking on new responsibilities. In addition to children, this is a group of people most often neglected and abused. Report any incidents of elder abuse to your state Adult Protective Services, either online or through their telephone hotline. Today's holiday can be observed by simply showing respect to your elders and all older persons in your realm of influence. Listen to their counsel, for their experience spans decades.

- LEV 19:32 ~ Stand when in the presence of the aged; show respect for the elderly and revere your God for I AM the Lord.

- 1 TI 5:1 ~ Do not speak harshly towards older people but treat them as you would your own parents.

- TIT 2:2 ~ Teach that which comes from sound doctrine. Teach the old men to be sober, worthy of respect, self-controlled, faithful, charitable, and patient.

- 1 PE 5:1–5 ~ Peter wrote to the elders as a fellow elder and witness of Christ's sufferings: Be shepherds to the flock that God has placed under your care, serving as overseers. Do this, not because you feel obligated or for money, but because you want to, as God desires. Be eager to serve, not lording over those God has entrusted to you, but as an example to the flock. And when the Chief Shepherd appears, you will receive a crown of glory that will never fade. Peter also addressed the younger people: Respect your elders. Serve each other. Clothe yourselves in humility. For God resists the proud and gives grace to the humble.

There will be workshops based on a particular theme each year, with promotional material, media events, and opportunities to volunteer or lend support to agencies like the Association for Adult Development and Aging (established in 1986) which advocates for the elderly, providing professional development and counseling. The American Society on Aging, (established in 1954) is another advocacy group where people can become involved.

In Biblical times the wise leaders of the church were often senior citizens. They were the elders of the church, who knew the scriptures and the laws backwards and forwards. For example, the high priests during the time of Christ were Caiaphas and his father-in-law Annas. Sometimes elders in the Bible were not all that wise, given that these two skirted the laws.

- EXO 24:1, 9–10 ~ God said to Moses, "Come to me, Moses, along with Aaron, Nadab, Abihu, and seventy of the elders of Israel, and worship me." Moses, Aaron, and the elders went to the foot of the mountain, and they saw God; and under His feet it looked like a roadway of transparent sapphire, just like heaven itself.

- JAM 5:13–16 ~ Is anyone among you suffering? Let him pray. Is anyone cheerful? Let him sing psalms. Is anyone sick? Let him call for the elders of the church to pray over him. And the prayers of faith will save the sick, and the Lord will raise them up, and forgive their sins.

- MAT 27:1 ~ The chief priests and elders conspired against Jesus to put Him to death.

- MAT 28:1–15 ~ On the morning of the Sabbath some women went to the tomb. An angel had moved the stone causing the ground to quake, whereupon he sat. His face was shining like

OCTOBER

lightning and his robe was white as snow. The guards began to shake, scared to death. The angel spoke to the women and told them not to fear, because the crucified Jesus they sought was not there; He had risen like He said He would. "Come and see where He was laid," the angel suggested. Next the angel directed the women to inform the disciples that Jesus would catch up with them in Galilee. The ladies left hastily and joyfully; they could hardly wait to spread the good news. As they were on their way, men from the night watch came into the city, and appeared before the chief priests relating what they had witnessed. An assembly of elders consulted together, then gave a large sum of money to the soldiers, ordering them, "You will testify that his disciples came by night and stole the body while you slept. If this comes to the governor's attention, we will persuade him not to make anything of it." So, the guardsmen took the money and did what they were told. And that tale continues to be reported among the Jews to this day.

- MAR 8:31–34 ~ Jesus explained that the Son of God had to suffer many things, be rejected by the elders, scribes, and chief priests, be killed, and rise from the dead after three days. And Peter took Him aside and rebuked the Lord. Then Jesus turned towards His disciples and rebuked Peter saying, "Get behind me Satan, for you do not cherish things of God but of men."

The Jewish council consisted of seventy elders of the church called the Sanhedrin. Among them were Nicodemus and Joseph of Arimathea. They believed in Jesus, but did so secretly, because of hostility and conspiracy against Jesus by the elders and Pharisees. Pilate gave the two men authority to take possession of the body of Christ and have Him interred.

- MAR 16:43–47; LUK 23:50–53; JOH 19:38–42 ~ There was a man named Joseph from Arimathea, who was a member of the Jewish high council; he was an upright and just man. He was against the decision of the council to condemn Jesus. He appealed to Pilate for the body of Jesus. Pilate allowed him to take the body. He was accompanied by Nicodemus who brought myrrh and aloe; the two men embalmed the body of Jesus, wrapped the body in new linens, and placed the body in Joseph's own tomb which was carved from solid rock, and in which no dead bodies had ever been laid.

- JOH 3:1–12 ~ Nicodemus, a Pharisee and authority over the Jews, came to see Jesus at nighttime. He said to Jesus, "Rabbi, we know that you are a teacher from God, for nobody can perform miracles without God being with him." Jesus responded, "Truly I tell to you, unless a man is born again, he cannot enter the kingdom of God." Nicodemus asked, "How can a man be born when he is old? Can he enter his mother's womb a second time and be reborn?" Jesus answered, "I tell you the truth, unless a man is born of water and of the Spirit he cannot enter into the kingdom of heaven. That which is born of the flesh is flesh; and that which is born of the Spirit is spirit. Do not be astounded that I said you must be born again. The wind blows wherever it wants; and you can hear it but you cannot see it, or tell where it came from or where it is going. It is the same with those who are born of the Spirit." Nicodemus wondered, "How can this be so?" Jesus replied, "Are you not a teacher in Israel? Yet do you not understand these things? Truthfully, we speak of what we know and testify to what we see, but there are many who do not receive our testimony. If I tell you about earthly things and you do not believe, how can you believe if I tell you about heavenly things?"

Heavenly Father of the ages, help people to be benevolent towards older people, assisting them when they struggle, being patient with them when they are slow, and showing them all due respect and courtesy. Let there be justice for older people who are being taken advantage of, or neglected, abused, swindled, or assaulted. Ensure that we notify authorities when we become aware of such things. Help the victims to be removed from harmful situations, and placed into a safe environment. In Jesus's name, Amen.

DAILY DEVOTIONAL EVENTS

October 2

International Day for Nonviolence is celebrated on the birthday of Mohandas Gandhi. The UN designated this holiday in 2007. This day is not unlike the International Day of Peace observed on 09/21 and has similar objectives. Again, we recognize the non-violent methods of Gandhi that helped bring about independence in India. This observance is for promoting communications, tolerance, and acceptance through discussion, compromise, and resolution. There will be the usual conference with distinguished speakers and focused theme, to create a dialogue that will generate mutual respect, equality, and sustained social justice and development.

- 2 SA 22:2–3 ~ David said, "The Lord is my rock, my fortress, and my deliverer. In Him I place my trust. He is my shield, the horn of my salvation, my high tower, my refuge, and my Savior. He saves me from violence."

- PSA 7:16 ~ The mischief and violence of the wicked will come back on their own heads.

- EZE 28:14–16 ~ You (Lucifer) were the anointed cherub; you lived upon the holy mountain of God. You were perfect from the day you were created until evil was found in you. Your great wealth made you violent inside and you became sinful.

- DAN 8:23 ~ In the latter days, when the evil ones are fully in power, a fierce king will arise from darkness.

- MIC 6:12 ~ The rich men are full of violence and lies.

- 2 TI 3:1–4, 12–13 ~ In the last days, perilous times will come. People will be self-centered, proud, boastful, envious, blasphemous, disobedient to parents, unthankful, and ungodly; people will be perverted, peace breakers, false accusers, unrestrained, fierce, and despisers of those who are good; they will be traitors, violent, arrogant, and lovers of pleasure rather than of lovers of God. Those who live a godly life in Christ will suffer persecution. For evil men and seducers will get worse and worse, deceiving and being deceived.

During the end times, violence and hostility will abound. There will be no chance to reason with the instigators, for their hatred is impenetrable. They will join with Satan in their disdain for humanity, executing actions of a demented mind. To them it is a duty to eradicate goodness and Christian godliness. The only recourse in dealing with them is death; and their death will be violent.

- REV 17:5, 9–11, 14 ~ On her head was written: Mystery, Babylon the great, the mother of prostitutes and all earthly abominations. The angel explained the mystery of the beast with seven heads as follows: The seven heads represent seven mountains on which the new Babylon sits. And there are seven kings, five have fallen, one is currently in power, and the seventh is yet to come and will reign for a short time. The beast is the eighth king and was also one of the seven; his capital is the great city that sits on seven mountains and over many waters, nations, and peoples.

- REV 18:2–7, 17, 21 ~ With a mighty voice the angel shouted, "Babylon the great has fallen, fallen; she has become a haven for demons and for every detestable creature. For her sins are piled up to heaven, and God has remembered her sins. Abandon her my people; do not participate in her sin so that you will not experience the plagues. Give back to her what she has done; pay her back double from her own cup. Give her as much torture and grief as she gave glory and luxury to herself. In just one hour the great riches of Babylon will come to naught. Babylon will be shamed and disgraced for such contemptible conduct." A mighty angel picked up a gigantic stone and cast it into the sea saying, "With such violence Babylon will be thrown down and disappear."

It will be futile to peacefully protest the oppressiveness that will pervade the world. When they see the opposition gathering in great numbers and demanding reforms they will be mowed down, because the powermongers fear that the sheer numbers standing against them will upset the status quo. The only way to fight against them is with spiritual weapons of war, in particular, the sword of the Spirit of God which is His Holy Word. In preparation for the coming scourge, the Word must be taken to all locales of the world. Yes, the righteous people have the numbers, but the enemy will have tanks, fighter jets, and nuclear weapons. And even though they will have the power of evil and the forces of technology, people of faith will have the power of God on their side. This is why the evil empire will be short-lived. There was an old Babylon that rose and fell rather quickly; the new Babylon will rise and fall much faster.

- JAM 5:1–3 ~ Go cry and moan you rich people, for the miseries that will come upon you. Your riches are corrupted and your clothes are worn out. Your disintegrating wealth will eat at you in the same fashion. You have heaped up riches for the last time.

- ISA 13:1, 9–10, 19 ~ The day comes when the Lord's wrath and anger will result in the desolation of Babylon and the destruction of the sinners there. The glory of Babylon will be like Sodom and Gomorrah when God destroyed those cities.

- JER 50:23–25, 28, 46 ~ Babylon will become a desolation. They were unaware that God would catch them and punish them for continuing to sin. They will flee from Babylon when the vengeance of the Lord is declared in Zion. The earth will be shaken, for the cry of Babylon's fall will be heard around the world.

- REV 14:8 ~ The angel said, "The great city of Babylon has fallen, because she caused all nations to drink the wine of the wrath of her fornication."

- REV 16:13–19 ~ I saw three evil spirits that looked like frogs come out of the dragon, the beast, and the false prophet. These were the demons that performed miracles, and coerced the kingdoms of the world to unite against God. They gathered the kings together at the place called Armageddon (in Hebrew). The seventh angel poured out his vial and a great voice came from the throne saying, "It is done." There was lightning and thunder, then a great earthquake, greater than any earthquake known to man. The great city was divided into three parts, while cities of every nation fell. God remembered what they had done; their sin did not go unpunished.

- REV 17:12–14 ~ Ten kings will obtain power for one hour with the beast. They will give their power and strength to the beast and will make war with the Lamb of God, only to be eliminated.

An exact timeline of the end times events cannot be found in the Bible because God chose not to make it clear; those things God wants clarified are obvious. All we know is that the signs are present, and this means it could occur in our generation. Since it is not fully elaborated, every generation has to be prepared for the end, and that means believing in Jesus Christ through the righteousness of faith. Chances are, God's elect will be spared the calamitous end.

- ACT 1:7 ~ Jesus said, "It is not for you to know the times or the seasons fixed by the power of God."

Heavenly Father, we pray that our faith does not waver despite the appearance of terrible times on the horizon, and the knowledge that things will get worse towards the end. Whether we are here to witness the end or not, let us never be afraid because you have claimed us. Let us openly carry the covering of Christ's blood which is our suit of armor; and help us to wield the sword of the Spirit to fend off the fiery advances of the evil one and his armies. We claim the blood of Jesus, so that the world will know we are His, Amen.

October 3

Feast of Trumpets is the Jewish festival of *Rosh Hashana*. It will vary from year to year, but on the Jewish calendar it is Tishrei 1–2. This ushers in the Jewish new year, with shouts of joy and trumpets. It also is a celebration of the birth of our world. Certainly, God deserves our thanks for creating this universe, our planet, human beings, and life. Whether you are Jewish or not, you would do well to celebrate the limitless gifts of God. The entirety of this universe was created with us in mind; this is known as the anthropic principle in cosmology. There are scientific and natural explanations for God being behind it all, not the least of which are the complexity and fine tuning which enables lifeforms on earth to thrive.

- EXO 15:11 ~ Who among the gods is like you, oh Lord? Who else is majestic in holiness, awesome in glory, and works such great wonders?

- 1 CH 16:8–12 ~ Give thanks to the Lord; call upon His name. Make known His wondrous deeds to everyone. Sing praises to Him and rejoice. Continuously seek the Lord with all your strength. Remember the marvelous things He has done, His wonders and His judgments.

- 1 CH 29:11 ~ Yours, oh Lord, is all greatness, power, glory, victory, and majesty. Everything in heaven and earth is yours, including the everlasting kingdom. You are exalted as head above all creatures.

- PSA 139:1–6 ~ Lord, you have searched me and know everything about me. You discern my thoughts, and are familiar with all my ways. I could never attain such knowledge. Even before I speak, you know what I will say.

- 2 PE 1:2–4 ~ May the Lord's grace and peace be multiplied to you, through the knowledge of God and of Jesus Christ our Lord. His divine power has given us everything we need for a life of godliness, through the knowledge of Him who called us to His glory and virtue. He has made wonderful and precious promises so that you can partake in His divine nature, and escape the corruption and sinful desires of this world.

Today and tomorrow, there is a raising of prayers to God Almighty, and the blowing of the ram's horn. It is like a prayer of confession and contrition, showing godly sorrow for one's sins, ending with the blast on the shofar in lieu of closing with an "amen". There will be ten holy days of repentance during this season. The next day is the Day of Atonement, the holiest day on the Jewish calendar (*Yom Kippur*), which we will cover in more detail next week.

- LEV 23:24–37 ~ The first day of the seventh month is the Feast of Trumpets. It is a high sabbath; do no work on that day and hold a holy convocation, including an offering by fire.

- PSA 51:17 ~ The sacrifices of God are a broken spirit; a broken and contrite heart, oh God, you will not despise.

- ISA 57:15 ~ This is what the Lord says, whose name is Holy, "I live in a high and holy place. I also live with those who have a contrite and humble spirit, reviving their heart and spirit."

- 2 CO 7:9–10 ~ I am glad that you were sorry for your sins and repented. Spiritual sorrow for one's sins works repentance unto salvation; but the sorrow of the world works death.

There are many variations associated with this celebration depending on religious persuasion. Regardless, it is God who is being celebrated for He is the creator, sustainer, and preserver of all life. We are His pride and joy, those who worship Him today and every day.

- DEU 11:16 ~ Guard your heart from deceptions that would cause you to turn aside, and serve other gods to worship them.

OCTOBER

- PSA 96:8 ~ Give God the glory He deserves. Bring your offerings and worship Him.
- MAT 4:10 ~ Jesus told Satan, "You must worship the Lord your God and serve only Him."
- JOH 4:24 ~ Jesus said, "God is Spirit and should be worshipped in spirit and in truth."

Seven trumpets will usher in phases of the tribulation ending with the last trumpet when the gates of heaven are opened. Those saved by the blood of Christ will be invited to enter.

- ISA 27:12–13 ~ In that day a great trumpet will sound, and those who were about to perish in Assyria, and the outcasts in Egypt, will be rescued and will worship the Lord at the holy mountain of Jerusalem.
- JOE 2:1, 15 ~ Blow the trumpet and sound the alarm; let everyone tremble, for the day of the Lord is at hand.
- ZEP 1:14–18 ~ The great day of the Lord is coming quickly, when mighty men will cry. It is a day of wrath, trouble, and distress, of destruction and desolation, gloom, clouds, and darkness. The trumpet will be a warning against the fenced cities and high towers. I will bring distress upon humankind; they will walk as blinded by their sins against the Lord. Their blood will be poured out like dust and their flesh like dung. Their riches will do them no good. The earth will be consumed at once by the fire of God's wrath to rid the land of them.
- MAT 24:22, 31, 40–42 ~ Unless those days are shortened, none will survive. But only for the elect's sake, those days will be shortened. And He will send His angels when the great trumpet sounds, to gather His elect from across heaven and earth. Two men will be working in the field, one will be taken; two women will be grinding in the mill, one will be taken. Watch and be ready, for you never know when the Lord may come.
- 1 CO 15:51–52 ~ Here is a mystery of God: We will not all sleep but we all will be changed. Suddenly, when the last trumpet sounds, Christ's own, whether dead or alive, will arise without corruption and be changed. Hence, the corruptible will have become incorruptible and the mortal will have become immortal.
- 1 TH 4:16–17 ~ The Lord will descend from heaven with a shout, with the voice of the archangel, and with a blast from the trumpet of God. Then the dead in Christ will rise first. Those who remain alive in Christ will rise to join the others in the clouds, meeting the Lord in the sky. Those chosen by Christ will live with Him forevermore.
- REV 8:2, 6 ~ There were seven angels standing before God and they were given seven trumpets; each angel was prepared to sound their trumpets in order.
- REV 10:7 ~ In the days when the seventh angel is about to sound his trumpet, the mystery of God will be accomplished, just as He announced through His servants the prophets.
- REV 11:14–15, 19 ~ The second woe had passed and the third woe was coming as the seventh angel sounded his trumpet. Voices in heaven were saying, "The kingdoms of earth now belong to Christ, and He will reign forever." Then the temple in heaven was opened…

Father, we shout with joy and praise for your wonderful deeds, especially the miracle of salvation awarded us through the life, death, and resurrection of Jesus Christ. Thank you, dear Father, for all we see was created by you for us to thrive, so we may love you and shine your light. Let our love grow and flourish as a tree of life that will stand strong, and bear good fruit, spreading the seeds of truth throughout our travels, trials, and tribulations. Help us to remain steadfast in the true faith until that day when the last trumpet sounds and you open the gates of heaven to invite us in. In Jesus's name, Amen.

October 4

World Smile Day is observed on the first Friday in October; it was promoted by commercial artist Henry Ball, the man who created the smiley face logo in 1963. The world's first smile day occurred in 1999 and seems to have caught on. After his death in 2001 the World Smile Foundation was established in Ball's honor with the motto, "Improving this world one smile at a time." The objective is to keep a smile on your face and influence others to smile, for smiling can be contagious. In 1883 Ella Wheeler coined this phrase in a poem: Laugh and the world laughs with you, cry and you cry alone. Sometimes we should smile and laugh together, and sometimes we should weep and mourn together. Either way, sometimes all a person needs is a warm smile to cheer them up; this is usually an expression from someone who has a warm heart.

- NUM 6:24–26 ~ God instructed Moses how to bless the people: May the Lord bless and keep you; may He make His face to shine upon you and be gracious unto you; may the Lord smile upon you and give you His peace.

- PSA 126:1–3 ~ When the Lord brought the captives back to Zion, it was like a dream. We were filled with laughter, singing songs. Even the heathens were saying, "The Lord did great things for them." The Lord has done great things and we are glad.

- PRO 15:13–14 ~ A merry heart has a cheerful smile, but a sorrowful heart breaks the spirit. The heart that has understanding seeks knowledge; but the mouth of a fool feeds on folly.

- PRO 17:22 ~ A merry heart is like medicine; but a broken spirit dries the bones.

We can rejoice and be glad, even when things are not going our way, because the setbacks in life teach us valuable lessons in patience, endurance, and steadfastness. You will not be alone during these trying times, as others will be feeling overwhelmed and burdened along with you. Let them see your smiling face, and you might be able to cheer them up and give them hope. They may ask, "What are you smiling about?" That will give you an opportunity to explain the scriptures below.

- PSA 37:7 ~ Find solace in the Lord and wait patiently for Him. Do not worry about evil people who prosper.

- LUK 21:19 ~ Those who are patient will possess their souls.

- ROM 5:3–5 ~ We rejoice in tribulations, knowing that tribulation works patience, and patience works experience, and experience works hope. And hope makes us unashamed, because the love of God fills our hearts, through the Holy Spirit that we have been given.

- ROM 12:12–13 ~ Rejoice in hope, be patient in troubled times, be constant in prayer; addressing the needs of the saints and being hospitable to everyone.

- JAM 1:2–3 ~ Brothers, count it joy when you fall into various trials, knowing that the testing of your faith produces patience.

- REV 2:10 ~ Jesus said, "Do not be afraid of suffering, imprisonment, and tribulation, for many will endure such hardships. Be faithful unto death and you will receive a crown of life."

It is difficult to remember the joy of our salvation, when we are troubled and facing uncertain times. However, we can be confident that our work will not be in vain. We can be certain that God's promises are true, and that we will live in perpetual bliss forever. Therefore, we always have something to look forward to and needn't feel hampered or dismayed so often. There is no reason to give up hope, because God will never leave us or forsake us; so, there is every reason to be happy. Do not forget to smile, and rejoice in the Lord always, and again, I say rejoice!

OCTOBER

- DEU 4:29–31 ~ If you will seek the Lord your God from this day forward, you will find Him, as long as you seek with all of your heart. When you experience tribulation, even during the latter days, turn to God and do what He commands of you. For He is a merciful God; He will neither forsake you nor destroy you, nor will He forget the covenant He swore to your ancestors.

- DEU 31:6 ~ Be courageous and strong; do not be afraid of anyone. For God goes with you; He will neither fail you nor forsake you.

- PSA 34:17–19 ~ The righteous cry, and the Lord hears and delivers them out of their troubles. The Lord is near to those with a broken heart, and He saves those with a contrite spirit. Many are the afflictions of the righteous, but the Lord delivers us from them all.

- PSA 50:15 ~ Call upon God in the day of trouble and you will be delivered, and you will glorify God.

- PSA 86:4–5, 12–13 ~ Gladden my soul, oh Lord, for to you I lift up my soul. For you Lord are good and always ready to forgive, and generous with your mercy to all who call upon you. I will praise you, oh Lord my God, with all of my heart; I will glorify your name forever. For great is your steadfast love toward me; you have delivered my soul from the depths of hell.

- ISA 61:10 ~ I will greatly rejoice in the Lord; my soul will be joyful in my God. For He has clothed me with the garments of salvation, he has covered me with the robe of righteousness, just like the groom is adorned with ornaments and the bride is adorned with jewels. Blessed be those whose sins are not counted against them.

- JER 9:24 ~ Whoever wants to rejoice, let them rejoice in the fact that they know God who is loving, kind, righteous, and just.

- HAB 3:18 ~ I will rejoice in the Lord and find joy in the God of my salvation.

- JOH 16:33 ~ Jesus said, "I have told you that I will bring you peace. In the world you will have tribulation; but be happy because I have overcome the world."

- 1 CO 15:58 ~ Be steadfast, immovable, and fruitful in the Lord; for your efforts will not be in vain.

- PHP 4:4 ~ Rejoice in the Lord, and again I say, rejoice!

- HEB 13:5 ~ Refrain from covetousness; be content with what you have, for God has said that He will never leave you or forsake you.

- 1 TH 5:21–22 ~ Examine all things and hold onto the good. Abstain from all appearance of evil.

- 2 TI 3:11 ~ Although Paul endured much hardship, persecution, and affliction, God always delivered him.

Heavenly Father, thank you for always being available to us every second of the day. Let this notion put a smile on our faces. Let us rejoice openly for your great deeds, and those of your Son Jesus. Have your Holy Spirit continue the good work you have started in us, and help us to be certain that you will bring it to completion. Enable us to be mindful of this when we feel overwhelmed or dismayed, so that our spirits will be lifted and our gladness reclaimed. Fill our hearts with joy and our minds with peace. Let us keep a smile on our faces and let that be an example to others of how your love works within our souls to make us content, patient, and happy. In Jesus's name we pray, Amen.

October 5

World Teacher's Day is another holiday established by the United Nations and has been observed since 1997. Today was selected to commemorate the 1966 UNESCO recommendations on the Status of Teachers, whereby teacher preparation, standards, rights, and responsibilities were adopted. Today we celebrate teachers, and their crucial contribution to society in the education and development of our kids. There will be a worldwide conference recognizing the influence of teachers, discussing policies for improving education, addressing issues faced by educators, identifying advances in technology, determining availability of resources, and empowering and equipping teachers and future teachers. Honors and awards will be part of the ceremonies. Over one-hundred member nations will be participating.

Good teachers mentor their students, exhibiting an example of uprightness, fairness, and caring. These are the teachers we remember, the ones we looked up to. The bad ones are less often remembered because they didn't have an impact on our success or growth. If you learned a lot and retained that learning, you will appreciate it when you get older. I still remember the names of several teachers that helped me in grade school, though I wasn't the most cooperative or conscientious student. I wish I could thank them. Because they gave me something that I had yet to value: knowledge and confidence. In college I began to value these things, and my grades improved, my interests were expanded. I would become a certified teacher and later a professor.

- PRO 1:2–4 ~ Try to know wisdom and instruction; to perceive the words of understanding; to receive the instruction of wisdom, justice, judgment, and equity; to give subtlety to the simple; to give knowledge and discretion to the young.

- PRO 19:20 ~ Listen to advice and accept instruction, and you will be wise.

- MAT 13:52 ~ Jesus said, "Every teacher who has been instructed about the kingdom of heaven is like a homeowner who has a treasure chest of things both old and new."

- EPH 4:11–13 ~ God gave some the abilities of apostles, prophets, evangelists, pastors, and teachers for the work of the ministry, the edifying of the saints, the perfecting of the body of Christ, and the unity of faith. Each can impart the knowledge of the Son of God, who was a perfect man, so that we could take on the characteristics of Christ.

- 2 TH 3:1 ~ Pray for teachers of the truth, and pray that the Word of God will be spoken freely and understood, like it was for you.

The quintessential textbook for all humanity is the Holy Bible. It is an expository of wisdom, truth, and understanding in the fields of history, science, politics, morality, divinity, self-help, philosophy, psychology, and much more. It is a handbook for life, preparing us for this world and for the world to come. God's Word is the final arbiter of truth, the epitome of reliability, and a comprehensive guide on how to become a child of God and recruit others.

Unfortunately, the Word of God is no longer accepted in public schools. Instead, books which have no business being read by children are being placed into libraries and recommended reading lists, introducing such things as alternative lifestyles and transgenderism, Marxism, and historically inaccurate accounts which serve only to bewilder young students and pollute their souls. The Bible warns about false teachers and false teachings. It is up to parents to discover the evil and corruption seeping into the curricula and the schools. They want to force kids into adult decisions before their brains are fully developed, while their hormones are also kicking in. They are disabling kids with identity confusion and unresolved developmental issues. Evil adults already have taken God out of school and now they are inserting the devil. Parents, be wary; be vigilant and investigatory regarding the schooling of your kids, from kindergarten to graduate school.

OCTOBER

- ISA 44:25 ~ God proves the false prophets to be liars and fools, causing their prophecies to be invalid.

- JER 23:32 ~ Their lies lead many people into sin. I did not send them and they have nothing important to say.

- MAT 15:14 ~ Stay away from false teachers, for they are like the blind leading the blind. And when the blind lead the blind, both fall into the ditch.

- 2 TI 3:13 ~ Evil people and false teachers will get worse, deceiving many. They themselves have been deceived by Satan.

- 2 TI 4:3–4 ~ People will seek teachers who conform to their own likes and dislikes; they will turn away from the truth and wander into myths.

- TIT 1:11 ~ They must be silenced, those who would ruin entire households, teaching things that are wrong for the sake of ill-gotten gain.

Why would adults push decadent ideas into these pliable minds? Why would they groom children to be sexual objects? Why would they want to redefine morality, history, and science? The only reasons are to exploit, abuse, molest, and take advantage of children; to defile their minds, destroy their moral compass, and make them evil, nasty, and violent. And who is behind this conspiracy? Satan, of course. These are dangerous times, especially for young people. They must be protected, and these deviant educators and administrators need to be found out and prohibited from contact with children. They should be incarcerated, but they mostly get away with it.

- PRO 19:18 ~ Discipline your children while there is hope, so you do not cause their death.

- ISA 5:20–21 ~ Woe to those who call evil good and good evil, who put darkness for light and light for darkness, who put bitter for sweet and sweet for bitter! Woe to those who are wise in their own eyes, and shrewd in their own sight.

- MAT 18:3–6 ~ Jesus said, "Unless you become converted and receive God as a little child, you will never enter the kingdom of heaven. Those who humble themselves like a child can become the greatest in God's kingdom. Whoever receives a child in my name receives me. But if anyone offends a child who believes in me, they would have been better off being tossed into the sea with a millstone tied to their neck."

- LUK 11:23 ~ Jesus said, "Whoever is not with me is against me, and whoever does not gather around me, scatters."

- JAM 1:25 ~ Those who study the perfect law of liberty and continue therein, not forgetting but continuing to do the work, these persons will be blessed for their deeds.

- 2 PE 2:2–3 ~ Many will follow their own insidious ways, and because of them the truth will be blasphemed. Through covetousness they will exploit with deceptive words. Their judgment has been decided and their damnation never sleeps.

Father, we pray for good teachers who are wise in your Word and teach only the truth. Derail the wayward designs of evil people who deliberately attempt to poison young minds against you and against their parents. Remove these devils from positions of authority and prevent them from teaching their vile ways to our children. Cause their depravity and venom to fall upon them and not the kids they were hired to instruct and nurture. Please God, raise up among us teachers, who will share your truth and ways with our students, as well as relate the basics needed to compete on the world stage in knowledge and skill. In the name of Jesus, Amen.

October 6

World Communion Sunday is a day for Christians throughout the world to band together, in unity of spirit, and celebrate the Eucharist. The idea goes back to 1930s when Presbyterian churches in the USA began to recognize a day of unity and Holy Communion. Through the Eucharist we receive Christ whose Holy Spirit indwells us via the bread and wine. Methodists recognized the observance, and in the 1940s the Federal Council of Churches adopted it. The holiday got a lot of traction during World War II. More denominations have since stepped aboard to hail the sacrifice of Christ, which occurred the afternoon following His institution of Holy Communion. Nowadays, evangelical establishments across the globe will be celebrating this day with communing together as the collective body of Christ, and communing with Christ through this blessed sacrament. What an excellent way to obtain Christian unity and oneness with Christ. Of course, the secular world will try to dismiss the part about Holy Communion, by focusing on world peace and communication.

True Christian denominations incorporate Holy Communion into their services, it is a key doctrine that is universal. Who is eligible to partake of this sacrament? Well, anyone who can examine themselves, confess their sins, and repent with a contrite heart; believing that Jesus Christ shed His blood and died to save them, desiring the body and blood of Christ to purify them through the bread and wine, and inviting the Holy Spirit to indwell them. Participation should lead to a serious attempt to spend more time learning about and worshipping God and less time sinning.

- GEN 14:18–19 ~ King Melchizedek (meaning King of Peace), priest of the most-high God, shared bread and wine with Abraham.

- ISA 44:24–26 ~ The Lord said, "I am the Lord who makes all things... and who confirms the Word of my Servant..."

- MAT 26:26–28 ~ Jesus took bread, blessed it, broke it into pieces, and distributed it to the apostles saying, "Take this bread and eat, for this is my body." Then He took a cup of wine, thanked God, and passed the cup to the apostles saying, "Take and drink from this cup, for this is my blood of the New Covenant, shed for you and for many for the remission of sins."

- 1 CO 1:5–8 ~ You are enriched by Christ in everything you say and everything you know. Even as the testimony of Christ was confirmed among you who wait for the day of His return, so He will confirm you until the end, ensuring that you receive all your spiritual needs, and be found blameless upon that day.

- 1 CO 2:14 ~ Worldly people do not receive things of the Spirit of God, for such things are foolishness to them; neither can they know the meaning for it must be spiritually discerned.

- 1 CO 10:16–17, 21 ~ The cup of blessing that we bless, does it not represent our communion with the blood of Christ? The bread that we break, does it not represent our communion with the body of Christ? Although we are many, we have become one body for we all are partakers of that one bread. You cannot drink from the cup of the Lord and from the cup of devils (you cannot be one with Christ if you commune with devils).

- 1 CO 11:25–29 ~ Jesus commanded the apostles on the first Holy Communion to partake of the sacrament often to remember Him. Thus, as often as you eat the bread and drink the wine of Holy Communion, you proclaim the death of Christ until His return. But if you participate in this holy sacrament unworthily (without sincerely repenting of your sins and desiring a communion with Christ), you will become one of those who are found guilty of Christ's crucifixion. Examine yourself before partaking of Holy Communion, because if you partake unworthily, you will be eating and drinking damnation upon yourself.

OCTOBER

William Tyndale was executed on this same date in 1536 for translating and publishing the Holy Bible into English. He followed in the footsteps of Martin Luther, and also his countryman John Wycliffe, who promoted the translation of scriptures and was excommunicated in 1415. Tyndale was another great reformer, bringing the Protestant message to England. Being proficient in Hebrew and Greek, he translated the New Testament and later the Old Testament. He also took advantage of the newly invented printing press, and the safety of doing business in Germany (it was forbidden in England), succeeding in putting God's Word into the hands of the populous. The Catholic regime couldn't bear to let people discover and learn the scriptures for themselves; they wanted parishioners to rely exclusively on them for guidance. Tyndale maintained that the Bible was the authoritative source, not popes and bishops. So, they arranged for a friend to betray him and he was executed as a heretic. But his works survived and helped in the undertaking of King James in 1611 to begin development on the King James Bible, releasing it in just five years. Meanwhile, Catholics and Protestants had been warring in the British Isles, a conflict that continued for centuries; in some circles, that animosity lingers.

It is a lot more common in America to see leaders from different evangelical denominations standing together to pray, teach, and worship. They all believe in the essential doctrines of the true Christian faith, including communion. A church that does not believe in the triune God, or the saving work of Christ, or the importance of faith above works, or salvation being a free gift through God's grace, or the sixty-six canonical books of the Holy Bible, is not likely to offer communion because they do not agree on these Biblical teachings. Test the doctrinal statements of the churches you attend to ensure they adhere to the dogma listed above.

- 1 CO 1:8–10 ~ Who will confirm you until the end, that you may be blameless in the day of our Lord Jesus Christ? God is faithful, by whom you were called into the fellowship of His Son, our Lord. I urge you, my brothers, in the name of our Lord Jesus Christ, to be in agreement with one another so that there will be no divisions among you. Be perfectly joined together in mind and thought.

- GAL 1:8–10 ~ Anyone, including angels, who preaches anything contrary to what Jesus and the apostles preached is cursed. We have said it before and I say it again, if anyone preaches a gospel that is different than the one you have received from us, that person is cursed. Am I trying to persuade people or God? For if I sought to please men, I would not be the servant of Christ.

- 1 TI 1:3–7 ~ Do not teach false doctrine, or recognize any myths or irrelevant genealogies, which only serve to raise questions, without providing any answers concerning the faith. The goal is to love with a pure heart, a right conscience, and a sincere faith. Some have wandered away from these principles and turned to meaningless jabber; desiring to be teachers of the Law yet knowing nothing about the Law or about what they purport to be true.

- REV 22:18–19 ~ For I testify to everyone who hears the words of the prophecy of this book, that if anyone adds to these words, God will add unto that person the plagues mentioned in this book. If anyone subtracts from the words of this prophecy, God will take away their name from the Book of Life, and they will not share in the inheritance.

We come to you today, most holy Father, to pray for your church on earth, that your Word would have free course wherever it is sent. Help us all to grow in true knowledge of you, your words, your works, and your ways so that we can be conversant, engaging others in dialogue who are eager to know the truth and learn the Bible. Help us to make disciples as Jesus commanded, so that they can make disciples; enabling the truth to reach more and more ears, and increasing exponentially the membership in the body of Jesus Christ. In His name we pray, Amen.

October 7

World Habitat Day falls on the first Monday of the month. The United Nations designated this holiday in 1985 to investigate how urbanization affects humanity and the environment. The underlying belief is that everybody deserves a decent place to live. The objectives are to decrease inequality, promote urban development, and improve living conditions for the homeless, for those living in slums, and for impoverished people whether in the inner city or rural areas.

- DEU 15:11 ~ There will never cease to be poor in the land. Therefore, open wide your hand to your brother, the needy, and the poor.

- PSA 33:8–10 ~ Let all the earth fear the Lord; let all the inhabitants of the world stand in awe of Him. For He spoke and it was done. Many are the woes of the wicked, but the Lord's unfailing love surrounds those who trust in Him.

- PSA 140:12 ~ The Lord will uphold the cause of the afflicted and the rights of the needy.

- PRO 14:31 ~ Whoever oppresses the poor insults the Lord; but those who are generous to the needy honor Him.

- PRO 29:7 ~ A righteous person knows the rights of the poor, but a wicked person does not possess such knowledge.

- LUK 14:13–14 ~ Jesus said, "When you have a banquet, invite the poor, crippled, lame, and blind and you will be blessed because they cannot repay you. But you will be repaid at the resurrection of the just."

- GAL 6:9–10 ~ Do not become weary of doing good, for you will be rewarded at the right time. When opportunity arises, do something nice for someone, especially people in the faith.

Today is a day for helping people in need. Consider donating to charities that provide for the needy in your area, in the nation, or abroad. Become an advocate for the homeless, needy, and destitute in your locality if you have time; or you can volunteer at churches that serve the poor and homeless, or at a food bank. Do what you can with your time, talents, and treasure to help those less fortunate than you.

When it comes to the homeless, give them food and tell them about Jesus if they will listen. But keep in mind that many of them live on the streets by choice. Though they often are mentally ill and/or addicted, most will not be interested in being institutionalized, or taking medication, or living in a house; they value the little freedom that they have on the street. Having worked with the homeless, I discovered that many are actually content with their lifestyle, while others have lost everything and desperately need support and encouragement. Yes, many of them are begging for money to support bad habits, but most will accept wholesome food. If you pass by homeless people frequently, consider keeping some sandwiches, fruit, or snacks with you to hand out to them. Some will accept the offer, others will not. Remember to be cautious, however, for some of them can become violent without provocation.

- HEB 6:10 ~ God is not unjust. He will not forget your work and the love you have shown in His name as you helped His people and continue to help them.

- HEB 13:2 ~ Do not forget to help strangers, for you may be ministering to angels without knowing it.

Father, help us to help others in your name. Let us be generous to the poor, needy, and homeless, giving them food to nurture their bodies and food to nurture their souls. Remind us that when we minister to others, we are serving you. In the name of Jesus who served us, Amen.

October 8

Great Chicago Fire Burned for two days beginning on the evening of 10/08/1871. The fire killed an estimated three hundred people, left 100,000 people without homes, and destroyed thousands of wooden buildings. Fueled by a long drought and high winds, the devastation could have been worse if not for rainfall the next evening. A popular rumor was that Mrs. O'Leary's cow kicked over a lantern igniting the straw in her barn. A number of eyewitnesses reported balls of fire falling from the sky suggesting a meteorite or comet had broken into pieces. Most people are unaware of an even more devastating fire that occurred almost simultaneously, leveling Peshtigo WI, which was by far the most destructive and deadly fire in US history. Other fires occurred in Manistee, Holland, and Port Huron MI during that exact timeframe. In total, these fires killed around two thousand more people. The primary contributing factors were the dryness, heat, and wind. How all these fires were ignited the same night remains a mystery.

One of the casualties of the Chicago fire was the church of D. L. Moody, as well as his home, and homes of fellow congregants. He had just finished the Sunday evening service. Moody and his family barely made it out of town alive; others in attendance were not so lucky. He took it hard. Moody was a traveling evangelist who drew crowds upwards of 100,000 people. Over the course of his ministry, he may have covered a million miles preaching as many as six sermons per day. As many as a million people possibly witnessed one of his powerful revivals.

Moody was a nondenominational Protestant who preached Christ and stressed the inerrancy of the Holy Bible. He was like a modern-day St. Paul: both were shipwrecked during their many travels and engagements. Paul traveled an estimated 20,000 miles by foot, beast, and ship. Jesus also put in hundreds of miles by foot during His ministry on earth.

- MAT 9:35–38 ~ Jesus healed every illness and disease wherever He went. As He traveled about, Jesus was moved with compassion for the multitudes, because they were weary and scattered like sheep with no shepherd. Jesus said, "The harvest is plentiful but the laborers are few. Pray, therefore, that the Lord will send laborers into the harvest."

- GAL 1:15–19; GAL 2:9 ~ God singled me out since birth and called me by His grace. He was pleased to reveal His Son to me, so I might preach to the heathen. Immediately, I took the message into Arabia, before returning to Damascus. Finally, after three years I visited Jerusalem to meet Peter, and stayed with him fifteen days. I also met with James, the Lord's brother. James, Peter, and John were pillars of the Christian church; they saw the grace that was given to me, and offered the right hand of fellowship to me and also Barnabas who was with me. We agreed that we would preach to the Gentiles and they would preach to the Jews.

- 1 TH 3:1 ~ Pray for the evangelists, so that God's Word may have free course, and be glorified in others even as it was with you.

- 2 TI 4:5 ~ Always be watchful, willing to endure afflictions, doing the work of the evangelist, doing whatever is necessary for the continuance of the ministry.

- 1 PE 4:10–11 ~ Whoever has received the gift of salvation in Christ should share that gift with others, as a steward of God's eternal grace. If you preach, do so as a messenger of God. If you minister, do so with the ability God gives you. Do this to glorify God through His Son Jesus Christ.

Father, we pray for evangelists who take your Word to those who need to hear it. We pray for missionaries who take your love and truth to remote places on earth. We pray for churches and congregations which endured dreadful fires, that they overcome. We pray that you lead us to study your Word diligently so we too can share Jesus in our lives. In His name, Amen.

October 9

Fire Prevention Day was inaugurated in 1919 in a joint resolution between the US and Canada for an annual observance in support of fire prevention. President Wilson established fire prevention week the following year. It was no coincidence that the chosen day and week coincided with the Chicago fire of 1871. The National Fire Prevention Association (NFPA) has become an international sponsor for this holiday. There will be presentations by fire departments everywhere to teach and disseminate information geared towards both children and adults. This is a great opportunity to meet your local fire department and thank them for their service. There also will be national observances and themes, as well as educational television shows and NFPA events. Everyone should be familiar with fire safety, and the hazards and evacuation plans associated with the places they frequent. Families and businesses are encouraged to develop a fire prevention and escape plan for their homes and offices.

Fire is represented in the Bible as purification, like the smelting of metal which removes impurities. Jesus baptizes with the Holy Spirit and with fire, analogous to our cleansing and purifying from sin. We have to undergo such refinement before we can enter into the kingdom of heaven and be presented by Christ as holy unto God.

- EXO 19:18 ~ Sinai was blanketed in smoke while the Lord descended with fire; and the whole mount quaked.
- 1 KI 18:31–38 ~ Elijah had the pagans drench the altar with water three times before calling fire from heaven which consumed the sacrifice, the altar, the water, and everything around it.
- ZEC 2:4 ~ Jerusalem will be a town without walls, for I will be a wall of fire around her, and I will be the glory in the middle of her.
- ZEC 13:8–9 ~ Two thirds will be cut off and die; the other one third will be brought through the refiner's fire to be tested for purity. Those who call on my name will be heard, and I will say, "These are my people," and they will say, "The Lord is my God."
- MAL 3:1–3 ~ I will send a messenger to prepare the coming of the Lord; but who can endure His coming? For He is like a refiner's fire which completely removes all impurities and imperfections.
- MAT 3:11 ~ John told the people, "Indeed, I baptize you with water unto repentance. But He who comes after me is mightier than I; I am not worthy of carrying His shoes. He will baptize you with the Holy Spirit, and with fire."
- ACT 2:3–4 ~ There appeared cloven tongues of fire, sitting upon each of the evangelists' heads. They were filled with the Holy Spirit and began to speak in other languages, as the Spirit directed them.
- 1 CO 3:13 ~ Everyone's work will be seen for what it is because the light will illuminate it; it will be revealed by the fire which tries every person's work as well as his or her dedication.
- HEB 12:28–29 ~ Since we will receive a kingdom which cannot be destroyed, let us have grace to willingly serve God with reverence and awe, for He is a consuming fire.

Fire also is represented in the Bible as judgment. God brought fire upon evil people and cities to eliminate the iniquity and decadency. At the end, God will throw the evildoers and the unrighteous into the lake of fire as judgment for sin. This represents a purification of the human race, through the elimination of people who chose to reject the atonement of Christ and pay the price of sin on their own. They didn't want or need a savior and they did not want or need God to

OCTOBER

tell them what they must do. Instead, they chose to do everything their way and be their own gods, and God respected that choice, which disappoints God tremendously for He knows they will be lost to Him forever (1 TI 2:4; 2 PE 3:9).

- GEN 19:24–25 ~ God rained fire and brimstone upon Sodom and Gomorrah. He destroyed those cities, the plains, the inhabitants, and everything that was alive or growing.

- DEU 32:22–24 ~ God says, "A fire is kindled by my anger and shall burn into the lowest depths of hell; and as it grows it shall consume the earth. They will be wasted with hunger, devoured with fire, and poisoned with pestilence."

- 2 KI 22:17 ~ God says, "Since they have forsaken me, worshipped other gods, and angered me by their evil works, my wrath will burn against them and that fire will never be extinguished."

- ISA 33:14 ~ The sinners in Zion are afraid; fear has surprised the hypocrites. Who among us will inherit the devouring fire? Who will burn forever?

- ISA 66:24 ~ Their punishment will not end, neither will their fire be quenched, for they have been a contempt to humankind.

- EZE 28:18 ~ Lucifer defiled the sanctuaries with abominations. He will be consumed by the fire within him and his terrible deeds will come to an end.

- EZE 38:22–23 ~ I will send plagues and swords upon them, with rainstorms of hail, fire and brimstone. The world will behold my greatness, and realize that I alone am God.

- MAT 25:41 ~ The Lord will say to those on the left, "Depart from me you cursed ones, into the everlasting fire prepared for the devil and his angels."

- LUK 17:16–30 ~ Jesus said, "As it was in the days of Noah, so it will be when the Son of man returns. The people ate, drank, and married until Noah and his family entered the ark, the flood came, and the rest drowned. Likewise, it will be as the days of Lot; they ate, drank, bought, sold, planted and built, until Lot and his family departed; then it rained fire and brimstone destroying the rest. Accordingly, perilous times will draw closer in the last days."

- REV 20:7–10, 14 ~ When the thousand years are over, Satan will be cut loose from his prison to deceive the nations in all four corners of the earth, Gog and Magog, and muster them for battle, the number of which is as the sand of the sea. They will surround the camp of the saints and the beloved city; but fire will come down from heaven and consume them all. And the devil who deceived them was thrown into the lake of fire and brimstone, where the beast and the false prophet were, to be tormented day and night forever. Death and hell were cast into the lake of fire. This is the second death. Whoever's name was not written in the Book of Life inherited the lake of fire.

- REV 21:8 ~ The fearful, the unbelieving, the murderers, prostitutes, sorcerers, idolaters, and liars were thrown into the lake of fire which was the second death.

Father, we thank you that you have cleansed us from all sin with the blood of your only Son. We thank you that you will continue to purify us through your Holy Spirit until the end when we will be fully sanctified. Then we will be permitted to enter into your kingdom free from iniquity, and inherit new bodies that will never die, with cleansed souls that cannot sin, even as Christ could not sin in His body. Help those who are in danger of hellfire to respond to the invitation you give to all people; equip and prepare us to be messengers in the world, inviting people to partake of the atonement offered by the Lamb of God, who is Jesus Christ the Lord, and in who's name we pray today and always, Amen.

October 10

World Mental Health Day recognizes the importance of mental health and celebrates mental health workers. This observance was sponsored by the World Health Organization in 2013 to support mental health providers and those suffering from mental health illnesses. The annual theme and guidelines are established by the World Federation for Mental Health to engage agencies and institutions in developing policies, resources, and innovations to enhance the efficacy of mental health services. Health care organizations and associations will be holding events and trainings today. If you suffer from mental problems, consider making an appointment with a social worker, psychotherapist, psychologist, or psychiatrist, depending on your needs.

Having spent half of my career as a clinician, I have found the holistic approach, which integrates physical, mental, and spiritual health, produces the best mental health outcomes in the shortest amount of time (Barber, 2016). Rarely, however, is the spiritual component addressed in counseling or therapy. Faith-based counseling is not for everyone, though it can work within any religious faith system, including agnostic. The reason for this is simple: if you want to get better you must believe you can get better; otherwise, you won't even give individual, group, marital, or family counseling a try. Clients need to believe in something: self, God, counseling, change. But if the individual needing treatment does not believe he or she can get better, or does not have any faith in the therapist or the therapeutic process, progress will be little to none.

Faith is the cure for unbelief no matter what faith system you prefer. There is a plethora of scientific evidence proving the utility of faith and prayer in producing positive outcomes in both physical healing and recovery and mental healing and recovery. Further, spiritually-oriented approaches are compatible with traditional psychotherapeutic methods such as cognitive-behavioral, client-centered, psychoanalytic, and existential (*ibid*). So, what kind of spiritual interventions could be helpful in a mental health setting? Answers are found in the Holy Bible.

- PRO 3:5–7 ~ Trust in the Lord with all your heart and do not rely on your own understanding. In all your ways acknowledge Him and He will make your paths straight.

- PSA 50:15 ~ Call on me in the day of trouble, and I will deliver you, and you will glorify me.

- PSA 55:22 ~ Cast your burdens on the Lord, and He will sustain you. He will never let the righteous be shaken.

- PSA 145:14–16 ~ The Lord raises those who fall and lifts those who are down. The eyes of all wait for Him and he gives them what they need when they need it. He opens His hand and satisfies the desires of every living thing.

- MAT 6:31–34 ~ Jesus said, "Do not worry about your worldly needs; your Father in heaven knows what you need. Instead, seek first the kingdom of heaven and the righteousness of God, and this you will receive, as well as all your earthly needs. Do not be concerned about tomorrow for it will bring its own problems; you have enough to deal with today without worrying about tomorrow."

- LUK 17:20–21 ~ Jesus said, "The kingdom of heaven will not appear while you are looking around for it, because the kingdom of heaven is with you."

- JOH 4:24 ~ Jesus said, "God is spirit, so those who worship Him must worship in spirit and truth."

- 2 CO 4:16 ~ We do not lose heart. Though our outer self is wasting away, our inner self is being renewed day by day.

OCTOBER

- PHP 4:8 ~ Whatever is true, honest, just, pure, lovely, uplifting, virtuous, and praiseworthy—think about these things.

- PHP 4:13 ~ I can do all things through Christ who strengthens me.

- GAL 5:22–23 ~ The fruit of the Spirit is love, joy, peace, patience, kindness, goodness, faithfulness, gentleness, self-control; against such things there is no law.

- JAM 5:13–16 ~ Is anyone among you suffering? Let him pray. Is anyone cheerful? Let him sing praises. Is anyone among you sick? Let him call for the elders of the church, and let them pray over him, anointing him with oil in the name of the Lord. And the prayer of faith will save the one who is sick, and the Lord will raise him up. And if he has committed sins, he will be forgiven. Therefore, confess your sins to one another and pray for one another, that you may be healed. The prayer of a righteous person has great power and yields results.

To be completely (wholly) healthy, one must be well in body, mind, and spirit. Regarding the spiritual component, sixty-five percent of Americans still claim to have a Judeo-Christian foundation. Sometimes all that is necessary is for them to become more active in their prayer life, Bible study, and church attendance to experience changes in attitude, performance, and wellbeing. Spiritual regeneration was one of the treatment goals for the majority of people I treated over the course of twenty-five years; many of them did not identify as Christian but were renewed nevertheless. People that do not believe in God will submit that they have a conscience that knows what is right and proper; this is akin to one's higher power, for with it resides one's moral standards. All persons, regardless of religious persuasion, possess this knowledge. When asked where their ethics come from, most will say God or the Holy Bible.

- PSA 51:10–12 ~ Create in me a clean heart, Lord, and renew an upright spirit within me. Do not remove me from your presence and do not take your Holy Spirit from me. Restore to me the joy of your salvation, and uphold me with your free Spirit.

- 2 CO 1:3–4 ~ Blessed be the God and Father of our Lord Jesus Christ, the Father of mercies and God of all comfort, who comforts us in all our affliction, so that we may be able to comfort those who are in any affliction, with the comfort which we ourselves are comforted by God.

- EPH 4:22–24 ~ Put off your old self, which belongs to your former manner of life and is corrupt through deceitful desires. Be renewed in the spirit of your minds, by putting on the new self, created after the likeness of God in true righteousness and holiness.

- 1 TH 5:14 ~ We urge you, brothers, admonish the idle, encourage the fainthearted, help the weak, and be patient with everyone.

- TIT 3:5–7 ~ God saved us, not because of works done by us in righteousness, but according to His own mercy, by the washing of regeneration and renewal of the Holy Spirit, whom He poured out on us richly through Jesus Christ our Savior, so that being justified by His grace we might become heirs according to the hope of eternal life.

Faith is the cure for doubt, hope is the cure for despair, love is the cure for fear, patience is the cure for exasperation. All of these gifts are spiritual in nature and available to everybody. I call them tools for change. The fruits of the Spirit listed in the Bible are all tools for change, and they all wield spiritual power. That is, they represent higher powers insofar as the positive is greater in power than the negative; for instance, love casts out fear so it must be the higher power between the two. This is why introducing spirituality in therapy is so important, for it is the part of holistic health that gets the least attention, though it produces the greatest impact on mental health.

If a practitioner wants to employ faith-based techniques, it behooves them to receive advanced training in spirituality as well as religions other than their own. They also need to get a feel for the client's faith system during the intake interview. When I was in practice I provided these trainings, and they were rated very highly; but I give God the credit because every principle I taught could be related to His Word. Very few therapists actually specialize in faith-based psychotherapy like I did, because they are not familiar with the techniques and the research. Seventy-five percent of my clients selected the faith-based approach when this was among the alternatives offered to them. Of all the spiritual powers that can be applied during the course of mental health counseling, I always started with the four discussed below.

Love is most important, because mental health patients need love to quell the fear, worry, and anxiety; it also raises their self-esteem. Love is the greatest of all spiritual powers; love defeats a multitude of evils and solves most of our problems. Clients need to love themselves, and love others as themselves. Of course, loving God is critical for without Him we cannot do anything well. Everyone needs God's love, which cures all illnesses and heals all wounds, whether they are physical, mental, or spiritual.

- PRO 8:13, 17, 21, 36 ~ To fear God is to hate evil. God loves those who love Him and seek Him, and He gives them wealth and treasures. All who hate God love death.

- JER 29:11 ~ For I know the plans I have for you, declares the Lord, plans for welfare and not for evil, to give you a future and a hope.

- AMO 5:15 ~ Hate evil, love goodness, and establish justice.

- MAT 22:37–40 ~ Jesus said, "Love the Lord your God with all your heart, mind, and soul: this is the first and greatest commandment. The second is like unto the first: Love your neighbor as yourself. All the laws and the prophets depend on these two commandments."

- 1 CO 13:2–8, 13 ~ Even if you have the gift of prophecy, can understand mysteries, and have a faith to move mountains, you are nothing without love. Even if you give all you have to the poor, you profit nothing if you do not have love. Love is patient. Love is kind. Love is never envious or conceited. Love is not rude, self-seeking, or angered, nor does is it find pleasure in sin. Love does not think of sinful things nor is it provoked by evil. Love rejoices in the truth. Love always protects, always trusts, always hopes, and always endures. Love never fails. Faith, hope and love abide, but the greatest of these three is love.

- COL 3:14 ~ Above all, put on love, which binds everything together in perfect harmony.

- 1 JO 4:16, 18–19 ~ We know and believe in God's love for us, because God is love. Those that live in love live in God and He lives in them. There is no fear in love, but perfect love casts out fear, because in fear there is torment. Those who fear are not made perfect in love. We love God because He loved us first.

Once people begin to care about themselves and their future, they will desire to get better and to succeed. This is where faith comes in. If they care, they can believe; if they do not care, they will not even try. Those who believe will be inclined to make an effort. Love gives them the desire to grow and make changes, faith gets them believing that growth and change are possible. Faith removes the doubt and helps us overcome our unbelief. Without faith, there is no hope.

- PRO 29:25 ~ The fear of man is a trap; but those who trust in the Lord will be safe.

- HOS 6:2 ~ After two days He will revive us, and the third day He will raise us up to live in His presence.

- HAB 2:4 ~ Those whose souls are not upright will fail; but the just will live by faith.
- MAT 17:20 ~ Jesus said, "If you had faith the size of a mustard seed you could move mountains; nothing would be impossible."
- MAT 21:22 ~ Jesus said, "If you believe, you can receive anything you ask through prayer."
- HEB 11:1, 3, 6 ~ Faith is the assurance of things hoped for, the evidence of things not seen. By faith we understand that the world was created by the Word of God, such that things we see were made from things which do not appear. Without faith, it is impossible to please God, for whoever would wish to come to Him must believe He exists and that He rewards those who seek Him.
- HEB 11:7–38 ~ With faith, the prophets and patriarchs were able to endure hardships and perform great feats, such as subduing kingdoms, escaping certain death, overcoming incredible odds, healing the sick, and even raising the dead.

With faith, the person believes things will get better. And as they see things improve, they begin to experience hope. They see hope looming on the horizon, though they are not sure what it will look like when they get there. Hope makes the client more determined to get there. Although the change hasn't happened yet, believing gives the person some assurance that it not only can happen, it will happen. This is the power of hope: knowing the things in which we believe are real and that they will create a new and improved reality with time.

- JOB 11:18, 20 ~ You will be confident because there is hope; you will be protected, so take rest in your safety. But the wicked will not escape; their hope will be like taking their last breath.
- PSA 31:24 ~ Be strong and let your heart take courage, you who hope in the Lord.
- PSA 130:5 ~ I wait for the Lord; my soul waits for Him and in His Word I will hope.
- PRO 13:12 ~ Hope deferred makes the heart sick, but a desire fulfilled is a tree of life.
- LAM 3:21–22 ~ I have hope because the steadfast love of the Lord never ceases and His mercies never end.
- ROM 8:24–25 ~ We are saved because we hope. But hope that is seen is not hope, for who hopes for things they can see? However, if we hope for what we cannot see, we must be patient.
- ROM 15:13 ~ May the God of hope fill you with all joy and peace in believing, so that by the power of the Holy Spirit you may abound in hope.
- GAL 5:5–6 ~ Through the Spirit, by faith, we wait for the hope of righteousness. Circumcision is of no avail; instead, it is faith working through love.
- 1 TI 6:17 ~ Tell the rich people in the world not to act so proud or to set their hopes on uncertain earthly riches. Tell them to set their hope and trust in God, who furnishes everything in this world for us to enjoy.

We hope for things we cannot see because we are looking toward the future. This is where patience comes in. We know that change is a process and that problems will eventually pass, but this doesn't happen overnight. We have to be patient and willing to wait, until we are ready. God knows when we are ready and His timing is always perfect. Patience will defeat the exasperation one feels when they haven't reached the goal yet; but the closer one gets, the stronger will be their hope. Notice how each preceding tool prepares one for the next phase, becoming ever stronger in spirit. And it makes them happier having positive, workable goals.

- ECC 8:6–7 ~ For every purpose under heaven there is a season, a time designated by God, although misery and trials may continue to occur. Since we do not know what that purpose is, who but God will be able to tell us when?

- ISA 40:31 ~ Those who wait for the Lord will renew their strength; they will mount up with wings like eagles; they will run and not grow weary; they will walk and not faint.

- LUK 21:19 ~ Jesus said, "The result of your patience is to possess your soul."

- ROM 5:3 ~ Paul said that he rejoices in his tribulations, knowing that tribulation produces patience.

- ROM 12:12 ~ Rejoice in hope, be patient in tribulation, and be constant in prayer.

- JAM 1:2–4 ~ My brothers, count it all joy when you fall into different temptations, for the trying of your faith produces patience. But let patience have her perfect work so that you may be perfect, and never wanting.

- JAM 5:10–11 ~ My friends, consider the prophets who spoke in the name of the Lord as an example of patience during times of suffering. Blessed be those who have persevered in this way. Remember Job, whose perseverance was rewarded with God's mercy and compassion.

To be completely whole we need to exercise our bodies, minds, and spirits. There are things people can to do that will work for them and can be fun as well. Physical exercise is even more fun when you do it with a partner who also needs the exercise. Go to the gym together, or go for a run or walk. Everyone needs some aerobic exercise, as well as toning and maintenance. This activity releases natural healing capabilities and improves mental health. Exercise the mind by solving puzzles, doing something creative like art or music, writing in a journal, learning new things, challenging your memory. If the mind is active, more things will get done, you can react more quickly and accurately, and this will improve your self-esteem. Spiritual activity keeps us connected to God, the highest power. Through His Spirit we receive all spiritual powers, including those discussed in this lesson. If you have good spiritual health, mental and physical health will follow.

Heavenly Father, we thank you for behavioral health professionals everywhere. We pray that those who need treatment will seek it and find a skilled helper. Let there be facilities, practitioners, inpatient, outpatient, and outreach programs to reach those who are unaware of the services available to them but are in desperate need of help. Remind us to maintain our own health by exercising or bodies, minds, and spirits. Help us to stick with our exercise programs and not get lazy; also, help us to not overdo it. Empower us with gifts of the Holy Spirit, and show us how to use our spiritual powers to defeat the things that bring us down, thereby lifting up ourselves and others as we continue down the path of righteousness. For the sake of your Son Jesus Christ in whose name we pray and on whose path we will stay, Amen.

October 11

Day of Atonement, known as *Yom Kippur*, occurs on the Jewish calendar (Tishrei 10) ten days after Rosh Hashana (Feast of Trumpets). This is a holy day, for it represents a cleansing from sin. In the Old Testament, atonement was achieved through frequent blood offerings upon the altar. But God had a plan to offer permanent atonement by sending His Messiah, which is referenced throughout the Old Testament. The New Testament represents the New Covenant in Christ who is that Messiah foretold from ages past.

- EXO 24:8 ~ Moses took blood from the sacrifice and sprinkled it on the people saying, "This is the blood of the everlasting covenant revealed by the Lord in these His words."

- PSA 89:27, 45 ~ I will make Him, my firstborn, higher than all the kings of the earth. The days of His youth will be shortened, and He will be covered with shame.

- ISA 11:12 ~ The Spirit of the Lord will rest upon Him; the spirit of wisdom and understanding, the spirit of counsel and might, the spirit of knowledge, and the fear of God.

- ISA 53:4–12 ~ He took upon Himself all of our grief and sorrows; yet we treated Him as an outcast. He was tortured for our sins and punished for our peace, and through His wounds we are healed. He was slaughtered like a lamb. He was buried like a criminal but in a rich man's grave. He was made an offering for sin, although He never committed a single act of sin or spoke an evil word. Therefore, His days will be prolonged and His name will be made great. He will be exalted, for He emptied his soul unto death.

- ZEC 9:9–10 ~ Rejoice, for here comes your righteous king riding on a donkey's colt. He will bring peace to all nations.

- MAT 2:4–6 ~ Herod gathered together the chief priests and scribes, demanding to know where the Messiah would be born. They replied that it would be Bethlehem of Judea, for it was written (MIC 5:2–4) "Bethlehem is not insignificant among the cities of Judea, for from there will come a governor who will rule my people, Israel."

- LUK 24:46–48 ~ Jesus taught, "It was written that Messiah would suffer, but would rise from the dead in three days. It was written that He would preach repentance and forgiveness of sins among all nations, beginning with Jerusalem. You are witnesses of these things."

- JOH 4:25–26 ~ The woman said to Jesus, "I know that the Messiah comes, who is called Christ. When He comes, He will explain everything." Jesus replied, "I who speak to you am He."

- JOH 8:56–58 ~ Jesus said, "Abraham rejoiced to see my coming; it made him very happy." The Jews replied, "Sure, you are not even fifty years old, and you are claiming to have seen Abraham." Jesus answered, "I tell you the truth, before Abraham was, I AM."

- 1 TI 3:16 ~ Without question, the mystery of godliness is great. For God was manifested in the flesh, justified in the Spirit, worshipped by angels, preached to the Gentiles, believed by the world, and has now ascended into heaven in His glory.

In the Jewish tradition, today is a celebration of God's forgiveness of the Israelites, after sinning while Moses was receiving the Ten Commandments. He came down from Mt. Sinai with the tablets and discovered the people worshipping a golden calf, after which he broke the tablets because they had broken God's covenant. Moses divided the people into two groups, and ordered those who would follow him to slay those who rebelled; three thousand men were slain by the sword (EXO 32). Moses returned to the mountain to plead with God, and God forgave the sin of the Israelites; Moses carved new tablets and God wrote the Ten Commandments on them a second time. Yom Kippur is a high sabbath that is celebrated by the Jews to this day; they will feast and then they will fast for a full day plus one hour.

- LEV 17:11 ~ The life of all flesh resides in the blood, and I have given it for you upon the altar to make atonement for your souls, for it is the blood that makes atonement for the soul.

- LEV 23:27–28 ~ On the Day of Atonement will be a holy convocation, you will do no work on that day; you will deny yourselves sustenance, and you will make sacrifices before the Lord to make atonement for your sins.

- LEV 25:9 ~ On the tenth day of the seventh month is the Day of Atonement; you will sound the trumpet throughout the land.

Atonement provided God's forgiveness through sacrificial offerings made on this day in accordance with the laws handed down to Moses by God Himself. The blood of the sacrifice provided temporary atonement, which is why the sacrifices had to be made repeatedly. Atonement was illustrated in the ram sacrificed by Abraham in lieu of his son Isaac and in the lamb sacrificed to spare the firstborn of Israel on the first Passover. With the New Testament came the New Covenant in Jesus Christ who is the Passover Lamb.

- JER 23:5–6; JER 31:31–34 ~ The days are coming when I will raise a righteous descendant of my servant David, a king that will reign with wisdom and justice. I will make a New Covenant with my people. It will not be like the covenant I made when I brought my people out of Egypt, which they broke. The New Covenant will be this: Instead of writing my laws on stone, I will write my laws into the minds and upon the hearts of my people. I will be their God and they will be my people; they will know me from the least to the greatest, because I will forgive and forget their sins.

- MIC 6:6–7 ~ How am I to appear before God? Shall I come before Him with offerings and sacrifices? Will He be pleased with thousands and thousands of sacrifices? Shall I sacrifice my firstborn, the fruit of my body, to atone for the sin of my soul?

- MAT 26:26–28 ~ Jesus took bread, blessed it, broke it into pieces, and distributed it to the apostles saying, "Take this bread and eat it, for this is my body." Then He took a cup of wine, thanked God, and passed the cup to the apostles saying, "Each of you drink from this cup of wine, for this is my blood of the New Covenant, shed for you and for many for the remission of sins."

- HEB 9:11–15, 18–22 ~ Christ came as the high priest and king over all good things to come, to prepare a greater and more perfect church, not made by hands like a building. Christ obtained eternal redemption for us, not by the blood of burnt offerings but by His own precious blood. If the blood of burnt offerings purified the hearts of men, how much more will the blood of Christ purify us! Through the Holy Spirit, Christ offered Himself, who was without blemish, and who purged our consciences from dead works to serve the living God. By this cause, Christ has become the mediator of the New Covenant. By His death, we are redeemed from the sins committed under the first covenant, so that those who are called might receive the promise of God's eternal inheritance. Even the first covenant included blood, for after Moses read from the Book of the Law, He sprinkled blood from the offering over the book and the people, saying, "This is the blood of the covenant which God has commanded for you to keep." Moses also sanctified the tabernacle in this manner. Under the Law, all acts of disobedience are purged with blood, for without the shedding of blood there is no remission of sins.

- HEB 10:1–4, 8–18 ~ The Law, even with sacrifices for sin offered continuously throughout the year, could never make anyone perfect; otherwise, the practice could have been discontinued, since they would have rid themselves of the knowledge of sin. With these sacrifices came a reminder of sins every year, since it is impossible for the blood of animals to take away sins. When Christ prayed to God saying, "You did not desire or take pleasure in sacrifices, sin offerings, and burnt offerings given in accordance with the Law" He added, "Behold, I have come to do your will." God did away with the first covenant in order to establish the second. By one complete offering Christ has made perfect those who will be sanctified. We are sanctified by the offering of the body of Jesus Christ, one sacrifice for all people. No offering for sin will ever be needed again. Every priest stood daily in service, offering repeatedly the same sacrifices which could never take away sins. So Christ offered a single sacrifice to last for all time, and now He sits at the right hand of God, waiting for the time when His enemies would be made a stool under His feet. For by a single offering, He has perfected for all time those who are to be sanctified. The Holy Spirit also bore witness saying, "This is the covenant I will make with them after those days. I will put my laws into their hearts and write them upon their minds. And I will remember their sins and lawlessness no more." Where there is forgiveness, there is no need for any other offering for sin.

The atonement of Christ, which takes away our sins, is the only way to make it into heaven and receive eternal life. Without His sacrifice, nobody could be saved. But in order to receive His forgiveness, one must believe that Christ died and rose from the dead to save us from sin and death. Those who believe will confess and repent of their sins before God in prayer or worship. Unless a person exhibits true contrition and godly sorrow for their wrongdoing, they will not be inclined to ask God for forgiveness, and they will not believe that they need a savior. Some religions teach that one can earn their place in eternity through their own doing. But the only good works that can earn salvation are the works of Christ whose life, death, and resurrection purifies the souls of all who believe. People who have this saving faith will be compelled to prove it through their conduct and their deeds, which includes forgiving others even as we have been forgiven.

- MAT 6:9–15 ~ Jesus taught us to pray like this: "Our Father in heaven, your name is holy. Let us come to your kingdom. Let your will be done on earth as it is in heaven. Provide us our daily needs. Forgive us our sins, as we forgive others who sin against us. Lead us away from temptation and deliver us from evil. For the kingdom, power, and glory are yours forever, Amen." Then Jesus said, "If you forgive others, your heavenly Father will forgive you. If you do not forgive others, your heavenly Father will not forgive you."

- LUK 6:37 ~ Jesus said, "Do not judge others and you will not be judged; do not condemn others and you will not be condemned. Forgive others and you will be forgiven."

We thank you, Father, Son, and Holy Spirit for the atonement that covers our sins with the blood of Jesus. We thank you for your Word that teaches us the way to heaven through Christ, and the way we should conduct ourselves through His example. Help us to remember today and every day your promises made in accordance with the Old Covenant of the Law and the New Covenant of Grace. For we are saved because of your undeserved favor, by faith and not by works of the law. Nevertheless, help us to obey your laws to the best of our ability, and demonstrate our faith through our actions, to include prayer and confession, public worship, participation in the sacraments, and forgiving others who have done us wrong. Keep us strong and steadfast in your love, always abiding in you, even as your Holy Spirit abides in us. In the name of Jesus Christ, whose blood sets us free to be people of God, we praise and thank you, Amen.

October 12

National Farmer's Day recognizes the contribution that farmers make to our nation and our people. Although they represent but a fraction of the population, without them we would not eat. Theirs is a tough job, working continuous hard days in the fields to provide food for us and for countries around the world. This day falls near the closing of the fall harvest. Its origin is unknown but the observance goes back 150 years or more, and was formerly known as Old Farmer's Day. Today we celebrate the people who grow our food and get it to the market in a timely manner. We take it for granted when we go to the grocery store and find what we are looking for, without paying any mind to the toil that went into getting it there.

- GEN 8:22 ~ As long as the earth remains, seeding and harvest, cold and hot, summer and winter, and day and night will not cease.

- DEU 8:10 ~ When you have eaten and are full, then bless the Lord your God for the good land He has provided.

- DEU 28:8, 11–12 ~ The Lord will order a blessing on you and your barns; everything you set your hand to do He will bless in the land that He gave you. The Lord will give you plentiful goods, be it the fruit of your body, your cattle, your ground, or the land He gave your fathers. God will open to you His treasure: the heaven to give rain on the land in season. He will bless the work of your hand and you will provide to many nations without having to borrow.

- ECC 11:4–6 ~ Those who depend on the wind will not sow; and those who depend on the clouds will not reap. Since you do not know the ways of the wind, or how bones grow in the womb, you cannot know the works of God who makes it all. Sow your seed in the morning and keep working into evening, for you do not know whether you will prosper, or whether it will be this or that or perhaps both.

- ISA 30:22–23 ~ You must rid yourselves of idols and toss them into the trash. Then you will see rain upon your seed and will sow into the ground; and the food you produce will be rich and plentiful, and your cattle will graze in large fields.

- JOE 2:24–25 ~ Be glad, children of Zion, and rejoice in the Lord your God, for He has given you rain for the early season and for the late season. And your threshing floors will be covered with wheat, and the vats shall overflow with wine and oil.

- LUK 10:2–3 ~ Jesus said, "The harvest is plentiful but the laborers are few. Pray that the Lord of the harvest would send more laborers to help. Keep in mind, I am sending you out like lambs among wolves."

- 1 CO 3:6–9 ~ Paul planted, Apollos watered, and God gave the increase. Neither he who plants nor he who sows is anything, because only God can make things grow. The man who plants and the man who waters have one purpose, and each will be rewarded according to their labor. For we all are laborers with God in His plantation; and you are God's building.

- 2 TI 2:6 ~ The hard-working farmer should be first to sample the crops.

- HEB 6:7–6 ~ The earth that drinks the rain which falls on it and produces a crop for those who farmed it becomes a blessing from God. But the land that produces thorns and thistles is in danger of being cursed. In the end it will be burned.

  Father, thank you for those who grow our goods, keeping stores stocked with produce. As they sow and reap, so let us sow seeds of truth and the Gospel of Christ. May your Holy Spirit nurture those seeds, to grow into a tree of life within their hearts. In Jesus's name, Amen.

OCTOBER

October 13

National Train Your Brain Day is all about learning new things and mastering old things. In particular, people should learn how to maximize their potential with respect to using their brains efficiently. To begin with, your brain needs exercise; if you exercise it regularly, you will be operating at a higher level of functioning than you would otherwise. We have the potential to continue learning until senility sets in, barring any other brain damage; this phase will occur earlier for those who do not exercise their brains. Certainly, working puzzles and brain teasers, solving problems in math or science, memorizing things and planning things in advance will keep your brain active and attentive, and give you more control over your thoughts. Mindfulness is the best way to control your thoughts: most importantly, being aware of God's omnipresence.

- 1 CH 28:9 ~ Know your God and serve Him with a whole heart and a willing mind. For the Lord searches all hearts and understands every thought and plan.

- PSA 139:1–6 ~ Lord, you have searched me and you know everything about me. You discern my thoughts, and are familiar with all my ways. I could never attain such knowledge. Even before I speak, you know what I will say.

- PRO 16:3 ~ Commit your works to God and He will establish your thoughts.

- PRO 22:17 ~ Incline your ear to hear the words of the wise and apply your mind to knowledge.

- PRO 23:19 ~ Hear and be wise, and direct your mind in the true way.

- ECC 7:25 ~ I directed my mind to know the truth, to investigate matters, to seek wisdom and find answers; and to know the evil of folly and the foolishness of madness.

- ECC 8:5 ~ Those who obey the commandments will meet no harm, and the mind of a wise person will know the time and the way.

- ROM 3:20 ~ Nobody can be justified in His sight by works of the Law; rather, through the Law we become conscious of sin.

- ROM 8:4–6 ~ Walk, not according to the flesh, but according to the spirit. Those who live according to the flesh set their minds on evil, but those who live according to the spirit set their minds on God. To set the mind on flesh results in death, but to set the mind on God results in peace and life.

- 2 CO 10:3–5 ~ Although we are human flesh and blood, we do not make war with flesh and blood. For the weapons we use are not of this world, because we have the Spirit on our side to bring down the strongholds of the enemy. We break down the arguments and the influences of those high and mighty people who stand against God; we take captive human thoughts, making them obedient to Jesus Christ.

- 1 TI 4:12 ~ Be an example of the believers in thoughts, in conversation, in love, in spirit, in faith, and in purity.

- HEB 6:19 ~ We have Jesus as a sure and steadfast anchor for our souls.

- 1 PE 2:19–21 ~ It is commendable if a man suffers unjustly because he is conscious of God. If you suffer for doing good and you endure it, you are favored by God. This is one reason you are called, because Christ suffered for you, giving you an example to follow.

You can increase brain power and speed by connecting the conscious mind with the unconscious mind. The part we actively exercise, which dominates during waking hours, is the conscious mind. Vastly larger and more advanced is the unconscious mind, where memory resides,

DAILY DEVOTIONAL EVENTS

automatic processes are regulated, dreaming takes place (REM), and programmed routines are organized. We are asleep when many of these activities are occurring; but make no mistake, you are processing data even when you sleep. The unconscious is capable of parallel processing, meaning it can handle many different data sets simultaneously whereas the conscious realm allows only linear processing and timesharing.

Are there ways of exercising the subconscious part of the brain? Well, yes there are. One, you can speed up processes by making them automatic through practice, skill development, and mastery; this enables one to perform separate processes by multitasking. Two, you can reprogram unwanted processes or programs by tapping into the unconscious realm. This can be achieved through meditation, introspection, self-hypnosis, ideation, and reframing. Three, certain drills facilitate data transfer between hemispheres of the brain, data sharing between visual and auditory memory, and data conveyance from higher levels to lower levels of consciousness. Some forms of cognitive therapy assist these processes (EMDR, NLP, hypnosis). The objective is to connect information between both hemispheres of the brain, and connect the conscious and unconscious domains of the mind, enabling one to explore the lower echelons of consciousness, to improve memory, and to automate processes.

Try this simple exercise when you have a break at work or after a long stretch of mental activity. Sit back, relax, breathe deeply and slowly, and think of your favorite place or a place you would like to visit in your mind. This distracts the conscious mind as you drift away from the external world, blocking outside stimuli and focusing inwardly. After a few hours of hard work, stop and explore your unconscious domain where the data you just collected have a chance to incubate. Your unconscious mind will organize and store this learning as you enjoy a pleasant and safe place inside of yourself. Studies have shown that employees who take a short break every two hours are more productive over the course of their workday. Instead of hanging out in the lounge drinking coffee on your break, use the time to rest the conscious part of your brain once in a while, as you exercise the unconscious domain, meditating on anything except work.

- LAM 3:19–22 ~ When I think about my sorrows, it brings my soul down. When I am down, I bring to mind that I always will have hope. Because of the Lord's great love, we are not consumed, and His compassion never fails.

- LAM 3:40 ~ Search out and examine your ways, and turn back to the Lord.

- JOS 1:8 ~ The book of the Law must never leave your mouth, and you should meditate on it day and night, so that you can act in accordance with all that is written therein. Then your ways will be prosperous and you will enjoy success.

- PSA 19:14 ~ Let the words of my mouth and the meditation of my heart be acceptable to you Lord.

- PSA 77:5–6 ~ I have considered the days of old, the years from ancient times. I recalled my song in the night. I meditated with my heart, and my spirit made diligent search.

- PSA 119:27 ~ Lord, make me understand your rules of conduct and I will meditate upon your wondrous works.

- PRO 2:2 ~ Make your ear attentive to wisdom and your heart to understanding.

- PRO 15:28 ~ The mind of the righteous ponders how to answer, but the mouth of the wicked pours out evil.

- PRO 16:23–24 ~ The mind of a wise person makes speech judicious, adding persuasiveness to words. Pleasant words are sweet to the soul and health to the body.

- PRO 27:23–24 ~ Pay attention to your business, for riches do not endure forever, and an earthly crown does not endure to every generation.

- ROM 12:3 ~ Do not think of yourself more highly than you should, but rather evaluate yourself with a clear mind, in accordance with the measure of faith God has given to you.

- 1 CO 9:25 ~ Those who strive to master a task must train hard and discipline themselves. They do so to obtain an earthly crown that will not last; but we strive for a crown that will last forever.

It is unknown the origin of today's observance but it has become a popular one. The brain is a fascinating thing, so complex that we still do not understand it fully, but it can outperform mega-computers in data processing speed. Skilled operations become automatic over time, enabling one to concentrate more attentional resources on operations requiring cognitive control. The brain has what is called plasticity, meaning it is quite versatile in reassigning tasks to different parts of the brain, connecting information clusters, updating internal models, establishing causality from repetition, and so on. The brain is proficient in far more areas than people realize.

Today you might consider developing a brain exercise routine; start by making a list of functions or processes you would like to improve. Then sample different approaches to exercise the brain at multiple levels of consciousness. The list below introduces ideas to start from.

- Conduct a decision analysis by weighing alternatives based on their costs and benefits.
- Practice attention and awareness scenarios, like noticing everybody you pass by today.
- Prepare a problem-solving scheme using a flow diagram or other illustration.
- Hone sensory-perceptual faculties by narrowing your focus with each of your five senses.
- Flag information inputs to pause a program, recognizing triggers to behavior worth ceasing.
- Employ relaxation and breathing exercises to calm down so you can create internal imagery.
- Analyze habitual programs to modify, by rehearsing alternative responses in your mind.
- Widen cognitive borders by solving different types of brain teasers each week.
- Recopy and outline notes on tasks: procedures, knowledge, skills, and resource requirements.
- Retrieve stored information or events using visual, auditory, and/or kinesthetic data cues.
- Write down your favorite Bible verses and commit them to memory.

Consider planning an activity for home or office to celebrate this day, playing team trivia or group brain games. Relate it to the job or the family when there is room for discussion. Just as physical exercise is more fun with friends, family, and colleagues, mental exercises are more fun with others too, and they improve cross-communications with all members of the group.

- PRO 27:17 ~ As iron sharpens iron, so also one person can sharpen another.

Omniscient Father, your wisdom exceeds that of all humankind put together. You bestow your wisdom on us as if feeding a baby. You have given us capabilities of which we were unaware until we sought your truth and learned your ways. Help us to be more productive using the talents, knowledge, and skills we have acquired to glorify you. Let us exercise our brains for the duration of our lives to keep them sharp, and be ready to respond when expected occasions arise. Help us to recreate routines and practice reprogramming to make our brains more useful, to make our words more accurate, and to make our actions more effective. Remind us that the study of your Word and faith in Christ are a composite of the wisdom found in your salvation. Let us meditate on these lofty things when we need solace, and not waste our time reliving meaningless events or dwelling on the past. In the name of Jesus, who is the truth of your Word in human form, Amen.

October 14

Indigenous Peoples Day is the second Monday of the month; it replaced Columbus Day which had been a federal holiday since 1937. On the five-hundredth anniversary of his first landing in the Americas on 10/12/1492, people and states renamed the day. Columbus's legacy fell into disrepute among many Americans due to his alleged exploitation and maltreatment of the indigenous peoples in the Caribbean. It is debatable whether or not Columbus was a ruthless butcher, although the discovery and exploration of the New World introduced deadly diseases such as small pox which wiped out many of the natives. Despite his flaws, and who doesn't have flaws, Columbus's contribution to the mass exodus from Europe to America should not be discounted. Holidays, observances, statues and monuments recognizing achievements made by ordinary, sinful people are not intended to bring them glory but to acknowledge their achievements. They often remind us of dark episodes in our history so that we will not forget. God has commanded His people to never worship humans, angels, oneself, idols, or graven images. Throughout our history, Americans have glorified God, giving Him the credit for our extraordinary accomplishments, as did the patriots who were heroes of the revolution.

- 1 CH 16:29 ~ Give to the Lord the glory due His name. Bring an offering and come before Him. Worship the Lord in the beauty of holiness.

- PSA 44:8 ~ It is good to brag about God and praise His name always.

- ISA 10:33 ~ Those who appear to be high and mighty will be cut down, and those who are proud will be humbled.

- JER 9:23 ~ The wise man must not glory in his wisdom, neither the mighty man glory in his might, nor the rich man glory in his riches. But let people who glorify, glory in this: that they understand and know me, and that I am the Lord who exercises loving kindness, judgment, and righteousness on the earth, for in these things I delight.

- MAT 5:16 ~ Let your light shine before others, so they may see your good works and glorify your Father who is in heaven.

- MAT 6:2 ~ When you help the needy, do not sound your trumpet as the hypocrites do in the churches and in the streets, so they might receive praise from others. The truth is, that is all the reward they will receive.

- ACT 3:12–13, 16 ~ Peter did not take credit for healing the lame man. Rather, he attributed the miracle to faith in Jesus Christ, emphasizing the power that exists through faith in the name of Jesus Christ. That faith was shared by Peter and the man who was healed.

- 2 CO 10:17–18 ~ Let those who rejoice, rejoice in the Lord. Those who commend themselves will not receive approval, only those who are commended by God.

- GAL 6:14 ~ God forbid that I should glory, except in the cross of our Lord Jesus Christ, by whom the world is crucified unto me, and I unto the world.

- 1 TI 1:17 ~ All glory and honor belongs now and forever to our eternal, immortal, and invisible King, who is the only wise God.

In recent decades, certain radical groups have made it their mission to rewrite our history by discounting Columbus, the Mayflower pilgrims, our founding fathers, and even Abraham Lincoln, calling them racists. They were not racists or white supremacists, they were people of faith, who believed in a sovereign God and the theology of the Bible. The Spaniard conquistadors were warriors, not evangelists, though part of their mission was to convert the natives to

OCTOBER

Catholicism; and yes, they were not too civil about it. Unpatriotic radicals who tear down statues and defame our heritage also lack civility; what they have in common is disdain for the Holy Bible, the Christian faith, and the lessons learned throughout our history, without which we would not be the most powerful nation that ever existed on earth. The USA has learned from these mistakes, having freed the slaves, and granted rights to all people born in the USA. In fact, indigenous peoples have extra rights insofar as the tribes and reservations are allowed self-government and are not taxed, though individual employees and those receiving gaming distributions do pay federal income tax.

- DEU 10:19 ~ Love the strangers in your midst for you were once strangers in the land of Egypt.
- DEU 31:12 ~ Gather the people together including men, women, and children, as well as the strangers among you, so that everyone can hear, learn, fear the Lord your God, and obey all the words of His Law.
- ISA 56:6–7 ~ Even those who are strangers to God's people Israel will be part of God's house if they obey Him.
- EZE 47:22 ~ The land will be divided as an inheritance for the house of Israel, as well as the strangers who lived among them and had children among them. Thus, the land will be shared by the twelve tribes as well as their companions.
- EPH 2:18–22 ~ Through Christ we have access by one Spirit to the Father. Thus, we are no longer strangers or foreigners, but fellow citizens with the saints in the household of God.

It is appropriate that we celebrate indigenous peoples, which also are celebrated on 08/09 with an international observance by the UN. There is no doubt that native Americans suffered; but those who abused, murdered, or discriminated against them were not representative of the values we hold dear in the USA. There are bad actors in every society, and there were atrocities committed by both sides. Nobody is blameless; we all are sinners and we all have treated others unfairly. As a nation, we have recognized our past sins and we have become stronger in doing so.

- ECC 7:20 ~ Surely there is not a righteous person on earth who does good and never sins.
- JER 14:20 ~ We acknowledge our wickedness, Lord, and the sins of our ancestors, for we all have sinned against you.
- ROM 3:23–24 ~ All people have sinned and come short of God's glory, and all people are justified freely by His grace through the redemption that is in Jesus Christ.
- ROM 5:18–21 ~ By one man, sin came into the world bringing death, and death was subsequently passed along to humankind for all have sinned. Therefore, while the sin of one man brought judgment and condemnation upon humanity, so the righteousness of one man brought the free gift of justification and life. Thus, by the disobedience of Adam we became sinful, and by the obedience of Christ we can become righteous.
- 2 CO 7:9–10 ~ I am glad that you were sorry for your sins and repented. Spiritual sorrow for one's sins works repentance unto salvation, but the sorrow of the world works death.

Heavenly Father, we pray for our nation that we may unite as one people and one nation under God, regardless of heritage, history, or preferences. We pray that we never forget our past, but continue to learn from it and teach it to our children, lest we forget how we got here and where we came from. Let younger generations appreciate that flawed people became revered because they overcame the odds and their shortcomings. Thank you for enabling flawed people as ourselves to overcome our faults through Jesus. We ask in His name, who overcame a world of sin, Amen.

October 15

Spread the Word Day seems appropriate for the ides of October which occurs exactly six months after the ides of March. This is the season of the Feast of Tabernacles (which we will cover in two days). Tabernacles represent God's church on earth both in the Old and the New Testaments. Jesus is the head of that church, for He is the bridegroom. [The late harvest season (*Sukkot*) is likely the time period of Christ's birth in 5 BC. This is based on King Herod's death around the early harvest season, in March of 4 BC. This is also based on Christ's death on Passover in AD 30, exactly 33.5 years from His birth; that would put the death of John the Baptist during the October harvest season at age 33.5, six months before the death of his cousin Jesus.]

God's Word is truth and it is our duty as His children to spread the Word and make disciples using our abilities and gifts (MAT 28:19–20). God communicates His love to us through His Word of truth spoken by the breath of His Holy Spirit. Through the written Word and the living Word, God speaks directly to humanity. God also communicates with us in His creation, where we can learn more about Him by studying the universe and nature. Jesus Christ, begotten of the Holy Spirit, is the Word made flesh. Christ was sent to personally convey God's Word to humans, as is clearly evident in interrelation of the Old and New Testaments. God has appointed Christians to be ministers of His Word to the world, for we are His church on earth.

- JER 23:28 ~ God says, "Whoever has my Word should speak that Word faithfully so others might hear it."

- JOH 1:1, 14 ~ In the beginning was the Word, and the Word was with God, and the Word was God. And the Word became flesh, and lived on earth, and we saw His glory, the glory the Father's only Son.

- JOH 8:31–32 ~ Jesus said, "If you believe in my words then you are indeed my disciples; and you will know the truth, and the truth will set you free."

- JOH 15:26 ~ Jesus said, "I will send the Comforter to you and He will testify about me; the Comforter is the Holy Spirit of truth which proceeds from the Father."

- 1 CO 2:13–15~ We teach using words taught by the Holy Spirit, not by human wisdom. Spiritual truths can only be interpreted by those who possess the Spirit. But the naturalist cannot receive things of the Spirit such things are foolishness to those without spiritual discernment. But a spiritual person judges all things, yet are judged by nobody.

- 2 TI 4:2–5 ~ Paul instructed Timothy to preach the Word; always be prepared to correct, rebuke, and encourage with patience and sound doctrine. For the time will come when people will turn away from sound doctrine and pursue their own lusts, finding teachers that tell them what they want to hear. They will wander from the truth and rely on myths. Always be watchful, willing to endure afflictions, doing the work of the evangelist, doing whatever is necessary for the continuance of the ministry.

The Bible was authored by God, but written by holy men who were directed by the Holy Spirit concerning what to write. Since the Word comes from God, it is perfect. Therefore, everything in the Holy Bible is true, because God is incapable of telling a lie.

- DEU 4:1–2 ~ Listen, Israel, to the statutes and judgments God has commanded you to keep so that you might live. Do not add to or subtract from these commandments God has given to you.

- PRO 30:5–6 ~ Every word of God is true; do not attempt to add to His words or He will rebuke you and you will be proven false.

OCTOBER

- MAT 24:35 ~ Jesus said, "Heaven and earth will pass away, by my words will remain forever."
- JOH 6:68–69 ~ Simon Peter answered Jesus, "Lord, who else can we turn to? You alone have the words of eternal life. We believe and we are positive that you are the Christ, the Son of the living God."
- GAL 1:8 ~ Anyone, including the angels, who preaches anything contrary to what Jesus Christ and the apostles preached are cursed.
- 2 PE 1:16, 21 ~ We did not follow cleverly devised fables when we told people about the power and coming of Jesus Christ, for we were eye witnesses to His majesty. No prophecy ever came from the impulse of man, but holy men spoke as they were directed by God.
- 1 JO 1:1–3 ~ That which was from the beginning, the very Word of life, we heard, we saw, and we touched. For life was revealed, and we have seen it, and bear witness, and show you that eternal life, which was with the Father, visited us. That which we have seen and heard we declare to you, so that you can become one of us; for truly our fellowship is with the Father, and with his Son Jesus Christ.
- 1 JO 5:6–8, 20 ~ There are three recorded in heaven: the Father, the Word, the Holy Spirit. These three are one. The same bear witness: the Spirit, the Water, the Blood. The Spirit is the witness, because the Spirit bears the truth. We know Jesus Christ who is true so we may know God who is true. We live in Him who has shown us His Son, the source of eternal life.
- REV 22:18–19 ~ For I testify to everyone who hears the words of the prophecy of this book, that if anyone adds to these words, God will add unto that person the plagues mentioned in this book. If anyone subtracts from the words of this prophecy, God will take away their name from the Book of Life, and they will not share in the inheritance.

Anyone attempting to change God's Word, add or subtract words, or alter their meaning are committing blasphemy. To refute what God says is akin to calling Him a liar. Those rejecting His truth have rejected the atonement of Christ and have committed the only unpardonable sin.

- LEV 24:16 ~ Whoever blasphemes the name of the Lord will surely be put to death; the entire congregation will certainly stone that person whether a stranger or a native to the land.
- MAT 12:31–32 ~ Jesus said, "All manner of sin and blasphemy can be forgiven, except blasphemy directed against the Holy Spirit. Whoever speaks against the Holy Spirit will not be forgiven, neither in this world nor in the world to come."
- ROM 1:25 ~ They changed God's truth into a lie and worshipped and served the creature rather than the Creator who is blessed forever, Amen.

Beware of false prophets, teachers, and cults which deviate from the true Word. If they do not acknowledge Jesus Christ as God in the flesh, if they do not confess Him as Savior, if they do not believe in the inerrancy of the Holy Bible—they are lost and condemned. It is essential to learn the truth directly from God in order to recognize untruth.

- ISA 59:4, 13 ~ They know they are being disobedient to God; they carefully plan their lies and mischief.
- LAM 2:14 ~ Your prophets have said foolish things and seen false visions.
- MAT 7:21 ~ Not everyone who acts or appears righteous is righteous.
- ACT 20:30 ~ From among yourselves will come those speaking perverse things to gain followers.

- 2 CO 11:13–14 ~ They have fooled people into thinking they are Christ's apostles. But that is not surprising, for even Satan disguises himself as an angel of light.
- 1 JO 4:1–3 ~ Test the prophets by asking them if they acknowledge Jesus Christ as God's Son who came as a human being to save humankind from sin.
- 1 JO 5:20–21 ~ Remain in Christ who is true. Stay away from anything or anyone who would distort God's truth or attempt to take God's place in your heart.
- JDE 1:4 ~ False teachers have infiltrated the churches, claiming that once you become Christians you can do whatever you want without being punished.

Jesus Christ is the Messiah, Redeemer, New Covenant, and Savior of humankind. Only He can provide salvation, through His death which atoned for the sin of the world, and His resurrection which provides eternal life for all believers. Nonbelievers will not be there with us in heaven for they have declined God's offer of salvation by faith in Christ.

- GEN17:2, 7 ~ God said to Abraham: Walk in righteousness and be blameless and I will make a covenant with you. I will multiply you exceedingly, and the everlasting covenant will be with your descendants from generation to generation.
- 2 SA 7:12–14 ~ God said to David through the prophet Nathan: I will raise up one of your descendants to build my kingdom. He will be my Son and I will be His Father; and my throne will be established forever
- DAN 7:13–14 ~ Daniel saw in a dream the Son of Man descending from the heavens. He was given all dominion and glory, to rule all peoples, nations, and languages. His kingdom was everlasting.
- MAL 3:1 ~ Malachi informed that the Messiah would be the messenger of the New Covenant.
- LUK 1:68–73 ~ The Lord God has redeemed His people just like He promised to David and Abraham as foretold by the prophets. The mercy that He showed to our ancestors was in accordance with the covenant that God told them to remember.
- JOH 5:24–25 ~ Jesus said, "Truly I tell you, whoever hears my Word and believes in Him who sent me will receive eternal life. They will not be condemned, but will pass from death into life. Truly I say that the hour is coming when the dead will hear my voice, and those who listened to me will live."
- ACT 4:12 ~ There is no salvation in any other; for there is no other name under heaven, given to people, whereby we can be saved.
- GAL 4:6 ~ Because you are God's children, He has sent the Spirit of His Son into your hearts.

Father, we thank you for your Word living within us by the power of your Holy Spirit. We thank you Jesus, for showing us the Word so we might believe and receive eternal life. Help us to be consistent in the study of your truth so we can expose that which is false and untrue. Equip us to take the truth with us wherever we go, and share it whenever there is an appropriate occasion to do so. Let all who seek the truth find it in the Holy Bible, so they will know the truth that sets people free from sin and death. Silence and stifle evil people and demons who seek to destroy truth and perpetuate lies. Strengthen us to call them out and rebut their deceitfulness so others will see them as the liars that they are and steer clear of them and their philosophy. Help us to restore honesty in our government and fill offices with people who believe and tell the truth. In the name of Jesus who is the life, the truth, and the way, Amen.

October 16

Boss's Day is observed on this date, unless it falls on a weekend, then it is celebrated on the nearest weekday. Today we celebrate bosses who we admire and who have mentored us. Being retired, I bring to mind great bosses throughout my career. I also think about God who is the greatest boss. If you do not like your boss, plan a luncheon or something anyway; sometimes it helps to get to know the boss better in a relaxed atmosphere; however, before planning an event or dinner, you might check with the boss first, keeping in mind it is a work day. Regardless, this is a good day to connect with your boss and build that relationship. This holiday is optional, since not all businesses will be celebrating; in fact, some people are against observing this holiday for various reasons. But many other countries and businesses have adopted the holiday and it is growing in acceptance. At least buy your boss a greeting card; yes, they do make cards and gifts in recognition of Boss's Day; in fact, this observance got a boost in 1979 by Hallmark.

The idea for this observance was submitted to the US Chamber of Commerce in 1958 by a secretary named Patricia Bays Haroski; she selected this day because it was her father's birthday, and he was the boss. She appreciated her boss as should everybody who has a job. The holiday was approved in her native Illinois by the governor in 1962.

- PRO 10:4–5, 26 ~ Whoever slacks off will become poor, but the diligent will become rich. Whoever gathers during the summer is wise; whoever sleeps during the harvest is shameful. As vinegar is to the teeth and smoke to the eyes, so is a sloth to an employer.

- MAT 20:1–16 ~ The kingdom of heaven is like the owner of a vineyard who spent the entire day hiring laborers to toil in his fields. At the end of the day, he paid them a full day wage. The ones who had worked all day were mad because the others who had not worked as long received the same payment. The owner replied, "I did not treat you unfairly; you received the agreed upon wages. It is not against the law for me to spend my money the way I please. You should not have an evil eye simply because I was generous to the others." Likewise, in heaven the last will be first and the first will be last, for many are called, but few are chosen.

- MAT 25:14–30 ~ The kingdom of heaven is like an investor who was traveling to a far country. He called his servants together and gave each of them some of his fortune to invest for him. He gave them varying amounts, depending on their abilities. After a year or so the investor returned to see how his money had been invested. The man who had received five portions doubled his money, as did the man who had received two portions. The boss was very happy saying, "Since you have been faithful with but a few things, I will make both of you rulers over many things." The man who had received one portion did not invest it but stashed it away for fear of losing it. The boss was irate saying, "The least you could have done is put it in the bank where it would have yielded a modest amount of interest." Then he ordered the portion be taken away from him and given to the man who had made the most of his investment. The boss said, "To those who have, more will be given; to those who do not have, the rest will be taken away." Then the unwise servant was thrown into the dungeon.

- COL 3:22–23 ~ Workers, obey your bosses, not only when they are watching or to garner favor, but always with a sincere heart, as if working for the Lord.

- EPH 6:9 ~ Bosses, do the same to your workers, not being overbearing, knowing that your Master is in heaven for He is master of everyone.

We thank you, Father, for giving us opportunities and jobs where we can make a gainful living in a field we enjoy. Help us show appreciation to our bosses and employers, and help them to show appreciation to their workers. For we all are working for you, in Jesus's name, Amen.

October 17

Feast of Tabernacles, also known as Feast of Booths (*Sukkot*), occurs on the Jewish calendar during the month of Tishrei, 15–21. This is the seventh and last of the major feasts God commanded Israel to observe; it begins near the end of the fall harvest, five days after the Day of Atonement. This celebration is often associated with the rebuilding of God's house, reflected in the assembly and disassembly of the tabernacle every time the Israelites relocated while in the wilderness of Sinai. This was a temporary dwelling for the Holy Spirit who traveled with them; the sojourners also built temporary dwellings, or booths. This is a time for fellowship, when the congregation together looks forward to living permanently with the Lord in heaven where He dwells. Traditionally, the men of Israel (males over twenty years old) made a pilgrimage to Jerusalem to celebrate this feast, where they housed in temporary dwellings or booths. Like the week of unleavened bread, this feast begins and ends on a high sabbath.

- LEV 23:34–36, 39–42 ~ The fifteenth day of the seventh month begins the seven days of the feast of tabernacles. There will be a holy convocation on the first day so there will be no work. For seven days make sacrifices by fire, until the eighth day when you will have another holy convocation, a solemn assembly. After you have gathered the fruit of the land, keep this feast, beginning and ending on a high sabbath. On the first day, collect boughs of large trees, willow and palm branches from the stream, and rejoice seven days, with a holy convocation on the eighth day. You will dwell in booths for seven days.

- PSA 76:2 ~ In Salem is God's tabernacle; in Zion is His home.

- PSA 118:15–16 ~ Shouts of joy and victory resound in the tabernacles of the righteous saying, "The right hand of the Lord is lifted high; His right hand has done mighty things."

- JOH 1:14 ~ The Word became flesh and lived among us. And we witnessed His glory, the glory of the Father's only Son, full of grace and truth.

- HEB 8:1–2 ~ In summary, we have a High Priest, who sits at the right hand of God in heaven and who serves in the sanctuary, the true tabernacle set up by the Lord and not by man.

The Israelites took the tabernacle wherever they went, breaking it down and setting it up countless times. The inner sanctum was the Holy of Holies which held the Ark of the Covenant, containing the stone tablets of the Ten Commandments. Only the high priest could enter the holiest chamber. The connection between the Old and New Covenants is the Holy Spirit, who is connected to the Father and to the Son in an eternal triad. We ourselves are temples, or booths, where the Holy Spirit of the Lord can dwell. A gathering of Christians is like a church filled with booths, each a part of the collective body of Christ. The entirety of those alive and dead in Christ comprises His Church, analogous to a bride being prepared for nuptials, the groom being the only begotten Son of God: the Lamb of God, the New Covenant.

- EXO 26:33 ~ Hang the curtain and place the Ark of the Covenant behind it; the curtain will separate the holy place from the most holy place.

- JER 31:31–33 ~ The days are coming when I will make a New Covenant with my people. It will not be like the covenant I made when I brought my people out of Egypt, which they broke. The New Covenant will be this: Instead of writing my laws on stone, I will write my laws inside the hearts of my people.

- MAT 26:26–28 ~ As they were eating, Jesus took bread, blessed it and said, "Take and eat, this is my body." Then He took the cup, gave thanks and said, "Take and drink, this is my blood of the new covenant, shed for you for the remission of sins."

- HEB 9:2–4 ~ A tabernacle was erected, containing a candlestick, a table, and the twelve loaves in the sanctuary. Inside the second curtain was the holiest place. It held the Ark of the Covenant with the tablets of the covenant (Ten Commandments).

- HEB 9:11–16 ~ Christ came as the high priest of good things to come, by a greater and more perfect tabernacle, not made by human hands. It was not dedicated by the blood of animals, but through His own blood, Christ entered into the holiest place, having obtained eternal redemption for sins. If the blood of sacrifices could sanctify and purify in accordance with the old covenant, how much more the blood of Christ can purify and sanctify, purging our consciences from dead works to serve the living God! He is mediator of the new covenant, that by His death there is forgiveness of sins committed under the old covenant, so we might receive the promise of an eternal inheritance.

- HEB 9:18–21 ~ Even the first covenant included blood, for after Moses read from the Book of the Law, He sprinkled blood from the offering on the book and the people, saying, "This is the blood of the everlasting covenant which God has commanded for you to keep." Moses also sanctified the tabernacle and the vessels in this manner.

Both the first and the last Jewish feasts continued for a period of eight days, one week plus one day, during the early harvest season and the late harvest season. These two festivals revealed a harvesting of God's people Israel in the Old Testament, and a harvesting of Christians who have been grafted into the Branch in the New Testament (ZEC 6:11–13; JOH 15:1–6). God's feasts started with Passover and a week of unleavened bread, and ended with Tabernacles after a week of sacrifice followed by a high sabbath day, representing the first and the last, the alpha and omega. You know, we have a calendar filled with holidays, but few are actually holy like this one.

The first coming of Christ is represented in the late harvest, when He came as a baby. His departure from earth is depicted in the early harvest, when He died and rose again. After forty days, He ascended to sit at God's right hand, leaving behind His Holy Spirit to continue building His Church on earth. The faith of Christians also is built by the Holy Spirit, who dwells within us. He is our life force forever, which we possess by claiming the blood of Christ. His blood covers us like the blood of the sacrifice sprinkled on the people by Moses after reading from the Book of the Law. Messiah will return before you know it, to claim us, for we are His, the true Christian Church, the seed of Abraham, the body of Christ: those sanctified by His Holy Spirit.

- ACT 2:42 ~ And they continued conscientiously in the apostles' doctrine and fellowship, in the breaking of bread, and in prayers.

- HEB 10:24–25 ~ Let us encourage one another to promote love and good works. Let us never cease to fellowship with one another in God's house as others are in the habit of doing.

- 1 JO 1:3–4 ~ That which we have seen and heard we declare to you, so that you can become one of us; for truly our fellowship is with the Father, and with His Son Jesus Christ. These things we write to you so that you may be filled

Father, we praise and thank you for giving us your Word so we could know you, and we praise and thank you for sending your Son so we could live with you. We praise and thank you for your Holy Spirit who teaches us your will and your wisdom, and who brings us all the way home. We proclaim Christ who is the resurrection and the life, and we claim His blood as a covering for our sins. Let your Holy Spirit indwell us as we now open our hearts and minds to receive Him. May we be temples of your Holy Spirit on earth; let us not defile that temple with the wicked ways of the world, or be influenced by demons and Satan. Instead, let your Spirit drive them from our midst wherever we go. In the name of the Father, Son, and Holy Spirit we pray, Amen.

October 18

Crown of Life Day is added to remind us of the prize given by our Lord for winning the human race. That is, believers who remain steadfast in the true Christian faith will receive everlasting life when Christ comes back to retrieve His people. What must one do to obtain this crown? Just believe that Christ gave His life for you and then came back to life again, so you can come back to life after you die, and live forever with Him in heaven. If you choose not to believe, that is your prerogative, but you will be giving up your inheritance. If you choose to believe, never giving up but persevering, you receive that crown of life. [from Barber, 2020a.]

- PRO 27:23–24 ~ Pay attention to your business, for riches do not endure forever, and an earthly crown does not endure to every generation.

- 1 CO 9:24–27 ~ Do you understand that there are many competitors in a race but only one will receive first prize? Therefore, run with the intention of winning that prize. Those who strive to master a task must train hard and discipline themselves. However, they do so to obtain an earthly crown that will not last; but we strive for a crown that will last forever. Therefore, I run like a man with a purpose. I do not fight like a boxer beating the air. Instead, I beat my body into shape, making it serve God's purpose, so that my preaching will not cause me to be disqualified for the prize.

- 2 TI 4:6–8 ~ Paul wrote: I am ready to sacrifice myself, for my time of departure is near. I have fought a good fight and I have finished the race, and my faith is still intact. Hereafter a crown of righteousness awaits me, which the Lord, the righteous judge, will give to me. He will give it, not only to me, but also to everyone who lovingly awaits Christ's coming.

- JAM 1:12 ~ Blessed be those who persevere despite their trials and temptations, because they will receive the crown of life which the Lord has promised to anyone who loves Him.

The term equity has been misused in recent years; it means fairness. Progressives have changed the meaning: equal outcomes for everyone. The purpose is to replace the word equality, which means equal opportunities for everyone. Anyone who competes, whatever the arena, does so to come out ahead, to better their previous performance, to win the game, to get promoted. What is the point of competing if everyone gets the same prize? Must institutions of higher learning water down their curricula and standards, so everyone gets a diploma or certification? I hope I don't get the surgeon who actually didn't pass microbiology. Not everyone wins in this world; and nobody wins the crown of righteousness: it was won for you by Jesus Christ. If equity applies to anything, it is to all of those who accept His free gift of eternal life.

Accepting the crown means acknowledging the captain of your team who is Christ, and your coach who is the Holy Spirit. And every time you are in the field, your Father in heaven is watching from the bleachers; He never misses a game. Christians are compelled to try improving, to get better; to please our heavenly Father by quitting certain behaviors, or acquiring new behaviors and skills. Doing nothing will earn a worthless token; that is what equity is all about, winners and losers being treated as equal. Rest assured, people are not equal; nobody is, because God has given us special abilities and talents that are unique. If you want to master these talents, or if you want to acquire skills that you do not currently possess, you have to train, practice, and persist. Those who try hard and work hard are winners in the human race.

- PRO 13:11~ Wealth obtained by pride will diminish; but those who achieve by way of hard work will see their wealth increase.

- 2 CO 9:8 ~ God is able to bless you abundantly, that in all things and at all times you have what you need, so you can abound in good works.

OCTOBER

- PHP 3:13–14 ~ Brothers, I have not yet taken hold of the prize for which God has called me in the name of Jesus Christ. But I press on, forgetting what is behind and focusing on what lies ahead.

- 2 TI 2:3–5 ~ Endure your hardships with us, like a good soldier of Jesus Christ. Soldiers do not involve themselves with civilian affairs but follow the orders of their commander. Similarly, if a person strives to master the task, he or she does not receive the victor's crown without obeying the rules.

- HEB 12:1–3 ~ Since we are being watched by numerous spectators, let us discard everything that hinders us such as the sin that trips us up, and run the race that has been set before us with perseverance. Let us fix our eyes on Jesus, the author and perfecter of our faith, who for the joy set before Him endured the cross, scorning its shame, and who now sits on His throne at the right hand of God. Remember Him, who endured great opposition from sinful men, so that you will not grow faint and lose heart.

- REV 3:11 ~ Jesus said, "I am coming soon. Hold tight to what you have so that nobody can take away your crown."

The crown of glory is the Lord Himself, who we wear like a halo around our heads. Some people who see Christ in us may turn away their heads, because they despise Him and His followers; they may scoff at you if you say, "Jesus saves." Nevertheless, put Him on like a garment, clothed in His righteousness and blanketed in His love, and protected by the armor of God as you persevere in your faith through this life and into the next (EPH 6:10–18).

- JOB 29:14 ~ I put on righteousness, and it clothed me; justice was my robe and crown.

- PSA 8:4–5 ~ Who is man that you, Lord, would be mindful of him? For you have made him a little lower than the angels, and have crowned him with glory and honor.

- PSA 73:24 ~ You guide me with your counsel, and afterward you will lead me into glory.

- PSA 103:2–4 ~ Praise the Lord, oh my soul, let everything in me praise Him who forgives sins, heals diseases, and redeems my life from destruction. He crowns me with love and tender mercy.

- ISA 28:5 ~ On that day the Lord of hosts will be a crown of glory and a diadem of beauty for the remnant of His people.

- ISA 61:10 ~ I will greatly rejoice in the Lord; my soul will be joyful in my God. For He has clothed me with the garments of salvation, he has covered me with the robe of righteousness, just like the groom is adorned with ornaments and the bride is adorned with jewels. Blessed be those whose sins are not counted against them.

- REV 3:5 ~ Jesus said, "Those who overcome will be clothed in white raiment. Their names will never be blotted out of the Book of Life, for I will acknowledge them before our Heavenly Father and His angels."

God showed us His Son Jesus to guide us along the correct route. Jesus left behind His Spirit to sustain us so that we can endure the race. He will hold you up so you do not fall. Though the pace is grueling and the path steep, the Lord will go the distance with you. As the race gets longer, the will gets stronger, nourished by the omnipresent power of the Holy Spirit.

- 1 CH 16:8–12, 23–25, 29–31, 35–36 ~ Give thanks to the Lord; call upon His name; make known His wondrous deeds to everyone. Sing praises to Him and rejoice. Continuously seek the Lord with all your strength. Remember all the great things He has done. Sing to the Lord all the earth; tell others about His salvation. Declare His glory to the nations. For great is the Lord and greatly is He to be praised. He is to be held in awe above all gods. Give to the Lord His due glory, with praise and offerings. Worship the Lord in holy array; tremble before Him all the earth. Let the heavens be glad and the earth rejoice, and let everyone say, "The Lord reigns." Give thanks to the Lord for He is good and His steadfast love endures forever. Ask God to deliver, gather, and save you, so that you may give eternal thanks and glory to Him. Blessed be the Lord from everlasting to everlasting.

- PSA 55:22 ~ Place your burdens upon the Lord and He will sustain you; He will never allow the righteous to fall.

- ISA 41:10 ~ Do not fear for I am with you. Do not be dismayed for I am your God. I will strengthen you and I will help you. Yes, I will hold you up with the right hand of my righteousness.

- ISA 58:11 ~ The Lord will guide you continuously. He will satisfy your soul when it thirsts and He will put meat on your bones. You will be like a watered garden, and like a wellspring where the waters never fail.

- JOH 14:6 ~ Jesus said, "I am the way, the truth, and the life; the only way to the Father is through me."

- JOH 15:2 ~ Jesus said, "Every branch in me that does not bear fruit is removed. Every branch in me that bears fruit, God prunes it, so that it can bear more fruit."

- COL 1:26–27 ~ The mystery, which was hidden for ages and generations, is now made evident to the saints, to whom God will show the riches of His glory which is Christ in you, the hope of glory.

- 1 TH 3:11 ~ May God our Father and our Lord Jesus Christ direct you along the path we have followed.

- 2 TH 3:5 ~ May the Lord direct your hearts into the love of God and into the patient waiting for Christ's coming.

- EPH 3:16 ~ I pray that God, according to the richness of His glory, with strengthen you and impart the power of His Spirit into your innermost being.

- 1 PE 5:10 ~ And after you have suffered for a while, may the God of all grace, who through Christ called you into His eternal glory, restore you and strengthen you so that you can be firm and steadfast.

Jesus Christ is adorned with the royal crown, Himself being the Prince of Peace. So also, are Christians adopted into the royal family as princes and princesses, to wear a crown of righteousness bought for us by Jesus Christ on the cross. As soon as He is part of you and you are part of Him, you can achieve anything. Who would not want God to be a part of their life? Well, I guess those who choose to go their own way and dismiss Jesus, like the men Jesus forgave who mocked, tormented, tortured, and placed a crown of thorns on His head. The executioners joked about His majesty and kingship, yet that crown of thorns was more elegant than every crown that ever adorned the head of a king throughout history.

- PRO 4:7–9 ~ Wisdom is the principal thing; therefore, seek wisdom, and with it receive understanding. Make this your priority, for with wisdom comes honor. And you will obtain a garland of grace, and a crown of glory.

- ISA 28:5 ~ In that day the Lord of Hosts will be a crown of glory, a garland of beauty to the remnant of His people.

- ISA 62:3 ~ You will be a crown of glory in the Lord's hand: a royal coronet in the hand of God.

- MAT 27:29; MAR 15:17; JOH 19:2~ They clothed Him with purple. They constructed a crown of thorns and placed it on His head. They put a reed in His right hand, and bowed before Him on bended knee. They mocked Him, saying, "Hail, King of the Jews!"

Ours is a crown of righteousness worn by everyone who trusted in the blood of Christ to cover their sins. God is supreme and He reigns forever. And the saints will reign with Christ in His kingdom forever, sharing in His glory. What did we do to deserve this? Not a thing. It is because of what Christ did for us and the fact that we know it is true. Materialistic people strive for worldly riches, fame, fortune, and crowns of gold. Such things come and go; they do not last, and are valueless in heaven.

- HOS 6:2 ~ After two days He will revive us, and the third day He will raise us up to live in His presence.

- 2 TI 2:12 ~ If we suffer with Him, we also will reign with Him; if we deny Him, He also will deny us.

- 1 PE 5:2–4 ~ Be shepherds of God's flock, serve them and be an example to them; and when the Chief Shepherd appears you will receive a crown of glory that will never fade away.

- REV 2:10 ~ Jesus said, "Do not be afraid of suffering and tribulation, for the devil will throw some of you into prison to test your faith, and you will be tormented for ten days. Be faithful, even unto death, and I will give you a crown of life."

- REV 3:11 ~ Behold, I come quickly. Hold fast to what you have so that nobody can take your crown away from you.

- REV 4:4, 10–11 ~ Surrounding the throne were twenty-four seats of honor, and upon the seats sat twenty-four elders clothed in white raiment; and they had crowns of gold on their heads. The elders fell down before Him who sat on the throne, and worshipped Him who abides forever and ever; and they cast their crowns of gold before the throne saying, "You alone are worthy, oh Lord, to receive glory, honor, and power; for you have created all things and for your pleasure all things that exist were created."

Heavenly Father, we thank you for your enduring love, grace, and mercy, which you have bestowed upon us for believing in Jesus. We could never earn your favor, but you have blessed us all the same, with a blessing that will endure for eternity. Praise be to God: Father, Son, and Holy Spirit, who has crowned us with the righteousness Christ imputed upon us when He nailed our sins to the cross. Those sins died with Jesus, but He rose again because sin and death had no power over Him. By conquering death, He gave us a new life; and though we have not received it yet, we know by faith that it is there. Thank you, Father, that we can trust in this and all of your promises, as we run the race and fight the fight of faith, persevering until the end when you call us home to receive the victor's crown. Oh Lord, how we look forward to that day. Let us never be afraid because we already can see our destiny which lies beyond the trials and temptations of this world. In the name of Jesus we pray, Amen.

October 19

Cornwallis Surrendered to Washington on this day in 1781 in Yorktown VA; this marked the end of the American Revolution. In his embarrassment, Cornwallis refused to meet with Washington and surrender his sword, so Washington appointed General Lincoln to accept the sword of General O'Hara. Still, it would take two more years before British troops were permanently removed, and the British crown recognized the USA as a sovereign nation at the Treaty of Paris. Britain also made peace treaties with France and Spain at that gathering. The US defeated the greatest army in the world, twice. Clearly, Providence played a role in our victory, just as God was aiding the Israelites when they defeated enemies, often with an inferior force.

- DEU 20:1, 4 ~ When you go into battle against your enemies, and see horses and chariots, and you realize you are outnumbered, do not be afraid. For the Lord goes with you. He is the one who rescued you out of Egypt. He goes with you to fight for you and to save you.

- JDG 6:12; JDG 7:19–23 ~ An angel of the Lord appeared to Gideon saying, "The Lord is with you, valiant man." As the angel instructed, Gideon took one hundred men, surrounded the enemy camp, blew trumpets, broke pots, and made noise around the camp. The enemy stood up, and many fled; others fought amongst themselves. The Midianites that fled were pursued and killed.

- 1 SA 17:45–47 ~ David told Goliath, "You have come with a sword, a spear, and a shield, but I come in the name of the Lord of hosts, the God of the armies of Israel, whom you have defied. Today the Lord will deliver you into my hand, for I will strike you down and take your head as a trophy. And everyone will know that there is a God in Israel who saves, not with a sword or spear. This battle belongs to the Lord, for He will give you to us."

- 2 SA 5:24 ~ David enquired of the Lord who said, "Take a compass and pass around them near the mulberry trees. When you hear the sound in the tops of the trees, attack the Philistines." David did this and massacred Philistines from Geba to Gazer.

- 2 KI 6:15–17 ~ The servant awoke and found they were surrounded by the Syrians, who were coming for Elisha the prophet. He told the servant not to fear as his army was greater than theirs. Then Elisha prayed, "Lord, I pray you would open his eyes that he may see." And the Lord opened the young man's eyes and he beheld a mountain full of horses and chariots of fire surrounding the Syrian army. Then Elisha prayed, "Lord, smite these people with blindness." And the Lord did so, and they escaped.

- 2 CH 20:15–17, 23–24 ~ Listen Judah, the inhabitants of Jerusalem, and King Jehoshaphat, for the Lord says, "Do not be afraid or dismayed from this great multitude coming against you, because the battle is not yours but God's. Go against them tomorrow as they descend from the cliff to the brook. Stand your ground and you will see the salvation of the Lord. And the armies of Ammon, Moab, and Mt. Seir ended up fighting amongst themselves. When the men of Judah came to the high ground, they saw countless dead bodies below; none survived.

- PSA 20:7–8 ~ Some trust in chariots and some trust in horses, but we trust in the name of the Lord our God. They are brought down and fallen, but we are risen and stand upright.

- PSA 60:12 ~ With God we fight valiantly, for He is the one who treads upon our enemies.

- 1 CO 15:57 ~ Thank God who gives us the victory through our Lord Jesus Christ.

Father, we thank you for helping us drive away our enemies; this country has survived because we trusted you. Help us to remain faithful to you so that you will remain faithful to us. Remind us that the battle belongs to you, Father, through Christ the Lord, Amen.

October 20

International Human Solidarity Day was declared by the United Nations in 2005 to promote human rights and socioeconomic development in emerging and impoverished countries around the world in order to "maintain international peace and solidarity". Basically, it is another globalist initiative asserting peace and unity, like many holidays established by the UN. A certain percentage of member contributions goes into a discretionary trust fund for the UN in pursuit of peace and eliminating poverty. The USA pays the most at 22%, followed by China at 12%, then Japan at 8.5%, Germany at 6%, the United Kingdom at 5%, and so on. It is one thing to preach peace, unity, harmony, diversity, and solidarity; it is yet another to actually achieve these things among nations who do not believe as we do, or do not see eye to eye with us. If Jesus Christ is the unifying factor, such things are achievable; when people and nations disagree about Jesus, there will be discord. Missionaries who travel to impoverished countries to spread goodwill, distribute food, help obtain fresh water, and reflect Christ, are doing the Lord's work. It is debatable, the degree to which the UN is doing the Lord's work.

- 2 CH 30:12 ~ In Judah, the hand of God was on the people giving them unity of mind to carry out the orders of their leaders in accordance with the Word of the Lord.

- PSA 133:1 ~ How good and pleasant it is for people of the faith to live together in unity!

- JER 6:14; JER 8:11, 15 ~ They kept saying "peace, peace" but there was no peace. We looked for peace but none came; we hoped for health but got trouble instead.

- MIC 3:2, 5 ~ You hate good and love evil. You talk of peace but make war.

- ROM 10:12 ~ There is no difference between a Jew and a Greek when it comes to the spiritual riches they can obtain through Christ.

- MAT 7:1–2 ~ Do not judge others or you will be judged. And you will be judged according to the same standards by which you judge others.

- EPH 4:3 ~ Keep the unity of the Spirit through the bond of peace.

- PHP 1:27–28 ~ Whatever happens, conduct yourselves in a manner worthy of the Gospel of Christ. Then, whether I am with you or absent, I will find that you have continued to stand firm in one spirit, contending fearlessly in unity for the faith of the Gospel.

- COL 3:14 ~ Above all, put on love, which binds all things together in perfect harmony.

- 1 TH 5:3 ~ When they talk of peace and safety, total destruction will come.

- JAM 2:13 ~ Whoever shows judgment without mercy will receive no mercy. Whoever shows mercy will receive mercy, because mercy prevails against judgment.

- 1 JO 4:5–6 ~ They who are of the world speak of worldly things, and the world listens to them. We are of God; those who know God will listen to us. Those who are not of God will not listen. We know the difference between the spirit of truth and the spirit of error.

Father, we ask for peace, harmony and solidarity within our country, between countries, and across cultures through faith in God who brings spiritual solidarity. For you are the Rock of Ages who holds all things together, and separates from yourself that which is contrary to your divine nature, which includes this sinful world and worldly strivings. We pray for your Spirit upon us when we break bread with others, when we meet together at work, social events, or church, and when we are witnessing Christ which should be everywhere and with anyone who is ready to receive an otherworldly message from your Son, in whose name we pray, Amen.

October 21

Magellan Found Passage Between Atlantic, Pacific on this day in 1520. Columbus and others proved there was a continent between Europe and Asia, not knowing if there was a path around the Americas. Magellan was a Portuguese captain funded by the Spanish government to explore a new route to the Spice Islands in Indonesia, and avoid the risky alternate route around the Cape of Good Hope. This took him on a westerly voyage around South America. Magellan had to quell a mutiny by some of his captains, killing one and leaving another in Argentina. He made it through the strait which now bears his name with one ship; the second ship was wrecked and the third taken by deserters. The crew was malnourished with scurvy when they finally landed in Guam. From there they sailed to the Philippine Islands, where Magellan tried to convert the natives and was impaled by a poison projectile in a fight with a rival tribe. The *Victoria* was the only ship that made it back to Spain, rounding the Cape of Good Hope in 1522; it was captained by navigator del Cano, who was the first to circumnavigate the globe, by completing this voyage. Less than ten percent of the original 240 crewmembers returned. Del Cano was acclaimed by King Charles; he would attempt a second trip across the Pacific, dying at sea in 1525. The Strait of Magellan remained a shipping route until the completion of the Panama Canal in 1914.

Exploration can be a risky business, largely because of uncertainty, which equates to a fear of the unknown. The less information we have the more uncertain we are and the greater the risk that our actions and decisions will not be successful. The more we know, the less uncertain we are and the more confident we will be that our decisions and actions should yield positive results. Thus, if you want to reduce uncertainty, gather more information. The only sure thing in this world, however, is Jesus Christ; through Him we have the secure hope of eternal life.

- DEU 29:29 ~ The secret things belong to the Lord, but those things that He reveals belong to us and to our children forever, so that we may follow the words of His Law.

- PRO 3:5–6 ~ Trust in the Lord with all your heart; do not depend on your own understanding. In all things acknowledge Him and He will direct you in the right path.

- PRO 30:15–16, 18–19 ~ There are four things that are never satisfied: the grave, the barren womb, the dry earth which thirsts for water, and fire. There are four things that are amazing: the flight of an eagle, the slithering of a snake, the sailing of a ship on the high seas, and the love between a young man and woman.

- COL 4:2 ~ Continue to pray and wait for the answer, giving thanks for the result.

- HEB 6:17–19 ~ Since God wanted to make the unchanging nature of His purpose very clear to the heirs of His promise, He confirmed it with an oath. First, God's Word is always true, and second, He gives His Word. That is, He backed up His promise with His Word of honor. He did this to emphasize the promise so that we, who cling to that hope, could be encouraged. We have this hope as an anchor for our souls, firm and secure, and penetrating to the depths of our being.

Thank you, Father, for the knowledge of your promises in which we hope, for they are backed up by your Word which is always true. Let us cling to that assurance as we look forward to what is to come, and not be overburdened by things past and present. Help us to open your Word of truth for anyone who is receptive to knowing how to become a child of God. Be with those who seek the truth, who explore the possibilities, who take risks to discover new information, and who explore new frontiers; let them find the truth so it can be shared with all people. Please do not allow the facts to be smothered by those who would control what we are allowed to see or know. We pray in the name of Jesus who is our hope of salvation, Amen.

October 22

Beware the Son of Perdition Day is suggested to increase awareness that the end of times may be upon us and we need to be prepared. Will it happen in our generation, the next, or when? Well, we just don't know; that's why we need to be ready, regardless of our generation. The second coming of Christ will not occur until the Antichrist is revealed. And who might that be?

- 2 TH 2:1–10 ~ I implore you brothers, as we await the coming of our Lord to gather us unto Himself, that you do not feel unsettled or afraid about some prophecy, teaching, or account as if it was from us or as if the day of Christ had arrived. Do not let anyone deceive you, for there will be a falling away prior to the revealing of the son of perdition who opposes everything that is of God; he will exalt himself above all others including God, demanding worship as he sits in the temple pretending to be God. Remember when I explained these things while I was with you? Now you know what is being held back, until the designated time when the evil son is revealed. The mystery of iniquity already is at work. But the one letting it proceed will continue to do so until he is moved out of the way. Then the wicked one will be revealed, whom the Lord will consume with the spirit of His mouth and destroy with the brightness of His coming. The man of lawlessness arrives first, to do the work of Satan with evil power, fake signs, and lying wonders; through deceptions of unrighteousness, people will perish because they did not obtain the love of the truth that could save them.

- 2 TH 2:11–12 ~ For this reason God will send them a strong delusion, allowing them to believe the lie. They will be damned for not believing the truth, while finding pleasure in unrighteousness instead.

- JDE 1:11–13 ~ These people speak evil of that which they know nothing about; but by what they know instinctively, as animals, they corrupt themselves. Woe unto them, for they have taken the wayward path of Cain, consumed by greed for an earthly reward like Balaam, only to perish in their rebellion as with Core. These people tarnish your charitable feasts, while they engorge themselves without concern. They are clouds without water carried away by the wind, trees without fruit that wither away—twice dead, plucked up by the roots. They are as raging waves foaming with shame, or wandering stars which are resigned to blackness forever.

Prophets have warned repeatedly not to fall for lies and deceptions being disseminated throughout the world via false prophets. But we must not be nervous or fearful because this is merely an initiation of the end. There will be a massive departure from faith, spirituality, godliness, and morality. Be watchful, and be ready; because things only get worse from there.

So, who exactly is that son of perdition, the lawless one who performs the works of Satan? Well, he is often referred to as Antichrist. Of course, anyone denying Jesus as God in the flesh, who died to save us from our sins and was raised to life to save us from death, is an antichrist. A distinction is made between an antichrist and The Antichrist, also referred to as The Beast in the book of Revelation.

- ISA 32:6–7 ~ The vile person comes speaking blasphemy and working evil and hypocrisy, opposing God Himself. His instruments are wickedness, lies, and dishonor.

- 1 JO 2:18, 22 ~ You have heard that the antichrist comes; in fact, many antichrists are here already. This is a sign that the days are nearing an end. Whoever denies that Jesus is the Christ is a liar; whoever denies both Jesus Christ and the Father is an antichrist.

- REV 13:1–18 ~ While standing on the seashore I saw a beast rise out of the sea, with seven heads and ten horns; a crown was on each horn, and on each head was the name of blasphemy. And the dragon (Satan) gave him power. One of the heads was wounded but healed itself. The world marveled at the beast and worshipped the beast, and they worshipped the dragon that gave power to the beast. The people said, "Who is like the beast? Who can possibly oppose him?" The beast spoke blasphemy against God for 3.5 years. He waged war against anyone who was holy, and defeated them. He gained power over all races, peoples, and nations. Everyone except the righteous honored the beast. Then another beast with two horns arrived, speaking like the dragon. He exercised the same power as the first beast, performing magic feats such as bringing fire down from heaven. He convinced the people to worship the first beast, and to make a graven image of it. And the second beast brought the image of the beast to life. He caused everyone to receive the mark of the beast on their right hand or forehead; only those with the mark could buy and sell goods. They tracked down and murdered anyone who did not receive the mark and worship the beast. The beast's number is the number of a man: 666.

Unfortunately, many will sell out and buy into the deception, corruption, and depravity. I wonder, who in their right mind would fall for this? But then again, they are not in their right minds if they are delusional, one of the central criteria in diagnosing psychosis. Apparently, the world will develop this "shared psychosis" which is a rare phenomenon indeed. But this is inevitable since it has been prophesied in the Bible. You sure don't want to align with them, knowing the ultimate consequence will be eternal damnation.

The Bible speaks of many mysteries that humankind cannot fathom, until and unless God reveals the solution (ACT 1:7). There are revelations in the Bible which explain mysteries, while other riddles remain unresolved. For example, the mystery of salvation is explained succinctly throughout the Bible, to include the involvement of all three persons of the Holy Trinity, a mystery not easily comprehended. Understanding any mystery of scripture requires the counsel of the Holy Spirit, without which one can neither understand the concept of our triune God, nor tell the difference between true prophecy or miracles and contrived prophecy or miracles.

- MAR 4:11 ~ Jesus said to His disciples, "You have been given the ability to understand the mystery of the kingdom of God. To the unbelievers, God's mystery is seen in parables, for Isaiah wrote (ISA 6:9) that they would see but not perceive, and they would hear but not understand."

- ROM 16:25–26 ~ Christ has the power to save you according to the revelation of God's mystery, which was kept secret since the world began but which is now evident by the scriptures. According to God's will the mystery is made known to all nations on earth for the obedience of faith.

- 1 CO 2:7–16 ~ We speak the wisdom of God as a mystery, even the hidden wisdom of God, which He ordained and which none of the rulers of this world knew, otherwise they would not have crucified Christ. It is written: Eyes have not seen, nor ears heard, nor the heart discerned the things that God has prepared for those who love Him (ISA 64:4). God has revealed these things to us by His Spirit; for the Spirit searches everything, even the deepest things of God. These things we speak, not in the words which humanity teaches, but which the Holy Spirit teaches, comparing spiritual things with spiritual. But natural people do not receive spiritual things of God for these things are foolishness to them; neither can they know these things because they need to be discerned spiritually. But those who are spiritual analyze everything and are judged by nobody. Nobody knows the mind of God that they can instruct Him, but those who are spiritual have the mind of Christ.

- EPH 3:3–6, 9–11 ~ In a revelation, God showed me the mystery of Christ, and I must share that mystery with the world. It is a mystery that was hidden but is now revealed through His apostles and prophets by the Holy Spirit. For the Gentiles will be fellow heirs with the Jews, and will partake of the promise that came true through Christ by the Gospel. All people can know the mystery which God hid from the beginning of the world, and the eternal purpose for which Jesus Christ our Lord has come.

- COL 1:26–27; COL 2:2–3 ~ The mystery, hidden from ages past, has now been revealed to the saints, to whom God will give the riches of His glory. It is for anyone who turns to Christ for their hope, including the Gentiles. The riches come from assured understanding and knowledge of the mystery of God, and of the Father, and of Christ, in whom all the treasures of wisdom and knowledge abide.

Then there is the mystery of our transformation into glorified bodies to live with the Lord Jesus forever upon His return. This change will defy physical laws, and will occur only once.

- 1 CO 15:51–58 ~ Here is a mystery of God: We will not all sleep (die) but we will all be changed. Upon Christ's return, in a single moment when the great trumpet sounds, Christ's own, whether alive or dead will arise into heaven to receive new, incorruptible bodies. Hence, the corruptible will have become incorruptible and the mortal will have become immortal. Then at the end, when Christ delivers the kingdom of God to the Father, He will destroy death, at which time the statement "death is swallowed up in victory" will be true. The godly will receive spiritual bodies which will never die. The flesh is of the earth, the spirit is of heaven; thus, flesh and blood will not inherit the kingdom of heaven. Therefore, be confident in your faith because your labor is not in vain.

- 1 JO 3:2 ~ Dear friends, now we are the children of God, and what we will become is not yet known. But we do know this: when He returns for us, we will become like Him, for we shall see Him as He really is.

Let's zero in on the passage in this lesson regarding the "holding back" of the man of lawlessness until the designated time (2 TH 2:7). Apparently, God is preparing to reveal something about lawlessness and evil that we cannot comprehend as yet. And we may not comprehend it until the "restrainer" has "moved out of the way." Eventually, evil will be eliminated, this we know. But before that occurs, there will be a final empire of malevolence, commandeered by the Beast, or Satan. The introduction of Satan's protegee, the son of perdition, is being delayed for reasons known only to God. Perhaps God is holding back time for those still looking for Him, before the scales are tipped and the majority of the last generation give into the grand delusion. Further, God may be waiting until Antichrist is revealed, after which those denying His Son will feel the full extent of His wrath. It is possible that believers never will comprehend the full wrath of God, for we will be moved away from it (JER 30:7; REV 3:10).

- GEN 7:1 ~ The Lord said to Noah, "You and your family must come into the ark, for you alone do I find righteous in this generation."

- DEU 1:35 ~ Surely, not one person from this evil generation will see the good land which God promised to their fathers.

- PSA 78:8 ~ Listen everyone, don't be like your fathers, a stubborn and rebellious generation that did not possess an upright heart and a steadfast spirit.

- DAN 7:23–25 ~ The four beasts represent four kings that will come (REV 13 & 17). The fourth beast, which represents the fourth king, is different: exceedingly terrible. The ten horns represent ten kings; three of them fall, while one replaces them. This evil one will speak great things against God and will make war with the saints, defeating them. He will change the times and the rules. He will reign for a time, times, and half a time (3.5 years).

- MAT 23:33 ~ Jesus said, "You, generation of snakes. How can you escape the damnation of hell?"
- REV 10:7 ~ When the seventh angel sounds his trumpet, the mystery of God will be finished, as He declared to the prophets and the saints.
- REV 17:5, 9–11, 15 ~ On her head was written: Mystery, Babylon the Great, the mother of prostitutes and all earthly abominations. This is the great city that sits on seven mountains and over many waters, nations, and peoples. The seven heads represent seven mountains on which the new Babylon sits. There are seven kings, five have fallen, one is currently in power, and one is yet to come; the seventh will reign for a short time. The beast is the eighth king and was one of the seven.

Tracking history, we find five kingdoms or empires which had fallen when St. John penned Revelation (see REV 17 above): Egyptian, Assyrian, Babylonian, Medio-Persian, and Grecian. The sixth empire existing while John was alive was the Roman. The seventh empire which was a short reign could have been Nazi Germany (some suggest Ottoman, but that was hardly a short conquest, and they never occupied Europe). Regardless, the logical conclusion is that the eighth and final empire will be that of the Beast, and it comes next. John mentioned this would be a repeat of one of the seven previous empires. John also wrote about a New Babylon, strikingly similar to the Old Babylon (some people also refer to the last kingdom as the revived Roman empire). Maybe the eighth is a repeat of all seven fallen empires since each fell due to deception, corruption, and depravity; in other words, all fell because of Satan's greed for control, a motive adopted by the evil emperors whom Satan influenced and/or possessed.

Once the son of perdition is revealed, we can expect all of the trials and tribulations associated with the beginning of sorrows. Thank God that His chosen will be spared the horrific end when Christ returns to gather us unto Himself.

Heavenly Father, help us to be watchful and waiting for the return of your Son Jesus. Especially help us to be prepared for that day when the son of perdition is revealed, so that we do not follow or give into this adopted son of Satan or any of his followers. Seal us for eternity so that we will be immune from the mark of the beast. Please do not let us fall for their scams or fake miracles; instead, give us the boldness and strength to call them out. Though these things may not happen in our lifetime, help us to be at a high state of readiness nevertheless. Jesus's last words to us in the Bible were "Behold, I come quickly." Let our response be the same as St. John: "Amen, come Lord Jesus."

October 23

Repel the Devil and Demons Day is a follow-on from the previous lesson. This study is about how to use the power of the Holy Spirit to resist, repel, defeat, and evacuate demons in our midst, especially Satan the chief of demons (LUK 11:15–19). We are surrounded by the devil and his minions: powerful spirits of evil that rebelled against God. Evil entities are referred to in the Bible as devils, demons, familiar spirits, and unclean or foul spirits. Long before humans came on the scene, Lucifer opposed God and was tossed out of heaven to the earth, along with one third of the angels who likewise committed mutiny in God's realm (ISA 14:12–19; EZE 11:14–18; REV 12:3–9). The devils landing on earth are still among us by the way. Demons are innumerable, millions or better; in other words, they are everywhere. St. John had a vision of thousands of angels singing, even ten thousand squared (REV 5:11–12). If there are a million-plus angels still in heaven, the devils that fell would represent up to half of that number which would be one third of all the angelic beings initially created by God.

On one occasion, Jesus encountered an individual possessed by thousands of demons. Recall the account of Legion (MAR 5:1–11; LUK 8:26–36) in which a man was possessed by a legion of demons (a Roman legion was about 6000 soldiers). Nobody could control or subdue this maniac, for he was dangerous and the people greatly feared him. The demons had exclusive control over the poor soul. But Jesus had mercy on the man and cast the hoard of demons into a herd of swine, which made them so crazy they ran off a cliff and drowned in the sea below. There are many occasions where Jesus evacuated demons, including His close companion Mary Magdalene from whom Jesus cast out seven (LUK 8:2). Clearly demons and the Holy Spirit cannot coexist, and demons are immensely afraid of Christ.

- LUK 4:33–36 ~ In the synagogue was a man possessed by the spirit of an unclean devil. When he saw Jesus, he cried out with a loud voice saying, "Leave us alone; what have you to do with us? I know who you are, the Holy One of God." Jesus rebuked the demon saying, "Keep quiet and come out of him." The devils threw him to the ground in front of everyone and immediately came out of the man, who was unhurt. All the people were amazed saying amongst themselves, "What a Word is this! For with authority and power He commands the unclean spirits and they obey."

- 1 CO 10:21 ~ You cannot drink the cup of the Lord and the cup of devils; you cannot partake at the Lord's table and the table of devils.

- JAM 2:19 ~ It is well for you to believe that there is one God; the devils also believe, and tremble.

- JAM 4:7 ~ Submit yourselves to God. Resist the devil and he will flee from you.

- 1 PE 5:8–9 ~ Be sober and vigilant; because your adversary the devil, like a roaring lion walks about seeking whom he may devour.

Being possessed by a single demon has got to be extremely annoying. Imagine being possessed by thousands, or Satan himself! This concept is horrifying to say the least. But anyone bearing the name of Christ will have the Holy Spirit and therefore, power over Satan and his army of demons. We are protected from invasion by demons, who are terrified of the Holy Spirit.

- LEV 19:31 ~ Stay away from those with familiar spirits and do not seek sorcerers to be defiled by them, for I am the Lord your God.

- 1 CO 3:16; 1 CO 6:19 ~ Do you not know that you are the temple of God, and the Holy Spirit dwells within you? This is God's gift, for you belong to Him.

- 2 CO 11:14 ~ Do not marvel when Satan disguises himself as an angel of light.

- EPH 6:11–12 ~ Put on the whole armor of God so you are able to stand against the wiles of the devil. For we wrestle, not against flesh and blood, but against principalities and powers, against rulers of darkness in this world, against spiritual wickedness in high places.

Those possessed by demons are spiritually empty, which is a welcome mat for evil spirits. That is to say, without the indwelling of the Holy Spirit the person becomes a target. A person cannot be possessed by an evil spirit if he or she possesses the free gift of God's Holy Spirit. Thus, to answer two age-old questions: Christians (e.g., doers of the Word and not just hearers) can neither be possessed by demons nor claimed by Satan.

- MAT 12:43–45; LUK 8:27–33 ~ When an unclean spirit departs from a person, he walks through dry places, seeking rest and finding none. Then he says, "I will return to the house I left." When he returns, he finds the house empty, swept, and tidy. Then he goes and finds seven other spirits more wicked than he and enters the person to live there, leaving the person worse off than before. This shall be the case in the wicked generation to come.

- GAL 5:16–17 ~ I tell you this: Walk in the Spirit and you will not fulfill the lust of the flesh. For the flesh fights against the spirit and the spirit against the flesh as these two are contrary, such that you cannot do the things you should.

- 1 JO 4:1–4 ~ Beloved, do not believe every spirit, but test them to see if they are from God; because many false prophets have entered the world. This is how you can recognize the Spirit of God: every spirit which confesses that Jesus Christ came in the flesh is of God; every spirit which does not confess Christ is not of God. This is the spirit of antichrist who you have heard is coming and already is in the world. You are of God, little children, and have overcome them, because greater is He that is in you than he that is in the world.

How does one become spiritually empty? Well, either invite the Holy Spirit to dwell within you or try to fill the emptiness with worldly things. The problem is, those seeking to fulfill the flesh will never be satisfied, for they will be hungry, thirsty, sleepy, horny and unfulfilled over and over. You cannot satisfy the flesh, but the Holy Spirit satisfies completely. If you seek spiritual blessings, you will receive them as well as everything you need to sustain your body and life (MAT 6:25–34). Filling your heart with things of the world will lead to a spiritual void. Hence, without God you can become empty, and susceptible to the evil in this world: every temptation of the flesh, bad people, and foul spirits. In short, with God you can do anything, without Him—well good luck with that (MAT 19:25–26; LUK 1:37; JOH 15:5).

Take, for example, addiction, where the more you indulge yourself, the less gratified you become. A person can become addicted to any substance or behavior; because while all things are available for our use, they all can be harmful when abused. Once the abuse becomes a habit the person loses control, whereas the addiction proceeds without conscious intervention or awareness and is very resistant to change. The condition is not unlike demon possession, insofar as any worldly strategy for filling an empty heart is destined to fail and opens the person to evil spirits. Interestingly, the famous Swiss psychiatrist Carl Jung pointed out almost a century ago that alcohol was like an evil spirit which represented the opposite end of a continuum from the Holy Spirit. Alcoholics Anonymous and the twelve-step process advanced by Bill Wilson was largely based on the philosophy of, and in collaboration with, Dr. Jung.

The impetus of twelve-step programs is to enable your higher power to take control, implying that the person has lost control to the world or worldly cravings. Christians recognize God's Holy Spirit as the highest power, from whom all knowledge of right and wrong proceeds.

Even an agnostic will admit that their conscience doesn't lie to them about moral choices and therefore represents a higher power within them; many are unaware that such knowledge was conferred upon them and all human beings via God's Holy Spirit. Any healing that takes place and self-control that is regained are among God's gifts to those who ask. Truth is ingrained into your own spirit or higher power, not the least of which is knowledge of forgiveness and salvation. Not surprisingly, twelve step programs conducted in conjunction with therapy and support have been scientifically proven to be the most effective treatment for addiction.

As Jung proposed, the path to recovery involves education, edification, and grace. God supplies the grace component, often by way of the proverbial wakeup call. Who do you suppose is trying to get the addict's attention but God Himself? When they turn control over to the highest power, they can defeat the demons of addiction not to mention Satan. Ever wonder where we get cliches such as "the demon of addiction" or "chasing the dragon" or "the devil made me do it"? Well now you know.

- 1 CO 10:23 ~ All things are lawful for me but not all things are expedient, and not all things can edify.

Unfortunately, there are many people, especially in their youth, who deliberately conger familiar spirits. They engage in seances, channeling, demonism, even devil worship, some proclaiming themselves satanists. Maybe people do this for entertainment, exploitation, kicks, or to explore the spirit world. Little do they know they are dabbling with the occult and asking demons to participate. Beware of occultism and demonology as such things are an abomination to the Lord and an invitation to Satan and his minions. One must be very ignorant or very dark inside to enjoy such things. Evil can be compelling to those thinking it will be fun, empowering, or educational. Anyone looking for demons eventually will find them; and once found it is very hard to get rid of them. The more lost and blind people feel on the inside, the more likely they will believe there is no way out and nowhere to go. This is spiritual emptiness. Of course, the Holy Spirit is the only way out, while there are countless ways into the pit.

- LEV 20:6 ~ The Lord says to the soul who follows those who have a familiar spirit or seeks out wizards, lusting after them: I will set my face against that soul and cut them off from their people.

- 1 SA 15:23 ~ Rebellion is as the sin of witchcraft, and stubbornness is as the iniquity of idolatry. Because you have rejected the word of the Lord, He has rejected you (Saul) as king over Israel.

- ISA 8:19 ~ When they suggest that you seek those with familiar spirits or wizards who whisper and mutter, reply to them, "Should we not ask God; why seek the dead, on behalf of the living?

- EZE 12:24 ~ There shall nevermore be vain visions or flattering divinations within the house of Israel.

- MAT 6:22–23 ~ The light of the body is the eye; if your eye is pure, your whole body will be full of light. But if your eye is evil your whole body will be full of darkness, and how great is that darkness.

Demons are out there and you would be advised to steer clear of them and anyone who converses with them. Are we surrounded by demons? Yes, but for the fact they are outnumbered by the angels of God, with God Himself abiding everywhere and in control of everything. Actually, the demons are the ones who are surrounded. Besides, all true Christians possess the Spirit of God (ROM 8:9) and the mind of Christ (1 CO 2:16), rendering demons powerless against members of the body of Christ. Remember this: the proliferation of evil in the last days will be enhanced, which will include people succumbing to foul spirits and demonic influences. Beware and be careful, and hold fast to the Holy Spirit lest they influence you.

- DEU 18:10–12 ~ God says there should never be among you those who pass their son or daughter through the fire, or use divinations, or observe times (e.g., astrologers); or an enchanter, witch, charmer, or anyone who seeks counsel from familiar spirits, wizards or necromancers. Those who do these things are an abomination to the Lord; and because of their abominations, the Lord your God will drive them out before you.

- 1 TI 4:1–2 ~ The Spirit expressly states that in the latter times some will depart from the faith, giving heed to seducing spirits and doctrines of devils; hypocrites speaking lies, having their conscience seared with a hot iron.

- REV 18:1–2 ~ I saw another angel come down from heaven, having great power; and the earth was illuminated with his glory. And he cried mightily with a loud voice saying, "Babylon the great has fallen, fallen, and become the habitation of devils, the stronghold of every foul spirit, and a cage for every unclean and hateful bird."

If you call upon the Holy Spirit in the name of Jesus Christ, you can command any demon to clear out; when they try to invade your mind or imbed impure thoughts, do this and see what happens. Continue to tap into God's power and you will become stronger, and the influences of evil coming against you will become weaker. In fact, the demons will begin to fear you because they see Christ in your heart and the Holy Spirit in your eyes. And they will run from you like pigs jumping off a cliff.

In conclusion, ask yourself this question: Is there anything from this world that you want so bad you would sell your soul to obtain it? Jesus said you could win the entire world and it would not cover the cost of forfeiting your soul (MAT 16:26). He also said that those who patiently await His return will keep their souls (LUK 21:19). Have you noticed people in politics, media, entertainment, and government who are sell-outs, both here in the USA and abroad? They would do anything to control wealth, power, and others to the degree they would sacrifice truth, morality, justice, faith, and even their souls. They would betray their loved ones, country, and God to enjoy the forbidden pleasures of this world for a finite period of time, in exchange for an eternity in hell, separated from the glorious love of God forevermore.

Do not fear or envy the sell-outs for they are to be pitied. Jesus warned the Jewish leaders during His ministry that they could not escape the fiery furnace (MAT 23:13–33); neither will self-righteous lying traitors who sell-out their countries and friends, ultimately relinquishing their souls. And what will Satan do with all those lost souls? Nothing, because he will burn along with them; he's just looking for company. Woe unto the one who lets the devil inside, that son of perdition referred to as antichrist, and everyone else who thinks they will rule in hell with Satan. They'll be destroyed with the fallen, be they human or demon, in the lake of fire.

Dear Father in heaven, you are our pride and joy. We love you so much, and we are so grateful that you love us even more. Help us to share that love, and the power over fear that comes with it. Such fear is the tool Satan uses to scare people into submission. Help them to see the power of your love so that they too can rebuke the demons by invoking the name of Jesus Christ. We invite your Holy Spirit to indwell us, creating a barrier between us and the thousands of demons out there. Help us to boldly and fearlessly stand against them, to call them out, and to cast them out. May your church on earth, the body of Christ, unite together as one, creating an army of Christian soldiers equipped and ready to wage war against Satan and his demonic army, and to soundly overthrow them. We invoke the name of Jesus as we pray in His name, Amen.

October 24

United Nations Day commemorates the anniversary of the United Nations, chartered in 1945. After World War II, representatives from fifty-one countries met together in San Francisco for the cause of world peace. This resulted in the creation on this date of the organization we call the United Nations; it evolved from the League of Nations which was established in 1919, and disbanded in 1946. In New York City, J. D. Rockefeller donated the land to build the UN campus, which became their headquarters in 1952. They have grown to 193 member nations.

The UN promotes socioeconomic reforms, provides peaceful resolutions to conflicts in the world, and endeavors to maintain international peace, security, human rights, and justice. Global conferences are held throughout the year to address issues and settle disputes. It has become a powerful political organization with a progressive ideology. Perhaps, the UN itself could use some reforms to heighten their legitimacy and reinforce their original goals.

Nations of the world can be united by faith in Christ. Unfortunately, many nations of the world despise Christians and Christianity. They are generally led by corrupt regimes which have no interest in unification much less the truth. The UN includes all nations, regardless of their leadership and motives; this was not the case during its inception. How can we unite as nations when there is hatred between certain peoples? Maybe the UN should consider adopting and promoting the following principles to attain unity.

- PSA 133:1 ~ Behold, how good and how pleasant it is for brothers and sisters of the faith to live together in unity!
- DAN 7:13–14 ~ I saw visions in the night, and One like the Son of man came in the clouds of heaven before the Ancient of Days. And there was given to Him dominion, and glory, and a kingdom, that all people, nations, and languages, should serve Him. His dominion is everlasting and will never pass away, and His kingdom will never be destroyed.
- ROM 6:7 ~ If we are united with Christ in death, we will be united with Him in the resurrection.
- ROM 15:5 ~ May the God who gives endurance, encouragement, and hope give you a spirit of unity as you follow Christ.
- 2 CO 6:14 ~ Do not be unequally yoked together with unbelievers; for what fellowship has righteousness with unrighteousness? What communion can there be between light and darkness?
- EPH 4:2, 12–13 ~ Be humble, gentle, and patient, holding up each other in love. Try earnestly to stay united in the Spirit through the bond of peace. The objective is to prepare God's people for works of service in order to edify the church. This will continue until we reach unity in the faith and in the knowledge of the Son of God, and become mature, attaining the whole measure of the fullness of Christ.
- PHP 2:2 ~ Make my joy complete by being like-minded, having the same love and being one in spirit and in purpose.
- COL 3:14 ~ Above all, put on love, which binds all things together in perfect harmony.
- 2 TI 2:22 ~ Flee from youthful lusts and follow righteousness, faith, love, and peace in unity with others who call on the Lord with a pure heart.
- REV 7:9, 14 ~ I saw a gigantic choir in white robes; they were from various nations, kindreds, and tongues, and had come from great tribulation. They had washed their robes in the blood of Christ.

Realistically, nations of the world are not destined to unite in Christ. Regrettably, they will unite in the latter days under Satan. However, the dominion of Christ is all-encompassing and eternal, for those who have been cleansed by His blood; while the dominion of Satan will perish and be gone forever, for they chose the wrong side by denying Christ.

- ISA 34:1–4, 8 ~ Come here, every nation; listen people of the world, and all things that come from the world. The Lord's anger is upon all nations and armies; He will utterly destroy and slaughter them. For the day of the Lord's vengeance is coming and the year of retribution is near, when He will uphold the cause of Zion.

- NAH 3:1–6 ~ Woe to the bloody city, full of lies and robbery. You prey on everyone; always present are the sounds of battle. Look at all the corpses. Because of the multitude of your abominations with the well-known prostitute, that witch who buys and sells nations and families, I will pour abominable filth upon you for everyone to see.

- 2 TI 3:1–7, 12–13 ~ There will be a time of great distress. People will love themselves and money. They will be abusive, arrogant, conceited, disobedient, treacherous, slanderous, ungrateful, unholy, inhumane, haters of good and lovers of pleasure. They will capture weak and wayward women, swayed by impulses. They are always learning but unable to come to the knowledge of the truth. Indeed, all who live a godly life in Christ Jesus will suffer persecution. Evil people and impostors will progress from bad to worse, as will the deceivers and the deceived.

- REV 13:5–7 ~ The beast spoke blasphemy against God for 3.5 years. He waged war against anyone who was holy, and defeated them. He gained power over all races, peoples, and nations.

- REV 14:8; REV 17:15 ~ The angel spoke, "The great city of Babylon has fallen, because she caused all nations to drink the wine of the wrath of her fornication." Another angel spoke, "This is the great city that sits on seven mountains and over many waters, nations, and peoples."

- REV 20:7–9 ~ When the thousand years are over, Satan will be cut loose from his prison to deceive the nations in all four corners of the earth, Gog and Magog, and muster them for battle, the number of which is as the sand of the sea. They will surround the camp of the saints and the beloved city; but fire will come down from heaven and consume them all.

The United Nations was a great idea at the start. Nations came together with a common goal: world peace. But the conditions for admittance became relaxed as the influence and power of the UN grew. Almost all countries of the world are now members, but not all of them want peace. And the agenda has become politicized by nations with the greatest clout. For example, the only nation not admitted is Taiwan; and the reason they are not recognized is because China has designs on annexing Taiwan permanently, whereas the Taiwanese are not interested in being annexed. Obviously, peace has nothing to do with it, but the thirst for power has everything to do with it.

Dear Father, the world is divided; half are for you and half are against you. And the number of those leaving the faith are increasing in proportion to the numbers of people denying you as sovereign in their life and in the universe. Let there be an awakening for those who are unsure where they stand. Let your Word reach those who are looking for the truth, especially in countries where the truth is stymied. Reveal yourself to them so they may follow you, despite the aggressive attempts by their leaders to prevent the mere speaking of your name. Show the lost souls the power of your love through your Holy Spirit; let them feel the love and see the light through divine revelation, the Holy Bible, and Jesus, in whom we pray, Amen.

October 25

International Artist Day recognizes creative people, who produce artistic works using any kind of medium. This day was selected because it was Pablo Picasso's birthday (1881). The idea was started in 2004 by Canadian artist Chris MacClure, whose style reflects romanticism and realism.

You can celebrate this occasion by supporting local artists in your area. Take your kids to an art museum and discuss the works of art that they like or dislike and why. Read the biography of a famous artist. Sign up for an art history class or a studio class like painting, pottery, printmaking, weaving, or sculpture. With younger kids, teach them how to make sculpture using papier mâché or modeling clay; or make a collage after clipping pictures from magazines; or try fingerpainting, water colors, or drawing with crayons or colored pencils. Buy them an art or craft kit, and show them how to turn their doodles into a masterpiece. Stimulate your artistic bone today individually or collectively, with family and friends. Everybody can find something that enables self-expression in a creative fashion; it's just a matter of trying out different things and discovering those that fit or work for you. Keep practicing and you might find you are good at it.

Ingredients of a work of art include design, color, contrast and light, texture, perspective and depth, composition, dimensions, shapes and lines. Educate yourself about each component. Imagine and diagram the layout when you decide what you want to create. Start small and work bigger. Begin critiquing art on each element above. Learn about the different genres of painting such as realism, surrealism, impressionism, romanticism, pop, and abstract; or architecture such as classical, gothic, renaissance, baroque, rococo, art nouveau, art deco, and modern.

Who is your favorite artist and what is your favorite genre? When I studied art, I was influenced largely by surrealism, especially the work of Dali. But when it comes to my favorite artist of all, I would pick God. There is artistry in every aspect of nature, the cosmos, and life itself. Critique God's works and discover how fantastic are the colors, how intricate the designs, how varied the textures, how everything and everyone has a unique shape and appearance, how every shade and pigment is represented from blinding light to total darkness. Art appreciation education starts by being an observant participant, as you experience every environment using all of your sensory-perceptual capacities.

- GEN 1:3–5 ~ And God said, "Let there be light" and there was light. And God saw the light, that it was good, so He divided the light from the darkness. God called the light day and the darkness He called night. And the evening and the morning was the first day.

- GEN 1:1–27 ~ God created the heavens and earth, day and night, oceans and land, and all living creatures, and He created humankind in His image.

- GEN 2:7 ~ God formed man from the dust of the earth, and breathed into his nostrils the breath of life, and man became a living soul.

- GEN 37:3 ~ Jacob loved Joseph over all of his children because he came from his old age; he made his son a coat of many colors.

- EXO 25:18 ~ God commanded Moses concerning the construction of the Ark of the Covenant that there should be two cherubim of gold, one at each end of the mercy seat.

- EXO 35:35 ~ God filled them with skill to work as engravers, designers, embroiderers, and weavers: all of them were skilled workers and designers.

- 1 KI 6:21, 23, 27 ~ Solomon built the temple and overlaid it with gold. Within the sanctuary he made two cherubim from olive trees. They were placed facing each other, with their wings against the walls, so that the wingtips of each cherub touched those of the other.

- 1 CH 29:11 ~ Yours, oh Lord, is all greatness, power, glory, victory, and majesty. Everything in heaven and earth is yours, including the everlasting kingdom. You are exalted as head above all creatures.

- JOB 32:8 ~ There is a spirit in a man, through which the inspiration of the Almighty gives him understanding.

- PSA 19:1–2 ~ The heavens declare the glory of God and the sky proclaims the work of His hands. Day after day they speak, and night after night they reveal knowledge.

- PSA 50:1–5 ~ Almighty God, who is the Lord, has spoken to all the earth from the rising of the sun to its setting. Out of Zion, the perfection of beauty, God has shined. God will come and will not be silent. A devouring fire will burn before Him, and around Him is a mighty tempest. He will call everyone for judgment, and will gather the saints of the covenant to Himself.

- PSA 139:14 ~ I will praise God for I am fearfully and wonderfully made; marvelous are His works and your soul knows it well.

- PRO 20:12 ~ The hearing ear and the seeing eye: the Lord made both of them.

- PRO 22:28 ~ Do you know someone who is skilled at their work? They will serve kings, not low-ranking officials.

- ECC 3:11 ~ He made everything beautiful in its time; also, He put eternity into everyone's heart. Nobody can find out the works God makes from the beginning to the end.

- ISA 10:15 ~ Should the axe boast itself as greater than the one who uses it to chop the wood? Should the saw magnify itself over the one who uses it to shape the wood?

- ISA 64:8 ~ Now Lord, you are our Father and we are the clay; you are the potter and we are the works of your hand.

- JER 1:5 ~ I knew you before I formed you in your mother's womb; I sanctified you before you were delivered from your mother's womb. I ordained you to be a prophet to all nations.

- 2 CO 5:17 ~ Therefore, if anyone is in Christ, he or she is a new creation; old things have passed away and all things have become new.

- COL 1:16–17 ~ For by Him all things were created that are in heaven and earth, whether visible or invisible, including thrones, dominions, principalities, and powers. All things were created by Him and for Him. He is before all things, and because of Him all things exist.

- COL 3:23 ~ Whatever you do, do it with all your heart, as if working for the Lord and not a human boss.

- HEB 11:3 ~ Through faith we understand that the worlds were framed by the Word of God, so that things which are seen were made from things that do not appear.

    Father Creator, how splendid are your works; we cannot fathom the complexity, synchronicity, dimensionality, depth, breadth, height, or extent of it. We do know it is beautiful, spectacular, and extraordinary, far and above what the human race is capable. Help us continue to strive and understand your creation by searching your Word, examining our surroundings and the universe, communicating your love with fellow believers, and cultivating our faith and nurturing the faith of others. May we be a beacon to illuminate your great works and words as we reveal your Holy Spirit to those lacking vision; sharing the truth of your Word and the Gospel of Christ to receptive persons. Remind us to listen when your Spirit speaks, and know what to say and to do, in obedience to your will and in service to one another. We ask in the name of Jesus, Amen.

October 26

Make a Difference Day is observed the fourth Saturday of the month. It was promoted by USA Weekend magazine in 1992 and caught on quickly. The holiday was cosponsored by Points of Light, a nonprofit organization founded by President G. H. W. Bush. This has become an international observance, having spread to dozens of other countries. There is no official sponsor anymore, since communities and countries independently promote public services on this weekend. This is the beginning of the giving season, which continues the rest of the year.

Help and serve your community, nation, and world. Help people at your workplace; volunteer at a charity or church; contribute financially to a worthy cause. Everybody can do these things; simply place others and the greater good high on your list of priorities. Definitely, God would be first on that list, and then everybody else second (MAT 22:37–40). Remember, we are to give of our time, talent, and treasure as an appropriate response to God's love and our prosperity. Donate in proportion to how you are being blessed by others and by God, and you will find that your possessions and your abilities increase (MAL 3:6–10). Give something back wherever you find yourself, even if it the last dollar bill in your pocket (MAR 12:41–44).

Actions have consequences, good and bad. Well-practiced behaviors have more predictable results. The more training, skill, tools, and experience, the better the outcomes. If you want to make a difference, help people who need your help or ask for your help, as long as you are able to help. I mean, if someone asks me to help them push a car, I cannot because I have an ailing back, like many others my age. You do not want your effort to make a difference in the wrong direction. This is where education and experience come in handy. The more abilities you have and the greater the degree to which you have mastered them, the more targeted will be your duties in your vocation, in your community, and in the ministry of Christ.

- PSA 41:1 ~ Whoever helps the poor will be blessed by God, and God will deliver them when they experience a time of trouble.

- PRO 1:2–7 ~ Try to know wisdom and instruction; to perceive the words of understanding; to receive the instruction of wisdom, justice, judgment, and equity; to give subtlety to the simple; to give knowledge and discretion to the young. A wise person will listen and will increase in learning; a person of understanding will seek wise counsel, and will try to understand a proverb and its interpretation, or the words of the wise and the hidden meaning of what they say. Remember, the fear of God is the beginning of understanding; only fools despise wisdom and instruction.

- PRO 19:7 ~ Those who are kind to the poor are lending to the Lord, who will reward their generosity.

- ISA 30:21 ~ Whether you veer to the left or to the right, your ears will hear a word behind you saying, "This is the way, walk in it."

- LUK 2:17–18 ~ The shepherds spread the word to everyone they met about the marvelous things they had seen and experienced regarding Christ's birth.

- ROM 2:21–22 ~ If you teach others, do you not teach yourself also? Do you not practice what you preach?

- ROM 5:3–4 ~ Being justified by faith we achieve peace with God through Christ, in whom we have access by that faith to the grace in which we stand, rejoicing in the hope of glory. Therefore, we rejoice in time of tribulation, knowing that it teaches us patience, we gain experience, and it strengthens our hope.

- 2 TI 2:24–26 ~ A servant of the Lord does not waste time arguing, but is gentle to everyone, able to teach, and not resentful. Such disciples gently instruct those who are in opposition to them, hoping that God will grant them repentance for acknowledging His truth, so that they may escape the devil's traps who would otherwise capture them for his own purpose.

- 1 JO 4:6 ~ We are of God. Those who know God will listen to His messengers; those who are not of God will not listen. We know the difference between the Spirit of truth and the spirit of untruth.

Certainly, God's wisdom has the most to do with how you can make an excellent difference in people's lives including yours. We are obliged to learn all we can about God the Father, Son, and Holy Spirit. Further, everyone has innate abilities, some which have yet to be realized. Discover, cultivate, and employ those abilities, and learn other abilities that bolster these abilities. For example, I never had heard of statistics till I had to take the course for my master degree; I found out I was good at it. I took several more stat classes for my doctorate degree. I ended up conducting experimental research for defense contractors; I also taught college-level statistics and coauthored a textbook on statistics. Honestly, if God had allowed me to choose in advance from a list of gifts, I doubt I would have selected statistics; but God knew I could use this gift to do good. So, when you seek wisdom and knowledge, take elective courses in things that appear challenging or fascinating, instead of things that look easy or that you already know about.

- EXO 31:3 ~ I have filled him with the Spirit of God, with talent and intelligence, with knowledge and abilities.

- 1 CO 12:7–11 ~ The Spirit is manifested in some way for everyone to use productively. Some people have received wisdom, some knowledge, some faith, all from the same Spirit. Some people have the ability to heal, others to work miracles, others to prophesy, others to discern spirits, others to speak foreign tongues. But all of them are working with the same Spirit, who divides power among His people as He chooses.

- HEB 6:10 ~ God is just and will not forget your works of love that you showed to His people and continue to do so.

- 1 PE 4:10–11 ~ Whoever has received the gift of salvation in Christ should share that gift with others, as a steward of God's eternal grace. If you preach, do so as a messenger of God. If you minister, do so with the ability God gives you. Do this to glorify God through His Son.

What we say and do has an impact at many levels. We all have spheres of influence in our lives to include ourselves, our inner circle (family, friends), community (office, school, church), society (culture, religion), nature (the planet), and God. Each sphere affects the one encompassing it, continuing all the way from you to God; and each sphere affects the ones within it, continuing from God to you (Barber, 2016). Perhaps you have heard of the butterfly effect, which postulates that a single event in spacetime can reverberate throughout the universe. Because of the synergy in God's creation, everything affects everything though this cannot be measured or observed directly. The bottom line is this: if you help someone, they might help someone else, because the behavior of helping multiplies; eventually, it comes back around to you again. So, what goes around indeed comes around, in time. The more you are a blessing to others, the more you will be blessed. On this day, you might want to contemplate how you can have a positive impact on each and all the spheres of influence in your environment.

- DEU 11:26–28 ~ Behold, I set before you a blessing and a curse: a blessing if you obey the commandments of the Lord your God; a curse if you disobey and turn away from the way I have commanded you this day, to never go after other gods which you have not known.

- PRO 22:9 ~ Generous people will be blessed when they share with the poor.

- JOH 1:16 ~ From Christ's fullness we all have received grace upon grace.

- LUK 6:38 ~ Give and it shall be given to you in abundance, overflowing; for the same measure that you give is returned unto you.

- LUK 12:48 ~ Jesus said, "To whomever much is given, much will be required. To those who have committed much, of them more will be asked."

- ROM 12:1 ~ I implore you brothers and sisters, by the mercies of God, that you present yourselves as living sacrifices, holy and acceptable to Him; this is your reasonable service.

- GAL 6:9–10 ~ Do not become weary of doing good, for you will be rewarded at the right time. When opportunity arises, do something nice for someone, especially people in the faith.

- COL 3:24 ~ If you help others, you are serving Christ.

- HEB 13:1–2, 16 ~ Let brotherly love continue. Help strangers, for you may be ministering to angels for all you know. Do good and share, for such sacrifices are pleasing to the Lord.

- 2 PE 1:5–8 ~ Supplement your faith with virtue, your virtue with knowledge, your knowledge with self-control, your self-control with steadfastness, your steadfastness with godliness, and your godliness with brotherly love. If these are yours and they abound, they will keep you from being fruitless and ineffective.

Remember, the negative things you do and say will affect others negatively, as well as adjoining spheres of influence. This could produce a ripple effect all the way to heaven, not to mention causing a multiplicative effect on earth. If the boss yells at you, you get angry; when you get home you might yell at your spouse; then your spouse gets mad and yells at your kid, who gets mad and takes it out on the dog. Anger is contagious just like love is contagious.

- EZR 9:14 ~ Should we break God's commandments again, and join in affinity with the kinds of people who commit such abominations? Would God not be angry with us until He consumed us, so that nobody would remain or escape?

- PRO 14:29 ~ Being slow to anger shows understanding; those who are hasty produce folly.

- PRO 15:1, 18 ~ A gentle answer repels anger but a harsh word provokes anger. An angry person creates conflict, but a calm person creates peace.

- PRO 22:24–25 ~ Do not make friends with an angry person or associate with someone who has a quick temper, for you risk learning their ways and falling into the same trap.

- JAM 1:19–20 ~ Be eager to listen, slow to speak, and slow to anger; for the anger of humankind cannot work with the righteousness of God.

Father God, help us to eagerly seek learning for as long as we live, especially from your Holy Word. Help us to grow in knowledge and wisdom so we can impart truth, wisdom, and understanding to others. Equip us with abilities and skills necessary to make a difference in our families, communities, nation, and world, for we know when we serve others, we are serving you. Help us to notice the needs of others so we can help them in their time of need, knowing that you will help us in our time of need. Let us have a positive impact within our spheres of influence that reverberates all the way to heaven, and let our love have a multiplicative effect in our world. In the name of Jesus, who is love in the flesh, Amen.

October 27

Reformation Sunday is the last Sunday of the month (prior to 10/31), and recognizes the day Luther posted ninety-five theses on the castle church door in Wittenberg Germany, the pivotal point of the Protestant Reformation (10/31/1517). At the time, the Roman Catholic church was corrupted by avarice (greed), lust (for power), and pride (piety of the leadership): three of the seven deadliest sins postulated by the likes of Pope Gregory I (sixth century) and St. Thomas Aquinas (thirteenth century). The worst violations were charging a fee, called an indulgence, in lieu of penance (defined as self-deprecation due to remorse from sin), to purchase freedom from purgatory (a type of prison or penalty to expiate sins, where sinners serve time before being admitted into heaven). First of all, there is no such place as purgatory; once you die, you either are saved or you aren't. You either go to Abraham's bosom, or Hades; there is no passage from one place to the other. Second, forgiveness of sins cannot be bought; there is no penance or punishment that will abate sin. Penance is more a way of showing remorse for one's sins through contrition, confession, punishment, and absolution. Yes, we must confess and repent of our sins to God, and true godly sorrow will result in a desire to change. But material payment to the church or inflicting self-punishment are not scriptural. Third, forgiveness for the sins of the world already has been paid in full by Jesus Christ through His death and resurrection. No charge for sins should be levied by any church upon any believer. There are two choices: accept the payment made by Christ or pay the debt of sin with your own life. This essential doctrine of the true Christian faith cannot be clearer (you'd think) for any denomination claiming to be Christian.

- ISA 38:18–19 ~ Those who die cannot praise God, only the living can. Once you are dead, you no longer can hope for the truth; you can hope only while you are alive.

- HOS 13:14 ~ God says, "I will ransom you from the power of the grave to be redeemed from death. Then I will destroy death."

- LUK 16:19–31 ~ Jesus told the parable of the rich man and the poor man: There was a rich man who lived a life of pleasure and luxury. A poor man lay at his gate who was weak, hungry, and afflicted, desiring mere crumbs off the rich man's plate. The two men died. The poor man was taken to Abraham's bosom, and the rich man was exiled in Hades. The rich man called out to Abraham asking if he would let the poor man dip his finger into water to wet his parched tongue. But Abraham reminded him how thoughtless and unmerciful he had been to the poor man, and told him that nobody could pass through the chasm separating them. The rich man implored that his family be warned, to prevent them from the same fate. Abraham informed the rich man that his family would have to rely on the Word of God like everybody else; for even a visit from the dead would not persuade them to change their ways.

- LUK 23:43 ~ Jesus told the repentant thief beside Him, "Today you will be with me in paradise."

- 2 CO 4:7 ~ We keep treasure in jars of clay, that shows the unsurpassed power which belongs to God and is not from us.

- 2 CO 5:1, 6–8 ~ We know that when this temple, which is our body, is dissolved, we will have a home in heaven; not a house made by hands but one that is eternal. This gives us the confidence we need, for we are living here in the flesh and absent from the Lord. We must walk by faith not by sight. I am not afraid; indeed, I yearn to be absent from this body and present with the Lord.

At the first ecumenical Council of Nicaea (AD 325), the sixty-six books of the Bible were canonized, and the essential doctrines of the Christian faith were established in the Nicene Creed;

these were accepted by the *Holy* Catholic church, the dominant church at the time (catholic means universal). Interestingly, the abovementioned heretical doctrines (purgatory, indulgences, penance) were introduced into *Roman* Catholic dogma circa twelfth century. Though agreement had been reached on essential doctrines, as stated in the Nicene Creed, the Roman Catholic church (established in the fifth century after splitting from Constantinople) adopted traditions that were unsupported Biblically. To justify their use, apocryphal books favoring them were added to the Catholic Bible. The true canon of scripture, thirty-nine books from the OT and twenty-seven from the NT, remains intact. Apocryphal books were added at the Council of Trent (1546), thirty years after Luther publicly challenged the Roman Catholic leaders in the Diet at Worms; those additional books were never canonized by any ecumenical council or church body.

- JER 33:8 ~ God will cleanse them of their sins and pardon them.

- MIC 7:18 ~ Who is like you, God, who pardons sin and ignores the evil done by your people? God does not stay angry forever, but finds pleasure in giving mercy.

- ROM 3:20, 23–24, 28 ~ By works of the Law will no person be justified in God's sight, for with the Law comes the knowledge of sin. All have sinned and come short of God's glory. We are justified freely by the grace of God through the redemption found in Jesus Christ. In conclusion, a person is justified by faith not by works of the Law.

- ROM 4:13, 16; ROM 9:6–7 ~ For the promise that he should be the heir of the world, was not to Abraham or to his seed through the Law, but through the righteousness of faith. Therefore, it is by grace through faith that the promise is given to all the seed; not only to those who obey the Law, but also to those who demonstrate the faith of Abraham who was the father of us all. Not everyone who is a descendant of Jacob is of the house of Israel. That is, just because someone is from the lineage of Abraham, it does not necessarily make them children or heirs.

- GAL 2:16 ~ Nobody is justified by works of the Law but by faith in Jesus Christ. Therefore, in Him we will place our faith, and not in our ability to adhere to the Law.

- EPH 2:8–9 ~ You are saved by the grace of God because of your faith in Jesus Christ. Salvation is a gift of God, it cannot be earned through good works, so nobody should brag.

- PHP 1:15–18 ~ Some indeed preach Christ out of envy and rivalry; others preach out of good will. One preaches Christ in order to be controversial, insincerely pretending to be an authority to draw attention to themselves. Another preaches out of love, the way I preach in defense of the Gospel. But whether in pretention or in truth, Christ is being preached, and for this I rejoice.

- TIT 3:5–7 ~ He has saved us, not because of our works of righteousness, but according to His mercy, through the washing of regeneration and renewing by His Holy Spirit, which He abundantly bestowed upon us through Jesus Christ our Savior. Being justified by grace, we have become heirs according to the hope of eternal life.

- HEB 10:10, 18 ~ We are sanctified by the offering of the body of Jesus Christ, one sacrifice for all people. No more offering for sin will ever be needed again.

In many churches today you will hear Martin Luther's greatest hymn being sung by the congregation, *A Mighty Fortress Is Our God*. Luther composed quite a number of hymns. The reader is encouraged to study Martin Luther if you are not familiar with him, and the Protestant Reformation in general, if you want to meet all the key players. Luther was quite an interesting and talented man, himself a Catholic priest, theologian, and professor. His break with the church of Rome was not intentional. He challenged the leadership to debate him on these issues using scripture alone. They could not prove him wrong; but instead of reforming their ways, they tried to eliminate Luther. He survived, and the rest is history, a history well worth learning about.

- DEU 12:32 ~ Make sure you do what God tells you; do not add to it or take away from it.

- PSA 34:18 ~ The Lord is near those with a broken heart; He saves those with a contrite spirit.

- ISA 29:13 ~ The people honor me with their lips but have removed their heart from me, and their knowledge of me is taught using principles invented by men.

- MAR 7:7–9 ~ Jesus said, "Isaiah prophesied about these hypocrites. In vain they worship God, teaching as doctrine the commandments of men. They set aside my commandments and substitute their own traditions."

- ROM 4:16 ~ The fulfillment of God's promise in your life depends entirely on trusting Him and His ways, and embracing Him and His works. The promise is received purely as a gift. That is the only way everyone can have a chance, including those who recognize religious traditions and those who are unaware of them.

- ROM 8:11 ~ The Spirit of Him who raised Jesus Christ from the dead will abide in you, and also will restore your mortal bodies from the dead.

- 2 TH 2:15 ~ Fellow Christians, stand fast in your faith and hold onto those traditions that you have been taught in God's Word, through the prophets and apostles.

- HEB 9:14–15 ~ How much more the blood of Christ, who offered Himself as the unblemished sacrifice, will purify our flesh and restore our consciences to serve the living God! For this reason, Christ has become the mediator of the New Covenant, because through His death He redeemed us from sin committed under the Old Covenant, so that we may receive our eternal inheritance.

There is nothing we can do to earn forgiveness or to purchase our freedom from sin and death. If this were possible, we would not need a savior. The Bible tells us that those who die in Christ will be with Him in paradise when they die (LUK 23:42; 2 CO 5:8). Once Jesus sets you free, you are definitely free forever (JOH 8:36). When a Christian dies, his or her soul immediately departs from the dead corpse and enters the presence of the Lord. There are no stops between the grave and Abraham's bosom. Beyond the grave, there is no hope for reconciliation with the Lord after a soul enters Hades (LUK 16:26). There were countless other objections with the Roman church raised by Luther and other evangelists and reformers. This caused a bit of warfare between the Protestants and Catholics, which is mostly resolved today though not for everybody. Despite such errors in theology, I do not believe that Catholics are condemned, as long as they believe they are saved by the grace of God through faith in Christ Jesus. However, this essential doctrine renders false any doctrine that is contrary.

Heavenly Father, we thank you for giving us the truth and a clear path to heaven through the righteousness of Christ. We praise you Father and Son, for the free gift of eternal life, given to all who believe in Jesus Christ as their personal Savior. Help people who are unsure of your truth to read it for themselves in the Holy Bible so they will not be confused by errant teachings or philosophies. Help Christian denominations to resolve their differences solely with the Word, and by the power of your Holy Spirit who conveys truth directly to our hearts and souls. Prevent us from believing in worldly traditions when they do not concur with the Holy Bible. Help those who seek your knowledge and truth to hear your Holy Spirit in the Word, where they will find Jesus Christ in whose name we pray, Amen.

October 28

National First Responders Day was established by Congress in 2019; the bill was introduced with bipartisan senators but it took two years getting through the House. The idea got its start when officer Sean Collier was murdered in 2013; he was shot by one of the suspects of the Boston Marathon bombing. His surviving brother Andrew started a movement to create this observance. It took several years but his determination made it happen. Today we honor men and women who run towards disaster rather than from it. This includes police, firefighters, paramedics, military, search and rescue personnel, and other emergency workers regardless of branch of government, job title, or official status. We have heroes such as these facing danger every day so that we can feel safe. This day is for showing our appreciation to their dedication, something we often take for granted. Say thanks to every person in uniform that you see today, and tell them you appreciate their service. Look for events in your area if you want to participate or volunteer your time to this cause.

- DEU 31:6 ~ Be strong and courageous, do not worry or be afraid; for the Lord your God is with you. He will never fail you or forsake you.

- PRO 3:27–31 ~ Do not withhold goodness from those who deserve it, when it is within your power to do so. Do not say to your neighbor, "Leave now; come again some other time and I will help," when you already have the means. Do not devise evil against your neighbor, since he lives securely alongside you. Do not cause strife with people where there is none. Do not envy oppressors or choose their ways.

- LUK 17:11–18 ~ Jesus healed ten lepers. After showing themselves to the priest that they were healed, only one of them returned to thank and praise Jesus. Jesus questioned why the other nine had not returned to give thanks to God.

- 1 CO 3:13–14 ~ Everyone's work will be seen for what it is because the light will illuminate it; it will be revealed by the fire which tries every person's work as well as his or her dedication. If that which is built endures, the builder will be rewarded. If it burns down, the builder will suffer the loss but will be saved from the flames.

- 2 CO 1:11 ~ You have helped us with your prayers. Many people will thank God for our ministry and for the favor God has granted us on behalf of your support and prayers.

- COL 4:5–6 ~ Be wise in the way you act towards outsiders and make the most of every opportunity. Let your speech always be full of grace, seasoned with salt, so that you can know how you ought to respond to others.

First responders rescue people from immediate danger countless times in their career. Their dedication to service is unmatched. They should be paid an additional stipend for hazardous duty, instead of being defunded by brainless politicians who want the money for pointless initiatives. Those who exhibit self-sacrifice to others are the true heroes of society and illustrate the sacrifices made by Christ and His apostles. They deserve your respect and thanks.

- PSA 121:7 ~ The Lord will protect you from evil and preserve your soul.

- SOS 1:5–9 ~ Notice, the characteristics the king admires in the maiden are her dedication and sense of duty, not her physical attractiveness. He overlooks the fact that her skin has been darkened by the sun from laboring in the fields where she tends flocks that are not her own.

- ROM 13:4–5 ~ If you do what is evil, be afraid, for God's minister will not bear the sword in vain, because he is sent to execute wrath upon those who do evil. Subject yourselves to them, not just to avoid their wrath but for the sake of your conscience.

- JOH 12:25 ~ Jesus said, "Those who love their lives on this earth will lose their lives, but those who hate their lives on this earth will keep their lives, unto life eternal."

- JOH 15:12–13 ~ Jesus said, "Love each other as I have loved you. No greater love exists than to give one's life for their friends."

- 1 CO 13:7 ~ Bear all things, believe all things, hope all things, endure all things.

- PHP 2:3–4 ~ Hold people in higher esteem than yourself. Let nothing be done through strife or vanity, but in lowliness of mind let everyone esteem others above themselves. Do not take care of only your things, but take care of the things of others.

- HEB 6:10 ~ God is just and will not forget your works of love that you showed to His people and continue to do so.

- 1 JO 3:16–17 ~ By this we know love, because Christ laid down His life for us. We also ought to lay down our lives for our brothers and sisters.

When God comes to our aid, we thank Him. God watches over us and sends His angels to keep us from harm and danger. If anyone deserves our appreciation it is God. Those individuals who protect and defend us reflect the love of God and should be appreciated as well. Remember them in your prayers as you give thanks and praise to the Lord for our unsung heroes.

- DEU 11:26–28 ~ Behold, I set before you a blessing and a curse: a blessing if you obey the commandments of the Lord your God; a curse if you disobey and turn away from the way I have commanded you this day, to never go after other gods which you have not known.

- PSA 91:11–12 ~ God gives His angels charge over you to protect you in all that you do. They will take you up in their hands so that you do not dash your foot on a stone.

- PSA 95:2 ~ Let us go before God with thanksgiving; make a joyful noise to Him with singing.

- ISA 41:10 ~ Do not fear for I am with you. Do not be dismayed for I am your God. I will strengthen you and I will help you. Yes, I will hold you up with the right hand of my righteousness.

- MAT 25:40, 45 ~ Jesus said, "Whenever you have done something to help another person, you have done it to me as well; whenever you have not done something to help another person, you have not done it to me."

- PHP 1:3–6, 9–11 ~ I thank God every time I remember you. I pray for you all the time with joy because of our partnership in the Gospel, being confident that He who began a good work in you will carry it onto completion until the day Christ returns. And this is my prayer: that your love will abound more and more in knowledge, depth, and insight, so that you will be able to discern what is best, and can remain pure and blameless until Christ comes. Being filled with the fruits of righteousness, which come from Jesus Christ for the glory of God.

We thank you, Father, for our first responders, and anybody who puts their lives in jeopardy to protect us. Just as Christ took our place in death, let us be ready to make personal sacrifices for others. Protect and defend the brave men and women who regularly risk their lives and personal wellbeing in their vocation. Truly, those who choose these jobs are dedicated to helping and are not expecting special compensation. May we show our appreciation to them today and every day, so they know people do care, and do understand their sacrifices and trauma, physical and mental. We know, heavenly Father, that you will not ignore their works of service and that you will reward those who help anyone out of love for Jesus. In His name, Amen.

October 29

Stock Market Crashed (Black Tuesday) on this day in 1929, sparking the Great Depression. The economy was in decline and panicking people dumped their stock—millions of shares in one day, and billions of dollars lost. Wages were already low; unemployment and debt were high. The US and most modernized countries landed into a depression that lasted a decade. That's what happens when you have too much spending, borrowing, and speculating on the one hand, and layoffs, pay cuts, tax hikes, and high interest rates on the other. We recently experienced a recession in the land, and if the government keeps blowing money, increasing the deficit, imposing tax hikes, raising interest rates, paying debts by printing more money, and forcing people out of work, we may experience another great depression. Such a scenario has been prophesied to occur in the latter days. It is eventual, because their zero-sum game will not work; but it will result in everyone being left with zero, including those who fleeced the masses to bankroll their extravagant lifestyles.

- DEU 11:26–28 ~ Behold, I set before you a blessing and a curse: a blessing if you obey the commandments of the Lord your God; a curse if you disobey and turn away from the way I have commanded you this day, to never go after other gods which you have not known.

- PSA 37:21 ~ The wicked borrow and do not pay back, but the righteous show mercy and give.

- PRO 22:7, 16 ~ The rich rule over the poor, and the borrower becomes the lender's slave. Those who oppress the poor to increase their own wealth and those who give to the rich eventually will become needy.

- PRO 23:4–5 ~ Do not labor to be rich, do not rely on your own wisdom. Do not set your eyes on something that is not there, because riches will certainly find wings and fly away like an eagle.

- ECC 10:18 ~ Because of laziness and idleness the building decayed and collapsed.

- MAT 6:24 ~ Jesus said, "Nobody can serve two masters, for they will end up loving one and despising the other; you cannot love God and money at the same time."

- LUK 12:15 ~ Jesus said, "Beware of earthly cravings, for your life does not consist of the abundance of the things which you can possess while living on this earth."

- LUK 12:19–20 ~ The greedy man said to his soul, "Soul, you have ample goods; take it easy; eat, drink and be merry." But God said to him, "Fool, tonight your soul is required of you. And all your goods, who will possess them now?"

- 2 TH 3:10–12 ~ When we were with you, we gave you this rule: if a man does not work, he should not eat. We have heard that some of you are lazy. They are not busy, they are busybodies. We urge these people, in the name of Christ, to settle down and to earn the bread that they eat.

- 1 TI 6:9–10, 17 ~ Those who long to be rich will fall into temptation and a snare, and into many foolish lusts which will drown them in destruction and damnation. For the love of money is the root of all evil. Those who have coveted after money have departed from the faith and brought upon themselves much pain and sorrow. Tell those who are rich in this present world not to be conceited or fix their hopes on the uncertainty of riches, but to focus on God who richly supplies all things for us to enjoy.

- REV 6:5–6 ~ When the third seal was removed, the third being spoke, "Come." And a black horse came with a rider holding scales in his hand. Then I heard, "One measure of wheat for a day's wages and three measures of barley for a day's wages, and do not touch the wine and the oil."

We can see the signs that the end could be near; one of the signs is the economic disaster looming on the horizon. So what can we do to prepare? Should we save up our money, and stash it away for a rainy day? Obviously not, since money will not be worth the paper it is printed on. It matters not how much money you have in the bank, or the accumulation of your possessions, for you cannot eat them. Those who are God's children need only to depend on Him for everything they need. If you are here for the next great depression, remember that God will provide if your trust is in Him.

- PSA 23:1 ~ The Lord is my Shepherd; He provides everything I need.

- PSA 34:10 ~ Lions may grow weak and hungry, but those who seek the Lord will lack no good thing.

- PSA 37:25 ~ I was young and now I am old, but I have never seen the righteous man forsaken or his children begging for bread.

- PRO 3:9–10 ~ Honor the Lord with your profits, and with the first fruits of your income, and your barns be filled and your winepresses will burst with new wine.

- PRO 10:3 ~ The Lord does not let the righteous go hungry, but He frustrates the cravings of the wicked.

- MAT 6:20–21 ~ Lay up for yourselves treasures in heaven, where they cannot rust, or rot, or be stolen by thieves. For where your treasure is, there your heart will be.

- MAT 6:34 ~ Seek first the kingdom of God and His righteousness and all of these things will be added unto you.

- MAT 21:22 ~ Jesus said, "Whatever you ask the Lord in prayer, believe and you will receive it."

- 1 CO 1:3–8 ~ Grace and peace be unto you from God our Father and from the Lord Jesus Christ. I thank God continuously on your behalf, for the grace He has given to you through Christ. You are enriched by Christ in everything you say and everything you know. Even as the testimony of Christ was confirmed among you who wait for the day of His return, so He will confirm you until the end, ensuring that you receive all your spiritual needs, and be found blameless upon that day.

- 2 CO 9:8 ~ God is able to bless you abundantly, that in all things and at all times you have what you need, so you can abound in good works.

- PHP 4:19 ~ God will supply your every need according to the riches of His glory.

Father, we thank you that we have everything we need to sustain us, physically, mentally, and spiritually; help us always to rely exclusively on you for all of our needs. Help us to seek your righteousness and your kingdom, and not dwell on worldly things, so we can be assured of your provision, protection, and preservation. Let us never be selfish or stingy, and help us to be satisfied with what you have blessed us with and responsible with all that you provide. Remind us to share what we have with others, giving in proportion to the degree that you have prospered us. We pray for all who are needy, not just for their daily bread but for the bread of life; we pray that they are filled, both in their bodies and their spirits. Let us give generously in support of the needy, sharing the love of Christ with them; let us also be ready to take the Gospel to whomever you would send us. In the name of Jesus, who is love personified, we pray, Amen.

October 30

Internet Day has been observed on October 29, since 2005, but it is not an official observance, so today will do. This commemorates the day in 1969 when graduate students at UCLA sent a digital message over the telephone line to students at Stanford; the systems crashed before the entire message could be transmitted but a proof of concept was achieved. However, it was five years earlier (1964), when an MIT scientist named J. Licklider posited a secure alternative to the telephone in the event of a Soviet offensive; he envisioned a system comprised of computers that could network together; this became known as ARPAnet. But the birth of the internet was mostly the work of a British software engineer named Tim Berners-Lee who invented the necessary tools: hypertext (which became known as HTML), uniform resource identifier (or URL), and hypertext transfer protocol (HTTP on a web address). By 1989, Lee was proposing a global hypertext system that could transfer documents by posting them on the internet; he developed the software for the server and web browser the following year. Berners-Lee established the World Wide Web Consortium at the MIT Computer Science Laboratory in 1994, developing web standards and protocols so that everyone could have access (see also the lesson on 08/01).

The internet was initially intended for use by the government. In 1974, Stanford computer scientist Vinton Cerf, in conjunction with the Defense Advanced Research Projects Agency (DARPA evolved from ARPA) developed transmission control protocol (TCP) enabling computers to interface with each other on a global network. This new capability was expanded to include academia, business, and personal use, again thanks to Berners-Lee who advocated for releasing internet software to the public. Soon, commercial networks became available, which opened the door to everyone, given the personal computer also had arrived on the scene. By the 1990s, we had browsers, email, dial-up modems, and thousands of internet service providers (ISP). Now, providers and websites are a dime-a-dozen, with applications for all kinds of uses; and they all have one thing in common: they want your money.

It is more important to connect with God, and people of God, than to connect with the world. For the world does not know God, and many who profess that they do are not talking about the same God as the Holy Bible. It is advisable to disconnect when the motivations of your connections are nefarious.

- 1 KI 8:53 ~ For the Lord separated Israel from all other peoples of the earth to be His inheritance, just as He promised to His servant Moses when He brought our fathers out of Egypt.

- PSA 80:14–15 ~ Please return to us God. Look down from heaven and visit us, and the vineyard your right hand has planted, the Branch you have made strong for yourself.

- ISA 4:2 ~ One day the Branch of the Lord will appear, beautiful and glorious; and the fruit of the earth will be excellent and lovely for those of Israel who escaped.

- ZEC 3:8–9 ~ The Branch is God's servant who will build God's temple, who will bear God's glory, and who will sit on God's throne as ruler and priest.

- JOH 15:1–6 ~ Jesus said, "I am the true vine; others are branches of this vine. If you do not abide in the Branch you will die. Now that you have been cleansed by the Word which I have spoken to you, you can live in me as I live in you. Just as a branch cannot bear fruit when separated from the vine, neither can you unless you stay connected to me. I am the vine and you are the branches. If you stay connected to me you will bear much fruit, but apart from me you can do nothing. Branches of the vine which do not bear fruit are chopped off and burned in the fire."

- ROM 11:16 ~ If the root is holy, so are the branches.

- COL 1:19–22 ~ God was pleased to have His fullness living in Christ, so that through Him, everything on earth and in heaven could be reconciled to Himself, by the peace that came through the shedding of Christ's blood on the cross. Before, you were separated from God; you were His enemies because of your sinful minds and evil deeds. But now, God has reconciled you by the body of Christ through His death, to be presented holy, blameless, and pure in the sight of God.

- JDE 1:18–19 ~ It was foretold that there will be mockers in the last times, who walk after ungodly lusts. They have separated themselves, for they are sensual and possess not the Spirit.

An explosion of technologies has indeed given worldwide access to the web. We have seen a proliferation of platforms produced by big tech giants for social interaction; these platforms also can spy on you and gather your personal data. The service is mostly free, but they also get your personal information for free, and some of them profit from this (we should be charging them). Anybody with an electronic device (computer, phone, tablet, etc.) can easily access most anything on the internet. Unfortunately, that also includes stuff that should not be allowed like illicit pornography, criminal behavior, terrorism, and cyberbullying, none of which can be considered free speech since they are violations of the law.

This is but one part of the global conspiracy to control you in every way possible. They have the means to censor, repress, and remove you, if you happen to disagree with what they say, do, or want. How is it that our government gives them immunity when they violate the First Amendment? You mustn't dare call them out, this illegitimate coalition of government, big business, and big tech/media. They assume they have cornered the market on experts and intelligence, but they are not as smart as they think. All of this is classic fascism, which has failed every time it has been tried, and it will fail again. The greatest enemy to fascism is faith in God; we are the ones they want silenced, just like globalists have intended to silence Christ and Christians throughout the ages.

- ECC 4:1 ~ I saw the oppression that occurred under the sun; I saw the tears of those who were down and out and noticed that they had no comforter. Even though they had power, they had no comforter.

- ECC 9:11 ~ I noticed that the race is not always to the swift, or the battle to the strong; neither bread to the wise nor wealth to the educated nor favor to the skilled; but time and chance happen to them all.

- ISA 8:12–13 ~ Do not join conspiracies or alliances with people who are afraid; do not fear the things they fear; do not be afraid at all. Sanctify the Lord of hosts; let Him be your fear.

- MIC 7:3 ~ They are skilled at doing evil. Rulers require gifts and judges require bribes for their services. Those in power dictate their desires; together they conspire against others.

- MAT 27:1 ~ The chief priests and elders conspired against Jesus to put Him to death.

- JOH 18:31 ~ Pilate told the chief priests and elders to judge Jesus according to their law. The Jewish leaders told Pilate it was unlawful for them to put a man to death.

- EPH 4:14–16 ~ We will no longer be helpless as children, swayed by false teachings and influenced by the trickery of deceitful schemes. Instead, we will speak the truth out of love, and we will grow in every way in Christ, who is our head. In Christ, the whole body is joined and held together just as our bodies are joined and held together by ligaments and joints. Christ is the head of this body, in which all members work together as an integrated system; through Him the body is nurtured and grows in His love.

- 1 TI 6:3:5 ~ If anyone teaches false doctrines, and disagrees with the true and godly teachings of Christ, they are arrogant and lack understanding. Their contrary positions cause envy, strife, insulting, skepticism, and controversy. They are devoid of the truth, supposing that financial gain is a godly pursuit. Avoid such people.

Thus, the internet has been a blessing, but it is becoming a curse. If the internet is not regulated it will get worse. But who in our government has the guts to take a stand against this long-prepared battle plan and the elites pushing it? There are innumerable bureaucrats who have imbedded themselves which need to be thrown out; they are like parasites who suck the blood out of our constitutional republic, working for the globalist organizers and not the people.

What if the entire system imploded? No internet, no electronic devices, no electricity for that matter? As fast as this age of information technology has grown, it could die quickly. Cyber warfare has become the norm, so be careful and watch out for imposters when you surf the web. Do not be eager to download something on your computer, for you might get malware downloaded along with it. It is wise to become informed of the dangers lurking in places like the so-called dark web, and many other sites and locales associated with the internet.

- GEN 1:2–5 ~ Darkness covered the earth and God commanded there to be light, and He saw that the light was good, and He separated the light from the darkness.

- EZE 32:27–29 ~ The fallen of the untrue have gone to hell with their weapons of war. They were the terror of the mighty in the land of the living, but now they join with those who go down to the pit.

- ROM 12:2 ~ Do not conform to this world, but become transformed by the renewing of your mind. Then you will be able to test and prove God's good, acceptable, and perfect will.

- 2 CO 6:14 ~ Do not be joined with unbelievers, for what fellowship can there be between righteousness and unrighteousness? What communion can there be between light and darkness?

- EPH 2:19–22 ~ You are no longer foreigners but fellow citizens of God's kingdom and members of His household, built on the foundation laid by the prophets and apostles with Jesus Christ as the chief cornerstone. In Him the entire building is joined together and grows into a holy temple. In Him you also are being built together to become a place for God's Holy Spirit to live.

Most merciful Father, let us never become disconnected from your love and grace through Jesus Christ; let us remain grafted to the Branch and to bear good fruit. Help us to steer clear of internet sites that promote evil and evil people; help parents to diligently monitor what their kids are viewing on the web, which has become a web of sin. Help us to select leaders that will thwart the designs of the fascists who are hungry for power; take them down from their ivory towers and expose their lies and conspiracies. Help us to identify the so-called deep state operatives who want to run our country into the ground by taking over the government. Protect the innocent especially our youth. We pray that they do not get sucked into the devious and pernicious web of evil that has become a major part of the internet, government, and some school boards and administrators. We ask these things in the name of Jesus, Amen.

October 31

Halloween occurs on the eve of All Saints Day. All Hallows Day (aka All Saints Day) became a religious observance with the early church in the fourth century; it was celebrated in March to venerate "hallowed" martyrs of Christianity. All Hallows Eve (Halloween), was originally a Celtic holiday when they honored their dead by setting a place for them at the table. To continue the tradition, certain ceremonial foods were eaten to include the English soul cake; people would go door to door wearing costumes and asking for a soul cake, and a prayer for their dear departed. Some would place jack-o-lanterns to shoo away evil spirits, since only their honored dead were invited. Such superstition has carried on in certain arenas: the idea that spirits can be dead, or the dead can return as spirits. If anything, these are occultist views and an invitation to demonism or fallen angels (aka familiar spirits); these spirits are not human and they are not dead.

- 1 SA 28:7 ~ King Saul ordered his servants to find a woman possessed by a familiar spirit so he could consult with her. They told him there was such a witch in Endor.

- JOB 7:7–10 ~ Remember, life is like the wind; after death, my eyes can no longer look for the good. Those who have seen me will see me no more for I will not exist. Like a cloud at the mercy of the wind, life vanishes. Those who go to their grave shall rise up no more. They will not return to their houses and nobody will know them any longer.

- PSA 146:4 ~ His breath leaves, and he returns to the ground; in that day his thoughts also perish.

- ECC 9:5–6, 10 ~ The living know that they will die, but the dead know nothing, neither can they receive any reward for they have been forgotten. Their love, hate, and envy have perished with them; they have no involvement forever with anything under the sun. Whatever your hands find to do, do it with your might; for there is no work, device, knowledge, or wisdom in the grave where you are going.

- ISA 8:19 ~ If anyone suggests consulting familiar spirits, or listening to sorcerers who search for paranormal visions and murmurings, answer them saying, "Should we not be consulting with the Lord God; should we not be seeking the living instead of the dead?"

- ISA 38:18 ~ The grave cannot praise God; death cannot celebrate Him. Those who go down to the pit cannot hope for His faithfulness.

- JOH 5:28–29 ~ The time is coming when all who are in the grave will hear His voice and come forth. Those who have been faithful and good will arise to everlasting life, and those who have been unfaithful and evil will arise to receive everlasting condemnation.

- HEB 4:10 ~ A person who has entered into his or her rest has ceased from their own works, as God did from His.

- REV 12:3–4 ~ A great wonder appeared in heaven: a red dragon with seven heads and ten horns. Its tail pulled one third of the stars (angels) in heaven down with it, and they were thrown to the earth.

All Saints Day was officially instituted by Pope Boniface IV in the seventh century; the date was changed to 11/01 by Pope Gregory III in the eighth century to overlap pagan holidays. This notion of venerating saints became a Catholic ritual, recognizing martyrs and those canonized as saints. This became an official Roman Catholic event on the liturgical calendar around the twelfth century. Now their calendar includes All Hallows Eve (10/31), Feast of All Saints (11/1), and Feast of All Souls (11/2), a day dedicated to prayer for souls supposedly being held in purgatory. These are among the very objections that Martin Luther listed on his ninety-five theses

OCTOBER

which he nailed to the Wittenberg church door on this date in 1517. Luther opposed the ideas of offering prayers to the dead and offering prayers for the dead. For the study on Reformation Day see the lesson on 10/27.

- MAT 6:6, 9 ~ Jesus said, "When you pray, go to a quiet place and shut the door; pray to the Father in secret and He will reward you openly. Pray like this: Our Father in heaven, hallowed be your name."

- JOH 13:13 ~ Jesus said, "Whatever you ask in my name that I will do, so the Father can be glorified in the Son."

- ACT 10:25–26 ~ When Peter arrived, Cornelius met him, fell to his feet and worshipped him. Peter helped him to his feet saying, "Stand up. I too am a mere man like you."

- 1 TI 2:5 ~ There is one God, and one mediator between God and humankind, the man Jesus Christ.

Halloween has returned to its pagan roots with costumes, trick-or-treating, jack-o-lanterns, and ghosts. This is not to say that one must never have fun on Halloween; but if your kids are going trick-or-treating, you'd best go with them. Because there are degenerates out there who want to despoil our children, harm or torment them, and teach them the ways of the occult. Many Christians hold events in their churches with programming geared towards the kids; recognizing Reformation Day above All Hallows Eve.

The community of saints includes everyone who lives or has died in Christ. We are the body of Christ and His church on earth. We will be rejoined with all saints on the last day, when those who are in Christ, whether dead or alive, will gather together in the sky to be escorted by the Lord into His kingdom. The church does not have the authority to designate or canonize saints, for all who die bearing the name of Christ are saints, appointed by our Father in heaven who alone knows the hearts of everybody.

- ACT 26:9–11 ~ Paul admitted that he did many things in Jerusalem that were contrary to the name of Jesus of Nazareth. "I shut them in prison by the authority of the chief priests, and ordered the death of many saints."

- ROM 8:27 ~ He who searches hearts knows what is in the mind of the Spirit who makes intercession for the saints according to His will.

- 1 CO 1:1–3 ~ Paul, called to be an apostle of Jesus Christ through the will of God, wrote this letter to Sosthenes: Unto the church of God at Corinth, to those who are sanctified in Christ and called to be saints with everyone else who calls upon the name of Christ, grace be unto you and peace from God our Father and from the Lord Jesus Christ.

- 1 TH 4:16–17 ~ The Lord will descend from heaven with a shout, with the voice of the archangel, and with a blast from the trumpet of God. Then the dead in Christ will rise first. Those who remain alive in Christ will rise to join the others in the clouds, meeting the Lord in the sky. Those chosen by Christ will live with Him forevermore.

Father, we pray that our kids will not get caught up with traditions from secular society or get involved in unscriptural practices regarding the dead. Instruct those who are misguided, and call upon, pray to, or pray for the dead. Let them know that you are alive but the dead are not, and that demons and the demon-possessed are everywhere. Let everyone know that such evil can be challenged by invoking the name of Christ, which will scare them away when we wield the sword of the Spirit. Thank you that we can possess the Holy Spirit by keeping our focus on Jesus, thereby receiving revelation, understanding, guidance, and power. In His name we pray, Amen.

November 1

All Saints Day is for remembering the saints who have gone before us to be with the Lord in heaven. Martyrs for Christ were revered in the early church. They were honored every year on the anniversary of their passing. There were a great many soldiers for Jesus who were martyred making it very difficult to remember each one and the day of their departure, so a single day was selected for the remembrance of Christian martyrs since the fourth century. The original day for commemorating these fallen believers and evangelists was during the early harvest, but this date was moved to 11/01 by the Catholic pope in the eighth century. All Saints Day is observed by Protestants and Catholics alike, but not necessarily as a church-sponsored occasion.

This is a good day to remember those who have passed who were special to you because they helped build you up in your faith in Christ. I was lucky to have two parents who attended weekly services, including Sunday school for every age group. My mother's parents were particularly devout and I learned a lot from them. My grandmother's grandfather was a Lutheran minister and missionary, who immigrated to the US in the 1800s and established Lutheran churches in northern Wisconsin. A few of my grandmother's siblings helped me with my first Christian book. My great-grandmother, who I never knew, was a strong, wise, and faithful woman of vision. These are the saints in my life who I venerate on this day: my royal lineage in Christ.

Who exactly are the saints? They are children who have been adopted by God our Father and are with Him now.

- DAN 12:1 ~ At that time, Michael the great prince who protects the children of God, will arise. It will be a time of trouble, unlike any before or after. You will be delivered, everyone whose name is written in the book.

- MAT 13:37–43 ~ Jesus summarized His parable saying, "The field represents the world. The harvest represents the end of the world. The reapers are the angels. The good grain represents the children of God, and the evil weeds represent the children of Satan. Jesus Christ is the sower of the grain. The enemy that sows the weeds is Satan. The weeds will be gathered by the angels and burned in the fire; all things that are offensive and evil will be thrown into the furnace where there is weeping and gnashing of teeth. The righteous will shine like the sun in the kingdom of their Father."

- JOH 1:12 ~ To all who have received Christ, and believed in His name, He has given the privilege to become children of God.

- ROM 9:4–8 ~ Who are the Israelites, to whom God gave the Law and granted the adoption, and with whom God made the covenants and promises? Christ came for them and for all people. It is not as if God's Word had no effect, for they who are of Israel are not all from Israel. Those who are of Abraham's seed are not all his children. In other words, those who are the children of the flesh are not children of God; those who cling to God's promises, they are counted as children.

- GAL 4:4–7 ~ When the time was right, God sent His Son, who was born of a woman under the Old Covenant of the Law, to redeem those who were under the Law. He did this so that everyone could receive the honor of becoming adopted children of God. If you are a child of God, you are no longer His servant, but a fellow heir of God through Christ.

- EPH 1:5, 11–14, 18 ~ We were predestined to become adopted children of God by Jesus Christ, according to His marvelous will; in order that we who first put our hope in Christ, might be for the praise of His glory. In Christ we obtain an inheritance in heaven, because we listened to the truth and trusted in Him for our redemption and salvation. I hope your eyes will be opened

NOVEMBER

and you will become enlightened, so you will feel the hope of His promise, and experience the glory of the inheritance of the saints.

- HEB 2:10–11 ~ Through His suffering, many people are saved to become glorified with Him as children of God. Both He that sanctifies and those who are sanctified are one; therefore, Christ is not ashamed to call them His brothers and sisters.

- 1 JO 3:2–3 ~ Dear friends, now we are the sons of God, and what we will become is not yet known. But we do know this: when He returns for us, we will become like Him, for we shall see Him as He really is. Everyone who has this hope in Him are purified even as He is pure.

- REV 7:9–17 ~ I beheld a great multitude, which nobody could count, from all nations, lineages, peoples, and languages, standing before the throne and the Lamb; they were clothed in white robes and held palm branches in their hands. They spoke as one in a loud voice, "Salvation to our God who sits on the throne, and to the Lamb." Angels standing around the throne, the elders, and the four living beings fell on their faces worshipping God, and saying, "Amen, blessing, glory, wisdom, thanksgiving, honor, power, and might be unto God forever and ever, Amen." Then an elder asked me, "Who are these arrayed in white robes, and where did they come from?" I replied, "Sir, you know." He said to me, "These people came out of great tribulation, and have washed their robes, and made them white with the blood of the Lamb. They are before the throne of God and serve Him day and night in His temple; and He who sits on the throne lives among them. They will never be hungry, thirsty, sunburned, or exhausted, for the Lamb in the middle of the throne will feed them and lead them to fountains of living water. And God will wipe away all the tears from their eyes."

Will we recognize our loved ones in heaven? I submit that we will recognize everyone in heaven, including the apostles, prophets, patriarchs and matriarchs. How did Peter, James, and John know it was Moses and Elijah who were transfigured with Christ? They were allowed a brief glimpse through a window into heaven, where Jesus stood in all of His glory shining like a star, alongside the two great prophets in a gloried state (refer to the lesson on Transfiguration Sunday, 03/10). All of the saints will be glorified like Jesus, to inherit the kingdom of heaven.

- PSA 17:15 ~ In righteousness I will see God's face; when I awaken, I will be satisfied because I will recognize Him.

- PSA 149:1 ~ Praise the Lord, sing unto Him a new song; let the entire congregation of saints praise Him.

- MAT 17:1–3 ~ Jesus was transfigured in the presence of Peter, James, and John; His face glowed like the sun and His clothes were bright as light. Appearing and talking with Jesus were Moses and Elijah.

- ROM 8:16–17 ~ The Spirit Himself bears witness with our spirits that we are children of God; and if children then heirs of God, and equal heirs with Christ, provided we suffer with Him so that we also may be glorified with Him.

- PHP 3:21 ~ Christ will change our vile bodies into bodies like His glorified body.

Abba Father, how we look forward to being reunited with our loved ones in heaven. It will be a privilege to dialogue with Moses, Elijah, and the prophets; it will be splendid to see Mary and Joseph, and the apostles. We especially cannot wait to see you face to face, and embrace our brother Jesus. Let us always bring to mind the glory we will receive with Christ in your kingdom, whenever we feel despairing, down, fearful, or sad. Help us to bring glory to your name by praising you, the Holy Spirit, and your Son, the promise of the resurrection. In His name we pray, Amen.

November 2

National Author's Day is observed on the first day of November, to recognize people who take the time to write books, essays, poems, stories, reports, and articles which are interesting, inspirational, thought provoking, educational, historical, and/or unique. Oftentimes, writing can be hard work: it takes considerable research; fact finding and validation; imagination and creativity; proofing and editing; and resources like time, attention, and equipment. If you want to become an author, a worthwhile investment is education in composition, grammar, formatting, and language arts. Regardless, there needs to be more emphasis on literacy in general and writing in particular in the public schools; recent statistics show America to be far down on the list of nations with respect to basic proficiencies such as reading, writing, math, and science.

This holiday idea was hatched in 1928 by Nellie McPherson, president of the Illinois Women's Club. She wrote a letter to an author whose book she loved; the author replied with a signed copy of another of his works. She took her idea to the General Federation of Women's Clubs who approved her proposal the following year. The US Department of Commerce endorsed the holiday in 1949, making it official. Her granddaughter Sue Cole now carries the torch, promoting the holiday and encouraging people to write letters to their favorite authors. Note that this holiday focuses on authors, while National Book Lover's Day (08/09) focuses on books.

- JOB 19:23–26 ~ Oh that my words were written, oh that my words were printed in a book; or carved into rock to last forever. For I know that my Redeemer lives, and that He will stand upon the earth on the last day. And though my body may be consumed by worms in the grave, yet in my flesh I will see God!
- HAB 2:2 ~ Write the vision plainly on tablets so that those who read it can run with it.
- LUK 1:1–4 ~ Seeing how many have taken time to compile a narrative of the things that were accomplished among us, just as those who were eyewitnesses and ministers of the word have provided to us, it seemed fitting for me, having investigated everything carefully from the beginning, to write it out for you in chronological order, most excellent Theophilus, so you can be certain of the things you have been taught.
- ROM 15:4 ~ Everything that was written before was for our learning, so that through patience and the encouragement of the scriptures we might have hope.
- 2 TH 3:17 ~ I, Paul, have written this salutation in my own hand as a sign of genuineness in every letter I write.

Everybody that can read can also write. Start a journal or diary today; this is good mental exercise and good writing practice. List your favorite books and authors. Consider joining a book club or chat room. Search websites that sell, publish, market, or help people create written works to explore what might interest you. Renew your library card; while you're at it, see what events or exhibitions are being held at public libraries near you. Writing can be fun; do it with your kids and take turns reading aloud what everybody wrote. If you are in college, enroll in American and/or English Literature classes; this is how I got started. Find your genre, style, or application and feed it. The better you can write, the more successful you will be in academic, vocational, and social arenas. You do not have to be published to be an author; just increase your output: prose, poetry, research papers, project reports, lists, whatever. The key ingredient is thought, preferably "outside the box". Express your thoughts in a poem, story, play, history, or outline.

For more advanced activities, practice critiquing written works; try writing a critique. Discover different applications of writing (basic vs. applied research, for example). Learn about software applications and tools, imbedding book data, industry requirements, and preparing works for public consumption. These are basic steps for becoming a published author. Or, you can express yourself through artistic writing for your own enjoyment and satisfaction. People need to keep challenging themselves, and not become stagnant. Writing helps to achieve that as well as being an entertaining, educational, and therapeutic pastime.

- DEU 32:7 ~ Remember the days of old and the years of many generations; ask your father and he will show you, or ask the elders and they will teach you.

- DAN 1:17 ~ For these four young men, God gave them learning and skill in all literature and wisdom; and Daniel was able to understand visions and dreams.

- JOH 21:25 ~ There are many other things that Jesus did; it would take so many volumes of books the world could not contain them.

I started writing stories and poems at an early age. Some of my early poems became songs that I composed while in college. Meanwhile, I was taking literature classes as electives; I ended up with enough credits for a minor in English (my major was Art). In time, I honed my style and grew in my proficiency. In graduate school, I landed jobs with defense contractors producing dozens of technical repots as a research scientist; many of those reports were published by the government or contractor. Nonfiction has been my forte, I guess, but it is very time consuming, considering all the research, analysis, and homework required. But intensive study goes into every lengthy literary work. Sometimes the research is fun: looking up scriptures to fit the narrative of these holidays has been a pleasant challenge for me. In researching this book, I discovered holidays I hadn't even heard of. I had to search numerous sources to get the facts right; you would be surprised the inconsistency between the various information sources on the internet. I had to compile notes from them all until the information converged into facts.

- DEU 13:44 ~ You must inquire, probe, and investigate it thoroughly to see if it is true, and whether detestable things like idolatry are being committed among you.

- JOS 1:8 ~ This book of the Law will never leave your mouth, and you will meditate on it day and night, so you can act in accordance with all that is written therein. Then your ways will be prosperous and you will enjoy success.

- ECC 7:25 ~ I directed my mind to know the truth, to investigate matters, to seek wisdom and find answers; and to know the evil of folly and the foolishness of madness.

- ACT 10:42–43 ~ Peter preached, "Christ commanded us to preach to the people and to testify that it was He who was ordained by God to be the judge of the living and the dead. All the prophets have been witnesses, instructing that faith in Christ provides remission of sins."

- 1 CO 2:10–16 ~ God has revealed these things to us by His Spirit; for the Spirit searches everything, even the deepest things of God. These things we speak, not in the words which humanity teaches, but which the Holy Spirit teaches, comparing spiritual things with spiritual. But natural people do not receive spiritual things of God for these things are foolishness to them; neither can they know these things because they need to be discerned spiritually.

- 1 TH 5:21 ~ Examine everything carefully and hold onto that which is good.

- 2 TI 3:14–17 ~ Continue in what you have learned and are convinced of, knowing from whom you have learned it. Remember how, from the beginning, you understood the scriptures which are able to make you wise unto salvation through faith in Christ. All scripture is inspired by God. God's Word provides the doctrine of truth, refutes that which is false, and instructs all people in the ways of righteousness, so that a true follower can become thoroughly equipped for every good work.

Not to be repetitive, but my favorite author is God and my favorite book is the Holy Bible. I hope everyone will take the time to study God's Word; for I believe by the seventh reading they will agree that the Bible is the best book of all time. I developed this devotional guide to demonstrate to the reader how everything relates to God's Word, and vice-versa.

The Holy Bible is presented in a variety of genres: history, prophecy, biography, geography, genealogy, drama, adventure, science, politics, law, comedy, self-help, advice, wisdom, morality, philosophy, and so forth. The Bible is represented by a variety of styles: narrative, testimony, prose, poetry, allegory, letters, presentations, education, and revelation. Writers of the books of the Bible were told by God what to convey, though their writing styles are unique, and their identities well-established. We know who wrote New Testament books and epistles because the information is evident in the book itself; the only exception is Hebrews which is often attributed to Paul because the style is similar to his and he mentions others who were with him in Rome; perhaps those words were dictated to Paul's companions during his incarceration.

- JER 30:3–4 ~ "Write in a book all of the words that I have spoken to you. For the days are coming when I will restore the fortunes of my people Israel and Judah," says the Lord. "I will bring them back to the land I gave their fathers so they can possess it."

- JER 31:33–34 ~ The New Covenant will be this: Instead of writing my laws on stone, I will write them into the hearts of my people. They will not have to instruct others to know me, because everyone will know me, for I will forgive their sins and remove those sins forever.

- MAT 24:35 ~ Jesus said, "Heaven and earth will pass away, by my words will remain forever."

- JOH 5:37–38, 46–47 ~ Jesus said, "The Father Himself, who sent me to do these things, has been a witness for me, even though you have neither seen Him nor heard His voice. The reason you do not have His Word inside you is because you did not believe in Him who God sent. But, if you believed Moses, you would believe me, for Moses has been my witness in his writings."

- ROM 10:10, 17 ~ Those who believe with their hearts are justified. Those who confess with their lips are saved. Faith comes by hearing and hearing by the Word of God.

- 1 TH 2:13 ~ We thank God that you received His Word and accepted it as the Word of God and not the word of men. The Word of God is at work in believers like you.

- 2 PE 1:16, 21 ~ We did not follow cleverly devised fables when we told people about the power and coming of Jesus Christ, for we were eye witnesses to His majesty. No prophecy ever came from the impulse of man, but holy men spoke as they were directed by God.

- REV 1:19 ~ The angel told John, "Write down these things which you have seen, as well as those that will take place in the future."

Father, help us to use our gifts and knowledge to spread the truth of your Word and the good news of the Gospel of Jesus Christ. Give citizens and parents the strength and influence to reinstate essentials like reading and writing into public school curricula, so that the competency of our children in the basics is not ignored in favor of indoctrinating them into a secular and globalist ideology. Help our students to be conversant in the truth and able to communicate it verbally and in writing, with good speech and effective composition. Awaken this nation as a whole, so the people can see the perverse nature of those who would redefine what we stand for, clearly outlined in our founding documents: peace, justice, equality, individuality, opportunity, and morality. In the name of Jesus we pray, Amen.

November 3

Keep Your Promise Day is proposed for celebrating promises kept. Have you ever made a promise that you did not keep? I guess everyone has. I have, and I remember feeling very guilty about it, so much that I wanted to go back in time and fix it; but that was not possible. Guilt is a motivator, if it is healthy guilt. If you did something wrong and you felt guilty, that is a healthy reaction. Anyone with a conscience should feel guilt when they have gone back on their word. The guilt reminds us that God, who never goes back on His Word, is in control. Guilt motivates us to discontinue the behavior that caused the guilt and try to make amends to those we hurt.

Unhealthy guilt is another story; this is when you feel guilty for something you didn't do, or when you carry a fault endlessly without forgiving yourself. It is very difficult to make amends to someone you have not harmed, much less to yourself. A good example of unhealthy guilt is survivor's guilt; for example, a combat soldier who witnessed the fall of a comrade may feel guilty and suffer from post-traumatic stress. There is no way to resolve unearned guilt until the individual accepts that Christ has taken the guilt upon Himself. People need to know, God forgives regardless of what one has done, or not done; those accepting God's forgiveness can begin the healing process by forgiving themselves. Forgiving will come a lot easier with Christ.

- PSA 32:5 ~ I confessed my sins to God, I did not try to hide them, and He forgave me.
- PSA 130:3–4 ~ Lord, if you enumerated our sins, who could stand? But there is forgiveness with you that you may be feared.
- EZE 18:20 ~ The righteousness of a godly man will be credited to him alone, and the wickedness of an evil man will be charged only to him.
- 1 CO 4:3–5 ~ To be judged by another person is insignificant to me. In fact, I cannot judge myself because I do not know me as well as the Lord does. Therefore, do not judge anyone before the Lord returns. He will bring to light all that is hidden, even the secrets of our hearts. Then everyone will praise God.
- 2 CO 7:9–10 ~ I am glad that you were sorry for your sins and repented. Spiritual sorrow for one's sins works repentance unto salvation; but the sorrow of the world works death.
- 1 JO 1:9 ~ If we confess our sins, God is faithful and just to forgive us our sins and cleanse us from unrighteousness.

God presents promises to those who believe in Him and trust Him completely. Clearly, the greatest of God's promises is eternal life, which includes an inheritance in His kingdom. The only thing people must do to receive these gifts is believe that they will, whereas disbelief will ensure that they will not. This requires faith in God's Word, the Bible, and God's Son who is the Word in human form, whom God gave to us as an offering for the sin of the world. Christ accepted all the guilt and shame to be put on Him, setting us free of it. It is our belief in the salvation of Christ that gives us confidence in God's promises, and the hope of everlasting life with Him, without which we would not think it possible.

- DEU 4:29–31 ~ If, from this time forward, you will seek the Lord, provided you seek Him with all your heart and soul, you will find Him. If you are in tribulation, even in the later days, and you turn to God and are obedient to Him, God who is merciful will not forsake you or destroy you. God will never forget the covenant He made with your ancestors.
- ISA 64:4 ~ Since the world began, nobody has heard, seen, or perceived, except God, the wonderful things He has prepared for those who wait for Him.

- JOH 14:2–3~ Jesus said, "In my Father's house are many mansions; I go to prepare such a place for you. I will return for you, so that where I am you can be also."
- ROM 10:9 ~ If you confess with your mouth that Jesus is Lord and believe in your heart that God raised him from the dead, you will be saved.
- EPH 1:13 ~ You were included with Christ when you listened to the words of truth and believed the good news of salvation, being marked by the Holy Spirit who has guaranteed your inheritance in God's kingdom.
- TIT 1:2 ~ Our faith and knowledge rests on the hope of eternal life which God, who cannot lie, promised before the beginning of time.
- 2 PE 3:13 ~ We, according to God's promise, look for new heavens and a new earth, wherein dwells righteousness.

Once you accept the free gifts of salvation and eternal life, you must make an effort to improve. You cannot ignore your conscience or try to repress the guilt; instead, confess and repent and God will forgive you, again and again. But if you continue to commit the same sin repeatedly, then your confession will not be sincere. Because true godly sorrow comes with a promise to try harder, to obey God's will by following His Son. God gives everyone the power, strength, and motivation to become more like Christ, equipping us for works of righteousness. He empowers us to face and overcome trials, tribulation, and adversity if we invite His Holy Spirit to indwell us. With this power we can and will do better, knowing we will never reach the mark until we are welcomed into God's kingdom spotless, clothed in the righteousness of Christ.

- DEU 31:6 ~ Be strong and courageous; do not be fearful or dismayed. For the Lord God goes with you; he will never fail you or forsake you.
- JOB 14:14 ~ If a person dies, can he or she live again? All the days of my appointed time I will wait, until my change comes.
- MAT 11:28–30 ~ Jesus said, "Come to me all who are weary and burdened and I will give you rest. Take my yoke upon you and learn from me, for I am gentle and humble in heart; and you will find rest for your souls. For my yoke is easy and my burden is light."
- ROM 8:28 ~ All things work together for good to those who love God and are called according to His purpose.
- 1 CO 10:13 ~ The temptations before you are common to humanity. God is faithful and will not cause you to be tempted beyond your ability to endure, and He will always provide a way to escape the temptation.

God also promises prosperity, provision, and protection to those who remain faithful. These promises come with peace, joy, and a purpose which unbelievers cannot comprehend. Our lives are given greater meaning, direction, and importance; this equates to spiritual growth through sanctification by the Holy Spirit. The power vested by Him authorizes us to forgive sins..

- PSA 37:4–5 ~ Find your delight in the Lord and He will give to you the desires of your heart. Commit yourself to the Lord and trust in Him, and He will make your desires come to pass.
- LUK 12:8–9 ~ Jesus said, "Whoever confesses me to others, I will confess them before God and His angels; but whoever denies me to others, I will deny them before God and His angels."
- JOH 20:23 ~ If you forgive anyone's sins, they are forgiven. If you do not forgive someone's sins, they are not forgiven.

NOVEMBER

- ACT 4:21,24,31–32 ~ Finally, after several threats, the Sanhedrin released Peter and John because they couldn't decide how to punish them, and because the people were praising the Lord for enabling these men of God to heal the lame man. The apostles returned home and told everyone what had occurred. And when the people heard what had happened, they raised their voice to God with one accord, and worshipped Him saying, "Lord, you alone are God, who made heaven, earth, the sea, and all living things." After their song of prayer, the meeting place began to shake and everybody was filled with the Holy Spirit boldly speaking the words of God. And all the believers were of one heart and mind. Nobody claimed any possessions of their own, but everyone shared their possessions with one another.

- 2 CO 5:21 ~ He made Christ who knew no sin to become sin for us, so that we could receive the righteousness of God that was in Him.

- 2 TH 2:13 ~ We will give thanks to God always for you brothers, beloved of the Lord, because God chose you from the beginning to receive salvation through sanctification of the Spirit and belief in the truth.

- 1 PE 1:2–5 ~ Christians are chosen by God in advance through sanctification of the Spirit, to be obedient to Christ and cleansed by His blood. Blessed be God the Father of our Lord Jesus Christ. According to His abundant mercy, He recreated in us the living hope, brought by the resurrection of Christ from the dead, to receive an incorruptible and undefiled inheritance reserved in heaven and lasting forever. Through faith, He has shielded us by His power until the coming of our salvation which is ready to be revealed on the last day.

God will deliver on His promises each time we come to Him in prayer, often in ways that we do not realize. His answers to our prayers take the form of blessings. God wants to be our Father and give us good things; and He wants us to be His children and ask for good things. Talk to God as you would a parent and He will treat you as His own child. Be obedient to Him and He will reward you, expanding your horizons and entrusting you with greater responsibilities. We can have any good thing that we desire simply by going to our heavenly Father and asking; therefore, our response should be giving to others who ask for our help and support. By cheerfully giving ourselves, our time, our love, and our forgiveness, we are sowing seeds of faith that will expand God's kingdom through the power of the Holy Spirit.

If a person chooses not to believe, dismisses the Holy Bible, refuses to follow Christ, is not interested in being God's child or living with Him in heaven forever—well there are promises which God makes to those people too. And those promises are very bad news.

- PSA 52:5 ~ God will destroy the evil ones forever. He will uproot them from the living.

- PRO 24:20 ~ Evil people have no future. Their light will be extinguished.

- PRO 29:16 ~ The righteous will see the downfall of the wicked.

- ISA 26:14 ~ They are dead and will not live; they will not rise. They have been visited with destruction and all memory of them has been wiped out.

- OBA 1:15 ~ The day of the Lord is near for the wicked. As they have done, so shall it be done to them; it will come back upon their heads.

- MAT 25:30, 41 ~ Jesus said, "God will cast the worthless people into outer darkness where there is weeping and gnashing of teeth. They will depart into the eternal fire prepared for the devil and his angels."

- ROM 8:6–8 ~ To set the mind on the flesh results in death, but to set the mind on the Spirit results in life and peace. Because, the carnal mind is enmity against God and will not submit to God's laws, indeed it cannot. Those who are pleasing the flesh cannot please God.
- PHP 1:6 ~ The Lord who has begun a good work in you will bring it to completion until the day Christ returns.
- GAL 6:7–8 ~ Do not be deceived; for God cannot be mocked. Whatever a man sows that will he also reap. People who sow to please their sinful flesh will reap destruction. People who sow to please the Holy Spirit will reap eternal life.
- 2 TH 1:8–9 ~ God will inflict vengeance upon those who do not know Him and who do not obey the Gospel of Jesus Christ. They will suffer the punishment of eternal destruction and exclusion from the glory of the Lord.
- 2 PE 2:12 ~ These people speak blasphemously about things they know nothing about. They are like animals that cannot reason, creatures of instinct, born to be captured and destroyed.

God is able to make good on every promise, and He has made so many it is hard to keep track of them all; especially seeing how everything in the universe He created for us. We owe it to Him to be respectful and thankful. Place your trust in God and learn about His wonderful promises, extended exclusively to Christians. The world cannot make such promises, neither can it deliver the things God promises. People frequently are unable to deliver on their own promises. But if you do make a promise as in a vow, God will hold you to it; and if you do not honor that vow, there will be consequences. The Israelites lost their land because they violated a covenant with God. Or, look what happened to Samson, when he violated the oath of a Nazarite (NUM 6:1–8; JDG 13:5); but he returned to God, he was forgiven, and he completed his mission.

- LEV 5:4 ~ Anyone who vows to do something foolish, whether sincere or not, is guilty.
- NUM 30:2 ~ If you take an oath before God to do something or not to do something, you should never break that oath.
- MAT 5:34, 37 ~ Jesus said, "Do not swear oaths. To declare something with the addition of an ultimatum is the same as taking an oath. Answer people with a simple yes or no. To strengthen a promise with a vow makes it suspect."
- HEB 6:16 ~ When someone takes an oath, they are calling upon God to force them to comply and to punish them if they do not.
- JAM 5:12 ~ Do not swear by heaven or by earth, or on anything else. A simple yes or no will suffice, and you will avoid sin and condemnation.

Father, we thank you for making good on all of your promises; help us to rely on you entirely, trusting in the salvation of Christ our Lord. Let us make good on our promises and vows to you and others. Help us to avoid making empty promises or swearing to do something without giving it further thought; help us not to swear at all, especially by using your name in vain. Though we are permitted to make vows in a court of law or at the altar of the Lord, remind us not to violate that oath and enable us to correct it when we do. Forgive us when we have given our word and taken it back again; help us to stop doing that. Let us never give our word of honor and later betray that honor. Help us to follow through with our promises, oaths, and responsibilities. May we never make any foolish promises. Encourage us as we cling to your promises, patiently waiting for answers to our prayers, until the day when we will receive our inheritance as a child of the living God. In the name of Jesus, who bought for us an inheritance in heaven equal to His own, Amen.

November 4

Use Your Common Sense Day occurs on the anniversary of the birth of humorist Will Rogers (11/04/1879), who once said, "Common sense ain't common." This holiday is relatively new; it was the brainstorm of motivational speaker and author Bud Bilanich in 2015. Common sense is defined in the dictionary as practical thinking and sound judgment. Of all the species indigenous to planet earth, only humans possess this capability. Aristotle (fourth century BC) was perhaps the first to differentiate between human reasoning and animal impulses or instincts.

All too often, people do not take the time to think things over or to use discretion before jumping to conclusions; to be thoughtful rather than reactive, to weigh the available information before deciding or believing. A person with common sense will seek out and examine evidence, making an educated decision; which simply put, means they are exercising thoughtfulness. You may be familiar with the pamphlet *Common Sense* published by physician and philosopher Thomas Paine in 1776, where he posited good reasons for becoming an independent nation, which included freedom, justice, self-governance, and equality. These are good reasons to reject globalism, socialism, communism, and fascism; only the unrighteous strive for such things.

The Bible is filled with wisdom, and provides instructions concerning how to make wise judgments and informed deductions. Mainly, the Bible teaches us to think before we react, speak, or take action. If you ponder what Jesus would do in the same situation, that would be a good place to begin.

- JOB 9:2–3, 8, 10–12, 14 ~ How can a man be just under God? If one would contend with Him, they could not answer even one out of a thousand. God alone spreads out the heavens and treads upon the ocean waves. He does things beyond finding out, with wonders that cannot be numbered. He goes before me and I see nothing; He passes by and I do not perceive. He takes away and who can stop Him? Who is going to ask God, what are you doing? How should I answer God, and choose the right words to reason with Him? Even if I was righteous, I would not answer, but would make an appeal before my judge.

- JOB 21:34 ~ How can you comfort me with your nonsense, because in your answers there remains falsehood?

- PRO 3:5–6 ~ Trust in the Lord with all your heart, and do not depend on your own understanding. In all things acknowledge Him and He will direct you in the right path.

- PRO 8:1, 14, 32–33 ~ I, wisdom, call to you. Counsel and sound judgment are mine; I understand all things and I have great power. Listen my children, for blessed are those who keep my ways. Listen to instruction and be wise; do not despise wisdom.

- PRO 14:30 ~ A sound mind gives life to the flesh, but envy rots the bones.

- PRO 14:33 ~ Wisdom abides in the minds of those with understanding, but it is not known in the minds of fools.

- PRO 15:28 ~ The mind of the righteous ponders how to answer, but the mouth of the wicked pours out evil.

- ECC 7:12, 25 ~ Wisdom is a defense, and money is a defense; but wisdom gives life to those who possess it. I applied my heart to know, to search, and to seek wisdom, and the reasons for things, and to know the wickedness of folly, foolishness, and madness.

- ISA 43:26 ~ Review the past; let us argue the matter together. State your case so that you may be proven innocent.

- 1 TI 6:7 ~ We brought nothing into this world and we can bring nothing out of it.

    Wisdom in the Holy Bible, is the only source of available truth coming directly from the mouth of God. We are reminded to turn to God for counsel and advice when faced with a dilemma or a risky situation that we must face. We also are reminded to collaborate with other Christians and not seek answers exclusively from people possessing only worldly wisdom.

- EXO 23:1–3 ~ Do not present a false report or present a wicked person to testify maliciously. Do not go along with the crowd in doing wrong. When you testify, do not support an evil cause to displace judgment.

- PRO 13:16 ~ A prudent person acts with knowledge, but a fool flaunts his folly.

- ISA 41:21–23 ~ Present your case and bring strong evidence, says the Lord. Let your idols tell us what will happen in the future. You are less than nothing, and your works are meaningless; whoever follows you is detestable.

- MAT 7:14 ~ Straight is the gate and narrow the way leading to life, and not many will find it.

- JOH 7:24 ~Do not judge according to appearance but judge with righteous judgment.

- LUK 10:16 ~ Those who listen to my disciples whom I have sent will listen to me; whoever rejects those who I have sent reject me. And those who reject me reject Him who sent me."

- ROM 12:16–21 ~ Be of the same mind one toward another. Do not be high-minded, but humble yourself before others, even those of low estate. Do not pretend to be wise in your own conceit. Do not recompense evil for evil. Always be honest in all things. Live peaceably with all people. Do not seek revenge when someone has done you wrong but rather hold back your wrath. For it is written: Vengeance is mine; I will repay, says the Lord. Therefore, if your enemy is hungry, feed him; if he is thirsty, give him a drink. In doing so you heap hot coals upon his head. Do not be overcome with evil, but overcome evil with goodness.

- ROM 16:25–26 ~ Christ has the power to save you according to the revelation of God's mystery, which was kept secret since the world began but which is now evident by the scriptures. According to God's will the mystery is made known to all nations on earth for the obedience of faith.

- 1 CO 15:33 ~ Do not be deceived; bad company corrupts good character.

- 1 TI 4:2–5 ~ Preach the Word; be prepared to correct, rebuke, and encourage with patience and sound doctrine. For the time will come when people will turn away from sound doctrine and pursue their own lusts, finding teachers that say what they want to hear. They will wander from the truth and rely on myths. Be watchful, willing to endure afflictions, doing the work of the evangelist, and whatever is necessary for the continuance of the ministry.

    Heavenly Father, help us to think things through before we act or respond; help us to be thorough in collecting evidence so we can make calculated decisions. Let us be vigilant and observant, assessing information from the context of the situation and from others who are present. Remind us that you are there, for your Holy Spirit is eager to listen and advise. Let us not ally with people whose intentions are evil, who invent evidence, who produce false witnesses, who bring false charges, who strive to upend justice, who refuse to listen to reason. Protect us from those people who would try to take us down or destroy our reputation when we do not agree with them. In the meantime, equip us with the power and wisdom to remain steadfast in the faith, and to be ready to give an answer to those who question the truth of your Word, or who sincerely want to know about our hope and joy that come from your promises. In the name of Jesus we pray, Amen.

November 5

Election Day is the Tuesday after the first Monday in November (November 2 to November 8), established by Congress in 1845 as the official day for national, and many state and local elections. At the end of election day, voting ceases and the tallies of popular and electoral votes are counted. Fair elections provide the opportunity for citizens to select who should govern via the democratic process; that is, the electorate gets to pick who will represent us in office in accordance with the will of the constituency. This was most eloquently stated by President Lincoln in his Gettysburg Address: "That this nation, under God, shall have a new birth of freedom, and that government of the people, by the people, for the people, shall not perish from the earth." Amen to that, Mr. President.

Whether you vote for a conservative or a liberal; whether you consider yourself a Democrat, Republican, Libertarian, Independent or whatever; regardless of your demographics or other individual proclivities, you should always vote your conscience. This is the part of you that knows right from wrong, good from evil. And how did you acquire that knowledge? It was endowed upon you by God; your conscience is the reservoir of certain truths, some of which were planted there by the Holy Spirit. Personally, I dislike politicians who consistently lie. I'm sure they all have lied at some point, who hasn't? But there are professional liars out there who do not deserve your vote; this requires one to fact check everything being put out. Research multiple sources and see if there is any divergence. Even then, you should check it against what the Holy Bible says, the final arbiter of truth; it is the only source that we always can rely upon. Unfortunately, it is not the media and certainly not the internet that we should be trusting.

In olden days, God chose rulers, kings, prophets, and priests; Christ selected apostles. God also appoints us to be disciples and carry on His message of truth. It is reasonable that we select the kind of people God would choose: honest, upright, faithful, loyal, kind, truthful, trustworthy. That should narrow the field considerably. It would be nice if God would choose our leaders, selecting people that love Him above all, who love this country and its people, and who love all humankind. God chooses His elect; if you choose God, you are included. He chooses you to be His children and to live in heaven with Him and our brother Jesus Christ.

- ISA 65:9 ~ God will bring forth a seed from Jacob and Judah; then my elect will inherit the mountains of the Holy Land.

- ISA 65:22–24 ~ God says, "They will not build houses for someone else to live in; they will not plant crops for others to eat; for my elect will enjoy the fruits of their labor. They will not labor in vain or produce fruit for nothing, for they are my offspring. When they call, I answer; when they speak, I hear."

- JER 2:2–5 ~ The Lord said to Jerusalem through the prophet, I remember how you were kind in your youth, how you loved me like a wife. Israel was holy to the Lord and represented the first fruits of His increase, when you followed Him into the wilderness. Those who try to destroy God's elect will have evil and disaster come upon them. The Lord wonders, what fault did your fathers see in me that you would leave me for your vanities?

- DAN 12:2 ~ God's elect will be delivered, all whose names are written in the Book of Life.

- MAT 24:31 ~ Jesus said, "At the great sound of the trumpet, God will send His angels to gather His elect together from the four winds and from one end of heaven to the other."

- MAR 13:22, 27 ~ Jesus said, "False prophets and antichrists will come, showing signs and miracles, to deceive even the elect if they could. God will send His angels to gather His elect from everywhere, even the outermost parts of the earth and the heavens."

- LUK 18:7–8 ~ Will God not avenge His elect, who plead with Him day and night, when He feels it is the right time? However, when the Son of God returns, will He find such a persistent faith on the earth?

- ROM 11:7–8 ~ The Israelites did not find what they were looking for; but God's elect found it. Thus it is written, "They have eyes that do not see and ears that do not hear."

- EPH 1:3–7 ~ Praise to God, the Father of our Lord Jesus Christ, who has chosen us before the foundation of the world to be holy and blameless before Him in love. We were destined to be God's adopted children, in accordance with His good will and grace, through Jesus Christ, in whom we have redemption and forgiveness through His blood.

- COL 3:12 ~ As God's elect, holy and blessed, we should be merciful, kind, humble, meek, and patient.

- 2 TI 2:10 ~ Therefore, I endure all things for the elect's sake, that they also may obtain the salvation which is in Christ Jesus with eternal glory.

- 1 PE 1:2 ~ You have been chosen in advance by God the Father, and sanctified by His Holy Spirit, through the shedding of the blood of His Son Jesus Christ, to whom you have become obedient. May God bless you with His abundant grace and peace.

Do you want to be elected? I'm not talking about running for office, I'm talking about running in the human race and winning. What do you have to do to win? Vote for Jesus Christ.

- ISA 40:31 ~ Those who wait on the Lord will be renewed in their strength. They will mount up with wings of eagles; they will run and not tire, and walk and not faint.

- HEB 12:1–3 ~ Since we are being watched by numerous spectators, let us discard everything that hinders us such as the sin that trips us up, and run the race that has been set before us with perseverance. Let us fix our eyes on Jesus, the author and perfecter of our faith, who for the joy set before Him endured the cross, scorning its shame, and who now sits on His throne at the right hand of God. Remember Him, who endured great opposition from sinful men, so that you will not grow faint and lose heart.

- 2 TI 4:6–8 ~ I am ready to sacrifice myself as my time of departure is near. I have fought a good fight and I have finished the race, and my faith is still intact. Hereafter a crown of righteousness awaits me, which the Lord, the righteous judge, will give to me. He will give it, not only to me, but also to everyone who lovingly awaits Christ's coming.

- 2 PE 1:2–4 ~ Grace and peace be multiplied to you through the knowledge of God, and of Jesus our Lord. His divine power has given us everything we need for life and righteousness through our knowledge of Him who called us by His own glory and goodness. He has given us His very great and precious promises, so that through them we may participate in the divine nature and escape the corruption of this world and its evil desires.

Dear Father, Abba Father, to your altar we come in prayer. We pray for our leaders and all who are in authority, that they would hear the voice of your Holy Spirit and be moved to speak and write; to legislate, execute and uphold your laws and the moral laws of our nation, its citizenry, and the world population. All peoples, tongues, tribes, and territories need to hear your voice, Father, who controls all things from the beginning to the end, and before and after, and hereafter for those who hear and perceive. May we dwell in your house as a family, along with the hosts of heaven. There is plenty of work left to be done; please send workers and advisors, for the harvest of lost souls is plentiful, as are the wayward rulers that must be brought down. May we overcome, even as Christ has overcome the world and its sin. In His name we pray, Amen.

November 6

National Stress Awareness Day is observed on the first Wednesday of the month. This holiday was introduced by Carole Spiers, founder of the International Stress Management Association (ISMA) in 1998 to further the cause of stress reduction, management, and awareness. Stress causes anxiety, which is the number one mental health problem in the USA; anxiety can be linked to a number of physical maladies like heart disease, hypertension, headaches, and exhaustion. Anxiety is an affective disorder; like depression it creates a disturbance in emotions and mood. Many people treated for anxiety problems also suffer from depression, for both are affective in nature and interrelated. A primary symptom of affective disorders is worrying, but then again, who doesn't worry? The opposite of is peace of mind. Both anxiety and peace are states of mind, meaning they are temporal, unlike traits that are persistent (such as personality traits). Inner peace is greater in power and can therefore defeat anxiety and stress triggered by external factors.

- PSA 119:165 ~ Those who love God's Law have great peace; nothing can make them stumble.

- ISA 26:3–6 ~ Those people whose minds are focused on God and trust in Him will be kept in perfect peace. Trust in Jehovah forever for an everlasting covenant. He will bring down the lofty city and those who live up high, and lay them all down low.to the ground, into the dust. They will be trampled underfoot, with the tracks of the poor and needy.

- LUK 1:79 ~ Jesus came to give light to those who are in darkness or in the shadow of death, and to guide us in the way of peace.

- JOH 14:27 ~ Jesus said, "Peace I leave you; my peace I give you; I do not give as the world gives, so never let your hearts be troubled or afraid."

- JOH 16:33 ~ Jesus said, "I have told you that I will bring you peace. In the world you will have tribulation; but be happy because I have overcome the world."

- ROM 8:6 ~ To set the mind on the flesh results in death, but to set the mind on the Spirit results in life and peace.

We get stressed when we are under pressure from work, school, home, and/or many other situations or circumstances, be they separation or loss, social or geopolitical, medical or spiritual, behavioral or performance related. Extreme reactions to stressful thoughts or events include panic disorder, obsessive-compulsive disorder, and post-traumatic stress disorder. People with anxiety and depression disorders can get some relief from anxiolytics (anti-anxiety medication) like benzodiazepines (Valium, Paxil, Ativan, Xanax, Clonazepam) or from antidepressants, most of which tweak serotonin, a neurotransmitter in the brain; some medications tweak multiple neurotransmitters. There are many other types of medications which I won't get into but you can look them up if you are interested (tricyclics, beta blockers, MAO inhibitors).

Everyone has to deal with multiple stressors at times; we get anxious, mostly because we want the situation to pass or end. We get impatient and sometimes try to force the issue when it would be better not to react. A person suffering from a serious anxiety disturbance may have a tendency to react emotionally; the most common responses to their fears are fight, flight, and freeze. The person wants to get away so they run from the situation; others will freeze in their tracks, still others will fight like mad. Obviously, none of these are rational responses because the person has retreated into the emotional region of the brain. It is very difficult to be reasonable and emotional at the same time. Reason occurs in the prefrontal cortex of the brain; emotion occurs in the limbic system (especially the amygdala and hypothalamus) which is a deeper area in the brain. The limbic system is where habitual fear responses are initiated, producing an automatic emotional reaction to a situational trigger or memory.

- PRO 12:20 ~ Deceit is in the heart of those who imagine evil things; but for the counselors of peace there is joy.

- PSA 37:7 ~ Find solace in the Lord and wait patiently for Him. Do not worry about evil people who prosper.

- JOH 1:33 ~ Jesus said, "I have told you these things so you can have peace. In the world you will have tribulation, but be of good cheer for I have conquered the world."

- ROM 15:13 ~ May the God of hope fill you with joy and peace through trusting Him, so you may abound in hope with the power of the Holy Spirit.

- EPH 4:3 ~ Maintain unity of the Spirit in the bond of peace.

- PHP 4:6–9 ~ Do not be anxious about anything but pray for everything. With thanksgiving let your requests be known to God. And the peace of God that surpasses all understanding will keep your hearts and minds in Jesus Christ.

- HEB 12:14 ~ Strive for peace with everyone, and for holiness; for without these things, nobody can see the Lord.

- JAM 1:3 ~ You learn patience when your faith is tested.

Stress and anxiety can be triggered by fear, anger, feeling trapped, and certain incidental conditions which are perceived to be present but not necessarily are. The best way to help loved ones who are anxious is to respond to them with a positive emotional response such as caring, loving, and nurturing, until their negative emotional reaction subsides and they can respond with reason again. Ways of coping and calming include relaxation and breathing exercises, meditation and visual imagery, yoga or exercise, massage, hot bath/shower, and a period of rest, or sleep. Taking a prescribed anxiolytic may help; sometimes these medications are taken daily, other times they can be taken on an as-needed basis. Certainly, one should never exceed the daily dosage because these medications can be habit forming; plus, they should never be taken in conjunction with alcohol or opiates, which can be deadly. Regardless, do not self-medicate.

- EXO 33:14 ~ The Lord said, "My presence will go with you and I will give you rest."

- PSA 4:8 ~ I will lie down in peace and sleep; for you, Lord, make me abide in safety.

- PSA 131:2 ~ Surely, I have calmed and quieted myself; like a weaned child with its mother is my soul within me.

- PSA 27:1 ~ The Lord is my light and my salvation, who else should I fear? The Lord is the strength of my life, of whom will I be afraid?

- PRO 3:24 ~ When you lie down you will not be afraid; yes, you will lie down and your sleep will be sweet.

- PRO 12:25 ~ Anxiety weighs down the heart but a kind word gladdens the heart.

- MAR 6:31 ~ Jesus said, "Many people are coming and going, let us depart to a private place and rest for a while."

- 2 CO 4:16–17 ~ Therefore, we do not lose heart; though outwardly we are wasting away, inwardly we are renewed every day. For our momentary troubles are achieving for us an eternal glory that far outweighs them.

The best treatment for stress is trusting in God to help us through the emotional phase. Prayer and spiritual meditation enable us to connect to the Holy Spirit who is the great Comforter.

He is the source of peace, whereas Jesus is the Prince of Peace. Certainly, mental health counseling should be considered; as a clinician I also incorporated spirituality during counseling if the client approved. Studies show that faith-based approaches used in combination with cognitive-behavioral therapy (CBT) were as good and sometimes better than CBT alone in producing a positive treatment outcome in a shorter time period. Thus, it is very effective in brief therapy. Ultimately, the comfort we get from the Holy Spirit is far more effective in the long run.

- DEU 31:6, 8 ~ Be strong and courageous, do not worry or be afraid; for the Lord your God is with you. He will never fail you or forsake you. Fear not and do not be dismayed.

- PSA 50:15 ~ Call upon God in the day of trouble, and you will be delivered, and you will glorify God.

- PSA 94:19 ~ When anxious thoughts overwhelm me, God's comfort gives my soul renewed joy.

- PSA 119:76 ~ Lord, I pray that your merciful kindness will be my comfort, according to your promise.

- MAT 6:25–34 ~ Jesus said, "Do not be anxious about your life, and do not worry about your next meal or what to wear. Look at the birds. They do not sow or reap but God feeds them just the same. Look at the lilies. They do not work or worry but Solomon himself was not clothed in such beauty. Are you not more important to God than birds or flowers? So do not worry about these things, because God knows that you need them. Besides, will being anxious about tomorrow add anything to your life? Seek first the kingdom of heaven and the righteousness of God, and all these things will be added unto you. Do not worry about tomorrow, because each day has enough trouble of its own. Let tomorrow worry about itself."

- MAR 4:19 ~ The worries of this world, the deceitfulness of riches, and the desire for other things enter a person and choke the Word, rendering it unfruitful.

Remember, spiritual powers are higher powers, and can defeat the negativity: peace defeats stress, joy defeats depression, love defeats fear, hope defeats despair. You do not need to be a therapist to help your loved one who is suffering from undesirable, self-destructive thoughts which are usually untrue. Truth is another great spiritual power which defeats self-deception. If people think they are worthless, tell them how precious they are to you, and to God (JER 31:3; JOH 3:16). If people think they are helpless, tell them they can do anything through Christ who strengthens them (JOB 42:4; PHP 4:13). If they feel hopeless, tell them that there is always hope due to the sacrifice of Jesus Christ (HEB 6:19; PSA 71:14).

Most merciful Father, we pray for all who suffer from stress, anxiety, depression, and despair; from hopelessness, helplessness, and worthlessness. Help them to find peace, joy, and love in your Word and through the comfort of the Holy Spirit who is always present. Help us to recognize when others are down or stressed, and provide comfort to them with the comfort that we ourselves have received from the Holy Spirit. Let us turn to you whenever we are feeling down, so we can be lifted up. Fill us with your truth which will defeat the negative self-messages that are untrue. Help us to remember that we are so important to you that you sent your Son Jesus to die for us. We pray these things in His name, Amen.

November 7

Lewis and Clark Spotted the Pacific Ocean for the first time on this date in 1805, arriving on the beach four days later. These military men were commissioned by President Jefferson, who persuaded Congress to agree to purchase the Louisiana territory from the French for $15 million in 1803; immediately, he wanted to explore these lands which extended west of the Mississippi River. The two trailblazers were fully equipped with supplies, horses, and forty-five men. The expedition experienced harsh terrain, raging rivers, extreme weather, hostile natives, pesky insects, starvation and disease. They also encountered some friendly natives, many of whom were very helpful to them, most notably a pregnant Shoshone woman named Sacagawea who joined their party as a guide and interpreter. They completed their mission in less than 2.5 years, traveling some 8000 miles by foot and boat, returning with journals, geographic and terrain maps, plant and animal specimens, seeds, information on Indian tribes (friendly and unfriendly), and no casualties.

Once again, one could argue that Providence was with this expedition. The Lord's blessing has been evident on many such occasions while this nation has evolved and grown. Through severe conditions and taxing mental and physical strain, Lewis and Clark traveled over half the continent and back in record time. One skirmish with Indians stealing horses and supplies resulted in two Indians being killed; that was the extent of any bloodshed. Contrast that with explorations by the Spanish conquistadors who massacred native Americans by the thousands. It is surprising that the Indians allowed any invasions into their land. A lot of them paid for it when they did. Let's hope God doesn't retract His protection on the USA, or lift His hand against us, due to our infidelity towards Him.

This brings to mind some of the great sojourners of the Bible such as Abraham. Here was a man, living in a land of pagans with multiple false gods, who earnestly sought the Lord. He was an upright man and spoke to God often, as He commands that we all do. Abraham was a man after God's own heart, trusting God always. When God told him to pack up and leave for a land that God would show him, he did not hesitate. He likely would have taken a route over the fertile crescent making the trip from Ur to Haran and then to Canaan (about a thousand miles give or take). What if you were in your mid-seventies, and received a directive from God to pack up and leave your home for a foreign country, and all you had were a few camels, some rations, supplies, bedding, and a handful of companions? Well, I guess times were different in Abraham's day; plus, he had an advantage, being the sole God-fearing man in the territory. Nevertheless, it took a lot of courage, not to mention mental, physical, and spiritual toughness.

- GEN 11:31—GEN 12:1–7 ~ Terah took his son Abram and grandson Lot (from Abram's brother Haran), and Abram's wife Sarai and left the land of Ur for the land of Canaan. They came to the village where Haran used to live and settled there until Abram's father died. Then the Lord said to Abram, "Leave your country and your kinfolk for a land that I will show you, and I will make you a great nation. I will bless you and make your name great; and you will be a blessing to others. I will bless those who bless you and curse those who curse you. And in you, all nations of the world will be blessed." So, Abram and Sarai departed as the Lord requested, and Lot went with them. Abram was seventy-five years old when he departed from Haran. Abram took his wife, his nephew, supplies, and some associates, and left Haran for the land of the Canaanites. When he arrived, the Lord appeared to Abram and said, "I will give this land to your seed." And Abram built an altar to the Lord.

- GEN 15:1–3 ~ God told Abraham in a vision, "Do not be afraid, because I will be your shield, and I will reward you for your faith." Abraham replied that he remained childless, and had no seed or heir. God said he would have an heir, and his seed would number as great as the stars.

NOVEMBER

In the New Testament we have the episode of Joseph and Mary, called to their city of origin for a Roman census in order to be taxed. They had to travel by donkey when Mary was very pregnant; it's almost one hundred miles from Nazareth to Bethlehem. There she gave birth to the baby Jesus in a stable with farm animals. Soon thereafter, they had to flee to Egypt because Herod was out to kill them; that's over four hundred miles. Once Herod had died, they traveled back to Nazareth which is another two hundred miles. Of course, the Lord was with them, in more ways than one, since their first child was the Son of God.

- PSA 80:8–17 ~ The vine, God's right hand, the Son of man who God has made strong for Himself, will be called out of Egypt, and He will be cut down. (Reference to the flight to Egypt to avoid Herod's decree, and the subsequent death of Christ: see MAT 2:13–15).

- JER 31:15 ~ In Ramah was heard the bitter weeping and mourning over the children who were killed. (Reference to Herod's failed attempt to kill the Christ child by butchering babies: see MAT 2:16–18).

- MIC 5:2–4 ~ Oh Bethlehem, you are such a small village but will be the birthplace of my king, who has been foretold from time eternal. God will forget Israel until the time has come for the chosen woman to bear the child; then the children of Israel will return. The Son will stand for and feed off the Lord, and will share His majesty. The children shall live in Him who is great, even to every corner of the earth.

- MAT 2:1–18 ~ Jesus was born in Bethlehem of Judea in the days of Herod the king. Wise men came from the east to Jerusalem asking Herod, "Where is He who is born king of the Jews? From the east we have seen His star and we have come to worship Him." Herod gathered together the chief priests and scribes, demanding to know where the Messiah would be born. They replied that it would be Bethlehem of Judea, for it was written, "Bethlehem is not insignificant among the cities of Judea, for from there will come a governor who will rule my people, Israel." After leaving Herod, the wise men followed the star. Finally, they stood directly under it. They found the young Christ child with Mary, His mother, and worshipped Him. They opened their treasures and presented to Him gifts of gold, frankincense, and myrrh. The angel of God told Joseph in a dream to take his family to Egypt to escape Herod's evil decree to kill all the male toddlers in Bethlehem. They stayed in Egypt until after Herod died, thereby fulfilling the prophecy: Out of Egypt God has called His Son. Herod killed all the babies in Bethlehem who were two years old and younger. This fulfilled the prophecy of Jeremiah (quoted above).

- LUK 2:4–5, 10–11, 15–16~ Joseph took his pregnant wife Mary from the city of Nazareth in Galilee to the city of David which is called Bethlehem, because he was a descendant of David; it was there that he and his family were to be taxed by the Romans. The angel said to the shepherds, "Do not be afraid because I bring you tidings of great joy which shall be for all people; for Christ the Savior is born today in the city of David." After the angels left, the shepherds said to each other, "Let us go to Bethlehem and see this great miracle which the Lord has made known to us." They hurried to Bethlehem and found Mary and Joseph, and the baby lying in a manger.

Heavenly Father, we pray for the faith of Abraham, and to hold onto that saving faith. Help us to be ready to go where you want, and do what you need done there. Give us the courage to carry out your will without hesitation, trusting always in your Son, and not worrying about how we are performing, because you are giving us the skill and resources to succeed. Please do not retract your protection of our country, or lift your hand against us, but let us be faithful unto you and continue forward with the mission until our time is up. In Jesus's name, Amen.

November 8

Rontgen Discovered the X-Ray on 11/09/1895, lifting medical science to a new level. Diagnosis and treatment were enhanced by making the inside of the patient visible when exposing it to high frequency light waves. Certain things would show up clearly, particularly bones, tumors, stones, and bullets. Still, it was yet to be understood the danger of radiation from x-rays. Rontgen never patented his discovery but donated the technology in the interest of medical science. He received the first Nobel Prize in physics in 1901 and donated the prize money to the University of Wurzburg. He is considered the father of diagnostic radiology. His name has been memorialized in the measurement of ionization caused by radioactive decay, which is used to quantify the dose of radiation when exposed to human tissue.

The Bible tells us that the universe was made from things we cannot see. Physicists suggest that particles, electromagnetic waves, dark matter, and many other invisible qualities exist in our universe. Of the entire electromagnetic spectrum, naturally visible waves constitute but a small fraction on the continuum, which falls between infrared (below red) and ultraviolet (above violet) on the spectrum: in other words, wavelengths between 750 nanometers (red) to 380 nanometers (violet) are visible light, with red light being much slower in frequency than violet, which is shorter in wavelength. Since the colors of light vary in frequency, they are refracted at different angles, which is why you see all the colors in order (red, orange, yellow, green, blue, indigo, violet) when light passes through a prism; the same phenomenon occurs when sunlight passes through water droplets producing a rainbow.

- GEN 9:12–17 ~ The rainbow will be a reminder of the everlasting covenant between God and all living things upon the earth, that He will never again send a flood to destroy the earth.

- EZE 1:26–28 ~ Above the firmament was a throne appearing as sapphire and a man sat upon it. The color of amber engulfed it as a fire, and the man's legs were as fire. A rainbow encircled it. The vision was in the likeness of the glory of the Lord. When I saw it, I fell to my face; and then the man spoke. [God was about to call Ezekiel to be His prophet (EZE 2).]

- REV 4:2–3 ~ I was taken up in spirit and saw a throne set in heaven, and one sitting on the throne. The throne appeared as stones of jasper and ruby, and the throne was surrounded by a rainbow that shown like an emerald.

- REV 10:1 ~ I saw a mighty angel descend from heaven, clothed in a cloud with a rainbow upon his head; his face shone like the sun, and his feet were pillars of fire.

The universe consists of a great many invisible qualities. In many cases we cannot see them, but we can observe their effects. Like x-rays, you cannot see them; but they will burn you if not employed properly by a certified technician. X-rays are considerably higher in frequency than ultraviolet; the highest frequency wavelengths are gamma rays. Slower waves on the spectrum include microwaves, radio waves, broadband, and alternating current (electrical circuits). Clearly, the shorter the wavelength (e.g., higher the frequency) the more damage it can do to human tissue; long term exposure is hazardous to your health for all frequencies above and including ultraviolet.

- PRO 24:20 ~ Evil people have no future. Their light will be extinguished.

- JOH 3:8 ~ Jesus said, "The wind blows wherever it wants; and you can hear it but you cannot see it or tell where it has come from or where it is going. It is the same with those who are born of the Spirit."

- ROM 1:18–21 ~ God's wrath is revealed from heaven against the sinfulness of people, who know the truth of unrighteousness, because God made it known to them. The invisible qualities of God are clearly seen from the creation of the world, for through His many creations one can understand God, even His power and divine nature, so nobody has an excuse. Though they knew of God they did not glorify Him, neither were they thankful; instead, they became vain in their imaginations and their foolish hearts were darkened.

- 2 CO 4:18 ~ We do not focus on the things we can see, but on the things that we cannot see; for the things we can see are temporal, but the things we cannot see are eternal.
- 2 CO 11:13–14 ~ Beware of false and deceitful prophets who claim to be from Christ, for even Satan disguises himself as an angel of light.
- EPH 5:13 ~ But everything exposed by the light becomes visible for all to see, for it is light that makes things visible.
- COL 1:15–17 ~ Christ is the very image of the invisible God. He created all things on heaven and earth, visible and invisible whether thrones, dominions, rulers, or authorities. All things were created through Him. He is before all things, and He holds all things together.
- 1 TI 1:17 ~ All glory and honor belong now and forever to our eternal, immortal, and invisible King, who is the only wise God.
- HEB 11:1–3 ~ Faith is the assurance of things hoped for, the evidence of things not seen. By faith we understand that the world was created by the Word of God, such that things we see were made from things which do not appear.

Light is the most powerful physical phenomenon known to humankind. Furthermore, God is light; in Him there is no darkness. Jesus is the light of life, who offers us eternal life so that our light can never be extinguished. Thus, His light lives in us, and we can shine that light for others to see, which will shed light on the way to heaven which is Christ. Spiritual light, while it is invisible, creates an effect that one can see; like wind that we cannot see though it can wreak havoc.

- GEN 1:2–5 ~ Darkness covered the earth and God commanded there to be light, and He saw that the light was good, and He separated the light from the darkness.
- ISA 3:9 ~ It shows on their faces that they are guilty; they declare their sin like Sodom, they do not hide it. Woe unto their souls for they have recompensed evil unto themselves.
- ISA 60:1–2 ~ Arise and shine, for your light has come; yes, the glory of God has come to you. Darkness covers the earth and great darkness covers its people. But the Lord will arise and come to you, and you will see His glory. And the Gentiles will come to His light, and kings will come to the brightness of His rising.
- MAT 5:14–16 ~ Jesus said to His followers, "You are the light of the world; a city on a hill cannot be hidden. A person does not light a candle and cover it, but places it on a candlestick so it will light the house. Let your light shine before others, so they can see your goodness, and glorify our Father in heaven."
- MAT 6:23 ~ Jesus said, "If your eye is not sound, your whole body will be full of darkness. So, if the light within you is darkness, how great is that darkness."
- LUK 11:35–36 ~ Jesus said, "Be careful, so that the light in you does not become darkness. If your whole body is full of light and has no darkness, it will be wholly bright as when a lamp with its rays gives light."
- JOH 8:12 ~ Jesus said, "I am the light of the world; those who follow me will not walk in darkness, but will have the light of life."

- 2 CO 4:6 ~ God commanded light to shine out of darkness. This same light shines in our hearts and radiates that light through the knowledge of Jesus Christ.

- EPH 5:8–14 ~ You were once in darkness, but now you are in the light of the Lord. Live as children of light and discover what pleases the Lord, for the fruit of the light consists of goodness, righteousness, and truth. Have nothing to do with the fruitless deeds of darkness, but rather expose them. For it is shameful even to mention what the disobedient do in secret. But everything exposed by the light becomes visible for all to see, for it is light that makes things visible. This is what is meant by the saying, "Wake up you sleepers; rise from the dead and Christ will shine on you."

- 1 PE 2:9 ~ You are a chosen generation, a royal priesthood, a holy nation, a unique people. So, praise Him who has called you out of darkness into his marvelous light.

- 1 JO 1:5 ~ God is light; in Him is no darkness at all.

- REV 22:5 ~ There will be no night, no need for a candle or the light of the sun, for the Lord God will provide the light; and His people will reign with Him forever and ever.

The electromagnetic spectrum is an interesting phenomenon; each partition provides a special capability, such as vision, television and radio, microwave ovens, electrical circuits, decontamination, lasers, and x-rays. We hear and see different wave patterns that our brain deciphers to describe the environment, giving us perception. Try to imagine all of the things going on around you that you cannot see, hear, or perceive.

- ISA 6:9–10 ~ God told Isaiah, "Go and speak to your people. They will hear but will not understand; they will see but will not perceive. For their heart is fat, and it makes their eyes heavy. They shut their eyes and ears so they cannot see or hear, and therefore they cannot understand in their heart, become converted, and be healed."

- ISA 64:4 ~ Since the world began, nobody has heard, seen, or perceived, except God, the wonderful things He has prepared for those who wait for Him.

- MAT 13:10–17 ~ The disciples asked Jesus why he spoke in parables. Jesus replied, "You know the mysteries of the kingdom but others are not so lucky. I speak to them in parables because they have eyes but do not watch and they have ears but do not listen. In them the prophecy of Isaiah is fulfilled: Their hearts have hardened; they hear but do not understand; they see but do not perceive. They have closed their eyes and ears so they cannot understand with their heart and become converted. You are blessed because your eyes and ears are open to me. Many people have longed to hear and see what you have heard and seen."

- 1 CO 2:9 ~ It is written: Nobody has ever heard or seen, or even imagined, the wonderful things God has prepared for those who love Him.

Omniscient Father, how amazing is your creation. We can only begin to understand the part we can perceive with our five senses, much less the part we cannot see or sense. We cannot even imagine heaven, for it will be greater and better than anything we have ever perceived; there is nothing on this planet or in this universe that can help us to describe it but we know it will be more wonderful and amazing than anything imaginable. We praise you, awesome Father, and your Son who enlightens us, and your Spirit who teaches us things that can only be ascertained within our own spirits. Help us to stay connected to you in spirit and in truth, so that we can know your perfect will and obey, with help from the Spirit of Christ living in our hearts. In His name, Amen.

November 9

World Freedom Day commemorates the destruction of the Berlin Wall which began on this day in 1989. President Reagan urged Russian premier Gorbachev to tear down the wall in 1987; he got his wish less than two years later. By 1991 the Soviet Union was essentially dismantled by Gorbachev; this event ended the cold war which lasted some forty years. World Freedom Day became a national holiday in 2001, during the presidency of G. W. Bush. It was a major blow to communism in Europe, setting East Germany free after over twenty years of oppression. For more information take a look at the lesson for August 13, describing the building of the Berlin Wall in 1961.

I could think of dozens of ways to celebrate this day, but I will leave that up to the reader. Certainly, every day is a good day to contemplate how great it is to live in a free country. There are many nations that do not celebrate this day because the people are not free, mostly communist dictatorships. Our freedoms are spelled out in the founding documents. Many of these freedoms are designated as unalienable, seeing how they were endowed upon humanity by God Himself. Most important are the freedoms of life, liberty, and the pursuit of happiness enumerated in the Declaration of Independence. It is a deadly sin to the Lord our God to deny these basic rights to anyone. The Constitution and the Bill of Rights explicitly state many other rights assured to US citizens: freedom of religion, speech, the press, and to bear arms; to not have your home commandeered; to not be put in double jeopardy, to not be denied due process of the law; to have legal representation and a trial by jury; also, freedom from cruel and unusual punishment, freedom from slavery, equal protection under the law; freedom from discrimination, and freedom to vote your conscience. The only way to lose any of these rights is to violate the laws associated with them. There are valid restrictions on these rights so that they are not abused or used to take advantage of others who have the same rights. Beware of governments who want to restrict these rights, whether endowed by God or guaranteed under our Constitution.

- GAL 5:13 ~ Brothers, you have been called to be free men, but do not use that freedom as an excuse to engage in lusts of the flesh, but in love serve one another.

- 2 TH 3:1 ~ Pray for Christian teachers and ministers, and pray for the freedom to openly speak God's Word.

- 1 PE 2:13–17 ~ Submit to the laws of the land, for it is God's will that you are lawful and upright, thereby silencing those ignorant people who would talk behind your back. Be free, but do not use your freedom to conceal evil. Instead, you must serve the Lord, respect all people, love your fellow Christians, fear God, and honor those in authority.

All people of every nation have the free will to seek, love, and obey God to the best of their ability. This results in an incomprehensible freedom to live forever with the Lord upon death. Yes, there are those denied human rights who are forced to worship the Lord in secret, but they are loved by God just as much. If they believe, they will be saved, and they can have that lasting hope despite living in a part of the world where there is no other hope.

- PSA 119:44–47 ~ I will obey God's laws continuously and forevermore; I will walk in freedom, for I have sought His rules. I will boldly testify before kings, and I will delight in God's commandments that I have loved.

- PRO 1:30–33 ~ Since they did not take heed, they will eat the fruit of their ways and be full of the fruit of their schemes. The waywardness of simple-minded people will be their demise, and the complacency of fools will destroy them. But whoever chooses to listen will be safe and at peace, free from fear of harm.

- ISA 61:1 ~ The Spirit of God is upon me, because He has directed me to preach the good news to the humble, to heal the broken hearted, to free the slaves, and to release those who are bound in chains and in prison.

- MAL 4:2 ~ For those who honor my name, the sun of righteousness will arise with healing in His wings. And they will go out leaping like a calf freed from its stall.

- JOH 8:31–32, 36 ~ Jesus said, "If you believe in my words then you are indeed my disciples; and you will know the truth and the truth will set you free. If the Son of God sets you free, you will definitely be free."

- ACT 2:38 ~ Peter said, "Repent and be baptized every one of you, in the name of Jesus Christ for the remission of your sins, and you will receive the free gift of the Holy Spirit."

- ROM 5:18 ~ Thank God, though you were servants of sin you have obeyed in your heart the doctrine delivered unto you; being made free from sin you became servants of righteousness.

- ROM 6:14, 17–18, 23 ~ Now sin has no hold over you, for you are not under the Law, you are under Grace. Thank God that we, who were servants of sin, have obeyed in our hearts the doctrine that delivers us, being made free from sin, and now serving righteousness instead. For the wages of sin is death; but the free gift of God is eternal life through Christ the Lord.

- ROM 8:1–2, 8–9, 18, 21 ~ There is now no condemnation for those who are in Christ Jesus, who walk after the Spirit and not the flesh. For the law of the Spirit of life in Christ has made us free from the law of sin and death. Those who live in the flesh cannot please God. If you are in the Spirit, it is because God's Spirit dwells within you. As for people who do not have the Spirit of Christ, Christ has no part of them or they in Him. For the sufferings we endure are nothing compared to the glory we will receive in Him. Thus, we have been freed from chains of corruption to glorious liberty as children of God.

- 1 CO 7:22 ~ Those who were servants when called by Christ have become free, and those who were free when called by Christ have become servants. You were bought with a great price, so do not become a slave to humankind, but remain responsible to God and the purpose for which He called you.

- EPH 1:4–5 ~ For He chose us before the creation of the world to be holy and blameless in His sight. In love, He predestined us to be adopted children through Jesus Christ, in accordance with His pleasure and will.

- 1 PE 4:10 ~ Even as you have received the free gift, share that gift with others, as good stewards of the endless grace of God.

Heavenly Father, we thank you for creating us free, and for giving us free will. Remind us never to abuse our rights and freedoms by sinning against you or any human being; help us never to violate the rights of others. We freely accept your promises by dedicating our lives to you, through your Son Jesus Christ. Let us never stray from the path He has revealed to us. Let us be messengers of your freedom and the right to be called your children. Help those who live in parts of the world where there is no freedom of religion, where they cannot worship you publicly, and where they are persecuted for loving you. Bring down the tyrants and despots that would deny people their God-given rights and freedoms. Let the oppressed people go free, and for those who are unable to escape, give them the hope of salvation and the peace that surpasses all understanding, through Christ our Savior. Give patriots the courage and strength to defend our rights if the government attempts to confiscate any freedom or otherwise seize control of our great nation which was founded on your Holy Word. We pray this in the name of Jesus, Amen.

November 10

First Bibles Placed by Gideons in Montana on this day in 1908. Gideons International was founded in 1899. A member named Archie Bailey was passing through Superior MT and stayed at the hotel. He asked the clerk if he could leave a Bile at the desk, and she suggested he leave a Bible in every room. He ordered twenty-five Bibles for the hotel; thus began the placement of Bibles by the Gideons. In 1898, three traveling businessmen met and started the organization: John Nicholson, Samuel Hill, and Will Knights. They discovered that a similar organization in England was leaving Bibles in hotel rooms. The Gideons picked up on the idea and since then they have placed over two billion Bibles in hotels, hospitals, prisons, and other places. Their objective was to spread the Word and they have been very successful at it. I often have opened these Bibles myself, having traveled a great deal over the years.

The Gideons is a group that takes the great commission given by Jesus Christ seriously. They have grown to over 250,000 members in hundreds of locations around the world. No doubt, the Bibles placed by the Gideons have been a welcome sight to thousands of people who needed some comfort as they sat alone in a hotel room far from home.

- ISA 55:10–11 ~ The rain and snow that falls from heaven does not return to heaven but waters the earth, causing the plants to bud and seed, and providing food. So also, God's Word does not return to Him void, but accomplishes what He wishes and prospers where He sends it.

- MAT 28:18–20 ~ Jesus said to His apostles just before leaving them, "All power in heaven and earth is given to me. Go and teach all nations the things I have taught you, baptizing them in the name of the Father, Son, and Holy Spirit. And remember, I will be with you always, even until the end of time."

- 1 CO 3:6–9 ~ Paul planted, Apollos watered, and God gave the increase. Neither he who plants nor he who sows is anything, because only God can make things grow. The man who plants and the man who waters have one purpose, and each will be rewarded according to their labor. For we all are laborers with God in His plantation; and you are God's building.

- 2 CO 9:8 ~ God is able to bless you abundantly, that in all things and at all times you have what you need, so you can abound in good works.

- HEB 4:9–12 ~ There remains a rest for the people of God. Those entering their rest have ceased their works as God did. Let us labor to obtain that rest, else we fall due to unbelief. For the Word of God is living and active, sharper than any double-edged sword, dividing the soul and spirit, and discerning the thoughts and intentions of the heart.

- 1 TI 6:12–13 ~ Fight the good fight of faith. Keep a firm grasp on eternal life, for this is why you were called, and why you testified before many witnesses and before God.

- 2 TI 2:1–4 ~ Be strong, my son, in the grace found through Christ Jesus. The things you heard me proclaim before many witnesses you must commit to faithful people who are able to teach others. You will endure hardship as a good soldier of Jesus Christ. Remember, people engaged in warfare do not get entangled in the affairs of the world so they can please Him who has called you to be a soldier.

Father in heaven, equip us with your Word of truth that we may carry it everywhere we go, sharing it with those who seek the truth, who are lost, and who want to know you. We pray that people living in countries where your Word is forbidden will hear and receive it. Bless foundations like the Gideons who share your Word wherever they go. Embolden us as Christian soldiers to boldly proclaim Christ to the world. In His name we pray, Amen.

November 11

Veterans Day occurs on this date every year; it is a day of gratitude for those who have served in our military. Also called Armistice Day, it commemorates the signing of the armistice ending World War I (1918). The purpose was to honor those who fought in that bloody war. The day was especially dedicated to survivors, many of whom returned with deeper wounds: physical, mental, and spiritual. We honor those who died in the line of duty every year on Memorial Day at the end of May. The least we can do is show our appreciation to veterans who are still with us.

Today, we honor those who have served, whether during war or peace, for they will give the last full measure for their country when called into action. Military life is tough; personal sacrifices are made by servicemen and women, spending many a day separated from loved ones. Whether in the line of fire, at a hospital, or in an office, you can be sure the workload will be heavy and the dedication genuine. Anyone doing the bidding of our elected government with dignity and honor deserves to be showered with dignity, honor, and thanks; they also can use our prayers. We should say a prayer every day for those in uniform who serve or have served our great nation. And when we send them into battle, pray that the Lord goes with them.

- DEU 20:1–4 ~ When you go into battle against your enemies, and you see horses and chariots, and you realize you are outnumbered, do not be afraid. For the Lord your God is with you, just like He was when He brought you out of Egypt. Before you go into battle the priest will speak to the people, "Hear, oh Israel, as we approach into battle against our enemies, let your hearts be strong and fear not; do not tremble or be terrified. For the Lord is going with you to fight against them and to save you.

- JDG 6:12 ~ An angel of the Lord appeared to Gideon and said, "The Lord is with you, mighty man of valor."

- 1 SA 17:36–37, 45–47 ~ David told King Saul, "I have killed a lion and a bear, and this uncircumcised Philistine (Goliath) will join them, since he has defied the armies of the living God. The Lord that delivered me from the lion and the bear will deliver me from this Philistine." And Saul said to David, "Go, and may the Lord be with you." Upon arriving at the battleground, David told Goliath, "You have come with a sword, a spear, and a shield, but I come in the name of the Lord of hosts, the God of the armies of Israel, whom you have defied. Today the Lord will deliver you into my hand, for I will strike you down and take your head as a trophy. And everyone will know that there is a God in Israel who saves, not with a sword or spear. This battle belongs to the Lord, for He will give you to us."

- 2 KI 6:15–17 ~ The servant awoke and found they were surrounded by the Syrians, who were coming for Elisha the prophet. He told the servant not to fear as his army was greater than theirs. Then Elisha prayed, "Lord, I pray you would open his eyes that he may see." And the Lord opened the young man's eyes and he beheld a mountain full of horses and chariots of fire surrounding the Syrian army. Then Elisha prayed, "Lord, smite these people with blindness." And the Lord did so, and they escaped.

Fighting for one's country is a very high calling. Those people who disrespect the uniform deserve to spend a summer at boot camp. Many denigrate the military, but the shame will fall on them. Those who engage in stolen valor are particularly loathsome; they should spend a year in a jail cell, which is the length of an average deployment in a war zone. I am proud to be a veteran; I consider it a privilege to have served. I have the utmost respect for veterans today and always. Do not be afraid to approach people you encounter in uniform and thank them personally. I would be willing to bet that it will make their day.

NOVEMBER

Remember this: at times, the people in power are not honorable; they send their countrymen and women into hell for personal gain. Those who fight under such circumstances are not guilty, so don't blame them. It's pretty obvious who will have to answer to God. Whether a war is justified or not, that is up to God. But there is such a thing as a just war, and that is when you will find God fighting on your side. Still, it is necessary to maintain the best military and keep them at the highest readiness. Nobody knows in advance when it will be necessary to deploy our military. But you can bet they will respond when ordered to do so, whether their superiors turn out to be right or wrong. But those who wage wars for ill-gotten gain will be subject to the wrath of God. They will be defeated, sooner or later. But those who honorably sacrificed themselves in battle will not face God's wrath, though their leaders might.

- PSA 23:4 ~ Even when I walk through the valley of the shadow of death, I will not be afraid of any evil, for God will be with me to comfort me.

- ECC 4:28 ~ Strive for the truth unto death and the Lord will fight with you.

- JOH 15:13 ~ Nobody demonstrates a greater love than when they lay down their life for their friends.

- ROM 14:7–9 ~ Nobody can live for themselves or die for themselves; whether we live or die it is for the Lord because we belong to Him. Christ died and rose from the dead to be the Lord of the living and the dead.

- 2 CO 10:4–5 ~ The weapons we fight with are not of this world, but have divine power to demolish strongholds. We cast down vain imaginations, and every pretension that is raised against the knowledge of God, capturing every thought to make it obedient to Christ.

- GAL 2:20 ~ I am crucified with Christ; nevertheless, I am alive. But it is not really me who lives, but Christ who lives in me. The life I now have in the flesh I live by faith in Christ who loved me and gave Himself for me.

- JAM 4:1–3 ~ Where do you think arguments and wars come from? They come from the lusts that battle inside you. You lust but have not; you kill and desire to have; you make war and you will not. But you have not because you ask not. When you do ask you receive not, because you ask for the wrong reasons, so you can indulge in your lusts.

The most important fight is inside oneself; and it is a life and death decision so you'd better pick carefully: either the world, or Satan, or God. The first two choices lead to your death; the third leads to eternal life. If you have chosen God, you will not be one to pick fights, but you may have to finish them. The fight of faith extends for the duration of your life; and either way, you can expect to die. But if you die in Christ, your spirit and soul will be taken immediately into heaven. Though your dead body remains in the grave, it too will be resurrected like that of Christ when He returns. Your new, glorified body will never die, and you will keep your soul forever. I don't know about you but I'd say this sure beats the alternative.

Merciful Father, we come to you in prayer for the sake of those who take our place in strife, who keep the peace in time of turmoil, and face the enemy head on in battle. We are beholden to them and to you, Lord, for our freedom, protection, security, and preservation. As you have given yourself for us, help us to likewise give ourselves to you, and to others, even unto death; knowing that death has no hold over us for you have overcome it. Watch over us, and give your angels charge over us, in particular those who are sent into danger, and sometimes have to bleed on our behalf. They are examples of your Son who laid down His life so that we might live free. Thank you for everyone who give their lives for freedom. And for the blood you shed on our behalf, Lord Jesus, we will be eternally grateful. In your name we pray, Amen.

DAILY DEVOTIONAL EVENTS

November 12

Billy Sunday Preached to 70,000 in Boston on this day in 1916. He was one of a string of evangelists to bring the Gospel of Jesus Christ to thousands of people at a time. He was a professional baseball player who turned preacher about five years after his conversion in 1886. He was ordained and trained in the Presbyterian church in 1903. His style was rough and rowdy, prancing around the stage, tossing chairs, even cursing sometimes. He championed women's suffrage, abolishing child labor, and vilified evolutionists and evolution theory. He supported Catholics and Jews which also made him a controversial figure. He supported the prohibition of alcohol, having once been an alcoholic himself. He preached hundreds of revivals, and tens of thousands of sermons (as many as twenty per week), welcoming people to come forward and commit themselves to Christ after every sermon. He was influenced largely by D L Moody (late 1800s) one of the most famous evangelists of all time. These men paved the way for the greatest contemporary evangelist ever, Billy Graham. Collectively, these three men brought millions of people to faith in Jesus Christ. The masses of people that evangelists were drawing to their revivals gave rise to the megachurch. The introduction of television enabled the broadcasting of sermons from megachurch pastors and assorted TV evangelists, which have multiplied in the past fifty years. Consequently, the days of evangelists like Billy Sunday and Billy Graham may be gone, though the world needs men like them who fight the good fight everywhere they go.

While many have come to Christ through revivals, attendance in church has hit historic lows. The pandemic contributed to this decline. Smaller churches have been dying out more rapidly in favor of the megachurches. The churches in America number about half of what it was one hundred years ago. The amount of people affiliated with a church or religion has been dropping; these numbers are replaced by the numbers of unaffiliated, non-believing individuals including agnostics and atheists. College graduates are leaving the church in which they were raised or are disregarding religion altogether largely because institutions of higher learning are indoctrinating students into secularism. Still, about seventy percent of Americans purport to have a solid Christian foundation including frequent prayer, scriptural study, and/or church attendance; about twenty-five percent are uncommitted or unaffiliated with any religion. Baby boomers represent the largest percentage of active Christians. There was a rise in religious activity such as church attendance and prayer with the so-called "Great Awakening" of the 1950s, followed by an abrupt decline in the 1960s and 1970s. Interestingly, according to recent research, only thirty-eight percent indicated belief in absolute standards of right and wrong, verses fifty-nine percent asserting that circumstances determine right and wrong (*www.pewresearch.org*)

God's Word emphasizes the importance of Christian fellowship. Churches provide Bible study, prayer, socialization, edification, and education, in addition to listening to the preaching of the Gospel of Jesus Christ. Many Christians today believe it unnecessary to attend church regularly, but this is mostly an excuse for people who are lazy or uncommitted. While there is nothing wrong with watching church services or evangelists preach on television, this does not provide the fellowship and edification available through human interaction. The pandemic exacerbated this effect, making many people complacent about school, church, and work; many would just as soon do things at home with a computer without getting dressed or going out.

- DEU 31:12 ~ Gather the people together including men, women, and children, as well as the strangers among you, so that everyone can hear, learn, fear the Lord your God, and obey all the words of His Law.
- MAT 18:20 ~ Jesus said, "Where two or more are gathered together in my name, I am there with you."

NOVEMBER

- ACT 1:14 ~ All of them continued with one accord in prayer and meditation.

- EPH 2:19–22 ~ You are no longer foreigners but fellow citizens of God's kingdom and members of His household, built on the foundation laid by the prophets and apostles with Jesus Christ as the chief cornerstone. In Him the entire building is joined together and grows into a holy temple. In Him you also are being built together to become a place for God's Holy Spirit to live.

- EPH 4:3, 11–13, 16 ~ Keep the unity of the Spirit through the bond of peace. Remember, Christ assigned some of you to be apostles, some prophets, some evangelists, some pastors, and some teachers, to prepare God's people for works of service. This He did so that the body of Christ can grow, until all reach a oneness of the Spirit and unity in the knowledge of the Son of God, and become mature in the faith attaining the whole measure of the fullness of Christ. In Christ, the entire body is fitly joined and held together by every supporting ligament, and grows and builds itself up in love as each component performs its function.

- HEB 10:25 ~ Do not cease to assemble together, as some are in the habit of doing, but continue to meet with one another and encourage each other, even more as the day of our Lord approaches.

Remember the Sabbath Day and keep it holy: this is the fourth commandment. God commands that we set aside a day each week for rest and worship. It doesn't matter which day, but most people worship on either Saturday or Sunday. In the Old Testament, this meant a holy convocation, which is an assembly of the entire congregation; no work was allowed on that day. Can a person be condemned for not obeying this commandment? No, all sin can be forgiven except blasphemy against the Holy Spirit. But reduced church attendance will lead to complacency, and possibly no church attendance. The absence of Christian fellowship is detrimental to your walk with Jesus.

- LEV 23:3–8 ~ Six days shall work be done, but the seventh day is the Sabbath of rest, a holy convocation. You will do no work because it is the Lord's Sabbath in all your dwellings. There are feasts of the Lord, also holy convocations, which you will observe in their seasons. The fourteenth day of the first month (Nisan) is the Lord's Passover. The fifteenth day of Nisan begins the feast of Unleavened Bread; seven days you must eat unleavened bread. The first day of that period will be a holy convocation: you will do no work on that day. You will present burnt offerings to the Lord throughout the celebration. The seventh day will be another holy convocation: you will do no work on that day.

- PSA 100:4 ~ Enter into God's gates with thanksgiving and into his courts with praise. Be thankful and bless His name.

- PSA 122:1 ~ I was glad when they said to me, "Let us go to God's house."

- COL 2:16 ~ Do not let anyone judge you according to what you eat or drink, or with respect to the holy day or Sabbath.

Dear Heavenly Father, help us to find a good church and attend regularly: a place where we will feel fulfilled, lifted, refreshed, and strengthened. We need to hear your Word, we need the support of Christian fellowship and unity, and we need to be replenished often by the sacrament of Holy Communion. These are things we cannot obtain staying at home. Help us to remember that all of our days belong to you, especially a day each week to honor the Sabbath. Help our church to be a place that always fills us with your Holy Spirit, reenergizing our spirits; a place that will never stray from the truth of your Word; and a place where the Holy Trinity is recognized, worshipped, and glorified. In the name of Jesus Christ our Lord we pray, Amen.

November 13

Birth of Augustine (also Augustin), Bishop of Hippo, occurred on this day in AD 354. His name is recognized more than other early church fathers. An apologist, theologian, philosopher, teacher, and prolific writer, he underwent a serious conversion well into adulthood, rapidly becoming a clergyman and church leader. He was quite the intellectual, influenced by Greek philosophers, especially Plato. He left his home in Africa (present day Algeria) for Rome, becoming a professor at Milan. His integration of spirituality with Platonic philosophy was not well received so he returned home after a few years, somewhat disgruntled. Being idle and lost, he reluctantly agreed to enter church service, where he was able to articulate his unique understanding of Christianity and deliver impassioned sermons. He became a bishop soon thereafter and remained so until his death in AD 430. Unlike many of the early church fathers, a great deal of his writings survived, such as *Confessions*, which was in large part an autobiography. Another popular work during his lifetime was *The City of God*. He wrote incessantly and many documented sermons endured. In his writings and his sermons, he helped to explain the nature and origin of sin, end of time events or eschatology, the sacraments, predestination, the Holy Trinity, and issues concerning sex and marriage.

From the first to the fifth centuries AD, a number of early church fathers quoted the New Testament and its authors. They were apologists and theologians who preached, wrote, and lived the teachings of Christ. Some of them were personally trained by apostles. If we had lost the original manuscript evidence used to create the canonical books of the New Testament, the compilation of more than 36,000 quotations from these post-apostolic evangelists would be enough to recreate the New Testament. It is worthwhile to study these early Christian leaders who kept the scriptures alive and distributed them around the world. The following list includes notable contributors to the growth of the early church (chronologically ordered): Polycarp, Papias, Clement, Ignatius, Justin Martyr, Irenaeus, Clement, Tertullian, Hippolytus, Origen, Cyprian, Athanasius, Eusebius, Ambrose, Jerome, Augustine.

Thanks to the early evangelists, Christianity spread quickly and was translated into several languages by AD 200. With the proliferation of reliable translations, in different tongues, for over two centuries, it became easy to weed out counterfeits; that is, agreement across multiple sources exposed fake revelations and inaccurate texts. New Testament scriptures were scrutinized, authenticated, and standardized during the canonization process. Any manuscripts that were inconsistent with established doctrine and teaching, or were works of unknown origin, or came from unreliable sources, were excluded from the canon. God ensured that His Word would survive from generation to generation. Proof of this was finding a complete scroll of Isaiah among the Dead Sea Scrolls, which happened to be identical to the modern version though separated by two thousand years.

- NUM 23:18 ~ God is not a man that He would lie; nor is He the son of man that he should repent. Has He said, and then not done it? Has he spoken and it did not come to pass?

- PSA 119:89 ~ Forever, Lord, your Word is settled in heaven.

- ISA 40:8 ~ The grass withers and the flower fades, but the Word of God will stand forever.

- MAL 3:6 ~ God says, "I am the Lord, I never change."

- MAT 24:35 ~ Jesus said, "Heaven and earth will pass away, but my words will remain true forever."

- HEB 13:8 ~ Jesus Christ is the same yesterday, today, and forever.

NOVEMBER

- JAM 1:17 ~ Every good thing comes from God; every perfect gift comes from above, from the Father of lights. God never varies, and in Him there is no darkness, not even a shadow.

    Some people argue that God does not leave the heavenly realm and insert Himself into the goings on down here. Their deist position is that God has been letting things carry on after Christ ascended into heaven. This is clearly not the case. The hand of Providence has not only preserved the scriptures but also has helped this country grow and thrive. Similar to Israel, who God prospered until they turned away, after which He allowed them to be conquered and scattered; God's warnings to Israel apply today to the USA, and any nation that seeks Him, receives His help, and then turns their backs on Him.

- JER 2:1–19 (see also EZE 20) ~ The word of the Lord came to Jeremiah saying: Go and cry into the ears of Jerusalem saying, "The Lord says I remember you and the fidelity of your youth, when you loved me like a spouse and you followed me into the wilderness through a land that was never sown. Israel was holy to me as were the first fruits you offered to me. Those who came upon you to devour you were held accountable and punished, for I would bring disaster upon them. Now hear this: What defect did your fathers find in me that they strayed far from me, walking after vanity and becoming worthless? They never asked, 'Where is the Lord who brought us out of Egypt, leading us through the wilderness: an arid expanse of desert and rough terrain, where no man had trodden or lived.' I brought you into a country of plenty, with good fruit and good land. But after you entered there, you defiled my land and made my heritage an abomination. Your priests did not ask of me and your governors did not know me; leaders sinned against me and prophets sought counsel from Baal and practiced idolatry. Therefore, I accuse you and your children's children. Look around and see what is going on. Has any nation changed their gods? But my people have replaced me with useless idols. Be astonished at this, oh heavens, and be terrified, says the Lord. For my people have committed two crimes. They have forsaken me, the fountain of living waters, then dug wells that cannot hold water. Is Israel a servant or a slave? Why are they now plundered? The lions have roared and made you a wasteland; your cities are burned and abandoned. Have you not brought this upon yourselves, seeing how you have forsaken the Lord your God after He showed you the way? Now you have gone the way of Egypt and you drink their water and the water of the Assyrians. Your own wickedness will punish you and your backsliding ways will rebuke you. This is an evil thing you have done, forsaking the Lord your God, and now you no longer fear me." Thus says the Lord of hosts.

    God cautioned Israel multiple times through the prophets Isaiah, Jeremiah, and Ezekiel, who said the Assyrians were going to invade them and the Babylonians were going to conquer them. Do you know what they did to Jeremiah when he forewarned them? They threw him into a cistern and held him there for a very long time. But God promised He would restore Israel if they returned to Him and He did just that. Israel regained their heritage and name in 1948. Can you see that God is sending us the same warning? God helped the USA become the greatest nation on earth and now a great many of our people would sooner disregard Him for their idols such as material wealth, worldly possessions, power over others, and physical pleasures.

    Heavenly Father, please wake up this nation; open our eyes so we can see your face again. We have wandered very far, and we need to return to you straightaway so you can heal our land. Truthful forecasters, evangelists, and representatives will be declaring your name and voicing your admonitions upon this wickedness. Do not let the hateful, demented, and evil ones silence the speech of your messengers; instead, cause their voices to be amplified and continue. May we reverse course and get back on the path that you set before us. Our leaders are sidetracked and need your divine intervention. We desperately pray for help, Father, Son, and Holy Ghost, Amen.

November 14

Choose Wisely Day is introduced to encourage the studious examination of alternatives, and selection of the most cost-effective among them. Obviously, you can simplify that analysis by choosing the alternative closest to God's will, or what you know in your heart He would choose for you. This requires that we prioritize our choices in light of what Jesus would do; we can find out what that is by studying the Holy Bible. We always have God's Word as a guide that spells out correct choices very succinctly.

God gives us freedom to make our own choices, including whether or not we want Him in control and an integral part of our lives. God chooses those who choose Him, and He cherishes them as His children. We have our own ability and will; we examine and we select what is right or what is wrong. Everybody has a conscience by which they know the right thing to do before taking action, though we all are spiritually weak due to sin, and choose the wrong way too often. However, even people who deny God know the right choices because they have observed how right choices produce better outcomes than wrong choices. Thus, we learn causality through trial and error, and usually know beforehand the relative likelihood of a decision or action resulting in positive or negative results, because these choices align with right and wrong, respectively.

- DEU 7:7–10 ~ The Lord did not pour His love upon you, or choose you because you were greater in number than other people, for you were the fewest of all people. But because the Lord loved you, and in order to keep the promise that He made with your fathers, He brought you out with a mighty hand, and redeemed you from bondage in the land of Egypt. Know therefore that the Lord is your God; He is faithful and keeps the covenant, and bestows mercy on those who love Him and keep His commandments. But He repays those who hate Him to their face, and utterly destroys them for everyone to see.

- JOS 24:15, 21–22 ~ Joshua announced, "If serving the Lord seems undesirable to you, then choose who you will serve. As for me and my household, we will serve the Lord." The people said to Joshua, "We promise to serve the Lord." Joshua replied, "You are witnesses before me and your countrymen that you have chosen the Lord, and have promised to serve Him." They responded, "Yes, we are witnesses."

- JOH 15:16, 19 ~ Jesus said to His disciples, "You did not choose me, I chose you and ordained you, so that you could bear fruit that would not wither. Anything you ask of the Father in my name will be given to you. If you were of the world, only the world would love you; but I have chosen you out of the world, and that is why the world hates you."

Why did God give us choices? He could have programmed us to do the right thing all the time. But then, how would be able to love Him back? Robots cannot show genuine love if you program them to say "I love you". God created humans to love, for He loved us first; and it is His desire that we choose to love Him back. Humans have children essentially for the same reason. If you love God, you will love His Son Jesus Christ, for they are one. To choose Christ is to choose life; to reject Christ is to choose death.

- DEU 30:19–20 ~ I call heaven and earth as witnesses that I have set before you both life and death, blessings and curses. I recommend that you choose life so that you and your children may live, and so you may love the Lord your God, listen to Him, and cling to Him. Because He is your life; and He will bless you with many years of prosperity in the land He promised your forefathers, Abraham, Isaac, and Jacob.

- MAT 20:16 ~ Jesus said, "The last will be first and the first will be last, for many are called but few are chosen."

NOVEMBER

- 1 CO 10:13 ~ The temptations you endure are common to humanity. But God is faithful and fair, and He will not cause you to suffer temptation beyond your ability to withstand it. And He will always provide you a way to escape from temptation.

- PHP 1:22–25 ~ If I live in the flesh, that will mean fruitful labor for me. But which shall I choose? For I am torn between two alternatives. I long to depart from this life and be with Christ which is far better. But for now, it is necessary for me to remain here and to help you progress in the faith.

Choosing is a thought process that precedes a behavior. By reflecting on the decision, and praying about it, you become reassured of what to say and do, and when. Listen to the Holy Spirit who is with you, and you always will know the truth and the right path to follow. Of course, you can choose to do the opposite but you probably will not like the long-term effects. Negative results often proceed from not being thoughtful or careful, or truthful to oneself.

- JOB 9:14 ~ How should I answer God, and choose the right words to reason with Him?

- PRO 6:3 ~ Commit your works to the Lord and He will establish your thoughts.

- ROM 12:2 ~ Do not conform to the ways of this world, but be transformed by the renewing of your mind, and you will be able to determine what is good, acceptable, and perfect in accordance with God's will.

- 1 CO 2:16 ~ For who has known the mind of God to instruct Him? But we have the mind of Christ.

- PHP 4:8 ~ Whatever is true, honest, fair, pure, lovely, uplifting, virtuous, and praiseworthy—think on these things.

The devil knows your weaknesses and will continue to exploit them if you give in. Most people are aware of their errors and misdeeds. The best strategy is to revise your thinking and change your behavior. This requires one to be mindful constantly; the moment you provide an opening, temptation is bound to enter. Train your brain to think pure thoughts and dismiss thoughts that lead to sin. Satan will implant the temptation; it is best to reject it before considering it. This requires cognitive intervention whenever a bad habit or thought enters your mind. We sin in thought, word, and deed. The most difficult thing to do is to control the thought. No doubt you have heard the expression, "Let your conscience be your guide." Where do you think your conscience came from? It was implanted into your soul from conception. It is the Holy Spirit that speaks to your inner sanctum, which is your conscience and your higher power. Basically, it is your moral compass which is your knowledge of right and wrong.

- 1 KI 20:40 ~ The king declared, "Since you were so busy doing this and that, the man you were supposed to guard escaped. His penalty will be yours, for you have decided it yourself."

- MAT 5:27–28 ~ Jesus said, "You know that you should not commit adultery. I tell you that whoever looks at a woman with lust has committed adultery in his heart."

- MAT 6:21, 33 ~ For where your treasure is there your heart will be also. Seek first the kingdom of God and His righteousness, and everything you need will be added unto you.

- EPH 2:3–4 ~ In times past we also engaged in lusts of the flesh, fulfilling desires of the body and of the mind; we were by nature children of wrath, just like the rest. But because of God's great love for us we were made alive in Christ, even when we were dead in our sins. It is by that grace that you also can be saved.

DAILY DEVOTIONAL EVENTS

- TIT 1:15 ~ To the pure all things are pure. But to the defiled and unbelieving there is nothing pure; even their minds and consciences are defiled.
- JAM 1:15 ~ When lust is conceived it brings forth sin; and sin, when finished, brings forth death.

God will prosper those who choose Him, who work hard, and who place spiritual riches above worldly wealth. The abundance of God's blessings will increase in accordance with your faith. You will find everything you need to complete your mission on the path of righteousness. Of course, you can choose to opt out of God's blessings and do it your way, but I wouldn't recommend it.

- PSA 115:13–14 ~ God will bless anyone who acknowledges Him, both great and small. He will increase you more and more, you and your children.
- PRO 13:21–22 ~ Evil pursues sinners; but to the righteous, good shall be their reward. A good man leaves an inheritance to his children's children; but the wealth of the sinner is laid up for the just.
- LUK 12:16–21 ~ Jesus spoke a parable to them: The land of a certain rich man produced plentifully, and the man thought to himself, "What shall I do? I do not have enough room for all the fruits of my labor. I know what I will do. I will tear down the barns and build bigger ones." And the man decided, "Since I have so much wealth, I will take it easy and eat, drink, and be merry." Then God said to him, "You fool, tonight your soul will be required. And who will possess all those things for which you have worked so hard?" Jesus concluded: Those who accumulate treasures for themselves are not rich towards God.
- ROM 8:28 ~ All things work towards good for those who love God and are called according to His purpose

Granted, there are some things that we cannot choose. For example, we cannot choose our gender, ethnicity, age, DNA, or relatives. Furthermore, we cannot control the past, other people, the weather, the truth, and the universe. Interestingly, we have no need to change or control any of these things to be successful in the vocation of our choice. And even when bad things happen, we learn and keep moving forward. Exceptionalism is available to everyone if they accept Christ and receive His Spirit. The Lord promises us good things in this life and better things in the next life; and all He wants from us is our love and faith. Choose God to be your Father, receive His parental love and mercy, love Him above all others, and He will choose you to be His child forever. This is the winningest strategy of them all.

Dear Father, it feels so good to call you Father, because we love you; you are first in our lives. Thank you for loving us and calling us to be your children, because that is what we are through your Son Jesus Christ who calls us His brothers and sisters. Thank you that we have been adopted into your royal family with an inheritance in your kingdom that lasts forever. Help us to be available to others and share this good news with them. Let us make choices that are in accordance with your will so that we may be blessed. Equip us to witness to others about how blessed we are, so they will seek you and pray for your blessings upon them. Remind us to think carefully before we react, decide, or take action, as we open our hearts to your Holy Spirit for guidance and direction. In the name of your Son Jesus Christ, whose path we choose to follow; a path that leads all the way to the pearly gates of heaven, Amen.

November 15

National Philanthropy Day recognizes the importance of charity and philanthropy. We who are blessed should share some of our wealth and time to help those who are struggling. This holiday was introduced by attorney and philanthropist Douglas Freeman in the early 1980s and was made official by President Reagan in 1986. Freeman encouraged wealthy people in his circle to donate to worthy causes and help those less fortunate. This holiday is sponsored by the Association for Fundraising Professionals (AFP) to recognize people and organizations that help out, whether through donations, scholarships, volunteer work, administrative services, or spreading overall goodwill. The AFP will be holding national events, awards ceremonies, and other activities, as will state and local chapters if you want to get involved. Otherwise, make a donation to a charity.

We are a generous nation because we have been so richly blessed; and the reason for that is our Judeo-Christian roots which have taught us to be giving and compassionate. When we help others, we are doing the work of God who gives His mercy and grace generously to all who seek Him. As God has blessed us abundantly, so we can bless others abundantly with what we have.

- PSA 103:8 ~ The Lord is merciful and gracious, slow to anger, and generous in mercy.

- PRO 11:27 ~ People that diligently seek good will find favor, but people that seek mischief will have mischief come upon them.

- MAT 6:2 ~ When you help the needy, do not sound your trumpet as the hypocrites do in the churches and in the streets, so that they can receive praise from others. The truth is, that is the only reward they will receive.

- LUK 2:8–14 ~ The angels told the shepherds about Jesus's birth and praised God saying, "Glory be to God in the highest, and on earth, peace and good will towards all people."

- ACT 2:44–45 ~ And the believers were as one, for they had everything in common. They sold their possessions and goods and gave generously to the needy.

- ACT 20:35 ~ In your labors give to the needy, remembering the words of Jesus Christ, "It is more blessed to give than to receive."

- 2 CO 9:7 ~ Everyone should give whatever they think is fair in their heart. Giving should be done voluntarily, not out of obligation, for God loves a cheerful giver.

- 1 TH 5:14–22 ~ Warn those who are unruly, comfort the feeble minded, support the weak, and be patient towards everyone. Never render evil for evil but follow that which is good in yourself and others. Rejoice always; pray without ceasing; give thanks in everything, for this is God's will in your life. Quench your thirst for the Spirit; do not hate the words of the prophets. Test all things keeping hold of the good. Refrain from anything that is evil.

- TIT 3:4–6 ~ With kindness and love, God our Savior appeared and saved us, not because of our works of righteousness, but because of His mercy; by the washing of regeneration, and renewing of the Holy Spirit, generously poured out for us through Jesus Christ our Savior.

Heavenly Father, you have been so generous with your blessings, mercy, and abundant love and we thank you sincerely. Help us to follow your example and be generous with what we have; surely, we have more than we need, whether it is love, time, or money. Let there be an outpouring of generosity on this day so that the hungry might be fed, the homeless sheltered, the destitute forgiven their debts, the enslaved set free, the hopeless gaining hope, and the outcasts brought home. Let every one of us do our part to reduce starvation, disease, disaster, and suffering. We pray in the name of your Son Jesus, who gave everything to save us, Amen.

November 16

Your Birthday Day has been scheduled for today; celebrate it as you normally would. It just so happens this also is my birthday. Everyone deserves to have their special day and today is a special day, not because of me, but because today only comes once per year. We can thank God today and every day that we have awakened to a brand-new day, full of experiences, excitement, and entertainment. I normally do not celebrate my birthday but I am going to celebrate yours today. And I assure you, I thank God you are here. May God bless you this day, and may you rejoice and be glad. But, allow me to ask, respectfully: given that you have been born, are you born again? You see, we are born in water from our mother's womb, and we are born again in the Spirit of our Lord when we accept Christ as Savior. And we will be born anew when Christ brings us home, giving us immortal bodies and everlasting life. There are many things to celebrate today: your birthday, being born again, and your rebirth in heaven with a perfect body!

- PRO 10:27 ~ Fearing the Lord prolongs your days; but the years of the wicked are shortened.

- PSA 118:24 ~ This is the day the Lord has made; let us rejoice and be glad in it.

- EZE 36:26 ~ I will give you a new heart and put inside you a new spirit; I will remove your heart of stone and replace it with a heart of flesh.

- JOH 3:3–6 ~ Jesus said, "Unless a person is born again, he cannot see God's kingdom." Nicodemus asked, "How can someone be born when they are old?" Jesus answered, "Unless a person is born of water and of the Holy Spirit he cannot enter into God's kingdom. Those who are born of the flesh are flesh, and those who are born of the Spirit are spirit."

- PHP 4:4 ~ Rejoice in the Lord always and again I say rejoice.

- 1 TH 5:21–22 ~ Examine all things and hold onto the good. Abstain from all appearance of evil.

- 1 PE 1:3–4, 9, 22–23~ Through God's mercy we have been born again to a living hope by the resurrection of Jesus Christ, to receive His inheritance which is imperishable, undefiled, unfailing, and kept in heaven for all believers. The outcome of faith in Jesus is salvation of the soul. You have purified your soul by obeying the truth through the Spirit, and by fervently loving one another with a pure heart. You have been born again, not of corruptible seed but of incorruptible, by the Word of God which lives and abides forever.

- 1 JO 4:7–8 ~ Let us love one another, for love is from God, and those who love are born of God and know Him. If you do not love God, you cannot know Him because God is love.

- 1 JO 5:4–5 ~ Everyone who is born of God overcomes the world; this is the victory, that by faith we can overcome the world. So, who can overcome the world? Anyone who believes that Jesus Christ is the Son of God.

Would you like to know how they partied during the Roman empire? Consider King Herod who threw a party for himself on his birthday (MAT 14:1–11; MAR 6:14–28). The grand finale was John the Baptist's head brought before the assemblage on a silver platter. You see, the evil king was sleeping with his brother's wife; her daughter also lived in the palace. Herod coaxed the lass into a provocative dance for up to half of his kingdom. So, she did it. Her mom, Herodias, told her daughter to ask for John's head and she got it, for Herodias despised the baptizer, though Herod feared him. John had warned the monarchs they were living in adultery and should be aware of the fires of hell. Talk about partying down, in the demonic sense of the word; and hell is exactly where they went.

NOVEMBER

- MAT 6:26–28 ~ In order not to lose face, Herod summoned the executioner, which caused the king great anxiety; but he had sworn an oath. The man returned with John's head on a platter, presenting it to the girl; she gave it to her mother. John's disciples heard of this and obtained the body, burying him in a tomb.

- MAR 6:18–22 ~ John told Herod he was violating the law taking his brother's wife Herodias; she hated John and wanted him put to death. But Herod feared John knowing he was honest and holy, and he listened to John. Herod's birthday came and he had a banquet for his lords, captains, and rich friends of Galilee. Then came the daughter of Herodias, and danced, and pleased Herod and his guests; and he offered her up to half of his kingdom.

Those who love God celebrate birthdays differently than pagans. Take Christmas for example: it is a solemn but praiseworthy occasion celebrated with worship, singing, and feasting. It is one of the two highest celebrations for those who love Christ, the other being Easter when Christ proved His deity with His victory over sin and death. Today we celebrate Christ as well; and we will celebrate Him tomorrow, and the rest of our days on earth, and for an eternity in heaven. Would you like to know how they party in heaven? Then ensure Christ is first in your life before your last day on earth, or you may end up where Herod and Herodias went.

- JOB 19:25–26 ~ I know that my Redeemer lives and that He will stand upon the earth. And although my flesh will have been destroyed, yet in my flesh I will see God.

- PSA 17:15 ~ In righteousness I will see God's face; when I awaken, I will be satisfied because I will recognize Him.

- PSA 118:16–17 ~ The righteous rejoice, for the Lord's right hand has done mighty things. I will not die, but live, and I will declare the works of the Lord.

- ISA 9:6 ~ A child is born for us; a Son is given to us. The government will be upon His shoulders. His name will be called Wonderful Counselor, Mighty God, Everlasting Father, and Prince of Peace.

- LUK 2:8–14 ~ The angels told the shepherds about Jesus's birth and praised God saying, "Glory be to God in the highest, and on earth, peace and good will toward all people."

- GAL 4:4–7 ~ When the time was right, God sent His Son, who was born of a woman under the Old Covenant of the Law, to redeem those who were under the Law. He did this so that everyone could receive the honor of becoming an adopted child of God. If you are a child of God, you are no longer His servant, but a fellow heir of God through Christ.

- COL 1:12–15 ~ We give thanks to the Father who has given us an inheritance with the saints in the kingdom of His dear Son, in whom we have received redemption and forgiveness. He is the very image of the invisible God, and the firstborn of every creature.

- COL 3:4, 10 ~ When Christ appears, who is our life, all Christians will appear with Him in glory. For we have become new people, renewed in God's image, by our knowledge of Him through Christ.

- 1 JO 3:2 ~ Dear friends, now we are the sons of God, and what we will become is not yet known. But we do know this: when He returns for us, we will become like Him, for we shall see Him as He really is.

Thank you, Father; thank you Jesus; thank you Holy Spirit. We give thanks to you for all good things. We give thanks that you made us, you saved us, and you adopted us. We praise you every day because we know we will see you face to face soon enough. In Jesus's name, Amen.

DAILY DEVOTIONAL EVENTS

November 17

International Students Day started as a memorial after the Nazis invaded Czechoslovakia. There were protests and demonstrations occurring at several universities and colleges. The Nazis commandeered universities and arrested over a thousand students and professors who were taken to concentration camps; then they executed nine activists without a trial. That fateful day was 11/17/1939. The following year, soldiers, students, and administrators reestablished the Central Association of Czechoslovak Students and opted to memorialize this day. The idea spread to England where students and soldiers joined the commemoration. By 1941, the idea had spread through the British Isles and into Europe. On the fiftieth anniversary (1989) a demonstration was organized in Prague protesting against the Communist Party of Czechoslovakia; by nightfall it became violent and many protestors were injured. This ignited a movement called the Velvet Revolution which advocated for democracy. A global demonstration was organized in 2004 and again in 2009 across Europe. Today's observance continues to be remembered around the world; in the Czech Republic it is named Struggle for Freedom and Democracy Day.

- LEV 19:17 ~ Do not hate your brother in your heart, but protest to your neighbor to prevent him from suffering evil.
- PRO 17:10 ~ A word of protest will go farther with one who has good sense, than a hundred blows will go with a foolish person.
- PRO 27:5 ~ An open reproof is better than love kept secret.
- PRO 28:23 ~ A person who rebukes another will garner more favor than flattering words.
- PRO 31:9 ~ Speak your mind, judge righteously, and defend the rights of the poor and needy.

Today we remember those young adults who were murdered, who died in concentration camps, or who otherwise gave their lives fighting against the Nazis during World War II. We also recognize the importance of higher education and the need to provide educational opportunities worldwide, especially where there is tyranny. For those in foreign lands seeking higher education, there are many roadblocks which students do not experience in a modernized world. The impetus of this holiday is to create educational accessibility across the globe. You may want to determine if your local college or university is sponsoring events on this memorable occasion.

- PRO 4:13 ~ Grab hold of instruction and do not let go, for she is your life.
- PRO 9:9–10 ~ Give instruction to a wise person and he or she will become wiser. Teach wise people and they will increase in learning. The fear of the Lord is the beginning of wisdom.
- PRO 16:16–17 ~ How much more valuable is wisdom than gold, and understanding than silver. The highway of the upright is to depart from evil; those who stay on it preserve their souls.

A key element of any university is diversity amongst the student population and the faculty. Many students come to the USA from abroad to conduct their studies here. As a result, the notion of international education represents students of diverse cultures, backgrounds, and nationalities learning together. The term university also implies unity; today is a day that students around the world can unite, interact, and develop friendships under the common causes of freedom, mutual respect, and educational rights. This day presents an opportunity for unity and diversity to come together in harmony in institutions of higher learning everywhere.

- PSA 133:1–2 ~ Behold, how good and how pleasant it is for brothers and sisters of the faith to live together in unity! It is like expensive ointment poured out on the head and running down one's face and garments, as with Aaron the priest.

- ECC 4:9–12 ~ Two are better than one because the reward of their labor is greater. If one falls, the other lifts him up. But it is unfortunate when alone, for if you fall there is nobody to lift you up. Similarly, two people lying together produce more warmth. Plus, two are better able to defend themselves. As the saying goes, a rope of three strands is not easily broken.

- ROM 2:10–11 ~ Glory, honor, and peace is given to all who do good, regardless of race. For there is no prejudice with God.

- ROM 12:16 ~ Live in harmony with one another. Do not be arrogant, but associate with the lowly. Never think yourself wise in your own sight.

- ROM 16:17–18 ~ I urge you, my brothers, identify those who cause divisions among you, and who place obstacles in your way that are contrary to the doctrine you have learned. Avoid them completely. They do not serve the Lord Jesus but their own vices, and with fancy words and persuasive speeches they deceive the hearts of the simple.

- 1 CO 14:26 ~ When you come together, everyone has a song, a doctrine, a language, and an interpretation. Let all things be done for mutual edification.

- EPH 4:3 ~ Keep the unity of the Spirit through the bond of peace.

- PHP 2:2 ~ Make my joy complete by being like-minded, having the same love and being one in spirit and in purpose.

- COL 4:5–6 ~ Be wise in the way you act towards outsiders and make the most of every opportunity. Let your speech be full of grace, seasoned with salt, so that you can know how you ought to respond to others.

International educational goals begin with disseminating wisdom, knowledge, and understanding. By definition it means teaching fundamentals that will generate future employment: that is, coursework with substance and depth. Instruction should not include an ideologue's ridiculous blather or political opinions. I experienced this as far back as the 1970s and now it is markedly worse. Having been an educator for over twenty years, I can tell you that the problem is pervasive in the USA; internationally, our excellency has fallen far below previous standards. Additionally, institutions at every level have relaxed the rules and are graduating some that should be held back or change fields. Learning is a stepwise process; we mustn't skip any step, and every step going up means that one can stand firmly on the step below. This would provide equal opportunity and quality in education which are sorely lacking.

First and foremost, today's goal is to make higher education available. This does not mean there should be no entry requirements, for the term itself implies the individual is ready to go higher. But everyone deserves basic education, and the ability to excel. Those who make it to higher levels such as graduate school should get there by merit. Let us make college level courses available to everyone, regardless of demographic; the only requirement should be the person has completed the necessary prerequisites. This illuminates the greater need to provide all levels of schooling for all kids and young adults, particularly in locales where education is sporadic. Unfortunately, this would mean a regime change in some places where leaders are resistant to growth and change in order to keep their power and control.

Father, we pray that young people in all parts of the world may be given the opportunity to obtain a proper education. Help us to turn our education systems around so they produce quality learners and qualified graduates, preparing them to make a living with their skills, thereby contributing to our society and the world. Let us be charitable to countries that welcome the aid and are well-intentioned concerning equal access to education. In Jesus's name, Amen.

November 18

Women Arrested for Voting included Susan B. Anthony and fourteen others, on this day in 1872; they had voted illegally during the reelection of U. S. Grant (11/05/1872). The state of New York argued that men alone were enfranchised to vote; Susan Anthony pointed out rights guaranteed to all natural born citizens in the Fourteenth Amendment. She was found guilty by an all-men jury, fined, refused to pay, and the judge declined to punish her to prevent an appeal to the Supreme Court. The other fourteen women were not charged. It would take four decades (1920) for the Nineteenth Amendment to be added to Constitution, declaring it unlawful to discriminate against voters on the basis of sex. Sadly, Susan passed in 1906 (see lesson 02/15).

Today, we again celebrate the courage of Susan B. Anthony for standing up for women's rights in a world dominated by men. Throughout the history of humankind, women have been treated unfairly, and they still are in many countries, especially under despots and certain religious theocracies. Obviously, women and men were created in the likeness of God and are therefore equally loved by Him and given the same mental faculties; but the sexes were created differently for a good reason. Women have been liberated by most sophisticated societies, largely because they have been given educational and career incentives. Curiously, women have been trending higher than men when it comes to voter turnout in America. It is unfortunate that it took 150 years from the beginning of our independent republic until the USA upheld the right of women to vote. New Zealand was first (1893); perhaps they were inspired by Ms. Anthony who was fighting the good fight. We waited until 1865 to abolish slavery, fighting a civil war over it. Many modern nations have yet to outlaw slavery: India and China have millions of slaves.

In the Old Testament, females often were not counted, such as during a census of the Levites, for only men could be priests (NUM 3:15). Men were bound by their oaths, but the oath of a woman could be nullified by her father or husband (NUM 30:2–13). Women had to be virgins when they married but not men (DEU 22:13–21). Men could serve a certificate of divorce to their wives but wives had no means of divorcing their husbands (DEU 24:1). St. Matthew wrote that Jesus fed five thousand men, not counting women and children (MAT 14:20–21); the same is true in the reporting of Jesus feeding four thousand men, not counting women and children (MAT 15:38). Additionally, St. Paul instructed that women should remain silent during a holy convocation and should not be teaching the Law (1 CO 14:34–35; 1 TI 2:11–12); recall that Paul received his training in Jewish Law from a leader of the Sanhedrin named Gamaliel (ACT 5:29–39). This is not to say that women were second-class citizens, given that women held prominent roles in the Bible to include judge, prophetess, and evangelist (see lesson 07/31). Many of those Old Testament traditions were rejected by Christ. For example, spouses were allowed to divorce only in cases of infidelity or abandonment (MAT 19:9; 1 CO 7:15). St. Paul also proclaimed that women and men are equal in Christ (GAL 3:28); and both sexes receive an equal inheritance in God's kingdom (HEB 2:10–11).

Muslim men traditionally have treated females as second-class citizens, as stated in the Koran (Surah 2:227–230; Surah 4:10–12; Surah 4:129–130; Surah 16:72; Surah 33:57). Sons inherit two times that of daughters. The husband inherits his deceased wife's estate, but the wife inherits only a quarter of her deceased husband's estate. Husbands can have up to four wives; men can have sex with their wives and their slaves. The Koran explains how men who make it to paradise lounge around drinking wine and enjoying the services of seventy-two virgins (Surah 52:14–20; Surah 55:52–68; Surah 56:7–48; Surah 83:22–25). There is no mention in the Koran about women and what paradise would look like to them for believing in Islam.

Father, we pray that the rights of women would be respected here and abroad. Let there be equal opportunities for learning and other rights regardless of sex. In Jesus's name, Amen.

November 19

International Men's Day is a celebration of the accomplishments and contributions of men in society, culture, and family. This observance began to show up in the early 1990s to bring attention to issues affecting men and boys, fathers and husbands, such as health, safety, roles, responsibility, and accountability. There is a significant need for positive male role models in the lives of children. Absent fathers and associated broken homes are the most critical issues of our time. The family is the core unit of society and the father should be available always. Kids who grow up without a solid father figure are prone to crime, drugs, dropping out, and behavioral health problems. Today's date was established by organizers who met in Trinidad and Tobago, an event that was supported by the United Nations, though they have yet to make this observance official. Recall that International Women's Day (March 8) was approved by the UN in 1977.

Men seem to be under attack these days by the culture warriors, but for the wrong reasons. There are more important issues than so-called "masculine toxicity". The real problems are deadbeat dads, corrupt oligarchs, and crooked politicians (which are not all male). The Bible appointed fathers to be the spiritual leaders of the household, a responsibility often shunned.

- DEU 1:13 ~ Take the wise men of understanding and notoriety, and make them rulers.
- DEU 22:5 ~ Women should not wear men's clothes; men should not wear women's clothes.
- PSA 12:8 ~ The wicked are all around when vile men are exalted.
- ISA 2:6, 11, 19 ~ The people practice divination and fortunetelling. They please themselves with children of strangers. The pride of men will be humbled, and the Lord alone will be exalted on that day. And people will hide from the terror of the Lord when He comes.
- JOE 2:28 ~ I will pour out my Spirit on humankind, and your sons and daughters will prophesy, your old men will dream dreams, and your young men will see visions.
- MIC 7:2–6 ~ All the godly and upright men are gone. The wicked lie in ambush for blood. They do evil with diligence. Princes and judges ask for bribes. Great men speak of and pursue the evil desires of their souls. Even the best of them is like a thorn. Their confusion and punishment await them. Nobody can be trusted; even family and friends become the enemy.
- JOH 3:19 ~ The light came into the world, but men loved darkness rather than light, because their deeds were evil.
- ACT 20:30 ~ Even from among yourselves men will come, speaking perverse things to get others to follow them.
- ROM 1:27 ~ Men gave up natural relations with women in favor of passion for each other. Men performed shameless acts with other men, thereby receiving in their own persons the due penalty for these evil deeds.
- TIT 1:14 ~ Pay no attention to Jewish fables and the commandments of men that turn people from the truth.
- TIT 2:2 ~ Men should be sober, calm, moderate, faithful, charitable, and patient.

Father, we pray for men, old and young, that they would be godly and generous fathers, husbands, workers, and leaders. Help them to fulfill their responsibilities with honor, integrity, and enthusiasm, so that their reputation will be one of a righteous, devout, and wise gentleman of God. We pray for all men who exemplify you, Father, and who, guided by the Holy Spirit, walk in Christ in whose name we pray, Amen.

November 20

World Children's Day was initiated through a United Nations resolution in December of 1954, called Universal Children's Day, to provide education, protection, welfare, and equal opportunity for children around the world so they can become high achievers and realize their full potential. Certainly, such an agenda elevates world peace and prosperity, teaching our children to appreciate cultural diversity and to acknowledge the relative worth of all humankind, rather than being manipulated, inhibited, brainwashed, or prejudiced against anyone of particular ethnicity, nationality, gender, age, or status. A day of celebrating children goes back to 1857 with Rose Day, which evolved into Flower Sunday, before being called Children's Day. The official day to acknowledge and propagate this vision was changed to November 20, when in 1959 the United Nations adopted their *Declaration of the Rights of the Child*. In 1989, the UN held a Convention of the Rights of the Child promulgating specific rights and needs of children, and urging all nations to declare children's rights as international law. In 2012, another UN initiative emphasized children's right to an education, to include instruction in the basics. Communities and nations are encouraged to advocate for children's rights today as well as all days henceforth. Being an international observance, anybody can participate whether in small groups, families, community events or global events; if you go, don't forget to bring the children.

Children are oftentimes viewed as an investment; yes, we must be invested in their developmental training, physical and mental wellbeing, and moral upbringing. However, all too often they are treated like a commodity that can be bought and sold. Children are the most exploited group of all time. The most heinous crimes imaginable are committed against children. It is time to speak out against unfair child labor, discrimination, exploitation, slavery, and trafficking. We must raise awareness of such things. We must shut down the child trafficking business once and for all. We must prevent the sexualization of kids in our schools. We must keep pedophiles, molesters, and abusers behind bars; statistically, they are the most likely criminals to reoffend.

- PSA 7:16 ~ His mischief returns upon his own head, and on his own skull his violence descends.

- PSA 127:3–4 ~ Children are a heritage unto the Lord, and the fruit of the womb is His reward. As arrows are in the hand of a mighty man so are the children of his youth.

- PSA 146:9 ~ The Lord preserves strangers and relieves the fatherless and the widows. But the way of the wicked he turns upside down.

- PRO 11:5 ~ The Lord tests the righteous, but His soul hates the wicked and the ones who love violence.

- PRO 19:18 ~ Discipline your child while there is hope; let not your soul hold back because of his or her crying.

- PRO 22:6 ~ Instruct your children in the way they should go and when they mature, they will not depart from it.

- MAT 18:6 ~ Jesus said, "But whoever causes one of these little ones who believe in me to sin, it would be better for him to have a great millstone tied around his neck and to be drowned in the depth of the sea."

- MAR 9:37 ~ Jesus said, "Whoever receives a child in my name, he receives me; and whoever receives me receives Him who sent me."

- COL 3:20–21 ~ Children, obey your parents in all things for this pleases the Lord. Parents, do not provoke your children to anger, lest they become discouraged.

- EPH 6:2–4 ~ Children, honor your father and mother which is the first commandment that comes with a promise: so that things will go well with you and you may live long upon the earth. Parents, raise your children in the nurture and discipline of righteousness.

We have a Mother's Day and a Father's Day, and we have the lesser-known Children's Day. Yeah, children deserve to be celebrated. Children also have rights which apply exclusively to them—from conception to delivery, throughout childhood and continuing into adulthood. Remember these rights are inalienable, since they are given by God. Nobody has the right to deny these rights, although godly parents may impose restrictions on children until they reach maturity.

- JOB 31:15 ~ Did He who formed me in the womb not make others the same way? Was it not the same God who formed every one of us within our mother's womb?

- PSA 22:10 ~ The Lord called me, even as I was in the womb, and I have been His since I was born.

- PSA 100:3 ~ The Lord is God. He is the One that made us, not we ourselves. We are His people and the sheep of His pasture.

- PSA 139:13, 15–16 ~ The Lord controlled my very being, even when I was in my mother's womb. My essence was never concealed from Him, for He knew me even as I was being secretly made and as I developed inside my mother. He saw me when I was still imperfect, and in His book were written all the members of my body while they were being formed and were yet undeveloped.

- ISA 44:2, 24 ~ The Lord made you and formed you in the womb…

- ISA 46:3–4 ~ God says, "Listen all of you in the house of Jacob and the remnants of Israel, for you were mine since you were conceived and lived in the womb; when you are old and gray, I still will be the one who keeps you. I made you, I sustain you, and I will deliver you."

- ISA 49:5 ~ The Lord formed me from the womb to be His servant.

- JER 1:5 ~ God said to Jeremiah, "I knew you before I formed you in your mother's womb; I sanctified you before you were delivered from your mother's womb. I ordained you to be a prophet to all nations."

- LUK 1:13–15, 44 ~ God told Zachariah that his wife Elisabeth would bear a son, and to call him John. That son would be filled with the Holy Spirit, even from his mother's womb. Elisabeth said to Mary, "The moment you said hello, the baby in my womb leaped with joy."

- 1 CO 7:4 ~ A spouse does not have exclusive power over his or her body.

Father in heaven, we implore that you protect the children of the world from violence and exploitation. Concerning those children whose parents have abandoned them, please place nurturing parental figures in their lives to teach and raise them. Bring to swift justice anyone who would harm a child mentally, emotionally, physically, sexually, and/or spiritually. Strengthen our law enforcement agencies to prioritize crimes directed at children, and ensure powerful punishment is levied against those who abuse, neglect, and exploit little ones. Enable us to place into office leaders who will crack down on crimes against children, and keep career criminals who abuse children from reoffending. Please help people to gain awareness of these issues, especially parents, so they can take precautions to include teaching kids to react immediately when certain warning signs are present. Help parents also to value the child in the womb. If they are not in a position to raise their child, help them to find good and godly people who would be thrilled to raise them. We ask this in the name of your only begotten Son, Jesus Christ, Amen.

November 21

World Television Day is a UN sanctioned occasion commemorating the meeting of the World Television Forum in 1996. This observance is part of their multimedia campaign to produce and stream programming in multiple languages for social media platforms and broadcast partners. You can access this programming through the UN social media channels. Certainly, TV has brought global news into every home with an electronic device. Television has been exploited for good and for evil, by shaping the narrative and public opinion. In the last two decades, that agenda has been centered on a single ideology, namely globalism. People make decisions based on information, and they trust the media to be an arbiter of truth; but lately it has been an arbiter of misinformation if not downright deceit. It behooves one to gather information from multiple sources and networks, disciplines, political agendas, and opinions; diligently sifting through the mess of all possible extremes for the hidden truth. Among the various misleading presentations, truth will be exposed, enabling one to draw an accurate conclusion that lies within all the clutter.

- PRO 1:4–7 ~ A wise person will listen and will increase in learning; a person of understanding will seek wise counsel, and will try to understand a proverb and its interpretation, or the words of the wise and the hidden meaning of what they say. Remember, the fear of God is the beginning of understanding; only fools despise wisdom and instruction.
- 1 CO 1:10 ~ By the name of Christ, be united in one mind and be of one opinion.
- 1 CO 2:7 ~ We speak the hidden wisdom of God in a mystery, the mystery that brings us glory which He ordained before the world was made.
- 1 CO 4:5 ~ Do not judge anyone before the Lord returns. God will bring to light all that is hidden, even the secrets of our hearts. Then everyone will praise Him.
- COL 2:2–3 ~ Be comforted, and bound together in love, and to the wealth of understanding and acknowledgment of the mystery of God, the Father, and Christ, in whom all the treasures of wisdom and knowledge are hidden.
- 1 JO 4:4–6 ~ We are of God. Those who know God will listen to His messengers, and those who are not of God will not listen. We know the difference between the Spirit of truth and the spirit of untruth.

In Biblical times there were few avenues to obtain information; it was largely by word of mouth since most of the population was illiterate. Consequently, numerous false prophets and counterfeit manuscripts proliferated, as the canon of the New Testament was being authenticated. However, bits and pieces of truth were often embedded within the lies. Biblical scholars have determined that these counterfeit and secular sources, when combined, converge on central truths aligned with the Biblical narrative. Despite concerted efforts to smother or distort the Word, the fakes collectively upheld much of the Bible, while enabling the weeding out of random drivel.

- LEV 19:16 ~ Do not go around spreading gossip or rumors.
- PRO 10:18 ~ Those who disguise their hatred with lies and those who slander another are fools.
- PHP 1:15–18 ~ Some indeed preach Christ out of envy and rivalry; others preach out of good will. One preaches Christ in order to be controversial, insincerely pretending to be an authority to draw attention to themselves. Another preaches out of love, the way I preach in defense of the Gospel. But whether in pretention or in truth, Christ is being preached, and for this I rejoice.
- 2 TH 2:15 ~ Stand strong and hold onto the traditions you have been taught whether by word of mouth or by epistle.

NOVEMBER

- JAM 3:5–6 ~ The tongue, although a little member, boasts great things; how great a matter a little fire can kindle. For the tongue is like fire, creating a world of sin; the tongue defiles the entire body, setting on fire the course of nature and the burning with hellfire.

There were countless scientists, inventors, and engineers who contributed to the invention of television; most notably were P. Farnsworth who converted images into electrical wave patterns, and V. Zworykin who invented the cathode ray tube. RCA combined the two technologies to produce the first television set in 1927. The BBC soon became the only network in England circa 1936. Another precipitating event was the 1939 World's Fair in New York when NBC broadcast the opening ceremonies and a speech by President F. D. Roosevelt. CBS and ABC broadcasting networks split off at that point. By the 1940s there were two dozen stations televising news reports and theatric productions. By the 1950s, half of Americans had a black and white TV. Color televisions were introduced in the 1960s; by the 1970s black and white televisions were ancient history. Since the 1980s, color television screens have become progressively larger. Now, most homes have more than one television set.

God broadcasts important messages in the Bible. When He speaks from heaven it is hard to miss. People of faith also broadcast, televise, and disseminate the truth of God and His works. Christians boast of our Lord and the wonders of His creation, loudly proclaiming His magnificence all over the world. Many networks provide Christian programming, and there is quite a variety. Unfortunately, such programming is censored in numerous locations around the world.

- ISA 6:1–3 ~ I saw the Lord sitting on His throne high in the heavens. Above Him were seraphim, each having six wings: two covered the face, two covered the feet, and two wings for flying. They shouted, "Holy, Holy, Holy is the Lord of hosts; the whole earth is full of His glory."

- MAT 3:16–17 ~ After John baptized Jesus, He came out of the water and the heavens were opened before Him while the Spirit of God descended like a dove and lighted upon Him. And a voice from heaven was heard saying, "This is my beloved Son in whom I am well pleased."

- LUK 9:28–31, 34–35 ~ Jesus took Peter, James, and John to the mountaintop to pray. While Jesus prayed, His countenance changed and His clothes shined as lightning. Moses and Elijah appeared with Jesus in glorious splendor; they were speaking of His departure which would occur during His upcoming visit to Jerusalem. While Peter spoke, a cloud enveloped them and they were afraid. A voice spoke from the cloud saying, "This is my Son whom I have chosen; listen to Him."

- 1 TH 4:16–18 ~ The Lord will descend from heaven with a shout, with the voice of the archangel, and with a blast from the trumpet of God. Then the dead in Christ will rise first. Those who remain alive in Christ will rise to join the others in the clouds, meeting the Lord in the sky. Those chosen by Christ will live with Him forevermore. Therefore, comfort one another with these words.

Father, we thank you for the many conveniences that we take for granted, such as television. We pray that this technology will be used to further your kingdom by reaching remote areas of the globe with the Gospel of Jesus Christ. We pray that the truth will be told, and that the programming will be geared towards godliness, integrity, and responsible reportage. Help parents to be unremitting in monitoring what their kids are viewing, blocking the programs that are immoral, deceitful, profane, or misleading. Let there be proper censorship of disinformation and appropriate dissemination of the facts in our media outlets. If it be your will, let us return to honesty in the press, which was the purpose of that cherished freedom; without a free and honest press we will not be free as a nation. In the name of Jesus who spoke the Gospel truth, Amen.

November 22

National Bible Week occurs during the week of Thanksgiving, starting the Sunday before and ending the Sunday after that hallowed occasion. In 1940 the National Bible Association was founded in New York City, to broadcast Bible readings and teachings that would bring comfort to the country, influencing President Roosevelt to establish National Bible Week the second week in December. To usher in the first Bible week, a program was hosted at the White House on December 7, 1941. A reading was underway when breaking news of Japan's attack on Pearl Harbor was announced. The rest of the day consisted of news updates and Bible readings. Everyone in the nation tuned into NBC for a mix of bad news from Hawaii, and good news from God's Word. Thereafter, Bible Week was observed in November, and Pearl Harbor Day was reserved for December. Bible Week was declared by every President after FDR, but that string ended with Obama who ignored Bible Week but held a Ramadan celebration at the White House.

Most of our presidents and the vast majority of the founders and framers of our constitutional republic have been God-fearing men. However, some of our presidents have claimed to be men of faith, but did not reflect that in their extracurricular activity or dialogue. Presidents are sinners like everybody, but people of faith in high positions must lead by example. They also should be willing to express their religious views and exercise their religious freedom as exhibited in the following quotes (from Barber, 2020b).

- John Adams: *The highest glory of the American Revolution was this: it connected, in one indissoluble bond, the principles of Christianity... Our Constitution was made only for a moral and religious people. It is wholly inadequate to the government of any other.*

- Benjamin Franklin: *God governs in the affairs of man... Here is my Creed. I believe in one God, the Creator of the Universe. That He governs it by His Providence. That He ought to be worshipped.*

- Alexander Hamilton: *I have carefully examined the evidences of the Christian religion, and if I was sitting as a juror upon its authenticity, I would unhesitatingly give my verdict in its favor. I can prove its truth as clearly as any proposition ever submitted to the mind of man.*

- John Hancock: *Continue steadfast and, with a proper sense of your dependence on God, nobly defend those rights which heaven gave, and no man ought to take from us... That the kingdom of our Lord and Savior Jesus Christ may be established in peace and righteousness among all the nations of the earth.*

- Patrick Henry: *It cannot be emphasized too strongly or too often that this great Nation was founded not by religionists, but by Christians; not on religions, but on the Gospel of Jesus Christ.*

- John Jay: *The Bible is the best of all books, for it is the word of God and teaches us the way to be happy in this world and the next.*

- Thomas Jefferson: *We all agree in the obligation of the moral principles of Jesus and nowhere will they be found delivered in greater purity than in His discourses... Can the liberties of a nation be thought secure when we have removed their only firm basis, a conviction in the minds of the people that these liberties are the Gift of God?*

- James Madison: *Cursed be all learning that is contrary to the cross of Christ.*

- George Mason: *The laws of nature are the laws of God, whose authority can be superseded by no power on earth... That religion, or the duty which we owe to our Creator, and the manner of discharging it, can be directed only by reason and conviction, not by force or violence; and therefore, all men are equally entitled to the free exercise of religion, according to the dictates of conscience; and that it is the mutual duty to all to practice Christian forbearance, love, and charity towards each other*

- James Monroe: *When we view the blessings with which our country has been favored, those which we now enjoy, and the means which we possess of handing them down unimpaired to our latest posterity, our attention is irresistibly drawn to the source from whence they flow. Let us then, unite in offering our most grateful acknowledgments for these blessings to the Divine Author of All Good.*

- Benjamin Rush: *The only means of establishing and perpetuating our republican form of government is the universal education of our youth in the principles of Christianity by means of the Bible.*

- Joseph Story: *I verily believe Christianity necessary to the support of civil society. One of the beautiful boasts of our municipal jurisprudence is that Christianity is a part of the Common Law.*

The Holy Bible is celebrated this week by readings, the sharing of favorite passages, singing hymns and worshipping, intercessory prayer, and focused studies from the Word of God. Many churches will have special readings on the Sundays before and after Thanksgiving. Bible Week ushers in the holy season of Advent which leads up to Christmas; Hanukkah is also celebrated by many Jews during this timeframe.

- DEU 28:1, 15–16 ~ God said, "If you listen diligently to the voice of the Lord, and observe His commandments, I will place you high above all nations of the earth. But if you do not listen to the Lord and you do not observe His commandments and statutes that I have commanded you to follow, curses will come upon you and overtake you; you will be cursed in the city and in the country.

- PSA 34:17 ~ The righteous cry, and the Lord hears and delivers them out of their troubles.

- PSA 50:15 ~ Call upon God in the day of trouble and you will be delivered, and you will glorify God.

- ROM 10:17 ~ Faith comes by hearing and hearing by the Word of God.

- EPH 1:5, 11, 13 ~ We were predestined to become adopted children of God by Jesus Christ, according to His marvelous will. In whom you trusted when you heard the Word of truth, the Gospel of your salvation; when you believed you were sealed by the Holy Spirit of promise.

- COL 3:16 ~ Remember what Christ taught you and let His words enrich your lives and make you wise. Teach His words to each other. Sing them openly and spiritually in psalms and hymns with thankful hearts.

- 1 TH 3:1 ~ Pray for the evangelists, so that God's Word may have free course, and be glorified in others even as it is with you.

- JAM 1:22 ~ Be doers of the Word and not merely hearers of the Word, thereby deceiving yourselves.

Heavenly Father, we pray that your Word will be spoken freely within our nation and proclaimed freely throughout the world; not just this week but every week, so that all can know the truth and find salvation in Jesus Christ. Let people find encouragement in your words so they will invite your Spirit to come into their hearts; and help them to find a Bible believing church, where every week is Bible Week. In the name of the Word made flesh we pray, Amen.

November 23

Pascal Converted After Vision of Crucifixion on this day in 1654. Blaise Pascal was a physicist, mathematician, inventor, and Christian apologist. His genius began to show early in his life; he was a teenager when he invented a mechanical digital calculator to help his accountant father, and he sold fifty of them. Born into the Catholic faith, he was not altogether religious, though he did dialogue with intellectuals from the clergy. He was barely into his thirties when he experienced the vision. It began with fire, then the appearance of Abraham, Isaac, and Jacob. He felt joyful and at peace. He identified Christ as God, and discovered the dignity of the human soul. He was afraid that he had forsaken God and His Son, and that God might forsake him. He prayed to God for eternal life and never again to be separated from Him. He renounced his sins and submitted to Christ, promising Him that he would keep His words forever. He recorded the two-hour vision on paper; then he sewed the paper into his jacket so it would remain close to his heart. He switched his focus from science and math to Christian apologetics (defense of the faith). Unfortunately, this great thinker was ill most of his life, dying before his fortieth birthday. Though he didn't seek fame, he became famous nevertheless.

- NUM 12:6 ~ If there is a prophet among you, I will make myself known to him in a vision and will speak to him in a dream.

- PRO 15:28 ~ The righteous heart studies the situation before giving an answer; however, a wicked mouth pours out evil words.

- ECC 7:12, 25 ~ Wisdom is a defense, and money is a defense; but wisdom gives life to those who possess it. I applied my heart to know, to search, and to seek wisdom, and the reasons for things, and to know the wickedness of folly, foolishness, and madness.

- HOS 12:10 ~ God spoke through the prophets, gave them many visions, and told parables through them.

- JOE 2:28 ~ I will pour out my Spirit upon all people. Your sons and daughters will prophesy, your old men will dream dreams, and your young men will see visions.

- ACT 11:1–18 ~ Peter had a vision that God would proclaim His Gospel to the Gentile nations.

Pascal was one of the great thinkers and philosophers of all time. He established that all angles in a triangle adds up to 180 degrees, and advanced his theorem in geometry which is still taught today. He determined the dynamics for the roulette wheel as he experimented with the concept of perpetual motion. He helped to employ and describe atmospheric and barometric pressure; he explained hydraulic resistance which is essential to braking systems and shock absorbers. He devised methods of calculating probabilities and expected values using statistics. These are but a glimpse of his numerous accomplishments during his short life.

- JER 8:9 ~ The wise will be put to shame; they will be dismayed and trapped by their foolishness. Since they have rejected the Word of the Lord, what kind of wisdom do they really have?

- 1 CO 1:19–21, 27 ~ It is written: I will destroy the wisdom of the wise and bring to nothing the understanding of the prudent. Where is wisdom? Has God not made foolish the wisdom of this world? The world through its wisdom cannot know God. But God has chosen foolish things of the world to confound the wise, and weak things to confound the mighty.

- 1 CO 2:7, 13–16 ~ We speak the wisdom of God as a mystery, even the hidden wisdom of God, which He ordained before the world to our glory. These things we speak, not in the words which humanity teaches, but which the Holy Spirit teaches, comparing spiritual things with spiritual. But natural people do not receive spiritual things of God for these things are foolishness to them; neither can they know these things because they must be discerned spiritually. But those who are spiritual analyze everything and are judged by nobody. Nobody knows the mind of God that they can instruct Him, but those who are spiritual have the mind of Christ.

As an apologist, Pascal proposed his famous "Pascal's Wager" declaring it pragmatic to live one's life as if God exists, for by doing so you lose nothing if God is not real; but if He is real, you gain eternal life. Conversely, if you live your life as if there is no God and there isn't, you lose nothing; but if He does exist you lose everything. Pascal also pointed out that those believing in God are generally happier, more hopeful, and more at peace than those who do not believe. Pascal's snippets of wisdom are quoted often; below are a few of my favorites.

- *People almost invariably arrive at their beliefs not on the basis of proof but on the basis of what they find attractive.*
- *Truth is so obscure in these times, and falsehood so established, that unless we love the truth, we cannot know it.*
- *Jesus is the God whom we can approach without pride and before whom we can humble ourselves without despair.*
- *The knowledge of God is very far from the love of Him.*

- JOB 21:34 ~ How can you comfort me with your nonsense, because in your answers there remains falsehood?

- PRO 25:2 ~ It is the glory of God to conceal things, but the glory of kings to search them out.

- ECC 3:9–12 ~ What do people gain from all their hard work? I have seen the struggle that God has given to the human race to keep them occupied. He has made everything beautiful in its time. He has placed eternity into our hearts. Still, humans cannot discover what He has done from the beginning to the end. There is no goodness in a person, but to rejoice and try to do good every day.

- MAR 4:22 ~ Nothing is hidden except for it to be revealed; nothing is kept secret except for it to come to light.

- HEB 11:1, 6 ~ Faith is the assurance of things hoped for, the evidence of things not seen. Without faith it is impossible to please God, for whoever would draw near to Him must believe that He exists and that He rewards those who seek Him.

- 1 JO 4:6–8 ~ We are of God; those who know God will listen to us. Those who are not of God will not listen. We know the difference between the spirit of truth and the spirit of error.

Heavenly Father, we know that you are real, true, and we love you with all our heart and soul. Help those who are not so sure to bet their lives on Jesus, for this is a guaranteed win, and the prize is a crown of life. Bring to those who require more proof a vision or a dream, something to get their attention so that they will want to seek you and learn about your words and promises. Help them to hear your Holy Spirit when He speaks, and to know that you are always with them in Spirit. Show them who you are in a manner that will convince them to delve into your Word, and receive you into their hearts, to live the rest of their lives in faith towards you and fervent love towards one another. Help intellectuals to learn the truth and see the proof in your Word. Help those of us who know you and love you to grow stronger each day in faith, hope, and love. We pray these things in the name of the Father, Son, and Holy Spirit, Amen.

November 24

Celebrate Your Unique Talent Day is self-explanatory. Everyone has a repertory of gifts and talents that God has given them; and these gifts vary from person to person. There is no historical or official recognition of this holiday, but it has become a trendy one. Since there is no known precedent that I could find, I will officially designate this holiday to be observed annually for the following reasons (each of these events occurred on November 24).

- 1877 – Author Anna Sewell published *Black Beauty.*
- 1901 – Artist Henri de Toulouse-Lautrec was born.
- 1947 – Author John Steinbeck published *The Pearl.*
- 1950 – Broadway musical *Guys and Dolls* opened.
- 1957 – Football legend Jim Brown set the club record for yards rushing.
- 1960 – Basketball legend Wilt Chamberlain set NBA rebound record.
- 1966 – The Beatles began recording *Sgt. Pepper's Lonely Hearts Club Band* album.
- 1982 – Baseball infielder Cal Ripken was named American League rookie of the year.
- 1991 – Vocalist Freddie Mercury of the band *Queen* died.

No doubt, we could add to the above list. All of these talented people had a profound influence on civilization, and upon innumerable individuals as well, giving them inspiration to excel and persevere. It matters not which gift you excel at, because all gifts will contribute to the betterment of society, culture, and people's lives; not to mention yourself and your life. Everybody is talented, regardless of age, sex, ethnicity, socioeconomic status, or what have you: we all have potential for greatness, thankfully, not in the same things. We also have equal ability to serve the Lord, in more than a few disciplines. Give God the glory for your abilities and achievements; thank Him for gifting you with unique talents. Praise Him who created you.

- PRO 19:21 ~ People develop their own plans, but it is the Lord's purpose that will prevail.

- ECC 8:6–7 ~ For every purpose under heaven there is a season, a time designated by God, although misery and trials may continue to occur. Since we do not know what that purpose is, who but God will be able to tell us when?

- ROM 12:4–6 ~ Just as our body has many members, each with a separate purpose, so we, being part of the body of Christ, have different responsibilities. We all have different gifts that the Lord our God in His grace has given us to use for His glory.

- 2 CO 4:6 ~ God, who commanded the light to shine out of darkness, has shined in our hearts, so that we can share the light of the knowledge of God's glory in Jesus Christ.

- HEB 12:28 ~ Since God has given us the kingdom, let us please Him by serving Him with thankful hearts, with holy fear, and with awe.

- 1 PE 4:10–11 ~ Whoever has received the gift of salvation in Christ should share that gift with others. Be a witness or a messenger with whatever abilities God has given you.

- 2 PE 1:3 ~ His divine power has granted to us all things pertaining to life and godliness, through the knowledge of Him who called us to His own glory and excellence.

What would be a good way to celebrate this day? Prepare a list of the talents that you believe you possess; ask family and friends what they think about your list and add to it. Choose some gifts that you want to cultivate, to master, possibly to employ as a vocation or for profit. Identify talents you wish you had, and identify some that you would make the effort to learn, exercise, and possibly add to your previous list of talents. Remember, God gives us all personal

NOVEMBER

talents, and you are probably aware of some of them; but you might have additional gifts that you have yet to realize. Do you want to find out what they are? Then study different things, research the requirements for certain jobs, try out new things: enough to determine if they are something worth pursuing. It may be harder to master things which you are not innately talented at, but with desire and effort, everyone has ability to master just about anything. You are never too old or too young to learn new things. I am living proof that you can teach an old dog new tricks.

- PSA 119:73 ~ Your hands made me and formed me; give me understanding to know your commands.

- ISA 64:8 ~ You, oh Lord, are our Father. We are the clay and you are the potter; we are the works of your hand.

- JER 29:11 ~ I know the plans I have for you, declares the Lord; plans to prosper you and protect you; plans to give you hope and a future.

In ancient Greece, a talent was a measure of weight; for example, a talent of silver was about twenty-five kilos (roughly twelve pounds) of silver. Talent carried weight and still does.

- MAT 25:14–30; LUK 19:12–26 ~ Jesus told the following parable: The kingdom of heaven is like a man traveling to a far country who called his servants together. He entrusted them with five talents, two talents, and one talent of gold, respectively, in accordance with their ability. The servant with five and the servant with two put their money to work and doubled their money. The master told each of them, "Well done, good and faithful servant; since you have been fruitful with a few things, I will make you ruler over many things, and you will receive the joy of the Lord." The servant with one talent had hidden it in the ground for fear of losing it. He said to his master, "I know you are a stern man, reaping that which you did not sow and gathering where you did not seed; and I was afraid. But here is your talent." The master replied, "You wicked and lazy servant; you at least could have put the money in the bank where it would have yielded modest interest." The master took the talent from him and gave it to the man who had ten talents, saying, "For everyone who has, more will be given; but from those who do not have, even that will be taken away." Then he threw the unfaithful servant into outer darkness where there will be weeping and gnashing of teeth.

- LUK 12:47–48 ~ Servants who know the Lord's will and do not prepare or obey their master will be punished severely; but those who disobey out of ignorance will receive a lesser punishment. Of those who have been given much, much will be required; and of those who have been entrusted much, more will be demanded.

- 2 CO 9:6–7, 10 ~ Whoever sows sparingly will reap sparingly; whoever sows bountifully will reap bountifully. It depends on the purpose one has in their heart. So, when you give, do not give begrudgingly or out of obligation, but give cheerfully, for that pleases God very much. He who provides seed to the sower and bread for food will multiply your store of seed and will enlarge your harvest in the name of righteousness.

God has given you talents to use for His glory. If you do not use them, you may lose them. Because every talent needs to be cultivated, exercised, and/or practiced. If you use it for the glory of God, you may obtain even more gifts. And with this comes more responsibility.

Father, we thank you for making us unique, different from every other human being, filled with talent, interests, and motivation to do your will and exercise our gifts. Let us use those gifts to the glory of your holy name, and for the advancement of our livelihood, of society and of humanity. Help us to likewise learn and cultivate our spiritual gifts to spread the truth and make disciples for Jesus. In His name we pray, Amen.

November 25

Expose the Grand Delusion Day is declared for unmasking the lies being perpetuated by people who have lost their spiritual sight, and therefore, cannot contemplate or acknowledge God. To these people, God is a myth. They choose to believe their own myths because they neither want God nor expect to be held responsible for their atrocities. Bottom line: they choose to believe there will be no judgment or accountability as they continue their decadent and ungodly lifestyles. They slacken the laws and legalize sinful behavior to justify their actions and beliefs. They deliberately choose to ignore the truth and subdue their consciences to placate their sinful lusts and greed. Consider these scriptures from the Holy Bible.

- ISA 66:4 ~ I will choose their delusions; I will bring their fears upon them. Because, when I called nobody answered; when I spoke, nobody listened. Instead, they were evil before my eyes, and they chose to do the things which I despise.

- 2 TH 2:8–12 ~ After the wicked one is revealed the Lord will consume him with the spirit of His mouth, and will destroy him with the brightness of His coming. Not only the one who acts on behalf of Satan, with power, signs, and wonders, but also followers who likewise possess deceptiveness and unrighteousness, hating the truth that could save them. For this reason, God will send them a strong delusion, and allow them to believe their lies. Those who will not believe the truth and find pleasure in unrighteousness will be damned.

Beware and prepare when evil encompasses the righteous, for Satan is establishing a stronghold, deceiving many with fake miracles, changing the laws, perverting the truth, and promoting wickedness. You will see an abandonment of decency and integrity, law and order, and charity and compassion for others. The focus will center on globalism, and assorted desires of the flesh. These priorities will replace godliness, ethics, and spirituality causing a massive falling away from the faith. Like Jesus said, you cannot love God and mammon (material things).

- DAN 11:23–24 ~ He will make alliances deceptively, and will plunder. He will corrupt people. He will forecast devices against his enemies. He will employ the power of forces. He will honor with money, pleasure, and luxury.

- HAB 1:4 ~ The law becomes loose and justice is not served, for the wicked encompass the righteous and wrong judgment proceeds.

- MAT 6:24 ~ Nobody can serve two masters, for they will end up loving one and despising the other. You cannot serve God and money at the same time.

- 2 TH 2:3–4 ~ There will be a vast falling away when the man of lawlessness comes, who is the son of perdition. He exalts himself to be a god or an object of worship, taking the seat in the temple of God.

Current events suggest a rapid regression away from God and His will, centered on one's own will and the will of those in power. People will be playing God, pretending to be sovereign or in control, and greedy for more power and control. Rather than being justified by faith in God, they will justify themselves in total disregard for God and people of faith. Those striving for riches, power, pleasure, and domination will never be satisfied; but regarding those who rely on the Lord, He will provide (MAT 6:25–34).

- ECC 5:10 ~ Those who love money will never be satisfied with it; those who love abundance will never have enough.

- HAB 1:11 ~ They are blown with the wind and pass on, those guilty men who relish in their own power as their god.

- GAL 6:7–8 ~ Do not be deceived; for God cannot be mocked. Whatever a man sows that will he also reap. People who sow to please their sinful flesh will reap destruction. People who sow to please the Holy Spirit will reap eternal life.

- 2 TI 3:1–4 ~ There will be a time of great distress. People will love themselves. They will be abusive, arrogant, conceited, disobedient, treacherous, slanderous, ungrateful, unholy, inhumane, haters of good and lovers of pleasure more than lovers of God.

Psychologically speaking, a delusion is a false belief or belief system; it is a common symptom of psychosis. Simply put, psychosis is an extreme mental disorder characterized by impaired intellectual and social functioning, and a significant departure from reality and truth. Spiritually speaking, the strong delusion addressed by the apostle Paul fits exactly the above descriptions. There may be organic reasons why a person is mentally ill such as a chemical imbalance in the brain, for which medication may help. Then there are people who choose to believe the lie over accepting truth; they deliberately distort reality to correspond with personal preferences. This fabricated reality becomes very resistant to factual information and associated disconfirming evidence, resulting in the relativism of truth and the conviction that truth can never be absolute. But indeed, for something to be absolutely true it must be true for everyone and for all time. God's truth will always remain relevant and will never change. A partial truth is indefinite and therefore subject to variations in interpretation, never approaching factuality or consistency with known reality.

- PRO 12:17 ~ Those who speak truth reveal righteousness, but a false witness reveals deceit.

- PRO 17:4 ~ An evildoer gives heed to false lips; and a liar gives ear to a filthy tongue.

- PRO 21:6–7 ~ Obtaining wealth by lying is a vanity tossed about among those who seek death; for the robbery committed by the wicked will destroy them.

- PRO 26:28 ~ A lying tongue hates the ones affected by it, and a flattering mouth works ruin.

- JOH 8:44 ~ Jesus told the unbelievers, "You evil people belong to your father, the devil, and the evil of your father is what you do. He was a murderer and a liar from the start. He never tells the truth; in fact, he is the father of lies."

- ROM 1:18–25 ~ The wrath of God is being revealed from heaven against the wickedness of men, who suppress the truth through unrighteousness, though the things that are known about God are clear to them because God has made these things clear. Since the creation of the world, God's invisible qualities have been obvious, including His eternal power and His divine nature. Therefore, they have no excuse; because, while they knew God, they neither glorified Him nor gave thanks to Him. Their thinking became futile and their foolish hearts were darkened. Though they claimed to be wise, they were foolish, exchanging the glory of God for graven images. God allowed them to become depraved, who turned God's truth into a lie and worshipped and served the creature rather than the Creator who is blessed forever.

For those accepting the strong delusion, everything becomes make-believe, lies are passed off as truth, and arguments fail to comport with actuality. The grandiose claims, blatant fabrications, false narratives, fake news, cancellation of truth and the people who tell it, these are components of a calculated scheme to swindle the masses out of their wealth, livelihood, prospects, education, freedom, self-determination, and dreams in order to subjugate the citizenry, take away their choices and freedoms, confiscate their property, and remove their ability to retaliate or defend themselves. It is Marxism any way you look at it, though called by any number of names such as democratic-socialism, globalism, progressivism, fascism, critical theory, collectivism, and the like. This is a charade and they know it, but they want you to take their propaganda seriously. The whole purpose of propaganda is to disseminate lies ad nauseum, assuming that people will come to accept it if not believe it. However, these charlatans are deceiving themselves if they think patriots are that stupid not to see through their fantasies and their play acting. I mean, some of the tall tales they tell are so inane they are laughable but for the fact that they are very dangerous.

- PRO 29:12 ~ If a ruler listens to lies, his entire cabinet will be evil.

- JER 9:3–5 ~ They bend their tongues like the bow, dispelling lies. They do not champion the truth but proceed from one evil to another. "They do not know me," says the Lord. Take heed of those around you and be careful who you trust, for a brother can be a deceiver and a neighbor a slanderer. They deceive people by avoiding the truth. They have trained their tongues to speak lies, and weary themselves with their sinful ways.

- HOS 4:1–2 ~ Listen to the Lord you children of Israel for He has a warning to the inhabitants of the land, because there is no truth, mercy, or knowledge of God anywhere to be found. Instead, there is cursing, lying, killing, stealing, and adultery; they break all laws such that bloodshed will follow bloodshed.

- ROM 1:25, 30–32 ~ They exchanged God's truth with lies and worshipped and served the creation rather than the Creator. They were filled with all kinds of wickedness, evil, disobedience, covetousness, boastfulness, insolence, malice, murder, deceit, slander, strife, and malignity. They were faithless, heartless, ruthless, and foolish. They enjoyed doing evil, even though they were warned that such wickedness would lead to death.

    Contemplate this illustration from recent developments. When you leave town on vacation do you take preventive measures to ensure your home is secure? Certainly, you would not leave your doors wide open which would welcome all kinds of nefarious people to enter your abode and steal your belongings, wreck your house, or burn the place down. This is exactly what happened when a movement sought to eliminate police, while civic leaders neglected to enforce the law. Anarchists barged in and engaged in looting, arson, assault, and murder while utter chaos burgeoned. When security, order, and justice are abandoned it incentivizes such mayhem and lawlessness. When the federal government opened our border, crowds of illegal immigrants stormed into the country. Officials claimed this was normal, which would be accurate insofar as they removed the restrictions and sent out an invitation. But this was yet another giant deception, since the situation was far from normal given the record numbers that breached the boundary the moment restrictions were lifted. What could possibly be the motivation for allowing this? Would you call it equitable, or humanitarian, or inclusive, or legal?

- MAT 24:42–44 ~ Be watchful, for you never know when the Lord will come. If the man of the house knew when the burglar would come, he could have prevented his house from being burglarized. So be ready and watchful, for the Lord will come at a time when you least expect Him.

- ROM 13:1–5 ~ Everyone is subject to the higher powers, for all power comes from God; that is, all powers that exist have been ordained by God. Anyone who resists these powers are resisting the ordinance of God, and those who resist God receive damnation as punishment. Those who do what is right have no fear of the authorities, only those who do wrong are afraid of them. Do what is right and the authorities will commend you. Governments are God's servants; they are there to make sure you do what is right. But if you do what is evil, beware, for they do not carry a sword in vain, but to execute judgment on those who commit evil. Submit to those who are in authority, not just because you will be punished if you do not, but also as a matter of keeping a clear conscience.

Although the Bible encourages people to acquiesce to government, there may come a time when corruption grows so rampant that inhabitants will feel they have no recourse but to revolt. The warning signs are readily apparent: promoting division and bigotry, eliminating civil rights, discouraging gainful employment, growing monopolies, destroying the middle class and small businesses, creating a welfare state by forcing the populace into dependency on the government, recklessly blowing money and distributing it to people who haven't earned it, silencing dissention, and the list goes on. It's ironic how foreigners have flooded the border, many from nations that imposed socialism and dictatorships, hoping to be part of the land of the free and to realize the American Dream. What a shock it must be for those who arrived only to realize they could inherit the very thing from which they fled. Well, maybe if they become citizens and vote they will vote against this nonsense. Never in the history of humankind has a totalitarian government endured, because economic collapse occurs quickly then chaos ensues.

It is easy to recognize fakery and deception, unless you are distracted by the smoke and mirrors. But these bad actors are not only bad people, they are bad at acting out their delusion. It doesn't pass the smell test. They will pool the money, might, resources, infrastructure, technology, communication networks, media outlets, and corporate entities to grab everything in sight as long as they receive no resistance. The coveted result is two classes of people: the oligarchy and the general public; or as Marx put it, the bourgeoisie and the proletariat. Nothing in-between, just the rich ruling the poor, which is simply another form of slavery; remember, it's all about control. Do not fall for the lie that everyone benefits which is impossible. The steps recently being taken follow the same radical game plan to the letter, with the primary objective to take your freedoms by force, which is the power and security of the populace. How else can they control you unless they revoke your liberties? Ironic seeing how they are obviously out of control given their numerous vices, irrational proposals, and foolhardy power grabs.

Is there an occasion when revolution can be a righteous cause? I suppose the American Revolution would fit the scenario. This country prospered and progressed as long as we remained one nation under God, indivisible, with liberty and justice for all. One might characterize the civil rights movement as revolutionary. Our nation again finds itself divided, with individual rights being compromised, no equal representation under the law, and justice being doled out unevenly and unfairly. It is painful to be experiencing class warfare, crony capitalism, educational indoctrination, and cancel culture. This is the same game plan used by the Nazis, Stalinists, Marxists, and communists. Our framers had it right, and our founding documents are still applicable, producing the best system of government ever implemented. The USA is our republic, but can we keep it? Only if we get government back into the hands of the people, and get control of our lives out of the hands of government.

- EXO 18:20–21 ~ Moses's father-in-law counseled him suggesting he choose capable men who feared God to help him govern the land. They needed to be instructed in God's ordinances and laws, and shown the way in which they should walk and the work that they should perform. They had to be truthful, hating covetousness.

- 1 SA 15:23 ~ Samuel told King Saul that rebellion was like the sin of witchcraft and stubbornness like the sin of idolatry. And because the evil king had rejected the counsel of the Lord, God had rejected Saul as king.

- 2 SA 23:3 ~ The Spirit of the Lord spoke to David telling him that a person who would govern others must be just, and rule in the fear of God.

- NEH 4:20–21 ~ If you hear the trumpet sound, come quickly; our God will fight for us. So, we continued our work (on the city wall) with half of us holding weapons.

- PRO 24:21–22 ~ Dear children, fear the Lord and the king, but do not meddle with those driven by change, for their calamity will rise suddenly. And who knows what ruin that both will bring?
- PRO 29:2 ~ When the righteous are in authority the people rejoice; when the wicked rule, the people mourn.
- JOE 3:10 ~ Beat your plowshares into swords and your pruninghooks into spears. Let the weak say, "I am strong."
- ACT 5:29 ~ As a united front, Peter and the apostles declared, "We must obey God above men."
- 2 TI 4:3–4 ~ The time will come when people will not endure sound doctrine, but will follow their own lusts. They will collect and listen to teachers with wayward teachings. They will turn away from the truth and toward fables.

Administrations whose leadership are in rebellion to God are insufferable. God often intervenes for His people when unscrupulous rulers go astray in this manner. This occurred many times in the Old Testament, as well as during the American Revolution which resulted in a nation founded upon the Holy Bible and a Judeo-Christian philosophy. But we are departing from this underpinning and wandering into forbidden territory in the eyes of God. I pray God will intervene on our behalf once again and help us avoid bloodshed. But even though He guided and assisted the founders and freedom fighters, it was not without bloodshed. Evil always results in bloodshed. If you don't agree, you don't know Jesus Christ. What are Christians to do? For starters, be patient and tell the truth. God will reveal your direction if you allow the Holy Spirit to speak to your heart. As for those falling for the grand delusion, they have created their own reality which is false, and they have chosen to believe it while disregarding what is real and true; in short, they have begun to believe their lies and now are determined to cancel the rest of us.

- EXO 14:14 ~ The Lord will fight for you and you will hold your peace.
- PSA 118:8 ~ It is better to trust in the Lord than to put your confidence in humankind.
- LUK 12:11–12 ~ Jesus said, "When they bring you before the authorities, do not worry about what to say or do, for the Holy Spirit will provide the information when you need it."
- 1 CO 2:12–13 ~ We have received, not the spirit of the world, but the Spirit of God, so that we may know the things that God has given to us for free. We speak of these things, not in the words that the world teaches, but in words that the Holy Spirit teaches, comparing spiritual things with spiritual.
- 2 CO 3:3, 17–18 ~ The Spirit of the living God has written His Word into our hearts; it is not written in ink or on tablets of stone. The Lord is that Spirit, and wherever that Spirit is found there is liberty. All of us can see His glory when we look into the mirror, for we have been changed into His image by God's Holy Spirit.

While the Bible does not address the idea of righteous revolution specifically, there are examples when God's people had to reclaim their inheritance. God does not authorize governments or establishments to take from the people that which He promised or gave such as inalienable rights and the opportunity to support and raise a family via hard work. Consider the church of Corinth in the first century, which was shifting from faith towards a more secular footing (1 CO 3). The church was divided between those following Apollos and those following Paul. Paul wrote to the church saying, "I planted the seed and Apollos watered it, but God is the one who makes things grow. The one who plants and the one who waters are one, for we are working together for God and you are the building" (1 CO 3:4–6). The body of Christ is the church, and here was a church divided, just as we are divided as a nation. Paul's direction to the Corinthians was to reunite into a building erected upon Christ. We are commissioned by Christ to do our share of the work in the harvesting of souls by exercising spiritual gifts. The keyword here is giving, of ourselves, to the causes of faith and truth. Paul reminded us that we are the temple of the Holy Spirit who lives in us (1 CO 3:16) and who directs our path and our service.

What can we learn from this example? First, we must come together in unity of faith, regardless of denomination, remembering that God is in charge and His Word is our foundation. Secularists seek to destroy the church, because it is their greatest threat; this has become their religion. If the body of Christ unites with the Holy Spirit binding us together, we will be a most formidable opponent. Second, we can employ our spiritual knowledge, talents, and influence in whatever societal function that we are involved, and shine the light of Christ. By doing what is right and moral, we expose that which is wrong and immoral. Third, we need to appoint leaders who will obey God's rules rather than altering them. God used to select leaders for His people because they listened to their Heavenly Father, which is why He gave authority to fathers as spiritual leaders in the home, and why He empowered our forefathers to build this great republic. We must not abandon our principles of love, faith, honor, truth, and reverence toward God.

- PRO 12:7 ~ The wicked are overthrown and are eliminated; but the house of the righteous remains standing.

- ISA 41:10 ~ Do not fear for I AM with you; do not be dismayed for I AM God. I will strengthen you and I will help you; yes, I will hold you up with the right hand of my righteousness.

- 1 CO 3:18–23 ~ Do not deceive yourself. If anyone among you seems to be wise in this world, let them become a fool, in order to become wise. For the wisdom of this world is foolishness to God. As it is written: He catches the wise in their own craftiness, and also, the Lord knows the thoughts of the wise that they are vain. Therefore, let nobody glory in the ways of the world, for all things are yours. Whether Paul, or Apollos, or Cephas (Peter), or the world, or life or death, or things past, present or future—all is yours, just as you are Christ's and He is God's.

Secularists and socialists are trying to cancel our culture, but they cannot cancel God, and they cannot silence anyone through whom the Holy Spirit speaks and acts. What are they afraid of? Truth, they cannot handle it, for it exposes their sin, hypocrisy, lies, and treachery. That is why the Church of Jesus Christ has become their greatest foe, since it stands for truth, faith, justice, freedom, and morality, the very pillars of our free society which they would bring down to gain an advantage. The other aspect of truth they deny is judgment. They do not want to be held accountable, so they pretend to occupy the moral high ground, constantly engaging in virtue signaling. Bottom line: they are afraid because they are guilty as sin and they know it, so they live in denial, though the fear never leaves their hearts because it is not a godly fear but a human fear. Like a drug addict they are hooked on power, perversion, fame, and material riches. They hate the thought of losing, but their paranoia will destroy them. Their souls are hanging in the balance for everyone who sells out (DAN 5:17–27). God has given everybody a conscience. Some choose not to listen to it because they know the consequences of evil yet refuse to face the music. Hence, the big lie overwhelms their thoughts, diverting their attention toward unholy strivings, exchanging spiritual treasures for material ones, and forfeiting an eternal reward for temporary gratification of their sinful flesh.

- ROM 2:14–15 ~ When the Gentiles, who were not given the law, do by nature the things required of the law, though they have not the law they are a law unto themselves. They exhibit the work of the law written upon their hearts, their conscience also bearing witness; because their thoughts either accuse them or excuse them for things they say and do.

- 1 TI 1:3–7 ~ Do not teach false doctrine, or recognize any myths or irrelevant genealogies, which only serve to raise questions, without providing any answers concerning the faith. The goal is to love with a pure heart, a right conscience, and a sincere faith. Some have wandered away from these principles and turned to meaningless jabber; desiring to be teachers of the Law yet knowing nothing about the Law or about what they purport to be true.

- 1 TI 4:1–2 ~ The Holy Spirit explicitly states that in the latter days some will depart from the faith, conferring with seducing spirits and following the doctrine of devils; speaking lies of hypocrisy, and possessing a conscience seared by a hot iron.

- TIT 1:15 ~ To the pure all things are pure, but to the corrupt and unbelieving nothing is pure; their minds and consciences are corrupt and evil.

Everyone alive will have to take a side in the coming standoff; I hope you choose wisely if it happens in your lifetime. Remember this: if you cherish freedom, the truth will set you free (JOH 8:31–32, 36).

- 1 CO 7:22 ~ Those who were servants when called by Christ have become free, and those who were free when called by Christ have become servants. You were bought with a great price, so do not become a slave to humankind, but remain responsible to God and the purpose for which He called you.

- HEB 12:25–29 ~ Do not refuse to listen to the one who speaks for God. If they could not escape after they refused His warning on the earth, they certainly could not escape after they refused to heed the warning coming out of heaven, when His voice shook the earth. God promises to shake the earth again, and not only the earth but the heavens also. And this Word, yet once more, will signify the ejection of things humans created, so things that are not dislocated may remain. Therefore, since we will receive a kingdom which cannot be moved, we should use this grace to serve God acceptably with reverence and godly fear. For our God is a consuming fire.

- 1 PE 2:19 ~ Be thankful if you must unfairly endure grief or suffering because you maintain an upright conscience toward God.

Sovereign Father, we implore you to save our people and heal our land. We believe in your promises, acknowledging how you brought this nation through catastrophes, crises, and wars of the past. We see the backsliding going on now, and we feel powerless to do anything about it. But our hope and faith remain in you. Help the people of our nation to reunite under the flag of freedom carrying the banner of Jesus Christ. Like you, oh Father, are one with Christ and the Holy Spirit, let us be indivisible as a nation and a church; and let your church be one with Christ empowered by the Holy Spirit. With your blessing we can prevail and reclaim our heritage, and throw the deceitful and arrogant derelicts out of office, removing them from positions of power and leadership. Together we will stand, but divided we will fall, and that is exactly what these deluded globalists are trying to achieve. Help them to see the light and the fact that they are merely pawns being pushed around the gameboard by Satan. What they need is a dose of truth; it is our prayer that they will get that proverbial wakeup call and return to their senses before this escalates into another bloody revolution. In the name of Jesus we pray, Amen.

November 26

Admonition Day is proposed to admonish those who would eliminate our liberties and steer this country into the sewer. Do you wonder why the USA is facing such calamitous times? May I suggest it is because God is admonishing us for disregarding Him and going our own way. Assuredly, this has been brewing a long time, while for decades our beloved country has crept towards socialism and totalitarianism. This is what the new progressivism is all about, but it is hardly a move towards progress. Quite the opposite; we are regressing: going back to the very ways and behaviors that our founders sought to escape. People are fleeing from other countries because of corrupt and oppressive governments, flocking to the USA only to find themselves in the same predicament. The odds cannot be predicted, but evangelicals still outnumber the rest, so it is time to admonish the government bureaucrats that are irreligious and antichristian, and make them pay who abuse the system, They are striving to tip the scales by indoctrinating our youth, and we cannot allow it.

God loves all people; in particular, God is attentive to those He has called to be His own. In Old Testament times God called the Jews; ever since New Testament times Jesus calls everyone to follow Him. Thus, the messages and warnings God gave to the Hebrews are every bit as applicable to Christians today, around the world. God has promised to prosper those who follow His ways and adhere to His laws. God also has promised that destruction will befall those who reject His ways and laws and follow the ways of the world. We the people of faith need to unite and stand strong in the Holy Spirit, for this conflict has become the Lord's battle. That is why the enemy promotes division, because unification is our best shot at defeating this scourge.

- EXO 20:20 ~ Moses addressed the people saying, "Do not fear, for God will come to reprove you, so that His fear will be your focus, thereby influencing you not to sin."

- LEV 26:40–42, 44 ~ God instructed, "If they confess their sins and the sins of their fathers; if they repent for walking contrary to the ways I have taught them; if they accept the punishment for their sins, then I will remember my covenant with Abraham, Isaac, and Jacob, and I will not detest them or discard them."

- DEU 30:19–20 ~ Moses said, "I have presented you with life and death, blessing versus cursing. I recommend that you choose life so you and your descendants may live. I hope you choose to love God, obey his Law, and cling to Him; for He is your life and He is your time, and you will live in the land which God promised to you and your ancestors."

- PSA 33:12 ~ Blessed is the nation whose God is the Lord, and blessed are the people He has chosen for His own inheritance.

- EPH 1:4 ~ God has chosen us to be His own before the foundation of the world, that we should be holy and without blame as we come to Him in love.

Individuals and groups of people who openly and deliberately despise the Lord, deny His sovereignty, and distort the truth are playing with fire (ISA 66:24). God eliminated entire nations for doing such things, to include driving the Israelites out of their land and into captivity. Who can say if God is not admonishing the USA for the same reasons: snubbing God, disobeying His commandments, pretending to be gods, following the wayward ways of our neighbors and other peoples, and blaspheming the Holy Spirit with lies and deception?

- LEV 18:24–25, 28 ~ Do not defile yourselves by doing any of these things, for because of this, other nations are defiled; and that is why I am driving them out before you. Even the land has become defiled by them, so I will punish the land for its sin, and the land will vomit out its inhabitants. And if you defile the land, it will vomit you out as well.

- NEH 9:32–33 ~ Our God is great and mighty, an awesome God who keeps His covenant of mercy. Do not think our problems are trivial, those hardships that have come upon our nation since the Assyrians ruled. God has been fair in punishing us this way, for we have been wicked.

- JOB 31:26–28 ~ If my heart was enticed by worldly things and celestial bodies, or if I was infatuated with myself, I would be guilty of denying God and worthy of His punishment.

- 1 TI 5:24–25 ~ Some people's sins will be exposed and they will be punished; for others, their punishment will come later. Likewise, some people's good deeds will be exposed and they will be rewarded; others will be rewarded later.

- HEB 10:26–29 ~ If we sin willingly, after having received the knowledge of the truth, there can be no further sacrifice for sins, but only the expectation of judgment and raging fire. A worse punishment awaits those who think themselves worthy, yet have walked over the Son of God, insulted the Spirit of Grace, and treated as unholy the blood of the covenant that sanctified them.

- JDE 1:4 ~ False teachers have infiltrated the churches, claiming that once you have become Christians you can do whatever you want without being punished. They deny the Lord and turn God's grace into lust.

    Some have strayed beyond the point of no return; for them there will be no repentance and therefore no forgiveness. At times, God removes evil people and regimes so they will not persuade others or despoil the innocent. There are a great many who are not sure what to think or believe; or otherwise, have not made up their minds about God and the Bible. Perhaps this is why Jesus has not returned yet, but time is running out. If you are not sure whose side you are on, you'd better decide without delay. If you side with God, you should not be ashamed or afraid to declare it.

- PSA 50:3–5 ~ God will come with a terrible fire burning all around Him. He will call everyone from heaven above to the earth below for judgment. He will gather the saints unto Himself.

- ISA 29:20 ~ The evil foe will come to nothing; the foe will be consumed and the wicked will be cut off from God.

- JER 8:12 ~ They shall be punished, for they were not ashamed when they committed their abominations.

- JER 51:6 ~ Flee from Babylon and save your lives. Do not get caught in her punishment, for this is the time of the Lord's vengeance.

- DAN 7:10 ~ A stream of fire flowed before Him. Millions ministered to Him. Hundreds of millions stood before Him. The judgment was set and the books were opened.

- MIC 7:2–6 ~ All the godly and upright men are gone. The wicked lie in ambush for blood. They do evil with diligence. Princes and judges ask for bribes. Great men speak of and pursue the evil desires of their souls. Even the best of them is like a thorn. Their confusion and punishment await them. Nobody can be trusted; even family and friends become the enemy.

- ROM 1:32 ~ People commit evil acts, knowing full well that their acts are worthy of the death penalty. Yet they continue to be evil and to find pleasure in others who do the same.

- 2 TH 1:8 ~ With flaming fire God will take vengeance on those that don't know Him and that don't obey the Gospel of Jesus Christ.

- REV 16:19 ~ The great city was divided into three parts and the cities of great nations fell. God remembered what they had done; their sin did not go unpunished.

NOVEMBER

There are natural consequences for sin, and these include the shame we feel in our own conscience as well as the reproving we receive from our parents, society, and/or government. But God also reproves us for He is our Father and the perfect example of parenting. So, punishment is not irrational or inappropriate, since God has given us the handbook for parenting, and in His Holy Word He commands us to reprove our children and one another.

- DEU 8:5 ~ Consider this: just as a father punishes his son, so also God punishes you.

- PSA 141:1–5, 8–10 ~ Lord I cry out to you; hear my prayer. I offer it as incense and lift it up with my hands toward you. Please warn me before I open my mouth. Let me not be inclined toward any evil thing, or associate with those who work wickedness, or be enticed by their luxuries. If I am admonished by righteous men, it will be a blessing to be reproved by them, and I bid your blessing upon them. My eyes are fixed upon you, Lord God, in you I will trust to never leave my soul destitute. Keep me from snares being laid for me and protect me from traps set by workers of iniquity. Let the wicked fall into their own nets, that I may escape.

- PRO 29:15, 17 ~ Punishment provides wisdom; but children left to themselves shame their parents. Correct your children when they are wrong, and you will be able to rest at night, and they will be your pride and joy.

- 2 TH 3:14–15 ~ If there are people among you who fail to conform to the Word as we have taught it to you, make note of them and stay away from them, so that they will feel ashamed of their behavior. However, do not consider them as an enemy, but admonish them as you would a brother or sister.

- 2 TI 3:1–5, 12–13 ~ Know this, that perilous times will come in the last days. People will love only themselves. They will be covetous, boasters, blasphemers, arrogant, disobedient to parents, unthankful and ungodly, void of natural affection. They will be promise breakers, false accusers, undisciplined, fierce despisers of goodness; traitors, reckless, conceited, lovers of worldly pleasures more than God; displaying a form of godliness but denying the power thereof. Stay away from people like this. Unfortunately, everybody that lives a godly life in Christ Jesus will suffer persecution. The evil men and seducers will grow continually worse, deceiving and being deceived.

Our Father in heaven admonishes us just as a parent admonishes his or her own children, for we are the children of God. He deserves our love and respect, even when He punishes us, because it is an act of love. That is, He loves us so much He sometimes must take drastic measures to keep us on the right path which was laid by His only Son Jesus Christ, the example of pure love, and who He gave as a sacrifice for sins so that we might live (ISA 53).

- JOB 5:17 ~ Blessed is a person corrected by God; never despise the discipline of the Lord.

- PRO 3:5–6, 11–12 ~ Trust in the Lord with all you heart and do not depend on your own understanding. In all you do acknowledge Him and He will direct you in the way you should go. Do not despise the Lord's discipline and do not resent His correction, for the Lord corrects those He loves just as any father who delights in his child.

- PRO 13:24 ~ Parents that do not discipline their children must hate them, for a loving parent has to punish their children sometimes.

- HEB 12:7–11 ~ If you endure punishment, God treats you as His own child, for what child is never disciplined by their parents? But if you are never punished then you have no parents and you are nobody's child. If we have natural parents correcting us, and if we respect them, should we not subject ourselves even more to the Father of all spirits, and live? For our parents punish us largely to make themselves feel better, but God punishes us so that we will profit from it, by sharing in His righteousness. While being punished may make one feel sorrowful, later it yields the peaceful fruit of righteousness.

God admonishes us to reprove us, so that we can be restored in spiritual health in preparation for His kingdom which is coming soon. In like manner, we are to admonish and discipline our children, ourselves, and others as directed by God who admonishes us. Admonition results in reprimand, which promotes repentance and rehabilitation, leading to forgiveness and restoration, and ending with reconciliation and righteousness.

- PSA 23:1–6 ~ The Lord is my Shepherd; He provides everything I need. He lets me graze in green pastures beside still waters. He restores my soul. He leads me in paths of righteousness for His namesake. Even when I walk through the valley of the shadow of death, I will not be afraid; His rod and staff protect and comfort me. He prepares a table before me in the presence of my enemies. He anoints my head with oil; my cup overflows. Surely goodness and mercy will always follow me, and I will live in the house of the Lord forever.

- PSA 32:5 ~ I acknowledged my sin to you Lord, and my iniquity I did not hide. I said, "I will confess my transgressions to the Lord." And you forgave the guilt of my sin. Amen.

- ISA 66:4 ~ I will choose their delusions; I will bring their fears upon them. Because when I called nobody answered; when I spoke, nobody listened. Instead, they were evil before my eyes, and they chose to do the things that I despise.

- JER 30:17 ~ Those who devoured you will be devoured and will become captives; those who preyed upon you will become the prey, because they called you an outcast and said, "Here is Zion which nobody cares about." But God will restore you and heal your wounds.

- GAL 6:1–2 ~ Brothers, if someone is overtaken by sin, you who are spiritual should restore that person in the spirit of humility, considering that you also can be tempted. Bear one another's burdens to fulfill the law of Christ.

- 2 TH 1:8–9 ~ God will inflict vengeance upon those who do not know Him and who do not obey the Gospel of Jesus Christ. They will suffer the punishment of eternal destruction and exclusion from the glory of the Lord.

- 1 PE 5:10–11 ~ After you have suffered for a while, may the God of all grace, who through Christ called you into His eternal glory, restore you and strengthen you so that you can remain firm and steadfast. To Him be glory and dominion forevermore, Amen.

Our Father in heaven, admonish us when we defy you, and help us to admonish one another in like manner. Please help us now; we are desperately in need of your guidance. We need people to stand up and realize that this country is going downhill fast and is about to fly off the rails. Help us to be obedient to you and to obey all reasonable and worthwhile laws of the land, admonishing those who refuse to walk the line and who are driving this runaway train off a cliff. Help us to regain control and get back on the tracks that you laid for us when this nation was founded. We also need your help gaining control over our education system which has abandoned the learning essentials in favor of a program of indoctrinating children into the ways of decadency and immorality. Please protect our youth from these evil deceivers, exposing their lives and their depraved ideology. Let the truth prevail, and let righteousness, honesty, and integrity flourish in all of our institutions and organizations. We need to reverse course soon, and we pray for your help in accomplishing this, before the enemy gains a stronghold in our beloved land, destroys our heritage, and drains our economy dry. As always, we pray this in Jesus's name, Amen.

November 27

Thanksgiving Day is a national holiday that occurs every fourth Thursday in November. President Lincoln declared a national day of thanksgiving and praise to our Heavenly Father during the Civil War in 1863. It has been celebrated ever since. President Washington also declared such a holiday in 1789, to give God the glory for our freedom, blessings, and His bounteous goodness. Many recognize the first Thanksgiving to have occurred after the *Mayflower* landed at Plymouth Rock, Massachusetts in 1620. The pilgrims were blessed by a plentiful autumn harvest in 1621, during which the settlers and Native Americans shared their crops and game through feast and fellowship for three days. Technically, however, the first day for annual thanksgiving was dedicated two years earlier when the good ship *Margaret* landed in Virginia in November, 1619. They drifted up the James River and settled at a site reserved in a land grant from England, disembarking on 12/04/1619. The settlers assembled and dedicated the land, declaring a day of thanksgiving that would be observed annually in worship, thanks, and prayer to Almighty God for bringing them to their destination safely. Our Judeo-Christian nation has a lot to be thankful for, and who but God should receive our thanks?

- 1 CH 16:25, 34–35 ~ Great is the Lord, and greatly should He be praised; He is to be feared above all gods. Let us give thanks to the Lord for He is good and His mercy endures forever. Ask God to gather His people together and deliver us from the wicked, so that we can give Him thanks and praise.

- 1 CH 23:30 ~ Give thanks and praise to the Lord every morning and every evening.

- NEH 9—10 ~ Nehemiah spoke a great prayer of worship and thanksgiving to God for bringing the Israelites back home. A written agreement was prepared binding the people in obedience to God and His rules. The leaders and priests affixed their seal to this agreement, and all the people swore an oath of allegiance to the Lord.

- PSA 95:1–3 ~ Come and sing with us to the Lord; let us make a joyful noise to the rock of our salvation. Let us come before God with thanksgiving; make a joyful noise to Him with psalms. For the Lord is a great God and a great King above all gods.

- PSA 100:4–5 ~ Enter into God's gates with thanksgiving and into his courts with praise. Be thankful and bless His name. For the Lord is good and His mercy endures to all generations.

- PSA 122:6–7 ~ Pray for peace in Jerusalem; may those prosper who love God. Peace be within your walls and security within your towers.

- PSA 150:2, 6 ~ Praise God for His mighty acts and His excellent greatness. Let everything that breathes praise the Lord.

- PHP 4:6–7 ~ Do not have anxiety about anything, but pray for everything. With thanksgiving let your requests be known to God. And the peace of God which surpasses all understanding will keep your heart in mind in Jesus Christ. Therefore, stand fast and hold onto the traditions which you learned through your hearing and reading.

- 2 TH 2:13–15 ~ We must always give thanks to God, because He has chosen you from the beginning for salvation, through sanctification of the Spirit and belief in the truth. Wherein He has called you by the Gospel to obtain the glory of our Lord Jesus Christ.

- 1 TI 2:1 ~ Prayers, intercessions, and thanks should be given to God by all people.

- HEB 13:15 ~ Let us continually offer to God the sacrifice of praise; praise and thanks are the fruits of our lips.

Suffice it to say that there have been many occasions to give thanks to God for bringing every one of us safely through the trials and tribulations of life, not to mention the challenges this nation has encountered over four centuries. Therefore, we should be giving praise and thanks to God every day. But a day of national thanksgiving is appropriate given the countless times the hand of Providence lifted us up when we faced perilous times. The fact is, our nation is encountering perilous times once again, and we desperately need God's grace and mercy as much as ever, to lift us up once again in His loving arms and save us from devastation by people who do not love this country or the Lord, and intend to take us down.

Hopefully, we can get people who fear God, love this country, and adhere to our Constitution to lead us. This is how we successfully made it this far. Thanksgiving Day holds a strong tradition in the USA and is based on faith and trust in our benevolent and compassionate Lord and Savior. That faith was the foundation of the patriarchs and is the basis for our legal and governmental systems. If our leaders and governors do not have faith, how can we have faith in them? We need men and women of faith to lead us forward from here.

- DEU 1:13 ~ Take the wise men of understanding and notoriety, and make them rulers.
- JOB 11:18, 20 ~ You will be confident because there is hope; you will be protected, so take rest in your safety. But the wicked will not escape; their hope will be like taking their last breath.
- JOB 34:17 ~ Shall someone who hates what is right govern others? Can a just person be condemned?
- PSA 37:3–8 ~ Trust in the Lord and do good and you will have security. Take delight in the Lord and you will receive the delights of your heart. Commit yourself to the Lord and He will vindicate you. Wait patiently for the Lord and do not worry. Refrain from anger and from doing anything evil.
- PRO 29:2 ~ When the righteous are in authority, the people rejoice; but when the wicked rule, the people mourn.
- PRO 29:26–27 ~ Many people seek favor from their rulers, but all judgment comes from God. An unjust person is disgusting to a just person; an upright person is disgusting to an evil person.
- HOS 8:4 ~ They have set up kings, but not by me; they appointed princes, but I did not recognize them. They made idols from their silver and gold, so they will be cut off.
- JAM 4:10–12 ~ Humble yourselves before God and He will exalt you. Do not speak evil of one another or judge one another, for you will be guilty of speaking evil of the Law and of judging the Law. If you judge the Law you cannot be a doer of the Law. There is only one lawgiver, who is able to save and to destroy.

Praise be to you heavenly Father for blessings too numerous to mention and gifts too numerous to count. Help us to remember that all good things come from you. Please guide and direct this land, and our people, that we may proceed on the pathway you laid which is in Christ the Lord, and in which our forefathers also walked. Help us to elect people of your choice, who will govern in accordance with your Law, and our best interest. We give thanks to you Father, Son, and Holy Spirit this day. Let us remember to give thanks and praise to you every day, even forevermore. Help us as a nation to unite once again, regardless of ethnicity and status, and glorify your name with worship, praise, and thanksgiving, just like the early settlers did when they arrived here. For you blessed this land because of them, Father, and we need your blessing again. We ask this in the name of your Son Jesus, Amen.

November 28

Black Friday always occurs the day after Thanksgiving. This holiday is not to be confused with the original Black Friday which was the gold crash of 1869. Today's observance began in the 1980s with retailers who wanted to take advantage of the day after Thanksgiving, traditionally part of a four-day weekend. Thus, to bolster sales for Christmas shoppers who used this opportunity to shop on their day off, the stores began offering specials and staying open later. The increase in sales helped retailers to get out of the red and "into the black" meaning a return to profitable status. Now they have included Cyber Monday to make it a five-day shopping spree. It seems somewhat sacrilegious to have a materialistic day after a religious day. We commemorate the giving of thanks by the first settlers to the New World, and then we spend like crazy to save money on Christmas gifts, or things we want ourselves. Like most spiritually oriented holidays, it seems there are one or more corresponding pagan or agnostic days.

The Bible tells us to focus on spiritual riches, not on worldly wealth or material possessions. This battle between spirituality and materialism is as old as humankind. Those who love the world and things of the world cannot love God at the same time (LUK 16:13). This is the idolatry of wealth: when material things take a front seat, pushing God away. Therefore, it is necessary that we examine our priorities. Yes, we give gifts during Christmas to celebrate the birth of Christ; we also give gifts when celebrating certain birthdays and anniversaries. There is nothing wrong with giving gifts and sharing love. What is wrong is to give a gift expecting to receive one, or to give a gift out of a sense of obligation (2 CO 9:6–7).

- ECC 5:10–12 ~ Whoever loves riches will never have enough, and whoever loves money will never be satisfied with their income. This is vanity. As goods increase, so do those who consume them. And of what benefit are belongings to the owner except the enjoyment of looking at them? The sleep of the hard worker is sweet; but the abundance of the rich prevents them from sleeping.

- JOB 20:15 ~ Those who swallow down riches will vomit them up again, just like God rids himself of those who relish in their riches.

- PRO 11:4, 28 ~ Riches will not profit anyone in the day of wrath; only righteousness can save a person from death. Those who trust in their riches will fail, but those who trust in God will flourish.

- PRO 23:5 ~ Do not set your eyes on something that is not there, because riches will certainly find wings and fly away like an eagle.

- DAN 11:43 ~ Satan has the power over gold, silver, and worldly riches.

- MAT 6:19–21 ~ Jesus taught, "Do not collect your treasures here on earth where they can be corrupted by insects or rust or stolen by thieves. Instead, store your treasures in heaven where they cannot be corrupted or stolen. Where your treasures are, there your heart will be also."

- MAT 21:12–13; MAR 11:15–17; LUK 19:45–46 ~ Jesus entered the temple and drove out those who bought and sold inside the temple, overturning the tables of the moneychangers selling pigeons. Jesus said, "It is written: My house is a house of prayer (ISA 56:7), but you have made it a den of robbers (JER 7:11)."

- MAR 4:19 ~ Jesus said, "Earthly desires, the deceitfulness of wealth, and other lusts of this world choke the Word, and it becomes useless to those who are enticed by these things."

- LUK 12:15–21 ~ Jesus said to them, "Beware of greed, for a person's life does not consist of the abundance of their possessions." Then He told them the parable about the rich man who had such an abundance of wealth that he decided to build bigger warehouses to store his goods. The man said to himself, "Now that you have it made, take it easy; eat, drink, and be merry." But God said to him, "You fool! This very night your soul will be demanded from you, then who will enjoy your prosperity?" Jesus concluded, "This is how it will be for those who store up worldly things for themselves but are not rich toward God."

- 1 CO 6:20 ~ You were bought with a great price, so glorify God in your bodies and your spirits, for you belong to Him.

- COL 3:2 ~ Set your mind on things above, not earthly things.

- 1 TI 6:5 ~ Those who teach that material wealth is godly have perverse minds, devoid of the truth. They would exploit the truth to gain riches. Stay away from them.

In the end times, greed will be pervasive. People will be bought and sold like merchandise (2 PE 2:3). Those who have much will oppress those who do not, because the former will hoard all the wealth and goods, while the latter will have to depend on the Lord for their sustenance, else they become totally dependent on the federation. When you see leaders of government, education, media, and business sell out to the globalists and their agenda, while seeking to silence and cancel everyone else, the end is nigh. There will be two classes, the rich and the poor, for the middle-class will have been obliterated. These will be dark and dreary days every day, until the end of days. Beware of those who intend to control all the wealth, for they intend to control the lives of all people, especially their adversaries, namely Christians, who they hate and persecute (REV 2:10).

- PSA 49:6–8, 15 ~ They trust in their wealth, and brag about their riches; but none of them have the means to redeem anyone, or to give a ransom for another. The ransom is extremely costly, and no amount of money is enough to buy eternal life. Only God can redeem my life from the grave.

- NAH 3:1–6 ~ Woe to the bloody city, full of lies and robbery. You prey on everyone; always present are the sounds of battle. Look at all the corpses. Because of the multitude of your abominations with the well-known prostitute, that witch who buys and sells nations and families, I will pour abominable filth upon you for everyone to see.

- LUK 17:16–30 ~ As it was in the days of Noah, so it will be when the Son of man returns. The people ate, drank, and married until Noah and his family entered the ark, the flood came, and the rest drowned. Likewise, it will be as the days of Lot; they ate, drank, bought, sold, planted, and built, until Lot and his family departed; then it rained fire and brimstone destroying them all. Accordingly, perilous times will draw closer in the last days.

- REV 13:15–18 ~ And the second beast brought the image of the beast to life. He caused everyone to receive the mark of the beast on their right hand or forehead; only those with the mark could buy and sell goods. They tracked down and murdered anyone who did not receive the mark and worship the beast. The beast's number is the number of a man: 666.

Heavenly Father, help us make our love, faith, and other spiritual gifts, our highest priority. Let us not be hung up on material possessions or worldly wealth. May we prosper in accordance with your will, and use our prosperity as a means of helping those less fortunate. Prepare us for perilous times to come, reminding us that you will provide. Let us depend on you exclusively for all our needs: spiritual, mental, and physical. You have been our fortress and shield in times of trouble, and our intention is to continue with that strategy. We pray for spiritual riches on earth as well as those being stored up for us in heaven, as we trust in your promises and words. In Jesus Christ whose name we trust with our lives, Amen.

November 29

Kennedy Assassination Investigated by the Warren Commission started on this day in 1963, one week after the tragedy. Former Vice President L. B. Johnson appointed Chief Justice Earl Warren to lead the commission, consisting of senators, congressmen, and lawyers. They were given authority to subpoena and interrogate witnesses, and to obtain documentation prepared by the CIA, FBI, Secret Service, and other agencies. They gathered news stories, personal records of suspects, photographs and video footage, autopsy and medical reports, and literally tons of paperwork. They produced a 188-page document a year later, concluding that Lee Harvey Oswald acted alone, ruling out conspiracy theories which were many. Another investigation was held by the House Select Committee on Assassinations; their final report was released in 1979. The only conclusion that differed from the Warren report was the likelihood of a second shooter. To this day, there continues to be conspiracy theories, and many films and documentaries have been produced about them. Some additional information was added to the body of knowledge but nothing conclusive. A great many documents were classified, to be released fifty years after the Warren report; twenty years past the deadline and the government still refuses to release any information. This fuels suspicion about the accuracy and completeness of what was disseminated to the public in the beginning.

- ISA 8:12 ~ Do not join in any conspiracies or alliances with people who collude; do not fear the things that they fear and do not let it cause you dismay.

Apparently, US presidents are frequently targeted by crazed psychopaths and political extremists. Lincoln was the first president to be assassinated (1865); next was Garfield (1881), followed by McKinley (1901), then Kennedy (1963). One unsuccessful attempt was made on Andrew Jackson (1835) but the gun misfired; Teddy Roosevelt (1912) was hit by a bullet that was blocked by items in his breast pocket. Another close call was Reagan (1981) who was seriously wounded but survived; his attacker was declared insane and eventually released from a mental institution in 2016. We cannot begin to second guess the will of God in these cases. The Bible records numerous conspiracies to commit murder. Many men of God were conspired against, but God protected them. Others were conspired against and God let them die.

- 2 SA 15:12, 31; 2 SA 17:23; 2 SA 18:12–15 ~ Absalom recruited Ahithophel, King David's advisor, to conspire against his father David. Someone warned David that Ahithophel was conspiring with Absalom. David prayed, "Lord, turn the counsel of Ahithophel into foolishness." Ahithophel committed suicide. Absalom was killed by Joab, David's general.

- DAN 5:23–31 ~ Daniel told King Belshazzar his days were numbered, for Babylon would fall. That night, the king was assassinated, and Darius the Mede seized power.

- ACT 9:20–25 ~ After his vision of Christ, Paul (formerly Saul) began preaching Christ in the synagogues. Those who heard him were amazed, saying, "Is this not the man who persecuted the followers of Jesus, bringing them to Jerusalem for trial." Meanwhile, Paul increased in strength and surprised the Jews in Damascus, providing proof that Jesus was the Christ. And the Jews conspired together to kill Paul. They were going to ambush him as soon as he walked out of the city gates, but the disciples lowered him over the city wall in a basket.

- ACT 23:11–12, 23 ~ God assured Paul that he would not be harmed, for he was to testify of Christ in Rome, just as he had in Jerusalem. The next morning, the Jews conspired amongst themselves swearing that they would not eat or drink until they had killed Paul. So, the commander had Paul relocated to the governor's barracks.

Jesus proclaimed Satan a murderer and a compulsive liar. Satan also has influenced a great many people to commit murder. Perhaps Satan induced Cain to commit the first murder. Satan influenced the hypocritical Jewish leaders who wanted Christ eliminated (MAT 23:13–29). This is how Satan, who hates God's people, conspires with humans: getting them to think evil and hateful thoughts. Apparently, if you hate somebody bad enough you commit murder in your heart (1 JO 3:15). Heinous crimes will worsen, as the days are numbered for this world.

- GEN 4:6–7 ~ Before killing his brother Abel, God said to Cain, "What are you angry about and why has your face fallen? If you do well, will you not be accepted? And if you do not do well, sin is crouching at the door: it wants to control you but you must control it."

- MIC 7:3 ~ They are skilled at doing evil. Rulers require gifts and judges require bribes for their services. Those in power dictate their desires; together they conspire against others.

- JOH 8:44 ~ Jesus told the unbelievers, "You evil people belong to your father the devil, and the evil of your father is what you do. He was a murderer and a liar from the start. He never tells the truth; in fact, he is the father of lies."

- REV 13:15 ~ They tracked down and murdered anyone that did not receive the mark and worship the beast.

- REV 5:11–12 ~ Then I looked I saw a multitude of angels, numbering thousands upon thousands, literally millions of angels encircling the throne. And they sang aloud with one voice, "Worthy is Christ the Lamb who was slain, to receive power and wealth, and wisdom and strength, and honor, glory and praise."

- REV 13:8 ~ The Lamb was slain since the creation of the world.

- REV 21:8 ~ Murderers will take part in the lake of fire which is the second death.

Jewish priests and leaders conspired to commit murder against Jesus. They convinced His friend Judas to betray Him; then they manipulated the gutless prefect Pontius Pilate to do their dirty work. Behind it all was Satan convincing the Jewish leaders to do his dirty work.

- HOS 6:9 ~ The priests commit murder by giving their consent, and they commit lewdness.

- MAT 2:11–14 ~ The Pharisees left and conspired against Jesus to kill Him.

- MAT 27:1 ~ The chief priests and elders conspired against Jesus to put Him to death.

- MAR 3:6 ~ The Pharisees sought council with the Herodians to assassinate Jesus.

The most popular conspiracy theory is "the devil made me do it". But he and other demons can only interject the temptation. It is people who choose to act on that temptation. Some fall into possession: willing fools who would channel evil spirits. In a way, all murderers are possessed by Satan because they are allowing evil to control their thoughts, convincing them of the lies that lead to abominable crimes such as murder. Thus, most if not all evil conspiracies include Satan as a coconspirator. No doubt, there was an evil conspiracy in the assassination of President Kennedy. Will we ever know the real truth? Well, we could get a better feel for who was responsible if the government would release the stuff they're holding back. The reluctance to do so implies they are covering for certain people or agencies. Transparent they are not. Maybe we will never know if any of the myriad of suggested conspiracies resulted in JFK's untimely death.

Lord God Almighty, you invented life and you invented death. Nothing escapes you, but we are often left with theories, not facts. We pray we will find the truth if we continue to seek it out. Let us not be misled by unfounded conspiracies. Help us to resist them and help us to rebuke the demons and those who conspire with the devil. Bring to light what is hidden, we pray, and bring to justice those who participate in evil conspiracies and murder. In Jesus's name, Amen.

November 30

Presence of the Lord Day is a new holiday for celebrating the fact that true Christians will be present with the Lord immediately upon the death of this mortal body. It also is an opportunity to acknowledge that God is always with us, even until the end of time. Have you ever asked yourself these questions: "Where do we go from here? Where will I be when I die?" If you are not sure, you will find answers in God's Word. Our life force is found in the living spirit, which energizes the body. Upon death, that spirit returns to God because He gave it to us and we belong to Him. Thus, a believer that dies will automatically travel in spirit to our Father in heaven along with his or her soul. In the meantime, we need to listen to the Word of the Lord who is ever-present and who is trying to get our attention even as we are now pondering these words.

- GEN 35:18 ~ Rachel died and her soul departed.
- ECC 12:7 ~ Upon death, the spirit returns to God who gave it.
- LUK 8:55 ~ The girl's spirit returned to her when Jesus brought her back to life.
- JOH 6:63 ~ Jesus said, "It is the spirit that gives life, not the flesh." Jesus spoke the words of spirit and life.
- 2 CO 3:6 ~ God has made us able ministers of the new testament, not of the letter of the Law, but of the Spirit, for the letter kills, but the Spirit gives life.
- 2 CO 5:8 ~ We are confident, and would prefer to be absent from this body and present with the Lord.

Those who by God's grace have been saved through Christ because of their faith in Him, will go directly to Him after they die. God's chosen people will live in peace forever in paradise with our merciful Lord. It will be wonderful there, where exists no sorrow, pain, suffering, or distress. However, those who do not believe God's Word, trusting in His Son Jesus Christ, will go to the other place, where all hope is lost; where body and soul are ultimately destroyed.

- PRO 24:20 ~ Evil people have no future. Their light will be extinguished.
- ECC 9:10 ~ Whatever your hand finds to do, do it with your might; for there is no work, device, knowledge, or wisdom in the grave where you are going.
- ISA 51:11 ~ Those redeemed by the Lord will return singing praises; they will have everlasting joy, and all sorrow and grief will be gone forever.
- ISA 64:4 ~ Since the world began, nobody has heard, seen, or perceived, except God, the wonderful things He has prepared for those who wait for Him.
- JER 18:11–12 ~ God warned them that He was going to destroy them unless they turned from their evil ways. But they said, "It is hopeless. Let us continue with our own plans. We will follow the imaginations of our evil hearts."
- LUK 16:19–31 ~ Jesus told the parable of the rich man and the poor man: There was a rich man who lived a life of pleasure and luxury. A poor man lay at his gate who was weak, hungry, and afflicted, desiring mere crumbs off the rich man's plate. The two men died. The poor man was taken to Abraham's bosom, and the rich man was exiled in Hades. The rich man called out to Abraham asking if he would let the poor man dip his finger into water to wet his parched tongue. But Abraham reminded him how thoughtless and unmerciful he had been to the poor man, and told him that nobody could pass through the chasm separating them. The rich man implored that his family be warned, to prevent them from the same fate. Abraham informed

the rich man that his family would have to rely on the Word of God like everybody else; for even a visit from the dead would not persuade them to change their ways.

- LUK 23:43 ~ Jesus said to the repentant thief, "I tell you the truth, today you will be with me in paradise."

- ACT 2:26–27 ~ My heart is glad and my tongue rejoices; my body abides in hope. For the Lord will not destroy my soul in hell.

- 2 PE 2:4; JDE 1:6 ~ God did not spare the angels that sinned, but sent them to hell, imprisoning them in chains of darkness to be held for judgment.

- REV 7:15–17 ~ They will live before the throne of God and will serve Him day and night in the temple. They will never be hungry, thirsty, hot or cold again. The Lamb among them will feed them, will lead them to fountains of living waters, and will remove all their sorrows.

God will allow His people to keep their souls forever. Thus, when Christ returns, Christians will possess that life-giving spirit that awakens and preserves our bodies, as well as our minds so we can think for ourselves continuously and still have a mind for Christ. This is our reward for the obedience of faith. It is God's gift to His elect for believing in Him and following His Son Jesus Christ to their heavenly home. And we will be free forever, with greater freedoms than we enjoy here in the land of the free, which is becoming the land of the forgotten.

- ISA 55:3 ~ Listen up and come to me, pay attention so your soul might live. I will make an everlasting covenant with you, to give you all the faithful love and mercies I showed to David.

- LUK 21:19 ~ Jesus said, "Be patient and you will keep your souls."

- 1 CO 15:42–46 ~ This is the way it will be with the resurrection of the dead. It is sown in corruption it is raised in incorruption. It is sown in dishonor it is raised in glory. It is sown in weakness it is raised in power. It is sown a natural body it is raised a spiritual body. The spiritual did not come first; the natural came first and then the spiritual. Flesh and blood cannot inherit the kingdom, and neither can corruption inherit perfection.

- HEB 10:39 ~ We do not shrink back and we are not destroyed, because those who have faith keep their souls.

- 1 PE 1:2, 4 ~ Christians are chosen by God in advance, through sanctification of the Spirit, to be obedient to Christ and cleansed by His blood. Blessed is God the Father of our Lord Jesus Christ. According to His abundant mercy, He recreated in us the living hope, brought by the resurrection of Christ from the dead, to receive an incorruptible and undefiled inheritance reserved in heaven and lasting forever.

When the Lord returns, it will be to call the righteous home and to pronounce judgment upon the wicked. Christians who are both alive and dead will be called home. Our spirits will be reunited with our physical bodies, which will be changed into glorified bodies that will never die.

- JOB 19:25–26 ~ I know that my Redeemer lives and that He will stand upon the earth. And although my flesh will have been destroyed, yet in my flesh I will see God.

- PSA 118:16–17 ~ The righteous rejoice, for the Lord's right hand has done mighty things. I will not die, but live, and I will declare the works of the Lord.

- EZE 36:26 ~ I will give you a new heart and put inside you a new spirit; I will remove your heart of stone and replace it with a heart of flesh.

NOVEMBER

- LUK 20:34–39 ~ Jesus answered them saying, "The people of this age get married. In the next age, those who are considered worthy of taking part in the resurrection will not marry, and will never die, for they will be like the angels. They are God's children, the children of the resurrection. When Moses encountered the burning bush, He learned that the dead arise, for he referred to the Lord as the God of Abraham, Isaac, and Jacob. God is not a God of the dead, but of the living; for to Him all are alive." Some teachers of the Law responded, "Well said, Teacher."

- 1 CO 15:51–58 ~ Here is a mystery of God: We will not all sleep (die) but we will all be changed. Upon Christ's return, in a single moment when the great trumpet sounds, Christ's own, whether alive or dead will arise into heaven to receive new, incorruptible bodies. Hence, the corruptible will have become incorruptible and the mortal will have become immortal. Then at the end, when Christ delivers the kingdom of God to the Father, He will destroy death, at which time the statement "death is swallowed up in victory" will be true. The godly will receive spiritual bodies which will never die. The flesh is of the earth, the spirit is of heaven; thus, flesh and blood will not inherit the kingdom of heaven. Therefore, be confident in your faith because your labor is not in vain.

- COL 3:4 ~ When Christ, who is your life, appears again, you will appear with Him in glory.

- 2 PE 1:2–4 ~ Grace and peace be multiplied unto you through knowledge of God and of Jesus Christ, our Lord. By God's divine power we have received all things pertaining to life and godliness, because we know Him who called all people to righteousness and glory. We cling to His precious promise, that His people will receive a divine nature, and escape the corruption and lust of the world.

- 1 JO 3:1–2 ~ How great is God's love that we should be called His children. The world does not know us because it didn't know Him. We are His children, but we do not know yet what that really entails; we do know, however, that we will be like Him, for we will see Him as He really is.

There are differing views concerning the rapture and the resurrection. The three most common views of the rapture, are the pre-, mid-, and post-tribulation rapture. The two prevailing positions on the thousand-year reign include millennialism and amillennialism. The former holds that there is a physical resurrection of the just prior to the millennium, and a second physical resurrection of the unjust after the millennium. The latter viewpoint holds that the first resurrection is a spiritual one occurring upon death, and the second a physical resurrection of all humankind on the last day, with the millennium being the unspecified period between the end of Christ's first advent and the beginning of His second. Thus, the former camp views the millennium as beginning with Christ's return, and the latter see it as ending with Christ's return. Regardless of a person's viewpoint on these issues, the truth is that believers are either raptured or resurrected to receive an inheritance in heaven. The unbelievers will be resurrected, only to die a second death in the lake of fire. Is it not a requirement to take any position on eschatology for that will not save you; if it was crystal clear there wouldn't be so many theories about it.

- PSA 52:5 ~ God will destroy the evil ones forever. He will uproot them from the living.

- ISA 26:14 ~ They are dead and will not live; they will not rise. They have been visited with destruction and all memory of them has been wiped out.

- DAN 12:2 ~ Those who sleep in the ground will awaken, some will arise to receive everlasting life and some will arise to everlasting shame and contempt.

- LUK 17:34–37 ~ Jesus said concerning His second coming, "Two men will be in bed, one will be taken and the other will be left behind; two women will be grinding grain together, only one will be taken; two men will be working in the field, only one will be taken."

- JOH 5:28–29 ~ The time is coming when all who are in the grave will hear His voice and come forth. Those who have been faithful and good will arise to everlasting life, and those who have been unfaithful and evil will arise to receive everlasting condemnation.

- 1 TH 4:16–17 ~ The Lord will descend from heaven with a shout, with the voice of the archangel, and with a blast from the trumpet of God. Then the dead in Christ will rise first. Those who remain alive in Christ will rise to join the others in the clouds, meeting the Lord in the sky. Those chosen by Christ will live with Him forevermore.

- REV 20:4–6, 13–15 ~ I saw thrones, and sitting on them were judges. I saw the souls of those who had been beheaded for their testimony of Jesus, who had not worshipped the beast or its image, nor received its mark on their foreheads or hands. They came to life again and reigned with Christ one thousand years. This was the first resurrection. The rest of the dead did not live again until after the thousand years. Blessed and holy are those who share in the first resurrection for they will not be victims of the second death. At the second resurrection the rest of the souls were raised to be judged by God. Death and Hell, and those who were not recorded in the Book of Life, were cast into the lake of fire; this was the second death.

Once you have died, there is no more hope for salvation (HEB 9:27). You must believe in Christ; never reject Him or you might miss His return. If you die in your sins, without repentance or forgiveness, you cannot be saved and you will not go to heaven. After the resurrection, the evil and unrepentant ones will be judged, found guilty, and condemned. The penalty will be death, for they will die again, becoming engulfed in the lake of fire with Satan and the other lost souls. Those who died believing in Christ will be with Him immediately in spirit, and in paradise. When the righteous are resurrected, they will be found innocent of their sin, for they will have been cleansed of all unrighteousness by the blood of the Lamb. Believers will receive glorified bodies uncorrupted by sin that will last for eternity; for without sin, there is no death. They will live as brothers and sisters with Jesus in a heavenly house with God our Father.

Heavenly Father, we come into your presence with a contrite heart, ashamed of our sins and our disobedience. We ask you to forgive us once again for all of our sins, including those we remember and those we have forgotten: sins which are too numerous even to count. Though we sincerely believe in the saving grace of your Son, and His sacrifice made in our stead, we cannot cease sinning; as hard as we try, we are unable. Thank you again, that you have wiped our transgressions from the record as we must always come before you in humble repentance. Strengthen us in the true faith, and help us to remember that you are always here. Whatever we are doing, help us to acknowledge your presence as often as we think about you, speaking to you in prayer and listening to your Holy Spirit who lives inside our hearts. Help us to love you above all others and to love our neighbors as ourselves as you have commanded. Increase in us true knowledge of you dear Father who loves us, Holy Spirit who comforts us, and Jesus Christ who redeems us. Let us always look to that day when we will join you in the highest heaven; help us to walk in your ways for all of our days until the last day when Christ brings us home. Praise be to you oh Lord, Amen.

December 1

National Christmas Lights Day is the day for stringing colored lights on trees and houses, to begin the Christmas cheer. Advent is underway, and we are less than four weeks from the night we celebrate the light that shone in Bethlehem over two thousand years ago. Messiah was that light. The wise men followed His star and found the baby Christ who would become the Savior of the world: God's only Son. His coming was proclaimed in the Old Testament and fulfilled in the New Testament. God's Holy Spirit spoke through the Bible and through His Word which became a man. Thus, the spectacular light of life is found in all three persons of the Holy Trinity.

- PSA 119:105 ~ God's Word is a lamp unto my feet, and a light unto my path.

- ISA 60:1–2 ~ Arise and shine, for your light has come; yes, the glory of God has come to you. Darkness covers the earth and great darkness covers its people. But the Lord will arise and come to you, and you will see His glory. And the Gentiles will come to His light, and kings will come to the brightness of His rising.

- MAT 2:9 ~ The wise men departed after visiting King Herod. And the star that they had followed all the way from the east shone before them, pointing the way to Bethlehem. Finally, they stood directly under the star. There they found the young Christ child. When they saw the child, they rejoiced with great enthusiasm.

- LUK 1:79 ~ The baby Jesus was born to give light to those who sit in darkness and in the shadow of death, and to guide their feet into the way of peace.

- JOH 3:19 ~ The light came into the world, but men loved darkness rather than light, because their deeds were evil. Those practicing evil hate the light and avoid the light which exposes their evil deeds. But those who enter the light will show their deeds to be from God.

- EPH 1:13 ~ You were included with Christ when you listened to the words of truth and believed the good news of salvation, being marked by the Holy Spirit who has guaranteed your inheritance in God's kingdom.

There is a continuum of light from complete darkness to eternal light; the former reflects total separation from God and the latter represents living in the presence of God. Light can consume darkness, but darkness cannot consume light. Therefore, there is no darkness in heaven where the light of the Lord shines forever; similarly, there is no light in hell.

- GEN 1:2–5 ~ Darkness covered the earth and God commanded there to be light, and He saw that the light was good, and He separated the light from the darkness.

- MAT 6:22–23 ~ Jesus said, "The eye is the lamp of the body. If your eye is sound, your whole body will be full of light. If your eye is not sound, your whole body will be full of darkness. So, if the light within you is darkness, how great is that darkness."

- LUK 11:35–36 ~ Be careful, so that the light in you does not become darkness. If your whole body is full of light and has no darkness, it will be wholly bright as when a lamp with its rays gives light.

- JOH 12:35 ~ Jesus said, "The light will be with you a little longer. Walk while you have the light, before the darkness overtakes you; those who walk in darkness do not know where they are going."

- 1 CO 4:5 ~ Judge nothing before the Lord returns, for He will bring to light all that is hidden in darkness, and will reveal the motivations of the heart. Then everyone will praise God.

- 1 JO 1:5 ~ God is light; in Him is no darkness at all.
- 1 JO 2:10–11 ~ Those who love others abide in the light and will not stumble. Those who hate others abide in darkness and do not know where they are going because the darkness has blinded their eyes.

The tradition of attaching candles to Christmas trees began centuries ago; in fact, Martin Luther was known for this. Of course, they had to ensure the evergreen tree didn't catch fire, but I bet it looked beautiful. Stringed electrical lights were invented in the early 1880s by Edison's colleague Edward Johnson. General Electric marketed them quite profitably by the early 1900s. Nowadays there are contests to see who can produce the most elaborate display of lights, which only adds to the materialism and commercialism that pervades the holiday season.

However, lights do add tremendously to the Christmas Spirit. Where there is light there is life. But nothing can live in darkness. The colorful display of lights reminds us of the life that was given to die for us, whose light shined on Christmas day, but was snuffed out on the cross. But His light returned with His Spirit, and shines forever in those who invite Christ to live inside them. If you have the light of life, you have eternal life.

- JOH 8:12 ~ Jesus said, "I am the light of the world; those who follow me will not walk in darkness, but will have the light of life."
- ROM 13:12 ~ The night is gone and the day is at hand. Let us cast away the works of darkness and put on the armor of light.
- 2 CO 4:4–6 ~ The god of this world has blinded the eyes of unbelievers so they cannot see the light of the Gospel of the glory of Christ who is the image of God. We proclaim Christ as Lord to draw people to Him. God commanded light to shine out of darkness. This same light shines in our hearts and radiates His glory through the knowledge of Jesus Christ.
- EPH 5:8–14 ~ You were once in darkness, but now you are in the light of the Lord. Live as children of light and discover what pleases the Lord, for the fruit of the light consists of goodness, righteousness, and truth. Have nothing to do with the fruitless deeds of darkness, but rather expose them. For it is shameful even to mention what the disobedient do in secret. But everything exposed by the light becomes visible for all to see, for it is light that makes things visible. This is what is meant by the saying, "Wake up you sleepers; rise from the dead and Christ will shine on you."

The light of life through God's Messiah was shown to Abraham, with the appearance of Melchizedek, King of Salem (translated "King of Peace" from the Hebrew). Melchizedek was God's High Priest, who is the Holy Spirit. Christ is the Prince of Peace, begotten of the Holy Spirit; He is the only other priest from the priestly order of Melchizedek. Christ proclaimed that meeting, recorded in the book of Genesis, by saying, "Abraham rejoiced to see my day." He was referring to this amazing occurrence foreshadowing the coming of Messiah, and making known to Abraham God's plan of salvation through one of his descendants. Melchizedek shared bread and wine with Abraham, literally a type of Holy Communion; in return, Abraham gave Him tithes of all he owned, being the first reference to tithing.

- GEN 14:18–20 ~ Melchizedek, King of Salem, meaning Peace, brought wine and bread to dine with Abraham. Melchizedek was the priest of the most-high God. He blessed Abraham, and Abraham gave him a tenth of all he owned.
- GEN 18:1–3 ~ The Lord appeared to Abraham along the plains of Mamre as he sat in his tent. Abraham looked up and saw three men standing there at the tent door. When Abraham saw

them, he bowed before them and said, "My Lord, if I have found favor in your sight, please promise, I pray, that you would never leave me."

- PSA 110:1, 4 ~ The Lord said to my Lord, "Sit at my right hand and I will make your enemies your footstool. He is priest forever, after the order of Melchizedek."

- JOH 8:56–58 ~ Jesus said, "Abraham saw my day and rejoiced." The Jews replied, "You are not even fifty years old and you claim to have seen Abraham." Jesus declared, "I tell you the truth, before Abraham was, I AM."

- GAL 3:8–13, 21–24 ~ The scriptures foretold that God would justify sinners through faith, announcing the Gospel in advance to Abraham, and promising him many descendants, one of whom would be a blessing to all nations. Those who live by faith will be blessed as Abraham was. But nobody is justified in God's sight by works of the Law, for it is written that the just will live by faith. Christ has redeemed us from the curse of the Law, being made a curse in our place, for it is written that cursed is he who is crucified on a cross. Is the Law, therefore, in opposition to God's promise? Absolutely not! For no law was given that could bring life. The scriptures tell us that the world is a slave to sin, and that the promise of life is given to all believers in Jesus Christ. Before faith in Christ came, everyone was a prisoner to the Law, kept there until faith was revealed in Christ. Hence, the Law is our teacher to bring us to faith in Christ, so that we might be justified by that faith.

- HEB 5:9–10 ~ God made Christ perfect and the author of eternal salvation for all who obey Him. He was called by God to be the high priest after the order of Melchizedek.

- HEB 7:1–28 ~ Melchizedek was the first King of Righteousness, and the King of Salem, meaning peace. Melchizedek had no parents or ancestors, no beginning or end. Melchizedek was made like the Son of God, being a priest and king continually. Consider how great He was, for Abraham paid tithes to Him, and always counted on His promises. Under the Levitical priesthood, the people received the Law. But the priesthood was changed, and this required a change in the Law. The new priesthood was fashioned by the power of eternal life, not the Law over sinful man. The Law made nothing perfect, but the bringing of a better hope did; that hope draws us to God through the testament of Jesus Christ, who is priest forever after the order of Melchizedek. Since Christ lives forever, the priesthood will never again change, for He is the holy, pure, and perfect high priest. The daily sacrifice of the Levitical priesthood has been replaced with the sacrifice of Christ, once and for all.

Father of Light, we pray that your light which lives in us will never be extinguished, and that we would never stray down a path unless it is illuminated by your love, life, and light. Though we have moments of doubt, ensure we always see the way out of trouble by looking for your light, and listening to your Spirit who is with us. Help us to recognize the darkness in our way and expose dark spirits of the evil one, his evil minions, and his evil followers. Let your light shine brightly in our hearts to repel those spirits of darkness; let our light consume that darkness so it cannot enter our homes. In the name of Jesus, whose life we celebrate by shining pretty lights outside our homes and inside our homes in order to remind us of the reason for the season, Amen.

December 2

International Day for the Abolition of Slavery was adopted by the United Nations on this day in 1949, when they held a Convention for the Suppression of the Traffic in Persons and of the Exploitation of the Prostitution of Others. Briefly stated, it was a convention to end slavery and exploitation in the world. Forced marriage, labor, prostitution, and servitude involve mostly women and children. Hundreds of millions of people worldwide have been forced against their will into slavery. Those perpetrating such immoral acts are themselves slaves to sin; for it is Satan who is controlling and exploiting them.

- ISA 59:13 ~ They know they are being disobedient to God; they carefully plan their lies.
- MAT 18:6 ~ Whoever causes a little child that believes in me to sin, it would be better for him if a millstone was hung around his neck, and he was drowned in the depths of the sea.
- 1 TI 6:5 ~ They are corrupt and have no knowledge of the truth. They think it is godly to exploit others for money.
- 2 TI 3:13 ~ Evil people and false teachers will get worse, deceiving many; they themselves have been deceived by Satan.
- 2 PE 2:2–3, 14, 18–19 ~ Many will join them in their sexual misconduct, bringing the way of truth into disrepute. In their greed, these teachers will exploit with false narratives. Their condemnation has been a long time coming, since their destruction does not sleep. They have eyes full of adultery, insatiable for sin, enticing wayward souls. They boast of their folly, alluring people with lustful passions who are vulnerable. They promise freedom while they are slaves to depravity. People become slaves to whatever is controlling them.

Human trafficking is a felonious enterprise and every bit as lucrative as the drug trade. Many women and children crossing our borders are kidnapped and exploited by the cartels for sale to the highest bidder. These crimes are seldom prosecuted or reported; their names are forgotten. Slavery exists everywhere; there has never been a people that was never enslaved and which never enslaved others. And though the US fought a war to end slavery, it is still here among segments of the aristocracy and criminal syndicates. The Bible says: heartless monsters such as they must be put to death. The best way to abolish slavery: identify and eliminate the offenders.

- EXO 21:16 ~ Kidnappers must be executed, regardless of whether they are in possession of a kidnapped victim or were guilty of selling victims into slavery.
- DEU 24:7 ~ Anyone caught kidnapping or enslaving their neighbor will be put to death. You must purge the evil among you.
- TIT 1:11 ~ They must be silenced, those who would ruin entire households, teaching things that are wrong for the sake of ill-gotten gain.

Many countries force children into servitude, hard labor, crime, and the military; their governments are complicit with these atrocities. It is a mystery to me why the US does business with them. The Bureau of International Labor Affairs at the Department of Labor identified seventy-eight countries in violation of child labor laws. Yet the UN does not sanction member states who are guilty. In addition to child labor, China forces Muslim people into slave labor; the US should ban their products from import, but instead we trade with China more than any other country. It is stunning the extensiveness of exploitation of women and children around the world.

Father, we pray for abolition of slavery in the world and swift justice upon perpetrators. Help our nation to stop sanctioning this atrocity both here and abroad. In Jesus's name, Amen.

December 3

International Day of Persons with Disabilities is a UN observance started in 1992, designed to provide innovations, technologies, programs, and support to ensure equal opportunities, rights, and inclusiveness for disabled people. In my experience, the disabled want to be treated like everybody else; most do not want to draw attention to their handicap but to their humanity. It is okay to open the door for a person in a wheelchair, but don't be surprised if they'd rather do it themselves. A common fallacy is that they are incapable of doing certain jobs, which is true to some extent. But in most cases, the handicapped person can learn just as easily as anybody, and they can perform jobs where they meet the entry level requirements. Of course, there are more limitations for those who are mentally handicapped. But even those people can be trained to do jobs that others decline to do, such as cleaning, landscaping, and manual labor.

Many businesses have made accommodations to improve accessibility and increase employment of the disabled, seeing how it is the law. The Americans with Disabilities Act was passed in 1990 under President Bush Sr., prohibiting discrimination on the basis of a handicap or disability. People with an impediment know their own limitations, but even then, some are able to transcend their shortcomings, by turning their weaknesses into strengths. And how do they do it? The same way anybody overcomes setbacks or inadequacies: desire, hard work, perseverance.

- PRO 3:5–6 ~ Trust in God with all your heart and do not depend on your own understanding. In all your ways acknowledge God and He will direct you in the way to go.

- ISA 40:30–31 ~ Even youths faint and become weary, and young men stumble and fall. But those who trust the Lord will be renewed in their strength; they will soar on wings like eagles. They will run and not grow weary; they will walk and not feel faint.

- EPH 4:1–3 ~ I Paul, a prisoner for the Lord, implore that you stay worthy of the vocation for which you are called, with humbleness, kindness, and perseverance; loving one another, staying unified in the Spirit, and bonded together in peace.

- EPH 6:18 ~ Pray always in the Spirit, and continue to watch for the Lord with perseverance.

- 2 TH 3:5 ~ May the Lord direct your hearts into God's love and Christ's perseverance.

- 1 TI 4:16 ~ Keep a close watch on your life and your doctrine and persevere in them, for you will prove yourself worthy as well as those who will listen.

- HEB 12:1 ~ Since we are being watched by numerous spectators, let us discard everything that hinders us such as the sin that trips us up, and run the race that has been set before us with perseverance.

- JAM 1:12 ~ Blessed be those who persevere despite their trials and temptations, because they will receive a crown of life which the Lord has promised to anyone who loves Him.

- JAM 5:10–11 ~ Remember the prophets as examples of patience in the face of suffering. We consider those who have persevered to be blessed by God.

Significant effort pays off no matter what your gifts or flaws. Make no mistake, we all have both. But some people must overcome debilities others do not; this influences them to be all the more determined when they undertake a task or goal. They will strive, and prove themselves as capable as those who do not have to overcome infirmities. That deserves honest respect.

- PRO 2:10–13 ~ When wisdom enters your heart and knowledge is pleasant to your soul, discretion will preserve you and understanding will keep you, to deliver you from evil and from those who speak evil.

- PRO 13:11 ~ Wealth obtained by pride will diminish; but those who achieve by way of hard work will see their wealth increase.

- LUK 14:16–24 ~ Jesus told a parable about the kingdom of heaven: The kingdom of heaven is like the king whose son was to be married. The king sent servants to gather the invited guests for the wedding, but they gave lousy excuses not to come. The king sent servants a second time, but those on the guest list ignored them, beat them, and even murdered them. The king found out and sent his armies to destroy the murderers and burn their cities. Then he sent servants into the streets to gather anybody and everybody, good or bad, rich or poor, the downtrodden, handicapped, and underprivileged until the banquet hall was filled. Nobody on the original guest list was welcome.

- 1 CO 3:8–9 ~ Everyone is rewarded according to their labor, for all are laborers for God.

- 2 CO 12:9–10 ~ The Lord said, "My grace is sufficient for you, because my strength is made perfect in weakness." Therefore, I gladly rejoice in my infirmities, so that the power of Christ may rest upon me. I take pleasure in infirmities, accusations, neediness, persecutions, and distress that I endure for Christ's sake; for when I am weak, then I become strong.

- HEB 11:7–38 ~ With faith, the prophets were able to endure anything and performed great feats, such as subduing kingdoms, escaping certain death, overcoming incredible odds, healing the sick, and even raising the dead.

- REV 14:13 ~ I heard a voice in heaven saying, "Blessed are those who die in the Lord; they will find rest from their hard work, for their actions precede them."

God illuminates our weaknesses and limitations to prepare us for greater challenges; this may require additional training and skill development. By revealing that some things have a threshold or limit, we realize that God's blessings are limitless, such as His everlasting love, comfort, and support. This should motivate one to perform their best in all circumstances.

- MIC 4:7 ~ I will make a remnant from the handicapped and a great nation from the outcasts. The Lord will rule over them in mount Zion henceforth, even forevermore.

- LUK 1:37 ~ With God, nothing is impossible.

- 2 CO 9:8 ~ God is able to bless you abundantly, that in all things and at all times you have what you need, so you can abound in good works.

- 1 TH 5:14–22 ~ Warn those who are unruly, comfort the feeble minded, support the weak, and be patient towards everyone. Never render evil for evil but follow that which is good in yourself and others. Rejoice always; pray without ceasing; give thanks in everything, for this is God's will in your life. Quench your thirst for the Spirit; do not hate the words of the prophets. Test all things keeping hold of the good. Refrain from anything that is evil.

- JAM 1:2–4 ~ My brothers, count it all joy when you fall into different temptations, for the trying of your faith produces patience. But let patience have her perfect work so that you may be complete, and never wanting.

Father, we pray for those with disabilities and handicaps, that they will persevere: never giving up but depending on you completely, knowing that with you they can do anything. We pray that companies and businesses would carefully consider the qualifications of people with disabilities and not hesitate to hire them when it is clear they can perform the work. Let these people have a chance to prove themselves, with a repertoire of abilities that others might not have. Let us ensure that all people are respected for their work. In Jesus's name we pray, Amen.

December 4

Extraordinary Work Team Recognition Day is an annual observance of unknown origin, which started relatively recently (about five years ago). Team building has been a major component of business and industry for over one hundred years. But the psychology of group dynamics and criteria for effective teams is a fairly modern science in social psychology. Certainly, teamwork is necessary in a variety of settings, including sports, military or police operations; in committees, research and study groups; in juries, families, organizations, sales, construction, etc. Teams have individual and group responsibilities, rules, goals, leaders, specialties, budgets, schedules, evaluations, reporting, and rewards that are different than that of non-group performance.

In the corporate world, some goals require participation by more than one person, which is the main reason work teams are constructed. The team is a collection of unique individuals with a common interest or goal. The team meets regularly to strategize, collaborate, plan, execute, and evaluate. A successful team requires members to be committed, accountable, cooperative, cohesive, supportive, and selfless. There are certain attributes that are detrimental to team success such as groupthink, social loafing, polarization, risky shift, autonomy, and leveraging. If you are unfamiliar with these terms, I recommend researching them, especially if you are organizing a team or you are a member of a team (Barber, 2016).

- PRO 22:29 ~ Do you know someone who is diligent in business matters? That person will serve kings, and will be able to avoid obnoxious people.

- PRO 27:23–24 ~ Pay attention to your business, for riches do not endure forever, and an earthly crown does not endure to every generation.

- MAT 18:20 ~ Jesus said, "When two or more people are gathered together in my name, I will be there with them."

- PHP 2:14 ~ Conduct your business without arguing or complaining.

- COL 1:20 ~ Christ established an everlasting peace through His blood which was shed on the cross, thereby causing all things on earth and in heaven to exist together in harmony with Him.

- COL 2:2 ~ My hope is that people's hearts will be comforted, being bound together in love, and that they receive the riches of understanding and acknowledgement of the mystery of God, and of the Heavenly Father, and of Jesus Christ.

Jesus Christ had a team of twelve backing Him; He also organized teams of two to carry out His missions. Their mission was to take the Gospel truth to every corner of the world. They were ordinary men (and women) who did extraordinary things; first as a group and then individually. Among the apostles, only John avoided a martyr's death. The betrayer Judas Iscariot would precede Jesus in death; to replace him, Matthias was selected by lot, with the apostles (TIT 1:1–3); but Jesus chose Paul to be His twelfth apostle (ACT 9:1–25; ROM 1:1; 1 CO 15:9–10).

- MAT 10:2–4; MAR 3:14–19; LUK 6:13–16; ACT 1:13 ~ Jesus had twelve apostles: Peter (previously Simon) and his brother Andrew; James and John (sons of Zebedee); Philip and Bartholomew (also Nathanael); Thomas, Matthew (the publican), James (son of Alphaeus), Thaddaeus (also Lebbaeus), Simon (the zealot), and Judas Iscariot.

- LUK 10:1, 16–17 ~ Jesus appointed seventy disciples to preach in every city, sending them in teams of two. Jesus said, "Those who listen to you will be listening to me; those who despise you will be despising me, and those who despise me despise Him who sent me." The seventy men returned after their ministry with joy, telling how demons obeyed them when they invoked the name of Jesus Christ.

- ACT 2:42–43; ACT 4:33 ~ Those who listened remained steadfast in the doctrine and fellowship of the apostles, in the breaking of bread together and in prayer. Everyone was awestruck, for many wonders and signs were performed by the apostles. And with great power the apostles bore witness of the resurrection of the Lord Jesus; and exceeding grace was bestowed upon them.

- EPH 4:11–16 ~ God gave abilities of apostles, prophets, evangelists, pastors and/or teachers for the work of the ministry, the edifying of the saints, the perfecting of the body of Christ, and the unity of faith. They imparted the knowledge of the Son of God who was a perfect man, so that we could put on the characteristics of Christ. We will no longer be helpless as children, swayed by false teachings and influenced by the trickery of deceitful schemes. Instead, we will speak the truth out of love, and we will grow in every way in Christ, who is our head. In Him, the whole body is joined and held together just as our bodies are held together by ligaments and joints. Christ is the head of this body, in which all members work together as an integrated system; through Him the body is nurtured and grows in His love.

We who are members of the body of Christ are also part of a team. We work together with other Christians just like our own body parts work together to complete tasks.

- ROM 12:4–8 ~ Just as our body has many members, each with a separate purpose, so we, being part of the body of Christ, have certain responsibilities. We have different gifts which God in His grace has given us. Some people can minister, some can teach, some can provide guidance and counseling. If you have the gift of prophecy do so in proportion to your faith. If you have the gift of giving, do so generously. If you have the gift of governing, do so with diligence. If you have the gift of mercy, show it cheerfully.

- 1 CO 3:9 ~ We are laborers working together with God. You are the mission field; you are God's building.

- 1 CO 12:4–13, 20–31 ~ There are a variety of spiritual gifts, but only one Spirit. There are different ways of administering but only one Lord. There are different operations, but the same God works through them. The Spirit is manifested in some way in everyone to use productively. Some people have received wisdom, some knowledge, some faith, all from the same Spirit. Some have the ability to heal, others work miracles, or prophesy, or discern spirits, or speak foreign tongues; but all of them are working with the same Spirit, who divides power among everyone as He chooses. Just as the body is one though it has several members, likewise we are all members of the body of Christ, regardless of race or status. There should be no inner conflict in this body; but all members should equally care for one another. If one member suffers, all suffer; if one member is honored all members rejoice. For the body is not one member, but many. God placed each member in the body for a particular purpose. Every member of the body, no matter how minor, is needed. God has assembled the body to eliminate division within it, and so that all members would receive equal recognition and importance. Just as with our physical body, each member of the body of Christ has a specific function. We cannot all be apostles, prophets, teachers, healers and helpers. But we all hold dear our best gifts, especially the gift of God's excellent Holy Spirit.

Heavenly Father, you give everyone the ability to learn and communicate; thank you that we have communication between your Spirit and our spirits. Help us to be evenly yoked to our spouses like a team of oxen, sharing the load together; and let our families work well together as an integrated team. May our places of worship be filled with people who work with one another to bring others into the fold. Help us to work well with others whenever the mission warrants it, whether doing our work or your work. In Jesus's name, Amen.

December 5

International Volunteer Day is one of many UN observances organized annually; it was inaugurated in 1985 to recognize the work of volunteers across the globe. Objectives include promoting voluntary service; recognizing the contributions of volunteers in the community, nation, and world; and creating networks of communication to share ideas, hold events, and develop initiatives. Volunteering is something everyone can do to give back to community, humanity, and God. Even if you work fulltime, you can find time to serve at your church, your kid's school, nursing home, hospital, emergency shelter, animal shelter, library, food bank, soup kitchen, environmental cleanup, nonprofit organization, and the list goes on. We are encouraged by God to give of our time, talents, and treasure. Volunteering is giving of yourself to help people, animals, the environment, or agencies, in service to the needy, rundown communities, or habitats.

- DEU 16:17 ~ Everyone should give as they are able, in accordance with the blessings which God has given them.

- PSA 41:1–2 ~ Blessed be those who consider the poor, for the Lord will deliver them in time of trouble. The Lord will preserve them and their lives; and they will be blessed upon the earth and will not be subjected to the will of their enemies.

- PRO 11:24 ~ One person gives freely and gains even more; another withholds the surplus but comes to poverty.

- ISA 58:10–11 ~ When you pour out your soul to the hungry and satisfy the needs of the afflicted, then will your light shine in the darkness, and your darkness become as the daylight at noon. And the Lord will guide you continually, and satisfy your soil, and put fat on your bones. You will be like a watered garden, and like a spring of water that does not run out.

- MAT 5:15–16 ~ Jesus said, "You do not light a candle and then cover it, because it is supposed to give light. Let the light inside you shine before others, and people will see in your actions that you live to glorify your Father in heaven."

- MAT 25:40, 45 ~ Jesus said, "Whenever you have done something for even the least significant of human beings, you have done it unto me; and whenever you have not done something for even the least of these, you have not done it for me either."

- JOH 20:21 ~ Jesus said, "Peace, brothers. Just as the Father sent me, now I am sending you."

- ACT 20:35 ~ In your labors, give to the needy, remembering the words of Jesus Christ, "It is more blessed to give than to receive."

- ROM 12:1 ~ I implore you brothers and sisters, by the mercies of God, that you present yourselves as living sacrifices, holy and acceptable to Him; this is your reasonable service.

- 2 CO 9:7 ~ Everyone should give whatever they think is fair in their heart. Giving should be done voluntarily, not out of obligation, for God loves a cheerful giver.

- GAL 6:9–10 ~ Do not get weary of doing good; if you keep it up you will reap in due season. In every opportunity, do good to other people, especially those who belong to the family of believers.

- EPH 2:10 ~ We are God's workmanship, created in Christ to do good works, which God prepared in advance for us to do.

- 1 PE 4:9–10 ~ Use hospitality with one another, without resentment. As everyone has received gifts, even so minister the same to others as good stewards of the manifold grace of God.

- 1 JO 3:17–18 ~ Whoever has it good and sees their neighbor in need, but neglects to help them, how can the love of God be in them? Dear children, let us not love with words and talk but with actions and with truth.

    Jesus said that whatever you do and whatever you fail to do for another person, will affect Him in the same manner. So, if you do good, you will be blessed; and if you fail to do good you will not be blessed. When you see someone in need and you help them, you help further the kingdom of Christ; when you have extra and do not share it with the needy, you are not furthering the kingdom but you are bringing poverty upon yourself.

- PSA 82:3–4 ~ Defend the poor and fatherless; do justice to the afflicted and needy. Rescue the weak and destitute; deliver them from the hand of the wicked.

- PRO 3:27–28 ~ Do not withhold good from them to whom it is due, when it is in the power of your hand to do it. Do not tell your neighbor to go away and come back tomorrow, even though you already have it.

- PRO 19:17 ~ Those who show compassion to others are lending to the Lord, and that which was given will be paid back.

- MAT 23:23–24 ~ "Woe to you teachers of the Law and you Pharisees, hypocrites everyone. You tithe but yet you neglect the more important matters of the law such as justice, mercy, and faith. You should have practiced the latter without neglecting the former. You are blind guides, which would strain at a gnat but swallow a camel."

- LUK 6:31 ~ Do unto others as you would like them to do unto you.

- 2 CO 3:6 ~ God has made us able ministers of the New Testament, not of the letter of the Law, but of the Spirit, for the letter kills, but the Spirit gives life.

- 1 TI 4:12–16 ~ Paul wrote to Timothy: Do not let anyone put you down because you are young, but set an example for the believers through your speech, life, love, faith, and purity. Devote yourself to the public reading of scripture, and to preaching and teaching. Never neglect your gift, which was given to you in a prophetic message when the elders laid their hands upon you. Be diligent in these matters, and give yourself completely to them, so that everyone may see your progress. Keep a close watch on your life and your doctrine and persevere in them, for you will prove yourself as well as those who will listen.

- 1 PE 2:19–21 ~ It is commendable if a man suffers unjustly because he is conscious of God. If you suffer for doing good and you endure it, you are favored by God. This is one reason you are called, because Christ suffered for you, giving you an example to follow.

- 1 PE 5:1–4 ~ Peter wrote to the elders as a fellow elder and witness of Christ's sufferings: Be shepherds to the flock that God has placed under your care, serving as overseers. Do this, not because you must or for money, but because you want to, as God desires. Be eager to serve, not lording over those God has entrusted to you, but as an example to the flock. And when the Chief Shepherd appears, you will receive a crown of glory that will never fade.

    Gracious and merciful Father, help us to imitate your Son by being gracious and merciful to others. Let us not be hesitant to share what extra we have in terms of time, goods, service, and help. Remind us that our volunteering to help will be in service to you, so that you receive the glory for our good deeds; let us trust only in the good deeds done by Jesus whose righteousness will become ours in the next life. Equip us to take on additional tasks in the conduct of your work on earth, performing them with the aid and power of your Holy Spirit, as we give aid and empower the lowly, needy, destitute, and afflicted, just like Jesus showed us, in whose name we pray, Amen.

December 6

St. Nicholas Day is remembered annually on this date in reverence to the fourth century bishop of Myra. He was born in Lycia of Asia Minor in the late third century. His Christian faith led him into the ministry where he began a winter tradition of giving out monetary gifts to the poor, and assisting people who were afflicted or suffering. He would drop coins into their shoes and socks; this tradition of placing gifts and money in stockings is practiced today on Christmas Eve, hanging stockings from the fireplace for St. Nick to leave small gifts and money. Eastern Orthodox countries continue to venerate Nicholas of Myra, the legendary miracle worker, who is the patron saint of Greece and Russia. He died on this day in the year AD 346 (12/19 on a Julian calendar).

The idea of Santa Claus was a spinoff of this godly and generous man, through tales of a portly man who rides a sleigh of reindeer delivering toys. Santa means saint, and Claus is the last syllable of Nicholas (Nick being the first syllable). So, Santa Claus, or St. Nick, are merely nicknames for Nicholas, who was a real person. Santa Claus, on the other hand, is a fictional character. The invention of Santa Claus presents another example of the commercialization of Christmas. Unless of course, people are celebrating the Feast of St. Nicholas which is primarily a Roman Catholic and Eastern Orthodox observance, though some Protestants also venerate the kindly bishop. It would be wise to explain to your kids the difference between St. Nicholas and Santa Claus before introducing them into your holiday rituals; one is for fun but one was for real.

- ISA 29:13 ~ These people come near to me with their mouth and honor me with their lips, but their hearts are far from me. Their worship of me consists only of rules taught by men.

- JER 10:1–4 ~ Do not learn the ways of the heathen and do not be discouraged by signs in the heavens like them; for the customs of other peoples are vain. They will cut down a tree and carve the wood, then deck it out with silver and gold, nailing it down so it cannot be moved.

- COL 2:8, 20–22 ~ Beware that you are not swayed by errant philosophies or vain deceptions, originating from worldly traditions and principles and not from Christ. You are in Christ and not the world, so why submit to its rules? You are not subject to ordinances that are the doctrines and commandments of men. Those traditions are destined to die out. People may appear reasonable with their self-imposed worship, false humility, and harsh treatment of the body, but these lack value in restraining the sinful flesh.

- GAL 4:9–11 ~ Now that you know God, or rather are known by Him, how can you turn back to the weak and worthless ways of the world, and become a slave once more? You observe curious days, months, seasons, and years! I fear that my time with you was wasted.

- 2 TH 2:15 ~ Fellow Christians, stand fast in your faith and hold onto those traditions that you have been taught in God's Word, through the prophets and apostles.

- 1 TI 1:4–5 ~ Give no heed to fables and endless genealogies, which only raise questions rather than edifying people in the true faith. The conclusion of the commandments is to love others with a pure heart and a clear conscience, with unwavering faith, from which some have swerved off the path into vain babbling.

- JAM 1:17 ~ Every good gift and every perfect gift is from above, from the Father of lights, in whom there is no variance nor any turning to the side like moving shadows.

Heavenly Father, guide us to celebrate and worship in accordance with your will and your Word, and not adopt unscriptural rituals, or base our religion on fictional characters. Let us keep our focus on you, and not the festive decorations, acknowledging true people of God that remind us of Christ whom we adore. In His name we pray, Amen.

December 7

Pearl Harbor Day is the day we remember the 2,403 lives lost and 1,178 injured when Japan attacked Pearl Harbor, HI on this day in 1941. The US Navy also lost about twenty ships and three hundred airplanes. Congress declared war on Japan the next day and the US entered World War II. In August of 1945, the US would drop two atomic bombs on Japan resulting in their immediate surrender. Today's observance became official under President Clinton in 1994.

- PSA 144:1–2 ~ David wrote: Blessed be the Lord, my rock; who trains my hands for war and my fingers for battle. He is my steadfast love and my fortress; my stronghold, my deliverer, my shield. I take refuge in the Lord who subdues people under me.
- PRO 21:15–16 ~ When justice is done it is a joy to the righteous but terror to the evildoers. The person who wanders from the path of understanding will join the congregation of the dead.
- ECC 3:8 ~ There is a time to love and a time to hate; a time for war and a time for peace.
- ISA 2:4 ~ God will judge between the nations and decide disputes for many peoples; they will beat their swords into plowshares and their spears into pruning hooks. Nations will not take up the sword against nation, neither will they learn war anymore.
- JER 51:20 ~ The Lord is my battle axe, my weapons of war; for with Him I break the nations into pieces and with Him I destroy kingdoms.
- JOE 3:9–12 ~ Proclaim this among the Gentile nations: Prepare for war; rouse the warriors. Let all the fighting men draw near and attack. Beat your plowshares into swords and your pruning hooks into spears. Let the weak say I am strong. Assemble yourselves, all of you heathens, and gather around this place; bid your mighty ones to come. Wake up all you heathens and come to the valley of Jehoshaphat, for there will I sit and judge you.
- MIC 7:8 ~ Do not rejoice over me, oh enemy of mine. For when I fall, I will get back up; when I sit in darkness, the Lord will be my light.
- MAT 5:9 ~ Blessed be the peacemakers for they will be called sons of God.
- MAT 24:6 ~ You will hear of wars and rumors of wars. Do not be alarmed for this must take place, but the end is not yet.
- ROM 8:37 ~ In all these things we are more than conquerors through Him who loved us.
- JAM 4:1–2 ~ What causes quarrels and conflict among you? Is it not your passions which are at war within you? You desire and do not have, so you murder. You covet but cannot obtain, so you quarrel and fight. You do not have because you do not ask.
- 1 PE 4:12 ~ Beloved, do not think it strange concerning the fiery trial which comes to test you for it is not that unexpected.

Father, we ask for your protection; shield us from the enemy abroad and help us defeat the enemy from within. Enable our leaders to be adept at diverting war and conflict with other nations, and help us eradicate those who incite violence inside our borders. Let your vengeance be poured out over the wicked; remind us to yield to your judgment, for vengeance is yours alone. Please do not let us take down our guard, become complacent, or react without preparation; rather, give us insight, awareness, vigilance, and resolve so that we are able to ward off the murderers, terrorists, insurrectionists, anarchists, and warmongers. Help us to restore and maintain peace in the world and within our borders to the extent possible, and let us always remember where our peace of mind comes from which is Jesus Christ, the Prince of Peace, in whose name we pray, Amen.

December 8

National Christmas Tree Day is a good day for putting up the Christmas tree. The president and first lady will light up the national tree in Washington DC tonight. Putting up the tree is a solemn ritual celebrated all around the world: selecting the tree and decorating it, with a star on top to remind us of the Star of Bethlehem. It is a spiritual moment for the family, where the Holy Spirit abides with us as we start to experience the spiritual joy of Christmas, getting us into the mood for the holy season which begins with Advent and continues into Epiphany.

Numerous countries celebrate by decorating their Christmas tree in the traditional style of that country. You can research this and find how individual countries decorate their trees with special kinds of ornaments. A nativity scene beneath the tree is a common addition. Most historians place the origin of the Christmas tree to fifteenth century Germany, largely based on the popular hymn *Oh Christmas Tree* (*O Tannenbaum*). Martin Luther is often credited with the introduction of the Christmas tree inside the home, and the placing of candles to represent the light of Christ. Traditionally, an evergreen tree is used as it stays green after being cut. The tree represents life and the light represents Christ. Thus, those claiming that the tree is akin to a graven image are mistaken; further, the suggestion that the Christmas tree was lifted from an ancient pagan practice is erroneous.

- HOS 14:4–9 ~ I will heal their lapsing, and love them freely; for my anger has been turned away from them. I will be as the dew to Israel; he will blossom like a lily and spread his roots like the cedars of Lebanon. His branches will reach out and his beauty will be as an olive tree with the aroma of cedar. Those who dwell under his shadow will return; they will revive as the corn, and grow as a vine with the scent of wine. Ephraim will say, "Why do we need idols?" For it is I who will answer and look after you. I am like a green fir tree; and you will receive your fruit from me. Who is wise that they can understand these things? Who is prudent to discern them? For the ways of the Lord are right, and the righteous will walk in them. But the transgressors will stumble over them.

Many scholars place the birth of Jesus during the Feast of Tabernacles which occurs in conjunction with the late harvest towards the end of October. During this observance, tree branches are cut to build temporary shelters or booths (e.g., tabernacles). [Note: The December date for Christmas was appointed by the Roman Church circa fourth century, possibly by emperor Constantine, to overlap pagan observances associated with the winter solstice.]

- LEV 23:34–36, 39–42 ~ On the fifteenth day of the seventh month is the Feast of Tabernacles lasting seven days; the first day will be a holy convocation so do not work. Present offerings by fire each day; the eighth day will be another holy convocation with an offering by fire to the Lord. On the first day take healthy boughs and branches from trees like palms and willows, and carry them rejoicing before the Lord. This will be an annual observance for all generations. The people of Israel will dwell in booths these seven days.

The Tree of Life represents everlasting life provided to all believers who place their trust in Christ. Again, we see this represented in the evergreen tree which does not lose its color and continues to bear fruit unless it dies and withers.

- GEN 3:22 ~ God said, "Humans are like the higher-order beings because they have the knowledge of right and wrong. They can eat from the Tree of Life and they can live forever."

- REV 2:7; REV 22:14, 17 ~ Blessed be those who keep God's commandments for they will be allowed to enter the gates of heaven and partake of the everlasting waters and of the Tree of Life. And they will never die again.

As we prepare to celebrate the birth of our Lord, many things come to mind. Not only is He both man and God, He is also the firstborn and only begotten of God. He was born into this world to give light and show us the love of the Father. Christ proved He was God by His birth, ministry, death, and resurrection from the dead. His entire life was a miracle, from the immaculate conception to His ascension into heaven. With His resurrection, Christ has become the firstborn of the dead, the first to be raised to remain with the Father for eternity; and because He lives, so will all who believe in Him be raised to live with the Father as the firstborn of Christ.

- JOH 14:18–21 ~ Jesus said, "I will not leave you without a comforter. In a little while the world will not see me anymore. But you will see me, and because I live, you will live also. On that day you will know that I am in the Father, and He is in me; and you are in me and I am in you. Those who know and keep my commandments are the ones who love me, and those who love me are loved by my Father; and I will love them and reveal myself to them."

- 1 CO 15:20–26, 44 ~ Christ arose from the dead, becoming the first to rise. Just as death came by a man, by a man has come the resurrection of the dead. Like Adam, we die, and like Christ, we will rise from the dead, Christ being the first. Christ will reign, and all His enemies will be destroyed; the last enemy to be destroyed will be death. It is our natural body that dies, it is our spiritual body that lives on after death.

- COL 1:12–20 ~ Give thanks to the Father, who has allowed us to partake of His inheritance, given to the saints who abide in His light. He has ransomed us from the power of darkness and delivered us to the kingdom of His dear Son Jesus Christ, who has redeemed us and forgiven us through His own precious blood. Christ is the very image of the invisible God; He is the firstborn of all living creatures. Through Him, all things were created on earth and in heaven, whether visible or invisible, including all thrones, dominions, principalities, and powers. All things were created by Him and for Him. He is before all things, and because of Him all things exist. He is the head of the body, which is the church. He is the beginning, the firstborn of the dead, and the supreme being above all things. God was pleased to allow His fullness to live in Christ. Christ established an everlasting peace through His blood which was shed on the cross, thereby causing all things on earth and in heaven to exist together in harmony with God.

- COL 2:9–10 ~ In Jesus Christ the whole deity of God lives. And you are complete in Him who is the head of all governments and powers.

- 1 JO 5:4–6, 9–10 ~ Whoever is born of God overcomes the world; the victory that overcomes the world is found in faith. Jesus Christ overcame the world; anyone believing in Him will also overcome the world. Christ is He, who came by water and blood. The Holy Spirit is He who bears witness, because the Spirit is truth. If we believe a person witnessing for another, we should believe God's witnessing even more; and God has given witness of His Son. Those who believe that Jesus is God's Son have God's witness in themselves; those who do not believe are calling God a liar, because they do not believe God's testimony concerning His Son.

Thank you Father, for your Son, who fulfilled the Law on our behalf, died to pay the penalty of our sin, and rose from the dead to prove His power over death. And because He lives, we also will live. Thank you that we will partake of the Tree of Life in heaven where sin and death do not exist. Help us to remember today the noble and humble birth of Christ, and His miraculous and glorious resurrection, both of which demonstrate His humanity and His deity, without which nobody could be saved. Let the Christmas tree be a reminder that this life is fleeting, and though we will die because of sin, our light will never be extinguished, just as the light of life found in Christ Jesus will never fade and cannot be hidden or snuffed out. In the name of Jesus we pray, Amen.

December 9

International Anti-Corruption Day is dedicated to fighting corruption in government and institutions. It was established by the UN Convention Against Corruption in 2003 due to rampant bribery, election fraud, crime, drug trafficking, and lack of accountability in government, leadership, business, and the media. Corruption degrades safety, security, peace, development, economy, human rights, laws, justice, and freedom; leading to chaos, civil war, poverty, and death. Each year, the UN will select a theme and an agenda to address this plague on society.

Corruption in politics and government breeds corruption among the governed. Similarly, corruption among the populace will result in a corrupt government. Satan prospers when corrupt and evil governments prosper. Corruption is a byproduct of our sinful flesh which craves worldly possessions and power. But those who accept the Spirit of God to guide and direct them will be able to control their flesh. Those who do not control the flesh will lose control, and ultimately, will lose their souls.

- PSA 12:8 ~ Wickedness is everywhere when vile men are exalted.

- PSA 14:1 ~ Only a fool would say in his or her heart that there is no God. Such people are corrupt and have done terrible things in the eyes of the Lord.

- PRO 29:2, 11–12 ~ When the righteous people increase, the people can rejoice. But when the unrighteous rule, the people mourn. Fools speak everything that is on their minds; people who are wise keep the matter until later. If a ruler listens to lies, his entire cabinet will be evil.

- MAT 6:19–21 ~ Jesus taught, "Do not collect treasures on earth where they can be corrupted by insects or rust, or stolen by thieves. Instead, store your treasures in heaven where they cannot be corrupted or stolen. For where your treasures are, there your heart will be also."

- MAT 7:17 ~ A good tree bears good fruit; a corrupt tree bears evil fruit.

- 1 CO 15:33 ~ Do not be deceived; evil associations corrupt good character.

- GAL 6:8 ~ Those who sow to the flesh will reap corruption to their flesh; those who sow to the Spirit, will from the Spirit reap eternal life.

- EPH 4:25, 29 ~ Quit lying; speak only the truth about one another, for we are part of one another. Do not let corrupt words leave your lips, but speak only good things about others.

- 1 TI 6:5 ~ Corrupt minds that are devoid of the truth will argue that godliness is a way of obtaining wealth. Stay away from them.

- TIT 1:15 ~ To the pure all things are pure, but to the corrupt and unbelieving nothing is pure; their minds and consciences are corrupt and evil.

- JAM 5:1–3 ~ Go cry and moan, you rich people, for the miseries that will come upon you. Your riches are corrupted and your clothes are worn out. Your disintegrating wealth will eat at you in the same fashion. You have heaped up riches for the last time.

- 2 PE 2:19–21 ~ They speak great words of emptiness and allure through lusts of the flesh, to attract those who have already escaped from them. They promise freedom but are themselves slaves to corruption, and are condemned. If a person has escaped the corruption of the world through the knowledge of our Lord and Savior Jesus Christ, and becomes entangled again and overcome, that person's end is worse than the beginning. It would have been better for them not to have known the way of righteousness, than to have known it and turned their backs on the sacred instructions given to them.

- JDE 1:10 ~ They speak evil of those things that they do not understand. However, the things they know naturally by instinct only serve to corrupt them.

   People become corrupted when they allow the temptations of this world to obscure their vision and ignore the guidance of the Lord. Apparently, they see the desires of the flesh as more important than their lives. For they would deny that they will be held accountable; indeed, they believe they are justified in their actions and beliefs. This is a classic example of the grand delusion, for they have deceived themselves to the extent that they believe their own lies (see lesson on 11/25). It takes considerable effort to hide the truth from oneself, especially when it is staring them in the face. But the desires of the flesh have taken precedent over the truth of the spirit, and therefore the spirit of light within them becomes darkness, such that they pollute the truth and they despise God for it. To them, all truth is relative, so they invent their own truth.

- PRO 28:13 ~ Whoever covers up their sins will not prosper; but those who confess and forsake their sins will obtain mercy.

- ISA 55:6–7 ~ Seek the Lord while He may be found; call upon Him while He is near. Let the wicked forsake their evil ways and their unrighteous thoughts, and return to the Lord; and He will have mercy on them and will pardon them abundantly.

- JER 9:23–24 ~ Wise people must not glory in their wisdom; mighty people must not glory in their might; rich people must not glory in their riches. Instead, glory only in the fact that you know God who exercises love, mercy, righteousness, and judgment upon the earth, for it pleases God when we glorify Him.

- ROM 8:5–8, 13–14 ~ Those who pursue things of the flesh belong to the flesh; those who pursue things of the spirit belong to the Spirit. To have a carnal mind is death; to have a spiritual mind is life and peace. People with a carnal mind hate God; they disregard God's Law for they are in complete opposition to Him. Therefore, those who live for the flesh cannot please God. If you live for the flesh you will die. If you live for the Spirit, you can control the flesh, and you will live. For whoever is led by the Spirit of God become children of God.

- JAM 4:1–4 ~ Where do you think arguments and wars come from? They come from the lusts that battle inside you. You lust but have not; you kill and desire to have; you make war and you will not. But you have not because you ask not. When you do ask you receive not, because you ask for the wrong reasons, so you can indulge in your lusts. You adulterers, do you not realize that friendship with the world is enmity against God? Whoever would choose to be a friend of the world cannot be a friend of God.

- 1 TH 5:22 ~ Test all things keeping hold of the good. Refrain from anything that is evil.

   Father, we pray that corrupt people be removed from office and positions of power; help us and other nations to elect godly leaders. Expose the corruption in our leaders and government so people will see them for who they really are, what they really believe, and how their true motives and intentions will bring destruction upon us. Open our eyes to the evils in people, whether in the media, business, or government, and help us to bring them down and remove them from our midst and from positions of power; let them be the ones who are prosecuted and imprisoned for their many crimes, which include the indiscriminate persecution of Christians and people of faith on earth. Strengthen the faithful so that we can stand united in truth, representing a formidable force that will strike fear into the hearts of the corrupt and godless people, causing them to flee and hide. Let your truth prevail over the relativism that they are endorsing. We pray that nations being brought down by corruption are revived. Let there be a revival and renewal in our land, in our people, and in your church. In Jesus's name, Amen.

December 10

Human Rights Day commemorates the anniversary of the *Universal Declaration of Human Rights* by the United Nations in Paris, 1948. Dignitaries from several nations acknowledged that inalienable rights belong to every human being, regardless of sex, ethnicity, age, nationality, birth, religion, status, viewpoint, and demographic. The declaration was translated into five hundred languages. While most member nations have agreed to rights shared by all human beings, many do not practice that doctrine. Like most UN observances, there will be events, workshops, and conferences across the globe to develop plans and initiatives that will increase awareness and compliance with human rights and its enforcement.

- ISA 3:9 ~ It shows on their faces that they are guilty; they declare their sin like Sodom, they do not hide it. Woe unto their souls for they have recompensed evil unto themselves.

- GAL 5:13–14 ~ Brothers, you have been called to be free men, but do not use that freedom as an excuse to engage in lusts of the flesh, but in love serve one another. For all the Law is fulfilled by loving your neighbor as yourself.

- TIT 2:11–12 ~ For the grace of God that brings salvation has appeared to all people. It teaches us to say no to wickedness and worldly pleasures. It teaches us to live in a self-controlled, upright manner.

- 1 PE 2:16 ~ Be free, but do not use your freedom to conceal evil, rather in service to God.

The declaration begins by stating how all human beings are born free, with equal dignity and rights. Everyone has a conscience, intrinsically knowing right from wrong; and all human beings can reason. Also recognized is the brotherhood of humankind, that we are all connected in spirit and in blood. Though a clear reference to Biblical principles, the Bible and God are not acknowledged anywhere in the document. However, the very definition of inalienable rights implies they are given by God, for only He has the right to deny them. Further, many of these rights are delineated in the founding documents of the USA. The following are among the rights deemed inalienable (abridged). These rights are typical of a wholly democratic republic. [Go to *www.un.org* for the entire document.].

- Life, liberty, security, privacy
- Freedom of thought, belief, religion, worship, participation
- Freedom of opinion and expression; freedom of assembly; freedom of choice
- Right to vote, work, equal pay, join a union; right to rest and relaxation, and days off
- Equal access to services, financial aid, security when disabled, ill, or unemployed
- Freedom from slavery, torture, cruelty, inhuman or degrading treatment or punishment.
- Right to law and order, morality, respect
- Freedom from arbitrary arrest, detention, or exile
- Equal protection under the law; right to a fair trial or hearing; presumption of innocence
- Freedom from discrimination; right of nationality
- Freedom of movement; freedom to leave the country and return; right of asylum
- Right to marry and raise a family; freedom from forced marriage; freedom to divorce
- Right to own property and not have property confiscated
- Right to an education, school choice, normal development
- Freedom to rebel against tyranny

- PSA 40:4 ~ Blessed be those who trust in the Lord rather than giving their respect to the proud and deceitful.

- PSA 82:3 ~ Give justice to the weak and fatherless; ensure the rights of the afflicted and destitute.

- PRO 2:6–9 ~ The Lord gives wisdom; from His mouth come knowledge and understanding. God stores up sound wisdom for the righteous and is a shield to those with integrity. He guards the paths of justice and preserves the way of the saints. Thus, you will understand righteousness, justice, equity, and every good path.

- PRO 31:8–9 ~ Speak out for those who have no voice, for the rights of the destitute. Speak up, judge righteously, and defend the rights of the poor and needy.

- ROM 8:18, 21 ~ If we suffer with Christ, we also will be glorified with Him. For the sufferings we endure are nothing compared to the glory we will receive in Him. Thus, we have been freed from chains of corruption to glorious liberty as children of God.

- 2 CO 3:3, 17 ~ The Spirit of the living God has written His Word into our hearts; it is not written in ink or on tablets of stone. The Lord is that Spirit, and wherever that Spirit is, there is liberty.

- GAL 3:28 ~ Paul wrote, "There is no such thing as Jew or Greek, slave or free, male or female, for we are all equal in Jesus Christ."

- EPH 2:19 ~ You are no longer strangers or foreigners, but fellow citizens with the saints in the household of God.

- PHP 2:3–8 ~ Do not do anything through strife or vanity; instead, be humble, and regard others as better than yourselves. Do not focus on yourself, focus on others just like Christ did, who although He was equal with God, He took on the form of a man. Instead of exalting Himself, He became the servant of all. He humbled Himself before others, and was obedient unto death, even death on the cross.

- JAM 1:22, 25 ~ Do not merely listen to the Law, do what it says. Whoever considers the perfect law of liberty, and continues focusing on doing what is right and not just hearing what is right, that person will be blessed because of their actions.

Clearly, the Bible teaches that all humans are created equal and in the image of God, and God would that all people seek Him and follow His Son. The violation of human rights is most often found where God and Christ are unwelcome. The subjugation and discrimination of people of varying demographic identities has continued since the dawn of civilization, which is ironic because violating one's rights is about as uncivilized as you can get. What's worse is the earnest effort to divide people according to categories, in order to gain control over them and others. Divide and conquer is the objective of globalism by people devoid of the Spirit (JDE 1:19).

Heavenly Father, you created every man, woman, and child to be treated equal from the start; because every human being is equally loved by you. Today we pray for those whose rights are being violated by leaders, movements, protestors, and groups, that they would find freedom in Christ, despite their sufferings. We pray for justice upon those who hide behind political barriers to truth, as they engage in riotous or violent behavior. We pray that the tyranny and greed of the evil powermongers would be thwarted, and their reign of terror ended. We pray for our country, that the divisiveness being staged by the new world order be reversed, and that we would return to unity as one nation under God, and one planet of equally human beings. In the name of your Son Jesus Christ who is the great equalizer, we pray, Amen.

December 11

Hawking Won Fundamental Physics Prize on this day in 2012 in recognition of his work on quantum mechanics, black holes, and the birth of the universe. This is the most prestigious prize for lifetime achievement in the field of physics (three million dollars in US currency). Consider Stephen Hawking, who despite a debilitating affliction (ALS) that struck him at the age of twenty-one, he persevered, though he wasn't expected to live into his thirties. He became a quadriplegic, requiring around the clock care and a feeding tube to eat. At the age of seventy-six he passed, being one of the most renowned astrophysicists of all time. Despite his handicaps, he obtained his doctorate at Cambridge University, taught graduate school, wrote numerous books on cosmology, and discovered attributes of the universe that baffled even the experts. Further, he was married twice and had three children. How would all of this be possible for a person who could not use his limbs or speak? As it turned out, he was able to perform slight movements in his face to select letters on a keyboard, from a device attached to his glasses; his thoughts would be typed into a computer and a synthesizer would read his words in a robotic voice. What was the key to his success? Hawking once said that his life proves that one should never lose hope. He was right. Hope requires faith; and it is faith in God which proves that our hope is not in vain. Regrettably, Hawking did not confess God or give Him the glory, so it is unclear if he was saved. He certainly believed in himself, and this was his primary source of hope.

- JOH 10:9–10 ~ Jesus said, "I am the door; whoever enters will be saved, free to come and go and find pasture. The thief comes only to steak and destroy. I have come so you can have life, and have it more abundantly. I am the good shepherd who gives His life for the sheep."

- ROM 8:24–25 ~ We are saved because we hope. But hope that is seen is not hope, for who hopes for things they can see? But if we hope for what we cannot see, we must be patient.

- PHP 4:13 ~ I can do all things through Christ who strengthens me.

- HEB 11:1 ~ Faith is the assurance of things hoped for, the evidence of things not seen.

Hawking certainly helped us understand this universe, which is unique, complicated, expanding, and perfectly fine-tuned for life. Hundreds of components in the universe are tweaked to the nth degree such that a miniscule variation in any direction would cause life on earth to cease to exist. Our solar system is unique, our planet is unique, and humanity is unique, for we were created with capabilities that far exceed those of other lifeforms indigenous to Earth. Each and every individual is unique and amazing, with talents, personality, abilities, and importance that differ from all other individuals. All humans are very special to God, and loved perfectly.

- PSA 8:4–5 ~ Who are humans, Lord, that you, would be mindful of us, and our children that you would visit them? For you have made humans a little lower than the angels, and have crowned us with glory and honor.

- ECC 3:11 ~ God has made everything beautiful in its time. He also has set eternity in the human heart, though nobody can find out what God has done from the beginning to the end.

- ACT 17:23–26 ~ Paul addressed the men of Athens saying, "As I walked through the city, I observed your objects of worship and one caught my eye with its inscription: To the unknown God. Today I proclaim to you this God, who made heaven and earth and everything in it. The Lord of heaven and earth does not live in temples made by man, nor is He served by human hands as if He needed anything, since He gives all things to humankind: life, breath, and all we have. From one blood, God made all the nations to dwell upon the earth. He determined the appointed times, boundaries, and dwelling places beforehand."

- 1 CO 12:7–10, 28 ~ The manifestation of the Holy Spirit is given to everyone, and is exhibited in unique abilities and attributes including wisdom, faith, healing, miracles, prophesy, discerning spirits, interpreting tongues, and more.

- 1 CO 14:12 ~ Try to excel in those gifts which edify the church.

- PHP 1:9–11 ~ I pray that your love abounds continuously in knowledge and judgment; that you approve of excellent things and remain sincere, without offense, until the Lord returns; being filled with fruit of righteousness through Christ, to the glory and praise of God.

- PHP 4:8 ~ Whatever is true, honorable, just, pure, lovely, and gracious, if there is any excellence, if there is anything worthy of praise, think on these things.

- HEB 11:7–38 ~ Because of their great faith, men of God were able to endure hardship, setbacks, torment, and affliction; yet they performed remarkable feats of subduing kingdoms, escaping certain death, overcoming incredible odds, healing the sick, and raising the dead.

- 1 PE 2:5–9 ~ You are living stones, built into a spiritual house; a holy priesthood, to offer spiritual sacrifices acceptable to God through Jesus Christ. You are a chosen generation, a royal priesthood, a holy nation, a special people; for you have been selected to give praise to Him who called you out of darkness into His marvelous light.

We all have potential for greatness, only not in the same things. You see, our ancestry, history, experience, knowledge, education, skill set, abilities, and possibilities are unique, making our interests, vocation, roles, responsibilities, and calling equally unique. We can glorify the Lord using all these gifts to perform missions and reach goals exceeding our wildest dreams, which God ordained in advance for us to do. Sometimes, all we lack is believing we can. With God anybody can, if they believe God is in charge. And like Hawking, believe in yourself also.

- EST 4:14 ~ Mordecai told Esther, "If you keep silent at this time, relief and deliverance will rise for the Jews from another place, but you and your father's house will perish. And who knows whether you have not come into this kingdom for such a time as this?"

- PRO 3:5–6 ~ Trust the Lord with all your heart and do not lean on your own understanding. In all your ways acknowledge Him and He will make your paths straight.

- PRO 23:7 ~ As a man thinks in his heart, so is he. Eat and drink he says, but his heart is not with you.

- JER 29:11 ~ For I know the plans I have for you, declares the Lord, plans for welfare and not for evil, to give you a future and a hope.

- HAB 2:2–3 ~ And the Lord answered me: Write the vision; make it plain on tablets, so he may run who reads it. For the vision awaits its appointed time; it hastens towards the goal and will not fail. If it seems slow, wait for it; it will surely come without delay.

- MAT 13:31–32 ~ Jesus said, "The kingdom of heaven is like a mustard seed that a farmer sows in the field. It is the smallest of seeds, but it grows larger than all the garden plants and becomes a tree enabling the birds to make nests in its branches."

- 1 CO 12:31 ~ If you eagerly desire the greater gifts, I will show you the most excellent way.

Father, remind us how you created us to do great things in your name. Let us never forget how you made us to be uniquely talented and gifted so we can serve you and others, and make a decent living. With confidence in your Word, give us the will to perform amazing things. May we use our potential to bring glory to you on behalf of your Son, in whose name we pray, Amen.

December 12

Washington DC Became US Capitol on this day in 1800 to situate the seat of our federal government. This location was President Washington's choice; he was familiar with the area since his home was close by. It was a seaworthy port adjacent to Georgetown, MD and Alexandria, VA marking the border between the northern and southern states. Its location was a strategic gateway to the interior. This moved the seat from Philadelphia to Washington; it was surnamed District of Columbia to honor Columbus. Before the switch, Congress met at various places, notably New York, prior to problems that led to the move from Pennsylvania.

The Capitol building, the president's residence, and other office buildings had scarcely been built when the war of 1812 erupted; two years later the British burned our capitol city. Once again, we had to stave off the Brits and reconstruct. Since then, all three branches of government have been located in DC; the buildings have been repaired, extended, and rebuilt over the years. We need to conserve all of the sites, monuments, and historic establishments at our capitol. And we need to preserve our three-pronged government with its checks and balances for generations down the road. Additionally, it may behoove us to not have all three branches in one place (DC).

Historical sites in DC will take your breath away if you are visiting for the first time; if you haven't been, it's worth the trip and the kids will love it. The museums are awesome, the monuments and statues are many, and Arlington cemetery causes you to take pause. Standing in the halls of Congress and seeing all the bronzes of great founders and presidents is educational and inspirational. Certainly, a White House tour would be humbling if you can get in. It takes three to five days to take in the plethora of things to do in DC. You will probably want to go back again; but maybe not this time of year, for the winters are unpredictable.

In the Old Testament, monuments were built to commemorate events, and mark historic sites, much like our memorials in Washington. Altars made of stone were common indicators.

- GEN 8:15–21 ~ God told Noah to disembark from the ark and bring out all the wildlife so they could breed and replenish the earth. There Noah built an altar to the Lord. Noah took every clean animal and bird and offered burnt offerings before the Lord. And the Lord promised never to curse the earth again because of man, since the imagination of man's heart was evil from his youth.

- GEN 13:4–6 ~ Abram returned to the alter he had built when first entering the land of promise; Lot was with him. There they parted with their flocks for they had prospered greatly.

- GEN 22:9 ~ They came to the place God led them, and there Abraham built an altar and placed the wood; then he bound Isaac and laid him upon the wood. Before he could sacrifice his son, an angel called and told Abraham to hold back, for the Lord was pleased that he loved Him so much he was willing to give his own son to God. There was a ram caught in a thicket, and Abraham sacrificed the ram as a burnt offering to the Lord.

- EXO 17:14–16 ~ The Lord told Moses to write a memorial in a book and rehearse it with Joshua, for God intended to wipe out the Amalekites. Moses built an altar and named it "the Lord is my banner" because pagan hands were lifted against the throne of God and they were utterly defeated. And the Amalekites would have God as their enemy for generations to come."

- JOS 8:30–32 ~ Joshua built an altar to the Lord on Mt. Ebal using uncut stones in accordance with instructions given earlier by the Lord to Moses. There Joshua presented burnt and fellowship offerings to the Lord for their victories. Then Joshua engraved stones with a copy of the law of Moses in the presence of the Israelites.

- JDG 6:22–24 ~ The Lord said to Gideon that he could be at peace for he would not die at the hand of the Midianites. So, Gideon built an altar and called it the "the Lord is Peace;" and it remains in Ophrah to this day.
- 2 SA 24:25 ~ David built an altar to the Lord and made burnt offerings and peace offerings to ward off the plague God was going to bring upon Israel.

The temple was the seat of Jewish government throughout the Bible. Like our capitol building, it was built and destroyed and rebuilt a couple of times. Jerusalem was the capital city of the Israelites where David settled. The first temple was built by King Solomon as God had commanded his father, David. It would later be destroyed by the Babylonians, along with the rest of the city. The second temple was erected during the reign of Cyrus of Persia (EZR 1). That temple would be destroyed by Titus of Rome in accordance with Jesus's own prophecy. Presumably, a third temple will be built; perhaps it will be the Dome of the Rock in Jerusalem, currently claimed by Moslems and Jews. The last temple will be desecrated by Satan in the end times; it too will be decimated before Satan receives his reward of eternal fire.

- 2 SA 5:6–9 ~ David took the stronghold of Zion (in Jerusalem); and there he lived and built the city up; it was called the City of David.
- 1 KI 6:21, 23, 27; 1 KI 9:10–13 ~ Solomon built the temple and overlaid it with gold. Within the sanctuary he had two cherubim carved from olive trees. They were placed facing each other, with their wings against the walls, so that the wingtips of each cherub touched those of the other. [Like the Ark of the Covenant.]
- DAN 9:26 ~ After sixty-two weeks, Messiah will be cut off; then the great prince and his army will come to destroy the city and the sanctuary. The end will come as a flood and there will be war until all is desolated.
- MAT 24:1–2; MAR 13:2; LUK 21:5–6 ~ As they left the temple the disciples approached Jesus, who said to them, "Do you see all of these buildings? I tell you the truth, there will not be one stone left upon another; all will be thrown down."
- 2 TH 2:3–4, 9–12 ~ The man of lawlessness comes, who is the son of perdition. He exalts himself as if a god, or an object of worship, taking the seat in the temple of God. He brings about the acts of Satan through deception and magic. God will let people believe the lies and carry on with their wickedness, and be condemned to hell.

Jesus was tried by members of the Sanhedrin at the second temple; they were the Jewish leadership, headed by the high priest Caiaphas and his father-in-law Annas. They accused Jesus of blasphemy, then took Him before the Roman authority, which was the prefect Pontius Pilate. They requested that Jesus be executed since they did not have the authority to carry it out. Pilate tried to pawn Jesus off on Herod, King of Judea, a counterpart to the Roman authority. Herod toyed with Jesus and sent Him back to Pilate. Thus, there were several leaders who had power and authority, and none of them knew what to do with Jesus. So, Pilate deferred to a riotous mob and permitted them to render the verdict, sentencing Jesus to death by crucifixion at their request. Who was in control during this episode of history? God was! Local and regional authorities were out of control.

- JOH 18:12–13, 31–32 ~ The representatives of the Jews took Jesus, bound Him and took Him away. But Pilate told them to take Jesus back and judge Him themselves. They replied, "It is against the law for us to put a man to death"
- MAT 27:24; JOH 19:10–11 ~ Pilate told Jesus, "Do you realize I have the power to crucify you or release you?" Jesus replied, "You can do nothing to me without being given the power

by God. The ones who delivered me to you for crucifixion, they have committed a greater sin than you." Pontius Pilate washed his hands in a symbolic gesture, denying any responsibility for the crucifixion of Christ, presuming that he was innocent of Christ's blood.

Zion will again be the Lord's capitol city, located in the New Jerusalem in heaven. That is where the throne of Christ will be, as well as everybody who trusted in Him.

- PSA 76:2 ~ In Salem is God's tabernacle; in Zion is His home. [Note: Jerusalem means city of peace.]

- PSA 125:1 ~ Those who trust in the Lord will be like mount Zion, which cannot be removed, but abides forever.

- ISA 2:3; ISA 11:1–4, 10; ISA 42:1, 6; ISA 44:28 ~ God said to Isaiah: From Zion I have sent the Law. From Jerusalem I will send the Word. I will raise up a descendant of Jesse, and the Spirit of the Lord will be upon Him. He will possess the Spirit of wisdom, understanding, counsel, and might. He will be faithful to God and will judge with righteousness. I have given Him to you as a covenant to the people, to be a light to all nations; and all nations, including Jews and Gentiles alike, shall seek Him. He is my appointed shepherd and He will do everything I ask. He will build Jerusalem, and lay the foundation of the temple.

- ISA 9:6–7 ~ For unto us a child is born; unto us a Son is given. The government will be upon His shoulders. His name will be called Wonderful Counselor, Mighty God, Everlasting Father, and Prince of Peace. There will be no end to His government or the peace He brings. He will inherit the throne of David, and will rule with judgment and justice henceforth, even forevermore. The zeal of the Lord of Hosts will see to it.

- ZEC 8:3–8 ~ I (God) will return to Zion and I will live in Jerusalem; and Jerusalem will be called the city of truth, and Zion will be called the holy mountain. Children will be playing in the streets. It will be marvelous for my people and also for me. I will save my people from the corners of the earth and bring them to Jerusalem. They will be my people and I will be their God, in truth and in righteousness.

- HEB 12:22–23 ~ You have come to Zion, to the city of the living God, the heavenly Jerusalem. You have come to the company of innumerable angels, to the general assembly and church of the firstborn, all of whom are written in heaven. You have come to live with God, the judge of all, and with the spirits of all honest people made perfect, and to Jesus Christ the mediator of the New Covenant.

- REV 7:15–17 ~ They will live before the throne of God and will serve Him day and night in the temple. They will never be hungry, thirsty, hot or cold again. The Lamb among them will feed them, will lead them to fountains of living waters, and will remove all of their sorrows.

- REV 11:19 ~ The temple in heaven was opened. Inside was the ark of the testament. I saw lightning and I heard voices and thundering; and there was an earthquake and enormous hail.

Thank you, Father, that you will bring us to the new Mt. Zion in the new Jerusalem, to live forever with you, Christ, and the Holy Spirit in your kingdom. It will be a glorious time, and a beautiful sight. Help us during our trials, tribulations, and sufferings to keep this in mind so that we can endure all things, knowing our inheritance awaits us. Help us to show others and teach them, so they too can find peace in this tumultuous world, looking forward to the world to come. Help our nation to stand tall against the globalist powers and leaders; let us never capitulate to them but remain a shining light on the hill, revealing liberty to all the nations, that they avoid being deceived. In the name of Jesus we pray, whose death sets us free to be people of God, Amen.

December 13

Body, Mind, and Spirit Day is recommended to acknowledge that we have three components to our being, which is one of the many ways we have been created in God's image. Your life is found in your spirit (JOB 33:4; JOH 3:6; JOH 6:63). Everyone is likewise created with a body and a soul. Humans have one soul which we alone possess among creatures native to planet Earth. The soul enables observation, learning, analysis, ethical processing, and associated selection, and is generally associated with the mind, the will, and reasoning. The soul becomes you, a person distinctive from everyone else; well, except for the fact that people are alike in at least two distinct ways: we are created in God's own image and are loved unconditionally by Him. God also possesses a spirit and a soul, and He became a carnal man named Jesus Christ: therefore, God exists in physical (human) form, as well as spiritually and mentally. The three persons of the Holy Trinity, Father, Son, and Holy Spirit, are indivisible, unlike humans who can lose their soul and their body, and consequently give up their ghost or spirit upon death. Though we were created in the image of God and are more like Him than other creatures, it is irresponsible to ascribe attributes of humans to God. We are like Him in some respects but He is not like us; and though a man, Christ was unlike any other human, and we can only strive for His perfection in heaven.

Our body, soul, and spirit, need nurturing and exercise in order to maintain holistic health. That is, to be completely whole you need to tap into all three areas. If you want to be functioning at the highest possible level, practice exercising each domain. We each are given a body to live in this world, a mind to understand it, and a spirit which is our life force. Upon death, your spirit returns to God (ECC 12:7). Thus, we have physical, mental, and spiritual means by which we can worship and serve the Lord. The body is our natural, carnal component; and in it resides a sinful nature, also unlike other creatures indigenous to planet Earth. The mind can receive inputs from desires of the flesh as well as desires of the spirit. God wants us to follow the spirit within us, which is our connection to Him, else we find ourselves entangled in the depravity of the world and its iniquity.

- GEN 2:7–8, 16–18 ~ God formed man from the dust of the earth, and breathed into his nostrils the breath of life, and man became a living soul. And God planted a garden in Eden where he placed the humans He had created. And God commanded the man that he may eat from any tree in the garden except the tree of the knowledge of good and evil. And then God said, "It is not good for man to be alone, so I will make hm a helper.

- JOB 32:8 ~ There is a spirit in every person through which the inspiration of the Almighty enables each one of us to understand.

- ROM 7:21–25 ~ I am aware of a law within me compelling me to do good, while evil is also present in my mind. I delight in the Law of God placed there for my edification, but I see another law in my body waging war against God's Law and making me a captive to the law of sin. What a wretched person I am! Who will deliver me from this body of death? Thank God through Jesus Christ our Lord! Although in my mind I serve the Law of God, in my flesh I am a slave to sin.

Thus, within our minds is the knowledge of God and His will, and His Word; if you take the time to learn it you are smart. This is the soul wherein resides the conscience, the moral compass, the knowledge of right and wrong, and God's command to value all life, especially humankind. Unfortunately, our defiled flesh will compel us to follow it into sin, and succumb to the temptations of evil spirits, wicked people, and a corrupt world. But if we are guided by the Holy Spirit, we will be inclined do the right thing and love others as we love ourselves. Hence, it is necessary for us to remain mindful of the circumstances, our instructions from God delineated

DECEMBER

in the Bible, and the thoughts we are thinking; then we can proceed in accordance with what our higher power is telling us. Yes, we know in advance what to do and what not to do, and we know that the consequences of our decisions, words, and actions likely will be positive or negative, respectively. It merely requires that we think carefully before choosing a course of action, with the spirit guiding us and not the flesh.

- JOH 12:23, 26–33 ~ Jesus said, "The hour has come for the Son of man to be glorified. Anyone who serves me follows me, so that where I am there they will be; those who serve me will be honored by my Father. My soul is troubled, but what can I say? Should I ask the Father to save me from this hour? This is the reason I have come to this hour. Father, glorify your name." Then a voice from heaven stated, "I have glorified it and I will glorify it again."

- ROM 8:3–7 ~ For what the Law could not do because of the weakness of human flesh, God accomplished by sending his own Son in the likeness of human flesh to be a sin offering. Thus, He condemned the sin of the flesh so that the righteous requirements of the Law could be found in those who do not live according to the flesh but according to the spirit. For those who follow their flesh are mindful of the things of the flesh; but those who follow their spirit are mindful of the things of the Spirit. To be carnally minded is death; but to be spiritually minded is life and peace. The carnal mind is averse towards God; it will not subject itself to the laws of God, indeed it cannot.

- PHP 2:3–11 ~ Do not do anything through strife or vanity; instead, be humble, and regard others as better than yourselves. Do not focus on yourself, focus on others like Christ did, who although He was equal with God, took on the form of a man. Instead of exalting Himself He became the servant of all. He humbled Himself before others and was obedient unto death, even death on a cross. Therefore, God has highly exalted His Son, giving Him a name above every other name, so at the name of Jesus every knee should bow, whether in heaven, on earth, or under the earth, and every tongue confess that Christ is Lord to the glory of God the Father.

- PHP 4:6–8 ~ Do not worry about anything, but pray for everything with thanksgiving, humbleness, and eagerness. Focus your mind on things that are true, honest, just, pure, lovely, admirable, virtuous, and praiseworthy.

- HEB 8:10; HEB 10:16 ~ For this is the covenant that I will make with the house of Israel after those days, says the Lord: I will put my laws into their minds and write them upon their hearts. And I will be their God, and they will be my people.

In order to remain mindful of God's will for our lives, we need to remain connected to His Holy Spirit, which is the same Spirit that breathed into us our energy and existence, and is our life force. God always keeps humankind in mind. In fact, everything He created, to include the entire universe and all its inhabitants, was initiated with humans in mind. Why else would God become a human? If God is always mindful of us, we should reciprocate by being continuously mindful of Him as best we can. It is necessary to know Him, to study His Word, to remember His promises, and to worship Him in spirit and in truth (JOH 4:24; JOH 16:13).

- 1 CH 16:14–15 ~ God is Lord, and His judgments are found in all the earth. He remains mindful of His covenant and the promises He decreed to a thousand generations.

- PSA 8:3–6; PSA 144:3 ~ When I ponder the heavens and the works of your hands, the moon and stars and all that you have set into motion, I wonder: who are we humans that you Lord would keep us in your thoughts, and that you would visit our offspring as well? For you made humans a little lower than angels, and have crowned us with glory and honor. You gave humans dominion over all of your creation. (also HEB 2:6–8).

- EPH 2:1–6 ~ You were dead in trespasses and sins, when in times past you walked according to the course of this world, according to the prince of the power of the air, the spirit that now works in the children of disobedience; among whom we also engaged in such lusts, fulfilling carnal desires of flesh and mind, by nature as the children of wrath along with many others. But God, rich in mercy and abundant in love, though we were dead in sins, revived us together with Christ; for by His grace, we have been saved. He has raised us up together, and we will sit together in heavenly places with Jesus.

Clearly, being steadfast in the faith and staying attentive to God's Holy Spirit is difficult. Fortunately, He is there at all times, ready to lead us and renew us in the righteousness of Christ. He intercedes for you, strengthens you, protects you, and sustains you. All you need to do is invite Him into your heart in the name of Jesus, and He will never leave you or forsake you (DEU 31:6).

- ROM 8:25–28 ~ If we hope for what we cannot see, we must be patient. The Holy Spirit helps us with our problems. We really do not know what we should pray for, so the Spirit intercedes for us in ways that words could never express. God, who searches the hearts of everyone, knows the mind of the Spirit, because the Spirit intercedes for God's people according to God's will. We can be sure that God will provide good things to those who love Him, and are called according to His purpose.

- ROM 12:2 ~ Do not be conformed to this world but be transformed by the renewing of your mind, so you may prove what is the good, acceptable, and perfect will of God.

- 1 CO 2:16 ~ Who has known the mind of God that they can instruct Him? But we have the mind of Christ.

- EPH 4:22–24 ~ Get rid of the old self, which is polluted with deceitful lusts. Become renewed by the spirit of your mind, putting on the new self which is like God, created in righteousness and true holiness.

You cannot be spiritually minded and carnally minded at the same time (LUK 16:1–15). You must choose whom you will serve. That is, you must put God first and others second, including yourself. If your focus is exclusively on the world or yourself, you will not be mindful of God; instead, you will become distracted from His presence during your daily activities.

- DEU 6:5 ~ You must love the Lord your God with all your heart, soul, and might.

- MAT 22:37–40; MAR 12:30–31~ Jesus said, "Love the Lord your God with all your heart, mind, and soul: this is the first and greatest commandment. The second is like unto the first: Love your neighbor as yourself. All the laws and the prophets depend on these two commandments."

- ROM 1:28 ~ Since they did not retain the knowledge of God, God allowed them to develop a reprobate mind, and do those things which should not be done.

- 2 CO 4:3–6, 13–14 ~ If the Gospel is hidden, it is hidden to those who are lost. The prince of this world has blinded the minds of unbelievers, preventing the light of the glorious Gospel of Christ, who is the picture of God, from shining down upon them. What we preach is not about ourselves but Jesus Christ our Lord. We are your servants for His sake. God commanded the light to shine out of darkness and that light has shined in our hearts. We shine the light of the knowledge of the glory of God whose face is Jesus Christ. We have the spirit of faith. As it is written: I believed, and therefore I have spoken; we also believe, and therefore speak. Knowing that He who raised up the Lord Jesus will, through Jesus, raise us up as well, to present us before God

DECEMBER

- JAM 1:8; JAM 4:8 ~ A double minded man is unstable in all his ways. Draw near to God, and He will draw near to you. Cleanse your hands you sinners; and purify your hearts, those of you who are double minded.

  What happens if you do not choose God? You will lose your soul and perish. If you have chosen God, you have believed in His Son who took your place in death; otherwise, you will die from your sin because you did not receive the atonement of Christ. For those going their own way, death is the price they will pay and it is permanent. For those following Jesus Christ, life is permanent; then we will truly emulate Christ.

- LEV 17:11 ~ The life of all flesh resides in the blood, and I have given it to you upon the altar to make atonement for your souls, for it is blood that makes atonement for the soul.

- NUM 15:30–31 ~ Anyone who sins defiantly, whether a resident or a stranger, blasphemes the Lord; for that person has despised the word of the Lord, and broken His commandments. Those souls will be cut off completely; their iniquity will be upon them.

- MAT 10:26–28 ~ Jesus said, "Do not fear those who hate you, for everything that is hidden now will be revealed later; everything that is unknown will become known. What I tell you in darkness you will speak in the light. What you hear in private will be proclaimed from the rooftops. Do not fear anyone who can kill your body but not your soul; fear the One who can destroy both your body and your soul in hell.

- LUK 12:16–21 ~ Jesus spoke a parable to them: The land of a certain rich man produced plentifully, and the man thought to himself, "What should I do? I do not have enough room for all the fruits of my labor. I know what I will do. I will tear down the barns and build bigger ones." And the man decided, "Since I have so much wealth, I will just take it easy and eat, drink, and be merry." But God said to him, "You fool, tonight your soul will be required. And who will possess all those things for which you have worked so hard?" Jesus concluded: Those who accumulate treasures for themselves are not rich towards God.

  Consider the value of your soul. It is the most precious possession you have in this life; it is your essence of individualism and excellence, your identity and personality, made in the image of God to love and be loved. The soul is a marvelous gift which God bestowed the moment His Spirit infused into your soul the breath of life, which will last for eternity if you accept His invitation to freedom.

- MAT 16:25–26; MAR 8:35–38 ~ Jesus said, "Whoever seeks to save his or her life will lose it; but whoever would lose his or her life for my sake will find it. What does it profit a person who gains the world but loses their soul? What can a person give in return for their soul?"

- LUK 21:19 ~ In your patience you will possess your soul.

  My career involved extensive study in psychology, counseling, and behavioral health. I was a research psychologist, psychotherapist, and professor of psychology, counseling, and religion. Did you know, the word "psychology" originates from the Greek word *psyche*, meaning soul? Thus, psychology is the study of the mind, or soul. This has been my life's work. While I studied extensively the mind, I could not have understood it sufficiently without studying the Holy Bible. This helped me to understand our need to be whole: body, soul and spirit. In my experience as a clinician, the spiritual component seemed the part most neglected. This is why I integrated spirituality with psychotherapy, as well as appropriate medical follow up. Patients who agreed to this approach attained holistic health more completely and quickly than those focused exclusively on their mental health or behavioral issues. But many people deny they have a spirit and a soul, or they misunderstand what these represent, unaware that they are integral to wholeness, life, overall health, and knowledge of the truth.

- 1 TH 5:23 ~ May the God of peace sanctify you wholly, so that your entire spirit, soul, and body can be preserved blameless until the coming of our Lord Jesus Christ.
- 2 TI 1:7 ~ God has not given us a spirit of fear, but of power, love and a sound mind.

If your body and soul are destroyed in hell, you will cease to exist. And your spirit—well it always belonged to God and He will keep it, since you will have forfeited it for having chosen death. However, if you place your trust in Jesus Christ and remain steadfast in your faith, you will keep your soul forever and receive a new incorruptible body that will never die, into which God will again breathe His life-giving Spirit at the resurrection. Once your body, mind, and spirit are reunited in heaven, you will be whole forever; the potential and possibilities will be endless, and your holistic health will be certain and everlasting. But there will be no hope beyond the grave for those people experiencing the second death (ECC 9:10; 1 CO 15:12–20; 1 TH 4:13–14; REV 20:14–15). It is imperative that every living soul consider what is at stake here. It is not just your life it is your chance at eternal life. It can be over in a flash of time, or a blink of the eye. Are you ready for Christ's return which could take place any second now? Or would you rather live it up until you die?

- EXO 33:5 ~ The Lord said to Moses, "Tell the children of Israel they are a stiff-necked people. If I came into the midst of them for just a moment, I could destroy them."
- JOB 20:4–5 ~ You have known from days of old, ever since man was placed upon the earth, that the triumph of the wicked is short and the joy of the hypocrite lasts only a moment.
- JOB 21:13 ~ They spend their days in wealth, and in a moment go down to the grave.
- PSA 73:19 ~ How they are brought to desolation; in a moment, utterly consumed with terror.
- LUK 4:5 ~ The devil took Jesus to a high mountain and showed Him all the kingdoms of the world in a single moment of time. The devil said, "All of this power and glory I will give you, including the power that is delivered to me and to whom I will give it. If you will worship me it all will be yours." Jesus answered, "Get behind me, Satan; for it is written that you must worship the Lord your God and serve only Him."
- 2 CO 4:17–18 ~ Our manageable afflictions, which are for a moment, work for us an exceedingly greater glory. So we focus, not on things which are seen, but on things which are not seen; for the things which are seen are temporal, but things not seen are eternal.
- COL 1:9–10 ~ We have not stopped praying for you and asking God to fill you with the knowledge of His will, through all spiritual wisdom and understanding. This is so you might live your lives worthy of the Lord and may please Him in every way, bearing good fruit and growing in the knowledge of God; being strengthened with all power according to His glorious might so that you will be able to endure hardship with great patience and joyfulness.

Dear Father in heaven, we thank you for creating us and sustaining us, and we pray for continued health, including spiritual, mental, and physical wellness. Please make us whole and please keep us safe and sound. Help us to be happy and to remember where that joy comes from, which is your promise of eternal life with you in your kingdom. Help us to treasure all of our talents and gifts and bear these and other fruits of the spirit as we share your Word with others, and serve those less fortunate. Help us to treasure spiritual things above material things, and to be generous with both. Enable us to be prosperous and productive in ways that bring glory to your name. In the name of Jesus whose name is above all other names, Amen.

December 14

Responsibility Day is submitted to preserve the commitment to one's duties including God, country, family, spouse, children, boss, neighbor, church, fellow Christians, and basically everyone, including oneself. You might consider developing an action plan that includes each of these categories so that nobody is left out.

To be sure, many people have their priorities out of order by placing themselves first. Yes, it is important to take care of oneself: body, mind, and spirit; all three areas need to be nurtured, without which we would not have the energy and willpower to take care of the other responsibilities. But we often forget the most important area, our spiritual self, which gets damaged by sin. We must take responsibility for our sins by confessing them to God, repenting in true contrition, making amends to those we have wronged, and effecting proper corrections regarding our behavior. If we are spiritually healthy, the mind and body will follow, and we will be more mindful of our responsibilities to others.

- GEN 3:12–19 ~ When God uncovered the sin of Adam and Eve, Adam tried to blame Eve, and Eve tried to blame Satan. Neither of them confessed, and God punished them both, as well as Satan who tempted them.

- EXO 32:21–25 ~ Aaron tried to make excuses for his sin by explaining to Moses that the people coerced him into constructing the golden calf.

- PRO 28:13 ~ Whoever tries to hide their sins will not prosper; but whoever confesses their sins and forsakes them will obtain mercy.

- MAT 7:1–2 ~ Do not judge others or you will be judged. And you will be judged according to the same standards by which you judge others.

- MAT 27:24 ~ Pontius Pilate washed his hands in a symbolic gesture, denying any responsibility for the crucifixion of Christ, claiming that he was innocent of Christ's blood.

- LUK 6:41–42 ~ Jesus taught, "Why do you look at the speck of sawdust in your brother's eye and pay no attention to the plank in your own eye? How can you help your brother remove the speck from his eye, when you fail to see the plank in your own eye? You hypocrite! First get rid of the plank in your own eye and then you will see clearly enough to remove the speck from your brother's eye."

- ROM 12:3–5 ~ Do not think of yourself more highly than you should, but rather evaluate yourself with a clear mind, in accordance with the measure of faith God has given to you. Just as our body has many members, each with a separate purpose, so we, being part of the body of Christ, have different responsibilities.

Our first responsibility is to God. We are to love Him, praise Him, worship Him, listen to Him, honor His Law and do His will. If we are obedient to Him, God will assign duties to us to further His kingdom. God our Father has given us certain skills and privileges, and with those skills and privileges come responsibilities and duties.

Responsibility is a gift from God, given to us in proportion to our faith. If we are not using God's gifts responsibly, He will correct us just like any conscientious parent corrects their children. The Lord will never give us more than we can manage or handle. But the more responsibilities we accept, the more responsibilities we will be given, and the more we do what is expected of us, the more that will be expected. If we do not act responsibly with the gifts and duties God has assigned to us, they will be taken away and given to someone else.

- GEN 4:7 ~ The Lord said to Cain, "If you do what is right, will you not be accepted? But if you do what is wrong, sin is crouching at your door."

- LEV 26:40–44 ~ If anyone confesses their sins, repents, and accepts responsibility, God will remember the covenant He made with Abraham, Isaac, and Jacob, and He will not discard them but He will forgive them.

- JOB 34:10–11 ~ Listen, you who have understanding. Far be it from God to do evil or for the Almighty to be wrong. He repays people for what they have done, and brings upon them what their conduct deserves.

- PRO 12:13–14 ~ An evil man is trapped by his sinful talk, but a righteous person escapes trouble. From the fruit of his lips a man is filled with good things as surely as the work of his hands rewards him.

- ECC 12:12 ~ The conclusion of the whole matter is this: fear God and keep His commandments. This is the entire duty of the people.

- LUK 12:48; LUK 19:26 ~ Those disobeying in ignorance will receive a lesser punishment. Of those who have been given much, much will be required; and of those who have been entrusted with much, more will be demanded. To those who have, more will be given, and to those who have not, the little they have will be taken away.

- 1 CO 10:13 ~ God will not allow us to be tempted beyond our ability to withstand it, and He will always provide us an escape from temptation.

- 1 CO 13:11–12 ~ When I was a child I understood as a child and I thought like a child; but when I became a man, I put away childish things. For now, we see only a dim reflection in the mirror, but someday it will be face to face. Now I know only in part, but then I will know fully, even as I am fully known.

- 2 CO 9:6 ~ Those who sow sparingly will reap sparingly, and those who sow bountifully will reap bountifully.

- EPH 4:12–13 ~ We are to prepare God's people for works of service, so that the body of Christ may be edified, until we reach unity in the faith and in the knowledge of the Son of God; as we mature, we attain the whole measure of the fullness of Christ.

- 1 TI 6:20–21 ~ Guard everything that has been entrusted to your care. Turn away from godless chatter and the opposing ideas of what is falsely called knowledge, which some have professed and in doing so have wandered from the faith.

- JAM 4:17 ~ Whoever knows the right thing to do and fails to do it, that for them is sin.

We answer to our Father in heaven, not to the world. We must ensure that we are following Jesus to know we are on the right path. Part of our responsibility is to help others find their way when they are heading in the wrong direction. Our primary responsibility is to God's kingdom, because we have been appointed overseers of His flock. When one sows the seeds of faith, it enlarges the mission field, because the Holy Spirit cultivates where His people plant.

- EZE 3:18–21 ~ God says, "I have told the wicked that they will surely die. If you do not warn the wicked to turn from their sin and be saved, you will also die since you will be partly responsible for their death. But if you do warn the wicked and they still do not turn from their wickedness, they will die in their sin but you will have saved yourself. If the righteous turn from righteousness to sin, they will die because their righteousness will no longer be remembered. If you do not warn them, you will die as well. But if you warn the righteous not to sin, and they do not sin, their souls will be saved and so will yours."

- ACT 20:28 ~ Keep watch over yourselves and the flock of which the Holy Spirit has made you overseers. Feed the church of God which he purchased with His own blood.

- ROM 14:19 ~ Let us do things that promote peace and which lead to mutual edification.

- ROM 15:1–7 ~ We who are strong ought to bear with the failings of the weak. When we do the right thing, it should not be to please ourselves, but to please others and to build them up in the Lord. Even Christ did not please Himself, but as it is written of Him, "The insults of those who would insult you have fallen on me." Everything that was written in the past was for our instruction, so that through endurance and the encouragement of the scriptures we might have hope. May the God who gives endurance, encouragement, and hope give you a spirit of unity as you follow Christ. Give glory to God the Father of our Lord Jesus Christ with one voice and one heart. Accept each other as Christ accepted you, so that God may be praised.

- 1 CO 14:12 ~ Since you are eager to have spiritual gifts, try to excel in those gifts which edify the church.

- 2 CO 3:5 ~ We are not self-sufficient enough to claim responsibility for what we have, because all of our sufficiency comes from God.

- GAL 6:1 ~ If someone is overtaken by sin, you who are spiritual should restore that person in the spirit of meekness, considering you also are a sinner and can be overcome by temptation.

- EPH 6:7 ~ With good will, serve others as if you are serving the Lord.

- COL 3:16 ~ Let the Word of Christ abide in you richly in all wisdom. Teach and admonish one another in psalms, hymns, and spiritual songs, singing to God with grace in your hearts.

- 1 TH 5:14 ~ We encourage you to warn those who are unruly, comfort the feeble minded, support the weak, and be patient towards everyone.

- 1 TI 5:8 ~ If a person does not provide for his relatives, especially his own family, he has denied the faith and is worse than an unbeliever.

- 1 PE 5:2–3 ~ Feed God's flock which is among you; be overseers of the kingdom. Do this, not out of obligation but willingly; do this not for ill-gotten gain but with a clear conscience. Do not act like lords over God's heritage but set an example to the flock.

Heavenly Father, who has given us the example of Jesus Christ to follow, help us to do so with dedication and resolve, so that your name will be glorified. Let us never forget or neglect our duties, or get distracted by our own wants and needs. Instead, let us cling to your promises, knowing we will want for nothing if we trust in you completely. Help us to be aware of the needs of others and make their needs our priorities, especially the needs of our spouses, children, and parents. Since you have blessed us abundantly, let us gladly share with others; since you have given us our life and time, help us to give of our time to bless the lives of others. No matter what our occupation or calling, help us to fulfill our responsibilities cheerfully, faithfully, and thoroughly; not seeking any glory for ourselves but crediting our accomplishments to you who has given us all things to enjoy and to employ. Let us also be encouraging to others, giving credit where credit is due, especially to those who work for us and with us in our vocations, whether worldly or heavenly. Fill us with your Holy Spirit so that our spirit will be strong, and our mind will be sound, and our bodies will be durable. In the name of Jesus we pray, Amen.

December 15

National Cat Herders Day recognizes managers that have a knack for delivering order out of chaos. They handle the difficult jobs requiring a certain type of personality, talent, expertise, and patience to deal with out-of-control situations or people. The phrase "herding cats" has unknown origin but got a boost from Monty Python's *Life of Brian* (1979) in a scene where two shepherds are imagining a "herd of cats" instead of sheep. About five years later, Tom and Ruth Roy suggested a day for appreciating people with tough jobs; they have been attributed to inventing the actual holiday. Research showed a significant increase in the use of the phrase in the mid-1980s, indicating that the idea was catching on. Since then, people have capitalized on this catch phrase using it in titles to books, songs, videos, and in conversations. The holiday received significant impetus from a Super Bowl commercial in 2000, showing cowboys herding cats.

Everyone knows that cats are very independent, and training even one to obey can be a challenge. But adding six more cats that intend to do their own thing, and getting all seven to cooperate, this would be an admirable feat. It is difficult and frustrating training diverse people with various agendas and intentions; teaching them to learn and work together is a greater feat.

The Bible has many stories illustrating this phenomenon. Consider Moses, who had to lead two million people out of Egypt. They were an onerous group, who rebelled, complained, and flip-flopped constantly. In fact, they were so cantankerous that they worshipped a golden calf while Moses was receiving the Ten Commandments from God. Unfortunately for them, their mistrust of Moses and God would result in all but two men over the age of twenty dying in the wilderness. Forty years of their lives would be spent wandering the wasteland of Sinai. No doubt, the number of the Israelites must have been reduced significantly by the time they crossed the Jordan River.

- EXO 6:13 ~ The Lord spoke to Moses and Aaron, giving them authority over the children of Israel, and the Egyptian pharaoh, to bring the Israelites out of the land of Egypt.

- EXO 32::9 ~ The Lord said to Moses, "I have seen these people, and indeed they are a stiff-necked people."

- NUM 1:1–3, 20–49 ~ The Lord told Moses to count the men over twenty years old who could go to war. From the tribe of Reuben were 46,500 men; from Simeon were 59,300; from Gad were 45,650; from Judah were 74,600; from Issachar were 54,400; from Zebulun were 57,400; from Ephraim were 40,500; from Manasseh were 32,200; from Dan were 62,700; from Asher were 41,500; from Naphtali were 53,400. This totaled 603,550 fighting men, not counting women, children under twenty, men who could not fight, and the Levites who served as priests in charge of the tabernacle.

- NUM 14:26–31 ~ The Lord spoke to Moses and Aaron: How long must I bear this evil congregation who are constantly complaining to me? Go tell them, "As I live, I will do to you as you have spoken about me. The bodies of those who have complained will die in this desert, all of you who were numbered that were twenty years and older, except Caleb and Joshua. By no means will you enter the land I promised. But your little ones whom you said would be the victims will be the ones I will bring into the land which you have despised."

- ACT 7:35–36, 39–41, 52 ~ Stephen spoke to the crowd: This Moses, whom the Israelites rejected saying, "Who made you ruler and judge?" is the same one God sent to be their deliverer. He brought them out, and showed them many signs and wonders in the land of Egypt, at the Red Sea, and in the wilderness those forty years. But our fathers did not obey, pushing him away, for their hearts remained in Egypt. They were impatient, wondering what had become of Moses, and they made the golden calf and sacrificed to it. Which of the prophets did your forefathers not persecute? They were killing the ones who prophesied of the coming of Messiah; and now you have betrayed and murdered Him as well.

Another example of a man that could herd cats was Jesus Christ. He chose twelve ordinary men with diverse backgrounds to be His apostles, and taught them for over three years; and they became disciplined evangelists who took the Gospel message to the world. They were quite the ragtag group starting out; most of them were fishermen, one was a tax collector, and one was an anarchist. One was a thief who stole from the treasury; he also would betray Jesus and commit suicide. He would be replaced by a man who was once a Pharisee and member of the Sanhedrin (Paul); he was the only apostle who had advanced education in the Law and the Bible, though all were reasonably devout Jews. By the end of their training, they knew the scriptures, and they knew Jesus was the Messiah; maybe Judas knew, for even demons know, and tremble (JAM 2:19).

- MAT 10:2–4; MAR 3:13–19; LUK 6:12–16 ~ One day Jesus went up into a mountain to pray to the Father, and continued there all night. When morning came, He called His disciples together, and chose twelve whom He named apostles. They included Simon, (aka Peter), Andrew his brother, James and John (Zebedee), Philip and Bartholomew (aka Nathanael), Matthew and Thomas, James (Alphaeus), Simon (the zealot), Thaddaeus (Lebbaeus), and Judas Iscariot, who would become a traitor.

- JOH 14:12 ~ Jesus promised, "Truly I tell you, those believing in me will do the works that I do; and greater works than these shall they do, when I have gone to be with my Father."

- ACT 2:43; ACT 4:33 ~ Fear came upon every soul, for many wonders and signs were performed by the apostles. And with great power the apostles bore witness to the resurrection of the Lord Jesus; and exceeding grace was bestowed upon them.

- 1 CO 4:9 ~ God put us, the apostles, on display, like those who die in the arena; for we were made to be a spectacle to the world, and to angels, and to men.

- 1 CO 9:1–2 ~ Paul wrote: Am I not an apostle? Am I not free? Have I not seen Jesus Christ our Lord? Are you not the result of my work in the Lord? Though I may not be considered an apostle to others, doubtless I am to you; for you represent the proof of my apostleship in the Lord.

- 1 CO 15:3–11 ~ Paul wrote: Christ died for our sins in accordance with the scriptures, He was buried, and He arose from the dead the third day, appearing to Peter and the twelve. After that, He was seen by over five hundred people at the same time most of whom are still alive. Then He appeared to James, and again to the remaining apostles. Eventually, He also appeared to me, the misfit of the family. For I am the least of the apostles; indeed, I am not worthy to be called an apostle because I persecuted the church of God. But by the grace of God, I am what I am, and the grace which He bestowed upon me was not in vain. Because I worked harder than all of them; but it was not me, it was the grace of God which lived in me. Therefore, whether it was them or me, this is what we preached, and this is what you believe.

Father in heaven, with the power of your Holy Spirit we have the ability to bring people to Christ, to teach the Holy Bible, to heal, to bless, and to work miracles; because it is not us doing these great works but Christ who lives in us. Thank you for the privilege to serve you, the only true and living God. Though we are ordinary people, we can do all things through Christ. Give us the boldness to take on the evil in this world and cut it asunder with the sword of the Spirit which is your Word of truth. Let us never be dismayed, but encouraged, as we walk with Jesus and follow His example in our lives and relationships. In His name we pray, Amen.

December 16

Boston Tea Party occurred on this day in 1773. England had imposed burdensome taxes on the colonists, without providing any assistance or adequate governance. The Americans protested severe taxation without any representation in Parliament, which was one of our founding principles. The English crown had imposed the Stamp Act followed by the Townshend Act such that they were taxing commonly used goods like paper, glass, paint, tea, etc. Eventually they replaced these acts with the Tea Act (May, 1773). In response, the colonists stopped buying tea through Britain, smuggling tea from the Dutch.

Recall, a few years earlier was the Boston Massacre (March 5). The Sons of Liberty was formed about that time, and included such notables as Sam Adams, John Hancock, Patrick Henry, and Paul Revere. On this day they rallied American rebels from the thirteen colonies and disguised themselves as Native Americans. Three ships in the harbor, permitted by the loyalist governor to unload their cargo, were raided. Hundreds of crates of tea were broken open and tossed overboard. England retaliated with further impositions to recover losses and pay debts but those measures backfired, resulting in more ships being boarded and tea being dumped into the ocean. September 1774 began meetings of the first Continental Congress resulting in boycotting goods from England, declaring the right to self-government, and establishing a militia.

Taxation without representation was a problem for Judeans during the Roman occupation of the Holy Land. The people were burdened with imposing taxes, but they had no representation per se. Though the Jewish leadership was allowed to handle many of the local disputes, other crimes were either brought before the Roman appointed tetrarchs (such as the Herodians) or the territorial governor (like Pilate, Felix, and Festus). Because of this imposition, tax collectors (called publicans) were despised, especially since many of them were crooked and overtaxed the citizens. The apostle Matthew was a tax collector (MAT 9:9–13), and so was Zacchaeus (LUK 19:1–10), a man who Christ converted. Also, the apostle Simon (the zealot) belonged to a group of anarchists who sought to overthrow the Roman government and protested the paying of taxes.

- LUK 2:1–5 ~ A decree was issued by Caesar Augustus that all inhabitants of the empire should be taxed. Cyrenius was the governor of Syria at the time. Everyone had to travel to their city of origin to be placed on the tax rolls. Joseph took his pregnant wife Mary from the city of Nazareth in Galilee to the city of David which is called Bethlehem, because he was a descendant of David; it was there that he and his family were to be taxed by the Romans.

- LUK 3:12–13 ~ Some publicans came to be baptized by John asking, "Master, what should we do?" John answered, "Do not collect more than required."

- LUK 18:9–14 ~ Jesus told the parable of the Pharisee and the publican. Two men went to the temple to pray: a Pharisee and a publican. The Pharisee said, "Thank you Lord that I am not a sinner like other men, such as that tax collector, because I give tithes and I fast twice a week." The publican bowed low before the altar and beat on his breast saying, "God be merciful to me a sinner." Only the publican returned home justified by God. Those who exalt themselves will later be humbled, and those who humble themselves will later be exalted.

It is lawful to pay taxes, but that implies the government is using the revenue to provide protection and other authorized services. But today we are faced with the same dilemma: taxation without representation, which itself is a crime, as is overtaxing; both are akin to larceny. When the government starts blowing money on things other than governing, something is wrong. For example, do you want your tax money to fund illegal aliens, especially when the government has committed a crime by letting them in without vetting or restricting them? Isn't protection the main responsibility of government? Yet they allow foreigners to overrun our communities.

DECEMBER

- MAT 17:24–27 ~ They came to Capernaum, and a tax collector came to Peter saying, "Does your master pay tribute?" Peter answered yes. Then he began to enter the place where they had gathered, and Jesus stopped him saying, "What do you think, Simon? Who do the kings of the earth collect their taxes from, the people or strangers?" Peter answered, "Strangers." "Then the children are exempt," Jesus said. "Nevertheless, to avoid offending them, go to the sea and drop a line, hook the first fish you see, open its mouth, and you will find a coin. Take that coin to the tax collector and pay the taxes for you and for me."

- LUK 20:20–26 ~ The Jewish leaders sent spies to gather incriminating evidence against Jesus that they could take to the governor. They asked Him, "Master, we know your teachings are true and that you accept all people. Tell us, is it lawful to pay taxes to Caesar?" Jesus knew their motive and said, "Why do you tempt me? Take out a penny. Whose image is on the coin?" They answered, "Caesar's." Jesus replied, "Render under Caesar what is Caesar's and unto God what is God's." And they were taken aback by His reply and held their peace.

- ROM 13:1–6 ~ Everyone is subject to the higher powers, for all power comes from God; that is, all powers that exist have been ordained by God. Anyone who resists these powers are resisting the ordinance of God, and those who resist God receive damnation as punishment. Those who do what is right have no fear of the authorities, only those who do wrong are afraid of them. Do what is right and the authorities will commend you. Governments are God's servants; they are there to make sure you do what is right. But if you do what is evil, beware, for they do not carry a sword in vain, but to execute judgment on those who are evil. Submit to those who are in authority, not just because you will be punished if you do not, but also as a matter of keeping a clear conscience. This is why you should pay your taxes, because governments are God's servants who work fulltime in governing.

The framers would be rolling over in their graves if they saw our government overtaxing the citizenry. The government's disinterest and inability to protect our border and our citizenry from insurgency by undocumented people is neglecting the primary function of defense. They are the equivalent of the British who were doing nothing to earn our taxes; that's when the first Continental Congress was formed. This was not unlike the oppressive Romans who subjugated the land of Judea. Their persecution of Christians was as sinister as the current activism against Christianity today. This is the very thing prophesied from olden days: the final global empire.

- REV 17:5, 9–15 ~ On her head was written: Mystery, Babylon the great, the mother of prostitutes and all earthly abominations. The angel explained the mystery of the beast with the seven heads: The seven heads represent seven mountains on which the new Babylon sits. There are seven kings, five have fallen, one is currently in power, and the seventh is yet to come; it will reign for a short time. The beast is the eighth king and was one of the seven. Ten kings will obtain power for one hour with the beast. They will give their power and strength to the beast and make war with the Lamb of God, only to be defeated. This is the great city which sits on seven mountains, and over many waters, nations, and peoples.

Merciful Father, we pray for this nation. Open our eyes; alert us about the fork in the road that leads toward destruction. We started out a God-fearing people, and despite our flaws, remain under the umbrella of your grace; let us abide forever in that grace. Help our government to reverse this disastrous course; redirect our path back to you. Please let us never be overtaken by evil leagues and leaders; nor join any global empire led by evil people and Satan. If war breaks out, we pray that it be your battle, and we will fight on your side. Prepare us and strengthen us to fight tyranny in any form, as sons of liberty. For that is what we are, children of the most high God, made free by Jesus Christ, without whom there is no liberty. These things we ask in His name, Amen.

December 17

Wright Brothers Day is celebrated today to acknowledge the achievement of Orville and Wilbur Wright, the first to achieve self-propelled flight. It was in 1903 near Kitty Hawk NC, when history was made and aviation was born. The brothers started building model aircraft while boys and graduated to bigger and better things when they became men. Their businesses in bicycle building and document printing funded their education in aeronautics and aircraft design. They consulted engineers to reduce the size of the motor and still generate enough momentum to turn the propellor and stay aloft. The Dayton Ohio boys searched for the ideal place to test their aircraft, where the winds and terrain were favorable, and moved their operation to North Carolina in 1900. They invented a wind tunnel to test the aerodynamics of different wings, while mastering the art of gliding with controls. They had attempted motor-powered flights several times before achieving success in 1903. Traveling about ten feet off the ground into a strong headwind, they took turns flying their plane. Wilbur achieved a maximum distance on the fourth flight of 852 feet in one minute. They returned to Dayton to work on design improvements and in 1905 flew a plane that remained airborne for forty minutes. They kept the design under wraps until achieving a patent, and soon signed a contract with the US Army to build flying machines and train pilots at Ft. Meyer, VA in 1908. The Wright Company opened a factory in Dayton in 1909 to continue their work. They were involved in a number of lawsuits and patent disputes, when the untimely death of Wilbur from typhoid fever occurred in 1912. Orville finally sold the company in 1915. The original Wright Flyer airplane eventually went on display at the Smithsonian, proving to the world how they were the first in flight despite the many claims that others had beat the Wright Brothers to the punch, among them the Smithsonian who issued a formal retraction.

The Bible mentions three events involving flying objects with and without the presence of angels. Who knows, maybe this would explain UFOs (see 07/02 lesson).

- 2 KI 2:11–14 ~ Elijah and Elisha walked and talked; then horses and a chariot of fire separated them, and Elijah went up by a whirlwind into heaven.
- EZE 1:5–14; EZE 10:1–22 ~ Ezekiel had a vision of four cherubim. Each had four faces (lion, ox, eagle, human), four wings, and human hands. They glowed with radiance and moved like lightning.
- DAN 7:3, 6 ~ Daniel also had a vision of four beasts; one was described as having four wings and four heads.
- ZEC 5:1–2 ~ Zechariah looked up and saw a flying scroll, twenty cubits by ten cubits in size.
- REV 4:6–8 ~ John had a vision of four beasts surrounding Christ's throne. They had eyes all around them, and they had six wings. Each had a different face: lion, ox, eagle, or human. They sang praises to God, day and night.

Someday the chosen of the Lord will fly like angels.

- ISA 40:31 ~ But those who trust the Lord will be renewed in their strength; they will soar on wings like eagles. They will run and not grow weary; they will walk and not feel faint.
- MAL 4:2 ~ For those who honor my name, the Sun of righteousness will arise with healing in His wings. And they will go out leaping like a calf freed from its stall.
- LUK 20:36 ~ Those who are accounted worthy will become like angels and will never die.

Father, when we trust in you, our strength is renewed. What more could we ask? We do not know what we will be in heaven, but we will see you in our flesh. Thank you, Jesus, Amen.

December 18

Salt of the Earth Day is a new holiday based on the following quote by Jesus.

- MAT 5:13–16 ~ Jesus said, "You are the salt of the earth, but if the salt has lost its flavor, how can it be made salty again? It is no longer good for anything, except to be thrown out and trampled down. You are the light of the world. A city built on a hill cannot be hidden. People do not light a lamp and then cover it; instead, they put it on a stand so it will provide light to everyone in the room. In the same manner, let your light shine before others so they can see your good deeds and praise your Father in heaven."

In Old Testament times, salt was added to a sacrificial offering to make it savory for the Lord, just as salt adds flavor to food. God did not want bland or mediocre offerings nor does He want His people to be tasteless. Salt is also used to preserve food. If we are the salt of the earth, it is because we have taste and we are preserved. We do not amble through life professing a weak or mediocre faith, but a vibrant faith that is backed up by our behavior. Otherwise, our faith would lose its flavor over time, our heart could become spoiled, our spirit could become dark.

- LEV 2:13 ~ Season your grain offerings with salt; never leave out the salt of the covenant from your grain offerings, but add salt to all your offerings.
- NUM 18:19 ~ The part set aside from the holy offerings presented to the Lord, I have given this to your sons and daughters as your regular share. It is an everlasting covenant of salt before the Lord for you and your offspring.
- JOB 6:6 ~ Can tasteless food be eaten without salt? Is there flavor in the white of an egg?
- PSA 121:7–8 ~ The Lord will preserve you from all evil. The Lord will preserve your going out and your coming in from this time forward even forevermore.
- MAR 9:49 ~ Jesus said, "Everyone will be salted with fire, and every sacrifice will be salted with salt."

Salt as a preservative is analogous to Christ's love which is His light living within us, preserving us in the true faith until His return. That salt brings out the best in us, enabling us to shine the light of Christ with the love that He placed into our hearts. Christ's blood sweetened the sacrificial offering for the sin of humanity before God. Our response is a change of heart and a clear conscience, which should be visible in our attitudes and behaviors. God's Holy Spirit is the preservative which keeps our desires and thoughts pure, day after day, even forevermore.

- 2 CH 13:5 ~ Do you not you know that the Lord God of Israel gave the kingship of Israel to David and his descendants forever through a covenant of salt?
- JER 23:5–6 ~ The days are coming when I will raise a righteous descendant of my servant David, a king that will reign with wisdom and justice in all the earth.
- JOH 1:1, 14 ~ The Old Covenant was the Word of God, provided in the Book of the Law. The New Covenant is the Word made flesh, which is Jesus Christ.

We are to illuminate the Word for others to see, because nobody can read or see in the dark. Let us capitalize on occasions for others to discover the truth, so they too can walk in the light. We are seasoned with God's love, and through our love we are able to season others, so they can season many more, and we all can be preserved in the true faith for eternity.

- ROM 13:12 ~ The night is gone and the day is at hand. Let us cast away the works of darkness and put on the armor of light.

- 2 CO 4:6 ~ God commanded light to shine out of darkness. This same light shines in our hearts and radiates light through knowledge of Jesus Christ.

- COL 4:5–6 ~ Be wise in the way you act towards outsiders and make the most of every opportunity. Let your speech always be full of grace, seasoned with salt, so that you can know how you ought to respond to others.

Jesus tells all of His followers that they are the salt of the earth because they possess the truth of His Word, the love of His Spirit, and the light of His life. We are seasoned with God's love, grace and mercy, thereby enriching our lives, just as seasoning enhances the flavor of food. But nobody seasons their food and then throws it away; rather they present that food for consumption, just as the sacrificial offerings in Old Testament times were to be presented.

God gives all Christians openings to witness, serve, and enlighten people who are stumbling around in the darkness of sin. Just as the light of Christ shows us the way to heaven, our light can illuminate the pathway home so others can find their way. That light also illuminates sin in this dark world, and drives out the darkness in our midst. Once you see the light and start reflecting it, you always will find your way, nevermore to be blinded by darkness.

- MAT 6:22–23 ~ Jesus said, "The eye is the lamp of the body. If your eye is sound, your whole body will be full of light. If your eye is not sound, your whole body will be full of darkness. So, if the light in you becomes darkness, how great is that darkness."

- LUK 22:53 ~ Jesus told His accosters, "When I taught daily in the temple, you did not lay a hand on me; but this is your hour and the power of darkness."

- JOH 3:17–21 ~ Jesus said, "Those who believe in God's Son are not condemned, but those who do not believe are condemned already. God sent His light into the world, but people loved the darkness rather than the light for they were evil. Everyone who follows evil hates the light, and they avoid the light because it will uncover their evil deeds. Everyone who follows the truth will come to the light, and the light will show that their ways are godly."

- ROM 1:21 ~ Though they knew God, they did not glorify Him or give thanks to Him, but became vain in their imaginations and their foolish hearts were darkened.

- EPH 4:17–18 ~ Testify to the truth in the Lord and do not walk with vanity in your mind as other Gentiles do, whose understanding has been darkened, having alienated themselves from the life God gives, because their ignorance has blinded their hearts.

- EPH 5:8–15 ~ You were once in darkness, but now you are in the light of the Lord. Live as children of light and discover what pleases the Lord, for the fruit of the light consists of goodness, righteousness, and truth. Have nothing to do with the fruitless deeds of darkness, but rather expose them. For it is shameful to even mention what the disobedient do in secret. But everything exposed by the light becomes visible for all to see, for it is light that makes things visible. This is what is meant by the saying, "Wake up you sleepers; rise from the dead, and Christ will shine on you." So be very careful how you live. Live like the wise not the unwise, making the most of every opportunity, because the days are evil.

Holy Father, your love is the ingredient that makes our lives fulfilling, and your Son makes our lives eternal. In Christ we will always have direction, purpose, and meaning. Your Spirit shines in us bringing out the best in us, as well as preserving us in our Christian faith while sanctifying our souls. Help us to be salt and light, bringing clarity and spice to our thoughts, decisions, behavior, and lives. We pray that we may live in that elevated state all of our days on the earth, and be forever inspired by the love of Jesus to perform works of love in His name, Amen.

December 19

First Christian Revival in America was held by Jonathan Edwards on this day in 1734. A revival is a spiritual awakening that leads many to receive the Spirit of Christ, to be renewed and/or reborn. This method became a trend that would include the likes of D. L. Moody, Billy Graham, and other notable evangelists (see 09/01 lesson). The format evolved from mega-events in stadiums, into megachurches where thousands of eager souls could congregate indoors.

Edwards was a fiery young pastor at a church in a relatively small community outside of Boston. His energetic personality and enthusiastic delivery brought large numbers to his revivals, often requiring services to be held outdoors. His famous sermon *Sinners in the Hands of an Angry God* was printed as a booklet (1941). This energetic style of preaching marked the start of a movement called the Great Awakening, which would occur in waves in the USA and abroad. Evangelists were adopting the same kind of zeal as the initiators of the Protestant Reformation. Edwards would be joined by British preacher George Whitefield in 1739; they held one another in awe with respect to their grasp of the Holy Spirit. Whitefield's traveling ministry drew crowds numbering in the tens of thousands. He covered five thousand miles and averaged one revival per day in a single year. Others to join this crusade were D. Brainard, S. Davies, and G. Tennent.

The message of these revivalists was simple: everyone is a sinner and needs a savior. We are redeemed by acknowledging our sins before God and asking His forgiveness. We receive salvation by God's grace through faith in Christ our Savior, with whom we can develop a personal relationship. Those who do not accept or desire the Lord will burn in hell.

Revival can be the key to deliverance. We become renewed in our faith and our spiritual strength every day when we have experienced a rebirth in Jesus Christ. That is, we are born again by the power of the Holy Spirit, to lead a life worthy of repentance, in which case we will be reborn yet again on the last day to receive a new body and a new life in heaven with our Lord.

- PSA 51:10 ~ Create in me a clean heart, Lord, and renew an upright spirit within me.

- PSA 80:14–19 ~ Return to us Almighty God! Look down from heaven and see! Watch over this vineyard that your right hand has planted, and the Branch you have raised up for yourself. The vine has been cut down and burned in the fire; at your rebuke your people perish. Let your hand rest on the man at your right, the Son of man who you have raised for yourself. Do this so we will not turn our backs on you. Revive us so we can call on your name. Turn us back, Lord of hosts, and let your face shine on us so we can be saved.

- ISA 57:15 ~ This is what the Lord says, the one whose name is Holy, "I live in a high and holy place; I also live with those who have a contrite and humble spirit, to revive that heart and spirit."

- ROM 12:2 ~ Do not conform to the ways of this world, but be transformed by the renewing of your mind, and you will be able to determine what is good, acceptable, and perfect according to God's will.

- EPH 4:23–24 ~ With respect to your former ways, you were taught to put off your old self which was corrupted with deceitful desires, and be renewed in the spirit of your minds. So put on the new self, the one created to be like God in true righteousness and holiness.

- TIT 3:5–7 ~ He has saved us, not because of our works of righteousness, but according to His mercy, through the washing of regeneration and renewing by His Holy Spirit, which He abundantly bestowed upon us through Jesus Christ our Savior. Being justified by grace, we have become heirs according to the hope of eternal life.

- 1 PE 1:3–6 ~ Blessed is God and Father of our Lord Jesus Christ, who according to His abundant mercy has given us rebirth in living hope, through the resurrection of Christ from the dead, to receive an inheritance that is incorruptible and undefiled, and that will never fade away. This is reserved for you who are kept by the power of God through faith for salvation, ready to be revealed on the last day. In this you greatly rejoice, though for now you are grieved by various trials.

    We are guilty of sin; and try as we might, we still end up missing the mark. Since we believe, we become aware of our shortcomings, transgressions, and guilt as often as we have wronged someone or otherwise have been disobedient to God; oftentimes that understanding occurs immediately. This is the best time to make confession to the Lord, otherwise we may forget, or get into the habit of overlooking sin until it is too late to correct an error. Complacency is your enemy; steadfastness is your friend. Forgiveness is not automatic, and it is not something to be taken for granted. Without confession and repentance, how can there be godly sorrow? Christ wants to forgive you of those sins you have committed. There is just one catch: you have to ask Him in faith to save you. Ask for the Holy Spirit and you will receive Him. Seek God and you will find Him. Knock on heaven's door, and Jesus Christ will open it for you Himself.

- PSA 51:17 ~ The sacrifices of God are a broken spirit; a broken and contrite heart, oh God, you will not despise.

- PSA 85:8, 10 ~ Let me listen to what the Lord has to say, for He speaks peace to His people, to His saints, and to all who turn their hearts to Him. Steadfast love and truth will meet; righteousness and peace will kiss each other.

- PSA 119:4–5 ~ God, you have established your precepts that must be fully obeyed. Oh, that my ways were steadfast in obeying your decrees!

- PSA 130:3–4 ~ If you, Lord, counted our sins against us, who would be able to stand? But there is forgiveness with you, that you may be feared.

- PRO 1:28–33 ~ They will call me but I will not answer; they will look for me but not find me. They hated knowledge and chose not to fear the Lord, ignoring my advice and spurning my reprimand. Since they did not take heed, they will eat the fruit of their ways and be full of the fruit of their schemes. The waywardness of simple-minded people will be their demise, and the complacency of fools will destroy them. But whoever chooses to listen will be safe and at peace, free from fear of harm.

- MAT 7:7 ~ Jesus told the world, "Ask and you will receive, seek and you will find, knock and the door will be opened."

- LUK 24:46–48 ~ Jesus taught, "It was written that Messiah would suffer, but would rise from the dead in three days. It was written that He would preach repentance and forgiveness of sins among all nations, beginning with Jerusalem. You are witnesses of these things."

- ROM 3:23–24 ~ For all have sinned and come short of God's glory. But we are justified freely by the grace of God through the redemption found in Jesus Christ.

- ROM 10:9–10 ~ If you confess the Lord Jesus with your mouth, and believe in your heart that God raised Him from the dead, you will be saved. For with the heart, we believe unto righteousness; and with the mouth confession is made unto salvation.

- 2 CO 7:10 ~ Do not regret godly sorrow which produces repentance leading to salvation. But worldly sorrow produces death.

DECEMBER

- JAM 2:10 ~ Whoever disobeys one point of the Law disobeys all points of the Law.

　　Confession is made to God our Father in sincere contrition for our disobedience. Forgiveness is granted through faith, which is a gift of the Holy Spirit. Salvation is sealed by Christ the Lamb, whose death and resurrection freed us from sin and death. All three persons of the Holy Trinity take part in our adoption, whereby we become children of God and brothers and sisters of Christ in the kingdom of heaven. We find relationship with God Almighty: baptized of, by, and with His Holy Spirit. Those who reject, deny, or avoid Him will inherit the lake of fire.

　　Revival is a straightforward and powerful method, especially with large groups of people gathered in one place looking for answers. This is how the enlightenment era gained momentum: its efficiency of time and space, and its effectiveness in getting good results. I bet witnessing the preaching of the Lord Jesus would be far more invigorating, however. Wouldn't that be something to behold? But we will, someday. Jesus preached the truth of righteousness by faith; fire and brimstone was the other side of that coin. Always with humility and certainty, Christ put everyone in their place then, and now. God showed the world His Son, the only way to paradise; Jesus also made it clear what would happen if people chose not to believe in Him (JOH 3:16).

- DEU 32:22–24 ~ God says, "A fire is kindled by my anger and shall burn into the lowest depths of hell; and as it grows it shall consume the earth. They will be wasted with hunger, devoured with fire, and poisoned with pestilence."

- PRO 8:36 ~ Whoever sins against God hurts his own soul; whoever hates God loves death.

- ISA 26:14 ~ The wicked will die, never to live again; they will be destroyed completely, along with any memory of them.

- LUK 20:46–47 ~ Jesus said, "Beware of the Pharisees. They enjoy wearing fancy robes, being greeted in the marketplace, sitting in the places of honor in church, and reserving the nicest rooms for their banquets; yet they cheat widows out of their homes, and for a show, say long prayers. They will receive the greater damnation."

- 1 TI 6:9–10 ~ Those who long to be rich will fall into temptation and a snare, and into many foolish lusts which will drown them in destruction and damnation. For the love of money is the root of all evil. Those who have coveted after money have departed from the faith and brought upon themselves much pain and sorrow.

- REV 21:8 ~ The fearful, unbelieving, abominable, murderous, promiscuous, idolatrous, lying, and demonic will have their part in the lake that burns with fire and brimstone; this is the second death.

　　Omnipotent Father, we earnestly pray for another revival in this country and in the world. Our leaders have lost their way, though many profess to know you. The masses have ignored your precepts and ordinances, and our governments have likewise watered down the laws of the land, whereas they do not enforce the laws, or prevent criminal behavior, or provide a deterrent to lawlessness. We need a rebirth, a full reversal of course, a renewal by your Holy Spirit, and we need it fast. Let us halt our backsliding ways immediately; help us to make a full stop and take a long look at what lies at the end of this path being forced upon us. Let us return now to your light and to your truth; illuminate the path that goes back to you, lest we continue in darkness and reach the point of no return. Let there be another wave of evangelists who will take your Word to every corner, making disciples and creating another great awakening by your Holy Spirit in all people of faith. And for those who are intent on remaining on this wayward course, do not let them take anyone else with them; for their inheritance is the lake of fire. We pray these things in the name of Jesus Christ, your Son and our Savior, who is the way back home, Amen.

December 20

National Underdog Day occurs annually on the third Friday of the month. Underdogs are competitors who are at a disadvantage, whether in sports, business, politics, science, school, combat, or historically. The suggestion for a holiday to honor underdogs came from Peter Moeller, who shared the idea with a calendar maker in 1976, and it stuck. The term originated long ago from shipbuilding. The man underneath the wooden plank ("dog") was the underdog; the man above who was sawing the "dog" was the overdog. The underdog had the dirtier job, always covered with sawdust. The term was later applied to the losing dog in a dogfight. The connotation in both examples: it's better being on top, namely, the top dog. With effort, skill, and practice, sometimes the underdog becomes the overdog, the top dog, or the big dog. For all practical purposes, nobody stays on top forever, not in this life. But that is no reason to give up.

Everybody likes watching come-from-behind victories, whether in horse racing, fighting, team sports, or any contest. Some people root for the underdog, hoping others get their shot at the spotlight for a change. Personally, I get tired watching sports where the same teams are always in the finals. Naturally, all contestants want to be winners, but most started at the bottom of the dogpile. Nobody begins at the top, but some make it there faster. Regardless, everybody can reach the pinnacle of success in a chosen field or endeavor. Competition is good for you; it makes you work harder. But the most important fight is between good and evil. If you win this clash, it's because Jesus won the victory for you. And the prize is a crown of life.

- 1 CH 29:11 ~ Yours, oh Lord, is the greatness, the power, the glory, the victory, and the majesty; for all that is in heaven and on earth is yours. Yours is the kingdom, Lord, and you are to be exalted as head above all.

- 1 CO 9:24–27 ~ Do you understand that there are many competitors in a race but only one receives first prize? Then, run with the intention of winning. Those who strive to master a task train hard and discipline themselves. But, they do so to obtain an earthly crown that will not last; we strive for a crown that lasts forever. Therefore, I run like a man with a purpose. I do not fight like a boxer beating the air. Instead, I beat my body into shape, making it serve God's purpose, so that my preaching will not cause me to be disqualified for the prize.

- 2 TI 2:3–5 ~ Endure hardship like a good Christian soldier. Those who fight wars need not get caught up with the affairs of this life, but rather should concern themselves with the affairs of Jesus Christ who chose them to be a soldier. In any competition you must discipline yourself and follow the rules if you ever expect to win the championship.

- 2 TI 4:5–8 ~ Paul wrote: I have fought a good fight and finished the race, and my faith is still intact. Hereafter, a crown of righteousness awaits me, which the Lord, the righteous judge, will give to me; and not just me, but everyone who lovingly awaits Christ's coming.

- JAM 1:12 ~ Blessed be those who persevere despite their trials and temptations, because they will receive the crown of life which the Lord has promised to anyone who loves Him.

Winners trust in God for all things, giving God the credit for their victories. Losers should take credit, even when their contribution was negligible. Cheaters never win, because their victory is tarnished. For example, does anyone credit the male, who claims to be transitioning into a female, as a winner when he can lift more weight than the biological women? And yet they give him the prize anyway. How ridiculous is that? Strangely, in these times trophies are given out to winners and losers, as if they are equal. And games are often decided by officials cheating or players throwing the game. Whatever happened to fair play? Satan is the king of cheaters, and he thinks he is stealing souls from God, but Satan and these losers will be losing their souls.

DECEMBER

- PSA 45:4 ~ In your majesty, Lord, ride forth victoriously on behalf of truth, humility, and righteousness; may your right hand reveal your awesome works.

- PRO 11:3, 14 ~ The integrity of righteous people can guide them, but the perverseness of wicked people will destroy them. For lack of guidance a nation falls, but many advisors assure the victory.

- MAT 10:38–39 ~ Jesus said, "If you want to be worthy of me, you must bear your cross every day and follow me. Whoever finds their life will lose it; whoever loses their life for my sake will find it."

- MAT 16:26 ~ Jesus said, "What does a person profit if they gain the whole world but lose their soul? What can a person give in exchange for their soul?"

There are many great underdog stories in the Bible. Realistically, they aren't exactly underdog stories because God had a hand in these victories; which proves that with God, everybody is a winner, as long as you are on His team. If you are on the opposing team, you may win a battle or two but you will lose the war in the end. Similarly, even if you are on God's team, He may let you lose a battle or two to strengthen you and whip you into shape. Either way, determination pays off; but with God it pays in a very big way, and the glory of it never fades.

- JDG 7:19–23 ~ As the angel instructed, Gideon took one hundred men, surrounded the Midianite camp, blew trumpets, broke pots, and made noise around the encampment. They shouted, "A sword for the Lord and for Gideon!" The enemy stood up startled out of their sleep, and many fled. Then three hundred trumpets sounded; the disoriented men turned against each other with their swords. The Midianites that fled were pursued and killed.

- 1 SA 17:45–47 ~ David told Goliath, "You have come with a sword, a spear, and a shield, but I come in the name of the Lord of hosts, the God of the armies of Israel, whom you have defied. Today the Lord will deliver you into my hand, for I will strike you down and take your head as a trophy. And everyone will know that there is a God in Israel who saves, not with a sword or spear. This battle belongs to the Lord, for He will give you to us."

- PSA 98:1 ~ Oh, sing to the Lord a new song, for He has done marvelous things. His right hand, which is His holy arm, has won for Him the victory.

- ISA 25:8 ~ The Lord will swallow up death in victory. He will wipe away the tears and He will remove the disgrace from His people. For the Lord has said so.

- COL 1:9–11 ~ We have not stopped praying for you and asking God to fill you with the knowledge of His will, through all spiritual wisdom and understanding. This is so you might live your lives worthy of the Lord and may please Him in every way, bearing good fruit and growing in the knowledge of God; being strengthened with all power according to His glorious might so that you will be able to endure hardship with great patience and joyfulness.

- 1 JO 5:4–5 ~ Whoever is born of God overcomes the world; the victory that overcomes the world is found in faith. Jesus Christ overcame the world; anyone believing in Him will also overcome the world.

Beloved Father, help us to fight the good fight of faith, and endure the burdens, challenges, and setbacks like good Christian soldiers. May we continue to train hard, work hard, and make you proud, never giving up but persevering until we successfully complete the race we must run. With you on our side, we will never grow weary or faint, and we will never give up or give in. We know that you will strengthen us when we are nearing exhaustion. We thank you, Father, that we are winners in the arena of life, through Christ our Lord, Amen.

DAILY DEVOTIONAL EVENTS

December 21

Winter Solstice falls around the third week of December in the northern hemisphere (usually 12/21 or 12/22) marking the first day of winter. The night will be the longest, as the position of the sun is lower in the sky and farther from earth. The tilt and rotation of the earth produce less light and colder temperatures. While the winter solstice is occurring in the northern hemisphere the summer solstice is occurring in the southern hemisphere. For more information, consult the lesson on the summer solstice (06/20).

Celebrations of Christmas and Hanukkah will often overlap within this timeframe; so will a number of pagan holidays and observances. Ancient Romans held a self-indulgent week of debauchery and promiscuity to honor Saturn, the god of agriculture and prosperity. Also celebrated this time of year was Mithra the Persian god of light (e.g., the sun). Thus, the pagans celebrated the winter solstice when there was no planting to be done and the amount of light was the least. During our summer solstice, the Incas would have been celebrating their winter solstice with animal sacrifices. Likewise, China and Japan have winter solstice celebrations.

- DEU 6:14–15 ~ Never follow other gods, for there is only one Lord among you and He is a jealous God; His anger will burn against you and He will destroy you if you follow false gods.

- DEU 32:17, 39 ~ Those pagans were sacrificing to demons, not gods; new gods were invented by people. Besides God, there are no others.

- JDG 10:14 ~ Go and cry to the false gods that you have chosen; see if they will deliver you in the time of your tribulation.

- JDG 16:28–30 ~ Remember when Samson called to the Lord and said, "Oh Lord God, strengthen me one more time, I pray, so that I may see with my own eyes your vengeance upon the Philistines." Then he caused the entire temple to collapse, killing all of the pagan worshippers.

- ISA 42:17 ~ Those who trust in idols and false gods will be utterly put to shame.

- ISA 44:9–11 ~ Only fools would create their own gods and idols.

- JOE 3:14 ~ Multitudes are gathering in the valley of decision, for the day of the Lord is coming when he will judge the pagans.

- HAB 2:18–19 ~ What value does a graven image have since it was a human that carved it? And what good is an image that teaches lies? For the one who makes it puts his trust in his own creation; he makes idols that cannot speak. Woe to him that says to the wood or to the stone, "Wake up and come to life." Can it give him guidance? It may be covered with gold and silver but it has no life in it.

- MAT 6:7 ~ Jesus said, "When you pray, do not use vain repetitions like the pagans do, for they think they will be heard for their many words."

- 2 CO 10:20 ~ When pagans offer something as a sacrifice, they sacrifice to demons.

Heavenly Father, the greatest commandment is to love you above all other gods, idols, or objects of worship. Therefore, we praise, worship, and adore you alone. Help us to cast out all forms of idolatry from our lives and from our nation. Help us to remember that we must never let anything in this world come between you and us. Let your Holy Spirit enrich our lives and make us wise, with the knowledge of truth and salvation, which you have granted to us on behalf of your Son Jesus Christ in whose name we pray, Amen.

December 22

Forefathers' Day is celebrated on this day to commemorate the *Mayflower* landing at Plymouth Rock on 12/21/1620. Descendants of these brave pilgrims organized the Old Colony Club in 1769 to keep this observance and its significance alive. Another association of Plymouth descendants and friends is the Mayflower Society (1897). Over time, people have merged today's holiday with Thanksgiving Day. Fewer Americans acknowledge this observance as separate. The *Mayflower* landing in Massachusetts was of equal importance with the *Margaret* landing in Virginia in 1619 when the first day of thanksgiving was held near Jamestown VA (see the lesson on 11/27). Folks near Plymouth take Forefather's Day seriously, with rituals, proclamations, and a traditional menu including succotash.

- DEU 4:1–2 ~ Listen, Israel, to the statutes and judgments I taught you; obey them so you may live, and possess the land which God promised to your forefathers. Do not add to the words which God has commanded you to obey and do not diminish from them either, but keep them.

- DEU 8:18–19 ~ Remember God, for it is He who gives you the power to prosper, thereby confirming His covenant which he swore to your forefathers, and which still applies to this day. But if you forget God, and follow, serve, or worship other gods, you surely will be destroyed.

- PRO 1:18–19 ~ Those who are greedy for riches and oppress others to obtain riches are ambushing their own lives and will succeed in destroying themselves.

- 1 CO 10:1–4 ~ You should know that our forefathers drank of the same spiritual drink, which came from the same spiritual Rock, and that Rock is Jesus Christ.

- 2 TI 1:2–7 ~ Paul wrote to Timothy: I thank God, whom I serve with a pure conscience as my forefathers did; for night and day I remember you and you are constantly in my prayers. Recalling your tears, I have longed to be with you, because that would fill me with joy. I am reminded of your sincere faith which first appeared in your relatives, and now I am persuaded lives in you. For this reason, I must remind you to fan the flames of God's gifts to you, for God did not give us a spirit of fear, but of power, love, and a sound mind.

Religious persecution and financial subjugation were major problems in seventeenth century England, largely imposed by the corrupt Church of England, such that pilgrims escaped to the Netherlands. But that was not an improvement, so the wayfarers organized another journey to the New World, knowing full well the dangers and risks. Two ships set sail; the second, dubbed the *Speedwell*, was determined unseaworthy, so they returned to dock; then all the willing passengers crowded aboard the *Mayflower* for a two-month voyage originating in Plymouth England. Unsanitary and cramped conditions caused illness and death enroute.

The original destination was an expansive land grant in Virginia, where the *Margaret* landed two years earlier; but conditions drove them farther north near Cape Cod. The Mayflower Compact was prepared by William Bradford and signed by most of the male colonizers prior to disembarking; this document was not unlike the US Constitution in its intent and the desire for self-government. Miles Standish was appointed to maintain law and order. One hundred two pioneers and thirty crew members went ashore. All the while, Bradford kept meticulous journals of this momentous episode in US history.

- DEU 26:7–9 ~ When we cried to the Lord, He heard us and looked into our affliction, burden, and oppression. He brought us out of Egypt with a mighty hand and terrible wrath, and with many signs and wonders; and He brought us to this place, a land that flows with milk and honey.

- ROM 8:35–39 ~ What can separate us from the love of Christ: tribulation, distress, persecution, famine, nakedness, peril, or sword? As it is written, for your sake we face death on a daily basis; we are sent as sheep to the slaughter. But we have conquered these things through Him who loved us. For I am convinced that neither death nor life, neither angels nor demons, neither the present nor the future, nor any powers, neither height nor depth, nor anything in all creation can separate us from the love of God that is in Jesus Christ our Lord.

When the sojourners arrived at Plymouth Rock, winter had begun in the northeast and there was no shelter or food. Half of the travelers perished from exposure, malnutrition, and disease. But with Spring came Chief Massasoit (aka Ousamequin) of the Wampanoag tribe, and Squanto of the Pokanoket people who served as liaison and tutored the settlers how to fish, hunt, and plant. The natives and the pilgrims formed a peace which remained in force for a generation. More ships would come and more communities would emerge, eventually being swallowed up in what would become Boston. This abridged version of the events hardly gives justice to the accomplishments, suffering, and determination of the first American settlements. It is recommended that the reader research this further, particularly the writings of William Bradford.

- HEB 11:13–16 ~ The children of Abraham kept the faith, though they died before seeing the land of God's promise come to pass. Nevertheless, they were convinced and they embraced God's promise, confessing their status as strangers and pilgrims on the earth. They plainly declared that they sought a country of their own. They could have returned to their old country, but the desire for a better country that was heavenly was their hope, where God would not be ashamed to be called their God, as He was preparing a city for them.

- 1 PE 2:9–12 ~ You are a chosen generation, a royal priesthood, a holy nation, a unique people; So, praise Him who has called you out of darkness into his marvelous light. In times past you were not a people, but you now are the people of God; you had not obtained mercy but now you have. Beloved, abstain from the passions of the flesh which wage war against your soul. Display good conduct among the Gentiles, even though they accuse you of evil; for after witnessing your good deeds and character they will glorify God when He visits them.

You can see the parallels between the journey to America with the journey of the Israelites. Both were intent on starting a new life governing themselves, with God as their ruler and king. They relied on God's promises to get them through some terrible times, and by faith they overcame. The Jews were God's chosen people and they would inherit the land of promise communicated to their forefathers Abraham, Isaac, and Jacob. The first Americans also were chosen by God to establish His church in the New World, where they could freely practice their religion, govern themselves, and maintain God's sovereignty in their lives. And like the Israelites, Americans prospered, as long as they kept the covenant. And when they broke the covenant, they were punished by God. This scenario is being repeated in our great land, for the leaders have followed the gods of wealth, riches, power, and fame, while the citizenry has become lazy and unconcerned. We could return to prosperity like the Jews returned to the Holy Land and prospered. God promises to enrich us when we are loyal, but we can lose everything if we betray Him and are disloyal. The time to act is now because we are running out of time.

Heavenly Father, we thank you for this great land and the forefathers who built this nation into the greatest country the world has ever seen. But our arrogance has replaced you in our lives with lusts of the flesh, human pride, and greed for riches and luxury. We have been duly warned; let us heed that warning and return to you now, for we have seen the destruction ahead and how this recent detour could lead to our demise. Instill courage into our hearts to stand against tyranny, subjection, and persecution, and take our country back whether through love, force, or both. May we live in peace and prosperity, with your Word as our Law and your Son as our King, Amen.

December 23

Image of God Day is proposed to acknowledge and affirm that we are made in the image of God and His Spirit lives in us. Yes, God created humankind in His own image. There are no other creatures on this planet to which that applies. Actually, we are like God in many ways, though some will wrongly ascribe human attributes to God. Like God, we exist spiritually, mentally, and physically. One might argue that animals do too, but their mental capabilities are markedly inferior to humans. All other earthly creatures operate by instinct; that's all they can think about Animals have no capacity to reason, make moral choices, conceptualize, analyze complex problems, apply logic, imagine the possibilities, and all other forms of higher-order thinking. That is, they do not possess a soul and are therefore, not condemned creatures since they do not sin. They cannot contemplate sin. However, animals can be taught to do things that are unnatural by sinful people.

- GEN 1:26–27 ~ God said, "Let us make humans in our image, after our likeness. And let them have dominion over the fish of the sea, over the fowl of the air, over the cattle, and over all the earth and everything that creeps upon the earth." So, God created humankind in His own image; in the image of God, He created us all, males and females alike.

- GEN 9:6 ~ Whoever sheds the blood of another human being will have their blood shed as well; for everyone was made in the image of God.

Jesus Christ is the image of God. He has been with God since the beginning (ISA 48:16; JOH 1:1–14), in other words, forever. Christ came to earth in human form so we could know Him. Thus, God can be seen in Christ, and in the entirety of His creation (ROM 1:20). And the Holy Spirit can be found in God's Word (ZEC 7:12; JOH 16:12–13; 2 PE 1:20–21), and in Jesus Christ (LUK 1:26–35). Can you imagine the Holy Trinity? If you can, you will understand Christianity; this is a mystery resolved only through your spirit by faith in God.

- 2 CO 4:2–4 ~ We have renounced the hidden things of dishonesty, not engaging in trickery, nor presenting the Word of God deceitfully; but through truthfulness we consign ourselves to everybody's conscience in the sight of God. For if our gospel is hidden it is concealed from those who are lost, in whom the god of this world has blinded their disbelieving minds to obscure the light of the glorious Gospel of Christ, the very image of God, from shining upon them.

- COL 1:12–20 ~ Give thanks to the Father, who has allowed us to partake of His inheritance, given to the saints who abide in His light. He has ransomed us from the power of darkness and delivered us to the kingdom of His dear Son Jesus Christ, who has redeemed us and forgiven us through His own precious blood. Christ is the very image of the invisible God; He is the firstborn of all living creatures. Through Him, all things were created on earth and in heaven, whether visible or invisible, including all thrones, dominions, principalities, and powers. All things were created by Him and for Him. He is before all things, and because of Him all things exist. He is the head of the body, which is the church. He is the beginning, the firstborn of the dead, and the Supreme Being above all things. God was pleased to allow His fullness to live in Christ. Christ established an everlasting peace through His blood which was shed on the cross, thereby causing all things on earth and in heaven to exist together in harmony with Him.

- HEB 1:1–2 ~ God, who spoke throughout history to the prophets, has in these past days spoken to us by His Son Jesus Christ, whom He appointed heir of all things and by whom He also made the worlds. Who, being the brightness of His glory and the express image of His person, and upholding all things by the Word of His power when He had by Himself purged our sins, He sat down at the right hand of His Majesty in heaven.

Jesus came to us to reveal God, to fulfill His promises, and to testify to the truth conveyed to us by the Holy Spirit in His Word; Christ is the Word in human form. Yes, He was God incarnate, but also the image of man; who was seen, heard, felt, and experienced even to this day by those who seek Him and bear witness to His sacrifice, His resurrection, and His glory. Jesus had two natures: He was fully man and fully God, making Him the perfect man.

- ROM 8:1–3 ~ Those who are in Christ are no longer condemned, because through Him, the law of the Spirit of life sets us free from the law of sin and death. For what the law could not do, in that it was weakened because of our sinful flesh, God sent His own Son in the likeness of sinful flesh to be an offering for sin, thereby condemning the sinfulness of humanity.

- PHP 2:5–11 ~ Keep your thoughts on Jesus Christ who, although He was God in the flesh, did not glorify Himself but became a servant. In the form of a man, He humbled Himself, becoming obedient unto death, even death on a cross. Therefore, God has exalted Him and given Him a name above all other names. Everyone should bow at the name of Jesus Christ, whether they are in heaven or on earth. Every tongue should confess that Jesus Christ is Lord, to the glory of God the Father.

When we receive Christ, we become conformed into His image. Through the process of sanctification, believers become more like Him, and are able to think and do as He would, with a moral compass that always points towards true north (ROM 9:1; 1 CO 2:16; 1 TI 1:5), that is, heavenward where God the Father awaits our arrival (GAL 4:4–7; EPH 1:3–7).

- PSA 17:15 ~ As for me, I will behold His face in righteousness. When I awaken, I will be delighted to see His likeness.

- ROM 6:3–5 ~ Do you not know that anyone who is baptized into Jesus Christ has been baptized unto death? Therefore, we who were baptized will be buried with Him, and as He was raised from the dead, so also, we will receive a new life. For if we have been united together in the likeness of His death, we likewise will be united together in the likeness of His resurrection.

- ROM 8:28–31 ~ We know that all things work together for good to those who love God and are called according to His purpose. For God knew them in advance and predestined them to be conformed into the image of His Son, and to be among the firstborn of His brothers. Whomever He predestined, He called; and whomever He called He justified; and whomever He justified, He also glorified. Therefore, if God is with us, who can be against us?

- 1 CO 15:49 ~ As we have borne the image of the earthy, we also will bear the image of the heavenly.

- 2 CO 3:18 ~ We, who with faces beaming, reflect as a mirror the glory of the Lord, will be changed into that same image with continuous glory by the Spirit of the Lord.

- COL 3:10 ~ We have put on the new self, which is renewed in knowledge in the likeness of our Creator.

Given the wondrous things the Lord has done for humanity, is seems odd that people would worship any other. Time and again God warned Israel about the idolatry of their pagan neighbors, who would invent their own gods, create images of them, and even worship them. Even more outrageously, God's people Israel disobeyed this commandment and worshipped the graven images of their enemies. And they aren't the only ones. Actually, anyone worshipping anything or anyone other than God are idolators. But then, who has never been guilty of idolatry, loving the world and material things? Precisely, that's why we need a Savior and the reason we worship God alone.

DECEMBER

- EXO 20:4; LEV 26:1 ~ You must not fashion any graven image, or any likeness of anything that is in heaven above, or that is on the earth, or that is in the water. You must not set up any image of stone and bow down to it, for I alone am God.

- HAB 2:18 ~ What does it profit those who fashion images, and teach lies, and trust in the work of their own hands in the producing of dumb idols?

- ROM 1:18–25 ~ The wrath of God is being revealed from heaven against the wickedness of men, who suppress the truth through unrighteousness, though the things that are known about God are clear to them because God has made these things clear. Since the creation of the world, God's invisible qualities have been obvious, including His eternal power and His divine nature. Therefore, they have no excuse; because, while they knew God, they neither glorified Him nor gave thanks to Him. Their thinking became futile and their foolish hearts were darkened. Though they claimed to be wise, they were foolish, exchanging the glory of God for graven images. God allowed them to become depraved, who turned God's truth into a lie and worshipped and served the creature rather than the Creator who is blessed forever.

In the end times, most of humanity will become idolatrous again, engaging in the worshipping of idols, the world, and other material or physical things. This is one of Satan's great deceptions. In fact, all worship that is not given to God is lost, as will be the idolators, for their adulation goes to the lake of fire along with Satan and demons. Strangely enough, in the last days Satan will present himself as a messiah, and he will have an idol fashioned in his image; and many will follow him, worship him, and be condemned with him.

- REV 13:11–15 ~ A beast came out of the earth and this beast had the authority of Satan. And he deceived people into worshipping the beast by performing miraculous feats. The beast ordered the people to construct an image of the beast, who was wounded and yet lived. He was able to invigorate the image of the beast, so that the image could speak. Everyone was expected to worship the image of the beast; the penalty for not worshipping it was execution.

- REV 14:9–11 ~ Those who worship the beast and his image, and those who receive the mark of the beast on their hand or forehead, will receive God's wrath. They will be tormented with fire and brimstone in the presence of the Lamb and His holy angels. The smoke from that torment will ascend from hell forever; and they will have no rest day and night.

- REV 16:2 ~ And the first angel poured out his vial upon the earth; and offensive and painful sores came upon people who had the mark of the beast, and upon those who worshipped his image.

- REV 19:20; REV 20:10 ~ The beast (antichrist) was taken, and with him the false prophet that had performed miracles before him and through which he had deceived those who had received the mark of the beast. Also taken were those who worshipped the image of the beast; they all were thrown alive into the lake of fire. Then Satan was thrown into the lake of fire along with them.

Satan, the fallen cherub, who dragged a third of the angels of heaven down with him, has been dragging human beings by the millions down with them. God created angels to minister to Him and to perform assigned tasks. Apparently, a great many of them left the employ of God and chose to join Satan in mutiny. They are lost and they are damned, for they are irredeemable. By the way, angels were not created in the image of God and do not inherit the kingdom as an adopted child of God. Though they are greater than humans in power and stature, at the resurrection God's chosen (the true believers) will gain a place higher than the angels. The angels that remained loyal to God will be there when we arrive in heaven, to live with us in unity.

- 1 CO 6:3 ~ Do you not know that you will be judging angels? How much more should we judge the things of this life!

- HEB 1:3–6 ~ Christ is the radiance of God's glory, and the exact image of His being, sustaining all things by His powerful Word. After He had provided purification from our sins, He sat down at the right hand of His Majesty in heaven. Therefore, He is superior to the angels, and His name is above all names. Did God ever say to an angel, "You are my son, today I have begotten you?" Or did He ever say, "I will be his Father and he will be my son?" Further, when God brought forth His firstborn He said, "Let all the angels worship Him."

- 2 PE 2:4; JDE 1:6 ~ God did not spare the angels who sinned and abandoned God but sent them into hell, where they are held in chains and darkness to await the judgment.

Appearances can be deceiving. Make sure you are not misled by false teachers and fake prophets. Especially, be ready and watchful, for the end times are coming and may already be upon us. There will be no more messiahs so do not follow anyone claiming to be Christ, pretending to be a prophet, or performing miracles, signs, and wonders to gain converts. They are working for Satan, just like the demons that he persuaded to follow him in forsaking God. When the true Messiah returns, time is up; there will be no further chance at redemption, after which fallen angels and fallen humans will end up in the same dreadful place.

- 2 CO 5:12 ~ We are not commending ourselves again to you, but giving you an opportunity to be prideful on our behalf, so you also can answer those who take pride in appearance but not in heart.

- 2 CO 10:7 ~ Do you examine things according to the outward appearance? If anyone claims to be in Christ, let them remember that we also claim Christ and belong to Him.

Do you imagine yourself living eternally in heaven or dying eternally in hell? Or are you among those who believe in neither heaven nor hell? Be advised, only one of these three groups are associated with the living.

Our Father in heaven, you are holy; your love knows no bounds, your truth is absolute, your creation is beautiful, and you have been patient with us since we arrived on the scene. And we are beautiful too, because you made us in your image. You made us to be elevated above the angels, adopted into your family as equal heirs with your only Son, Jesus Christ. You call us your children and Jesus calls us His brothers and sisters. And we did nothing to deserve this but for the fact that we love you and we want to live with your forever. If you hadn't have loved us first, we would not even know the meaning of the word. We cannot begin to fathom just how fortunate we are to have such an exalted place in your kingdom. And we cannot begin to thank you enough that it was Jesus's suffering, death, and resurrection that earned for us that status. We worship you and we praise you, and we are here to serve you in whatever capacity you wish; let us be conscientious in that service here on earth, and forevermore in heaven. Fill us with the love and peace that only you can provide, as we depend upon you for everything. You are responsible for all things good; help us to love the good and reject the evil. Help us to proudly proclaim your love, your works, and your words to anyone who will listen. Help us to minister to others in their need, especially those who are lost and need someone to show them the way, even as you have shown us the way through Jesus Christ, your Son, our Lord, who is the Way, the Truth, and the Life, and in whose name we pray, Amen.

December 24

Christmas Eve was my favorite day as a youngster; now I feel blessed every day. Though we were poor, there were presents under the tree for a week or two for us kids, parents, and grandparents. We would go to church, have a great homecooked meal, and gather under the tree just before midnight. The day was filled with carols, singing, festivities, hugs, lights, and love. It was the same way when I became a parent; we would begin on Christmas Eve and continue through Christmas Day. What a wonderful tradition we have of sharing gifts, and love, in honor of the baby Jesus, a gift directly from God our Father to every human being that will ever live on earth.

- ISA 7:14–17 ~ The Lord Himself will provide the sign: A virgin will become pregnant and bear a son, and will call His name Immanuel meaning God with us. He will eat curds and honey until He knows enough to reject the wrong and choose the right. But before the boy shall know to refuse the evil and choose the good the land will be laid to waste.

- ISA 9:6–7 ~ A child is born for us; a Son is given to us. The government will be on His shoulders. His name will be called Wonderful Counselor, Mighty God, Everlasting Father, and Prince of Peace. There will be no end to His reign and His peace.

- LUK 2:1–20 ~ It occurred when Caesar Augusts decreed that the world should be taxed, and all had to travel to their hometown to be enrolled. Joseph took his wife Mary, who was pregnant, from Galilee of Nazareth to Bethlehem of Judea, the city of David, for he was from that lineage. Soon after they arrived it was time for Mary to give birth. She delivered her firstborn Son, wrapped Him in cloths, and laid Him in a manger, for there was no room for them in the inn. There were shepherds watching their flocks that night in the hills nearby. An angel of the Lord appeared to them, and the glory of God shined all around them. The shepherds were terrified. The angel told them, "Do not be afraid, I bring you good news that will be of great joy to all people on earth. Today, in the city of David, a Savior is born who is Christ the Lord. This is a sign for you: You will find a baby wrapped in cloths and lying in a manger." Suddenly, a great multitude of angels appeared in the heavens, praising God and singing, "Glory to God in the highest, and on earth peace and goodwill toward all people." When the angels departed, the shepherds said to each other, "Let us go to Bethlehem and see this great miracle which the Lord has made known to us." They hurried to Bethlehem and found Mary and Joseph, with the baby lying in a manger. Afterwards, they spread the word to everyone they met concerning the marvelous things they had seen and experienced. And everyone who heard was amazed at what the shepherds said. But Mary kept these things in her heart and pondered them. The shepherds returned to their flocks, glorifying and praising God for everything they had heard and seen, just as the angel had revealed.

- JOH 1:14–17 ~ The Word was made flesh and lived among us; and we saw the glory of the only begotten Son of the Father, full of grace and truth. John the Baptist said that Jesus would come after him, that He ranks before him, and that He came before him as well. Of His fullness we all have received, Grace for grace. For the Law was given by Moses, but Grace and Truth came through Jesus Christ.

Our Father, who sent His Son to earth to be our Messiah, the same who has been one with you and the Holy Spirit since the beginning of time; we thank and praise you Holy Trinity. We love your Word, where you foretold of Christ's coming in hundreds of passages in the Bible so we would be sure. The Old Testament is your testimony to us, declaring the coming of your firstborn and only Son; and the New Testament is Christ's testament to you, Holy Father. Both of you, Holy Father and Son, have written your Word into our hearts by your Holy Spirit, who indwells us as we follow your Son to you and your household. In the name of our Triune God we pray, Amen.

December 25

Christmas Day has been an annual observance worldwide since the late third century AD. Rome observed a pagan festival coincident with the winter solstice. To compete if not counteract pagan observances, this time period was selected as the day to celebrate the birth of Jesus Christ. Some historical accounts attribute the date selection to emperor Constantine, who legalized Christianity in the early fourth century AD. Christmas has been a federal holiday since 1870. It is unlikely that late December was when Christ was born; however, this timeframe could overlap the visit of the wise men which we celebrate on 01/06.

- NUM 24:17 ~ I shall send Him, but not now. A star will rise out of Jacob (Israel), a ruler to strike down Moab and the children of Seth.

- DEU 18:15, 1 8 ~ God said, "I will raise up a prophet like me from among your brothers. You must listen to Him. I will put my words in His mouth and He will tell the people everything I ask of Him."

- 2 SA 7:12–16 ~ God said to David, "I will make one of your descendants a strong king who will rule forever. I will be His Father and He will be my Son."

- PSA 89:27, 45 ~ I will make Him, my firstborn, higher than all the kings of the earth.

- ISA 42:1 ~ Behold, the chosen One, my delight; God's Spirit is upon Him.

- MIC 5:2–4 ~ Oh Bethlehem, you are such a small village but will be the birthplace of my king, who has been foretold from time eternal. God will forget Israel until the time has come for the chosen woman to bear the child; then the children of Israel will return. The Son will stand for and feed off the Lord, and will share His majesty. The children shall live in Him who is great, even to every corner of the earth.

- MAT 2:4–6 ~ Herod gathered together the chief priests and scribes, demanding to know where the Messiah would be born. They replied that it would be Bethlehem of Judea, for it was written, "Bethlehem is not insignificant among the cities of Judea, for from there will come a governor who will rule my people, Israel."

- LUK 1:26–35 ~ God sent the angel Gabriel to the city of Nazareth in Galilee, to speak to a virgin named Mary, who was engaged to a man named Joseph a descendant of David. The angel came to her and said, "You are highly favored by God and He is with you; you will be blessed above all other women." Mary trembled with fear. Gabriel said, "Do not be afraid, for you please God very much. You are going to conceive and bear a son, and you will name Him Jesus. Your child will be great, the Son of the Most High. God will give to Him the throne of his ancestor David. He will reign over the house of Jacob (Israel) forever; His kingdom will never end." Mary replied, "How can I bear a child since I have never had sex with a man?" Gabriel replied, "The Holy Spirit will come upon you and impregnate you. Thus, your child rightly will be called the Son of God."

- GAL 4:4 ~ When the set time came, God sent His Son, born of a woman and born under the Law, to redeem those under the Law, so that we might receive adoption as sons and daughters.

Father, we pray that all people put Christ back into their Christmas activities and not discount the magnificent miracle of the birth of your Son by the virgin Mary. We pray your blessing on Christians everywhere who are celebrating the coming of Messiah with their friends and families. Let doubters receive a vision of the manger scene, the lowly stable where Christ entered this universal plane when time seemed to stand still. Jesus came to show humankind who you are Father; and everyone who saw Him were seeing you. We will be seeing you soon, Amen.

December 26

Saint Stephen's Day recognizes the first Christian martyr, a man selected by the apostles to be a minister to the Christians in Jerusalem. He was stoned to death by an angry mob, with the approval of the Jewish leadership, which included a Pharisee named Saul of Tarsus (later to become St. Paul). Saul arrested and prosecuted Christians until his conversion, in which he was personally called by Jesus Christ to take the Gospel to the Gentiles, not long after the death of Stephen. This is likely why Paul referred to himself as the chief of sinners (1 TI 1:15), because of what he did to followers of Jesus prior to becoming an apostle of Christ.

Also known as the Feast of St. Stephen, this observance is held the day after Christmas by the Catholic church in the west, and two days after Christmas by the Catholic church in the east. This observance is also practiced by many Protestant churches and denominations.

- ACT 6:1–15 ~ There was a dispute in the church about favoritism being shown to certain widows. The twelve apostles gathered together to choose godly men of good character, who were filled with the Holy Spirit and wisdom, to attend to the needs of these congregations. Those chosen for this ministry were Stephen, a man full of faith and strong in the Spirit; and Philip, Prochorus, Nicanor, Timon, Parmenas, and Nicolaus of Antioch. They were brought before the apostles who laid hands on them. The Word of God continued to be preached, and the number of disciples multiplied in Jerusalem, many of whom became deacons. Stephen, full of grace and power, was performing miracles and prophesying. Some of the members of a Jewish sect called the Synagogue of the Freemen could not tolerate his wisdom and the Spirit who talked through him; they stirred up many others from among the Cyrenians, Alexandrians, Cilicians, and Asians. They accosted Stephen and brought him before the council, calling false witnesses to say, "This man never stops speaking against this holy place and the law. We heard him say that Jesus of Nazareth would destroy this temple and change the customs of Moses." As they were gazing at him, Stephen's face shown like that of an angel.

- ACT 22:20 ~ Paul declared, "When the blood of the martyr Stephen was shed, I stood there giving my approval, keeping the coats of those who killed him."

The story of St. Stephen is a rather short one, but a very significant one. Stephen was a man filled with the Holy Spirit, and he knew the scriptures thoroughly. For this reason, his last sermon is recorded in the Bible.

- ACT 7:1–60 ~ The high priest said, "Are these things so?" Stephen said, "Brothers and fathers, hear me. The God of glory appeared to our father Abraham when he was in Mesopotamia, telling him to leave his land and relatives for a land God would show him. Abraham left the land of the Chaldeans and went to Haran, until his father died. Then God led him to this land. But he had no inheritance here, for God promised it to his offspring, though he had no children at the time. God said his offspring would be sojourners in a foreign land, where they would be enslaved four hundred years. But God would judge that land and its people, and free His people to worship in this place. God gave Abraham the covenant of circumcision. Abraham became the father of Isaac, and circumcised him on the eighth day, and Isaac became the father of Jacob, and Jacob became the father of the twelve patriarchs. The sons of Jacob were jealous of their brother Joseph, and sold him into slavery in Egypt; but God rescued him and gave him favor and wisdom before Pharaoh, who made him ruler over Egypt and his household. Then came a famine in Egypt and Canaan. When Jacob heard there was grain in Egypt, he sent our fathers there. On their second visit Joseph made himself known to his brothers, and Joseph's family became known to Pharaoh. Joseph sent for his father and his relatives, seventy-five persons in all. Jacob went to Egypt where he and our forefathers died; they were carried back to Shechem and laid in the tomb Abraham had bought there. As time passed, the people increased and multiplied in Egypt until another king arose who did not know Joseph. He dealt harshly with our people and destroyed our infants. This is when Moses was born; and he was beautiful in God's sight. Pharaoh's daughter adopted him and he was instructed in the wisdom of the Egyptians; and Moses was mighty in his words and deeds. When he was forty years old, he visited his Hebrew brothers. After seeing one of them harmed, he defended the man and killed the Egyptian oppressor. The next day he saw two of his people quarreling and tried to reconcile them. But the man who was wronging his neighbor asked him, 'Who made you ruler and judge? Do you want to kill me like you did the Egyptian.' Moses fled to the land of Midian, where he became the father of two sons. After forty more years, an angel appeared to him in the wilderness of Sinai, through the burning bush. When Moses saw it, he was amazed and went up the mountain to get a closer look. There he heard the voice of the Lord saying, 'I am the God of your fathers, the God of Abraham, Isaac, and Jacob. Take off your sandals for the place where you are standing is holy ground. I have seen the affliction of my people in Egypt, and I have heard their groaning. I will deliver them, and that is why I am sending you back to Egypt.' Moses would lead the Israelites out, performing wonders and signs in Egypt, at the Red Sea and in the wilderness for forty years. Moses received messages from God to give to our people. But they turned against God asking Aaron to craft the golden calf, for they had no idea what had become of Moses; and they offered sacrifices to the idol. God turned away and gave them over to worship the host of heaven, as written in the book of the prophets. Our fathers had the tabernacle in the wilderness, and brought it into this land with Joshua, when they dispossessed the nations which God drove out before them. So it was, until the days of David who found favor in the sight of God, and who asked to build a temple to the Lord; but it was Solomon who would build God's house. However, the Most High does not dwell in buildings made by hands. As the prophet said, 'Heaven is my throne, and the earth is my footstool.' You stubborn people, uncircumcised in heart and ears; you always resist the Holy Spirit, just as your fathers did. Which of the prophets did your fathers not persecute? They killed those who prophesied the coming of Messiah, whom you have now betrayed and murdered; you, who received the law from angels and did not keep it." When they heard these things, they were enraged and ground their teeth at him. Stephen, full of the Holy Spirit, gazed into heaven and saw the glory of God, with Jesus standing at His right hand. And Stephen said, "Behold, I see the heavens opened, and the Son of man standing at the right hand of God." The crowd cried out with a loud voice, covering their ears, and rushed at him. They dragged him outside the city and stoned him. The witnesses had placed their coats at the feet of a young man named Saul. As they were stoning Stephen, he called out, "Lord Jesus, receive my spirit." He fell to his knees and cried out with a loud voice, "Lord, do not hold this sin against them." And when he had said this, he fell asleep.

Heavenly Father, we thank you for great prophets and evangelists like Stephen, who gave himself for Jesus, just as Jesus gave Himself for him, and for all Christians. Let us be willing to give ourselves for Jesus, and not fear the evil ones who cannot stand to hear the truth of your Word. Do not let us turn away from you under any circumstances, like your people did in the wilderness of Sinai, and like many people today who likewise pretend to be pious and godly, but are equally lost, distracted by earthly desires and riches. We have Christ to show us the way, and we pray that we never lose our way no matter what. In the name of Jesus Christ, the Messiah, who was rejected then and who we worship and adore now and forevermore, Amen.

ANDREW V BARBER

December 27

Feast of Dedication (*Hannukah*) is an eight-day celebration occurring on the Jewish calendar from Kislev 25 to Tevet 3. The dates vary on the Gregorian calendar because of the inexactness of the lunar calendar. The second temple in Jerusalem had been desecrated by the Greek conqueror Antiochus Epiphanes: the town was raided, the people massacred, and the temple defiled by the sacrifice of pigs to the Greek god Zeus. This prompted a rebellion led by Mattathias and Judas Maccabeus, who incorporated guerilla warfare tactics to break the grip of the pagan Greeks and Syrians. Eventually they drove out the troublemakers and rededicated the holy temple around 164 BC. When they lit the candelabra in the sanctuary, there was only enough olive oil to last one day. Miraculously, the lamp remained lit for eight days in a row.

- JOH 10:22–25 ~ It was winter in Jerusalem during the Feast of Dedication. Jesus walked into the temple at Solomon's porch. The Jews gathered around Him asking, "Why do you cause us to doubt? If you are the Christ, tell us plainly." Jesus answered, "I told you and you did not believe. The works I do in my Father's name bear witness of me."

Thus, the candelabra representing the seven Jewish feasts in the Torah became eight, with the inclusion of the Feast of Dedication (aka Feast of Lights). This history is recorded in the Books of Maccabees: apocryphal books which were never officially canonized. Jewish historian Josephus also made reference to these events. The Jewish faction known as "reformed" Jews recognize this feast, while other factions (e.g., orthodox Jews) do not. This is why some menorahs have seven candles and others nine. Traditionally one candle is lit each day until the last day when the ninth candle in the center is also lit. Hannukah is a joyful and lively celebration. The festivities include worship, singing, feasting, games, readings, and fellowship.

- EXO 25:31–37 ~ Make a lampstand of pure gold; it will be one piece of hammered gold on the base, stem, cups, buds, and flowers. Six branches will extend, three from either side, with almond blossom cups, each with bud and flower. On the lampstand itself will be four such cups. Make seven lamps to set upon them, to shed their light forward.

- ZEC 4:1–14 ~ An angel woke me at night asking, "What do you see?" I replied, "I see a lampstand of gold with a bowl on top and seven lamps. There are two olive trees, one on either side." The angel asked, "Do you know what this means?" I answered, "No, my Lord." He explained, "This is a message from the Lord to Zerubbabel: not by might or power, but by my Spirit. Who are you, mighty mountain? In the sight of Zerubbabel, you will be leveled. Then the capstone will emerge with shouts of blessings." [Note: Jesus is the capstone of the arch, the chief cornerstone.] "The hands of Zerubbabel will lay the foundation of the temple, and he will finish it. Then everyone will know that the Lord of hosts has sent me to you. Who dares to despise the day of small things, while the seven eyes of the Lord watch over all the earth, rejoicing when they see the plumbline in the hand of Zerubbabel?" Again, the angel spoke, "What are these two olive trees on either side of the lampstand that pour out their oil into the bowls through the golden pipes?" I replied, "I do not know, my Lord." He said, "These are the two anointed ones who serve the Lord over all the earth." [Note that Zerubbabel was a priest and prophet who helped restore and rebuild the second temple (EZR 3:8). He also was an ancestor of both Joseph and Mary (MAT 1:12–13; LUK 3:27).]

- REV 11:3–6 ~ I will give power to my two witnesses. These are the two olive trees and the two candlesticks. They have the power to breathe fire, to stop the rain, to turn water into blood, and to send plagues.

We thank you, heavenly Father, for your Word which explains mysteries and ties all things together. Let us always continue to study the Bible and discover its hidden truth, Amen.

December 28

Holy Innocents Day remembers the butchering of the little boys after King Herod's evil decree, in an attempt to destroy the Christ child. But His parents were warned by an angel and the family already had fled Bethlehem for Egypt. Originally observed during the season of Epiphany, the two observances were separated around the fifth century in parts of Europe. The Roman Catholic Church calls it the Feast of Holy Innocents, ascribing martyrdom to every child murdered on that day. Some consider these children to be the first martyrs for Christ, but the fact that they were innocent implies they did not choose their fate. Either way, it can be assumed that these innocents were taken up to heaven. Many Protestant churches also recognize this occasion, with a dedicated service, often with a special message for the children.

- JOB 4:7–8 ~ Consider this: Who among the innocent ever perished? When were the righteous ever destroyed? I have seen for myself, that those who plow evil and those who sow trouble reap the same.

- ISA 59:3–7 ~ Your hands are defiled with blood and sin. Your lips have spoken lies and wickedness. They conceive evil and rely on foolishness and lies. They run to evil and hasten to shed innocent blood. Desolation and destruction ride their highways.

- JER 31:15 ~ In Ramah was heard the bitter weeping and mourning, Rachel weeping for her children, refused to be comforted because they were dead.

- MAT 2:1–18 ~ Jesus was born in Bethlehem of Judea in the days of Herod the king. Wise men came from the east to Jerusalem asking Herod, "Where is He who is born king of the Jews? From the east we have seen His star and we have come to worship Him." This troubled Herod deeply, as well as his friends. Herod gathered together the chief priests and scribes, demanding to know where the Messiah would be born. They replied that it would be Bethlehem of Judea, for it was written, "Bethlehem is not insignificant among the cities of Judea, for from there will come a governor who will rule my people, Israel." Herod took the wise men aside, asking them when the star appeared. Then he sent them to Bethlehem saying, "Go and search for the young child, and when you find him, send word to me so that I too may worship him." After leaving Herod, they watched the star, until they stood directly under it. There they found the young Christ child with Mary, His mother, and worshipped Him. They opened their treasures and presented to Him gifts of gold, frankincense, and myrrh. Then, being divinely warned in a dream not to return to Herod, they departed for their country using a different route. The angel of God told Joseph in a dream to take his family to Egypt and escape Herod's evil decree to kill all the male toddlers in Bethlehem. They stayed in Egypt until after Herod died, thereby fulfilling the prophecy: Out of Egypt God has called His Son. Herod murdered all the babies in Bethlehem who were two years old and younger. This fulfilled the prophecy of Jeremiah who wrote, "In Ramah was heard the bitter weeping and mourning, Rachel weeping for her children because their lives were taken."

- REV 12:4–5 ~ The dragon stood before the woman, in an attempt to devour the child that she was about to deliver. She gave birth to a Son, who would rule all nations; and her child was brought up to God to sit on His throne.

Interestingly, a similar decree was issued by an Egyptian king, when Satan convinced Pharaoh to kill baby boys but spare the girls born among the Hebrew slaves. For Satan wanted to destroy Moses just like he tried to destroy Jesus. Here is yet another parallel between the Old and New Testaments. Secular kings were jealous of God's people, and hated them because they prospered. These kings feared being challenged by male children who could grow up into strong fighting men that might become their adversaries. They loved their extravagant lifestyles so badly that they sanctioned the murder of children to keep it. They were constantly afraid of losing it all (JOB 20:15; ECC 5:10–14; 1 TI 6:10); but they did anyway, relatively quickly. They never realized that Satan was the adversary, which is true for everybody (1 PE 5:8).

- EXO 1:15–22; EXO 2:1–10 ~ The king of Egypt spoke to the Hebrew midwives, Shiphrah and Puah. He told them to kill the male babies but not the females. But the midwives feared God, and did not obey the king. The irate king called them back and asked why they disobeyed him. The women explained that Hebrew mothers deliver their babies quickly, before the midwives arrive. Therefore, God intervened for the midwives, and the people multiplied, becoming stronger. Pharaoh again issued a decree that male babies were to be thrown into the river, but not females. There was a Levite man who took a wife and she conceived and bore a son; he was a healthy child so his mother hid him. Knowing she could not keep him a secret forever, she placed him in an ark made of bulrushes and pitch, and put the boy in the ark and floated it down the river. The boy's sister watched from afar, to see what would become of him. The daughter of Pharoah went to bathe in the river and saw the ark and sent her maid to fetch it. She saw the child who started crying; and Pharoah's daughter said, "This one is Hebrew." The boy's sister came along and suggested to her a woman that could nurse the child. So, Pharoah's daughter sent for the women who happened to be the boy's mother. She was paid to nurse and nurture the boy. When he was fully weaned, the woman brought the child to Pharoah's daughter, who named him Moses, because she drew him out of the water.

It is intriguing how the ignorant pharaoh sought to subdue the Hebrews by killing male babies, because it would be the one adopted by his own daughter that would ruin him. Pharaoh would lose the majority of his army as well, due to his disdain for God's people Israel (EXO 14:28). As for Herod, he would die soon after murdering the innocents; he was eaten up inside by worms (ACT 12:23). God will avenge the innocents who suffer at the hands of madness. These evil kings were desperately fearful, though they did not fear the one true God who will destroy their bodies and souls in hell (MAT 10:28).

- MAT 18:3–6 ~ Jesus said, "Unless you become converted and receive God as a little child, you will never enter the kingdom of heaven. Those who humble themselves like a child can become the greatest in God's kingdom. Whoever receives a child in my name receives me. But if anyone offends a child who believes in me, they would have been better off being tossed into the sea with a millstone tied to their neck."

- LUK 18:15–17 ~ People brought children and babies to Jesus for His blessing. The disciples tried to prevent them from bringing the children but Jesus told them, "You must allow the little children to come to me, and never forbid them from entering my presence, for only those who can demonstrate such trust and faith as a little child will inherit the kingdom of God. I tell you the truth, unless you receive the kingdom of God like a child does, you will never enter there."

Heavenly Father, you love children more than their own parents are able, because your love is perfect and unconditional. We pray for the protection of children, and that parents will be vigilant and dutiful in raising their children. The little ones in the world today are growing up in a world of uncertainty, confusion, and without proper supervision. They are not taught to love you and they are not schooled in your Word; furthermore, they are not taught morality at home or at school. Father, open parents' eyes to the dangers facing their children to be more proactive in their learning, development, and education. Please do not allow the innocents to fall into the hands of evil adults who wish to exploit them and placate their lustful designs. Bring swift justice upon the crazy fools that would defile a child, especially those in our own justice system who turn a blind eye to crime whenever it suits them, which is complicity. Bring swift justice on those who permit or excuse such behavior. We ask these things in the name of Jesus, if it be your will, Amen.

December 29

Still Need to Do Day is a secular observance that is set aside to take care of personal business that has been on hold during the holiday season. Many people will be returning gifts, doing repairs about the home, cleaning up the garage, or going back to work to get caught up. It is a good idea to keep a to-do list for occasions such as these. I always have a list, without which I would simply forget, and more rapidly as I age. There is no official history of this occasion, but it has been around for about five years, and it's probably here to stay. Given that there are several observances ascribed to this date, this one seems the most practical. It is not a good idea to procrastinate in doing something worthwhile or necessary, meaning it is probably long overdue.

- PRO 14:23 ~ All hard work brings a profit; but mere talk leads to poverty.

- ECC 9:10–11 ~ Whatever your hand finds to do, do it with your might; for there is no work, device, knowledge, or wisdom in the grave where you are going. I returned, and realized that the race does not belong to the swift, nor the battle to the strong, nor sustenance to the wise, nor riches to the intelligent, nor favor to the skilled, but time and chance happen to everyone.

- ECC 11:4 ~ Watchers of the wind will not sow; watchers of the clouds will not reap.

- LUK 9:62 ~ Jesus said, "Nobody who puts their hands on the plow and then looks back is fit for service in the kingdom of God."

- 1 CO 14:40 ~ Ensure all things are done properly and in the right order.

- JAM 4:16–17 ~ If you boast about your great plans, your boasting is evil. When someone knows what is proper, but does not do it, that for them is sin.

When it comes to knowing the Lord and the true meaning of Christ's birth, it is wise to be sure. Those who entertain themselves during the holidays but neglect spending time in church or in worship are missing the point. Today is a good day to figure this out before putting Christ on the back burner for another year. The to-do list can wait if you have left this undone.

- DEU 32:35 ~ To God belongs vengeance and recompense. The evil nation will slide in due time, for the day of their calamity is at hand; that which comes upon them will come fast.

- 1 CH 16:29 ~ Give to the Lord the glory due Him; bring your offerings and worship Him.

- LUK 12:35–37 ~ Keep your pants on and the candles burning. Be like those who wait for the master to return from the wedding feast, so when he comes and knocks, you will be ready to let him in. Blessed are the servants who the master finds watching, ready to serve when he arrives.

- JOH 9:4 ~ Jesus declared, "While it is day, we will do the work of Him who sent me, since the night approaches when nobody can work."

- GAL 6:9–10 ~ Let us not grow weary in doing well; for in due season, we will reap if we do not give up. When the opportunity arises, let us do good to all people, especially those in the household of faith.

- EPH 5:15–17 ~ See that you live prudently, not as fools but as wise; making the most of every opportunity, because the days are evil. Therefore, do not be unwise, but be wise in understanding the will of the Lord.

- HEB 12:11~ In the moment, all discipline may seem painful; but it yields the peaceful fruit of righteousness to those trained by it.

As we ponder the mystery of Christmas, which has now passed, and look towards the new year, it is a good time to establish our goals and priorities. What do we need to do that we have put off? Maybe it is a new year resolution that we keep making but never follow through. Maybe it is a promise we have made to a loved one or to God about how we intend to modify our behavior or quit a bad habit. I remember making a resolution for five years straight to quit smoking. Finally, one day my wife and I decided to wean ourselves off of cigarettes and nicotine by vaping; it is like titrating yourself off of a medication you no longer need. Little by little we reduced our consumption, reaching zero nicotine in about a year's time.

For those of you who neglected to attend church services, you missed all the great decorations, spirit filled carols, worshipping and fellowshipping, the Christmas cheer, and the joy and peace that goes with the pageant and the program. Perhaps you need to get with the program.

- GEN 2:15 ~ The Lord God brought the man into the garden of Eden to work it and nurture it.

- PRO 16:3 ~ Commit your works to the Lord and your plans will be established.

- ECC 3:13 ~ Everyone should eat and drink and enjoy the results of all their labor for this is a gift from God.

- MAT 13:1–23 ~ Jesus told a parable about sowing to the Spirit: A sower of seeds left seeds by the wayside where the birds ate them. He left seeds in the rocky ground where there was insufficient soil for them to grow. He left seeds among the weeds and thorns where they were choked to death. He also left seeds on fertile ground where they grew and bore fruit. The seeds represent the Word of God. If the Word is left by the wayside, it will be snatched away by the wicked one. If the Word is given to those with a heart of stone, it will never take root in their hearts. If the Word is given to corrupt and worldly people, it will be choked out by the lusts of the flesh. But if the Word is received by someone who listens and understands, it will take root in his or her heart and that person will bear much fruit.

- JOH 16:12–14 ~ Jesus informed them, "I have many things to tell you but you are not ready for them yet. Nevertheless, the Spirit of Truth comes; He will guide you into all truth. He does not draw attention to Himself but to me. He hears and He speaks, and He will show you things to come."

- ROM 14:5–8, 22–23 ~ Whatever you believe and whatever you do, let it be for God. If you eat or if you fast, do it for Him. For nobody lives to themselves and nobody dies to themselves. Regardless of whether we live or die, we belong to the Lord. If you have faith, maintain it between you and God. Blessed is the person who is not condemned by the same things for which he or she has given approval. If you have any doubts, do not do it; for whatever is not of faith is of sin.

- PHP 1:9–11 ~ I pray that your love abounds continuously in knowledge and judgment; that you approve of things which are excellent and that you remain sincere and without offense until the Lord returns; being filled with the fruit of righteousness that comes through Christ, to the glory and praise of God.

Father, we thank you for the joyous season that we are in, especially we rejoice for the coming of your Son, our Lord. We also thank you for our loved ones whom we shared quality time together, and for the family of saints we worshipped with. Help us to use our time wisely, and give you the glory when we are successful. Let today be an opportunity for us to reevaluate our situation and what needs to be finished, ensuring our priorities are in alignment with yours. Thank you for the chance to labor with your Holy Spirit in our daily duties, our duties to the church, and especially our duties to you, Father, on behalf of the baby Jesus, Amen.

December 30

True Wisdom Day is a brand-new holiday designed to keep a clear head about what is true and what is real. With all the festivities of the holiday season, we get distracted easily, if not fooled. There will be much celebration during the next few days and there will be much recovering as well. The main thing is that we do not lose our focus.

There is God's wisdom, and then there is the world's wisdom. When the two are in discord, which one do you think is truly wise? Well, the only kind of wisdom must, by definition, be based on truth. And God's truth is rock solid. It is amazing to me the degree to which some are inclined to invent their own truth and put it out as fact. Unfortunately, it is becoming increasingly more difficult to fact-check what you hear or read, unless you can find it in the Holy Bible which is the sole source of absolute truth known to humankind, seeing how it came from the breath of God Himself. You certainly cannot depend on the internet or media anymore where truth is often censored since certain people dislike the truth.

- JAM 3:13–18 ~ Whoever is wise among you should show it with good conversation and meekness. But if you are bitter and envious, do not glory in it and do not tell lies. Such behavior is not from God but is from this world, sensual and evil. For where there is envy and strife, there is confusion and wickedness. But the wisdom from above is first pure, peaceable, gentle, easily approachable, full of mercy and good deeds, impartial, and never hypocritical. And the fruit of righteousness is sown in peace by those who promote peace.

Consider the scripture above concerning the wisdom of the world versus the wisdom from above. Apparently, the wisdom of the world is not wisdom at all, since it is tainted with bitterness, envy, deceit, discord, confusion, and evil intent. Sound familiar? Those who strive for control and power will use false contentions to persuade people to believe things that are untrue. These schemers are conniving, diabolical, hypocritical, divisive, dishonest, and manipulative. They appear to be wise but only in their own eyes, or in the eyes of those who are likewise unbelievably ignorant of the truth. Whereas the wisdom of God is pure, which is to say, unadulterated, incontrovertible, and not subject to misinterpretation.

It is impossible to successfully argue against real truth because it represents reality. Therefore, people who are in denial will attempt to stifle the truth and those who tell it. They have no proof so they invent it while discounting actual evidence. Choosing to believe an obvious hoax or lie is mentally unsound and irrational, if not delusional. Those who prefer lies over truth are of the devil, the father of lies, whose primary mission has been to distort or cancel the truth of God and His Word. Satan succeeded in casting doubt on God's Word in the Garden of Eden and has been doing it ever since in order to lead people away from God. Therefore, those who tell lies religiously are following the religion of Satan. Those who believe these liars are equally lost because they have not sought the wisdom from above.

- 1 CO 1:19–27, 31 ~ It is written: God will destroy the wisdom of the wise and bring to nothing the understanding of the prudent. Where is wisdom? Has God not made foolish the wisdom of this world? The world through its wisdom cannot know God. The Jews want a sign and the Gentiles want wisdom. But we preach to them about Christ's crucifixion, which to the Jews is an obstacle and to the Gentiles is foolishness. But Christ is the power and wisdom of God to all who are called, both Jews and Gentiles. The foolishness of God is wiser than the wisdom of humankind. The weakness of God is stronger than the strength of many people. You can see that not many of those who are wise, mighty, and noble by earthly standards are called by God. But God has chosen the foolish things of this world to confuse the wise, and the weak things of this world to confound the mighty. Those who glory, let them glory in the Lord only.

- 1 CO 2:7–16 ~ We speak the wisdom of God as a mystery, even the hidden wisdom of God, which He ordained and which none of the rulers of this world knew, otherwise they would not have crucified Christ. It is written: Eyes have not seen, nor ears heard, nor the heart discerned the things that God has prepared for those who love Him. God has revealed these things to us by His Spirit; for the Spirit searches everything, even the deepest things of God. These things we speak, not in the words which humanity teaches, but which the Holy Spirit teaches, comparing spiritual things with spiritual. But natural people do not receive spiritual things of God for these things are foolishness to them; neither can they know these things because they need to be discerned spiritually. But those who are spiritual analyze everything and are judged by nobody. Nobody knows the mind of God that they can instruct Him, but those who are spiritual have the mind of Christ.

- JDE 1:10 ~ They speak evil of those things that they do not understand. However, the things they know naturally by instinct only serve to corrupt them.

The bottom line is this: If you are of the world and pursue lusts of the flesh you are sensually minded and materialistic, but if you are of Christ and pursue the righteousness of God you are morally minded and spiritually motivated. To be spiritual is to listen to God's Holy Spirit, the impeccable source of true knowledge, wisdom, and truth. If you don't know what the Holy Spirit is telling you, read the Holy Bible; pray to the Father in the name of Jesus for guidance, and walk in the ways of the Lord through Christian worship and fellowship. For starters, try listening to your conscience, for it will not lie to you, because it is founded on the righteousness of God in whose image we have been created. Persons whose moral compass has gone haywire are not listening to God at all but to their own ego.

- PRO 2:2–6, 10–12 ~ Incline your ears to wisdom and apply your heart to understanding. If you cry for knowledge and ask for understanding, if you seek wisdom as you would for treasures, then you will understand the fear of the Lord and find knowledge of God. For God gives wisdom, knowledge, and understanding. When wisdom enters your heart and knowledge is pleasant to your soul, discretion will preserve you and understanding will keep you to deliver you from evil.

- PRO 14:6, 8, 16, 29 ~ A scornful person seeks wisdom but does not find it; however, knowledge comes easy for those who understand. The wisdom of the prudent is to understand where they are going, but the folly of fools is deceit. Wise people shy away from and depart from evil, but the fool rages on with confidence. Those who are slow to anger have great understanding, but those who are hasty produce folly.

- ISA 11:2 ~ The Spirit of the Lord will rest upon Him (the Messiah), the spirit of wisdom and understanding, the spirit of counsel and might, the spirit of knowledge, and the fear of God.

- HOS 6:2 ~ After two days He will revive us, and the third day He will raise us up to live in His presence.

- JOH 16:13 ~ Jesus said, "When the Spirit of truth comes, He will guide you in all truth. He will not speak of Himself, but will show you things to come."

Yes, there are natural ways of learning truth and establishing facts, because God has revealed many truths in His creation. And He has given human beings discerning minds enabling us to distinguish what is right, true, virtuous, and genuine. For example, we often hear pundits say "follow the science" since it is possible to observe God's creation and establish certain patterns, facts, and laws. This is precisely why God promulgated laws, order, and consistency in the universe and why we can come to know the truth from God's book of nature as well as God's book of scripture. That way we can verify truth because it will be consistent with both sources. Why then, I wonder, do people cry out to follow the science and then cherry-pick what they consider to be reliable sources of truth?

As a scientist by trade, I find it disconcerting what some of these so-called experts espouse as scientific or factual, while completely ignoring much of the vigorous scientific work being conducted and published. Actually, much of the robust empirical evidence out there is being buried, shunned, discredited, or otherwise rejected. How unscientific can you get? Clearly, there is a nefarious purpose behind such diversions and deviations from truth and science. For example, now that the pandemic is behind us, we find that the truth was being deliberately smothered in lieu of pseudoscience, whereas countless lives would otherwise have been spared severe illness or death.

- PSA 1:1–3 ~ Blessed is he that does not walk in the counsel of the ungodly, or stand in the path of sinners, or sit in the seat of the scornful. His delight is the Law of the Lord and he meditates upon it day and night. He will be like a tree planted by flowing rivers, that brings forth fruit in due season; his leaf will not wither, and whatever he does will prosper.

- 1 CO 6:9–11 ~ Do you realize that the wicked will not inherit the kingdom of God? Do not be deceived, for sinners, fornicators, idolaters, adulterers, homosexuals, perverts, thieves, greedy people, drunkards, slanderers, and swindlers will not inherit the kingdom. And many of us were sinners just like them. But we have been washed clean, sanctified, and justified in the name of our Lord Jesus Christ, by the Spirit of our God.

- 1 TI 6:20–21 ~ Paul wrote to Timothy: Guard carefully those things of which you have been entrusted. Avoid profane and vain babble. Ignore opposing arguments that are falsely called scientific knowledge, which are professed to be truths by those who have consequently become diverted from the true faith.

The best way to succeed and prosper is to meditate on the truth revealed by God in His Word every day, and you will grow in true wisdom, knowledge, and understanding. This does not discount learning obtained through formal education, scientific study, and experience. But listening to the Holy Spirit will bring meaning to all of those endeavors, and collectively will increase in you true wisdom from on high. Those relying on the wisdom of the world will eventually fail and lose, because theirs' is not true wisdom but manufactured wisdom. They will try to censor anyone wielding the Sword of the Spirit which is the Word of God, because it defeats their arguments, lies, scams, and tricks. They cannot stand against truth; and that sword will slice their flaky foundation into pieces, as it pierces into the depths of their souls. In short, truth is painful to them if not devastating; that is why they ignore, distort, or avoid it at all costs.

- JOS 1:8 ~ This book of the Law shall not depart from your speech; if you meditate on it day and night you will be observant to do those things written therein. This will make your ways prosperous and you will obtain good success.

- ROM 1:18–25 ~ The wrath of God is being revealed from heaven against the wickedness of men, who suppress the truth through unrighteousness, though the things that are known about God are clear to them because God has made these things clear. Since the creation of the world God's invisible qualities have been obvious, including His eternal power and divine nature. Therefore, they have no excuse; because, while they knew God, they neither glorified Him nor gave thanks to Him. Their thinking became futile and their foolish hearts were darkened. Though they claimed to be wise, they were foolish, exchanging the glory of God for graven images. God allowed them to become depraved, who turned God's truth into a lie and worshipped and served the creature rather than the Creator who is blessed forever, Amen.

- 1 CO 12:7 ~ For the manifestation of the Holy Spirit is shown to everybody for the advancement of humankind.

- TIT 2:11 ~ The grace of God which brings salvation appears to everyone.

We humanoids are often fickle and untrustworthy. For example, do you know anyone who promised something; or gave their word of honor; or took a vow and swore to it; or testified to tell the truth with their hand on the Holy Bible—and then broke that oath, vow, or promise? Not only do I know people that have done that, I have done it myself. Yeah, I made a vow that I didn't keep. I felt guilty as sin, and I repented with a contrite heart. And God forgave me of this and all of my sins, many of which were much worse, and most of which I can't even remember.

I advise everyone not to make a habit of spreading false information and swearing to it, or you will be among those speeding down the highway to hell. I doubt if they even care, since they have denied the One who can cleanse their souls and save them from sins leading to death. They have no idea what that means, as they plunge headfirst into the lake of fire which is the fate of the damned. They will lose everything, including their souls. But God promises to take anyone back who is truly sorry, reforms their ways, and places their faith in Jesus Christ. Thank goodness God never goes back on His Word; the fact is, He cannot. He is perfect in righteousness and truth, which is why temptation could not sway Jesus either and why those who have rejected His salvation need to think twice before they sell out to the grand delusion (2 TH 2:8–12).

Our Father in heaven, you are the source of all truth, and your truth is absolute as are all of your glorious attributes. We see the wisdom of the world waning, where education is being watered down with propaganda and introductions to immorality. Evil people have taken your name out of the schools, from preschool to graduate school; the truth is being smothered and erroneous teachings are being presented. We beseech you that your Holy Spirit would activate parents and teachers of faith to intervene on behalf of our children and our nation to force educational institutions into teaching the essentials and telling the truth. We ask that power be taken away from the unbelieving tricksters, who claim to have the moral high ground but are actually working for Satan. We ask that people of integrity and faith be appointed and elected to positions of authority and leadership so that truth can be reintroduced into our society and into the soul of our country. Just as you chose the leaders and prophets of old, and just as Jesus appointed His apostles, we pray that you would intervene and choose the leaders of our schools and government so that our foundation of faith can be established once again, and so that our freedoms can be restored and reinforced. Help us to expose the liars and the deviant philosophies being proliferated, and replace their disinformation with reality and truth, so that people will value the truth and so justice will prevail. There was a time when our citizenry stood for honesty and justice, for generosity and diplomacy, for morality and discipline, for accountability and decency, for loyalty and honor, for equality and integrity. Please help us to return as a united front to those tenets in support of faith, liberty, lawfulness, and legitimacy. Repair the demented minds of misguided people and embolden those who still cling to your words, so that we can reunite into one nation under God, shining as a light on a hill that draws good people to come. We bring all of these petitions to you Holy Father, in the name of Jesus your Son, Amen.

December 31

New Years' Eve, the last day of the year when we party like crazy before chalking the year down to history. Those who follow the Gregorian calendar celebrate the new year on 01/01. Different dates are celebrated where a different calendar is followed. Today, people usually will attend or host a party somewhere. But be careful of places and people who are using the final countdown as a reason to engage in debauchery, promiscuity, criminality, and immorality.

- PRO 23:21 ~ The drunkard and the glutton will come to poverty.

- LUK 21:34 ~ Jesus said, "Be careful. Do not let overindulgence, drunkenness, and worrying get the better of you, so when that fateful day comes you will not be caught by surprise."

- ROM 13:13–14 ~ Be honest, as in the daylight; do not engage in rioting, drunkenness, overindulgence, promiscuity, fighting, and jealousy. Build your life around Jesus Christ, do not indulge in the lusts of the flesh.

- 1 CO 5:11, 13 ~ Do not associate with someone who claims to be a Christian but is sexually promiscuous, greedy, idolatrous, slanderous, a drunkard, or a swindler; do not even eat at the same table with them. You must expel the wicked from among you.

- EPH 5:18, 29 ~ Do not get drunk, which is excess; instead, fill yourself with the Holy Spirit. Nobody hates their own bodies; instead, they nourish and cherish their bodies, just as Christ nourishes and cherishes the church.

- PHP 4:5 ~ Let your moderation be an example to others.

- 1 PE 4:1–3 ~ Even though Christ has done away with sin, you must not continue to sin as you have in the past when you engaged in sexual sin, lust, drunkenness, overindulgence, orgies, and idolatry.

New Years' Eve is like a person with a split personality, much like the addict who has a normal side and a monster side. The monster comes out when getting high or drunk or when going through withdrawals. Either way, nobody likes the monster, except maybe other monsters. So, you know what to look out for, and what not to become. The last thing we need are more monsters in public places. Go ahead and enjoy festivities, music, dancing, dining: whatever is on the agenda. But know your limits; if you do not know your limits, stay home.

- ISA 3:9 ~ It shows on their faces that they are guilty; they declare their sin like Sodom, they do not hide it. Woe unto their souls for they have recompensed evil unto themselves.

- JER 23:14, 17 ~ I have seen horrible things. They commit adultery, tell lies, and support evildoers so that nobody returns to being good. It is like Sodom and Gomorrah. They say you will find peace for being evil and following your fantasies.

- JOE 3:3 ~ They gamble for my people, and trade a boy for a harlot, and sell a girl to get intoxicated.

- HAB 2:15 ~ Woe to those who get their neighbors drunk so that they can seduce them.

- GAL 5:19–21 ~ The works of the flesh include adultery, fornication, perversion, lust, idolatry, witchcraft, hatred, quarreling, rivalry, dissension, rage, fighting, sedition, heresy, jealousy, murder, drunkenness, orgies, and the like. Those who engage in such activities will not inherit the kingdom of God.

The end of the year is near, but some will not see the new year because they threw discretion into the wind. For those people, there will be no hope, so I hope they had life figured

DECEMBER

out before their time ran out. Not only is the new year close at hand, but so also is the new heaven and the new earth. That's right, the return of the Lord could be right around the corner. And like those who were not ready for the new year, there will be many not ready for the coming of Christ. It is well worth the time to sit down with your family and discuss the importance of faith and repentance. Whether we die or Christ comes, either way it will be over and there will be no more second chances after that.

- ISA 26:19–21 ~ Your dead will live, oh Lord, along with my dead body they will arise. Awake and sing you who abide in the dust, for your dew is as the dew of the morning, when the earth gives birth to her dead. Come, my people, and enter into your chambers, and shut the doors behind you. Hide yourself for a little while until the indignation has passed over. Behold, the Lord comes out of His place to punish the inhabitants of the earth for their iniquity: the earth will disclose the blood shed upon her, and will cease to conceal her slain.

- HOS 6:2 ~ After two days the Lord will revive us, and on the third day He will restore us, so that we may live in His presence.

- LUK 18:1–8 ~ Jesus taught the parable about the unjust judge: There was a judge who neither feared God nor had a high regard for his fellow man. A widow appealed to him to avenge her of an enemy who had done her wrong. The judge did nothing. The widow continued to bother the judge until her persistence finally paid off and the judge awarded her a fair settlement. God also will avenge His elect who plead with Him day and night, even though He does it in His own time. However, when the Son of God returns, will He find such a persistent faith on the earth?

- ACT 1:8–11 ~ Jesus told the apostles, "The Holy Spirit will come upon you and give you power; and you will be my witnesses in Jerusalem, Judea, Samaria, and the far corners of the earth." Then Jesus ascended into heaven and disappeared into the clouds. As the apostles gazed into heaven, two angels appeared with them and said, "Men of Galilee, why do you gaze into heaven? This same Jesus who you saw ascend into heaven into the clouds will return in the same manner in which He left."

- 2 CO 5:19–21 ~ God was in Christ, and reconciled the world to Himself. He has not imputed our sins upon us, but rather has given us the message of reconciliation. So now we have become ambassadors for Christ, as though God was speaking His message through us, so that you too may be reconciled to Him. For He gave us His Son Jesus Christ, who knew no sin, to bear our sins, so that we could receive the righteousness of God that was in Him.

- ROM 10:9–10 ~ If you confess the Lord Jesus with your words, and believe in your heart that God raised Him from the dead, you are saved. For with the heart the people believe unto righteousness, and with the mouth they confess unto salvation.

- JAM 1:12–15 ~ Blessed are people that endure temptation, for when they are judged, they will receive the crown of life that God promises to all who love Him. Do not say that you are tempted by God, because God cannot be tempted by evil, neither does He tempt anyone; but people are tempted when they are drawn by their own lust and enticed to commit sin. When lust conceives, it brings sin, and sin, when it is finished, brings death.

Father, we pray that people will know their limits and not invent an excuse to go beyond them tonight. We pray that those who attend a gala find a safe ride home. We pray that those who have not investigated your Word or are unaware of your promises will take the time to seek the truth before it is too late. We pray that the new year will bring these people a new lease on life, which only can be found through Jesus Christ, in whose name we pray, Amen.

DAILY DEVOTIONAL EVENTS

INDEX

Abbreviation	iv	Babylon	24, 63, 89, 448, 536, 601
Abortion	48, 378	Banning	364
Abraham	116, 171, 196, 320, 519, 685	Baptism	vii, 30, 183
Acceptance	44, 412	Bastille	428
Addiction	(see Alcoholism, Drugs)	Beast	(see Satan)
Admonition	726	Beginning	1, 86, 352, 489
Advent	vii, 740	Bell, A.	156
Affirmation	140	Berlin Wall	499, 690
Air	551	Bible	114, 279, 523, 692, 713
Airborne	v, 504	Biography	288
Alamo	154	Birds	11
Alcoholism	347, 414, 647	Birthday	703
Angels	400, 482, 504	Bombs	432, 578, 750
Animals	(see Wildlife)	Books	57, 202, 213, 357, 488, 671
Annunciation	187	Boone, D.	338
Anointing	xi, 50, 295	Boss	145, 542, 632
Anthony, S.	109, 526, 707	Boys	90
Antichrist	642, 646	Brain	68, 441, 624
Appleseed, J.	163	Caesar	168
Appreciation	9, 145, 223, 234, 568	Calendars	vi, 95, 134
Arbor	244	Camera	390
Archaeology	4, 26, 72, 231	Cancer	81
Armed Forces	(see Military)	Canonization	57, 525
Armor	159, 294, 531	Catastrophe	89, 527, 612
Artistry	71, 225, 652	Charity	19, 506, 547, 702
Ascension	ix, 196, 274	Children	35, 202, 306, 519, 709, 795
Ash Wed.	viii, 108	Chocolate	562
Assassinated	69, 168, 734	Choices	4, 79, 81, 378, 616, 699
Athletics	448, 472	Christmas	vii, 752, 790, 791
Atonement	278, 519, 582, 620	Citizenship	328, 570
Authors	v, 3, 671	Civil War	159, 215, 404
Automobile	551, 593	Cleaning	277, 797
Awareness	65, 456, 591, 682	Code	247, 306, 591

Colt, S.	136	Earth	16, 182, 237, 260, 333, 438
Columbus	230, 627	Easter	175, 196, 242
Communicate	65, 156, 204, 324, 468	Education	55, 335, 364, 587, 606, 705
Communion	viii, 192, 240, 609	Edwards, J.	778
Communism	123, 499, 690	Elderly	514, 552, 599
Computers	463, 497, 664	Elections	119, 680
Conservation	182, 237	Emancipation	1, 215, 368, 743
Constitution	33, 74, 255, 359, 378, 570	Emergency	262, 660
Corruption	25, 754	Empires	24, 64, 231, 435, 536, 644
Cousins	446	Employee	145, 542, 632
Cowboys	454	Encourage	508, 560
Creation	72, 134, 142, 166, 237	End Times	86, 367, 431, 602, 642, 736
Creativity	180, 236, 652	Enforcement	21, 383
Crime	301, 434, 538, 754	Environment	237, 333, 551, 611
Crown	635	Epiphany	vii, 13, 16, 795
Crucifixion	viii, 193, 239, 715	Equality	158, 526, 634
Crusade	430, 540, 778	Equinox	vi, 176, 584
Dance	251	Evangelism	302, 388, 540, 629, 695, 778
Death	44, 48, 79, 81, 242, 344, 350	Evidence	3, 166, 213, 291, 697, 778
Dedication	660, 794	Evolution	440
Delusion	492, 719	Executions	409, 436, 477
Democracy	359, 428, 570, 565, 705	Experiment	150, 390, 715
Demons	482, 642, 646	Exploration	221, 230, 554, 627, 641, 685
Devotion	398, 404	Faith	37, 46, 258, 331, 588, 776
Dinosaur	16, 291	Family	286, 446, 452, 552
Disability	44, 547, 744	Farmers	623
Division	37, 151, 588	Fasting	5
DNA	142, 446	Fathers	234, 362, 784
Doctors	195, 272	Fear	315, 394, 558
Doctrine	37, 57, 303, 380, 525, 657	Feast	x, 184, 239, 354, 603, 633
Dream	28, 226, 440, 529	Fiction	3, 202, 488
Drug Abuse	384	Fire	612, 613
Duty	90, 398, 404, 768, 797	Firefighters	262, 613, 660
Early Church	173, 388, 697	First Fruits	x, 196, 242

Flag	357	Heaven	167, 221, 260, 489, 736
Flight	221, 775	Hell (Hades)	350, 489, 642
Flood	323, 527	Helping	112, 164, 212, 546, 654, 748
Flowers	223, 296	Heritage	231
Fools	200	Heroes	174, 208, 598
Forgiveness	380, 411, 620	Holocaust	63
Freedom	1, 33, 74, 152, 154, 170, 690	Holy Bible	iv, xiii, 114, 279, 692
Friendship	97, 324, 341	Holy Spirit	ix, 30, 50, 187, 295, 309, 450
Gandhi	69, 601	Honesty	253
GI Bill	374	Hope	28, 331, 386, 508, 556, 615
Gideons	692	Human	48, 510, 640, 756
Girls	83, 84, 164	Humanitarian	131, 165, 211, 510
Give Up	(see Quitting)	Humbleness	5, 128
Giving	(see Charity)	Humor	233, 263
Globalism	123, 319, 640, 719, 732	Husbands	60, 234, 568
Glory	128, 161, 442, 635	Image of God	48, 786
Gold Star	208, 598	Independence	1, 406
Good Friday	viii, 193	Indigenous	230, 328, 627
Goodness	165, 412	Infinity	485
Government	114, 119, 123	Information	9, 66, 170, 468, 565
Graham, Billy	540	Innocents	795
Grandparents	552	Innovation	40, 236, 247, 593
Gregorian	vi, 134	Inspire	71
Groundhog	77	Internet	468, 664
Guilt	411, 475, 674	Inventions	35, 135, 512, 523, 593, 711
Guns	136	Irenaeus	388
Halloween	667	Islam	319, 430, 578
Handicap	(see Disability)	Joan of Arc	321
Hanukkah	xii, 354	Juneteenth	368
Happiness	178, 233, 605	Justice	122, 434
Hard Work	(see Labor)	Keller, H.	386
Health	211, 615, 763	Kids	(see Children)
Hearing	148	Kindness	25, 112
Heart	71, 99, 106, 596, 762	King, M. L.	32, 529

INDEX

Knowing	264	Mental	615, 624, 763
Labor	145, 542	Military	93, 293, 463, 693
Lake of Fire	(see Hell)	Mind	473, 763
Latter Days	(see End Times)	Mindfulness	297, 424, 591, 678
Laughter	233, 263	Ministry	211, 464
Law	21, 256, 285, 477	Missing	306
Laziness	542	Money	662, 732
Leadership	93, 771	Moody, D.L.	612
League	23, 650	Morse, S.	156, 247
Leap Year	134, 144	Mothers	281, 598
Liberty	(see Freedom)	Mountain	161, 494
Library	26, 213	Murder	378, 538, 556, 734
Life	48, 635	Museum	26
Light	13, 370, 687, 740	Music	71, 79, 372, 563
Lighting	40, 740	Mutilation	84
Liturgical	vii	Napoleon	366
Loneliness	422	Nations	23, 650
Love	60, 106, 329, 572	Native	(see Indigenous)
Lucifer	(see Satan)	Neighbor	165, 594
Lunar	95, 438	New Year	1, 95, 803
Luther, M.	58, 380, 588, 657	Newton, I.	166, 407
Magna Carta	359	Nicholas	750
Mardi Gras	105	Nurses	272, 283
Maritime	159, 299	Obedience	584
Marriage	60, 106, 234, 568	Occult	415, 436, 646
Martyrs	69, 250, 321, 388, 697, 792	Palm Sunday	186
Marxism	123, 719	Paradise	(see Heaven)
Massacre	152, 154, 554	Parents	455, 552
Materialism	42, 554, 732, 800	Passover	x, 239
Mayflower	730, 784	Patrick, St.	171
Maundy	192	Patriotism	226, 484, 504, 558, 693, 784
Meditation	297, 424, 682	Peace	131, 189, 418, 579, 640, 682
Memorial	249, 313	Pearl Harbor	751
Men	234, 708	Pen Pal	324

DAILY DEVOTIONAL EVENTS

Pentecost	xi, 295	Resurrection	ix, 196, 746
Perdition	(see Hell)	Revelation	161, 457
Perseverance	508, 744	Revival	540, 695, 778
Pets	219, 341	Revolution	428, 639, 773
Philanthropy	131, 702	Rights	109, 355, 690, 707, 756
Photography	(see Camera)	Rocks	16, 426
Pioneers	338, 784	Sabbath	xii
Plants	163, 223	Sacrifice	174, 208, 250, 547
Poetry	71, 180	Safety	(see Security)
Police	21, 285, 660	Saints	171, 667, 669, 792
Pony Express	204	Salt	776
Potential	35, 55, 385	Satan	52, 642, 646
Poverty	19	Science	3, 35, 134, 166, 485
Prayer	7, 37, 147, 258	Scientists	166, 408, 687, 715, 758
Presence	736	Scouting	90, 164
Presidents	119, 170, 713, 734	Security	66, 501, 591, 756
Privacy	66	Seed	163, 223, 521
Promises	674	Self-Control	99
Protest	69, 601, 705	Seniors	(see Elderly)
Psychology	413, 624, 766	Service	110, 165, 376, 558
Purim	184	Shavuot	(see Hanukkah)
Puzzle	68, 441, 624	Shroud	72, 390
Quitting	508	Siblings	217
Radio	512	Signs	77, 89, 357, 642
Reconcile	549	Simplicity	424
Red Cross	272	Sin	344
References	xiii	Slavery	1, 215, 743
Reformation	303, 380, 523, 657, 667	Sloth	(see Laziness)
Rejoice	470	Smile	178, 233, 605
Relaxation	297, 502, 682	Solstice	370, 783
Religion	46	Sorrow	86
Religious	33, 93, 150, 364, 713	Soul	418, 667, 669
Reprobate	473	Space	221, 260, 438
Responsible	see Duty	Speech	99, 529, 565

INDEX

Sports	83, 472	Trumpets	603
Spouse	60, 208	Trust	97, 461
Steadfastness	574	Truth	57, 253, 264, 629, 719, 799
Stephen	792	Tyndale, W.	524, 610
Sticks, Stones	99	UFO	400
Stress	297, 418, 682	UN	23, 650
Students	55, 335, 705	Underdog	781
Suicide	556	United States	545, 554, 760, 784
Sunday, Billy	695	Unity	23, 37, 640, 705
Tabernacles	633	Unleavened	240
Talent	35, 71, 717	Valentine	106
Taxes	228	Veterans	693
Teachers	55, 607	Vexation	531
Teamwork	746	Vigilance	164, 306, 591
Telephone	156	Violence	301, 319, 579, 601
Television	711	Vision	28, 236, 484, 489, 715
Temple	536, 794	Volunteer	748
Term Limits	138	Walking	206
Terrorism	558, 578, 579	Warfare	154, 159, 209, 516
Testaments	114	Water	17, 182
Thankful	25, 730	Wesley, J.	303
Thanksgiving	730	Wildlife	219, 440, 546
Theater	191	Winning	448
Theodosius	140	Wisdom	678, 799
Tolerance	84	Witchcraft	437
Tourism	270	Wives	60, 568, 568
Trafficking	384	Women	83, 109, 147, 158, 464, 526
Transfigure	161	Words	99, 629
Treaty	23, 189, 434, 516, 545, 639	Workers	123, 145, 249
Trees	244, 752	World Wars	209, 639, 751
Trinity	x, 305, 309, 525	Worry	315, 394
Trivia	9	Wycliffe, J.	303, 610

DAILY DEVOTIONAL EVENTS